# CORPORATE FINANCE AND STRATEGY

## An Active Learning Approach

# CORPORATE FINANCE AND STRATEGY

## An Active Learning Approach


**Cheng Few Lee**
Rutgers University, USA

**John Lee**
Center for PBBEF Research, USA

**Michael Lee**
Center for PBBEF Research, USA



World Scientific

NEW JERSEY • LONDON • SINGAPORE • BEIJING • SHANGHAI • HONG KONG • TAIPEI • CHENNAI • TOKYO

*Published by*

World Scientific Publishing Co. Pte. Ltd.

5 Toh Tuck Link, Singapore 596224

*USA office:* 27 Warren Street, Suite 401-402, Hackensack, NJ 07601

*UK office:* 57 Shelton Street, Covent Garden, London WC2H 9HE

**Library of Congress Cataloging-in-Publication Data**

Names: Lee, Cheng F., author. | Lee, John C., author. | Lee, Michael., author.

Title: Corporate finance and strategy : an active learning approach / by Cheng Few Lee, Rutgers University, USA, John Lee, Center for PBBEF Research, USA, Michael Lee, Center for PBBEF Research, USA.

Description: New Jersey : World Scientific, [2022] | Includes bibliographical references and index.

Identifiers: LCCN 2021028031 (print) | LCCN 2021028032 (ebook) | ISBN 9789811239038 (hardcover) | ISBN 9789811239045 (ebook) | ISBN 9789811239052 (ebook other)

Subjects: LCSH: Corporations--Finance. | Capital investments.

Classification: LCC HG4011 .L393 2022 (print) | LCC HG4011 (ebook) | DDC 658.15--dc23

LC record available at https://lccn.loc.gov/2021028031

LC ebook record available at https://lccn.loc.gov/2021028032

**British Library Cataloguing-in-Publication Data**

A catalogue record for this book is available from the British Library.



For any available supplementary material, please visit
https://www.worldscientific.com/worldscibooks/10.1142/12337#t=suppl

Desk Editors: Balasubramanian Shanmugam/Lai Ann

Typeset by Stallion Press
Email: enquiries@stallionpress.com

Printed in Singapore

# Preface

This book is an updated and expanded version of our previous books in financial management, corporate finance, financial planning, analysis, and forecasting, which will be discussed in the acknowledgement section in further detail. Our title, *Corporate Finance and Strategy: An Active Learning Approach,* describes both the objective of this textbook and the method we have chosen to achieve the objective. Our goal is to introduce business and finance students to that area of finance that deals with processing alternative types of information and making financial decisions within the corporate framework but under different economic environments. Our method is to blend current academic thinking with respect to financial theory with real-world and case like examples. Whenever practical, we use real information about the financial theory or decision under discussion.

Understanding the relationship of financial theory and decision-making is important because managers are continually faced with the task of using theory to make financial decisions. Therefore, we concentrate initially on presenting financial theory along with supporting examples; we then provide numerous questions and problems that allow students to apply their newly gained knowledge.

This text is designed to be used in either a one-semester or two-semester introductory corporate finance course at the MBA level or intermediate-level undergraduate program in financial management. It can also be used for the introductory financial management course in certain undergraduate programs. Chapters 1 to 13 provide the basic topics of financial management and can be covered in a single semester. Chapters 14 to 27 provide the instructor with the specialized subject matter appropriate to the second course of a two-semester sequence or to supplement a one-semester course.

We have attempted to make the book more approachable by the extensive use of numerical examples, exhibits, tables, and diagrams. Some topics require frequent summaries that highlight key technical terms and procedures, as in the discussion of present value and of stock and bond valuations in Chapters 4 and 5. Other topics, such as cash budgeting and short-term financial planning presented in Chapter 18, lend themselves more to extensive case examples. We have made every attempt to tailor our presentation of the material to the nature of the topic being discussed.

Our text contains 27 chapters and is divided into eight parts. Part I, Overview and Background, includes Chapters 1 through 3 and introduces topics such as shareholder wealth, the role of finance in the firm and its relationship to other business disciplines, the financial markets, financial statement analysis in terms of Johnson & Johnson, and some of the basics of financial planning. Excel programs are used to perform real-world financial ratio analysis.

Part II, Valuation Principles and Applications, includes Chapters 4 and 5. We introduce time value of money concepts and then apply them to fixed rate mortgage, annual percentage rate, bond, and bond and stock valuation. Excel programs are extensively used to perform these analyses.

Part III, Capital Budgeting and Risk Return Trade-off, introduces capital budgeting in a progression that starts with the basics and moves to more complex topics in Chapters 6 through 9. Integrating strategy and marketing, we review the financial tools of capital budgeting. We then discuss how to estimate future cash flows and evaluate project risk.

Part IV, Cost of Capital, Financing Choices, and Dividend Decisions, includes Chapters 10 through 13. We show how to estimate a project's cost of capital. We review the capital structure decision and discuss the choices that managers face when considering a debt or equity offering. We discuss the theory and practice as well as determining an appropriate dividend payout policy.

Part V, Long-Term Financing, discusses long-term financing which includes debt financing, common stock, preferred stock, and warrants and convertibles. In addition, we also discuss leasing in

Chapter 17. Part VI, Short-Term Financing and Financial Planning, reviews a variety of short-term issues and long-term financial analysis, planning, and forecasting in Chapters 18 through 21. In Chapter 21, we use Johnson & Johnson's annual report data in terms of "Excel programs" to perform "financial analysis and forecasting." Part VII, Options, Futures, and Corporate Finance, discusses options, futures, swap, and synthetic options in Chapters 22 through 24. Part VIII, Other Topics, discusses mergers, divestitures, bankruptcy, workouts, and corporate reorganization in Chapters 25 and 26. In Chapter 27, we discuss important issues related to international financial management.

This book is designed for a corporate finance course for both senior business students or MBA students who already have basic financial management, statistics, and basic computer courses. We use an active instead of a passive approach to write this book. We strongly suggest that the instructor assigns students homework (10–15%), three projects (30–35%), and a midterm and final examination (40–50%). The syllabi and detailed suggestion for this course will be presented in the instructor's manual.

## Ancillary Material

A complete set of ancillary materials is available to adopters of *Corporate Finance and Strategy*:

1. An instructor's manual, written by Cheng-Few Lee, Wen-Chi Yeh, and Matthew Gregory, from Rutgers University and authors of this text, features detailed chapter outlines as well as solutions to end-of-chapter discussion questions and problems.
2. PowerPoints and Excel programs, prepared by Cheng-Few Lee, Wen-Chi Yeh, and Matthew Gregory.

PowerPoints feature chapter outlines, graphs, tables, and important material from each chapter. Excel programs are important tools to conduct the active teaching approach of *Corporate Finance and Strategy*.

# About the Authors

**Professor Cheng-Few Lee** is a Distinguished Professor of Finance and Economics at Rutgers Business School, Rutgers University, and was chairperson of the Department of Finance from 1988–1995. He has also served on the faculty of the University of Illinois (IBE Professor of Finance) and the University of Georgia. He has maintained academic and consulting ties in Taiwan, Hong Kong, China, and the United States for the past five decades. He has been a consultant to many prominent groups, including the American Insurance Group, the World Bank, the United Nations, The Marmon Group Inc., Wintek Corporation, Polaris Financial Group, and others.

Professor Lee founded the *Review of Quantitative Finance and Accounting* (RQFA) in 1990 and the *Review of Pacific Basin Financial Markets and Policies* (RPBFMP) in 1998, and he serves as managing editor for both journals. He was also a co-editor of the *Financial Review* (1985–1991) and *The Quarterly Review of Economics and Finance* (1987–1989). In the past 50 years, Professor Lee has written numerous textbooks ranging in subject matters from financial management to corporate finance, security analysis and portfolio management to financial analysis, planning and forecasting, and business statistics. In addition, he has edited several popular books, *Encyclopedia of Finance* (with Alice C. Lee), *Handbook of Quantitative Finance and Risk Management* (with Alice C. Lee and John Lee), *Handbook of Financial Econometrics and Statistics* (with John Lee), *Handbook of Financial Econometrics, Mathematics, Statistics, and Machine Learning* (with John Lee), and *Handbook of Investment Analysis, Portfolio Management and Financial Derivatives* (with Alice C. Lee and John Lee). Professor Lee has also published more than 240 articles in more than 20 different journals on finance, accounting, economics, statistics, and management. Professor Lee has been ranked the most published finance professor worldwide during the period 1953-2008.

Professor Lee was the intellectual force behind the creation of the new Masters of Quantitative Finance program at Rutgers University. This program began in 2001 and has been ranked as one of the top fifteen quantitative finance programs in the United States. Professor Lee started the Conference on Financial Economics and Accounting in 1989. This conference is a consortium of Rutgers University, New York University, Temple University, University of Maryland, Georgia State University, Tulane University, Indiana University, and University of Toronto. This conference is the most well-known conference in finance and accounting. In addition, Professor Lee also started the conference on Pacific Basin Finance, Economics, Accounting, and Management (PBFEAM) in 1993.

**John C. Lee** is a Microsoft Certified Professional in Microsoft Visual Basic and Microsoft Excel VBA. He has a Bachelor's and a Master's degrees in accounting from the University of Illinois at Urbana-Champaign.

John has worked for over 30 years in both the business and technical fields as an accountant, auditor, systems analyst, and business software developer. He is the author of the book *Essentials of Excel, Excel VBA, SAS and Minitab for Statistical and Financial Analyses*, which is a companion text to *Statistics of Business and Financial Economics*, 2nd and 3rd editions, of which he is one of the co-authors. In addition, he has also coauthored the textbooks *Financial Analysis, Planning and Forecasting*, 3rd edition (with Cheng F. Lee and Alice C. Lee), and *Security Analysis, Portfolio Management, and Financial Derivatives* (with Cheng F. Lee, Joseph Finnerty, Alice C. Lee, and Donald Wort). He has also coauthored two forthcoming books, titled *Microsoft Excel VBA, Python and R For Financial Statistics, and Portfolio Analysis* and *Microsoft Excel VBA, Python and R For Financial Derivatives, Financial Management, and Machine Learning*. John has been a Senior Technology Officer at the Chase Manhattan Bank and Assistant Vice President at Merrill Lynch. Currently, he is the Director of the Center for PBBEF Research.

# Acknowledgments

This book is an updated and expanded version of the following three books:

1. *Foundations of Financial Management* (with Joseph E. Finnerty and Edgar A. Norton), West Publishing Company, 1997.
2. *Corporate Finance: Theory, Method, and Applications* (with Joseph E. Finnerty), Harcourt Brace Jovanovich, Publishers, 1990.
3. *Financial Analysis, Planning and Forecasting* (with John C. Lee), 3rd edition. World Scientific Publishing Co., 2017.

In addition, this book also incorporates some information from the following four books:

1. *Security Analysis, Portfolio Management, and Financial Derivatives* (with Cheng F. Lee, Joseph Finnerty, Alice C. Lee, and Donald Wort), World Scientific, 2013.
2. *Statistics for Business and Financial Economics*, 3rd edition (with John C. Lee and Alice C. Lee), Springer Academic Publishers, 2013.
3. *Essentials of Excel, Excel VBA, SAS and Minitab for Statistical and Financial Analyses* (with John C. Lee, Jow-Ran Chang, and Tzu Tai), Springer International Publishing, 2016.
4. *Encyclopedia of Finance*, 3rd edition (with Alice C. Lee), Springer Academic Publishers, Forthcoming, 2022.

We would like to appreciate the following professors who have given their comments and suggestions for the previous seven books and the current version of this book.

Mike Alderson
Texas A&M University

Dwight C. Anderson
Louisiana Tech University

V. Ravi Anshuman
Boston College

John Baber
University of North Carolina-Charlotte

Stephen P. Baginski
University of Georgia

Randy P. Beatty
University of Southern California

William Bernaek
University of Georgia

Ted Bos
University of Alabama at Birmingham

John S. Bowdidge
South Missouri State University

Denis O. Boudreaux
University of Southwestern Louisiana

Edward L. Bubnys
Suffolk University

Ching-Fu Chang
National Chengchi University

Andrew H. Chen
Southern Methodist University

Carl R. Chen
University of Dayton

C.W. Chen
Hong Kong University of Science and Technology

Hong-Yi Chen
National Chengchi University

Ren-Raw Chen
Fordham University

Sheng-Syan Chen
National Taiwan University

Son-Nan Chen
Shanghai Jiao Tong University

Indudeep S. Chhachhi
Western Kentucky University

Chin-Chen Chien
National Cheng Kung University

Wan-Jiun Paul Chiou
Northeastern University

Chen C. Chu
Memphis State University

James P. D'Mello
Western Michigan University

Victor J. Defeo
Washington University

Anand S. Desai
University of Florida

Kevin Dougherty
University of Wisconsin-Parkside

John W. Ellis
Colorado State University

Timothy Gallagher
The Tuck School of Business at Dartmouth

James A. Gentry
University of Illinois at Urbana-Champaign

A. Steven Graham
University of Mississippi

Theoharry Grammatikos
University of Wisconsin-Madison

Manoj Gupta
Wichita State University

Scott E. Harrington
The Wharton School, the University of Pennsylvania

Kim Wai Ho
Nanyang Technological University

Chin-Wen Hsin
Yuan Ze University

Chengru Hu
State University of New York at Canton

Dar-Yeh Hwang
National Taiwan University

Michael B. Imerman
Claremont Graduate University

James F. Jackson, Jr.
Oklahoma State University

S. V. Jayanti
Cleveland State University

Frank C. Jen
State University of New York at Buffalo

Dana Johnson
Virginia Polytechnic Institute and State University

James M. Johnson
Northern Illinois University

Stephen A. Johnson
University of Texas at El Paso

Robert Johnston
George Mason University

Joan C. Junkus
De Paul University

William Kelly
Clemson University

Dong Cheol Kim
Rutgers University

Daniel P. Klein
Bowling Green University

Robert Kleinman
Oakland University

Nan-Ting Kou
Shandong University of Technology

Douglas Lamdin
University of Maryland-Baltimore

Han Hsing Lee
National Yang Ming Chiao Tung University

Thomas Liao
St. John's University

Annie H. Lin
ROLM Systems

Fang-Chi Lin
National Pingtung University

Jeng-bau Lin
National Taiwan
Chung-Hsing University

Yun Lin
Shih Hsin University

James T. Lindley
University of Southern
Mississippi

Te-Chien Lo
National Dong Hwa University

Don Manual
Auburn University

Jose Mercado-Mendez
Central Missouri State
University

Allen D. Morton
Western Connecticut State
University

Ron Moy
St. John's University

Chien-Chung Nieh
Tamkang University

Paul Newbold
University of Illinois at
Urbana-Champaign

Henry R. Oppenheimer
University of Rhode Island

James E. Owers
Georgia State University

Frank H. Page
Indiana University

Oded Palmon
Rutgers University

Paul S. Peyser
George Washington University

Ehud Ronn
University of Texas at Austin

Louis O. Scott
University of Georgia

Calvin Sealey
University of North Carolina at
Charlotte

Lemma Senbet
University of Maryland

James Seward
Dartmouth College

R. Shafiqur
Portland State University

Wei-Kang Shih
Public Company Accounting
Oversight Board (PCAOB)

David B. Smith
University of Nebraska-Lincoln

Duane Stock
The University of Oklahoma

Paul Swanson
University of Cincinnati

Robert Taggart, Jr.
University of Boston

William K. Templeton
Butler University

Daniel L. Tompkins
University of Michigan-Dearborn

Emery A. Trahan
Northeastern University

Tzu Tai
Wells Fargo & Company

Chiung-Min Tsai
Central Bank of the Republic of China (Taiwan)

Michael C. Walker
University of Cincinnati

Chih-Wei Wang
National Central University

Alan M. Weatherford
Cal Poly State University-SLO

Dan G. Weaver
Rutgers University

Shelly E. Webb
Xavier University

John K.C. Wei
Indiana University

David Whiteford
University of Illinois at Urbana-Champaign

Walter J. Woerheide
Rochester Institute of Technology

Chunchi Wu
The State University of New York at Buffalo

C.C. Young
National Taiwan University

Kent Zumwalt
Colorado State University

We are grateful to these individuals for giving so generously of their time and wisdom. However, any shortcomings, errors, or omissions that remain are our own responsibility.

To prepare this book, we appreciate the help from Natalie Krawczyk, Wen-Chi Yeh, Matthew Gregory, Yuanyuan Xiao, and Michelle Lee. We also appreciate the help of the editor, Balasubramanian Shanmugam, from World Scientific.

**Cheng Few Lee**
**John Lee**
**Michael Lee**
2022

# Contents in Brief

# Contents

Appendix 4B — Book Value, Replacement Cost, and Tobin's $q$ . . . 202

## Part IV Cost of Capital, Financing Choices, and Dividend Decisions 481

# PART I
# Overview and Background

# Chapter 1

# Introduction and Overview of Financial Management

## Contents



## 1.1 Introduction

Finance is an interesting and dynamic field that affects virtually everyone. Advertised interest rates for car loans, mortgages, and bank accounts reflect financial market trends. News broadcasts describe the ups and downs of the stock market, bond market, and other financial markets.

Finance is much more than the events in the financial markets, however. Rather than being a narrow discipline, finance cuts across many boundaries. Financial managers work with marketing, production, and human resource personnel to address challenges facing the firm. They also work with top management to evaluate and plan a firm's strategy.

Consider these applications of finance within a firm:

- To help determine corporate strategy, a firm's chief financial officer (CFO) evaluates trends in the global economy and the industry, as well as the firm's capabilities and needs.
- Working with the marketing department to evaluate future sales growth, a financial analyst estimates the increase in assets that will be needed to satisfy forecasted demand.
- Working with quality and operations managers as well as a marketing team, a financial manager evaluates alternative plans to determine precisely what equipment needs to be purchased and what buildings need to be constructed to meet production and sales goals.
- A team of financial analysts examines how best to finance the firm's expansion. This may involve negotiations with international bankers of Wall Street investment bankers.
- The human resources department works with financial managers to develop incentives for production workers and the sales force so their actions will reflect the firm's overall strategy.
- A firm's treasurer coordinates cash collection activities in dozens of bank accounts across the globe, as well as ensuring that the firm's bills, debt interest, stock dividends, and employees are paid on time.

The tools of finance have many applications outside the corporate world as well. What you'll learn in this course has a number of applications. For example, financial concepts will help you to determine the answers to questions such as these:

- Is it better to buy a car or lease it?
- What type of home mortgage i.e., fixed rate or variable rate mortgage best meets your needs?

- How should you invest money to meet future needs, such as buying a house, paying for children's college education, and allowing enough money for retirement?

First, this chapter introduces some important issues and concepts in finance. We'll review the place of finance within the firm and how it relates to other company functions such as accounting and marketing. Also, we'll discuss how business decisions should be made to promote the goal of maximizing the wealth of the firm's owners, as well as some of the problems that inhibit achievement of that goal.

This chapter also discusses organizational structure and taxes for a firm. If the organization's policies and structure are not in line with its strategy and desired goals, most likely the goals will not be met. For example, suppose a firm has a goal to maximize shareholder wealth but management bonuses are based upon sales revenues. Chances are, sales revenues will be the focus of management's attention, rather than shareholder wealth.

It's easy to specify a goal for a firm, such as maximizing shareholder wealth; it's quite another matter to achieve it. There are some basic concepts and tools that can help managers maximize shareholder wealth. We explore these in future chapters. But first, in this chapter we examine the impact that people, a firm's managers and workers, and the firm's organizational structure can have on a firm's financial decisions. How a firm is organized and how a firm's workers are motivated affect how well the firm is able to return value to shareholders.

If a firm's managers are not successful in increasing shareholder value, angry shareholders may seek new managers. This chapter reviews several issues dealing with the topic of corporate governance, that is, just who really runs a firm: its owners or its managers. The chapter also discusses several tools that can be used to make company managers think and act in ways that coincide with the goal of shareholder wealth maximization.

How a firm is organized also affects how much of its income is paid out in the form of taxes. Taxes represent a cash outflow from the firm. Shareholder wealth can be increased if the firm's managers take actions to (legally) minimize the firm's tax obligations.

In Section 1.2, we discuss the concept and definition of finance. Organization charts for a company are discussed in Section 1.3.

In Section 1.4, we discuss the goal of a firm. Corporate governance is discussed in Section 1.5. Forms of different business organizations are discussed in Section 1.6. Tax rates are reviewed in Section 1.7. In Section 1.8, the outline of the book is discussed. Finally, Section 1.9 is the summary.

## 1.2 What is Finance?

*Finance* is the study of how to manage assets and obtain funds in order to maximize the wealth of the owner. Thus, the broad field of finance deals with such varied topics as designing a personal retirement plan, managing inventory, investing excess cash, borrowing money, or attracting bank depositors. Business operations generate profits when the firm can raise funds at a lower cost than the return generated by the investment of the funds.

Businesses purchase assets with the hope that they will generate future cash flows. The cash flows may be in the form of income, future cost savings, and/or changes in company value. To finance asset purchases, firms sell liability and equity securities, including bonds, stocks, mortgages, and loans. Investors are willing to buy the securities in order to receive future cash flows, which help the investors meet their own future needs. The value of an asset depends on three cash flow characteristics:

- amount,
- pattern over time, and
- risk.

Investors will pay more for an asset that promises larger cash flows after shorter time periods with lower risks. Values are lower for assets that generate smaller, later, and/or more uncertain cash flows.

### 1.2.1 *Areas of finance*

Within the general field of finance, there are several areas of study. Each examines the management of assets, liabilities, and equity from a different perspective or setting. One area of study deals with *financial intermediaries*, such as banks and insurance companies, which collect funds from savers and lend them to or invest them in businesses or people that need cash.

A second area within finance is the study of *investments*. Students of investment learn how to analyze the investor's stake in stocks, bonds, and other financial instruments. This analysis focuses on evaluating the cash flow from such financial assets to decide whether they represent attractive investments. As in the other fields of finance, the analysts also must plan how to manage the assets in an investment portfolio to meet future liabilities (such as college tuition, a new car or house, or retirement income).

The third field within finance is *financial management*, the subject of this book. This field studies how an organization should manage its assets, liabilities, and equity to produce a good or service.

No field within finance stands alone. Many decision methods and analytical tools are shared by these three fields. Moreover, all students of finance must understand the environment of business. This requires a familiarity with the appropriate tax laws; other laws and regulations that affect financial transactions; social, political, and economic trends; changes in technology and ways of doing business; and the ever-increasing globalization of business and financial markets.

## 1.3 Finance in the Organization Chart

In all but the smallest of firms, a top manager with the title *CFO* or *vice president of* finance usually reports to the president. Managers of two areas usually report to the CFO: the firm's *treasurer* and its *controller*, as shown in Figure 1.1. The firm's treasurer oversees the traditional functions of financial analysis: capital budgeting, short-term and long-term financing decisions, and current asset management. The controller traditionally manages accounting, cost analysis, and tax planning.

The influence of the financial manager has increased substantially in recent years, so that now the CFO is often second only to the chief executive officer (CEO) in the corporate hierarchy. Further, the CFO serves as the heir apparent for the CEO in many organizations. As an illustration of this importance, in 1993, AT&T's CFO, Alex Mandl, was responsible for the decisions and negotiations when

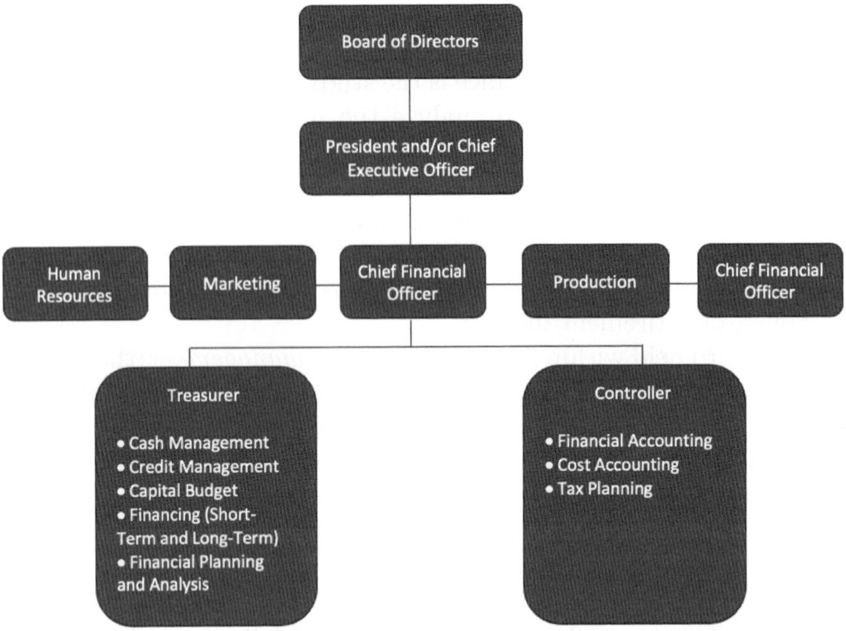


Figure 1.1 The Position of Finance in a Typical Organization Chart.

the corporation acquired McCaw Cellular, a major component of AT&T's strategy for the 1990s and beyond. In late 1995, he was appointed president and chief operating officer for AT&T.

### 1.3.1 *The place of finance in the organization*

A firm's strategy for business success is plotted by its top officers and, in the case of a corporation, its board of directors. Often, this strategy will be reflected in the composition of the firm's balance sheet, as seen in Figure 1.2. Those involved in planning the firm's strategy follow the structure provided by the balance sheet in answering several basic questions:

1. The *capital budgeting* question: What fixed or long-term assets should the firm purchase to produce its product?
2. The *capital structure* question: How should the firm finance these purchases?

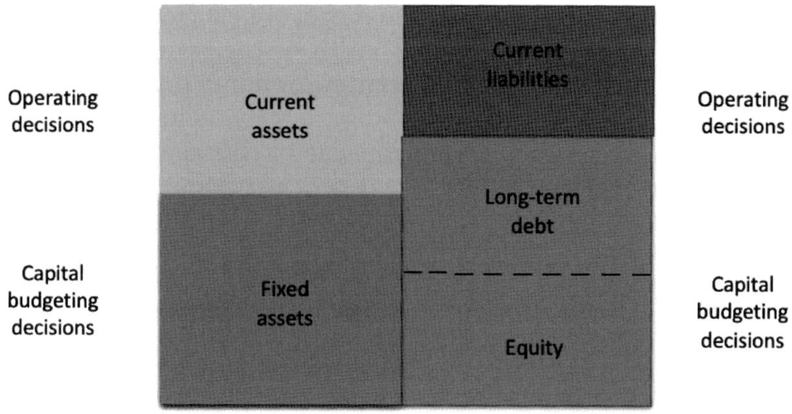


Figure 1.2 The Balance Sheet.

3. The operations or *net working capital* question: How should the firm manage inventory, collect payments from customers, pay suppliers, and manage its cash account?

It is important to realize that the methods by which financial decisions are analyzed depend upon the decision maker's point of view. Different levels of management treat financial decisions in different ways. The board of directors or senior managers usually take a long-range view of the company and of the effects of various decision alternatives. For example, their overriding consideration in setting the dividend will be its long-range impact on the company's stock price, the firm's investment decisions, and the ability of the firm to maintain that dividend over time.

In comparison, operating managers generally focus on short-term goals and the effects of various decision alternatives on the firm's current operations. For example, operations management includes making cash management decisions. This analysis places primary emphasis on short-term objectives, such as cash liquidity, the need to maintain sufficient inventory to meet expected sales demand, and the need to maintain good supplier relations.

### 1.3.2 *The role of the financial analyst*

The position of the financial analyst in the corporate structure and the scope of his or her work are interdependent. The financial analyst is a staff member who diagnoses the effects of management proposals and/or decisions on the financial health of the firm. Acting as an internal consultant, the financial analyst examines profitability, cash flows, and operations; conducts studies; interprets information; and designs financial controls. Although some of this analysis is focused entirely within the firm, the analysts also must examine the dynamic economic, social, political, and competitive environments that are external to the firm, in an attempt to gauge their impact on the firm's well-being. This information as input for upper-level management's decisions; generally, he or she does not set policy or make decisions. Major decisions are made by top management, which may include the CFO and treasurer of the firm.

In addition to the above, the financial analyst must perform many tasks on a periodic basis. These activities include analyzing the company's liquidity and profitability and supervising its day-to-day financial operations, including accounts receivable, accounts payable, and cash balances. The analyst must also contribute to longer term projects by analyzing the firm's capital structure and major investment alternatives.

The analyst also completes specific projects that are either self-initiated or, more commonly, requested by others. For example, if the analyst notices a marked variation from a normal financial ratio, he or she may try to determine the underlying cause of the variation and report it to management as part of the control function. Also, the analyst may examine the effect of a current economic force on the company, such as how a tax policy change might affect the firm's cash flows and stock value. The financial analyst may assist operations management in determining whether to lease or purchase a specific asset. Some problem analyses are critical to the success of the entire company, such as the decision whether to expand or sell off one of the operating divisions; others are as commonplace as deciding whether to purchase Treasury bills or certificates of deposit (CDs) with surplus cash.

Within the company's organization structure, the position of financial analysts may be centralized or decentralized or have elements of both. Centralizing the analyst function places it at corporate headquarters, separate from the operational units for which it performs most of its analyses. Decentralizing the position places analysts in each of the firm's divisions to do division-specific work.

Centralization allows the firm to pool expertise, promote interaction among the analysts, and maintain objectivity, as the analyst views a divisional issue from a companywide point of view consistent with the firm's overall strategy.

However, certain circumstances create advantages for a decentralized financial analyst function. A decentralized organization is useful: (1) when the analyst's role is to advise the operating manager, who has some independence to make division-level decisions; (2) when the operations of the division are complex and the analyst must possess specialized expertise to make useful recommendations; and (3) when the larger firm is really a holding company for different, independent organizations (e.g., one corporation may operate a banking division, another may run an insurance division, and so on).

### 1.3.3 *Relationships between finance and the other business disciplines*

Nearly all managers perform aspects of financial management. This means that all managers must develop the skills necessary to apply the principles of finance to their specific functional situations, while recognizing the consequences of their decisions for their organizations. This text will provide an overview of both financial theory and practice and introduce the tools and concepts that all managers need.

The field of economics provides the basic framework within which managers make firm-level decisions, since microeconomic decisions are implemented in the context of a dynamic, global macroeconomy. The accounting function quantifies, to a certain extent, the economic relationships within the firm and provides data on which management bases its planning, controlling, and operating decisions. The field of finance links the economic principles with the quantitative data provided by a firm's accountants and its management information system to give managers practical tools to facilitate decision making.

Like accounting, finance deals with value and the monetary resources of the organization: like marketing, finance is oriented toward the future, dealing with management, strategy, and planning issues that together help strengthen a firm's market position; like economics, finance employs the theory of rational decision making; like quantitative management science, finance does use some highly structured models and methods; and, like management science, finance is concerned with methods of decision making, strategy implementation, and employee incentives and compensation. This integrating feature of the discipline of finance creates an inclusive point of view from which to survey the operations of the entire business enterprise. The impact of these business disciplines on finance, and the impact of financial concepts on these disciplines, will become clear as you progress through this text.

This central position of the finance function affords you the opportunity to gain some useful knowledge, regardless of your background or future career plans. A truly successful financial manager must possess an open mind, free of preconceptions. The individual must be ready to adapt to changing environments and changing information, using any and all techniques of analysis from many diverse areas to work toward a useful decision. Hence, an understanding of finance can enhance whatever career path you choose.

Finance differs from the pure science of physics, mathematics, and logic because its value comes, not from its internal symmetry, consistency, or beauty, but rather from its usefulness in solving many different types of problems. It has been said that finance is difficult and challenging. We believe that any difficulty comes not from the subject matter *per se*, but rather from the need of the financial manager or student of finance to examine financial problems from several points of view at once. At times, alternative perspectives lead to competing interpretations and answers. Determining the "best" solution can be a matter of individual judgment. A good financial analyst or financial manager is able to bring qualitative as well as quantitative judgment to bear on financial problems and tailor the various analyses to fit the situation. Financial decision making is in this respect both an art and a science.

## 1.4 The Goal of a Firm

The firm must operate to achieve a purpose or goal; otherwise, decisions will be made carelessly, allowing better informed, more serious competitors to put the firm out of business. Although many firms may have *mission statements* espousing goals of quality, customer service, fair prices, and so on, such qualitative statements are really only a means to an end. The firm's managers need a definite benchmark against which to evaluate the alternative means for attaining these goals. We argue that the goal of any firm is a financial one, namely the maximization of the owners' (or the common shareholders') wealth.

A firm is a collection of assets, and the value of those assets depends upon the size, timing, and risk of their cash flows. Of all the possible goals of a firm, only shareholder wealth maximization fully considers the size, timing, and risk of the cash flow generated by the firm's activities.

A firm purchases its assets with funds obtained from sources listed on the right-hand side of the balance sheet-liabilities and owners' equity. Thus, the value of a firm belongs to its creditors and owners. Creditors have a fixed claim on the firm that does not change with variations in the value of the firm's assets over time. As the shareholders have a residual claim on the firm's assets, variations in a firm's value are reflected mainly in the fluctuating value of the owners' or shareholders' wealth in the firm. Therefore, decision alternatives should be evaluated in light of their impact on shareholders' wealth. Alternatives that increase shareholders' wealth should be chosen; alternatives that harm shareholders' wealth should be rejected. Some mandatory projects, such as the need to retrofit factories due to regulation changes, may be costly and harm shareholder wealth. In such cases, if several alternatives exist, the project that hurts stockholder wealth the least should be chosen.

This view is consistent with the process of raising funds and investing them to earn rates of return in excess of their cost. If the firm is able to do this, the excess return will accrue to the firm's owners, the shareholders.

Economics teaches that the goal of a firm is to maximize its economic profit, which is a function of the difference between the return earned on its assets and the opportunity cost of buying those assets. The workings of the financial markets will ensure that the cost to a firm of raising capital is equal to the capital's opportunity cost; otherwise, available funds will flow to other firms that can offer investors higher expected returns at lower risk. Should returns earned by the firm exceed this cost, the profit belongs to the firm's owners.

Thus, the financial goal of maximizing shareholder wealth is similar to the concept of maximizing economic profit.

### 1.4.1 *Measuring shareholder wealth*

Shareholder wealth is measurable and observable daily in the financial sections of newspapers (at least for publicly traded firms). *Shareholder wealth* is nothing more than the market value of a firm's common stock. This market value of the shareholders' claim on a firm is equal to:

$$\begin{aligned}\text{Shareholder wealth} &= \text{Common stock price}\\ &\quad \times \text{Number of common shares outstanding}\end{aligned} \tag{1.1}$$

This relationship allows analysts to keep track of changes in shareholder wealth for competing firms in an industry on a regular basis to see which is most successful at returning value to its shareholders. As long as the number of common stock shares outstanding does not change appreciably, the market's perception of the firm and its management's actions will be reflected in the firm's stock price.

A measure to identify successful firms that is growing in popularity is market value added (MVA). MVA measures the value created by the firm's managers. It equals the market value of the firm's stocks and debts minus the amount of money investors paid to the firm (their book value) when these securities were first issued. That is, MVA equals[1]:

$$\begin{aligned}&\text{Market value of stock} + \text{Market value of debt} - \text{Book value of stock}\\ &\quad - \text{Book value of debt}\end{aligned} \tag{1.2}$$

Stern Stewart & Company, a financial consulting firm, regularly reports firms' MVAs. Based upon Stern Stewart's method, which is presented in Eq. (1.2), we calculate MVA of Dow Jones 30 in terms of 2018 data. We present the MVA values for these 30 companies in Table 1.1. In Table 1.1, columns 3 and 4 present market value and

[1]Usually, a firm's market value of debt closely approximates its book value, so a close estimate of MVA is the market value of equity less the book value of equity.

Table 1.1 Ranking Firms by MVA: Dow Jones 30, 2018.

| Company Name | Stock Ticker | Market Value of the Stock ($) | Book Value of the Stock ($) | Value Added ($) | Ranking of Value Added |
|---|---|---|---|---|---|
| 3M Company | MMM | 94,040,000,000 | 10,084,658,400 | 88,085,341,600 | 21 |
| American Express | AXP | 104,680,000,000 | 23,173,470,000 | 81,506,530,000 | 22 |
| Apple Inc. | AAPL | 908,310,000,000 | 97,934,000,000 | 807,366,000,000 | 2 |
| The Boeing Company | BA | 189,940,000,000 | 5,511,206,800 | 195,841,206,800 | 10 |
| Caterpillar Inc. | CAT | 66,150,000,000 | 15,080,475,600 | 52,119,524,400 | 26 |
| Chevron Corporation | CVX | 230,570,000,000 | 156,522,000,000 | 76,938,000,000 | 23 |
| Cisco Systems, Inc. | CSCO | 222,300,000,000 | 36,508,400,000 | 187,921,600,000 | 13 |
| The Coca-Cola Company | KO | 227,590,000,000 | 18,147,500,000 | 212,382,500,000 | 9 |
| DuPont de Nemours, Inc. | DD | 51,150,000,000 | 126,450,000,000 | 74,180,000,000 | 30 |
| Exxon Mobil | XOM | 294,360,000,000 | 191,322,900,000 | 115,487,100,000 | 20 |
| Goldman Sachs Group | GS | 72,660,000,000 | 80,861,614,200 | 9,428,384,800 | 29 |
| The Home Depot, Inc. | HD | 226,750,000,000 | 2,145,000,000 | 233,225,000,000 | 7 |
| IBM Corporation | IBM | 119,330,000,000 | 17,661,868,800 | 56,824,411,200 | 25 |
| Intel Corporation | INTC | 202,810,000,000 | 76,140,000,000 | 127,550,000,000 | 18 |
| Johnson & Johnson | JNJ | 348,850,000,000 | 61,206,600,000 | 287,273,400,000 | 5 |
| JPMorgan Chase & Co. | JPM | 334,790,000 | 252,703,800 | 380,930,086,200 | 3 |
| McDonald's | MCD | 165,840,000,000 | 6,551,344,800 | 170,321,344,800 | 16 |

(*Continued*)

Table 1.1 (*Continued*)

| Company Name | Stock Ticker | Market Value of the Stock ($) | Book Value of the Stock ($) | Value Added ($) | Ranking of Value Added |
|---|---|---|---|---|---|
| Merck & Co., Inc. | MRK | 217,580,000,000 | 27,571,200,000 | 191,488,800,000 | 11 |
| Microsoft | MSFT | 1,040,000,000,000 | 102,567,400,000 | 944,802,600,000 | 1 |
| Nike, Inc. | NKE | 128,160,000,000 | 7,200,000,000 | 121,250,000,000 | 19 |
| Pfizer Inc. | PFE | 192,730,000,000 | 62,653,500,000 | 138,866,500,000 | 17 |
| Procter & Gamble | PG | 289,760,000,000 | 46,359,700,000 | 248,540,300,000 | 6 |
| The Travelers Companies, Inc. | TRV | 38,130,000,000 | 25,416,345,600 | 13,503,654,400 | 28 |
| UnitedHealth Group | UNH | 231,460,000,000 | 53,238,046,800 | 187,341,953,200 | 14 |
| United Technologies Corporation | UTX | 110,050,000,000 | 41,131,233,000 | 72,788,767,000 | 24 |
| Verizon | VZ | 229,470,000,000 | 56,498,400,000 | 175,551,600,000 | 15 |
| Visa Inc. | V | 394,760,000,000 | 23,611,800,000 | 371,138,200,000 | 4 |
| Walmart Inc. | WMT | 300,470,000,000 | 82,165,500,000 | 230,794,500,000 | 8 |
| Walgreens Boots | WBA | 46,810,000,000 | 24,430,096,000 | 23,888,904,000 | 27 |
| Walt Disney Company | DIS | 244,140,000,000 | 75,692,000,000 | 188,618,000,000 | 12 |

book value, respectively. Column 5 presents MVA for the Dow Jones 30 company. The last column in the table presents the ranking in terms of absolute value of MVA.

### 1.4.2 *Why not measure performance by some other criterion?*

Many possible criteria can be used to evaluate firm performance. Total sales, the growth rate of the firm, market share, management's strategy, or earnings per share frequently are suggested as bases for evaluating and analyzing firms. We argue, however, that shareholder wealth is the best measure of firm performance for several reasons.

First, shareholder wealth is an objective, market-determined measure. It is not subject to manipulation (except in violation of securities laws)[2] or limited to subjective evaluation. The value of a firm's stock is based on the joint decision of many investors, who generally are forward-looking and trade in markets that determine unbiased prices.

Second, any accounting performance measure (such as sales, earnings, or firm growth) is vulnerable to distortion by accounting principles, whose application may be somewhat subjective (such as when to recognize revenue or how quickly to depreciate assets). Rather than present an unbiased view of firm performance, accounting statements may be oriented toward the perspective that management wants to present. Additionally, accounting-based performance measures are always *historical.* They tell us where the firm has been. In contrast, shareholder wealth is a forward-looking measure, incorporating the market's objective assessment of the firm's prospects for the future.

Third, growth for the sake of growth or merely to increase market share may have dangerous long-run implications. It would be folly to invest scarce capital in plant, equipment, and workers with no plan for how these investments will pay for themselves and return capital (plus interest) to the financial markets. The firm may win the short-term market-share battle but lose the long-term war as poor returns on investments hurt its ability to raise capital, repay loans, and pay bills and workers. The firm may find it difficult to maintain

---

[2] *Ibid.*

its short-sighted market-share gains as leaner and more financially responsible rivals counterattack at the firm's weak points to reclaim their lost customers. Thus, sacrificing financial value for market share does not lead to successful, long-term business. Maximizing shareholder value does.

Fourth, a shareholder wealth orientation ensures adequate consideration of risk in a firm's decisions. A basic principle of finance is the risk/return tradeoff. Higher risk investments must offer higher expected returns; otherwise, investors will purchase assets that offer the same return with less risk, or a higher return for the same risk.[3] Projects that attempt to increase a firm's earnings or cash flow may favorably affect the *size* and *timing* of cash flows, but they may ignore the *risk* component. Increases in a firm's exposure to risk, even in the face of rising earnings, may lead to a *lower* firm and shareholder value. Attempts to maximize returns without considering risk may harm the firm's long-run viability and value to shareholders, creditors, and employees.

Fifth, shareholder value is the best performance measure because it represents the firm's performance from the perspective of those who have their capital most at risk — namely, its owners. Bond holders or bankers are not owners, but creditors; they receive their interest and principal payments before shareholders receive any cash from the firm. Although a very important component of any successful firm, employees resemble creditors; in exchange for their labor, they receive income from the firm's owners. Overemphasizing customer quality, satisfaction, or service may lead to happy customers, but uncontrolled cost increases to meet these needs without sufficient revenues may ultimately lead to the firm's demise. Lenders, fearing nonpayment, may cut off lines of credit; employees, fearing cutbacks, may leave to take others jobs; and the financial market, upset with the firm's poor use of capital, may downgrade its value, harming its owners.[4]

Focusing on shareholder value rectifies all of these potential problems. Smart managers make decisions to service customers in a

[3]Chapters 5, 10, and 11 examine risk more closely. Some related evidence from the financial markets is discussed in Chapters 7 and 8.

[4]Methods by which to evaluate the attractiveness of different strategies and projects are discussed in Chapter 9.

cost-efficient manner. They treat and pay employees fairly; otherwise, unmotivated and unhappy employees become unproductive, cost-increasing employees who prevent the firm from satisfying its goals. By focusing on firm value, managers work to maintain stable relationships with financing sources so funds will be available to finance future growth or retrenchment needs.

Some may wonder whether focusing on shareholder wealth may be detrimental to the nonfinancial aspects of the firm. Quite the opposite, focusing on shareholder wealth is the best means of helping the long-term survival of the firm in a dynamic, global economy. Shareholder value simultaneously considers all of the influences on the firm; decisions that are made to maximize shareholder wealth reflect the best interests of all of the firm's constituents or stakeholders.

In particular, decisions to maximize shareholder wealth may benefit employees. Managers realize that a happy, stable work force both increases productivity and reduces costs. Human resource departments of firms often conduct studies to compare the benefits and costs of offering programs to meet workers' needs. For example, an on-site day care center for workers' preschool-aged children can benefit both the employees and shareholders by reducing employee absenteeism and job turnover. Similarly, innovations in flexible worker scheduling and career planning can add value to the firm by reducing employee turnover and the subsequent costs of hiring and training new workers. Wellness programs encourage healthy eating and exercise habits among employees and can reduce both absenteeism costs and health insurance premiums. Workers for some firms periodically leave the factory and visit customers to learn more about customers' needs. This results in better motivated workers who can appreciate the importance of their job to the customer.

Shareholder wealth as a measure of firm performance is objective and forward-looking, and it incorporates all influences on the firm and its stakeholders. No other measure of firm performance is so inclusive and practical as a means for evaluating a firm's strategies.

### 1.4.3 *What about ethics?*

Critics frequently argue that emphasizing shareholder wealth may lead managers to focus on quick fixes to problems, even resorting to unethical behavior in an effort to maintain firm value. Remember, however, that today's stock prices mainly reflect expectations about future cash flows. Some managers do make decisions to ignore product quality, worker safety, the well-being of communities, or use deceitful selling practices. As long as these practices are not discovered or publicized, they may help keep shareholder value higher than it should be. But let's take a closer look at this accusation.

Emphasizing shareholder value as a performance measure probably does not affect such abusive practices. Unethical managers will make improper decisions regardless of the performance measure. By inflating firm revenues, keeping costs artificially low, or diverting scarce resources to less productive uses, unethical practices would improve virtually any performance measure. Thus, to blame ethical lapses on financial measures of firm performances is inappropriate.

In fact, focusing on firm value may help to keep management's eyes on the longer-term consequences of their actions. Firms engaged in unethical or careless behavior run the danger of exposure. Such revelations can harm the firm's reputations and shareholder value for extended periods, as customers and employees feel their trust has been violated. Recent examples include Union Carbide (Bhopal gas leak), Drexel Burnham Lambert (Dennis Levine and the insider trading scandal), Salomon Brothers (government bond auction improprieties), E. F. Hutton (check-kiting) and Archer Daniels Midland (alleged price-fixing). The consequent bad publicity and legal proceedings can continue to depress a firm's performance well into the future. Typically, the risk of having unethical behavior exposed is not worth the minimal additional return it may offer. In fact, some evidence suggests that firms with a social conscience may gain more in the marketplace.[5]

### 1.4.4 *Criterion for nonpublic firms*

An obvious question to ask is which criterion to employ for organizations that have no observable market prices (for example, a small, closely held company or a nonprofit organization). The answer lies in the characteristics that causes any productive asset to have value. Management needs to balance the risks, timing, and sizes of the organization's cash flows to maximize what the decision maker

[5]See J. Martin, "Good Citizenship is Good Business," *Fortune*, 1994, pp. 15–16.

believes would be the market value of the owners' equity if it were traded in the financial markets.

Owner-managers of small firms face a different situation, however. Since they own their firms, they seek to maintain their own wealth, but this wealth may defy clear expression in dollar terms. Nonmonetary benefits may be personally important to the owner-manager, such as maintaining control of the firm, keeping the business in the family, or having adequate leisure time. From a purely monetary perspective, the owner-manager may not be maximizing the financial wealth of the firm, but as the owners, they have to answer only to themselves as long as they make timely payments to their creditors and employees! Their decisions will attempt to maximize their total personal wealth, which includes both monetary and nonmonetary components.

## 1.5 Corporate Governance

Suppose that a large corporation has several billions of dollars of cash. It is not investing it in the firm; it is not increasing its dividends; it is not repurchasing shares of outstanding stock. It is just sitting on it, investing it in short-term securities. Management argues that the cash is needed as a "cushion" against difficult times ahead in the next recession. Is this thinking in line with shareholder wealth maximization?

Next, consider the case of a corporation's CEO who has total compensation one year of over $100 million. How does this pay package help maximize shareholder wealth?

In many firms, particularly large corporations, people other than the owners make the business decisions. In other words, there is a separation of ownership and control. Professional managers, not the shareholders, control the operations, determine corporate strategies, and put together the compensation package. This arrangement may result in a special kind of ethics problem if managers make choices to benefit themselves rather than shareholders.

### 1.5.1 *The principal-agent problem*

The principals, or owners of the firm, hire agents, or managers, to run the firm in the best interests of the principals. But ethical

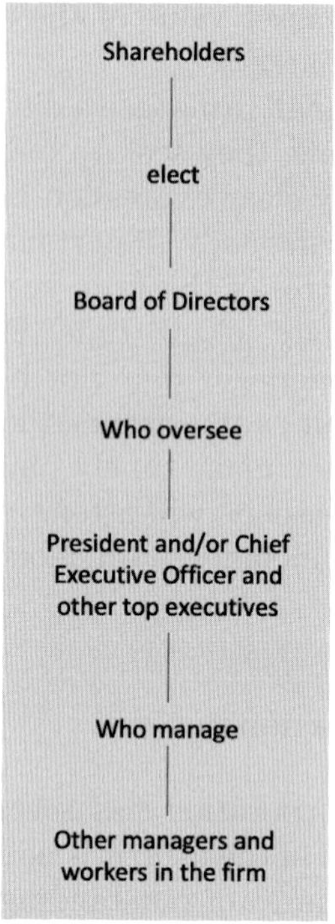


Figure 1.3 A Typical Organization Chart for a Corporation.

lapses, self-interest, or the owners' lack of trust in the managers can lead to conflicts of interest and suspicions between the two parties. This problem in corporate governance is called the principal-agent problem.

As outlined in Figure 1.3, the shareholders of a firm elect a board of directors. In theory, the board's role is to oversee managers and ensure that they are working in the best interests of the shareholders. In practice, however, the board often has a closer relationship with management than with the shareholders. For example, it is not unusual for the firm's top executives to sit on the firm's board of directors, and the firm's top executives often nominate candidates for board sets. These relationships can obscure loyalties and make the board a toothless watchdog for shareholders' interests.

Managers, acting as agents, may pursue their own self-interest by increasing their salaries, the size of their staffs, or their perquisites (better known as "perks"), which might include club memberships and use of company planes or luxurious company cars. Managements, in conjunction with the board, may seek to fend off takeovers that would allow shareholders to sell their shares at a price above the current market price, or they may try to preempt such merger or acquisition attempts by seeking changes in the corporate charter that would make such takeovers difficult to pursue. Examples of such delaying tactics, proxy defenses, or poison pills include:

- Provisions that require super-majorities (for example, two-thirds) of existing shareholders to approve any takeover;
- The decision to place some, rather than all, board sets up for election ever year, thus delaying the ability of an acquirer to control the firm;
- Provisions to allow the board to authorize and issue large quantities of stock or to repurchase outstanding bonds in the event of a takeover attempt;
- Provisions that stipulate expensive payouts to existing managers in the face of any successful buyout;
- The establishment of advance notice requirements, so shareholders must meet deadlines for presenting business or director nominations at shareholder meetings; and
- Restrictions on the ability of shareholders to call special meetings.[6]

Some managers also may try to use their privileged access to private information about the firm for their own personal gain. By buying shares of stock before good news is announced and selling it prior to the release of bad news, insider trading allows them to profit inordinately as compared to the market as a whole. Such actions are illegal in the U.S., but it is sometimes difficult to prove that an executive's stock purchases or sales were caused by his or her access to private information.

Because of these difficulties, the principal-agent problem imposes agency costs on shareholders. Agency costs are the tangible and intangible expenses borne by shareholders because of the self-serving actions of managers. Agency costs can be explicit, out-of-pocket expenses (sometimes called direct agency costs) or more implicit ones

[6]See V. Anand, "New Proxy Defenses Gain Popularity," *Pensions and Investments*, 1995, p. 9.

(sometimes called implicit agency costs). Examples of explicit agency costs include:

- the costs of auditing financial statements to verify their accuracy;
- the purchase of liability insurance for board members and top managers;
- the monitoring of managers' actions by the board or by independent consultants.

Implicit agency costs include restrictions placed against managerial actions (e.g., the requirement of shareholder votes for some major decisions) and covenants or restrictions placed on the firm by a lender. Such covenants are placed on the firm to protect the lender's position and to ensure that available cash flow will be directed to repay the loan.

The end result of self-serving behaviors by management and shareholder attempts to limit them is a reduction in firm value. Investors will not pay as much for the firm's stock because they realize that the principal-agent problem and its attendant costs lower the firm's value. Agency costs will decline, and firm value will rise, as principals' trust and confidence in their agents rises. We will discuss some ways of reducing agency costs in the next section.

### 1.5.2 *Reducing agency problems*

Two basic approaches can be used to mitigate the consequences of managers making self-serving decisions. First, their incentives can be aligned to more closely match those of shareholders. Second, closer oversight and increased information flows to owners can make managers more accountable.

#### 1.5.2.1 *Incentives*

Agency problems decline in owner-controlled firms. When owners manage the firm, there is no conflict with agents! Consequently, firms will be managed to better maximize the wealth of the owners. Thus, one way to help managers make decisions that are in shareholders' best interests is to relate the managers' personal wealth to shareholder value. Some firms require top managers to purchase sizable portions of company stock. Others tie managerial compensation to stock performance, often by awarding managers stock options as part of their compensation. The option allows managers to purchase, at a future time, a stated number of the firm's shares at a specific price. If the firm's stock price rises, the value of the shares, and therefore the managers' wealth, also rises. Decisions that detract from the best interest of shareholders will affect management by making the stock options less valuable. More and more firms are basing the compensation of their top managers on the firm's stock price. This trend is also spreading to non-U.S. firms as well.

Business periodicals and the press usually publicize the largest CEO salaries for the previous year; such salaries can reach \$20, \$30, and \$50 million or more.[7] However, the news reports often fail to recognize that much of this CEO income comes from exercising stock options. A CEO can make a lot of money on stock options if he or she performs the job well and raises the stock price. Big headlines were made in 1994 when it was announced that Michael Eisner, the CEO of Walt Disney Company, had 1993 compensation of \$203,010,590, the highest ever for an executive. In the case of Eisner, he took over Disney when it was experiencing severe marketing and financial trouble. He worked to turn the company around and develop new animated films and marketing strategies. The resulting increase in the price of Disney stock increased the wealth of Disney's shareholders and the value of Eisner's stock options also dramatically rose.

There are some questions of ethics regarding such pay packages. Compensation packages typically are negotiated with the firm's board of directors. If there is a lack of independence and oversight on the board, it may be a weak negotiator and overly generous in designing stock option compensation schemes. Some studies have shown that the size of executive compensation packages is growing more rapidly than share price performance, and that executive compensation is more a function of firm size than its stock performance. International studies also have shown that American and British executives earn relatively more than their executive counterparts in other countries. But recent trends in European corporations show that their executives are receiving more stock options. Some also are

---

[7]See, for example, J. A. Byrne, "CEO Pay: Ready for Takeoff," *Business Week*, 1995, pp. 88–119.

receiving higher paychecks, which has resulted in protests by workers and some politicians.

Other methods also exist to align managers' incentives with shareholder value. One way is to allow an innovative manager to become the top officer of a corporate subsidiary. This decentralizes the management structure and can increase managers' accountability and entrepreneurial behavior. Thermo Electron Corporation "spins out" new companies when managers develop interesting new product ideas. Thermo Electron retains majority ownership in the new enterprise and offers new stock to the public. The manager of the new subsidiary can use the proceeds of the stock sale to finance research or engineering studies and to develop and market a new product. The employees responsible for the original idea can run their own firm and benefit from any subsequent increases in shareholder value.

Taking agent ownership to the next level, employee ownership can help align the incentives of all the firm's workers with those of the shareholders. Employee stock ownership plans (ESOPs), if correctly implemented, can make all employees think and act like owners. As part of the ESOP, employee participation groups (comprised of members elected by fellow employees) meet regularly to discuss ways to increase productivity and the firm's value and, therefore, the value of the employees' stake. About 10,000 firms, many of them privately owned, currently have ESOPs in place.

ESOPs can be difficult to implement for an international firm. Some countries ban stock options or limit ownership of foreign shares. For a firm residing in such a country, an ESOP plan needs to be designed to meet specific, local requirements.

#### 1.5.2.2 *Monitoring and increased information flows*

Another means of reducing agency problems is to increase managers' accountability. ESOPs help to monitor managers' actions and self-interest. As owners, employees receive regular financial updates about the firm, sometimes monthly. Information and ideas are exchanged at employee participation groups to inform workers/owners about the condition of their company.

Some firms are taking steps to draw on the strengths and expertise of their boards. Firms seem to be increasing the number of independent directors (i.e., individuals who are not part of the firm's management) on their boards. Such independent directors may be more inclined to carefully analyze management's strategies and proposals and their effects on shareholder value.

Board members usually serve on committees that review management's actions. Compensation committees sometimes have exacerbated agency problems in the past by offering overly generous executive pay packages. More compensation committees now are using outside consultants to recommend levels of executive pay, options, and benefits.

The Securities and Exchange Commission (SEC), a major U.S. regulatory body that oversees financial markets, is examining its executive pay disclosure rules. To help keep shareholders informed on compensation matters, it may soon require that shareholder reports include information on how executive pay packages are determined. This change probably would increase the use of outside, independent consultants to set appropriate levels of management compensation.

Meanwhile, major institutional investors, such as pension funds and mutual funds, are becoming more vocal investors. Some are taking active roles in overseeing the performance of the companies in which they hold stock by requesting meetings with management, criticizing management actions, and suggesting shareholder votes on issues of importance to the firm. A wide, dispersed base of individual shareholders can leave managers with a loss of discretion in running the firm, but if vocal institutional investors own a large portion of outstanding shares, management may pay more attention to issue of importance to shareholders.

Other countries also are moving toward greater disclosure of management compensation information. In 1993, firms listed on the Toronto Stock Exchange were required to list the individual compensation they paid to their CEOs and the next four highest paid officers. In addition, stockholders in a firm now receive information on its stock performance, as well as information on the performance of a stock market index and the shares of comparable firms.

Institutional oversight of management has been common in several countries outside of the U.S. for some time, For example, in Japan, commercial banks, other financial institutions, and corporations own a majority of the stock of Japanese firms, including the firms' supplier and major customers; a similar situation also exists in Germany. Representatives of these investors typically sit on a firm's board to oversee management's actions, give advice, and maintain smooth working relationships between the firm, its constituents, and the financial markets. Compared with the U.S., agency problems are less acute in such countries.

In summary, the principal-agent problem arises when owners aren't managers. In the next section, we discuss the various ways the U.S. firms can be organized. As part of our discussion, we examine the capital-raising implications and the agency cost consideration of these different organizational forms.

## 1.6 Forms of Business Organizations

There are three basic ways to organize a business: as a sole proprietorship, a partnership, or a corporation. A firm's organizational form affects how it is taxed. In addition, the form of the business influences its susceptibility to agency concerns and its ability to raise capital.

### 1.6.1 *Proprietorship*

Proprietorships outnumber all other forms of business organizations in the U.S. A proprietorship is simply a business owned by the one person. Setting up a business is fairly simple and inexpensive — seldom more complicated than applying for a city or state license. All income is taxed as personal income to the proprietor. Depending on this person's filing status and income level, this can be an advantage or a disadvantage. For example, depending upon the owner's level of taxable income, a proprietorship may owe more or less tax than a corporation with the same level of taxable income.

As the firm has one owner, this person's expertise determines much of the success of the firm. If additional expertise is needed, the owner must hire someone. The life of the proprietorship ends when the owner dies; in general, a proprietorship is not an asset that can be easily valued and sold.

Agency costs are nil in proprietorships, as the manager is the owner, and he or she presumably will make decisions that reflect his or her best interests. The ability to raise capital is limited to the owner's personal wealth and credit line (although generous friends or relatives may help him or her).

Proprietorships have unlimited liability, which makes the proprietor solely responsible for all debts of the business. Should bankruptcy occur, the owner's personal assets — financial holdings, cars, house — may be forfeited to settle any debts. Losses may exceed what the proprietor has invested in the firm.

### 1.6.2 *Partnerships*

A partnership brings two or more individuals together to invest their time, energy, and talents to the firm. Organizing a partnership is relatively simple, although some legal documents may be needed to spell out the percentage ownership, rights, and duties of each partner. By drawing on the strengths of two or more individuals, each can specialize in his or her own area to help the firm achieve success. Also, the combined financial resources of two or more individuals may increase the firm's ability to raise and borrow capital.

As with a proprietorship, partnership income is taxable to each partner at his or her own personal tax rate. The partnership ends upon the death of any partner; unless other arrangements have been made, firm assets may need to be sold to settle the deceased partner's estate.

As the partners presumably manage their firms, agency costs can be zero, as long as they agree on the firm's goals, work together amicably, and trust and respect each other as professionals. Should intractable differences of opinion or suspicions arise, arguments, and even court battles, can result.

Partnerships suffer from other drawbacks. As with a proprietorship, it is difficult to value and transfer ownership in a partnership. In addition, partners are jointly and severally liable for the debts of the partnership. That means each partner may have to pay more than his or her proportional ownership share to settle the firm's debts in case of failure. Each partner has unlimited liability. Anyone thinking of joining a partnership should seriously consider the risk.

The liability risks just noted describe a general partnership. A limited partnership addresses the liability concern by identifying at least one general partner as having unlimited liability; the remaining limited partners face liability limited to their investment in the firm, in other words, their personal assets cannot be demanded to settle the firm's debts. However, they also are limited in that they cannot participate in the operations of the firm. Operating decisions may be made only by the general partners.

### 1.6.3 *Corporations*

Proprietorships are the most numerous forms of business organizations, but in terms of market value, corporations are the dominant form. A corporation is a legal person in the eyes of the law, separate in concept from its owners and managers. As a person, it has rights, duties, privileges, and obligations.

We've already reviewed some of the agency problems that can arise when owners and managers are not the same people. However, the corporate organizational form has several advantages, as well.

As a separate legal entity, its life does not depend on that of its owners. Unlike a proprietorship or partnership, the death of a shareholder does not force the corporation to stop doing business. Shares of ownership in the corporation, especially those listed on stock exchanges such as the New York Stock Exchange, can be traded at easily discernible prices.[8] Issuing shares gives a corporation access to much larger pools of capital than a partnership or proprietorship. As a legal entity, it can borrow money in its own name. Also, as owners of a corporation have limited liability, the most they can lose is their investment.

A major disadvantage of the corporate organizational form is the taxation of earnings. Depending upon the income level, corporate income may be taxed at higher rates that proprietor or partnership income. In addition, corporate dividends are taxed twice. As corporations pay dividends from after-tax earnings, they represent funds that have been taxed once at the corporate level. Investors than pay taxes on these dividends again, as part of their personal income.

Two special forms of corporate organization in the U.S. allow dividends to escape double taxation. A Subchapter S corporation (named for the section of the tax code that discusses this organization) must have fewer than 35 shareholders, none of which is another

[8] Shares of small corporations or corporations that are not listed on stock exchanges may be fairly difficult to value and trade, just as partnership interests are.

corporation. Income from a Subchapter S corporation flows untaxed to the shareholders; thus, it is taxed only once as personal income of the shareholders.

A limited liability company (LLC) organizational form has been authorized by the laws of more than 35 states as the end of 1995. Similar to a Subchapter 5 corporation, it offers owners limited liability and its income is taxed only once as personal income of the shareholder. Unlike a Subchapter 5 corporation, however, an LLC can have an unlimited number of shareholders, including other corporations. The LLC can sell shares without completing the costly and time-consuming process of registering them with the SEC, which is a requirement for standard corporations that sell their securities to the public. The LLC structure has drawbacks in that, should an owner leave, all others must formally agree to continue the firm. Also, all of the LLC's owners must take active roles in managing the company. To protect partners from unlimited liability, some partnerships, including large accounting firms such as Coopers & Lybrand, Ernest & Young, and Price Waterhouse, having changed their organizational form to LLC.

Many countries' laws recognize the corporate form of organization. U.S. corporations may use the suffixes "Inc." or "Corp." to designate themselves. British corporations use the suffix "PLC," for public limited company, in which limited refers to shareholders' liability in the firm. The suffix "AG" following the names of firms in Germany, Austria, Switzerland, or Liechtenstein is an abbreviation for Aktiengesellschaft, which means corporation. Some countries allow corporations to sell bearer shares, which allow the owners to remain anonymous. A history of social upheavals, wars, and high taxation in Europe led to the evolution of bearer shares to allow owners to remain anonymous and thus escape taxation from their governments or identification if their governments were overthrown. Suffixes of "NV" (Naamioze Vennotschap) in the Netherlands and "SA" (Societe Anonyme) in France and Belgium designate such firms.

It is up to the firm's owners to weigh the pros and cons and determine which organizational form best suits the needs of their firm. As we've seen, each has its own implications for taxation, control by the owners, ability to trade ownership positions, limitations on liability, firm life, and raising capital.

## 1.7 Tax Rates

The rate at which income is taxed depends upon the organizational form, typically corporate versus noncorporate. But how income to a proprietorship or member of partnership is taxed depends upon the individual's situation, such as if they are married or single.

For individuals, some examples of 2018 tax rates are shown in Table 1.2. The combined state and federal tax rate is shown in Table 1.3.

### 1.7.1 *Average and marginal tax rates*

The average tax rate is the tax bill of a firm divided by its earnings before income taxes (i.e., pretax income). For individuals, it is their tax bill divided by their taxable income. In either case, it represents the percentage of total taxable income that is paid in taxes. The marginal tax rate represents the proportion of each additional

Table 1.2 Personal Income Tax Rate.

| **Federal Tax Brackets: 2018 Tax Brackets (For Taxes Due April 15, 2019)** | | |
|---|---|---|
| **Tax Rate (%)** | **Single ($)** | **Head of Household ($)** |
| 10 | Up to 9,525 | Up to 13,600 |
| 12 | 9,526 to 38,700 | 13,601 to 51,800 |
| 22 | 38,701 to 82,500 | 51,801 to 82,500 |
| 24 | 82,501 to 157,500 | 82,501 to 157,500 |
| 32 | 157,501 to 200,000 | 157,501 to 200,000 |
| 35 | 200,001 to 500,000 | 200,001 to 500,000 |
| 37 | 500,001 or more | 500,001 or more |
| **Tax Rate** | **Married Filing Jointly or Qualifying Widow** | **Married Filing Separately** |
| 10 | Up to 19,050 | Up to 9,525 |
| 12 | 19,051 to 77,400 | 9,525 to 38,700 |
| 22 | 77,401 to 165,000 | 38,701 to 82,500 |
| 24 | 165,001 to 315,000 | 82,501 to 157,000 |
| 32 | 315,001 to 400,000 | 157,001 to 200,000 |
| 35 | 400,001 to 600,000 | 200,001 to 300,000 |
| 37 | 600,001 or more | 300,001 or more |

Table 1.3 Corporate Combined State and Federal Tax Rate.

| State | Corporate Tax Rate (%) | Combined States and Federal Corporate Tax Rate (%) |
|---|---|---|
| Alabama* | 6.5 | 25.1 |
| Alaska | 9.4 | 28.4 |
| Arizona | 4.9 | 24.9 |
| Arkansas | 6.5 | 26.1 |
| California | 8.8 | 28.0 |
| Colorado | 4.6 | 24.7 |
| Connecticut | 8.3 | 27.5 |
| Delaware | 8.7 | 27.9 |
| District of Columbia | 9.0 | 28.1 |
| Florida | 5.5 | 25.3 |
| Georgia | 6.0 | 25.7 |
| Hawaii | 6.4 | 26.1 |
| Idaho | 7.4 | 26.8 |
| Illinois | 9.5 | 28.5 |
| Indiana | 6.0 | 25.7 |
| Iowa* | 12.0 | 29.5 |
| Kansas | 7.0 | 26.5 |
| Kentucky | 6.0 | 25.7 |
| Louisiana* | 8.0 | 26.0 |
| Maine | 8.9 | 28.1 |
| Maryland | 8.3 | 27.5 |
| Massachusetts | 8.0 | 27.3 |
| Michigan | 6.0 | 25.7 |
| Minnesota | 9.8 | 28.7 |
| Mississippi | 5.0 | 25.0 |
| Missouri* | 6.3 | 25.4 |
| Montana | 6.8 | 26.3 |
| Nebraska | 7.8 | 27.2 |
| Nevada | 0.0 | 21.0 |
| New Hampshire | 8.2 | 27.5 |
| New Jersey | 9.0 | 28.1 |
| New Mexico | 5.9 | 25.7 |
| New York | 6.5 | 26.1 |
| North Carolina | 3.0 | 23.4 |
| North Dakota | 4.3 | 24.4 |
| Ohio | 0.0 | 21.0 |
| Oklahoma | 6.0 | 25.7 |
| Oregon | 7.6 | 27.0 |
| Pennsylvania | 9.99 | 28.9 |
| Rhode Island | 7.0 | 26.5 |

(*Continued*)

Table 1.3 (*Continued*)

| State | Corporate Tax Rate (%) | Combined States and Federal Corporate Tax Rate (%) |
|---|---|---|
| South Carolina | 5.0 | 25.0 |
| South Dakota | 0.0 | 21.0 |
| Tennessee | 6.5 | 26.1 |
| Texas | 0.0 | 21.0 |
| Utah | 5.0 | 25.0 |
| Vermont | 8.5 | 27.7 |
| Virginia | 6.0 | 25.7 |
| Washington | 0.0 | 21.0 |
| West Virginia | 6.5 | 26.1 |
| Wisconsin | 7.9 | 27.2 |
| Wyoming | 0.0 | 21.0 |
| **Average** | **6.3** | **25.9** |
| **Weighted Average** | **6.0** | **25.7** |

*Note*: *State allows a deduction against taxable income for federal liability.
*Source*: Tax Foundation (https://taxfoundation.org/us-corporate-income-tax-more-competitive/).

dollar of income that the government claims as taxes. The "tax rate" column in Table 1.2 shows the marginal tax rates for individuals at different income levels; Table 1.3 shows the combined state and federal tax rate.

## 1.8 Outline of the Book

This text discusses both the theory and practice of financial management. Where possible, we present perspectives of practicing financial managers. We also relate the finance function to the other functional areas of business to help you appreciate the interrelationships of the business specialties within the firm. We address global issues where appropriate to infuse an international perspective in the chapters. Firms of all sizes and organizational firms are doing business globally, so we hope to prepare you for this stimulating and challenging trend. This book uses an active, instead of passive, approach to teach finance, which has been discussed in Chapter 9 of Lee (2017). Lee and Lee (2017) also used active approach to discuss financial analysis, planning, and forecasting.

Part I of the text, "Overview and Background," began with this chapter; it continues in the succeeding two chapters. Chapter 2 discusses information and the environment for financial management, and Chapter 3 discusses developing a long-term financial plan.

Part II, "Valuation Principles and Applications," presents the time value of money concepts that underline all financial analysis. Many practical examples show how to apply these tools to common business and personal situations. Chapter 4 investigates the concepts and methods of present value. Chapter 5 discusses how present value concepts can be used to evaluate bonds, stocks, and preferred stocks.

Part III, "Capital Budgeting and Risk Return Trade-off," continues to discuss the application of time value money concepts in the context of the firm's capital budgeting process. These chapters review tools for analyzing a firm's investments, as well as methods for evaluating a project's cash flow and risk. Chapter 6 discusses capital budgeting under certainty, and Chapter 7 shows how risk can be estimated and the basic concepts of portfolio analysis. Chapter 8 discusses risk and return trade-off analysis and capital asset pricing model. Finally, Chapter 9 discusses capital budgeting under uncertainty.

Part IV, "Cost of Capital, Financing Choices, and Dividend Decisions," reviews the costs to the firm of raising funds in the financial markets for investments in its projects. These chapters discuss issues relevant to determining an appropriate financing mix for the firm. They also examine issues surrounding the firm's decision to issue dividends. Chapter 10 discusses the cost of capital, Chapter 11 talks about capital structure and valuation, Chapter 12 discusses the dividend puzzle, and Chapter 13 discusses the interactions of investment, dividend, and financing policies.

Part V, "Long-term Financing," discusses long-term financing related to issuing bonds, common stock, and preferred stock. Options, warrants, and convertible securities are also presented in this part. In addition, leasing financing is discussed this in this part. Chapter 14 discusses long-term debt financing, Chapter 15 talks about common stock, preferred stock, and financing decisions, and Chapter 16 discusses warrants and convertible securities. Finally, the theory and practice of leasing is discussed in Chapter 17.

Part VI, "Short-term Financing and Financial Planning," examines some of the day-to-day operating issues that financial managers face. These include managing a firm's cash, factors that affect its credit policy, and sources of short-term financing. Chapter 18 discusses short-term financial analysis and planning. Credit, cash, marketable securities, and inventory management are all talked about in Chapter 19. Short-term financing is discussed in Chapter 20, and Chapter 21 talks about financial planning and strategy.

Part VII, "Options, Futures, and Corporate Finance," discusses the use of financial options and other financial derivative instruments to manage the risks faced by the firm. Portfolio insurance and synthetic options are also discussed in this part. Options, futures, swaps, and risk management are discussed in Chapter 22. Option pricing theory and firm valuation are talked about in Chapter 23. Finally, Chapter 24 explores portfolio insurance and synthetic options.

Part VIII, "Other Topics," discusses other important subject in financial management. Mergers and divestitures are discussed in Chapter 25. Bankruptcy, workouts, and corporate reorganization is explored in Chapter 26. Finally, international financial management is discussed in Chapter 27.

## 1.9 Summary

Finance plays an integral role in helping to determine a firm's strategy, which assets it should purchase, how it should raise funds, and how it should manage the firm's working capital accounts. The value of a firm is determined by the size, timing, and risk of its cash flows.

The goal of a firm is to maximize shareholder wealth. This is an objective, future-oriented measure of a firm's performance that incorporates perspectives from all of the firm's constituencies. Future chapters build upon this concept as we examine how to practically apply financial concepts.

Agency problems can result from self-serving managers who focus more on their own interests than on maximizing shareholders' wealth. Several means of mitigating and correcting these agency problems are available, including restructuring managers' incentives, monitoring managers' actions, and increasing information flows. Ross *et al.* (2019) and Lee and Lee (2022) have explained these issues in further details.

The three most basic forms of business organization are the proprietorship, the partnership, and the corporate form. The financial implications and concerns differ for each form, as do the tax consequences.

## References

Lee, C.-F. *From East to West: Memoirs of a Finance Professor on Academia, Practice, and Policy* (World Scientific, Singapore, 2017).

Lee, C.-F. and A. C. Lee. *Encyclopedia of Finance*, 3rd edn. (Springer, 2022, Forthcoming).

Lee, C.-F. and J. C. Lee. *Financial Analysis, Planning and Forecasting*, 3rd edn. (World Scientific, Singapore, 2017).

Ross, S., R. Westerfield, J. Jaffe, and B. Jordan. *Corporate Finance*, 12th edn. (McGraw-Hill Education, 2019).

## Questions and Problems

1. Why is it important to have a broad business perspective, rather than a narrow one, when using financial tools to examine business problems?
2. What affects the value of an asset?
3. How would you respond to someone who argues: "The proper way to evaluate management is to see how closely it follows its stated strategy?"
4. Are the *Fortune* 500 rankings, based upon firms' sales revenues, a good measure of firm success? Why or why not?
5. "It is inappropriate to focus on financial measures of success. We can only evaluate a firm's performance by seeing how it treats its workers, its customers, and the environment, and by observing the ethical standards of its management and work force." Do you agree or disagree? Explain.
6. What are the implications for agency costs, taxes, and capital raising for the proprietorship, partnership, and limited partnership organizational forms?
7. Why might some businesses consider Subchapter S Corporation and the limited liability company organizational forms advantageous over the corporate form? What advantages does the corporate form have over them?

8. Why might some argue that agency problems are less of a concern in Germany and Japan? How might close relationships between firms and their bankers and suppliers affect shareholder wealth?
9. How does executive compensation — both its amount and its form — relate to the principal-agent problem? What are some ways of reducing agency costs with respect to executive compensation issues?
10. "Unethical managers are responsible for the agency problem." Do you agree or disagree? Explain.
11. A new CEO is quoted as saying, "I want people I know and trust sitting on my board. There's nothing wrong with corporate officers, friends, and family being on the board. They know the business better than some outsider." Do you agree or disagree? Explain.

Chapter 2

# Information and Environment for Financial Management

## Contents

## 2.1 Introduction

Economic, financial, market, and accounting information is important in understanding and applying sound financial management. For the financial decision-maker, financial management is central in tying together national economic policies with individual financial decisions made at the firm level. In turn, the financial decisions made at the firm level affect both the real (product) markets as well as the financial (capital) markets.

In Section 2.2, we discuss economic policies and information. In Section 2.3, financial market information is discussed. A brief review of financial statements is given in Section 2.4. A critique of accounting information is offered in Section 2.5. In Section 2.6, an analysis of static ratio is provided. In Section 2.7, an analysis of cost–volume–profit (CVP) is given. The relationships among economic, financial, and accounting information is discussed in Section 2.8. And, Section 2.9 offers a summary. Appendix 2A shows how Excel can be used to calculate financial ratios. Appendix 2B discusses two possible methods to estimate sustainable growth rate (SGR). Finally, Appendix 2C shows how to compute the degree of operating leverage (DOL), degree of financial leverage (DFL), and degree of combined leverage with Excel (DCL).

## 2.2 Economic Policies and Information

National economic goals and policies affect the goals of financial management and financial decisions through real markets and financial markets as shown in Figure 2.1, which indicate the economic environment faced by a firm. The goal of financial management and financial decision making has been briefly discussed in Chapter 1. National economic goals and policies and financial market information are explored in the second and third section of this chapter.

The Employment Act of 1946 stated four main objectives for the U.S. economy:

1. Full employment
2. Economic growth

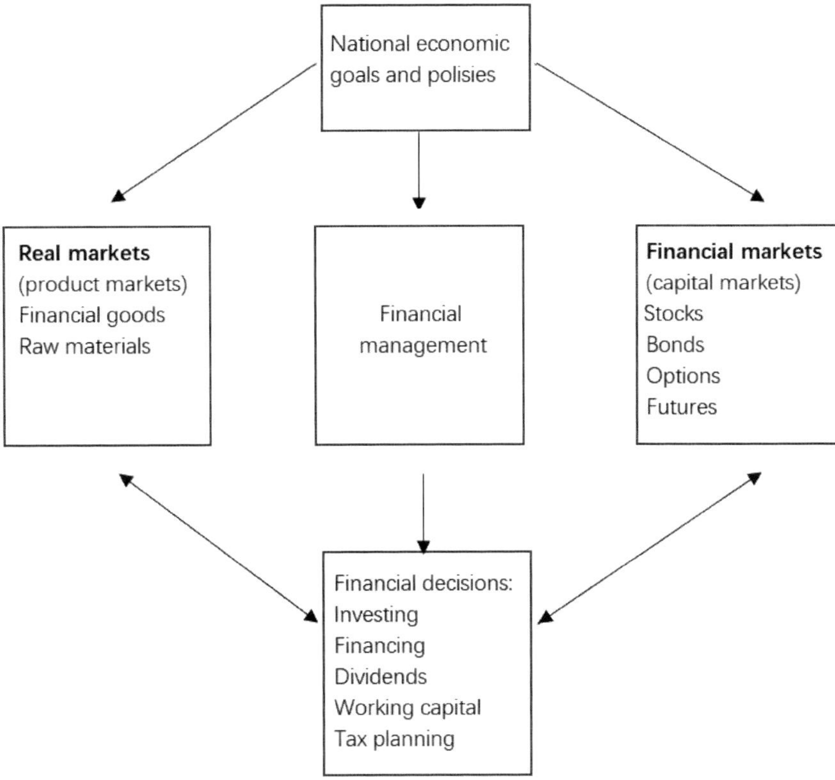


Figure 2.1 Interrelationships between Real and Financial Markets.

3. Stable price levels
4. Balanced balance of payments.

These goals were reaffirmed by the Full Employment and Balanced Growth Act of 1978, also known as the Humphrey–Hawkins Act. To achieve these goals, the branches of government have different responsibilities and tools, such as monetary policy, fiscal policy, federal deficit management, and antitrust policy.

The federal government affects economic activities through monetary and fiscal policies. The Federal Reserve System uses the discount rate, reserve requirements, and open-market operations as the basic tools with which to execute its monetary policies. The president and

Congress can jointly use tax revenue and government expenditures to manage both aggregate demand and general economic activity.

### 2.2.1 *Monetary policy*

The Federal Reserve has four instruments of credit control with which to administer monetary policy:

1. Open-market operations of repurchasing or selling government securities.
2. Determination of Federal Funds Rate.
3. Setting of reserve requirements for banks.
4. Establishment of margin requirements for carrying and purchasing financial securities.

These instruments generally are divided into two categories: (1) those that affect all financial markets and (2) those that affect specific areas of the economy. Instruments 1–3 are general tools, while instrument 4 is a selective tool.

The principal use of these instruments is to regulate the money supply defined as M1, M2, M3, and M4. M1 is the traditional definition of the money supply: currency and coin plus demand deposits (checking accounts) at commercial banks, negotiable order of withdrawal (NOW) accounts, share draft accounts (credit unions), and savings accounts that automatically transfer funds into a checking account when the checking account is overdrawn. The two components have elements of the traditional savings account but also have readily spendable characteristics.

The definition of M2 is M1 plus most forms of savings account balances plus shares in money market mutual funds. Changes in M1 and M2 directly affect interest rates and indirectly affect a firm's market value. Hence, most financial managers are interested in how these measures change over time and in the current government policy concerning these factors.

Most recently, money supply has been expanded from M1 and M2 to M3 and M4. M3 is a measure of the money supply that includes M2 as well as large time deposits, institutional money market funds, short-term repurchase agreements and larger liquid assets.

The M3 measurement includes assets that are less liquid than other components of the money supply and are referred to as "near, near money," which are more closely related to the finances of larger financial institutions and corporations than to those of small businesses and individuals.

Money supply can be defined as narrow money (M0) and broad money (M4). M0 = the level of notes and coins in circulation + banks operational balances at the Bank of England. M4 money supply is defined as a measure of notes and coins in circulation (M0) + bank accounts. It is a broader definition because it includes bank accounts and not just notes and coins in circulation.

During the 2007 and 2008 financial crisis, the Federal Reserve used open-market operations of repurchasing or selling government securities. Quantitative easing (QE1, QE2, and QE3) is continually used to save the financial market. Beginning in March 2020, in order to deal with COVID-19 the Federal Reserve cut the federal fund rate to make the short-term and long-term Treasury rate go to historical lows to save the financial market.

### 2.2.2 *Fiscal policy*

Fiscal policy involves the use of government taxing and spending to achieve a macroeconomic objective. Government taxing and spending affects both consumer and corporate income.

Taxes are either direct or indirect. Direct taxes included personal income tax and corporate income tax, both of which are important factors in determining a firm's market value and are discussed in subsequent chapters. Indirect taxes include sales tax and value added tax (VAT). These taxes generally are passed on to the ultimate consumer and have little direct effect on the firm's value.

To stimulate economic activity, the Trump administration cut both corporate and personal income tax. This resulted in a historically low U.S. unemployment rate in 2019 and a historically high stock market. Unfortunately, when COVID-19 occurred in the beginning of 2020, the unemployment rate reached a historical high. The government passed the Coronavirus Aid, Relief, and Economic Security Act (CARES Act) to help both individuals and companies.

### 2.2.3 *Leading economic indicators (LEIs)*

LEIs are economic variables whose time series reaches peaks and troughs before aggregating economic activity does. Examples are the housing industry and the heavy durables industry, such as furniture and automobiles. Generally, if activity in the housing market increases, after a short lag the general economy will follow, because the increased demand for housing will bring an increased demand for construction materials, workers, and home furnishings. The lag occurs because it takes time for the first evidence of increased housing demand (increased housing starts) to affect overall economic activity.

The National Bureau of Economic Research (NBER) publishes 47 series of economic data on leading movements in the business cycle. A *lead* must be greater than three months. Series that lead or lag economic activity by three months or less are considered coincident to the current level of economic activity. The Index of Leading Indicators consists of 12 of the 47 NBER indicators, as follows:

1. Average weekly working hours of manufacturing workers.
2. Average weekly initial claims for unemployment insurance.
3. Real value of new orders for manufacturers' consumer goods and materials.
4. Index of new business formations.
5. Index of 500 common stock prices.
6. Contracts and orders for plant and equipment in 1972 dollars.
7. Index of new private housing starts authorized by local building permits.
8. Vendor performance (the percentage of companies receiving delivery later than the industry average).
9. Net change in inventories on hand and on order in 1972 dollars.
10. Change in sensitive materials prices.
11. Change in total consumer and business credit outstanding.
12. Real money supply measure M2.

Unlike econometric modeling, the LEI approach to forecasting does not require assumptions about what causes economic behavior. Instead, it relies on statistically detected patterns among economic variables, which are used to forecast turning points in overall economic activity. In effect, using the leading indicators is a simple way to perform the difficult task of predicting the future.

The stock market crash of October 19, 1987 had a major impact on the LEI for the last quarter of 1987. The large decline in stock prices causes the index to decline substantially, which, in turn, caused consumer sentiment to turn negative. Consumers then began to cut back on their spending plans, which had an adverse economic impact on the Gross National Product (GNP) performance during the first quarter of 1988. This is an example of the importance of the LEI.

This brief overview of macroeconomics indicates that an understanding of economics is integral to the understanding of finance. For a more detailed explanation of macroeconomics can be found in any macroeconomics textbook.

## 2.3 Financial Market Information

Information from financial markets is useful in evaluating and understanding a firm's performance. Primary sources of market information are the stock market, the bond market, and the options and futures markets.

To obtain external sources of funds, a firm issue equity (stock) or debt (bonds). To do this, the firm uses such instruments as common stock, corporate bonds, preferred stock, convertible bonds, and convertible preferred stock. (Stocks and bonds are discussed in detail in Chapters 14, 15, and 16.) These instruments are issued in the private placement market or through public underwriting. Once the firm has issued these securities, they can be traded either in organized exchanges or in the less formal over-the-counter (OTC) markets. The major organized exchange, the New York Stock Exchange (NYSE) is in New York City. The OTC market is in reality a communication network and does not have a specific geographic location.

Besides the prices and values of stocks and bonds, option price quotations are also a useful source of market information. The major markets for options trading are the Chicago Board of Options Exchange (CBOE), the American Stock Exchange, the Philadelphia Stock Exchange, the Pacific Stock Exchange and the NYSE. (Options are covered in detail in Chapter 22.)

The interest rates or yields to maturity of debt claims issued by corporations also provide useful financial market information.

### 2.3.1 *The stock market*

The stock market consists of primary and secondary markets. The *primary market* for corporate stock offerings is the market in which issues of preferred stock or common stock are initially sold to investors by the firm to acquire new capital for internal uses. (The underwriting process carried out by investment banking firms is described in detail in Chapter 15.)

The *secondary market* for securities and stocks is where outstanding issues are traded between investors. Secondary issues are those which have already been sold and are being traded between current and potential owners. The proceeds from a secondary market transaction do not go to the company but to the owner (seller) of the security. The purpose of the secondary stock market (which comprises the NYSE, AMEX, and OTC) is to provide liquidity to investors who acquire securities from the primary market. Without this liquidity, the transactions of the primary market would be seriously affected and the ability of firms to acquire capital seriously handicapped because investors would be reluctant to tie up their funds in securities that are not easily convertible to cash if necessary.

### 2.3.2 *The bond market*

Bonds, like stocks, are issued at the primary level by corporations or by federal or local governments to raise long-term capital, but they are also traded in the secondary markets for the benefit of the bondholder who wants liquidity.

There are two secondary bond markets: the corporate bond market and the government bond market. Corporate bonds are issued by industrial, manufacturing, financial, public utility, and railroad companies. These bonds vary greatly in quality and are graded according to their riskiness by credit-rating agencies, such as Moody's and Standard and Poor's. For the most part, the grades are determined by the default risk of the bond issuer; that is, the probability that the bond investor will not receive promised interest or principal payments.

Government bonds are issued at the federal, state, and municipal levels. The federal government issues both long-term bonds and notes (1–30 years) and short-term treasury securities (91–182 days). Several government agencies, such as the Federal Home Loan Bank, the Federal Land Bank, the Federal National Mortgage Association, and the World Bank, also issue notes and bonds. Some bonds are expressly guaranteed by the U.S. government and others are indirectly guaranteed, so that usually there is little concern about their riskiness.

Municipal bonds issued by the state and local government agencies have a special tax exempt status from the federal government. This means that interest received by the investor of these securities is exempt from federal income tax and also may be exempt from state income tax. Capital gains, however, are fully taxable at the federal and state levels. Because the creditworthiness varies among issuers of municipal bonds, rating agencies assign ratings to the individual issues.

All government bonds are traded on the OTC markets by dealers specializing in a specific bond. For example, banks sell municipal bonds because they are excluded from the equity markets by the Glass-Steagall Act of 1933 and because they often have commercial interactions with local government agencies.

Information about current interest-rate levels in these markets for various maturities of securities provides the financial manager not only with estimates of current capital costs but also of future costs.

### 2.3.3 *The option market*

The trading of equity options began on April 26, 1973, on the CBOE. Today, the American Stock Exchange, the Philadelphia Stock Exchange, the Pacific Stock Exchange and the NYSE also list and trade equity options. Most of the companies for which options are traded are listed on the NYSE, because they tend to be the largest firms with the greatest number of shareholders, who might want to protect the value of their investments by purchasing or writing options. Information about investor's short-term expectations of equity price, bond price, commodity price, etc. movements is reflected in the option prices reported by these markets.

### 2.3.4 *Other markets*

Commodities and financial futures are traded on the New York Future's Exchange (NYFE), Chicago Board of Trade (CBOT), and Chicago Mercantile Exchange (CME). In addition to traditional commodities (such as grains and hog bellies), financial futures, stock index futures, options on the stock index, and options on index futures as well as foreign exchange are also traded. Price and volume information about the trading of such commodities conveys specific information that the financial manager will find useful.

## 2.4 Financial Statements: A Brief Review

Corporate annual and quarterly reports generally contain four basic financial statements: balance sheet, statement of earnings, statement of retained earnings, and statement of changes in financial position. Using Johnson & Johnson (JNJ) annual consolidated financial statements as examples, we discuss the usefulness and problems associated with each of these statements in financial analysis and planning. Annual financial statements can be classified as either a calendar year or fiscal year. Since JNJs financial statement ends on December 31, we can regard JNJs annual financial statements as calendar year financial statements. Finally, the use of annual versus quarterly financial data is addressed.

### 2.4.1 *Balance sheet*

The balance sheet describes a firm's financial position at one specific point in time. It is a static representation, such as a snapshot, of the firm's financial composition of assets and liabilities at one point in time. The balance sheet of JNJ, shown in Table 2.1, is broken down into two basic areas of classification — total assets (debit) and total liabilities and shareholders' equity (credit).

On the debit side, accounts are divided into six groups: current assets, marketable securities (MS) — noncurrent, property, plant and equipment (PP&E), intangible assets, deferred taxes on income, and other assets. Current assets represent short-term accounts, such as cash and cash equivalents, MS and accounts receivable, inventories, deferred tax on income, and prepaid expense. It should be noted that

Table 2.1 Consolidated Balanced Sheets of JNJ Corporation and Subsidiaries.

| **Consolidated Balance Sheets — USD ($) in Millions** | **2012** | **2013** | **2014** | **2015** | **2016** | **2017** | **2018** | **2019** |
|---|---|---|---|---|---|---|---|---|
| **Assets** | | | | | | | | |
| *Current assets* | | | | | | | | |
| Cash and cash equivalents | 14,911 | 20,927 | 14,523 | 13,732 | 18,972 | 17,842 | 18,107 | 17,305 |
| MS | 6,178 | 8,279 | 18,566 | 24,644 | 22,935 | 472 | 1,580 | 1,982 |
| Accounts receivable trade, less allowances for doubtful accounts | 11,309 | 11,713 | 10,985 | 10,734 | 11,699 | 13,490 | 14,098 | 14,481 |
| Inventories | 7,495 | 7,878 | 8,184 | 8,053 | 8,144 | 8,765 | 8,599 | 9,020 |
| Deferred taxes on income | 3,139 | 3,607 | — | — | — | — | — | — |
| Prepaid expenses and other receivables | 3,084 | 4,003 | 3,486 | 3,047 | 3,282 | 2,537 | 2,699 | 2,392 |
| *Total current assets* | **46,116** | **56,407** | **55,744** | **60,210** | **65,032** | **43,088** | **46,033** | **45,274** |
| PP&E, net | 16,097 | 16,710 | 16,126 | 15,905 | 15,912 | 17,005 | 17,053 | 17,658 |
| Intangible assets, net | 28,752 | 27,947 | 27,222 | 25,764 | 26,876 | 53,228 | 47,611 | 47,643 |
| Goodwill | 22,424 | 22,798 | 21,832 | 21,629 | 22,805 | 31,906 | 30,453 | 33,639 |
| Deferred taxes on income | 4,541 | 3,872 | 6,202 | 5,490 | 6,148 | 7,105 | 7,640 | 7,819 |
| Other assets | 3,417 | 4,949 | 3,232 | 4,413 | 4,435 | 4,971 | 4,182 | 5,695 |
| **Total Assets** | **121,347** | **132,683** | **130,358** | **133,411** | **141,208** | **157,303** | **152,954** | **157,728** |

*(Continued)*

Table 2.1 (*Continued*)

| **Consolidated Balance Sheets — USD ($) in Millions** | **2012** | **2013** | **2014** | **2015** | **2016** | **2017** | **2018** | **2019** |
|---|---|---|---|---|---|---|---|---|
| **Liabilities and Shareholders' Equity** | | | | | | | | |
| *Current liabilities* | | | | | | | | |
| Loans and notes payable | 4,676 | 4,852 | 3,638 | 7,004 | 4,684 | 3,906 | 2,769 | 1,202 |
| Accounts payable | 5,831 | 6,266 | 7,633 | 6,668 | 6,918 | 7,310 | 7,537 | 8,544 |
| Accrued liabilities | 7,299 | 7,685 | 6,553 | 5,411 | 5,635 | 7,304 | 7,610 | 9,715 |
| Accrued rebates, returns and promotions | 2,969 | 3,308 | 4,010 | 5,440 | 5,403 | 7,201 | 9,380 | 10,883 |
| Accrued compensation and employee related obligations | 2,423 | 2,794 | 2,751 | 2,474 | 2,676 | 2,953 | 3,098 | 3,354 |
| Accrued taxes on income | 1,064 | 770 | 446 | 750 | 971 | 1854 | 818 | 2,266 |
| *Total current liabilities* | **24,262** | **25,675** | **25,031** | **27,747** | **26,287** | **30,537** | **31,230** | **35,964** |
| Long-term debt | 11,489 | 13,328 | 15,122 | 12,857 | 22,442 | 30,675 | 27,684 | 26,494 |
| Deferred taxes on income | 3,136 | 3,989 | 2,447 | 2,562 | 2,910 | 8,368 | 7,506 | 5,958 |
| Employee related obligations | 9,082 | 7,784 | 9,972 | 8,854 | 9,615 | 10,074 | 9,951 | 10,663 |
| Other liabilities | 8,552 | 7,854 | 8,034 | 10,241 | 9,536 | 9,017 | 8,589 | 11,734 |
| **Total Liabilities** | **56,521** | **58,630** | **60,606** | **62,261** | **70,790** | **97,143** | **93,202** | **98,257** |

| | | | | | | | | |
|---|---|---|---|---|---|---|---|---|
| *Shareholders' equity* | | | | | | | | |
| Preferred stock — without par value | — | — | — | — | — | — | — | — |
| Common stock — par value $1.00 per share | 3,120 | 3,120 | 3,120 | 3,120 | 3,120 | 3,120 | 3,120 | 3,120 |
| Accumulated other comprehensive income | (5,810) | (2,860) | (10,722) | (13,165) | (14,901) | (13,199) | (15,222) | (15,891) |
| Retained earnings | 85,992 | 89,493 | 97,245 | 103,879 | 110,551 | 101,793 | 106,216 | 110,659 |
| Stockholders' equity before Treasury Stock | 83,302 | 89,753 | 89,643 | 93,834 | 98,770 | 91,714 | 94,144 | 97,888 |
| Less: common stock held in treasury, at cost | 18,476 | 15,700 | 19,891 | 22,684 | 28,352 | 31,554 | 34,632 | 38,417 |
| **Total shareholders' equity** | **64,826** | **74,053** | **69,752** | **71,150** | **70,418** | **60,160** | **59,752** | **59,471** |
| **Total Liabilities and Shareholders' equity** | **121,347** | **132,683** | **130,358** | **133,411** | **141,208** | **157,303** | **152,954** | **157,728** |

deferred tax on income in this group is a current deferred tax and will be converted into income tax within one year.

Property encompasses all fixed or capital assets such as real estate, plant and equipment, special tools, and the allowance for depreciation and amortization. Intangible assets refer to the assets of research and development (R&D).

The credit side of the balance sheet in Table 2.1 is divided into current liabilities, long-term liabilities, and shareowner's equity. Under current liabilities, the following accounts are included: accounts, loans, and notes payable; accrued liabilities; accrued salaries and taxes on income. Long-term liabilities include various forms of long-term debt, deferred tax liability, employee-related obligations, and other liabilities. The stockholder's equity section of the balance sheet represents the net worth of the firm to its investors. For example, as of December 31, 2012, JNJ had $0 million preferred stock outstanding, $3,120 million in common stock outstanding, and $85,992 million retained earnings. Sometimes there are preferred stock and hybrid securities (e.g., convertible bond and convertible preferred stock) on the credit side of the balance sheet.

The balance sheet is useful because it depicts the firm's financing and investment policies. The use of comparative balance sheets, those that present several years' data, can be used to detect trends and possible future problems. Table 2.1 presents the consolidated balance sheet of JNJ from eight periods: December 31, 2012, December 31, 2013, December 31, 2014, December 31, 2015, December 31, 2016, December 31, 2017, December 31, 2018, and December 31, 2019. The balance sheet, however, is static and therefore should be analyzed with caution in financial analysis and planning.

### 2.4.2 *Statement of earnings*

JNJ's statement of earnings is presented in Table 2.2 and describes the results of operations for a 12-month period ending December 31. The usual income-statement periods are annual, quarterly, and monthly. Both the annual and quarterly reports are used for external as well as internal reporting. The monthly statement is used primarily for internal purposes, such as the estimation of sales and profit targets, judgment of controls on expenses, and monitoring progress

Table 2.2 Consolidated Statements of Earnings of JNJ Corporation and Subsidiaries.

| (Dollars in Millions Except Per Share Figures) | 2012 | 2013 | 2014 | 2015 | 2016 | 2017 | 2018 | 2019 |
|---|---|---|---|---|---|---|---|---|
| **Sales to Customers ($)** | 67,224 | 71,312 | 74,331 | 70,074 | 71,890 | 76,450 | 81,581 | 82,059 |
| Cost of products sold | 21,658 | 22,342 | 22,746 | 21,536 | 21,685 | 25,354 | 27,091 | 27,556 |
| Gross profit | 45,566 | 48,970 | 51,585 | 48,538 | 50,101 | 51,011 | 54,490 | 54,503 |
| Selling, marketing and administrative expenses | 20,869 | 21,830 | 21,954 | 21,203 | 20,067 | 21,520 | 22,540 | 22,178 |
| Research expense | 7,665 | 8,183 | 8,494 | 9,046 | 9,143 | 10,594 | 10,775 | 11,355 |
| Purchased in-process R&D | 1,163 | 580 | 178 | 224 | 29 | 408 | 1,126 | 890 |
| Interest income | (64) | (74) | (67) | (128) | (368) | (385) | (611) | (357) |
| Interest expense, net of portion capitalized | 532 | 482 | 533 | 552 | 726 | 934 | 1,005 | 318 |
| Other (income) expense, net | 1,626 | 2,498 | (70) | (2,064) | 210 | (42) | 1,405 | 2,525 |
| Restructuring | — | — | — | 509 | 491 | 509 | 251 | 266 |
| Earnings before provision for taxes on income | 13,775 | 15,471 | 20,563 | 19,196 | 19,803 | 17,673 | 17,999 | 17,328 |
| Provision for taxes on income | 3,261 | 1,640 | 4,240 | 3,787 | 3,263 | 16,373 | 2,702 | 2,209 |
| **Net earnings** | **10,514** | **13,831** | **16,323** | **15,409** | **16,540** | **1,300** | **15,297** | **15,119** |
| **Basic net earnings per share ($)** | **3.50** | **3.76** | **3.67** | **4.62** | **6.04** | **0.48** | **5.70** | **5.72** |
| **Diluted net earnings per share ($)** | **3.46** | **3.73** | **3.63** | **4.57** | **5.93** | **0.47** | **5.61** | **5.63** |

toward longer-term targets. The statement of earnings is more dynamic than the balance sheet, because it reflects changes for the period. It provides an analyst with an overview of a firm's operations and profitability on a gross, operating, and net income basis. JNJ's income includes sales, interest income, and other income/expenses. Costs and expenses for JNJ include the cost of goods sold, selling, marketing, and administrative expenses, depreciation, depletion, and amortization. The difference between income and cost and expenses results in the company's Net Earnings. A comparative statement of earnings is very useful in financial analysis and planning because it allows insight into the firm's operations, profitability, and financing decisions over time. For this reason, JNJ presents the statement of earnings of six consecutive years: 2012, 2013, 2014, 2015, 2016, 2017, 2018, and 2019. Armed with this information, evaluating the firm's future is easier.

The last four rows of Table 2.2 present basic net earnings per share, diluted net earnings per share, basic average shares outstanding, and diluted average shares outstanding. All of this information is useful for financial analysis, planning, and forecasting.

### 2.4.3 *Statement of equity*

JNJ's statements of equity are shown in Table 2.3. These are the earnings that a firm retains for reinvestment rather than paying them out to shareholders in the form of dividends. The statement of equity is easily understood if it is viewed as a bridge between the balance sheet and the statement of earnings. The statement of equity presents a summary of those categories that have an impact on the level of retained earnings: the net earnings and the dividends declared for preferred and common stock. It also represents a summary of the firm's dividend policy and shows how net income is allocated to dividends and reinvestment. JNJ's equity is one source of funds for investment, and this internal source of funds is very important to the firm. The balance sheet, the statement of earnings, and the statement of equity allow us to analyze important firm decisions on the capital structure, cost of capital, capital budgeting, and dividend policy of that firm.

Table 2.3 Consolidated Statements of Equity of JNJ Corporation and Subsidiaries (2012–2019) (Dollars in Millions).

| **Consolidated Statements of Equity — USD ($) in Millions** | **Total** | **Retained Earnings** | **Accumulated Other Comprehensive Income** | **Common Stock Issued Amount** | **Treasury Stock Amount** |
|---|---|---|---|---|---|
| **Balance at December 30, 2012** | **$ 64,826** | **85,992** | **(5,810)** | **3,120** | **(18,476)** |
| Net earnings | 13,831 | 13,831 | — | — | — |
| Cash dividends paid | (7,286) | (7,286) | — | — | — |
| Employee compensation and stock option plans | 3,285 | (82) | — | — | 3,367 |
| Repurchase of common stock | (3,538) | (2,947) | — | — | (591) |
| Payments for repurchase of common stock | 3,538 | — | — | — | — |
| Other | (15) | (15) | — | — | — |
| Other comprehensive income (loss), net of tax | 2,950 | — | 2,950 | — | — |
| **Balance at December 29, 2013** | **$ 74,053** | **89,493** | **(2,860)** | **3,120** | **(15,700)** |
| Net earnings | 16,323 | 16,323 | — | — | — |
| Cash dividends paid | (7,768) | (7,768) | — | — | — |
| Employee compensation and stock option plans | 2,164 | (769) | — | — | 2,933 |
| Repurchase of common stock | (7,124) | — | — | — | (7,124) |
| Other | (34) | (34) | — | — | — |
| Other comprehensive income (loss), net of tax | (7,862) | — | (7,862) | — | — |
| **Balance at December 28, 2014** | **$ 69,752** | **97,245** | **(10,722)** | **3,120** | **(19,891)** |
| Net earnings | 15,409 | 15,409 | — | — | — |
| Cash dividends paid | (8,173) | (8,173) | — | — | — |
| Employee compensation and stock option plans | 1,920 | (577) | — | — | 2,497 |
| Repurchase of common stock | (5,290) | — | — | — | (5,290) |

(*Continued*)

Table 2.3 (*Continued*)

| Consolidated Statements of Equity — USD ($) in Millions | Total | Retained Earnings | Accumulated Other Comprehensive Income | Common Stock Issued Amount | Treasury Stock Amount |
|---|---|---|---|---|---|
| Other | (25) | (25) | — | — | — |
| Other comprehensive income (loss), net of tax | (2,443) | — | (2,443) | — | — |
| **Balance at January 03, 2016** | **$ 71,150** | **103,879** | **(13,165)** | **3,120** | **(22,684)** |
| Net earnings | 16,540 | 16,540 | — | — | — |
| Cash dividends paid | (8,621) | (8,621) | — | — | — |
| Employee compensation and stock option plans | 2,130 | (1,181) | — | — | 3,311 |
| Repurchase of common stock | (8,979) | — | — | — | (8,979) |
| Other | (66) | (66) | — | — | — |
| Other comprehensive income (loss), net of tax | (1,736) | — | (1,736) | — | — |
| **Balance at January 01, 2017** | **$ 70,418** | **110,551** | **(14,901)** | **3,120** | **(28,352)** |
| Net earnings | 1,300 | 1,300 | — | — | — |
| Cash dividends paid | (8,943) | (8,943) | — | — | — |
| Employee compensation and stock option plans | 2,077 | (1,079) | — | — | 3,156 |
| Repurchase of common stock | (6,358) | — | — | — | (6,358) |
| Other | (36) | (36) | — | — | — |
| Other comprehensive income (loss), net of tax | 1,702 | — | 1,702 | — | — |
| **Balance at December 31, 2017** | **$ 60,160** | **101,793** | **(13,199)** | **3,120** | **(31,554)** |

| | | | | | |
|---|---|---|---|---|---|
| Net earnings | 15,297 | 15,297 | — | — | — |
| Cash dividends paid | (9,494) | (9,494) | — | — | — |
| Employee compensation and stock option plans | 1,949 | (1,111) | — | — | 3,606 |
| Repurchase of common stock | (5,868) | — | — | — | (5,868) |
| Other | (15) | (15) | — | — | — |
| Other comprehensive income (loss), net of tax | (1,791) | — | (1,791) | — | — |
| **Balance at December 30, 2018** | **$ 59,752** | **106,216** | **(15,222)** | **3,120** | **(34,362)** |
| Net earnings | 15,119 | 15,119 | — | — | — |
| Cash dividends paid | (9,917) | (9,917) | — | — | — |
| Employee compensation and stock option plans | 1,933 | (758) | — | — | 2,691 |
| Repurchase of common stock | (6,746) | — | — | — | (6,746) |
| Other | (1) | (1) | — | — | — |
| Other comprehensive income (loss), net of tax | (669) | — | (669) | — | — |
| **Balance at December 29, 2019** | **$ 59,471** | **110,659** | **(15,891)** | **3,120** | **(38,417)** |

### 2.4.4 *Statement of cash flows*

Another extremely important part of the annual and quarterly report is the statement of cash flows. This statement is very helpful in evaluating a firm's use of its funds and in determining how these funds were raised. Statements of cash flow for JNJ are shown in Table 2.4. These statements of cash flow are composed of three sections: cash flows from operating activities, cash flows from investing activities, and cash flows from financing activities. The statement of cash flows can be compiled by either the direct or indirect method. Most companies, such as JNJ, compile their cash flow statements using the indirect method. For JNJ, the sources of cash are essentially provided by operations. Application of these funds includes dividends paid to stockholders and expenditures for PP&E, etc. Therefore, this statement reveals some important aspects of the firm's investment, financing, and dividend policies; making it an important tool for financial planning and analysis.

The cash flow statement shows how the net increase or decrease in cash has been reflected in the changing composition of current assets and current liabilities. It highlights changes in short-term financial policies. It should be noted that the balance of cash flow statement should be equal to the first item of the balance sheet (i.e., cash and cash equivalents). Furthermore, it's well known that investment policy, financial, dividend, and production policies are four important policies in the financial management and decision-making process. Most of the information of these four policies can be obtained from the cash flow statement. For example, cash flow associated with operation activity gives information about operation and production policy. Cash flow associated with investment activity gives information about investments policy. Finally, cash flow associated with financial activity gives information about dividend and financing policy.

The statement of cash flows can be used to help resolve differences between finance and accounting theories. There is value for the analyst in viewing the statement of cash flow over time, especially in detecting trends that could lead to technical or legal bankruptcy in the future. Collectively, the balance sheet, the statement of retained earnings, the statement of equity, and the statement of cash flow present a fairly clear picture of the firm's historical and current position.

Table 2.4 Comparative Cash Flow Statement (2012–2019).

| (Dollars in Millions) | 2012 | 2013 | 2014 | 2015 | 2016 | 2017 | 2018 | 2019 |
|---|---|---|---|---|---|---|---|---|
| **Cash flows from operating activities** | | | | | | | | |
| Net earnings | 10,514 | 13,831 | 16,323 | 15,409 | 16,540 | 1,300 | 15,297 | 15,119 |
| **Adjustments to reconcile net earnings to cash flows** | | | | | | | | |
| Depreciation and amortization of property and intangibles | 3,666 | 4,104 | 3,895 | 3,746 | 3,754 | 5,642 | 6,929 | 7,009 |
| Stock based compensation | 662 | 728 | 792 | 874 | 878 | 962 | 978 | 977 |
| Noncontrolling interest | 339 | — | 87 | 122 | — | — | — | — |
| — Venezuela adjustments | — | 108 | — | — | — | — | — | — |
| Asset write-downs | 2,131 | 739 | 410 | 624 | 283 | 795 | 1,258 | 1,096 |
| Net gain on sale of assets/businesses or equity investment | — | −417 | −2,383 | −2,583 | −563 | −1,307 | −1,217 | −2,154 |
| Deferred tax provision | −39 | −607 | 441 | −270 | −341 | 2,406 | −1,016 | −2,476 |
| Accounts receivable allowances | 92 | −131 | −28 | 18 | −11 | 17 | −31 | −20 |
| **Changes in assets and liabilities, net of effects from acquisitions** | | | | | | | | |
| Increase in accounts receivable | −9 | −632 | −247 | −433 | −1,065 | −633 | −1,185 | −289 |
| (Increase)/decrease in inventories | −1 | −622 | −1,120 | −449 | −249 | 581 | −644 | −277 |
| (Decrease)/increase in accounts payable and accrued liabilities | 2,768 | 1,821 | 1,194 | 287 | 656 | 1,725 | 3,951 | 4,060 |
| Decrease/(increase) in other current and noncurrent assets | −2,172 | −1,806 | 442 | 65 | −529 | −411 | −275 | −1,054 |
| Increase in other current and noncurrent liabilities | −2,555 | 298 | −1,096 | 2,159 | −586 | 8,979 | −1,844 | 1,425 |
| **Net cash flows from operating activities** | **15,396** | **17,414** | **18,710** | **19,569** | **18,767** | **21,056** | **22,201** | **23,416** |

*(Continued)*

Table 2.4 (*Continued*)

| **(Dollars in Millions)** | **2012** | **2013** | **2014** | **2015** | **2016** | **2017** | **2018** | **2019** |
|---|---|---|---|---|---|---|---|---|
| **Cash flows from investing activities** | | | | | | | | |
| Additions to PP&E | −2,934 | −3,595 | −3,714 | −3,463 | −3,226 | −3,279 | −3,670 | −3,498 |
| Proceeds from the disposal of assets | 1,509 | 458 | 4,631 | 3,464 | 1,267 | 1,832 | 3,302 | 3,265 |
| *Acquisitions, net of cash acquired* | −4,486 | −835 | −2,129 | −954 | −4,509 | −35,151 | −899 | −5,810 |
| Purchases of investments | −13,434 | −18,923 | −34,913 | −40,828 | −33,950 | −6,153 | −5,626 | −3,920 |
| Sales of investments | 14,797 | 18,058 | 24,119 | 34,149 | 35,780 | 28,117 | 4,289 | 3,387 |
| Other (primarily intangibles) | 38 | −266 | −299 | −103 | −123 | −234 | −464 | 44 |
| **Net cash used by investing activities** | **−4,510** | **−5,103** | **−12,305** | **−7,735** | **−4,761** | **−14,868** | **−3,176** | **−6,194** |
| **Cash flows from financing activities** | | | | | | | | |
| Dividends to shareholders | −6,614 | −7,286 | −7,768 | −8,173 | −8,621 | −8,943 | −9,494 | −9,917 |
| Repurchase of common stock | −12,919 | −3,538 | −7,124 | −5,290 | −8,979 | −6,358 | −5,868 | −6,746 |
| Proceeds from short-term debt | 3,268 | 1,411 | 1,863 | 2,416 | 111 | 869 | 80 | 39 |
| Retirement of short-term debt | −6,175 | −1,397 | −1,267 | −1,044 | −2,017 | −1,330 | −2,479 | −100 |
| Proceeds from long-term debt | 45 | 3,607 | 2,098 | 75 | 12,004 | 8,992 | 5 | 3 |
| Retirement of long-term debt | −804 | −1,593 | −1,844 | −68 | −2,223 | −1,777 | −1,555 | −2,823 |
| Proceeds from the exercise of stock options | 2,720 | 2,649 | 1,543 | 1,005 | 1,189 | 1,062 | 949 | 954 |
| Other | −83 | 56 | — | −57 | −15 | −188 | −148 | 575 |
| **Net cash used by financing activities** | **−20,562** | **−6,091** | **−12,499** | **−11,136** | **−8,551** | **−7,673** | **−18,510** | **−18,015** |
| Effect of exchange rate changes on cash and cash equivalents | 45 | −204 | 310 | 1,489 | −215 | 337 | −241 | −9 |
| Increase/ (Decrease) in cash and cash equivalents | −9,631 | 6,016 | 6,404 | 791 | 5240 | −1,148 | 283 | −802 |
| Cash and cash equivalents, beginning of year | 24,542 | 14,911 | 20,927 | 14,523 | 13,732 | 18,972 | 17,824 | 18,107 |
| **Cash and cash equivalents, end of year** | **14,911** | **20,927** | **14,523** | **13,732** | **18,972** | **17,824** | **18,107** | **17,305** |

| | | | | | | | | |
|---|---|---|---|---|---|---|---|---|
| **Supplemental cash flow data** | | | | | | | | |
| **Cash paid during the year for** | | | | | | | | |
| Interest | 616 | 596 | 603 | 617 | 730 | 960 | 1,049 | 576 |
| Interest, net of amount capitalized | 501 | 491 | 488 | 515 | 628 | 866 | 963 | 492 |
| Income taxes | 2,507 | 3,155 | 3,536 | 2,865 | 2,843 | 3,312 | 4,570 | 2,970 |
| Supplemental schedule of noncash investing and financing activities | | | | | | | | |
| Treasury stock issued for employee compensation and stock option plans, net of cash proceeds | 615 | 743 | 1,409 | 1,486 | 2,043 | 2,062 | 2,095 | 995 |
| Conversion of debt | — | 22 | 17 | 16 | 35 | 16 | 6 | 1 |
| Acquisitions | | | | | | | | |
| Fair value of assets acquired | 19,025 | 1,028 | 2,167 | 1,174 | 4,586 | 36,937 | 1,047 | 7,228 |
| Fair value of liabilities assumed | −1,204 | −193 | −38 | −220 | −77 | −1,786 | −148 | −1,418 |
| Net cash paid for acquisitions | 4,486 | 835 | 2,129 | 954 | 4,509 | 35,151 | 899 | 5,810 |

### 2.4.5 *Interrelationship among four financial statements*

It should be noted that the balance sheet, statement of earnings, statement of equity, and statement of cash flow are interrelated. These relationships are briefly described as follows:

(1) Retained earnings calculated from the statement of equity for the current period should be used to replace the retained earnings item in the balance sheet of the previous period. Therefore, the statement of equity is regarded as a bridge between the balance sheet and the statement of earnings.
(2) We need the information from the balance sheet, the statement of earnings, and the statement of equity to compile the statement of cash flow.
(3) Cash and cash equivalents item can be found in the statement of cash flow. In other words, the statement of cash flow describes how the cash and cash equivalent changed during the period. It is known that the first item of the balance sheet is cash and cash equivalent.

### 2.4.6 *Annual versus quarterly financial data*

Both annual and quarterly financial data are important to financial analysts; which one is the most important depends on the time horizon of the analysis. Depending upon pattern changes in the historical data, either annual or quarterly data could prove to be more useful. It is well-known that understanding the implications of using quarterly data versus annual data is important for proper financial analysis and planning.

Quarterly data has three components: trend-cycle, seasonal, and irregular or random components. It contains important information about seasonal fluctuations that "reflects an intra-year pattern of variation which is repeated constantly or in evolving fashion form year to year." Quarterly data has the disadvantage of having a large irregular, or random, component that introduces noise into analysis.

Annual data has both the trend-cycle component and the irregular component, but it does not have the seasonal component. The irregular component is much smaller in annual data than in quarterly data. While it may seem that annual data would be more useful for long-term financial planning and analysis, seasonal data reveals important permanent patterns that underlie the short-term series in financial analysis and planning. In other words, quarterly data can be used for intermediate-term financial planning to improve financial management.

Use of either quarterly or annual data has a consistent impact on the mean-square error of regression forecasting, which is composed of variance and bias. Changing from quarterly to annual data will generally reduce variance while increasing bias. Any difference in regression results, due to the use of different data, must be analyzed in light of the historical patterns of fluctuation in the original time-series data.

## 2.5 Critique of Accounting Information

### 2.5.1 *Criticism*

At first glance, accounting information seems to be heavily audited and regulated, automatically determining what numbers are presented. However, careful analysis makes it apparent that accountants work with a fairly broad framework of rules that increase the distance between accounting and financial valuation. This leeway in accounting rules also tends to make accounting information more random. In addition, Hong (1977) shows that the selection of "last in, first out" (LIFO) or "first in, first out" (FIFO) methods for tax and depreciation based upon historic cost generally introduces a bias in a firm's market-value determination. This combination of discrepancy, bias, and randomness means that accounting information does not represent the "true" information. As a result, both time-series and cross-sectional comparisons of accounting information are difficult to analyze.

A major problem with the use of accounting information rises due to errors made in classifying transactions into individual accounts. There are several types of classification error.

One classification error occurs when a bookkeeper enters an item into the wrong account. This is dealt with by modern auditing through the use of sampling techniques, where the auditor certifies that the probability of a material error, an error that would alter a manager's or investor's decision, is within an acceptable limit.

The difference between accountancy and finance theory is another case of classification error. An accountant defines income as the change in shareholder's wealth due to operations of the firm; this includes the use of accruals in wealth determination. The finance discipline defines a firm's income as cash income, or the difference between cash revenues and cash expenses (those payments made to generate current revenue). Due to the accruals used in accounting, accounting income is numerically different from cash income because of the difference in timing.

Another problem with accounting information derives from depreciation costs. There are various accepted ways to spread the cost of an asset over its useful life.[1] The choice of a depreciation method can cause a wide variation in net income.[2] A straight-line method will reduce income less than an accelerated method in the first years of depreciation. In the later years, accelerated depreciation will reduce income less than a straight-line method.

The use of historical costs for pricing an asset acquisition also causes problems in using accounting information. Such reliance on historical cost is particularly troublesome in times of high inflation, because historical cost values are no longer representative of the underlying values of the assets and liabilities of the firm.

---

[1]Depreciation is a procedure that allocates the acquisition costs of the asset to subsequent periods of time on a systematic and rational basis. There are several widely used methods of allocating the acquisition costs: straight-line, declining balance, and sum-of-the-years digits.

[2]There is a limit on the ability of the firm to manipulate its financial statements by repeatedly changing accounting methods, for depreciation, inventory valuation, or any other of the numerous decisions permitted by generally accepted accounting principles (GAAP). The limitation on constant changes in accounting methods is provided by several sources. Accounting Principle Board 20 requires that any changes must be justified on the basis of fair representation and the change and the justification must be disclosed.

The American Institute of Certified Public Accountants, through the Auditing Standards Board, requires that the auditor certify that accounting principles have been consistently observed in the current period in relation to the preceding periods [AU 150.02].

The accounting profession is attempting to deal with this problem through the use of supplementary disclosure of selected financial statement items, as required by Financial Accounting Standard Board 33, for large, publicly traded firms.[3] Accountants are also developing replacement cost and other inflation-adjusted accounting procedures.

### 2.5.2 *Methods for improvement*

Three possible methods for improving the representativeness or accuracy of accounting information in financial analysis and planning is the use of alternative information, statistical tools, and finance and economic theories.

#### 2.5.2.1 *Use of alternative information*

Of the many types of alternative information that is used to improve accounting data, the most practical and consistent type is market information. Stock prices and replacement costs can be used to adjust reported accounting earnings. According to the theory of efficient capital markets, the market price of a security represents the market's estimate of the value of that security. Furthermore, the market value (or the "intrinsic" value) of a common stock represents the firm's "true" earning potential perceived by investors. An example of the use of market information to complement accounting information is the use of the option-pricing model in capital budgeting under uncertainty in Chapter 9.

#### 2.5.2.2 *Statistical adjustments*

Another method of improving accounting information is the use of statistical tools. By using a time-series decomposition technique suggested by Lee *et al.* (2013), quarterly earnings can be divided into three components: trend-cycle, seasonal, and irregular components. This decomposition procedure can be used to remove some undesirable noise associated with accounting numbers. Therefore,

[3]Financial Accounting Standards Board Statement #33, Stamford CT, June 1974.

this statistically adjusted accounting earnings data can be used to improve its usefulness in determining a firm's intrinsic value.

For long-term financial planning and analysis, the trend-cycle component is the major source of information. The seasonal and irregular components introduce noise that clouds the analysis, and this noise can be removed. For short-term (or intermediate term) planning and analysis, the seasonal component also produces valuable information. Thus, both trend-cycle and seasonal components should be used in working capital management. Note that the source(s) of noise can also be eliminated by moving average or other statistical methods.

#### 2.5.2.3 *Application of finance and economic theories*

The third method of improving accounting information is the use of finance and economic theories. For example, there is the Modigliani and Miller valuation theory, the capital-asset pricing theory, and the option pricing theory, which will be discussed in Chapters 8, 11, and 22. By applying these theories, one can adjust accounting income to obtain a better picture of income measurement, i.e., finance income (cash flow). Also, the use of finance theory combined with market and other information gives an analyst another estimate of income measurement. In addition, the various earnings estimates can shed additional light on the firm's value determination. To do these kinds of empirical tests, Lee and Zumwalt (1981) use a multiple regression model to investigate the association between six alternative accounting profitability measures and the security rate-of-return determination. Their empirical results suggest that accounting profitability information is an important extra-market information component of asset pricing. In other words, it is shown that different accounting profitability measures should be used by security analysts and investors to determine the equity rates of return for different industries.

## 2.6 Static Ratio Analysis

In order to make use of financial statements, an analyst needs some form of measurement for analysis. Frequently, ratios are used to relate one piece of financial data to another. The ratio puts the two pieces of data on an equivalent base, which increases the usefulness of the data. For example, net income as an absolute number is meaningless to compare across firms of different sizes. However, if one creates a net profitability ratio (NI/Sales), comparisons are easier to make. Analysis of a series of ratios will give us a clear picture of a firm's financial condition and performance.

Analysis of ratios can take one of two forms. First, the analyst can compare the ratios of one firm with those of similar firms or with industry averages at a specific point in time. This is a type of cross-sectional analysis technique that may indicate the relative financial condition and performance of a firm. One must be careful, however, to analyze the ratios while keeping in mind the inherent differences between a firm's production functions and its operations. Also, the analyst should avoid using "rules of thumb" across industries because the composition of industries and individual firms varies considerably. Furthermore, inconsistency in a firm's accounting procedures can cause accounting data to show substantial differences between firms, which can hinder ratio comparability. This variation in accounting procedures can also lead to problems in determining the "target ratio" (to be discussed later).

The second method of ratio comparison involves the comparison of a firm's present ratio with their past and expected ratios. This form of time-series analysis will indicate whether the firm's financial condition has improved or deteriorated. Both types of ratio analysis can take one of the two following forms: static determination and its analysis, or dynamic adjustment and its analysis.

### 2.6.1 *Static determination of financial ratios*

The static determination of financial ratios involves the calculation and analysis of ratios over a number of periods for one company, or the analysis of differences in ratios among individual firms in one industry. An analyst must be careful of extreme values in either direction, because of the interrelationships between ratios. For instance, a very high liquidity ratio is costly to maintain, causing profitability ratios to be lower than they need to be. Furthermore, ratios must be interpreted in relation to the raw data from which they are calculated, particularly for ratios that sum accounts in order to arrive at the necessary data for the calculation. Even though this analysis must be performed with extreme caution, it can yield important conclusions in the analysis for a particular company. Table 2.5 presents six alternative types of ratios for JNJ. These six ratios are short-term solvency, long-term solvency, asset management, profitability ratios, market value ratios, and policy ratios. We now discuss these six ratios in detail.

#### 2.6.1.1 *Short-term solvency, or liquidity ratios*

Liquidity ratios are calculated from information on the balance sheet; they measure the relative strength of a firm's financial position. Crudely interpreted, these are coverage ratios that indicate the firm's ability to meet short-term obligations. The current ratio (ratio 1 in Table 2.5) is the most popular of the liquidity ratios because it is easy to calculate, and it has intuitive appeal. It is also the most broadly defined liquidity ratio, as it does not take into account the differences in relative liquidity among the individual components of current assets. A more specifically defined liquidity ratio is the quick or acid-test ratio (ratio 2), which excludes the least liquid portion of current assets, inventories. In other words, the numerator of this ratio includes cash, MS, and receivables. Cash ratio (ratio 3) is the ratio of the company's total cash and cash equivalents (MS) to its current liabilities. It is most often used as a measure of company liquidity. A strong cash ratio is useful to creditors when deciding how much debt they're willing to extend to the asking party (Investopedia.com).

The net working capital to total asset ratio (ratio 4) is the NWC divided by the total assets of the company. A relatively low value might indicate relatively low levels of liquidity.

#### 2.6.1.2 *Long-term solvency, or financial leverage ratios*

If an analyst wishes to measure the extent of a firm's debt financing, a leverage ratio is the appropriate tool to use. This group of ratios reflects the financial risk posture of the firm. The two sources of data from which these ratios can be calculated are the balance sheet and the statement of earnings.

The balance-sheet leverage ratio measures the proportion of debt incorporated into the capital structure. The debt–equity ratio measures the proportion of debt that is matched by equity; thus this ratio

Table 2.5 Alternative Financial Ratios for JNJ (2016–2019).

| Ratio Classification | Formula | JNJ 2019 | JNJ 2018 | JNJ 2017 | JNJ 2016 |
|---|---|---|---|---|---|
| **I. Short-term Solvency, or Liquidity Ratios (times)** | | | | | |
| (1) Current Ratio | (current asset)/(current liabilities) | 1.26 | 1.47 | 1.41 | 2.47 |
| (2) Quick Ratio | (cash + MS + receivables)/(current liabilities) | 0.94 | 1.08 | 1.04 | 2.04 |
| (3) Cash Ratio | (cash + MS)/(current liabilities) | 0.54 | 0.63 | 0.60 | 1.59 |
| (4) Net Working Capital to Total Asset | (net working capital)/(total asset) | 0.06 | 0.10 | 0.08 | 0.27 |
| **II. Long-term Solvency, or Financial Leverage Ratios (times)** | | | | | |
| (5) Debt-to-Asset | (total debt)/(total asset) | 0.62 | 0.61 | 0.62 | 0.50 |
| (6) Debt-to-Equity | (total debt)/(total equity) | 1.65 | 1.56 | 1.61 | 1.01 |
| (7) Equity Multiplier | (total asset)/(total equity) | 2.65 | 2.56 | 2.61 | 2.01 |
| (8) Times Interest Paid | (EBIT)/(interest expenses) | 54.49 | 17.91 | 18.92 | 28.28 |
| (9) Long-term Debt Ratio | (long-term debt)/(long-term debt + total equity) | 0.31 | 0.32 | 0.34 | 0.24 |
| (10) Cash Coverage Ratio | (EBIT + depreciation)/(interest expenses) | 76.53 | 24.80 | 24.96 | 33.45 |
| **III. Asset Management, or Turnover (Activity) Ratios (times)** | | | | | |
| (11) Day's Sales in Receivables (Average Collection Period) | (account receivable)/(sales/365) | 64.41 | 63.08 | 64.41 | 59.40 |
| (12) Receivable Turnover | (sales)/(account receivable) | 5.67 | 5.79 | 5.67 | 6.14 |
| (13) Day's Sales in Inventory | (inventory)/(cost of goods cold/365) | 119.48 | 115.86 | 126.18 | 137.08 |
| (14) Inventory Turnover | (cost of goods sold) (inventory) | 3.05 | 3.15 | 2.89 | 2.66 |

*(Continued)*

Table 2.5 (*Continued*)

| | Formula | JNJ 2019 | JNJ 2018 | JNJ 2017 | JNJ 2016 |
|---|---|---|---|---|---|
| (15) Fixed Asset Turnover | (sales)/(fixed assets) | 4.65 | 4.78 | 4.50 | 4.52 |
| (16) Total Asset Turnover | (sales)/(total assets) | 0.52 | 0.53 | 0.49 | 0.51 |
| (17) Net Working Capital Turnover | (sales)/(net working capital) | 8.81 | 5.51 | 6.09 | 1.86 |
| **IV. Profitability Ratios (percentage)** | | | | | |
| (18) Profit Margin | (net income)/(sales) | 18.42 | 18.75 | 1.70 | 23.01 |
| (19) Return on Assets (ROA) | (net income)/total assets) | 9.59 | 10.00 | 0.83 | 11.71 |
| (20) Return on Equity (ROE) | (net income)/(total equity) | 25.42 | 25.60 | 2.16 | 23.49 |
| **V. Market Value Ratios (times)** | | | | | |
| (21) Price-earnings (PE) Ratio | (mkt price per share)/(earnings per share) | 30.08 | 25.96 | 289.33 | 18.70 |
| (22) Market-to-Book Ratio | (mkt price per share)/(book value per share) | 6.48 | 5.71 | 6.25 | 4.39 |
| (23) Earnings Yield | (earnings per share)/(mkt price per share) | 0.03 | 0.04 | 0.00 | 0.05 |
| (24) Dividend Yield | (dividend per share)/(mkt price per share) | 0.02 | 0.02 | 0.02 | 0.03 |
| (25) Price/Earnings to Growth (PEG) Ratio | (PE ratio)/(earnings growth rate) | 343.85 | 267.28 | −2277.37 | 166.27 |
| (26) Enterprise Value-EBITDA Ratio | (enterprise value)/(EBITDA) | 18.97 | 17.68 | 18.81 | 14.46 |
| (27) Dividend Payout Ratio | (dividend payout)/(net income) | 0.66 | 0.62 | 6.88 | 0.52 |
| **VI. Policy Ratios (percentage)** | | | | | |
| (5) Debt-to-Asset | (total debt)/(total asset) | 62.30 | 60.93 | 61.76 | 50.13 |
| (27) Dividend Payout Ratio | (dividend payout)/(net income) | 65.59 | 62.06 | 687.92 | 52.12 |
| (28) SGR | [(1-payout ratio) × ROE]/[1 − (1 − payout ratio) × ROE] | 9.59 | 10.76 | −11.27 | 12.67 |

reflects the composition of the capital structure. The debt–asset ratio (ratio 5), on the other hand, measures the proportion of debt-financed assets currently being used by the firm. Other commonly used leverage ratios include the equity multiplier ratio (7) and the time interest paid ratio (8).

Debt-to-equity (6) is a variation on the total debt ratio. Its total debt divided by total equity.

Long-term debt ratio (9) is long-term debt divided by the sum of long-term debt and total equity.

Cash coverage ratio (10) is defined as the sum of EBIT and depreciation divided by interest. The numerator is often abbreviated as EBITDA.

The income-statement leverage ratio measures the firm's ability to meet fixed obligations of one form or another. The time interest paid, which is earnings before interest and taxes over interest expense, measures the firm's ability to service the interest expense on its outstanding debt. A more broadly defined ratio of this type is the fixed-charge coverage ratio, which includes not only the interest expense but also all other expenses that the firm is obligated by contract to pay. (This ratio is not included in Table 2.5 because there is not enough information on fixed charges for these firms to calculate this ratio.)

#### 2.6.1.3 *Asset management, or turnover (activity) ratios*

This group of ratios measures how efficiently the firm is utilizing its assets. With activity ratios, one must be particularly careful about the interpretation of extreme results in either direction; very high values may indicate possible problems in the long term, and very low values may indicate a current problem of low sales or not taking a loss for obsolete assets. The reason that high activity may not be good in the long term is that the firm may not be able to adjust to an even higher level of activity and therefore may miss out on a market opportunity. Better analysis and planning can help a firm get around this problem.

The days-in-accounts-receivable or average-collection-period ratio (11) indicates the firm's effectiveness in collecting its credit sales. The other activity ratios measure the firm's efficiency in generating sales with its current level of assets, appropriately termed turnover ratios. While there are many turnover ratios that can be calculated, there are three basic ones: inventory turnover (14), fixed assets turnover (15), and total assets turnover (16). Each of these ratios measure a different aspect of the firm's efficiency in managing its assets.

Receivables turnover (12) is computed as credit sales divided by accounts receivable. In general, a higher accounts receivable turnover suggests more frequent payment of receivables by customers.

In general, analysts look for higher receivables turnover and shorter collection periods, *but this combination may imply that the firm's credit policy is too strict,* allowing only the lowest risk customers to buy on credit. Although this strategy could minimize credit losses, it may hurt overall sales, profits, and shareholder wealth.

Day's sales in inventory ratio (13) estimates how many days, on average, a product sits in the inventory before it is sold.

Net working capital turnover (17) measures how much per dollar of net working capital can generate dollar of sales. For example, if this ratio is 3, this means the per dollar of net working capital can generate $3 of sales.

#### 2.6.1.4 *Profitability ratios*

This group of ratios indicates the profitability of the firm's operations. It is important to note here that these measures are based on past performance. Profitability ratios are generally the most volatile, because many of the variables affecting them are beyond the firm's control. There are three groups of profitability ratios; those measuring margins, those measuring returns, and those measuring the relationship of market values to book or accounting values.

Profit-margin ratios show the percentage of sales dollars that the firm was able to convert into profit. There are many such ratios that can be calculated to yield insightful results, namely: profit margin (18), return on asset (19), and return on equity (20).

Return ratios are generally calculated as a return on assets or equity. The return on assets ratio (19) measures the profitability of the firm's asset utilization. The return on equity ratio (20) indicates the rate of return earned on the book value of owner's equity. Market-value analyses include (i) market-value/book-value ratio and

(ii) price per share/earnings per share (P/E) ratio, and other ratios as indicated in Table 2.5.

Overall, all four different types of ratios (as indicated in Table 2.5) have different characteristics stemming from the firm itself and the industry as a whole. For example, the collection-period ratio (which is Accounts Receivable times 365 over Net Sales) is clearly the function of the billings, payment, and collection policies of the pharmaceutical industry. In addition, the fixed-asset turnover ratios for those firms are different, which might imply that different firms have different capacity utilization.

#### 2.6.1.5 *Market value ratios*

A firm's profitability, risk, quality of management, and many other factors are reflected in its stock and security prices. Hence, market value ratios indicate the market's assessment of the value of the firm's securities.

The PE ratio (21) is simply the market price of the firm's common stock divided by its annual earnings per share. Sometimes called the *earnings multiple*, the PE ratio shows how much the investors are willing to pay for each dollar of the firm's earnings per share. Earnings per share comes from the income statement. Therefore, earnings per share is sensitive to the many factors that affect the construction of an income statement, such as the choice of GAAP to management decisions regarding the use of debt to finance assets. Although earnings per share cannot reflect the value of patents or assets, the quality of the firm's management, or its risk, and stock prices can reflect all of these factors. Comparing a firm's PE ratio to that of the stock market as a whole, or with the firm's competitors, indicates the market's perception of the true value of the company.

Market-to-book ratio (22) measures the market's valuation relative to balance sheet equity. The book value of equity is simply the difference between the book values of assets and liabilities appearing on the balance sheet. The price-to-book-value ratio is the market price per share divided by the book value of equity per share. A higher ratio suggests that investors are more optimistic about the market value of a firm's assets, its intangible assets, and the ability of its managers.

Earnings yield (23) is defined as earnings per share divided by market price per share and is used to measure return on investment. Dividend yield (24) is defined as dividend per share divided by market price per share, which is used to determine whether this company's stock is an income stock or a gross stock. A gross stock dividend yield is very small or even zero. For example, the stock from a utility industry dividend yield is very high.

PEG ratio (25) is defined as PE ratio divided by earnings growth rate. The PEG ratio is used to determine a stock's value while taking the company's earnings growth into account and is considered to provide a more complete picture than the PE ratio. While a high PE ratio may make a stock look like a good buy, factoring in the company's growth rate to get the stock's PEG ratio can tell a different story. The lower the PEG ratio, the more the stock may be undervalued given its earnings performance. The PEG ratio that indicates an over or underpriced stock varies by industry and by company type, though a broad rule of thumb is that a PEG ratio below one is desirable. Also, the accuracy of the PEG ratio depends on the inputs used. SGR is usually used to estimate earnings growth rate. In Appendix 2B, we introduce two possible methods to calculate it. However, using historical growth rates, for example, may provide an inaccurate PEG ratio if future growth rates are expected to deviate from historical growth rates. To distinguish between calculation methods using future growth and historical growth, the terms "forward PEG" and "trailing PEG" are sometimes used.

Enterprise value is an estimate of the market value of the company's operating assets, which means all the assets of the firm except cash. Since market values are usually unavailable, we use the right-hand side of the balance sheet and calculate the enterprise value as:

$$\begin{aligned}\text{Enterprise value} = {} & \text{Total market value of equity} \\ & + \text{Book value of total liabilities} - \text{Cash}\end{aligned}$$

Notice that the sum of the value of the market values of the stock and all liabilities equals the value of the firm's assets from the balance sheet identity. Total market value of equity = market price per share times basic number of shares outstanding.

Enterprise value is often used to calculate the Enterprise value-EBITDA ratio (26):

$$\text{EBITDA ratio} = \text{Enterprise value/EBITDA}$$

where EBITDA is defined as earnings before interest, taxes, depreciation, and amortization.

This ratio is similar to the PE ratio, but it relates the value of all the operating assets to a measure of the operating cash flow generated by those assets.

#### 2.6.1.6 *Policy ratios*

Policy ratios include debt-to-asset ratio, dividend payout ratio, and SGR. Debt-to-asset ratio has been discussed in Group 2 of Table 2.5. Dividend payout ratio is defined as (dividend payout)/(net income). The dividend payout ratio is the ratio of the total amount of dividends paid out to shareholders relative to the net income of the company. It is the percentage of earnings paid to shareholders in dividends. The amount that is not paid to shareholders is retained by the company to pay off debt or to reinvest in core operations. It is sometimes simply referred to as the 'payout ratio.'

SGR is defined as $[(1 - \text{payout ratio})*\text{ROE}]/[1 - (1 - \text{payout ratio}) \times \text{ROE}]$. Appendix 2B will discuss SGR in further detail.

Table 2.5 summarizes all 28 ratios for JNJ during 2016, 2017, 2018, and 2019. Appendix 2A shows how to use Excel to calculate the first 26 ratios with the data of 2018 and 2019 from JNJ Financial Statement.

#### 2.6.1.7 *Estimation of the target of a ratio*

An issue that must be addressed at this point is the determination of an appropriate proxy for the target of a ratio. For an analyst, this can be an insurmountable problem if the firm is extremely diversified, and if it does not have one or two major product lines in industries where industry averages are available. One possible solution is to determine the relative industry share of each division or major product line, then apply these percentages to the related industry averages. Lastly, derive one target ratio for the firm as a whole with which its ratio can be compared. One must be very careful in any such analysis, because the proxy may be extremely over- or underestimated. The analyst can also use Standard Industrial Classification (SIC) codes to properly define the industry of diversified firms. The analyst can then use 3- or 4-digit codes and compute their own weighted industry average.

Often an industry average is used as a proxy for the target ratio. This can lead to another problem, the inappropriate calculation of an industry average, even though the industry and companies are fairly well defined. The issue here is the appropriate weighting scheme for combining the individual company ratios in order to arrive at one industry average. Individual ratios can be weighted according to equal weights, asset weights, or sales weights. The analyst must determine the extent to which firm size, as measured by asset base or market share, affects the relative level of a firm's ratios and the tendency for other firms in the industry to adjust toward the target level of this ratio. One way this can be done is to calculate the coefficients of variation for a number of ratios under each of the weighting the schemes and to compare them to see which scheme consistently has the lowest coefficient variation. This would appear to be the most appropriate weighting scheme. Of course, one could also use a different weighting scheme for each ratio, but this would be very tedious if many ratios were to be analyzed. Note, that the median rather than the average or mean can be used to avoid needless complications with respect to extreme values that might distort the computation of averages. Dynamic financial ratio analysis is to compare individual company ratios with industry averages over time. In general, this kind of analysis needs to rely upon regression analysis. Lee and Lee (2017, Chapter 2) have discussed this kind of analysis in detail.

## 2.7 Cost–Volume–Profit Analysis

CVP *analysis* is a method by which a firm's income statement is examined for operating efficiency, financial leverage, and control. It is one of the tools that aid the manager in the planning and control process. The key variables of CVP analysis are volume, price per unit, variable cost per unit, and fixed cost per unit. *Break even analysis* is the basic type of CVP analysis and is especially useful when a firm is considering expansion of its plant and equipment or its product lines. Ratio information is necessary for performing this type of analysis. Thus, CVP analysis can be considered a type of ratio analysis.

### 2.7.1 *Deterministic break-even analysis*

*Deterministic break-even analysis* is an analytical technique that describes the relationships among fixed costs, variable costs, and profits. A firm with both fixed and variable costs suffers a loss until a certain sales volume, the break-even level, is attained. Above this sales level, the firm covers its fixed and variable costs and earns a profit from its operations.

*Deterministic break-even analysis* is a basic concept taught in microeconomics, accounting, and finance courses. The basic equation describing net profit — the earnings after interest and tax (EAIT) — is basically an income statement:

$$\text{Net profit} = EAIT = (Q(P - V) - F)(1 - \tau_C) \tag{2.5}$$

where $Q$ = the quantity of goods sold; $P$ = the price per unit sold; $V$ = variable cost per unit sold; $F$ = total amount of fixed costs; and $\tau_C$ = the corporate tax rate.

When net profit is 0, the amount produced and sold just covers the cost of production (the fixed cost and the variable cost for the quantity produced). Because the firm produces no income, it does not have to pay taxes, so at the break-even point the $(1 - \tau_C)$ in Eq. (2.5) is dropped and the equation becomes $Q(P - V) - F = 0$ or, rearranging,

$$Q^* = \frac{F}{(P - V)} \tag{2.6}$$

where $Q^*$ is the number of production units required to generate zero profit. This equation is used to calculate the break-even quantity. In Figure 2.2, the fixed costs are \$15 million, variable costs are \$5 per

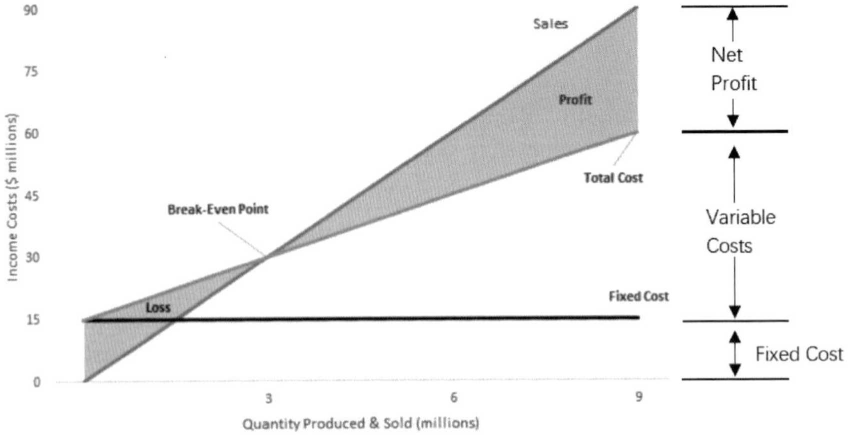


Figure 2.2 Linear Break-Even Chart.

unit and the selling price is \$10 per unit. Using Eq. (2.6), we find that the break-even quantity is 3 million units:

$$Q^* = \frac{\$15 \text{ million}}{(\$10/\text{unit} - \$5/\text{unit})} = 3 \text{ million units}$$

There are two types of break-even points: linear and nonlinear. These are depicted in Figure 2.2 (linear) and Figure 2.3 (nonlinear). Figure 2.2 shows the break-even point occurring at 3 million units produced at a cost of \$30 million. Units produced and sold prior to this point are sold at a loss. At the break-even point, sales revenue just covers the cost of goods sold. Beyond the break-even point, the firm earns a profit.

Multiple break-even points occur because the product market is not perfect. As the quantity sold and produced increases, the firm may be forced to reduce its product prices or input prices (materials, labor, capital) may increase with increases in production, such as the cost of overtime labor. This nonlinearity in the price or the cost function, or both, produces a nonlinear break-even situation.

Economies of scale can be constant (linear) or they can increase or decrease (not strictly linear). Nonlinear representation of the variable costs and income curves may be more accurate than linear representations, but ambiguities may arise when we try to interpret or use

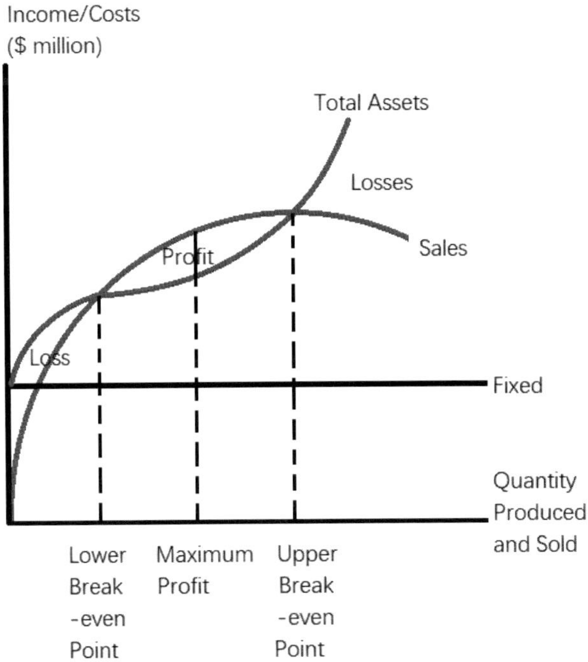


Figure 2.3 Nonlinear Break-Even Chart.

these nonlinear curves. As Figure 2.3 depicts, there exists a trade-off between accurate representation of the real world and the usefulness of the information generated by a simplified model.

In finance we are more interested in sales revenue than in the number of units produced and sold. To find sales revenue, we change Eq. (2.6) to a dollar amount:

$$\hat{Q} = PQ^* = \frac{F}{1 - \frac{V}{P}} \tag{2.7}$$

where $\hat{Q}$ is break-even sales in dollars; $F$ is the fixed cost per unit; $V$ is the variable cost per unit; and $P$ is the selling price per unit.

There is an important relationship between the break-even point and the DOL used by a firm. DOL is determined as

$$\text{DOL} = \frac{\text{\% Change in profits}}{\text{\% Change in sales}} = \frac{Q(P - V)}{Q(P - V) - F} \tag{2.8}$$

The first part of Eq. (2.8) is the basic definition of DOL: the ratio of percentage change in profits to percentage change in sales. The second part of the equation is obtained by substituting the definition of profits and sales from Eq. (2.5). Based on the definition of the break-even quantity and Eq. (2.6), Eq. (2.8) can be rewritten as

$$\text{DOL} = \frac{1}{1 - \frac{Q^*}{Q}} \tag{2.9}$$

The implications of Eq. (2.9) are as follows:

- If $Q > Q^*$, then DOL $> 0$. In this case, the change in profits is in the same direction as the change in sales (when sales increase, profits increase).
- If $Q < Q^*$, then DOL $< 0$. Here, the change in losses is in the opposite direction as the change in sales (if sales increase, losses will decrease).

DOL is important to the financial manager. The higher the DOL, the greater the increase in profits for a given increase in sales. For example, consider firms A and B in the same industry. Firm A is highly capital intensive with a large DOL, while firm B is highly labor intensive with a small DOL. The decisions regarding strategies to increase sales for firm A will have a greater impact on profitability than will similar decisions for firm B.

In addition to DOL, we also analyze DFL and DCL. Appendix 2C has carefully defined the definition of DOL, DFL, and DCL. This appendix also shows how to use Excel to calculate DOL, DFL, and combined leverage.

### 2.7.2 *Stochastic analysis*

Stochastic financial analysis involves the use of random variables. (The word *stochastic* refers to chance or probability.) For example, net profit is a random variable because a component of its equation, the quantity to be sold in the future, is estimated (in contrast to the price per unit and variable cost per unit, which generally are known with certainty). Stochastic CVP analysis with only one random variable is the simplest form because we do not have to be concerned about the interdependence of the variables. Stochastic CVP analysis becomes more complicated when more random variables are involved (such as price (P) and variable costs (V)).

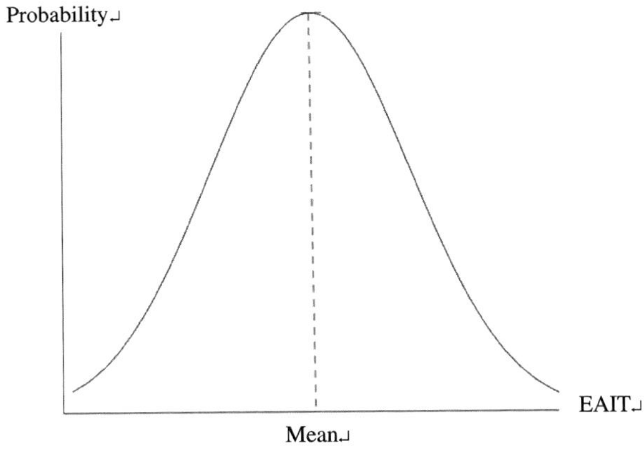


Figure 2.4 Normal Distribution of EAIT.

Equation (2.5) can be generalized so that $Q$ is a stochastic variable ($\tilde{Q}$). Profit then becomes a stochastic variable also.

$$\text{Net profit} = \text{EAIT} = (\tilde{Q}(P - V) - F)(1 - \tau_C) \tag{2.10}$$

Stochastic CVP analysis is useful to the financial manager because of the increasing importance of moving from point (certainty) estimates to interval (uncertainty) estimates. Particularly in the current dynamic business environment, stochastic CVP formulation allows calculation of not only a point estimate but also of the related interval estimate based on the probability distribution of quantity sold. The application of probability models (discussed in Chapters 6, 7, and 8) greatly enhances the degree of realism in such analysis.

In stochastic analysis, EAIT is depicted with a normal curve (see Figure 2.4) because its input variable, $\tilde{Q}$, is the source of the uncertainty. The concept of the normal distribution is discussed in Chapter 6 and is especially important in understanding capital budgeting under uncertainty, which is presented in Chapter 8.

## 2.8 Relationships among Economic, Financial, and Accounting Information

The best way to describe the relationships among economic, financial, and accounting information is in terms of how they affect or describe income. Income can be described in terms of accounting earnings, based on the recording of transactions according to GAAP. Accounting uses accruals and deferrals rather than cash flows. Accountants measure the firm's net income by matching its revenues with the costs incurred in generating those revenues.

Economic earnings are more abstract in that they are defined as the maximum value that an individual or firm can consume in a given period and sill be as well off at the end of the period as in the beginning. This is the historic definition of economic earning as given by Hicks (1946). Accounting earnings measures only the changes in wealth caused by *realized* gains and losses. This includes obvious gains or losses instead of those gains and losses that are not yet realized but are inevitable. Economic income measures the change in wealth based on both realized and unrealized gains and losses. For this reason, economic and financial information and its effects on the firm provide a different measure of income and value than does accounting information.

Financial income is based on cash flow changes in wealth. The definition of cash income is cash revenue less cash expenses. Therefore, the definition of financial income is the change in wealth (net cash flow), or net cash income less cash investment outlays.

Theoretically, economic income should be used rather than accounting earnings for the determination of the firm's value. The reason is that economic income represents the firm's true earnings and cash flow. However, economic income, as theoretically defined, is not directly observable and thus accounting earnings are generally used as a measurement. The relationship between economic income and accounting earnings is shown by the following:

$$A = E + e, \tag{2.11}$$

where $A$ = accounting earnings; $E$ = economic income; and $e$ = errors.

Suppose the accounting earnings of two firms are equal — for example, \$1 per share. Firm A has economic earnings of \$0.80 per share and an error component of \$0.20 per share, while firm B has economic earnings of \$0.50 per share and an error component of \$0.50 per share. The market will value the earnings of firm A higher than firm B by giving firm A a larger P/E ratio, which makes firm A's stock price higher than firm B's stock price even though both firms report numerically the same accounting earnings. The larger the portion of economic earnings, the greater the firm's value.

Equation 2.11 is also useful in analyzing the market value of a firm, because the financial analyst is continually using accounting information and adjusting it based on other information to determine financial value or worth.

## 2.9 Summary

This chapter reviews economic, financial, market, and accounting information to provide some environmental backgrounds to understand and apply sound financial management. Also covered are financial ratios, CVP analysis, break-even analysis, and degree of leverage (DOL) analysis. Financial ratios are an important tool by which managers and investors evaluate a firm's market value as well as understand the reasons for the fluctuations of the firm's market value. Factors that affect the industry in general and the firm in particular should be investigated. The best way to understand the common factors is to study economic information associated with the fluctuations or to look at the leading indicators. Accounting information, market information, and economic information are the three basic sources of data used in the financial decision-making process. In addition to analyzing the various types of information at one point in time and over time, the financial analyst is also interested in how the information changes over time. This area of study is known as *dynamic analysis and a detailed discussion can be found in Lee and Lee* (2017).

## References

Deakin, E. B. "Distribution of Financial Accounting Ratios," *The Accounting Review*, 52 (1976, pp. 90–96).

Dornbusch, R., S. Fisher and R. Startz. *Macroeconomics*, 13th edn. (McGraw-Hill, 2018).

Hicks, J. R. *Value and Capital*, 2nd edn. (London: Oxford University Press, 1965).

Hilliard, J. E. and R. A. Leitch. "Cost-Volume-Profit Analysis under Uncertainty: A Log Normal Approach," *The Accounting Review*, 51 (1975, pp. 69–80).

Hong, H. "Inflation and the Market Value of the Firm: Theory and Tests," *The Journal of Finance*, 32(4) (1977, pp. 1031–1048).

Johnson & Johnson 2016, 2017, 2018, and 2019 Annual Reports.
Lee, C. F. and J. Lee. *Financial Analysis and Planning: Theory and Application* (World Scientific: Singapore, 2017).
Lee, C. F. and C. C. Wu. "Expectation Formulation and the Financial Ratio Adjustment Processes," *Accounting Review,* 63 (April 1988, pp. 292–306).
Lee, C. F. and J. K. Zumwalt. "Associations between Alternative Accounting Profitability Measures and Security Returns," *Journal of Financial and Quantitative Analysis* (March 1981).
Lee, C. F., J. Lee and A. C. Lee. *Statistics for Business and Financial Economics*, 3rd edn. (Springer Academic Publishers, 2013).
Lev, B. "Industry Averages as Targets for Financial Ratios," *Journal of Accounting Research*, 7 (Autumn 1969, pp. 290–300).
Wei, S. "A General Discussion Model for Cost-Volume-Profit Analysis under Uncertainty," *The Accounting Review*, 54 (October 1979, pp. 687–706).

## Appendix 2A — Calculate 27 Financial Ratios with Excel

In this appendix, we use the data of 2018 and 2019 fisical year of JNJ annual report as the example and show how to calculate the 27 basic financial ratios across five groups. The following figure lists 20 basic input variables from the Financial statements of fisical year 2019 and 2018. The colunm A is the name of input variable. The column B shows the value of each variables in 2019 and column C shows that in 2018.

| | | | | |
|---|---|---|---|---|
| 1 | **Johnson and Johnson** | | | |
| 2 | **Input financial variables** | **2019** | **2018** | |
| 3 | Cash and Cash equivalents | 17,305 | 18,107 | In Millions |
| 4 | Marketable securities | 1,982 | 1,580 | In Millions |
| 5 | Account Receivables | 14,481 | 14,098 | In Millions |
| 6 | Inventory | 9,020 | 8,599 | In Millions |
| 7 | Current Asset | 45,274 | 46,033 | In Millions |
| 8 | Fixed Asset | 17,658 | 17,035 | In Millions |
| 9 | Total Asset | 157,728 | 152,954 | In Millions |
| 10 | Current Liability | 35,964 | 31,230 | In Millions |
| 11 | Long term debt | 26,494 | 27,684 | In Millions |
| 12 | Total Liability | 98,257 | 93,202 | In Millions |
| 13 | Total Equity | 59,471 | 59,752 | In Millions |
| 14 | Sales | 82,059 | 81,581 | In Millions |
| 15 | Cost of Goods Sold | 27,556 | 27,091 | In Millions |
| 16 | Interest Expense | 318 | 1,005 | In Millions |
| 17 | Provision for taxes on income (taxes expense) | 2,209 | 2,702 | In Millions |
| 18 | Net Income | 15,119 | 15,297 | In Millions |
| 19 | Dividend payout | 9,917 | 9,494 | In Millions |
| 20 | Basic average shares outstanding | 2,645.1 | 2,681.5 | In Millions |
| 21 | Depreciation and amortization of property and intangible | 7,009 | 6,929 | In Millions |
| 22 | Price of last trading day | 145.75 | 127.27 | Dollars per share |

## 2A.1 Liquidity Ratio

First, we focus on the Liquidity ratio, which measures relative strength of a firm's financial position. It usually includes current ratio, quick ratio, cash ratio and networking capital to total asset ratio. The formula for each ratio is defined as follows:

$$\text{Current ratio (CR)} = \frac{\text{Current asset}}{\text{Current liability}}$$

$$\text{Quick ratio} = \frac{\text{Cash} + \text{MS} + \text{Receivables}}{\text{Current liability}}$$

$$\text{Cash ratio} = \frac{\text{Cash} + \text{MS}}{\text{Current liability}}$$

$$\text{Net working capital to total asset} = \frac{\text{Net working capital}}{\text{Current asset}}$$

The following figure shows how to calculate these ratios based on the formulae with Excel. To compute the Current ratio, we only need to find the cell in which the value of current asset locates (B7) and the cell in which the value of current liability belongs to (B10) and then find an empty cell to input "=B7/B10," which means dividing current asset by current liability. The Excel will show the results "1.26."

SUM | fx =B7/B10

| | A | B | C | D | E | F | G | H | I |
|---|---|---|---|---|---|---|---|---|---|
| 1 | **Johnson and Johnson** | | | | | **Financial Ratio** | | | |
| 2 | **Input financial variables** | **2019** | **2018** | | | **Liquidity ratio** | | **2019** | **2018** |
| 3 | Cash and Cash equivalents | 17,305 | 18,107 | In Million | | Current Ratio | =B7/B10 | =B7/B10 | 1.47 |
| 4 | Marketable securities | 1,982 | 1,580 | In Million | | Quick Ratio | =(B3+B4+B5)/B10 | 0.94 | 1.08 |
| 5 | Account Receivables | 14,481 | 14,098 | In Million | | Cash Ratio | =(B3+B4)/B10 | 0.54 | 0.63 |
| 6 | Inventory | 9,020 | 8,599 | In Million | | Net working capital to total asset | =(B7-B10)/B9 | 0.06 | 0.10 |
| 7 | Current Asset | 45,274 | 46,033 | In Million | | | | | |
| 8 | Fixed Asset | 17,658 | 17,035 | In Million | | | | | |
| 9 | Total Asset | 157,728 | 152,954 | In Million | | | | | |
| 10 | Current Liability | 35,964 | 31,230 | In Million | | | | | |
| 11 | Long term debt | 26,494 | 27,684 | In Million | | | | | |
| 12 | Total Liability | 98,257 | 93,202 | In Million | | | | | |
| 13 | Total Equity | 59,471 | 59,752 | In Million | | | | | |
| 14 | Sales | 82,059 | 81,581 | In Million | | | | | |
| 15 | Cost of Goods Sold | 27,556 | 27,091 | In Million | | | | | |
| 16 | Interest Expense | 318 | 1,005 | In Million | | | | | |
| 17 | Provision for taxes on income (taxes expense) | 2,209 | 2,702 | In Million | | | | | |
| 18 | Net Income | 15,119 | 15,297 | In Million | | | | | |
| 19 | Dividend payout | 9,917 | 9,494 | In Million | | | | | |
| 20 | **Basic average shares outstanding** | 3,120 | 3,120 | In Million | | | | | |
| 21 | Depreciation and amortization of property and intangible | 7,009 | 6,929 | In Million | | | | | |
| 22 | Price of last trading day | 145.75 | 127.27 | Dollars per share | | | | | |

Similarly, we can compute the Quick ratio and Cash Ratio as the following two figures instruct. Compared with calculating the current ratio, the only difference for computing the Quick ratio or the Cash ratio is that different numerator is used. We have to use the sum of Cash and cash equivalent and MS [=(B3 + B4)] as the numerator in order to calculate the Cash ratio or use the sum of Cash and cash equivalent, MS and Accounting receivables [=(B3 + B4 + B5)] as the numerator in order to calculate the Quick ratio.

SUM =(B3+B4+B5)/B10

| | A | B | C | D | E | F | G | H | I |
|---|---|---|---|---|---|---|---|---|---|
| 1 | **Johnson and Johnson** | | | | | **Financial Ratio** | | | |
| 2 | **Input financial variables** | **2019** | **2018** | | | **Liquidity ratio** | | **2019** | **2018** |
| 3 | Cash and Cash equivalents | 17,305 | 18,107 | In Million | | Current Ratio | =B7/B10 | 1.26 | 1.47 |
| 4 | Marketable securities | 1,982 | 1,580 | In Million | | Quick Ratio | =(B3+B4+B5)/B10 | B5)/B10 | 1.08 |
| 5 | Account Receivables | 14,481 | 14,098 | In Million | | Cash Ratio | =(B3+B4)/B10 | 0.54 | 0.63 |
| 6 | Inventory | 9,020 | 8,599 | In Million | | Net working capital to total asset | =(B7-B10)/B9 | 0.06 | 0.10 |
| 7 | Current Asset | 45,274 | 46,033 | In Million | | | | | |
| 8 | Fixed Asset | 17,658 | 17,035 | In Million | | | | | |
| 9 | Total Asset | 157,728 | 152,954 | In Million | | | | | |
| 10 | Current Liability | 35,964 | 31,230 | In Million | | | | | |
| 11 | Long term debt | 26,494 | 27,684 | In Million | | | | | |
| 12 | Total Liability | 98,257 | 93,202 | In Million | | | | | |
| 13 | Total Equity | 59,471 | 59,752 | In Million | | | | | |
| 14 | Sales | 82,059 | 81,581 | In Million | | | | | |
| 15 | Cost of Goods Sold | 27,556 | 27,091 | In Million | | | | | |
| 16 | Interest Expense | 318 | 1,005 | In Million | | | | | |
| 17 | Provision for taxes on income (taxes expense) | 2,209 | 2,702 | In Million | | | | | |
| 18 | Net Income | 15,119 | 15,297 | In Million | | | | | |
| 19 | Dividend payout | 9,917 | 9,494 | In Million | | | | | |
| 20 | **Basic average shares outstanding** | 3,120 | 3,120 | In Million | | | | | |
| 21 | *Depreciation and amortization of property and intangible* | 7,009 | 6,929 | In Million | | | | | |
| 22 | Price of last trading day | 145.75 | 127.27 | Dollars per share | | | | | |

SUM =(B3+B4)/B10

| | A | B | C | D | E | F | G | H | I |
|---|---|---|---|---|---|---|---|---|---|
| 1 | **Johnson and Johnson** | | | | | **Financial Ratio** | | | |
| 2 | **Input financial variables** | **2019** | **2018** | | | **Liquidity ratio** | | **2019** | **2018** |
| 3 | Cash and Cash equivalents | 17,305 | 18,107 | In Million | | Current Ratio | =B7/B10 | 1.26 | 1.47 |
| 4 | Marketable securities | 1,982 | 1,580 | In Million | | Quick Ratio | =(B3+B4+B5)/B10 | 0.94 | 1.08 |
| 5 | Account Receivables | 14,481 | 14,098 | In Million | | Cash Ratio | =(B3+B4)/B10 | B10 | 0.63 |
| 6 | Inventory | 9,020 | 8,599 | In Million | | Net working capital to total asset | =(B7-B10)/B9 | 0.06 | 0.10 |
| 7 | Current Asset | 45,274 | 46,033 | In Million | | | | | |
| 8 | Fixed Asset | 17,658 | 17,035 | In Million | | | | | |
| 9 | Total Asset | 157,728 | 152,954 | In Million | | | | | |
| 10 | Current Liability | 35,964 | 31,230 | In Million | | | | | |
| 11 | Long term debt | 26,494 | 27,684 | In Million | | | | | |
| 12 | Total Liability | 98,257 | 93,202 | In Million | | | | | |
| 13 | Total Equity | 59,471 | 59,752 | In Million | | | | | |
| 14 | Sales | 82,059 | 81,581 | In Million | | | | | |
| 15 | Cost of Goods Sold | 27,556 | 27,091 | In Million | | | | | |
| 16 | Interest Expense | 318 | 1,005 | In Million | | | | | |
| 17 | Provision for taxes on income (taxes expense) | 2,209 | 2,702 | In Million | | | | | |
| 18 | Net Income | 15,119 | 15,297 | In Million | | | | | |
| 19 | Dividend payout | 9,917 | 9,494 | In Million | | | | | |
| 20 | **Basic average shares outstanding** | 3,120 | 3,120 | In Million | | | | | |
| 21 | Depreciation and amortization of property and intangible | 7,009 | 6,929 | In Million | | | | | |
| 22 | Price of last trading day | 145.75 | 127.27 | Dollars per share | | | | | |

For the net working capital to total asset ratio,we firstly need to calculate "Net working capital" and then divide it by current asset. As net working capital is defined as "Current asset minus current liability," we compute this ratio by inputing "=(B7−B10)/B9," which gives us 0.06 in the figure below.

SUM =(B7-B10)/B9

| | A | B | C | D | E | F | G | H | I |
|---|---|---|---|---|---|---|---|---|---|
| 1 | **Johnson and Johnson** | | | | | **Financial Ratio** | | | |
| 2 | **Input financial variables** | **2019** | **2018** | | | **Liquidity ratio** | | **2019** | **2018** |
| 3 | Cash and Cash equivalents | 17,305 | 18,107 | In Million | | Current Ratio | =B7/B10 | 1.26 | 1.47 |
| 4 | Marketable securities | 1,982 | 1,580 | In Million | | Quick Ratio | =(B3+B4+B5)/B10 | 0.94 | 1.08 |
| 5 | Account Receivables | 14,481 | 14,098 | In Million | | Cash Ratio | =(B3+B4)/B10 | 0.54 | 0.63 |
| 6 | Inventory | 9,020 | 8,599 | In Million | | Net working capital to total asset | =(B7-B10)/B9 | B9 | 0.10 |
| 7 | Current Asset | 45,274 | 46,033 | In Million | | | | | |
| 8 | Fixed Asset | 17,658 | 17,035 | In Million | | | | | |
| 9 | Total Asset | 157,728 | 152,954 | In Million | | | | | |
| 10 | Current Liability | 35,964 | 31,230 | In Million | | | | | |
| 11 | Long term debt | 26,494 | 27,684 | In Million | | | | | |
| 12 | Total Liability | 98,257 | 93,202 | In Million | | | | | |
| 13 | Total Equity | 59,471 | 59,752 | In Million | | | | | |
| 14 | Sales | 82,059 | 81,581 | In Million | | | | | |
| 15 | Cost of Goods Sold | 27,556 | 27,091 | In Million | | | | | |
| 16 | Interest Expense | 318 | 1,005 | In Million | | | | | |
| 17 | Provision for taxes on income (taxes expense) | 2,209 | 2,702 | In Million | | | | | |
| 18 | Net Income | 15,119 | 15,297 | In Million | | | | | |
| 19 | Dividend payout | 9,917 | 9,494 | In Million | | | | | |
| 20 | **Basic average shares outstanding** | 3,120 | 3,120 | In Million | | | | | |
| 21 | Depreciation and amortization of property and intangible | 7,009 | 6,929 | In Million | | | | | |
| 22 | Price of last trading day | 145.75 | 127.27 | Dollars per share | | | | | |

## 2A.2 Financial Leverage Ratio

In this section, we compute the financial leverage ratios, which reflect financial risk posture of a firm, with Excel. There are six ratios which are commonly used in financial analysis.

$$\text{Debt to asset} = \frac{\text{Total liability}}{\text{Total asset}}$$

$$\text{Debt to equity} = \frac{\text{Total liability}}{\text{Total equity}}$$

$$\text{Equity multiplier} = \frac{\text{Total asset}}{\text{Total equity}}$$

$$\text{Times interest paid} = \frac{\text{EBIT}}{\text{Interest expense}}$$

$$\text{Long term debt ratio} = \frac{\text{Long term debt}}{\text{Long term debt+Total equity}}$$

$$\text{Cash coverage ratio} = \frac{\text{EBIT+Depreciation}}{\text{Interest expense}}$$

For the first four ratios, their calculations are quite simple. We input "=B12/B9" to get 0.62 for the Debt to Asset ratio, "=B12/B13" to get 1.65 for the Debt to Equity ratio, "=B9/B13" to get 2.65 for the Equity Multiplier, "=(B18 + B16 + B17)/B16" to get 55.49 for the Times interested paid.

The following figure shows how to calculate the Long term debt ratio. We input "=B11/(B11 + B13)" in an empty cell, where (B11 + B13) equals the sum of long term debt and total equity. Excel gives us 0.31.

SUM | × | ✓ | *fx* | =B11/(B11+B13)

| | A | B | C | D | E | F | G | H | I |
|---|---|---|---|---|---|---|---|---|---|
| 1 | **Johnson and Johnson** | | | | | **Financial Ratio** | | | |
| 2 | **Input financial variables** | **2019** | **2018** | | | | | **2019** | **2018** |
| 3 | Cash and Cash equivalents | 17,305 | 18,107 | In Million | | | | | |
| 4 | Marketable securities | 1,982 | 1,580 | In Million | | | | | |
| 5 | Account Receivables | 14,481 | 14,098 | In Million | | | | | |
| 6 | Inventory | 9,020 | 8,599 | In Million | | | | | |
| 7 | Current Asset | 45,274 | 46,033 | In Million | | | | | |
| 8 | Fixed Asset | 17,658 | 17,035 | In Million | | **Financial Leverage ratio** | | | |
| 9 | Total Asset | 157,728 | 152,954 | In Million | | Debt to Asset | =B12/B9 | 0.62 | 0.61 |
| 10 | Current Liability | 35,964 | 31,230 | In Million | | Debt to Equity | =B12/B13 | 1.65 | 1.56 |
| 11 | Long term debt | 26,494 | 27,684 | In Million | | Equity Multiplier | =B9/B13 | 2.65 | 2.56 |
| 12 | Total Liability | 98,257 | 93,202 | In Million | | Times Interest Paid | =(B18+B16+B17)/B16 | 55.49 | 18.91 |
| 13 | Total Equity | 59,471 | 59,752 | In Million | | Long term debt ratio | =B11/(B11+B13) | B13) | 0.32 |
| 14 | Sales | 82,059 | 81,581 | In Million | | Cash coverage ratio | =(B18+B17+B16+B21)/B16 | 77.53 | 25.80 |
| 15 | Cost of Goods Sold | 27,556 | 27,091 | In Million | | | | | |
| 16 | Interest Expense | 318 | 1,005 | In Million | | | | | |
| 17 | Provision for taxes on income (taxes expense) | 2,209 | 2,702 | In Million | | | | | |
| 18 | Net Income | 15,119 | 15,297 | In Million | | | | | |
| 19 | Dividend payout | 9,917 | 9,494 | In Million | | | | | |
| 20 | **Basic average shares outstanding** | 3,120 | 3,120 | In Million | | | | | |
| 21 | Depreciation and amortization of property and intangible | 7,009 | 6,929 | In Million | | | | | |
| 22 | Price of last trading day | 145.75 | 127.27 | Dollars per share | | | | | |

Similarly, the Cash coverage ratio can be computed based on the formula by inputting "=(B18 + B17 + B16 + B21)/B16." Then we obtain 77.53 as the value of this ratio.

SUM | =(B18+B17+B16+B21)/B16

| | A | B | C | D | E | F | G | H | I |
|---|---|---|---|---|---|---|---|---|---|
| 1 | **Johnson and Johnson** | | | | | **Financial Ratio** | | | |
| 2 | **Input financial variables** | **2019** | **2018** | | | | | **2019** | **2018** |
| 3 | Cash and Cash equivalents | 17,305 | 18.107 | In Million | | | | | |
| 4 | Marketable securities | 1,982 | 1,580 | In Million | | | | | |
| 5 | Account Receivables | 14,481 | 14.098 | In Million | | | | | |
| 6 | Inventory | 9,020 | 8,599 | In Million | | | | | |
| 7 | Current Asset | 45,274 | 46,033 | In Million | | | | | |
| 8 | Fixed Asset | 17,658 | 17,035 | In Million | | **Financial Leverage ratio** | | | |
| 9 | Total Asset | 157,728 | 152,954 | In Million | | Debt to Asset | =B12/B9 | 0.62 | 0.61 |
| 10 | Current Liability | 35,964 | 31,230 | In Million | | Debt to Equity | =B12/B13 | 1.65 | 1.56 |
| 11 | Long term debt | 26.494 | 27,684 | In Million | | Equity Multiplier | =B9/B13 | 2.65 | 2.56 |
| 12 | Total Liability | 98,257 | 93,202 | In Million | | Times Interest Paid | =(B18+B16+B17)/B16 | 55.49 | 18.91 |
| 13 | Total Equity | 59,471 | 59,752 | In Million | | Long term debt ratio | =B11/(B11+B13) | 0.31 | 0.32 |
| 14 | Sales | 82,059 | 81,581 | In Million | | Cash coverage ratio | =(B18+B17+B16+B21)/B16 | B16 | 25.80 |
| 15 | Cost of Goods Sold | 27,556 | 27,091 | In Million | | | | | |
| 16 | Interest Expense | 318 | 1,005 | In Million | | | | | |
| 17 | Provision for taxes on income (taxes expense) | 2,209 | 2,702 | In Million | | | | | |
| 18 | Net Income | 15,119 | 15,297 | In Million | | | | | |
| 19 | Dividend payout | 9.917 | 9,494 | In Million | | | | | |
| 20 | **Basic average shares outstanding** | 3,120 | 3.120 | In Million | | | | | |
| 21 | Depreciation and amortization of property and intangible | 7,009 | 6,929 | In Million | | | | | |
| 22 | Price of last trading day | 145.75 | 127.27 | Dollars per share | | | | | |

## 2A.3 Asset Efficiency Ratios

These ratios mainly reflect how a firm is utilizing its asset. We list 7 common ratios used in financial analysis. They are Day's sales in receivables, Receivables Turnover, Day's sales in Inventory, Inventory Turnover, Fixed Asset Turnover, Total Asset Turnover, Net working capital turnover.

$$\text{Day's sales in receivables} = \frac{\text{Account receivable}}{\frac{\text{Sale}}{365}}$$

$$\text{Receivables turnover} = \frac{\text{Sales}}{\text{Account receivable}}$$

$$\text{Day's sales in inventory} = \frac{\text{Inventory}}{\frac{\text{COGS}}{365}}$$

$$\text{Inventory turnover} = \frac{\text{COGS}}{\text{Inventory}}$$

$$\text{Fixed asset turnover} = \frac{\text{Sales}}{\text{Fixed assets}}$$

$$\text{Total asset turnover} = \frac{\text{Sales}}{\text{Total assets}}$$

$$\text{Net working capital turnover} = \frac{\text{Sales}}{\text{Net working capital}}$$

It is very simple to compute Receivable turnover by inputting "=B14/B5," to calculate Inventory Turnover by inputting "=B15/B6," to obtain Fixed Asset Turnover via inputting "=B14/B8" and to get Total Asset Turnover via inputting "=B14/B9." Excel will show all these values.

The following two figures shows that we calculate the Day's sales in Receivables by inputting "=B5/(B14/365)" and that we calculate the Day's sales in Inventory by inputting "=B6/(B15/365)." The key point here is to add a bracket to denominator when we calculate "Sales/365."

SUM | × ✓ $f_x$ | =B5/(B14/365)

| | A | B | C | D | E | F | G | H | I |
|---|---|---|---|---|---|---|---|---|---|
| 1 | **Johnson and Johnson** | | | | | **Financial Ratio** | | | |
| 2 | **Input financial variables** | **2019** | **2018** | | | **Liquidity ratio** | | **2019** | **2018** |
| 3 | Cash and Cash equivalents | 17,305 | 18,107 | In Million | | | | | |
| 4 | Marketable securities | 1,982 | 1,580 | In Million | | **Asset Efficiency ratio** | | | |
| 5 | Account Receivables | 14,481 | 14,098 | In Million | | Day's sales in receivables | =B5/(B14/365) | 365) | 63.08 |
| 6 | Inventory | 9,020 | 8,599 | In Million | | Receivables Turnover | =B14/B5 | 5.67 | 5.79 |
| 7 | Current Asset | 45,274 | 46,033 | In Million | | Day's sales in Inventory | =B6/(B15/365) | 119.48 | 115.86 |
| 8 | Fixed Asset | 17,658 | 17,035 | In Million | | Inventory Turnover | =B15/B6 | 3.05 | 3.15 |
| 9 | Total Asset | 157,728 | 152,954 | In Million | | Fixed Asset Turnover | =B14/B8 | 4.65 | 4.79 |
| 10 | Current Liability | 35,964 | 31,230 | In Million | | Total Asset Turnover | =B14/B9 | 0.52 | 0.53 |
| 11 | Long term debt | 26,494 | 27,684 | In Million | | Net working capital turnover | =B14/(B7-B10) | 8.81 | 5.51 |
| 12 | Total Liability | 98,257 | 93,202 | In Million | | | | | |
| 13 | Total Equity | 59,471 | 59,752 | In Million | | | | | |
| 14 | Sales | 82,059 | 81,581 | In Million | | | | | |
| 15 | Cost of Goods Sold | 27,556 | 27,091 | In Million | | | | | |
| 16 | Interest Expense | 318 | 1,005 | In Million | | | | | |
| 17 | Provision for taxes on income (taxes expense) | 2,209 | 2,702 | In Million | | | | | |
| 18 | Net Income | 15,119 | 15,297 | In Million | | | | | |
| 19 | Dividend payout | 9,917 | 9,494 | In Million | | | | | |
| 20 | **Basic average shares outstanding** | 3,120 | 3,120 | In Million | | | | | |
| 21 | Depreciation and amortization of property and intangible | 7,009 | 6,929 | In Million | | | | | |
| 22 | Price of last trading day | 145.75 | 127.27 | Dollars per share | | | | | |

SUM | × ✓ $f_x$ | =B6/(B15/365)

| | A | B | C | D | E | F | G | H | I |
|---|---|---|---|---|---|---|---|---|---|
| 1 | **Johnson and Johnson** | | | | | **Financial Ratio** | | | |
| 2 | **Input financial variables** | **2019** | **2018** | | | **Liquidity ratio** | | **2019** | **2018** |
| 3 | Cash and Cash equivalents | 17,305 | 18,107 | In Million | | | | | |
| 4 | Marketable securities | 1,982 | 1,580 | In Million | | **Asset Efficiency ratio** | | | |
| 5 | Account Receivables | 14,481 | 14,098 | In Million | | Day's sales in receivables | =B5/(B14/365) | 64.41 | 63.08 |
| 6 | Inventory | 9,020 | 8,599 | In Million | | Receivables Turnover | =B14/B5 | 5.67 | 5.79 |
| 7 | Current Asset | 45,274 | 46,033 | In Million | | Day's sales in Inventory | =B6/(B15/365) | 365) | 115.86 |
| 8 | Fixed Asset | 17,658 | 17,035 | In Million | | Inventory Turnover | =B15/B6 | 3.05 | 3.15 |
| 9 | Total Asset | 157,728 | 152,954 | In Million | | Fixed Asset Turnover | =B14/B8 | 4.65 | 4.79 |
| 10 | Current Liability | 35,964 | 31,230 | In Million | | Total Asset Turnover | =B14/B9 | 0.52 | 0.53 |
| 11 | Long term debt | 26,494 | 27,684 | In Million | | Net working capital turnover | =B14/(B7-B10) | 8.81 | 5.51 |
| 12 | Total Liability | 98,257 | 93,202 | In Million | | | | | |
| 13 | Total Equity | 59,471 | 59,752 | In Million | | | | | |
| 14 | Sales | 82,059 | 81,581 | In Million | | | | | |
| 15 | Cost of Goods Sold | 27,556 | 27,091 | In Million | | | | | |
| 16 | Interest Expense | 318 | 1,005 | In Million | | | | | |
| 17 | Provision for taxes on income (taxes expense) | 2,209 | 2,702 | In Million | | | | | |
| 18 | Net Income | 15,119 | 15,297 | In Million | | | | | |
| 19 | Dividend payout | 9,917 | 9,494 | In Million | | | | | |
| 20 | **Basic average shares outstanding** | 3,120 | 3,120 | In Million | | | | | |
| 21 | Depreciation and amortization of property and intangible | 7,009 | 6,929 | In Million | | | | | |
| 22 | Price of last trading day | 145.75 | 127.27 | Dollars per share | | | | | |

In order to calculate the Net Working capital Turnover, we input "=B14/(B7-B10)" since "B7-B10" equals to the working capital of JNJ in 2019. Excel shows the final value of 8.81.

SUM =B14/(B7-B10)

| | A | B | C | D | E | F | G | H | I |
|---|---|---|---|---|---|---|---|---|---|
| 1 | **Johnson and Johnson** | | | | | **Financial Ratio** | | | |
| 2 | **Input financial variables** | **2019** | **2018** | | | **Liquidity ratio** | | **2019** | **2018** |
| 3 | Cash and Cash equivalents | 17,305 | 18,107 | In Million | | | | | |
| 4 | Marketable securities | 1,982 | 1,580 | In Million | | **Asset Efficiency ratio** | | | |
| 5 | Account Receivables | 14,481 | 14,098 | In Million | | Day's sales in receivables | =B5/(B14/365) | 64.41 | 63.08 |
| 6 | Inventory | 9,020 | 8,599 | In Million | | Receivables Turnover | =B14/B5 | 5.67 | 5.79 |
| 7 | Current Asset | 45,274 | 46,033 | In Million | | Day's sales in Inventory | =B6/(B15/365) | 119.48 | 115.86 |
| 8 | Fixed Asset | 17,658 | 17,035 | In Million | | Inventory Turnover | =B15/B6 | 3.05 | 3.15 |
| 9 | Total Asset | 157,728 | 152,954 | In Million | | Fixed Asset Turnover | =B14/B8 | 4.65 | 4.79 |
| 10 | Current Liability | 35,964 | 31,230 | In Million | | Total Asset Turnover | =B14/B9 | 0.52 | 0.53 |
| 11 | Long term debt | 26,494 | 27,684 | In Million | | Net working capital turnover | =B14/(B7-B10) | B10) | 5.51 |
| 12 | Total Liability | 98,257 | 93,202 | In Million | | | | | |
| 13 | Total Equity | 59,471 | 59,752 | In Million | | | | | |
| 14 | Sales | 82,059 | 81,581 | In Million | | | | | |
| 15 | Cost of Goods Sold | 27,556 | 27,091 | In Million | | | | | |
| 16 | Interest Expense | 318 | 1,005 | In Million | | | | | |
| 17 | Provision for taxes on income (taxes expense) | 2,209 | 2,702 | In Million | | | | | |
| 18 | Net Income | 15,119 | 15,297 | In Million | | | | | |
| 19 | Dividend payout | 9,917 | 9,494 | In Million | | | | | |
| 20 | **Basic average shares outstanding** | 3,120 | 3,120 | In Million | | | | | |
| 21 | Depreciation and amortization of property and intangible | 7,009 | 6,929 | In Million | | | | | |
| 22 | Price of last trading day | 145.75 | 127.27 | Dollars per share | | | | | |

## 2A.4 Profitability Ratios

These ratios reflect the profitability of a firm's operations. Profit Margin, Return on Asset and Return on Equity are widely used in empirical research.

$$\text{Profit margin} = \frac{\text{Net income}}{\text{Sales}}$$

$$\text{Return on equity} = \frac{\text{Net income}}{\text{Total equity}}$$

$$\text{Return on asset} = \frac{\text{Net income}}{\text{Total asset}}$$

Similar to the skills used before, we only need to divide one variable (X1) by another one (X2) with inputting "=X1/X2" to obtain the ratios. The figure below gives an example of how to calculate the Profit Margin (0.18). ROA and ROE can be obtained in a similar way.

SUM =B18/B14

| | A | B | C | D | E | F | G | H | I |
|---|---|---|---|---|---|---|---|---|---|
| 1 | **Johnson and Johnson** | | | | | **Financial Ratio** | | | |
| 2 | **Input financial variables** | **2019** | **2018** | | | | | **2019** | **2018** |
| 3 | Cash and Cash equivalents | 17,305 | 18,107 | In Million | | | | | |
| 4 | Marketable securities | 1,982 | 1,580 | In Million | | **Profitability ratio** | | | |
| 5 | Account Receivables | 14,481 | 14,098 | In Million | | Profit Margin | =B18/B14 | =B18/B14 | 0.19 |
| 6 | Inventory | 9,020 | 8,599 | In Million | | ROA | =B18/B9 | 0.10 | 0.10 |
| 7 | Current Asset | 45,274 | 46,033 | In Million | | ROE | =B18/B13 | 0.25 | 0.26 |
| 8 | Fixed Asset | 17,658 | 17,035 | In Million | | | | | |
| 9 | Total Asset | 157,728 | 152,954 | In Million | | | | | |
| 10 | Current Liability | 35,964 | 31,230 | In Million | | | | | |
| 11 | Long term debt | 26,494 | 27,684 | In Million | | | | | |
| 12 | Total Liability | 98,257 | 93,202 | In Million | | | | | |
| 13 | Total Equity | 59,471 | 59,752 | In Million | | | | | |
| 14 | Sales | 82,059 | 81,581 | In Million | | | | | |
| 15 | Cost of Goods Sold | 27,556 | 27,091 | In Million | | | | | |
| 16 | Interest Expense | 318 | 1,005 | In Million | | | | | |
| 17 | Provision for taxes on income (taxes expense) | 2,209 | 2,702 | In Million | | | | | |
| 18 | Net Income | 15,119 | 15,297 | In Million | | | | | |
| 19 | Dividend payout | 9,917 | 9,494 | In Million | | | | | |
| 20 | **Basic average shares outstanding** | 3,120 | 3,120 | In Million | | | | | |
| 21 | Depreciation and amortization of property and intangible | 7,009 | 6,929 | In Million | | | | | |
| 22 | Price of last trading day | 145.75 | 127.27 | Dollars per share | | | | | |

## 2A.5 Market Value Ratios

The last group includes market value ratios, which indicate an assessment of value of a firm's stock. We calculate six ratios in this section.

$$\text{Price} - \text{Earnings ratio(PE)} = \frac{\text{Price per share}}{\text{Earnings per share}}$$

$$\text{Market} - \text{Book ratio(MB)} = \frac{\text{Price per share}}{\text{Book value per share}}$$

$$\text{Earnings yield} = \frac{\text{Earnings per share}}{\text{Price per share}}$$

$$\text{Dividend yield} = \frac{\text{Dividend per share}}{\text{Price per share}}$$

$$\text{PEG ratio} = \frac{\text{PE}}{\text{Earnings growth rate}}$$

$$\text{Dividend payout ratio} = \frac{\text{Dividend payout}}{\text{Net income}}$$

$$\text{Enterprise} - \text{EBDTA ratio} = \frac{\text{Enterprise value}}{\text{EBITDA}}$$

The following two figures show how to compute PE ratio and MB ratio. Since price per share is input into cell B22, we only need to find EPS or book value per share. According to the definition of EPS, it is computed via dividing net income by total shares(=B18/B20). Similarly, book value per share can be obtained by inputing "=B9/B20." In order to calculate PE ratio or MB ratio in one step,we directly input "=B22/(B18/B20)," and "= B22/(B13/B20)," respectively. The values are 30.0774 and 6.4825, respectively.

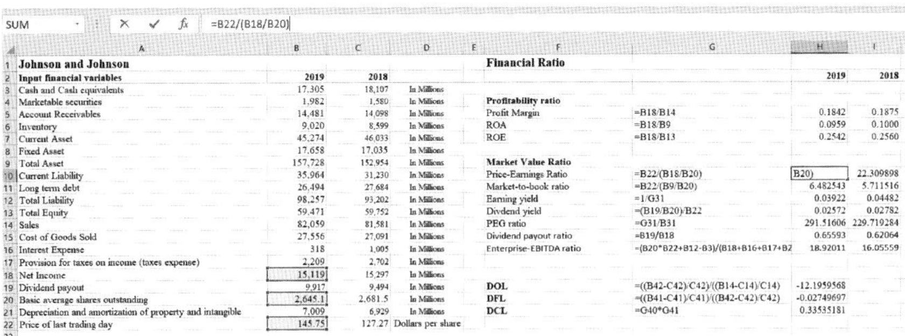

SUM =B22/(B18/B20)

| | A | B | C | D | E | F | G | H | I |
|---|---|---|---|---|---|---|---|---|---|
| 1 | **Johnson and Johnson** | | | | | **Financial Ratio** | | | |
| 2 | **Input financial variables** | **2019** | **2018** | | | | | **2019** | **2018** |
| 3 | Cash and Cash equivalents | 17,305 | 18,107 | In Millions | | | | | |
| 4 | Marketable securities | 1,982 | 1,580 | In Millions | | **Profitability ratio** | | | |
| 5 | Account Receivables | 14,481 | 14,098 | In Millions | | Profit Margin | =B18/B14 | 0.1842 | 0.1875 |
| 6 | Inventory | 9,020 | 8,599 | In Millions | | ROA | =B18/B9 | 0.0959 | 0.1000 |
| 7 | Current Asset | 45,274 | 46,033 | In Millions | | ROE | =B18/B13 | 0.2542 | 0.2560 |
| 8 | Fixed Asset | 17,658 | 17,035 | In Millions | | | | | |
| 9 | Total Asset | 157,728 | 152,954 | In Millions | | **Market Value Ratio** | | | |
| 10 | Current Liability | 35,964 | 31,230 | In Millions | | Price-Earnings Ratio | =B22/(B18/B20) | B20) | 22.309898 |
| 11 | Long term debt | 26,494 | 27,684 | In Millions | | Market-to-book ratio | =B22/(B9/B20) | 6.482543 | 5.711516 |
| 12 | Total Liability | 98,257 | 93,202 | In Millions | | Earning yield | =1/G31 | 0.03922 | 0.04482 |
| 13 | Total Equity | 59,471 | 59,752 | In Millions | | Divdend yield | =(B19/B20)/B22 | 0.02572 | 0.02782 |
| 14 | Sales | 82,059 | 81,581 | In Millions | | PEG ratio | =G31/B31 | 291.51606 | 229.719284 |
| 15 | Cost of Goods Sold | 27,556 | 27,091 | In Millions | | Dividend payout ratio | =B19/B18 | 0.65593 | 0.62064 |
| 16 | Interest Expense | 318 | 1,005 | In Millions | | Enterprise-EBITDA ratio | =(B20*B22+B12-B3)/(B18+B16+B17+B2 | 18.92011 | 16.05559 |
| 17 | Provision for taxes on income (taxes expense) | 2,209 | 2,702 | In Millions | | | | | |
| 18 | Net Income | 15,119 | 15,297 | In Millions | | | | | |
| 19 | Dividend payout | 9,917 | 9,494 | In Millions | | **DOL** | =((B42-C42)/C42)/((B14-C14)/C14) | -12.1959568 | |
| 20 | Basic average shares outstanding | 2,645.1 | 2,681.5 | In Millions | | **DFL** | =((B41-C41)/C41)/((B42-C42)/C42) | -0.02749697 | |
| 21 | Depreciation and amortization of property and intangible | 7,009 | 6,929 | In Millions | | **DCL** | =G40*G41 | 0.33535181 | |
| 22 | Price of last trading day | 145.75 | 127.27 | Dollars per share | | | | | |

SUM | × ✓ fx | =B22/(B13/B20)

| | A | B | C | D | E | F | G | H | I |
|---|---|---|---|---|---|---|---|---|---|
| 1 | **Johnson and Johnson** | | | | | **Financial Ratio** | | | |
| 2 | **Input financial variables** | **2019** | **2018** | | | | | **2019** | **2018** |
| 3 | Cash and Cash equivalents | 17,305 | 18,107 | In Millions | | | | | |
| 4 | Marketable securities | 1,982 | 1,580 | In Millions | | **Profitability ratio** | | | |
| 5 | Account Receivables | 14,481 | 14,098 | In Millions | | Profit Margin | =B18/B14 | 0.1842 | 0.1875 |
| 6 | Inventory | 9,020 | 8,599 | In Millions | | ROA | =B18/B9 | 0.0959 | 0.1000 |
| 7 | Current Asset | 45,274 | 46,033 | In Millions | | ROE | =B18/B13 | 0.2542 | 0.2560 |
| 8 | Fixed Asset | 17,658 | 17,035 | In Millions | | | | | |
| 9 | Total Asset | 157,728 | 152,954 | In Millions | | **Market Value Ratio** | | | |
| 10 | Current Liability | 35,964 | 31,230 | In Millions | | Price-Earnings Ratio | =B22/(B18/B20) | 25.499261 | 22.309898 |
| 11 | Long term debt | 26,494 | 27,684 | In Millions | | Market-to-book ratio | =B22/(B9/B20) | B20) | 5.711516 |
| 12 | Total Liability | 98,257 | 93,202 | In Millions | | Earning yield | =1/G31 | 0.03922 | 0.04482 |
| 13 | Total Equity | 59,471 | 59,752 | In Millions | | Divdend yield | =(B19/B20)/B22 | 0.02572 | 0.02782 |
| 14 | Sales | 82,059 | 81,581 | In Millions | | PEG ratio | =G31/B31 | 291.51606 | 229.719284 |
| 15 | Cost of Goods Sold | 27,556 | 27,091 | In Millions | | Dividend payout ratio | =B19/B18 | 0.65593 | 0.62064 |
| 16 | Interest Expense | 318 | 1,005 | In Millions | | Enterprise-EBITDA ratio | =(B20*B22+B12-B3)/(B18+B16+B17+B2 | 18.92011 | 16.05559 |
| 17 | Provision for taxes on income (taxes expense) | 2,209 | 2,702 | In Millions | | | | | |
| 18 | Net Income | 15,119 | 15,297 | In Millions | | | | | |
| 19 | Dividend payout | 9,917 | 9,494 | In Millions | | **DOL** | =((B42-C42)/C42)/((B14-C14)/C14) | -12.1959568 | |
| 20 | Basic average shares outstanding | 2,645.1 | 2,681.5 | In Millions | | **DFL** | =((B41-C41)/C41)/((B42-C42)/C42) | -0.02749697 | |
| 21 | Depreciation and amortization of property and intangible | 7,009 | 6,929 | In Millions | | **DCL** | =G40*G41 | 0.33535181 | |
| 22 | Price of last trading day | 145.75 | 127.27 | Dollars per share | | | | | |

Additionally, the Earnings yield is simply the reciprocal of PE so that we get it (1/30.0774 = 0.03325), and Dividend yield can be computed via inputing "=(B19/B20)/B22" and equals 0.0218. The following figure shows the result.

SUM | × ✓ fx | =(B19/B20)/B22

| | A | B | C | D | E | F | G | H | I |
|---|---|---|---|---|---|---|---|---|---|
| 1 | **Johnson and Johnson** | | | | | **Financial Ratio** | | | |
| 2 | **Input financial variables** | **2019** | **2018** | | | | | **2019** | **2018** |
| 3 | Cash and Cash equivalents | 17,305 | 18,107 | In Millions | | | | | |
| 4 | Marketable securities | 1,982 | 1,580 | In Millions | | **Profitability ratio** | | | |
| 5 | Account Receivables | 14,481 | 14,098 | In Millions | | Profit Margin | =B18/B14 | 0.1842 | 0.1875 |
| 6 | Inventory | 9,020 | 8,599 | In Millions | | ROA | =B18/B9 | 0.0959 | 0.1000 |
| 7 | Current Asset | 45,274 | 46,033 | In Millions | | ROE | =B18/B13 | 0.2542 | 0.2560 |
| 8 | Fixed Asset | 17,658 | 17,035 | In Millions | | | | | |
| 9 | Total Asset | 157,728 | 152,954 | In Millions | | **Market Value Ratio** | | | |
| 10 | Current Liability | 35,964 | 31,230 | In Millions | | Price-Earnings Ratio | =B22/(B18/B20) | 30.077386 | 25.958188 |
| 11 | Long term debt | 26,494 | 27,684 | In Millions | | Market-to-book ratio | =B22/(B9/B20) | 2.883065 | 2.596090 |
| 12 | Total Liability | 98,257 | 93,202 | In Millions | | Earning yield | =1/G31 | 0.03325 | 0.03852 |
| 13 | Total Equity | 59,471 | 59,752 | In Millions | | Divdend yield | =(B19/B20)/B22 | B22 | 0.02391 |
| 14 | Sales | 82,059 | 81,581 | In Millions | | PEG ratio | =G31/B31 | 343.8547149 | 267.284791 |
| 15 | Cost of Goods Sold | 27,556 | 27,091 | In Millions | | Dividend payout ratio | =B19/B18 | 0.65593 | 0.62064 |
| 16 | Interest Expense | 318 | 1,005 | In Millions | | Enterprise-EBITDA ratio | =(B20*B22+B12-B3)/(B18+B16+B17+B2 | 21.72752 | 18.20759 |
| 17 | Provision for taxes on income (taxes expense) | 2,209 | 2,702 | In Millions | | | | | |
| 18 | Net Income | 15,119 | 15,297 | In Millions | | | | | |
| 19 | Dividend payout | 9,917 | 9,494 | In Millions | | | | | |
| 20 | **Basic average shares outstanding** | 3,120 | 3,120 | In Millions | | | | | |
| 21 | Depreciation and amortization of property and intangible | 7,009 | 6,929 | In Millions | | | | | |
| 22 | Price of last trading day | 145.75 | 127.27 | Dollars per share | | | | | |

For enterprise – EBITDA ratio, we firstly calculate enterprise value on the numerator according to the definition "Total market value of equity + Book value of Total Liability-Cash" and then input "=B20*B22 + B12-B3" into an empty cell. Next, we divide enterprise value by EBITDA, which is "=B18 + B16 + B17 + B21." So the one-step formula is "=(B20*B22 + B12 − B3)/(B18 + B16 + B17 + B21)." Excel gives us the value of 21.7275.

SUM | × ✓ fx | =(B20*B22+B12-B3)/(B18+B16+B17+B21)

| | A | B | C | D | E | F | G | H | I |
|---|---|---|---|---|---|---|---|---|---|
| 1 | **Johnson and Johnson** | | | | | **Financial Ratio** | | | |
| 2 | **Input financial variables** | **2019** | **2018** | | | | | **2019** | **2018** |
| 3 | Cash and Cash equivalents | 17,305 | 18,107 | In Millions | | | | | |
| 4 | Marketable securities | 1,982 | 1,580 | In Millions | | **Profitability ratio** | | | |
| 5 | Account Receivables | 14,481 | 14,098 | In Millions | | Profit Margin | =B18/B14 | 0.1842 | 0.1875 |
| 6 | Inventory | 9,020 | 8,599 | In Millions | | ROA | =B18/B9 | 0.0959 | 0.1000 |
| 7 | Current Asset | 45,274 | 46,033 | In Millions | | ROE | =B18/B13 | 0.2542 | 0.2560 |
| 8 | Fixed Asset | 17,658 | 17,035 | In Millions | | | | | |
| 9 | Total Asset | 157,728 | 152,954 | In Millions | | **Market Value Ratio** | | | |
| 10 | Current Liability | 35,964 | 31,230 | In Millions | | Price-Earnings Ratio | =B22/(B18/B20) | 30.077386 | 25.958188 |
| 11 | Long term debt | 26,494 | 27,684 | In Millions | | Market-to-book ratio | =B22/(B9/B20) | 2.883065 | 2.596090 |
| 12 | Total Liability | 98,257 | 93,202 | In Millions | | Earning yield | =1/G31 | 0.03325 | 0.03852 |
| 13 | Total Equity | 59,471 | 59,752 | In Millions | | Divdend yield | =(B19/B20)/B22 | 0.02181 | 0.02391 |
| 14 | Sales | 82,059 | 81,581 | In Millions | | PEG ratio | =G31/B31 | 343.8547149 | 267.284791 |
| 15 | Cost of Goods Sold | 27,556 | 27,091 | In Millions | | Dividend payout ratio | =B19/B18 | 0.65593 | 0.62064 |
| 16 | Interest Expense | 318 | 1,005 | In Millions | | Enterprise-EBITDA ratio | =(B20*B22+B12-B3)/(B18+B16+B17+B2 | B21) | 18.20759 |
| 17 | Provision for taxes on income (taxes expense) | 2,209 | 2,702 | In Millions | | | | | |
| 18 | Net Income | 15,119 | 15,297 | In Millions | | | | | |
| 19 | Dividend payout | 9,917 | 9,494 | In Millions | | | | | |
| 20 | **Basic average shares outstanding** | 3,120 | 3,120 | In Millions | | | | | |
| 21 | Depreciation and amortization of property and intangible | 7,009 | 6,929 | In Millions | | | | | |
| 22 | Price of last trading day | 145.75 | 127.27 | Dollars per share | | | | | |

For the dividend payout ratio, it is computed as "=B19/B18," and excel gives us 0.6559. The PEG ratio equals to PE ratio divided by SGR. Since we already have PE ratio, we only need to find the value of SGR. Based on the formula: SGR = ROE∗(1 − dividend payout ratio), we input sustainable growth rate = H7∗(1−H15). Therefore, we get PEG ratio by inputting "=H10/(H7∗(1−H15))," which equals to 343.8547. The result is as follows

SUM | × ✓ *fx* | =H10/(H7*(1-H15))

| | A | B | C | D | E | F | G | H | I |
|---|---|---|---|---|---|---|---|---|---|
| 1 | **Johnson and Johnson** | | | | | **Financial Ratio** | | | |
| 2 | **Input financial variables** | **2019** | **2018** | | | | | **2019** | **2018** |
| 3 | Cash and Cash equivalents | 17,305 | 18.107 | In Millions | | | | | |
| 4 | Marketable securities | 1,982 | 1,580 | In Millions | | **Profitability ratio** | | | |
| 5 | Account Receivables | 14,481 | 14.098 | In Millions | | Profit Margin | =B18/B14 | 0.1842 | 0.1875 |
| 6 | Inventory | 9,020 | 8,599 | In Millions | | ROA | =B18/B9 | 0.0959 | 0.1000 |
| 7 | Current Asset | 45.274 | 46.033 | In Millions | | ROE | =B18/B13 | 0.2542 | 0.2560 |
| 8 | Fixed Asset | 17,658 | 17,035 | In Millions | | | | | |
| 9 | Total Asset | 157.728 | 152.954 | In Millions | | **Market Value Ratio** | | | |
| 10 | Current Liability | 35,964 | 31,230 | In Millions | | Price-Earnings Ratio | =B22/(B18/B20) | 30.077386 | 25.958188 |
| 11 | Long term debt | 26.494 | 27.684 | In Millions | | Market-to-book ratio | =B22/(B9/B20) | 2.883065 | 2.596090 |
| 12 | Total Liability | 98,257 | 93,202 | In Millions | | Earning yield | =1/G31 | 0.03325 | 0.03852 |
| 13 | Total Equity | 59,471 | 59.752 | In Millions | | Divdend yield | =(B19/B20)/B22 | 0.02181 | 0.02391 |
| 14 | Sales | 82,059 | 81,581 | In Millions | | PEG ratio | =H10/(H7*(1-H15)) | 1-H15)) | 267.284791 |
| 15 | Cost of Goods Sold | 27.556 | 27.091 | In Millions | | Dividend payout ratio | =B19/B18 | 0.65593 | 0.62064 |
| 16 | Interest Expense | 318 | 1.005 | In Millions | | Enterprise-EBITDA ratio | =(B20*B22+B12-B3)/(B18+B16+B17+B2 | 21.72752 | 18.20759 |
| 17 | Provision for taxes on income (taxes expense) | 2,209 | 2,702 | In Millions | | | | | |
| 18 | Net Income | 15,119 | 15,297 | In Millions | | | | | |
| 19 | Dividend payout | 9,917 | 9.494 | In Millions | | | | | |
| 20 | **Basic average shares outstanding** | 3,120 | 3,120 | In Millions | | | | | |
| 21 | Depreciation and amortization of property and intangible | 7,009 | 6.929 | In Millions | | | | | |
| 22 | Price of last trading day | 145.75 | 127.27 | Dollars per share | | | | | |

## Appendix 2B — Two Possible Methods to Estimate SGR

SGR can be either estimated by (i) using both external and internal source of fund or (ii) using only internal source of fund.

We present these two methods in detail as follows:

**Method 1:** The SGR with both external and internal source of fund can be defined as (Lee 2017):

$$\text{SGR} = \frac{\text{Retention rate} * \text{ROE}}{1 - (\text{Retention rate} * \text{ROE})}$$

$$= \frac{(1 - \text{Dividend payout ratio}) * \text{ROE}}{1 - [(1 - \text{Dividend payout ratio}) * \text{ROE}]}$$

$$\text{Dividend payout ratio} = \text{Dividends/Net income} \qquad (2.1\text{B})$$

**Method 2:** The SGR: Considering internal source of fund

$$\begin{aligned}
\text{ROE} &= \text{Net income/Total equity} \\
\text{ROE} &= (\text{Net income/Assets}) \times (\text{Assets/Equity}) \\
\text{ROE} &= (\text{Net income/Sales}) \times (\text{Sales/Assets}) \times (\text{Assets/Equity}) \\
\text{SGR} &= (\text{Net income/Sales}) \times (\text{Retention rate}) \times (\text{Sales/Assets}) \\
&\quad \times (\text{Assets/Equity}) \\
&= \text{ROE} \times (1 - \text{Dividend payout ratio}) \qquad (2.2\text{B})
\end{aligned}$$

**Example:**

With the data from JNJ financial statement of 2019 fiscal year, we estimate obtain

ROE = Net income/Total equity = 15,119/ 59,471 = 0.2542.
Dividend payout ratio = Dividends/Net income = 9,917/ 15,119 = 0.6559.

According to the Method 1,

$\text{SGR} = (1 - 0.6559) \times 0.2542/1 - [(1 - 0.6559) \times 0.2542] = 0.0959.$

According to the Method 2,

$\text{SGR} = 0.2542 \times (1 - 0.6559) = 0.0875.$

**The difference between Method 1 and Method 2:**

Technically, as $ROE \times (1 - D)$ is the numerator of $ROE \times (1 - D)/1 - ROE \times (1 - D)$ and $1 > [1 - ROE \times (1 - D)] \geq 0$, it is easy to prove $ROE \times (1 - D)/1 - ROE \times (1 - D) \geq ROE \times (1 - D)$. In addition, we can transform $ROE \times (1 - D)/1 - ROE \times (1 - D)$ into Retained Earnings/Equity − Retained Earnings and transform $ROE \times (1 - D)$ into Retained Earnings/Equity. It is obvious to see Retained Earnings/Equity − Retained Earnings ≥ Retained Earnings/Equity since Equity − Retained Earnings ≤ Equity. If we use equity value at the end of this year, then (Equity − Retained Earnings) can be interpreted as the equity value at the beginning of this year under the condition of no external finance.

Consequently, the SGR from Method 1 is usually greater than that from Method 2. The numerical result 0.0959 > 0.0875 confirms this.

**How to calculate SGR with two methods with Excel:** We compute the SGR with Method 1 by inputting "=((1 − B26)∗ H28)/(1 − ((1 − B26)∗H28))" and then obtain 0.0958558 and with Method 2 by inputting "=H28∗(1 − H36)" and then obtain 0.087471204. The following figures show the calculation.

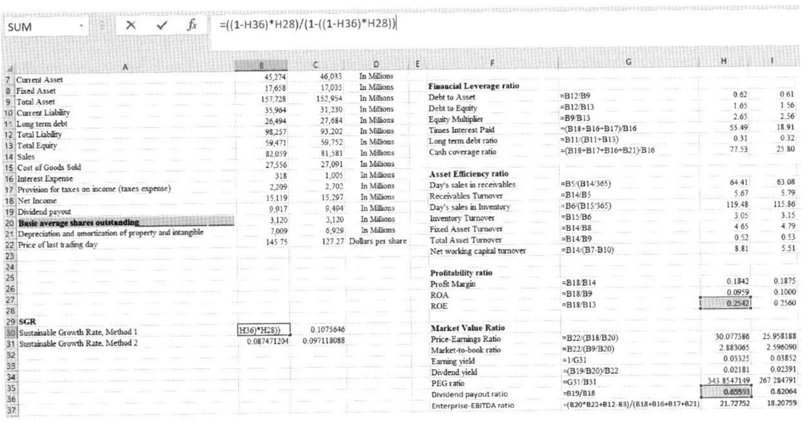

SUM | =((1-H36)*H28)/(1-((1-H36)*H28))

| | A | B | C | D | E | F | G | H | I |
|---|---|---|---|---|---|---|---|---|---|
| 7 | Current Asset | 45,274 | 46,033 | In Millions | | | | | |
| 8 | Fixed Asset | 17,658 | 17,035 | In Millions | | **Financial Leverage ratio** | | | |
| 9 | Total Asset | 157,728 | 152,954 | In Millions | | Debt to Asset | =B12/B9 | 0.62 | 0.61 |
| 10 | Current Liability | 35,964 | 31,230 | In Millions | | Debt to Equity | =B12/B13 | 1.65 | 1.56 |
| 11 | Long term debt | 26,494 | 27,684 | In Millions | | Equity Multiplier | =B9/B13 | 2.65 | 2.56 |
| 12 | Total Liability | 98,257 | 93,202 | In Millions | | Times Interest Paid | =(B18+B16+B17)/B16 | 55.49 | 18.91 |
| 13 | Total Equity | 59,471 | 59,752 | In Millions | | Long term debt ratio | =B11/(B11+B13) | 0.31 | 0.32 |
| 14 | Sales | 82,059 | 81,581 | In Millions | | Cash coverage ratio | =(B18+B17+B16+B21)/B16 | 77.53 | 25.80 |
| 15 | Cost of Goods Sold | 27,556 | 27,091 | In Millions | | | | | |
| 16 | Interest Expense | 318 | 1,005 | In Millions | | **Asset Efficiency ratio** | | | |
| 17 | Provision for taxes on income (taxes expense) | 2,209 | 2,702 | In Millions | | Day's sales in receivables | =B5/(B14/365) | 64.41 | 63.08 |
| 18 | Net Income | 15,119 | 15,297 | In Millions | | Receivables Turnover | =B14/B5 | 5.67 | 5.79 |
| 19 | Dividend payout | 9,917 | 9,494 | In Millions | | Day's sales in Inventory | =B6/(B15/365) | 119.48 | 115.86 |
| 20 | **Basic average shares outstanding** | 3,120 | 3,120 | In Millions | | Inventory Turnover | =B15/B6 | 3.05 | 3.15 |
| 21 | Depreciation and amortization of property and intangible | 7,009 | 6,929 | In Millions | | Fixed Asset Turnover | =B14/B8 | 4.65 | 4.79 |
| 22 | Price of last trading day | 145.75 | 127.27 | Dollars per share | | Total Asset Turnover | =B14/B9 | 0.52 | 0.53 |
| 23 | | | | | | Net working capital turnover | =B14/(B7-B10) | 8.81 | 5.51 |
| 24 | | | | | | | | | |
| 25 | | | | | | **Profitability ratio** | | | |
| 26 | | | | | | Profit Margin | =B18/B14 | 0.1842 | 0.1875 |
| 27 | | | | | | ROA | =B18/B9 | 0.0959 | 0.1000 |
| 28 | | | | | | ROE | =B18/B13 | 0.2542 | 0.2560 |
| 29 | **SGR** | | | | | | | | |
| 30 | Sustainable Growth Rate, Method 1 | H36)*H28)) | 0.1075646 | | | **Market Value Ratio** | | | |
| 31 | Sustainable Growth Rate, Method 2 | 0.087471204 | 0.097118088 | | | Price-Earnings Ratio | =B22/(B18/B20) | 30.077386 | 25.958188 |
| 32 | | | | | | Market-to-book ratio | =B22/(B9/B20) | 2.883065 | 2.596090 |
| 33 | | | | | | Earning yield | =1/G31 | 0.03325 | 0.03852 |
| 34 | | | | | | Divdend yield | =(B19/B20)/B22 | 0.02181 | 0.02391 |
| 35 | | | | | | PEG ratio | =G31/B31 | 343.8547149 | 267.284791 |
| 36 | | | | | | Dividend payout ratio | =B19/B18 | 0.65593 | 0.62064 |
| 37 | | | | | | Enterprise-EBITDA ratio | =(B20*B22+B12-B3)/(B18+B16+B17+B21) | 21.72752 | 18.20759 |

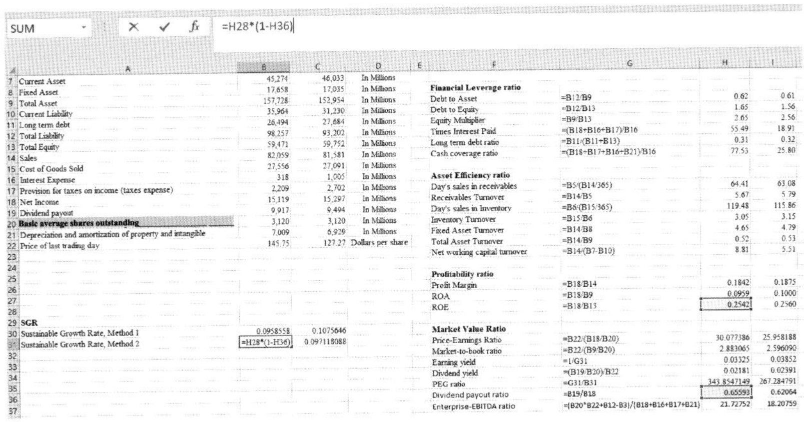

SUM | =H28*(1-H36)

| | A | B | C | D | E | F | G | H | I |
|---|---|---|---|---|---|---|---|---|---|
| 7 | Current Asset | 45,274 | 46,033 | In Millions | | | | | |
| 8 | Fixed Asset | 17,658 | 17,035 | In Millions | | **Financial Leverage ratio** | | | |
| 9 | Total Asset | 157,728 | 152,954 | In Millions | | Debt to Asset | =B12/B9 | 0.62 | 0.61 |
| 10 | Current Liability | 35,964 | 31,230 | In Millions | | Debt to Equity | =B12/B13 | 1.65 | 1.56 |
| 11 | Long term debt | 26,494 | 27,684 | In Millions | | Equity Multiplier | =B9/B13 | 2.65 | 2.56 |
| 12 | Total Liability | 98,257 | 93,202 | In Millions | | Times Interest Paid | =(B18+B16+B17)/B16 | 55.49 | 18.91 |
| 13 | Total Equity | 59,471 | 59,752 | In Millions | | Long term debt ratio | =B11/(B11+B13) | 0.31 | 0.32 |
| 14 | Sales | 82,059 | 81,581 | In Millions | | Cash coverage ratio | =(B18+B17+B16+B21)/B16 | 77.53 | 25.80 |
| 15 | Cost of Goods Sold | 27,556 | 27,091 | In Millions | | | | | |
| 16 | Interest Expense | 318 | 1,005 | In Millions | | **Asset Efficiency ratio** | | | |
| 17 | Provision for taxes on income (taxes expense) | 2,209 | 2,702 | In Millions | | Day's sales in receivables | =B5/(B14/365) | 64.41 | 63.08 |
| 18 | Net Income | 15,119 | 15,297 | In Millions | | Receivables Turnover | =B14/B5 | 5.67 | 5.79 |
| 19 | Dividend payout | 9,917 | 9,494 | In Millions | | Day's sales in Inventory | =B6/(B15/365) | 119.48 | 115.86 |
| 20 | **Basic average shares outstanding** | 3,120 | 3,120 | In Millions | | Inventory Turnover | =B15/B6 | 3.05 | 3.15 |
| 21 | Depreciation and amortization of property and intangible | 7,009 | 6,929 | In Millions | | Fixed Asset Turnover | =B14/B8 | 4.65 | 4.79 |
| 22 | Price of last trading day | 145.75 | 127.27 | Dollars per share | | Total Asset Turnover | =B14/B9 | 0.52 | 0.53 |
| 23 | | | | | | Net working capital turnover | =B14/(B7-B10) | 8.81 | 5.51 |
| 24 | | | | | | | | | |
| 25 | | | | | | **Profitability ratio** | | | |
| 26 | | | | | | Profit Margin | =B18/B14 | 0.1842 | 0.1875 |
| 27 | | | | | | ROA | =B18/B9 | 0.0959 | 0.1000 |
| 28 | | | | | | ROE | =B18/B13 | 0.2542 | 0.2560 |
| 29 | **SGR** | | | | | | | | |
| 30 | Sustainable Growth Rate, Method 1 | 0.0958558 | 0.1075646 | | | **Market Value Ratio** | | | |
| 31 | Sustainable Growth Rate, Method 2 | =H28*(1-H36) | 0.097118088 | | | Price-Earnings Ratio | =B22/(B18/B20) | 30.077386 | 25.958188 |
| 32 | | | | | | Market-to-book ratio | =B22/(B9/B20) | 2.883065 | 2.596090 |
| 33 | | | | | | Earning yield | =1/G31 | 0.03325 | 0.03852 |
| 34 | | | | | | Divdend yield | =(B19/B20)/B22 | 0.02181 | 0.02391 |
| 35 | | | | | | PEG ratio | =G31/B31 | 343.8547149 | 267.284791 |
| 36 | | | | | | Dividend payout ratio | =B19/B18 | 0.65593 | 0.62064 |
| 37 | | | | | | Enterprise-EBITDA ratio | =(B20*B22+B12-B3)/(B18+B16+B17+B21) | 21.72752 | 18.20759 |

## Appendix 2C — How to Compute DOL, DFL, and DCL with Excel

In this appendix, we first define the definitions of DOL, DFL, and DCL in terms of elasticity definition, then we show how Excel program can be used to calculate these three variables in terms of financial statement data. In Chapter 11, we will theoretically and empirically discuss these three variables in further detail.

How Excel program can be used to calculate these three variables in terms of financial statement data.

1. The definition of DOL is:

$$\text{DOL} = \frac{\%\ \text{Change in EBIT}}{\%\ \text{Change in Sale}} \tag{2.1C}$$

To calculate the DOL, we firstly compute the percentage change in EBIT by inputting "(B4 − C4)/C4." Then, compute the percentage change in Sale by inputting "(B3 − C3)/C3." Put them together, we input "=((B4 − C4)/C4)/((B3 − C3)/C3)" to get DOL = −6.3626.

SUM | × ✓ *fx* | =B18/B20

| | A | B | C | D | E | F | G | H | I |
|---|---|---|---|---|---|---|---|---|---|
| 1 | **Johnson and Johnson** | | | | | **Financial Ratio** | | | |
| 2 | **Input financial variables** | **2019** | **2018** | | | **Liquidity ratio** | | **2019** | **2018** |
| 3 | Cash and Cash equivalents | 17,305 | 18,107 | In Millions | | Current Ratio | =B7/B10 | 1.26 | 1.47 |
| 4 | Marketable securities | 1,982 | 1,580 | In Millions | | Quick Ratio | =(B3+B4+B5)/B10 | 0.94 | 1.08 |
| 5 | Account Receivables | 14,481 | 14,098 | In Millions | | Cash Ratio | =(B3+B4)/B10 | 0.54 | 0.63 |
| 6 | Inventory | 9,020 | 8,599 | In Millions | | Net working capital to total asset | =(B7-B10)/B9 | 0.06 | 0.10 |
| 7 | Current Asset | 45,274 | 46,033 | In Millions | | | | | |
| 8 | Fixed Asset | 17,658 | 17,035 | In Millions | | **Financial Leverage ratio** | | | |
| 9 | Total Asset | 157,728 | 152,954 | In Millions | | Debt to Asset | =B12/B9 | 0.62 | 0.61 |
| 10 | Current Liability | 35,964 | 31,230 | In Millions | | Debt to Equity | =B12/B13 | 1.65 | 1.56 |
| 11 | Long term debt | 26,494 | 27,684 | In Millions | | Equity Multiplier | =B9/B13 | 2.65 | 2.56 |
| 12 | Total Liability | 98,257 | 93,202 | In Millions | | Times Interest Paid | =(B18+B16+B17)/B16 | 55.49 | 18.91 |
| 13 | Total Equity | 59,471 | 59,752 | In Millions | | Long term debt ratio | =B11/(B11+B13) | 0.31 | 0.32 |
| 14 | Sales | 82,059 | 81,581 | In Millions | | Cash coverage ratio | =(B18+B17+B16+B21)/B16 | 77.53 | 25.80 |
| 15 | Cost of Goods Sold | 27,556 | 27,091 | In Millions | | | | | |
| 16 | Interest Expense | 318 | 1,005 | In Millions | | **Asset Efficiency ratio** | | | |
| 17 | Provision for taxes on income (taxes expense) | 2,209 | 2,702 | In Millions | | Day's sales in receivables | =B5/(B14/365) | 64.41 | 63.08 |
| 18 | Net Income | 15,119 | 15,297 | In Millions | | Receivables Turnover | =B14/B5 | 5.67 | 5.79 |
| 19 | Dividend payout | 9,917 | 9,494 | In Millions | | Day's sales in Inventory | =B6/(B15/365) | 119.48 | 115.86 |
| 20 | **Basic average shares outstanding** | 3,120 | 3,120 | In Millions | | Inventory Turnover | =B15/B6 | 3.05 | 3.15 |
| 21 | Depreciation and amortization of property and intangible | 7,009 | 6,929 | In Millions | | Fixed Asset Turnover | =B14/B8 | 4.65 | 4.79 |
| 22 | Price of last trading day | 145.75 | 127.27 | Dollars per share | | Total Asset Turnover | =B14/B9 | 0.52 | 0.53 |
| 23 | | | | | | Net working capital turnover | =B14/(B7-B10) | 8.81 | 5.51 |
| 39 | | | | | | | | | |
| 40 | **DOL, DFL, DCL** | | | | | **DOL** | =((B42-C42)/C42)/((B14-C14)/C14) | -12.195957 | |
| 41 | EPS | =B18/B20 | 4.902884615 | | | **DFL** | =((B41-C41)/C41)/((B42-C42)/C42) | 0.16283921 | |
| 42 | EBIT | 17,646 | 19,004 | | | **DCL** | =G40*G41 | -1.98598 | |

SUM | × ✓ *fx* | =B18+B16+B17

| | A | B | C | D | E | F | G | H | I |
|---|---|---|---|---|---|---|---|---|---|
| 1 | **Johnson and Johnson** | | | | | **Financial Ratio** | | | |
| 2 | **Input financial variables** | **2019** | **2018** | | | **Liquidity ratio** | | **2019** | **2018** |
| 3 | Cash and Cash equivalents | 17,305 | 18,107 | In Millions | | Current Ratio | =B7/B10 | 1.26 | 1.47 |
| 4 | Marketable securities | 1,982 | 1,580 | In Millions | | Quick Ratio | =(B3+B4+B5)/B10 | 0.94 | 1.08 |
| 5 | Account Receivables | 14,481 | 14,098 | In Millions | | Cash Ratio | =(B3+B4)/B10 | 0.54 | 0.63 |
| 6 | Inventory | 9,020 | 8,599 | In Millions | | Net working capital to total asset | =(B7-B10)/B9 | 0.06 | 0.10 |
| 7 | Current Asset | 45,274 | 46,033 | In Millions | | | | | |
| 8 | Fixed Asset | 17,658 | 17,035 | In Millions | | **Financial Leverage ratio** | | | |
| 9 | Total Asset | 157,728 | 152,954 | In Millions | | Debt to Asset | =B12/B9 | 0.62 | 0.61 |
| 10 | Current Liability | 35,964 | 31,230 | In Millions | | Debt to Equity | =B12/B13 | 1.65 | 1.56 |
| 11 | Long term debt | 26,494 | 27,684 | In Millions | | Equity Multiplier | =B9/B13 | 2.65 | 2.56 |
| 12 | Total Liability | 98,257 | 93,202 | In Millions | | Times Interest Paid | =(B18+B16+B17)/B16 | 55.49 | 18.91 |
| 13 | Total Equity | 59,471 | 59,752 | In Millions | | Long term debt ratio | =B11/(B11+B13) | 0.31 | 0.32 |
| 14 | Sales | 82,059 | 81,581 | In Millions | | Cash coverage ratio | =(B18+B17+B16+B21)/B16 | 77.53 | 25.80 |
| 15 | Cost of Goods Sold | 27,556 | 27,091 | In Millions | | | | | |
| 16 | Interest Expense | 318 | 1,005 | In Millions | | **Asset Efficiency ratio** | | | |
| 17 | Provision for taxes on income (taxes expense) | 2,209 | 2,702 | In Millions | | Day's sales in receivables | =B5/(B14/365) | 64.41 | 63.08 |
| 18 | Net Income | 15,119 | 15,297 | In Millions | | Receivables Turnover | =B14/B5 | 5.67 | 5.79 |
| 19 | Dividend payout | 9,917 | 9,494 | In Millions | | Day's sales in Inventory | =B6/(B15/365) | 119.48 | 115.86 |
| 20 | **Basic average shares outstanding** | 3,120 | 3,120 | In Millions | | Inventory Turnover | =B15/B6 | 3.05 | 3.15 |
| 21 | Depreciation and amortization of property and intangible | 7,009 | 6,929 | In Millions | | Fixed Asset Turnover | =B14/B8 | 4.65 | 4.79 |
| 22 | Price of last trading day | 145.75 | 127.27 | Dollars per share | | Total Asset Turnover | =B14/B9 | 0.52 | 0.53 |
| 23 | | | | | | Net working capital turnover | =B14/(B7-B10) | 8.81 | 5.51 |
| 39 | | | | | | | | | |
| 40 | **DOL, DFL, DCL** | | | | | **DOL** | =((B42-C42)/C42)/((B14-C14)/C14) | -12.195957 | |
| 41 | EPS | 4.84583333 | 4.902884615 | | | **DFL** | =((B41-C41)/C41)/((B42-C42)/C42) | 0.16283921 | |
| 42 | EBIT | B17 | 19,004 | | | **DCL** | =G40*G41 | -1.98598 | |

SUM | fx =((B42-C42)/C42)/((B14-C14)/C14)

| | A | B | C | D | E | F | G | H | I |
|---|---|---|---|---|---|---|---|---|---|
| 1 | **Johnson and Johnson** | | | | | **Financial Ratio** | | | |
| 2 | **Input financial variables** | **2019** | **2018** | | | **Liquidity ratio** | | **2019** | **2018** |
| 3 | Cash and Cash equivalents | 17,305 | 18,107 | In Millions | | Current Ratio | =B7/B10 | 1.26 | 1.47 |
| 4 | Marketable securities | 1,982 | 1,580 | In Millions | | Quick Ratio | =(B3+B4+B5)/B10 | 0.94 | 1.08 |
| 5 | Account Receivables | 14,481 | 14,098 | In Millions | | Cash Ratio | =(B3+B4)/B10 | 0.54 | 0.63 |
| 6 | Inventory | 9,020 | 8,599 | In Millions | | Net working capital to total asset | =(B7-B10)/B9 | 0.06 | 0.10 |
| 7 | Current Asset | 45,274 | 46,033 | In Millions | | | | | |
| 8 | Fixed Asset | 17,658 | 17,035 | In Millions | | **Financial Leverage ratio** | | | |
| 9 | Total Asset | 157,728 | 152,954 | In Millions | | Debt to Asset | =B12/B9 | 0.62 | 0.61 |
| 10 | Current Liability | 35,964 | 31,230 | In Millions | | Debt to Equity | =B12/B13 | 1.65 | 1.56 |
| 11 | Long term debt | 26,494 | 27,684 | In Millions | | Equity Multiplier | =B9/B13 | 2.65 | 2.56 |
| 12 | Total Liability | 98,257 | 93,202 | In Millions | | Times Interest Paid | =(B18+B16+B17)/B16 | 55.49 | 18.91 |
| 13 | Total Equity | 59,471 | 59,752 | In Millions | | Long term debt ratio | =B11/(B11+B13) | 0.31 | 0.32 |
| 14 | Sales | 82,059 | 81,581 | In Millions | | Cash coverage ratio | =(B18+B17+B16+B21)/B16 | 77.53 | 25.80 |
| 15 | Cost of Goods Sold | 27,556 | 27,091 | In Millions | | | | | |
| 16 | Interest Expense | 318 | 1,005 | In Millions | | **Asset Efficiency ratio** | | | |
| 17 | Provision for taxes on income (taxes expense) | 2,209 | 2,702 | In Millions | | Day's sales in receivables | =B5/(B14/365) | 64.41 | 63.08 |
| 18 | Net Income | 15,119 | 15,297 | In Millions | | Receivables Turnover | =B14/B5 | 5.67 | 5.79 |
| 19 | Dividend payout | 9,917 | 9,494 | In Millions | | Day's sales in Inventory | =B6/(B15/365) | 119.48 | 115.86 |
| 20 | **Basic average shares outstanding** | 3,120 | 3,120 | In Millions | | Inventory Turnover | =B15/B6 | 3.05 | 3.15 |
| 21 | Depreciation and amortization of property and intangible | 7,009 | 6,929 | In Millions | | Fixed Asset Turnover | =B14/B8 | 4.65 | 4.79 |
| 22 | Price of last trading day | 145.75 | 127.27 | Dollars per share | | Total Asset Turnover | =B14/B9 | 0.52 | 0.53 |
| 23 | | | | | | Net working capital turnover | =B14/(B7-B10) | 8.81 | 5.51 |
| 39 | | | | | | | | | |
| 40 | **DOL, DFL, DCL** | | | | | **DOL** | =((B42-C42)/C42)/((B14-C14)/C14) | C14)/C14) | |
| 41 | EPS | 4.84583333 | 4.902884615 | | | **DFL** | =((B41-C41)/C41)/((B42-C42)/C42) | 0.16283921 | |
| 42 | EBIT | 17,646 | 19,004 | | | **DCL** | =G40*G41 | -1.98598 | |

2. The definition of DFL is:

$$\text{DFL} = \frac{\%\ \text{Change in EPS}}{\%\ \text{Change in EBIT}} \tag{2.2C}$$

To calculate the DOL, we firstly compute EPS (Net income/Total shares) by inputting "=B5/B6." And then we compute the percentage change in EPS by inputting "(B7−C7)/C7," which is the percentage change in EPS. Then, compute the percentage change in EBIT in inputting "(B4−C4)/C4." Put them together, we input "=((B7−C7)/C7)/((B4−C4)/C4)," to get DFL = 0.312132932.

SUM | fx =((B41-C41)/C41)/((B42-C42)/C42)

| | A | B | C | D | E | F | G | H | I |
|---|---|---|---|---|---|---|---|---|---|
| 1 | **Johnson and Johnson** | | | | | **Financial Ratio** | | | |
| 2 | **Input financial variables** | **2019** | **2018** | | | **Liquidity ratio** | | **2019** | **2018** |
| 3 | Cash and Cash equivalents | 17,305 | 18,107 | In Millions | | Current Ratio | =B7/B10 | 1.26 | 1.47 |
| 4 | Marketable securities | 1,982 | 1,580 | In Millions | | Quick Ratio | =(B3+B4+B5)/B10 | 0.94 | 1.08 |
| 5 | Account Receivables | 14,481 | 14,098 | In Millions | | Cash Ratio | =(B3+B4)/B10 | 0.54 | 0.63 |
| 6 | Inventory | 9,020 | 8,599 | In Millions | | Net working capital to total asset | =(B7-B10)/B9 | 0.06 | 0.10 |
| 7 | Current Asset | 45,274 | 46,033 | In Millions | | | | | |
| 8 | Fixed Asset | 17,658 | 17,035 | In Millions | | **Financial Leverage ratio** | | | |
| 9 | Total Asset | 157,728 | 152,954 | In Millions | | Debt to Asset | =B12/B9 | 0.62 | 0.61 |
| 10 | Current Liability | 35,964 | 31,230 | In Millions | | Debt to Equity | =B12/B13 | 1.65 | 1.56 |
| 11 | Long term debt | 26,494 | 27,684 | In Millions | | Equity Multiplier | =B9/B13 | 2.65 | 2.56 |
| 12 | Total Liability | 98,257 | 93,202 | In Millions | | Times Interest Paid | =(B18+B16+B17)/B16 | 55.49 | 18.91 |
| 13 | Total Equity | 59,471 | 59,752 | In Millions | | Long term debt ratio | =B11/(B11+B13) | 0.31 | 0.32 |
| 14 | Sales | 82,059 | 81,581 | In Millions | | Cash coverage ratio | =(B18+B17+B16+B21)/B16 | 77.53 | 25.80 |
| 15 | Cost of Goods Sold | 27,556 | 27,091 | In Millions | | | | | |
| 16 | Interest Expense | 318 | 1,005 | In Millions | | **Asset Efficiency ratio** | | | |
| 17 | Provision for taxes on income (taxes expense) | 2,209 | 2,702 | In Millions | | Day's sales in receivables | =B5/(B14/365) | 64.41 | 63.08 |
| 18 | Net Income | 15,119 | 15,297 | In Millions | | Receivables Turnover | =B14/B5 | 5.67 | 5.79 |
| 19 | Dividend payout | 9,917 | 9,494 | In Millions | | Day's sales in Inventory | =B6/(B15/365) | 119.48 | 115.86 |
| 20 | **Basic average shares outstanding** | 3,120 | 3,120 | In Millions | | Inventory Turnover | =B15/B6 | 3.05 | 3.15 |
| 21 | Depreciation and amortization of property and intangible | 7,009 | 6,929 | In Millions | | Fixed Asset Turnover | =B14/B8 | 4.65 | 4.79 |
| 22 | Price of last trading day | 145.75 | 127.27 | Dollars per share | | Total Asset Turnover | =B14/B9 | 0.52 | 0.53 |
| 23 | | | | | | Net working capital turnover | =B14/(B7-B10) | 8.81 | 5.51 |
| 39 | | | | | | | | | |
| 40 | **DOL, DFL, DCL** | | | | | **DOL** | =((B42-C42)/C42)/((B14-C14)/C14) | -12.195957 | |
| 41 | EPS | 4.84583333 | 4.902884615 | | | **DFL** | =((B41-C41)/C41)/((B42-C42)/C42) | C42)/C42) | |
| 42 | EBIT | 17,646 | 19,004 | | | **DCL** | =G40*G41 | -1.98598 | |

3. The definition of DCL is:

$$\text{DCL} = \frac{\%\ \text{Change in EPS}}{\%\ \text{Change in EBIT}} * \frac{\%\ \text{Change in EBIT}}{\%\ \text{Change in sale}}$$

$$= \frac{\%\ \text{Change in EPS}}{\%\ \text{Change in sale}} \tag{2.3C}$$

To calculate the DCL, we firstly compute the percentage change in EPS by inputting "(B7−C7)/C7," which is the percentage change in EPS. Then, compute the percentage change in sale in inputting "(B3−C3)/C3." Put them together, we input "=((B7−C7)/C7)/((B3−C3)/C3)," to get DFL = −1.986.

Alternatively, we can also input "=B10∗B11" to get the same result since DCL = DFL ∗ DOL = −1.986.

SUM | =H40*H41

| | A | B | C | D | E | F | G | H | I |
|---|---|---|---|---|---|---|---|---|---|
| 1 | **Johnson and Johnson** | | | | | **Financial Ratio** | | | |
| 2 | **Input financial variables** | **2019** | **2018** | | | **Liquidity ratio** | | **2019** | **2018** |
| 3 | Cash and Cash equivalents | 17,305 | 18,107 | In Millions | | Current Ratio | =B7/B10 | 1.26 | 1.47 |
| 4 | Marketable securities | 1,982 | 1,580 | In Millions | | Quick Ratio | =(B3+B4+B5)/B10 | 0.94 | 1.08 |
| 5 | Account Receivables | 14,481 | 14,098 | In Millions | | Cash Ratio | =(B3+B4)/B10 | 0.54 | 0.63 |
| 6 | Inventory | 9,020 | 8,599 | In Millions | | Net working capital to total asset | =(B7-B10)/B9 | 0.06 | 0.10 |
| 7 | Current Asset | 45,274 | 46,033 | In Millions | | | | | |
| 8 | Fixed Asset | 17,658 | 17,035 | In Millions | | **Financial Leverage ratio** | | | |
| 9 | Total Asset | 157,728 | 152,954 | In Millions | | Debt to Asset | =B12/B9 | 0.62 | 0.61 |
| 10 | Current Liability | 35,964 | 31,230 | In Millions | | Debt to Equity | =B12/B13 | 1.65 | 1.56 |
| 11 | Long term debt | 26,494 | 27,684 | In Millions | | Equity Multiplier | =B9/B13 | 2.65 | 2.56 |
| 12 | Total Liability | 98,257 | 93,202 | In Millions | | Times Interest Paid | =(B18+B16+B17)/B16 | 55.49 | 18.91 |
| 13 | Total Equity | 59,471 | 59,752 | In Millions | | Long term debt ratio | =B11/(B11+B13) | 0.31 | 0.32 |
| 14 | Sales | 82,059 | 81,581 | In Millions | | Cash coverage ratio | =(B18+B17+B16+B21)/B16 | 77.53 | 25.80 |
| 15 | Cost of Goods Sold | 27,556 | 27,091 | In Millions | | | | | |
| 16 | Interest Expense | 318 | 1,005 | In Millions | | **Asset Efficiency ratio** | | | |
| 17 | Provision for taxes on income (taxes expense) | 2,209 | 2,702 | In Millions | | Day's sales in receivables | =B5/(B14/365) | 64.41 | 63.08 |
| 18 | Net Income | 15,119 | 15,297 | In Millions | | Receivables Turnover | =B14/B5 | 5.67 | 5.79 |
| 19 | Dividend payout | 9,917 | 9,494 | In Millions | | Day's sales in Inventory | =B6/(B15/365) | 119.48 | 115.86 |
| 20 | **Basic average shares outstanding** | 3,120 | 3,120 | In Millions | | Inventory Turnover | =B15/B6 | 3.05 | 3.15 |
| 21 | Depreciation and amortization of property and intangible | 7,009 | 6,929 | In Millions | | Fixed Asset Turnover | =B14/B8 | 4.65 | 4.79 |
| 22 | Price of last trading day | 145.75 | 127.27 | Dollars per share | | Total Asset Turnover | =B14/B9 | 0.52 | 0.53 |
| 23 | | | | | | Net working capital turnover | =B14/(B7-B10) | 8.81 | 5.51 |
| 39 | | | | | | | | | |
| 40 | **DOL, DFL, DCL** | | | | | **DOL** | =((B42-C42)/C42)/((B14-C14)/C14) | -12.195957 | |
| 41 | EPS | 4.84583333 | 4.902884615 | | | **DFL** | =((B41-C41)/C41)/((B42-C42)/C42) | 0.16283921 | |
| 42 | EBIT | 17,646 | 19,004 | | | **DCL** | =G40*G41 | =H40*H41 | |

## Questions and Problems

1. Define the following terms:

   a. Real versus financial market
   b. $M_1$, $M_2$, $M_3$, and $M_4$
   c. LEI
   d. NYSE, AMEX, and OTC
   e. Primary versus secondary stock market
   f. Bond market
   g. Options and futures markets

2. Briefly discuss the definition of liquidity ratios, financial leverage ratios, asset management ratios, profitability ratios, market value ratios, and policy ratios. What can we learn from examining the financial ratio information of JNJ from 2016 to 2019 as listed in Table 2.5?

3. a. Please discuss the differences among constant return to scale, increasing return to scale, and decreasing return to scale.
   b. Discuss the major difference between the linear and nonlinear break-even analysis.
4. ABC Company's financial records are as follows:

   Quantity of goods sold = 10,000
   Price per unit sold = \$20
   Variable cost per unit sold = \$10
   Total amount of fixed cost = \$50,000
   Corporate tax rate = 50%
   Interest expense = \$20,000

   Using the above information, please answer the following questions.

   a. Calculate EAIT.
   b. What is the break-even quantity?
   c. What is the DOL, DFL, and DCL?
   d. Should the ABC Company produce more for greater profits?

5. ABC Company's predictions for next year are as follows:

| | | | | Variable | |
|---|---|---|---|---|---|
| | Probability | Quantity | Price (\$) | Cost/ Unit (\$) | Corporate Tax Rate |
| State 1 | 0.3 | 1,000 | 10 | 5 | 0.5 |
| State 2 | 0.4 | 2,000 | 20 | 10 | 0.5 |
| State 3 | 0.3 | 3,000 | 30 | 15 | 0.5 |

   In addition, we also know that the fixed cost is \$15,000. What is the next years expected EAIT?
6. Use an example to discuss three alternative depreciation methods.
7. XYX, Inc. currently produces one product that sells for \$330 per unit. The company's fixed costs are \$80,000 per year; variable costs are \$210 per unit. A salesman has offered to sell the company a new piece of equipment which will increase fixed costs to \$100,000. The salesman claims that the company's break-even number of units sold will not be altered if the company

purchases the equipment and raises its price (assuming variable costs remain the same).

a. Find the company's current break-even level of units sold.
b. Find the company's new price if the equipment is purchased and prove that the break-even level has not changed.

8. Consider the following financial data of a corporation:

Sales = \$500,000
Quantity = 25,000
Variable cost = \$300,000
Fixed cost = \$50,000

a. Calculate the DOL at the above quantity of output.
b. Find the break-even quantity and sales levels.

9. On the basis of the following firm and industry norm ratios, identify the problem that exists for the firm:

| **Ratio** | **Firm** | **Industry** |
|---|---|---|
| Total asset utilization | 2.0 | 3.5 |
| Average collection period | 45 days | 46 days |
| Inventory turnover | 6 times | 6 times |
| Fixed asset utilization | 4.5 | 7.0 |

10. The financial ratios for Wallace, Inc., a manufacturer of consumer household products, are given below along with the industry norm:

| | **Firm** | | | |
|---|---|---|---|---|
| **Ratio** | **1986** | **1987** | **1988** | **Industry** |
| Current ratio | 1.44 | 1.31 | 1.47 | 1.2 |
| Quick ratio | 0.66 | 0.62 | 0.65 | 0.63 |
| Average collection period | 33 days | 37 days | 32 days | 34 days |
| Inventory turnover | 7.86 | 7.62 | 7.72 | 7.6 |
| Fixed asset turnover | 2.60 | 2.44 | 2.56 | 2.8 |
| Total asset utilization | 1.24 | 1.18 | 1.40 | 1.20 |
| Debt to total equity | 1.24 | 1.14 | 0.84 | 1.00 |

| | | | | |
|---|---|---|---|---|
| Debt to total assets | 0.56 | 0.54 | 0.46 | 0.50 |
| Times interest earned | 2.75 | 5.57 | 7.08 | 5.00 |
| Return on total assets | 0.02 | 0.06 | 0.07 | 0.06 |
| Return on equity | 0.06 | 0.12 | 0.12 | 0.13 |
| Net profit margin | 0.02 | 0.05 | 0.05 | 0.05 |

Analyze Wallace's ratios over the three-year period for each of the following categories:

a. Liquidity
b. Asset utilization
c. Financial leverage
d. Profitability

11. Below are the Balance Sheet and the Income Statement for Nelson Manufacturing:

**Balance Sheet for Nelson on 12/31/88**
**Assets**

| | |
|---|---|
| Cash and MS | $125,000 |
| Accounts receivable | 239,000 |
| Inventories | 225,000 |
| Prepaid expenses | 11,000 |
| Total current assets | $600,000 |
| Fixed assets (net) | 40,000 |
| Total assets | $1,000,000 |
| **Liabilities and Stockholder's Equity** | |
| Accounts payable | $62,000 |
| Accruals | 188,000 |
| Long-term debt maturing in 1 year | 8,000 |
| | $258,000 |
| Long-term debt | 221,000 |
| Total liabilities | $479,000 |
| Stockholder's equity | |
| Preferred stock | 5,000 |
| Common stock (at par) | 175,000 |
| Retained earnings | 341,000 |
| Total stockholder's equity | $521,000 |
| Total liabilities and shareholder's equity | $1,000,000 |

**Income Statement for Nelson for Year Ending 12/31/88**

| | |
|---|---|
| Net sales | $800,000 |
| Less: Cost of goods sold | 381,600 |
| Selling, general, and administrative expense | 216,800 |
| Interest expense | 20,000 |
| Earnings before taxes | $181,200 |
| Less: Tax expense (40%) | 72,480 |
| Net income | $108,720 |

a. Calculate the following ratios for Nelson.

| | Nelson | Industry |
|---|---|---|
| (1) Current ratio | | 3.40 |
| (2) Quick ratio | | 2.43 |
| (3) Average collection period | | 88.65 |
| (4) Inventory turnover | | 6.46 |
| (5) Fixed asset turnover | | 4.41 |
| (6) Total asset utilization | | 1.12 |
| (7) Debt to total equity | | 0.34 |
| (8) Debt to total assets | | 5.25 |
| (9) Times interest earned | | 12.00 |
| (10) Return on total assets | | 0.12 |
| (11) Return on equity | | 0.18 |
| (12) Net profit margin | | 0.12 |

b. Identify Nelson's strengths and weaknesses relative to the industry norm.

12. The following is financial information for Company XYZ.

| | | | |
|---|---|---|---|
| Anticipated sales | = $400,000, | DFL | = 4/3 |
| Variable cost | = $200,000, | Combined leverage effect | = 2 |
| Quantity sold | = $100,000 units, | Profit margin | = 5% |
| Total debt | = $200,000, | Leverage ratio | = Total |
| | | debt/total asset | = 1/2 |

Common stock outstanding = 10,000 shares,
Current price per share = $40,
Retention rate = 1/2

Using the above information, please calculate the following:

(a) The DOL
(b) The total fixed cost
(c) The total interest expense
(d) The break-even quantity
(e) The EAIT
(f) The return on total assets
(g) EPS
(h) The P/E ratio for common stock
(i) The return on equity
(j) The payout ratio for dividend
(k) The growth rate
(l) Total assets turnover
(m) The required rate of return
(n) Analyze the financial situation of Company XYZ
(o) If the probabilistic concepts are applied to break-even analysis, how should the analysis in question O be revised?

Solution:

(a) The DOL

$$\text{DOL} = \frac{\text{DCL}}{\text{DFL}} = \frac{2}{\frac{4}{3}} = 1.5 \qquad (2.1\text{C})$$

(b) The total fixed cost

$$\text{DOL} = \frac{Q(P-V)}{Q(P-V)-F} = 1.5 = 1 + \frac{F}{\text{EBIT}} \qquad (2.2\text{C})$$

from (2.1C) we know $F = 0.5$ EBIT
By definition,

$$\begin{aligned}\text{EBIT} &= Q(P-V) - F \\ &= QP - QV - F = 400{,}000 - 200{,}000 - F \quad (2.3\text{C})\end{aligned}$$

By (2.2C) and (2.3C), we can solve EBIT = 133,333.33
Substitute EBIT into (2.1C), we obtain F = 66666.665.

(c) The total interest expense

$$\text{DFL} = \frac{\text{EBIT}}{\text{EBIT} - I} = \frac{4}{3}$$

we obtain

$$\text{EBIT} = 4I \tag{2.4C}$$

Substitute EBIT into (2.4C), we can solve $I = 66{,}666.665$.

(d) The break-even quantity

$$\text{Break-even quantity} = \frac{F}{(P - V)} = \frac{F}{2} = 33333.33$$

(e) The EAIT

$$\begin{aligned}\text{EAIT} &= \text{Profit margin} * \text{Anticipated sales}\\ &= 0.05 * \$400{,}000 = \$20{,}000\end{aligned}$$

(f) ROA

$$\begin{aligned}\text{ROA} &= \frac{\text{EAIT}}{\text{Total asset}}\\ &= \frac{20{,}000}{D + D * \left(\frac{E}{D}\right)} = \frac{20{,}000}{200{,}000(1+1)} = 0.05\end{aligned}$$

(g) EPS

$$\text{EPS} = \frac{\text{EAIT}}{\text{Outstanding share}} = \frac{20{,}000}{10{,}000} = 2.0$$

(h) P/E ratio

$$\text{P/E ratio} = \frac{\text{Price per share}}{\text{EPS}} = \frac{40}{2.0} = 20$$

(i) ROE

$$\text{ROE} = \text{ROA}\left(\frac{\text{Total assets}}{\text{Total equity}}\right) = \left(\frac{\text{Total assets}}{\text{Total assets} - \text{Total debt}}\right)$$

$$\text{ROA} = \left(\frac{1}{1 - \frac{\text{Total debt}}{\text{Total assets}}}\right) ROA = 0.05\left(\frac{1}{1 - \frac{1}{2}}\right) = 0.1$$

(j) Payout ratio

$$\text{Payout ratio} = 1 - \text{Retention rate} = 1 - 1/2 = 1/2$$

(k) Growth rate

Using growth rate = Retention rate (ROE), then growth rate is equal to $0.5 * 0.1 = 0.05$.

When external financing is allowed, then the growth rate can be calculated as follows:

$$\begin{aligned}&\text{Growth rate}\\&\quad = \text{Retention rate (ROE)}/(1 - \text{Retention rate (ROE)})\\&\quad = \left(\frac{1}{2} * 0.1\right)/(1 - 0.05) = 0.0526\end{aligned}$$

(l) Total assets turnover

$$\begin{aligned}&\text{Total assets turnover}\\&\quad = \text{Sales/Total assets}\\&\quad = \$400{,}000/\$200{,}000/(200{,}000 * 2) = 1\end{aligned}$$

(m) The required rate of return

By definition:

$$\frac{\text{Required rate of return} = \text{Dividends per share in period one}}{\text{Price per share in current period} + \text{Growth rate}}.$$

From previous calculations and information given, we know that price share in the current period is equal to \$40. Growth rate is equal to 0.05. Dividend per share in the current period is equal to \$1, therefore required rate of return is equal to $\$1*(1+0.05)/\$40+0.05 = 0.026 + 0.05 = 0.076$.

(n) Analyze the financial situation of Company XYZ.

(o) If the probabilistic concepts are applied to break-even analysis, how the analysis in N should be revised.

13. Here is ABC Company's next year's prediction:

| Economy | Probability | ROA (%) | Debt ($) | Equity ($) | Tax Rate (%) | Interest Rate (%) |
|---|---|---|---|---|---|---|
| State 1 | 0.1 | 12 | 500 | 1,000 | 40 | 8 |
| State 2 | 0.5 | 14 | 500 | 1,000 | 40 | 8 |
| State 3 | 0.4 | 15 | 500 | 1,000 | 40 | 8 |

a. Calculate next year's expected after-tax return on equity.
b. How much is the after-tax return on equity?
c. Assume the debt prediction was wrong. Instead, debt will increase to \$1,000 next year, Answer: Questions a and b.
d. Compare your results under each scenario. How sensitive are the results to errors in the forecasted level of debts?

The Expanded Version of the Solution:

a. E(ROA) = (0.1)(12) + (0.5)(14) + (0.4)(15) = 14.2%.
b. Two Alternative Methods to Solve Expected ROE

Method 1: Adjusted ROE Method
E(Cost of Debt) = (1 – 0.40) (8%) = 4.8%

$$14.2\% - \frac{500}{1000 + 500}(4.8\%) = 12.6\%$$

$$\text{E(ROE)} = \frac{12.6}{1000/1500} = 18.9\%$$

Please note that 12.6 is ROA adjusted for interest rate cost.
(1000)(0.189) = \$189

Method 2: Adjusted Revenue Method
Total Revenue = 14.2% ∗ \$1,500 = \$213
\$500 ∗ 1.04 ∗ 0.08 = \$41.6
(\$213 – \$41.6)/1000 = 17.14%

c. E(ROA) = 14.2%
E(Cost of Debt) = 4.8%

$$14.2\% - \frac{1000}{1000 + 1000}(4.8) = 11.8\%$$

$$E(\text{ROE}) = \frac{11.8}{1000/2000} = 23.6\%.$$

Then,
$(1000)(0.236) = \$236.$

d. If the expected return on assets is held constant, then as debt is increased, the expected rate of return on equity will increase. Errors in forecasting the expected level of debt may cause the expected return on equity to be biased.

## Chapter 3

# Developing a Long-term Financial Plan

## Contents



## 3.1 Introduction

All managers, whether they are part of a firm's financial staff or not, need to be familiar with the firm's external environment. Domestic and international economic conditions influence a firm's financing, marketing, operating, and organizational decisions. Financial statements can help provide information that managers and analysts both inside and outside the firm can use to evaluate its strengths and weaknesses. But financial statements serve another important purpose for a firm's managers: the relationships among the financial statements data helps managers plan for the firm's future. The planning process must consider the firm's external and internal environment to properly evaluate goals, strategies, and plans and put them into action.

A full discussion of the planning process is far beyond the scope of this book, but this chapter will introduce the use of financial statements information as part of the firm's overall planning process. We will discuss several basic financial planning models to show how information from accounting, marketing, and economics can be combined with investment, financing, and dividend policies to develop plans and estimate how future financial statements may look. As part of this process, managers also must evaluate the effect of risk on the firm. In this chapter, we review two sources of risk, business risk and financial risk.

Planning is an important process in any organization; as a rule, following a plan improves a firm's chances of reaching its destination, even if that destination changes to reflect a new situation. The alternative, limping for crisis to crisis, leaves a firm at risk, randomly reacting to monetary economic and competitive developments.

But planning helps a firm with more than its overall course; it also simplifies the process of raising capital. As a firm grows, it must obtain financing to expand its current plant and distribution channels. Only in rare situations can a firm finance growth from current profits alone. Most firms seek financing from banks, private investors, or the public debt and equity markets. In order to obtain the funds, the firm must show evidence of a well-conceived plan for using the funds to improve its prospects. The investors want to know how and when the firm expects to generate income to reward them with adequate returns for risking their capital. A carefully developed financial plan will detail much of this information and increase the likelihood that the firm will obtain the funds it requests.

In this chapter, we begin with an overview of financial planning in Section 3.2. Our emphasis will be on long-term financial planning and analysis. In Chapter 21 we will discuss some other long-term financial planning models in detail. Short-term financial planning, which is related to long-term financial planning, will be discussed in chapters 18, 19, and 20. In Section 3.3 we discuss forecasting growth rates and outside financing, and in Section 3.4 we discuss forecasting external financial needs. Section 3.5 goes over the percentage of sales method, and in Section 3.6 we talk about risk consideration. In Section 3.7, we discuss the types of risk and their effects on returns. Finally, in Section 3.8 we summarize the chapter.

## 3.2 Overview of Financial Planning

*Financial planning* is the process of analyzing alternative investment, financing, and dividend strategies in the context of various potential economic environments. Planning involves forecasting both the outcomes of different strategies and their risk. Thus, financial planning models are tools to help managers improve their forecast of important accounts of financial statements and better understand the interactions of investment, financing, and dividend decisions.

In developing a long-term financial plan, these three decisions (policies) can be described more explicitly as follows.

1. *The firm's investment decision.* This refers to the amount of cash needed for the firm's investment in a new asset (it is also called the *capital budgeting decision*). In addition, it also refers to the amount of working capital needed on an ongoing basis (also referred to the *working capital decision*).
2. *The firm's financing decision.* This refers to new borrowing or new equity issued for financing the firm's investment in new assets. This decision is influenced by the degree of financial leverage (DFL) the firms chooses to employ and how it plans to raise the necessary new funds.
3. *The firm's dividend decision.* This refers to the amount of cash the firm thinks is necessary and appropriate to pay equity holders as cash dividends.

At the most basic level, a planning model is a tool that uses inputs supplied by managers in the form of economic, accounting, market, and policy information. Depending on its sophistication, the output of the financial planning and forecasting model may include simple estimates of growth rates or complex pro forma financial statements, with projected financial statements data, and forecast of stock price, earnings per share (EPS), dividends per share, new equity issues, and new debt issues.[1]

[1]In this chapter, we develop a simple, but useful long-term planning technique — the percentage of sales method. The output of this method includes only items from the pro forma financial statements.

An abstraction of reality, the model itself represents the links that exist between the firm's external environment, management policy, and internal accounting relationships. The model is constructed using data from past years to estimate the links between different variables. For example, an economic forecast of a weaker U.S. dollar may lead to higher levels of overseas sales for the firm's products. This, in turn, may imply the need to expand production facilities and to finance the expansion. Thus, the projected balance sheet will reflect higher levels of assets and debt and/or equity financing. The model will qualify these relationships. For example, if management forecast a 10% decline in the value of the dollar, the model's output may estimate that sales will increase by 14%, that assets will need to expand by 7%, and that additional debt and equity financing must be raised in accordance with the financing policy that management has built into the model.

To help achieve their goal of maximizing shareholder wealth, it is useful for managers to develop financial planning models to facilitate forward thinking and planning.

In the real world, however, shareholders wealth is not determined by financial models. Unexpected economic and political events or unexpected strategies from competitors can cause financial plans and future stock prices to deviate from projections. The process of planning for the future, designing contingency plans, and mulling over possible future scenarios in planning meetings can only help managers to understand their firm better. Moreover, these activities help managers refine the instincts they need to help their firm compete more effectively in a dynamic and global environment. With their common limitations in mind, we'll review a few basic financial planning concepts and simple planning model.

## 3.3 Forecasting Growth Rates and Outside Financing

An old adage says that it takes money to make money. Unfortunately, a firm may succeed so well that it runs out of money. It may find itself unable to increase it assets quickly enough to keep up with a sales growth. A firm that tries to expand its asset base aggressively may find itself short of cash, unable to repay creditors, and facing bankruptcy. It is well known that accounting income does not represent cash flow. Should cash receipts lag the payments made to expand production and purchase supplies, the firm can find itself in a financial bind should banks be hesitant to lend additional funds. One simple financial planning tool, the *growth rate model*, works to determine just how quickly a firm's asset can grow without running short of cash. In this section, we will discuss two alternative ways to estimate asset growth rates, i.e., the internal growth rate, and the sustainable growth rate. Then, we'll show how the growth rate estimates can be used to determine the amount of required new funds.

### 3.3.1 *Internal growth rate*

The *internal growth rate* measures how quickly a firm can increase its assets base over the next year without raising outside funds. It does not measure divisional growth or break down total growth into domestic or international components. More detailed analysis must be done to estimate the forces that determine growth rates. The internal growth rate gives a general, companywide value.

The internal growth rate model assumes that the firm can only finance its growth by its internal funds. Consequently, the cash used to finance growth must come from only retained earnings. Therefore, retained earnings can be expressed as:

$$\begin{aligned}\text{Retained earnings} &= \text{Earnings} - \text{Dividends}\\ &= \text{Profit margin} \times \text{Total sales} - \text{Dividends}\\ &= p(S + \Delta S) - p(S + \Delta S)(1 - b)\\ &= pb(S + \Delta S)\end{aligned}$$

where $p$ = the profit margin on all sales; $S$ = annual sales; $b$ = retention rate; and $\Delta S$ = the increase in sales during the year.

Because retained earnings is the only source of new funds, the use of cash represented by the increase in assets must equal the retained earnings:

$$\begin{aligned} \text{Uses of cash} &= \text{Sources of cash} \\ \text{Increases in assets} &= \text{Retained earnings} \\ \Delta ST &= p(S + \Delta S)b \\ &= pbS + pb\Delta S \\ \Delta S[T - pb] &= pSb \\ \frac{\Delta S}{S} &= \frac{pb}{T - pb} \end{aligned} \tag{3.1}$$

where $T$ = the ratio of total assets to sales. If we divide both the numerator and denominator of Eq. (3.1) by $T$ and rearrange the terms, then we can show that the internal growth rate is:

$$\begin{aligned} g &= \frac{\Delta S}{S} \\ &= \frac{pb/T}{1 - pb/T} \\ &= \frac{b \times ROA}{1 - b \times ROA} \end{aligned} \tag{3.2}$$

where $ROA$ is the return on assets. The internal growth rate is the maximum growth rate that can be achieved without debt or equity kind of external financing. But note this assumption of not issuing new debt or common stock to finance growth is inconsistent with the basic assumption of the constant discount rate models that the firm maintains a constant market-based leverage ratio. Hence, this model cannot be used to estimate the growth rate and be employed by the Gordon Growth Model.

$b$ is the firm's retention rate and ROA is its return on assets. The internal growth rate divides the product of these values by one minus this product.[2] The retention rate represents the proportion of every $1 of EPS that is retained by the firm; in other words, it is to one minus the *dividend payout ratio.*

[2] An end-of-chapter problem (Problem 1) invites you to derive this relationship.

**Example 3.1.** Growing on Your Own

Q: If historically, 40% of a firm's earnings has been paid out as dividend and the firm has average a 15% return on asset over the past several years, how quickly can the firm growth without needing to tap outside financing sources?

A: A 40% dividend payout ratio means that the firm's reaction rate is 1.0 – 0.40 = 0.60. Of every dollar of net income, the firm distributes $0.40 as dividends and retains $0.60. With a 15% ROA, Eq. (3.1) tells us that the internal growth rate for the firm is:

$$\text{Internal growth rate} = \frac{(0.60)(0.15)}{1-(0.60)(0.15)} = 0.0989 \quad \text{or} \quad 9.9$$

If the firm relies only on new additions to retained earnings to finance asset acquisition, the firm can increase its asset base by a little under 10% next year.

Most managers plan and think in terms of sales rather than asset size, so it may help to relate the internal growth rate to sales growth. Suppose that a firm has internal growth rate of 10%; what percentage sales growth does this imply?

We can roughly estimate a sales growth rate by recalling the total asset turnover ratio from Chapter 2. The total asset turnover ratio equals sales divided by total assets. If management can assume that this ratio will remain constant into the foreseeable future, the growth in sales will equal the internal growth rate computed above.[3]

The internal growth rate makes the restrictive assumptions that the firm will pursue no outside sources of financing. Should the firm grow at its internal growth rate, its retained earnings account will continually rise (assuming profitable sales), while its dollar amount of debt outstanding will remain constant. Thus, the firm's debt-to-equity ratio declines over time, until debt falls below its correct proportion in management's ideal finance mix.

---

[3]This implies that $1+g_s = 1+g_a$, or that sales growth will equal the asset growth rate.

### 3.3.2 *Sustainable growth rate*

Perhaps a more realistic assumption would be to allow management to borrow funds over time to maintain steady capital structure ratios. As the stockholders' equity account rises from new additions to retained earnings, the firm issues new debt to keep its debt-to-equity ratio constant over time. This allows the firm to finance faster asset and sales growth, gaining funds from both new debt and additions to retained earnings. This rate of growth is the *sustainable growth rate*. It measures how quickly the firm can grow when it uses both internal equity and debt financing to keep its capital structure. Higgins (1977, 1981, and 1992) has developed a sustainable growth rate under the assumption that firms can generate new funds by using retained earnings or issuing debt, but not issuing new shares of common stock. Growth and its management present special problems in financial planning. From a financial perspective, growth is not always a blessing. Rapid growth can put considerable strain on a company's resources, and unless management is aware of this effect and takes active steps to control it, rapid growth can lead to bankruptcy. Assuming a company is not raising new equity, the cash to finance growth must come from retained earnings and new borrowings. Further, because the company wants to maintain a target debt-to-equity ratio equal to $L$, each dollar added to the owners' equity enables it to increase its indebtedness by $\$L$. Since the owners' equity will rise by an amount equal to retained earnings, the new borrowing can be written as:

$$\begin{aligned}\text{New borrowings} &= \text{Retained earnings}\\ &\quad\times \text{Target debt-to-equity ratio}\\ &= pb(S+\Delta S)L\end{aligned}$$

The use of cash represented by the increase in assets must equal the two sources of cash (retained earnings and new borrowings):

$$\begin{aligned}\text{Uses of cash} &= \text{Sources of cash}\\ \text{Increases in assets} &= \text{Retained earnings} + \text{New borrowing}\end{aligned}$$

$$\begin{aligned}
\Delta ST &= pb(S + \Delta S) + pb(S + \Delta S)L \\
&= pb(1 + L)S + pb(1 + L)\Delta S \\
\Delta S[T - pb(1 + L)] &= pb(1 + L)S \\
g &= \frac{\Delta S}{S} \\
&= \frac{pb(1 + L)}{T - pb(1 + L)}
\end{aligned} \tag{3.3}$$

In Eq. (3.3) the $\Delta S/S$ or $g$ is the firm's sustainable growth rate assuming no infusion of new equity. Therefore, a company's growth rate in sales must equal the indicated combination of four ratios, $p, b, L$, and $T$. In addition, if the company's growth rate differs from $g$, one or more of the ratios must change. For example, suppose a company grows at a rate in excess of $g$, then it must either use its assets more efficiently, or it must alter its financial policies. Efficiency is represented by the profit margin and asset-to-sales ratio. It therefore would need to increase its profit margin ($p$) or decrease its asset-to-sales ratio ($T$) in order to increase efficiency. Financial policies are represented by payout or leverage ratios. In this case, a decrease in its payout ratio $(1 - b)$ or an increase in its leverage ($L$) would be necessary to alter its financial policies to accommodate a different growth rate. It should be noted that increasing efficiency is not always possible and altering financial policies are not always wise.

If we divide both the numerator and denominator of Eq. (3.3) by $T$ and rearrange the terms, then we can show that the sustainable growth rate can be shown as

$$\begin{aligned}
g &= \tfrac{\Delta S}{S} \\
&= \tfrac{pb(1+L)/T}{1-pb(1+L)/T} \\
&= \tfrac{b\times ROE}{1-b\times ROE}
\end{aligned} \tag{3.4}$$

Please note that, in the framework of internal growth rate and sustainable growth rate presented above, the source of cash is taken from the end of period values of assets and assumed that the required financing occurs at the end of the period.

**Example 3.2.** Sustainable Growth

**Q**: Suppose that the firm in Example 3.1 maintains a debt-to-equity of 1.0, since management feels that this rate minimizes financing cost. What is the firm's sustainable growth rate?

**A**: To begin, we'll use the information from Example 3.1 and the debt-to-equity ratio to compute the firm's return on equity. Then we'll apply Eq. (3.4).

It is well known that ROE = ROA × Equity multiplier and the equity multiplier equals total assets divided by equity. A debt-to-equity ratio of 1.0 means that the amount of debt equals the amount of equity; if we arbitrarily let debt equal 1.0 and equity equal to 1.0, the firm's total asset will equal 2.0 (debt plus equity). Therefore, the firm's equity multiplier is

$$\frac{TA}{SE} = \frac{2.0}{1.0} = 2.0$$

Since the firm has a return on assets of 15%, its ROE equals

$$\text{ROA} \times \text{Equity multiplier} = 15\% \times 2 = 30\%$$

With a retention rate of 0.60 from Example 3.1 the sustainable growth rate equals:

$$\begin{aligned}\text{Sustainable growth rate} &= \frac{(0.60)(0.30)}{1 - (0.60)(0.30)} \\ &= 0.2195 \text{ or } 21.95\%\end{aligned}$$

Thus without outside equity financing, the firm can increase sales and assets by slightly under 10%; by maintaining a constant capital structure, the firm can grow by nearly 22%.

### 3.3.3 *Effects of unexpectedly higher (or lower) growth*

The internal and sustainable growth rates are planning tools. These formulas cannot make a firm grow by certain amount. Changing global competition, political, and credit market conditions can cause actual growth to deviate from planned growth.

The growth formulas in Eqs. (3.2) and (3.4) suggest that there are four basic influences on growth: dividend policy (which affects the retention rate), profit margin, total asset turnover, and the equity multiplier (DuPont analysis shows us that these last three factors affect ROA and ROE). Should actual growth differ from planned growth, one or more of these four factors will have to be adjusted either to prevent financial difficulty or absorb excess funds.

**Dividend Policy.** A reduction in the dividend payout ratio implies a higher retention rate and the ability for the firm to grow more quickly, if all else remains constant. Thus, a fast-growing firm may decide to cut its dividend in an effort to finance its rapid growth. More mature, slower growing firms usually increase dividends as growth opportunities diminish.

**Profit Margin.** Higher profit margins generate more net income, larger additions to retained earnings, and a faster growth, when all else is held constant. Should growth outpace the planned rate, the firm can seek to finance the unexpected growth by raising its prices and/or reducing expenses in an attempt to increase its profit margin. If growth falls short of the planned rate, the firm may have to reduce prices, and therefore its profit margin, to stimulate sales.

**Total Asset Turnover.** More equity is determined by the firm's financing policy. A firm that uses a larger amount of financial leverage can support a faster sustainable growth rate, when all else remains constant. If actual growth exceeds the sustainable growth rate, a firm can finance the difference by taking on additional debt. Growth below the planned rate may lead to smaller additions to debt and an unplanned reduction in financial leverage.

One or more of these four variables must deviate from planned levels to accommodate a deviation of actual growth from planned growth. If a firm's actual growth exceeds the planned rate, management will have to reduce dividends, increase profit margins, increase asset efficiency, use more debt, or determine some combination of these options. If growth slows, the firm will need to increase dividends, reduce its profit margin, decrease asset turnover, reduce its use of debt, or choose some combination of these alternatives.

## 3.4 Forecasting External Financing Needs

A firm's financial manager must plan ahead. If the firm's product market conditions are such that the firm's growth is projected to be above the firm's internal growth rate, outside funds may have to be obtained. To understand the process of estimating fund needs, let's look at the following situation.

Below is a simplified balance sheet for Blues Industries. Currently, production is running only 80% of capacity; current sales are $50 million. The profit margin is 5%, and the dividend payout ratio is 50% of net income. Sales are expected to rise 10% next year to 55 million. The current asset and current liability accounts are expected to rise proportionately with the sales growth rate. Will Blues need to obtain outside financing?

**Blues Industries Balance Sheet**

| | | | |
|---|---|---|---|
| Current assets | $25 million | Current liabilities | $7.5 million |
| Fixed assets | 25 million | Long-term debt | 20.0 million |
| Total assets | $50 million | Stockholders' equity | 22.5 million |
| Total liabilities and equity | | | $50.0 million |

If current sales are $50 million while the plant operates at 80% of capacity, full capacity sales are $50 million/0.80, or $62.5 million. With expected sales of only $55 million next year, no growth in fixed assets is expected. But external funds may still be needed for working capital needs if Blues' internal growth rate is less than the 10% (0.05 [profit margin] × 50 million [sales]/$50 million [asset]). Thus, Blues' internal growth rate is:

$$\text{IGR} = \frac{(b)(ROA)}{1-(b)(ROA)} = \frac{(0.5)(0.05)}{1-(0.5)(0.05)} = 0.0256 \text{ or } 2.6\%.$$

The expected growth rate of 10% exceeds the internal growth rate. Despite the no-growth situation in fixed assets, outside financing may still be needed because of the increase in working capital associated with sales growth.

Current assets and current liabilities are anticipated to grow at a rate equal to the 10% sales growth rate. Therefore, next year's current assets are expected to grow by \$2.5 million, to \$7.5 million. Current liabilities are expected to grow by \$0.75 million, to \$8.25 million. The difference between the current asset growth and current liability growth, \$2.5 million − \$0.75 million, or \$1.75 million needs to be financed through the use of additions to retained earnings or through outside financing. We can compute the expected addition to retained earnings from our estimate of next year's sales, profit margin, and dividend payout. With a 5% profit margin on sales of \$55 million, net income is forecast to be \$2.75 million. One-half of that will be paid as dividends, leaving \$1.375 million as the expected addition to retained earnings. The difference between the increase in current assets on one hand and the increase in current liabilities and retained earnings on the other equals Blues' need for additional financing.

| | | | | | | |
|---|---|---|---|---|---|---|
| External Financing | = | Change in assets | − | Change in liabilities | − | Change in equity |
| External Financing | = | \$2.5 million (increase in current assets) | − | \$0.75 million (increase in current liabilities) | − | \$1.375 million (increase in retained earnings) |

(3.5)

Solving, we see the need for external financing is +\$0.375 million. Thus, despite the fact that no increase in fixed assets is anticipated, Blues still needs to obtain \$375,000 to finance the forecasted increase in current assets.

The technique illustrated in the above example for determining the required amount of outside financing can be applied to all growth scenarios, including cases in which the firm is already operating at full capacity. For example, if Blues were already operating at full capacity when sales were \$50 million, a 10% sales growth forecast would mean that both assets and sales would grow by 10%. Total assets would rise \$5 million, to \$55 million; current liabilities would rise, as before, by \$0.75 million. The expected addition to retained earnings would equal \$1.375 million, just as it did above. The difference between the increase in total assets on one hand and the increase in total liabilities and retained earnings on the other would equal Blue's need for additional financing:

| Change in assets | = | Change in liabilities | + | Change in equity | + | External financing |
|---|---|---|---|---|---|---|
| \$5 million (increase in total assets) | = | \$0.75 million (increase in current liabilities) | + | \$1.375 million (increase in retained earnings) | + | External financing |

Solving, the need for outside financing is +\$2.875 million. Blues can plan ahead for these funds by arranging for a bank loan, bond sale, equity issue, or some combination of these.

## 3.5 Percentage of Sales Method

The percentage of sales method is a more complex financial planning model than the internal growth, sustainable growth, or external financing needs models. *The percentage of sales method* generates a set of *pro forma or forecasted balance sheets and income statements* for the firm. The analyst projects what will happen to the firm's accounts over time, which supports an estimate of the firm's external financing needs for a particular period.

The first step of the percentage of sales method is implied by the method's name. Using historical data, the analyst divides each balance sheet and income statement item by sales revenue.[4] The resulting ratios are examined to see which accounts have maintained fairly constant relationships of trends with respect to sales.

The second step of the percentage of sales method is to estimate future sales levels. This estimate can rely on market research studies or on an analysis of internal or sustainable growth rates, as discussed in the previous section.

In the third step the analyst can construct projected financial statements. This process begins by placing the sales forecast at the top of the income statement. To forecast the value of income

[4]Recall that dividing all the income statement items by sales gives us the common-size income statement. The percentage of sales method also requires the balance sheet accounts to be divided by sales, as the sales forecast will be used to estimate the next period's balance sheet accounts.

statement items having a steady or predictable relationship to sales, the analyst assumes this relationship will continue. For items that do not have a consistent relationship to sales, other assumptions will be needed to forecast their values. For example, current credit market conditions may suggest holding interest expense constant or projecting it to grow at a predetermined rate; projected taxes will reflect the firm's tax rate.

Similarly, the analyst projects balance sheet accounts based upon their relationship with sales revenue. Accounts that lack consistent relationships to sales may be assumed to be held constant or to change in a manner consistent with recent trends and future market projections.

The analyst estimates retained earnings by adding the forecasted addition to retained earnings to the existing retained earnings balance. The forecasted addition to retained earnings is the net income on the *pro forma* (projected) income statement less any dividends, that is:

$$\begin{array}{l} \text{Projected} \\ \text{retained} \\ \text{earnings} \end{array} = \begin{array}{l} \text{Existing} \\ \text{retained} \\ \text{earnings} \end{array} + \begin{array}{l} \text{Projected} \\ \text{net income} \\ \phantom{x} \end{array} - \begin{array}{l} \text{Estimated} \\ \text{dividend} \\ \text{payment} \end{array} \qquad (3.6)$$

The accounting identity requires that total assets equal total liabilities and equity; in the first pass, however, the percentage of sales method will rarely produce this equality. To balance the *pro forma* balance sheet, the analyst inserts a plug figure, so that:

$$\text{Total assets} = \text{Total liabilities} + \text{Stockholders' equity} + \text{Plug} \qquad (3.7)$$

The plug figure, sometimes labeled "external funds needed" or "external funds required," typically represents an addition to or subtraction from notes payable to restore equality to the balance sheet equation. A positive plug figure suggests that additional short-term borrowing will be needed to finance the firm's growth plans. (Of course, this need for funds also can be met by issuing long-term debt or equity.) A negative plug figure suggests that project operating results will generate excess cash which the firm can use to reduce its short-term or long-term borrowing or to repurchase stock.

Table 3.1 JNJ, Consolidated Statements of Earnings, 2016–2018 (Dollars and Shares in Million Except Per Share Amounts).

| | 2018 | 2017 | 2016 |
|---|---|---|---|
| **Sales to Customers** | $81,581 | 76,450 | 71,890 |
| Cost of goods sold | 27,091 | 25,439 | 21,789 |
| Gross profit | 54,490 | 51,011 | 50,101 |
| Selling, general, and administrative expense | 22,540 | 21,520 | 20,067 |
| Research and development expense | 10,775 | 10,594 | 9,143 |
| In-process research and development | 1,126 | 408 | 29 |
| Interest Expense | (611) | (385) | (368) |
| Interest expense, net of portion capitalized | 1,005 | 934 | 726 |
| Other (income) expense, net | 1,405 | (42) | 210 |
| Restructuring | 251 | 309 | 491 |
| Earnings before provision for taxes on income | 17,999 | 17,673 | 19,803 |
| Provision for taxes on income | 2,702 | 16,373 | 3,263 |
| **Net Income (Loss)** | **$15,297** | **1,300** | **16,540** |

*Source*: JNJ, 2018 Annual Report.

### 3.5.1 *Percentage of sales analysis of JNJ*

To illustrate percentage of sales analysis, let's consider again the financial statements for JNJ, Inc. Table 3.1 presents the consolidated statements of earnings and Table 3.2 presents the consolidated balance sheets for JNJ for 2016, 2017, and 2018.

Table 3.3 shows the year-to-year percentage growth in JNJ sales as well as income statement and balance sheet items expressed as percentages of sales for the period from 2016 to 2018. Note that a number of accounts show fairly consistent or predictable relationships to JNJ's sales from 2016 to 2018. Note also that sales grew at a rate of 2.59%, 6.34%, and 6.71% for this period, respectively. We use the average sales growth over these three years, 5.22%, as forecasted sales growth rate. We also assume that the 2020 and 2019 percentage of sales ratios will be the average of their values from 2016 to 2018, as reported in Table 3.3.

Based upon forecasted sales and these percentage of sales proportions, Table 3.4 presents a *pro forma* income statement and balance sheet for JNJ for 2019 and 2020. Here we describe the approach taking 2019 as an example. And the case of 2020 is the same.

Table 3.2 JNJ and Subsidiaries, Consolidated. Balance Sheets, at Dec. 30, 2018, Dec. 31, 2017 and Jan. 1, 2017 (Dollars in Millions Except Share and Per Share Amounts).

| | 2018 | 2017 | 2016 |
|---|---|---|---|
| **Assets** | | | |
| **Current assets** | | | |
| Cash and cash equivalents | $18,107 | 17,824 | 18,972 |
| Marketable securities | 1,580 | 472 | 22,935 |
| Accounts receivable trade, less allowances for doubtful accounts | 14,098 | 13,490 | 11,699 |
| Inventories | 8,599 | 8,765 | 8,144 |
| Prepaid expenses and other receivables | 2,699 | 2,537 | 3,282 |
| Assets held for sale | 950 | — | — |
| **Total current assets** | **46,033** | **43,088** | **65,032** |
| Property, plant and equipment, net | 17,035 | 17,005 | 15,912 |
| Intangible assets, net | 47,611 | 53,228 | 26,876 |
| Goodwill | 30,453 | 31,906 | 22,805 |
| Deferred taxes on income | 7,640 | 7,105 | 6,148 |
| Other assets | 4,182 | 4,971 | 4,435 |
| **Total Assets** | **152,954** | **157,303** | **141,208** |
| **Liabilities and Shareholders' Equity** | | | |
| **Current liabilities** | | | |
| Loans and notes payable | $2,796 | 3,906 | 4,684 |
| Accounts payable | 7,537 | 7,310 | 6,918 |
| Accrued liabilities | 7,601 | 7,304 | 5,635 |
| Accrued rebates, returns and promotions | 9,380 | 7,210 | 5,403 |
| Accrued compensation and employee related obligations | 3,098 | 2,953 | 2,676 |
| Accrued taxes on income | 818 | 1,854 | 971 |
| **Total current liabilities** | **31,230** | **30,537** | **26,287** |
| Long-term debt | 27,684 | 30,675 | 22,442 |
| Deferred taxes on income | 7,506 | 8,368 | 2,910 |
| Employee related obligations | 9,951 | 10,074 | 9,615 |
| Long-term taxes payable | 8,242 | 8,472 | — |
| Other liabilities | 8,598 | 9,017 | 9,356 |
| **Total Liabilities** | **93,202** | **97,143** | **70,790** |

(*Continued*)

Table 3.2 (*Continued*)

| | 2018 | 2017 | 2016 |
|---|---|---|---|
| **Shareholders' equity** | | | |
| Preferred stock — without par value | — | — | — |
| Common stock — par value $1.00 per share | 3,120 | 3,120 | 3,120 |
| Accumulated other comprehensive income | (15,222) | (13,199) | (14,901) |
| Retained earnings | 106,216 | 101,739 | 110,551 |
| | 94,114 | 91,724 | 98,770 |
| Less: common stock held in treasury, at cost | 34,362 | 31,554 | 28,352 |
| **Total shareholders' equity** | **59,752** | **60,160** | **70,418** |
| **Total Liabilities and Shareholders' Equity** | **$152,954** | **157,303** | **141,208** |

*Source*: JNJ Annual Reports of 2017 and 2018.

The 2019 sales revenue estimate shows a 5.22% increase over the 2018 sales figure reported in Table 3.1. Cost of goods sold is assumed to maintain its percentages of sales, which is 32.26%.

General, selling, and administrative expenses, historically 27.90% of sales, is estimated by multiplying the 2018 sales estimate by 0.2790. Research expense is estimated by assuming it will increase to 13.26% of sales. Interest expense is assumed to remain unchanged from the prior year's level, and other expenses will be close to their 3-year averages. An average tax rate of 20% gives the firm's tax bill, leaving net income.

The level of some of these variables is sometimes unrelated to sales volume. For example, interest expense is determined by the firm's current loans adjusted for any anticipated changes (for example, new issues or debt repurchases). Research is a policy variable determined by management. For simplicity, in this example we assume a constant relationship to sales.

The

2019 forecasted balance sheet is similarly constructed by multiplying 2018 estimated sales by each account's percentage of sales from Table 3.3. Cash and marketable securities are projected at 35.45% of 2018 sales. Accounts receivable and inventory are forecasted to equal 17.07% and 11.11% of sales, respectively. Prepaid expenses and deferred taxes are estimated to be 9.47% and 9.47% of sales.

Table 3.3 Percentage of Sales for Selected Financial Statement Accounts.

| | **2016** (%) | **2017** (%) | **2018** (%) | **2019** (%) | **2020** (%) |
|---|---|---|---|---|---|
| Annual increase in sales | 2.59 | 6.34 | 6.71 | 5.22 | 5.22 |
| Cost of goods sold | 30.31 | 33.28 | 33.21 | 32.26 | 32.26 |
| Selling, general, and administrative expense | 27.91 | 28.15 | 27.63 | 27.90 | 27.90 |
| Research and development expense | 12.72 | 13.86 | 13.21 | 13.26 | 13.26 |
| In-process research and development | 0.04 | 0.53 | 1.38 | 0.65 | 0.65 |
| Earnings before provision for taxes on income | 27.55 | 23.12 | 22.06 | 24.24 | 24.24 |
| Cash and securities | 58.29 | 23.93 | 24.13 | 35.45 | 35.45 |
| Account receivable | 16.27 | 17.65 | 17.28 | 17.07 | 17.07 |
| Inventories | 11.33 | 11.47 | 10.54 | 11.11 | 11.11 |
| Prepaid expense | 4.57 | 3.32 | 3.31 | 3.73 | 3.73 |
| Deferred taxes on income | 8.55 | 9.29 | 9.36 | 9.07 | 9.07 |
| Net fixed assets | 105.96 | 149.40 | 131.06 | 128.81 | 128.81 |
| Account payable | 9.62 | 9.56 | 9.24 | 9.47 | 9.47 |
| Accrued liabilities | 7.84 | 9.55 | 9.32 | 8.90 | 8.90 |
| Accrued rebated, returns and promotions | 7.52 | 9.43 | 11.50 | 9.48 | 9.48 |
| Accrued compensation and employee related obligations | 3.72 | 3.86 | 3.80 | 3.79 | 3.79 |
| Accrued taxes on income | 1.35 | 2.43 | 1.00 | 1.59 | 1.59 |
| Miscellaneous liabilities | 30.44 | 47.00 | 42.04 | 39.83 | 39.83 |
| Tax rate | 20.00 | 20.00 | 20.00 | 20.00 | 20.00 |
| Dividend payout ratio | −52.12 | −687.92 | −62.06 | −267.37 | −267.37 |

Table 3.4 JNJ, Inc. Percentage of Sales *Pro Forma* Financial Statements, 2019–2020 ($ Million).

| **Income Statement** | **2019** | **2020** | **Percentage** |
|---|---|---|---|
| Sales to customers | 85,836 | 90,312 | (5.22% increase) |
| Cost of goods sold | 27,694 | 29,138 | (32.26% of sales) |
| Gross profit | 58,142 | 61,174 | |
| Selling, general, and administrative expense | 23,946 | 25,195 | (27.90% of sales) |
| Research and development expense | 11,383 | 11,976 | (13.26% of sales) |
| In-process research and development | 559 | 588 | (0.65% of sales) |
| Interest Expense | (611) | (611) | (Constant at 2018 level) |
| Interest expense, net of portion capitalized | 1,005 | 1,005 | (Constant at 2018 level) |
| Other (income) expense, net | 524 | 524 | (Average over last 3 years) |
| Restructuring | 350 | 350 | (Average over last 3 years) |
| Earnings before provision for taxes on income | 20,808 | 21,894 | (24.24% of sales) |
| Provision for taxes on income | 4,162 | 4,379 | (20% tax rate) |
| Net Income (Loss) | 16,647 | 17,515 | |
| **Consolidated Balance Sheets — USD ($) in Millions** | **2019** | **2020** | |
| **Assets** | | | |
| **Current assets** | | | |
| Cash and securities | 30,431 | 32,018 | (35.45% of sales) |
| Accounts receivable trade, less allowances for doubtful accounts | 14,649 | 15,413 | (17.07% of sales) |
| Inventories | 9,537 | 10,035 | (11.11% of sales) |
| Deferred taxes on income | 7,785 | 8,191 | (9.47% of sales) |
| Prepaid expenses and other receivables | 3,202 | 3,369 | (3.73% of sales) |

(*Continued*)

Table 3.4 (*Continued*)

| **Consolidated Balance Sheets — USD ($) in Millions** | **2019** | **2020** | |
|---|---|---|---|
| **Total current assets** | **65,605** | **69,027** | |
| Total fixed assets | 110,563 | 116,329 | (128.81% of sales) |
| **Total Assets** | **176,168** | **185,356** | |
| **Liabilities and Shareholders' Equity** | | | |
| **Current liabilities** | | | |
| Loans and notes payable | 3,351 | 3,351 | (Average of last 2 years) |
| Accounts payable | 8,133 | 8,557 | (9.47% of sales) |
| Accrued liabilities | 7,642 | 8,041 | (8.90% of sales) |
| Accrued rebates, returns and promotions | 8,138 | 8,563 | (9.48% of sales) |
| Accrued compensation and employee related obligations | 3,257 | 3,427 | (3.79% of sales) |
| Accrued taxes on income | 1,367 | 1,439 | (1.59% of sales) |
| **Total current liabilities** | **31,888** | **33,376** | |
| Long-term debt | 27,684 | 27,684 | (Constant at 2018 level) |
| Miscellaneous liabilities | 34,185 | 35,967 | (11.87% of sales) |
| Total liabilities | **93,757** | **97,028** | |
| **Shareholders' equity** | | | |
| Common stock — par value $1.00 per share | 3,120 | 3,120 | (Constant at 2018 level) |
| Accumulated other comprehensive income | –15,222 | –15,222 | (Constant at 2018 level) |
| Retained earnings | 114,539 | 123,296 | **(See text discussion)** |

(*Continued*)

Table 3.4 (*Continued*)

| **Consolidated Balance Sheets — USD ($) in Millions** | **2019** | **2020** | |
|---|---|---|---|
| Less: common stock held in treasury, at cost | 34,362 | 34,362 | (Constant at 2018 level) |
| **Total shareholders' equity** | **136,799** | **145,556** | |
| **Total Liabilities and Shareholders' Equity** | **230,556** | **242,584** | |
| **Plug** | **–54,388** | **–57,228** | |
| | **176,168** | **185,356** | |

Accounts payable are assumed to remain equal to 9.47% of sales; likewise, most of the other accounts are estimated using the percentages from Table 3.3. Long-term debt and common stock are two accounts that we assume will remain constant at the 2018 level. Due to their variability, we assume loans and notes payable will equal the average of the prior two years' amounts.

The retained earnings value for 2019 comes from applying Eq. (3.6):

Retained earnings of 2018 ($106,216) + Estimated net income of 2019 ($16,647) – Estimated dividends of 2019 [(0.50) ($16,647)] = $114,539.5 ≈ Retained earnings 2019.

Completing the balance sheet in Table 3.4 leaves assets that are less than liabilities plus equity. We use Eq. (3.5) to find the plug:

$$\text{Total assets} = \text{Total liabilities} + \text{Stockholders' equity} + \text{Plug}$$

$$\$176{,}168 = \$93{,}757 + \$136{,}799 + \text{Plug}$$

$$\text{Thus, Plug} = -\$54{,}388$$

The percentage of sales method provides a useful, broadbrush projection of future financial statements. Its ease of use can mislead a naïve analyst, however. Always remember that the specific flow of cash into and out of the firm over the course of the year is unknown. Thus, the firm's actual borrowing needs during the year may far exceed the amount suggested by year-end *pro forma* financial statements.

Managers cannot count on such analysis as solid truth. These simple financial planning models, as well as more complex models, depend heavily on accounting relationships. As such, they do not examine the size and timing of cash flows. Managers still must complete the detailed work of estimating daily, weekly, and monthly cash needs using methods that we will discuss in Chapter 20.

These financial planning models also fail to consider changes in the firm's risk that may arise from varying capital structures or profit margins. Managers may simulate analysis of the sensitivity of a financial planning model to changing conditions by varying the model's inputs.

Remember, again, that these models are merely planning tools. Managers must assess the implications of a financial plan on the firm's strategy choices, cash flows, and risk before they put any plan into action. The following sections discuss various methods of evaluating a firm's risk based on financial statement relationships.

## 3.6 Risk Considerations

Any planning process must incorporate the one uncertainty in planning for the future: risk. The projected plan is not likely to happen exactly as it was forecast. Changes in monetary policy by the Fed, an unexpected strengthening of the U.S. dollar, a new product introduction by a competitor, or myriad other influences, either positive or negative, will create actual cash flows and financial statements that differ from what was projected. The remainder of this chapter's discussion focuses on the manger's perspective of risk, namely, how to measure a firm's risk and the causes of risk. These tools also are useful for other types of analyses, such as investment analysis or strategic analysis.

We'll first introduce the concept of firm risk using tools that are familiar from your statistics course: the average (or mean) and the standard deviation. We then examine influences such as business risk and financial risk, which cause a firm's income and cash flows to

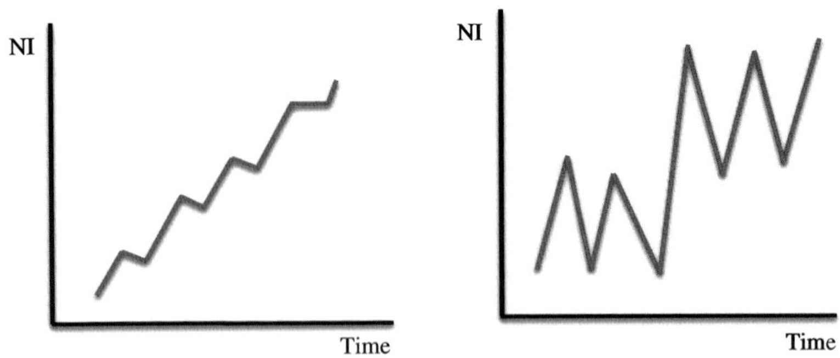


Figure 3.1 Net Income for Two Firms Over Time.

vary. Then we'll examine how financial statement analysis can give us some practical insight into the magnitude of business and financial risk faced by a firm.

### 3.6.1 *Ex-post return and risk for a single asset*

Figure 3.1 shows the net income over time for firms A and B. Firm A's profit rises fairly steadily in value, whereas firm B's shows more fluctuation. The risk of an item is reflected in its variability from its average level. For comparison, a stock analyst may want to determine the level of return and the variability in returns for these two assets to see whether investors in the higher risk asset earned a higher return over time. A financial analyst may want to examine historical differences between risk and profit on different types of new product introductions or projects undertaken in different countries.

If historical, or ex-post data are known, an analyst can easily compute historical average return and risk measures. If $X_t$ represents a data item for period $t$, the *arithmetic average* $X$, over $n$ periods is given by:

$$\bar{X} = \frac{\sum_{i=1}^{n} X_i}{n} \tag{3.8}$$

The historical risk of an asset can be measured by its variability of its net income in relation to this average. The *variance*, $\sigma^2$, from a sample of data is computed by summing the squared deviations and dividing by $n-1$:

$$\sigma^2 = \frac{\sum_{i=1}^{n}(X_i - \bar{X})^2}{n-1} \tag{3.9}$$

Squaring the terms can make the variation difficult to interpret. What do units like percent-squared or dollars-squared tell the analyst about an asset's risk? Therefore, analysts often prefer the *standard deviations*, $\sigma$, which is simply the square root of the variance.

$$\sigma = \sqrt{\sigma^2} \tag{3.10}$$

The standard deviation formula gives units of measurement that match those of raw data.

Standard deviation can be given a statistical interpretation to help give the analyst an intuitive feel for the possible range of returns that can occur. As shown in Figure 3.2, if the underlying distribution of data is approximately normal, then we expect 68% of the data terms to fall within one standard deviation of the mean, that is, $\overline{X} \pm 1\sigma$. About 95% of observed returns will fall within two standard deviations of the average $\overline{X} \pm 2\sigma$. Actual returns should fall within three standard deviations of the mean, $\overline{X} \pm 3\sigma$, about 99% of the time. Thus, if the mean and standard deviations are known, a rough range for future values can be estimated.

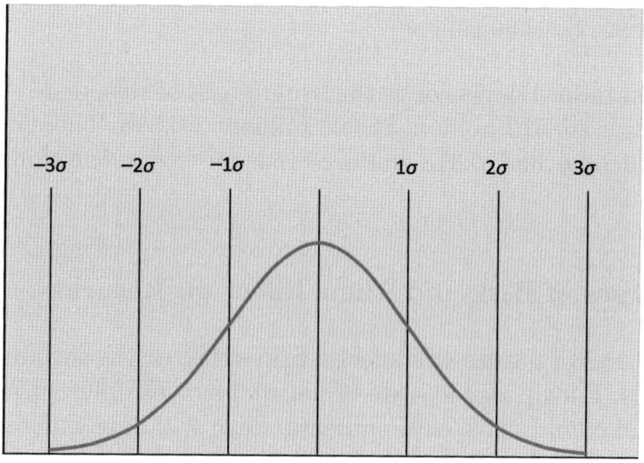


Figure 3.2 Normal Distribution.

One problem with using the standard deviation as a measure of risk is that we cannot get an intuitive feel for risk by looking at the standard deviation alone. Firm A's profits may have a higher standard deviation than firm B, but because firm A's mean return is much higher, firm A's actually may have lower risk. The *coefficient of variation* (CV) allows us to make comparisons because it controls for the size of the average. The CV measures risk-per-unit of return. The coefficient variation is computed as the standard deviation divided by the mean:

$$CV = \sigma\sqrt{X} \tag{3.11}$$

**Example 3.3.** Average, Variance, and Standard Deviation

**Q:** JNJ, Inc.'s net income in 1992 was \$1,030 million; in 1993 it was \$1,787 million; in 1994, it was \$2,006 million. What was JNJ's average net income during these three years? What was the variance, standard deviation, and CV of J&J's profit?

**A:** Equation (3.8) calculates the arithmetic average rate of return by adding the three profit figures and dividing the sum by 3: [\$1,030 + \$1,787 + \$2,006]/3 = \$1,608 million. Using this arithmetic average, we can compute the variance using Eq. (3.9):

$$\sigma^2 = \frac{(\$1,030 - \$1,608)^2 + (\$1,787 - \$1,608)^2 + (\$2,006 - \$1,608)^2}{3-1}$$

$$= \$262,264.50 \text{ million}^2$$

The standard deviation is the square root of this, or \$512 million. The CV is \$512 million/\$1,608 million = 0.318. Therefore, JNJ's net income had 0.318 units of risk for every one dollar of net income.

## 3.7 Types of Risk and Their Effect on Returns

Future states of nature will affect a firm's risk, or the variability of its cash flows. Each possible state of nature involves different macroeconomic and competitive environments. Each will have different effects on the firm's ability to generate cash flows and compete in the marketplace. In this section, we'll discuss how changes in the firm's economic and competitive environment can affect the firm.

Within the firm, there are two general risks, business risk and financial risk. *Business risk* deals with a firm's operating structure. It is directly affected by the type of assets used by the firm and the markets in which it competes. *Financial risk* is determined by how the firm decides to finance its assets.

### 3.7.1 *Business risk*

Business risk is determined by the products the firm sells and the production processes it uses. The effects of business risk are seen ultimately in the variability of earnings before interest and taxes (EBIT) over time. In fact, one popular measure of a firm's business risk is the standard deviation of EBIT. To control for the effects of a firm's size, another popular method of gauging business risk is to find the standard deviation over time of the firm's operating return on assets, that is, EBIT/Total Assets.

Table 3.5 shows a simplified income statement. Because business risk is measured by variability in EBIT, line items that affect business risk appear on the top half of the income statement. This suggests that a firm's business risk is affected by three major influences: unit volume fluctuations, fixed costs (including depreciation expenses), and the relationship between the firm's selling price and its variable costs.

*Unit Volume Variability.* Variability in the quantity of output sold can lead to variability in EBIT through variations in sales revenue and total variable costs such as raw material costs and labor costs.

Table 3.5 Simplified Income Statement.

| | |
|---|---|
| Impact of business risk (Top half of income statement) | Sales = Price × Quantity sold<br>− Costs[Variable cost(cost per unit × quantity)<br>+ fixed cost(fixed constant)]<br>−Depreciation(also a fixed cost) |
| | = EBIT(EBIT or operating income) |
| Impact of financial risk (Bottom half of income statement) | − Interest expense<br>= Earnings before taxes (EBIT) − Taxes<br>= Earnings after taxes(EAIT or net income) |

Table 3.6 Scenario 1: Impact of Sales and Fixed Costs on EBIT; Fixed Costs = \$200.

| | **Base Case** | **Number of Units Sold Rises by 10%** | **Number of Units Sold Falls by 10%** |
|---|---|---|---|
| Sales | \$1,000 | \$1,100 | \$900 |
| Variable costs | 750 | 825 | 675 |
| Fixed costs | 200 | 200 | 200 |
| EBIT | \$50 | \$75 | \$25 |

The net effect of fluctuating volume leads to fluctuations in EBIT and contributions to business risk.

*Fixed Costs.* The second factor affecting business risk is the firm's fixed costs. Fixed costs, such as rent, lease payments, and depreciation, remain the same whether the firm's sales, production, or profitability levels rise or fall. The effect of fixed costs on the firm's operating structure is to magnify, or leverage, the impact of a change in sales on EBIT.

Table 3.6 shows the effects of fixed costs and varying output levels on EBIT and business risk. Suppose the firm can sell its product for \$10 a unit, and the variable cost is \$7.50 a unit. The sales forecast projects sales of 100 units. Table 3.6 shows that fixed costs of \$200 would give an EBIT of \$50. Should the quantity sold rise 10%, to 110 units, sales and variable costs rise by 10%; however, EBIT rises 50%, to \$75. Should the actual quantity sold fall to 90 units (a 10% reduction), both sales and variable costs fall 10%, but EBIT falls 50%, to \$25. With fixed costs of \$200, a 10% change in quantity sold would result in a 50% change in EBIT.

Table 3.7 presents a scenario identical to Table 3.6, except the level of fixed costs is \$100. As in Table 3.6, a given percentage change in quantity sold leads to a larger percentage change in EBIT. Business risk is less with the lower level of fixed costs, however, as EBIT varies by only 16.67% as quantity changes by 10%.

Tables 3.6 and 3.7 illustrate how business risk reacts to the amount of a firm's fixed costs; Table 3.6, with its higher fixed costs, shows more variability in EBIT than Table 3.7.

Table 3.7 Scenario 2: Impact of Sales and Fixed Costs on EBIT; Fixed Costs = $100.

| | Base Case | Number of Units Sold Rises by 10% | Number of Units Sold Falls by 10% |
|---|---|---|---|
| Sales | $1,000 | $1,100 | $900 |
| Variable costs | 750 | 825 | 675 |
| Fixed costs | 100 | 100 | 100 |
| EBIT | $150 | $175 | $125 |

**Example 3.4.** Zero Fixed Operating Costs

**Q:** What happens to business risk if a firm has zero fixed costs?
**A:** Alter the scenario given in Tables 3.6 and 3.7 to assume that fixed costs equal zero:

| | Base Case | Number of Units Sold Rises by 10% | Number of Units Sold Falls by 10% |
|---|---|---|---|
| Sales | $1,000 | $1,100 | $900 |
| Variable Costs | 750 | 825 | 675 |
| Fixed Costs | 0 | 0 | 0 |
| EBIT | $250 | $275 | $225 |

EBIT still fluctuates, but the percentage change in each case, 10%, is the same as the percentage change in sales. The fixed costs in Tables 3.6 and 3.7 magnify the effects of the sales change. Zero fixed costs produce no magnification effect on EBIT; the percentage change in EBIT is the same as the percentage change in sales.

The Price-Variable Cost Margin. The third factor affecting business risk is the firm's ability to maintain a constant, positive difference between price and per-unit variable cost:

$$\text{Margin} = \frac{\text{Price} - \text{Variable cost-per-unit}}{\text{Price}} \tag{3.12}$$

Tables 3.6 and 3.7 and Example 3.4 all assumed a constant margin of 25% to isolate the effects of fluctuating sales levels and fixed costs on business risk. The next example shows how varying margins influence business risk.

**Example 3.5.** On the Margin

**Q:** Assume that unit sales 10% higher than predicted would create competitive conditions that would allow the firm to increase its margin from 25% to 40%. Also assume that unit sales 10% lower than expected would include competitors to cut their prices to stimulate demand, dropping the firm's margin to 10%. Using the base case from Table 3.6, what impact would change in sales volume and margin have on EBIT?

**A:** With unit sales 10% higher than expected, variable costs in Table 3.6 were \$825; using Eq. (3.10) a 40% margin would imply total sales revenues such that:

$$0.40 = \frac{\text{Sales} - \$825}{\text{Sales}}$$

This would provide sales equal to \$1,375. Likewise, according to Table 3.6, a 10% decline in unit sales led to variable costs of \$675; a margin of 10% would provide sales revenues of \$750. This information on total sales implies the following calculations for EBIT:

| | **Base Case** | **Number of Units Sold Rises by 10%** | **Number of Units Sold Falls by 10%** |
|---|---|---|---|
| Sales | \$1,000 | \$1,375 | \$750 |
| Variable costs | 750 | 825 | 675 |
| Fixed costs | 200 | 200 | 200 |
| EBIT | \$50 | \$350 | –\$125 |

When the number of units sold rises by 10%, the increased margin results in a 600% increase in EBIT! If sales volume slumps, leading competitors to cut prices, EBIT falls to –\$125, a loss of 350%. Obviously, changing price-cost margins can have significant effects on EBIT variability and business risk. These effects are likely to be pro-cyclical, as margins will rise in good times and shrink in bad. Thus, rising margins can make good times even better, while declining margins can make bad times disastrous.

### 3.7.2 *Degree of operating leverage*

We have seen that a firm's business risk is affected by its level of fixed costs, or in financial terminology, its *operating leverage.* A quick way to approximate a firm's exposure to business risk is to compute its degree of operating leverage. The DOL is a measure of the sensitivity of EBIT to a change in unit volume in sales, *assuming a constant price-variable cost margin.* Formally,

$$\text{DOL} = \frac{\text{Percentage change in EBIT}}{\text{Percentage change in unit sales}} \tag{3.13}$$

In Table 3.6 (which assumed a constant margin), a 10% change in unit volume caused a 50% change in EBIT ([\$75 − \$50]/\$50 = 50%). Thus, the firm had a DOL of 50%/10%, or 5.0. That number means that a 1% change in unit volume would lead to a 5.0 times 1%, or 5,0% change in EBIT. The leverage effect, as seen in Table 3.6, works both ways; it magnifies both increases and decreases in sales into larger increases or decreases in EBIT.

Table 3.7 shows a lower level of fixed costs; this means it has a lower degree of operating leverage. When unit volume changed by 10%, EBIT changed 16.67%. This gives a DOL of 16.67%/10%, or 1.667.

There is a more straightforward way to compute a firm's degree of operating leverage. If the firm's revenue, total variable costs, and fixed costs are known, the DOL can be computed as:

$$\text{DOL} = \frac{\text{Sales revenue} - \text{Variable costs}}{\text{Sales revenue} - \text{Variable costs} - \text{Fixed costs}} \tag{3.14}$$

Or, stated with variables, the formula for DOL can be written as:

$$\frac{Q(p-v)}{EBIT} = \frac{Q(p-v)}{Q(p-v)-F}$$

where $Q$ = quantity of goods sold; $p$ = price per unit; $v$ = variable cost per unit; $F$ = total fixed cost; EBIT = earnings before interest and taxes.

For the base case data in Table 3.6:

$$\text{DOL} = \frac{\$1{,}000 - \$70}{\$1{,}000 - \$750 - \$200} = \frac{\$250}{\$50} = 5.0$$

For Table 3.7:

$$\text{DOL} = \frac{\$1{,}000 - \$750}{\$1{,}000 - \$750 - \$100} = \frac{\$250}{\$150} = 1.667$$

These formulas make computing the degree of operating leverage seem fairly straightforward, but these calculations assume constant margins. Any careful analysis of business risk should include analysis of competitive conditions and other influences on the firm's margins.

**Example 3.6.** Operating Leverage

**Q:** With sales of $1,000, the base case gave a DOL of 5.0; that is, a 1% change in unit volume led to a 5% change in EBIT, assuming constant margins. Calculate the firm's new DOL after Part (a) unit sales rose by 10% to 1,100 units, and Part (b) sales fell by 10% to 900 units.

**A:** (a) A 10% increase in unit sales would give a new sales revenue figure of $1,100, variable costs of $825, and fixed costs of $200. Using Eq. (3.14):

$$\text{DOL} = \frac{\$1{,}100 - \$825}{\$1{,}100 - \$825 - \$200} = \frac{\$275}{\$75} = 3.67$$

At this higher level of revenue, a 1% increase in unit volume would cause EBIT to increase by 3.67%.

(b) If sales were to fall by 10%, revenues would be $900, with variable costs of $675, and fixed costs of $200. Thus,

$$\text{DOL} = \frac{\$900 - \$675}{\$900 - \$675 - \$200} = \frac{\$225}{\$25} = 9.0$$

A 1% decrease in volume would cause EBIT to decrease by 9%.

Why does a firm's DOL change as its level of unit sales varies? Recall the basic definition of DOL: it is the percentage change in EBIT that corresponds to a 1% change in unit sales. For lower levels of sales, EBIT is small. At the firm's *break-even point*, where revenues equal total costs, EBIT is zero. Therefore, any change in sales from the break-even point results in an infinite percentage change in EBIT and a DOL value of infinity.[5] As sales volume grows, the level of EBIT also grows, but the resulting percentage change in EBIT becomes smaller and smaller, leading to reductions in the firm's degree of operating leverage. With constant margins and fixed costs, this implies that firm growth causes business risk to decline. Using the same level of fixed costs in the same price-variable cost margin as in Table 3.6, Table 3.8 illustrates how DOL changes at different sales levels.

Table 3.8 EBIT and Degree of Operating Leverage for Different Sales Levels.

| % | **Sales ($)** | % | **EBIT ($)** | **DOL** |
|---|---|---|---|---|
| | 1210 | | 102.50 | 2.95 |
| +10 | | | | |
| | 1100 | | 75.00 | 3.67 |
| +10 | | +50 | | |
| Base case | 1000 | | 50.00 | 5.00 |
| –10 | | –50 | | |
| | 900 | | 25.00 | 9.00 |
| –10 | | –90 | | |
| | 810 | | 2.50 | 81.00 |
| –1.23 | | –100 | | |
| | 800 | | 0.00 | $\infty$ |

[5]From Eq. (5.12a), we can redefine DOL as

$$\text{DOL} = \frac{1}{1 - \frac{Q^*}{Q}}$$

where $Q^*$ represents the break-even quantity. Therefore if a firm operates below the break-even point, then the DOL will be negative. For example, if DOL $= -3.0$, then a 1% increase in sales volume will result in a 3% reduction of loss. If $Q^* = Q$, then DOL equals infinity.

### 3.7.3 *Financial risk*

Business risk, or variability in EBIT, arises, in part, because of fixed costs in the firm's operating structure. *Financial risk* occurs as a result of fixed costs in a firm's financial structure. A firm's financial structure is the combination of debt and equity that it uses to finance assets. Equity dividends, including preferred stock dividends, are considered to be a variable financing cost, as the firm can reduce the dollar amount of dividends or eliminate them entirely if its cash flow is poor. Shareholders may be unhappy, but even preferred shareholders can do little to force the firm to pay dividends.

Interest on debt, however, is a fixed financing cost. Debt holders have legal rights if the firm does not pay interest in full when it is due. To remain a going concern, it must pay interest regardless of changes in sales or EBIT. Just as operating leverage arises from fixed operating costs, financial leverage arises from fixed financing costs.[6]

Turn back to Table 3.5 and notice that financial risk affects the bottom half of the income statement (i.e., specifically, how changes in EBIT affect net income). Since many analysts examine firms' EPS and the impact of earnings-per-share changes on stock prices, many prefer to think of financial risk as the relationship between a firm's operating income, EBIT, and its EPS. The fixed interest expense magnifies or leverages the effects of changes in EBIT on the firm's EPS.

To see this, let's continue the example from Table 3.6, focusing on the relationship between EBIT and EPS. Suppose the firm in Table 3.6 has a fixed interest expense of \$10, a 40% tax rate, and 100 shares of stock outstanding.[7] Table 3.8 shows the impacts of operating income and fixed interest expense on EPS. Fixed interest expense magnifies a 50.0% change in EBIT into a 62.5% change

---

[6]We consider all debt that requires payment of interest in cash as a fixed financial cost. Some may argue this point, as many firms have variable rate bank loans and even long-term debt with adjustable coupon rates. The variability in interest payments on such instruments depends on financial market conditions, however, *not* the firm's recent sales performance or profitability. Whatever the interest cost is, it is considered fixed at a point in time and cannot be altered by management.

[7]Although taxes may be ever present, they are not a fixed cost. The total tax bill is variable; it rises and falls with the firm's taxable income.

Table 3.9 Impact of Financial Leverage on EPS.

| | **Base Case ($)** | **EBIT Rises by 50% ($)** | **EBIT Falls by 50% ($)** |
|---|---|---|---|
| EBIT | 50 | 75 | 25 |
| −Interest | 10 | 10 | 10 |
| =EBIT | 40 | 65 | 15 |
| −Tax (40v) | 16 | 26 | 6 |
| =Net Income | 24 | 39 | 9 |
| EPS | 0.24 | 0.39 | 0.09 |

in EPS. Example 3.7 shows how a different level of fixed interest affects EPS.

**Example 3.7.** Financial Risk

**Q:** (a) Referring to Table 3.9, what happens to the percentage change in EPS if the interest expense increases to $20?
(b) What happens to financial risk if the firm is financed entirely by equity?

**A:** (a) Suppose the interest expense rises to $20 rather than $10 as shown in Table 3.9:

| | **Base Case** | **EBIT Rises by 50%** | **EBIT Falls by 50%** |
|---|---|---|---|
| EBIT | $50 | $75 | $25 |
| − Interest | 20 | 20 | 20 |
| = EBT | $30 | $55 | $5 |
| − Tax (40%) | 12 | 22 | 2 |
| = Net income | $18 | $33 | $3 |
| EPS | $0.18 | $0.33 | $0.03 |

The larger fixed interest expense results in greater variability in EPS. A 50.0% change in EBIT now leads to an 83.33% change in EPS. The firm faces greater financial risk when it includes more financial leverage, that is, more debt, in its financial structure.

(b) Now let's answer the second part of the question, namely what happens to financial risk if no debt is used to finance the firm. Returning to Table 3.8, we reduce interest expense to zero.

| | **Base Case** | **EBIT Rises by 50%** | **EBIT Falls by 50%** |
|---|---|---|---|
| EBIT | $50 | $75 | $25 |
| − Interest | 0 | 0 | 0 |
| = EBIT | $50 | $75 | $25 |
| − Tax (40%) | 20 | 30 | 10 |
| = Net Income | $30 | $45 | $15 |
| EPS | $0.30 | $0.45 | $0.15 |

When the firm has no interest expense, it has no financial risk and no financial leverage. When EBIT changes by 50%, net income and EPS also change by 50%. No magnification effect occurs.

Table 3.8 and Example 3.7 show that financial leverage (that is, fixed interest expense) magnifies a given percentage change in EBIT to produce an even larger percentage change in EPS. Thus, fixed financial costs have much the same effect on the bottom half of the income statement that fixed operating costs have on the top half.

### 3.7.4 *Degree of financial leverage*

A firm's financial risk reflects its interest expense, or in financial jargon, its financial leverage. A quick way to determine a firm's exposure to financial risk is to compute its DFL. The DFL measures the sensitivity of EPS to changes in EBIT:

$$\text{DFL} = \frac{\text{Percentage change in EPS}}{\text{Percentage change in EBIT}} \tag{3.15}$$

This definition clearly suggests that DFL represents the percentage change in EPS due to a 1% change in EBIT. As illustrated in Table 3.8, when EBIT rose or fell by 50.0%, EPS rose or fell by 62.5%. The firm's DFL was thus 62.5%/50.0%, or 1.25. This value means that the firm's EPS rises (or falls) by 1.25% for every 1% increase (or decreases) in EBIT from its base case value of \$50.

**Example 3.8.** DFL, Part I

**Q:** Compute the DFL for these situations reviewed in Example 3.7, that is, when interest expense equals Part (a) \$20, and Part (b) \$0.

**A:** (a) In example 3.7, when EBIT changed by 50.0%, EPS changed by 83.33%. Thus, when EBIT equals \$50 and the firm has a \$20 interest expense, the DFL is 83.33%/50.0%, or 1.67. A 1% change in EBIT leads to a 1.67% changes in EPS.

(b) When the firm is financed only be equity, interest expense is zero. From Example 3.7, if EBIT changes by 50%, EPS also changes by 50%. When no financial leverage is present, the DFL is 50%/50%, or 1.00. EPS will change by the same percentage as EBIT.

There is a more straightforward method to compute a firm's DFL that avoids handling percentage changes in variables. This formula is given in Eq. (3.16):

$$\text{DFL} = \frac{\text{EBIT}}{\text{EBIT} - \text{I}} = \frac{\text{EBIT}}{\text{EBT}} \tag{3.16}$$

DFL equals the firm's EBIT divided by EBIT minus interest expense (I), or earnings before taxes (EBT).

**Example 3.9.** Degree of Financial Leverage, Part II

**Q:** Use the shortcut formula in Eq. (3.14) to find the DFL when EBIT equals \$50 and interest expense equals Part (a) \$10, Part (b) \$20, and Part (c) \$0.

**A:** (a) When EBIT equals \$50 and interest expense equals \$10, as in Table 3.8,

$$\text{DFL} = \frac{\$50}{(\$50 - \$10)} = 1.25$$

(b) When interest expense is \$20, as in Example 3.7:

$$\text{DFL} = \frac{\$50}{(\$50 - \$20)} = 1.67$$

(c) When the interest expense is zero, as in the second part of Example 3.7:

$$\text{DFL} = \frac{\$50}{(\$50 - \$0)} = 1.00$$

This example shows that Eq. (3.14) results in the same measures for the DFL as Eq. (3.13).

How is the firm's DFL affected when its level of EBIT rises or falls over time? We already know that DFL is 1.25 when EBIT equals \$50 and interest expense equals \$10. If EBIT increases to \$75, the firm's new DFL is:

$$\text{DFL} = \frac{\$75}{(\$75 - \$10)}$$

Or about 1.15; a 1% change in EBIT now changes EPS by only 1.15%. If EBIT falls to \$25, the firm's DFL is:

$$\text{DFL} = \frac{\$25}{(\$25 - \$10)} = 1.67$$

If EBIT equals \$25, a 1% change in EBIT results in a 1.67% change in EPS.

DFL changes with the level of EBIT for much the same reason that DOL changes with sales volume. When EBIT is about the same as the firm's interest expense, EPS is small. A slight change in EBIT can therefore lead to a large percentage change in EPS, resulting in a large DFL. If the firm's interest expense does not change while EBIT continues to grow, the percentage increase in EPS becomes smaller and smaller, resulting in lower values for the firm's DFL.

### 3.7.5 *Total risk*

Table 3.5 showed that business risk affects the top half of the income statement. Operating leverage magnifies the effect of changing sales to produce a percentage change in EBIT larger than the change in sales, assuming constant profit margins. Financial risk affects the bottom half of the income statement. Financial leverage magnifies any change in EBIT to produce a percentage change in EPS larger than the change in EBIT. The total earnings risk, or total variability in EPS, is a combination of the effects of business risk and financial risk. Operating leverage and financial leverage combine to magnify a given percentage change in sales to a potentially much greater percentage change in earnings.

Together, operating and financial leverage produce an effect called *combined leverage.* A firm's *degree of combined leverage* (DCL) is the percentage change in EPS that results from a 1% change in sales volume:

$$\text{DCL} = \frac{\text{Percentage change in EPS}}{\text{Percentage change in sales}} \tag{3.17}$$

The relationship between the degrees of operating and financial leverage and the DCL is a multiplicative one. DFL times DOL results in Eq. (3.15) as follows:

$$\frac{\text{Percentage change in EPS}}{\text{Percentage change in EBIT}} \times \frac{\text{Percentage change in EBIT}}{\text{Percentage change in sales}}$$
$$= \frac{\text{Percentage change in EPS}}{\text{Percentage change in sales}} = \text{DCL}$$

From Eqs. (3.14) and (3.16), we can explicitly define the DCL as:

$$\text{DCL} = \frac{Q(p-v)}{EBIT - I} \tag{3.18}$$

Please note that all notations used in Eq. (3.18) have been defined in either Eqs. (3.14) or (3.16).

Thus, a firm's DCL is simply the product of its degree of operating leverage and its DFL. The DCL represents the impact on EPS of the combined efforts of operating leverage and financial leverage if profit margins remain constant.

**Example 3.10.** Combined Leverage

**Q:** Based upon the information in Tables 3.6 and 3.9, what is the DCL for the firm when sales revenue is at its base case of \$1,000?

**A:** From the information in Table 3.6, the firm's degree of operating leverage is 50%/10% or 5.00. From Table 3.8, the firm's DFL is 62.5%/50% or 1.25. The firm's DCL thus equals 5.00 times 1.25, or 6.25. A 1% change in sales revenue results in a 6.25% change in EPS.

Table 3.10 DCL, Sales, and EPS.

| | Base Case | Number of Units Sold Rises by 10% | Number of Units Sold Falls by 10% |
|---|---|---|---|
| Sales | \$1,000 | \$1,100 | \$900 |
| Variable cost | 750 | 825 | 675 |
| Fixed cost | 200 | 200 | 200 |
| EBIT | \$50 | \$75 | \$25 |
| – Interest | 10 | 10 | 10 |
| EBT | \$40 | \$65 | \$15 |
| – Tax (40%) | 16 | 26 | 6 |
| Net income | \$24 | \$39 | \$9 |
| EPS | \$0.24 | \$0.39 | \$0.09 |

The firm's DCL is apparent in Table 3.10, which combines information from Tables 3.6 and 3.9 to construct a complete income statement.

Table 3.10 verifies that a 10.0% change in sales revenues results in a 62.5% change in EPS. Using the definition of the DCL, from Eq. (3.15), DCL equals 62.5% divided by 10%, or 6.25.

**Example 3.11.** Forecasting Earnings

**Q:** Assume the firm is currently at its base case, as shown in Tables 3.6 and 3.9. Suppose, as well, that a competitive analysis reveals that the firm will sell 5% less product this year, with no change in margin. Project the firm's new EPS.

**A:** This can be answered by setting up a new income statement and working through to determine the new EPS, but it is easier to use our knowledge of the firm's DCL to determine the change in earnings. Since DCL equals 6.25 we know that a 1% change in sales will result in a 6.25% change in earnings; therefore a 5% decline in sales will result in a 5 times 6.25, or 31.25% decline in EPS. As the current EPS is \$0.24, the new EPS will be (\$0.24) (1 – 0.3125) = \$0.165, or about 16.5 cents a share.

Like the degree of operating leverage and the DFL, the DCL is not constant, as the firm's sale rise and fall over time. We know DOL declines as sales increase and DFL declines as EBIT rises. Thus, a firm's DCL will fall as it sales and EBIT increases, as long as the firm's margin, fixed operating costs and financial costs remain constant.

**Example 3.12.** Finding the DCL

**Q:** From the previous example, we know that the firm's DCL is 6.25% when sales revenues equal $1,000. What will be the firm's new DCL if Part (a) sales rise by 10%, and Part (b) sales fall by 10%?

**A:** We can find the DCL values by multiplying together the appropriate degree of operating leverage and DFL values.

(a) If sales were to rise by 10%, Table 3.6 showed that sales revenue would be $1,100 and EBIT would be $75. In Part (a) of Example 3.6, we computed a 3.67 DOL for this case. Incidentally, following Example 3.9 we computed the DFL when EBIT equals $75; it was approximately 1.15. Thus, if sales revenues were to rise 10% to equal $1,100, the DCL would be:

$$(3.67)(1.15) = 4.22$$

A 1% change in sales would cause earnings to change by 4.22%.

(b) If sales were to fall by 10%, Table 3.6 showed that sales revenue would be $900 and EBIT would be $25. In Part (b) of Example 3.6, we computed DOL for this case; it was 9.00. Shortly after Example 3.9, we computed DFL when EBIT equals $25; it was approximately 1.67. Thus, if sales revenue were equal to $900, the DCL would be:

$$(9.00)(1.67) = 15.00$$

A 1% change in sales would cause earnings to change by 15.00%.

Table 3.11 summarizes the firm's degree of operating, financial, and combined leverage values at sales levels of $900, $1,000, and $1,100. It illustrates that if fixed costs do not change, DOL, DFL, and DCL all decline as the firm grows.

This section has introduced the concepts of business risk and financial risk. The DCL uses a firm's operating leverage and financial leverage and the assumption of constant margins to estimate a

Table 3.11 DOL, DFL, and DCL.

| Sales | $900 | $1,00 | $1,100 |
|---|---|---|---|
| DOL | 9.00 | 5.00 | 3.67 |
| × DFL | 1.67 | 1.25 | 1.15 |
| = DCL | 15.00 | 6.25 | 4.22 |

relationship between changes in sales and changes in earnings. The financial planning process can use this information to determine the risk or potential variability that exists behind the numbers appearing in projected financial statements.

### 3.7.6 *The value of financial statement analysis*

Financial statements, by their nature, look backward. They report the firm's assets, liabilities, and equity as of a certain past date, or a firm's revenues, expenses or cash flows over some past time period.

But knowledge of a firm's operating and financial structure can help the analyst to predict the effects of future events on the firm's cash flows. Together with projections or likely future scenarios, knowledge of the firm's operating and financial leverage can help analyst gauge the risk and expected cash flows of the firm. The analyst also must combine knowledge of the firm's strategy, operating and financial leverage characteristics, and possible macroeconomic and microeconomic scenarios to determine an appropriate market price for the firm's stock. Combining what is known about the firm with data that reflects potential future scenarios allows the analyst to evaluate the risks facing the firm and then to develop an expected return forecast based upon these risks. The final outcome of the process is the market's determination of the firm's current security price.

## 3.8 Summary

Two basic types of financial planning models are available to help managers analyze the interactions of company decisions: (1) the internal growth and sustainable growth rate models, and (2) the percentage of sales method. Both types of models show how financial statement ratios and accounting relationships can support internal analysis for firm planning. However, the simplicity and ease of use of these models have a cost: they don't indicate the size, timing, and risk of cash flows. Neither do they clearly indicate the effects of different marketing, pricing, and production strategies on asset growth, inventory levels, and receivables.

| | | | |
|---|---|---|---|
| Cash | $2 | Accounts payable | $5 |
| Receivables | 6 | Notes payable | 4 |
| Inventory | 8 | Long-term bonds | 8 |
| Fixed assets | 25 | Stockholders' equity | 24 |
| Total assets | $41 | Total liabilities and equity | $41 |

The percentage of sales method and other more advanced financial planning methods can be performed on either mainframe computers or PCs. Spreadsheet programs can facilitate planning by allowing the analyst to change various inputs (for example, the sales growth rate assumption, or the cost of goods sold percentage) and then quickly see the effects of these changes and assumptions on company plans. The expanded version of percentage sales method will be discussed in Chapter 21, entitled, "Financial Planning and Strategy."

Financial managers can gauge the risk faced by the firm by adjusting forecasted inputs during the planning process. Business risk, measured by the variability in EBIT, arises from the firm's fixed operating costs, changes in unit volume, and changes in the firm's price-cost margin. Financial risk is the extra variability in net income caused by the firm's fixed interest obligations. Managers can estimate the effect of sales variability on operating income and net income by computing a firm's degree of operating leverage, financial leverage, and combined leverage.

## Key Terms

Arithmetic average
Break-even point
Business risk
Combined leverage
Degree of combined leverage (DCL)
Degree of financial leverage (DFL)

Degree of operating leverage (DOL)
Dividend payout ratio
Financial leverage
Financial planning
Financial risk
Internal Growth rate
Operating Leverage
Percentage of Sales method
*Pro Forma* Financial Statements
Retention rate
Standard deviation
Sustainable growth rate
Variance

## Self-Test Problems

1. **Internal and Sustainable Growth Rates.** A balance sheet and income statement are given below for Mrs. Plain's Cookies. Assuming a 60% earnings retention rate, find the internal growth rate and sustainable growth rate.

Mrs. Plains' Cookies
Balance Sheet, December 31, 1996
(All numbers in millions of dollars)

Mrs. Plains' Cookies
Income Statement 1996
(All numbers in millions of dollars)

| | |
|---|---|
| Sales | $50 |
| Cost of goods sold | 25 |
| Depreciation | 10 |
| EBIT | $15 |
| Taxes | 5 |
| **Net income** | $10 |

A: Equation (3.1) tells us how to find the internal growth rate:

$$\text{IGR} = \frac{\text{RR} \times \text{ROA}}{1 - (\text{RR} \times \text{ROA})}$$

The given information tells us that the net income is \$10 and the total assets are \$41; the return on assets is \$10/\$41 or 0.244. With a retention rate of 0.60, the internal growth rate equals:

$$\text{IGR} = \frac{0.60 \times 0.244}{1 - (0.60 \times 0.244)} = 0.172 \quad \text{or} \quad 17.2$$

With no outside financing, Mrs. Plains' Cookies can afford to expand sales and assets at 17.2% rate.

The Eq. (3.2) shows us how to find the sustainable growth rate:

$$\text{SGR} = \frac{\text{RR} \times \text{ROE}}{1 - (\text{RR} \times \text{ROE})}$$

The given information tells us that net income is \$10 and stockholders' equity is \$24; the return on equity is \$10/\$24, or 0.417. With a retention rate of 0.60, the sustainable growth rate equals:

$$\text{SGR} = \frac{0.60 \times 0.417}{1 - (0.60 \times 0.417} = 0.333 \quad \text{or} \quad 33.3\%$$

By obtaining sufficient outside debt to maintain a constant debt-to-equity ratio, Mrs. Plains' Cookies can expand sales and assets at a 33.3% rate.

**2. Retention rate and ROA.** An aggressive marketing plan for MRS. Plains' Cookies forecast a 40% increase in sales. How can this growth be financed using only internal sources of funds?

A: The internal growth rate is only 17.2%. To finance a 40% growth rate, Mrs. Plains' will have to increase the earnings retention rate and/or the firm's return on assets. ROA can be increased by increasing the profit margin and/or the firm's total asset turnover.

Can the firm finance 40% growth by cutting its dividends? Let's see what retention ratio, along with the firm's current ROA of 24.4%, is necessary for the firm to growth at 40%. We can determine this by setting the internal growth rate to 0.40 (40% in decimal terms), setting ROA equal to 0.244, and solving the equation for the required level of RR:

$$\text{IGR} = \frac{\text{RR} \times \text{ROA}}{1 - (\text{RR} \times \text{ROA})}$$

$$0.407 = \frac{\text{RR} \times 0.244}{1 - (\text{RR} \times 0.244)}$$

After doing the algebra, we find the value of earnings retention necessary to finance 40% growth internally is 1.17, or 117%! Since earnings retention cannot exceed 100%, it is obvious we can't finance this high growth solely by eliminating the dividend. Suppose we plan to increase the earnings retention rate to 80%; what level of ROA is needed to finance 40% growth internally?

Again, we will use internal growth rate formula. Substituting 0.80 for the retention ratio and 0.40 for the growth rate, we have:

$$\text{IGR} = \frac{\text{RR} \times \text{ROA}}{1 - (\text{RR} \times \text{ROA})}$$

$$0.40 = \frac{0.80 \times \text{ROA}}{1 - (0.80 \times \text{ROA})}$$

Solving this equation for ROA, the solution is 0.357 or 35.7%. With an 80% retention rate, an ROA of 35.7% is needed to finance 40% growth with internal funds. This can be accomplished by raising prices, reducing expense, or seeking to improve production efficiency by increasing total asset turnover.

**3. DOL, DFL, and DCL.** A simplified income statement for Zavor Services appears below. Compute and interpret its degree of operating leverage, DFL, and DCL.

Zavor Services
Income Statement, 1995

| | |
|---|---|
| Sales | 1,050,000 |
| Variable costs | 767,000 |
| Fixed costs | 75,000 |
| EBIT | \$208,000 |
| Interest expense | 110,000 |
| EBT | \$98,000 |
| Taxes (30%) | 29,400 |
| Net income | \$68,600 |

A: Using Eqs. (3.12) and (3.14), we can compute the degree of operating leverage and the degree of financial leverage from this single income statement. The degree of operating leverage is computed from Eq. (3.12) as:

$$\begin{aligned} \text{DOL} &= \frac{\text{Sales} - \text{Variable cost}}{\text{Sales} - \text{Variable cost} - \text{Fixed costs}} \\ &= \frac{\$1{,}050{,}000 - 767{,}000}{\$1{,}050{,}000 - 767{,}000 - 75{,}000} \\ &= \frac{283{,}000}{208{,}000} \\ &= 1.36 \end{aligned}$$

This means a 1% change in sales revenue is expected to result in a 1.36% change in EBIT.

The DFL is found by using Eq. (3.14):

$$\begin{aligned} \text{DOL} &= \frac{\text{EBIT}}{\text{EBIT} - 1} \\ &= \frac{\$208{,}000}{\$208{,}000 - 110{,}000} \\ &= \frac{\$208{,}000}{\$98{,}000} \\ &= 2.12 \end{aligned}$$

This means a 1% change in EBIT is expected to result in a 2.12% change in net income (or EPS).

The DCL equals the product of DOL and DFL:

$$\text{DCL} = \text{DOL} \times \text{DFL} = 1.36 \times 2.12 = 2.88$$

so a 1% change in sales is expected to change net income by 2.88%.

## References


Higgins, R. C. *Analysis for Financial Management*, 3rd edn. (Homewood, IL: Richard D. Irwin, Inc. 1992).

Higgins, R. C. "How Much Growth Can a Firm Afford?," *Financial Management*, 6 (Fall 1977, pp. 7–16).

Higgins, R. C. "Sustainable Growth under Inflation," *Financial Management*, 10 (Winter 1981, pp. 36–40).

Lee, C. F. and J. C. Lee. *Financial, Analysis, and Planning*, 3rd edn. (World Scientific Publishing Co., 2017).

Lee, C.-F. and A. C. Lee. *Encyclopedia of Finance*, 3rd edn. (Springer, 2022, Forthcoming).

Ross, S., R. Westfield and J. Jaffe. *Corporate Finance*, 12th edn. (McGraw-Hill, 2019).


## Questions and Problems

### Part A: Questions

1. Caldwell Company decides to increase its R&D spending. If everything else stays constant this year, explain what will happen to Caldwell's internal growth rate this year.
2. Fairly Dry Cleaners is expanding its present facilities. Assuming all other influences and ratios are the same before and after expansion, explain what should happen to fairly's internal growth rate.
3. Occasionally, firms repurchase shares of their outstanding stock. Explain how this affects their internal and sustainable growth rates.
4. The management of Albar Incorporate has decided to increase the firm's use of debt from 30% of assets to 45% of assets. How

will this affect its future internal growth rate? Its future sustainable growth rate?

5. How might a weaker U.S. dollar in a firm's export markets affect its sales growth? What would happen if actual growth was different from the internal growth rate?
6. In the context of the sustainable growth rate, discuss how marketing, finance, and growth are interrelated.
7. A booming economy creates an unexpectedly high sales growth rate for a firm with a low internal growth rate. How can the firm respond to this unplanned sales increase?
8. A tax increase creates slower than expected sales growth throughout the economy. How can a firm with a sustainable growth rate that exceeds the economy's growth rate adjust to unexpectedly slow sales?
9. How might changing from one generally accepted accounting principle to another affect a firm's net income, sales, retention ratio or assets? How might this affect its internal and sustainable growth rates? What recommendations would you offer for developing a growth forecasting model that would be less sensitive to these effects?
10. Is it possible for the sales growth rate to differ from the asset growth rate over time? Why or why not?
11. What are some of the disadvantages of using internal or sustainable growth rates as planning tools?
12. How is the percentage of sales method different from the internal growth rate method? How is it similar?
13. How will a percentage of sales method forecast be affected by changes in accounting principles?
14. Suppose a variable such as prepaid expenses is highly variable from one year to the next and is hard to predict. How can the percentage of sales method be used in such a case?
15. How might the following influences affect a firm's business risk (consider each separately)?
    a. Imports increase the level of competition.
    b. Labor cost decline.
    c. Health care cost (provided for all employees) increase.
    d. The firm's proportion of social security taxes and unemployment insurance taxes increases.
    e. Adoption of new technology allows the firm to produce the same output with a smaller number of employees.

f. The burden of paperwork required under government regulations rises.
g. The tax rate declines.
h. Interest rate rises
i. The firm stock price declines

16. How might the following influences affect a firm's financial risk (consider each separately)?

    a. Interest rates on the firm's short-term bank loans are reduced.
    b. The firm refinances a mortgage on one of its buildings at a lower interest rate.
    c. Tax rate decline.
    d. The firm's stock price increases.
    e. Interest rate in the economy rise.
    f. The firm suffers a sales and operating income decline

17. Explain why the relationship between the degree of operating leverage and the DFL is multiplicative rather than additive.
18. How might a firm try to reduce its business risk? Its financial risk?
19. How will a switch from FIFO to LIFO accounting affect a firm's business financial risks?
20. How will a change from accelerated to straight-line depreciation affect a firm's business and financial risks?
21. Explain how financial statements analyst can assist the evaluation of a firm's business and financial risk.
22. What are the ethical or agency cost implications of a divisional manager telling her staff "Our division's average sales growth rate has been 3%, but I think we can justify an 8% growth forecast for each of the next two years to top management. They are too concerned about strategic issues to pay close attention to our forecasts. The higher growth forecast will allow us to obtain a larger budget increase for next year.
23. To grow faster than the sustainable growth rate, a firm most do some combination of the following: increase profit margins, increase asset efficiency. Increase financial leverage, or reduce its dividend. Discuss the implications of each of this from ethical perspectives. Will faster growth lead to gains in shareholder wealth?

## Part B: Problems

1. **Financial Ratios and Internal Growth Rate.** Let S = last year's sales revenue; A = last year's total assets; D = last year's total liabilities; E = last year's stockholders' equity; NI/S = the firm's (presumably constant) profit margin, the ratio of net income to sales; g = the firm's expected sales growth rate; RR = the firm's (presumably constant) retention ratio. Using these symbols and relationships you are familiar with, find the following:
   a. What will this year's net income equal?
   b. How much will be added to stockholders' equity this year?
   c. What will year's level of assets?
   d. What will be the change in assets between last year and this year?
   e. The change in assets computed in Part (d) has to be financed. Assuming only internal financing is available, compute the firms' internal growth rate. (*Hint*: Set your answers to Part (b) and Part (d) equal to each other, and solve for g. The answer should be the same as Eq. (3.1), the internal growth rate.)
2. **Financial Ratios and Sustainable Growth Rate.** Using the same notation used in Problem 1, now assume that the firm will raise some funds externally in order to keep the firm's debt-to-equity (D/E) ratio constant.
   a. What will this year's net income equal?
   b. How much will be added to stockholders' equity this year?
   c. If the D/E ratio remains constant, how much external debt will the firm raise this year?
   d. What will be this year's level of assets?
   e. What will be the change in assets between this year and the last?
   f. The change in assets computed in Part (e) has to be financed. Assuming a constant debt-to-equity ratio, compute the firm's sustainable growth rate. (*Hint*: Add your answers in Parts (b) and (c) together and set them equal to the solution to Part (e); then solve for g. The answer should be the same as Eq. (3.2), the sustainable growth rate.)

3. **Estimated Retained Earnings.** Hall, Hall, and Hall have retained earnings of $30 million as of the end of last year. This year's sales are expected to be $215 million with a profit margin of 10%. Historically, Hall, Hall, and Hall have paid dividends equal to 60% of the year's net income. Estimate the level of retained earnings at the end of this year.
4. **Pay-out Ratio and Equity.** Danson and Wilson have stockholders' equity of 5$ million as of the end of last year. Their equity multiplier is 2.5. This year's sales are expected to be $21 million, with a return on assets of 10%.

   a. Historically, D&W has paid constant dividends of $1,000,000 to shareholders. Estimate the level of stockholders' equity at the end of this year.
   b. Historically, D&W has paid dividends equal to 40% of net income. Estimate the level of stockholders' equity at the end of this year.
   c. Historically, D&W has paid constant dividends of $2.5 million to stockholders. Estimate the level of stockholders' equity at the end of this year. Where will the money come from to pay this dividend?

5. **Growth Rates, Projected Financial Statements and Plug.** Below are recent financial statements from Moss and Mole Manufacturing.

**Moss and Mole Manufacturing**
**Balance Sheet, December 31, 1995**
**(All numbers are in thousands)**

| | |
|---|---|
| Sales | $260,000 |
| Costs of goods sold | 20,000 |
| Selling, general, and administrative expenses | 173,000* |
| EBIT | $67,000 |
| Interest expense | 12,000 |
| Earnings before taxes | $55,000 |
| Taxes | 17,000 |
| **Net Income** | $37,500 |

*Includes lease payment of $47,000 and depreciation of $8,000

a. Find M&MM's internal growth rate.

b. Find its sustainable growth rate.
c. Using the percentage of sales method, forecast the 1995 balance sheet and income statement assuming (1) a 10% sales growth rate, and (2) that the proportion of most of the financial statement items with respect to sales will be the same in 1996 as they were in 1995. Long-term debt, lease payment, depreciation, and interest will remain at their 1995 dollar level.
d. What is the "plug" figure in Part (c)? Why does it take on this value?
e. Repeat Part (c) assuming that the firm's average tax rate is expected to rise to 35% in 1996.

6. **The Plug and Projected Financial Statements.** Assume that M&MM (refer to the firm's financial statements in Problem 5) will stop leasing assets in 1996; instead, it will purchase them. The consequences of this action will be to eliminate all lease payments, increase fixed assets by $470,000 and increase depreciation by $10,000. The earnings retention rate is assumed to be 50%.

   a. Ignoring sales growth, forecast what 1996's balance sheet and income statement will look like. What is the "plug?"
   b. Now, incorporate a 10% sales growth into your projections. Forecast 1996's balance sheet and income statement.

7. **Growth Rates and Projected Financial Statements.** Bagle's Biscuits has the following financial statement (all numbers are in millions):

**Bagle's Biscuits**
**Balance Sheet, December 31, 1996**

| | |
|---|---|
| **Current Assets** | |
| Cash and marketable securities | $8.1 |
| Receivables | 20.8 |
| Inventories | 22.3 |
| Other current assets | 7.9 |
| **Total Current Assets** | $59.1 |

**Fixed Assets**

| | |
|---|---|
| Net fixed assets | $41.6 |
| Other assets | 34.2 |
| Total Assets | $134.9 |

**Liabilities & Stockholders' Equity**

| | |
|---|---|
| Current Liabilities | $50.2 |
| Long-term Debt | 13.8 |
| Other Liabilities | 19.2 |
| Stockholders' equity | 51.7 |
| Total Liabilities and equity | $134.9 |

**Bagle's Biscuits**
**Income Statement, 1996**

| | |
|---|---|
| Net Sales | $137.5 |
| Costs of goods sold | 51.4 |
| Gross profit | $86.1 |
| Selling & administrative expenses* | 54.3 |
| Research expense | 9.3 |
| Other expenses | 1.1 |
| EBIT | $21.4 |
| Interest expense | 12.4 |
| EBT | $9.0 |
| Income taxes | 1.0 |
| Net income | $8.0 |

*Remark: Depreciation and amortization expense is $5.6 and lease payments total $6.8

a. Find Bagle's internal growth rate.
b. Compute Bagle's sustainable growth rate.
c. Using the percentage of sales method, forecast the 1997 balance sheet and income statement assuming a 10% sales growth rate. Assume that, with the exception of "Other current assets," "Other expenses," and "Other liabilities," the proportion of the financial statement items with respect to sales will be the same in 1997 as they were in 1996. The levels of the "other" accounts are expected to remain the same in 1997 as they were in 1996.
d. Repeat Part (c) assuming improvements in production efficiencies will lower the cost of goods sold to 35% of sales in 1997 and that 1997's inventory level will shrink to $15 in 1997.

8. **Plug and Projected Financial Statements.** Assume that Bagle's Biscuits (refer to the firm's financial statements in Problem 7) has decided not to fund any further R&D on biscuits. This will reduce 1997's R&D expense to zero, reduce fixed assets by 5%, and cut leasing expenses in half. The earnings retention rate is assumed to be 60%.

   a. Ignoring sales growth, forecast what 1997's balance sheet and income statement will look like. What is the "plug"?
   b. Now incorporate a 10% sales growth into your projections. Forecast 1997's balance sheet and income statement.

9. **Growth Rates and Projected Balance Sheet.** Oakhill and Company's 1996 sales are $250 million; its return on equity is 10%; and no dividends are currently paid. Its balance sheet appears below (all numbers are in thousands):

**Oakhill and Company**
**Balance Sheet, December 31, 1996**

| **Assets** | | **Liabilities and Equities** | |
|---|---|---|---|
| Cash | $25,500 | Accounts payable | $35,000 |
| Accounts Receivables | 60,000 | Notes payable | 0 |
| Inventory | 4,500 | Long-term debt | 103,000 |
| Fixed assets | 85,000 | Stockholders' equity | 37,000 |
| **Total assets** | $175,000 | **Total liabilities and equity** | $175,000 |

a. What is Oakhill's internal growth rate?
b. What is Oakhill's sustainable growth rate?
c. Using the percentage of sales method, forecast Oakhill's 1997 balance sheet assuming 5% sales growth *and* a planned reduction in long-term debt to $80,000.
d. Forecast the 1997 balance sheet, assuming that along with the changes in Part (c), the firm wants to begin paying dividends. Use a 20% dividend pay-out ratio.

10. **External Financing Needed.** A simplified balance sheet for Redeye Industries is presented below. Currently, production is running only 80% of capacity; current sales are $200 million. The profit margin is 5%, and the dividend payout ratio is 50% of net income. Sales are expected to rise 10% next year, to $220 million. The current asset and current liability accounts are expected to rise proportionately. Will Redeye need to obtain outside financing?

**Redeye Industries**
**Balance Sheet, 1996**

| **Assets** | | **Liabilities and Equities** | |
|---|---|---|---|
| Current assets | $100 million | Current liabilities | $30 million |
| Fixed assets | 100 million | Long-term debt | 80 million |
| **Total assets** | $200 million | Stockholders' equity | 90 million |
| | | **Total liabilities and equity** | $200 million |

11. **Mean and Variance for Profit Margin.** Debrach's Duds and Reilly's Risers have had the following profit margins over the past six years:

| **Year** | **1** | **2** | **3** | **4** | **5** | **6** |
|---|---|---|---|---|---|---|
| Debrach's | 15% | 13% | 9% | 7% | 5% | 3% |
| Reilly's | 3% | 5% | 7% | 9% | 13% | 15% |

a. What is the average profit margin for each?
b. What is the variance of the profit margins for each?

c. Based solely upon your answers in Parts (a) and (b), which firm has the less variable profit margin?
d. What does this analysis tell you about the need to consider all information when evaluating risk?

12. **Mean and Standard Deviation of Returns.** The Exterminator Company has had stockholder returns of 3%, 15%, 20%, 8%, and 32% over the past five years. What has been an investor's arithmetic average return over this time frame? Find the standard deviation of these returns and CV.
13. **DOL, DFL, and DCL.** The income statements for Mount Lewis Copy Centers for 1995 and 1996 appear below:

**Mount Lewis Copy Centers**
**Income Statement**

| | **1995** | **1996** |
|---|---|---|
| Sales | $20,000 | $21,000 |
| Costs of goods sold | 10,000 | 10,500 |
| Leases | 2,500 | 3,000 |
| Depreciation | 2,000 | 2,100 |
| EBIT | $5,500 | $5,400 |
| Interest | 3,000 | 3,200 |
| EBT | $2,500 | $2,200 |
| Taxes (30%) | 750 | 660 |
| Net income | $1,750 | $1,540 |

a. Compute and interpret the degree of operating leverage, DFL, and DCL in 1995. Assume the components of the costs of goods sold are all variable costs.
b. Compute and interpret the degree of operating leverage, DFL, and DCL in 1996. Assume the components of the costs of goods sold are all variable costs.
c. Why did these numbers change between 1995 and 1996?

14. **DOL, DFL, and DCL.** Using the income statements from the Mount Lewis Copy Centers for 1995 and 1996 in Problem 13, find the percentage change in sales, EBIT, and net income. Use them to compute the degree of operating leverage, financial leverage, and combined leverage.
15. **DOL, DFL, and DCF.** Here's a recent income statement from TC1 Telecommunications Services, Inc. (numbers are in millions):

**TC1 Telecommunications Services, Inc.**
**Income Statement, 1996**

| | |
|---|---|
| Sales | $53.7 |
| Costs of goods sold | 20.2 |
| Depreciation | 13.9 |
| EBIT | $19.6 |
| Interest expense | 12.4 |
| EBT | $7.2 |
| Taxes (25%) | 1.8 |
| **Net Income** | $5.4 |

a. Compute TC1's degree of financial, operating, and combined leverage if half of the cost of goods sold is a variable cost and the other half is a fixed cost.
b. Assume during the current year TC1's sales rise to $59.5 million. What is your estimate of TC1's net income of this year?
c. Suppose TC1's actual net income is only $5 million. Why might the actual net income differ from your estimate in Part (b)?

16. **DOL.** Redo the analysis in Table 3.6, assuming the unit sales increase by 20%. What is the degree of operating leverage? What happens if unit sales decrease by 20%?
17. **DOL.**

a. Using the data in Table 3.6, assume that if unit sales rise by 10%, the unit price will be $9.50 to reflect a downward-sloping demand curve. What is the degree of operating leverage a unit sales change from 100 units to 110 units?

b. Based upon your answer in Part (a), how does a downward-sloping demand curve affect an analysis of operating leverage?

18. **DOL.**

a. Using the data in Table 3.6, assume that if unit sales fall 10% because of a lower priced competing product, the firm will cut its price to $9.00 in response. What is the degree of operating leverage as unit sales change from 100 units to 90 units?
b. Based upon your answer in Part (a), how might new entry or intense competitive rivalry affect business risk and operating leverage?

19. **DOL.**

a. Using the data in Table 3.6, assume that if unit sales rise 10%, the variable costs will rise to $8.23 per unit as suppliers raise their prices to reflect the firm's increased demand for raw materials. If the firm's price remains constant, what is the degree of operating leverage as unit sales change from 100 units to 110 units?
b. Based upon your answer in Part (a), how does a rising cost curve affect an analysis of operating leverage?

20. **DFL.**

a. Using the data in Table 3.8, assume the firm's average tax rate rises to 45% when EBT equals $65. What is the firm's DFL as EBIT rises from $50 to $75?
b. What is the firm's DFL if the *marginal* tax rate rises to 45% for all taxable income above $40?
c. In general, how do tax increases serve to increase or decrease the sensitivity of EPS to a change in operating income?

21. **Arithmetic Mean of Rates of Return.** (CFA 1993 Level I Exam) The annual rate of return for JSI's common stock has been:

| | **1989** | **1990** | **1991** | **1992** |
|---|---|---|---|---|
| Return | 14% | 19% | –10% | 14% |

What is the arithmetic mean of the rate of return for JSI's common stock over the four years?

22. **Standard Deviation of Rates of Return.** Using the data from Problem 21, what has been the standard deviation of the returns? How can we interpret this number?
23. **Normal Distribution and Internal Estimate.** An investment strategy has an expected annual return of 12%, an annual standard deviation of 12%, and investment returns are normally distributed. In any one year, there is a 68% chance that the investment returns will fall in what range? There is a 95% chance that investment returns will fall within what range?

# PART II

# Valuation Principles and Applications

# Chapter 4

# Present Values: Concepts and Methods

## Contents

## 4.1 Introduction

The concepts of present value, discounting, and compounding are frequently used in most types of financial analysis. Chapter 4 discusses the concepts of the time value of money and the mechanics of using various forms of the present value model. These ideas provide a foundation that is used throughout this book.

The first two sections of this chapter introduce the basic concept of the present value model. Section 2 discusses the basic concepts of present values, and Section 3 discusses the foundation of net present value (NPV) rules. Section 4 covers the compounding and discounting processes, and the use of present and future values tables is covered in Section 5. Section 6 discusses present values as basic tools for financial management decisions, Section 7 discusses liquidity preference, and Section 8 summarizes the chapter. Three hypotheses about inflation and the firm's value are given in Appendix 4A, book value, replacement cost, and Tobin's $q$ are discussed in Appendix 4B, Appendix 4C discusses continuous compounding and continuous discounting, Appendix 4D discusses applications of Excel for calculating time value of money, and Appendix 4E presents four time value of money tables.

## 4.2 Basic Concepts of Present Values

Suppose that we offered to give you either $1,000 today or $1,000 one year from today; which would you prefer? Surely you would choose the former! Even if you were in the happy position of having no immediate unfulfilled desires, you could invest $1,000 today and, at no risk, obtain an amount in excess of $1,000 in one year time. For example, you could purchase government securities due to mature in one year. Suppose that the annual interest rate on such securities is 8%. Then $1,000 today would be worth $1,080 a year from today.

This simple example illustrates a significant fact motivating our analysis in this chapter. Put simply, a dollar today is worth more than a dollar at some time in the future. There are two basic reasons for this: (1) human nature being what it is, immediate gratification has a higher value than gratification sometime in the future, and (2) inflation erodes the purchasing power of an individual's dollar the longer it is held in the form of cash. Therefore, we say that money has a *time value*. The time value is reflected in the interest rate that one earns or pays to have the right to use money at various points in time. Even in the absence of inflation, money has time value as long as it has an alternative use that pays a positive interest rate. When an author signs a contract with a publisher, one important element of the contract involves payment to the author of an advance on royalties. When the book is published and the royalties become due, the amount of the advance is subtracted from the royalties. Nevertheless, because of the preference to have money sooner rather than later, authors will negotiate, all other things being equal, for as large an advance as possible. Conversely, of course, publishers prefer to keep the advance payments to authors as low as possible.

We prefer to have $1,000 today rather than in the future because interest rates are positive. Why is interest paid on loans? There are two related rationales, even in the absence of inflation. These are the *liquidity preference* and the *time preference* theories. The liquidity preference theory asserts that rational people prefer assets with higher liquidity to assets with lower liquidity. Since cash is the most liquid asset of all, we can view interest payments as providing compensation to the lender for the sacrifice of some liquidity. The time preference theory asserts that people prefer current consumption to the same real level of consumption in the future and will sacrifice current consumption only in the expectation of being able to achieve, through interest payments, higher future consumption levels. Lenders view interest as a payment to induce consumers to give up the current use of their funds for a certain period of time. Borrowers view interest as a payment or rental fee for the privilege of being able to have the immediate use cash that they otherwise would have to save over time.

We answered the question posed at the beginning of this section by noting that if the risk-free annual interest is 8%, then $1,000 today will be worth $1,080 a year from now. This is calculated as follows:

$$(1 + 0.08)1{,}000 = \$1{,}080$$

We can turn this statement around to determine the value today of $1,000 received a year from now; that is, the present value of this future receipt. To do this, it is necessary to determine how much we would have to invest today, at 8% annual interest, to obtain $1,000 in a year's time. This is done as follows:

$$\frac{1{,}000}{1.08} = \$925.93$$

Therefore, to the nearest cent, given an interest rate of 8%, the present value of $1,000 a year from now is $925.93.

The concept of present value is crucial in corporate finance. Investors commit resources now in the expectation of receiving future earnings flows. To properly evaluate the returns from an investment, it is necessary to consider that returns are derived in the future. These future monetary amounts must be expressed in present value terms to assess the worth of the investment when compared to its cost or current market value. Additionally, the cast receipts received at different points in time are not directly comparable without employing the present value (PV) method.

## 4.3 Foundation of NPV Rules

We begin our study of procedures for determining present values with a simple example. Suppose that an individual, or a firm, has the opportunity to invest $C_0$ dollars today in a project that will yield a return of $C_1$ dollars in one year. Assume further that the risk-free annual interest rate, expressed as a percentage, is $r$. To evaluate this investment, we need to know the present value of the future return of $C_1$ dollars. In general, for each dollar invested today at interest rate $r$, we would receive in one year's time, an amount

$$\text{Future value per dollar} = (1 + r)$$

The term $(1+r)$ is an important enough variable in finance to warrant its own name. It is called a *wealth relative* and is part of all present value formulations. Returning to our discussion, it follows that the present value of a dollar to be received in our year is

$$\text{Present value per dollar} = \frac{1}{1+r}$$

Therefore, the present value of $C_1$ dollars to be received in the future is

$$\text{PV} = \frac{C_1}{1+r}$$

In assessing our proposed investment, the present value of the return must be compared with the amount invested. The difference between these two quantities is called the *NPV* of the investment. For convenience of notation, we will write

$$C_0 = -\text{Cost}$$

So that $C_0$, which is negative, represents the "cost" today. The NPV, then, is the sum of today's "cost" and the present value of the future return; that is

$$\text{NPV} = C_0 + \frac{C_1}{1+r}$$

Provided this quantity is positive, the investment is worth making.

As another example, suppose you are offered the opportunity today to invest \$1,000, with an assured return of \$1,100 one year from now and a risk-free interest rate of 8%. In our notation, then, $C_0 = -1{,}000$; $C_1 = 1{,}100$; and $r = 0.08$. The present value of the \$1,000 return is

$$\frac{C_1}{1+r} = \frac{1{,}100}{1.08} = \$1{,}018.52$$

where again we have rounded to the nearest cent. Thus, it requires \$1,018.52 invested at 8% to yield \$1,000 in one year. Therefore, the NPV of our investment opportunity is

$$\text{NPV} = C_0 + \frac{C_1}{1+r} = -1{,}000 + 1{,}018.52 = \$18.52$$

Offering you this investment opportunity then, is equivalent to an increase of \$18.52 in your current wealth.

This example is quite restrictive in that it assumes that all of the investment's returns will be realized precisely in one year. In the next section we see how this situation can be generalized to allow for the possibility of returns spread over time.

## 4.4 Compounding and Discounting Processes

In this section, we extend our analysis of present values to consider the valuation of a stream of cash flows. We consider two cases. In the first, a single payment is to be received at some specified time in the future; in the second, a sequence of annual payments is to be received. For each, we will consider both future and present values.

### 4.4.1 *Single payment case — Future values*

Suppose that \$1 is invested today for a period of $t$ years at a risk-free annual interest rate $r_t$, with interest to be compounded annually. How much money will be returned at the end of $t$ years? We find the answer by proceeding in annual steps. At the end of the first year, an amount of interest $r_1$ is added, giving a total of $\$(1 + r_1)$. Since interest is compounded, second-year interest is paid on this whole amount, so that the interest paid at the end of the second year is $\$r_2(1 + r_1)$. Hence, the total amount at the end of the second year is

$$\begin{aligned}\text{Future value per dollar after 2 years} &= (1 + r_1) + r_2(1 + r_1)\\ &= 1 + r_1 + r_2 + r_1r_2\end{aligned}$$

In words, the future value in two years comprises four quantities: the value you started with, \$1; the interest accrued on the principal during the first year, $r_1$; the interest earned on the principal during the second year, $r_1r_2$. If the interest rate is constant — that is, $r_1 = r_2 = r_t$ — then the compound term $r_1r_2$ can be written $r_t^2$. This assumes that the term structure of interest rates is flat. (Duration will be discussed in Chapter 5.) Continuing in this way, interest paid at the end of the third year is $\$r_3(1 + r_t)^2$, so that

$$\begin{aligned}\text{Future values per dollar after 3 years} &= (1 + r_t)^2 + r_3(1 + r_t)^2\\ &= 1 + r_1 + r_2 + r_3 + r_1r_2\\ &\quad + r_1r_3 + r_2r_3 + r_1r_2r_3\\ &= (1 + r_t)^3\end{aligned}$$

In words, the future value in three years comprises eight terms: the principal you started with; three terms for the interest on the principal each year, $r_1$, $r_2$, $r_3$; three terms for the interest on the interest,

$r_1r_2$, $r_1r_3$, $r_2r_3$; and a term for the interest during year 3 on the compound interest from years 1 and 2, $r_1r_2r_3$. Again, if $r_1 = r_2 = r_3 = r_t$, this can all be reduced to $(1 + r_t)^3$. It is interesting to note that as $t$ increases, the $r_t$ terms increase linearly whereas the compound terms increase geometrically. That is, for each year there is only one yearly interest payment, but for the compounding terms the number for $t = 4$ is 16 compounding terms, and for $t = 5$ it is 32 compounding terms. This compounding of interest on interest is an important concept to any investor. Large increases in value are not caused by yearly interest but by the reinvestment of the interest. The general line of reasoning should be clear. After $t$ years, where $t$ is any positive integer, we have

$$\text{Future value per dollar} = (1 + r_t)^t \tag{4.1}$$

To illustrate, suppose that \$1,000 is invested at an annual interest rate of 8%, with interest compounded annually, for a period of five years. At the end of this term, the total amount received, in dollars, will be

$$1{,}000(1 + 0.08)^5 = 1{,}000(1.08)^5 = 1{,}469.33$$

The total interest of \$469.33 consists of \$400 yearly interest (\$80 per year × 5 years) and \$69.33 of compounding. If $t = 64$ years, the future value is \$137,759.11, which consists of \$5,120 yearly interest (80 per year × 64) and \$131,639.11 of compounding.

### 4.4.2 *Continuous compounding*

There is no difficulty in adapting Eq. (4.1) to a situation where interest is compounded at an interval of less than one year. Simply replace the word *year* with the word *period* compounding (the interval) in the above discussion. For example, suppose the interest is compounded semiannually, with an annual rate of 8%. This implies that 4% is to be added to the balance at the end of each half year. Suppose, again, that \$1,000 is to be invested for a term of five years. Since this is the same as a term of ten half years, the total amount (in dollars), to be received is

$$1{,}000(1 + 0.04)^{10} = 1{,}000(1.04)^{10} = 1{,}480.24$$

The additional \$10.91 (\$480.24 – \$469.33) arises because the compounding effect is greater when it occurs ten times than when it occurs five times.

The extreme case is when interest is compounded continuously. (This is discussed in Appendix 4C in greater detail.) The total amount per dollar to be received after $t$ years, if interest is compounded continuously at an annual rate $r_t$, is

$$\text{Future value per dollar} = e^{tr_t} \tag{4.2}$$

where $e = 2.71828\ldots$ is a constant. If \$1,000 is invested for five years at an annual interest rate of 8%, with interest compounded continuously, the end-of-period return would be

$$1{,}000\, e^{5(0.08)} = 1{,}000\, e^{.4} = \$1{,}491.80$$

Many investment opportunities offer daily compounding. The formula we present for continuous compounding provides a close approximation to daily compounding.

### 4.4.3 *Single payment case — Present values*

Since many investments generate returns during several different years in the future, it is important to assess the present value of future payments. Suppose that a payment is to be received in $t$ years' time and that the risk-free annual interest rate for a period of $t$ years is $r_t$. In Eq. (4.1), we saw that future value at the end of $t$ years is $(1 + r_t)^t$ per dollar. Conversely, it follows that the present value of a dollar received at the end of $t$ years is

$$\text{Present value per dollar} = \frac{1}{(1 + r_t)^t} \tag{4.3}$$

For example, suppose that \$1,000 is to be received in four years. At an annual interest rate of 8%, the present value of this future receipt is

$$1{,}000 \times \frac{1}{(1 + 0.08)^4} = \frac{1{,}000}{(1.08)^4} = \$735.03$$

More generally, we can consider a stream of annual receipts, which may be positive or negative. Suppose that, in dollars, we are to receive $C_0$ now, $C_1$ in one year, $C_2$ in two years, and so on, finally in year $N$ we receive $C_N$. Again, let $r_t$ denote the annual rate of interest for a period of $t$ years. To find the NPV of this stream of receipts, we simply add the individual present values, obtaining

$$\text{PV} = C_0 + \frac{C_1}{(1+r_1)^1} + \frac{C_2}{(1+r_2)^2} + \cdots + \frac{C_N}{(1+r_2)^N} \tag{4.4}$$

$$\text{PV} = \sum_{t=0}^{N} \frac{C_t}{(1+r_t)^t}$$

Typically, the rate of interest, $r_t$, depends on the period $t$. When a constant rate, $r$, is assumed for each period, the NPV formula Eq. (4.4) simplifies to

$$\text{PV} = \sum_{t=0}^{N} \frac{C_t}{(1+r)^t} \tag{4.5}$$

### 4.4.4 *Annuity case — Present values*

An *annuity* is a special form of income stream in which regularly spaced equal payments are received over a period of time. Common examples of annuities are payments on home mortgages and installment credit loans.

Suppose that an amount $C$ dollars is to be received at the end of each of the next $n$ time periods (which could, for example, be months, quarters, or years). Assume further that, irrespective of the term, the interest rate period is fixed at $r$. Then the present value of the payment to be received at the end of the first period is $C/(1+r)$, the present value of the next payment is $C/(1+r)^2$, and so on. Hence, the present value of the $N$ period annuity is

$$\text{PV} = \frac{C}{(1+r)^1} + \frac{C}{(1+r)^2} + \cdots + \frac{C}{(1+r)^n} = \sum_{t=1}^{N} \frac{C_t}{(1+r)^t}$$

In fact, it can be shown[1] that this expression simplifies to

$$\text{PV} = C\left[\frac{1}{r} - \frac{1}{r(1+r)^N}\right] \tag{4.6}$$

Suppose that an annuity of \$1,000 per year is to be received for each of the next ten years. The total dollar amount is \$10,000, but because receipts stretch far into the future, we would expect the present value to be much less. Assuming an annual interest rate of 8%, we can find the present value of this annuity by using Eq. (4.6):

$$\$1{,}000\left[\frac{1}{0.08} - \frac{1}{0.08(1.08)^{10}}\right] = \$6{,}710$$

This annuity, then, has the same value as an immediate cash payment of \$6,710.

## Perpetuity

An extreme type of annuity is a *perpetuity*, in which payments are to be received forever. Certain British government bonds, known as "consols," are perpetuities. The principal need not be repaid, but a fixed interest payment to the bondholder is made every year. To find the present value of a perpetuity, we need only let the term — $N$, in the annuity case — grow infinitely large. Consequently, the second expression in brackets on the right-hand side of Eq. (4.6) becomes zero, so that the present value of perpetuity payments of $C$ dollars per period, when the per period interest rate is $r$, is

$$\text{PV} = \frac{C}{r}$$

For example, given an 8% annual interest rate, the present value of \$1,000 per annum in perpetuity is

$$\frac{\$1{,}000}{0.08} = \$12{,}500$$

---

[1]Let $x = 1/(1+r)$. Then

$$\text{PV} = C(x)(1 + x + \cdots + x^{N-1}) = C(x)\left(\frac{1-x^N}{1-x}\right) = C * \frac{1}{1+r} * \frac{1+r}{r}$$
$$\left[1 - \frac{1}{(1+r)^N}\right]$$

From which Eq. (4.8) follows.

Notice that this sets an upper limit on the possible value of an annuity. Thus, if the interest rate is 8% per annum, annuity payments of $1,000 per year must have a present value of less than $12,500, whatever the term.

We will now show how the present value annuity formula defined in Eq. (4.6) can be used in capital budgeting decision. Capital budgeting decision will be discussed in further detail in Chapter 6.

**Example 4.1.** A corporation must choose between two projects. Each project requires an immediate investment, and further costs will be incurred in the next year. The returns from these projects will be spread over a four-year period. The following table shows the dollar amounts involved.

| | | Year 0 | Year 1 | Year 2 | Year 3 | Year 4 |
|---|---|---|---|---|---|---|
| Project A | Costs | 80,000 | 20,000 | 0 | 0 | 0 |
| | Returns | 0 | 20,000 | 30,000 | 50,000 | 50,000 |
| Project B | Costs | 50,000 | 50,000 | 0 | 0 | 0 |
| | Returns | 0 | 40,000 | 60,000 | 30,000 | 10,000 |

At first glance, this data might suggest that, for project A, total returns exceed total costs by $50,000, while the same figure that project B is only $40,000, indicating a preference for project A. However, this neglects the timing of the returns. Assuming an annual interest rate of 8% over the four-year period, we can calculate the present values of the net receipts for each project as follows:

| | | Year 0 | Year 1 | Year 2 | Year 3 | Year 4 |
|---|---|---|---|---|---|---|
| Project A | Net returns | –80,000 | 0 | 30,000 | 50,000 | 50,000 |
| | Present values | –80,000 | 0 | 25,720 | 39,692 | 36,751 |
| Project B | Net returns | –50,000 | –10,000 | 60,000 | 30,000 | 10,000 |
| | Present values | –50,000 | –9,259 | 51,440 | 23,815 | 7,350 |

It is the sums of the present values that must be compared in evaluating the projects. For Project A, substituting $r = 0.08$ into Eq. (4.5),

$$\mathrm{NPV(A)} = -80{,}000 + \frac{0}{(1.08)^1} + \frac{30{,}000}{(1.08)^2} + \frac{50{,}000}{(1.08)^3} + \frac{50{,}000}{(1.08)^4}$$

$$= -80{,}000 + 0 + 25{,}720 + 39{,}692 + 36{,}751 = \$22{,}163$$

Similarly, for Project B,

$$\mathrm{NPV(B)} = -50{,}000 - \frac{10{,}000}{(1.08)^1} + \frac{60{,}000}{(1.08)^2} + \frac{30{,}000}{(1.08)^3} + \frac{10{,}000}{(1.08)^4}$$

$$= -50{,}000 - 9{,}259 + 51{,}440 + 23{,}815 + 7{,}350 = \$23{,}346$$

It emerges that if future returns are discounted at an annual rate of 8%, the NPV is higher for Project B than for Project A. Hence, Project B is preferred, because it provides larger cash flows in the early years, which gives the firm more opportunity to reinvest the funds, there by adding greater value to the firm.

By using Excel, we can calculate NPV values for Projects A and B as follows:

Both NPV method and internal rate of return (IRR) method can be used to do the capital budgeting decision. For example, Project A and Project B, the initial outlays and net cash inflow for year 0 to year 4 are presented in Table 4.1. In Table 4.1, we know that the initial outlay at year 0 for Projects A and B are \$80,000 and \$50,000 respectively. In year 1, additional investment for Project A and B are \$20,000 and \$50,000 respectively. The net cash inflow of Project A for the next four years are \$20,000, \$30,000, \$50,000 and \$50,000 respectively. The net cash inflow of Project B for the next four years are \$40,000, \$60,000, \$30,000 and \$10,000, respectively.

Table 4.1 Partial Inputs Information for NPV Method and IRR Method.

| | | Year 0 | Year 1 | Year 2 | Year 3 | Year 4 |
|---|---|---|---|---|---|---|
| **Project A** | Cost | –\$80,000 | –\$20,000 | 0 | 0 | 0 |
| | Return | 0 | \$20,000 | \$30,000 | \$50,000 | \$50,000 |
| **Project B** | Cost | –\$50,000 | –\$50,000 | 0 | 0 | 0 |
| | Return | 0 | \$40,000 | \$60,000 | \$30,000 | \$10,000 |

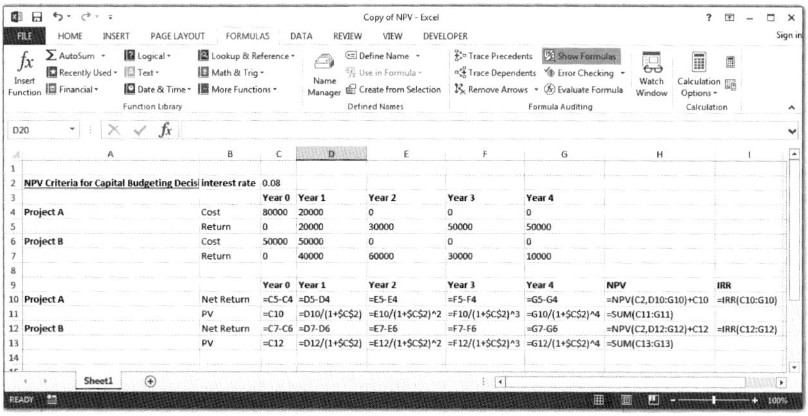

| | A | B | C | D | E | F | G | H | I |
|---|---|---|---|---|---|---|---|---|---|
| 1 | | | | | | | | | |
| 2 | **NPV Criteria for Capital Budgeting Decis** | **interest rate** | 0.08 | | | | | | |
| 3 | | | **Year 0** | **Year 1** | **Year 2** | **Year 3** | **Year 4** | | |
| 4 | **Project A** | Cost | 80000 | 20000 | 0 | 0 | 0 | | |
| 5 | | Return | 0 | 20000 | 30000 | 50000 | 50000 | | |
| 6 | **Project B** | Cost | 50000 | 50000 | 0 | 0 | 0 | | |
| 7 | | Return | 0 | 40000 | 60000 | 30000 | 10000 | | |
| 8 | | | | | | | | | |
| 9 | | | **Year 0** | **Year 1** | **Year 2** | **Year 3** | **Year 4** | **NPV** | **IRR** |
| 10 | **Project A** | Net Return | =C5-C4 | =D5-D4 | =E5-E4 | =F5-F4 | =G5-G4 | =NPV(C2,D10:G10)+C10 | =IRR(C10:G10) |
| 11 | | PV | =C10 | =D10/(1+$C$2) | =E10/(1+$C$2)^2 | =F10/(1+$C$2)^3 | =G10/(1+$C$2)^4 | =SUM(C11:G11) | |
| 12 | **Project B** | Net Return | =C7-C6 | =D7-D6 | =E7-E6 | =F7-F6 | =G7-G6 | =NPV(C2,D12:G12)+C12 | =IRR(C12:G12) |
| 13 | | PV | =C12 | =D12/(1+$C$2) | =E12/(1+$C$2)^2 | =F12/(1+$C$2)^3 | =G12/(1+$C$2)^4 | =SUM(C13:G13) | |
| 14 | | | | | | | | | |

Figure 4.1 Excel Calculation Functions for NPV Method.

The NPV of a project is computed by discounting the project's cash flows to the present by the appropriate cost of capital. The formula used to calculate NPV can be defined as follow:

$$\text{NPV} = \sum_{t=1}^{N} \frac{CF_t}{(1+k)^t} - I \tag{4.7}$$

where $k$ = the appropriate discount rate; $CF_t$ = Net Cash flow (positive or negative) in period $t$; $I$ = Initial outlay; $N$ = Life of the project.

Using the excel function, we can calculate NPV for both Projects A and B. We also can calculate Example above using Excel NPV function. NPV is a function to calculate the NPV of an investment by using a discount rate and a series of future payments (negative values) and income (positive values). The NPV function in Cell H10 is equal to

$$= \text{NPV}(\text{C2}, \text{D10} : \text{G10}) + \text{C10}$$

Based upon the NPV function on Figure 4.1, the NPV results are shown in Figure 4.2.

The IRR ($r$) is the discount rate which equates the discounted cash flows from a project to its investment. Thus, one must solve

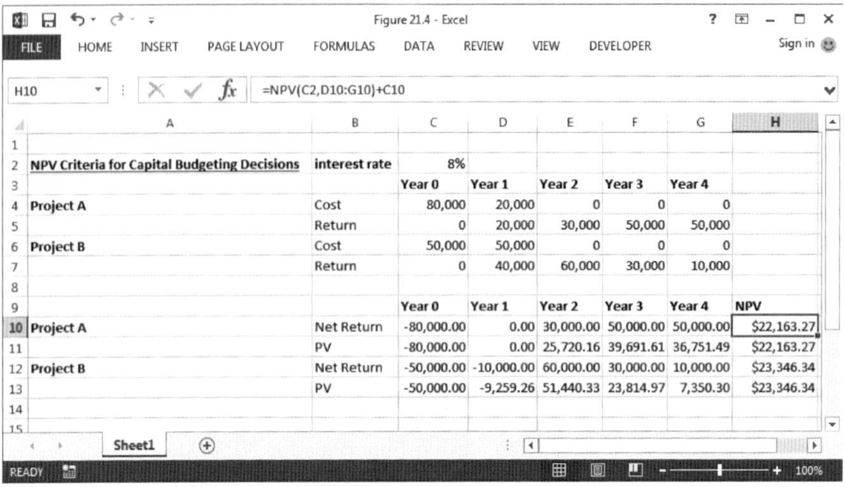


| | A | B | C | D | E | F | G | H |
|---|---|---|---|---|---|---|---|---|
| 1 | | | | | | | | |
| 2 | NPV Criteria for Capital Budgeting Decisions | interest rate | 8% | | | | | |
| 3 | | | Year 0 | Year 1 | Year 2 | Year 3 | Year 4 | |
| 4 | Project A | Cost | 80,000 | 20,000 | 0 | 0 | 0 | |
| 5 | | Return | 0 | 20,000 | 30,000 | 50,000 | 50,000 | |
| 6 | Project B | Cost | 50,000 | 50,000 | 0 | 0 | 0 | |
| 7 | | Return | 0 | 40,000 | 60,000 | 30,000 | 10,000 | |
| 8 | | | | | | | | |
| 9 | | | Year 0 | Year 1 | Year 2 | Year 3 | Year 4 | NPV |
| 10 | Project A | Net Return | -80,000.00 | 0.00 | 30,000.00 | 50,000.00 | 50,000.00 | $22,163.27 |
| 11 | | PV | -80,000.00 | 0.00 | 25,720.16 | 39,691.61 | 36,751.49 | $22,163.27 |
| 12 | Project B | Net Return | -50,000.00 | -10,000.00 | 60,000.00 | 30,000.00 | 10,000.00 | $23,346.34 |
| 13 | | PV | -50,000.00 | -9,259.26 | 51,440.33 | 23,814.97 | 7,350.30 | $23,346.34 |
| 14 | | | | | | | | |
| 15 | | | | | | | | |

Figure 4.2 Excel Calculation Results for NPV Method.

iteratively for the $r$ in Eq. (4.8):

$$\sum_{t=1}^{N} \frac{CF_t}{(1+r)^t} = I \tag{4.8}$$

where $CF_t$ = Net Cash flow (positive or negative) in period $t$; $I$ = Initial investment; $N$ = Life of the project; $r$ = IRR.

In addition, we can use Excel function IRR to calculate IRR. IRR is a function to calculate the IRR which is the rate of return received for an investment consisting of payments (negative values) and income (positive values) that occur at regular periods. The IRR function in Cell I10 is

$$= \text{IRR}(\text{C10} : \text{G10})$$

Based upon the IRR function on Figure 4.1, the IRR results in terms of excel calculations are shown in Figure 4.3.

The application of the both the NPV method and IRR method for capital budgeting decision will be discussed in further detail in Chapter 6.

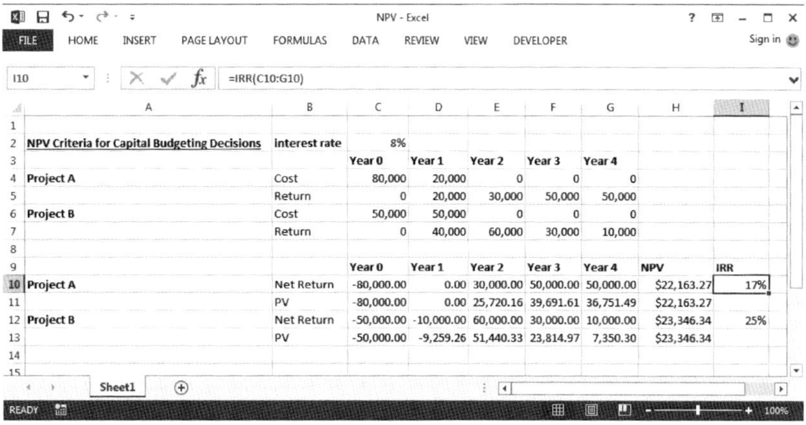


| | A | B | C | D | E | F | G | H | I |
|---|---|---|---|---|---|---|---|---|---|
| 1 | | | | | | | | | |
| 2 | NPV Criteria for Capital Budgeting Decisions | interest rate | 8% | | | | | | |
| 3 | | | Year 0 | Year 1 | Year 2 | Year 3 | Year 4 | | |
| 4 | Project A | Cost | 80,000 | 20,000 | 0 | 0 | 0 | | |
| 5 | | Return | 0 | 20,000 | 30,000 | 50,000 | 50,000 | | |
| 6 | Project B | Cost | 50,000 | 50,000 | 0 | 0 | 0 | | |
| 7 | | Return | 0 | 40,000 | 60,000 | 30,000 | 10,000 | | |
| 8 | | | | | | | | | |
| 9 | | | Year 0 | Year 1 | Year 2 | Year 3 | Year 4 | NPV | IRR |
| 10 | Project A | Net Return | -80,000.00 | 0.00 | 30,000.00 | 50,000.00 | 50,000.00 | $22,163.27 | 17% |
| 11 | | PV | -80,000.00 | 0.00 | 25,720.16 | 39,691.61 | 36,751.49 | $22,163.27 | |
| 12 | Project B | Net Return | -50,000.00 | -10,000.00 | 60,000.00 | 30,000.00 | 10,000.00 | $23,346.34 | 25% |
| 13 | | PV | -50,000.00 | -9,259.26 | 51,440.33 | 23,814.97 | 7,350.30 | $23,346.34 | |
| 14 | | | | | | | | | |

Figure 4.3 The Excel Calculation Results for IRR.

### 4.4.5 *Annuity case — Future values*

With an annuity of $C$ dollars per year, we can also calculate a future value (FV) by using Eq. (4.8):

$$\text{FV} = C(1+r)^N + C(1+r)^{N-1} + \cdots + C(1+r)^1 \tag{4.9}$$

This is very similar to the single value case discussed earlier; each of the terms on the right-hand side of Eq. (4.9) is identical to the values shown by Eq. (4.1).

### 4.4.6 *Annual percentage rate (APR)*

The APR is the actual or effective interest rate that the borrower is paying. Quite often, the stated or nominal rate of a loan is different from the actual amount of interest or cost the lender is paying. This results from the differences created by using different compounding periods. The main benefit of calculating the APR is that it allows us to compare interest rates on loans or investments that have different compounding periods.

The Consumer Credit Protection Act (Truth-in-Lending Act), enacted in 1968, provides for disclosure of credit terms so that the borrower can make meaningful comparison of alternative sources of credit. This act was the cornerstone for Regulation Z of the Federal Reserve. The finance charge and the annual percentage rate must be given explicitly to the borrower. The *finance charge* is the actual dollar amount that the borrower must pay if given the loan. The APR also must be explained to individual borrowers and the actual figure must be given.

Exhibit 4.1 shows the amount of interest paid and the APR for a $1,000 loan at 10% interest for 1 year, to be repaid in 12 equal monthly installments.

**Exhibit 4.1:** Interest Paid and APR.

Amount borrowed = $1,000

Nominal interest rate = 10% per year or 0.83% per month

$$\text{Annuity or monthly payment} = \frac{\text{Amount borrowed}}{\sum_{t=1}^{N} \frac{1}{\left(1+\frac{r}{12}\right)^t}} = \frac{1{,}000}{11.3745} = \$87.92$$

| Month | Payment | Interest | Principal Paid Off | Remaining Principal Unpaid |
|---|---|---|---|---|
| 0 | — | — | — | $1,000 |
| 1 | $87.92 | $8.33 | $79.58 | $920.42 |
| 2 | 87.92 | 7.67 | 80.25 | 840.17 |
| 3 | 87.92 | 7.00 | 80.91 | 759.26 |
| 4 | 87.92 | 6.33 | 81.59 | 677.67 |
| 5 | 87.92 | 5.65 | 82.27 | 595.40 |
| 6 | 87.92 | 4.96 | 82.95 | 512.45 |
| 7 | 87.92 | 4.27 | 83.65 | 428.80 |
| 8 | 87.92 | 3.57 | 84.34 | 344.46 |
| 9 | 87.92 | 2.87 | 85.05 | 259.41 |
| 10 | 87.92 | 2.16 | 85.75 | 173.66 |
| 11 | 87.92 | 1.45 | 86.47 | 87.19 |
| 12 | 87.92 | 0.73 | 87.19 | 0.00 |
| Total | $1,054.99 | $54.99 | $1,000.00 | |

$$\text{Average loan balance} = \frac{\text{Beginning balance} - \text{Ending balance}}{2}$$
$$= \frac{1{,}000 - 0}{2} = 500$$
$$\text{APR} = \frac{\text{Interest}}{\text{Average loan outstanding}} = \frac{54.99}{500}$$
$$= 10.9981\%$$

From Exhibit 4.1, we see that the total interest paid is \$54.99 and the APR is 10.9981%. The nominal rate and the APR will be different for all annuity arrangements, because the more frequent the repayment, the greater the APR. This calculation is useful to individuals in evaluating home mortgages and to corporations borrowing with term loans to finance assets. The procedure uses to construct Exhibit 4.1 can also be used to calculate fixed mortgage amortization. (See Questions and Problems 21 for further detail).

## 4.5 Present and Future Value Tables

In the previous section, we presented formulae for various present and future value calculations. However, the arithmetic involved can be rather tedious and time-consuming. Because present and future values are frequently needed, tables have been prepared to make the computational task easier. When using present value tables, keep in mind the following: (1) they cannot be used for $r < 0$, (2) the interest or discount rate must be constant over time for use of annuity tables, and (3) the tables are constructed by assuming that all cash flows are reinvested at the discount rate or interest rate.

### 4.5.1 *Future value of a dollar at the end of t periods*

Suppose that a dollar is invested now at an interest rate $r$ per period, with interest compounded at the end of each period. Equation (4.1) gives the future value of a dollar at the end of $t$ periods. Values of this expression for various interest rates, $r$, and number of periods, $t$, are tabulated in Table 4.1E, which presents the future value annuity. Table 4.3D of Appendix D presents the Excel approach to calculate this future value.

To illustrate, suppose that a dollar is invested now for 20 years at an annual rate of interest of 10% compounded annually. Table 4.1E shows that the future value — the amount to be received at the end of this period — is \$6,728. (It follows, of course, that the future value of an investment of \$1,000 is \$6,728.)

**Example 4.2.** Suppose you deposit \$1,000 at an annual interest rate of 12% for two years. How much extra interest would you receive at the end of the term if interest was compounded monthly instead of annually?

Annual compounding is straightforward. Table 4.1E shows that the future value per dollar for a term of two years at an annual interest rate of 12% is \$1.254. If the interest is compounded monthly, then the number of periods would be 4 and the monthly interest rate is 6%. According to Table 4.1E, the future value factor for 4 periods with interest rate to be 6% is 1.2625. Hence, the future value of \$1,000 is \$1,270.

Therefore, the extra interest we would receive (the gain in future value) from monthly compounding is

$$\$1{,}270 - \$1{,}254 = \$16$$

Using the information in Table 4.1E of Appendix 4E, we can construct graphs showing the effect over time of compound interest. Figure 4.4 shows the future values over time of a dollar invested at interest rates of 0, 4, 8, and 12%. At 0%, the future value is always \$1. The other three curves were constructed from the future values taken from the 4, 8, and 12% interest columns in Table 4.1E. Notice that these curves exhibit exponential growth; that is, as a result of compounding, annual changes in future values increase nonlinearly. Of course, the higher the rate of interest, the greater the growth rate; or the longer the time, the greater the compounding effect.

In Figure 4.5, we compare future values of a dollar over time under simple and annually compounded interest, both at a 10% annual interest rate. By simple interest, we usually mean the interest calculated for a given period by multiplying the interest rate times

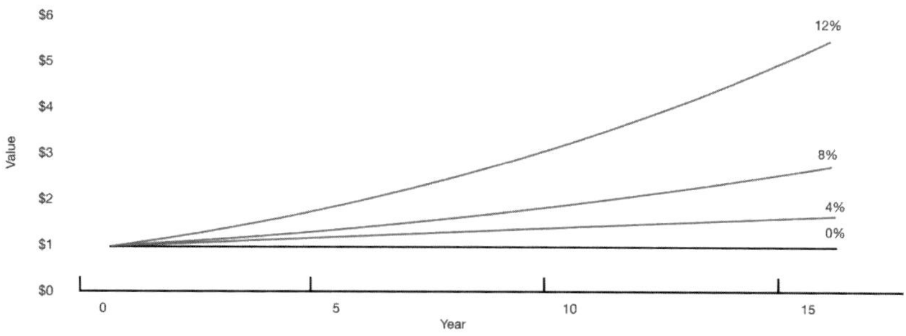


Figure 4.4 Future Value over Time of $1 Invested at Different Interest Rates.

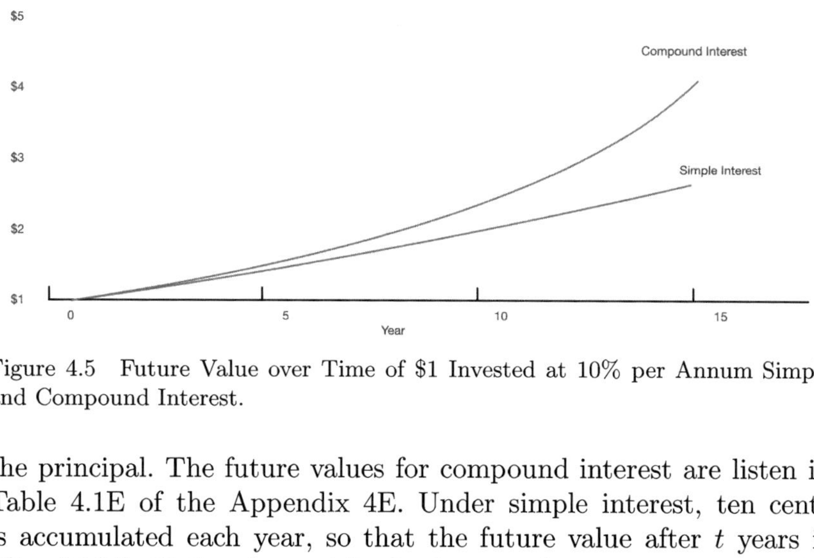


Figure 4.5 Future Value over Time of $1 Invested at 10% per Annum Simple and Compound Interest.

the principal. The future values for compound interest are listen in Table 4.1E of the Appendix 4E. Under simple interest, ten cents is accumulated each year, so that the future value after $t$ years is $\$(1+0.10\,t)$. Notice that, while the future values grow exponentially under compounding, they do so only linearly with simple interest, so that the two curves diverge over time.

### 4.5.2 *Future value of a dollar continuously compounded*

Table 4.2E in Appendix 4E shows the future value of a dollar invested for $t$ periods at interest rate $r$ per period, continuously compounded. The entries in this table are computed from Eq. (4.2), which states that future value is $e^{rt}$. Table 4.2E shows the corresponding future values for specific values of $rt$.

To illustrate, suppose a dollar is invested now for 20 years at an annual interest rate of 10%, with continuous compounding. The future value at the end of the term can be read from Table 4.2E, using $r = 0.10$, $t = 20$, $rt = 2$. From the table, we find, corresponding to an $rt$ value of 2, the future value is \$7.389.

Figure 4.6 compares, over time, the future value of a dollar invested at 10% per annum under both annual and continuous compounding. The two curves were constructed from the information in Tables 4.1E and 4.2E of Appendix 4E. Notice that, over time, the curves diverge, reflecting the faster growth rate of future values as the interval for compounding decreases.

### 4.5.3 *Present value of a dollar received t periods in the future*

Suppose that a dollar is to be received $t$ periods in the future and that the rate of interest is $r$, with compounding at the end of each period. The present value of this future receipt can be computed from Eq. (4.3). The results of various combinations of values of $r$ and $t$ are tabulated in Table 4.3E of the Appendix 4E at the back of this volume. For example, the table shows that the present value of a dollar to be received in 20 years' time, at an annual interest rate of 10% compounded annually, is \$0.149 (It follows that the present value of \$1,000 under these conditions is \$149.)

Using the information in Table 4.3E from Appendix 4E, we can construct graphs showing the effect over time of the discounting process involved in present value calculations. Figure 4.7 shows the present values of a dollar received at various points in the future, discounted at interest rates of 0, 4, 8, and 12%. Notice that the present values decrease the further into the future the payment is to be received; the higher the interest rate,the sharper the decrease. Comparison of Figures 4.4 and 4.7 reveals the connection between compound interest and present values. This is also clear from Eqs. (4.1) and (4.4). If the future value after $t$ years of a dollar invested today,

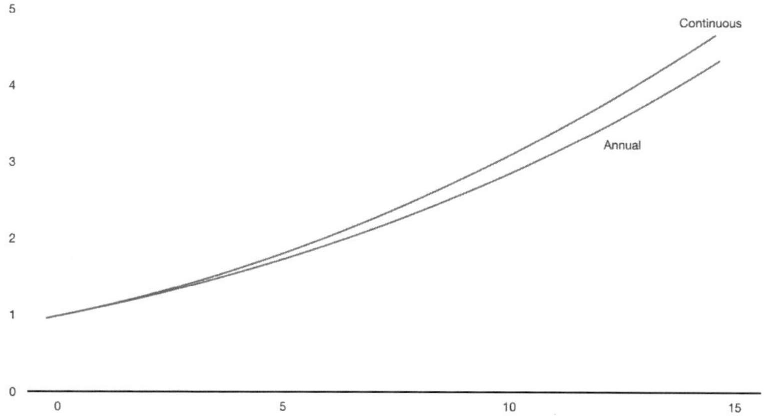


Figure 4.6 Future Value Time of $1 Invested at 10% Per Annum, Compounded Annually and Continuously.

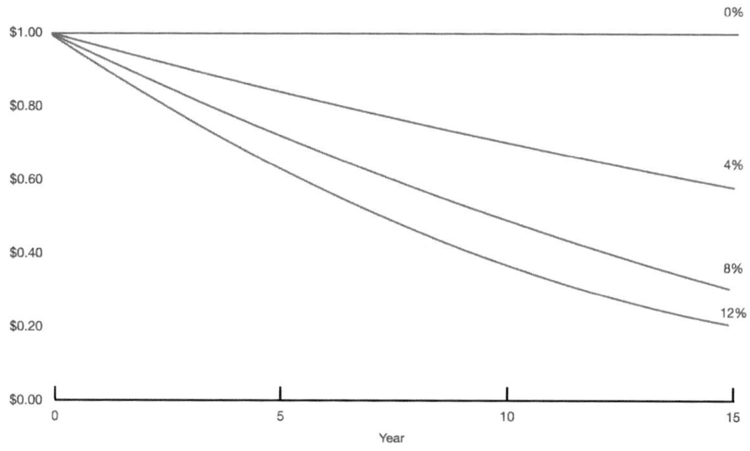


Figure 4.7 Present Value, at Different Discount Rates, of $1 to be Received in the Future.

at annual interest rate $r$, is K, then, using the same interest rate, the present value of K to be received in $t$ years' time is $1.

**Example 4.3.** A corporation is considering a project for which both costs and returns extends into the future, as set out in the following table (in dollars).

| Year | 0 | 1 | 2 | 3 | 4 | 5 |
|---|---|---|---|---|---|---|
| Costs | 130,000 | 70,000 | 50,000 | 0 | 0 | 0 |
| Returns | 0 | 20,000 | 25,000 | 50,000 | 60,000 | 75,000 |
| Year | 6 | 7 | 8 | 9 | 10 | |
| Costs | 0 | 0 | 0 | 0 | 0 | |
| Returns | 75,000 | 60,000 | 50,000 | 25,000 | 20,000 | |

Assuming that future returns are discounted at an annual rate of 8%, find the NPV of this project.

As in Example 4.1, we could solve this problem by using an equation; in this case, Eq. (4.5). However, we can save time and effort by obtaining the present value per dollar figures directly from Table 4.3E of the Appendix 4E of this book. Multiplying these figures by the corresponding net returns and then summing gives us the NPV:

$$\begin{aligned}\text{NPV} &= -130{,}000 - (50,000)(0.9259) - (25{,}000)(0.8573)\\ &\quad + (50{,}000)(0.7938) + (60{,}000)(0.7350) + (75{,}000)(0.6806)\\ &\quad + (75{,}000)(0.6302) + (60{,}000)(0.5835) + (50{,}000)(0.5403)\\ &\quad + (25{,}000)(0.5002) + (2000)(0.4632) = \$68,163.06\end{aligned}$$

### 4.5.4 *Present value of an annuity of a dollar per period*

Suppose that a dollar is to be received at the end of each of the next $N$ periods. If the interest rate per period is $r$, the present value of this annuity is obtained by using $C = 1$ in Eq. (4.8). These present values are tabulated for various interest rates in Table 4.4E in Appendix 4E. For example, at an annual interest rate of 6%, the present value of \$1 per year for 20 years is \$11,470. (It follows that the present value of an annuity of \$1,000 per year is \$11,470.)

## 4.6 Why Present Values are Basic Tools for Financial Management Decisions

An unrealistic feature of our discussion of present values has been the assumption that monetary amounts of future returns on an investment are known with certainty. However, in most management decision problems, while it is possible to estimate future returns, these estimates will not be precisely equal to the actual outcomes. In practice, then, it is necessary to take into account some element of risk. To do this, we discount future returns by using $r_t$, which is not the risk-free interest rate but rather the interest rate on some equivalent, equally risky security or investment. In principle, with this modification, a financial manager can compute the NPV of any risky project. Our aim in this section is to show that such present value calculations are important basic tools in the financial management decision-making process.

Another way to incorporate risk into the analysis is through *certainty equivalence.* Suppose that a project will yield an estimated \$10,000 next year, but that there is some risk attached, so that this result is not certain. Typically, an investor will be averse to risk and so would prefer an alternative project in which \$10,000 was certain to be realized. However, other investors may prefer the risky project with a sure return of some what less than \$10,000, being prepared to accept some risk in the expectation of a higher return. For example, the original project may be seen as equivalent to one in which are turn of \$9,000 is certain. We can then value the project by discounting the certainty equivalent return at the risk-free rate. (These concepts are covered in greater detail in Chapter 8.)

### 4.6.1 *Managing in the stockholders' interest*

Consider the dilemma of a corporate manager who makes investment decisions on behalf of the corporation's stockholders. Because stockholders do not constitute a homogeneous entity, the manager is faced with the problem of accommodating an array of tastes and preferences. In particular:

- Stockholders are not uniform in their time preferences for consumption. Some prefer relatively high levels of current consumption, while others prefer less current consumption in order to obtain higher consumption levels in the future.
- Stockholders have different attitudes toward the risk-return tradeoff. Some are happier than others to accept an element of risk in anticipation of higher potential returns.

Even if the manager is able to elicit accurate information about the various tastes and preferences of individual stockholders, the problem of making decisions for the benefit of all seems formidable. Fortunately, Irving Fisher, in 1930, developed a simple resolution. Essentially, Fisher demonstrated that, given certain assumptions, whatever the array of stockholder tastes and preferences, the optimal management strategy is to *maximize the firm's NPV.*

To illustrate, suppose that a particular stockholder has a current cash flow of \$50,000 and a future cash flow, next year, of \$64,800.[2] This stockholder could plan to consume \$50,000 this year and \$64,800 next year. However, this is not the only consumption pattern that can be achieved with these resources.

At the heart of our analysis is the assumption that there is access to the capital markets, in which cash on hand can be lent, or that an investor can borrow against future cash receipts. This allows our stockholder to consume either more or less than \$50,000 this year, which affects next year's consumption level. Moreover, the investor is not restricted to risk-free market instruments, but is free to opt for riskier securities with higher expected returns. For our conclusions to follow, we need to assume perfect competition in the capital markets; that is:

[2]The restriction of our analysis to two periods is convenient for graphical exposition. However, the same conclusions follow when this restriction is dropped.

1. Access to the market is open and free, with securities readily traded.
2. No individual, or group of individuals acting in collusion, has sufficient market power for the actions of the individual or group to significantly influence market prices.
3. All relevant information about the price and risk of securities is readily available, at no cost, to all.

Certainly, these assumptions are an idealization of reality. Nevertheless, they are sufficiently close to reality for our analysis to be appropriate.

Now, in considering the consumption patterns available to our individual investor, we will assume borrowing or lending at the risk-free rate, which, for purposes of illustration, is 8%. The investor may, instead, prefer to assume some level of risk, which trading in the capital market allows for, and for such an investor this example can be carried through in terms of certainty equivalent amounts.

Let us begin by computing the present value and future value of this investor's cash flow stream. At an interest rate of 8%, the present value is

$$\mathrm{PV} = 50{,}000 + \frac{64{,}800}{1.08} = 50{,}000 + 60{,}000 = \$110{,}000$$

This investor could consume \$110,000 this year and nothing next year by borrowing \$60,000 at 8% interest. All of next year's income will then be needed to repay this loan.

The future value, next year, of the cash flow stream is

$$\mathrm{FV} = (50{,}000)(1.08) + 64{,}800 = 54{,}000 + 64{,}800 = \$118{,}800$$

It follows that another option available to our investor is to consume nothing this year and \$118,800 next year. This can be achieved by investing all of this year's cash flow at 8% interest.

Our results are depicted in Figure 4.8, which represents possible two-period consumption levels. These levels are found by plotting current consumption on the horizontal axis and future consumption

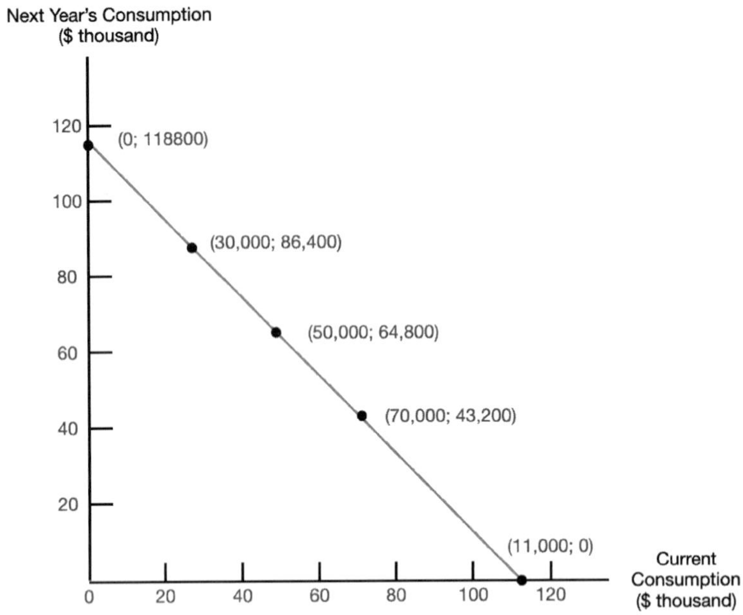


Figure 4.8 Trade-offs in Two-period Consumption Levels.

on the vertical axis; a point on the curve represents a specific combination of current and future consumption levels. Thus, our two extreme cases are (0; 118,800) and (110,000; 0).

Between these extremes, many combinations are possible. If the investor wants to consume only $30,000 of the current year's cash flow, the remaining $20,000 can be invested at 8% to yield $21,600 next year. Adding this to next year's cash flow produces a future consumption total of $86,400.

Conversely, $70,000 can be consumed this year by borrowing $20,000 at 8% interest. This requires repayment of $21,600 next year, leaving $43,200 available for consumption at that time.

The consumption possibilities discussed so far are listed in Table 4.2 and plotted in Figure 4.8. But these are not the only possibilities. Notice that the five points all lie on the same straight line. The reason is that at 8% annual interest, each $1 of current consumption can be traded for $1.08 of consumption next year, and vice versa; therefore, any pair of consumption levels on the line in Figure 4.8 is

Table 4.2 Consumption Possibilities as Plotted in Figure 4.8 (in dollars).

| | | | | | |
|---|---|---|---|---|---|
| Current Year | 0 | 30,000 | 50,000 | 70,000 | 110,000 |
| Next Year | 118,800 | 86,400 | 64,800 | 43,200 | 0 |

possible. The slope of the consumption trade-off line in Figure 4.8 is $-(1+r)$, i.e., $-1.08$.

### 4.6.2 *Productive investments*

So far, we have assumed that the only opportunities for our investor are in the capital market. Suppose that there are productive investment opportunities, which may yield, in certainty equivalent terms, rates of return in excess of 8% per annum. Each dollar invested now that produces a return in excess of \$1.08 in a year's time will increase NPV for the investor.

To illustrate, suppose the investor finds \$80,000 worth of such opportunities that will yield \$97,200 next year. (Notice that the amount invested can exceed the current year's cash flow, because any excess can be borrowed in the capital market.) The NPV of these investment opportunities is

$$\text{NPV} = -80{,}000 + \frac{97{,}200}{1.08} = \$10{,}000$$

These productive investments would raise the present value of our investor's cash flow stream from \$110,000 to \$120,000. Similarly, future value is raised by (1.08)(10,000)=\$10,800, from \$118,800 to \$129,600.

Taking advantage of such productive opportunities does not affect the investor's access to the capital market. Therefore, our investor could consume \$120,000 now and nothing next year, or nothing now and \$129,600 next year. It is also possible to have intermediate consumption level combinations by trading \$1 of current consumption for \$1.08 of future consumption.

This position is illustrated in Figure 4.9, which shows the shift in the consumption possibilities line resulting from the productive investments. As compared with the earlier position, it is possible

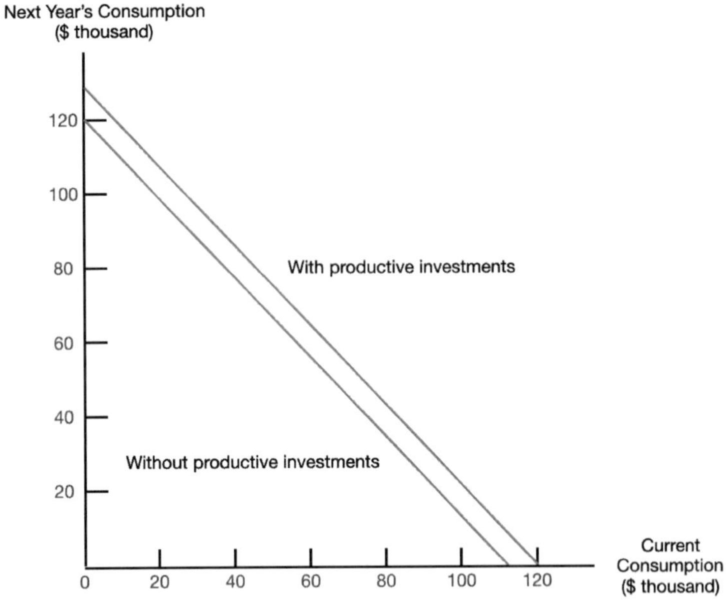


Figure 4.9 Trade-offs in Two-period Consumption Levels With and Without Productive Assets.

to consume more both now and in the future. Hence, we find that, whatever the time preference for consumption, the investor is better off as a result of a productive investment that raises NPV. Neither is it necessary to worry about the investor's attitude toward risk, as this too can be accommodated through capital market investments.

We have now established Irving Fisher's concept. Viewing this individuals stockholder's cash flows as shares of those of the corporation, it follows that, to act in the stockholders' interest, management's objective should be to seek those productive investments that increase the NPV of the corporation as much as possible. (The relationship between NPV of projects and the firm's value is discussed in Chapter 6.)

It follows from this discussion that the concept of NPV does considerably more than provide a convenient and sensible way of interpreting future receipts. As we have just seen, NPV provides a basis on which financial managers can judge whether a proposed productive investment is in the best interest of corporate stockholders. The manager's task is to as certain whether or not the project raises the firm's NPV by more than would competing projects, without having to pay attention to personal tastes and preferences of stockholders.

## 4.7 Liquidity Preference

In addition to the time preference discussed in the previous section, positive interest rates also indicate a liquidity preference on the part of some investors. Keynes (1936) gives three reasons why individuals require cash: (1) to pay bills (transaction balances), (2) to protect against uncertain adverse future events (precautionary balances), and (3) for speculative reasons (for example, if interest rates are expected to rise in the future, it may be best to stay liquid today to take advantage of the future higher rates). Each rationale for holding cash makes individuals more partial to maintaining liquidity. An incentive must be offered in the form of a positive interest rate to induce these individuals to give up some of their liquidity.

For a corporation, the management of cash and working capital is an important treasury function that takes these factors into consideration. (This is discussed in Chapters 14 and 20.)

## 4.8 Summary

In this chapter we have introduced the concept of the present value of a future receipt. For each dollar to be received in $t$ years at an annual interest rate over $t$ years of $r_t$, the present value is

$$\mathrm{PV} = \frac{1}{(1 + r_t)^t}$$

The rationale is that at interest rate $r_t$, present value is the amount that would need to be deposited now to receive one dollar in $t$ years.

Using the concept of present values, we can evaluate an investment for which returns are to be received in the future. Denoting $C_0$, $C_1$, $C_2, \ldots, C_n$ as the dollar returns in current and future years, and $r_t$ as the $_t$-year annual interest rate, NPV is given as

$$\mathrm{NPV} = \sum_{t=0}^{N} \frac{C_t}{(1 + r_t)^t}$$

We have seen that NPV is a basic tool for financial management decision-making. Under fairly reasonable assumptions, since stockholders have access to the capital market, it follows that to act in the interests of existing stockholders, the objective of management should be to maximize the NPV of the corporation.

## References

Beckwith, R. E. "Continuous Financial Process," *Journal of Finance and Quantitative Analysis*, 10 (June 1968, pp. 113–33).

Feldstein, M. and L. Summers. "Inflation and the Taxation of Capital Income in the Corporate Sector," *National Tax Journal* (December 1979, pp. 445–47).

Fisher, I. *The Theory of Interest* (New York: MacMillan, 1930).

French, K., R. Ruback and W. Schwert. "Effects of Nominal Contracting on Stock Returns," *Journal of Political Economy*, 91 (February 1983, pp. 70–96).

Grant, E. L., W. E. Ireson and R. S. Leavenworth. *Principle of Engineering Economy*, 8th edn. (Wiley, 1990).

Keynes, J. M. *The General Theory of Employment, Interest and Money* (London: Macmillan, 1936).

Saari, D. G. *Mathematics of Finance* (Springer International Publishing, 2019).

Tobin, J. and W. C. Brainard. "Asset Markets and the Cost of Capital," in *Economic Progress, Private Values, and Public Policy: Essays in Honor of William Fellner*, B. Balassa and R. Nelson (eds.) (Amsterdam: North-Holland, 1977).

Van Horne, J. and W. Glassmire. "The Impact of Unanticipated Changes in Inflation on the Value of Common Stocks," *The Journal of Finance* (December 1972, pp. 1083–1092).

## Appendix 4A — Three Hypotheses about Inflation and the Firm's Value

We began Chapter 4 by asking whether you would prefer to receive \$1,000 today or \$1,000 a year from now. One reason for selecting the first option is that, as a result of inflation, \$1,000 will buy less in a year than it does today. In Appendix 4A, we explore the possible effects of inflation on a firm's value. According to Van Horne and Glassmire (1972), unanticipated inflation affects the firm in three ways, characterized by thefollowing hypotheses:

1. Debtor-creditor hypothesis
2. Tax-effects hypothesis
3. Operating income hypothesis

The *debtor-creditor hypothesis* postulates that the impact of unanticipated inflation depends on a firm's net borrowing position. In periods of high inflation, fixed money amounts borrowed today will be repaid in the future in a currency with lower purchasing power. Thus, while the rate of interest on the loan reflects expected inflation rates over the term of the loan, a higher than anticipated rate of inflation should result in a transfer of wealth from creditors to debtors. Conversely, if the inflation rate turns out to belower than expected, wealth is transferred from debtors to creditors. Hence, according to the debtor-creditor hypothesis, a higher than anticipated rate of inflation should, all other things being equal, raise the value of firms with heavy borrowings.

The *tax-effects hypothesis* concerns the influence of inflation on those firms with depreciation and inventory tax shields. Since these shields are based on historical costs, their real values decline with inflation. Hence, unanticipated inflation should lower the value of the firms with such shields. The magnitude of these tax effects could be very high indeed. For example, Feldstein and Summers (1979) estimated that the use of depreciation and inventory accounting on a historical cost basis raised corporate tax liabilities by $26 billion in 1977.

In principle, the effects of general inflation should only be felt when parties are forced to comply with nominal contracts, the terms of which failto anticipate inflation. Hence, in theory, wealth transfers caused by general inflation should be due primarily to the debtor–creditor or tax-effects hypothesis discussed above. Apart from these considerations, if all prices move in unison, real profits should not be affected. Nevertheless, there is strong empirical evidence of a negative association between corporate profitability and the general inflation rate. One possible explanation, called the *operating income hypothesis*, is that high inflation rates lead to restrictive government fiscal and monetary policies, which in turn depress the level of business activity and, hence, profits. Further, operating income may be adversely affected if prices of inputs, such as labor and materials, react more quickly to inflationary trends than prices of outputs. Viewed in this light, we might expect firms to react differently to inflation, depending on the reaction speed in the markets in which the firms operate.

Van Horne and Glassmire suggest that, of these three effects of unanticipated inflation on the value of the firm, the operating in come effect is likely to dominate. Some support for this contention is provided by French, Ruback, and Schwert (1983), who find that debtor-creditor effects and tax effects are rather small.

## Appendix 4B — Book Value, Replacement Cost, and Tobin's *q*

An objective of financial management should be to raise the firm's NPV. We have not, however, discussed what constitutes a firm's value.

An accounting measure of value is the total value of all a firm's assets, including plant and equipment, plus inventory. Generally, in a firm's accounts, the book values of the assets are reported. However, this is an inappropriate measure for two reasons. First, it takes no account of the growth rate of capital goods prices since the assets were acquired, and second, it does not account for the economic depreciation of those assets. Therefore, in considering a firm's value, it is preferable to consider current accounting measures that incorporate inflation and depreciation. The relevant measure of accounting value, then, is replacement cost, which is the cost today of purchasing assets of the same vintage as those currently held by the firm.

However, this accounting concept of value is not the one used in financial management, as it does not incorporate the potential for future earnings through the exploitation of productive investment opportunities. If this broader definition is considered, the value of a firm will depend not only on the accounting value of its assets, but also on the ability of management to make productive use of those assets. In finance theory, the relevant concept of values of common stock, preferred stock, and debt, all of which are determined by the financial markets.[3]

The ratio of a firm's market value to the replacement cost of its assets is known as Tobin's $q$, as shown in Tobin and Brainard (1977). One reason for looking at this relationship is that if the acquisition of new capital adds more to the firm's value than the cost of acquiring that capital — that is, it has a positive NPV — then shareholders immediately benefit from the acquisition. On the other hand, if the addition of new capital adds less than its cost to market value, shareholders would be better off if the money were distributed to them as dividends. Therefore, the relationship between market value and replacement cost is crucial in financial management decision-making.

## Appendix 4C — Continuous Compounding and Continuous Discounting

In this appendix, we will show how continuous compounding and discounting can be theoretically derived. In addition, we also give some examples to show how these two processes to the real world.

### 4C.1 Continuous Compounding

In the general calculation of interest, the amount of interest earned plus principal is

$$\text{Principal} + \text{Interest} = \text{Principal} \times \left(1 + \frac{r}{m}\right)^{T} \tag{4.1C}$$

where $r$ = annual interest rate; $m$ = number of compounding periods per year; and $T$ = number of compounding periods ($m$) times the number of years $N$.

There are three variables: the initial amount of principal invested, the period interest rate, and the time period of the investment. If we assume that you invest \$100 for 1 year at 10% interest, you will

[3]In the next chapter, we will discuss the valuation of the financial instruments.

receive the following:

$$\text{Principal} + \text{Interest} = \$100\left(1 + \frac{0.10}{1}\right)^1 = \$110$$

For a given interest rate, the greater frequency with which interest is compounded affects the interest and the time variables of the above equation; the interest per period decreases, but the number of compounding periods increases. The greater the frequency with which interest is compounded, the larger the amount of interest earned. For interest compounded annually, semiannually, quarterly, monthly, weekly, daily, hourly, or continuously, we can see the increase of the amount of interest earned as follows:

$$\text{Principal} + \text{Interest} = P_0\left(1 + \frac{r}{m}\right)^T$$

| | | | |
|---|---|---|---|
| Annual | \$110 | = | $100\left(1+\frac{0.10}{1}\right)1$ |
| Semiannual | 110.25 | = | $100\left(1+\frac{0.10}{2}\right)2$ |
| Quarterly | 110.38 | = | $100\left(1+\frac{0.10}{4}\right)4$ |
| Monthly | 110.47 | = | $100\left(1+\frac{0.10}{12}\right)12$ |
| Weekly | 110.51 | = | $100\left(1+\frac{0.10}{52}\right)52$ |
| Daily | 110.52 | = | $100\left(1+\frac{0.10}{365}\right)365$ |
| Hourly | 110.52 | = | $100\left(1+\frac{0.10}{8760}\right)8760$ |
| Continuously | 110.52 | = | $100(e^{0.1(1)}) = 100(2.7183)^{0.1}$ |

In the case of continuous compounding, the term $\left(1+\frac{r}{m}\right)^T$ goes to $e^{rN}$ as $m$ gets infinitely large. To see this, we start with

$$P_0 + I = P_0\left(1 + \frac{r}{m}\right)^T$$

where $T = m(N)$ and $N =$ number of years.

If we multiply $T$ by $r/r$, we can rearrange Eq. (4.1C) as follows:

$$P_0 + I = P_0 \left[1 + \frac{r}{m}\right]^{\frac{mNr}{r}} = P_0 \left[\left(1 + \frac{r}{m}\right)^{\frac{m}{r}}\right]^{Nr} \quad (4.2C)$$

Let $x = m/r$, and substitute this value into Eq. (4.2C):

$$P_0 + I = P_0 \left[(1 + \frac{1}{x})^{x}\right]^{Nr} \quad (4.3C)$$

The term $(1 + 1/x)^x$ is equal to $e$ as

$$\lim_{x \to \infty} \left(1 + \frac{1}{x}\right)^x = e$$

This says that as the frequency of compounding becomes instantaneous or continuous, Eq. (4.1C) can be written as

$$P_N = P_0 + I = P_0 e^{rN} \quad (4.4C)$$

Figure 4.1C provides graphs of the value of $P = I$ as a function of the frequency of compounding and the number of years. We can see that for low interest rates and shorter periods, the differences between the various compounding methods are very small. However, as either $r$ or $N$ becomes large the difference becomes substantial. In general, as either $r$ or $N$ or both variables become larger, the frequency of compounding will have a greater effect on the amount of interest that is earned.

## 4C.2 Continuous Discounting

As we have seen in Chapter 4, there is a relationship between calculating future values and present values. Starting from Eq. (4.1C), which calculates future value, we can rearrange to find present value:

$$P_0 = \frac{P_0 + I}{(1 + \frac{r}{m})^T} \quad (4.5C)$$

As we mentioned earlier, as $m \to \infty$ we see that the term $(1+r/m)^T$ goes to $e^{Nr}$. Rewriting Eq. (4.5C),

$$P_0 = \frac{P + I}{e^{Nr}} = (P_0 + I)(e^{-Nr}) \quad (4.6C)$$

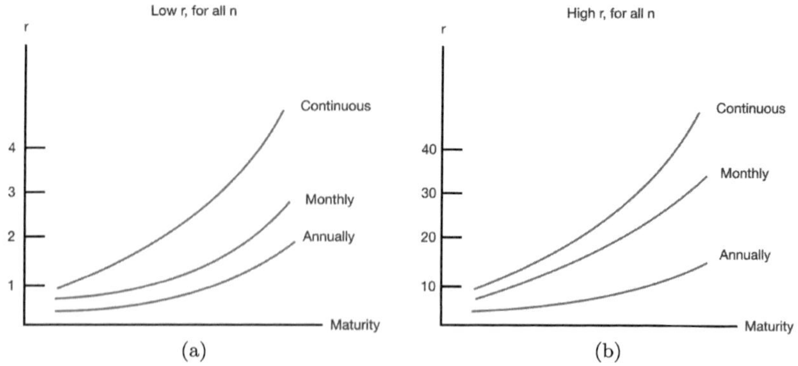


Figure 4.1C Graphical Relationships between Frequency of Compounding $r$ and $N$.

Equation (4.6C) tells us that the present value ($P_0$) of a future amount ($P+I$) is related by the continuous discounting factor $e^{-Nt}$. Similarly, the present value of an annuity of future flows can be viewed as the integral of Eq. (4.6C) over the relevant time period:

$$P_0 = \int_0^N F_t e^{-Nr} dt \tag{4.7C}$$

where $F_t$ is the future cash flow received in period $t$. In fact, $F_t$ can be viewed as a continuous cash flow. For most business organizations, it is more realistic to assume that the cast inflows and outflows occur more or less continuously throughout a given time period instead of at the end or beginning of the period as is the case with the discrete formulation of present value.

## Appendix 4D — Applications of Excel for Calculating Time Value of Money

In this appendix, we will show how to use Excel to calculate (i) the future value of a single amount, (ii) the present value of a single amount, (iii) the future value of an ordinary annuity, and (iv) the present value of an ordinary annuity.

### 4D.1 Future Value of a Single Amount

Suppose the principal is $1,000 today and interest rate is 5% per year.

Table 4.1D Future Value of Single Period.

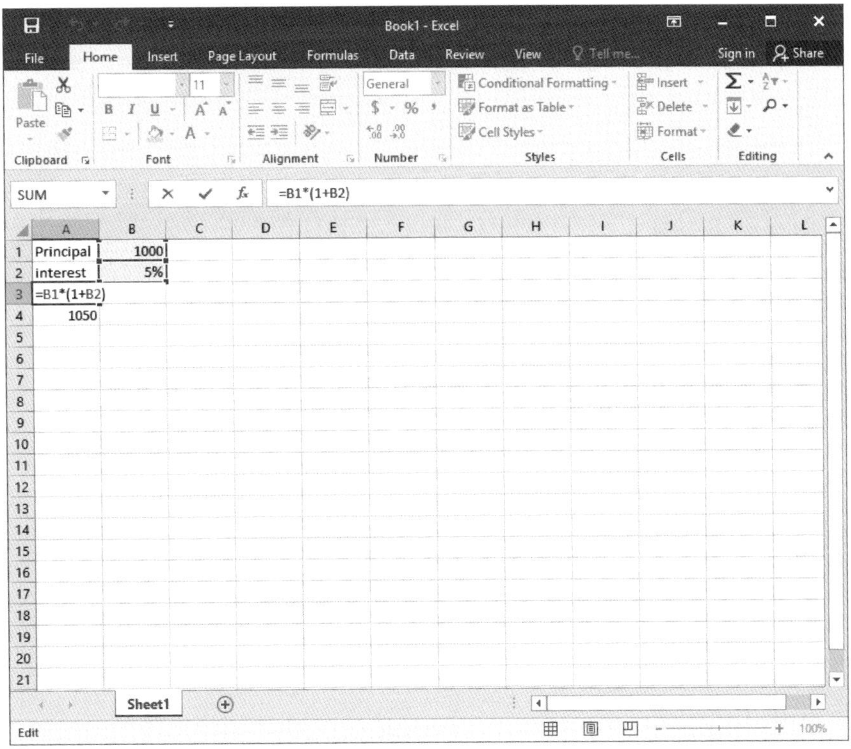


The future value of the principal can be calculated as $FV = PV(1+r)^n$, where $n$ is the number of years.

**Case 1**. Suppose there is only one period, i.e., $n = 1$. The future value in one year will be $1000(1 + 5\%)^1 = 1050$

We can use Excel to directly compute it by inputting "= B1* (1+B2)," as presented in Table 4.1D.

Or we can also use the function in Excel to compute the future value by inputting "=FV(B2,1,B1,0)."

There are five options in this function.

**Rate:** The interest rate per period.

**Nper:** The number of payment periods.

**PMT**: The payment in each period; If "pmt" is omitted, we should include the "pv" argument below.

Table 4.2D Future Value of Single Period in Terms of Excel Formula.

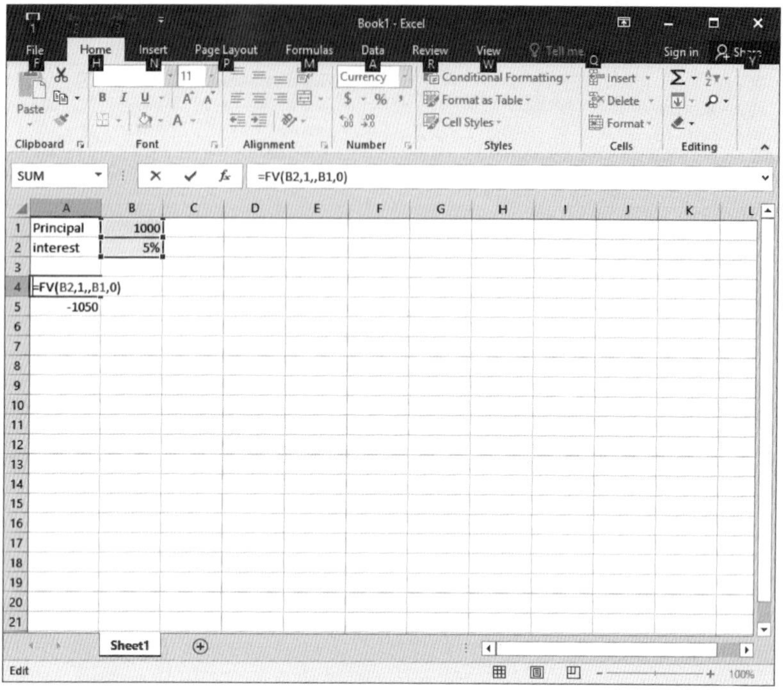


**PV:** The present value. If "pv" is omitted, it is assumed to be 0. Then we should include the "pmt" argument above.

**Type:** The number 0 or 1 shows when payments are due. If payments are due at the end of the period, Excel sets it as 0; If payments are due at the beginning of the period, Excel sets it as 1.

The FV function gives us the same amount as what we calculate according to the formula except the sign is negative. Actually, the FV function in Excel is to compute the Future value of the principal that one party should payback to another party. Therefore, Excel adds a negative sign to indicate the amount needed to pay back, as presented in Table 4.2D.

**Case 2**. Now suppose there are 4 periods. The future value of $1,000 at the end of the 4th year will be $1000(1 + 5\%)^4 = 1215.51$

We use two methods to compute the future value and obtain the same result.

Table 4.3D Compound Value of Multiple Periods.

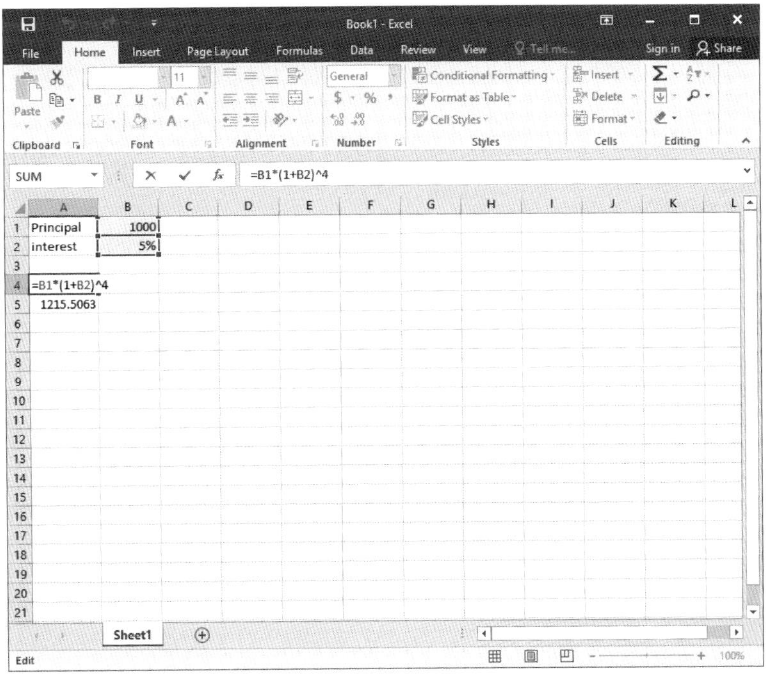


First, we calculate it directly according to the formula, as presented in Table 4.3D.

Second, we use FV function in Excel to calculate it, as presented in Table 4.4D.

The FV function gives us the same amount as what we calculate according to the formula except the sign is negative. Actually, the FV function in Excel is to compute the Future value of the principal that one party should payback to another party. Therefore, Excel adds a negative sign to indicate the amount needed to pay back.

## 4D.2 Present Value of a Single Amount

The present value of the future sum of money can be calculated as $PV = FV/(1+r)^n$, where $n$ is the number of years.

Table 4.4D Compound Value of Multiple Period in Terms of Excel Formula.

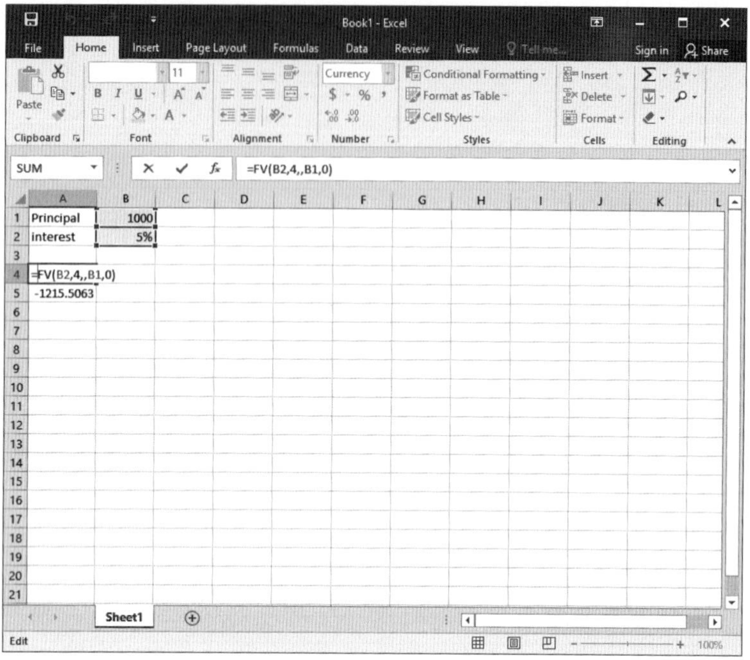


**Case 1**. Suppose a project will end in one year and it pays \$1000 at the end of that year. The interest rate is 5% for one year.

The present value will be $1000/(1 + 5\%)^1 = 952.38$.

We can use Excel to directly compute it by inputting "= B1/ (1+B2)," as presented in Table 4.5D.

Or, we can use the FV function which is quite similar to the FV function we used before. The result is presented in Table 4.6D.

**Case 2**. Suppose a project will end in four years and it would pay \$1000 only at the end of the last year. The interest rate is 5% for one year.

The present value will be $1000/(1 + 5\%)^4 = 952.38$.

We can use Excel to directly compute it by inputting "= B1/ (1+B2)^4," as presented in Table 4.7D.

Or we use the PV formula in Excel buy inputting "= PV(B2, 4,B1,0)," as presented in Table 4.8D.

Table 4.5D Present Value For Single Period.

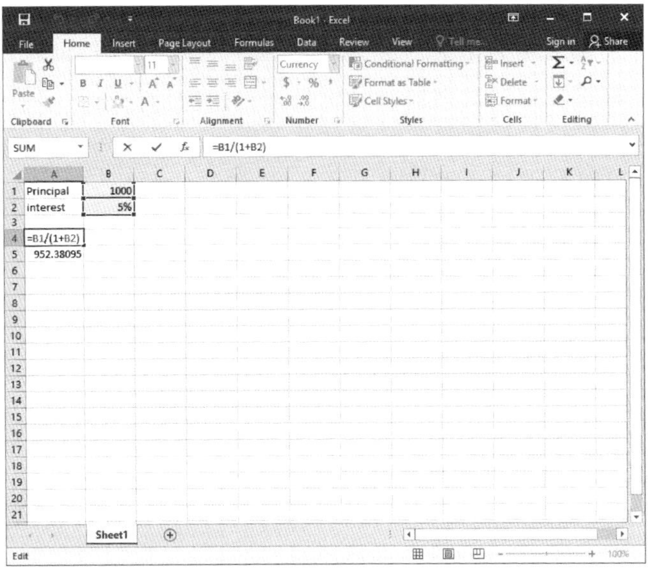


Table 4.6D Present Value of Single Period in Terms of Excel Formula.

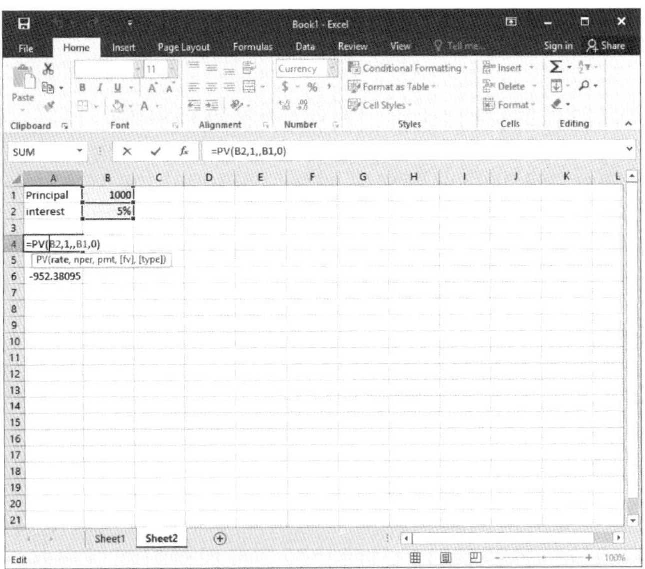

Table 4.7D Present Value for Multiple Periods.

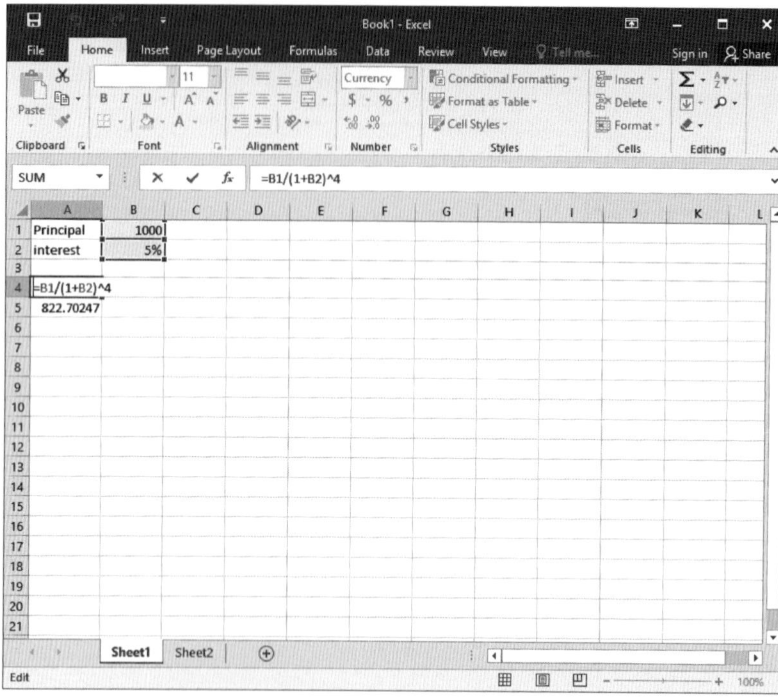


## 4D.3 Future Value of an Ordinary Annuity

Annuity is a series of cash flow of a fixed amount for n periods of equal length. It can be divided into Ordinary Annuity (the first payment occurs at the end of period) and Annuity Due (the first payment is at the beginning of the period).

### Case 1. Future Value of an Ordinary Annuity

The formula is FV $= \sum_{k=1}^{n} PMT(1+r)^{k-1}$, where $PMT$ is the payment in each period.

Suppose a project will pay you $1,000 at the end of each year for 4 years at 5% annual interest, and the following graph shows the process.

Table 4.8D Present Value for Multiple Periods in Terms of Excel Formula.

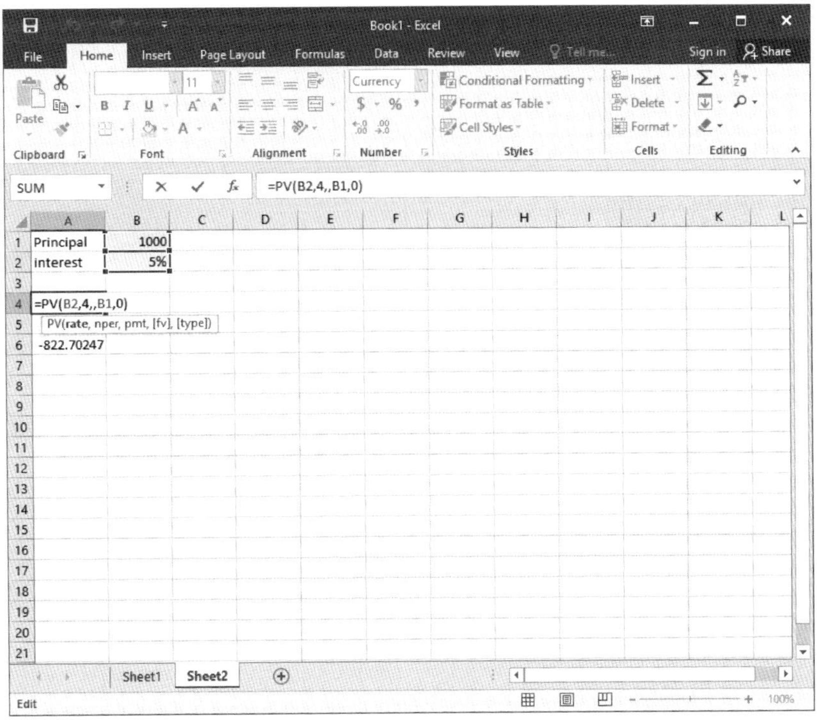


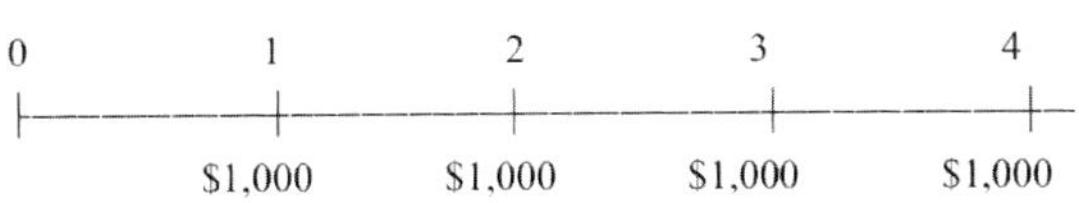


We still use two methods to calculate the future value of this ordinary annuity. First, we directly use the formula to compute it and obtain the value of 4,310.125. The result is presented in Table 4.9D.

Then we use FV function in Excel to compute the future value and obtain 4,310.125. Hence, the two methods give us the same result, as presented in Table 4.10D

## Case 2. Future Value of an Annuity Due

The formula is FV $= \sum_{k=1}^{n} PMT(1+r)^k$, where $PMT$ is the payment in each period.

Table 4.9D Future Value of Annuity.

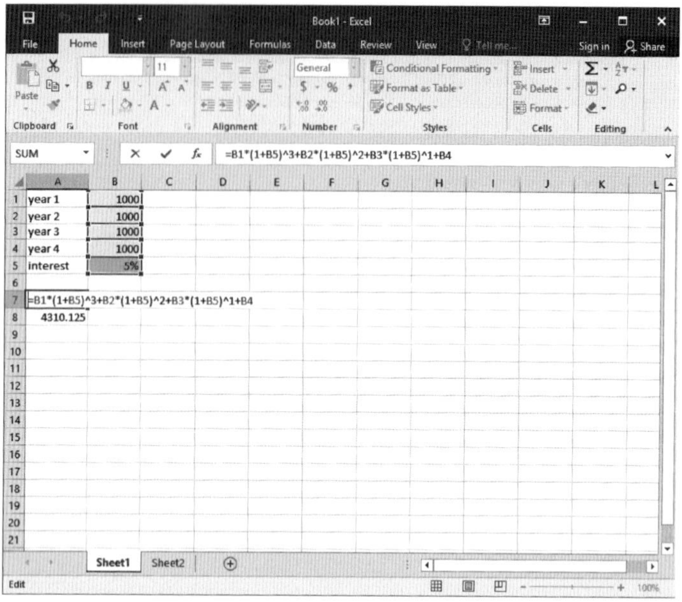


Table 4.10D Future Value of Annuity in Terms of Excel Formula.

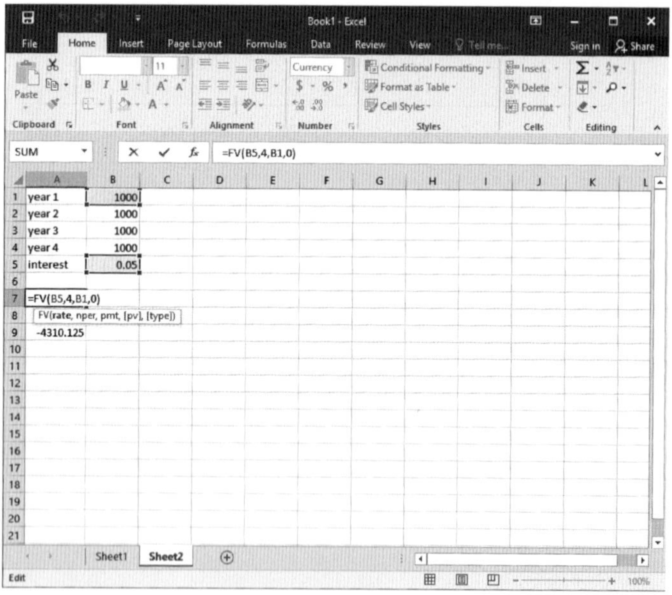

Table 4.11D Future Value of Annuity Due.

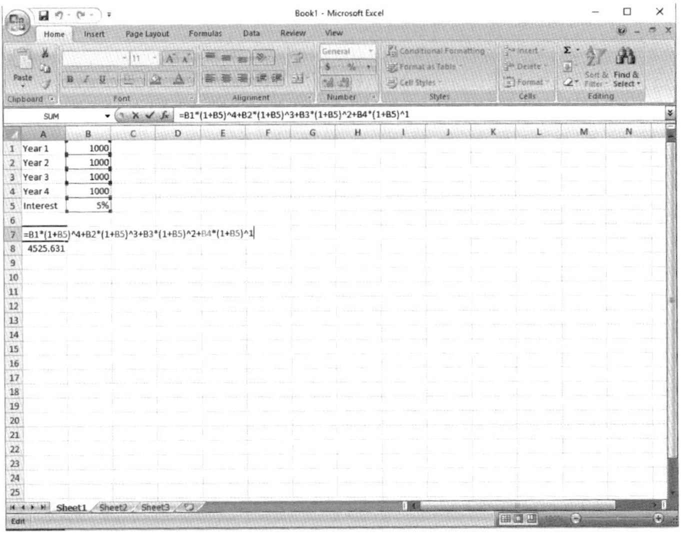


Suppose a project will pay you \$1,000 at the beginning of each year for 4 years at 5% annual interest, and the following graph shows the process.

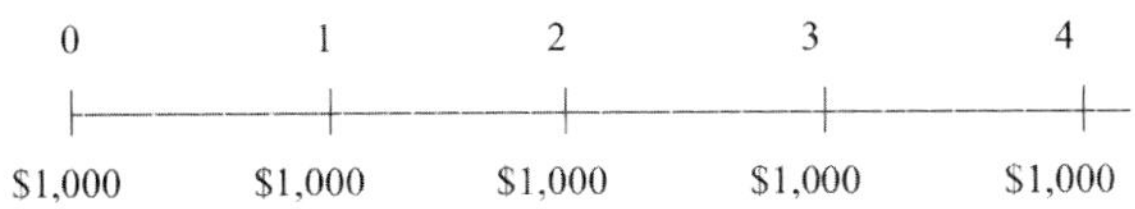


First, we directly use the formula to compute it and obtain the future value of 4,525.631. The result is presented in Table 4.11D.

Then we use FV function in Excel to compute the future value and obtain 4,525.63. The only difference between calculating annuity due and computing ordinary annuity is to choose "1" in "type term" of FV function rather than to choose "0." The two methods give us the same result, as presented in Table 4.12D.

## 4D.4 Present Value of an Ordinary Annuity

### Case 1. Present Value of an Ordinary Annuity

The formula is $\mathrm{FV} = \sum_{k=1}^{n} PMT/(1+r)^k$, where $PMT$ is the payment in each period.

Table 4.12D Future Value of Annuity Due in Terms of Excel Formula.

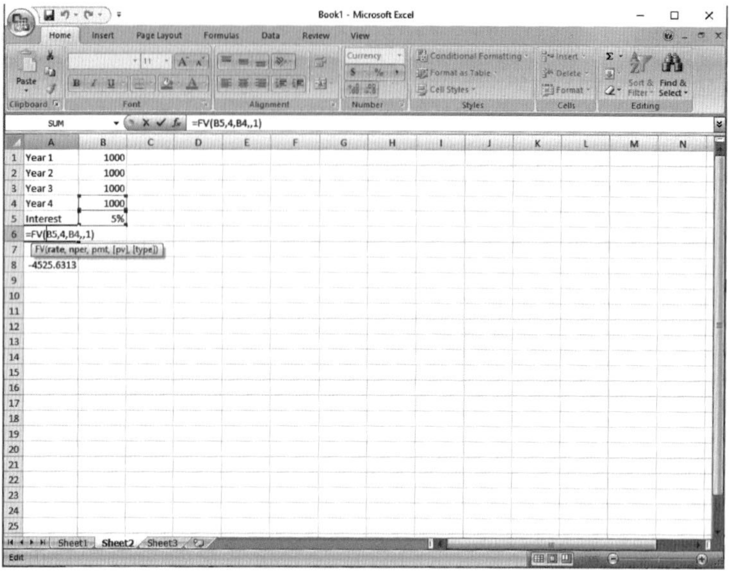


Suppose a project will pay you $1500 at the end of each year for 4 years at 5% annual interest.

According to this formula, we directly input "=B1/(1+B5) ^4+B2/(1+B5) ^3+B3/(1+B5) ^2+B4/(1+B5) ^1" to get the present value of 5,318.93, as presented in Table 4.13D.

In addition, we can use PV function in Excel directly and obtain the same amount as above, as presented in Table 4.14D.

## Case 2. Present Value of An Annuity Due.

The formula is $\text{PV} = \sum_{k=0}^{n-1} PMT/(1+r)^k$, where $PMT$ is the payment in each period.

Suppose a project will pay you $1,500 at the end of each year for 4 years at 5% annual interest.

According to this formula, we directly input "=B1/(1+B5)^3+B2/(1+B5)^2+B3/(1+B5)^1+B4/(1+B5)^0" to get the present value of 5,584.87, as presented in Table 4.15D.

Table 4.13D Present Value of Annuity.

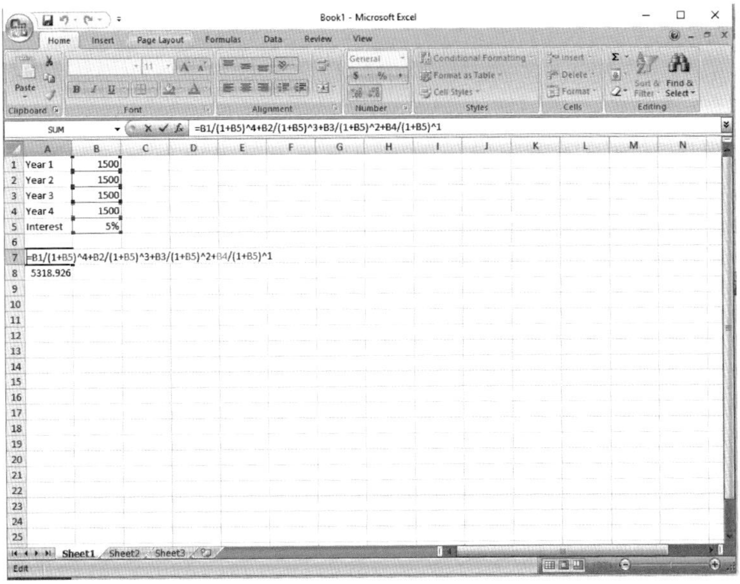


Table 4.14D Present Value of Annuity in Terms of Excel Formula.

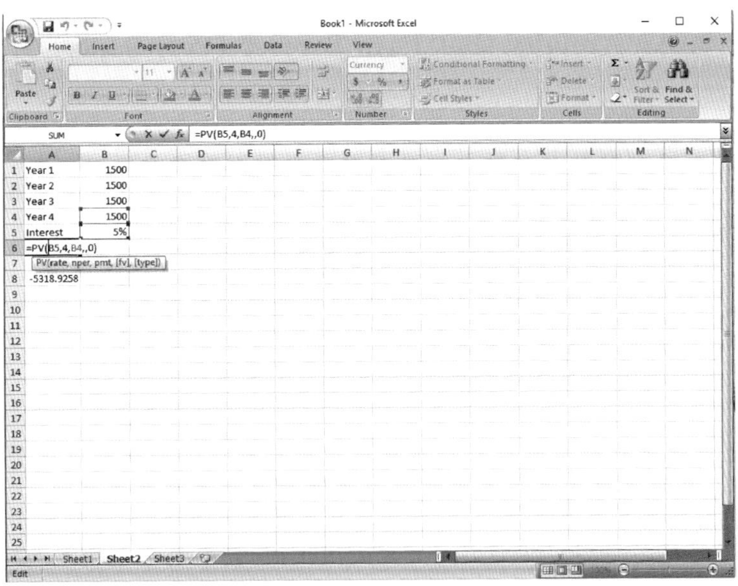

Table 4.15D Present Value of Annuity Due.

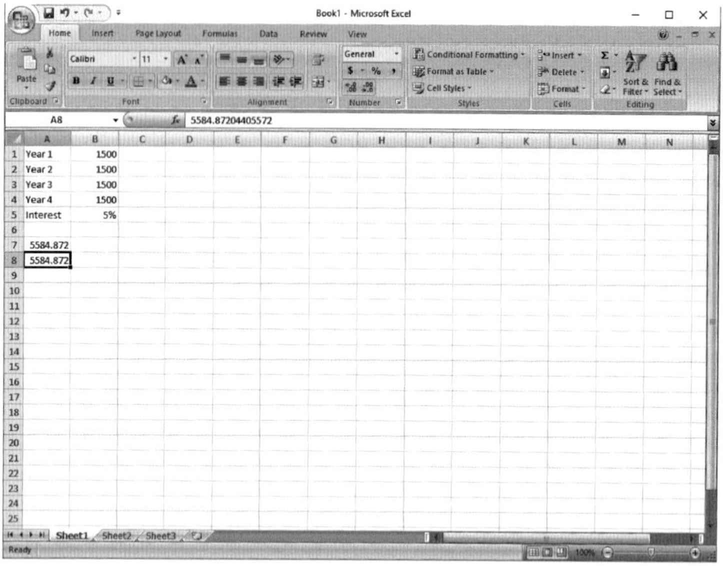


Similarly, the PV function gives us the same result as presented in Table 4.16D.

### Case 3. An Annuity that Pays Forever (Perpetuity)

$$\text{PV} = \frac{PMT}{r}$$

In Excel, we directly input "=B1/B2" to get PV=30,000, as presented in Table 4.17D.

## Appendix 4E — Tables of Time Value of Money

### 4E.1 Future Value Table (Annually Compounded)

Suppose that $k$ dollar(s) is invested now at an interest rate $r$ per period, with interest compounded at the end of each period.

Table 4.1E gives the future value of $k$ dollar(s) at the end of $t$ periods for various interest rates, $r$, and number of periods, $t$.

Assume the amount of money in dollar(s) is $1.

Table 4.16D Present Value of Annuity Due in Terms of Excel Formula.

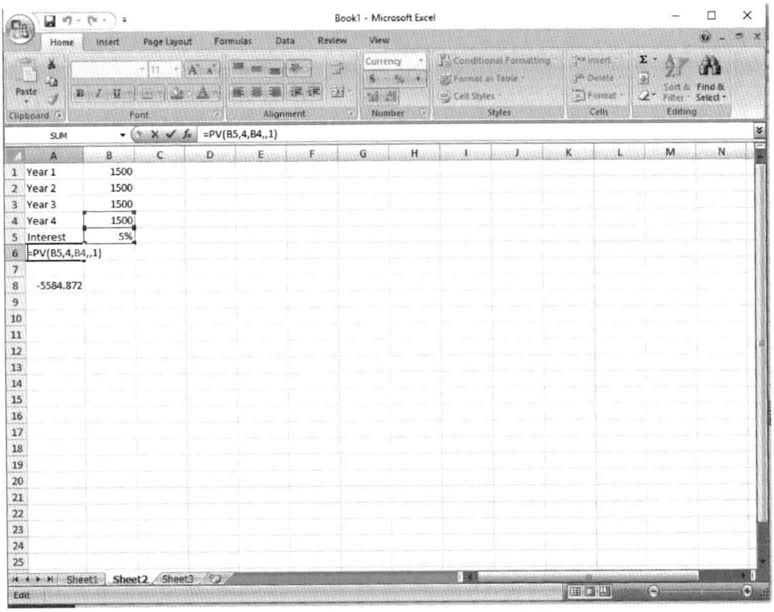


Table 4.17D Present Value of Perpetuity.

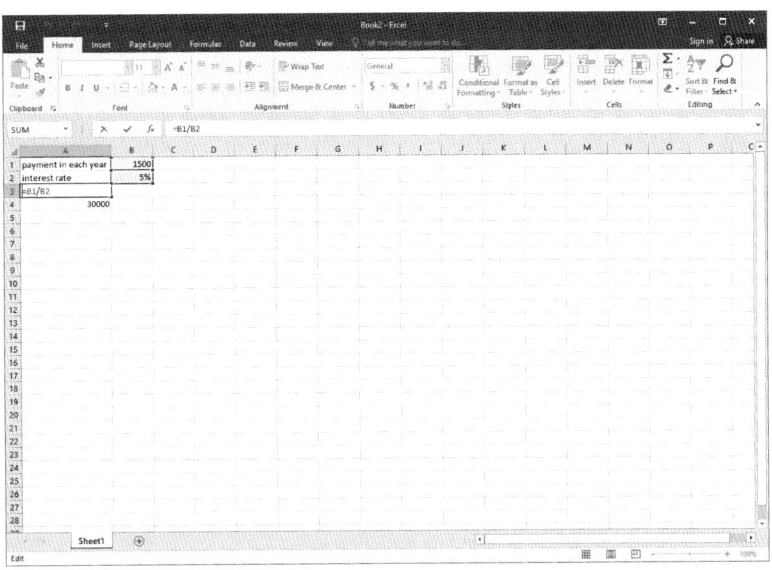

## 4E.2 Future Value Table (Continuously Compounded)

Suppose that $k$ dollar(s) is invested now at an interest rate $r$ per period, with interest continuously compounded.

Table 4.2E shows the future value of $k$ dollar(s) invested for $t$ periods at interest rate $r$ per period, continuously compounded.

Assume the amount of money in dollar(s) is \$1.

## 4E.3 Present Value Table — Present Value of a Dollar Received $t$ Periods in the Future

Suppose that $k$ dollar(s) is to be received $t$ periods in the future and that the rate of interest is $r$, with compounding at the end of each period.

Table 4.3E gives the present value of $k$ dollar(s) collected at the end of $t$ periods for various interest rates, $r$, and number of periods, $t$.

Assume the amount of money in dollar(s) is \$1.

## 4E.4 Present Value Table — Present Value of an Annuity of a Dollar per Period

Suppose that $k$ dollar(s) is collected, and the interest is compounded at the end of each period.

Table 4.4E gives the value of $k$ dollar(s) collected at the end of $t$ periods for various interest rates, $r$, and number of periods, $t$.

Assume the amount of money in dollar(s) is \$1.

Table 4.1E Future Value Table (Annually Compounded).

| $t/r$ | 2% | 4% | 6% | 8% | 10% | 12% | 14% | 16% | 18% | 20% |
|---|---|---|---|---|---|---|---|---|---|---|
| **1** | 1.0200 | 1.0400 | 1.0600 | 1.0800 | 1.1000 | 1.1200 | 1.1400 | 1.1600 | 1.1800 | 1.2000 |
| **2** | 1.0404 | 1.0816 | 1.1236 | 1.1664 | 1.2100 | 1.2544 | 1.2996 | 1.3456 | 1.3924 | 1.4400 |
| **3** | 1.0612 | 1.1249 | 1.1910 | 1.2597 | 1.3310 | 1.4049 | 1.4815 | 1.5609 | 1.6430 | 1.7280 |
| **4** | 1.0824 | 1.1699 | 1.2625 | 1.3605 | 1.4641 | 1.5735 | 1.6890 | 1.8106 | 1.9388 | 2.0736 |
| **5** | 1.1041 | 1.2167 | 1.3382 | 1.4693 | 1.6105 | 1.7623 | 1.9254 | 2.1003 | 2.2878 | 2.4883 |
| **6** | 1.1262 | 1.2653 | 1.4185 | 1.5869 | 1.7716 | 1.9738 | 2.1950 | 2.4364 | 2.6996 | 2.9860 |
| **7** | 1.1487 | 1.3159 | 1.5036 | 1.7138 | 1.9487 | 2.2107 | 2.5023 | 2.8262 | 3.1855 | 3.5832 |
| **8** | 1.1717 | 1.3686 | 1.5938 | 1.8509 | 2.1436 | 2.4760 | 2.8526 | 3.2784 | 3.7589 | 4.2998 |
| **9** | 1.1951 | 1.4233 | 1.6895 | 1.9990 | 2.3579 | 2.7731 | 3.2519 | 3.8030 | 4.4355 | 5.1598 |
| **10** | 1.2190 | 1.4802 | 1.7908 | 2.1589 | 2.5937 | 3.1058 | 3.7072 | 4.4114 | 5.2338 | 6.1917 |
| **11** | 1.2434 | 1.5395 | 1.8983 | 2.3316 | 2.8531 | 3.4785 | 4.2262 | 5.1173 | 6.1759 | 7.4301 |
| **12** | 1.2682 | 1.6010 | 2.0122 | 2.5182 | 3.1384 | 3.8960 | 4.8179 | 5.9360 | 7.2876 | 8.9161 |
| **13** | 1.2936 | 1.6651 | 2.1329 | 2.7196 | 3.4523 | 4.3635 | 5.4924 | 6.8858 | 8.5994 | 10.6993 |
| **14** | 1.3195 | 1.7317 | 2.2609 | 2.9372 | 3.7975 | 4.8871 | 6.2613 | 7.9875 | 10.1472 | 12.8392 |
| **15** | 1.3459 | 1.8009 | 2.3966 | 3.1722 | 4.1772 | 5.4736 | 7.1379 | 9.2655 | 11.9737 | 15.4070 |
| **16** | 1.3728 | 1.8730 | 2.5404 | 3.4259 | 4.5950 | 6.1304 | 8.1372 | 10.7480 | 14.1290 | 18.4884 |
| **17** | 1.4002 | 1.9479 | 2.6928 | 3.7000 | 5.0545 | 6.8660 | 9.2765 | 12.4677 | 16.6722 | 22.1861 |
| **18** | 1.4282 | 2.0258 | 2.8543 | 3.9960 | 5.5599 | 7.6900 | 10.5752 | 14.4625 | 19.6733 | 26.6233 |
| **19** | 1.4568 | 2.1068 | 3.0256 | 4.3157 | 6.1159 | 8.6128 | 12.0557 | 16.7765 | 23.2144 | 31.9480 |
| **20** | 1.4859 | 2.1911 | 3.2071 | 4.6610 | 6.7275 | 9.6463 | 13.7435 | 19.4608 | 27.3930 | 38.3376 |

Table 4.2E Future Value Table (Continuously Compounded).

| $t/r$ | **2%** | **4%** | **6%** | **8%** | **10%** | **12%** | **14%** | **16%** | **18%** | **20%** |
|---|---|---|---|---|---|---|---|---|---|---|
| **1** | 1.0202 | 1.0408 | 1.0618 | 1.0833 | 1.1052 | 1.1275 | 1.1503 | 1.1735 | 1.1972 | 1.2214 |
| **2** | 1.0408 | 1.0833 | 1.1275 | 1.1735 | 1.2214 | 1.2712 | 1.3231 | 1.3771 | 1.4333 | 1.4918 |
| **3** | 1.0618 | 1.1275 | 1.1972 | 1.2712 | 1.3499 | 1.4333 | 1.5220 | 1.6161 | 1.7160 | 1.8221 |
| **4** | 1.0833 | 1.1735 | 1.2712 | 1.3771 | 1.4918 | 1.6161 | 1.7507 | 1.8965 | 2.0544 | 2.2255 |
| **5** | 1.1052 | 1.2214 | 1.3499 | 1.4918 | 1.6487 | 1.8221 | 2.0138 | 2.2255 | 2.4596 | 2.7183 |
| **6** | 1.1275 | 1.2712 | 1.4333 | 1.6161 | 1.8221 | 2.0544 | 2.3164 | 2.6117 | 2.9447 | 3.3201 |
| **7** | 1.1503 | 1.3231 | 1.5220 | 1.7507 | 2.0138 | 2.3164 | 2.6645 | 3.0649 | 3.5254 | 4.0552 |
| **8** | 1.1735 | 1.3771 | 1.6161 | 1.8965 | 2.2255 | 2.6117 | 3.0649 | 3.5966 | 4.2207 | 4.9530 |
| **9** | 1.1972 | 1.4333 | 1.7160 | 2.0544 | 2.4596 | 2.9447 | 3.5254 | 4.2207 | 5.0531 | 6.0496 |
| **10** | 1.2214 | 1.4918 | 1.8221 | 2.2255 | 2.7183 | 3.3201 | 4.0552 | 4.9530 | 6.0496 | 7.3891 |
| **11** | 1.2461 | 1.5527 | 1.9348 | 2.4109 | 3.0042 | 3.7434 | 4.6646 | 5.8124 | 7.2427 | 9.0250 |
| **12** | 1.2712 | 1.6161 | 2.0544 | 2.6117 | 3.3201 | 4.2207 | 5.3656 | 6.8210 | 8.6711 | 11.0232 |
| **13** | 1.2969 | 1.6820 | 2.1815 | 2.8292 | 3.6693 | 4.7588 | 6.1719 | 8.0045 | 10.3812 | 13.4637 |
| **14** | 1.3231 | 1.7507 | 2.3164 | 3.0649 | 4.0552 | 5.3656 | 7.0993 | 9.3933 | 12.4286 | 16.4446 |
| **15** | 1.3499 | 1.8221 | 2.4596 | 3.3201 | 4.4817 | 6.0496 | 8.1662 | 11.0232 | 14.8797 | 20.0855 |
| **16** | 1.3771 | 1.8965 | 2.6117 | 3.5966 | 4.9530 | 6.8210 | 9.3933 | 12.9358 | 17.8143 | 24.5325 |
| **17** | 1.4049 | 1.9739 | 2.7732 | 3.8962 | 5.4739 | 7.6906 | 10.8049 | 15.1803 | 21.3276 | 29.9641 |
| **18** | 1.4333 | 2.0544 | 2.9447 | 4.2207 | 6.0496 | 8.6711 | 12.4286 | 17.8143 | 25.5337 | 36.5982 |
| **19** | 1.4623 | 2.1383 | 3.1268 | 4.5722 | 6.6859 | 9.7767 | 14.2963 | 20.9052 | 30.5694 | 44.7012 |
| **20** | 1.4918 | 2.2255 | 3.3201 | 4.9530 | 7.3891 | 11.0232 | 16.4446 | 24.5325 | 36.5982 | 54.5982 |

Table 4.3E Present Value Table — Present Value of a Dollar Received $t$ Periods in the Future.

| $t/r$ | 2% | 4% | 6% | 8% | 10% | 12% | 14% | 16% | 18% | 20% |
|---|---|---|---|---|---|---|---|---|---|---|
| **1** | 0.9804 | 0.9615 | 0.9434 | 0.9259 | 0.9091 | 0.8929 | 0.8772 | 0.8621 | 0.8475 | 0.8333 |
| **2** | 0.9612 | 0.9246 | 0.8900 | 0.8573 | 0.8264 | 0.7972 | 0.7695 | 0.7432 | 0.7182 | 0.6944 |
| **3** | 0.9423 | 0.8890 | 0.8396 | 0.7938 | 0.7513 | 0.7118 | 0.6750 | 0.6407 | 0.6086 | 0.5787 |
| **4** | 0.9238 | 0.8548 | 0.7921 | 0.7350 | 0.6830 | 0.6355 | 0.5921 | 0.5523 | 0.5158 | 0.4823 |
| **5** | 0.9057 | 0.8219 | 0.7473 | 0.6806 | 0.6209 | 0.5674 | 0.5194 | 0.4761 | 0.4371 | 0.4019 |
| **6** | 0.8880 | 0.7903 | 0.7050 | 0.6302 | 0.5645 | 0.5066 | 0.4556 | 0.4104 | 0.3704 | 0.3349 |
| **7** | 0.8706 | 0.7599 | 0.6651 | 0.5835 | 0.5132 | 0.4523 | 0.3996 | 0.3538 | 0.3139 | 0.2791 |
| **8** | 0.8535 | 0.7307 | 0.6274 | 0.5403 | 0.4665 | 0.4039 | 0.3506 | 0.3050 | 0.2660 | 0.2326 |
| **9** | 0.8368 | 0.7026 | 0.5919 | 0.5002 | 0.4241 | 0.3606 | 0.3075 | 0.2630 | 0.2255 | 0.1938 |
| **10** | 0.8203 | 0.6756 | 0.5584 | 0.4632 | 0.3855 | 0.3220 | 0.2697 | 0.2267 | 0.1911 | 0.1615 |
| **11** | 0.8043 | 0.6496 | 0.5268 | 0.4289 | 0.3505 | 0.2875 | 0.2366 | 0.1954 | 0.1619 | 0.1346 |
| **12** | 0.7885 | 0.6246 | 0.4970 | 0.3971 | 0.3186 | 0.2567 | 0.2076 | 0.1685 | 0.1372 | 0.1122 |
| **13** | 0.7730 | 0.6006 | 0.4688 | 0.3677 | 0.2897 | 0.2292 | 0.1821 | 0.1452 | 0.1163 | 0.0935 |
| **14** | 0.7579 | 0.5775 | 0.4423 | 0.3405 | 0.2633 | 0.2046 | 0.1597 | 0.1252 | 0.0985 | 0.0779 |
| **15** | 0.7430 | 0.5553 | 0.4173 | 0.3152 | 0.2394 | 0.1827 | 0.1401 | 0.1079 | 0.0835 | 0.0649 |
| **16** | 0.7284 | 0.5339 | 0.3936 | 0.2919 | 0.2176 | 0.1631 | 0.1229 | 0.0930 | 0.0708 | 0.0541 |
| **17** | 0.7142 | 0.5134 | 0.3714 | 0.2703 | 0.1978 | 0.1456 | 0.1078 | 0.0802 | 0.0600 | 0.0451 |
| **18** | 0.7002 | 0.4936 | 0.3503 | 0.2502 | 0.1799 | 0.1300 | 0.0946 | 0.0691 | 0.0508 | 0.0376 |
| **19** | 0.6864 | 0.4746 | 0.3305 | 0.2317 | 0.1635 | 0.1161 | 0.0829 | 0.0596 | 0.0431 | 0.0313 |
| **20** | 0.6730 | 0.4564 | 0.3118 | 0.2145 | 0.1486 | 0.1037 | 0.0728 | 0.0514 | 0.0365 | 0.0261 |

Table 4.4E Present Value Table — Present Value of an Annuity of a Dollar per Period.

| $t/r$ | 2% | 4% | 6% | 8% | 10% | 12% | 14% | 16% | 18% | 20% |
|---|---|---|---|---|---|---|---|---|---|---|
| **1** | 0.9804 | 0.9615 | 0.9434 | 0.9259 | 0.9091 | 0.8929 | 0.8772 | 0.8621 | 0.8475 | 0.8333 |
| **2** | 1.9416 | 1.8861 | 1.8334 | 1.7833 | 1.7355 | 1.6901 | 1.6467 | 1.6052 | 1.5656 | 1.5278 |
| **3** | 2.8839 | 2.7751 | 2.6730 | 2.5771 | 2.4869 | 2.4018 | 2.3216 | 2.2459 | 2.1743 | 2.1065 |
| **4** | 3.8077 | 3.6299 | 3.4651 | 3.3121 | 3.1699 | 3.0373 | 2.9137 | 2.7982 | 2.6901 | 2.5887 |
| **5** | 4.7135 | 4.4518 | 4.2124 | 3.9927 | 3.7908 | 3.6048 | 3.4331 | 3.2743 | 3.1272 | 2.9906 |
| **6** | 5.6014 | 5.2421 | 4.9173 | 4.6229 | 4.3553 | 4.1114 | 3.8887 | 3.6847 | 3.4976 | 3.3255 |
| **7** | 6.4720 | 6.0021 | 5.5824 | 5.2064 | 4.8684 | 4.5638 | 4.2883 | 4.0386 | 3.8115 | 3.6046 |
| **8** | 7.3255 | 6.7327 | 6.2098 | 5.7466 | 5.3349 | 4.9676 | 4.6389 | 4.3436 | 4.0776 | 3.8372 |
| **9** | 8.1622 | 7.4353 | 6.8017 | 6.2469 | 5.7590 | 5.3282 | 4.9464 | 4.6065 | 4.3030 | 4.0310 |
| **10** | 8.9826 | 8.1109 | 7.3601 | 6.7101 | 6.1446 | 5.6502 | 5.2161 | 4.8332 | 4.4941 | 4.1925 |
| **11** | 9.7868 | 8.7605 | 7.8869 | 7.1390 | 6.4951 | 5.9377 | 5.4527 | 5.0286 | 4.6560 | 4.3271 |
| **12** | 10.5753 | 9.3851 | 8.3838 | 7.5361 | 6.8137 | 6.1944 | 5.6603 | 5.1971 | 4.7932 | 4.4392 |
| **13** | 11.3484 | 9.9856 | 8.8527 | 7.9038 | 7.1034 | 6.4235 | 5.8424 | 5.3423 | 4.9095 | 4.5327 |
| **14** | 12.1062 | 10.5631 | 9.2950 | 8.2442 | 7.3667 | 6.6282 | 6.0021 | 5.4675 | 5.0081 | 4.6106 |
| **15** | 12.8493 | 11.1184 | 9.7122 | 8.5595 | 7.6061 | 6.8109 | 6.1422 | 5.5755 | 5.0916 | 4.6755 |
| **16** | 13.5777 | 11.6523 | 10.1059 | 8.8514 | 7.8237 | 6.9740 | 6.2651 | 5.6685 | 5.1624 | 4.7296 |
| **17** | 14.2919 | 12.1657 | 10.4773 | 9.1216 | 8.0216 | 7.1196 | 6.3729 | 5.7487 | 5.2223 | 4.7746 |
| **18** | 14.9920 | 12.6593 | 10.8276 | 9.3719 | 8.2014 | 7.2497 | 6.4674 | 5.8178 | 5.2732 | 4.8122 |
| **19** | 15.6785 | 13.1339 | 11.1581 | 9.6036 | 8.3649 | 7.3658 | 6.5504 | 5.8775 | 5.3162 | 4.8435 |
| **20** | 16.3514 | 13.5903 | 11.4699 | 9.8181 | 8.5136 | 7.4694 | 6.6231 | 5.9288 | 5.3527 | 4.8696 |

## Questions and Problems

1. Define following terms:

   a. Present values and future value
   b. Compounding and discounting process
   c. Discrete versus continuous compounding
   d. Liquidity preference
   e. Debtor-creditor hypothesis
   f. Operating income hypothesis

2. Discuss how the following four tables (Table 4.1E–Table 4.4E) listed at the end of the chapter are compiled.

   a. Present value table
   b. Future value table
   c. Present value of annuity table
   d. Compound value of annuity table

3. Suppose that \$100 is invested today at an annual interest rate of 12% for a period of 10 years. Calculate the total amount received at the end of this term as follows:

   a. Interest compounded annually
   b. Interest compounded semiannually
   c. Interest compounded monthly
   d. Interest compounded continuously

4. What is the present value of \$1,000 paid at the end of one year if the appropriate interest rate is 15%?
5. $CF_0$ is initial outlay on an investment, and $CF_1$ and $CF_2$ are the cash flows at the end of the next two years. The notation $r$ is the appropriate interest rate. Answer the following:

   a. What is the formula for the NPV?
   b. Find NPV when $CF_0 = -\$1{,}000$, $CF_1 = \$600$, $CF_2 = \$700$, and $r = 10\%$.
   c. If the investment is risk-free, what rate is used as a proxy for $r$?

6. ABC Company is considering two projects for a new investment, as shown in table below (in dollars). Which is better if ABC uses the NPV rule to select between the projects? Suppose that the interest rate is 12%.

| | | Year 0 | Year 1 | Year 2 | Year 3 | Year 4 |
|---|---|---|---|---|---|---|
| Project A | Costs | 10,000 | 0 | 0 | 0 | 0 |
| | Returns | 0 | 0 | 0 | 1,000 | 20,000 |
| Project B | Costs | 5,000 | 5,000 | 0 | 0 | 0 |
| | Returns | 0 | 10,000 | 5,000 | 3,000 | 2,000 |

7. Suppose that $C$ dollars is to be received at the end of each of the next $N$ years, and that the annual interest rate is $r$ over the $N$ years.
   a. What is the formula for the present value of the payments?
   b. Calculate the present value of the payments when $C = \$1,000$, $r = 10\%$, and $N = 50$.
   c. Would you pay $10,000 now ($t = 0$) for the annuity of $1,000 to be received every year for the next 50 years?
   d. If $1,000 per year is to be received forever, what is the present value of those cash flow streams?
8. Mr. Smith is 50 years old and his salary will be $40,000 next year. He thinks his salary will increase at an annual rate of 10% until his retirement at age 60.
   a. If the appropriate interest rate is 8%, what is the present value of these future payments?
   b. If Mr. Smith saves 50% of his salary each year and invests these savings at the annual interest rate of 12%, how much will he save by age 60?
9. Suppose someone pays you $10 at the beginning of each year for 10 years, expecting that you will pay back a fixed amount of money each year forever commencing at the beginning of Year 11. For a fair deal when annual interest rate is 10% how much should the annual fixed amount of money be?
10. ZZZ Bank agrees to lend ABC Company $10,000 today in return for the company's promise to pay back $25,000 five years from today. What annual rate of interest is the bank charging the company?
11. Which of the following would you choose if the current interest rate is 10%?
    a. $100 now
    b. $12 at the end of each year for the next 10 years

c. \$10 at the end of each year forever
d. \$200 at the end of the seventh year
e. \$50 now and yearly payments decreasing by 50% a year forever
f. \$5 now and yearly payments increasing by 5% a year forever

12. You are given an opportunity to purchase an investment which pays no cash in years 0 through 5, but will pay \$150 per year beginning in year 6 and continuing forever. Your required rate of return for this investment is 10%. Assume all cash flows occur at the end of each year.
    a. Show how much you should be willing to pay for the investment at the end of year 5.
    b. How much should you be willing to pay for the investment now?
13. If you deposit \$100 at the end of each year for the next five years, how much will you have in your account at the end of five years if the bank pays 5% interest compounded annually?
14. If you deposit \$100 at the beginning of each year for the next five years, how much will you have in your account at the end of five years if the bank pays 5% interest compounded annually?
15. If you deposit \$200 at the end of each year for the next 10 years and interest is compounded continuously at an annual quoted rate of 5%, how much will you have in your account at the end of 10 years?
16. Your mother is about to retire. Her firm has given her the option of retiring with a lump sum of \$50,000 now or an annuity of \$5,200 per year for 20 years. Which is worth more if your mother can earn an annual rate of 6% on similar investments elsewhere?
17. You borrow \$6,145 now and agree to pay the loan off over the next ten years in ten equal annual payments, which include principal and 10% annually compounded interest on the unpaid balance. What will your annual payment be?
18. Ms. Mira Jones plans to deposit a fixed amount at the end of each month so that she can have \$1,000 once year hence. How much money would she have to save every month if the annual rate of interest is 12%?
19. You are planning to buy an annuity at the end of five years from now. The annuity will pay \$1,500 per quarter for the next four years after you buy it ($t = 6$–$9$). How much would you have to pay for this annuity in year 5 if the annual rate of interest is 8%?

20. Air Control Corporation wants to borrow \$22,500. The loan is repayable in 12 equal monthly installments of \$2,000. The corporate policy is to pay no more than an annual interest rate of 10%. Should Air Control accept this loan?
21. If John buys a house, which worth \$600,000, and he decides to put 20% down payments. In addition, he borrows \$480,000 from PNC bank with fixed annual rate 4% for 15 years. Please follow the procedure of constructing Exhibit 4.1 to calculate the fixed mortgage amortization table.

**Solution**

If $C$ represents the monthly payment of the 15-year fixed mortgage rate, then we can follow Eq. (4.6) to calculate C as follows.

$$4\%/12 = 0.3333\%$$

$$480{,}000 = C\left[\frac{1}{0.003333} - \frac{1}{0.003333(1+0.003333)^{180}}\right]$$

$$C = 3550.50$$

Then the fixed rate amortization table can be presented as the following table. The monthly mortgage payment (the second column of the amortization table) is \$3,550.5 for each of the 180 months. In each month, the mortgagor is scheduled to make both interest and principal payments. Initially, the interest payments are a very large proportion of the mortgage payment. Towards the termination of the mortgage, the interest payments are a very small proportion of the mortgage payment.

Table A Monthly Mortgage Amortization Table

| Month | Mortgage Payment | Interest Payment | Principal Payment | Principal Balance |
|---|---|---|---|---|
| 0 | | | | 480,000 |
| 1 | 3550.5 | 1600 | 1950.5 | 478,050 |
| 2 | 3550.5 | 1593.498 | 1957.002 | 476,092 |
| 3 | 3550.5 | 1586.975 | 1963.525 | 474,129 |
| . | . | . | . | . |
| . | . | . | . | . |
| 179 | 3550.5 | 23.55384 | 3526.946 | 3,539 |
| 180 | 3550.51 | 11.79735 | 3538.713 | 0 |

# Chapter 5

# Valuation of Bonds and Stocks

## Contents



## 5.1 Introduction

The main purpose of this chapter is to discuss how to use time value of money concepts and methods, which have been discussed in Chapter 4, to determine the valuation of bonds and stocks. Some bonds pay coupon interest annually, some semiannually, and some pay no coupon interest at all. Some stocks pay no dividends, others pay the same dollar amount each year as a dividend, and some pay dividends that change every year. How much should investors be willing to pay for these securities? And what price can issue corporations expect to receive in selling them? Fortunately, basic techniques exist to help us to value, or determine a price on these assets.

In Chapter 11, we will use the valuation of bonds and stocks to discuss capital structure and other related issues.

We know how the process of discounting allows us to determine the present value of a future cash flow. This technique can be applied to the valuation of any asset, real or financial. In this chapter, our aim is to apply this discounting principle to the valuation of financial assets, such as bonds, preferred stocks, and common stocks. We begin with Section 5.2 discussing bond valuation, followed by Section 5.3, which explores stock valuation. Section 5.4 discusses growth rate estimation and its application, and preferred stock valuation is discussed in Section 5.5. Section 5.6 discusses risk, return, and market efficiency. Section 5.7 provides application examples, and Section 5.8 summarizes the chapter. Appendix 5A talks about the derivation of dividend discount model.

## 5.2 Bond Valuation

A bond represents a liability of a firm or government entity that arises from borrowing money. A typical bond pays a set amount of interest each year and repays the principal amount of the loan at maturity. The valuation principle states that the bond's value equals the present value of these expected future cash flows.

Four factors affect bond valuation: the bond's yield to maturity, par value, maturity date, and coupon rate. The *yield to maturity* is the effective annual rate of return demanded by investors on bonds of a given maturity and risk. The face value of a bond is called the *par value*. In general, this is the amount of money that the issuer has initially borrowed and promised to repay at a future *maturity date*. Most U.S. corporate bonds have a par value of $1,000 per bond. The *coupon interest rate* is the percentage of the par value to be paid annually, as interest, to the bond holder.

Most U.S. corporate bonds make interest payments semiannually, that is, every six months. *Eurobonds*, which are bonds denominated in U.S. dollars issued by firms in financial markets outside the U.S., typically pay interest annually. A bond's maturity date, par value, and coupon rate are all disclosed to investors prior to purchase; for the most part, these items are fixed and do not change over the life of a bond issue. The yield to maturity changes, however, depending upon economic and financial trends, market expectations, and firm-specific information affecting risk.

Suppose that a bond with par (face) value $F$ is purchased today and that the bond matures in $N$ years. Let us assume that interest payments of dollar amount $I$ are to be made at the end of each of the next $N$ years. The bondholder will then receive a stream of $N$ annual payments of $I$ dollars, plus a payment of $F$ dollars at the end of the $N$th year. Using the rate of interest $k$ to discount future receipts, the present value of the bond is

$$\mathrm{PV} = \sum_{t=1}^{N} \frac{I}{(1+k)^t} + \frac{F}{(1+k)^N} \tag{5.1}$$

The first term on the right-hand side of Eq. (5.1) is the present value of the stream of interest payments, while the second term is the present value of the future receipt of the par amount.

### 5.2.1 *Present value of future cash flows*

Cash flows arise from the receipt of coupon interest every six months and from the par value at maturity. Thus, cash flows from a bond have two components. First, the coupon interest payments resemble an annuity that occurs every six months over the bond's life. Second, the par value payment is a lump sum or single payment made when the bond matures.

The annual interest payments on a bond equal the coupon rate multiplied by the par value. Thus, the amount of each semiannual coupon payment is half of this amount. For example, a 10% coupon bond pays annual interest of 0.10 times $1,000, or $100; each semiannual coupon payment is half of $100, or $50.

The easiest way to compute the present value, or price, of a bond is to divide the analysis into two simpler present value problems that we already know how to solve. The complex cash flow pattern shown can be separated into two familiar cash flow patterns: (1) an annuity (the coupon payments), and (2) a lump sum (the principal payment). The first step in determining a bond's price is to compute the present value of the coupon annuity; the second part of the analysis involves computing the present value of the par value. The price of the bond will be the sum of these two present value calculations, as shown in Eq. (5.2):

$$\text{Bond price} = \text{PVAN(Coupon)} + \text{PV(Par Value)} \tag{5.2}$$

**Example 5.1.** Eurobonds-Annual Coupons

**Q:** A Eurobond with a coupon rate of 8% pays interest annually, has a par value of \$1,000, and matures 7 years from now. What current market price would we expect for this bond, assuming that bonds of similar risk and maturity have a 10% yield to maturity?

**A:** To find the price of the bond, first find the present value of the coupon annuity and add it to the present value of the par value. With an 8% coupon rate, annual interest payments for the bond are 0.08 times \$1,000, or \$80; with interest paid annually, the size of the coupon annuity is \$80 per year. With seven years until maturity and a 10% yield to maturity, the present value of the coupon annuity is:

$$\text{PVAN}_{\text{coupon}} = \sum_{t=1}^{7} \frac{\$80}{(1+10\%)^t} = \$389.47$$

The present value of the par value is:

$$\text{PV}_{\text{par}} = \frac{\$1{,}000}{(1+10\%)^7} = \$513.16$$

Thus, the current market price of the bond should be \$389.47 plus 513.16, or \$902.63.

**Semiannual Coupon Payments.**

Semiannual coupon payments would change our analysis in Example 5.1. We know that when cash flows occur more frequently than once a year, adjustments must be made to $n$, the number of periods, and to $r$, the discount rate. The number of periods, $n$, becomes the number of years multiplied by the number of cash flows per year. The interest rate also will need to be adjusted to determine the appropriate periodic interest rate. The method by which we compute the periodic interest rate depends, however, upon which type of annual interest rate is quoted. Bonds can have two interest rates that reflect their annual returns: they can be based on the effective annual rate

(EAR), or they can be quoted based upon the annual percentage rate (APR) concept. We discuss each of these in turn.[1]

**EAR or Yield to Maturity.**

When the EAR is quoted for bonds, it is called the bond's yield to maturity (YTM) or market interest rate. To properly discount the semi-annual coupons, we must determine the periodic interest rate that corresponds to the EAR.

We can calculate the EAR as:

$$\text{EAR} = \text{YTM} = (1 + \text{Periodic interest rate})^m - 1$$

in order to solve for the periodic interest rate:

$$\text{Periodic interest rate} = (1 + YTM)^{1/m} - 1$$

If the yield to maturity is given as 10% for a bond that makes coupon payments semiannually, the appropriate discount rate is:

$$(1 + 0.10)^{1/2} - 1 = 0.04881 \text{ or } 4.881\% \text{ per period.}$$

Let's use this in an example.

**Example 5.2.** Computing Price Using the Yield to Maturity
Revise Example 5.1 to assume semiannual coupon payments, which is the norm with most bonds issued in the U.S. Let's assume a yield to maturity of 10%. Recall that the bond has an 8% coupon rate and par value of $1,000; it matures in 7 years.

**Q:** What is the present value (i.e., the current market price) of this bond?

**A:** Annual interest payments for this bond are $80, so the periodic cash flow is $40. The number of periods is 14 (seven years times 2). Since the yield to maturity is given, the periodic interest rate is:

$$(1 + 0.10)^{1/2} - 1 = 0.044881\% \, \text{per period}$$

---

[1]With annual coupons, the EAR and APR are identical, as no immediate cash flows occur during the year. When coupons are paid semiannually, the yield to maturity and stated annual interest rate differ; the reason for this is that the EAR calculation assumes period-by-period compounding of interest, whereas the APR calculation does not.

The present value of the coupon annuity is:

$$\text{PVAN}_{\text{coupon}} = \sum_{t=1}^{14} \frac{\$40}{(1+0.04481)^t} = \$398.98$$

The present value of the par value is:

$$\text{PV}_{\text{par}} = \frac{\$1{,}000}{(1+0.04481)^{14}} = \$513.16$$

Thus, the current market price of the bond should be \$398.98 plus 513.16, or \$912.14. This is higher than the price of the bond in Example 5.1, \$902.63, since one-half of each year's coupon payments occurs earlier. Since some cash flows arrive sooner, their present value is higher when they are discounted at the same yield to maturity.

It is important to note that the present value of the par value is \$513.16 in both Examples 5.1 and 5.2. Regardless of the frequency of the coupon cash flows, the present value of the par value remains the same. When the EAR is 10%, the \$1,000 lump sum cash flow seven years from now is worth \$513.16 in present value terms, regardless of the frequency of the coupon payments.

### APR or Stated Annual Interest Rate.

When the bond interest rate is quoted as an APR, it is called a *stated annual interest rate* or *nominal interest rate.*[2] Given an APR, the periodic interest rate is APR/m, where m represents the number of periods or cash flows in a year. Recall that the APR assumes no period-by-period compounding of cash flows, so it fails to account for interest-on-interest. If a bond has a coupon rate of 8% with semiannual coupon payments and has a nominal interest rate of 10%, the bond's periodic cash flows should be discounted at 10%/2 or 5% per six-month period.

[2]The stated rate convention arises from the long-standing use of bond table books by traders. These tables report the correct semiannual rate of return but then multiply it by 2. Thus, stated rates are similar in concept to APRs.

**Example 5.3.** Computing Price with a Stated Annual Rate
Suppose the bond in Example 5.2 had 10% stated annual interest rate. What should its price be?

With no other facts changing, the bond will still pay \$40 every six months over the next 14 periods (seven years). It will repay its \$1,000 par value at maturity. Since the stated annual rate is equivalent to an APR, the periodic interest rate will be APR/m, that is, 10%/ 2 or 5%. The present value of the coupon annuity is:

$$\text{PVAN}_{\text{coupon}} = \sum_{t=1}^{14} \frac{\$40}{(1+0.05)^t} = \$395.95$$

The present value of the par value is:

$$\text{PV}_{\text{par}} = \frac{\$1{,}000}{(1+0.05)^{14}} = \$505.07$$

The current market price of the bond will be \$395.95 plus \$505.07, or \$901.01.

Why is the market price of the bond in Example 5.3 less than the \$912.14 price found in Example 5.2? Because in Example 5.2, the 10% market interest rate represents an EAR. In Example 5.3, the 10% stated rate (or APR) is equivalent to a yield to maturity (or EAR) of:

$$\begin{aligned} \text{EAR} &= (1+r)^m - 1 = (1+0.10/2)^2 - 1 \\ &= (1+0.05)^2 - 1 = 0.1025 \text{ or } 10.25\% \end{aligned}$$

It is well known that higher discount rates lead to lower present values; in Example 5.3, a higher EAR or yield to maturity of 10.25% leads to a lower price.[3]

[3]The stated annual rate for the bond in Example 5.2 with a 10% yield to maturity is 4.881% × 2, or 9.762%. Thus, it can be said the bond in Example 5.2 has a 10% yield to maturity or a 9.762% stated annual rate. Both methods of quoting the interest rate result in a periodic rate of 4.881%. As far as the bond in Example 5.3 is concerned, it can be said that it has a 10% stated annual rate or a yield to maturity of 10.25%. Both methods of quoting the interest rate result in a periodic rate of 5%.

### 5.2.2 *Interest rate, yield to maturity, and bond price*

A bond that sells below par value, such as the one in Example 5.2, is said to be selling at a discount and is called a *discount bond.* Someone who purchases the discount bond in Example 5.2 today and holds it to maturity will receive, in addition to the stream of coupon interest payments, a gain of \$87.86, the difference between the bond's price (\$912.14) and its principal repayment (\$1,000).

A bond's price will reflect changes in market conditions while it remains outstanding with its fixed 8% coupon rate. The bond in the above example will no longer be attractive to investors when alternative investments yield 10%. The bond's market price will have to fall in order to offer buyers a combined return of 10% from the coupon payments and the par value.

If the market yield to maturity falls, to say 6.09%, the price of the seven-year bond in Example 5.2 will rise to \$1,112.96 (check this on your own!), a price above the par value. The price of a discount bond will rise as it nears maturity if the market rate remains the same, since at maturity its price will equal par value. When a bond's price exceeds its par value, it is said to be selling at a premium, and it is called a *premium bond.* The price of a premium bond will fall as it nears maturity if the market rate remains the same, since at maturity its price will equal its par value. The investor who holds the bond until maturity will receive the above–market coupon payments of 8% per year, offset by a loss of \$112.96 (the difference between its purchase price and par value). In most cases when the bond sells at a premium, interest rates have fallen after the bond's issue. This bond's 8% coupon rate makes it very attractive to investors; buying pressure increases its price until its overall yield matches the yield to maturity of 6.09% of other bonds of similar risk and maturity.

When they originally are issued, most bonds sell at prices close to par and offer coupon rates close to the market rates on bonds of similar maturity and risk. Over the life of a bond its price will fluctuate as a result of interest rate fluctuations in the economy. Our discussion of discounts and premiums shows that bond prices will vary inversely to, or in the opposite direction of, interest rates. As interest rates rise in the economy, bond prices fall; as interest rates fall, bond prices rise. Since one rises as the other falls, we call this relationship between bond prices and interest rates the "seesaw effect."

**Calculating a Yield to Maturity.**
Bond price quotes are available in the marketplace, either from bond dealers or from the daily price listings found in secondary sources, such as *The Wall Street Journal.* Both investors and financial managers must calculate the yield to maturity on bonds, given known par values, coupon rates, times to maturity, and current prices. The yield to maturity can be determined from the PVIFA and PVIF formulas we used to compute bond price:

$$\text{Price} = \text{PVAN(Coupon)} + \text{PV(Par value) or}$$

$$\text{Price} = \$CF/2\left[\frac{1-\left(\frac{1}{1+k}\right)^{n}}{k}\right] + \text{Par}\left[\frac{1}{(1+k)^{n}}\right] \tag{5.3}$$

"The relationship between Interest Rates and Bond Prices — The Seesaw Effect"

where $r$ represents the periodic interest rate and $n$ is the number of semiannual periods until the bond matures and $k$ is the periodic interest rate. The yield to maturity equals $(1 + k)^2 - 1$; the stated annual rate equals $k \times 2$. But mathematics offers no simple technique for computing $r$.

For those seeking a quick estimate of the return, the approximation method may be used. Here, the average annual dollar return to the investor of a bond that matures in $n$ years is the coupon payment plus a straight-line amortization of the bond's premium (or discount):

$$\text{Average annual dollar return} = \text{Annual coupon} + \frac{\text{Price} - \text{Par}}{n}$$

The average amount invested in the bond is the average of its purchase price and par value:

$$\text{Average investment} = \frac{\text{Par} + \text{Price}}{2}$$

The approximate yield to maturity is the ratio of the average annual dollar return to the average investment.

$$\text{Approximate yield to maturity} = \frac{\text{Annual coupon} + \frac{\text{Price} - \text{Par}}{n}}{\frac{\text{Par}+\text{Price}}{2}}$$

Calculators and spreadsheets usually use a trial-and-error method for computing values of $r$. Various values of $k$ are used until one is found, such that the present value of the cash flows equals the price within some (pre-specified) error range.

### 5.2.3 *Credit risk, interest rate risk, and reinvestment rate risk*

Basically, investors in domestic bonds face three types of risk: credit risk, interest rate risk, and reinvestment rate risk. Inventors in foreign bonds are subject to two additional risks: political risk and exchange rate risk.

#### 5.2.3.1 *Credit risk*

The cash flows received by bond market investors are not certain; like individuals, corporate debtors may pay interest payments late or not at all. They may fail to repay principal at maturity. To compensate investors for this credit or default risk, rates of return on corporate bonds are higher than those on government securities with the same terms to maturity. Government securities are presumed to be free of credit risk. In general, as investors perceive a higher likelihood of default, they demand higher default-risk premiums. Since perceptions of a bond's default risk may change over its term, the bond's yield to maturity also may change, even if all else remains constant. Firms, such as Moody's and Standard & Poor's, provide information on the riskiness of individual bond issues.

Examples of bond rating categories are presented in Table 5.1. Higher bond ratings imply a lower risk of default and, given the risk/return tradeoff, lower expected return (ER) to investors. Lower bond ratings imply a higher level of default risk and higher ER. Investment quality bonds have ratings of BBB (or Baa) or higher. They are called investment quality as some institutional investors, such as pension funds and insurance companies, restrict themselves to

Table 5.1 Examples of Bond Rating Categories.

| | **Moody's** | **Standard & Poor's** | **Former Standard & Poor's** |
|---|---|---|---|
| Best quality, smallest degree of risk | Aaa | AAA | AAA |
| High quality, slightly more long-term risk than top rating | Aa1 | AA+ | |
| | Aa2 | AA | |
| | Aa3 | AA– | |
| Upper-medium grade, possible impairment in the future | A1 | A+ | |
| | A2 | A | A |
| | A3 | A– | |
| Medium-grade, lack outstanding investment characteristics | Baa1 | BBB+ | |
| | Baa2 | BBB | BBB |
| | Baa3 | BBB– | |
| Speculative issues, protection may be very moderate | Ba1 | BB+ | |
| | Ba2 | BB | BB |
| | Ba3 | BB– | |
| Very speculative, may have small assurance of interest and principal payments | B1 | B+ | |
| | B2 | B | B |
| | B3 | B– | |
| Issues in poor standing, may be in default | Caa | CCC | CCC |
| Speculative in a high degree, with marked shortcomings | Ca | CC | CC |
| Lowest quality, poor prospects of attaining real investment standing | C | C | C |
| | | D | D |

investing only in these low-default risk issues. Noninvestment quality bonds are called junk bonds or high-yield bonds to reflect their higher risk and higher ERs.

#### 5.2.3.2 *Interest rate risk*

The general level of interest rates in an economy does not remain fixed; it fluctuates. For example, interest rates will change in response to changes in investors' expectations about future inflation rates. From the "seesaw effect" shown in Eq. (5.3), a rise in interest rates renders the fixed coupon interest payments on a bond less attractive, lowering its price. Therefore, bond holders are subject to the risk of capital loss from such interest rate changes should the bonds have to be sold prior to maturity.

A long term to maturity, all else being equal, increases the sensitivity of a bond's price to a given change in interest rates, as the discount rate change compounds over a longer time period. Similarly, a lower coupon rate also increases the sensitivity of the bond's price to market interest rate changes. This occurs since lower coupons bonds have most of their cash flow occurring further into the future, when the par value is paid.

Because of interest rate risk, investors will demand a larger risk premium for a bond whose price is especially sensitive to market interest rate changes. Hence, we would expect higher yield to maturity for long-term bonds with low coupon rates than for short-term bonds with high coupon rates. A bond's *duration* is a measure of a bond's sensitivity to market rate changes that takes maturity coupons and other factors into account. Duration is computed by means of a complicated-looking formula. The concept of duration will be discussed in the following part.

#### 5.2.3.3 *Bond returns and duration*

For a bond, "yield to maturity" and "total return" are two different concepts. Total return for a fixed-income investment includes not only the income yield but also the interest on reinvested interest and price changes.

Compounded interest is the largest return component for investors that purchase and hold on to long-term bonds until they mature. For short-term investors that buy a bond hoping to sell it quickly at a higher price, fluctuations in a bond's price caused by market interest rate or bond rating changes are the largest return component.

As we've seen in this chapter, a bond's price moves inversely to prevailing interest rates. A measure of the price sensitivity of a bond to interest rate changes is called the bond's *duration*. Higher duration bonds have larger price reactions to interest rate changes; lower duration bonds have smaller price reactions. One method of computing duration calculates it as the weighted average of the time to receive a bond's cash flows; the weights are present values of each cash flow (coupon interest and par value) divided by the bond's price.

The concept of duration has many applications; areas in which duration is used frequently include bank asset and liability management, investment analysis, and pension fund management. A common risk management technique in these areas is to set the duration of a pension fund's asset equal to the duration of its liabilities. This way, as market rates fluctuate, the market value of the asset and liabilities will rise or fall together. By trying to set asset and liability durations equal to each other, the equity, or net worth will be little affected by changing interest rates. A further detailed analysis of duration and the relationship between duration and yield to maturity can be found in Chapter 14. In addition, applications of duration and yield to maturity and bond valuation will be further discussed in Chapter 14.

#### 5.2.3.4 *Reinvestment rate risk*

The return that an investor receives from a bond investment equals the bond's yield to maturity or EAR only if the coupon payments can be reinvested at a rate equal to the bond's yield to maturity. Recall the form of the interest factor in bond price Eq. (5.3): $(1+k)^n$. This assumes that all the cash flows are reinvested at the periodic rate $k$. Should future coupons be reinvested at a lower rate, the investor's actual yield will be less than the bond's yield to maturity. Thus, *reinvestment rate risk* occurs when fluctuating interest rates cause coupon payments to be reinvested at different interest rates. Another illustration of reinvestment rate risk occurs when maturing bank certificates of deposit (CD) are rolled over into new CDs. The risk benefits the investor when the new CD rate is higher than the maturing CD rate; it works against the investor when the new CD rate is lower.

#### 5.2.3.5 *Risk of nondomestic bonds*

Investors in nondomestic securities face a number of risks beyond those of domestic securities. Among these are political risk and exchange rate risk. *Political risk* can affect a bond investor in a number of ways. A foreign government may block currency exchanges, preventing the investor from repatriating coupon income. Social unrest may lead a foreign corporation to default on its bonds. Of course, exchange rate changes will cause fluctuations in the values of cash flows in terms of U.S. dollars; this is called *exchange rate risk.*

### 5.2.4 *Zero-coupon bonds*

*Zero-coupon bonds* pay no coupon interest and provide only one cash flow: payment of their par value upon maturity. Treasury bills are a form of zero-coupon debt. An investor purchases a T-bill at a price below par and receives no interest or other cash flows until maturity. At that time, the investor receives the par value of the T-bill. The return on the security is the difference between its discount price and its par value.

There are two reasons for the popularity of zero coupon bonds: (1) the investor does not face a reinvestment rate risk (there are no cash flows to be reinvested, so as interest rates fluctuate the investor is not forced to invest the cash flow at lower rates of interest) and (2) for certain investors (for example, those with Individual Retirement Arrangements (IRAs)) the tax of the bond return can be deferred until some future date. As these bonds provide no cash flows to reinvest, investors effectively lock in a given yield to maturity. However, under IRAs regulations, investors must pay yearly taxes on the *implicit* interest paid by the bonds; the IRAs has special rules for determining this value. In essence, investors must pay taxes on income they have not received. Thus, zero-coupon bonds are mainly purchased by tax-exempt investors who pay no tax on their investment returns, such as pension funds.

Issuing a zero-coupon bond also helps lower borrowing costs for the firm. The original discount can be expensed for tax purposes on a straight-line basis over the life of the bond. Thus, rather than cash outflows from coupon interest payments, the issuing firm receives annual cash inflows from tax savings. However, the issuer must plan for a large capital requirement at the maturity of these bonds.

Present value calculations to determine the price of a zero-coupon bond are straight-forward, as the following example illustrates.

**Example 5.4.** Zeroing in on Bonds
A zero-coupon bond with a par value of \$1,000 has a maturity date seven years from now. At what price would this bond provide a yield to maturity to match the current market rate of 10%?

This problem requires finding the present value of a single future cash flow. The price will equal:

$$P = \$1{,}000 \times \frac{1}{(1 + 10\%)^7} = \$1{,}000 \times 0.51316 = \$513.16$$

The current price of this bond should be \$513.16.

## 5.3 Stock Valuation

We now turn to the valuation of common stock. A stockholder receives income from two sources: (1) dividend payments and (2) capital gain from the change in stock price (which can, of course, be negative). The price of common stock reflects investors' expectations of these two income sources.

The principle for determining an appropriate stock price is the same as that for determining a bond price: find the present value of expected future cash flows. With bonds, this is a relatively straightforward process; the typical corporate bond has a definite life, fixed coupon payments and par value, and an easily discernible yield to maturity or stated annual interest rate.

Equity offers no such certainty. Common and preferred stocks generally are assumed to have infinite lives. For common stock, relevant cash flows (divided payments) are variable and depend upon firm growth, profitability, and investment opportunities. Finally, each firm can have its own required rate of return. Despite these difficulties, in this section we shall see that the present value of all future dividends should equal a stock's current price, and that some simplifying assumptions can make the task of determining stock value much easier. Our discussion in this section focuses on common stock. As we shall see, the method for valuing preferred stock is a special case of common stock valuation.

It may seem rather strange to treat the stock price as nothing more than the present value of all future dividends. Who buys stock with no intention of ever selling it, even after retirement? Investors generally buy stock with the intention of selling it at some future time, ranging from a few hours to 30 years or longer. Despite the length of any one investor's time horizon, we can show that the current price of common stock should equal the present value of all future dividends.

Let the present value, or current market price, of a share of common stock be denoted by $P_0$. Let $d_0$, $d_1$, $d_2$, ..., be the successive annual dividends and $P_1$, $P_2$, ..., be the price per share of stock at the end of successive year. Suppose that a share of stock is held for one year. At this year's end, after receiving dividend payment $d_1$, the stockholder could sell the stock for an amount $P_1$. If these future ERs are discounted at the required rate of return, $k$, the present value of the investor's cash flows comes to:

$$P_0 = \frac{d_1}{(1+k)} + \frac{P_1}{(1+k)} \tag{5.4}$$

Suppose that someone else purchases the stock at price $P_1$ at the end of the first year and holds it for one year. The purchase price should equal:

$$P_1 = \frac{d_2}{(1+k)} + \frac{P_2}{(1+k)}$$

Substituting this information into Eq. (5.4) gives us:

$$P_0 = \frac{d_1}{(1+k)^1} + \frac{d_2}{(1+k)^2} + \frac{P_2}{(1+k)^2}$$

Continuing in this way, looking $N$ years into the future, we have:

$$P_0 = \frac{d_1}{(1+k)^1} + \frac{d_2}{(1+k)^2} + \cdots + \frac{d_n}{(1+k)^n} + \frac{P_n}{(1+k)^n} \tag{5.5}$$

If we continue this process indefinitely, the time horizon $N$ becomes infinitely large. In that case, the final term on the right-hand side of Eq. (5.5) approaches zero, that is selling the stock in an infinite future would be worth nothing in terms of its present value. And we have the final result:

$$P_0 = \sum_{t=1}^{\infty} \frac{d_t}{(1+k)^t} \tag{5.6}$$

The present value of a share of stock is the sum of all future dividend payments, discounted to the present. It does not depend on the investment horizon of any individual investor.

What if the analyst encounters a corporation that currently pays no dividends and has no plans to pay dividends in the foreseeable future? Is the value of this company's stock zero? — No! Several reasons support the intuitively obvious answer. Firstly, just because the firm has no plans to pay dividends does not mean that it never will. To finance rapid growth, young firms often retain all their earnings; when they mature, they often begin paying out a portion of earnings as dividends. Second, at the very least, the firm's stock should be worth the per-share liquidation value of its assets. Otherwise, an arbitrageur could buy all the outstanding stock to purchase the firm and then make a profit by selling its real assets piece-by-piece. Most firms' values as going concerns exceed their liquidation values; the price of any such firm will reflect its going-concern value.

As it stands, Eq. (5.6) is difficult to use, since it requires estimation of all future dividend payments and investors' required return on the stock. Matters can be simplified considerably if the analyst can assume that the firm's dividends will remain constant or will grow at a constant rate over time.

### 5.3.1 *Constant dividend growth rate model*

If the firm's dividends are expected to remain constant, so that $d_0 = d_1 = d_2, \ldots$, we can treat its stock as a perpetuity. This is how we value *preferred stock*. If a common stock is expected to have constant dividends, the valuation process is identical to that of preferred stock. The present value of a perpetuity is the cash flow divided by the discount rate. For stocks with constant dividends, this means Eq. (5.6) becomes $P_0 = d_0/k$ since

$$P_0 = d_0 \times \left[\sum_{t=1}^{\infty} \frac{1}{(1+k)^t}\right] \quad \text{and}$$

$$\left[\sum_{t=1}^{n} \frac{1}{(1+k)^t}\right] = \frac{1}{k}$$

Many firms have sales and earnings that increase over time; their dividends may arise, as well. If we assume that a firm's dividends grow at an annual rate of $g$ percent, next year's dividend, $d_1$, will be $d_0(1+g)$; the dividend in two years' time will be $d_0(1+g)^2$. Generalizing,

$$d_t = d_0(1+g)^t$$

Substituting this into Eq. (5.6) and doing some algebra gives an equation for the present value of all future dividends:

$$P_0 = \frac{d_1}{(k-g)} \tag{5.7}$$

(Derivation of Eq. (5.7) can be found in Appendix 5A.)

where $d_1$ is equal to the current dividend $d_0$ times $(1+g)$ or $d_1 = d_0(1+g)$. Or, still more generally, the price at any future time $t$ is given by (See Appendix 5A for derivation of this formula):

$$P_1 = \frac{d_{t+1}}{k-g} \tag{5.8}$$

where $d_{t+1} = d_t(1+g)$.

This result, known as the *Gordon model,* or the *constant dividend growth model,* provides a straightforward tool for common stock valuation. The main assumption of constant growth in dividends may not be realistic for a firm that is experiencing a period of high growth or negative growth (that is, declining revenues). Neither will constant dividend growth be a workable assumption for a firm whose dividends rise and fall over the business cycle. Therefore, a consequence of the Gordon model is that if the dividend growth rate and the discount rate $k$ remain constant, the price per share of stock grows at the same rate as dividend per share.

The constant dividend growth model reveals that the following three factors affect stock prices, ceteris paribus: (1) The higher the dividend, the higher the stock price; (2) The higher the dividend growth rate, the higher the stock price; (3) The lower the required rate of return $k$, the higher the stock price.

The constant dividend growth model also assumes a dividend-paying stock; the model cannot give a value for a stock that does not pay dividends. Also, in the denominations of both Eqs. (5.7) and (5.8), the required rate of return, $k$, must exceed the estimated growth rate, $g$. Otherwise, the formula gives a nonsense result.

Finally, the constant dividend growth model assumes estimates for $k$, the required rate of return, and $g$, the dividend growth rate. Some methods for estimating the growth rate, $g$, will be discussed in this chapter and Chapter 21, including the internal growth rate (the rate at which the firm can grow without raising outside financing) and the sustainable growth rate, which has been discussed in Appendix 2B of Chapter 2. These estimates must be used circumspectly.

**Example 5.5.** Constant Dividend Growth

A corporation is currently paying dividends of \$5 per share on its common stock, and dividends are expected to grow at an annual rate of 6%. If investors discount future receipts at an annual rate of 10%, compute the stock's price.

Using the notation of Eq. (5.7), we have $k = 0.10$, $g = 0.06$, and $d_0 = \$5$. Next year's dividend, $d_1$, is expected to equal \$5 (1+0.06) = \$5.30. Substituting these values into Eq. (5.7) gives us:

$$P_0 = \frac{5.30}{0.10 - 0.06} = \$132.50$$

Under these conditions, the stock should sell for \$132.50 per share.

A shareholder earns returns from both dividend payments and price changes. If dividend payments grow at a constant rate, what happens to the price of the stock? The Gordon model reveals that, if the dividend growth rate and the discount rate remain constant, the price per share of stock will grow at the same rate as dividends per share.

### 5.3.2 *Rate of return and required rate of return*

Share price provides only a step toward fully evaluating a stock investment. The analyst also must compare the investment to others based on rate of return. Suppose that share of stock is purchased at price $P_0$ and sold after one year at price $P_1$. The total return to the investor is the sum of the dividend payment, $d_1$, and the capital gain, so that:

$$\text{Return} = d_1 + (P_1 - P_0)$$

The annual rate of return on this investment is therefore:

$$\text{Rate of return} = \frac{d_1 + (P_1 - P_0)}{P_0} \tag{5.9}$$

We have just seen how the Gordon model implies that stock prices grow at constant rate $g$, so that:

$$P_1 = (1 + g)P_0$$

Substituting this information into Eq. (5.9), the required rate of return calculation becomes:

$$\text{Required rate of return} = \frac{d_1 + [(1+g)P_0 - P_0]}{P_0} = \frac{d_1 + gP_0}{P_0}$$

$$= \frac{d_1}{P_0} + g \tag{5.10}$$

which is the same result as solving Eq. (5.7) for $k$; the discount rate. *This shows that under the Gordon model, the discount rate for future cash flows (Eq. (5.7)) is the investors' expected rate of return (Eq. (5.10)).* The required rate of return is sometimes called the *market capitalization rate*. From Eq. (5.10), we see that the market capitalization rate is the sum of the *dividend* yield, $d_1/P_0$, and the dividend growth rate, $g$, which is the same as the capital gains rate.

**Example 5.6.** Rate of Return

A share of common stock currently sells for \$120. Current dividends of \$6 per share are expected to grow at 7% per year. Find the rate of return required by investors in the stock.

Using the notation of Eq. (5.10), we have $P_0 = \$120$, $g = 0.07$, $d_0 = \$6$, and $d_1 = \$6\ (1{+}0.07) = \$6.42$. Substituting this information into Eq. (5.10), we obtain:

$$k = \frac{\$6.42}{\$120} + 0.07 = 0.1235$$

Hence, the required annual rate of return is 12.35%.

Investors in common stocks face a number of risks that bond holders do not. This additional risk leads them to require a higher rate of return on a firm's stock than on its debt securities. For example, in the event of corporate failure, the claims of stockholders have lower priority than those of bond holders, so the former face a greater risk of loss than the latter. Dividends can be variable and omitted, whereas bond cash flows have a legal obligation to be met.

If the general level of interest rates rises, investors will demand a higher required rate of return on stocks to maintain their risk premium differential over debt securities. From Eq. (5.7), as $k$ rises, the stock price will fall. Therefore, stockholders risk capital loss from any general upward movement of market interest rate.

Also, future dividends, or dividend growth rates, are not known with certainty at the time the stock is purchased. Operating and financial leverage, as we saw in Appendix 2C in Chapter 2, lead to variations in earnings. If poor corporate performance or adverse general economic conditions lead investors to lower their expectations about future dividend payments, this will lower the present value of shares of the stock, leaving the stockholder with the risk of capital loss. As discussed in more detail in investments courses, stock analysts systematically review economic, industry, and firm conditions in great detail to gain insight into corporate growth prospects and the appropriate level of return that an investor should require of a stock.

The rate of return required by investors in a common stock reflects all of these potential risks. The difference in risk as compared to other investments will lead to investors to demand larger risk premiums and therefore higher required returns from common stock investments than from other, less risky investments.

### 5.3.3 *Supernormal growth stocks*

In formulating the Gordon model, it was assumed that dividends per share would grow at a constant rate, strictly less than the market capitalization rate. That is, $g > k$ in Eq. (5.7). In practice, a corporation in an emerging industry may experience, for an initial period, abnormally high, or *supernormal*, growth rates. We would not expect these growth rates to be maintained indefinitely; rather, the industry will eventually enter a mature state, where constant growth at a lower rate is a reasonable expectation. The Gordon model can be adapted to deal with such supernormal growth stocks. The initial period is treated separately, with the constant growth assumption applied only to the mature phase of development.

Suppose, for example, that supernormal growth is expected for three years and that, thereafter, dividends are expected to grow at annual rate $g$. The valuation formula then becomes

$$P_0 = \frac{d_1}{(1+k)^1} + \frac{d_2}{(1+k)^2} + \frac{d_3}{(1+k)^3} + \sum_{t=4}^{\infty} \frac{d_t}{(1+k)^t} \tag{5.11}$$

Substituting $d_{t+1} = (1+g)d_t$ for $t = 4, 5, 6, \ldots$, we then have

$$P_0 = \frac{d_1}{(1+k)^1} + \frac{d_2}{(1+k)^2} + \frac{d_3}{(1+k)^3} + \frac{d_4}{(1+k)^3(k-g)} \tag{5.12}$$

**Example 5.7.** Supernormal Growth Stocks

Over the first three years, a corporation is expected to pay dividends of \$5, \$6, and \$6.75 per share of common stock. Thereafter, dividends per share are expected to grow at an annual rate of 7.5%. If investors require an annual rate of return of 12.5%, find the present value of a share of this stock.

In the notation of Eqs. (5.10) and (5.11), we have $r = 0.125$; $g = 0.075$; $d_1 = \$5$; $d_2 = \$6$; $d_3 = \$6.75$; and $d_4 = (1 + 0.075)(6.75) = \$7.25625$. Using Eq. (5.11), the present value is

$$P_0 = \frac{5}{1.125} + \frac{6}{(1.125)^2} + \frac{6.75}{(1.125)^3} + \frac{7.25625}{(1.125)^3(0.125 - 0.075)} = \$115.85$$

Under our assumptions, a share of this stock should sell for \$115.85.

## 5.4 Growth Rate Estimation and its Application

The purpose of this section is to show how growth rates can be mathematically estimated. The application of these estimated growth rates is briefly discussed.

### 5.4.1 *Compound-sum method*

One method of estimating the growth rate it to use the compounding process. Both discrete and continuous compounding are basic concepts in financial management and investment analysis. These concepts are expressed mathematically in Eqs. (5.13) and (5.14):

$$P_n = P_0(1 + i)^n \tag{5.13}$$

$$P_n = P_0 e^{in} \tag{5.14}$$

where $P_0 =$ the price at time zero; $P_n =$ the price at time $n$; $i =$ the compound interest rate; $e =$ a constant roughly equal to 2.718; and $n =$ number of periods for interest payment

Equation (5.13) describes a discrete compounding process and Eq. (5.14) describes a continuous compounding process.

The relationship between Eqs. (5.13) and (5.14) can be illustrated by using an intermediate expression such as

$$P_n = P_0\left(1 + \frac{i}{m}\right)^{mn} \tag{5.15}$$

where $m$ is the frequency of compounding in each year. If $m = 4$, Eq. (5.15) is a quarterly compounding process; if $m = 365$, it describes a daily process; and if $m$ approaches infinity, it describes a continuous compounding process. Thus Eq. (5.15) can be derived from Eq. (5.16) in the following manner. Based upon the definition

$$\lim_{m\to\infty}\left(1+\frac{1}{m}\right)^{m} = e = 2.718 \tag{5.16}$$

Equation (5.15) can be rewritten as

$$\lim_{m\to\infty} P_n = \lim P_0\left(1+\frac{1}{m/i}\right)^{m/i(in)} = P_0 e^{in} \tag{5.17}$$

The growth rate of earnings or dividends can be estimated either mathematically or statistically. Mathematically, the growth rate can be estimated by using either Eqs. (5.13) or (5.14). Rewriting Eq. (5.13) using the symbol for growth rate, $g$, in place of $i$ gives:

$$P_n = P_0(1+g)^n \tag{5.18}$$

From Eq. (5.18), it is clear that

$$(1+g)^n = \frac{P_n}{P_0} \tag{5.19}$$

Given values for $P_0, P_n$, and $n$, and using a compound sum table, the value of $g$ can easily be obtained. This approach is called the *compound-sum method* for estimating growth rates. While the advantage of this method is its simplicity, it ignores other information between the first and last period.

Suppose there are two firms whose dividend payments patterns are as shown in Table 5.2, using the compound-sum method the growth rate of firm ABC can be calculated as

$$(1+g)^m = \frac{P_m}{P_0} = \frac{1.77}{1.00}$$

Table 5.2 Dividend Behavior of Firms ABC and XYZ in Dividends per Share (DPS, Dollars).

| Year | ABC | XYZ |
|---|---|---|
| 2005 | 1.00 | 1.00 |
| 2006 | 1.00 | 1.10 |
| 2007 | 1.00 | 1.21 |
| 2008 | 1.00 | 1.33 |
| 2009 | 1.00 | 1.46 |
| 2010 | 1.00 | 1.61 |
| 2011 | 1.77 | 1.77 |

Using a compound-sum table where $m = 6$ and interest factor $=$ 1.77, $g = 10\%$. The compound-sum method also yields a growth rate of 10% for firm XYZ. Yet it is clear that the dividend behavior of these firms is distinctly different when looking at the dividends per share in Table 5.2.

### 5.4.2 *Regression method*

To use all the information available to the security analysts, two regression equations can be employed. These equations can be derived from Eqs. (5.13) and (5.14) by letting $i = g$ and taking the logarithm (ln):

$$\ln P_n = \ln P_0 + n \ln(1+g) \tag{5.20}$$

$$\ln P_n = \ln P_0 + gn \tag{5.21}$$

Both Eqs. (5.20) and (5.21) indicate that $P_n$ is linearly related to $n$. Using the data in Table 5.2 for companies ABC and XYZ, we can estimate the growth rates for their respective dividend streams. Graphs of the regression equations for ABC and XYZ are shown in Figure 5.1. The slope of the regression using Eq. (5.20) for ABC shows an estimated value for growth of about 6%. The estimate for XYZ is 9.5%. If Eq. (5.21) had been used to estimate the growth, then the antilog of the regression slope estimate would equal the growth rate.

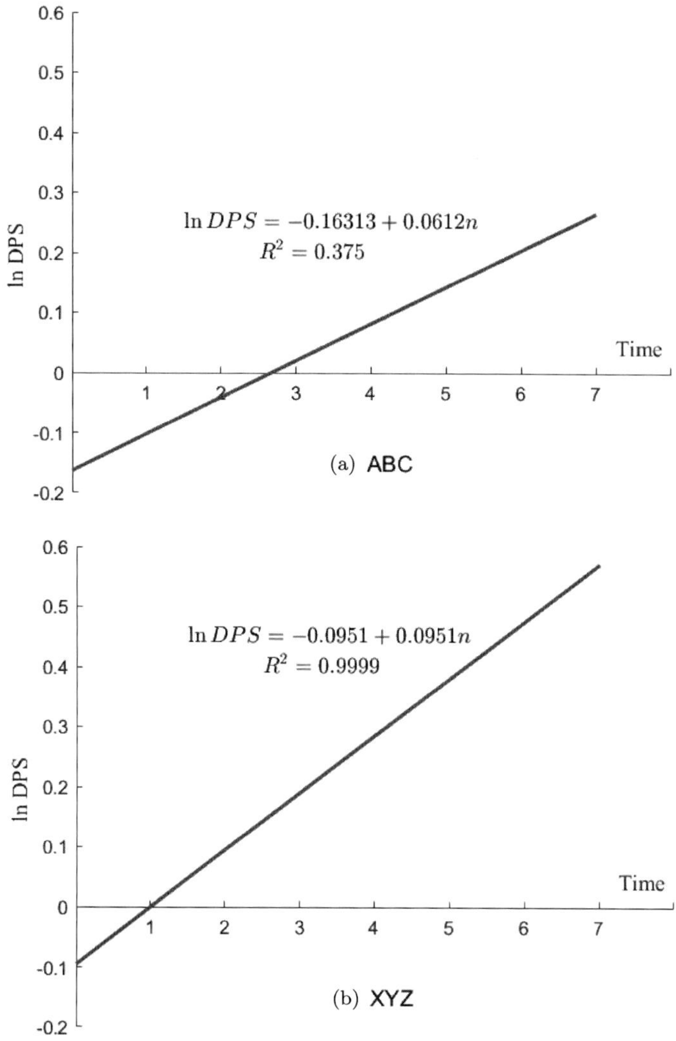


Figure 5.1 Regression Models for ABC and XYZ.

### 5.4.3 *One-period growth model*

Another method of estimating the growth rate involves the use of percentage change in some variable such as earnings per share, dividend per share, or price per share in a *one-period growth model.* The one-period growth model is the model in which the same growth will continue forever. If $b$ stands for the fraction of earnings retained within the firm (i.e., the retention rate), $r$ stands for the rate of return the firm will earn on all new investments, and $I_t$ stands for investment at $t$, a very simple expression for growth is obtained: growth in earnings arises from the return on new investments. Therefore, earnings can be written as

$$E_t = E_{t-1} + rI_{t-1} \tag{5.22}$$

where $E_t$ = earnings in period $t$; and $E_{t-1}$ = earnings in period $t-1$.

If the firm's retention rate is constant, then:

$$E_t = E_{t-1} + rbE_{t-1} = E_{t-1}(1 + rb) \tag{5.23}$$

Growth in earnings is the percentage change in earnings, or

$$\begin{aligned} g &= \frac{E_t - E_{t-1}}{E_{t-1}} = \frac{E_{t-1}(1 + rb) - E_{t-1}}{E_{t-1}} \\ &= rb \end{aligned} \tag{5.24}$$

Since a constant proportion of earnings is assumed to be paid out each year, the growth in earnings equals the growth in dividends, or

$$g_E = g_0 = rb$$

If firm M has a retention rate of 50% and an average return on investment of 20%, then the expected growth in dividends on earnings can be expressed as

$$g_E = g_0 = rb = (0.20)(0.50) = 0.1 \quad \text{or} \quad 10\%$$

Using this expression for growth, Eq. (5.8) can be rewritten as

$$P = \frac{D_1}{k - rb} \tag{5.25}$$

Alternatively, this model can be stated in terms of the capitalization rate:

$$k = \frac{D_1}{P_0} + rb \tag{5.26}$$

It is worthwhile to examine the implication of this model for the growth in stock prices over time. The growth in stock price is

$$g_P = \frac{P_{t+1} - P_t}{P_t} \tag{5.27}$$

Recognizing that $P_t$ and $P_{t+1}$ can be defined by Eq. (5.25), with the exception that $D_{t+1}$ must be replaced by $D(1+br)$:

$$g_P = br$$

Thus, under the assumption of a constant retention rate, for a one-period model, dividends, earnings, and prices are all expected to grow at the same rate.

Investors may use a one-period model in selecting stocks, but future profitability of investment opportunities plays an important role in determining the value of the firm and its earnings per share (EPS) and dividend per share (DPS). The rate of return on new investments can be expressed as a fraction, $c$ (perhaps larger than one), of the rate of return security holders require, or

$$r = ck$$

Substituting this into Eq. (5.26) and rearranging:

$$k = \frac{(1-b)E}{(1-cb)P_0} \tag{5.28}$$

If a firm has no extraordinary investment opportunities ($r = k$), then $c = 1$ and the rate of return that security holders require is simply the inverse of the stock's price/earnings ratio. On the other hand, if the firm has investment opportunities that are expected to offer a return above that required by the firm's stockholders ($c > 1$), the earnings/price ratio at which the firm sells will be below the rate of return required by investors.

An investor could predict next year's dividends, the firm's long-term growth rate, and the rate of return stockholders require for holding the stock. Equation (5.7) could then be solved for the theoretical price of the stock that could be compared with its present price. Stocks that have theoretical prices above actual price are candidates for purchase; those with theoretical prices below their actual price are candidates for sale or for short sale. Example 5.8 provides further illustration of the one-period growth model.

**Example 5.8.** The use of the one-period model can be illustrated by using the JNJ data from Table 5.3.

### Solution

At the end of 2018, JNJ's stock was selling for \$129.05 a share. The capitalization rate can be calculated using Eq. (5.26):

$$k = \frac{d_1}{P_0} + rb \quad \text{or} \quad k = \frac{d_1}{P_0} + g$$

The current dividend yield is expressed:

$$\frac{d_1}{P_0} = \frac{\$3.54}{\$129.05} = 0.0274 \quad \text{or} \quad 2.74\%$$

If JNJ's dividend is expected to grow at 10% per year:

$$k = 2.74 + 10.00$$

$$k = 12.74$$

Thus, the required rate of return as estimated is 12.74%.

Alternatively, Eq. (5.25) could be used to estimate the theoretical value of JNJ stock. If the dividend is expected to stay at \$3.54, and $k = 12.74$, then estimates for the retention rate and the ER for investment are required. For the sake of example, it is assumed that a retention rate of 50% and an ER from investment of 18% yields for $b$ times $r$. This gives an estimated value for the stock of

$$P = \frac{d_1}{k - br} = \frac{\$3.54}{0.1274 - 0.5 \times 0.18} = \$94.65$$

While JNJ's stock would seem to be overvalued selling at \$129.05 a share, notice the sensitivity of this valuation equation to both the estimate of the appropriate discount rate (required rate of return) and the estimate of the long-term growth rate. For example, if JNJ's required rate of return had been 11.74% rather than 12.74%, its theoretical price would have been \$129.05.

It seems logical to assume that firms that have grown at a very high rate will not continue to do so in the infinite future. Likewise, firms with very poor growth might improve in the future. Although a single growth rate could be found, it is difficult to estimate this single number. In order to give greater flexibility to this technique many analysts have turned to multiple period (two or three periods) growth-rate models. Each period has a specific growth rate associated with the firm's prospects in the short run and also the long run.

### 5.4.4 *Two-period growth model*

The simplest extension of the one-period model is to assume that a period of extraordinary growth will continue for a certain number of years, after which growth will change to a level at which it is expected to continue indefinitely. This kind of model is called the *two-period growth model.*

If it is assumed that the length of the first period is $n$ year, that the growth rate in the first period is $g_1$, and that $P_n$ is the price at the end of period $n$, the value of the stock can be written as

$$P = \frac{d_1}{1+k} + \frac{d_1(1+g_1)}{(1+k)^2} + \frac{d_1(1+g_1)^2}{(1+k)^3} + \cdots + \frac{d_1(1+g_1)^{n-1}}{(1+k)^n} + \frac{P_n}{(1+k)^n}$$

where $d_1$ = the current dividend per share; and $g_i$ = the growth rate during period $i$.

Using the formula for the sum of geometric progression as defined as the sum first term [1 − (common ratio)$^n$]/(1 − common ratio), where $n$ is the number of terms summed over, the value of the stock can be written as

$$P_0 = d_1 \left( \frac{1 - \left(\frac{1+g_1}{1+k}\right)^n}{k - g_1} \right) + \frac{P_n}{(1+k)^n} \tag{5.29}$$

After $n$ periods, it is assumed that the firm exhibits a constant growth forever. If $g_2$ is the growth in the second period and $d_{n+1}$ is the dividend in the $n+1$ period, then:

$$P_n = \frac{d_{n+1}}{k - g_2}$$

The dividend in the $n+1$ period can be expressed in terms of the dividend in first period:

$$d_{n+1} = d_1(1+g_1)^n(1+g_2)$$

Making substitutions for $P_n$ and $d_{n+1}$ the two-period model becomes:

$$P_0 = d_1 \left( \frac{1 - \left(\frac{(1+g_1)^n}{(1+k)^n}\right)}{k - g_1} \right) + \frac{d_1}{(k - g_2)} \left(\frac{1+g_1}{1+k}\right)^n (1+g_2) \tag{5.30}$$

This formula can easily be solved for the theoretical price of any stock. For example, Firm OPQ pays a dividend of \$1.00 per share which is expected to grow at 10% for five years and 5% thereafter.

The investors in OPQ require a rate of return of 15%. The current price of OPQ stocks using Eq. (5.30) should be

$$P = 1.00\left(\frac{1-\frac{(1+0.10)^5}{(1.15)^5}}{0.15-0.10}\right) + \frac{1.00}{0.15-0.05}\left(\frac{1+0.10}{1+0.15}\right)^5(1+0.05)$$

$$= 3.985 + 8.405 = \$12.39$$

### 5.4.5 *Three-period growth model*

A logical extension of the two-period model is the *three-period growth model*. The three-period growth model implies that there exist three different growth rates for the whole growth valuation process. The resulting model would assume that in the first period growth is expected to be constant at some level. A forecast must be of both the level of growth and the duration of period one. During period two, the growth changes from its value in period one to a different level. Both the duration and the pattern of change of growth in period two must be forecasted. The third and final period is the period of steady-state growth.

Look at Firm OPQ again. If instead of forecasting a growth rate of 5% during the second period, the three-period model is used to forecast at a 7% growth rate during the sixth through tenth years and at a 5% growth rate from the eleventh year thereafter, the price of OPQ stock can be calculated using Eq.(5.31).

$$P = d_1\left(\frac{1-\frac{(1+g_1)^n}{(1+k)^n}}{k-g_1}\right) + d_1(1+g_1)^n(1+g_2)\left(\frac{1-\frac{(1+g_2)^{M-n}}{(1+k)^{M-n}}}{k-g_2}\right)$$
$$+ \frac{D(1+g_1)^n(1+g_2)^{M-n}(1+g_3)}{(1+k)^M(k-g_3)} \tag{5.31}$$

where $M$ is the end of the second period and other terms are defined as before.

$$P = 1.00\left(\frac{1-\frac{(1.10)^5}{(1.15)^5}}{0.15-0.10}\right) + 1.00(1.10)^5(1.07)\left(\frac{1-\frac{(1.07)^5}{(1.15)^5}}{0.15-0.07}\right)$$

$$+\frac{1.00(1.1)^5(1.07)^5(1.05)}{(1.15)^{10}(0.15-0.05)}$$
$$= 3.985 + 6.520 + 5.862 = \$16.05$$

The additional information about the three periods of OPQ's growth yields a different answer for the theoretical market price of the shares. Since the firm experiences five years of growth at 7% during the second period, which is larger than the 5% growth assumed in the two-period model, the market price per share is \$3.66 per share higher when we use the three-period model.

In Example 5.9, a set of actual data is employed to show how these concepts can be used to help security analysts and portfolio managers analyze the expected value of a firm.

**Example 5.9.** To demonstrate how the concepts of growth rate and stock-valuation model discussed in the previous sections can analyze securities, the per-share values for price, earnings, and dividends of JNJ during 1997–2018 are used. (See Table 5.3.)

The mean and the SDs of the EPS are higher than the mean and SD of the DPS. As expected, on average JNJ earns more per share in earnings than they pay out in dividends; nevertheless, variability of the earnings stream is smaller than the variability of the dividend stream.

In comparing the dispersion of two different series there generally is a problem with simply comparing the magnitude of the respective SDs. The SD is an absolute measure of dispersion and as such is influenced by the numbers in the series. To compare the dispersion of two series, the CV, is usually employed. The CV is defined as the SD divided by the ER. The larger the CV, the greater the dispersion relative to the mean. In this case, the DPS still has a greater dispersion than the EPS series.

The expected value per share for JNJ is determined using the Gordon model as expressed in Eq. (5.31). To use this valuation approach, it is necessary to estimate the dividends per share in the next period, the capitalization rate, and the growth rate of dividends per share. The capitalization rate can be estimated by the earnings yield method, the weighted cost of capital method, or the capital asset pricing model (CAPM) method (discussed in Chapter 8). The

Table 5.3 Selected Financial Data for JNJ.

| Selected Financial Data for JNJ | | | | |
|---|---|---|---|---|
| **Year** | **Time X_1** | **EPS X_2** | **DPS X_3** | **PPS X_4** |
| 1997 | 1 | 2.41 | 0.85 | 65.88 |
| 1998 | 2 | 2.23 | 0.97 | 83.88 |
| 1999 | 3 | 2.94 | 1.09 | 93.25 |
| 2000 | 4 | 3.40 | 1.24 | 105.06 |
| 2001 | 5 | 1.84 | 0.70 | 59.10 |
| 2002 | 6 | 2.16 | 0.80 | 53.71 |
| 2003 | 7 | 2.40 | 0.93 | 51.66 |
| 2004 | 8 | 2.84 | 1.10 | 63.42 |
| 2005 | 9 | 3.46 | 1.28 | 60.10 |
| 2006 | 10 | 3.73 | 1.46 | 66.02 |
| 2007 | 11 | 3.63 | 1.62 | 66.70 |
| 2008 | 12 | 4.57 | 1.80 | 59.83 |
| 2009 | 13 | 4.40 | 1.93 | 64.41 |
| 2010 | 14 | 4.78 | 2.11 | 61.85 |
| 2011 | 15 | 3.49 | 2.25 | 65.58 |
| 2012 | 16 | 3.86 | 2.40 | 70.10 |
| 2013 | 17 | 4.81 | 2.59 | 91.59 |
| 2014 | 18 | 5.70 | 2.76 | 104.57 |
| 2015 | 19 | 5.48 | 2.95 | 102.72 |
| 2016 | 20 | 5.93 | 3.15 | 115.21 |
| 2017 | 21 | 0.47 | 3.32 | 139.72 |
| 2018 | 22 | 5.61 | 3.54 | 129.05 |
| Mean | | 3.6427 | 1.8550 | 80.6092 |
| Standard Deviation (SD) | | 1.4256 | 0.8986 | 25.5753 |
| Coefficient of Variation (CV) | | 0.3914 | 0.4844 | 0.3173 |

*Source*: Compustat

following numerical example uses a required return of 16% for JNJ and the compound-sum method of computing dividends per share growth rate. (Use of Eq. (5.20) yields a growth rate of 6.69%.) Substituting these values into Eq. (5.7) yields:

$$P_0 = \frac{3.54}{0.16 - 0.069} = \$38.06$$

This theoretical value is a smaller than the average price for the period (\$80.6092) and the current price (\$129.05). The primary

Table 5.4 Covariance Matrix.

| | **Time** | **EPS** | **DPS** | **PPS** | **lnEPS** | **lnDPS** | **lnPPS** |
|---|---|---|---|---|---|---|---|
| Time | 40.2500 | | | | | | |
| EPS | 5.0536 | 1.9401 | | | | | |
| DPS | 5.3516 | 0.6991 | 0.7708 | | | | |
| PPS | 88.9053 | 7.5722 | 16.0059 | 624.3639 | | | |
| lnEPS | 0.8821 | 0.6929 | 0.1135 | (1.2426) | 0.2914 | | |
| lnDPS | 3.0067 | 0.4349 | 0.4284 | 8.1082 | 0.0859 | 0.2479 | |
| lnPPS | 0.9842 | 0.1069 | 0.1820 | 7.1647 | (0.0040) | 0.0938 | 0.0835 |

Table 5.5 Correlation Matrix.

| | **Time** | **EPS** | **DPS** | **PPS** | **lnEPS** | **lnDPS** | **lnPPS** |
|---|---|---|---|---|---|---|---|
| Time | 1.0000 | | | | | | |
| EPS | 0.5719 | 1.0000 | | | | | |
| DPS | 0.9608 | 0.5717 | 1.0000 | | | | |
| PPS | 0.5608 | 0.2176 | 0.7296 | 1.0000 | | | |
| lnEPS | 0.2576 | 0.9216 | 0.2395 | (0.0921) | 1.0000 | | |
| lnDPS | 0.9519 | 0.6271 | 0.9801 | 0.6517 | 0.3195 | 1.0000 | |
| lnPPS | 0.5370 | 0.2658 | 0.7177 | 0.9925 | (0.0257) | 0.6518 | 1.0000 |

problems associated with this stock-valuation approach involve the adequacy of using averages of past data to estimate the future and using the compound-sum method to estimate the growth rate.

The data from Table 5.3 can be used to show how the growth rates of dividends and earnings per share can be estimates by the *regression method*. To estimate the related regression parameters and to provide a base for discussion of other implications, covariances and correlation coefficients for time, EPS, DPS, PPS, lnEPS, lnDPS, lnPPS are presented in Tables 5.4 and 5.5. The covariance matrix in Table 5.4 presents variances (elements on the diagonal) and covariances (elements off the diagonal). The correlation matrix in Table 5.5 presents correlation coefficients.

Conceptually, both the covariance and the correlation coefficient can be used to measure the extent to which two variables move together. The correlation coefficient is most commonly used because it is a standardized unit-free measure. Correlation coefficients range from −1.0 (perfect negative correlation) to +1.0 (perfect positive correlation). The concepts introduced here will be useful in understanding the diversification process discussed later in this book.

Some implications can be drawn from the size and the magnitude of the correlation coefficients in Table 5.5. The correlation coefficient between Time and PPS (column 1, row 4) is 0.5608, indicating that the price has increased over time. The coefficient between Time and DPS (column 1, row 3) is 0.9608, implying that dividends were generally increasing over time. The coefficient of correlation between Time and EPS (column 1, row 2) is 0.5719, which is positive, and this implies increased in earnings over time.

Following the format of Eqs. (5.31) and (5.32), the models for regressing lnEPS ($X_5$) and lnDPS ($X_6$) on time ($X_1$) can be defined:

$$X_5 = a_0 + a_1 X_1 + e_5 \tag{5.32}$$

$$X_6 = b_0 + b_1 X_1 + e_6 \tag{5.33}$$

where $a_0$, $a_1$ and $b_0, b_1$ = regression parameters; and $e_5$ and $e_6$ = error terms.

The formulas necessary to estimate the slopes $a_1$ and $b_1$ are represented by

$$a_1 = \text{COV}(X_1, X_5)/\text{Var}(X_1) \tag{5.34}$$

$$b_1 = \text{COV}(X_1, X_6)/\text{Var}(X_1) \tag{5.35}$$

Based on the information listed in Table 5.4, the estimates slopes are

$$a_1 = \frac{0.8821}{40.2500} = 0.0219\,(t\,\text{value} = 1.1921)$$

$$b_1 = \frac{3.0067}{40.2500} = 0.0747\,(t\,\text{value} = 13.8897)$$

The estimated student's $t$-statistic, shown in parentheses, is used to show whether the regression estimate is significantly different from zero. Given values of the regression estimate and the degrees of freedom, we see that $a_1$ is not significantly different from zero and that $b_1$ is statistically significant. This verifies the aforementioned implications, which were drawn from the correlation matrix — that is, the growth rate of earnings per share as estimated by $a_1$ is essentially zero (2.19%) and the growth rate of dividends per share as estimated by $b_1$ is positive at 7.47%.

Use of the regression-generated growth rate for dividends per share of 7.47% in the valuation equation yields:

$$P_0 = \frac{\$3.54}{0.16 - 0.0747} = \$41.50$$

which is closer to the average price for the period ($80.6092) and the 2018 price of $129.05 per share, compared to the result by the compound-sum method, i.e., $38.06. Thus, use of the regression method in this case is not as useful as the compound-sum method in valuing the shares of JNJ.

## 5.5 Preferred Stock Valuation

Most preferred stock entitles the stockholder to a fixed dividend payment in perpetuity. There is no opportunity for the dividend to grow, so the term $(1+g)^t$ is dropped from the valuation model. Denoting the annual dividend payment by $d_0$ and the required rate of return by $r$, we can substitute $d_0 = d_t$ for $t = 1, 2, 3, \ldots$, to obtain the preferred stock valuation:

$$P_0 = d_0 \sum_{t=1}^{\infty} \frac{1}{(1+k)^t} = \frac{d_0}{k} \tag{5.36}$$

**Example 5.10.** A share of preferred stock, yielding annual dividend payments of $5, sells $52. Find the rate of return required by investors in this stock.

The notation is $P_0 = \$52$ and $d_0 = \$5$. Because Eq. (5.36) implies

$$k = \frac{d_0}{P}$$

it follows that the required rate of return is

$$k = \frac{5}{52} = 0.0962$$

Therefore, investors in the stock require an annual rate of return of 9.62%.

In some instances, preferred stock contains a *participation provision.* In these cases, in addition to the fixed dividend, preferred stockholders are allocated a share of any dividend remaining after the common stockholders receive a common share dividend equal to the preferred payment. If there is such a participation provision, Eq. (5.36) is not appropriate for the valuation of preferred stock, because the dividend payments, $d$, will constitute only a lower limit on the dividend payments stockholders receive. We will not, however, pursue this elaboration in detail here.

An adjustable rate preferred stock (ARPS) is a recently developed financial instrument designed to place the risk of fluctuating interest rates on the investor. The ARPS concept allows the dividend rate on preferred stock to vary based on changes in the market rate of interest. For example, the ARPS rate may be set each quarter at 30 basis points above the 91-day Treasury bill rate, with an upper and lower bound, called a *collar*, set at some arbitrary level, such as 7% to 14%. ARPS appeals to corporate managers for two reasons: (1) dividends on ARPS, like the dividends on all preferred issues, enjoy an 80% exclusion from federal income tax, and (2) ARPS reflects current market return because of the quarterly adjustment in interest rates, thereby reducing the fluctuation in stock price.

The valuation of ARPS is different than the valuation shown in Eq. (5.36), as follows:

$$P_0 = \sum_{t=1}^{n} \frac{d_t}{(1+k)^t} + \frac{P_n}{(1+k)^n} \tag{5.37}$$

The major difference between Eqs. (5.36) and (5.37) is that in the case of preferred stock the $d$ is fixed, whereas for the ARPS the dividend is variable, $d_t$.

## 5.6 Risk, Return, and Market Efficiency

This chapter defines the value of an asset as the present value of the expected cash flows that arise from owning that asset. It is the size, timing, and risk of the cash flows that determine asset value.

To compute a present value, we need to know certain information in addition to the expected future cash flows from owning an asset. For example, we also must know the appropriate discount rate, or the required rate of return at which to discount expected cash flows back to the present. Chapter 8 will identify three components of required rate of return: the real risk-free rate of return, inflation expectations, and risk premium.

The first two components of required rate of return are the same for all investments; their combined effect is approximated by the yield on a short-term Treasury bill. Required returns differ as a result of different risk premiums; thus, finance professionals say that *risk drives return.* A low-risk investment will have a lower required return than a high-risk investment.

As security prices depend only on future expected cash flows and required returns, it stands to reason that prices should vary only because of changes in these variables. Should unexpected good news occur, such as higher than expected earnings or continued economic growth without expected inflationary pressures, we would expect to see asset prices rise. Should unforeseen bad news occur, such as higher than expected Federal Government budget deficits or lower than expected company sales, asset prices should fall.

Of course, the largest price changes affect the assets that are most sensitive to such news. Since the future cash flows of common stock are much less certain than those of bonds, we would expect common stock prices to be more sensitive than bond prices to news announcements. This sensitivity causes greater price swings and more price variability for stocks than for bonds. As compensation for this higher risk, investors demand higher risk premiums and higher required rates of return for common stock than for bonds. This suggests that stockholders should earn higher returns over time than owners of safer investments such as bonds.

### 5.6.1 *Historical returns and fluctuations*

Table 5.6 reports the average annual returns and SDs for different types of investments. The return distributions for small-company common stocks and all common stocks have large SDs, indicating much more risk than the bond investments. Clearly, however,

Table 5.6 Geometric Versus Arithmetic Average Returns: 1926–2011.

| Series | Geometric Mean (%) | Arithmetic Mean (%) | SD (%) |
|---|---|---|---|
| Small-company stocks | 11.9 | 16.5 | 32.5 |
| Large-company stocks | 9.8 | 11.8 | 20.3 |
| Long-term corporate bonds | 6.1 | 6.4 | 8.4 |
| Long-term government bonds | 5.7 | 6.1 | 9.8 |
| Intermediate-term government bonds | 5.4 | 5.5 | 5.7 |
| U.S. treasury bills | 3.6 | 3.6 | 3.1 |
| Inflation rate | 3.0 | 3.1 | 4.2 |

investors who undertake such risk earn higher rewards over the long haul, since stock returns reward investors more than conservative bond investments.

For an average risk stock under normal market conditions, the discount rate $k$ for finding the present value of future dividends should be close to the 12% compounded average annual rate of return earned by the stock market since 1926.

### 5.6.2 *Efficient capital markets*

Unexpectedly good or bad news can cause assets' prices to change. Good news surprises lead market participants either to reduce the risk premium they demand of an asset (thus decreasing its required return) or to increase their expectations for future cash flows. Either reaction leads to an increase in an asset's price. Bad news surprises lead the market to demand a higher risk premium (and required return) or to reduce its expectations for future cash flows; either reaction results in a falling asset price.

If a market adjusts prices quickly and in an unbiased manner after the arrival of important news surprises, it is said to be an *efficient market.* If the market for IBM stock is efficient, we should see a quick price change shortly after any announcement of an unexpected event that affects sales, earnings, or new products. A quick movement in the price of a stock such as IBM should take no longer than several minutes. After this price adjustment, future price changes should appear to be random. That is, initial price reaction to the news should be unbiased, or, on average, fully reflect the effects of the news. Every time IBM's stock price changes in reaction to new information, it should show no continuing tendency to rise or fall after the price adjustment. After new information hits the market and the price adjusts, no steady trend in either direction should persist.

Any consistent trend in the same direction as the price change would be evidence of an *inefficient market* that does not quickly and correctly process new information to properly determine asset prices. Likewise, evidence of price corrections or reversals after the immediate reaction to news implies an inefficient market that overreacts to news.

In an efficient market, it is difficult to consistently find stocks whose prices do not fairly reflect the present values of future expected cash flows. Prices will change only when the arrival of new information indicates that an upward or downward revision in this present value is appropriate.

This means that in an efficient market investor cannot consistently profit from trades made after new information arrives at the market. The price adjustment occurs so rapidly that no buy or sell order placed after the announcement can, in the long-run, result in return above the market's average return. An order to buy after the arrival of good news may result in large profits, but such a gain will occur only by chance, as will comparable losses. Stock price trends always return to their random ways after initially adjusting to the new information.

Efficient markets result from interactions among many market participants, all analyzing available information in pursuit of an advantage. Also, the information flows or news they analyze must be random, both in timing and content (i.e., in an efficient market, no one can consistently predict tomorrow's news). The profit motive leads investors to try to buy low and sell high on the basis of new information and their interpretation of it. Hordes of investors analyzing all available information about the economy and individual firms quickly identify incorrectly priced stocks; resulting market pressures immediately push those stocks to their correct prices. In an efficient market, this causes prices to move in a *random walk*, meaning that they appear to fluctuate randomly over time, driven by the random arrival of new information.

Although some studies refute this contention, the average performance of equity mutual funds usually is worse than that of overall market averages such as the S&P 500 on a year-by-year basis.

Based upon Fama (1970, 1991) and Bodie *et al.* (2018) different assumptions about information availability give rise to different types of market efficiency. A market in which prices reflect *all* public and privately available knowledge, including past and current information, is a *strong-form efficient market.* In such an efficient market, even corporate officers and other insiders cannot earn above-average, risk-adjusted profits from buying and selling stocks; even their detailed, exclusive information already is reflected in current stock prices. Few markets can ever pass the test of strong-form efficiency. U.S. laws prohibit *insider trading*, or trading based on important, nonpublic information. These laws reflect a public perception that it is unfair for someone with access to private information to use that position for their own profit. Remember that corporate officers should try to maximize shareholder wealth. Using inside information to benefit themselves at the expense of unknowing shareholders is a violation of the trust that should exist in the principal-agent relationships.

In a *semistrong-form efficient market*, all *public* information, both past and current, is reflected in asset prices. The U.S. stock market appears to be a fairly good example of a semistrong-form efficient market. For the most part, news about the economy or individual companies appears to produce quick stock price changes without subsequent trends or price reversals.

A *weak-form efficient market* is a market in which prices reflect all past information, such as information in last year's annual reports, previous earnings announcements, and other past news. Some investors, called *chartists* or *technicians,* examine graphs of past price movements, number of shares bought and sold, and other figures to try to predict future price movements. A weak-form efficient market implies that such investors are wasting their time; they cannot earn above-average, risk-adjusted profits by projecting past trends in market variables. Generally, evidence indicates that historical information is not helpful in predicting future stock price performance.

### 5.6.3 *Implications for financial managers*

Much evidence exists that the financial markets are fairly efficient. In terms of the above three categories, most researchers and analysts would conclude that the markets are generally semistrong-form efficient. Evidence shows that higher risk assets do earn higher returns and that stock price reactions to news events generally are rapid and unbiased (that is, no price drift occurs after the announcement).

This means that efficient markets provide valuable information to a firm's managers. Stock price adjustments in reaction to announcements by the firm tell managers if their decisions are perceived by the marketplace to be shareholder-wealth enhancing or destroying. Managers also can base their decisions on current market data, with a high degree of confidence that the interest rates the firm pays and the prices of its bonds and stocks reflect the current market opinion about the firm.

## 5.7 Application Examples

**1. Zero-Coupon Bond Yield.** Suppose a price quote specifies $250 for a zero-coupon bond with a par value of $1,000. The bond matures in 15 years. What is the yield to maturity on the bond, compounded annually?

A: We know that the present value is:

$$\text{PV} = \frac{\text{FV}}{(1+k)^n}$$

PV is the current price of $250; the future cash inflow is the par value of $1,000, paid at maturity. The number of years, $N$, is 15, and $r$ is the unknown. Plugging in the known information and solving for $r$, we obtain:

$$k = \left(\frac{1.000}{250}\right)^{\frac{1}{15}} - 1 = 1.0968 - 1 = 0.0968 \text{ or } 9.68\%$$

**2. Valuation.** Calculate the price of the following bond assuming that interest payments are made semi-annual and future cash flows are discounted at a 10% nominal annual rate.

| Par Value | Coupon Rate | Maturity |
|---|---|---|
| \$1,000 | 7% | 8 years |

A: Since coupons are paid semiannually, the number of periods is 8 years × 2, or 16. The nominal rate of APR of 10% means the periodic interest rate is 10/2% or 5%. Every six months, investors will receive an interest payment of [(0.07 × 1000)/2], or \$35. The bond's price will equal the present value of the coupon annuity plus the present value of the par value:

$$\text{Price} = \$35\left[\frac{1-\left(\frac{1}{1.05}\right)^{16}}{0.05}\right] + \$1{,}000\left(\frac{1}{1.05}\right)^{16}$$

$$= \$35(10.8377) + \$1{,}000(0.45811) = \$837.43$$

The bond should sell for \$837.43 in the market.

**3. Stock Valuation.** Ana List estimates that Mertz Company's dividend will grow at 5% a year into the foreseeable future. Mertz's dividend this year is \$1.80 a share.

a. If stock investors require a 15% return on stocks with Mertz's level of risk, what should the current price of Mertz stock be?
b. Suppose Mertz's price is \$25 a share and the current dividend is \$1.80 a share. If investors require a 15% return, what is the market's estimate for Mertz's constant dividend growth rate?

A: a. Since dividends are assumed to grow at a constant rate of 5% annually, we can use the constant dividend growth model. The current dividend is \$1.80; the required return is 15%; and the growth rate is 5%. Our estimate of Mertz's stock price will be:

$$P_0 = \frac{d_1}{k-g} = \frac{(\$1.80)(1.05)}{0.15-0.05} = \frac{\$1.89}{0.10} = \$18.90$$

According to this data, Mertz's stock should be \$18.90.

b. Here we are given the current market price and dividend, and the required return. We can work backward to determine the constant growth rate that is constant with this data:

$$P_0 = \frac{d_1}{k-g} = \frac{(\$1.80)(1+g)}{0.15-g} = \$25$$

Multiplying through and solving for $g$, the growth rate, we have:

$$\begin{aligned} \$1.80 + \$1.80(g) &= \$3.75 - \$25(g) \\ \$26.80(g) &= \$1.95 \\ g &= 0.73 \quad \text{or} \quad 7.3\% \end{aligned}$$

The market anticipates a 7.3% constant growth rate in Mertz's dividend into the foreseeable future.

## 5.8 Summary

A variety of factors influence the values of bond and stock issues. In assessing the values of these investments, we can use the notion of present value, discounting future cash flows at some appropriate discount rate. The rate at which the market discounts an investment's expected future receipts depends on its perceived degree of risk. More risk leads the market to demand a higher expected rate of return.

An analyst computes the price of a bond from its par value, term to maturity, coupon payments, and periodic interest rate. When computing prices, it is important to distinguish between the stated or nominal annual interest rate on a bond, which is similar to an APR, and the bond's yield to maturity, which is similar to an EAR.

The value of a share of common stock is the present value of all future dividend payments per share. The price of the stock will depend upon investors' perception of its risk and expectations about future dividend growth.

New information affecting future cash flows and investors' required rates of return will result in changes in asset prices. How quickly those price changes occur will depend on the efficiency of the market. In a strong-form efficient market, prices reflect all public and private information. In a semistrong-form efficient market, all past and current public information is reflected in current prices. In contrast, a weak-form efficient market reflects only past information.

## References

Babcock, G. C. "Duration as a Link between Yield and Value," *The Journal of Portfolio Management*, 10(4) (1984, pp. 58–65).

Bierwag, G. O., G. G. Kaufman and A. Toevs. "Single-Factor Duration Models in a Discrete General Equilibrium Framework," *The Journal of Finance*, 37 (May 1982, pp. 325–338).

Bodie, Z., A. Kane and A. Marcus. *Investments.* 11th edn. (McGraw-Hill/Irwin, 2018).

Cox, J., J. E. Ingersoll and S. A. Ross. "Duration and Measurement of Basis Risk," *Journal of Business*, 52 (January 1979, pp. 51–61).

Fama, E. "Efficient Capital Markets: A Review of Theory and Empirical Work," *The Journal of Finance*, 25 (May 1970, pp. 383–417).

Fama, E. "Efficient Capital Markets: II," *The Journal of Finance*, 25 (December 1991, pp. 1575–1617).

Reilly, F. K. and R. Sidhu, "The Many Uses of Bond Duration," *Financial Analysts Journal*, 36(4) (July–August 1980: pp. 58–72).

Hopewell, M. and G. G. Kaufman. "Bond Price Volatility and Terms to Maturity: A Generalized Respecification," *American Economic Review*, 63 (September 1973, pp. 749–753).

Lee, C. F. and A. C. Lee, *Encyclopedia of Finance*, 3rd edn. (Springer, 2022, forthcoming).

Lee, C. F., J. E. Finnerty, J. Lee, A. C. Lee and D. Wort. *Security Analysis and Portfolio Management, and Financial Derivatives* (World Scientific: Singapore, 2013).

Lee, C. F., J. C. Lee, J. R. Chang and T. Tai. *Essentials of Excel, Excel VBA, SAS and Minitab for Statistical and Financial Analyses* (Springer International Publishing, 2016.)

Lee, C. F., J. C. Lee and A. C. Lee. *Statistics for Business and Financial Economics*, 3rd edn. (Springer Academic Publishers, 2013).

Malkiel, B. "Expectations, Bond Prices, and the Term Structure of Interest Rates," *Quarterly Journal of Economics*, 76 (May 1962,

pp. 197–218).
Saunders, A. and M. Cornett. *Financial Institutions Management: A Risk Management Approach*, 10th edn. (McGraw-Hill/Irwin, 2021).

## Appendix 5A — Derivation of Dividend Discount Model

### 5A.1 Summation of Infinite Geometric Series

Summation of geometric series can be defined as:

$$\mathrm{S} = \mathrm{A} + \mathrm{AR} + \mathrm{AR}^2 + \cdots + \mathrm{AR}^{n-1} \tag{5.1A}$$

Multiply both sides of Eq. (5.1A) by R, we obtain

$$\mathrm{RS} = \mathrm{AR} + \mathrm{AR}^2 + \cdots + \mathrm{AR}^{n-1} + \mathrm{AR}^n \tag{5.2A}$$

Subtract Eq. (5.1A) by Eq. (5.2A), we obtain

$$\mathrm{S} - \mathrm{RS} = \mathrm{A} - \mathrm{AR}^n$$

It can be shown

$$\mathrm{S} = \frac{\mathrm{A}(1 - \mathrm{R}^n)}{1 - \mathrm{R}} \tag{5.3A}$$

If R is smaller than 1, and $n$ approaches to $\infty$, then $\mathrm{R}^n$ approaches to 0. i.e.,

$$\mathrm{S}_\infty = \mathrm{A} + \mathrm{AR} + \mathrm{AR}^2 + \cdots + \mathrm{AR}^{n-1} + \cdots + \mathrm{AR}^\infty \tag{5.4A}$$

Then

$$\mathrm{S}_\infty = \frac{\mathrm{A}}{1 - \mathrm{R}} \tag{5.5A}$$

### 5A.2 Dividend Discount Model

Dividend Discount Model can be defined as:

$$P_0 = \frac{D_1}{1+k} + \frac{D_2}{(1+k)^2} + \frac{D_3}{(1+k)^3} + \cdots, \tag{5.6A}$$

where $P_0$ = Present value of stock price per share

$D_t$ = dividend per share in period $t$ $(t = 1, 2, \cdots, n)$.

If dividends grow at a constant rate, say $g$, then, $D_2 = D_1(1+\text{g})$, $D_3 = D_2(1+g) = D_1(1+g)^2$, and so on.

Then, Eq. (5.6A) can be rewritten as:

$$P_0 = \frac{D_1}{1+k} + \frac{D_1(1+g)}{(1+k)^2} + \frac{D_1(1+g)^2}{(1+k)^3} + \cdots \text{ or}$$

$$P_0 = 7\frac{D_1}{1+k} + \frac{D_1}{1+k} \times \frac{(1+g)}{(1+k)} + \frac{D_1}{1+k} \times \frac{(1+g)^2}{(1+k)^2} + \cdots$$

Comparing Eq. (5.7A) with Eq. (5.4A),

i.e., $P_0 = S_\infty$, $\frac{D_1}{1+k} = \text{A}$, and $\frac{1+g}{1+k} = R$ as in the Eq. (5.4A).

Therefore, if $\frac{1+g}{1+k} < 1$ or if $k > g$, we can use Eq. (5.5A) to find out $P_0$

i.e.,

$$P_0 = \frac{D_1/(1+k)}{1-[(1+g)/(1+k)]} = \frac{D_1/(1+k)}{[1+k-(1+g)/(1+k)]}$$

$$= \frac{D_1/(1+k)}{(k-g)/(1+k)} = \frac{D_1}{(k-g)} = \frac{D_0(1+g)}{k-g}$$

.

## Questions and Problems

1. Define the following terms.

   a. Face value or par value of a bond
   b. Coupon rate
   c. Yield to maturity
   d. Zero coupon bond

2. What happens to bonds prices as interest rates rise? Does this relationship change as the term to maturity increases? When will a bond sell for a discount? When will it sell at a premium?
3. What is the relationship between stock prices and the growth rate of dividends?

4. Suppose you wish to value, in U.S. dollar terms, the cash flows from a German bond that is denominated in Deutsche marks. How can the process of bond valuation in this chapter be adapted to take non-U.S. dollar cash flows into consideration?
5. What is reinvestment rate risk? How is it related to interest rate risk? How is it different from interest rate risk?
6. Describe what is meant by an "efficient market." What are the expected characteristics on an efficient market? Can a market be weakly efficient by not semistrong efficient? Why or why not?
7. What is insider trading? Why might some argue that insider trading should be illegal? Why might some argue that it should be legal? Why might insider trading be more of a concern for stock investors than bond investors?
8. (CFA Level I exam, 1993) Assuming all other factors remain unchanged, which one of the following would reduce a firm's price/earnings ratio? Explain.
   a. The dividend payout ratio increases.
   b. Investors become less risk averse.
   c. The level of inflation is expected to decline.
   d. The yield on treasury bills increases.
9. (CFA Level I exam, 1993) The semistrong form of the efficient market hypothesis asserts that stock prices:
   a. fully reflect all historical price information
   b. fully reflect all publicly available information
   c. fully reflect all relevant information including insider information
   d. may be predictable
10. (CFA Level I exam, 1993) Assume that a company announces an unexpectedly large cash dividend to its shareholders. In an efficient market without information leakage, one might expect:
    a. an abnormal price change at the announcement
    b. an abnormal price increase before the announcement
    c. an abnormal price decrease after the announcement
    d. no abnormal price change before or after the announcement

11. (CFA Level I exam, 1993) Which one of the following would provide evidence against the semistrong form of the efficient market theory? Explain.
    a. About 50% of pension funds outperform the market in any year.
    b. All investors have learned to exploit signals about future performance.
    c. Trend analysis is worthless in determining stock prices.
    d. Low P/E stocks tend to have positive abnormal returns over the long-run.
12. (CFA Level I exam, 1992). List and briefly define the three forms of the efficient market hypothesis.
13. **Bond Valuation.** Yukon Mining Co. bonds have a par value of $1,000 and a 13-year percent coupon rate; they pay interest semiannually. Bonds with similar ratings have a 12% yield to maturity. If the bond has 15 years until maturity, what is its value?
14. **Yield to Maturity.** Find the yield to maturity on a zero coupon bond that has a $10,000 maturity value, matures in 20 years, and is currently selling for $1,250.
15. **Bond Valuation.** A corporate bond can be issued either at par, at a discount, or at a premium. ABC Company would like to issue a new corporate bond that will mature in 10 years and the discount rate for this bond is $r = 15\%$. Assume annual coupon payments. (a) What is the coupon rate needed for this bond to be issued at par? (b) If the par value of this bond is $1,000 and the coupon rate is 10%, then what is the bond's market value?
16. **Yield to Maturity.** HDTV, Inc., bonds are currently selling for $776 with a coupon rate of 9% and a maturity of 20 years. What is the yield to maturity, assuming annual coupons?
17. **YTM and the State Annual Rate.** Global Company has a Eurobond issue outstanding. It has a $900 market value. It matures in 5 years, pays an 8.5% coupon, and has a par value of $1,000. What is the bond's yield to maturity? Its stated annual rate?

18. **Constant Dividends.** Safety, Inc., has a policy of paying dividends of \$5 per share every year. This policy is not expected to change. What is the value of this stock of you require a 15% return?
19. **Stock Valuation.** CD Technologies anticipates constant dividend growth of 15%. The market currently requires a return of 22% on similar securities.

    (a) If next year's dividend is predicated to be \$1.75 per share, what is the current price of the stock? (b) What will be the price of the stock in year 5?

20. **Dividends per Share.** Reilly's Franks has an expected dividend growth rate of 3% and investors require an 11% return on their investment in Reilly's stock. If Reilly's has a current stock price of \$45, what is its current dividend? What is next year's expected dividend?
21. **Required Rate of Return.** Suppose ABC Company stock is currently selling for \$50 per share and pays a constant dividend of \$4 per share every year. What is the required return on this stock?
22. **Dividend Yield.** Suppose XYZ, Inc., stock is currently selling for \$72 per share and this year's dividend is \$6.25. What is the dividend yield on this stock?
23. **Growth Rate of Dividend.** Top Spin Tennis, Inc., stock is currently selling for \$100 per share and has just paid a dividend of \$6. Assume stockholders require a 10% return. If dividends are expected to grow at a constant rate, what is the growth rate of Top Spin dividends?
24. **Required Rate of Return.** Suppose LMNO Company has just paid a dividend of \$5. Dividends are expected to grow at a constant rate of 6% and the current price of the stock is \$132.50. What is the ER on the stock?
25. **Stock Valuation.** (CFA Level I exam, 1992) Peggy Mulroney recalled from her CFA studies that the constant dividend growth model was one way to arrive at a valuation for a company's common stock. She collected current dividend and stock price data for Eastover, shown below:

| | Current Share Price | Current Dividends Per Share | 1992 EPS Estimate | Current Book Value Per Share |
|---|---|---|---|---|
| Eastover | $28 | $1.20 | $1.60 | $17.32 |

a. Using 11% as the required rate of return (i.e., discount rate) and a projected growth rate of 8%, compute a constant dividend growth model value for Eastover's stock and compare the computed value for Eastover to its stock price indicated above.

b. Mulroney's supervisor commented that a two-stage constant dividend growth model may be more appropriate for companies such as Eastover. Mulroney believes that Eastover could grow more rapidly over the next three years and then settle in at a lower but sustainable rate of growth beyond 1994. Her estimates are shown below:

| Projected Growth Rates | |
|---|---|
| **Next 3 Years (1992, 1993, 1994)** | **Growth Beyond 1994** |
| 12% | 8% |

Using 11% as the required rate of return, compute the two-stage DDM value of Eastover's stock and compare that value to its stock price indicated above. Show calculations.

26. **Required Rate of Return.** (CFA Level I exam, 19990) The constant dividend growth model can be used both for the valuation of companies and for the estimation of the long-term total return of a stock. Assume:

$20 = The price of a stock today
8% = The expected growth rate of dividends
$0.60 = The annual dividend one year forward

a. Using only the above data, compute the expected long-term total return on the stock using the constant dividend growth model.
b. Briefly discuss three disadvantages of the constant growth dividend discount model.

27. **Yield to Maturity.** (CFA Level I exam, 1990) What is the yield to maturity of a bond with a 12% coupon, 10 years to maturity, and a price of $880? What assumptions must you make in order to solve for the yield to maturity?
28. **Bond Valuation.** (CFA Level I exam, 1990) Consider a five-year bond with a 10% coupon that has a present yield to maturity of 8%. If interest rates remain constant, what will be the price of the bond one year from now?
29. **Stock Valuation.** The Japanese Motor Company's stock is selling for 20,000 and pays a dividend of 1,000 annually. The dividend is expected to grow at a 5% annual rate. If the spot exchange rate is 110/$, what is the current U.S. price for the stock?
30. **Stock Valuation.** Gordon's Biscuit Company has just paid its shareholders a $5 dividend. Analysts expect the dividend to grow at a 10% rate into the foreseeable future. Investors require a 15 percent return on this stock.

    a. What should be the current price of Gordon's stock?
    b. What is the present value of the dividend over the next five years? What percentage is this of Gordon's current price?

31. Calculate the present value of each of the following bonds, assuming that interest payments are made annually at the end of the year and future receipts are discounted at 10% per annum.

| **Bond Bond** | **Par ($)** | **Coupon Rate (%)** | **Maturity (in Years)** |
|---|---|---|---|
| A | 1,000 | 12 | 3 |
| B | 1,000 | 10 | 4 |
| C | 1,000 | 9 | 5 |

32. XYZ Company's dividends per share are expected to grow indefinitely by 5% a year.

    a. If this year's dividend is \$5 payable at year end and the market capitalization race is 10%, what is the current stock price of XYZ Company?
    b. If this year's dividend is \$7 and the current market price is \$100, what is the market capitalization rate?

33. ABC Company has a retention ratio of 60% of earnings, which is expected to continue. Financial analysts predict that ABC's earnings per share next year will be \$12 and the company's investments will yield an annual rate of return of 20%. ABC's market capitalization rate is 15% per annum,

    a. What is the payout ratio?
    b. What is the present value of ABC's stock?
    c. How much of this present value should be attributed to future productive growth potential?
    d. What is the growth rate of dividends?
    e. How much will the expected dividend be five years from now?

34. This year, Alvarez, Inc. paid a dividend of \$2 on its common stock. It is predicted that dividends will grow at a rate of 5% a year in perpetuity. If the stockholders require a rate of return of 10% on their investment in Alvarez, how much would you pay for this stock?
35. You just bought a 10-year bond from ABC Company, with a par value of \$1,000 and a coupon rate of 10%. If another investor wants to exchange 20 shares of ABC's stock for your bond, what would you do? (Assume the appropriate discount rate is 15%.) The price of stock is equal to \$12 per share.
36. Zelta's bonds have a coupon rate of 10%, a par value of \$1,000, and five years remaining until maturity.

    a. If the bonds have a current (present) market value of \$850, what is the yield to maturity?
    b. If the bonds have a current yield to maturity of 8% what is the value of the bonds?

37. XYZ's common stock recently paid a dividend of \$1.50 (at $t = 0$) and has a current market price of \$24 per share. Dividends are

expected to grow at 8% indefinitely. What is the yield on the stock?

38. Jenner's common stock is currently selling at \$30 per share. Dividends of \$1 are expected to be paid at the end of the year ($t = 1$). The required rate of return on this stock is 12%.
    a. If dividends are expected to grow at a 10% rate indefinitely, find the value of the stock.
    b. If dividends are expected to grow at a 15% rate over the next three years, then at 11% for years 4 and 5, and 6% forever beginning in year 6:

    (1) Find the dividends for years 1 through 6.
    (2) Find the value of the stock at the end of year 5.
    (3) Find the value of the stock at the end of year 3.
    (4) Find the value of the stock now at $t = 0$.
    (5) Does the current value of the stock change if you plan on selling it at the end of year 5? at the end of year 3? Explain.

39. Find the yield on a zero coupon bond which currently sells for \$800 and has four years remaining until maturity at which time the holder of the bond will be paid the \$1,000 par value.
40. Carey Smith is considering investing in some preferred stock which pays an 8% dividend on a par value of \$100. If Carey's required rate of return on this type of investment is 9%, how much should she be willing to pay for it now?

# PART III

# Capital Budgeting and Risk Return Trade-off

## Chapter 6

# Capital Budgeting Under Certainty

### Contents



## 6.1 Introduction

To begin an examination of the issues in capital budgeting, we will assume certainty in both the cash flows and the cost of funds. Later, in Chapter 9, these assumptions will be relaxed to deal with uncertainty in estimation, and with the problems involved with inflation.

First, we will discuss a brief overview of the capital budgeting process in Section 6.2. Issues related to using cash flows to evaluate alternative projects will be discussed in Section 6.3. Alternative capital budgeting methods will be investigated in Section 6.4. Comparison of NPV and IRR methods will be explored in Section 6.5. Problems related to differences in economic life will be investigated in Section 6.6. A linear-programming method for capital rationing will be discussed in detail in Section 6.7. Finally, results of this chapter will be summarized in Section 6.8. Appendix 6A gives a manager's view on alternative capital budgeting models, Appendix 6B discusses derivation of crossover rate, Appendix 6C uses Excel to calculate NPV and IRR, and Appendix 6D solves the linear program model for capital rationing.

## 6.2 The Capital Budgeting Process

In his article "Myopia, Capital Budgeting and Decision Making," George Pinches (1982) assesses capital budgeting from both the academic and the practitioner's point of view. He presents a framework for discussion of the capital budgeting process, which we use in this chapter.

Capital budgeting techniques can be used for very simple "operational" decisions concerning whether to replace existing equipment, or they may be used in larger, more "strategic" decisions concerning acquisition or divestiture of a firm or division, expansion into a new product line, or increasing capacity.

The dividing line between operational and strategic decisions varies greatly depending on the organization and its circumstances. The same analytical techniques can be used in either circumstance, but the amount of information required and the degree of confidence in the results of the analysis depend on whether an operational or a strategic decision is being made. Many firms do not require capital budgeting justification for small, routine, or "production" decisions. Even when capital budgeting techniques are used for operating decisions, the tendency is not to recommend projects unless upper-level management is ready to approve them. Hence, while operating decisions arc important and can be aided by capital budgeting analysis, the more important issue for most organizations is the use and applicability of capital budgeting techniques in strategic planning.

In a general sense, the capital budgeting framework of analysis can be used for many types of decisions, including such areas as acquisition, expansion, replacement, bond refinancing, lease versus buy, and working capital management. Each of these decisions can be approached from either of two perspectives: the *top-down* approach, or the *bottom-up* approach. By *top-down*, we mean the initiation of an idea or a concept at the highest management level, which then filters down to the lower levels of the organization. By *bottom-up*, we mean just the reverse.

For the sake of exposition, we will use a simple four-step process to present an overview of capital budgeting. The steps are: (1) identification of areas of opportunity, (2) development of information and data for decisions regarding these opportunities, (3) selection of the best alternative or courses of action to be implemented, and (4) control or feedback of the degree of success or failure of both the project and the decision process itself. While we would expect these steps to occur sequentially, there are many circumstances where the order may be switched or the steps may occur simultaneously.

### 6.2.1 *Identification phase*

The identification of potential capital expenditures is directly linked to the firm's overall strategic objective; the firm's position within the various markets it serves; government fiscal, monetary, and tax policies; and the leadership of the firm's management. A widely used approach to strategic planning is based on the concept of viewing the firm as a collection, or portfolio, of assets grouped into strategic business units. This approach, called the Business Strategy Matrix, has been developed and used quite successfully by the Boston Consulting Group. It emphasizes market share and market growth rate in terms of stars, cash cows, question marks, and dogs, as shown in Exhibit 6.1.

**Exhibit 6.1:** Boston Consulting Group, Business Strategy Matrix.

| | | Relative Market Share | |
|---|---|---|---|
| | | Strong | Weak |
| Market Growth Rate | High | Stars | Question marks |
| | Low | Cash cows | Dogs |

**Exhibit 6.2:** Capital Budgeting and the Business Strategy Matrix.

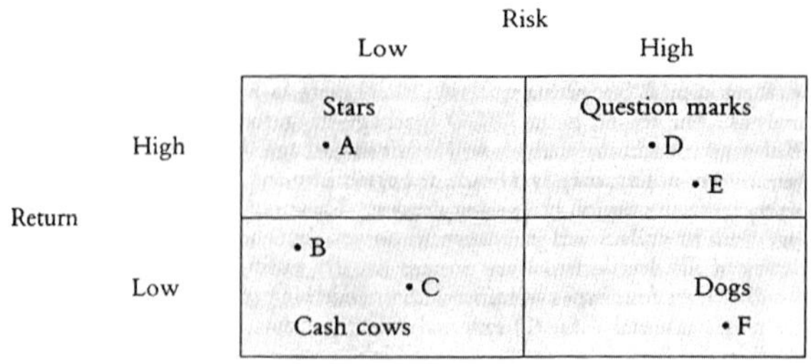


Given an organization that follows some sort of strategic planning relative to the Business Strategy Matrix, the most common questions are, How does capital budgeting fit into this framework? and, Are the underlying factors of capital budgeting decisions consistent with the firm's objectives of managing market share?

There are various ways to relate the Business Strategy Matrix to capital budgeting. One of the more appealing is presented in Exhibit 6.2.

This approach highlights the risk-and-return nature of both capital budgeting and business strategy. As presented, the inclusion of risk in the analysis focuses on the identification of projects such as A, which will add sufficient value (return) to the organization to justify the risk that the firm must take. Because of its high risk and low return, project F will not normally be sought after, nor will extensive effort be made to evaluate its usefulness. Marginal projects such as B, C, D, and E require careful scrutiny. In the case of projects such as B, with low risk but also low return, there may be justification for acceptance based on capital budgeting considerations, but such projects may not fit into the firm's strategic plans. On the other hand, projects such as E, which make strategic sense to the organization, may not offer sufficient return to justify the higher risk and so may be rejected by the capital budgeting decision-maker.

To properly identify appropriate projects for management consideration, both the firm's long-run strategic objectives and its financial objectives must be considered. One of the major problems facing the financial decision-maker today is the integration of long-run strategic goals with financial decision-making techniques that produce short-run gains. Perhaps the best way to handle this problem is in the project identification step by considering whether the investment makes sense in light of long-run corporate objectives. If the answer is no, look for more compatible projects. If the answer is yes, proceed to the next step, the development phase.

### 6.2.2 *Development phase*

The development, or information generation, step of the capital budgeting process is probably the most difficult and most costly. The entire development phase rests largely on the type and availability of information about the investment under consideration. With limited data and an information system that cannot provide accurate, timely, and pertinent data, the usefulness of the capital budgeting process will be limited. If the firm does not have a functioning management information system (MIS) that provides the type of information needed to perform capital budgeting analysis, then there is little need to perform such analysis. The reason is the GIGO (garbage-in, garbage-out) problem; garbage (bad data) used in the analysis will result in garbage (bad or useless information) coming out of the analysis. Hence, the establishment and use of an effective MIS is crucial to the capital budgeting process. This may be an expensive undertaking, both in dollars and in human resources, but the improvement in the efficiency of the decision-making process usually justifies the cost.

There are four types of information needed in capital budgeting analysis: (1) the firm's internal data, (2) external economic data, (3) financial data, and (4) nonfinancial data. The actual analysis of the project will eventually rely on firm-specific financial data because of the emphasis on cash flow. However, in the development phase, different types of information are needed, especially when various options are being formulated and considered. Thus, economic data external to the firm such as general economic conditions, product market conditions, government regulation or deregulation, inflation, labor supply, and technological change play an important role in developing the alternatives. Most of this initial screening data is nonfinancial. But even such nonfinancial considerations as the quality and quantity of the work force, political activity, competitive reaction, regulation, and environmental concerns must be integrated into the process of selecting alternatives.

Depending on the nature of the firm's business, there are two other considerations. First, different levels of the firm's management require different types of information. Second, as Ackoff (1970) notes, "most managers using a management information system suffer more from an overabundance of irrelevant information than they do from a lack of relevant information."

In a world in which all information and analysis were free, we could conceive of management analyzing every possible investment idea. However, given the cost, in both dollars and time, of gathering and analyzing information, management is forced to eliminate many alternatives based on strategic considerations. This paring down of the number of feasible alternatives is crucial to the success of the overall capital budgeting program. Throughout this process, the manager faces critical questions, such as, Are excellent proposals being eliminated from consideration because of lack of information? and, Are excessive amounts of time and money being spent to generate information on projects that are only marginally acceptable? These questions must be addressed on a firm-by-firm basis. When considered in the global context of the firm's success, these questions are the most important considerations in the capital budgeting process.

After the appropriate alternatives have been determined during the development phase, we are ready to perform the detailed economic analysis, which occurs during the selection phase.

### 6.2.3 *Selection phase*

Because managers want to maximize the firm's value for the shareholders, they need some guidance as to the potential value of the investment projects. The selection phase involves measuring the value, or the return, of the project as well as estimating the risk and weighing the costs and benefits of each alternative to be able to select the project or projects that will increase the firm's value given a risk target.

In most cases, the costs and benefits of an investment occur over an extended period, usually with costs being incurred in the early years of the project's life and benefits being realized over the project's entire life. In our selection procedures, we take this into consideration by incorporating the time value of money. The basic valuation framework, or normative model, that we will use in the capital budgeting selection process is based on present value, as presented in Eq. (6.1):

$$\mathrm{PV} = \sum_{t=1}^{N} \frac{\mathrm{CF}_t}{(1+k)^t} \tag{6.1}$$

where PV = the present value or current price of the investment; $\mathrm{CF}_t$ = the future value or cash flow that occurs in time $t$; $N$ = the number of years that benefits accrue to the investor; and $k$ = the time value of money or the firm's cost of capital.

By using this framework for the selection process, we are looking explicitly at the firm's value over time. We are not emphasizing short-run or long-run profits or benefits but are recognizing that benefits are desirable whenever they occur. However, benefits in the near future are more highly valued than benefits far down the road.

The basic normative model (Eq. (6.1)) will be expanded to fit various situations that managers encounter as they evaluate investment proposals and determine which proposals are best.

### 6.2.4 *Control Phase*

The control phase is the final step of the capital budgeting process. This phase involves placing an approved project on the appropriation budget and controlling the magnitude and timing of expenditures while the project is progressing. A major portion of this phase is the *postaudit* of the project, through which past decisions are evaluated for the benefit of future capital expenditures.

The firm's evaluation and control system are important not only to the post-audit procedure, but also to the entire capital budgeting process. It is important to understand that the investment decision is based on cash flow and relevant costs, while the *postaudit* is based on accrued accounting and assigned overhead. Also, firms typically evaluate performance based on accounting net income for profit centers within the firm, which may be inaccurate because of misspecification of depreciation and tax effects. The result is that

**Exhibit 6.3:** Relevant Time Perspective.

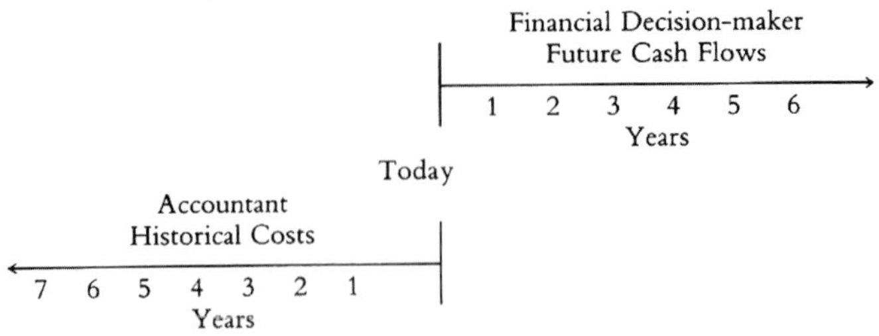


while managers make decisions based on cash flow, they are evaluated by an accounting-based system.

In addition to data and measurement problems, the control phase is even more complicated in practice because there is a growing concern that the evaluation, reward, and executive incentive system emphasizes a short-run, accounting-based return instead of the maximization of long-run value of cash flow. Thus, quarterly earnings per share, or revenue growth, are rewarded at the expense of longer-run profitability. This emphasis on short-run results may encourage management to forego investments in capital stock or research and development that have long-run benefits in exchange for short-run projects that improve earnings per share.

A brief discussion of the differences between accounting-based information and cash flow is appropriate at this point. The first major difference between the financial decision-maker who uses cash flow and the accountant who uses accounting information is one of time perspective. Exhibit 6.3 shows the differences in time perspective between financial decision-makers and accountants.

As seen in Exhibit 6.3, the financial decision-maker is concerned with future cash flows and value, while the accountant is concerned with historical costs and revenue. The financial decision-maker faces the question, what will I do? while the accountant asks, how did I do?

The second problem is one of definition. The financial decision-maker is concerned with economic income, or a change in wealth. For example, if you purchase a share of stock for $10 and later sell the stock for $30, from a financial viewpoint you have gained $20 of value.

It is easy to measure economic income in this case. However, when we look at a firm's actual operations, the measurement of economic income becomes quite complicated.

The accountant is concerned with accounting income, which is measured by the application of generally accepted accounting principles. Accounting income is the result of essential but arbitrary judgments concerning the matching of revenues and expenses during a particular period. For example, revenue may be recognized when goods are sold, shipped, or invoiced, or on receipt of the customer's check. A financial analyst and an accountant would likely differ on when revenue is recognized.

Clearly, over long periods economic value and accounting income converge and are equal because the problems of allocation to particular time periods disappear. However, over short periods there can be significant differences in these two measures. The financial decision-maker should be concerned with the value added over the life of the project, even though the *postaudit* report of results is an accounting report based on only one quarter or one year of the project's life. To incorporate a long-run view of value creation, the firm must establish a relationship between its evaluation system, its reward or management incentive system, and the normative goals of the capital budgeting system.

Another area of importance in the control or post audit phase is the decision to terminate or abandon a project once it has been accepted. Too often we consider capital budgeting as only the acquisition of investments for their entire economic life. The possibility of abandoning an investment prior to the end of its estimated useful or economic life has important implications for the capital budgeting decision. The possibility of abandonment expands the options available to management and reduces the risk associated with decisions based on holding an asset to the end of its economic life. This form of contingency planning gives the financial decision-maker and management a second chance to deal with the economic and political uncertainties of the future.

At any point, to justify the continuation of a project, the project's value from future operations must be greater than its current abandonment value. Given the recent increase in the number and frequency of divestitures, many firms now give greater consideration to abandonment questions in their capital budgeting decision-making.

An ideal time to reassess the value of an ongoing investment is at regular intervals during the post audit.

## 6.3 Cash-Flow Evaluation of Alternative Investment Projects

Investment should be undertaken by a firm only if it will increase the value of shareholders' wealth. Theoretically, Copeland and Weston (2003) show that the investment decisions of the firm can be separated from the individual investor's consumption-investment decision in a perfect capital market. This is known as Fisher's (1930) separation theorem. With perfect capital markets, the manager will increase shareholder wealth if he or she chooses projects with a rate-of-return greater than the market-determined rate-of-return (cost of funds), regardless of the shape of individual shareholders' indifference curves. The ability to borrow or lend in perfect capital markets leads to a higher wealth level for investors than they would be able to achieve without capital markets. This ability also leads to optimal production decisions that do not depend on individual investors' resources and preferences. Thus, the investment decision of the firm is separated from the individual's decision concerning current consumption and investment. Investment decision will therefore depend only on equating the rate-of-return of production possibilities with the market rate-of-return.

This separation principle implies that the maximization of the shareholders' wealth is identical to maximizing the present value of their lifetime consumption. Under these circumstances, different shareholders of the same firm will be unanimous in their preference. This is known as the unanimity principle. It implies that the managers of a firm, in their capacity as agents for shareholders, need not worry about making decisions that reconcile differences of opinion among shareholders: All shareholders will have identical interests. In fact, the price system by which profit is measured conveys the shareholders' unanimously preferred production decisions to the firm.

Looked at in another way, the use of investment decision rules, or capital budgeting, is really an example of a firm attempting to realize the economic principle of operating at the point where marginal cost equals marginal revenue to maximize shareholder wealth. In terms of investment decisions, the "marginal revenue" is the rate-of-return on investment projects, which must be equated with the marginal cost, or the market-determined cost of capital.

Investment decision rules, or capital budgeting, involve the evaluation of the possible capital investments of a firm according to procedures that will ensure the proper comparison of the cost of the project, that is, the initial and continuing outlays for the project, with the benefits, the expected cash flows accruing from the investment over time. To compare the two cash flows, future cash amounts must be discounted to the present by the firm's cost of capital. Only in this way will the cost of funds to the firm be equated with the benefits from the investment project.

The firm generally receives funds from creditors and shareholders. Both fund suppliers expect to receive a rate-of-return that will compensate them for the level of risk they take. Hence, the discount rate used to discount the cash flow should be the weighted-average cost of debt and equity. In Chapter 10, we will discuss the weighted cost of capital with tax effect in detail.

The weighted-average cost of capital is the same with the market-determined opportunity cost of funds provided to the firm. It is important to understand that projects undertaken by firms must earn enough cash for the creditors and shareholders to compensate their expected risk-adjusted rate-of-return. If the present value of annuity on the cash flow obtained from the weighted-average cost of capital is larger than the initial investment, then there are some gains in shareholders' wealth using this kind of concept. Copeland and Weston (2003) demonstrated that maximizing the discount cash flows provided by the investment project.

Before any capital-budgeting techniques can be surveyed, a rigorous definition of cash flows to a firm from a project must be undertaken. First the decision maker must consider only those future cash flows that are incremental to the project; that is, only those cash flows accruing to the firm that are specifically caused by the project in question. In addition, any decrease in cash flows to the company by the project in question (i.e., the tax-depreciation benefit from a machine replaced by a new one) must be considered as well.

The main advantage of using the cash-flow procedure in capital-budgeting decisions is that it avoids the difficult problem underlying the measurement of corporate income associated with the accrual method of accounting, for example, the selection of depreciation methods and inventory-valuation methods.

It is well-known that the equality between sources and uses of funds for an all-equity firm in period $t$ can be defined as:

$$R_t + N_t P_t = N_t d_t + WSMS_t + I_t \tag{6.2}$$

where $R_t$ = Revenue in period $t$; $N_t P_t$ = New equity in period $t$; $N_t d_t$ = Total dividend payment in period $t$; $\text{WSMS}_t$ = Wages, salaries, materials, and service payment in period $t$; $I_t$ = Investment in period $t$.

Equation (6.2) is the basic equation to be used to determine the cash flow for capital-budgeting determination.

Secondly, the definition of cash flow relevant to financial decision making involves finance rather than accounting income. Accounting regulations attempt to adjust cash flows over several periods (e.g., the expense of an asset is depreciated over several time periods); finance cash flows are calculated as they occur to the firm. Thus, the cash outlay ($I_t$) to purchase a machine is considered a cash outflow in the finance sense when it occurs at acquisition.

To illustrate the actual calculations involved in defining the cash flows accruing to a firm from an investment project, we consider the following situation. A firm is faced with a decision to replace an old machine with a new and more efficient model. If the replacement is made, the firm will increase production sufficiently each year to generate \$10,000 in additional cash flows to the company over the life of the machine. Thus, the before-tax cash flow accruing to the firm is \$10,000.

The cash flow must be adjusted for the net increase in income taxes that the firm must now pay due to the increased net depreciation of the new machine. The annual straight-line depreciation for the new machine over its five-year life will be \$2,000, and we assume no terminal salvage value. The old machine has a current book value of \$5,000 and a remaining depreciable life of five years with no terminal salvage value. Thus, the incremental annual depreciation will be the annual depreciation charges of the new, \$2,000, less the annual depreciation of the old, or \$1,000. The additional income to the firm from the new machine is then the \$10,000 cash flow less the incremental depreciation, \$1,000. The increased tax outlay from the acquisition will then be (assuming a 50% corporate income-tax rate) $0.50 \times$ \$9,000, or \$4,500.

Adjusting the gross annual cash flow of \$10,000 by the incremental tax expense of \$4,500 gives \$5,500 as the net cash flow accruing to the firm from the new machine. It should be noted that corporate taxes are real outflow and must be taken into account when evaluating a project's desirability. However, the depreciation allowance (dep) is not a cash outflow and therefore should not be subtracted from the annual cash flow.

The calculations of post-tax cash flow mentioned above can be summarized in Eq. (6.3):

$$\begin{aligned}\text{Annual After-Tax Cash Flow} &= \text{ICFBT} - (\text{ICFBT} - \Delta\text{dep})\tau \\ &= \text{ICFBT}(1-\tau) + (\text{dep})\tau \qquad (6.3)\end{aligned}$$

where ICFBT = Annual incremental operating cash flows; $\tau$ = Corporate tax rate; $\Delta$ dep = Incremental annual depreciation charge, or the annual depreciation charges on the new machine less the annual depreciation on the old.

Following Eq. (6.3), ICFBT can be defined in Eq. (6.4) as

$$\text{ICFBT} = \Delta R_t - \Delta \text{WSMS}_t \qquad (6.4)$$

Note that ICFBT is an amount before interest and depreciation are deducted and $\Delta$ indicates the change of related variables. The reason is that when discounted at the weighted cost of capital as defined in Eq. (12.18), we are implicitly assuming that the project will return the expected interest payments to creditors and the expected dividends to shareholders.

Alternative depreciation methods will change the time pattern but not the total amount of the depreciation allowance. Hence it is important to choose the optimal depreciation method. To do this, the net present value (NPV) of tax benefits due to the tax deductibility of the depreciation allowance can be defined as:

$$\text{NPV(Tax benefit)} = \tau \sum_{t=1}^{N} \frac{\text{dep}_t}{(1+k)^t}$$

where $\text{dep}_t$ = depreciation allowance in period $t$ and $N$ = life of project; it will depend upon whether the straight-line, double declining balance, or sum-of-years'-digits method is used.

The net cash inflow in period $t$ ($C_t$) used for capital budgeting decision can be defined as:

$$C_t = \text{CF}_t - \tau_c(\text{CF}_t - \text{dep}_t - I_t) \tag{6.5}$$

where $\text{CF}_t = [Q_t(P_t - V_t)]$; $Q_t$ = quantity produced and sold; $P_t$ = price per unit; $V_t$ = variable costs per unit; $\text{dep}_t$ = depreciation; $\tau_c$ = tax rate; and $I_t$ = interest expense.

## 6.4 Alternative Capital-Budgeting Methods

Several methods can be used by a manager to evaluate an investment decision. Some of the simplest methods, such as the accounting rate-of-return or net payback period, are useful in that they are easily and quickly calculated. However, other methods — the net present value, profitability index, and the internal rate-of-return methods — are superior in that explicit consideration is given by them to both the cost of capital and the time value of money.

For illustrating these methods, we will use the data in Table 6.1, which shows the estimates of cash flows for four investment projects. Each project has an initial outlay of $100, and the project life for

Table 6.1 Initial Cost and Net Cash in Flow for Four Projects.

| Year | A | B | C | D |
|---|---|---|---|---|
| 0 | −100 | −100 | −100 | −100 |
| 1 | 20 | 0 | 30 | 25 |
| 2 | 80 | 20 | 50 | 40 |
| 3 | 10 | 60 | 60 | 50 |
| 4 | −20 | 160 | 80 | 115 |

the four projects is four years. Since they are mutually exclusive investment projects, only one project can be accepted, according to the following capital budgeting methods.

### 6.4.1 *Accounting rate-of-return*

In this method, a rate of return for the project is computed by using average net income and average investment outlay. This method does not incorporate the time value of money and cash flow. The *ARR* takes the ratio of the investment's average annual net income after taxes to either total outlay or average outlay. The accounting rate-of-return method averages the after-tax profit from an investment for every period over the initial outlay:

$$\text{ARR} = \frac{\sum_{t=0}^{N} \frac{\text{AP}_t}{N}}{I} \tag{6.6}$$

where $\text{AP}_t$ = After-tax profit in period $t$; $I$ = Initial investment; $N$ = Life of the project.

By assuming that the data in Table 6.1 are accounting profits and the depreciation is \$25, the accounting rates-of-return for the four projects are:

Project A: –2.5%

Project B: 35%

Project C: 30%

Project D: 32.5%

Project B shows the highest accounting rate-of-return; therefore, we will choose Project B as the best one.

The ARR, like the payback method, which will be investigated later in this section, ignores the timing of the cash flows by its failure to discount cash flows back to the present. In addition, the use of accounting cash flows rather than finance cash flows distorts the calculations through the artificial adjustment of some cash flows over several periods.

### 6.4.2 *Internal rate-of-return method*

The internal rate of return (IRR, $r$) is the discount rate which equates the discounted cash flows from a project to its investment. Thus, one must solve iteratively for the r in Eq. (6.7):

$$\sum_{t=1}^{N} \frac{CF_t}{(1+r)^t} = I \tag{6.7}$$

where 3 $CF_t$ = Cash flow (positive or negative) in period $t$; $I$ = Initial investment; $N$ = Life of the project.

The IRR for the four projects in Table 6.1 are: Project A: IRR does not exist (since the cash flows are less than the initial investment); Project B: 28.158%; Project C: 33.991%; and Project D: 32.722%. It should be noted that Excel can be effectively used to calculate IRR. Appendix 6C shows how Excel can be used to calculate IRR.

Since the four projects are mutually exclusive and Project C has the highest IRR, we will choose Project C.

The IRR is then compared to the cost of capital of the firm to determine whether the project will return benefits greater than its cost. A consideration of advantages and disadvantages of the IRR method will be undertaken when it is compared to the net present value method.

### 6.4.3 *Payback method*

The payback method calculates the time period required for a firm to recover the cost of its investment. It is that point in time at which the cumulative new cash flow from the project equals the initial investment.

The payback periods for the four projects in Table 6.1 are

Project A: 2.0 years

Project B: 3.125 years

Project C: 2.33 years

Project D: 2.70 years

If we use the payback method, we will choose Project A.

Several problems can arise if a decision maker uses the payback method. First, any cash flows accruing to the firm after the payback period are ignored. Secondly, and most importantly, the method disregards the time value of money. That is, the cash flow returned in the later years of the project's life is weighted equally with more recent cash flows accruing to the firm.

Although there are several problems in using the payback method as a capital-budgeting method, the reciprocal or payback period is related to the internal rate-of-return of the project when the life of the project is very long. For example, assume an investment project that has an initial outlay of $I$ and an annual cash flow of $R$. The payback period is $I/R$ and its reciprocal is $R/I$. On the other hand, the IRR ($r$) of a project can be written as follows:

$$r = \frac{R}{I} - \left(\frac{R}{I}\right)\left[\frac{1}{(1+r)^N}\right] \tag{6.8}$$

where $r$ is the IRR and $N$ is the life of the project in years. Clearly, when $N$ approaches infinity, the reciprocal of payback period $R/I$ will approximate the annuity rate of return. The payback method provides a liquidity measure: i.e., sooner is better than later.

Equation (6.8) is the special case of the internal rate-of-return formula defined in Eq. (6.7). By assuming equal annual net receipts and zero semi-annual value, Eq. (6.7) can be rewritten as:

$$I = \frac{R}{1+r}\left[1 + \frac{1}{(1+r)} + \frac{1}{(1+r)^2} + \cdots + \frac{1}{(1+r)^{N-1}}\right] \tag{6.7$'$}$$

where $R = CF_1 = CF_2 = \cdots = CF_n$. Summing the geometric series within the square brackets and reorganizing terms, we obtain Eq. (6.8).

### 6.4.4 *NPV Method*

The NPV of a project is computed by discounting the project's cash flows to the present by the appropriate cost of capital. A net present value of the firm is

$$\text{NPV} = \sum_{t=1}^{N} \frac{\text{CF}_t}{(1+k)^t} - I \tag{6.9}$$

where $k$ = the appropriate discount rate, and all other terms are defined as above.

The NPV method can be applied to the cash flows of the four projects in Table 6.1. By assuming a 12% discount rate, the NPV for the four projects are as follows: Project A: –23.95991, Project B: 60.33358, Project C: 60.19367, and Project D: 62.88278. It should be noted that Excel can be more effectively used to calculate NPV for investment projects. Appendix 6C shows how to use Excel to calculate NPV.

Since Project D has the highest NPV, we will select Project D as the best one.

Clearly the NPV method explicitly considers both time value of money and economic cash flows. It should be noted that this conclusion is based upon the discount rate which is 12%. However, if the discount rate is either higher or lower than 12%, this conclusion may not be entirely true. This issue can be resolved by crossover rate analysis, which can be found in Appendix 6B. In Appendix 6B, we analyzed Projects A and B for different cash flow and different discount rates. The main conclusion for Appendix 6B can be summarized as follows.

NPV(B) is higher with low discount rates and NPV(A) is higher with high discount rates. This is because the cash flows of Project A occur early and those of Project B occur later. If we assume a high discount rate, we would favor Project A; if a low discount rate is expected, Project B will be chosen. In order to make the right choice, we can calculate the crossover rate. If the discount rate is higher than the crossover rate, we should choose Project A; if otherwise, we should go for Project B.

Based upon the concept of break-even analysis discussed in Eq. (2.6) of Chapter 2, we can determine the units of product that must be produced in order for NPV to be zero. If $\text{CF}_1 = \text{CF}_2 = \cdots = \text{CF}_N = \overline{\text{CF}}$ and NPV = 0, then Eq. (6.9) can be rewritten as:

$$\overline{\text{CF}}\left[\sum_{t=1}^{N}\frac{1}{(1+k)^t}\right] = I \tag{6.9$'$}$$

By substituting the definition of $\overline{\text{CF}}$ given in Eq. (6.5) into Eq. (6.9′), we can obtain the break-even point ($Q^*$) for capital budgeting as:

$$Q^* = \left\{\frac{[I - (\text{dep})\tau]/(1-\tau)}{\sum_{t=1}^{N} 1/[(1+k)^t]}\right\}\left(\frac{1}{p-v}\right) \tag{6.10}$$

A real-world example of an application of the NPV method to breakeven analysis can be found in Reinhardt (1973) and Chapter 13 of Lee and Lee (2017).

### 6.4.5 *Profitability index*

The Profitability Index is very similar to the NPV method. The PI is calculated by dividing the discounted cash flows by the initial investment to arrive at the present value per dollar outlay:

$$\text{PI} = \frac{\sum_{t=1}^{N}[\text{CF}_t/((1+k)^t)]}{I} \tag{6.11}$$

The project should be undertaken if the PI is greater than 1; the firm should be indifferent to its undertaking if PI equals one. The project with the highest PI greater than one should be accepted first. Obviously, PI considers the time value of money and the correct finance cash flows, as does the NPV method. Further, the PI and NPV method will lead to identical decisions unless ranking mutually exclusive projects and/or under capital rationing. When considering mutually exclusive projects, the PI can lead to a decision different from that derived by the NPV method.

For example:

| Project | Initial Outlay | Present Value of Cash Inflows | NPV | PI |
|---|---|---|---|---|
| A | 100 | 200 | 100 | 2 |
| B | 1000 | 1300 | 300 | 1.3 |

Projects A and B are mutually exclusive projects. Project A has a lower NPV and higher PI compared to Project B. This will lead to a decision to select Project A by using the PI method and select Project B by using the NPV method. In the case shown here, the NPV and PI rankings differ because of the differing scale of investment: The NPV subtracts the initial outlay while the PI method divides by the original cost. Thus, differing initial investments can cause a difference in ranking between the two methods.

The firm that desires to maximize its absolute present value rather than percentage return will prefer Project B, because the NPV of Project B ($300) is greater than the NPV of Project A ($100). Thus, the PI method should not be used as a measure of investment worth for projects of differing size where mutually exclusive choices have to be made. In other words, if there exists no other investment opportunities, then the NPV will be the superior method in this case because, under the NPV, the highest-ranking investment project (the one with the largest NPV) will add the most value to shareholders' wealth. Since this is the objective of the firm's owners, the NPV will lead to a more accurate decision.

The manager's views on alternative capital budgeting methods and related practical issues will be presented in Appendix 6A.

## 6.5 Comparison of the NPV and IRR Method

### 6.5.1 *Theoretical criteria*

If projects are mutually exclusive, the ranking of the investment alternatives by a capital-budgeting technique determines which of the projects will actually be undertaken. The IRR and NPV methods

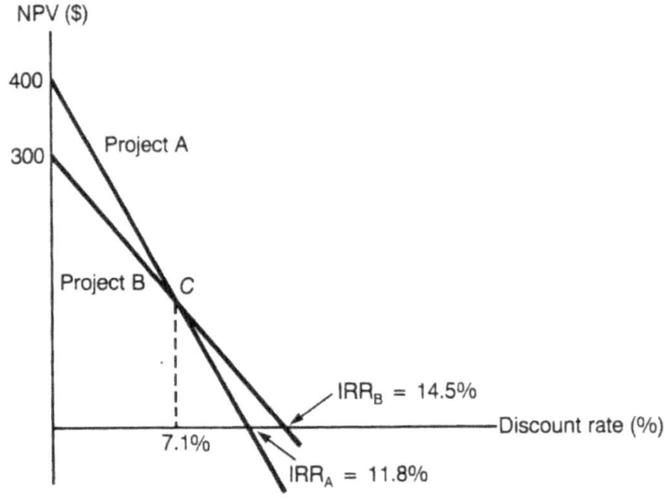


Figure 6.1 NPVs of Projects A and B at Different Discount Rates.

may lead to similar accept-reject decisions; in some instances, however, the NPV and IRR methods will provide different ranking for capital investment projects. Some choice must be made as to which method gives the more accurate rankings if projects are mutually exclusive.

Projects have different rankings if the cost of one project is greater than that of another or if the timing of cash flows differs among projects. To show the effect of differing cash-flow patterns, the present-value profile of two projects is shown in Figure 6.1. The NPV of each project will change depending on the rate-of-return used to discount the periodic cash flows. Thus, when moving along the horizontal axis to higher discount rates, the NPV of each project will fall. However, the NPV of the project with its largest cash flows in the future will be affected more severely by the increasing discount rate, and thus the NPV for Project A decreases more rapidly than Project B. The point at which the NPV is 0 for a project is the project's IRR.

As shown, the ranking derived from the NPV differs from that of the IRR if the discount rate is below the point C, the cross-over rate. Thus, the conflict between the NPV and IRR rankings on whether the discount rate used by the firm is less than the cross-over rate, or that rate which equates the project's NPVs.

When such a conflict arises, the decision maker should use the NPV-determined rankings. Again, the NPV measures the added value accruing to shareholder wealth when the project is undertaken. The project that maximizes this value (the project with the highest NPV) should be the project that is undertaken.

Although it is typically argued that the NPV is the superior method, the viability of the IRR should not be completely dismissed. Its value depends on certain other assumptions, such as the time horizon used by the firm. For instance, considering two mutually exclusive projects, firm policy sets a planning horizon for the firm of four or five years, regardless of what length the investment project's useful life may extend. Projects then must be considered under this time constraint, and the project with the highest terminal value at the end of the planning horizon will be the desired project to undertake. Although obviously the manager is not maximizing shareholder wealth by, in effect, ignoring the more long-term aspects of investment projects, he may be operating in a more realistic and practical manner: Many firms feel that planning horizons of ten years or longer are too fraught with uncertainty to be useful. Given such a time constraint, the IRR method will more accurately judge the desired project.

Since the NPV of projects with large future cash flows decrease rapidly under increasing discount rates, the IRR will favor projects with higher short-term terminal value. That is, projects with larger IRR values will also have time patterns of cash flows with higher short-term terminal values. The existence of such practical constraints as the one above mitigates some of the more theoretical disadvantages in the use of the IRR.

### (a) Multiple rates-of-return

One of the difficulties with using the IRR is the possibility of multiple rates of return. Each time the cash flows change sign (which may be necessitated, for instance, by the requirement to inject additional capital into the project in future years), there will be a new root solution to the IRR problem. For instance, a negative cash flow in the second year would result in a quadratic equation, and consequently multiple roots. For example:

| Year | 0 | 1 | 2 |
|---|---|---|---|
| Cash Flow | –50 | 750 | –800 |

$$\text{NPV} = 0 = -50 + \frac{750}{(1+\text{IRR})} - \frac{800}{(1+\text{IRR})^2}$$

$$-50(1+\text{IRR})^2 + 750(1+\text{IRR}) - 800 = 0$$

$$50\,\text{IRR}^2 - 650\,\text{IRR} + 100 = 0$$

The solution can be obtained using the quadratic formula:

$$\text{IRR} = 650 \pm \frac{\sqrt{(650)^2 - (50)(100)}}{100}$$

$$\text{IRR} = 0.1557 \quad \text{or} \quad 12.84$$

Thus, use of the IRR would result in an ambiguous capital-budgeting "solution" if the investment under consideration were such as to generate negative cash flows in some years. It is even possible that the IRR method could result in imaginary solutions (involving $\sqrt{-1}$), whose interpretation is problematic at best.

For example:

| Year | 0 | 1 | 2 |
|---|---|---|---|
| Cash Flow | −100 | 250 | −160 |

$$0 = -100 + \frac{250}{(1+\text{IRR})} - \frac{160}{(1+\text{IRR})^2}$$

$$0 = -100(1+\text{IRR})^2 + 250(1+\text{IRR}) - 160$$

$$0 = -10 - 20\,\text{IRR} - 10\,\text{IRR}^2 + 25 + 25\,\text{IRR} - 16$$

$$10\text{IRR}^2 - 5\text{IRR} + 1 = 0$$

$$\text{IRR} = \frac{5 \pm \sqrt{25 - 40}}{20}$$

$$\text{IRR} = \frac{1}{4} \pm \frac{1}{20}\sqrt{15}i$$

### (b) Reinvestment rate problem

Another of the difficulties involved with the IRR is the underlying assumption of differing reinvestment rates. When discounting cash flows in the NPV method at the cost of capital, the NPV implicitly assumes that the shareholders of the firm can reinvest the periodic cash flows accruing from the project at the cost of capital. With the IRR, however, the implicit assumption is that the shareholder can reinvest the cash flows at the IRR of each project. Thus, the IRR runs into difficulties in two ways: It divorces the discounting process from the cost of capital, and it implies that reinvestment rates are contingent on individual projects. In a world of certainty, where each project has the same risk, it is illogical to assume that shareholders can invest funds, for instance, at both 14% and 25%, depending on the IRR of the two projects.

### (c) Separability of projects

A third difficulty in using the IRR method is that its use leads to differing decisions when groups of projects are considered. It is desirable that a decision rule allow the manager to choose projects independently of each other; the IRR, however, may lead to the necessity of considering projects in all possible combinations. To illustrate, data for three projects are shown in Tables 6.2 and 6.2(a).

Assuming 12% discount rate:

## 6.5.2 *Practical perspective*

Doenges (1972) takes a closer look at the net-present-value and internal-rate-of-return methods and questions the common assertion

Table 6.2 NPV for Different Projects.

| | Year | | | | |
|---|---|---|---|---|---|
| **Projects** | **0** | **1** | **2** | **3** | **NPV** |
| A | −100 | 50 | 100 | 500 | 380.2537 |
| B | −200 | 600 | 100 | 50 | 451.02269 |
| C | −300 | 100 | 700 | 100 | 418.49945 |
| A+B | −300 | 650 | 200 | 550 | 831.27505 |
| B+C | −500 | 700 | 800 | 150 | 869.52214 |
| A+C | −400 | 150 | 800 | 600 | 798.75182 |

Table 6.2(a) IRR for Different Projects.

| | **>IRR** |
|---|---|
| A | 1.10438 |
| B | 2.18184 |
| C | 0.76360 |
| A | 1.67275 |
| B+C | 1.19227 |
| A+C | 0.87172 |

that NPV is superior simply because it assumes reinvestment of intermediate funds at a single discount rate. In contrast, a major premise of the internal-rate-of-return method is that intermediate cash flows be reinvested to earn a rate-of-return equal to the internal rate-of-return, without reference to the shareholders' required rate-of-return. The differing foundations upon which each method rests result in frequently conflicting decision signals.

Doenges proceeds to question the assumptions implicit in the "reinvestment problem" concerning the existence of an appropriate single reinvestment rate and the magnitude, duration, and time pattern of net cash flows. Although he questions the assumption of mutually exclusive alternatives caused by capital rationing, other studies have shown that capital rationing is, in fact, prevalent in the business world. If, however, the supply function of funds for the firm is upward sloping, as may be true for many firms, the appropriate discount rate would reflect this rising cost of capital rather than merely an opportunity cost as discussed in Chapter 10.

Doenges also raises a question that has often bothered academics. Although for practicality's sake, the firm's normal planning horizon is often used to evaluate investment alternatives, utilization of the projects' actual expected lives may more accurately reflect the real value of those projects. When the more easily workable time horizons are utilized, the financial analyst should at least recognize the possible effects of this incongruency. This is closely related to the abandonment-versus-retention issue raised in the article, and the effects of these calculations on investment acceptability must also be considered. The project-life problem will be discussed in Section 6.9 and the issues related to the abandonment value will be explored later.

Doenges also raises a very frequently voiced concern about risk and uncertainty. The manner, in which these are accounted for, if at all, in capital-budgeting decisions, may have a tremendous impact on those decisions. The issue of uncertainty will be discussed more completely in a later portion of this section.

The major difference between the NPV and IRR methods, however, is the assumption by net-present-value theorists that a single reinvestment rate exists. Especially in an economy subject to change such as ours, no one can predict with certainty what returns can be made on funds invested at some future date. Special opportunities can arise in which an alert financier can earn above-average returns. In contrast, recession or depression periods can produce negative returns. Thus, the assumption of limited variability in reinvestment rates can be seen to rest on a fairly tenuous foundation when viewed in a "real-world" perspective.[1]

Doenges presents an alternative that may be feasible in certain cases. When cash inflows from a project currently being considered are ear marked to be used as funding for some future project in the planning horizon, the projected returns from this future project can be considered as the reinvestment rate for the current project. Although this process would involve an abundance of uncertainty and more time-consuming analysis, it could shed new light on alternative projects. In any case, Doenges suggests that several potential reinvestment rates be considered when evaluating projects. This could eliminate some of the uncertainty involved in project analysis. Although Doenges does not say that the internal rate-of-return method is superior to net present value, he does provide some food for thought to net present value supporters.[2] He also questions many of the theoretical and practical assumptions on which capital budgeting decisions are based.

## 6.6 Different Lives and Equivalent Annual Cost

### 6.6.1 *Different lives*

Up to this section, we assumed that all investment projects have the same life. However, the traditional NPV technique may not be the appropriate criterion to select a project from mutually exclusive investment projects, if these projects have different lives. The underlying reason is that, compared with a long-life project, a short-life project can be replicated more quickly in the long run. In order to compare projects with different lives, we compute the NPV of an infinite replication of the investment project. For example, let Projects A and B be two mutually exclusive investment projects with the following cash flows.

| Year | Project A | Project B |
|---|---|---|
| 0 | −100 | −100 |
| 1 | 70 | 50 |
| 2 | 70 | 50 |
| 3 | | 50 |

By assuming a discount rate of 12%, the traditional NPV of Project A is 18.30 and the NPV of Project B is 20.09. This shows that Project B is a better choice than Project A. However, the NPV with infinite replications for Project A and B should be adjusted into a comparable basis.

In order to compare Projects A and B, we compute the NPV of an infinite stream of constant scale replications. Let NPV $(N, \infty)$ be the NPV of an $N$-year project with NPV $(N)$, replicated forever. This is exactly the same as an annuity paid at the beginning of the first period and at the end of every $N$ years from that time on. The NPV of the annuity is:

$$\text{NPV}(N, \infty) = \text{NPV}(N) + \frac{\text{NPV}(N)}{(1+K)^N} + \frac{\text{NPV}(N)}{(1+K)}2N + \cdots$$

In order to obtain a closed-form formula, let $(1/[(1+K)^N]) = \text{H}$. Then we have:

$$\text{NPV}(N,t) = \text{NPV}(N)(1 + \text{H} + \text{H}^2 + \cdots \text{H}^t) \qquad (6.12\text{a})$$

Multiplying both sides by H, this becomes

$$\text{H}[\text{NPV}(N,t)] = \text{NPV}(N)(\text{H} + \text{H}^2 = \cdots + H^t + H^{t+1}) \qquad (6.12\text{b})$$

Subtracting Eq. (6.12b) from Eq. (6.12a) gives:

$$\text{NPV}(N,t) - (\text{H})\text{NPV}(N,t) = \text{NPV}(N)(1 - H^{t+1})$$

$$\text{NPV}(N,t) = \frac{NPV(N)(1 - H^{t+1})}{1 - H}$$

And taking the limit as the number of replications, $t$, approaches infinity gives:

$$\lim_{t\to\infty} \text{NPV}(N,t) = \text{NPV}(N,\infty) = \text{NPV}\left[\frac{1}{1 - [1/(1+K)^N]}\right]$$

$$= \text{NPV}(N)\left[\frac{(1+K)^N}{(1+K)^N - 1}\right] \qquad (6.13)$$

Equation (6.13) is the NPV of an $N$-year project replicated at constant scale an infinite number of times. We can use it to compare projects with different lives because when their cash-flow streams are replicated forever, it is as if they had the same (infinite) life.

Using Eq. (6.13) for Projects A and B gives us the following:

**For Project A:**

$$\text{NPV}(2,\infty) = \text{NPV}(2)\left[\frac{(1+0.12)^2}{(1+0.12)^2 - 1}\right]$$

$$= (18.30)\left[\frac{1.2544}{0.2544}\right]$$

$$= 90.23$$

**For Project B:**

$$\begin{aligned}\text{NPV}(3,\infty) &= \text{NPV}(3)\left[\frac{(1+0.12)^3}{(1+0.12)^3-1}\right]\\ &= 20.09\left[\frac{1.4049}{0.4049}\right]\\ &= 69.71\end{aligned}$$

Consequently, we would choose to accept Project A over Project B, because, when the cash flows are adjusted for different lives, A provides the greater cash flow.

Alternatively, Eq. (6.13) can be rewritten as an annuity version as:

$$\text{KNPV}(N,\infty) = \frac{\text{NPV(N)}}{\text{Annuity factor}} \tag{6.14}$$

where the annuity factor is

$$[1-(1+K)^{-N}]/K$$

The decision rule from Eq. (6.14) is equivalent to the decision rule of Eq. (6.13).

The different project lives can affect the beta coefficient estimate. Lee and Lee (2013) have discussed this issue and its empirical implication in detail.

### 6.6.2 *Equivalent annual cost*

Equation (6.14) can be written as

$$\text{NPV}(N) = K \times \text{NPV}(N,\infty) \times \text{Annuity factor} \tag{6.15}$$

Ross *et al.* (2018) has discussed Equivalent Annual Cost. The Equivalent Annual Cost ($C$) can be calculated from

$$\text{NPV}(N) = C \times \text{Annuity factor} \tag{6.16}$$

From Eqs. (6.15) and (6.16), we obtain

$$\text{C} = K \times \text{NPV}(N,\infty) \tag{6.17}$$

Assume company A buys a machine that costs 1,000 and will be maintenance expense of $250 to be paid at the end of each of the four years. To evaluate this investment, we can calculate the present value of the machine. Assuming the discount rate 10%, we have

$$\mathrm{NPV(A)} = 1000 + \frac{250}{1.1} + \frac{250}{(1.1)^2} + \frac{250}{(1.1)^3} + \frac{250}{(1.1)^4} = 1792.47 \quad (6.18)$$

Equation (6.18) shows that payments of (1000, 250, 250, 250, 250) are equivalent to a payment of 1,792.47 at time 0. Using Eq. (6.16), we can equate the payment at time 0 of 1,749.47 with a four year annuity.

$$1792.47 = C \times A_{0.1}^{4} = C \times 3.1699$$
$$C = 565.47$$

In this example, following Eq. (6.11), we can find

$$\mathrm{NPV}(N, \infty) = 1749.47 \times (1 + 0.1)^4/[(1 + 0.1)^4 - 1] = 5{,}654.71$$

Then following Eq. (6.17), we obtain

$$C = K * \mathrm{NPV}(N, \infty) = 0.1 \times 5654.71 = 565.47$$

Therefore, the equivalent annual cost $C$ is identical to the equivalent annual NPV as defined in Eq. (6.17).

## 6.7 Capital-Rationing Decision

In this section we will discuss a capital-budgeting problem that involves the allocation of scarce capital resources among competing economically desirable projects, not all of which can be carried out due to a capital (or other) constraint. This kind of problem is often called "capital rationing." In this section, we will show how linear programming can be used to make capital-rationing decisions.

### 6.7.1 *Basic concepts of linear programming*

Linear programming is a mathematical technique used to find optimal solutions to problems of a firm involving the allocation of scarce resources among competing activities. Mathematically, the type of problem that linear programming can solve is one in which both the objective of the firm to be maximized (or minimized) and the constraints limiting the firm's actions are linear functions of the decisions variables involved. Thus, the first step in using linear programming as a tool for financial decisions is to model the problem facing the firm into a linear-programming form. To construct the linear-programming model, one must take the following steps.

First, identify the controllable decision variables involved in the firm's problem. Second, define the objective or criterion to be maximized or minimized and represent it as a linear function of the controllable decision variables. In finance, the objective generally is to maximize the profit contribution or the market value of the firm or to minimize the cost of production.

Thirdly, define the constraints and express them as linear equations or inequalities of the decision variables. This will usually involve (a) a determination of the capacities of the scarce resources involved in the constraints, and (b) a derivation of a linear relationship between these capacities and the decision variables.

Symbolically, then, if $X_1$, $X_2, \cdots, X_n$ represent the quantities of output, the linear-programming model takes the general form:

$$\text{Maximize(or minimize)} Z = c_1X_1 + c_2X_2 + \cdots + c_nX_n \quad (6.19)$$

$$\begin{aligned}
\text{Subject to: } a_{11}X_1 + a_{12}X_2 + \cdots + a_{1n}X_n &\leq b_1 \\
a_{21}X_1 + a_{22}X_2 + \cdots + a_{2n}X_n &\leq b_2 \\
\vdots \qquad\qquad\qquad & \vdots \\
a_{m1}X_1 + a_{m2}X_2 + \cdots + a_{mn}X_n &\leq b_m \\
X_j \geq 0, (j = 1, 2, \cdots, n)
\end{aligned}$$

Here $Z$ represents the objective to be maximized (or minimized), profit or market value (or cost), $c_1$, $c_2, \ldots, c_n$ and $a_{11}$, $a_{12}, \ldots, a_{mn}$ are constant coefficients relating to profit contribution and input, respectively; $b_1$, $b_2, \ldots, b_m$ are the firm's capacities of the constraining resources. The last constraint ensures that the decision variables to be determined are nonnegative.

Several points should be noted concerning the linear programming model. First, depending upon the problem, the constraints may also be stated with equal signs (=) or as greater-than-or-equal-to. Secondly, the solution values of the decision variables are divisible; that is, a solution would permit $x(j) = 1/2, 1/4$, etc. If such fractional values are not possible, the related technique of integer programming, yielding only whole numbers as solutions, can be applied. Thirdly, the constant coefficients are assumed known and deterministic (fixed). If the coefficients have probabilistic distributions, one of the various methods of stochastic programming must be used. Examples will be given below of the application of linear programming to the areas of capital rationing and capital budgeting.

### 6.7.2 *Capital rationing*

The XYZ Company produces products A, B, and C within the same product line, with sales totaling $37 million last year. Top management has adopted the goal of maximizing shareholder wealth, which to them is represented by gain in shareholder price. Wickwire plans to finance all future projects with internal or external equity; funds available from the equity market depend on share price in the stock market for the period.

Three new projects were proposed to the Finance Committee, for which the following net after-tax annual funds flows are forecast:

| | Year | | | | | |
|---|---|---|---|---|---|---|
| **Project** | **0** | **1** | **2** | **3** | **4** | **5** |
| X | −100 | 30 | 30 | 60 | 60 | 60 |
| Y | −200 | 70 | 70 | 70 | 70 | 70 |
| Z | −100 | −240 | −200 | 400 | 300 | 300 |

All three projects involve financing cost-saving equipment forwell-established product lines; adoption of any one project does not preclude adoption of any other. The following NPV

| **Investment** | **NPV** |
|---|---|
| X | 65.585 |
| Y | 52.334 |
| Z | 171.871 |

formulations have been prepared by using a discount rate of 12%.

In addition, the finance start has calculated the maximum internally generated funds that will be available for the current year and succeeding two years, not counting any cash generated by the projects currently under consideration.

| Year 0 | Year 1 | Year 2 |
|---|---|---|
| \$300 | \$70 | \$50 |

Assuming that the stock market is in a serious downturn, and thus no external financing is possible, the problem is which of the three projects should be selected, assuming that fractional projects are allowed.

The problem essentially involves the rationing of the capital available to the firm among the three competing projects such that share price will be maximized. Thus, assuming a risk-adjusted discount rate of 12%, the objective function becomes:

$$\text{Maximize}\, V = 65.585X + 52.334Y + 171.871Z$$
$$+ 0C + 0D + 0E$$

where V represents the total present value realized from the projects, and C, D, and E will represent idle funds in period 0, 1, 2, respectively. The constraint for period 0 must ensure that the funds used to finance the projects do not exceed the funds available. Thus,

$$100X + 200Y + 100Z + C + 0D + 0E = 300 \tag{6.20}$$

In this constraint, C represents any idle funds unused in period 0 after projects are paid for. Similarly, for period 1 and 2,

$$-30X - 70Y + 240Z - C + D + 0E = 70$$
$$-30X - 70Y + 200Z + 0C - D + E = 50$$

Here –D and –E are included in the second and third constraints, ensuring that idle funds unused from one period are carried over to the succeeding period. In addition, to prevent the program from repeatedly selecting only one project (the "best") until funds are exhausted, three additional constraints are needed:

$$X \leq 1, \quad Y \leq 1, \quad Z \leq 1 \tag{6.21}$$

The solution to the model if V = \$208.424, is:

$$X = 1.0, \quad Y = 0.6586, \quad Z = 0.6305 \tag{6.22}$$

The process of solving this linear program with Excel is illustrated in Appendix 6C.

To give an indication of the value of relaxing the funds constraint in any period (the most the firm would be willing to pay for additional financing), the shadow price of the funds constraints are given below[3]:

| Funds Constraint | Shadow Price |
|---|---|
| 1st period | 0.4517 |
| 2nd period | 0.4517 |
| 3rd period | 0.0914 |

It should be noted that the constraints related to $X \leq 1$, $Y \leq 1$, and $Z \leq 1$ are required in solving capital-rationing problems. If these constraints are removed, then we will obtain X = 2.4074, Y = 0, and Z = 0.5926. This issue has been discussed by Copeland and Weston (2003) and Weingartner (1963, 1977).

Thus, linear programming is a valuable mathematical tool with which to solve capital-budgeting problems when funds rationing is required. In addition, duality has been used by the banking industry to determine the cost of capital of funds. In Chapter 21, we will discuss capital rationing for four project cases. In addition, we will also discuss how to use linear programming in working capital management and long-term financial planning and forecasting.

## 6.8 Summary

Important concepts and methods related to capital-budgeting decisions under certainty were explored in this chapter. Cash-flow estimation methods were discussed before alternative capital-budgeting methods were explored. A comparison of the NPV and IRR methods was investigated in accordance with both theoretical and practical viewpoints. Issues relating different project lives were explored in some detail. Finally, capital-rationing decisions in terms of linear programming were discussed.

Following a survey by Graham and Harvey (2001) what we discussed in this chapter relative to the findings of this survey are present value techniques and firm risk. Furthermore, this survey analyzed how although larger firms use present value techniques and CAPM however, smaller firms concentrate on the payback criterion. Also, the survey findings suggest that firms are interested in the firm's risk and financial flexibility when evaluating new investments.

## Notes

1. Based upon a pure "efficient market" hypothesis and the concept of "opportunity cost," Copeland and Weston (2003) have argued that the logic of "reinvestment rates" used by the IRR rule is fallacious. However, if their two unrealistic assumptions do not hold, then their conclusion will not follow. Note that both short-run and long-run economic conditions should be considered in practical capital-budgeting decisions.
2. Dorfman (1981) has shown that the objective of determining the rate of growth of an enterprise in certain circumstances was best achieved by an IRR criterion instead of a NPV criteria. The reason was that when growth is the objective, the critical consideration in choosing among opportunities is the extent to which they generate funds available for reinvestment, and the best opportunity from this point of view is not necessarily the one with the highest NPV of cash flows.
3. Shadow price is the solution of the duality problem. This price is not a market price; it is the value to be imputed to the resources. These concepts and others, basic concepts of linear programming, will be explored further in Chapter 22.

## References

Ackoff, R. L. *A Concept of Corporate Planning* (Wiley, New York, 1970).

Bierman, H., Jr. and S. Smidt. *The Capital Budgeting Decision,* 1st edn. (Routledge, 2007).

Copeland, T. E. and J. F. Weston, *Financial Theory and Corporate Policy,* 4th edn. (Addison-Wesley Publishing Co., Reading, 2003).

Doenges, R. C. "The Reinvestment Problem in the Practical Prospective," *Financial Management*, 1 (Spring 1972, pp. 85–91).

Dorfman, R. "The meaning of internal rates of return," *The Journal of Finance*, 36(5) (1981, pp. 1011–1021).

Fisher, I. *The Theory of Interest* (MacMillan, New York, 1930).

Graham, J. R. and Harvey, C. R. "The Theory and Practice of Corporate Finance: Evidence from the Field," *Journal of Financial Economics*, 60(2–3) (2001, pp. 187–243).

Lee, C. F. and A. C. Lee. *Encyclopedia of Finance*, 2nd edn. (Springer, New York, 2013).

Lee, C. F. and J. C. Lee. *Financial Analysis, Planning, and Forecasting*, 3rd edn. (World Scientific Publishing Co., 2017).

Modigliani, F. and M. H. Miller, "The Cost of Capital, Corporation Finance, and the Theory of Investment," *American Economic Review*, 48 (June 1958, pp. 261–297).

Modigliani, F. and M. H. Miller, "Corporate Income Tax and the Cost of Capital: A Correction," *American Economic Review*, 53 (June 1963, pp. 433–443).

Myers, S. C. "Interaction of Corporate Financing and Investment Decision," *The Journal of Finance*, 29 (1974, pp. 1–25).

Pinches, G. "Myopia, Capital Budgeting, and Decision Making," *Financial Management*, 11 (1982, pp. 6–19).

Reinhardt, H. E. "Break-even Analysis for Lockheed's Tri Star: An Application," *The Journal of Finance*, 28 (September 1973, pp. 821–838).

Ross, S., R. Westerfield, J. Jaffe and B. Jordan. *Corporate Finance*, 12th edn. (McGraw-Hill Education, 2018).

Weingartner, H. M. *Mathematical Programming and the Analysis of Capital-Budgeting Problems* (Prentice-Hall, Englewood Cliffs, New Jersey, 1963).

Weingartner, H. M. "Capital Rationing: N Authors in Search of a Plot," *The Journal of Finance*, 32 (December 1977, pp. 1403–1432).

## Appendix 6A — Managers' View on Alternative Capital-Budgeting Methods

In an attempt to determine exactly what tools were needed by practitioners and what methods they were currently using in capital budgeting, Mao (1970), Hastie (1974), Fremgen (1973), Brigham and Pettway (1973), Schall, Sundem, and Geijsbeek (1978), and Oblak and Helm (1980) conducted surveys and field studies of companies. The papers that emerged from these studies provide great insight into the gulf that exists between theory and practice and attempt to explain the reasons for this gulf.

Mao (1970), in "Survey of Capital Budgeting: Theory and Practice," specifically examines three areas of capital budgeting and the disparity between theory and practice in each area. He first considers the objective of financial management, which, according to theory, is to maximize the market values of the firm's common shares. Price per share is, according to theory, a function of its expected earnings, the pure rate of interest, the price of risk, and the amount of risk as measured by covariance between its return and other returns. Of course, current theory does not provide any all-encompassing criteria by which to choose between alternative time patterns of share prices within the planning horizon, so the businessman has no way to accurately implement plans to increase share price.

Nevertheless, most executives interviewed implied that maximization of the value of the firm was their goal, although they phrased the idea in more operationally meaningful terms. However, in a break from theory, most executives didn't consider diversification by investors as having much impact on the value of the firm. According to theory, in a portfolio context only the nondiversifiable risk is relevant. While the major institutional investors, with large staffs of investment analysts, may fit into this portfolio context, many other investors will not. The executives saw consistent growth as a more important factor determining share value.

Mao next considered the theory and practice of risk analysis. The theoreticians measure risk by the variance of returns. Mao suggests, and I agree, that semi variance is a better measure of risk because it measures only downside risk. Management will not see the possibility of excess returns as a risk, but will focus on the risk of failing to earn an adequate return. The executives interviewed also emphasized downside risk and one called the chance of excess returns "a negative risk (a sweetener)." Those interviewed also expressed risk as a danger of insolvency when a large amount of capital was to be invested.

Theory recommends either of two methods for incorporating risk into investment analysis: the certainty-equivalent approach and the risk-adjusted discount-rate approach. When more than one investment may be made, the theory advocates the use of the portfolio approach.

The practitioners depended in general on a risk-adjusted discount rate approach to incorporate risk, although their actual methods may be more rudimentary than the purely theoretical approach dictates. Consideration is given to the human factors of enthusiasm and dedication to the project, qualities that are nonquantifiable. Interviews also disclosed a definitional difference between theorists and practitioners about the word diversification. In theory, every project should be evaluated in terms of its covariance with other projects in the portfolio. In practice, diversification is a much more subjective, long-range process where only major activities and their impact on diversification are considered.

Mao next revives a topic considered earlier: how to measure returns on projects. Theory immediately discounts payback period and accounting profit in favor of internal rate-of-return and net present value. Interview results show that only two of the eight companies use Internal Rate-of-Return alone, whereas six use payback and accounting profit alone or in conjunction with internal rate-of-return. Theorists have advanced two explanations for this incongruence. First, internal rate-of-return and net present value do not consider the effect of an investment on reported earnings. Stability of estimated EPS is important to management and investors alike, and these two criteria do not give management an indication of expected stability of earnings. Many companies neglect the net-present-value method because of the extreme difficulty of determining the appropriate discount rate. Individual company characteristics also determine, to a large extent, which measurement criteria are most appropriate. Lastly, Mao recommends types of research that can make theory more useful and meaningful to practitioners.

K. Larry Hastie (1974), himself a practitioner, also tries to give the academic world some advice on how to better aid the businessman. According to Hastie, in "One Businessman's View of Capital Budgeting," what is needed is not refinement or multiplication of measurement techniques but a re-evaluation of the assumptions inherent in the capital-budgeting process.

Hastie outlines the major problems practitioners face in capital budgeting. First, most companies are limited by capital rationing, so the problem becomes not one of finding adequate projects, but of choosing from among the acceptable projects. Theory offers no means of ranking projects with different risks, strategic purposes, and quality of analytical support. Ranking *per se* is not an adequate selection method unless the more qualitative criteria can somehow be incorporated into the process.

Judgments enter into any process in which uncertain profits must be estimated. Hastie highlights two types of errors in judgment that can lead to failure to achieve expected returns on projects. The first is caused by excessive pessimism or optimism, with only the second posing a serious problem. Overpessimism is akin to "upside" risk in that the company will not fail to meet its goal. Overoptimism is caused by poor judgment concerning future uncertainties, which in many cases could be cured only by hiring accurate fortune tellers.

Hastie also recognizes that, in many cases, it is not the measurement method but the financial analyst who fails. The financial analyst must have a good grasp of the quantitative and qualitative impacts of each project and must be able to communicate this information to the decision makers. Those preparing expenditure requests should be objective and realistic.

Hastie recommends several methods to improve capital-budgeting techniques. First, corporate strategy must be clarified and communicated so that projects incompatible with this strategy will not be needlessly analyzed. Second, analytical techniques must be evaluated. They should be understood by all who work with them and should generate the type of information used by the company in decision making. Hastie recommends the use of sensitivity analysis to isolate critical variables and give an expanded, more realistic range of estimated profits. What is essential is that those involved in the capital-budgeting process understand corporate strategy and policy and generate realistic data, which can effectively communicate to top-level management.

James Fremgen (1973) in "Capital Budgeting Practices: A Survey," continues the analysis of practitioner use of capital-budgeting techniques and offers some support for Hastie's position that measurement techniques are not the only important factor in capital budgeting. His survey again finds that payback period and accounting profit are widely used as selection criteria, contrary to theoretical approval of these methods, but also finds strong support for the use of internal rate-of-return. His results, however, do highlight a problem encountered when using the internal rate-of-return method — the multiple internal rate-of-return. His results also give some support to Doenges' recommendation that firms try to predict reinvestment rates for the funds to be received form projects being currently evaluated. Although of the 29% which projected reinvestment rates, the majority used current rates-of-return or costs of capital, some tried to estimate future reinvestment rates based on predicted future rate-of-returns or cost of capital.

A majority of those questioned used some technique to measure risk and uncertainty when analyzing investment projects. Again, however, a problem arises when deciding how to quantify this risk into the analysis. Most firms appear to require an unspecified amount of additional profit for additional risk. Of course, much of the analysis of projects is based on nonfinancial or nonquantitative judgments, and companies may feel that risk is best handled in this manner.

Fremgen confirmed the previously mentioned conclusion that capital rationing is a major influence on the capital-budgeting process. This rationing, commonly caused by a limitation on borrowing, was dealt with by most of the surveyed companies through ranking of projects. Although Hastie says this is not an adequate method of project selection, Fremgen makes little mention of nonfinancial, subjective methods of selection. Since project selection must be based on both financial and nonfinancial data, the results received must be due to wording of the question, which disallowed nonfinancial answers.

Providing impressive support for Hastie's position, Fremgen next described three stages of capital budgeting, only one of which dealt with financial analysis of the project. The results clearly reveal that financial analysis is considered neither the most critical nor the most difficult stage of the capital-budgeting process. More academic attention should be focused on the stage of project definition and estimation of cash flows, and the implementation and review stage of the process. Although these two stages are more difficult to adapt to quantitative methods, they would be more useful for the practitioner.

One final analysis of capital-budgeting theory and practice deals with a specific, fairly unique industry. Eugene Brigham and Richard Pettway (1973), in "Capital Budgeting by Utilities," studied the practices in this heavily regulated industry. Regulation has a profound effect on capital-budgeting practice, and the theory behind this regulation has become antiquated with the advent of double-digit inflation.

The regulators specify a target rate-of-return for utility companies, which then determine the rates they can charge consumers. However, inflation has caused the actual rate-of-return to fall below the "reasonable" rate-of-return, and, due to the lags in the regulatory process, new targeted rates-of-returns, when implemented, already have fallen behind inflation.

Another unique feature of the utility industry is that, due to legal requirements, they must make "mandatory" investments when needed to provide service upon demand. These mandatory investments, the major component of the capital budget, frequently offer rates-of-return below the utility's cost of capital. Although discretionary investments may provide higher returns, rarely can these excess returns counterbalance the effects of inflated operating costs, rising cost of capital, mandatory investments, and regulatory lags. Thus, the cost of capital exceeds the actual rate-of-return in the capital-investment budget.

Because of this unique situation, utilities must be very cautious when deciding which discretionary projects to accept. Projects with high rates of return are needed to help compensate for other losses. For mandatory investments, revenues are disregarded, and alternatives evaluated solely on the basis of costs on a discounted cash-flow basis. Due to the urgency of keeping costs as low as possible for mandatory investments, and profits as high as possible for discretionary investments, 94% of the companies use the discounted cash-flow method to project future financial results more accurately. Risk is also formally analyzed by over 50% of the utilities questioned.

Surprisingly, only 49% of these companies indicated that they have experienced capital rationing in the past five years, and most of these indicated that their response would be to apply for a rate increase to alleviate the problem. The most serious problem they face is securing permission to build new generating plants, a problem not shared with other industries. Since it is so crucial for rate determination, most utilities have ready cost-of-capital figures to use in capital-budgeting analysis.

Obviously, many of the problems facing the utility industry are unique to the industry, and the managers have developed different perspectives and policies on capital budgeting to cope with these problems. There is a message in this for all those involved with financial management. Regardless of the academician's recommendations, the competition's practices, and the market's signals, capital-budgeting policy and practice must be adapted to suit the individual firm's characteristics and needs. Theory and practice are helpful only to the extent that they can be successfully integrated into the individual company's financial structure. Theorists must try to recognize the needs of financial practitioners, but the practitioners must also realize that no mere formula will guarantee success, and realistic theories will help their financial analysis and planning decisions.

The reader should be aware that, in practice, most firms use a combination of capital budgeting techniques to arrive at investment decisions. For instance, in a survey of large firms, Schall, Sundem, and Geijsbeek (1978) found that 17% of those firms responding used four of the capital-budgeting techniques outlined above, and 34% used three of the four in making decisions. More surprisingly, although 86% of the firms used at least one of the discounting methods, the most popular technique was found to be the payback method, despite its disregard of several important factors. Perhaps the continued use of simpler methods combined with the more accurate NPV or IRR, points to the importance of ease of calculation for practitioners. In addition, despite the frequently noted ambiguities accompanying use of the IRR, the method enjoys a substantial and continuing popularity in practice. In their paper "Survey and Analysis of Capital-Budgeting Methods used by Multinationals," Oblak and Helm (1980) found that the IRR method and the payback method are two most popular capital-budgeting methods used by multinational firms. The continued use of IRR may be due to the fact that the rate-of-return of a project has a more intuitive appeal and is therefore easier to explain and justify within the firm than the more esoteric NPV criterion. The survey conducted by Graham and Harvey (2001) explains the existing and popular methods and processes of corporate finance.

This survey also mentioned John Lintner's (1956) groundbreaking research and study of the dividend policy. The goal of this survey conducted by Graham and Harvey was to establish new theories as well as alter current views of corporate finance. This survey also hopes to expose how other firms perform by offering recommendations that are not already being fully applied. The overall scope of this survey is very extensive and the concepts of capital budgeting, cost of capital, and capital structure are analyzed and discussed thoroughly. Furthermore, a large sample of about 4,440 firms is selected. Out of this sample, 392 chief financial officers responded to the survey, meaning that this survey has a response rate of about 9%. Another distinguishing factor of this survey is that the responses are analyzed according to firm characteristics. Overall the approach that this survey implements allows for a balance between clinical studies and large sample analyses.

## Appendix 6A References

Brigham, E. F. and Pettway, R. H. "Capital budgeting by utilities," *Financial Management*, 2(3) (1973, pp. 11–22).

Fremgen, J. "Capital-Budgeting Practices: A Survey," *Management Accounting*, 2 (May 1973, pp. 19–25).

Hastie, K. L. "One Businessman's View of Capital Budgeting," *Financial Management*, 3 (Winter 1974, pp. 36–44).

Lee, C. F. and A. C. Lee. *Encyclopedia of Finance*, 2nd ed. (Springer, New York, 2013).

Lintner, J. "Distribution of Incomes of Corporations among Dividends, Retained Earnings, and Taxes," *The American Economic Review*, 46(2) (1956, pp. 97–113).

Mao, J. C. T. "Survey of Capital Budgeting: Theory and Practice," *The Journal of Finance* (May 1970, pp. 349–60).

Oblak, D. J. and R. J. Helm, Jr. "Survey and Analysis of Capital-Budgeting Methods used by Multinationals," *Financial Management*, 9 (pp. 37–41).

Schall, L. D., G. L. Sundem and W.R. Geijsbeek, Jr. "Survey and Analysis of Capital-Budgeting Methods," *The Journal of Finance* (March 1978, pp. 281–287).

## Appendix 6B — Derivation of Crossover Rate

Suppose there are 2 projects under consideration. Cash flows of Projects A, B, and B–A as followed:

| Period | 0 | 1 | 2 | 3 |
|---|---|---|---|---|
| Project A | –10,000 | 10,000 | 1,000 | 1,000 |
| Project B | –10,000 | 1,000 | 1,000 | 12,000 |
| Cash flows of B–A | 0 | –9,000 | 0 | 11,000 |

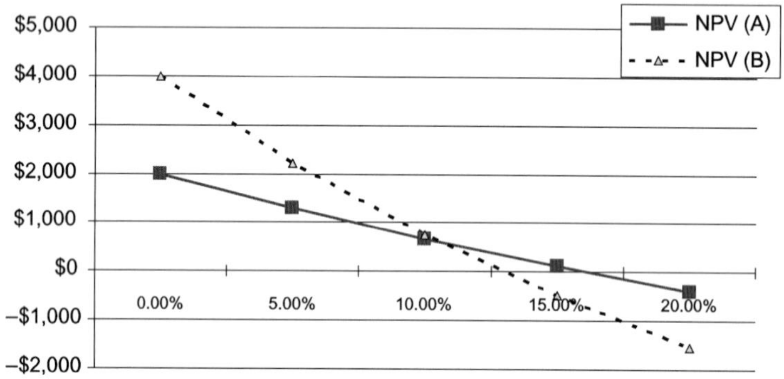


Figure 6.B1 NPV and IRR for Mutually Exclusive Projects.

NPV(B) is higher with low discount rates and NPV(A) is higher with high discount rates. This is because the cash flows of Project A occur early and those of Project B occur later. If we assume a high discount rate, we would favor Project A; if a low discount rate is expected, Project B will be chosen. In order to make the right choice, we can calculate the crossover rate. If the discount rate is higher than the crossover rate, we should choose Project A; if otherwise, we should go for Project B. *The crossover rate, Rc, is the rate such that NPV* (A) *equals to NPV* (B).

Suppose the crossover rate is $Rc$, then

$$\text{NPV(A)} = -10{,}000 + 10{,}000/(1 + Rc) + 1{,}000/(1 + Rc)^2 + 1{,}000/(1 + Rc)^3 \tag{6.1B}$$

$$\text{NPV(B)} = -10{,}000 + 1{,}000/(1 + Rc) + 1{,}000/(1 + Rc)^2 + 12{,}000/(1 + Rc)^3 \tag{6.2B}$$

$$\text{NPV(A)} = \text{NPV(B)}$$

Therefore,

$$-10{,}000 + \frac{10{,}000}{1+R_c} + \frac{1{,}000}{(1+R_c)^2} + \frac{1{,}000}{(1+R_c)^3} = -10{,}000 + \frac{1{,}000}{1+R_c} + \frac{1{,}000}{(1+R_c)^2} + \frac{12{,}000}{(1+R_c)^3}$$

Rearranging the above equation (moving all terms on the LHS to the RHS), we obtain (6.3B)

$$0 = [-10{,}000 - (-10{,}000)] + \left[\frac{1{,}000}{1+R_c} - \frac{10{,}000}{1+R_c}\right] + \left[\frac{1{,}000}{(1+R_c)^2} - \frac{1{,}000}{(1+R_c)^2}\right] + \left[\frac{12{,}000}{(1+R_c)^3} - \frac{1{,}000}{(1+R_c)^3}\right] \quad .....(6.3B)$$

Solving Eq. (6.3B) by trial and error method for $R_c$.
$R_c$ equals 10.55%.

In addition, the general equation of (6.3B) can be defined as

$$0 = CF_0(B-A) + \frac{CF_1(B-A)}{1+R_c} + \frac{CF_2(B-A)}{(1+R_c)^2} + \frac{CF_3(B-A)}{(1+R_c)^3}$$

where

$CF_0(B-A)$ = The different of net cash inflow between Project A and Project B at time 0.

$CF_1(B-A)$ = The different of net cash inflow between Project A and Project B at time 1.

$CF_2(B-A)$ = The different of net cash inflow between Project A and Project B at time 2.

Table 6.C1 Partial Inputs Information for NPV Method and IRR method.

| | | Year 0 | Year 1 | Year 2 | Year 3 | Year 4 |
|---|---|---|---|---|---|---|
| **Project A** | Cost | –\$80,000 | –\$20,000 | 0 | 0 | 0 |
| | Return | 0 | \$20,000 | \$30,000 | \$50,000 | \$50,000 |
| **Project B** | Cost | –\$50,000 | –\$50,000 | 0 | 0 | 0 |
| | Return | 0 | \$40,000 | \$60,000 | \$30,000 | \$10,000 |

$CF_3(B - A)$ = The different of net cash inflow between Project A and Project B at time 3.

In other word, $R_c$ is the IRR of the Project (B – A).

## Appendix 6C — Using Excel to Calculate NPV and IRR

Both NPV method and IRR method can be used to do capital budgeting decision. For example, Projects A and B, the initial outlays and net cash inflow for year 0 to year 4 are presented in Table 6.1C. In Table 6.1C, we know that the initial outlay at year 0 for Projects A and B are \$80,000 and \$50,000 respectively. In year 1, additional investment for Projects A and B are \$20,000 and \$50,000, respectively. The net cash inflow of Project A for the next four years are \$20,000, \$30,000, \$50,000, and \$50,000, respectively. The net cash inflow of Project B for the next four years are \$40,000, \$60,000, \$30,000, and \$10,000, respectively.

The net present value of a project is computed by discounting the project's cash flows to the present by the appropriate cost of capital. The formula used to calculate NPV can be defined as follows:

$$\mathrm{NPV} = \sum_{t=1}^{N} \frac{CF_t}{(1+k)^t} - I \tag{6.1C}$$

where $k$ = the appropriate discount rate; $CF_t$ = Net Cash flow (positive or negative) in period $t$; $I$ = Initial outlay; $N$ = Life of the project.

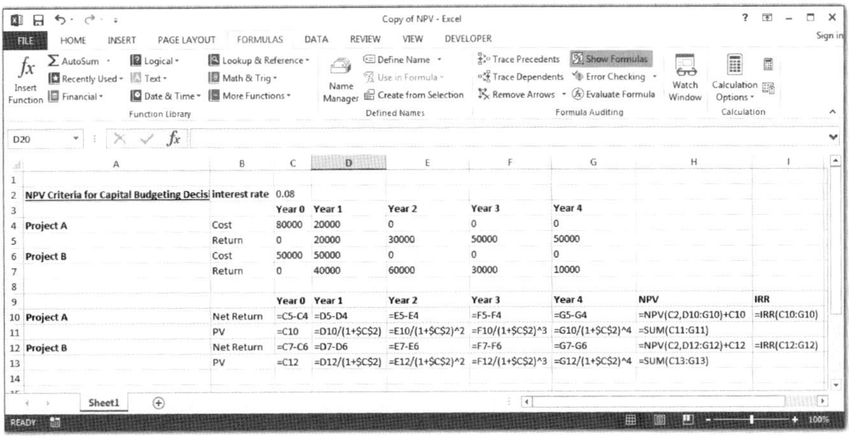

| | A | B | C | D | E | F | G | H | I |
|---|---|---|---|---|---|---|---|---|---|
| 1 | | | | | | | | | |
| 2 | NPV Criteria for Capital Budgeting Decisi | interest rate | 0.08 | | | | | | |
| 3 | | | Year 0 | Year 1 | Year 2 | Year 3 | Year 4 | | |
| 4 | Project A | Cost | 80000 | 20000 | 0 | 0 | 0 | | |
| 5 | | Return | 0 | 20000 | 30000 | 50000 | 50000 | | |
| 6 | Project B | Cost | 50000 | 50000 | 0 | 0 | 0 | | |
| 7 | | Return | 0 | 40000 | 60000 | 30000 | 10000 | | |
| 8 | | | | | | | | | |
| 9 | | | Year 0 | Year 1 | Year 2 | Year 3 | Year 4 | NPV | IRR |
| 10 | Project A | Net Return | =C5-C4 | =D5-D4 | =E5-E4 | =F5-F4 | =G5-G4 | =NPV(C2,D10:G10)+C10 | =IRR(C10:G10) |
| 11 | | PV | =C10 | =D10/(1+$C$2) | =E10/(1+$C$2)^2 | =F10/(1+$C$2)^3 | =G10/(1+$C$2)^4 | =SUM(C11:G11) | |
| 12 | Project B | Net Return | =C7-C6 | =D7-D6 | =E7-E6 | =F7-F6 | =G7-G6 | =NPV(C2,D12:G12)+C12 | =IRR(C12:G12) |
| 13 | | PV | =C12 | =D12/(1+$C$2) | =E12/(1+$C$2)^2 | =F12/(1+$C$2)^3 | =G12/(1+$C$2)^4 | =SUM(C13:G13) | |
| 14 | | | | | | | | | |

Figure 6.1C Excel Calculation Functions for NPV Method.

Using the Excel function, we can calculate NPV for both Projects A and B. We also can calculate he example above using Excel NPV function. NPV is a function to calculate the net present value of an investment by using a discount rate and a series of future payments (negative values) and income (positive values).

The NPV function in Cell H10 = NPV(C2,D10:G10) + C10

Based upon the NPV function in Figure 6.1C, the NPV results are shown in Figure 6.2C.

The IRR ($r$) is the discount rate which equates the discounted cash flows from a project to its investment. Thus, one must solve iteratively for the $r$ in Eq. (6.2C):

$$\sum_{t=1}^{N} \frac{CF_t}{(1+r)^t} = I \tag{6.2C}$$

where $CF_t$ = Net cash flow (positive or negative) in period $t$; $I$ = Initial investment; $N$ = Life of the project; $r$ = The internal rate of return.

In addition, we can use Excel function IRR to calculate IRR. IRR is a function to calculate the IRR which is the rate of return received for an investment consisting of payments (negative values)

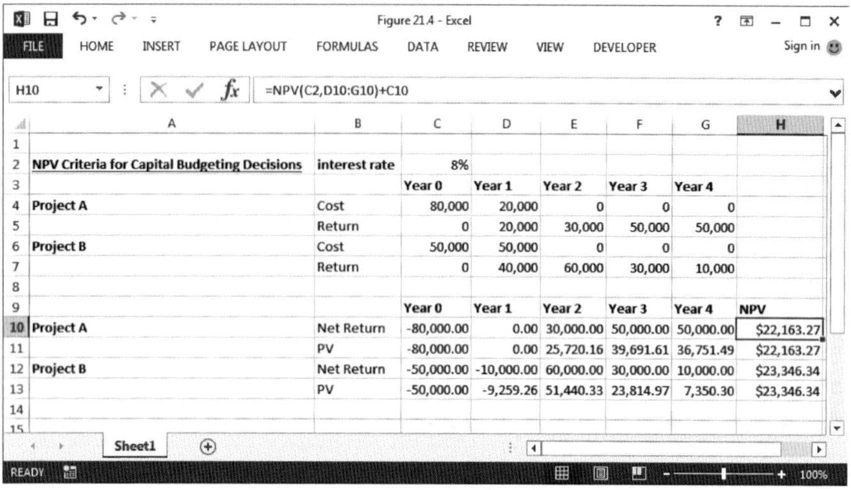


| | A | B | C | D | E | F | G | H |
|---|---|---|---|---|---|---|---|---|
| 1 | | | | | | | | |
| 2 | NPV Criteria for Capital Budgeting Decisions | interest rate | 8% | | | | | |
| 3 | | | Year 0 | Year 1 | Year 2 | Year 3 | Year 4 | |
| 4 | Project A | Cost | 80,000 | 20,000 | 0 | 0 | 0 | |
| 5 | | Return | 0 | 20,000 | 30,000 | 50,000 | 50,000 | |
| 6 | Project B | Cost | 50,000 | 50,000 | 0 | 0 | 0 | |
| 7 | | Return | 0 | 40,000 | 60,000 | 30,000 | 10,000 | |
| 8 | | | | | | | | |
| 9 | | | Year 0 | Year 1 | Year 2 | Year 3 | Year 4 | NPV |
| 10 | Project A | Net Return | -80,000.00 | 0.00 | 30,000.00 | 50,000.00 | 50,000.00 | $22,163.27 |
| 11 | | PV | -80,000.00 | 0.00 | 25,720.16 | 39,691.61 | 36,751.49 | $22,163.27 |
| 12 | Project B | Net Return | -50,000.00 | -10,000.00 | 60,000.00 | 30,000.00 | 10,000.00 | $23,346.34 |
| 13 | | PV | -50,000.00 | -9,259.26 | 51,440.33 | 23,814.97 | 7,350.30 | $23,346.34 |
| 14 | | | | | | | | |

Figure 6.2C Excel Calculation Results for NPV Method.

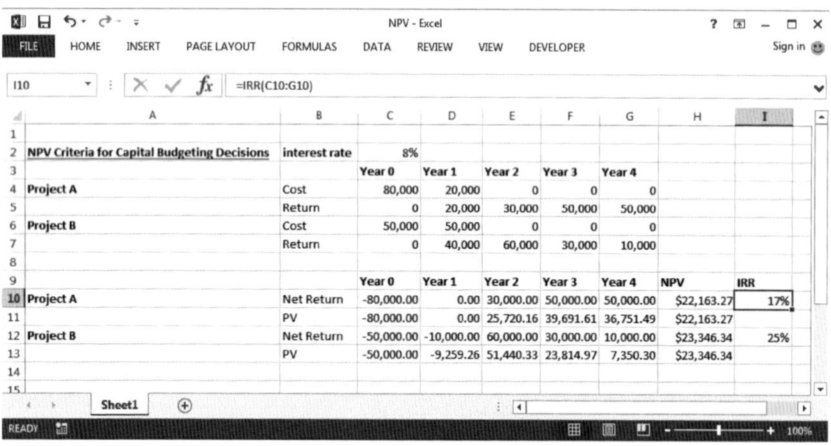


| | A | B | C | D | E | F | G | H | I |
|---|---|---|---|---|---|---|---|---|---|
| 1 | | | | | | | | | |
| 2 | NPV Criteria for Capital Budgeting Decisions | interest rate | 8% | | | | | | |
| 3 | | | Year 0 | Year 1 | Year 2 | Year 3 | Year 4 | | |
| 4 | Project A | Cost | 80,000 | 20,000 | 0 | 0 | 0 | | |
| 5 | | Return | 0 | 20,000 | 30,000 | 50,000 | 50,000 | | |
| 6 | Project B | Cost | 50,000 | 50,000 | 0 | 0 | 0 | | |
| 7 | | Return | 0 | 40,000 | 60,000 | 30,000 | 10,000 | | |
| 8 | | | | | | | | | |
| 9 | | | Year 0 | Year 1 | Year 2 | Year 3 | Year 4 | NPV | IRR |
| 10 | Project A | Net Return | -80,000.00 | 0.00 | 30,000.00 | 50,000.00 | 50,000.00 | $22,163.27 | 17% |
| 11 | | PV | -80,000.00 | 0.00 | 25,720.16 | 39,691.61 | 36,751.49 | $22,163.27 | |
| 12 | Project B | Net Return | -50,000.00 | -10,000.00 | 60,000.00 | 30,000.00 | 10,000.00 | $23,346.34 | 25% |
| 13 | | PV | -50,000.00 | -9,259.26 | 51,440.33 | 23,814.97 | 7,350.30 | $23,346.34 | |
| 14 | | | | | | | | | |

Figure 6.3C The Excel Calculation Results for IRR.

and income (positive values) that occur at regular periods. The IRR function in Cell I10, i.e., equal to IRR(C10:G10).

Based upon the IRR function on Figure 6.1C, the IRR results in terms of excel calculations are shown in Figure 6.3C.

## Appendix 6D — Solving the Linear Program Model for Capital Rationing

*The first step is to choose the cells which represents the unknowns: X, Y, Z, C, D and E.*

I use B15 to represent X, D15 represents Y, F15 represents Z, H15 represents C, J15 represents D, L15 represents E. Indeed, you can choose any cells to proxy for the unknowns based on your preference.

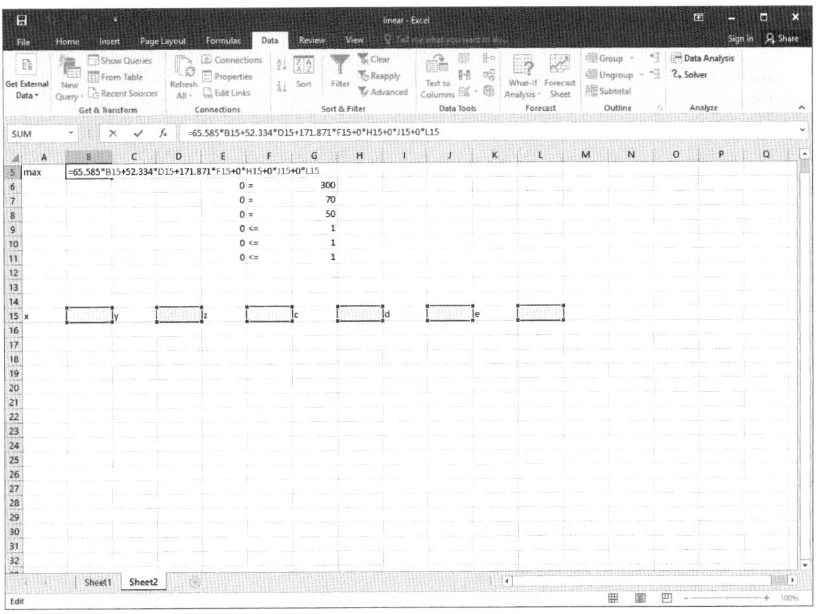


*The second step is to express the objective function.*

As our objective to maximize: V = 65.585X + 52.334Y + 171.871Z + 0C + 0D + 0E, V is our objective function. I then input the expression of the objective function in B5: "=65.585*B15+52.334*D15+171.871*F15+0*H15+0*J15+0*L15."

*The third step is to input the expression of the constraint.*

Our first constraint is: 100X + 200Y + 100Z + C + 0D + 0E = 300, so I input the left side of this equation "=100*B15+200*D15+100*F15+1*H15+0*J15+0*L15" in E6.

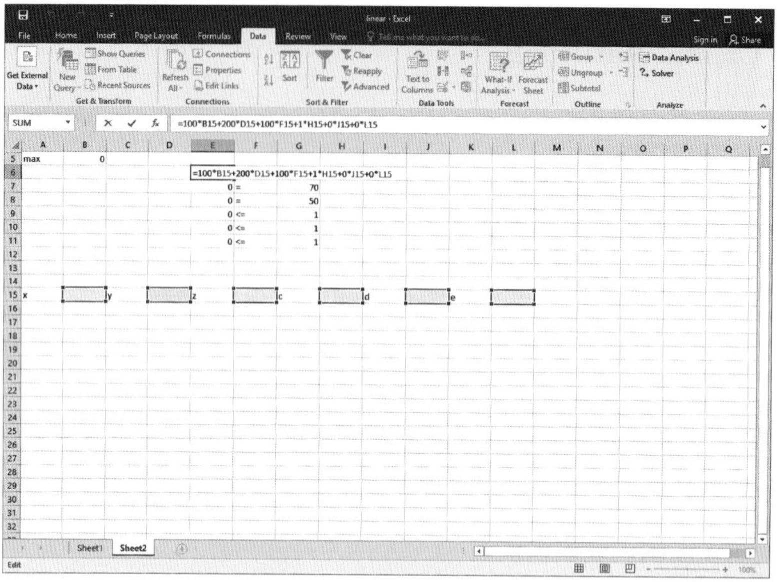

Our second constraint is: –30X – 70Y + 240Z – C + D + 0E = 70, so I input the left side of this equation "=–30*B15+(–70)*D15+240*F15+(–1)*H15+1*J15+0*L15" in E7.

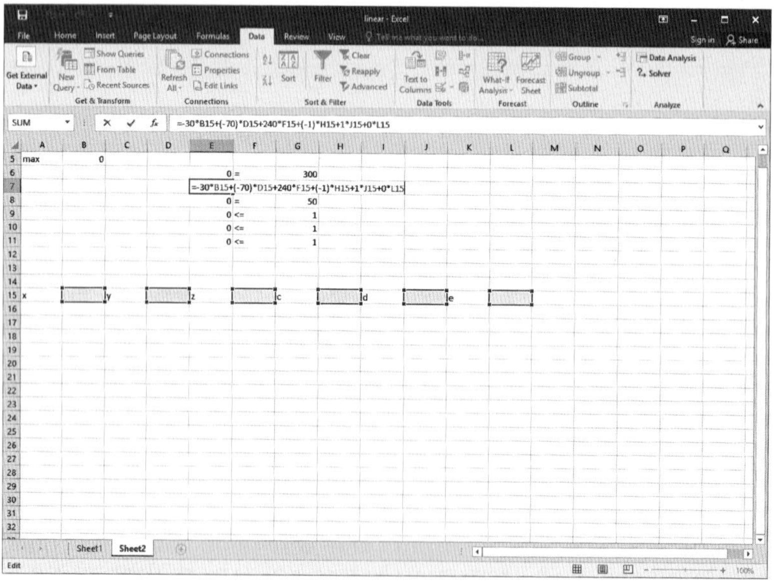

Our third constraint is: –30X – 70Y + 200Z + 0C – D + E = 50., so I input the left side of this equation "=–30*B15+(–70)*D15+200*F15+0*H15+(–1)*J15+1*L15" in E8.

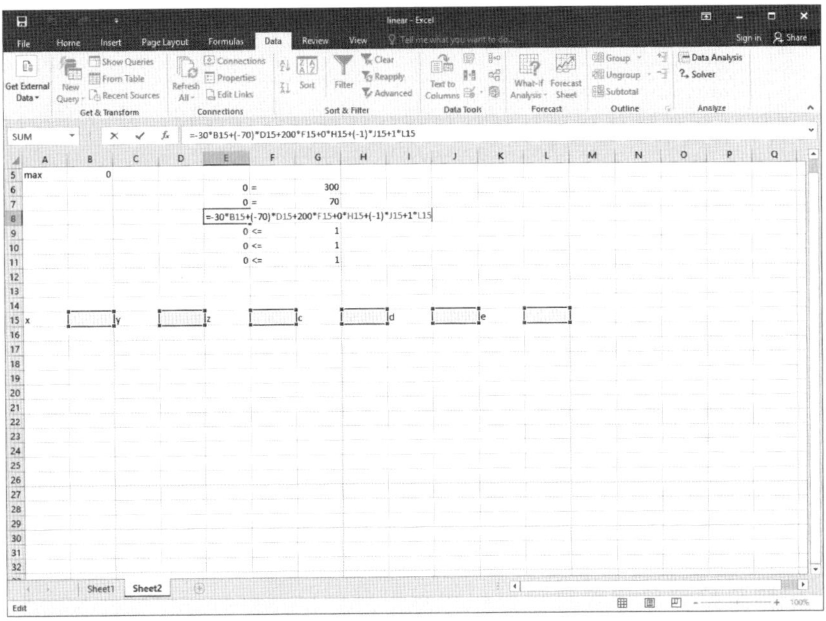

Additionally, we have constraints on X, Y and Z: X $\leq$ 1, Y $\leq$ 1, Z $\leq$ 1 and nonnegative. We will deal with them later.

*The fourth step is to click "data" and then open "Solver."*

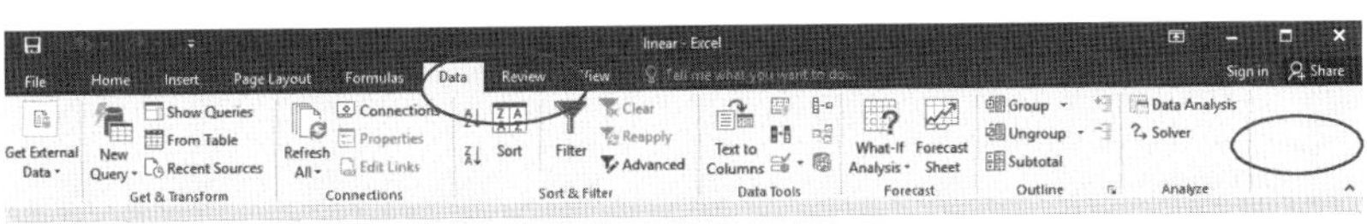

As our objective function is expressed in B5, we select "B5" in the place "set objective." Then we choose "Max" since we want to maximize the function.

Next we select B15, D15, F15, H15, J15 and L15 in the place "By changing variable cells" since we use these cells to represents our unknowns X, Y, Z, C, D, and E.

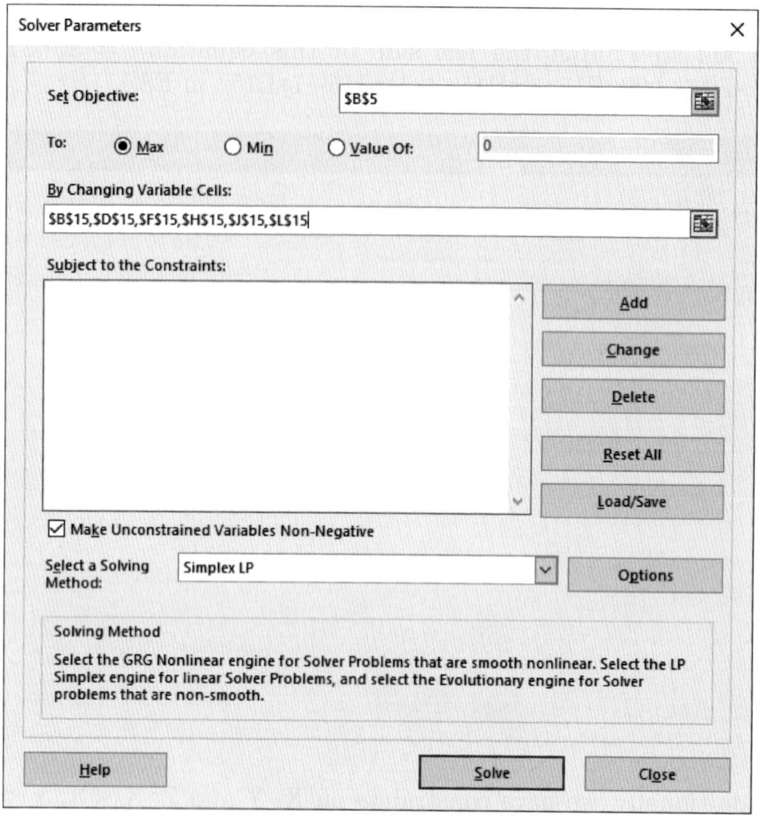


Next we add constraints via clicking "Add."

Our first constraint is expressed in E6, so we select in E6 in cell reference. Then we let E6 "=300" and click "Add."

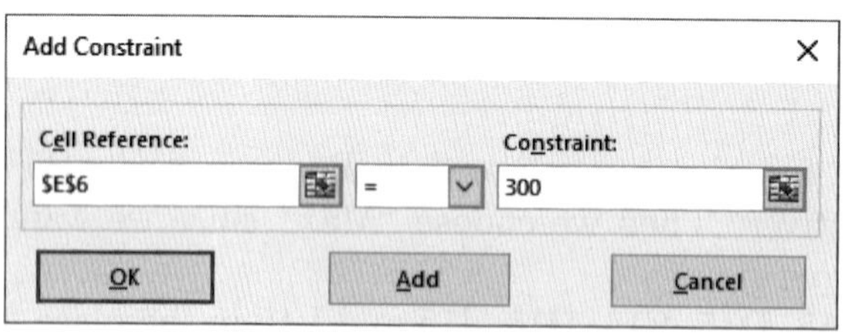


Our second constraint is expressed in E7, so we select in E6 in cell reference. Then we let E7 "=70" and click "Add."

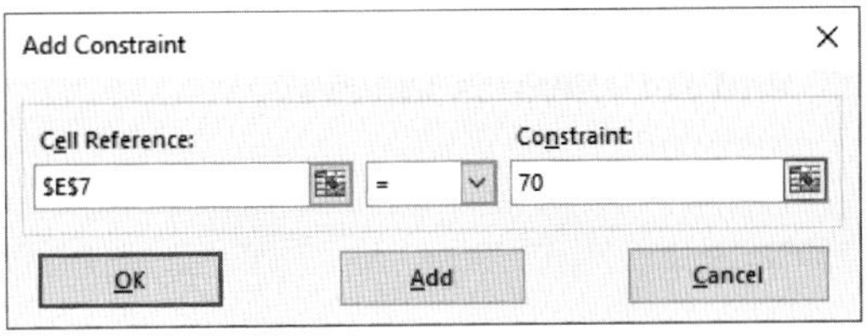


Our third constraint is expressed in E8, so we select in E6 in cell reference. Then we let E7 "=50" and click "Add."

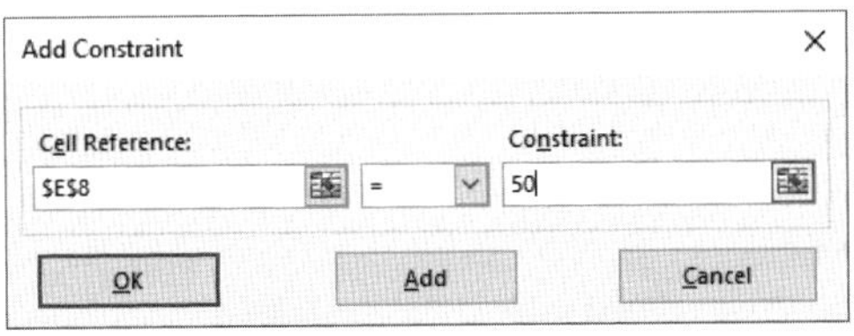


After we finish adding the three constraints, we have the followings display.

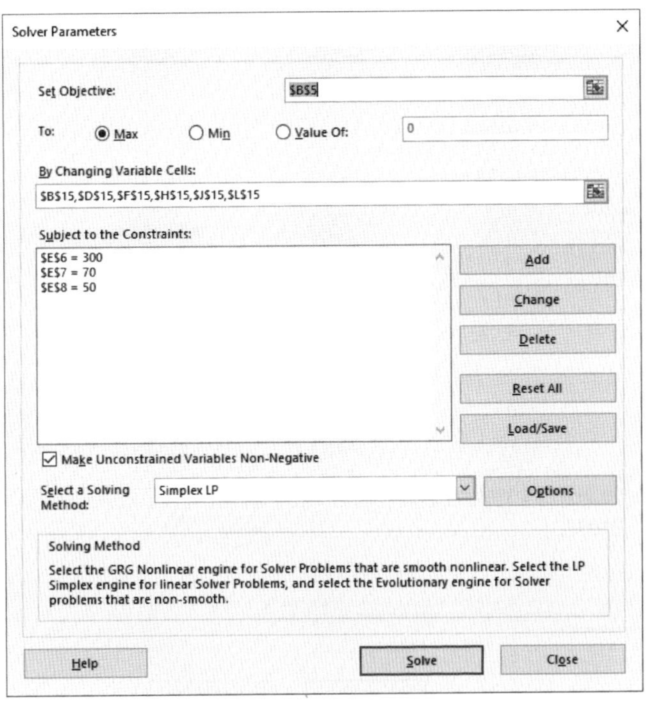

For additional constraints, X ≤ 1, Y ≤ 1, Z ≤ 1 and nonnegative, we continue clicking "add" and set them as follows:

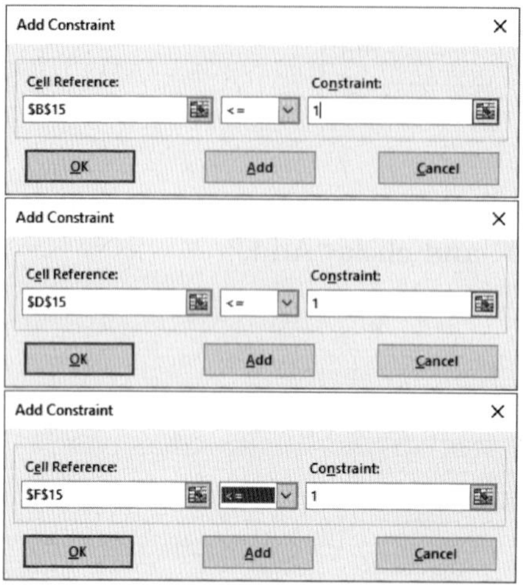


After adding all the constraint, we should select "Make Unconstrained variables nonnegative" because our X, Y, Z, C, D, E are nonnegative. The final display of setting the model is as follows:

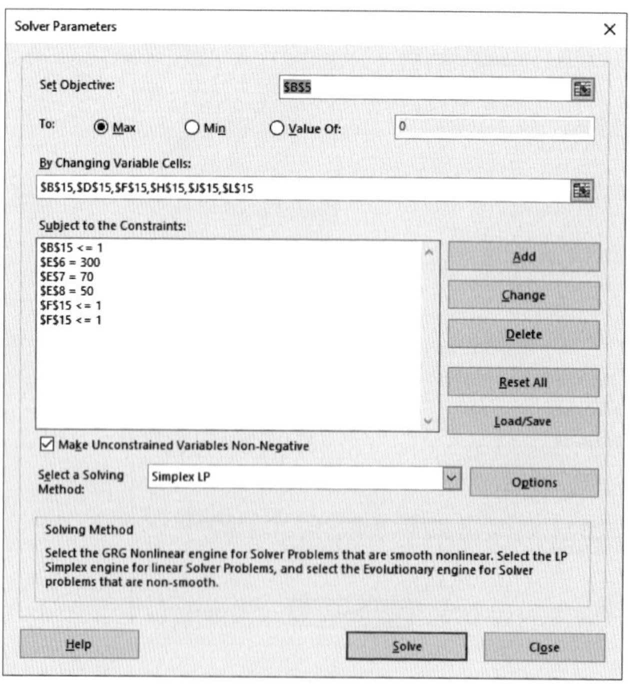

Now, we can click "solve" to get our final result. The Excel will give us the optimal weights X, Y, Z, C, D, and E in B15, D15, F15, H15, J15, and L15, respectively, and the maximum value of V in B5. The results are consistent with the solution shown in the example.

| | A | B | C | D | E | F | G | H | I | J | K | L |
|---|---|---|---|---|---|---|---|---|---|---|---|---|
| 5 | max | 208.4224 | | | | | | | | | | |
| 6 | | | | | 300 | = | 300 | | | | | |
| 7 | | | | | 70 | = | 70 | | | | | |
| 8 | | | | | 50 | = | 50 | | | | | |
| 9 | | | | | | | | | | | | |
| 10 | | | | | | | | | | | | |
| 11 | | | | | | | | | | | | |
| 12 | | | | | | | | | | | | |
| 13 | | | | | | | | | | | | |
| 14 | | | | | | | | | | | | |
| 15 | x | 1 | y | 0.658635 | z | 0.630522 | c | 5.220884 | d | 0 | e | 0 |
| 16 | | | | | | | | | | | | |
| 17 | | | | | | | | | | | | |
| 18 | | | | | | | | | | | | |
| 19 | | | | | | | | | | | | |
| 20 | | | | | | | | | | | | |
| 21 | | | | | | | | | | | | |

## Questions and Problems

1. Discuss the impact of project cash flows on a firm's market value. Which cash flows should be considered? What effect do accounting regulations have on the estimation of such flows?
2. Define the following terms:

   a. Net cash inflow
   b. Mutual exclusive versus independent project
   c. Opportunity cost versus cost of capital
   d. Accounting rate of return method
   e. Reinvestment rate
   f. Profitability index
   g. Capital rationing

3. Discuss the procedures involved in the cash-flow estimation with and without debt.
4. What is the capital budgeting process developed by Professor George Pinches (1982)?
5. What are the advantages and disadvantages of IRR method and NPV method for capital budgeting decisions?

6. Describe how linear programming method can be used to make the capital rationing decision.
7. Briefly discuss the various capital-budgeting methods. Which methods are theoretically and empirically more acceptable? Why?
8. Compare the NPV and IRR methods. Also discuss the situations when there is a conflict between the two results. Why do these conflicts occur?
9. Discuss some of the theoretical arguments against the use of the IRR method. Based upon the literature, are these arguments justifiable?
10. Discuss the effects of inflation on the capital-budgeting decision.
11. What major problems in performing capital budgeting are faced by practitioners? In what ways can alternative capital-budgeting techniques be improved?
12. Discuss and explain the processes involved in using linear programming to solve capital-rationing decisions. What assumptions must be made?
13. What are the implications for the capital-budgeting decision when comparing projects with unequal lives? How can we adjust for such a situation?
14. How can the NPV method be incorporated with break-even analysis to make the project decision analysis become more acceptable?
15. ZZZ Company is considering three projects. Which project is the best if the firm uses the accounting rate of return method for the selection method?

| | | **Net Income Year** | | | |
|---|---|---|---|---|---|
| **Project** | **Cost** | **1** | **2** | **3** | **4** |
| A | −100 | 50 | 50 | 60 | 60 |
| B | −100 | 10 | 50 | 60 | 80 |
| C | −100 | 120 | 40 | 30 | 10 |

a. In the question above, which of the three projects is best if ZZZ Company uses the payback method?

16. The ABC Company is considering two mutually exclusive investments. Project A has a cost of $25,000 and will produce after-tax net cash flows of $4,351 per year for ten years. Project B also has a cost of $25,000, and it is expected to produce cash flows of $6,990 per year for five years.

    a. Assuming that ABC's average cost of capital is 12% and that these two projects are both of average risk, which, if either, should ABC accept?
    b. Now assume that ABC's cost of capital rises to 14%. What is your decision now?
    c. Suppose ABC's cost of capital falls to 10%. How does this affect your decision?
    d. Draw the two projects' NPV profiles. Examine and explain the economic logic of why one project is better than the other.

17. ZZZ Company is considering three projects. Which project is the best if the firm uses NPV method for the selection method? Assume that the average cost of capital is equal to 10%.

| | | **Net Income Year** | | | |
|---|---|---|---|---|---|
| **Project** | **Cost** | **1** | **2** | **3** | **4** |
| A | −100 | 50 | 50 | 60 | 60 |
| B | −100 | 10 | 50 | 60 | 80 |
| C | −100 | 120 | 40 | 30 | 10 |

18. In Question 17 above, which of the three projects is best if ZZZ Company uses the profitability index method?

19. Calculate the IRR of Projects A and B:

| | | Net Income Year | | | | |
|---|---|---|---|---|---|---|
| **Project** | **Cost** | **1** | **2** | **3** | **4** | **5** |
| A | −200 | 40 | 60 | 50 | 100 | 1000 |
| B | −200 | 100 | 100 | 50 | 60 | 40 |

20. Let Projects X and Y be two mutually exclusive investment projects with a discount rate of 10% and the following cash flows:

| **Year** | **Project X** | **Project Y** |
|---|---|---|
| 0 | −100 | −100 |
| 1 | 80 | 20 |
| 2 | 70 | 30 |
| 3 | | 50 |
| 4 | | 100 |

a. Calculate NPV of the two projects.
b. Calculate NPV with infinite replication.

21. Projects A and B both involve the same initial investment and generate the same IRR, which exceeds the opportunity cost of capital. The cash flows of Project A are larger than those of B, but tend to occur later. Which has higher NPV?
22. The cash flows from ZZZ Company's project are $C_0 = 500{,}000$, $C_1 = 400{,}000$, and $C_2 = -1{,}200{,}000$. If the opportunity cost of capital is 12%, should ZZZ accept the project?
23. Lamy Enterprises is a manufacturer of high quality running shoes. Meredith Lamy, president, is considering computerizing the company's ordering, inventory, and billing procedures. She estimates that the annual savings from computerization include a reduction often ten employees with annual salaries of $15,000

each, $8,000 from reduced production delays caused by raw materials inventory problems. $12,000 from lost sales due to inventory stockouts, and $3,000 associated with timely billing procedures. The purchase price of the system is $200,000 and installation costs are $50,000. These outlays will be capitalized (depreciated) on a straight-line basis to a zero book salvage value which is also its market value at the end of five years. Operation of the new system requires two computer specialists with annual salaries of $40,000 per person. Also annual maintenance and operating (cash) expenses of $12,000 are estimated to be required. The corporation's tax rate is 40% and its required rate of return (cost of capital) for this project is 12%.

a. Find the project's initial net cash outlay.
b. Find the project's operating and terminal value cash flows over its 5-year life.
c. Evaluate the project using the NPV method.
d. Evaluate the project using the IRR method.
e. Evaluate the project using the PI method.
f. Calculate the project's payback period.
g. Find the project's cash flows and NPV (parts a through c) assuming that the system can be sold for $25,000 at the end of five years even though the book salvage value will be zero.
h. Find the project's cash flows and NPV (parts a through c) assuming that the book salvage value for depreciation purposes is $20,000 even though the machine is worthless in terms of its resale value.

24. Thompson's Tree Farm is considering the replacement of its large delivery tractor and trailer. The old truck originally cost $60,000 when it was purchased three years ago. It is being depreciated over a six-year life to a zero book value. Thompson believes that the useful remaining life of the old truck is five years after which it will have a resale value of zero. The company can sell the old truck now for $14,000.

The new truck will cost $90,000 and will be depreciated over a five-year period to a zero book salvage value. At the end of five years it will be sold for $20,000. The new truck will produce cash savings of $8,000 as a result of reduced maintenance and additional savings of $15,000 from delays caused by breakdowns on deliveries.

The company's tax rate is 40% and it uses straight-line depreciation. The required rate of return (cost of capital) for the project is 10%.

a. Find the project's initial net cash outlay.
b. Find the project's operating and terminal value cash flows for years 1 through 5.
c. Evaluate the project using the NPV.
d. Evaluate the project using the IRR.
e. Evaluate the project using the PI.
f. Calculate the project's payback period.

25. If a project's PI is 2.0 and its initial net cash outlay is $5,000, find its NPV.
26. Stephanie's Tack and Bridle Shop is considering opening a new (additional) store in a nearby city. Fixed operating costs are estimated to be $25,000 and variable costs will be 30% of sales. Annual revenues for the project are forecasted to be $90,000.

    The land for the store currently costs $40,000 and the building will cost $80,000 to construct. Depreciable equipment costing $20,000 must be purchased. The building and equipment will be depreciated over its 10-year life to a zero salvage value. At the end of 10 years the building and land will be sold for a combined price of $95,000. (The land value will be $70,000 and the value of the building will be $25,000.)

    The company's tax rate is 40%. Its required rate of return for the project is 14%; and, straight-line depreciation is used.

    a. Find the project's initial net cash outlay.
    b. Find the project's operating and terminal cash flows.
    c. Evaluate the project using the NPV, IRR, and PI methods.
    d. If the new store reduces annual cash flows at the existing store by $13,000, would your answers to parts a through c change? Explain.
    e. If $3,000 of Stephanie's existing overhead will be allocated to the new facility for accounting purposes, will your answers to parts a through c change? Explain.

27. AMCG Electric is required to install additional safety control equipment at its northwestern nuclear power plant. There are two different types of equipment that meet government standards. The Alpha equipment costs \$105,000, has a 10-year life over which it will be depreciated to a zero book salvage value. The Gamma equipment costs \$90,000 and will also be depreciated over a 10-year life to a zero book salvage value. The Alpha equipment will require \$10,500 per year in cash operating and maintenance expenses while the Gamma equipment will require only \$9,000. Neither machine will have any resale value at the end of its 10-year life. Given a required rate of return of 10% for this investment decision, which type of equipment should be purchased? The corporate tax rate is 40%.

## Chapter 7

# Risk Estimation and Diversification

**Contents**



## 7.1 Introduction

This chapter presents the basic concepts of risk in the context of business operations, corporate financing decisions, and diversification. Methods of measuring risk are explained by using basic statistical procedures. Also included are the concepts and applications of the dominance principle and portfolio theory.

We begin the chapter by discussing the types and classifications of risk in Section 7.2. This is followed by Section 7.3 on the concepts of portfolio analysis and its applications. In Section 7.4, we discuss the calculations of the market rate of return and the market risk premium. Determination of the commercial lending rate in accordance with risk and return concepts is discussed in Section 7.5. Section 7.6 discusses the dominance principle and the necessity of using performance measures to compare the performance of different portfolios. Finally, in Section 7.7, the results of this chapter are summarized. Appendix 7A discusses the estimation of market risk premium, while Appendix 7B explores the normal distribution. Appendix 7C discusses how minimum-variance approach can be used to derive the optimal weight for a two-security portfolio. Finally, in Appendix 7D we show how the Sharpe performance measure approach can be used to derive the optimal weight for a two-security portfolio.

## 7.2 Risk Classification

Earlier, we discussed the rates of returns on stocks. In this chapter, we discuss the risk associated with the rate of return. Risk is defined as the probability of success or failure, where success is making a profit and failure is losing money on an investment. In finance and accounting, we refer to risk as the degree of fluctuation associated with either return on investment (ROI) or the rates of return on securities. Depending on its sources, risk can be classified as business risk or financial risk. Sources of risk are useful for both corporate managers and shareholders to determine and assess a firm's market value.

### 7.2.1 *Business risk*

Business risk, sometimes called operating risk, refers to the degree of fluctuation of net income and cash flow associated with different types of businesses and operating strategies. The fluctuation of operating income represents a business risk. Business risk to shareholders generally arises from uncertainty about the firm's product markets, input markets, or operations. Business risk also can be inherent in the firm's commercial activities. If a firm is entirely equity funded, then the fluctuation of ROI, earnings per share (EPS), and rate of equity (ROE) can be used to determine business risk.

The possible ROIs of General Motors (company A) and Ford (company B) for the coming year are listed in Table 7.1.

Table 7.1 ROI and State of Economy.

| **State of Economy** | **State Occurring ($P_i$)** | **ROI ($A_1$) of GM($X_{AI}$) (%)** | **ROI ($B_i$) of Ford ($X_{Bi}$) (%)** |
|---|---|---|---|
| Boom | 0.20 | 15 | 14 |
| Normal | 0.60 | 12 | 11 |
| Recession | 0.20 | 4 | 3 |

In Table 7.1, we see that there is a 20% chance of a boom economy in the coming year, in which both GM and Ford will have a high ROI; and a 20% chance of a recession, which will mean low ROI for both GM and Ford.

The expected ROI and the variance of ROI for these two auto manufacturers can be calculated by Eqs. (7.1) and (7.2):

$$\text{Expected ROI} = \bar{X} = \sum_{i=1}^{n} X_i P_i \tag{7.1}$$

$$\text{Variance of ROI} = \sigma^2 = \sum_{i=1}^{n} (Xi - \overline{X})^2 P_i \tag{7.2}$$

where $P_i$ = probability of occurrence of the $i$th state of the economy and $X_i$ = ROI in the $i$th state of the economy.

Substituting the data of Table 7.1 into Eqs. (7.1) and (7.2), we have

$$\text{GM}: \ \bar{X}_{\text{A}} = (0.15)(0.2) + (0.12)(0.6) + (0.4)(0.2) = 11\%$$

$$\text{Ford}: \ \overline{X}_{\text{B}} = (0.14)(0.2) + (0.11)(0.6) + (0.3)(0.2) = 10\%$$

$$\begin{aligned}\text{GM}: \ \sigma^2_{\text{A}} &= (0.15 - 0.11)^2(0.2) + (0.12 - 0.11)^2(0.6)\\ &\quad + (0.4 - 0.11)^2(0.2) = 0.00136\end{aligned}$$

$$\begin{aligned}\text{Ford}: \ \sigma^2_{\text{B}} &= (0.14 - 0.10)^2(0.2) + (0.11 - 0.10)^2(0.6)\\ &\quad + (0.3 - 0.1)^2(0.2) = 0.00136.\end{aligned}$$

These results show that the expected ROIs are 11% for GM and 10% for Ford, with a variance of ROI for both firms of 0.00316. Thus, the absolute business risk is about the same for both firms.

To simultaneously compare these firms in terms of expected returns and risk, we use the coefficient of variation as indicated in Eq. (7.3):

$$\text{Coefficient of variation (CV)} = \frac{\sigma}{\bar{X}} \tag{7.3}$$

The CV for GM and Ford is determined as follows:

$$\text{GM: } \mathrm{CV}_A = \frac{\sqrt{0.00136}}{0.11} = \frac{0.369}{0.11} = 0.3353$$

$$\text{Ford: } \mathrm{CV}_B = \frac{\sqrt{0.00136}}{0.10} = \frac{0.0369}{0.10} = 0.3690$$

These coefficients of variation show that the risk per unit of return for Ford is greater than the risk per unit of return for GM. That is, even though both companies face the same business risk, when we simultaneously consider both risk and return, GM is superior. It should be noted that this result does not necessarily hold in a portfolio context, where the appropriation risk measure is not only the variance or the coefficient of variation but is also the correlation coefficient. (This is discussed in greater detail later in this chapter.)

If the probability distribution of the firms' ROI is normal, then the mean and standard deviation of ROIs for both GM and Ford can be used to calculate the probability that ROI will be greater or less than a certain amount. We will now discuss the method that is used to standardize the distribution in order to determine how many standard deviations a specific ROI is from the mean. Suppose we want to know the probability that the actual ROI for GM will be greater than 15.44%. In standardizing the distribution (see Appendix 7A), we obtain:

$$Z = \frac{15.44\% - 11\%}{3.69\%} = 1.20 \text{ Standard deviations}$$

Referring to the normal distribution table found in the appendix at the end of this book, we find that there is a 0.885 probability that actual ROI will be greater than 15.44%.

For a normal distribution, the actual ROI will lie within $\pm 1$ standard deviation of expected ROI 68.27% of the time the actual ROI will be within $\pm 2$ standard deviation of expected ROI 95.45% of the time and the actual ROI will lie within $\pm 3$

standard deviation of expected ROI 99.73% of the time. These interval estimates of ROI for both GM and Ford are shown below:

| | Interval | Chance of Occurrence (%) |
|---|---|---|
| GM | $0.11 - 0.037 < X < 0.11 + 0.037$ | 68.27 |
| | $0.11 - 0.074 < X < 0.11 + 0.074$ | 95.45 |
| | $0.11 - 0.111 < X < 0.11 + 0.111$ | 99.73 |
| Ford | $0.10 - 0.037 < X < 0.10 + 0.037$ | 68.27 |
| | $0.11 - 0.074 < X < 0.11 + 0.074$ | 95.45 |
| | $0.11 - 0.111 < X < 0.11 + 0.111$ | 99.73 |

This information is useful for investors because it enables them to make risk comparisons between GM and Ford. In this case, the standard deviations of ROI for both companies are the same, implying that the risk for each is the same. Hence, GM is preferable because it has a higher return for the same level of risk.

### 7.2.2 *Financial risk*

Financial leverage is the magnification of profit or loss through the use of debt financing. Financial risk refers to the risk of not being able to meet the fixed cash flow requirement of debt financing, which could lead to bankruptcy. Hence, financial risk is related to financial leverage. The amount of financial leverage is determined by the amount of short- and long-term debt that the firm employs in its capital structure. One of the ways to measure financial risk is by the firm's debt/equity ratio. The relationship between total risk and financial leverage (debt/equity) is indicated in Figure 7.1. Business risk is unrelated to the amount of financial leverage, as shown by line AB. But financial risk is directly related to the amount of leverage, as shown by line AC. The sum of business risk and financial risk is the firm's total risk. The combination of business risk and financial risk plays a central role in the theory and practice of corporate finance.

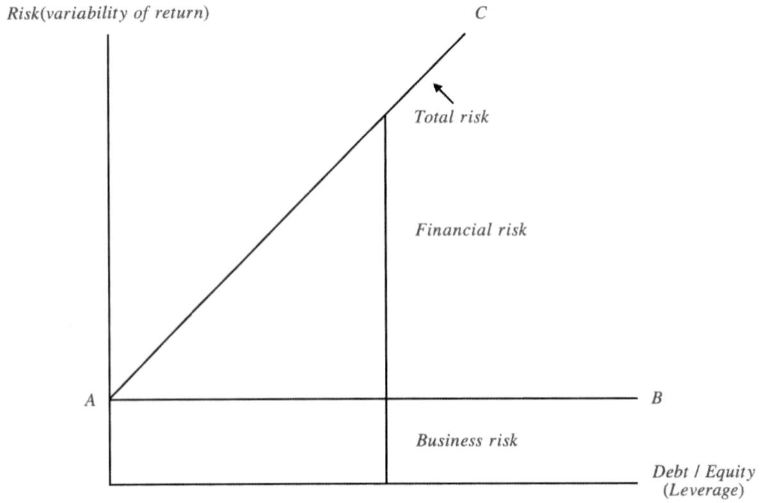


Figure 7.1 Relationship of Total Risk to Financial Leverage.

Business risk and financial risk are not necessarily constant over time. Both can be affected by fluctuations of the business cycle or by changes in the federal government's fiscal policy and the Federal Reserve System's monetary policy. Hence, economic information is relevant to the financial manager when assessing the riskiness of a given situation.

### 7.2.3 *Total risk*

Total risk refers to the combined effects of business risk and financial risk, as indicated in Figure 7.1. Total risk is defined as:

$$\text{Total risk} = \text{Business risk} + \text{Financial risk}$$

In the case of multinational firms, or firms with international investments, business risk can take on an international dimension. Exchange rate fluctuations, government stability, and segmented markets are some components of international risk. Exchange rate risk deals with the foreign exchange rate between the firm's home country and the foreign country where its investments are being made. The exchange rate is the price of foreign currency in terms of the domestic monetary unit. A change is the price of foreign currency in terms of the domestic monetary unit. A change in the exchange rate will produce a change in price of foreign goods in terms of domestic currency, as well as a proportionate change in the price of domestic goods in terms of the foreign currency.

For example on September 24, 2007, the exchange rate between the U.S. dollar and the Chinese Yuan was $1331 to 1 Yuan. Suppose that on September 25, 2007, the Yuan was devalued 10%, such that $.1198 was equal to 1 Yuan. For a U.S. consumer, an item costing 1,000 Yuan in China would cost $133.1 on September 24. On September 25, this same item would be $119.8. Therefore, the U.S. will import more goods from China because the depreciation in the value of the Chinese currency makes Chinese exports cheaper. For the Chinese consumer, an item worth $133.1 would cost 1,000 Yuan on September 24 and 1,110 Yuan on September 25. This increase in price, caused by the Yuan depreciation, would result in a decreased demand for American imports. Therefore, an appreciation in the Yuan would cause an opposite effect, an increase in demand for imports. It is apparent that firms with business dealings in foreign countries must be aware of foreign exchange fluctuations. A profit made in a foreign country could be easily translated into a loss with a sudden appreciation in the U.S. dollar.

A second type of international business risk is political risk, which refers to the political climate and conditions of the country. For instance, a country with an unstable government may experience wild fluctuations in interest rates because of a lack of confidence from the business community. Or there may be a chance that the government will expropriate plant and equipment or negate contracts. These are all political risks that a firm must include in its risk analysis when it operates internationally. Such risks are also included in the business risk component of total risk.

## 7.3 Portfolio Analysis and Application

A portfolio is any combination of assets or investments. Portfolio analysis is used to determine the return and risk characteristics for any combination of assets. As first described by Harry Markowitz (1959), portfolio analysis involves the identification of specific statistical characteristics that enable managers or investors to systematically reduce risk through diversification; that is, holding more than a single asset in a portfolio.

### 7.3.1 *Expected rate of return on a portfolio*

The rate of return on a portfolio is simply the weighted average of the returns of individual securities in the portfolio. This is a linear relationship. For example, suppose 40% of the portfolio is invested in security $a$ and 30% is invested in security $b$ and $c$, respectively. If the expected rate of return of securities $a$, $b$, and $c$ is 10%, 5%, and 12%, respectively, then the expected rate of return for this portfolio is:

$$\begin{aligned}\overline{R}_P &= W_a\overline{R}_a + W_b\overline{R}_b + W_c\overline{R}_c \\ &= (0.4)(0.1) + (0.3)(0.05) + (0.3)(0.12) \\ &= 0.091\end{aligned}$$

where $W_a$, $W_b$, and $W_c$ are the propositions of the portfolio invested in securities $a$, $b$, and $c$. The summation of these weights equals 1. $\overline{R}_a$, $\overline{R}_b$, and $\overline{R}_c$ represent expected rates of return on securities $a$, $b$, and $c$. $\overline{R}_p$ represents the expected rate of return of return for the portfolio, which is the weighted average of the securities' expected rates of return. In general, the expected return on an n-asset portfolio is defined by Eq. (7.4):

$$\overline{R}_p = \sum_{i=1}^{n} W_i\overline{R}_i \quad \text{where} \quad \left(\sum_{i=1}^{n} W_i = 1\right) \tag{7.4}$$

where $W_i$ is the proportion of the individual's investment allocated to security $i$, and $\overline{R}_i$ is the expected rate of return for security $i$.

If an investor chooses not to invest the entire portfolio in financial assets, then one of the investor's assets will be cash. Hence, the individual investor must hold 100% of his or her financial wealth in some form of profitable assets and cash.

### 7.3.2 Variance and standard deviation of a portfolio

A portfolio's risk is measured by its standard deviation, or variance. The standard deviation is the square root of the variance. To calculate a portfolio's standard deviation, we should first identify the covariance among the securities in the portfolio. The covariance between two such securities is defined as follows:

$$\begin{aligned}\mathrm{COV}(W_1R_1,\, W_2R_2) &= \frac{1}{N}\sum_{t=1}^{N}(W_1R_{1t} - W_1\overline{R}_1)\\ &\quad (W_2R_{2t} - W_2\overline{R}_2)\\ &= \frac{W_1W_2}{N}\sum_{t=1}^{N}(R_{1t} - \overline{R}_1)(R_{2t} - \overline{R}_2)\\ &= W_1\,W_2\mathrm{COV}(R_1, R_2) \qquad (7.5)\end{aligned}$$

where $R_{1t}$ is the rate of return for the first security in period $t$ and $R_{2t}$ is the rate of return for the second security in period $t$. $\overline{R}_1$ and $\overline{R}_2$ are average rates of return for the securities, while $\mathrm{COV}(R_1,\, R_2)$ represents the covariance between $R_1$ and $R_2$.

$$\begin{aligned}\sigma_P^2 = \mathrm{VAR}(W_1R_{1t} + W_2R_{2t}) &= \frac{1}{N}\sum_{t=1}^{N}[(W_1R_{1t} + W_2R_{2t})\\ &\quad -(W_1\overline{R}_1 + W_2\overline{R}_2)]^2 = W_1^2\sigma_1^2\\ &\quad +W_2^2\sigma_2^2 + 2W_1W_2\mathrm{COV}(R_1, R_2)\end{aligned} \qquad (7.6)$$

Now that we have shown how to find covariance and variance of a portfolio, we proceed to the standard deviation of returns for a portfolio, which is determined as follows:

$$\sigma_P = \sqrt{\frac{1}{N}\sum_{t=1}^{N}(R_{pt} - \overline{R}_P)^2} \qquad (7.7)$$

where $\sigma_p$ is the standard deviation of the portfolio's return, $R_{pt}$ is the portfolio's rate of return in period $t$, and $\overline{R}_p$ is the average

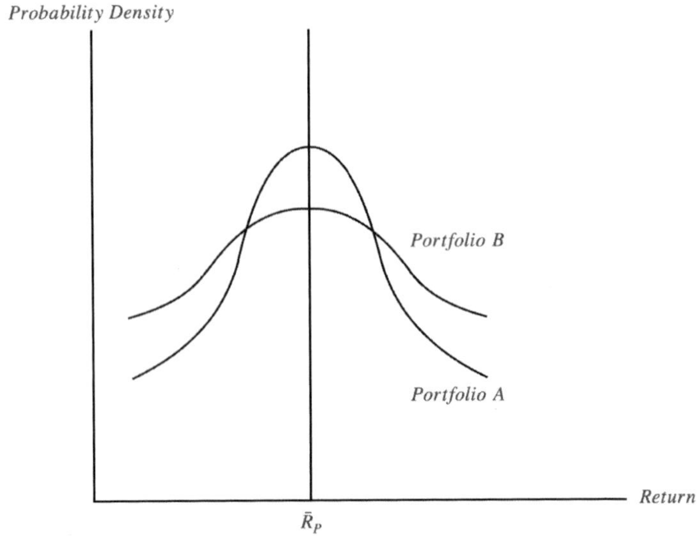


Figure 7.2 Probability Distribution of Returns for Two Portfolios.

portfolio rate of return. Figure 7.2 illustrates two possible distributions for two portfolios with the same expected return but with different degrees of risk. Portfolio B's variability is larger than portfolio A's. Consequently, investors regard portfolio B as riskier than portfolio A. Therefore, portfolio A is more attractive than portfolio B because it offers less risk with the same expected return.

### 7.3.3 *The two-asset case*

To explain the fundamental aspect of portfolio risk diversification, we consider the two-asset case. Following Eqs. (7.6) and (7.7), we define $\sigma_p$ as follows:

$$\sigma_P = \left[W_1^2\text{VAR}(R_1) + W_2^2\text{VAR}(R_2) + 2W_1W_2\text{COV}(R_1, R_2)\right]^{\frac{1}{2}} \tag{7.8}$$

where $W_1 + W_2 = 1$. The covariance term can be expressed in terms of the correlation coefficient between $R_1$ and $R_2$ and the respective standard deviations of $R_1$ and $R_2$:

$$\text{COV}(R_1, R_2) = \rho_{12}\sigma_1\sigma_2 \tag{7.9}$$

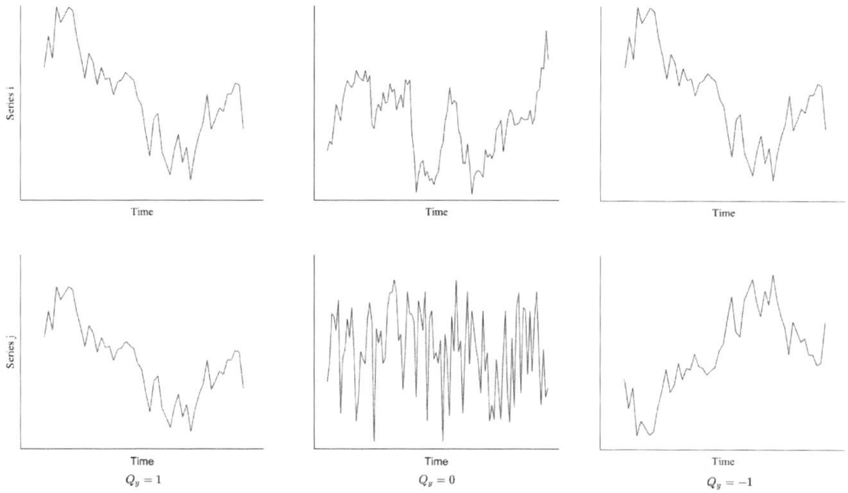


Figure 7.3 Relationship of Total Risk to Financial Leverage.

The correlation coefficient measures the degree of similarity of movement for a time series. The $\rho_{ij}$ is defined over the range of +1 to −1. Figure 7.3 depicts various values of $\rho_{ij}$. At $\rho_{ij} = 1$, the fluctuation of returns for both series over time is identical; at $\rho_{ij} = 0$, the returns are unrelated; and at $\rho_{ij} = -1$, the fluctuations are moving in opposite directions.

Equation (7.7) is a quadratic equation, and some value of $W_1$ minimizes $\sigma_p$. To obtain this value, we differentiate Eq. (7.8) with respect to $W_1$ and set this derivative equal to 0 to solve for $W_1$[1]:

$$W_1 = \frac{\sigma_2(\sigma_2 - \rho_{12}\sigma_1)}{\sigma_1^2 + \sigma_2^2 - 2\rho_{12}\sigma_1\sigma_2} \tag{7.10}$$

Equation (7.10) can be used to estimate the optimal weight of security 1. From the constraint $W_1 + W_2 = 1$, the optimal weight of security 2 can also be estimated. From estimated $W_1$ and $W_2$, we can estimate $\overline{R}_p$ and $\sigma_p$ for a two-security minimum-variance portfolio.

[1]In Appendix 7C, we have shown how to obtain optimal weights for a two-security portfolio. In addition, Appendix 7D discusses how the Sharpe performance measure approach can be used to derive the optimal portfolio weights.

### 7.3.4 The N-asset case

An expanded form of Eq. (7.8) for a portfolio of $N$ securities is $\rho_{ij}$, the correlation coefficient between $i$ and $j$, and $n$ is the number of securities included in the portfolio.

$$\sigma_p = \sqrt{\sum_{i=1}^{n} W_i^2\sigma_i^2 + \sum_{j=1}^{n}\sum_{i=1}^{n} W_iW_j\rho_{ij}\sigma_i\sigma_j}, \quad i \neq j \tag{7.11}$$

where $W_i$ and $W_j$ are the investor's investment allocated to securities, $i$ and $j$. $\rho_{ij}$ is the correlation coefficient between $i$ and $j$, and $n$ is the number of securities included in the portfolio.

Since Eq. (7.11) has $n$ securities, there are $n$ variance terms (that is, $W_i^2\sigma_i^2$) and $(n^2 - n)$ covariance terms (that is $W_iW_j\rho_{ij}\sigma_i\sigma_j$). If $n = 20$, Eq. (7.11) will have 20 variance terms and 380 covariance terms.

Using a matrix notation, we can express these terms as follows:

$$\begin{bmatrix} W_1^2\sigma_1^2 & \cdots & \cdots & W_1W_{20}\sigma_{1,20} \\ \vdots & W_2^2\sigma_2^2 & \vdots & \vdots \\ \vdots & \vdots & \ddots & \vdots \\ W_{20}W_1\sigma_{20,1} & \cdots & \cdots & W_{20}^2\sigma_{20}^2 \end{bmatrix}$$

This is a variance-covariance matrix for portfolio analysis. Lee *et al.* (2013), Elton *et al.* (2013), and Francis and Kim (2013) have used this kind of matrix to perform portfolio analysis. In addition, they also showed how to obtain the optimal ways for an N-asset portfolio.

### 7.3.5 The efficient portfolios

Under the mean-variance framework, by definition, a security or a portfolio will be efficient if

1. No other portfolio has the same expected return at a lower risk.
2. No other portfolio has a higher expected return at the same risk.

These two rules are called the *dominance principle*, which we discussed in detail later in this chapter.

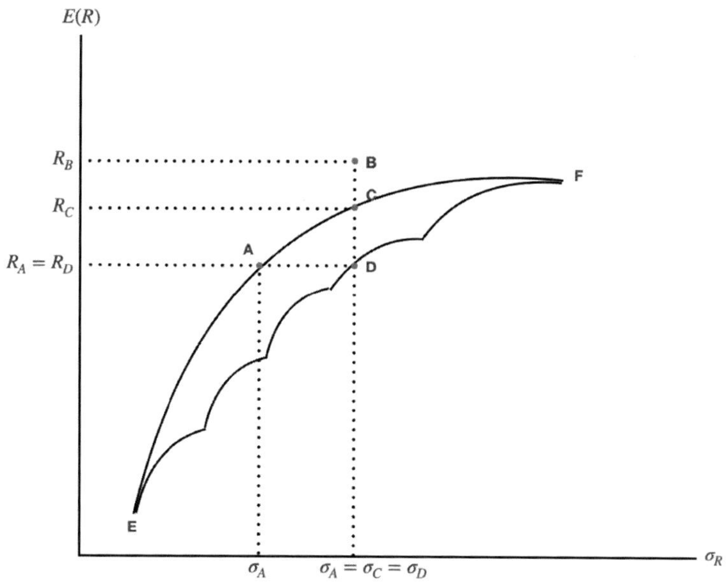


Figure 7.4 Efficient Frontier in Portfolio Analysis.

This suggests that given two investments, A and B, A is preferred to B if

$$\text{E(A)} > \text{E(B)} \quad \text{and} \quad \text{VAR(A)} = \text{VAR(B)}$$

or

$$\text{E(A)} = \text{E(B)} \quad \text{and} \quad \text{VAR(A)} < \text{VAR(B)}$$

where E(A) and E(B) are the expected returns of investments A and B, and VAR(A) and VAR(B) are their respective variances, or risk. The mean return and standard deviation of an investment can be calculated and plotted as a single point on a mean-standard deviation diagram, as shown in Figure 7.4.

All points below curve EF represent possible portfolio combinations. All points above EF are combinations of risk and returns that do not exist. Point D represents a portfolio of investments with return $R_D$ and risk $\sigma_D$. Therefore, point B represents a risk-and-return combination that cannot be obtained with any combination of existing investment opportunities.

The EF curve is also called the efficient frontier, because all points below the curve are dominated by a point found on the curve. The efficient frontier is defined as the set of portfolios that has the maximum return for every given level of risk or the minimum risk for every level of return. Suppose a firm is willing to assume a maximum risk $\sigma_D$ It can obtain a return of $R_D$ with portfolio D or move to point C on the frontier and receive a higher return of $R_C$ with that portfolio at the same level of risk. Therefore, portfolio C dominates portfolio D because it is preferred to portfolio D.

A similar argument could be made in terms of risk. If the firm wants to achieve a return of $R_A$, it would select portfolio A over D, because A represents the same return at a lower level of risk or standard deviation: $\sigma_A < \sigma_D$. Therefore, point D is not efficient but points A and C are. A decision-maker following these arguments would, therefore, select any point on the frontier as being preferable to any interior point.

The amount of curvature of the efficient frontier depends on the correlation between the two assets. If the correlation between assets equals +1, the combinations lie on the straight line. The lower the correlation coefficient, the more curved the efficient frontier.

**Example 7.1.** To show how the portfolio concepts and methods discussed in this section can be used in practical analysis, we evaluate the monthly rates of return during January 2010–December 2018 for Johnson & Johnson (JNJ) and International Business Machines Corporation (IBM).

The basic statistical estimates for these two firms are average monthly rates of return and the variance-covariance matrix. The average monthly rates of return are –0.0011439 for IBM and –0.008967 for JNJ.

The variance and covariance are listed in Table 7.2.

From Eq. (7.10), we have

$$W_{IBM} = \frac{\sigma_{JNJ}^2 - \text{COV}(R_{IMB}, R_{JNJ})}{\sigma_{IBM}^2 + \sigma_{JNJ}^2 - \text{COV}(R_{IMB}, R_{JNJ})}$$

$$= \frac{0.0016 - 0.0006}{0.0030 + 0.0016 - 0.0006} = 0.2512$$

$$W_{JNJ} = 1 - 0.2512 = 0.7488$$

Table 7.2 Variance–Covariance Matrix.

| | **IBM** | **JNJ** |
|---|---|---|
| IBM | 0.00298732 | |
| JNJ | 0.00060082 | 0.00160289 |

Using the weight estimates and Eqs. (7.5) and (7.8),

$$E(R_P) = -0.007002$$

$$\sigma_P^2 = 0.000226$$

$$\rho_{1,2} = 0.2746$$

When $\rho_{12}$ is less than 1, the combination of the two securities results in a total risk less than the sum of their weighted risk. This is the diversification effect. When $\rho_{12}$ equals to 1, the combination of the two securities has no diversification effect at all.

For the correlation coefficient of $\rho_{12} = 0.2746$, we see that a portfolio that combines JNJ and IBM. shows a greater diversification effect and a substantial reduction in risk then would holding each of the securities separately.

Depending on the correlation coefficient between securities, as long as the securities are not positively correlated, the risk of a portfolio as measured by the standard deviation of return will be less than the weighted average of the risks (standard deviations) of the individual securities. In notational form,

$$\sigma_P < W_1\sigma_1 + W_2\sigma_2, \quad \text{if} \quad \rho_{12} \neq 1$$

This will always be true and represents a significant fact that investors and managers must keep in mind when making financial decisions.

### 7.3.6 *Corporate application of diversification*

The effects of diversification are not necessarily isolated to security analysis and portfolio management but may have wider applications at the corporate decision-making level. Managers often justify undertaking multiproduct lines because of the effects of diversification.

Instead of putting "all eggs in one basket," the investment risks are spread out among many lines of services of products in hopes of reducing overall risk and maximizing returns. To what degree this diversification takes place in other types of corporate decisions depends on the decision-maker's preference for risk and return. The overall goal is to reduce business risk fluctuations of net income.

This type of corporate diversification can also be taken to the multinational level. For example, General Motors has overseas divisions throughout the world that all produce the same product — autos and auto parts. Because GM is a multinational corporation, it can take advantage of diversifying effects of different exchange rates and political and economic climates, because each overseas division is less than perfectly positively correlated with each other.

The strategy of diversifying at the corporate level has been criticized because shareholders can attain diversification in their own portfolios, which makes corporate diversification redundant. There is the agency theory argument that corporate diversification is in fact a form of risk-sharing between stockholders and bondholders, where the bondholders have less risky fixed-income securities due to corporate diversification and the shareholders suffer a loss in the value of their equity position. Finally, there is a reduction in the risk/return deals with options, which deals with mergers and divestitures.

## 7.4 The Market Rate of Return and Market Risk Premium

The market rate of return is the return expected from the market portfolio. This portfolio consists of all risky assets, such as stocks, bonds, options, bullion, real estate, and coins. Because risky assets are included, the market portfolio is a completely diversified portfolio. All unsystematic risks related to individual assets would, therefore, be diversified away. In general, *unsystematic risk* refers to those risks that are related uniquely to the firm (this topic is covered in more detail in Chapter 8). *Systematic risk* influences the rate of return for all risky assets.

The market rate of return can be calculated using one of several types of market indicator series, such as the Dow Jones 30, Standard and Poor's (S&P) 500, or the New York Stock Exchange Index, using the equation:

$$\frac{I_t - I_{t-1}}{I_{t-1}} = R_{mt} \tag{7.12}$$

where $R_{mt}$ = market rate of return; $I_t$ = market index at $t$; and $I_{t-1}$ = market index at $t-1$.

$R_{mt}$ is the market rate of return using the index $I_t$. This equation calculates the percent change in the market index during period $t$ and the previous period $t-1$. This change is the rate of return an investor would expect to receive in $t$ had he invested in $t-1$.

### 7.4.1 *The risk premium*

A risk-free investment is one in which the timing and amount of income streams are known. However, for most investments, investors are uncertain as to the timing and amount of income. Investment risk can be quite broad, ranging from relatively riskless Treasury bills to highly risky speculative stocks, which have been discussed in detail by Bodie *et al.* (2021).

The rational investor dislikes risk and uncertainty and thus requires an additional return on the investment to compensate for this uncertainty. This is called the *risk premium* and is added to the nominal risk-free rate. The risk premium should always be positive. This means that investors will not accept a lower return for investments with higher risk. When trying to estimate the correct risk premium, we cannot always rely on historic data. In actuality, risky investments do lose money and hence experience a negative risk premium. However, just because investments have lost money in the past does not mean that they will do so in the future.

**Example 7.2.** The market rate of return using S&P 500 was calculated using Eq. (7.12) to derive average quarterly returns. These returns are given in Table 7.3. The T-bill rate was deducted from the market return rate $(R_m - R_f)$ to derive the risk premium. For example, in the first two quarters of 2004, the risk premiums were low because of the low market returns. This allowed the T-bill rate to earn a higher return that the market and resulted in a negative risk premium. On the other hand, when the market return rates are higher than the riskless rates, the market premium is positive.

Table 7.3 Market Returns and T-bill Rates by Quarters 2016–2018.

| Year | Quarter | S&P 500 Index | (A) Market Return | $\frac{I_t - I_{t-1}}{I_{t-1}}$ Annualized 3-month T-bill Rates | (B) Quarterly 3-month T-bill Rates | (A − B) Quarterly Rates Premium |
|---|---|---|---|---|---|---|
| 15 | 4 | 164.92 | | | | |
| 16 | 1 | 159.17 | −3.49 | 9.52 | 2.38 | −5.87 |
| 2 | 153.17 | −3.77 | 9.87 | 2.47 | −6.24 | |
| 3 | 166.09 | 8.44 | 10.37 | 2.59 | 5.84 | |
| 4 | 167.23 | 0.69 | 8.06 | 2.02 | −1.33 | |
| 17 | 1 | 180.65 | 8.02 | 8.52 | 2.13 | 5.89 |
| 2 | 191.84 | 6.19 | 6.95 | 1.74 | 4.46 | |
| 3 | 182.07 | −5.09 | 7.10 | 1.78 | −6.87 | |
| 4 | 211.27 | 16.04 | 7.10 | 1.78 | 14.26 | |
| 18 | 1 | 238.90 | 13.08 | 6.56 | 1.64 | 11.44 |
| 2 | 250.84 | 5.00 | 6.21 | 1.55 | 3.45 | |
| 3 | 231.32 | −7.78 | 5.21 | 1.30 | −9.08 | |
| 4 | 242.17 | 4.69 | 5.53 | 1.38 | 3.31 | |
| Mean | 195.36 | 3.50 | 7.58 | 1.90 | 1.61 | |

Theoretically, it is not possible to have an *ex ante* negative risk premium, because taking on additional risk requires an increase in expected return. However, using short-run estimators, as in Table 7.3, may result in negative figures, which are not good estimators because they reflect the short-run fluctuations of the market, thus demonstrating that the *ex ante* expectations of market participants may not be realized ex post.

In Appendix 7A, we discuss long-run risk premium, which more accurately estimates future risk premiums. In the next chapter we will use the risk premium to calculate a firm's cost of capital.

## 7.5 Determination of Commercial Lending Rates

In this section we explain the process of estimating a lending rate that a financial institution would extend to a firm, or a borrowing rate a firm would feel is reasonable. The loan officers of the bank and the financial analysts of the firm need to consider the firm's business, financial, and total risks to make a fair analysis of the cost of borrowing for the firm or the rate the bank should charge when lending money to the firm.

The lending rate is based in part on the risk-free rate. Therefore, we must forecast the risk-free rate ($R_f$) for boom, normal, and recession economies.

The second component of the lending rate is the risk premium ($R_p$), which is calculated individually for each firm by examining the change in EBIT under the three economic conditions. The EBIT is an indicator to the lender as to the ability of the potential borrower to repay borrowed funds.

Tables 7.4 and 7.5 provide the information required for the analysis. In Table 7.4, column B lists probabilities relating to economic conditions for the entire economy, and column D lists probabilities of various levels of EBIT for the firm.

There are nine possible lending rates for the three economic conditions. The probabilities of these rates for the three economic conditions are elaborated in Table 7.5.

These tables show that during a boom the risk-free rate is 10%, but the risk premium can take on different values. There is a 40% chance that the risk premium will be 2%, a

Table 7.4 Input Information.

| Economic Condition | $R_t$ (%) | (A) Probability | (B) EBIT | (C) Probability | (D) $R_p$ (%) |
|---|---|---|---|---|---|
| Boom | 10 | 0.25 | \$2.5 m | 0.40 | 2 |
| | | | 1.5 | 0.30 | 3 |
| | | | 0.5 | 0.30 | 5 |
| Normal | 9 | 0.50 | \$2.5 m | 0.40 | 2 |
| | | | 1.5 | 0.30 | 3 |
| | | | 0.5 | 0.30 | 5 |
| Poor | 8 | 0.25 | \$2.5 m | 0.40 | 2 |
| | | | 1.5 | 0.30 | 3 |
| | | | 0.5 | 0.30 | 5 |

Table 7.5 Calculation Table.

| Economic Condition | (A) $R_t$ (%) | (B) Probability | (C) $R_p$ (%) | (D) Probability | (B × D) Probability of Occurrence | (A+C) Lending Rate (%) |
|---|---|---|---|---|---|---|
| Boom | 10 | 0.25 | 2 | 0.40 | 0.100 | 12 |
| | | | 3 | 0.30 | 0.075 | 13 |
| | | | 5 | 0.30 | 0.075 | 15 |
| Normal | 9 | 0.50 | 2 | 0.40 | 0.200 | 11 |
| | | | 3 | 0.30 | 0.150 | 12 |
| | | | 5 | 0.30 | 0.150 | 14 |
| Poor | 8 | 0.25 | 2 | 0.40 | 0.100 | 10 |
| | | | 3 | 0.30 | 0.75 | 11 |
| | | | 5 | 0.30 | 0.75 | 13 |
| | | | | | 1.000 | |

30% chance it will be 3%, and a 30% chance it will be 5%. By multiplying the two probabilities, $R_f$ and $R_p$, we get the joint probability of occurrence. Therefore, there is a 10% chance of receiving a 13% or 15% rate. This process also applies for normal and recession conditions.

For the problem set up in Table 7.5, the weighted average lending rate is

$$\overline{R} = (0.100)(12\%) + (0.75)(13) + (0.075)15 + (0.200)11 + (0.150)(12)$$

$$+ (0.150)(14) + (0.100)10 + (0.074)(13\%)$$
$$= 12.2\%$$

with a standard deviation of

$$\sigma = \big[(0.100)(12 - 12.2)^2 + (0.075)(13 - 12.2)^2 + (0.075)(15 - 12)^2$$
$$+ (0.200)(11 - 12.2)^2 + (0.150)(12 - 12.2)^2 + (0.150)$$
$$\times (14 - 12.2)^2 + (0.100)(10 - 12.2)^2 + (0.075)(11 - 12.2)^2$$
$$+ (0.075)(13 - 12.2)^2\big]^{0.5}$$
$$= (0.004 + 0.048 + 0.588 + 0.288 + 0.006 + 0.436 + 0.484$$
$$+ 0.108 + 0.048)^{0.5} = 1.42\%$$

If the lending rate distribution is normal (as discussed in Appendix 7B). Given the mean and standard deviation for such a distribution, in Figure 7.5 we see that 68.3% of the observations of a normal distribution are within a standard deviation of 1 of the mean, 95.4% are within a standard deviation of 2, and 99.7% within a standard deviation of 3.

Based on the mean and standard deviation of the estimated lending rate, we depict the expected lending rate and its standard deviation in Figure 7.5. The percentages in Figure 7.5, along with the mean and standard deviations, illustrate the normal distribution. The average lending rate is normally distributed with a mean of 12.2% and a standard deviation of +1.43%. This implies that almost all (99.7%) of the rates lie in the range from 7.91% to 16.49%. We also know 68.3% of the rates lie in the range of 10.77% to 13.63%.

This example is based on expected values for determining required rates of return. From a financial theory view point, equilibrium models such as capital asset pricing model (CAPM) and option pricing model (OPM) are superior for determining required rates of return.

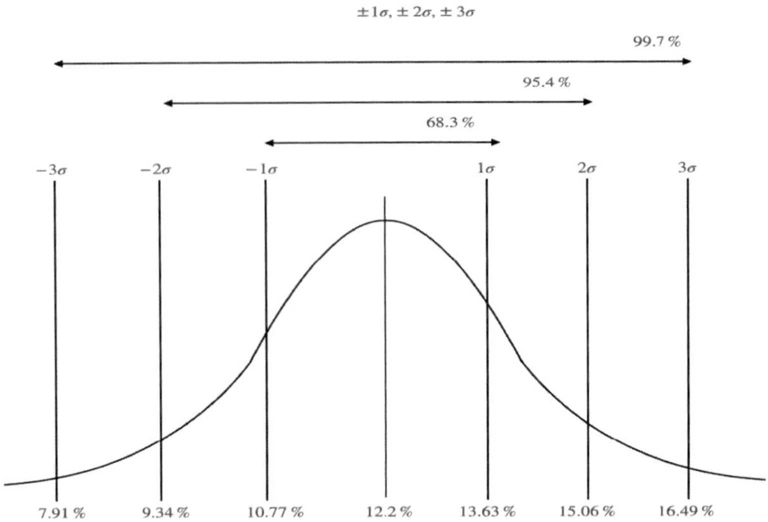


Figure 7.5 Probability Distribution of Lending Rate.

## 7.6 The Dominance Principle and Performance Evaluation

The *dominance principle* can be used to understand the risk/return trade-off. When making financial decisions, we are dealing with two-dimensional analysis — risk and return. The dominance principle allows us to hold one variable constant while we make comparisons based on the other variable. However, in some cases this may not be sufficient. When dealing simultaneously with different levels of risk and return, we need to use the method of *performance evaluation.*

As with efficient frontier analysis, we must assume an investor prefers returns and dislikes risks. For example, as depicted in Figure 7.6, if prepared to experience the risk associated with $\sigma_A$, an investor can obtain a higher expected return with portfolio $A(\overline{R}_A)$ than with portfolio $B(\overline{R}_B)$. Thus, $A$ dominates $B$ and would be preferred. Similarly, if satisfied with a return of $\overline{R}_B$, an investor would select portfolio $B$ over $C$ because the risks associated with $B$ are less: $\sigma_B < \sigma_C$. Points B and C were directly comparable because of a common return, $\mathrm{R_B} = \mathrm{R_C}$. How about portfolio $D$? How does its risk versus return compare with other portfolios in the figure, especially $B$? Portfolio $D$ is not directly comparable using the dominance

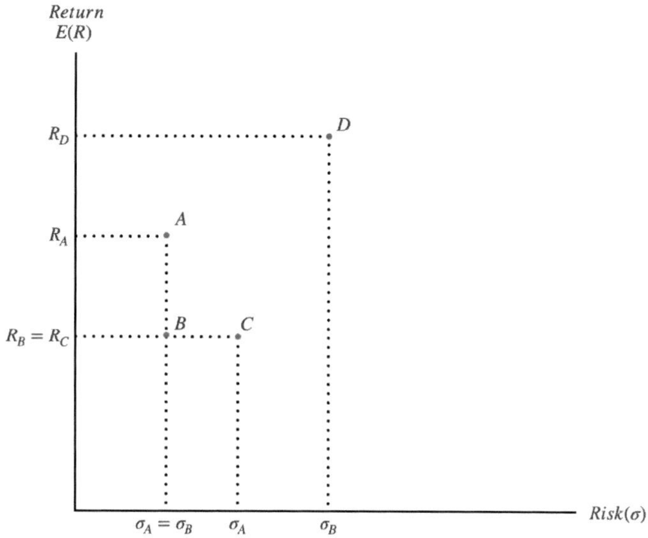


Figure 7.6 Relationship of Total Risk to Financial Leverage.

principle, and this is a basic limitation: portfolios without a common risk or return factor are not directly comparable. The problem can be solved using a technique called *stochastic dominance*, which is a subject covered in advanced corporate finance or investment courses. Stochastic dominance allows for joint consideration of the mean and variance.[2]

A simplified approach for comparing portfolios $A$ and $D$ is to use a performance measure. Basically, there are three portfolio performance measures: the Sharpe, Treynor, and Jensen methods. Here, we elaborate on the Sharpe measure, which is the most basic of the three. Using this method, we can compare the relative risk-return trade-off performance of portfolios $B$ and $D$ as follows:

$$SP^D = \frac{\overline{R}_D - R_f}{\sigma_D}$$

[2]Complete coverage of this topic can be found in a text by Levy and Sarnat (1984).

Table 7.6 Information for Two Mutual Funds.

| | **Smith Fund (%)** | **Jones Fund (%)** |
|---|---|---|
| Average return ($\overline{R}$) | 18 | 16 |
| Standard deviation ($\sigma$) | 20 | 15 |
| Risk-free rate $= R_f = 9.5\%$ | | |

$$SP^B = \frac{\overline{R}_B - R_f}{\sigma_B}$$

where $SP^D$ and $SP^B$ = Sharpe performance measures; $\overline{R}_D$ and $\overline{R}_B$ = average return of each respective portfolio; $R_f$ = average risk-free rate; and $\sigma_D$ and $\sigma_B$ = respective standard deviation of returns of each portfolio.

Because the numerator is the average return reduced by the risk-free rate, it represents the average risk premium of each portfolio. Dividing the risk premium by the total risk per portfolio results in a measure of the unit return (premium) per unit risk for each portfolio. The Sharpe performance measure equation would, therefore, allow direct comparison of any portfolio given its risks and returns.

**Example 7.3.** An insurance firm is considering two investment funds. From past performance, they calculate the average returns and variables for both funds, as listed in Table 7.6. The T-bill rate is 9.5%, which the firm uses as a measure of the risk-free rate.

Using this information, the Sharpe performance measure is calculated as

$$SP_S = \frac{0.18 - 0.095}{0.2} = 0.425$$

$$SP_J = \frac{0.16 - 0.095}{0.15} = 0.433$$

From these calculations, we see that the Jones fund will have a slightly better performance and thus would be the better alternative of the two investments.

## 7.7 Summary

In this chapter, we defined the basic concepts of risk and risk measurement. Based on the relationship of risk and return, we demonstrated the efficient portfolio concept and its implementation, as well as the dominance principle and performance measures. Interest rates and market rates of return were used as measurements to show how the commercial lending rate and the market risk premium are calculated. Following a surveyed paper by Graham and Harvey (2001), we discussed in this chapter that management evaluates firm risk, rather than project risk, when evaluating new investment opportunities. Also, firms focus on financial flexibility and credit ratings when issuing debt and EPS dilution and recent stock price appreciation when issuing equity.

## References

Bodie, Z., A. Kane and A. Marcus. *Investments*, 12th edn. (McGraw-Hill Book Company, New York, 2021).

Bowman, R. G. "The Theoretical Relationship between Systematic Risk and Financial (Accounting) Variables," *The Journal of Finance*, 34 (June 1979, pp. 617–30).

Cochrane, J. H. *Asset Pricing,* Revised edn. (Princeton University Press, 2005).

Elton, E. J., M. J. Gruber, S. J. Brown and W. N. Goetzmann. *Modern Portfolio Theory and Investment Analysis,* 9th edn. (Wiley, 2013).

Francis. J. C. and D. Kim. *Modern Portfolio Theory: Foundations, Analysis, and New Developments* (Wiley, 2013).

Ibbotson, R. *2020 SBBI Yearbook: Stocks, Bonds, Bills, and Inflation* (Duff & Phelps).

Ibbotson, R. G. and R. A. Sinquefield. *Stocks, Bonds, Bills, and Inflation* (Chicago: Morningstar, 2015).

Ibbotson, R., R. J. Grabowski, J. P. Harrington and C. Nunes. *2016 Stocks, Bonds, Bills, and Inflation (SBBI) Yearbook*, 1st edn. (Wiley, 2016).

Lee, C. F. and A. C. Lee. *Encyclopedia of Finance*, 3rd edn. (Springer, New York, 2022, Forthcoming).

Lee, C. F., J. C. Lee and A. C. Lee. *Statistics for Business and Financial Economics*, 3rd edn. (Springer Academic Publishers, 2013).
Lee, C. F, J. C. Lee, J. R. Chang and T. Tai. *Essentials of Excel, Excel VBA, SAS and Minitab for Statistical and Financial Analyses* (Springer International Publishing, 2016).
Lee, C. F., J. E. Finnerty, D. H. Wort, J. Lee and A. C. Lee. *Security Analysis, Portfolio Management, and Financial Derivatives* (World Scientific Publishers, Inc, 2013).
Markowitz, H. M. *Portfolio Selection: Efficient Diversification of Investments* (New York: John Wiley & Sons, 1959).
Modigliani, F. and G.A. Pogue. "An Introduction to Risk and Return," *Financial Analysts Journal*, 30 (May–June 1974, pp. 69–86).

## Appendix 7A — Estimation of Market Risks Premium

To estimate the market risk premium, we used historical returns for 1926–2015 for stocks and bonds; these are shown in Table 7.1A. The arithmetic risk premium estimated is based on this data is 7.88%, as shown in Table 7.2A. This is calculated as the difference between stock returns of 11.64% and T-bill returns of 3.75%, which was shown in Table 7.1A. The long-run market risk premium is one of the key inputs to estimating the cost of equity capital.

The risk premiums calculated by this method are used by both practitioners and academicians. The major potential weakness, however, is that these premiums assume the variance of market return and the risk-free rate are stationary over time. To deal with this problem, Merton (1980) has used the concept of Sharpe's performance measure, as discussed earlier, to generalize the above results. In general, Merton's method obtains a long-run risk premium that is greater than the above results.

## Appendix 7B — The Normal Distribution

In Chapter 7, we introduced the idea of thinking about the uncertainty involved in future corporate returns on assets by regarding

Table 7.1A Summary Statistics of Annual Returns (1926–2015).

| Series | Geometric Mean (%) | Arithmetic Mean (%) | Standard Deviation (%) |
|---|---|---|---|
| S&P 500 Index | 9.78 | 11.64 | 19.30 |
| U.S. treasury bills (3 Month) | 3.71 | 3.75 | 3.13 |
| Long-term corporate bonds (20 Year) | 7.04 | 7.08 | 3.07 |
| Long-term government bonds (20 Year) | 5.57 | 6.00 | 9.97 |

*Source*: Lee and Lee (2017). *Financial Analysis, Planning and Forecasting*, page 358.

Table 7.2A Derived Series: Summary Statistics of Annual Component Returns (1926–2015).

| Series | Geometric Mean | Arithmetic Mean | Standard Deviation | Distribution |
|---|---|---|---|---|
| Equity risk premia (stock — bills) | 5.95% | 7.88% | 19.34% | 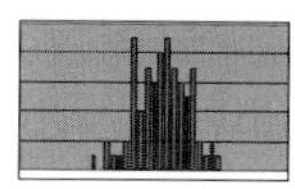 |
| Default premia (LT corps. — LT govts.) | 0.9 | 1.39 | 9.67 | 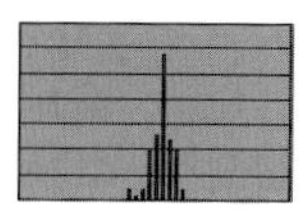 |
| Horizon premia (LT govts. — bills) | 1.18 | 1.63 | 9.76 | 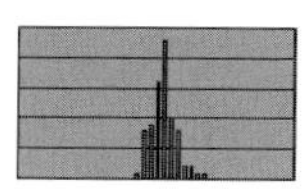 |
| Real interest rates (bills — inflation) | 0.55 | 0.64 | 4.12 | 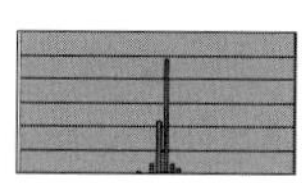 |

*Source*: Lee and Lee (2017). *Financial Analysis, Planning and Forecasting*, page 359.

such returns not as fixed numbers but rather as random variables. Specifically, we briefly discussed the possibility of using the normal distribution for this purpose. The normal distribution is generally described by its probability density function. If the random variable $X$ follows such a distribution function, the probability density function is:

$$f_x(x) = \frac{1}{\sigma\sqrt{2\pi}} e^{\frac{-(x-\mu)^2}{2\sigma^2}}$$

where $\mu$ is the mean, or expected value, of $X$, and $\sigma^2$ its variance. Here, $\pi = 3.14158$ and $e = 2.71828\cdots$ are physical constants.

Figure 7.1B shows a graph of this probability density function, exhibiting a characteristic "bell shape" centered on the mean. Probability density functions are constructed in such a way that the area under the curve, between any two possible values of the random variable, measures the probability that the random variable will take a value in the corresponding range, illustrated in Figure 7.1B.

The mean of a normal distribution determines the center of the distribution, but does not influence its dispersion. Therefore, two normally distributed random variables with the same variance but different means will have identical probability density functions, except that one will be shifted to the right of the other. This is shown graphically in Figure 7.2B.

The variance of a normal distribution determines the spread, or dispersion, about the mean, but does not affect the center of the

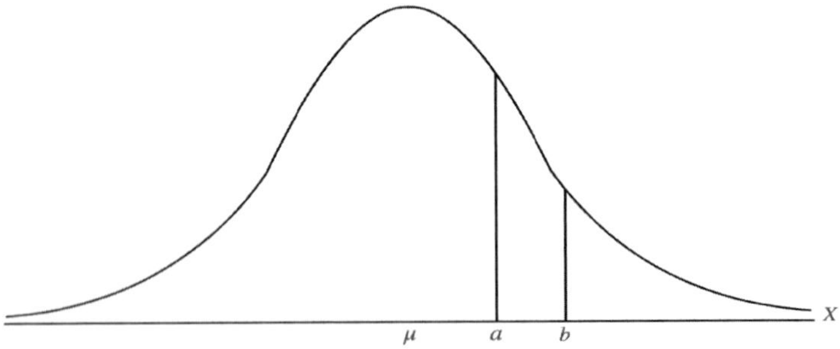


Figure 7.1B Probability Density Function for a Normal Distribution, Showing the Probability that a Normal Random Variable Lies between $a$ and $b$.

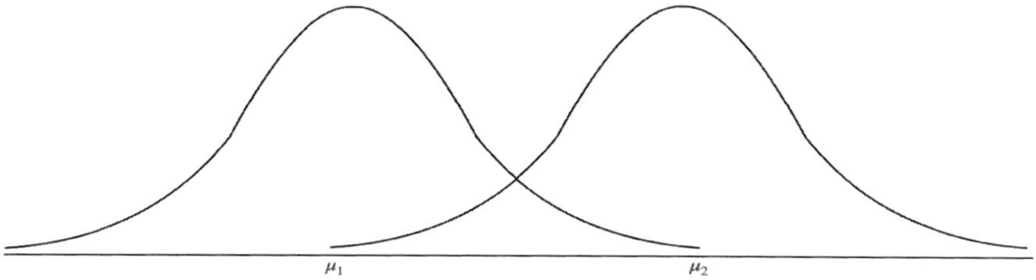


Figure 7.2B Probability Density Function of Normal Random Variables with Equal Variances: Mean $\mu_2$ is Greater than $\mu_1$.

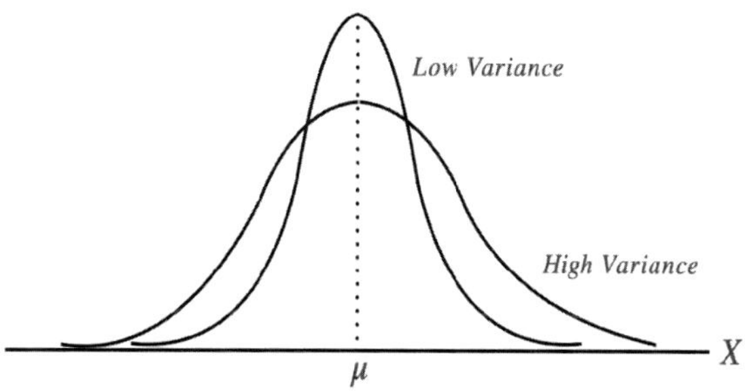


Figure 7.3B Probability Density Functions of Normal Distributions with Equal Means and Different Variances.

distribution. The higher the variance, the greater is the dispersion. Figure 7.3B shows the probability density functions of two normal distributions with identical means but different variances.

It follows that the greater the variance, the larger the probability that a normally distributed random variable differs from its mean by any fixed amount. For this reason, we associate variance with risk when considering the distribution of possible rates of return.

In fact, using the normal distribution table listed at the end of the book, it is possible to calculate the probability that a normally distributed random variable lies in any specified range. For convenience, we tabulate some useful values in Table 7.1B. The table shows the probability that a random variable lies between $\mu - K$ and $\mu + K$ for particular values of $K/\sigma$, where the standard deviation is $\sigma$, as depicted by the shaded area in Figure 7.4B.

**Example 7.1B.** An investor is interested in the prospects of a particular corporation. The investor expects the corporation to

Table 7.1B Probability, $P$, that a Normal Random Variable with Mean $\mu$ and Standard Deviation $\sigma$ lies between $K - \sigma$ and $K - \sigma$.

| P | $K/\sigma$ |
|---|---|
| 0.50 | 0.674 |
| 0.60 | 0.842 |
| 0.70 | 1.036 |
| 0.80 | 1.281 |
| 0.90 | 1.645 |
| 0.95 | 1.960 |

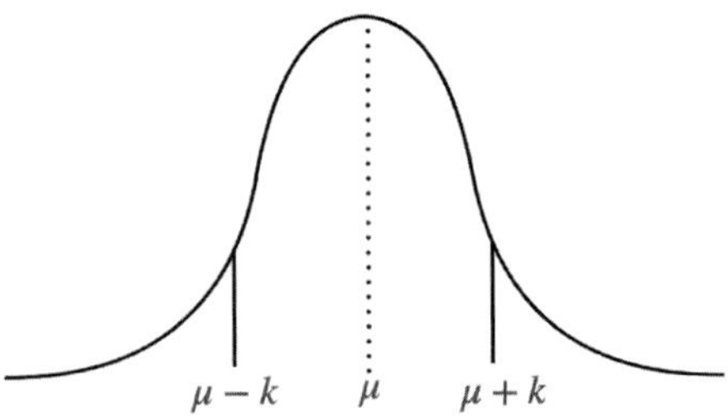


Figure 7.4B Probability that a Normal Random Variable is between $\mu - K$ and $\mu + K$.

achieve a rate of return on assets of 12% next year, and believes there is a 50% probability. If this uncertainty can be expressed as a normal distribution, find the mean and variance of that distribution.

The mean is the expected return, so that we have

$$\mu = 12$$

According to this investor, the probability is 0.50 that the actual return will be between 10.5 and 13.5%, so that, in our notation,

$$K = \frac{13.5 - 10.5}{2} = 1.5$$

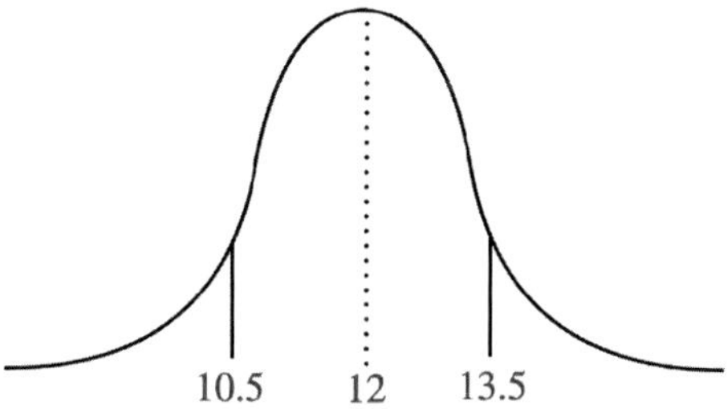


Figure 7.5B For a Normal Random Variable with Mean 12, Standard Deviation 4.95, the Probability is 0.5 of a Value between 10.5 and 13.5.

From Table 7.1B, we have

$$\frac{K}{\sigma} = 0.674$$

so that

$$\sigma = \frac{K}{0.674} = \frac{1.5}{0.674} = 2.2255$$

Finally, the variance is the square of the standard deviation, hence

$$\sigma^2 = (2.2255)^2 = 4.95$$

This is illustrated in Figure 7.5B.

You might want to extend these calculations to demonstrate that variance does indeed provide a useful measure of uncertainty. Suppose our investor is less uncertain about future prospects. This could be reflected in one of two ways:

(1) The investor may believe there is a 70% chance that next year's return on assets will lie between 10.5 and 13.5%.
(2) The investor may believe there is a 50% chance that next year's return on assets will be between 11 and 13%.

It is left as an exercise to the reader to verify that, in either case, assuming a normal distribution, this uncertainty will be described by a distribution with a mean of 12 and a variance of less than 4.95.

One important property of a normal distribution is that any linear function of a normal random variable also has a normal distribution. Specifically, suppose that the random variable $X$ has a normal distribution with mean $\mu$ and variance $\sigma^2$, and we define the random variable $Y$ as

$$Y = c + dX$$

where $c$ and $d$ are any constant fixed numbers. Then it can be shown that $Y$ has a normal distribution with mean $(c + d\mu)$ and variance $\mathrm{d}^2\sigma^2$.

## Appendix 7C — Minimum-Variance Approach to Derive Optimal Weight

If there is a two security portfolio, its variance can be defined as

$$\sigma_p^2 = w_1^2\sigma_1^2 + w_2^2\sigma_2^2 + 2w_1w_2\mathrm{Cov}(r_1, r_2) \tag{7.1C}$$

where $w_1$ and $w_2$ are weight associated with security 1 and 2, respectively.

$\sigma_1^2$ and $\sigma_2^2$ are variance of security 1 and 2 respectively.

The problem is choosing optimal $w_1$ to minimize the portfolio variance, $\sigma_p^2$

$$\underset{w_1}{\mathrm{Min}} \,.\, \sigma_P^2 \tag{7.2C}$$

We can solve the minimization problem by differentiating the $\sigma_p^2$ with respect to $w_1$, and setting the derivative equal to zero. i.e., we want to solve

$$\frac{\partial\sigma_p^2}{\partial w_1} = 0 \tag{7.3C}$$

Since, $w_1 + w_2 = 1$ or $w_2 = 1 - w_1$.

Therefore, the variance, $\sigma_p^2$, can be rewritten as

$$\begin{aligned}\sigma_p^2 &= w_1^2\sigma_1^2 + w_2^2\sigma_2^2 + 2w_1w_2\mathrm{COV}(r_1, r_2)\\ &= w_1^2\sigma_1^2 + (1 - w_1)^2\sigma_2^2 + 2w_1(1 - w_1)\mathrm{COV}(r_1, r_2)\end{aligned}$$

$$= w_1^2\sigma_1^2 + \sigma_2^2 - 2w_1\sigma_2^2 + w_1^2\sigma_2^2 + 2w_1\text{COV}(r_1, r_2) - 2w_1^2\text{COV}(r_1, r_2).$$

Now, the first order conditions of Eq. (E3) can be written as

$$2w_1\sigma_1^2 - 2\sigma_2^2 + 2w_1\sigma_2^2 + 2\text{COV}(r_1, r_2) - 4w_1\text{COV}(r_1, r_2) = 0$$

Rearrange the above equation

$$w_1\sigma_1^2 + w_1\sigma_2^2 - 2w_1\text{COV}(r_1, r_2) = \sigma_2^2 - \text{COV}(r_1, r_2)$$

$$[\sigma_1^2 + \sigma_2^2 - 2\text{COV}(r_1, r_2)]w_1 = \sigma_2^2 - \text{COV}(r_1, r_2)$$

Finally, we have

$$\boxed{w_1 = \frac{\sigma_2^2 - \text{COV}(r_1, r_2)}{\sigma_1^2 + \sigma_2^2 - 2\text{COV}(r_1, r_2)}}$$

## Appendix 7D — Sharpe Performance Approach to Derive Optimal Weight

In Appendix 7C, we derived the optimal portfolio weight in terms the minimum-variance approach. In this case, we assume that the investor is only concerned with the risk without considering the return. If the investor is concerned with both return and risk, then the Sharpe performance measure approach can be used to derive the optimal weights, which will be discussed in this appendix.

Solution for the weights of the optimal risky portfolio include two securities can be found by solving the following maximization problem:

$$\underset{w_1}{\text{Max}}\ S_p = \frac{E(r_p) - r_f}{\sigma_p}$$

where $E(r_p)$ = expected rates of return for portfolio $p$; $r_f$ = risk free rates of return; $S_p$ = Sharpe performance measure; $\sigma_p$ as defined in Eq. (7.1C) of Appendix C.

We can solve the maximization problem by differentiating the $S_p$ with respect to $w_1$, and setting the derivative equal to zero. i.e., we want to solve

$$\frac{\partial S_p}{\partial w_1} = 0 \tag{7.1D}$$

In the case of two securities, we know that

$$E(r_p) = w_1 E(r_1) + w_2 E(r_2) \tag{7.2D}$$

$$\sigma_p = [w_1^2 \sigma_1^2 + w_2^2 \sigma_2^2 + 2 w_1 w_2 \text{COV}(r_1, r_2)]^{1/2} \tag{7.3D}$$

$$w_1 + w_2 = 1 \tag{7.4D}$$

From above Eqs. (7.2D–7.4D), we can rewrite $E(r_p) - r_f$ and $\sigma_p$ as

$$\begin{aligned} E(r_p) - r_f &= w_1 E(r_1) + w_2 E(r_2) - r_f = w_1 E(r_1) + (1 - w_1) E(r_2) \\ &\quad - r_f \equiv f(w_1) \end{aligned} \tag{7.5D}$$

$$\begin{aligned} \sigma_p &= [w_1^2 \sigma_1^2 + w_2^2 \sigma_2^2 + 2 w_1 w_2 \text{COV}(r_1, r_2)]^{1/2} \\ &= [w_1^2 \sigma_1^2 + (1 - w_1)^2 \sigma_2^2 + 2 w_1 (1 - w_1) \text{COV}(r_1, r_2)]^{1/2} \\ &\equiv g(w_2) \end{aligned} \tag{7.6D}$$

Equation (7.1D) becomes

$$\frac{\partial S_p}{\partial w_1} = \frac{\partial \frac{f(w_1)}{g(w_2)}}{\partial w_2} = \frac{f'(w_1) g(w_2) - f(w_1) g'(w_2)}{[g(w_2)]^2} = 0 \tag{7.7D}$$

where

$$f'(w_1) = \frac{\partial f(w_1)}{\partial w_1} = E(r_1) - E(r_2) \tag{7.8D}$$

$$g'(w_1) = \frac{\partial g(w_1)}{\partial w_1} = \frac{1}{2} \times [w_1^2\sigma_1^2 + (1-w_1)^2\sigma_2^2$$
$$+ 2w_1(1-w_1)\mathrm{COV}(r_1, r_2)]^{\frac{1}{2}-1}$$
$$\times [2w_1\sigma_1^2 + 2w_1\sigma_2^2 - 2\sigma_2^2$$
$$+ 2\mathrm{COV}(r_1, r_2) - 4w_1\mathrm{COV}(r_1, r_2)] = [w_1\sigma_1^2 + w_1\sigma_2^2 - \sigma_2^2$$
$$+\mathrm{COV}(r_1, r_2) - 2w_1\mathrm{COV}(r_1, r_2)]$$
$$\times [w_1^2\sigma_1^2 + (1-w_1)^2\sigma_2^2 + 2w_1(1-w_1)\mathrm{COV}(r_1, r_2)]^{1/2} \quad (7.9\mathrm{D})$$

From Eq. (7.7D),

$$f'(w_1)g(w_1) - f(w_1)g'(w_1) = 0 \quad \text{or}$$
$$f'(w_1)g(w_1) = f(w_1)g'(w_1) \quad (7.10\mathrm{D})$$

Now, plugging $f(w_1)$, $g(w_1)$, $f'(w_1)$, and $g'(w_1)$ [Eqs. (7.5D–7.9D)] into Eq. (7.10D), we have

$$[E(r_1) - E(r_2)] \times [w_1^2\sigma_1^2 + (1-w_1)^2\sigma_2^2 + 2w_1(1-w_1)\mathrm{COV}(r_1, r_2)]^{1/2}$$
$$= [w_1E(r_1) + (1-w_1)E(r_2) - r_f] \times [w_1\sigma_1^2 + w_1\sigma_2^2 - \sigma_2^2$$
$$+ \mathrm{COV}(r_1, r_2) - 2w_1\mathrm{COV}(r_1, r_2)]$$
$$\times [w_1^2\sigma_1^2 + (1-w_1)^2\sigma_2^2 + 2w_1(1-w_1)\mathrm{COV}(r_1, r_2)]^{1/2} \quad (7.11\mathrm{D})$$

Multiplying by $[w_1^2\sigma_1^2 + (1-w_1)^2\sigma_2^2 + 2w_1(1-w_1)\mathrm{COV}(r_1, r_2)]^{1/2}$ on both hand sides of Eq. (7.11D), we have

$$[E(r_1) - E(r_2)] \times [w_1^2\sigma_1^2 + (1-w_1)^2\sigma_2^2 + 2w_1(1-w_1)\mathrm{COV}(r_1, r_2)]$$
$$= [w_1E(r_1) + (1-w_1)E(r_2) - r_f] \times [w_1\sigma_1^2$$
$$+ w_1\sigma_2^2 - \sigma_2^2 + \mathrm{COV}(r_1, r_2) - 2w_1\mathrm{COV}(r_1, r_2)] \quad (7.12\mathrm{D})$$

Rearrange all terms on both hand sides of Eq. (7.12D). i.e.,

**Left hand side of Eq. (7.12D):**

$$
\begin{aligned}
&[E(r_1) - E(r_2)] \times [w_1^2\sigma_1^2 + (1 - w_1)^2\sigma_2^2 + 2w_1(1 - w_1)\text{COV}(r_1, r_2)] \\
&\quad = [E(r_1) - E(r_2)] \times [w_1^2\sigma_1^2 + \sigma_2^2 - 2w_1\sigma_2^2 \\
&\quad + w_1^2\sigma_2^2 + 2w_1\text{COV}(r_1, r_2) - 2w_1^2\text{COV}(r_1, r_2)] \\
&\quad = [E(r_1) - E(r_2)] \times \{w_1^2[\sigma_1^2 + \sigma_2^2 - 2\text{COV}(r_1, r_2)] \\
&\quad + \ 2w_1[\text{COV}(r_1, r_2) - \sigma_2^2] + \sigma_2^2\} \\
&\quad = [E(r_1) - E(r_2)] \times \{w_1^2[\sigma_1^2 + \sigma_2^2 - 2\text{COV}(r_1, r_2)]\} \\
&\quad + [E(r_1) - E(r_2)] \times \{2w_1[\text{COV}(r_1, r_2) - \sigma_2^2]\} \\
&\quad + [E(r_1) - E(r_2)] \times \sigma_2^2 \\
&\quad = [E(r_1) - E(r_2)] \times [\sigma_1^2 + \sigma_2^2 - 2\text{COV}(r_1, r_2)]w_1^2 \\
&\quad + 2[E(r_1) - E(r_2)] \times [\text{COV}(r_1, r_2) - \sigma_2^2]w_1 \\
&\quad + [E(r_1) - E(r_2)] \times \sigma_2^2
\end{aligned}
$$

**Right hand side of Eq. (7.12D):**

$$
\begin{aligned}
&[w_1E(r_1) + (1 - w_1)E(r_2) - r_f] \times [w_1\sigma_1^2 + w_1\sigma_2^2 - \sigma_2^2 + \text{COV}(r_1, r_2) \\
&\qquad -2w_1\text{COV}(r_1, r_2)] = [w_1E(r_1) + E(r_2) - w_1E(r_2) - r_f] \\
&\qquad \times [w_1\sigma_1^2 + w_1\sigma_2^2 - 2w_1\text{COV}(r_1, r_2) - \sigma_2^2 + \text{COV}(r_1, r_2)] \\
&\quad = \{w_1[E(r_1) - E(r_2)] + [E(r_2) - r_f]\} \\
&\qquad \times \{w_1[\sigma_1^2 + \sigma_2^2 - 2\text{COV}(r_1, r_2)] + \text{COV}(r_1, r_2) - \sigma_2^2 \\
&\quad = w_1[E(r_1) - E(r_2)] \times w_1[\sigma_1^2 + \sigma_2^2 - 2\text{COV}(r_1, r_2)] \\
&\qquad + w_1[E(r_1) - E(r_2)] \times [\text{COV}(r_1, r_2) - \sigma_2^2] \\
&\qquad + [E(r_2) - r_f] \times w_1[\sigma_1^2 + \sigma_2^2 - 2\text{COV}(r_1, r_2)] + [E(r_2) - r_f] \\
&\qquad \times [\text{COV}(r_1, r_2) - \sigma_2^2] = [E(r_1) - E(r_2)] \times [\sigma_1^2 + \sigma_2^2 \\
&\qquad - 2\text{COV}(r_1, r_2)]w_1^2 + [E(r_1) - E(r_2)] \times [\text{COV}(r_1, r_2) \\
&\qquad - \sigma_2^2]w_1 + [E(r_2) - r_f] \times [\sigma_1^2 + \sigma_2^2 - 2\text{COV}(r_1, r_2)]w_1 \\
&\qquad +[E(r_2) - r_f] \times [\text{COV}(r_1, r_2) - \sigma_2^2]
\end{aligned}
$$

Subtracting $[E(r_1)-E(r_2)][\sigma_1^2+\sigma_2^2-2\text{COV}(r_1,r_2)]w_1^2$ and $[E(r_1)-E(r_2)][\text{COV}(r_1,r_2)-\sigma_2]w_1$ from both hand sides of Eq. (7.12D), we have

$$\begin{aligned}
&[E(r_1)-E(r_2)]\times[\text{COV}(r_1,r_2)-\sigma_2^2]w_1+[E(r_1)-E(r_2)]\times\sigma_2^2\\
&\quad=[E(r_2)-r_f]\times[\sigma_1^2+\sigma_2^2-2\text{COV}(r_1,r_2)]w_1+[E(r_2)-r_f]\\
&\quad\times[\text{COV}(r_1,r_2)-\sigma_2^2] \qquad (7.13\text{D})
\end{aligned}$$

Moving all the terms with $w_1$ on one side and leaving the rest terms on the other side from Eq. (7.13D), we have

$$\begin{aligned}
&[E(r_1)-E(r_2)]\times\sigma_2^2-[E(r_2)-r_f]\times[\text{COV}(r_1,r_2)-\sigma_2^2]\\
&\quad=[E(r_2)-r_f]\times[\sigma_1^2+\sigma_2^2-2\text{COV}(r_1,r_2)]w_1-[E(r_1)-E(r_2)]\\
&\quad\times[\text{COV}(r_1,r_2)-\sigma_2^2]w_1 \qquad (7.14\text{D})
\end{aligned}$$

Rearrange Eq. (7.14D) in order to solve for $w_1$ i.e.,

$$\begin{aligned}
&[E(r_1)-E(r_2)+E(r_2)-r_f]\times\sigma_2^2-[E(r_2)-r_f]\text{COV}(r_1,r_2)\\
&\quad=\{[E(r_2)-r_f]\sigma_1^2+[E(r_2)-r_f]\sigma_2^2-[E(r_2)-r_f][2\text{COV}(r_1,r_2)]\\
&\quad-[E(r_D)-E(r_E)]\text{COV}(r_1,r_2)+[E(r_1)-E(r_2)]\sigma_2^2\}\,w_1\\
&\quad=\{[E(r_1)-r_f]\sigma_2^2+[E(r_2)-r_f]\sigma_1^2\\
&\quad-[E(r_1)-r_f+E(r_2)-r_f]\text{COV}(r_1,r_2)]\}\,w_1
\end{aligned}$$

Finally, we have the optimum weight of security 1 as

$$w_1=\frac{[E(r_1)-r_f]\sigma_2^2-[E(r_2)-r_f]\text{COV}(r_1,r_2)}{\begin{array}{c}[E(r_1)-r_f]\sigma_2^2+[E(r_2)-r_f]\sigma_1^2-[E(r_1)-r_f\\+E(r_2)-r_f]\text{COV}(r_1,r_2)\end{array}}$$

In this appendix we discussed the Sharpe Performance Measure approach in terms of two securities cases. This kind of method can be extended to $n$ securities case. Chiou, Lee, and Chang (2009) have used this approach to investigate whether international diversification is beneficial to investors. In addition, Lee *et al.* (2013) and Bodie *et al.* (2021) have shown this approach in detail.

## Appendix 7E — Solving Example 7.1 with Excel

In this section, we briefly describe how to solve the problem presented in example 7.1.

First, we obtain the monthly adjusted close prices of JNJ and IBM for the periods from Jan. 2010 to Dec. 2018. Then we calculate the monthly log returns of each firm.

According to the monthly returns, we calculate in Excel the monthly average returns of both firms and the variance-covariance matrix of the two series of returns. Note that here we assume the annual risk-free rate is 3.2%, and then the monthly risk-free return is therefore 0.00266667.

**Mean returns**

| *IBM* | *JNJ* |
|---|---|
| −0.0011439 | −0.008967 |

**Variance-Covariance Matrix**

| | *IBM* | *JNJ* |
|---|---|---|
| IBM | 0.00298732 | |
| JNJ | 0.00060082 | 0.00160289 |

**Risk-free Returns**

| |
|---|
| 0.00266667 |

To obtain the variance–covariance matrix, we can use the incorporated function in Excel. Go to the 'data' tab, and click the 'data analysis'. (See below.)

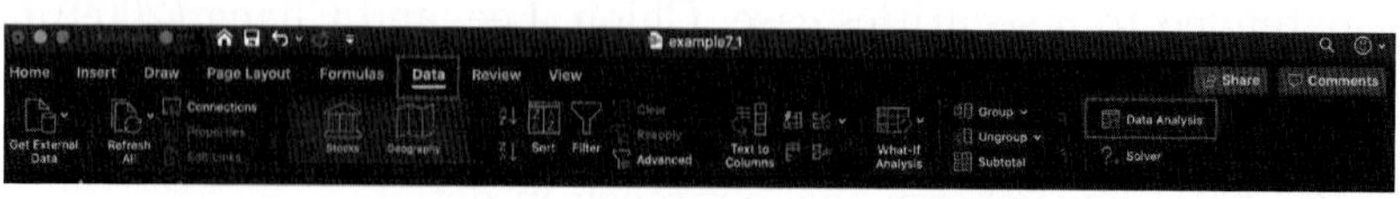

Then choose the option 'covariance' as shown below.

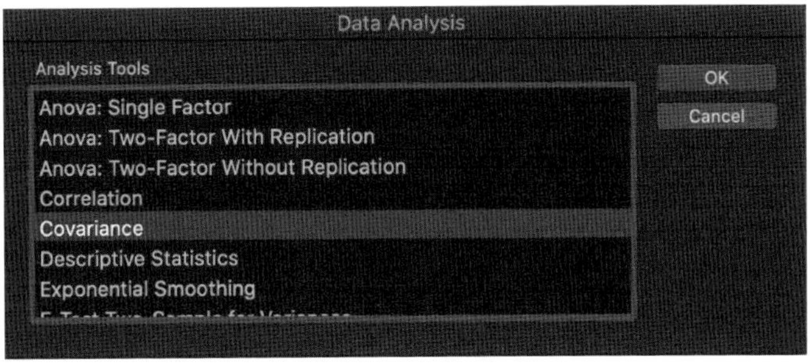


For the input, chose the columns of returns. That is the two columns of monthly returns we have for IBM and JNJ. Then for the output range, you may choose any cell in the sheet where you would like the output matrix to be shown.

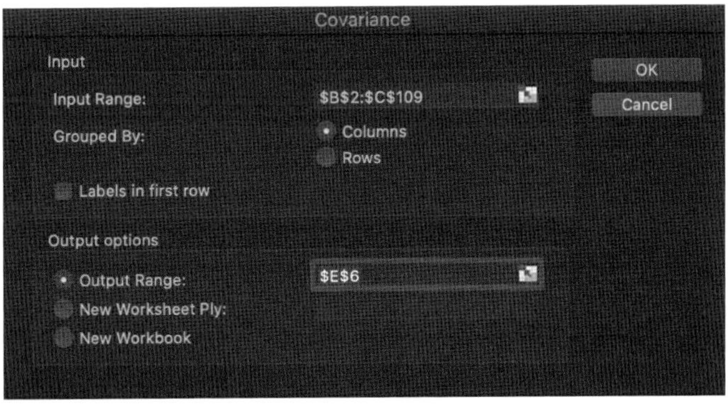


Once we obtain the variance, and the covariance, we are ready to compute the optimal weights of each stock based on the principle of variance minimization. (See the screenshot below.)

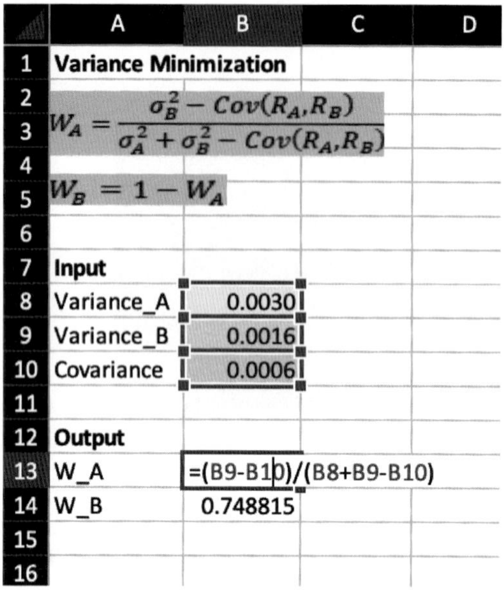


And then, the weight of the other stock is therefore one minus the weight of stock A.

## References

Bodie, Z., A. Kane and A. Marcus. *Investments*, 12th edn. (McGraw-Hill Book Company, New York, 2021).

Chiou, W. J. P., A. C. Lee and C.-C. A. Chang. "Do Investors Still Benefit from International Diversification with Investment Constraint?" *The Quarterly Review of Economics and Finance*, 49(2) (May 2009, pp. 448–483).

Lee, C. F. and A. C. Lee. *Encyclopedia of Finance*, 2nd edn. (Springer, New York, 2013).

Lee, C. F., J. Finnerty, J. Lee, A. C. Lee and D. Wort. *Security Analysis, Portfolio Management, and Financial Derivatives* (World Scientific, 2013).

## Questions and Problems

1. Define the following terms:

   a. Business risk, financial risk, and total risk
   b. Coefficient of variation
   c. Diversification
   d. Market risk premium
   e. Probability
   f. Efficient portfolio and efficient frontier
   g. Dominance principle

2. How can diversification concepts and methods be used in financial management?
3. Discuss the concepts and methods used to determine the commercial lending rate that are developed in detail in the text.
4. The average monthly rate of return, variance and covariance for GE and General Foods (GF) during the period 1982–1987 are listed as follows:

| | E($r$) | $\sigma^2$ | $\sigma_{12}$ |
|---|---|---|---|
| GE | 0.01 | 0.0035 | 0.0008 |
| GF | 0.008 | | |

   If the optimal weights used to calculate the portfolio are $W_1 = 0.6$ and $W_2 = 0.4$, then calculate the mean and standard deviation of this portfolio.
5. For each of the following investments, which would always be preferred by a rational investor?

   a. Portfolio A: $r = 10\%$ $\sigma = 20\%$
      Portfolio B: $r = 14\%$ $\sigma = 15\%$
      Portfolio C: $r = 15\%$ $\sigma = 15\%$
   b. Portfolio D: $r = 20\%$ $\sigma = 30\%$
      Portfolio E: $r = 20\%$ $\sigma = 25\%$
      Portfolio F: $r = 22\%$ $\sigma = 27\%$

6. Here is variance–covariance matrix of Companies X and Y.

| | $\sigma_x^2$ | $\sigma_{xy}$ |
|---|---|---|
| X | 0.005 | 0.0012 |
| | $\sigma_{xy}$ | $\sigma_y^2$ |
| Y | 0.0012 | 0.004 |

(Assuming that E($r$) of X and Y are 0.02 and 0.01, respectively.)

a. Calculate the optimal weights to construct an efficient portfolio.
b. Find the mean and the standard deviation of the portfolio.
c. Determine the coefficient of correlation.

7. An insurance company wants to choose between two investment opportunities. The company calculates the average returns and variances for two investments shown below. Using the Sharpe performance measure, choose the better investment opportunity for the insurance company.

| | 1 | 2 |
|---|---|---|
| Average return | 14% | 20% |
| Variance | 10% | 15% |

8. An investor puts 50% of his money in stock A and the balance in stock B. the standard deviation of returns on A is 10% and on B is 20%. Calculate the variance of portfolio returns when

a. The correlation between the returns is 0.
b. The correlation is 0.5.
c. The correlation is 1.
d. The correlation is –1.

9. The probability distribution of returns on two assets are given as follows.

| **Asset X** | | **Asset Y** | |
|---|---|---|---|
| **Probability** | **Return (%)** | **Probability** | **Return (%)** |
| 0.3 | −5 | 0.2 | −7 |
| 0.4 | 3 | 0.6 | 0 |
| 0.3 | 15 | 0.2 | 8 |

   a. Calculate the mean and variance of the returns for securities X and Y.
   b. If you had to choose either X or Y, which would you prefer?
   c. If the correlation coefficient of the returns of the two securities is .2, what is the covariance of returns for X and Y?
   d. Given the covariance value you computed in Part (c), find the mean and variance for a portfolio comprised of 30% of X and 70% of Y.

10. An investor is considering between Portfolios A and B. Portfolio A has an expected return of 0.20 and a Sharpe Performance measure of 0.5, while B has an expected return of 0.16 and a Performance measure of 0.4. The risk-free rate of interest is 5%.

    a. Which security would you prefer based on Sharpe's Performance measure? Explain this measure.
    b. Find the standard deviation for each of the two portfolios.

11. Zallex, Inc. is attempting to qualify their business risk for the coming year. Based on different states of the economy, their chief economist has devised the following forecasts:

| **State of Economy** | **Probability of State Occurring** | **ROI in State (%)** |
|---|---|---|
| Recession | 0.3 | 10 |
| Normal | 0.4 | 16 |
| Boom | 0.3 | 20 |

a. Find the mean (Expected) ROI.
b. Find the standard deviation of the ROI distribution.

12. Below are the mean and standard deviation of returns for securities K, L, and N.

| Security | Mean | Standard Deviation |
|---|---|---|
| L | 0.30 | 0.10 |
| K | 0.20 | 0.06 |
| N | 0.16 | 0.04 |

The correlation coefficient between L and K is 0.5; that for L and N is 0.2; and that for K and N is 0.3.
Find the expected return and standard deviation for a Portfolio in which L and K each makeup 30% and portfolio N accounts for 40% of the total portfolio.

13. Given the information in the Problem 12, answer the following:

a. Find the optimal weights for a portfolio of only securities K and L. Find the mean and the standard deviation of returns for the portfolio using these optimal weights.
b. Find the optimal weights for a portfolio of only securities K and N. Find the mean and the standard deviation of returns for the portfolio using these optimal weights.
c. Find the optimal weights for a portfolio of only securities L and N. Find the mean and the standard deviation of returns for the portfolio using these optimal weights.
d. Would you prefer portfolio KL, KN, or LN? Explain.
e. Draw the opportunity set and explain how the efficient frontier (set) is identified from the opportunity set.

14. Consider a risky portfolio. The end-of-year cash flow derived from the portfolio will be either $90,000 or $170,000 with equal probabilities of 0.5. The alternative risk free investment in T-bills pays 5% per year.

(a) How much would an investor pay for the portfolio if he requires a risk premium of 10%?

(b) Assume the portfolio can be purchased by the amount calculated in Part (a). What is the expected rate of return on the portfolio?
(c) Suppose that the investor's required risk premium increases to 15%. How much would this investor pay for the portfolio now?
(d) Based on the answers in Parts (a), (b), and (c), please discuss the relationship between the required risk premium on a portfolio and the price at which the portfolio will sell.

15. Suppose the utility function of John is $U = E(r) - 0.5A\ \sigma^2$. He is considering a portfolio that offers an expected rate of return of 10% and standard deviation of 15%. The T-bill rate is 5%. Please calculate the maximum level of risk aversion for which the risky portfolio is still preferred to the T-bill.
16. Alice is managing a risky portfolio with expected return of 16% and standard deviation of 25%. Assume the T-bill rate is 6%.

(a) One of Alice's clients chooses to invest 60% of a portfolio in your fund and 40% in a T-bill money market fund. What is the expected value and standard deviation of the rate of return of his portfolio?
(b) Suppose Alice includes the following three stocks in the given proportion:

Stock A 41%
Stock B 28%
Stock C 31%

What are the investment proportion of the client's overall portfolio, including the position in T-bills?
(c) What is the reward-to-variability ratio of Alice's risky portfolio? The client's?

17. Given the information in question 16, suppose that the client decides to invest in Alice's portfolio a proportion $y$ of the total investments budget so that the overall portfolio will have an expected return of 15%.

(a) What is the investment proportion $y$?
(b) What is the client's investment proportion in Alice's three stocks and the T-bill fund?

(c) What is the standard deviation of the rate of return of the client's portfolio?

18. Given the information in question 16, suppose that the client wants to invest in Alice's portfolio a proportion of $y$ that maximizes the expected return on the complete portfolio subject to the constraint that the complete portfolio's standard deviation will not be greater than 15%.

    (a) What is the investment proportion $y$ now?
    (b) What is the expected rate of return on the complete portfolio?

19. Suppose that the client's utility function is U =E(r) – 0.5A $\sigma^2$ and the degree of risk aversion A is equal to 4.

    (a) What proportion of $y$ of the total investment should be invested in Alice's fund?
    (b) What is the expected value of standard deviation of the rate of return on the client's optimized portfolio?

20. Gordon is managing a risky portfolio and a risk free asset with the following information.

$$E(r_P) = 14\%, \quad \sigma_P = 18\%, \quad r_f = 6\%$$

    (a) One of Gordon's clients wants to invest a proportion of her total investment budget in Gordon's risky fund to provide an expected rate of return on her overall or complete portfolio equal to 10%. What proportion should she invest in the risky portfolio P and what proportion in the risk free asset?
    (b) What will be the standard deviation of the rate of return on her portfolio?
    (c) Another client wants the highest return possible subject to the constraint that you limit his standard deviation to be no more than 12%. Which client is more risk averse?

21. Amanda is managing a risky portfolio with an expected rate of return of 16% and a standard deviation of 18%. Suppose the borrowing rate your client face is 8%. Assume that the S&P 500 index has an expected return of 15% and standard deviation of 20%. The risk free rate is 6%. What is the range of the risk aversion for which a client will neither borrow nor lend, that is, for which $y = 1$?

22. Daniel is managing a risky portfolio with an expected rate of return of 12% and a standard deviation of 16%. Assume that the S&P 500 index has an expected return of 16% and standard deviation of 30%. Also, the risk free rate is 6% but the borrowing rate Daniel's client faces is 9%. What is the largest percentage fee that a client who currently is lending ($y < 1$) will be willing to pay to invest in Daniel's fund? What about a client who is borrowing (What about a client who is borrowing ($y > 1$)?
23. Suppose that the risk premium ($\mathrm{E}(r_M) - r_f$) for the S&P 500 over T-bill from 1980–2005 is 8.5% and the standard deviation of this risk premium is 20%. Suppose that the S&P 500 is your portfolio.

    (a) If your risk-aversion coefficient is 3 and you believe that the entire 1980-2005 period is representative of future expected performance, what fraction of your portfolio should be allocated to T-bills and what fraction to equity?
    (b) If your financial advisor tells you that the risk premium of S&P 500 in this period should be 8.7% and you take his advice (assume that the standard deviation of the risk premium is still 20%). What is your answer to Part (a) now? Please draw comparison between these two scenarios.

24. Please use Appendix 7C to show step by step how the optimal weight for a 2-security portfolio can be derived. In addition, please discuss the potential application of this procedure in deriving the regression coefficients of simple regression in terms of ordinary least square method.

## Chapter 8

# Risk and Return Trade-Off Analysis

**Contents**



## 8.1 Introduction

In this chapter, we discuss the risk-return trade-off and the economic relationships between risk and return, using the risk estimation and diversification concepts presented in Chapter 7. We also explain how the market model can be used to estimate the systematic risk and Jensen performance measure. Applications of the beta coefficient and the economic relationships between risk and return are also discussed.

Section 8.2 of this chapter pertains to the capital market line (CML), the efficient-market hypothesis (EMH), and the capital asset pricing model (CAPM). Section 8.3 shows how a market model can be used to estimate the beta coefficient. Section 8.4 discuss the empirical evidence for the risk-return relationship, while Section 8.5 talks about the importance of the beta coefficient in financial management. The determination of systematic risk is discussed in Section 8.6, and applications and implications of the capital asset pricing model are discussed in Section 8.7. Liquidity and capital asset pricing model is discussed in Section 8.8. A generalized capital asset pricing model — arbitrage pricing theory (APT) is discussed in Section 8.9. Finally, Section 8.10 summarizes the chapter. A mathematical derivation of the capital asset pricing model is shown in Appendix 8A.

## 8.2 Capital Market Line, Efficient-Market Hypothesis, and Capital Asset Pricing Model

Based on the risk-return trade-off principle and the portfolio diversification process (discussed in Chapter 7), Sharpe (1964) and Lintner (1965) developed an asset pricing model that not only determines the value of an efficient portfolio, but also the value of an individual security. They focused on the pricing implications of those areas of risk that can be eliminated through diversification as well as those that cannot.

*Systematic risk* is the part of total risk that results from the tendency of stock prices to move together with the general market. *Unsystematic risk* is the result of variations peculiar to a firm or industry; for example, a labor strike or resource shortages.

Systematic risk' also referred to as *market risk*, reflect the fluctuations and change of the general market. Some stocks and portfolios are sensitive to movements in the market, while others show more independence and stability. A measure of a stock of portfolio's relative sensitivity to the market, based on its past record, has been designated by the Greek letter beta ($\beta$). The estimation and application of beta is discussed in the following section.

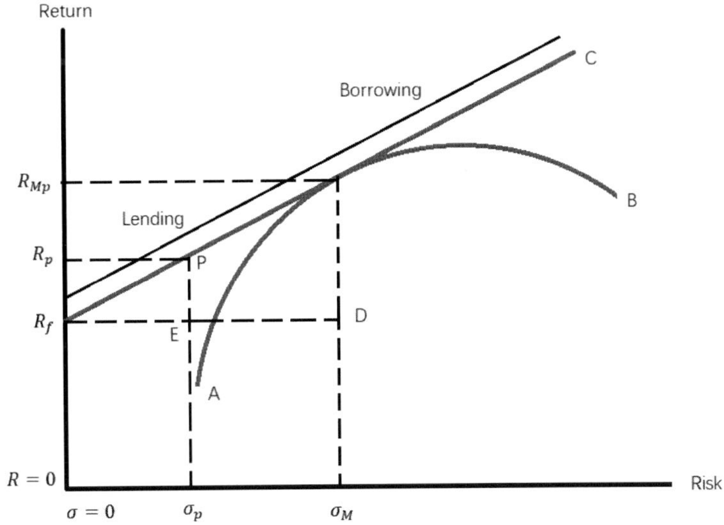


Figure 8.1 The Capital Market Line.

### 8.2.1 *Lending, borrowing, and the market portfolio*

In Chapter 7, we assumed the efficient frontier was constructed with risk assets only. In Figure 8.1, this is shown by the curve $AM_PB$. If there are both risk-free and risky assets, then investors have the choice of investing in either type of asset or in combinations of the two types.

In general, risk-free assets refer to government securities, such as Treasury bills (T-bills). These assets are backed by the federal government and are default free, and hence riskless; the cash flows are certain. An investor's portfolio can comprise different sets of investment opportunities including the risk-free asset with a return of $R_f$. The riskless asset has zero risk and is a point on the vertical axis of the risk-and-return area as shown in Figure 8.1.

With the additional opportunity to invest in risk-free assets that yield a return of $R_f$, the investor can create new combinations of portfolios that combine the risk-free asset with risky assets. The investor is thus able to achieve any combination of risk and return that lies along the line connecting $R_f$ and a point tangent to $M_p$, the market portfolio. All portfolios along the line $R_fM_pC$ represent the best attainable combinations of risk and return.

At point $R_f$, an investor has all available funds invested in the riskless asset and expects to receive the return of $R_f$. The portfolios along the line $R_f M_p$ are *lending portfolios* and contain combinations of investments in the risk-free asset and investments in a portfolio of risky assets, $M_p$. In a sense, the investor is lending the government money at the risk-free rate $R_f$; hence, the name lending portfolio.

At point $M_p$, the investor holds only risky assets; all the investor's wealth is in the risk-asset portfolio, which is the market portfolio. At $M_p$, investors receive a rate of return $R_m$ and undertake risk $\sigma_m$.

If investors can borrow money at risk-free rate $R_f$ and invest this money in risky portfolio $M_p$, they will be able to construct portfolios with higher rates of return but with higher risks along the line extending beyond $M_p$. The extent to which this is possible is regulated by the margin requirements imposed by the government. The higher the margin requirement, the shorter the line $M_pC$. The amount of money that can be borrowed by investors may also be limited by considerations of the creditworthiness of borrowers. The portfolios along segment $M_pC$ are called *borrowing portfolios*, because the investor must borrow funds to achieve these risk-and-return combinations. The new efficient frontier becomes $R_f M_p C$ and is referred to as the *capital market line* (CML). In short, the capital market line describes the relationship between expected return and total risk for efficient portfolios with the existence of risk-free assets.

### 8.2.2 *The capital market line*

We have just given a graphical illustration and verbal explanation of the capital market line. In equation form, the CML is

$$E(R_p) = R_f + [E(R_m) - R_f]\frac{\sigma_p}{\sigma_m} \tag{8.1}$$

where $R_f$ = the risk-free rate; $R_m$ = return on market portfolio $M_p$; $R_p$ = return on the portfolio consisting of combinations of the risk-free asset and portfolio $M_p$; $\sigma_p$ and $\sigma_m$ = standard deviations of the portfolio and the market; and the operator $E$ denotes expectations.

The interpretation of Eq. (8.1) can be explained geometrically. An investor has three investment choices; $R_f$, the riskless asset; $M_p$, the market portfolio; and any other efficient portfolio along the efficient frontier, such as portfolio $P$ in Figure 8.1.

The riskless asset offers a return of $R_f$, the market portfolio an average return of $R_m$ and risk of $\sigma_m$, and portfolio $P$ an average return of $R_p$ with risk of $\sigma_p$. The difference between $R_m$ and $R_f$, $(R_m - R_f)$ is called the *market risk premium.*

The investor in portfolio $P$ only needs to take on risk of $\sigma_p$, so the risk premium is $(R_p - R_f)$, which is less than risks of an investor who holds portfolio $M_p$.

By geometric theory, triangles $R_f\ PE$ and $R_f M_p D$ are similar and are, therefore, directly proportional. Thus,[1]

$$E(R_p) - R_f = [E(R_m) - R_f]\frac{\sigma_p}{\sigma_m}\frac{\sigma_p}{\sigma_m} \tag{8.2}$$

In equilibrium, all investors will want to hold a combination of the risk-free and risky assets at the tangency portfolio, $M_p$. At equilibrium, prices are such that the demand for all marketable assets equals their supply; therefore, tangency portfolio $M_p$ must represent the market portfolio. An individual security's proportional makeup in the market portfolio is the ratio of its market value (its equilibrium price times the total number of shares outstanding) to the total market value of all securities in the market, or

$$x = \frac{\text{Market value of an individual asset}}{\text{Market value of all assets}} \tag{8.3}$$

Thus, at equilibrium, prices are such that supply is equated to demand and all securities in the market will be represented in the market portfolio according to their market value.

### 8.2.3 *The efficient-market hypothesis*

Some critical assumptions which will be discussed in deriving the capital asset pricing model are concerned with the efficiency of capital markets. Therefore, the basic concepts of the *efficient-market hypothesis* (EMH) are discussed next. In the efficient-market hypothesis, it is assumed all investors cannot predict the future or direction

---

[1]Since $\Delta PR_fE \cong \Delta M_pR_fD$, therefore,

$$\frac{E(R_p) - R_f}{E(R_m) - R_f} = \frac{\sigma_p}{\sigma_m}$$

From this equation, we obtain Eq. (8.2).

of capital markets based upon past actions; that is, the short-run changes in stock prices cannot be predicted.

Following Fama (1970, 1976), there are several assumptions that must hold for the efficient-market theory to be accepted. First, there must be a large number of profit-maximizing investors who operate independently of each other. Second, new information must enter the market randomly and independently over time. Third, all investors adjust security prices accordingly when they receive new information, as quickly as possible. It is assumed that price adjustment would occur rapidly because of the large volume of investors participating in the market.

The last assumption is that any point in time, security prices reflect unbiasedly all available information. This supposition arises because stock prices are supposed to reflect all available public information at any given time.

Therefore, based on these criteria, an efficient market is one in which security prices adjust rapidly with the introduction of new information, and stock prices always reflect all currently available information, including all risks. In conclusion, the returns expected from any given security are consistent with the risk reflected in its price.

#### 8.2.3.1 *Weak-form efficient-market hypothesis*

This hypothesis assumes that all current stock prices fully reflect all historical and current stock market information. This includes information on prices, price sequences, and volume. The main conclusion is that there is no relationship between past price changes and future price changes, and all price changes are independent.

#### 8.2.3.2 *Semistrong-form efficient-market hypothesis*

This hypothesis states that security prices adjust rapidly after the release of any new public information and that prices reflect all of this information. This hypothesis is inclusive of the weak-form theory also, because public information includes market information as well as nonmarket information such as economic and political views, earnings, stock splits, and other fundamental corporate information.

The major implication of this hypothesis is that investors who act on public information after it is released will not be able to earn above-average profits, because security prices will already have changed to reflect this information.

#### 8.2.3.3 *Strong-form efficient-market hypothesis*

This hypothesis encompasses both the weak and semistrong forms in that it contends stock prices fully reflect all information — public, private or otherwise. Therefore, no group of investors will ever be able to consistently derive above-average profits. As a requirement, therefore, the strong form states that markets must be perfect in that all information must be available to everybody at the same time. Since all information is available to all groups, the strong-form hypothesis contends that no group will have monopolistic access to information and derive above-average profits.

A lot of empirical work has been done in the last two decades to test which efficient-market hypothesis is valid. Fama (1976) and others have concluded that the semistrong hypothesis best describes market behavior, Finnerty (1976) has shown that the stock market is not strong-form efficiency. In recent years, this has led to an increase in inside-trading prosecution by the securities and Exchange Commission.

### 8.2.4 *The capital asset pricing model*

To derive the *capital asset pricing model* (CAPM) we must first list a few assumptions concerning the investors and the securities market:

1. Investors are risk-averse.
2. The CAPM is a single-period model because it is assumed that investors maximize the utility of their end-of-period wealth.
3. All investors have the same efficient frontier; that is, they have homogenous expectations concerning asset returns and risk.
4. Portfolios and securities are characterized by their means and variances.
5. There is a risk-free asset with an interest rate $R_f$. This rate is available to all investors to either borrow or lend. The borrowing rate is equal to the lending rate.
6. All assets are marketable and perfectly divisible, and their supplies are fixed.

7. There are no transaction costs.
8. Investors have all information available to them at no cost.
9. There are no taxes or regulations associated with trading.

Given these assumptions and the derivation presented in Appendix 8A, the capital asset pricing model (CAPM) is defined as

$$E(R_i) = R_f + \beta_i[E(R_m) - R_f] \tag{8.4}$$

where $E(R_i)$ = the expected rate of return for asset $i$; $R_f$ = the risk-free rate; $\beta_i$ = the measure of systematic risk (beta) for asset $i$; and $E(R_m)$ = the expected return on the market portfolio.

Equation (8.4) implies that an asset's systematic risk $\beta_i$ is the only relevant risk measure of capital asset pricing for both individual asset and portfolio. Figure 8.2 depicts the risk-return trade-off relationship for the CAPM. This risk-return trade-off is also called the *security market line* (SML).

With the capital asset pricing model, we must assume that utility-maximizing investors will attempt to be somewhere along the CML and will attempt to put some portion of their wealth into the market portfolio of risky assets.

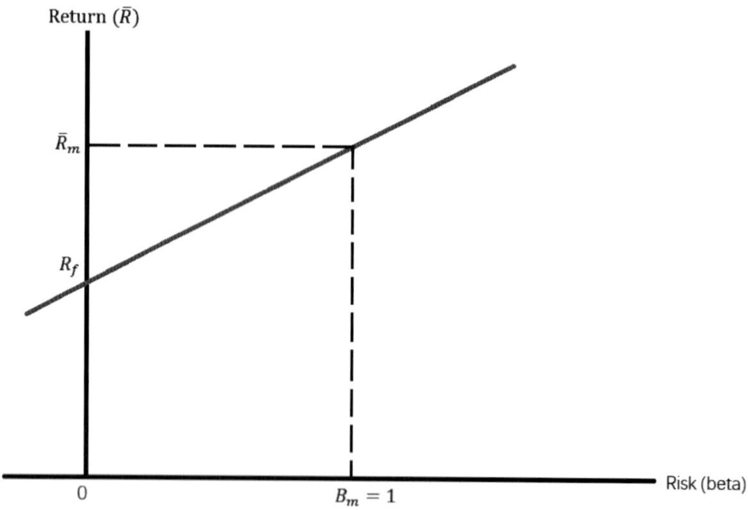


Figure 8.2 The Capital Asset Pricing Model (SML).

The CAPM implies that the market portfolio is the only relevant portfolio of risky assets. Hence, the relevant risk measurement of any security is its covariance with the market portfolio, the systematic risk of the market.

The relationship between the CML and the CAPM can be shown by starting with the definition of the beta coefficient:

$$\beta_i = \frac{\mathrm{COV}(R_i, R_m)}{\mathrm{VAR}(R_m)} = \frac{\rho_{i,m}\sigma_i\sigma_m}{\sigma_m^2} = \frac{\rho_{i,m}\sigma_i}{\sigma_m} \tag{8.5}$$

where $\sigma_i$ = standard deviation of ith security's rate of return; $\sigma_m$ = standard deviation of the market rate of return; and $\rho_{i,m}$ = the correlation coefficient of $R_i$ and $R_m$.

If $\rho_{i,m} = 1$, then Eq. (8.4) reduces to

$$E(R_i) = R_f + \frac{\sigma_i}{\sigma_m}[E(R_m) - R_f] \tag{8.6}$$

If $\rho_{i,m} = 1$, this is an efficient portfolio, or for an individual security, the returns and risks associated with the asset are similar to the market as a whole. The implications of this comparison are as follows:

1. Equation (8.4) is a generalized case of Eq. (8.2), because Eq. (8.4) includes the correlation coefficient, whereas Eq. (8.2) assumes that the correlation coefficient equals 1.
2. The security market line (SML), instead of the CML, should be used to price an individual security or an inefficient portfolio. The reason is that if we use the CML to price an inefficient portfolio, we would be pricing unsystematic risk. (The SML is discussed in detail later in this chapter.)
3. The CML prices the risk premium in terms of total risk, and the SML prices the risk premium in terms of systematic risk.

To apply the CAPM, we need to have estimates of the beta coefficient, the risk-free rate, and the market risk premium. Estimates of these quantities can be obtained from time-series data, this is discussed in the following section.

## 8.3 The Market Model and Beta Estimation

As stated above, the total risk of a portfolio or security can be viewed as the sum of its systematic and unsystematic risks. The equation that expresses these concepts states that the return on any asset at time $t$ can be expressed as a linear function of the market return at time $t$ plus a random error component. Thus, this relationship, called the *market model*, is

$$R_{i,t} = \alpha_i + \beta_i R_{m,t} + \epsilon_{i,t} \tag{8.7}$$

where $R_{i,t}$ = the return of the $i$th security at time $t$; $\alpha_i$ = the intercept of the regression; $\beta_i$ = the slope coefficient of the regression; $R_{m,t}$ = the market return at time $t$; and $\epsilon_{i,t}$ = the random error term.

This regression equation describes the risky asset's return relationship with the market portfolio return. Equation (8.7) is also called the *characteristic line* and is a statistical tool employed to measure systematic and unsystematic risk. The term $\alpha_i$ is called the *alpha coefficient* for security $i$. This is the intercept point where the characteristic line intercepts the y-axis. Since beta is the slope coefficient for this regression (market model), it demonstrates how responsive returns for the individual assets are to the market portfolio.

Alternatively, a market model can be define as follows:

$$R_{i,t} - R_{f,t} = \alpha_i + \beta_i (R_{m,t} - R_{f,t}) + \epsilon_{i,t} \tag{8.8}$$

where $R_{f,t}$ is the risk-free rate. All variables of Eq. (8.8) can be estimated from observed data. Equation (8.8) is the risk premium form of the market model and is similar to the market model indicated in Eq. (8.7).

The CAPM shown by Eq. (8.4) has $R_f$ as the intercept term. In Eq. (8.8), the intercept term of the characteristic line in terms of risk premium is $\alpha_i$, which has investment performance implications. The estimated $\alpha_i$, $\alpha_i$ is called the Jensen performance measure. The $\alpha_i$ is defined as

$$\hat{\alpha}_i = (\bar{R}_i - \bar{R}_f) - \beta_i(\bar{R}_m - R_f) \tag{8.9}$$

Table 8.1 Mean, Variance, and Covariance for Individual Firms and Market.

| | **Average Return** ($\bar{R}_i$) | **Variance** ($\sigma_i^2$) | **Covariance** [**COV**($\boldsymbol{R_i}$,$\boldsymbol{R_m}$)] |
|---|---|---|---|
| IBM | −0.0004436 | 0.00370575 | 0.00125605 |
| JNJ | 0.00952633 | 0.00160325 | 0.0007522 |
| KO | 0.00728444 | 0.00148232 | 0.00050345 |
| Market (GSPC) | 0.00932868 | 0.00100985 | |

where $\bar{R}_i$, $\bar{R}_m$, and $\bar{R}_f$ represent the average rate of return for security $i$, average market rate of return, and the risk-free rate.

**Example 8.1.** To show how Eqs. (8.7) and (8.8) can be applied, we use estimates from International Business Machines Corporation (IBM), Johnson & Johnson (JNJ), and Coca-Cola's (KO) monthly returns for the period from January 2012 to October 2019. Average return, variance, and covariance for these companies are provided in Table 8.1, as is the market average return and the variance of market return.

From the definition of the slope of the regression line

$$\beta_i = \frac{\text{COV}(R_i, R_m)}{\sigma_m^2}$$

We calculate the beta of IBM to be

$$\beta_{IBM} = \frac{0.00125605}{0.00100985} = 1.2438$$

the beta of JNJ to be

$$\beta_{JNJ} = \frac{0.0007522}{0.00100985} = 0.7449$$

and the beta of Coca-Cola to be

$$\beta_{KO} = \frac{0.00050345}{0.00100985} = 0.4985$$

To compare these three firms, we have various methods available. In a mean-and-variance framework, the three firms are related as you would expect: the higher the risk, the higher the return. This is shown in Figure 8.3.

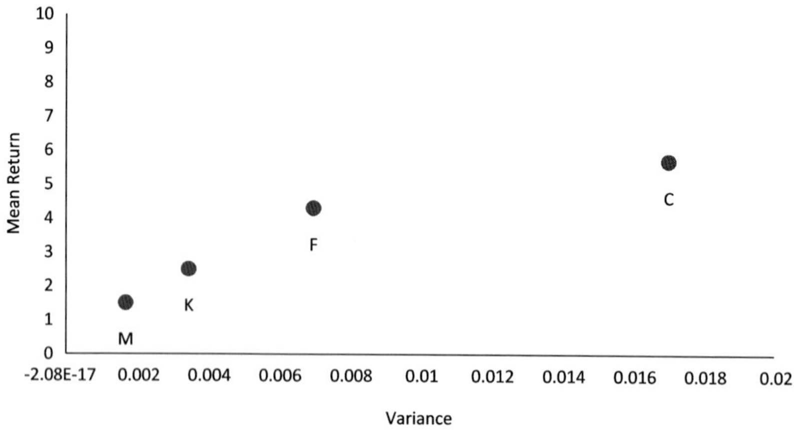


Figure 8.3 Mean–Variance Comparison.

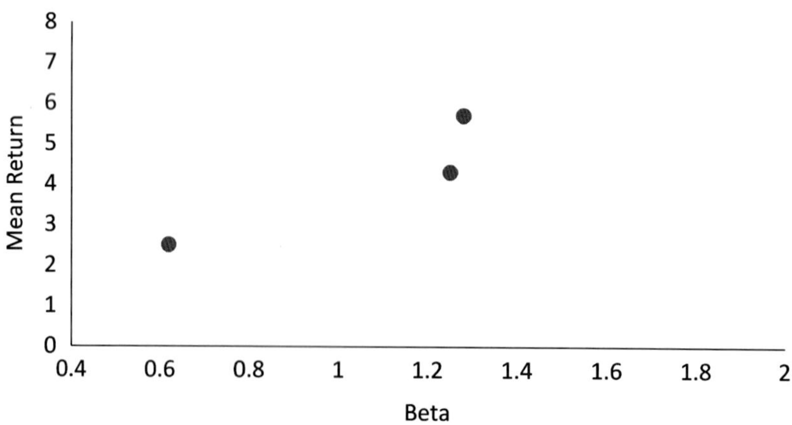


Figure 8.4 SML Comparison.

In a systematic risk-and-return framework, we find that the higher the beta, the higher the return. This is shown in Figure 8.4.

Using the Jensen performance measure, we can calculate the relative performance of each firm. If $R_f = 0.005$,

$$\begin{aligned}\hat{\alpha}_{IBM} &= (-0.0004436 - 0.005) - (1.2438)(0.00932868 - 0.005) \\ &= -0.0108276\end{aligned}$$

$$\begin{aligned}\hat{\alpha}_{JNJ} &= (0.00952633 - 0.005) - (0.7449)(0.00932868 - 0.005)\\ &= 0.00130207\\ \hat{\alpha}_{KO} &= (0.00728444 - 0.005) - (0.4985)(0.00932868 - 0.005)\\ &= 0.00012643\end{aligned}$$

The relative risk-return ranking shown by the Jensen measure ranks JNJ first, KO second, and IBM third.

## 8.4 Empirical Evidence for the Risk-Return Relationship

The validity of the CAPM can be shown through observations of actual portfolios held in the marketplace. As discussed in Chapters 7 and 8, there are two primary observations about the relationship between risk and return. First, the rate of return of efficient portfolios is a linear function of their riskiness as measured by their standard deviation and illustrated by the capital market line. Second an asset's rate of return is determined by its risk contribution to the market portfolio, and this is measured by beta, which has a linear relationship with the security's expected rate of return. This is illustrated by the security market line (SML).

We can use the performance of mutual funds to test the explanatory powers of the linear relationship between risk and return of the CML. Mutual funds are professionally managed and are one of the most visible type of portfolios. One study was performed by Sharpe (1966) to test a fund's performance and the relationship between its rate of return to risk over time. Sharpe computed average annual returns and the standard deviations of these returns for 34 mutual funds between 1954 and 1963. His model implies that portfolios with higher risks will receive higher returns. Sharpe found this to be true for all 34 funds. He calculated a correlation between average returns and their standard deviations to be 0.836, so that greater than 80% of the difference in returns was due to differences in risk.

Sharpe also found that there was a linear relationship between returns and risks except in the region of extra high risks. Sharpe used the CML instead of the SML in his study of efficient mutual funds. From the relationship in Eq. (8.6), we know that the results of that study would have been the same using either the SML or the CML. Sharpe's study gives basic support to his contention that the CML explains the relationship between portfolio theory and the determination of prices in the market.

Another study was performed by Jensen (1969), who studied the correlation of beta coefficients (market sensitivity) and the expected return of mutual funds. Based on his analysis of 115 mutual funds over a nine-year period, Jensen was able to conclude that high returns are associated with high volatility or high systematic risk. He also found evidence that beta coefficients were a valid and accurate measure of risk.

Both the Sharpe and Jensen studies on the risk-and-return relationship of mutual funds show that there is an empirical risk-return relationship among mutual funds. However, Sharpe used the capital market line to perform his empirical tests, while Jensen used the security market line, which was derived by Sharpe (1964).

The second implication of the risk-return relationship is that the risk premium on individual assets depends on the contribution of each asset to the riskiness of the entire portfolio and can be algebraically explained by the CAPM and written as

$$E(R_i) - R_f = [E(R_m) - R_f]\beta_i \tag{8.10}$$

where

$$\beta_i = \frac{\sigma_{im}}{\sigma_m^2} = \frac{\rho_{i,m}\sigma_i}{\sigma_m} \tag{8.5}$$

Equation (8.5) states that the riskiness of each asset depends on the covariance of its return ($\sigma_{im}$) relative to the variance of the market ($\sigma_m^2$). Therefore, if the correlation is 1 and the riskiness of the asset is equal to the riskiness of the market; that is, the standard deviation of the individual asset is equal to the standard deviation of the market. Then this implies that the risk premium on the individual asset will be equal to that of the market. If the correlation is 0, then the risk premium is 0 because the asset does not add any additional systematic risk to the portfolio.

To test the CAPM, a problem must first be resolved. The CAPM utilizes *expected* returns, whereas we can observe *actual* returns. The first step is to transfer nonmeasurable expected returns into a form that utilizes observable data. The empirical model used to test the CAPM is defined as

$$\overline{\overline{R}}_p - \overline{\overline{R}}_f = r_0 + r_1\beta_p + e_p \tag{8.11}$$

where $R_p - R_f$ = the observed excess return on portfolio $p$; $\beta_p$ = the estimated beta for portfolio $p$; and $e_p$ = the residual term associated with the cross-sectional regression.

Equation (8.11) predicts the following:

1. The intercept, $r_0$, will not be significantly different from 0. If it were, the CAPM might be misspecified.
2. The relationship with respect to beta is linear.
3. The estimated $r_1$ would be equal to $(R_m - R_f)$.

Another problem that is prevalent with testing whether theoretical models are valid representatives of real-world phenomena is the "joint hypothesis" problem. When we evaluate real-world problems using theoretical models, we cannot be sure that the conclusions reached are accurate or affected by a misspecification of the model used to perform the evaluation. Are the results obtained from using a correct model or are the results obtained because the model is incorrect?

Major empirical tests performed on the CAPM are Blume and Friend (1973), Friend *et al.* (1970), and Fama and Macbeth (1973). Their results were mixed. The empirical results of these researchers were summarized in Copeland, Weston, and Shastri (2003). Roll (1977, 1978) provided a critique on both the CAPM and the Jensen performance measure.

## 8.5 Why Beta is Important in Financial Management

Beta is used as a measurement of risk by gauging the sensitivity of a stock or portfolio relative to the market. A beta of 1 is characteristic of a broad market index, such as the NYSE index or the S&P 500. A beta of 2 indicates that the stock is expected to swing twice as far in either direction, given a fall or rise in the market average. If the market is expected to gain 15%, a security of beta = 2 is expected to gain 30%. Conversely, if the market is expected to fall 15%, then the stock is expected to fall 30%.

A beta of 0.5 indicates that the stock is more stable than the market and is expected to move half as much as the market. For example, if the market is expected to lose 20%, a stock with beta = 0.5 is expected to fall only 10%, and if the market is expected to gain 20%, the stock is expected to gain only 10%. High-beta stocks have been classified as *aggressive*, while low-beta stocks are referred to as *defensive*.

The CAPM approach requires a long-run view of decision-making. If the manager consistently follows the indications of the CAPM, short-run errors will tend to cancel out and the expectations will be realized. However, for any single decision, the *a priori* expectations may be very different from the actual results because of various random factors. Therefore, any judgement or evaluation of the efficiency of this method must be carried out over relatively long periods and numerous usages.

The CAPM has shown that risks are associated with portfolios. The relevant (systematic) risk of a security is dependent on the security's effect on portfolio risk. Therefore, the CAPM equation, $E(R_i) - R_f = [E(R_m) - R_f]\beta_i$, represents a description of how rates of return are established in the marketplace assuming that investors behave according to the model's assumptions. Thus, a stock's beta measures its contribution of risk to the portfolio and therefore is a measure of the stock's riskiness relative to the market.

In the previous section, we found that stock $i$ is presumed to bear a linear relationship with the market, as described by Eq. (8.7):

$$R_{i,t} = \alpha_i + \beta_i R_{m,t} + \epsilon_{i,t} \tag{8.7}$$

The regression coefficient $\beta_i$ is a market sensitivity index and is a measure of the volatility of stock $i$ against the market. This risk component is the stock's market or *nondiversifiable* risk. Therefore, the size of beta indicates the amount of systematic risk. The greater is beta, the greater is the stock's market or nondiversifiable risk.

There is a distinction between the market risk premium and an individual stock's risk premium. The CAPM asserts that the market risk premium is common to all stocks. However, the beta coefficient multiplied by the market risk premium determines the stock's risk premium. Hence, because each stock has a different beta, it will also have a unique risk premium.

The use of beta is of great importance to the financial manager because it is a key component in the estimation of the cost of capital. A firm's expected cost of capital can be derived from $E(R_i)$, where $E(R_i) = R_f + [E(R_m) - R_f]\beta_i$. This assumes that the manager has access to the other parameters, such as the risk-free rate and the market rate of return.

Beta is also an important variable because of its usefulness in security analysis. In this type of analysis, beta is used to measure a security's response to a change in the market and so can be used to structure portfolios that have certain risk characteristics.

## 8.6 Systematic Risk Determination

As mentioned above, systematic risk is nondiversifiable because it occurs in all industries and companies and affects entire markets. Systematic risk comprises several components; here we discuss a few of the basic ones.

There are two dimensions of risk that affect a firm's systematic risk. The first is *business risk*, which is the riskiness of a firm's operations if the firm takes on no debt. This is related to the types of investments the firm makes; that is, capital intensive versus labor intensive. The second is *financial risk*, the additional risk placed on the firm and its stockholders due to the firm's decision to be levered (taking on debt).

Business risk is inherent in a firm's operations. It can also be defined as the uncertainty inherent in the projection of future operating income or earnings before interest and taxes (EBIT). Fluctuations in EBIT are caused by a number of factors. On the national level, these can be economic factors such as inflationary or recessionary periods. At the industry level, factors such as the level of competition between similar industries, natural or man-made catastrophes during production, labor strikes, and price controls can cause EBIT fluctuations. There are a host of possibilities, all of which are reflected in the EBIT by raising or reducing its level.

Uncertainty regarding future income flows is caused by the company's business risk, which may fluctuate between industries, among firms, and over time. The extent of business risk is dependent on the firm and industry. Cyclical industries, such as steel and automobiles, have especially high business risks because they are dependent on the cycles of the economy. The retail food industry is considered stable because food is a necessary good and will be purchased regardless of the state of the economy.

Business risk is dependent on numerous factors; some of the more important are as follows:

1. *Demand variability*: Stable demand levels for the firm's product reduce business risk.
2. *Sales price variability*: Highly volatile prices result in high-risk volatile markets. Therefore, price stability reduces business risk.
3. *Supplier price variability*: Firms whose input prices are highly variable are exposed to higher levels of risk.
4. *Output price flexibility relative to input prices*: Because of inflation, a firm that raises its output prices with increasing input costs minimizes its business risk.

Financial risk refers to the use of fixed-charge securities such as debt or preferred stock. Financial leverage affects a firm's return on equity and the riskiness of these returns, as well as the firm's earnings per share and stock price.

### 8.6.1 *Business risk and financial risk*

A firm's capital structure affects the riskiness inherent in the company's common stock and thus affects its required rate of return and stock price. A company's capital structure policy requires choosing between risk and return. Taking on increasing levels of debt increases the riskiness of the firm's earning stream but results in a higher expected rate of return. High levels of risk tend to lower a stock's price, but high levels of expected rate of return tend to raise it. Therefore, striking a balance between risk and return affects the stock's price. (This issue of capital structure is discussed in Chapter 11.)

When a firm uses debt, or financial leverage, business risk and financial risk are concentrated on the stockholders. For example, if a firm is capitalized only with common equity, then the investors all share the business risk in proportion with their ownership of stock. However, if a firm is 50% levered (50% of the corporation financed by debt, the other half by common equity), then the investors who put up the equity will have to bear all business and financial risk as a result of leverage.

A generalization of the effects of leverage upon return on assets (ROA) and return on equity (ROE) and its effect on the stockholders can be summarized as follows:

1. Leverage, or debt, generally increases ROE.
2. The standard deviation of ROA ($\sigma_{\text{ROA}}$) measures business risk, while the standard deviation of ROE ($\sigma_{\text{ROE}}$) measures the risk borne by stockholders. $\sigma_{\text{ROA}} = \sigma_{\text{ROE}}$ if the firm is not levered; otherwise, with the use of debt, $\sigma_{\text{ROE}} > \sigma_{\text{ROA}}$, an indication that business risk is being borne by the stockholders.
3. The difference between $\sigma_{\text{ROA}}$ and $\sigma_{\text{ROE}}$ is the actual risk stockholders face and a measure of the increased risk due to financial leverage:

$$\text{Risk of financial leverage} = \sigma_{\text{ROE}} - \sigma_{\text{ROA}}$$

### 8.6.2 *Other financial variables*

Besides leverage, other financial variables are associated with the firm that can affect the beta coefficient. These are the growth rate, accounting beta, and variance of EBIT.

The growth rate is measured in terms of the growth in total assets or the growth in sales, and is determined by the percentage change between two periods. For example:

$$g_s = \frac{\text{Sales}_t - \text{Sales}_{t-1}}{\text{Sales}_{t-1}} \times 100\%$$

or

$$g_{\text{TA}} = \frac{\text{Total assets}_t - \text{Total assets}_{t-1}}{\text{Total assets}_{t-1}} \times 100\%$$

These equations give the firm's percentage growth.

The accounting beta is calculated from earnings per share data. Using EPS as an example, the accounting beta is calculated as follows:

$$\text{EPS}_{i,t} = a_0 + a_1\text{EPS}_{m,t} + E_{i,t} \tag{8.12}$$

where $\text{EPS}_{i,t}$ = earnings per share of firm $i$ at time $t$ and $\text{EPS}_{m,t}$ = earnings per share of market average at time $t$. The estimate of $a_1$ is the EPS type of accounting beta.

The variance of EBIT can be defined as

$$\sigma^2(\text{EBIT}) = \frac{\sum_{t=1}^{N} (\text{EBIT}_t - \overline{\text{EBIT}})^2}{N-1}$$

where $\text{EBIT}_t$ = earnings before interest and taxes in period $t$. The variance of EBIT can be used to measure the overall fluctuation of a firm's accounting earnings. In general, the more stable the firm's earnings, the better for the investors.

### 8.6.3 *Capital labor ratio*

Both capital, $K$, and labor, $L$, are two important inputs for the firm's production process. Mathematically, the relationship between the quantity produced and these two inputs is described in Eq. (8.13):

$$Q = f(K, L) \tag{8.13}$$

where $K$ = the machine (that is, capital) usage during a period (machine/year can be used to measure the amount of capital used) and $L$ = hours of labor input. The capital-labor ratio, $K/L$, can be used to measure the degree of capital intensity.

Corporations often choose between increasing their capital intensity by installing computers, using robotics in place of labor, or increasing their labor inputs. Small industries specializing in handcrafted goods will have to increase their capital ratio to increase production. However, the trend in recent years for many growth-oriented firms, whether manufacturers or other members of the business sector, is to increase efficiency through increased investments in capital. Auto manufacturers are finding that robots can assemble cars of high and consistent quality at only a fraction of the cost of assembly-line labor. Hence, many automobile firms are increasing their capital intensity ratio to be more profitable.

Capital intensity increases total risk and generally results in an increase in beta. Large investments are often needed to make a plant fully automated or a financial institution completely computerized. Taking on debt or issuing securities to finance these capitalizations increases the financial risk. If the capital-labor ratio is greater than 1 (that is, $K > L$), a firm is capital intensive. If the capital-labor ratio is less than 1, then there is a reduction in capital intensity and a shift toward human resource investments. Firms with capital intensity ratios greater than 1 tend to have high betas, as shown by Subrahmanyam and Thomadakis (1980) and Mandelker and Rhee (1984).

### 8.6.4 *Fixed costs and variable costs*

Business risk depends on the extent to which a firm builds fixed costs into its operations. Fixed costs do not decline when demand falls off. If fixed costs are high, then a slight drop in sales can lead to large decline in EBIT. Therefore, the higher a firm's fixed costs, the greater its business risk.

Firms with a high percentage of fixed costs have a high degree of operating leverage (as discussed in Chapter 2). An example of such costs is the highly skilled workers of an engineering firm. The firm cannot easily hire and fire experienced and highly skilled workers, so these workers must be retained and paid during periods of slack activity when revenues are low. Therefore, a firm that is highly levered can be characterized as one of which a small change in sales causes a large change in operating income.

Variable costs have the opposite effect because they are adjustable in meeting the changes in revenues that a firm may face. Should a drop in sales occur, variable costs can be reduced to meet the lower output demand.

The extent to which firms can control their operating leverage depends on the type of product or service they provide. Companies that require large investments in fixed assets (such as steel mills, auto manufacturers, and airlines) have large fixed costs and operating leverage. Therefore, the extent to which a company is willing to take on operating leverage must be considered during the capital budgeting decision. If the firm is risk averse, it may opt for alternatives with smaller investments and fixed costs, or it may use different types of financing arrangements (such as leases) to shift the burden of ownership and thereby reduce the investment required.

A company with a large percentage of fixed costs generally uses more capital-intensive types of technology in production. For example, an automobile manufacturer such as Ford has a higher percentage of fixed costs than a company in the food industry, such as Coca-Cola. Therefore, Ford's capital-labor ratio is expected to be higher than Coca-Cola's. The implication is that Coca-Cola is expected to have a lower beta than Ford.

### 8.6.5 *Market-based versus accounting-based beta forecasting*

Market-based beta forecasts are based on market information alone. The firm's historical betas are used as a measure of the firm's future beta. On the other hand, accounting-based beta forecasts rely on the relationship of accounting information — such as the growth rate, EBIT, and leverage — as a basis for forecasting beta. To use accounting information in beta forecast, we first relate the historical beta estimates cross-sectionally with accounting information:

$$\beta = a_0 + a_1 X_1 + a_2 X_2 + a_3 X_3 + \cdots + a_n X_n \tag{8.14}$$

where $X_j$ = $j$th accounting variables for individual firms ($j = 1, 2, \ldots, n$); $a_j$ = the coefficient associated with the $j$th variable; and $a_0$ = the intercept.

Lee, Newbold, Finnerty, and Chu (1986), using accounting information, have shown a relationship between market-based beta and accounting variables. Over the period 1961 to 1980, for a sample of 250 manufacturing firms, they estimated the regression equation shown in Table 8.2.

From these results, we can conclude that accounting information is related to the firm's measure of systematic risk. This information can be used to estimate the cost of capital or the risk-adjusted discount rate for those firms that are not actively traded and therefore do not have market data available. In other words, from

Table 8.2 Regression Results for the Accounting Beta.

$$\beta = a_0 + a_1 X_1 + a_2 X_2 + a_3 X_3 + \cdots + a_n X_n$$

| | **Coefficients** | ***t* Values** |
|---|---|---|
| Intercept ($a_0$) | 0.911 | 11.92 |
| Financial leverage ($a_1$) | 0.704 | 5.31 |
| Dividend payout ($a_2$) | −0.175 | −3.50 |
| Sales beta ($a_3$) | 0.03 | 3.02 |
| Operating income beta ($a_4$) | 0.011 | 2.18 |

Eq. (8.14) we can estimate beta coefficient in terms of accounting information. Alternatively, we can use accounting information to estimate accounting beta for example, accounting beta for earnings per share (EPS) can be estimated as follows.

$$EPS_{i,t} = \alpha_i + \beta_i EPS_{m,t} + e_{i,t} \tag{8.15}$$

where $EPS_{i,t}$ = earnings per share of firm $i$ at time $t$; $EPS_{m,t}$ = earnings per share of market average at time $t$; and $e_{i,t}$ = error term.

The estimate of $\beta_i$ is the EPS type of accounting beta.

## 8.7 Some Applications and Implications of the Capital Asset Pricing Model

Since its development, the uses of the CAPM have extended into all areas of financial analysis and planning. These specific uses are discussed in detail in subsequent chapters and are given a general overview here. The CAPM can be applied to the capital budgeting problem in determining the cost of capital and in assessing the riskiness of a project under consideration (Chapter 9). The CAPM can also be useful in a real asset problem, such as the lease-buy decision (Chapter 17).

The use of the CAPM can be extended into the valuation of the entire firm. Because of its impact on firm valuation, the CAPM has been of great use in the merger analysis area of financial analysis (Chapter 25). The CAPM has also been used to test various financial theories. By including a dividend term and considering its effects, the CAPM can be used to test the effects of the firm's dividend policy on the value of the firm's shares (Chapter 12). An area that has received a great deal of attention is the use of the CAPM in testing the efficient market hypothesis.

An application of the CAPM to the capital budgeting process concerns the valuation of risky projects. If accurate estimates can be made about the systematic risk of a project, then the CAPM can be used to determine the risk-adjusted discount rate necessary to compensate the firm for the project's risk. If the sum of the estimated cash flows discounted by the CAPM-calculated required rate of return is positive, then the firm should undertake the project.

This is one method that can be used to handle uncertainty. A more detailed discussion of this risk-adjusted-discount rate method as well as the certainty equivalent method is presented in Chapter 9.

Rubinstein (1973) demonstrated how the CAPM could be used to value securities and to calculate their risk-adjusted equilibrium price. First, the CAPM must be converted to price variables instead of expected returns, as follows:

$$E(R_i) = \frac{E(P_1) - P_0}{P_0}$$

where $E(R_i)$ = the expected returns of the CAPM model; $P_1$ = price of stock in period 1; and $P_0$ = price of stock in the previous period. Thus, the CAPM becomes

$$\frac{E(P_1) - P_0}{P_0} = R_f + [E(R_m) - R_f]\beta_i \tag{8.16}$$

or rearranging Eq. (8.16)

$$P_0 = \frac{E(P_1)}{1 + R_f + [E(R_m) - R_f]\beta_i} \tag{8.17}$$

Thus, the rate of return used to discount the expected end-of-period price contains a risk premium dependent on the security's systematic risk. (Eq. (8.16) is used in Chapter 9 to determine risk-adjusted discount rates for capital budgeting decisions under uncertainty.) The long-term market risk premium, $[E(R_m) - R_f]$, can be found in Ibbotson *et al.* (2016).

The CAPM can be used to choose between alternative projects under uncertainty. For example, the capital budgeting and business strategy relationship matrix, as used in Chapter 6, can be solved by using the CAPM relationship.

If the security market line (SML) is identified as shown in Figure 8.5, then the acceptance or rejection of Projects A, B, C, D, E, and F can be easily determined. Projects A, B, and D should be accepted because they offer a higher level of return for a given risk level than currently available in the market. Projects C, E, and F should be rejected because their returns are not sufficient to justify the amount of risk that each entails.

The Sharpe approach, used in Chapter 7, consists of drawing a capital market line and then evaluating the risk and return trade-off

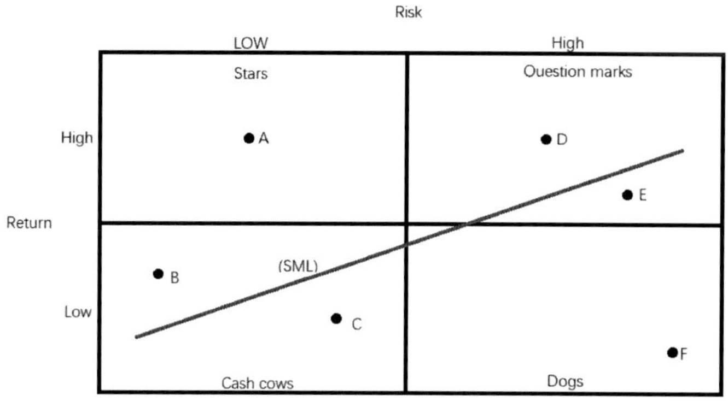


Figure 8.5 Capital Budgeting and Business Strategy Matrix.

of each project. The difference between the CML and the SML is the selection of either total risk or systematic risk as the appropriate risk measure.

CAPM has also been applied in the analysis of mergers. It has been shown that portfolio risk can be substantially reduced with the inclusion of securities whose returns are not perfectly correlated. This principle also applies with respect to mergers between firms. The merger of two firms with different product lines is considered a conglomerate merger. The managers of the merging firms consider the benefits of diversification for these types of firms to be positive. Suppose that one firm sells a product that is recession-resistant, while the other firm's product is highly cyclical. A decrease in earnings of one division of the conglomerate will be offset by the steady earnings of another division during changes in the business cycle. The overall result will be a relatively stable income stream despite shifting trends in the economy.

The application of the CAPM form of analysis in a perfect market setting is governed by the *value additivity principle* (VAP). According to the VAP, in equilibrium the total market value of any set of income streams received by investors in the market is the same regardless of how that set of streams is combined or divided into the debt or equity stream of one or more firms. In our merger discussion, we apply the CAPM form of the analysis, but we assume that real-world markets (both financial and product) in which the manager must operate are not perfect (VAP may not hold). This real-world approach will be stressed in the remainder of the text.

## 8.8 Liquidity and Capital Asset Pricing Model

Cochrane (2005) has introduced the liquidity factor into the CAPM model. In accordance with the liquidity effect, Acharya and Pedersen (2005) proposed the following model for liquidity considering the impact of liquidity risk on security pricing.

$$E(R_i) = kE(C_i) + \lambda(\beta + \beta_{L1} - \beta_{L2} - \beta_{L3}) \tag{8.18}$$

where $E(C_i)$ = expected cost of liquidity; $k$ = adjustment for average holding period over all securities; $\lambda$ = market risk premium net of average market liquidity; $\beta$ = systematic market risk; $\beta_{L1}, \beta_{L2}, \beta_{L3}$ = liquidity betas.

In their model, Acharya and Pedersen (2005) suggests that the overall risk of a security account for three kinds of liquidity risks are defined as follows.

$$\beta_{L1} = \frac{\text{COV}(C_i, C_M)}{\text{VAR}(R_M - C_M)}$$

$$\beta_{L2} = \frac{\text{COV}(R_i, C_M)}{\text{VAR}(R_M - C_M)}$$

$$\beta_{L3} = \frac{\text{COV}(C_i, R_M)}{\text{VAR}(R_M - C_M)},$$

where $R_M$ = market rate of return; $C_M$ = market average liquidity premium.

First, $\beta_{L1}$ measures the sensitivity of security illiquidity to market illiquidity. In general, investors demand higher premium for holding an illiquid security when the overall market liquidity is low. Further, $\beta_{L2}$ measures the sensitivity of security's return to market illiquidity. Investors are willing to accept a lower average return on security that will provide higher returns when market illiquidity is higher. Finally $\beta_{L3}$ measures the sensitivity of security illiquidity to the market rate of return. In general, investors are willing to accept a lower average return on security that can be sold more easily.

Liquidity is an important subject in finance research. It has been found liquidity will affect the asset pricing determination. Readers can refer this issue to Cochrane (2005) and Acharya and Pedersen (2005).

## 8.9 Arbitrage Pricing Theory

Ross (1976, 1977) has derived a generalized capital asset pricing relationship called *arbitrage pricing theory* (APT). To derive the APT, Ross assumed the expected rate of return on $i$th security $[\mathrm{E}(R_{it})]$ be explained by $k$ independent influences (or factors) as

$$E(R_{it}) = a + b_{j1}(\text{factor } 1) + b_{j2}(\text{factor } 2) + \cdots + b_{jk}(\text{factor } K) \tag{8.19}$$

where $b_{ij}$ is a sensitivity indicator that measures how responsive returns from asset $i$ are to factor (index) $j = 1, 2, \ldots, k$ factors. The theory doesn't say what factors should be used to explain the expected rates of return. These factors could be interest rates, oil prices, or other economic factors. The market portfolio itself might be a factor.

Using Eq. (8.19), Ross has shown that the risk premium of $j$th security can be defined as

$$E(R_i) - R_f = [E(F_i) - R_f]_{bi1} + \cdots + [E(F_k) - R_f]b_{ik} \tag{8.20}$$

where $E(F_i) - R_f$ represents the risk premium associated with the $i$th factor and measures the market price of risk for whatever risk is measured by $b_{ij}$. If $b_{i1} = 1$, and $b_{i2} = B_{i3} = \cdots = b_{ik} = 0$, and the first factor is the market, then Eq. (8.19) reduces to the CAPM as

$$E(R_i) - R_f = [E(R_m) - R_f]\beta_i$$

By comparing Eq. (8.20) with the CAPM equation, we can conclude that the APT is a generalized capital asset pricing model. Therefore, it is one of the important models for students of finance to understand. This model is generally discussed in upper-level financial management or investment courses. A more detailed discussion of APT can be found in Chapter 9 of Lee and Lee (2017), Lee *et al.* (2013), Bodie *et al.* (2021), and Francis and Kim (2013).

## 8.10 Summary

In this chapter, we have discussed the basic concepts of risk and diversification and how they pertain to the CAPM, as well as the procedure for deriving the CAPM itself. It was shown that the CAPM is an extension of the capital market line theory. The possible uses of the CAPM in financial analysis and planning were also indicated.

The concept of beta and its importance to the financial manager were introduced. Beta represents the firm's systematic risk and is a comparative measure between a firm's security or portfolio risk in comparison with the market risk. Systematic risk was further discussed by investigating the relationship between the beta coefficient and other important financial variables.

## References

Acharya, V. V. and L. H. Pedersen. "Asset Pricing with Liquidity Risk," *Journal of Financial Economics*, 77(2) (2005, pp. 375–410).

Blume, M. E. and I. Friend. "A New Look at the Capital Asset Pricing Model," *The Journal of Finance*, 28(1) (1973, pp. 19–33).

Bodie, Z., A. Kane and A. Marcus. *Investments*, 12th edn. (McGraw-Hill Book Company, New York, 2021).

Cochrane, J. H. *Asset Pricing*, Revised edn. (Princeton University Press, 2005).

Copeland, T. E., F. J. Weston and K. Shastri. *Financial Theory and Corporate Policy*, 4th International Edition (2003).

Fama, E. F. "Efficient Capital Market: A Review of Theory and Empirical Work," *The Journal of Finance*, 25 (May 1970, pp. 383–405).

Fama, E. F. *Foundations of Finance* (Basic Books, New York, 1976).

Fama, E. F. and J. D. MacBeth. "Risk, Return, and Equilibrium: Empirical Tests," *Journal of Political Economy*, 81(3) (1973, pp. 607–636).

Finnerty, J. E. "Insiders and Market Efficiency," *The Journal of Finance*, 31(4) (1976, pp. 1141–1148).

Francis. J. C. and D. Kim. *Modern Portfolio Theory: Foundations, Analysis, and New Developments* (Wiley, 2013).

Friend, I., M. Blume and J. Crockett. *Mutual Funds and Other Institutional Investors: A New Perspective* (McGraw-Hill Companies, 1970).

Ibbotson, R., R. J. Grabowski, J.P. Harrington and C. Nunes. *2016 Stocks, Bonds, Bills, and Inflation (SBBI) Yearbook*, 1st edn. (Wiley, 2016).

Jensen, M. C. "Risk, The Pricing of Capital Assets, and The Evaluation of Investment Portfolio," *Journal of Business* (April 1969, pp. 167–247).

Lee, C. F., and A. C. Lee. *Encyclopedia of Finance*, 2nd edn. (Springer, New York, 2017).

Lee, C. F., J. E. Finnerty, D. H. Wort, J. Lee and A. C. Lee. *Security Analysis, Portfolio Management, and Financial Derivatives* (World Scientific Publishers, Inc. 2013).

Lee, C. F., P. Newbold, J. E. Finnerty and C. C. Chu. "On Accounting-based, Market-based and Composite-based Beta Predictions: Methods and Implications," *Financial Review*, 21(1) (1986, pp. 51–68).

Lintner, J. "The Valuation of Risky Assets and the Selection of Risky Investments in Stock Portfolios and Capital Budgets," *Review of Economics and Statistics*, 47 (1965, pp. 13–37).

Mandelker, G. and S. Rhee. "The Impact of the Degree of Operating and Financial Leverage on Systematic Risk of Common Stock," *Journal of Financial and Quantitative Analysis*, 19(1) (March 1984, pp. 45–57).

Roll, R. "A Critique of the Asset Pricing Theory's Tests Part I: On Past and Potential Testability of the Theory," *Journal of Financial Economics*, 4(2) (1977, pp. 129–176).

Roll, R. "Ambiguity When Performance is Measured by the Securities Market Line," *The Journal of Finance*, 33(4) (1978, pp. 1051–1069).

Ross, S. A. "Arbitrage Theory of Capital Asset Pricing," *Journal of Economic Theory*, 8 (1976, pp. 341–360).

Ross, S. A. "Return, Risk and Arbitrage," *Risk and Return in Finance*, 1 (Cambridge, MA: Ballinger, 1977, pp. 187–208).

Rubinstein, M. E. "A Mean-Variance Synthesis of Corporate Financial Theory," *The Journal of Finance*, 18 (1973, pp. 167–187).

Sharpe, W. F. "Capital Asset Prices: A Theory of Market Equilibrium Under Conditions of Risk," *The Journal of Finance*, 19 (September 1964, pp. 425–442).

Sharpe, W. F. "Mutual Fund Performance," *Journal of Business*, 39(1) (January 1966, pp. 119–318).

Subrahmanyam, M. and S. Thomadakis. "Systematic Risk and the Theory of the Firm," *Quarterly Journal of Economics*, 94(3) (May 1980, pp. 437–451).

## Appendix 8A — Mathematical Derivation of the Capital Asset Pricing Model

In this appendix, we will first derive the CAPM, then we will discuss the chain rule and its application.

### 8A.1 Derivation of CAPM

Using the assumptions of efficient and perfect markets, stated earlier in Chapter 8, we can show how Sharpe derived the CAPM.

Sharpe (1964) used a general risky asset that did not lie on the CML and dubbed it $I$. The combinations of risk and return possible by combining security $I$ with the market portfolio, $M$, are shown by Figure 8.1A. The average return and standard deviation for any $I - M$ combination can be approached in the same way as for a two-asset case:

$$E(R_p) = w_i E(R_i) + (1 - w_i)E(R_m) \tag{8.1A}$$

$$\begin{aligned} \sigma_P &= [w_i^2 \sigma_i^2 + (1 - w_i)\sigma_m^2 + 2(1 - w_i)w_i \sigma_{im}]^{\frac{1}{2}} \\ &= (g(w))^{\frac{1}{2}} = f(g(w)) \end{aligned} \tag{8.2A}$$

where $w_i$ represents excess demand for *i's asset* or demand greater than its equilibrium weight in portfolio $M$, and $\sigma_{im}$ is the covariance of $i$ and $m$. Please note that Eq. (8.2A) is a compositive function.

The change in mean and standard deviation as the proportion $w_1$ changes are the partial derivatives

$$\frac{\partial E(R_p)}{\partial w_i} = E(R_i) - E(R_m) \tag{8.3A}$$

$$\begin{aligned} \frac{\partial(\sigma_p)}{\partial w_i} = \frac{1}{2}&[w_i^2 \sigma_i^2 + (1 - w_i)^2 \sigma_m^2 + 2w_i(1 - w_i)]^{-\frac{1}{2}} \\ &(2w_i \sigma_i^2 - 2\sigma_m^2 + 2w_i \sigma_m^2 \\ &+2\sigma_{im} - 4w_i \sigma_{im}) \end{aligned} \tag{8.3B}$$

When $w_i = 0$, the security is held in proportion to its total market value and there is no excess demand for security $I$. This is the key insight to Sharpe's paper, for when $w_i = 0$, it is possible to equate the slope of the curve *IMI'* with the capital market line and thus obtain an expression for the return on any risky security $I$. At equilibrium when $w_i = 0$, the slope along the *IMI'* curve will equal

$$\frac{\partial E(R_p)}{\partial \sigma_p} = \frac{\frac{\partial E(R_p)}{\partial w_i}}{\frac{\partial(\sigma_p)}{\partial w_i}} = \frac{\frac{E(R_i)-E(R_m)}{\sigma_{im}-\sigma_m^2}}{\sigma_m} \tag{8.4A}$$

The slope of the capital market line at point $M$ is

$$\frac{E(R_m) - R_f}{\sigma_m} \tag{8.5A}$$

By letting Eq. (8.4A) equal Eq. (8.5A), this equality is presented in Figure 8.1A.

Rearranging the terms to solve for $E(R_i)$ gives the equation for the security market line or CAPM

$$E(R_i) = R_f + [E(R_m) - R_f]\frac{\sigma_{im}}{\sigma_m^2} \tag{8.6A}$$

This represents the return on any risky asset $I$. At equilibrium, every risky asset will be priced so that it lies along the security market line. It should be noted that the term $\sigma_{im}/\sigma_m^2$ represents the beta coefficient for the regression of $R_i$ vs. $R_m$, so that Eq. (8.6A) can be rewritten as

$$E(R_i) = R_f + [E(R_m) - R_f]\beta_i \tag{8.7A}$$

## 8A.2 Chain Rule and Its Application

Equation (8.2A) is a compositive function. In this compositive function, there exists two layers. Function $f$ is the "outer layer" and function $g$ is the "inner layer." To take the partial derivative of Eq. (8.2A) with respect to $w$, the chain rule tells us to first differentiate the outer layer, leaving the inner layer unchanged

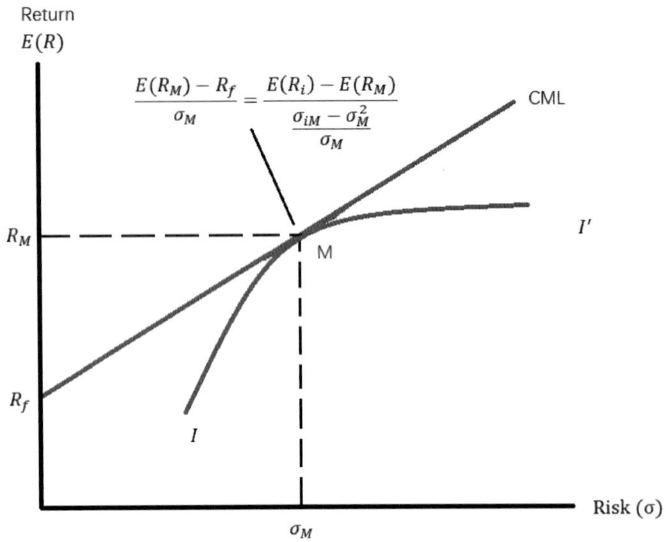


Figure 8.1A The Opportunity Set Provided by Combinations of Risky Asset/and Market Portfolio, M.

(the term $f'(g(w))$), then differentiate the inner layer (the term $g'(w)$). Using the procedure of chain rule, the detailed derivation of Eq. (8.3A(b)) is presented as follows.

$$
\begin{aligned}
\frac{\partial(\sigma_P)}{\partial w_i} &= \frac{\partial([w_i^2\sigma_i^2 + (1-w_i)^2\sigma_m^2 + 2(1-w_i)w_i\sigma_{im}]^{\frac{1}{2}})}{\partial w_i} \\
&= \frac{1}{2}[w_i^2\sigma_i^2 + (1-w_i)^2\sigma_m^2 + 2(1-w_i)w_i\sigma_{im}]^{-\frac{1}{2}} \\
&\quad * \frac{\partial}{\partial w_i}(w_i^2\sigma_i^2 + (1-w_i)^2\sigma_m^2 + 2(1-w_i)w_i\sigma_{im})^2 \\
&= \frac{1}{2}[w_i^2\sigma_i^2 + (1-w_i)^2\sigma_m^2 + 2(1-w_i)w_i\sigma_{im}]^{-\frac{1}{2}} \\
&\quad * \left[\frac{\partial}{\partial w_i}(w_i^2\sigma_i^2) + \frac{\partial}{\partial w_i}(1-w_i)^2\sigma_m^2 + \frac{\partial}{\partial w_i}(2(1-w_i)w_i\sigma_{im})\right]
\end{aligned}
$$

[2]This procedure is obtained by taking partial derivative with respect to the outer layer and then taking partial derivative with respect to the inner layer.

$$= \frac{1}{2}[w_i^2\sigma_i^2 + (1-w_i)^2\sigma_m^2 + 2(1-w_i)w_i\sigma_{im}]^{-\frac{1}{2}}$$
$$*[2w_i\sigma_i^2 + 2(1-w_i)(-1)\sigma_m^2 + 2\sigma_{im} - 4w_i\sigma_{im}]$$
$$= \frac{1}{2}[w_i^2\sigma_i^2 + (1-w_i)^2\sigma_m^2 + 2(1-w_i)w_i\sigma_{im}]^{-\frac{1}{2}}$$
$$*[2w_i\sigma_i^2 - 2\sigma_m^2 + 2w_i\sigma_m^2 + 2\sigma_{im} - 4w_i\sigma_{im}]$$

## Questions and Problems

1. Define the following terms:
   a. Systematic versus nonsystematic risk
   b. CML versus SML
   c. Sharpe versus Jensen performance measure
   d. Strong versus weak form market efficiency
   e. Market model and characteristic line
   f. Aggressive versus defensive stock
2. What is the relationship between the CAPM and the APT?
3. Briefly discuss the key variables used to describe the beta coefficient.
4. The risk-free interest rate of an investment is 5% and the expected return on the market is 11%. Answer these questions on the basis of CAPM.
   a. What is the risk premium on the market?
   b. XYZ Company has a beta of 2. What is the required rate of return on an investment made with the XYZ Company?
   c. If an investment with a beta of 1.5 is supposed to yield an expected rate of return of 11%, does the investment have positive NPV?
5. If the standard deviation of the market return is 15%, answer the following:
   a. What is the standard deviation of return on a well-diversified portfolio (zero nonsystematic risk) with a beta of 1.2?
   b. A portfolio still has some nonsystematic risk. If its standard deviation is 30% and its beta is 1.7, what is the nonsystematic risk portion?
   c. How much is the systematic risk of the portfolio in Question b?

6. ABC Company is a manufacturing firm that buys rare raw materials from other countries. However, the supply of these materials is very unstable, causing wide fluctuations in ABC's income. If the expected market rate of return is 10% and ABC Company's beta is 2, what is the company's expected rate of return?
7. Stock X has a beta of 1.2 and its expected price at time 1 is $100. Find its equilibrium price at time 0. (Assume $Rm = 12\%$ and $RF = 6\%$.)
8. If the stock's expected price at time 1 is $100 with certainty, what will be the price of X in Question 7 at time 0?
9. Here is a firm's data on business and financial risk:
   Variance of ROA = 5%
   Variance of ROE (with debt) = 7%

   a. How much is business risk?
   b. How much is financial risk?
   c. How much is the variance of ROE without debt?

10. Below are the statistics on the returns from three securities, the market, and the risk-free rate:

| **Security** | **Mean Return** | **Variance** | **Covariance** |
|---|---|---|---|
| Sellnex | 0.20 | 0.15 | 0.08 |
| Kally | 0.10 | 0.06 | 0.03 |
| Nikita | 0.13 | 0.10 | 0.05 |
| Market | 0.15 | 0.06 | |
| Risk-free Rate | 0.05 | | |

   a. Find the betas for the three securities.
   b. Find the required rate of return for the three securities according to the Security Market Line (SML).
   c. What is the average risk premium for the market return?
   d. Find the average risk premium for each of the three securities.
   e. Find Jensen's Performance Measure, alpha, for each of the three securities.
   f. Plot the mean and variance of the three securities. Does any one security dominate the other two?
   g. Plot the mean return against the expected rate of return along the Security Market Line. Which securities are "good" investments?

11. Draw the Security Market Line and the Capital Market Line. Then discuss how they are similar and how they differ.
12. AXEL, Inc. has security returns which have a correlation coefficient with the market of 0.6. The standard deviation of AXEL's returns is 5% while that for the market is 8%.

    a. Find AXEL's beta.
    b. If the risk-free rate of interest if 5% and the expected (mean) return on the market is 14%, what is the required rate of return for AXEL? (Use the CAPM)
    c. If an investor analyzes AXEL's stock and estimates an expected rate of return of 12%, is it a good investment?

13. A firm has a standard deviation of its ROE equal to 4%.

    a. What is its business risk if no debt financing is used?
    b. What is its business and financial risk if the standard deviation of ROA is 2%?

14. Joe's stock is expected to have a market price of $70 at the end of one year ($t = 1$). The stock's beta is 1.3, the return on the market is 14%, and the risk-free rate is 6%. What is the value of the stock now?
15. Compare and contrast the Security Market Line and the characteristic line. How are they similar and how do they differ?
16. The return on the market portfolio is 16% and its standard deviation is 6%. The risk-free rate of interest is 5%.

    a. Find the return and risk of an investment strategy in which the investor lends 40% of his/her investment at the risk-free rate and invests the remaining 60% in the market portfolio.
    b. Find the risk and return of an investment strategy in which the investor puts 130% of his/her investment in the market portfolio by borrowing at the current risk-free rate.
    c. Would the risk-averse investor prefer the strategy in Part (a) or Part (b)? Explain.

17. Please use chain rule to answer the following questions:

    i. $(2x + 3)^2$
    ii. $(3x^2 + 4x + 5)^3$
    iii. $(4x^3 + 2x^2 + 3x + 6)^2$

    *Note*: Please see Appendix 8A for the chain rule procedure.

18. Please show step by step how the capital market line can be derived.
19. Please use Appendix 8A to show how CAPM can be derived step by step.
20. Please discuss the relationship between the capital market line and CAPM.

# Chapter 9

# Capital Budgeting Under Uncertainty

## Contents



## 9.1 Introduction

In Chapter 6, we discussed an alternative method to deal with capital budgeting under certainty. In this chapter, we tackle the problem of developing a capital budget under conditions of uncertainty. We begin by investigating the sources of uncertainty and discuss the potential methods for capital budgeting under uncertainty, then we go on to explore the use of risk-adjusted discount rate, the certainty equivalent method, the implication of the statistical distribution model on cash flows, the simulation method, and the effect of inflation on the capital budgeting decision.

In Section 9.2, we discuss sources of uncertainty and methods for capital budgeting under uncertainty. The risk-adjusted discount rate method is discussed in Section 9.3, and the certainty equivalent method is discussed in Section 9.4. Section 9.5 talks about the statistical distribution method, and Section 9.6 mentions some simulation methods. Inflationary effects in the capital budgeting decision are discussed in Section 9.7, and finally the chapter is summarized in Section 9.8. Appendix 9A discusses the decision tree method for investment decisions, while Appendix 9B presents Hillier's statistical distribution method for capital budgeting under uncertainty.

## 9.2 Sources of Uncertainty and Methods for Capital Budgeting Under Uncertainty

In Chapter 6, Capital Budgeting under Certainty, we assumed most of the information needed is known. However, the information needed for capital budgeting is not always known with certainty. The uncertainties affect such variables as cost of capital, net cash flow, and life of machine. Therefore, capital budgeting procedures for conditions of uncertainty are needed to improve the precision of accurately assessing the value of risky investment projects.

There are three basic types of risk that affect capital budgeting decisions and are sources of uncertainty. These are (1) business risk — the risk inherent to the firm's cash flow without the use of debt; (2) financial risk — the additional risk placed on the firm's stockholders through the use of debt; and (3) inflation risk — risk arising from purchasing power instability.

Business risk is the uncertainty of future operating income or earnings before interest and taxes (EBIT) that is inherent in the firm's operations. This type of risk is an important determinant of a firm's capital structure. For example, we may look at a firm in the manufacturing industry. Usually, manufacturing firms produce a product that fits into one of three categories: (1) necessity goods — goods that the customer must purchase because they are necessities, such as food, clothing, and shelter; (2) inferior goods — goods of which smaller quantities are consumed with income increases; and (3) luxury goods — goods whose consumption increases with income. The type of goods a manufacturing firm produces influences how the firm will be affected by the business cycle; that is, product demand depends on the economic climate. In periods of recession, consumers purchase fewer luxury and inferior goods, but must still buy necessity goods. This is part of the business risk a firm must bear.

When a firm decides to leverage itself by taking on debt, it adds variability to the expected returns on stockholders' equity. This is financial risk, which results from the payment of interest on debt that is deducted from the variable returns on the firm's assets. The actual interest rate ($i_t$) that a firm pays for its debt comprises the risk-free rate ($R_f$) and a risk premium; the variability in interest rates arises from this risk premium. In times of inflation and economic instability, the risk premium is high, to compensate the lender for the financial and inflation risks that the lender incurs. In periods of low inflation and economic stability, the risk premium is smaller.

In evaluating an unlevered firm without inflation, only business risk is relevant. Therefore, financial risk is zero and the total risk premium comprises the business risk premium only. In the case of levered firms, the total risk premium comprises both business and financial premiums.

A third type of risk is inflation risk. During inflationary times, the purchasing power of the firm's funds and resources is reduced by a set percentage. The uncertainty and fluctuation of inflation and purchasing power are sources of risk in a firm's capital budgeting decisions and must therefore be incorporated into the firm's risk estimation.

In Chapter 6, we have discussed different methods for capital budgeting under certainty. From both theoretical and empirical points of view, we conclude that the NPV method should be accepted for capital budgeting under certainty. In this chapter, based upon the NPV method we introduce uncertainty information into capital budgeting decision. Overall, we will propose five different methods to deal with capital budgeting under uncertainty. These five methods are:

a. *Risk-Adjusted Discount-Rate Method*
In this method, we use risk-adjusted discount-rate instead of risk-free rate to discount the future net cash inflow. The risk-adjusted discount-rate can be estimated by CAPM, which is equal to risk-free rate plus risk-premium. The risk-premium is equal to beta coefficient times long-term market risk premium. Therefore, the NPV estimated by risk-adjusted discount-rate is smaller than the estimated risk-free rate. This method will be discussed in Section 9.3.

b. *Certainty Equivalent Method*
In this method, we use risk-free rate to calculate the net present value of future net cash inflow; however, we modify the future net cash inflow by a certain equivalent coefficient, which is smaller than 1. Therefore, the NPV obtained from this method is smaller than NPV value calculated by using risk-free rate and certainty net cash inflow. This method will be discussed in Section 9.4.

c. *Statistical Distribution Method*
Under this method we first calculate the expected value of NPV, then we calculate standard deviation associated with NPV. In other words, we assume the random NPV is normally distributed with mean $N\bar{P}V$ and standard deviation $\sigma_{NPV}$, then we can use this information to perform interval estimates for NPV. This method will be discussed in Section 9.5.

d. *Simulation Analysis Method*
Simulation is another approach to confront the problems of capital budgeting under uncertainty. Because uncertainty associated with capital budgeting is not restricted to one or two variables, every variable relevant in the capital-budgeting decision can be viewed as a random variable. Facing so many random variables, it may be impossible to obtain tractable results from an economic model. Simulation is a useful tool designed to deal with this problem and is the closest we can get to modeling in cases of uncertainty. From this simulation we can obtain the mean $\overline{NPV}$ and the standard deviation of $\sigma_{NPV}$. With this information we can perform capital budgeting in terms of interval analysis. This method will be discussed in Section 9.6.

e. *Decision-Tree Method*
A decision-tree approach to capital-budgeting decisions can be used to analyze some investment opportunities involving a sequence of investment decisions over time. The decision tree is an analytical technique used in sequential decisions, where various decision points are studied in relation to subsequent chance events. This technique enables one to choose among alternatives in an objective and consistent manner. Under this method, there are different NPV for different situations. By using these different NPV values we can calculate the mean $\overline{NPV}$ and standard deviation of $\sigma_{NPV}$. By using this information, we can make interval analysis of capital budgeting decision. This method will be discussed in Appendix 9A.

In sum, the first two methods are point estimation methods. The other three methods are interval estimation methods. It is well-known that the interval estimation method is better than the point estimation method. The first four methods will be discussed in Sections 9.3, 9.4, 9.5, and 9.6, respectively. The decision tree method will be discussed in Appendix 9A.

## 9.3 Risk-Adjusted Discount Rate Method

With uncertain future cash flows, a financial planner is confronted with a probability distribution of cash flows for each period rather than a single estimated amount. The *risk-adjusted discount method* was developed to deal with the problem of uncertain cash flows. The method extends the net present value framework (a certainty method) to the uncertainty case. In equation form, it is expressed as

$$\mathrm{NPV} = \sum_{t=1}^{N} \frac{\bar{X}_t}{(1+k_t)^t} - I_o \tag{9.1}$$

where NPV = the net present value of the capital budgeting project; $\bar{X}_t$ = the median or mean of the expected risky cash flow distribution $X_t$ in the period $t$; $k_t$ = the risk-adjusted discount rate appropriate to risk of cash flow $X_t$; $N$ = the life of the project; and $I_o$ = the amount of investment.

The model considers specifically the uncertainty associated with future cash flows. It is assumed that the actual cash flow can be a range of values with the distribution $X_t$. For Eq. (9.1), the median or mean is taken to be most representative of the distribution. The model does not specify how to measure the risk in the firm's cash flow; this must be estimated subjectively by the financial analyst. However, the model enables the analyst to study how risk affects the relationship among the variables.

For example, assuming investors are risk-averse, an increase in the riskiness of cash flows usually results in a larger discount rate to compensate for the risk of undertaking the particular investment. The use of a higher discount rate, $k_t$, decreases the value of the cash flows, and this increases the chance of a negative NPV and rejection of the project.

However, the requirement of estimating a discount rate is also a disadvantage of risk-adjusted discount method. Because the discount rate is assessed subjectively by the user, it differs from one person to another. Thus, the method does not allow objective determination of the value of a risky investment project unless $k_t$ can be objectively estimated.

Recent developments with the capital asset pricing model (CAPM), as discussed in Chapter 8, incorporate the capital market equilibrium pricing framework. This approach has helped derive an objective estimate of the appropriate risk-adjusted discount rate. However, this model assumes perfect capital markets and that all participants within the capital market have homogeneous expectations as to the prospects of all securities and investments. These assumptions may reduce the usefulness of the CAPM when it is used to estimate the discount rate.

To help explain the application of the risk-adjusted method, let us consider a firm that is evaluating an investment for a new product line. The firm estimates that faddish properties of this product give it a life of about four years. The current risk-free rate is 9%. Forecasts of inflation and economic trends indicate that a risk premium of 6% is appropriate in this case. (The risk-adjusted discount rate could be estimated by the CAPM method, as discussed in Chapter 10.)

The initial investment is \$2,000. In the first year, the expected cash inflow is \$650. In the second year, this amount increases to \$712.50. the firm expects the project cash flows to decline in the third year to \$475, and then rise in the fourth year to \$650. In this case, the expected cash flow is a mean cash flow.

With these estimates, let us estimate whether it would be advisable for the firm to undertake the project, given the set of economic circumstances. We know that $N = 4$ years; $k =$ the risk-free rate + estimated risk premium ($9\% + 6\% = 15\%$); and $I_o = \$2{,}000$. We also know the mean cash flows: $\bar{X}_1 = 650$; $\bar{X}_2 = 712.5$; $\bar{X}_3 = 475$; and $\bar{X}_4 = 650$. Therefore,

$$\begin{aligned}\text{PV} &= \frac{650}{(1+0.15)^1} + \frac{712.5}{(1+0.15)^2} + \frac{475}{(1+0.15)^3} + \frac{650}{(1+0.15)^4} \\ &= 650(\text{PVIF}_{1,15\%}) + 712.5(\text{PVIF}_{2,15\%}) + 475(\text{PVIF}_{3,15\%}) \\ &\quad + 650(\text{PVIF}_{4,15\%})\end{aligned}$$

$$= 650(0.8696) + 712.5(0.7561) + 475(0.6575) + 650(0.5718)$$

$$= 565.24 + 538.72 + 312.31 + 371.67 = 1787.94$$

$$\text{NPV} = 1787.94 - 2000 = \$(212.06)$$

In this case, the project will result in a negative NPV, which would decrease the net cash value of the firm and therefore should be rejected.

Some practical approaches to help estimate a risk-adjusted discount rate are the *pure play method* and the *accounting beta method.*

Frequently, the information required to determine a risk-adjusted discount rate is not available or is extremely expensive to generate, in which case the pure play technique is useful. Fuller and Kerr (1981) proposed this method to estimate the risk-adjusted discount rate. If a similar firm or project can be identified that closely resembles the firm or project being analyzed, then market information of the proxy project can be used to estimate the risk-adjusted discount rate, which can then be used in the NPV framework. The pure play method may be difficult to implement, in practice, because it may be impossible to find a proxy firm or project.

Another approach to estimate the risk-adjusted discount rate is the accounting beta approach. Normally, as we have seen in Chapter 8, betas, or risk measures, are found by regressing the historic returns of a particular firm or project against the returns on a market index. Instead of using the project's market returns, which may not be available, accounting measures of return (for example, EBIT/Total assets) can be regressed against a market index. The resultant estimate of this relationship is the accounting beta, as discussed in Chapter 8.

## 9.4 Certainty Equivalent Method

So far, we have shown that whenever returns on a project or security have a degree of risk, we can adjust for this risk by altering the valuation equation's denominator — the discount rate — such that a higher rate reflects a riskier situation. However, the numerator — cash flow — of the present value equation can also be adjusted to reflect risk. With the *certainty equivalent method*, we can explore this alternative.

The types of cash flows and how they are generated for specific investments and projects are discussed in Chapter 6. These are risk-free cash flows; that is, cash flows with variables (quantity sold, price, variable costs, fixed costs, etc.) that are assumed to be known. In real-life situations, these variables are not known with certainty, but must be estimated. Therefore, financial managers performing capital budgeting analysis are dealing with risky cash flows.

The certainty equivalent method adjusts the estimated value of the risk cash flow rather than the discount rate. This method uses the economic concept of utility theory, which formalizes the preferences of individuals and is a useful apparatus for analyzing decision-making. Utility is defined as the satisfaction that an individual received from various activities. The theory is easy to understand: more satisfaction is better than less. Theoretically, it is easy to make financial decisions that provide greater profits, return, or cash flow. Unfortunately, the obstacles to measuring utility have so far proved insurmountable. There are two major problems: (1) determining an appropriate unit of measurement for utility, and (2) holding external factors and the environment constant. Consequently, even though we like to discuss financial decision-making in terms of utility, it may not be easily applied to actual decisions.

The decision-maker evaluates risky cash flows by attaching an expected utility to them. This utility estimate is roughly equal to the utility derived from the same risk-free amount of cash flow. When the decision-maker performs this process for each cash flow, the result is a series of certainty equivalents. In this way, capital budgeting under uncertainty is reduced to capital budgeting under certainty, and the decision criteria applied to "certainty" investments can be used.

To begin our discussion of utility, we illustrate a utility function indifference curve in Figure 9.1. The curve plots a series of risk-return combinations to which the decision-maker would be indifferent.[1]

[1]Indifference curves are an important economic tool used in the area of consumption analysis. An indifference curve is defined as a combination of goods that provide the same level of utility to an individual. At any point on a given indifference curve, the individual received the same satisfaction from the consumption of goods. For a further discussion of this topic, see Nicholson and Snyder, *Intermediate Microeconomics and Its Application*, 14th edn. (Cengage Learning, 2014).

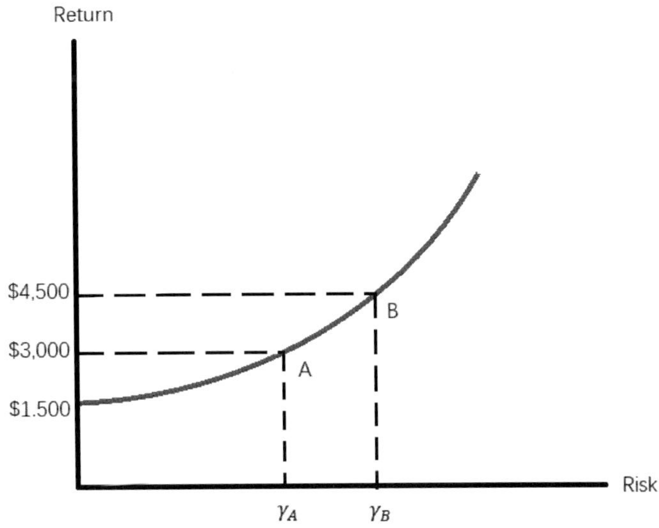


Figure 9.1 Certainty Equivalent Returns.

The indifference curve shows that this individual would be indifferent to any risk-return combination lying along the curve. Point $A$ represents an investment with a perceived risk measured by the risk coefficient $\gamma_A$ and an expected return of \$3,000. Point $B$ represents an investment with risk coefficient $\gamma_B$ and an expected return of \$4,500. Therefore, an individual whose indifference curve, or risk-return trade-off function, can be represented by Figure 9.1 would be indifferent with regards to a sure \$1,500, \$3,000 at risk $\gamma_A$, or \$4,500 at risk $\gamma_B$. In this discussion, the risk coefficient $\gamma$ could be measured for either total risk (variance of return) or systematic risk (beta). The utility function could come from the individual manager or decision-maker, or it could be a proxy for the perceived utility curve of the firm's shareholders. In this example, for the sake of generality, we do not specify which is to be used.

Given the indifference curve of a financial planner, or of investors in general, project value may be determined as follows:

1. Substitute the risk-free discount rate, $R_f$, for the risk-adjusted discount rate $k_t$ in the denominator of the Eq. (9.1).
2. Calculate the certainty equivalent adjustment factor, $\alpha$, by dividing the certainty equivalent (sure amount) of a risky return by the

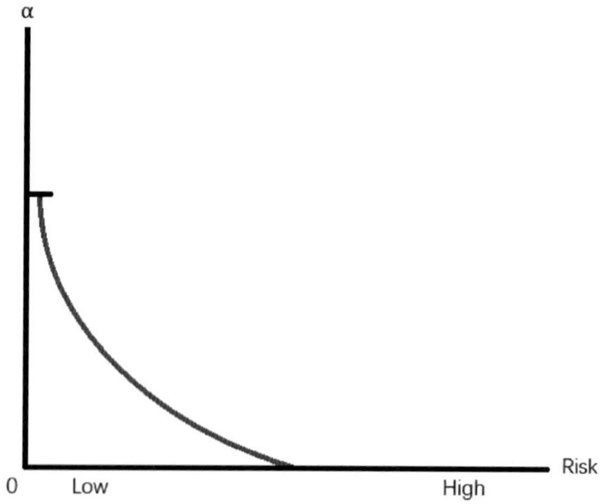


Figure 9.2 Certainty Equivalent Adjustment Factors.

risky return, $C_D$

$$\alpha_A = \frac{\text{Certain return}}{\text{Risky return}} = \frac{\$1{,}500}{\$3{,}000} = 0.5 \quad \text{for } \gamma_A$$

$$\alpha_B = \frac{\$1{,}500}{\$4{,}500} = 0.33 \quad \text{for } \gamma_B$$

3. Calculate $\alpha$ values for all ranges of cash flow ($C_t$); these will range from 1 ($\gamma = 0$) to 0 (large $\gamma$) assuming the investor is risk averse. Figure 9.2 illustrates this market-risk aversion.
4. Calculate the certainty equivalent given the market risk-aversion function and the degree of risk in the risky return:

$$\text{Certainty equivalent of } C_t = \alpha_t \bar{X}_t$$

5. Valuation of a project would then be

$$\text{NPV} = \sum_{t=1}^{N} \frac{\bar{X}_t}{(1+k_t)^t} - I_o = \sum_{t=0}^{N} \frac{\alpha_t \bar{X}_t}{(1+R_f)^t} - I_o \qquad (9.2)$$

With this model, the effects of different risks are incorporated into the yearly cash flows.

**Example 9.1.** A firm wishes to undertake a project for which cash flows are uncertain because of the economic climate. The firm's finance department has calculated an indifference curve from the risk-return projection provided by management. The project has a life of three years ($N = 3$ years) and an initial investment of \$300,000. The current market yield of government T-bills is 9% ($R_f = 9\%$), and the certain return of $\gamma = 1$ is \$60,000. What is the project's NPV assuming risk-adjusted cash flows given the following period cash flows?

| **Year** | **Cash Flow** ($\bar{X}_t$) |
|---|---|
| 0 | (150,000) |
| 1 | 75,000 |
| 2 | 150,000 |
| 3 | 200,000 |

The certainty adjustment factor ($\alpha_t$) for each period is calculated as follows:

$$\alpha_i = \frac{\text{Certain return}}{\text{Risky return}}$$

$$\alpha_1 = \frac{60{,}000}{75{,}000} = 0.8$$

$$\alpha_2 = \frac{60{,}000}{150{,}000} = 0.4$$

$$\alpha_3 = \frac{60{,}000}{200{,}000} = 0.3$$

The certainty equivalent of $\bar{X}_t$ for each period is calculated by multiplying the expected return by the certainty adjustment factor found above:

$$\text{Certainty equivalent of } C_t = \alpha_t \bar{X}_t$$

$$C_1 = 0.8(\$75{,}000) = \$60{,}000$$

$$C_2 = 0.4(\$150{,}000) = \$60{,}000$$

$$C_3 = 0.3(\$200{,}000) = \$60{,}000$$

$$\text{NPV} = \frac{\$60{,}000}{(1+0.09)^1} + \frac{\$60{,}000}{(1+.09)^2} + \frac{\$60{,}000}{(1+0.09)^3} - \$300{,}000$$
$$= \$60{,}000(2.531) - \$300{,}000 = -\$148{,}140$$

Hence, the project has a negative NPV and should be rejected.

### 9.4.1 *The CAPM approach to the certainty equivalent method*

So far, our theoretical discussion of the certainty equivalent method has dealt with an individual investor and the proverbial bird in the hand. We are asking the question that would you rather have a bird in the hand with complete certainty or take the chance of capturing two birds in the bush with a chance of success of less than 100%? Different people will answer this question in various ways. The ambiguity that arises when we try to apply individual utility theory to capital investment decisions leaves us in a precarious situation. We have no general rule or guideline that allows us to select unambiguously a good risky investment in a real-world situation. To present a useful method for determining the certainty equivalent term $\alpha_t$ in real-world situations, we can use the CAPM.

Following Eq. (8.4) in Chapter 8, the CAPM can be defined as

$$E(R_i) = R_f + [E(R_m) - R_f]\frac{\sigma_{im}}{\sigma_m^2}$$

where $R_i$ = project return rate; $R_f$ = risk-free rate; $R_m$ = market return rate; $\sigma_{im}$ = covariance between $R_i$ and $R_m$; and $\sigma_m^2$ = variance of $R_m$.

By definition,

$$R_i = \frac{X_i}{V_i}$$

and

$$E(R_i) = \frac{\bar{X}_i}{V_i}$$

where $X_i$ = cash flow for the $i$th firm; $\bar{X}_i$ = expected $X_i$; and $V_i$ = market value of the $i$th firm. Therefore,

$$\frac{\bar{X}_i}{V_i} = R_f + [E(R_m) - R_f]\frac{\mathrm{COV}(\frac{X_i}{V_i}, R_m)}{\sigma_m^2}$$

Multiplying both sides of this equation by $V_i$ and rearranging the terms, we obtain the market value of $i$th firm as

$$V_i = \bar{X}_i - [E(R_m) - R_f]\frac{\frac{\mathrm{COV}(X_i, R_m)}{\sigma_m^2}}{R_f} \tag{9.3}$$

To find the market value of a project, we redefine Eq. (9.3) as

$$V_i^0 = \bar{X}_i^0 - [E(R_m) - R_f]\frac{\frac{\mathrm{COV}(X_i^0, R_m)}{\sigma_m^2}}{R_f} \tag{9.4}$$

where $\mathrm{COV}(X_i^0, R_m) = \beta_i(\sigma_m^2)(I_0)$; $\beta_i = \mathrm{COV}\frac{(X_i^0, R_m)}{\sigma_m^2 I_0}$; $V_i^0$ = market value of the project; $X_i^0$ = cash flow of the project; $\bar{X}_i^0$ = expected $X_i^0$; and $I_0$ = initial investment. Combining the NPV equation with Eq. (9.4), we have

$$NPV^0 = V_i^0 - I_0$$

In Eq. (9.4), the numerator $\bar{X}_i^0 - [E(R_m) - R_f]\frac{\mathrm{COV}(X_i^0, R_m)}{\sigma_m^2}$ is analogous to the $\alpha_t \bar{X}_t$ of the certainty equivalent method. The major differences between these two numerators are (1) the $\alpha_t$ is determined uniquely for each individual; hence, each decision-maker may have a different estimate of $\alpha_t$; (2) the CAPM risk premium term $[E(R_m) - R_f]\frac{\mathrm{COV}(X_i^0, R_m)}{\sigma_m^2}$ is determined from information about the project and the market, and there is only one value for this expression; (3) the $\alpha_t X_t$ is based on utility theory; and (4) the $\bar{X}_i^0 - I_0[E(R_m) - R_f]\beta_i$ is based on rational behavior in markets.

**Example 9.2.** A firm is facing an investment decision with the following values:

$$\text{Risk-free rate } (R_f) = 9\%$$

$$\text{Market return rate } (R_m) = 12\%$$

$$\text{Cash Flow } (\bar{X}_i) = \$450$$

$$\text{Initial investment } (I_0) = \$3{,}000$$

$$\text{Beta } (\beta_i) = 0.70$$

$$\sigma_m^2 = 0.02$$

From Eq. (9.4), we get

$$V_i^0 = \frac{450 - (0.12 - 0.09) \times \frac{(0.70)(0.02)(3000)}{(0.02)}}{(0.09)} = \frac{450 - 63}{(0.09)} = \$4{,}300$$

$$NPV^0 = \$4{,}300 - \$3{,}000 = \$1{,}300$$

Since the cost of the project is \$3,000 and project value is \$4,300, the net present value is \$1,300 and the project should be accepted.

The CAPM approach for performing the certainty equivalent method might be easier to execute than the method of estimating certainty coefficient. The reason is because the information in terms of the CAPM approach is easier and can be more objectively obtained.

### 9.4.2 *Risk-adjusted discount rate versus certainty equivalent method*

The risk-adjusted discount rate method involves handling investment risks through adjustments of the discount rate (denominator). The certainty equivalent method involves handling investment risks through adjustments of the cash flows (numerator). The risk-adjusted method is simpler and thus is used more frequently. However, according to a paper published by Robichek and Myers (1966), the certainty equivalent method, although more complicated, is far superior theoretically, especially if risk is perceived as an increasing function of time.

Since both methods are used to evaluate future uncertain cash flows, the two models should yield the same value for a given stream of cash flows. Moreover, the present value of each period's cash flow should be the same under these two valuation models, for each period $t$:

$$PV_t = \frac{\alpha_t \bar{X}_t}{(1+R_f)^t} = \frac{\bar{X}_t}{(1+k_t)^t} \tag{9.5}$$

Rearranging the terms of this equation, we obtain

$$\alpha_t = \frac{(1+R_f)^t}{(1+k_t)^t} \tag{9.6}$$

and

$$\alpha_{t+1} = \frac{(1+R_f)^{t+1}}{(1+k_{t+1})^{t+1}} \tag{9.7}$$

From $\alpha_t$ and $\alpha_{t+1}$, we can write the risky discount rate, $k_t$, in terms of the risk-free rate $R_f$, and the certainty equivalent coefficient as

$$k_t = \frac{1+R_f}{\alpha_t^{\frac{1}{t}}} - 1$$

$$k_t = \frac{R_f}{\alpha_t^{\frac{1}{t}}} + RP$$

$$\text{where } RP = \frac{1-\alpha^{\frac{1}{t}}}{\alpha^{\frac{1}{t}}}$$

$RP$ represents risk premium and is a positive number because $\alpha^{\frac{1}{t}} < 1$. Equations (9.6) and (9.7) imply that $\alpha_t$ is a decreasing function of time, since $(1+k_t)^t$ accounts for the time value of money ($R_f$) and risk ($RP$) by one adjustment process. Note that $\alpha_t$ is a decreasing function of both time and risk premium ($RP$). Although $R_f$ and $RP$ values are constant over time, a given risk premium has a larger and larger impact on $\alpha_t$ as the time horizon is lengthened. This phenomenon occurs because the risk premium itself is compounded and there is a cumulative effect in the $t$-period discount factor $1/(1+R_f+RP)$. By comparing Eq. (9.6) to Eq. (9.7), we see that

$$\alpha_{t+1} < \alpha_t \tag{9.8}$$

Equation (9.8) implies that using a constant discount rate in capital budgeting analysis suggests that risk increases over time. Therefore, the risk-adjusted discount rate method with constant discount rate is not appropriate for capital budgeting projects that have constant risk.

## 9.5 The Statistical Distribution Method

Capital budgeting frequently incorporates the concept of probability theory. To illustrate, consider two projects — project $x$ and project $y$ — and three states of the economy — prosperity, normal, and recession — for any given time. For each of these states, we may calculate a probability of occurrence and estimate their respective returns, as indicated in Table 9.1.

The expected returns for projects $x$ and $y$ can be calculated by Eq. (9.9):

$$\begin{aligned}\bar{k} &= \sum k_i p_i \\ \bar{k}_x &= 6.25\% + 7.50\% + 1.25\% = 15.00\% \\ \bar{k}_y &= 10\% + 7.50\% - 2.50\% = 15.00\%\end{aligned} \tag{9.9}$$

Table 9.1 Means and Standard Deviation.

| State of Economy | Probability of State ($p_i$) | Return ($k_i$) (%) | $k_i p_i$(%) |
|---|---|---|---|
| **Project $x$** | | | |
| Prosperity | 0.25 | 25 | 6.25 |
| Normal | 0.50 | 15 | 7.50 |
| Recession | 0.25 | 5 | 1.25 |
| | 1.00 | | 15.00 |
| Standard Deviation $= \sigma_x = 7.07\%$ | | | |
| **Project $y$** | | | |
| Prosperity | 0.25 | 40 | 10.00 |
| Normal | 0.50 | 15 | 7.5 |
| Recession | 0.25 | −10 | − 2.5 |
| | 1.00 | | 15.00 |
| Standard Deviation $= \sigma_y = 17.68\%$ | | | |

and the standard deviation for these returns can be found through Eq. (9.10):

$$\sigma = \sqrt{\sum_{i=1}^{n} (k_i - \bar{k})^2 p_i}$$

$$\begin{aligned}\sigma_x &= [(0.25 - 0.15)^2(0.25) + (0.15 - 0.15)^2(0.50) \\ &\quad + (0.05 - 0.15)^2(0.25)]^{\frac{1}{2}} = 7.07\% \\ \sigma_y &= [(0.40 - 0.15)^2(0.25) + (0.15 - 0.15)^2(0.50) \\ &\quad + (-0.10 - 0.15)^2(0.25)]^{\frac{1}{2}} = 17.68\% \end{aligned} \tag{9.10}$$

Data in Table 9.1 can be used to draw histograms of projects $x$ and $y$ as depicted in Figure 9.3(a). If we assume that rates of return ($k$) are distributed continuously and normally, then Figure 9.3(a) can be drawn as Figure 9.3(b).

The concept of statistical probability distribution can be combined with capital budgeting to derive the statistical distribution method for selecting risky investment projects.

The expected return for both projects is 15%, but because project $y$ has a flatter distribution with a wider range of values, it is the riskier project. Project $x$ has a normal distribution with a larger collection of values nearer the 15% expected rate of return and therefore is more stable.

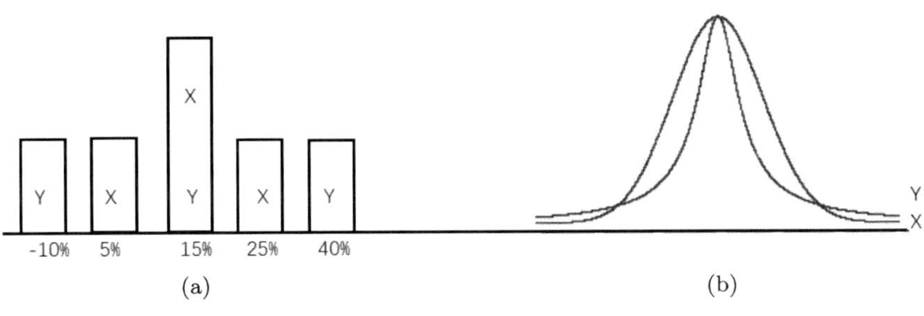


Figure 9.3 (a) Histogram of Projects X and Y. (b) Probability Density of Projects X and Y.

### 9.5.1 Statistical distribution of cash flow

From Eq. (6.5) of Chapter 6, the equation for net cash inflow can be defined as:

$$C_t = CF_t - \tau_c(CF_t - \text{dep}_t - I_t)$$

where $CF_t = [Q_t(P_t - V_t)]$; $C_t$ = net cash flow in period $t$; $Q_t$ = quantity produced and sold; $P_t$ = price; $V_t$ = variable costs; $dep_t$ = depreciation; $\tau_c$ = tax rate; and $I_t$ = interest expense. For this equation, net cash flow is a random number because $Q$, $P$, and $V$ are not known with certainty. We can assume that net $C_t$ has a normal distribution.

If two projects have the same expected cash flow, or return, as determined by the expected value (Eq. (9.9)), we may be indifferent between either project if we were to base our choice solely on return. However, if we also take risk into account, we get a more accurate picture of the type of distribution to expect, as shown in Figure 9.3.

With the introduction of risk, a firm is not necessarily indifferent between two investment proposals having equal NPV. Both NPV and its standard deviation ($\sigma_{NPV}$) should be estimated in performing capital budgeting analysis under uncertainty, NPV under uncertainty is defined as:

$$\text{NPV} = \sum_{t=1}^{N} \frac{\tilde{C}_t}{(1+k)^t} + \frac{S}{(1+k)^N} - I_o \tag{9.11}$$

where $\tilde{C}_t$ = uncertain net cash flow in period $t$; $k$ = risk-adjusted discounted rate; $S_t$ = salvage value; and $I_o$ = initial outlay.

The mean of the NPV distribution and its standard deviation is defined as

$$\text{NPV} = \sum_{t=1}^{N} \frac{\bar{C}_t}{(1+k)^t} + \frac{S}{(1+k)^N} - I_o \tag{9.12}$$

$$\sigma_{NPV} = \left[\sum_{t=1}^{N} \frac{\sigma_t^2}{(1+k)^{2t}}\right]^{\frac{1}{2}} \tag{9.13}$$

Table 9.2 Cash Flows and Standard Deviations.

| | Project A | | Project B | |
|---|---|---|---|---|
| **Year** | **Cash Flow** | **Std. Deviation** | **Cash Flow** | **Std. Deviation** |
| 0 | (\$60) | | (\$60) | |
| 1 | \$20 | 4 | \$20 | 2 |
| 2 | 20 | 4 | 20 | 2 |
| 3 | 20 | 4 | 20 | 2 |
| 4 | 20 | 4 | 20 | 2 |
| Salvage value | \$5 | | \$5 | |
| Assume a discount rate of 10% | | | | |

*Note*: Cash Flows Are Displayed in \$ Thousands.

for cash flows that are mutually independent ($\rho = 0$) cash flows. The generalized case for both Eqs. (9.12) and (9.13) is explored in Appendix 9B.

**Example 9.3.** A firm is considering two new product lines, Projects A and B, with the same life, mean returns, and salvage flow, as indicated in Table 9.2. Under the certainty methods (Chapter 6), both projects would have the same NPV:

$$\text{NPV}_A = NPV_B = \sum_{t=1}^{5} \frac{\bar{C}_t}{(1+k)^t}$$

$$\begin{aligned}\text{NPV} &= 20(PVIF_{10\%,1}) + 20(PVIF_{10\%,2}) + 20(PVIF_{10\%,3}) \\ &\quad + 20(PVIF_{10\%,4}) + 20(PVIF_{10\%,5}) - 60 + 5(PVIF_{10\%,5}) \\ &= 20(0.9091) + 20(0.8264) + 20(0.6830) + 20(0.6209) \\ &\quad - 60 + 5(0.6209) = 19.90\end{aligned}$$

However, because the standard deviations of Project A's cash flows are greater than Project B's, Project A is riskier than Project B. This difference can only be explicitly evaluated by using the statistical distribution method. To examine the riskiness between the two projects, we can calculate the standard deviation of their NPVs. If cash flows are perfectly positively correlated over time, then the standard deviation of NPV ($\sigma_{NPV}$) can be simplified as[2]:

$$\sigma_{NPV} = \sum_{t=1}^{N} \frac{\sigma_t}{(1+k)^t} \tag{9.13A}$$

$$\begin{aligned}
\sigma_{NPV(A)} &= (\$4)(PVIF_{10\%,1}) + (\$4)(PVIF_{10\%,2}) + \cdots + (\$4) \\
(PVIF_{10\%,5}) &= (4)(0.9091) + (4)(0.8264) + (4)(0.7513) \\
&\quad + (4)(0.6830) + (4)(0.6209) = 15.16 \text{ or } \$15{,}160 \\
\sigma_{NPV(B)} &= (\$2)(PVIF_{10\%,1}) + (\$2)(PVIF_{10\%,2}) + \cdots + (\$2) \\
(PVIF_{10\%,5}) &= (2)(0.9091) + (2)(0.8264) + (2)(0.7513) \\
&\quad + (2)(0.6830) + (2)(0.6209) = 7.58 \text{ or } \$7{,}580
\end{aligned}$$

With the same NPV, project B's cash flows would fluctuate \$7,580 per year, while project A's would fluctuate \$15,160. Therefore, project B would be preferred, given the same returns, because it is less risky.

Wang and Lee (2010) provide the fuzzy real option valuation approach to solve the capital budgeting decision under uncertainty environment. In Wang and Lee's model framework, the concept of probability is employed in describing fuzzy events under the estimated cash flow based on the fuzzy numbers, which can better reflect the uncertainty in the project. By using a fuzzy real option valuation, the managers can select fuzzy projects and determine the optimal time to abandon the project under the assumption of limited capital budget. Chapter 14 of Lee and Lee (2017) has discussed this in detail.

## 9.6 Simulation Methods

*Simulation* is another approach to capital budgeting decision-making under uncertainty. In cases of uncertainty, every variable relevant to the capital budgeting decision can be viewed as random. With so many random variables, it may be difficult or impossible to obtain an optimal solution with an economic or financial model.

---

[2]Equation (9.13A) is a special case of Eq. (9.1B), which is presented in Appendix 9B.

Any model of a business-decision problem can be used as a simulation model if it replicates or simulates business problems and conditions. However, true simulation models are designed to generate alternatives rather than find an optimal solution. A decision is then made through examination of these alternative results. Another aspect of the simulation model is that it focuses on an operation of the firm in detail, either physical or financial, and studies the operations of such a system over time. Simulation is also a useful tool for looking at how the real system operates and showing the effects of the important variables.

When uncertain, or random, variables play a key part in the operations of a system, the uncertainty will be included in the simulation and the model is referred to as a *probabilistic simulation*. Its counterpart, *deterministic simulation*, does not include uncertainty.

The easiest way to explain simulation is to present a simple simulation problem and discuss how it is used.

**Example 9.4.** A production manager of a small machine-manufacturing firm wants to evaluate the firm's weekly ordering policy for machine parts. The current method is to order the same amount demanded the previous week. However, the manager does not believe this is the most efficient or productive approach. The parts for assembly of one particular product cost \$20 per machine, and each machine is sold for \$60. The parts are ordered Friday morning and received Monday morning.

From experience, the manager knows that about 300–750 machines have been sold by its distributors per week and has tabulated this demand in Table 9.3.

Table 9.3 Weekly Demand Information.

| Demand Per Week | Relative Frequency |
|---|---|
| 350 Machines | 0.10 |
| 450 | 0.30 |
| 550 | 0.20 |
| 650 | 0.30 |
| 750 | 0.10 |
| | 1.0 |

The manager is considering two courses of action: (1) to order the amount that was demanded in the past or (2) to order the expected value based on past weekly demands for the product, which in this case is

$$(350)(0.10) + (450)(0.30) + (550)(0.20) + (680)(0.30) + (750)(0.10)$$
$$= 550 \text{ machines}$$

The manager would like to compare the results of these alternatives. The current procedure — ordering what was demanded the previous week — will be designated as Alternative A and the second procedure as Alternative B. These are defined as follows:

$$\text{Alternative A: } Q_n = D_{n-1}$$

$$\text{Alternative B: } Q_n = \mathit{550}$$

where $Q_n$ = amount ordered on day $n$ and $D_{n-1}$ = amount demanded the previous week. These alternatives can be compared to the firm's weekly profits on that particular machine as follows:

$$P_n = (S_n \times P_n) - (Q_n \times C) \tag{9.14}$$

where $P_n$ = profit in week $n$; $S_n$ = amount sold in week $n$; $P$ = selling price per machine; $Q_n$ = amount ordered at end of week $n$; and $C$ = cost per machine.

To further prepare this problem for simulation, there must be a method to generate weekly demand to compare these two alternatives. For this purpose, we will use a probability distribution and a random-number table. The relative-frequency values must be connected to probabilities. A specific number or numbers are then attached to each probability value to reflect the proportion of numbers from 00–99 that corresponds to each probability entry. In our example, the numbers from 00 to 09 represent 10% of the numbers, 10 to 30 represent 30% of these numbers, 40 to 59 represent 20%, and so on. Table 9.4 depicts the relative frequency, corresponding probability, and associated random numbers, for this problem.

Table 9.5 is a uniformly distributed table of random numbers.

We can easily carry out hand simulation to determine if Alternative A or B is optimal for the firm's planning and production needs. The basic procedure is as follows:

Table 9.4 Weekly Demands and their Probabilities.

| **Demand per Week** | **Relative Frequency** | **Probability** | **Random Interval** |
|---|---|---|---|
| 350 | 0.10 | 0.10 | 00–09 |
| 450 | 0.30 | 0.30 | 10–39 |
| 550 | 0.20 | 0.20 | 40–59 |
| 650 | 0.30 | 0.30 | 60–89 |
| 750 | 0.10 | 0.10 | 90–99 |

Table 9.5 Uniformly Distributed Random Numbers.

| | | | | | | | | |
|---|---|---|---|---|---|---|---|---|
| 06433 | 80674 | 24520 | 18222 | 10610 | 05794 | 37515 | 48619 | 02866 |
| 39208 | 47829 | 72648 | 37414 | 75755 | 1717 | 29899 | 78817 | 03500 |
| 89884 | 59051 | 67533 | 08123 | 17730 | 95862 | 08034 | 19473 | 03071 |
| 61512 | 32155 | 51906 | 61662 | 64130 | 16688 | 37275 | 51262 | 11569 |
| 99653 | 47635 | 12506 | 88535 | 36553 | 23757 | 34209 | 55803 | 96275 |
| 95913 | 11045 | 13772 | 76638 | 48423 | 25018 | 99041 | 77529 | 81360 |
| 55804 | 44004 | 13112 | 44115 | 01691 | 50541 | 00147 | 77685 | 58788 |
| 35334 | 82410 | 91601 | 40617 | 72876 | 33967 | 73830 | 15405 | 96554 |
| 59729 | 88646 | 76487 | 11622 | 96297 | 24160 | 09903 | 14041 | 22917 |
| 57383 | 89317 | 63677 | 70119 | 94739 | 25875 | 38829 | 68377 | 43918 |
| 30574 | 06039 | 07967 | 32422 | 76791 | 39725 | 53711 | 93385 | 13421 |
| 81307 | 13314 | 83580 | 79974 | 45929 | 85113 | 72208 | 09858 | 52104 |
| 02410 | 96385 | 79007 | 54039 | 21410 | 86980 | 91772 | 93307 | 34116 |
| 18969 | 87444 | 52233 | 62319 | 08598 | 09066 | 95288 | 04794 | 01534 |
| 87803 | 80514 | 66800 | 62297 | 80198 | 19347 | 73234 | 86265 | 49096 |
| 68397 | 10538 | 15438 | 62311 | 72844 | 60203 | 46412 | 05943 | 79232 |
| 28520 | 54247 | 58729 | 10854 | 99058 | 18260 | 38765 | 90038 | 94200 |
| 44285 | 09452 | 15867 | 70418 | 57012 | 72122 | 36634 | 97283 | 95943 |
| 80299 | 22510 | 33517 | 23309 | 57040 | 29285 | 07870 | 21913 | 72958 |
| 84842 | 5748 | 90894 | 61658 | 15001 | 94055 | 36308 | 41161 | 37341 |

1. Draw a random number from Table 9.5. It doesn't matter exactly where on the table numbers are picked, as long as the pattern for drawing numbers in consistent and unvaried; for example, the first two numbers of row 1, then row 2, then row 3, and so forth.
2. In Table 9.4, find the random-number interval associated with the random number chosen from Table 9.5.

3. Find the weekly demand ($D_n$) in Table 9.4 that corresponds to the random number ($RN$).
4. Calculate the amount sold ($S_n$). If $D_n > Q_n$, then $S_n = Q_n$; if $D_n < Q_n$, $S_n = D_n$.
5. Calculate weekly profit $[P_n = (S_n P) - (Q_n C)]$.
6. Repeat steps 1 to 5 until 20 days have been simulated.

The results of the above procedures are summarized in Table 9.6. There are nine columns in Table 9.6. Column a represents the week, column b represents the random number, column c represents the weekly demand, column d represents amount ordered for $n$th week for Alternative A, column e represents sales for Alternative A, column f represents profit of $n$th week for Alternative A, column g represents amount ordered for $n$th week for Alternative B, column h represents sales for Alternative B, and column i represents profit of $n$th week for Alternative B.

We will now explain how the random numbers in column b were obtained. The first nine random numbers were taken from the first two digits of the random numbers in row 1 of Table 9.5. The second nine numbers were obtained from the first two digits of the random numbers in row 6 of Table 9.5. The last three random numbers are from the first two digits of the first three random numbers in row 11. Column c is a number demand for nth week. The first number for number demand for Week 0 is 550, which is the average number of Table 9.4. The first random number, 06, is in the first random interval of Table 9.4, therefore, the demand is 350. The second random number, 80, is in the fourth random interval of Table 9.4, therefore the demand is 650. Similarly, we can obtain other random numbers in column c. Column d represents quantity order for Alternative A, which represents the demand number of the previous week. Column e and column h represent amount sold in week $n$ for Alternatives A and B, respectively. This sale number is determined in accordance with Procedure 4, which was mentioned above. Column g represents the weekly amount order for Alternative B, which is the average number (550) of Table 9.4. Column f and column i represent the weekly profit for Alternatives A and B, respectively, which was calculated using the formula in Eq. (9.14).

Through simulation, we can see that because there would be fewer machine parts in the inventory, the firm would earn, on average, an

Table 9.6 Simulation Results for Alternatives A and B.

| | | | **Alternative A** | | | **Alternative B** | | |
|---|---|---|---|---|---|---|---|---|
| **Week** | **RN** | **$D_n$** | **$Q_n$** | **$S_n$** | **$P_n(A)$** | **$Q_n$** | **$S_n$** | **$P_n(B)$** |
| (a) | (b) | (c) | (d) | (e) | (f) | (g) | (h) | (i) |
| 0 | | 550 | — | — | — | — | — | — |
| 1 | 06 | 350 | 550 | 350 | $10,000 | 550 | 350 | $10,000 |
| 2 | 80 | 650 | 350 | 350 | 14,000 | 550 | 550 | 22,000 |
| 3 | 24 | 450 | 650 | 450 | 14,000 | 550 | 450 | 16,000 |
| 4 | 18 | 450 | 450 | 450 | 18,000 | 550 | 450 | 16,000 |
| 5 | 10 | 450 | 450 | 450 | 18,000 | 550 | 450 | 16,000 |
| 6 | 05 | 350 | 450 | 350 | 12,000 | 550 | 350 | 10,000 |
| 7 | 37 | 450 | 350 | 350 | 14,000 | 550 | 450 | 16,000 |
| 8 | 48 | 550 | 450 | 450 | 18,000 | 550 | 550 | 22,000 |
| 9 | 02 | 350 | 550 | 350 | 10,000 | 550 | 350 | 10,000 |
| 10 | 95 | 750 | 350 | 350 | 14,000 | 550 | 550 | 22,000 |
| 11 | 11 | 450 | 750 | 450 | 12,000 | 550 | 450 | 16,000 |
| 12 | 13 | 450 | 450 | 450 | 18,000 | 550 | 450 | 16,000 |
| 13 | 76 | 650 | 450 | 450 | 18,000 | 550 | 550 | 22,000 |
| 14 | 48 | 550 | 650 | 550 | 20,000 | 550 | 550 | 22,000 |
| 15 | 25 | 450 | 550 | 450 | 16,000 | 550 | 450 | 16,000 |
| 16 | 99 | 750 | 450 | 450 | 18,000 | 550 | 550 | 22,000 |
| 17 | 77 | 650 | 750 | 650 | 24,000 | 550 | 550 | 22,000 |
| 18 | 81 | 650 | 650 | 650 | 26,000 | 550 | 550 | 22,000 |
| 19 | 30 | 550 | 550 | 550 | 22,000 | 550 | 550 | 22,000 |
| 20 | 06 | 350 | 550 | 350 | 10,000 | 550 | 350 | 10,000 |
| 21 | 07 | 350 | 550 | 350 | 10,000 | 550 | 350 | 10,000 |
| Total | | 11,200 | 11,050 | 9,250 | $336,000 | 11,550 | 9,550 | $350,000 |
| Weekly average | | 533.3 | 526.2 | 440.5 | $16,000 | 550 | 469 | $16,667 |

additional $667 per week using Alternative B rather than Alternative A. This is because an average of about 29 more machines are sold per week. Through the simulation of these two types of order techniques, we have found that Alternative B is the better of the two, but not necessarily the optimal choice. We may run simulations for other types of decision alternatives and may choose among these.

A simulation model is a representation of a real system, wherein the system's elements are depicted by arithmetic or logical processes. These processes are then executed either manually, as illustrated in Example 9.4, or by using a computer, for more complicated models, to examine the dynamic properties of the system. Simulation of the actual operation of a system tests the performance of the specific system. For this reason, simulation models must be custom-made for each situation.

Example 9.4 is a specific production management problem and serves as a learning tool on manual simulation. Simulation models have been developed for capital budgeting decisions, and by way of Example 9.4, we can see how such models can be utilized at the financial analysis and planning level.

### 9.6.1 *Simulation analysis and capital budgeting*

The following example shows how the simulation model developed by Hertz (1964, 1979) can be used in capital budgeting. Here we consider a firm that intends to introduce a new product; the 11 input variables thought to determine project value are shown in Table 9.7. Of these inputs, variables 1–9 are specified as random variables (that is, there is no predetermined sequence or order for their occurrence) with ranges as listed in the table. We could add a random element to variables 10 and 11, but the computational complexity and the insights gained do not justify the effort. Also, for ease of modelling, we use a uniform distribution to describe the probability of any particular outcome in a specified range. By using a set range for each of the nine random variables, we are not actually allowing the probabilities of each possible outcome to vary, but the spirit of varying probabilities is imbedded in the simulation approach. One further qualification of our model is that the life of the facilities is restricted to an integer value with the range as specified at the bottom of Table 9.7.

The uniform distribution density function[3] can be written as

$$f_x = \begin{cases} \dfrac{1}{\beta - \alpha} \end{cases} \tag{9.15}$$

[3]For a more detailed discussion of the properties of the uniform density function, see Hamburg (1983, pp. 100–101). Other more realistic distributions, such as log-normal and normal distributions, can be used to improve the empirical results of this kind of simulation.

Table 9.7 Variables for Simulation.

| **Variables** | **Range** |
|---|---|
| 1. Market size (units) | 2,500,000–3,000,000 |
| 2. Selling price ($/unit) | 40–60 |
| 3. Market growth | 0–5% |
| 4. Market share | 10–15% |
| 5. Total investment required ($) | 8,000,000–10,000,000 |
| 6. Useful life of facilities (years) | 5–9 |
| 7. Reside value of investment ($) | 1,000,000–2,000,000 |
| 8. Operating cost ($/unit) | 30–45 |
| 9. Fixed costs ($) | 400,000–500,000 |
| 10. Tax rate | 40% |
| 11. Discount rate | 12% |

*Source*: Lee and Lee (2017). *Financial Analysis, Planning and Forecasting*, page 683.

where $\beta$ is the upper bound on the variable value and $\alpha$ is the lower bound. Over the range $\alpha < x < \beta$, the function $f_x = 1/\beta - \alpha$; over the range $\beta < x < \alpha$, $f_x = 0$. With this in mind, note the way the values are assigned. For each successive input variable, a random-number generator selects a value from 01 to 00 (where 00 is the proxy for 100 using a 2-digit random-number generator) and then translates that value into a variable value by taking account of the specified range and distribution of the variable in question.

For each simulation, nine random numbers are selected. From these random numbers, a set of values for the nine key factors is created. For example, the first set of random numbers, as shown in Table 9.8, is 39, 73, 72, 75, 37, 02, 87, 98, and 10. The procedure of selecting these numbers is similar to Example 9.4, however, these random numbers are not based upon the uniform distribution random number as presented in Table 9.5. If we use the random numbers from Table 9.5, we can use the first two digits of the first row of this random table, then the random numbers are 06, 80, 24, 18, 10, 05, 37, 48, and 02.

The value of the market size factor for the first simulation can be obtained as follows:

$$2{,}500{,}000 + \frac{39}{100}(3{,}000{,}000 - 2{,}500{,}000) = 2{,}695{,}000$$

The value of sales price factor for the first simulation can be obtained as follows:

$$40 + \frac{73}{100}(60 - 40) = 54.6$$

The operating cost for the first simulation can be obtained as follows:

$$30 + \frac{98}{100}(45 - 30) = 44.7$$

Similar computations can be used to calculate the values of all variables except the useful life of the facilities. Because useful life of facilities is restricted to integer values, we use the following correspondence between random numbers and useful life of facilities:

| Random number | 01–19 | 20–39 | 40–59 | 60–79 | 90–99 | 00 |
|---|---|---|---|---|---|---|
| Useful life | 5 | 6 | 7 | 8 | 9 | 10 |

Since the random number for useful life is 02, it is within the range of 01–19, therefore, the useful life is 5 years.

For each simulation, a series of cash flows and its net present value can be calculated by using the following formula:

$$\begin{aligned}
(\text{Sales volume})_t &= [(\text{Market size}) \times (1 + \text{Market growth rate})^t] \\
&\quad \times (\text{Market share}) \\
\text{EBIT} &= (\text{Sales volume})_t \times (\text{Selling price} \\
&\quad - \text{Operating cost}) - (\text{Fixed cost}) \\
(\text{Cash flow})_t &= \text{EBIT}_t \times (1 - \text{Tax rate}) + \text{Depreciation} \\
\text{NPV} &= \sum_{t=1}^{N} \frac{(\text{Cash flow})_t}{(1 + \text{Discount rate})^t} - I_0
\end{aligned}$$

where $t$ represents the $t$th year and $N$ represents useful life.

The results in terms of cash flow for each simulation are listed in Table 9.9, with each period's cash flows shown separately. Now, we will discuss how the cash flow for the first simulation is calculated. For example, the cash flow for the first three periods are \$2,034,382.33,

\$2,116,529.56, and \$2,201,525.23 can be calculated as follows:

$$
\begin{aligned}
(\text{Sales volume})_1 &= [(\text{Market size}) \times (1 + \text{Market growth rate})^t] \\
&\quad \times (\text{Market share}) \\
&= [(2{,}695{,}000) \times (1 + 0.036)] \times (13.75\%) \\
&= 383{,}902.75 \\
\text{EBIT}_1 &= (383{,}902.75) \times (54.6 - 44.7) - (410{,}000) \\
&= 3{,}390{,}637.22 \\
(\text{Cash flow})_1 &= 3{,}390{,}637.22 \times (1 - 40\%) = 2{,}034{,}382.33 \\
(\text{Sales volume})_2 &= [(\text{Market size}) \times (1 + \text{Market growth rate})^t] \\
&\quad \times (\text{Market share}) \\
&= [(2{,}695{,}000) \times (1 + 0.036)^2] \times (13.75\%) \\
&= 397{,}732.249 \\
\text{EBIT}_2 &= (397{,}732.249) \times (54.6 - 44.7) - (410{,}000) \\
&= 3,527{,}549.27 \\
(\text{Cash flow})_2 &= 3{,}527{,}549.27 \times (1 - 40\%) = 2{,}116{,}529.56 \\
(\text{Sales volume})_3 &= [(\text{Market size}) \times (1 + \text{Market growth rate})^t] \\
&\quad \times (\text{Market share}) \\
&= [(2{,}695{,}000) \times (1 + 0.036)^3] \times (13.75\%) \\
&= 412{,}041.285 \\
\text{EBIT}_3 &= (412{,}041.285) \times (54.6 - 44.7) - (410{,}000) \\
&= 3{,}669{,}208.72 \\
(\text{Cash flow})_3 &= 3{,}669{,}208.72 \times (1 - 40\%) = 2{,}201{,}525.23
\end{aligned}
$$

In Table 9.9 for the first, sixth, and tenth simulation, we calculate cash flow for five periods. For the second and fifth simulation, we calculate cash flow for eight periods. For the third, seventh, and eighth simulation, we calculate cash flow for seven periods. For the fourth simulation, we calculate cash flow for six periods. Finally, for the ninth simulation, we calculate cash flow for nine periods.

Table 9.8 Simulation.

| **Variables** | **1** | **2** | **3** | **4** | **5** |
|---|---|---|---|---|---|
| VMARK 1 | (39)2,695,000 | (47)2,735,000 | (67)2,835,000 | (12)2,580,000 | (78)2,890,000 |
| PRICE 2 | (73)$54.6 | (93)$58.6 | (59)$51.8 | (78)$55.6 | (61)$52.2 |
| GROW 3 | (72)3.6% | (21)1.05% | (63)0.0315 | (03).0015 | (42)0.021 |
| SMARK 4 | (75)13.75% | (95)14.75% | (78)0.139 | (04)0.102 | (77)0.1385 |
| TOINV 5 | (37)8,740,000 | (97)9,940,000 | (87)9,740,000 | (61)9,220,000 | (65)9,300,000 |
| KUSE 6 | (02)5 years | (68)8 years | (47)7 years | (23)6 years | (71)8 years |
| RES 7 | (87)1,870,000 | (41)1,410,000 | (56)1,560,000 | (15)1,150,000 | (20)1,200,000 |
| VAR 8 | (98)$44.7 | (91)$43.65 | (22)$33.3 | (58)$38.7 | (17)$32.55 |
| FIX 9 | (10)$410,000 | (80)$480,000 | (19)$419,000 | (93)$493,000 | (48)$448,000 |
| TAX 10 | 0.4 | 0.4 | 0.4 | 0.4 | 0.4 |
| DIS 11 | 0.12 | 0.12 | 0.12 | 0.12 | 0.12 |
| NPV | $197,847.561 | $7,929,874.287 | $12,146,989.579 | $1,169,846.55 | $15,306,345 |

| Variables | 6 | 7 | 8 | 9 | 10 |
|---|---|---|---|---|---|
| VMARK 1 | (89)2,945,000 | (26)2,630,000 | (60)2,800,000 | (68)2,840,000 | (23)2,615,000 |
| PRICE 2 | (18)$43.6 | (47)$49.4 | (88)$57.6 | (39)$47.8 | (47)$49.4 |
| GROW 3 | (83)0.0415 | (94)0.047 | (17)0.0085 | (71)0.0355 | (25)0.0125 |
| SMARK 4 | (08)0.104 | (06)0.103 | (36)0.118 | (22)0.111 | (79)0.1395 |
| TOINV 5 | (90)9,800,000 | (72)9,440,000 | (77)9,540,000 | (76)9,520,000 | (08)8,160,000 |
| KUSE 6 | (05)5 years | (40)7 years | (43) 7 years | (81) 9 years | (71)1,710,000 |
| RES 7 | (89)1,890,000 | (62)1,620,000 | (28)1,280,000 | (88)1,880,000 | (71)1,710,000 |
| VAR 8 | (18)$32.7 | (47)$37.05 | (31)$34.65 | (94)$44.1 | (58)$38.7 |
| FIX 9 | (08)$408,000 | (68)$468,000 | (06)$406,000 | (76)$476,000 | (56)$456,000 |
| TAX 10 | 0.4 | 0.4 | 0.4 | 0.4 | 0.4 |
| DIS 11 | 0.12 | 0.12 | 0.12 | 0.12 | 0.12 |
| NPV | $−1,513,820.475 | $11,327,171.67 | $839,650.211 | $−6,021,018.052 | $563,687.461 |

*Note*: Definitions of variables can be found in Table 9.7.
*Source*: Reprinted from Lee and Lee (2017).

Table 9.9 Cash Flow Estimation for Each Simulation.

| Period | 1 | 2 | 3 | 4 | 5 |
|---|---|---|---|---|---|
| 1 | 2,034,382.335 | 3,368,605.531 | 4,260,506.327 | 2,376,645.064 | 4,549,425.961 |
| 2 | 2,116,529.563 | 3,406,999.889 | 4,402,631.377 | 2,380,653.731 | 4,650,608.707 |
| 3 | 2,201,525.239 | 3,445,797.388 | 4,549,233.365 | 2,384,668.412 | 4,753,916.289 |
| 4 | 2,289,636.147 | 3,485,002.261 | 4,700,453.316 | 2,388,689.114 | 4,859,393.331 |
| 5 | 2,380,919.049 | 3,524,618.785 | 4,856,436.695 | 2,392,715.848 | 4,967,085.391 |
| 6 | | 3,564,651.282 | 5,017,333.551 | 2,396,748.622 | 5,077,038.985 |
| 7 | | 3,605,104.120 | 5,183,298.658 | | 5,189,301.603 |
| 8 | | 3,645,981.714 | | | 5,303,921,737 |
| 9 | | | | | |
| | **6** | **7** | **8** | **9** | **10** |
| 1 | 1,841,398.655 | 1,820,837.760 | 4,344,679.668 | 439,076.864 | 2,097,642.448 |
| 2 | 1,927,975.899 | 1,919,614.735 | 4,383,680.045 | 464,802.893 | 2,127,282.979 |
| 3 | 2,018,146.099 | 2,023,034.228 | 4,423,011.926 | 491,442.196 | 2,157,294.016 |
| 4 | 2,112,058.362 | 2,131,314.436 | 4,502,681.491 | 519,027.194 | 2,187,680.191 |
| 5 | 2,209,867.984 | 2,244.683.815 | 4,502,681.491 | 547,591.459 | 2,218,446.194 |
| 6 | | 2,363,381.554 | 4,543,024.884 | 577,169.756 | |
| 7 | | 2,487,658.087 | 4,583,711.195 | 607,798.082 | |
| 8 | | | | 639,513.714 | |
| 9 | | | | 672,355.251 | |

*Note*: NPVs are listed in Table 9.8.
*Source*: Reprinted from Lee and Lee (2017).

The NPVs for each simulation are given under the input values listed in Table 9.8. From these NPV figures, we can calculate a mean NPV figure and standard deviation, from which we can analyze the project's risk and return profile. As we can see, this project's NPV can range from –$6 million to +$15 million, depending on the combinations of random events that could take place. The mean NPV is $4,194,647.409 with a standard deviation of $6,618,476.469. This indicates that there is a 70% chance that the NPV will be greater than 0. In addition, we can use this average NPV and its standard deviation to calculate interval estimate for NPV. In other words, by using simulation we can have interval estimate of NPV, which was used in both statistical distribution method and decision tree method.

Furthermore, if we change the range or distribution of the random variables, we can then perform sensitivity analysis to investigate the impact of a change of an input factor on the risk and return of the investment project.

Also, by using sensitivity analysis, we essentially break down the uncertainty involved in the undertaking of any project, thereby highlighting exactly what the decision-maker should be primarily concerned with in forecasting in terms of those variables critical to the analysis. The information obtained from simulation analysis is valuable in allowing the decision-maker to more accurately evaluate risky capital investments. Other simulation methods can be found in Chapter 30 of Lee *et al.* (2016).

## 9.7 Inflationary Effects in the Capital Budgeting Decision

At various times, inflation has been a significant economic problem. With the advent of double-digit inflation in the 1970s and the early years of the 1980s, inflation must be considered in any sound capital budgeting analysis. Financial managers can adjust for inflation through the estimated cash flow, the discount rate, or the capital intensity level, all inputs or variables of the capital budgeting decision. Incorporating inflation into the capital budgeting process affects financial decisions as well as increases the complexity of the capital budgeting procedure.

The general price escalation that accompanies inflation affects both consumers and corporate customers because of the decrease in purchasing power. For the corporation, inflation affects revenue and costs, because an increase in inflation also increases costs of materials, transportation, and labor. Inflation also affects depreciation tax credit. Depreciation tax laws are based on historical costs rather than current costs, which implies that depreciation write-offs will be underestimated during times of inflation, thereby resulting in a greater tax burden on the firm.

We can categorize firms as either *inflation-favorable* or *inflation-unfavorable*. Inflation-favorable firms are those whose revenues increase faster than costs during inflationary times and thus have a strong chance of remaining solvent. This is best exemplified by companies in the food industry. Despite hard economic times, food is a necessity that consumers must continue to purchase. Inflation-unfavorable firms are those whose costs rise much faster than revenue during inflationary times. Such firms must adopt defensive strategies during long periods of poor economic conditions. This is especially true of industries that produce consumer durables or luxury items such as cars, major appliances, and homes. The consumer can forego these items until times improve, and this action is detrimental to many of these companies.

### 9.7.1 *The implication of inflation for investment decisions*

Much of the emphasis given to capital budgeting adjustments for inflation involves re-estimation of the discount rate. Much less emphasis has been given to adjusting cash flows themselves, which may give rise to a bias in accept-reject decisions when expected future rates of inflation are incorporated into the discount rate but not into the cash flow estimates. This bias increases when expected inflation is high and may result in a large underestimation of the project's true value to the firm.

The traditional risk-adjusted discount rate used NPV, as discussed earlier in this chapter, can be written

$$\text{NPV} = \sum_{t=1}^{N} \frac{CF_t}{(1+k)^t} - I_0 \qquad (9.12\text{A})$$

where $CF_t$ is the expected nominal net cash flow at the end of period $t$; $N$ is the number of periods in which cash flows are related to the risk-adjusted discount rate $k$; and $I_0$ is the initial cash outlay.

Discount rate $k$ consists of two components, the risk-free rate $R_f$ and risk premium $\rho$, associated with the uncertainty attached to cash flows $CF_t$.

Cooley, Roenfeldt, and Chew (1975) developed a discount model that incorporates inflation into discount rate $k$. They state that in the presence of inflation, $R_f$ can consist of $I$ (the pure rate of return) and $\eta$ (an element of anticipated inflation) or $R_f = i + \eta$. Since $i$ is the pure rate of return, or the time value of real money used for discounting real cash flows, anticipated inflation can be estimated by subtracting $i$ from the current return on long-term U.S. Treasury securities. Therefore, the traditional discount rate consists of

$$k = R_f + \rho = i + \eta + \rho \tag{9.16}$$

### 9.7.2 *Calculating the NPV of real cash flows*

When considering actual investments, the future real values, instead of the nominal values, are important in determining which project to undertake, because nominal values can be misstated by the effects of inflation. To calculate the real future value, the nominal net cash flow expected in $t$ must be discounted by 1 plus the expected inflation rate, $\eta$ and raised to the power of $t$. This real net cash flow must then be discounted by the real rate, $i + \rho$, which excludes any inflationary element and results in the real net present value of the profit, or

$$\text{NPV}_R = \sum_{t=1}^{N} \frac{CF_t}{(1+\eta)^t(1+i+\rho)^t} - I_0 \tag{9.17}$$

By varying risk premiums and the inflation rate, Eq. (9.16) can be written as:

$$\text{NPV}_R = \sum_{t=1}^{N} \frac{CF_t}{(1+i+\rho_t)(1+i)^{t-1}\prod_{j=1}^{t}(1+\eta_j)} \tag{9.18}$$

**Example 9.5.** Table 9.10 illustrates the differences between the traditional NPV model, as depicted by Eq. (9.1), and the

Table 9.10 Capital Budgeting Information Under Inflation.

| | |
|---|---|
| Initial cost | $I = \$26{,}875$ |
| Expected average net cash inflows | $\bar{CF}_t = \$12{,}500$ for 3 years |
| Pure rate | $i = 6.25\%$ (constant) |
| Anticipated inflation | $\eta_1 = 12.5\%,\ \eta_2 = 10\%,\ \eta_3 = 7.5\%$ |
| | $\bar{\eta} = 10\%$ |
| Risk premium | $\rho_t = 8.75\%$ (constant) |
| Traditional $K_t = i + \bar{\eta} + \rho_t = 6.25 + 10 + 8.75 = 25\%$ | |

| A<br>Year ending $t$ | B<br>$CF_t$ | C<br>$(1+k)^t$ | D<br>$(1+i+\rho_t)$ | E<br>$(1+i)^{t-1}$ | F<br>$\pi(1+\eta_j)$ | G<br>(D) (E) (F) |
|---|---|---|---|---|---|---|
| 0 | −26,875 | — | — | — | — | — |
| 1 | +12,500 | 1.250 | 1.15 | 1.000 | 1.125 | 1.294 |
| 2 | +12,500 | 1.563 | 1.15 | 1.063 | 1.238 | 1.513 |
| 3 | +12,500 | 1.953 | 1.15 | 1.129 | 1.209 | 1.570 |

*Note*: For the non-inflation-adjusted case, we use the discount factors shown in column C to calculate the NPV,

$$\begin{aligned}\text{NPV}_T &= \sum_{t=1}^{N} \frac{CF_t}{(1+k_t)^t} - I_0 \\ &= \frac{12{,}500}{1.250} + \frac{12,500}{1.563} + \frac{12{,}500}{1.953} - 26{,}875 \\ &= 10{,}000 + 7{,}997 + 6{,}400 - 26{,}875 = -\$2{,}478\end{aligned}$$

For the inflation-adjusted case, we use the discount facts shown in column G, which are the products of columns D, E, and F, to calculate the real NPV.

$$\begin{aligned}\text{NPV}_R &= \sum_{t=1}^{N} \frac{CF_t}{(1+i+\rho_i)(1+i)^{t-1}\prod_{j=1}^{t}(1+\eta_j)} \\ &= \frac{12{,}500}{1.294} + \frac{12{,}500}{1.513} \\ &\quad + \frac{12{,}500}{1.570} - 26{,}875 = 9{,}660 + 8{,}262 + 7{,}962 - 26{,}875 = -\$991\end{aligned}$$

inflation-adjusted version, Eq. (9.16). The example shows an initial project cost of \$26,875 with expected cash inflows of \$12,500 per year for $N = 3$ years. The pure rate is assumed to be a constant of 6.25%, and inflation of 12.5%, 10%, and 7.5% for each of the three years, with a three-year average of 10%. The risk premium is assumed constant at 8.75%. The traditional NPV yields a negative \$2,478, while the inflation-adjusted method is a negative \$991. After inflation adjustment, the difference in NPV is \$1,487. Both procedures indicate this project should be rejected; however, because of the large differences in NPVs, the inflation-adjusted NPV could result in acceptance in the case of other projects. The differences in NPV will be further accentuated with longer time periods, higher rates of inflation, and larger rates of return.

This inflation-adjustment method of Cooley, Roenfeldt, and Chew has been developed further by Jensen (1987).

## 9.8 Summary

In this chapter, we have discussed uncertainty and how capital budgeting decisions are made under conditions of uncertainty. Presented were four methods of handling uncertainty: the certainty equivalent, the risk-adjusted discount rate, simulation, and statistical distribution. Each method is based on the NPV approach, so that, in theory, using any of the methods should yield similar results. However, in practice, the method used will depend on the availability of information and the reliability of that information. Also discussed were the impact of inflation on the capital budgeting decision and how the determination of real cash flows can help solve the capital budgeting decision in a highly inflationary environment.

## References

Bernhard, R. H. "Risk-Adjusted Value, Timing of Uncertainty Resolution and the Measurement of Project Worth," *Journal of Financial and Quantitative Analysis*, 19 (March 1984, pp. 83–98).

Bierman, H. and S. Smidt. *The Capital Budgeting Decision: Economic Analysis of Investment Projects*, 1st edn. (Routledge, 2007).

Cooley, P. L., R. L. Roenfeldt and I. K. Chew. "Capital Budgeting Procedures under Inflation," *Financial Management*, 4(4) (1975, pp. 18–27).

Fama, E. F. "Risk-Adjusted Discount Rates and Capital Budgeting Under Uncertainty," *Journal of Financial Economics*, 5(1) (1977, pp. 3–24).

Fuller, R. J. and H. S. Kerr. "Estimating the divisional cost of capital: An analysis of the pure-play technique," *The Journal of Finance*, 36(5) (1981, pp. 997–1009).

Gitman, L. J. and J. R. Forrester. "A Survey of Capital Budgeting Techniques Used by Major Firms," *Financial Management*, 6 (Fall 1977, pp. 66–71).

Hertz, D. B. "Risk Analysis in Capital Investments," *Harvard Business Review*, 42 (January/February 1964, pp. 95–106).

Hertz, D. B. "Risk Analysis in Capital Investments," *Harvard Business Review*, 57 (September/October 1979, pp. 169–181).

Hillier, F. S. "The Derivation of Probabilistic Information for the Evaluation of Risky Investments," *Management Science*, 9 (April 1963, pp. 443–457).

Jensen, R. E. "A Dynamic Analytic Hierarchy Process Analysis of Capital Budgeting Under Stochastic Inflation Rates and Risk Premium," *Advances in Financial Planning and Forecasting*, 2 (1987, pp. 269–302).

Lee, C. F. and A. C. Lee. *Encyclopedia of Finance*, 3rd edn. (Springer, New York, 2022, Forthcoming).

Lee, C. F., J. C. Lee, J. R. Chang, and T. Tai. *Essentials of Excel, Excel VBA, SAS and Minitab for Statistical and Financial Analyses* (Springer International Publishing, 2016).

Lee. C. F. and J. Lee. *Financial Analysis, Planning & Forecasting: Theory Application* (World Scientific, Singapore, 2017).

Lee, C. F. and S. Y. Wang "A Fuzzy Real Option Valuation Approach to Capital Budgeting Under Uncertainty Environment," *International Journal of Information Technology & Decision Making*, 9(5) (2010, pp. 695–713).

Myers, S. and S. M. Turnbull. "Capital Budgeting and the Capital Asset Pricing Model: Good News and Bad News," *The Journal of Finance*, 32 (May 1977, pp. 321–322).

Pinches, G. E. "Myopic, Capital Budgeting and Decision Making," *Financial Management*, 11 (Autumn 1982, pp. 6–19).

Robichek, A. A. and S. C. Myers. "Conceptual problems in the use of risk-adjusted discount rates," *The Journal of Finance*, 21(4) (1966, pp. 727–730).

Ross, S. A., C. S. Spatt and P. H. Dybvig. "Present Values and Internal Rates of Return," *Journal of Economic Theory* (August 1980, pp. 524–531).

Rubinstein, M. E. V. "A Mean Variance Synthesis of Corporate Financial Theory," *The Journal of Finance*, 28 (March 1973, pp. 167–181).

## Appendix 9A — Decision Tree Method for Investment Decisions

A *decision tree* is a general approach to structuring complex decisions and helps direct the user to a solution. It is a graphical tool that describes the types of actions available to the decision-maker and their consequences.

In capital budgeting decision-making, the decision tree is used to analyze investment opportunities involving a sequence of investment decisions over time. To illustrate the basic ideas of the decision tree, we will develop a problem involving numerous decisions.

First, we must enumerate some of the basic rules to implement this methodology: (1) the decision-maker should try to include only important decisions or events to prevent the tree from becoming a "bush;" (2) the decision tree requires subjective estimates on the part of the decision-maker when assessing probabilities; and (3) the decision tree must be developed in chronological order to ensure the proper sequence of events and decisions.

A decision point is represented by a box, or *decision node*. The available alternatives are represented by branches out of this node. A circle represents an *event node*, and branches from this type of node represent types of possible events.

The *expected monetary value* (EMV) is calculated for each event node by multiplying probabilities by conditional profits and then summing them. The EMV is then placed in the event node and represents the expected value of all branches arising from that node.

**Example 9.1A.** Figure 9.1A illustrates a decision tree for a packaging firm that sells paper and paperboard materials to customers for packaging such items as cans and bottles. The firm predicts that with the advent of shrink-wrap packaging, their products may be obsolete within a decade. The firm must first decide on one of four short-term plans: (1) do nothing, (2) establish a tie-in with a company that manufactures plastics packaging, (3) acquire such a company, or (4) develop its own plastics packaging. These four alternatives are the first four branches extending from the event node in Figure 9.1A. If the firm does nothing, it's short-term profits will be about the same as in previous years. If the firm decides to establish a tie-in with another firm, it foresees either a 90% successful introduction of

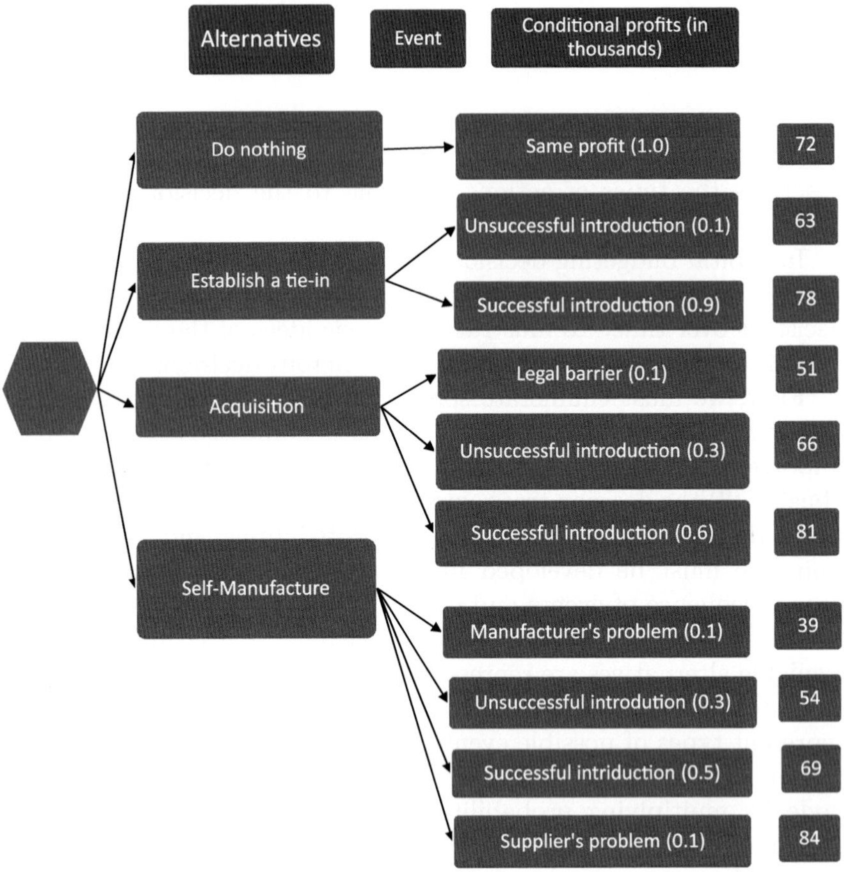


Figure 9.1A Decision Tree for Capital Budgeting Decision.

its new plastics line or a 10% possibility of failure. If the firm decides on acquisition, it foresees a 10% chance of encountering legal barriers, such as problems with antitrust laws; a 30% possibility of an unsuccessful introduction of the plastics line; and a 60% chance of success. If the firm decides to manufacture a plastics line on its own, it foresees many more problems. The firm anticipates a 10% chance of having problems with suppliers in developing a total packaging system for customers, a 30% chance of customers not purchasing the new materials, and a 50% chance of success in the development and introduction of the plastics line.

The third column in Figure 9.1A is *conditional profit*, the amount of profit the firm can expect to make with the advent of each preceding set of alternative and consequent events.

In Figure 9.1A the expected monetary values are shown in the event nodes. The financial planner decides which actions to take by selecting the highest EMV, which in this case is $76.5, as indicated in the decision node at the beginning of the tree. The parallel lines drawn across the nonoptimal decision branches indicate elimination of these alternatives from consideration.

In Example 9.1A, we have simplified the number of possible alternatives and events to provide a simpler view of the decision tree process. However, as we introduce more possibilities into this problem, and as it becomes more complex, the decision tree becomes more valuable in organizing the information necessary to make the decision. This is especially true when making a sequence of decisions rather than a single decision. A more detailed discussion on decision tree method for capital budgeting decision, can be found in Chapter 14 of Lee and Lee (2017).

## Appendix 9B — Hillier's Statistical Distribution Method for Capital Budgeting under Uncertainty

In Chapter 9, we discussed the calculation of the standard deviation of NPV (1) where cash flows are independent of each other as presented in Eq. (9.13) and (2) where cash flows are perfectly positively correlated as presented in Eq. (9.13A). In either case, the covariance term drops out of the equation for the variance of the NPV. Now we develop a general formula for the standard deviation of NPV that can be used for all cash flow relationships.

The general equation for the standard deviation of NPV ($\sigma_{NPV}$) with a mean of

$$NPV = \sum_{t=1}^{N} \frac{\bar{C}_t}{(1+k)^t} + \frac{\bar{S}_t}{(1+k)^N} - I_0$$

is

$$\sigma_{NPV} = \left[\sum_{t=1}^{N} \frac{\sigma_t^2}{(1+k)^{2t}} + \sum_{t=1}^{N}\sum_{\tau=1}^{N} W_t W_\tau \mathrm{COV}(C_\tau C_t)\right]^{\frac{1}{2}} \quad (\tau \neq t) \tag{9.1B}$$

Table 9.1B Variance and Covariance Metrics.

| | $W_1C_1$ | $W_2C_2$ | $W_3C_3$ |
|---|---|---|---|
| $W_1C_1$ | $W_1^2\sigma_1^2$ | $W_1W_2\text{COV}(C_1, C_2)$ | $W_1W_3\text{COV}(C_1, C_3)$ |
| $W_2C_2$ | $W_1W_2\text{COV}(C_2, C_1)$ | $W_2^2\sigma_2^2$, | $W_2W_3\text{COV}(C_2, C_3)$ |
| $W_3C_3$ | $W_1W_3\text{COV}(C_3, C_1)$ | $W_2W_3\text{COV}(C_2, C_3)$ | $W_3^2\sigma_3^2$ |

where $\sigma_t^2$ = variance of cash flows in the $t$th period; $W_t$ and $W_\tau$ = discount factors for the $t$th and $\tau$th period (that is, $W_t = 1(1+K)^t$ and $W_\tau = 1/(1+K)^\tau$; and $\text{COV}(C_t, C_\tau)$ = covariability between cash flows in $t$ and $\tau$ (that is, $\text{COV}(C_t, C_\tau) = \rho_{t\tau}\sigma_\tau\sigma_t$, where $\rho_{t\tau}$ = correlation coefficient between cash flow in $t$th and $\tau$th period).

Cash flows between periods $t$ and $\tau$ are generally related. Therefore, $\text{COV}(C_t, C_\tau)$ is an important factor in the estimation of $\sigma_{NPV}$. The magnitude, sign, and degree of the relationships of these cash flows depends on the economic operating conditions and the nature of the product or service produced.

Using portfolio theory to calculate the standard deviation of a set of securities, we have derived Eq. (9.1B), which can be explained by an example. Suppose we have cash flows for a three-year period, $C_1$, $C_2$, $C_3$, with discount factors of $W_1, W_2, W_3$. Table 9.1B shows for the calculation of $\sigma_{NPV}$.

The summation of the diagonal ($W_1^2\sigma_1^2$, $W_2^2\sigma_2$, $W_3^2\sigma_3^2$) results in the first part of Eq. (9.1B), or

$$\sum_{t=1}^{N}\sum_{\tau=1}^{N} W_tW_\tau\text{COV}(C_\tau, C_t) \quad t \neq \tau$$

This calculation is similar to the calculation of portfolio variance, as discussed in Chapter 6. However, in portfolio analysis, $W_t$ represents the percent of money invested in the $i$th security, and the summation of $W_t$ equals 1. In the calculation of $\sigma_{NPV}$, $W_t$ represents a discount factor. Therefore, the summation of $W_t$ will not necessarily equal 1.

Equation (9.1B) is the general equation for $\sigma_{NPV}$. Thus, Eq. (9.13) for $\sigma_{NPV}$ under perfectly correlated cash flows or independent cash flows is a special case derived from the general Eq. (9.1B).

Hillier (1963) combined the assumption of mutual independence and perfect correlation to develop a mode of $\sigma_{NPV}$ to deal with mixed situations. This model is presented in Eq. (9.2B), which analyzes investment proposals in which expected cash flows are a combination of correlated and independent flows.

$$\sigma = \left[\sum_{t=1}^{N} \frac{\sigma_{yt}^2}{(1+k)^{2t}} + \sum_{h=1}^{m}\left(\sum_{t=0}^{N} \frac{\sigma_{zt}^h}{(1+k)^t}\right)^2\right]^{\frac{1}{2}} \tag{9.2B}$$

where $\sigma_{yt}^2$ = variance for an independent net cash flow in period $t$ and $\sigma_{zt}^h$ = standard deviation for stream $h$ of a perfectly correlated cash flow stream in $t$. If $h = 1$, then Eq. (9.2B) is a combination of Eqs. (9.13) and (9.13A).

## Questions and Problems

1. Define following terms:
   a. Risk-adjusted discount rate method
   b. Certainty equivalent coefficient
   c. Simulation method for capital budgeting
   d. Decision tree method for capital budgeting
2. Discuss the major difference between the risk-adjusted discount rate method and the certainty equivalent method for capital budgeting decisions.
3. Analyze in detail the statistical distribution method for capital budgeting decisions.
4. A firm has an investment opportunity. Find its $NPV$ according to this information:

   Initial investment cost = \$2,000
   Cash flows for five years = \$600 per year
   Risk-free rate = 5%
   Risk premium on the investment = 10%.
5. A project is under consideration. The risk-free rate is 5%, and market risk premium is 7%. The beta of the project under consideration is 1.8, with expected net income of \$1,000 per year for three years. The initial investment cost is \$2,200.

a. Using CAPM, find the required rate of return on this project.
b. Should the project be accepted?
c. If the third year's net income is a certain \$1,000, should the project be accepted?

6. Project A's initial cost is \$2,000, and its cash flow at time 1 has the following probability distribution:

| Probability | Cash Flows |
|---|---|
| 0.3 | 1,000 |
| 0.4 | 3,000 |
| 0.3 | 4,000 |

a. If the risk-free rate is 5% and expected market rate of return is 10%, and the project's beta is 2, what is the *NPV* of the project?
b. If the beta of project B is 0, so that its cash flow is \$2,500 with certainty, how much initial cost is needed for project B for the analyst to be indifferent between project A and B?

7. A firm is considering an investment with the following values and estimates:

(a) Risk-free rate = percent
(b) Initial cost = \$6,500.

| **Cash Flows (Profit on Investment)** | | | |
|---|---|---|---|
| **Joint Probability Distribution** | | | |
| **Expected Market Rate of Return** | **\$400** | **\$600** | **\$800** |
| 0.1 | 0.2 | 0.1 | 0 |
| 0.15 | 0.1 | 0.2 | 0.1 |
| 0.20 | 0.0 | 0.1 | 0.2 |

Find the equilibrium market value of the investment. Would you accept or reject the opportunity?

8. A financial manager derived a 15% of required rate of return on his project using CAPM (risk-free rate was assumed 5%). If expected cash flow is \$1,000, how much is the certainty equivalent of the risky return?
9. Given the following information, which project is better according to the statistical distribution method?

| State of Economy | Probability | Return of A (%) | Return of B (%) |
|---|---|---|---|
| 1 | 0.3 | 25 | 30 |
| 2 | 0.4 | 15 | 15 |
| 3 | 0.3 | 5 | 0 |

If the expected market rates of return are 20, 10, and 0% for states 1, 2, and 3, and risk-free rate is 7%, what are required rates of return on projects A and B?

10. The following are facts about a small firm:

    Risk-free rate = 6%
    Expected return on the market = 12%
    Variance of market return = 2%
    Covariance of the net income of the firm with the market return is \$50
    Expected net income = \$450

    a. Find the firm's value using the certainty equivalent method.
    b. Find the firm's values using the risk-adjusted discount rate method.
    c. If the firm's value is considerably below it equilibrium value derived in a and b, what will happen?

11. Below is the probability distribution of cash flows for years 1 and 2 of projects L and K:

| Project L | | Project K | |
|---|---|---|---|
| **Year 1** | | **Year 1** | |
| **Probability** | **Cash Flow** | **Probability** | **Cash Flow** |
| 0.4 | 300 | 0.5 | 400 |
| 0.6 | 400 | 0.5 | 600 |
| **Year 2** | | **Year 2** | |
| 0.2 | 200 | 0.3 | 400 |
| 0.5 | 500 | 0.4 | 600 |
| 0.3 | 700 | 0.3 | 800 |

a. Find the expected value of the cash flows for years 1 and 2 for each of the projects.
b. Assume that the risk-free rate of interest is 6%, the expected return on the market is 12%, and the beta is 0.9 for L and 1.2 for K.

   i. Evaluate each of the projects using the risk adjusted discount rate method. Which one would be preferred?
   ii. Find the certainty equivalent coefficients (alpha) that would give the same present value of the mean cash flow in each year of project L's life.
   iii. Evaluate the projects using the certainty equivalent form of the Capital Asset Pricing Model.

12. For the cash flow distributions given in the preceding problem, the certainty equivalent cash flows for each project for each year are given below:

| **Project** | **Year** | **Certain Cash Flow** |
|---|---|---|
| L | 1 | 200 |
| | 2 | 300 |
| K | 1 | 300 |
| | 2 | 400 |

a. Find the certainty equivalent coefficients for each year of the projects' lives.
b. Evaluate project's L and K using the certainty equivalent method, given a risk-free rate of 6%.

13. Under what circumstances will the certainty equivalent method and the risk adjusted discount rate methods give the same present value of cash flows? When they give different present values, which one should be used?
14. Assume you are given the following information concerning the mean and standard deviation of cash flows:

| **Year** | **Expected Value of Cash Flow** | **Standard Deviation of Cash Flow** |
|---|---|---|
| 1 | 700 | 200 |
| 2 | 900 | 300 |

The project's initial outlay is \$500 and the discount rate for this project is 10%.

a. Find the $E\ (NPV)$ and standard deviation of $NPV$ given that the cash flows are independent from one another over time.
b. Find the $E\ (NPV)$ and standard deviation of $NPV$ given that the cash flows are perfectly positively correlated over time.
c. How does your answer to Part (b) compare to that a Part (a)? Explain.

15. Spider Enterprises is considering two mutually exclusive investment proposals. Both of the projects have two-year lives with their initial outlay at \$10,000. The probability distribution of cash flows for years 1 and 2 of the projects' lives are identical and given as follows:

| **Year 1** | | **Year 2** | |
|---|---|---|---|
| **Probability** | **Cash Flow** | **Probability** | **Cash Flow** |
| 0.1 | 4,000 | 0.3 | 4,000 |
| 0.8 | 6,000 | 0.4 | 6,000 |
| 0.1 | 8,000 | 0.3 | 8,000 |

Project A has a perfect correlation between the first and second year cash flow distributions while the correlation coefficient between the first and second year's cash flows for Project B is 0.5. The discount rate for this project is 8%.

a. Find the expected $NPV$ and standard deviation of the $NPV$ for Projects A and B.
b. The firm's existing assets have an expected $NPV$ of \$10,000 and a standard deviation of $NPV$ of \$5,000. The correlation coefficient between the cash flows of the existing assets and project A is 0.0 while the correlation coefficient between the existing assets and project B is 0.3. Find the $E\ (NPV)$ and standard deviation of $NPV$ for portfolios of:

   i. Project A and the existing assets.
   ii. Project B and the existing assets.

c. Should either project A or B be accepted? Explain.

16. Alpha Corporation is considering an investment which will be implemented in two stages if profitable. If Phase I is built now at a cost of \$5,000, high cash flows of \$5,000 for years 1 through

3 have an estimated 0.7 probability of occurrence, while low cash flows of $3,000 for years 1 through 3 have a 0.3 probability. At the end of year 3 Phase II can be implemented at a cost of $7,000. If the first three years' cash flows are high, it is estimated that Phase II will generate cash flows of $10,000 for years 4 through 10 with a 0.9 probability and $6,000 for years 4 through 10 with a 0.2 probability. On the other hand, if cash flows for years 1 through 3 are low and Phase II is implemented, then cash flows for years 4 through 10 have a 0.5 probability of being $4,000 and a 0.5 probability of being $1,000. If Phase II is not implemented at the end of year 3, then the cash flows earned in years 1 through 3 are estimated continue for years 4 through 10. Evaluate the project using the decision tree method. The discount rate for this project is 10%.

17. Please discuss five different capital budgeting decision methods under uncertainty.

**Table A** Variables for Simulation.

| Variables | Range |
|---|---|
| 1. Market size (units) | 2,500,000–3,000,000 |
| 2. Selling price ($/unit) | 40–60 |
| 3. Market growth | 0–6% |
| 4. Market share | 10–15% |
| 5. Total investment required ($) | 8,000,000–10,000,000 |
| 6. Useful life of facilities (years) | 5–9 |
| 7. Reside value of investment ($) | 1,000,000–2,000,000 |
| 8. Operating cost ($/unit) | 30–45 |
| 9. Fixed costs ($) | 400,000–500,000 |
| 10. Tax rate | 15% |
| 11. Discount rate | 6% |

*Source*: Lee and Lee (2017). *Financial Analysis, Planning and Forecasting*, page 683.

18. Simulation method for capital budgeting decision: Use the random number table, presented in Table 9.5 and variables for simulation presented in Table A to perform simulation.

1. Please perform five simulations for each variable as indicated in Table A.
   *Note*: Choose the first two digits from the nine random numbers in the first row of Table 9.5 to perform the first simulation. These random variables are 06, 80, 24, 18, 10, 05, 37, 48, and 02. Then, use the first two digits from the nine random numbers in the second row of Table 9.5 to perform the second simulation. Similarly, choose the first two digits from the nine random variables in the third, fourth, and fifth rows to perform simulation three, four, and five. Then, you need to create a table similar to Table 9.8.
2. Use the example of Table 9.9 to calculate cash flow for each simulation for five periods.
3. Calculate NPV for each simulation and obtain five NPVs.
4. Use five NPVs to calculate the mean value and standard deviation and perform interval estimate for this simulation analysis.

(b) Useful life of facilities is an integer indicated as below.

| **Random number** | **Years** |
|---|---|
| 01–19 | 5 |
| 20–39 | 6 |
| 40–59 | 7 |
| 60–79 | 8 |
| 80–99 | 9 |
| 00 | 10 |

# PART IV

# Cost of Capital, Financing Choices, and Dividend Decisions

# Chapter 10

# The Cost of Capital

## Contents



## 10.1 Introduction

Estimating the cost of capital is an important process in finance. First, the capital budgeting decision requires a reasonable estimate of the cost of capital. Second, many other business decisions, such as the issuance of bonds, the choice between purchasing or leasing a capital asset, and general investment policies, require an estimate of the cost of capital. Third, the aim of all financial managers is to maximize firm value through the minimization of costs, including the cost of capital. Therefore, the financial manager needs an accurate estimate of the cost of capital in many important financial decisions.

From an economic perspective, a firm's cost of capital is also an opportunity cost of funds. The rate of return required by an investor is the opportunity cost of investing in one project rather than another with equivalent risk. Various sources of funds include debt, preferred and common stock, and retained earnings. Each source represents varying amounts of risk and therefore requires varying rates of return in compensation. Additionally, a firm must be assured that an investment project undertaken with investors' money will be of greater value than the cost of these funds. Thus, the key issue in capital budgeting is to select investment projects that will compensate the providers of the various sources of funds for the risk undertaken and increase the wealth of the firm's shareholders. The cost of capital must be calculated in a manner consistent with these objectives.

In this chapter, we discuss several methods used to estimate the cost of capital. In Section 10.2, we compare the average earnings yield with the current earnings yield method. Section 10.3 discusses the discounted cash flow approach. In Section 10.4, we estimate the cost of the major components of the capital structure and form the weighted cost of capital. Section 10.5 covers the marginal cost of capital appraisal. Section 10.6 discusses Chase Manhattan model approach to cost of equity capital, and Section 10.7 provides a summary of the chapter. Appendix 10A discusses M&M Propositions 1 and 2, and Appendix 10B explores a mathematical approach to marginal cost of capital.

## 10.2 Average Earnings Yield Method Versus Current Earnings Yield Method

The *average earnings yield* is the most basic method used in estimating the cost of capital. It is related to the return on asset (ROA) ratio (net income divided by total assets). We use a valuation model proposed by Modigliani and Miller (1958), or M&M's Proposition 1, which defines the market value of a firm as

$$V = \frac{\bar{x}}{K} \tag{10.1}$$

where $\bar{x}$ = the average expected future earnings and $K$ = the cost of capital. Rearranging Eq. (10.1), we obtain an equation for the cost of capital:

$$K = \frac{\bar{x}}{V} \tag{10.2}$$

Average accounting earnings can be used as a measure for expected future earnings in Eq. (10.2) for firms in stable industries. This approach to the calculation of the cost of capital is similar to M&M's model, which is discussed later in this chapter.

The main weakness of the average earnings yield method is that the earnings growth rate is not explicitly incorporated into the cost of capital determination. This rate can be a large and significant variable in the case of growth firms. We can adjust for this by using the *current earnings yield* method. Lintner (1963) demonstrated that the current earnings yield is equal to the marginal cost of capital under conditions of certainty. Under uncertainty, a risk premium must be added to the marginal cost of capital estimate generated by the current earnings yield method. The current earnings yield method has not been very popular in terms of practical application, but it is useful nevertheless because it depicts the link between M&M's valuation theory and cost of capital determination.

The equation for current earnings yield is

$$Y = \frac{EPS}{P} \tag{10.3}$$

where $EPS$ = the current earnings per share and $P$ = the current price per share. This is the inverse of the price-earnings ratio, which is the market's assessment of the value of corporate earnings. Lintner derived the marginal cost of capital decision rule as

$$r > Y \text{ (Accept investment)} \tag{10.4}$$

where $r$ = the marginal internal rate of return on the investment project. Thus, Eq. (10.4) requires that an investment should not be accepted unless $r$ is larger than $Y$; that is, the yield of an investment must be greater than its cost of capital.

Lintner also showed that $Y$ is equal to the discount rate, $K$, as indicated by Eq. (10.2), in cases where profit opportunities are infinitely elastic such that there are constant returns to scale for investment.

Lintner also concluded that current earnings yield, with its inclusion of a growth variable, is more accurate and should be preferred to average earnings yield in estimating the cost of capital.

## 10.3 The Discounted Cash Flow Approach to Cost of Capital Determination

As we recall from Chapter 6, the discounted cash flow technique was developed to evaluate a project or investment by taking into consideration the time value of money. Essentially, the discounted cash flow (DCF) method is used to determine the cost of capital for a firm's retained earnings.

### 10.3.1 *Gordon dividend model*

The formula for deriving the cost of capital of retained earnings using the discount method is taken from the Gordon growth equation[1] for stock valuation, which was discussed in Chapter 5.

$$P_o = \frac{D_1}{K - g} \tag{10.5}$$

where $P_o$ = current price per share; $D_1$ = expected dividend per share (at beginning of the next period); $K$ = required rate of return for common equity; and $g$ = growth rate of dividends. Rearrangement of Eq. (10.5) yields an equation for the cost of equity capital, $K$,

$$K = \frac{D_1}{P_o} + g \tag{10.6}$$

where $D_1/P_o$ = current dividend yield. As you can see from Eqs. (10.5) and (10.6), $K$ can stand for either the required rate of return for common equity or the cost of equity capital.

---

[1]This originated with the constant growth model of J. B. Williams, *The Theory of Investment Value* (Cambridge: Harvard University Press, 1938).

In practice, a historical average value can be used to estimate the dividend per share or dividend yield indicated in Eq. (10.6).

### 10.3.2 *Growth rate*

While the dividend and price components of Eq. (10.6) are easily obtained from financial statements or financial newspapers, the estimation of the growth rate is more difficult. Generally, there are five methods to estimate the growth rates of dividends or earnings.[2]

The first of these methods is the simple growth rate between two successive periods, which is used to estimate the proportionate change in earnings per share (EPS):

$$g = \frac{EPS_t - EPS_{t-1}}{EPS_{t-1}} \tag{10.7}$$

where $EPS_t$ = earnings per share at time $t$; $EPS_{t-1}$ = earnings per share at time $t-1$; and $g$ = the estimate of the growth rate between period $t$ and $t-1$.

Equation (10.7) can be modified into the *arithmetic average*, where growth for short periods is estimated and averaged to derive a single growth estimate for the entire period:

$$\frac{g_1 + g_2 + \cdots + g_n}{n} = \bar{g} \tag{10.8}$$

where $g_1, g_2, \ldots, g_n$ = simple growth-rate estimates for each "short period" (say, 1 year); $\bar{g}$ = estimate of the average growth rate for the total period; and $n$ = number of growth rate estimates.

A third and slightly more accurate estimate can be obtained using the discrete compounded growth rate:

$$EPS_0(1+g)^n = EPS_n \tag{10.9}$$

Rearrangement yields an equation for the growth rate:

$$(1+g)^m = \frac{EPS_n}{EPS_0} \tag{10.10}$$

where $EPS_0$ and $EPS_n$ = earnings per share for periods 0 and $n$, and $n$ = time period used for compounding. Referring to the compound

[2]Brick *et al.* (2016) discussed alternative growth rate estimate in detail. In addition, Lee *et al.* (2011) and Chen *et al.* (2013) have also discussed the issue related to growth rate.

sum table in the back of this book, we can estimate $(1+g)^n$ and then $g$ itself.

When compound interest factors are not readily available, the compound growth rate can be found by taking the $n$th root of the interest factor, where $n$ equals the number of growth periods. This method is also called the *compound sum method of growth rate estimation*. The advantage of this method is its ease of understanding and calculation. However, it does not utilize all the information available. For example, if we have 10 years of EPS data for Companies A and B, the compound sum method uses only data from the first and tenth periods and ignores the data between these two periods.

Table 10.1 gives the 10-year EPS history of Company A and Company B and shows how their growth rates are calculated. Figure 10.1 approximately shows the 10-year growth paths of the two companies. Both companies begin and end at the same point, but A takes a much more even path than does B.

Table 10.1 Compound Growth Rate Estimation for Companies A and B.

| **Company A** | | **Company B** | |
|---|---|---|---|
| **Year** | **EPS** | **Year** | **EPS** |
| 0 | \$1.00 | 0 | \$1.00 |
| 1 | 1.10 | 1 | 1.20 |
| 2 | 1.21 | 2 | 1.21 |
| 3 | 1.33 | 3 | 1.72 |
| 4 | 1.46 | 4 | 1.46 |
| 5 | 1.67 | 5 | 2.48 |
| 6 | 1.77 | 6 | 1.77 |
| 7 | 1.94 | 7 | 3.58 |
| 8 | 2.14 | 8 | 2.14 |
| 9 | 2.36 | 9 | 5.15 |
| 10 | 2.59 | 10 | 2.59 |
| $(1+g)^{10} = \frac{EPS}{EPS} = \frac{2.59}{1}$ | | $(1+g)^{10} = \frac{EPS}{EPS} = \frac{2.59}{1}$ | |
| $g = 1.1 - 1$ | | $g = 1.1 - 1$ | |
| $g = 0.1 = 10\%$ | | $g = 0.1 = 10\%$ | |

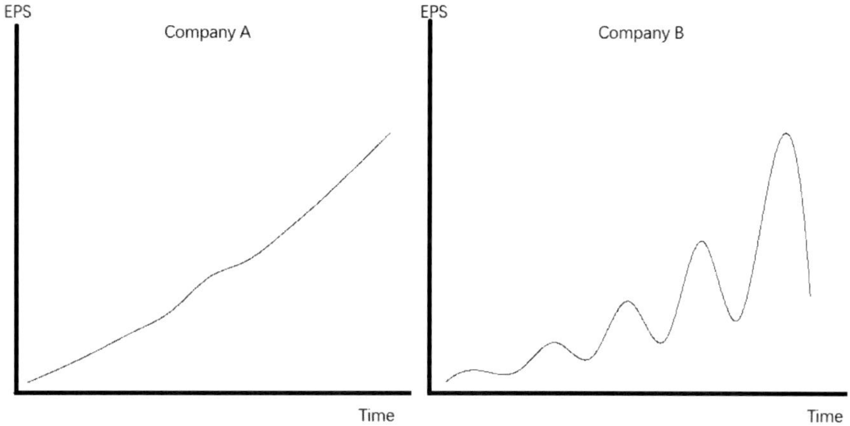


Figure 10.1 Compound Growth Rate Estimation for Companies A and B.

The fourth estimation procedure of the growth rate is obtained by using *ordinary least squares* (OLS) regression,[3] which yields growth rates for earnings per share or dividend per share. The equation is

$$LOG_e(EPS_t) = a_0 + a_1 t + \epsilon_t \tag{10.11}$$

or

$$= LOG_e(DPS_t) = b_0 + b_1 t + \epsilon_t \tag{10.12}$$

where $EPS_t$ = earnings per share at time $t$; $DPS_t$ = dividend per share at time $t$; $t$ = the time indicator $1, 2, \ldots, n$; $a_1$ and $b_1$ = the estimated growth rates for EPS and DPS; $a_0$ and $b_0$ = the intercept terms for EPS and DPS; and $\epsilon_t$ = the random error term.

The regression method includes all information rather than just the beginning and ending points used in the compound sum method. Also, a null hypothesis test can be performed to determine whether the growth rate, $a_1$ or $b_1$, obtained from the regression is statistically different from 0. Therefore, the regression method is more useful for

[3]Equation (10.11) utilizes continuous compounding, which can be derived in terms of the equation

$$\text{EPS}_t = \text{EPS}_{0e}^{gt}$$

The logarithmic transformation of this equation results in the regression Eq. (10.11) plus an error term.

Table 10.2 OLS Growth Rate Estimation Method.

| Company A | | Company B | |
|---|---|---|---|
| Year | EPS | Year | EPS |
| 0 | \$1.00 | 0 | \$1.00 |
| 1 | 1.10 | 1 | 1.20 |
| 2 | 1.21 | 2 | 1.21 |
| 3 | 1.33 | 3 | 1.72 |
| 4 | 1.46 | 4 | 1.46 |
| 5 | 1.67 | 5 | 2.48 |
| 6 | 1.77 | 6 | 1.77 |
| 7 | 1.94 | 7 | 3.58 |
| 8 | 2.14 | 8 | 2.14 |
| 9 | 2.36 | 9 | 5.15 |
| 10 | 2.59 | 10 | 2.59 |
| $\text{LOG}_e(\text{EPS}_t) = a_0 + a_1 t + \epsilon_t$ | | $\text{LOG}_e(\text{EPS}_t) = a_0 + a_1 t + \epsilon_t$ | |
| | $a_0 = 0.002$ | | $a_0 = 0.038$ |
| | $a_1 = 0.099 = 9.9\%$ | | $a_1 = 0.126 = 12.6\%$ |
| | $R^2 = 0.999$ | | $R^2 = 0.85$ |

the estimation of the growth rate, which is used in determining the cost of capital.

For Companies A and B, we can calculate the growth rates by the OLS method, as shown in Table 10.2.

The logarithms of the EPS or DPS observations are necessary to convert the constant percentage change in each time period from a nonlinear to a linear relationship.

Finally, an important and reliable source of estimated growth rates are analysts' expectations and earnings forecasts published by brokerage houses. These forecasts are usually based on internal rate of return on investment ($r$) and the firm's dividend retention ratio ($b$) as discussed in Chapter 5. An estimate of growth is $g = br$.

In general, when estimating cost of capital, the more different types of estimates we have, the better. This is especially true if the various techniques — which are based on different theories and use different types of information — provide similar estimates. However, if the various techniques yield widely different numbers, we are faced with the problem of deciding which estimate to rely on. This decision depends on the situation or case under consideration. Estimating a firm's cost of capital is an art, not a science. It is just as important to know which model is appropriate in a given circumstance (the art) as it is to know and understand the model or technique (the science).

## 10.4 The Weighted Cost of Capital

To calculate the *weighted average cost of capital* (WACC), you must first perform two fundamental procedures: (1) determine the relative proportions of various financial instruments in a firm' capital structure and (2) calculate the proper cost of each of these capital components. The first step is the determination of the components of a firm's financial structure — the *capital components*. These are found on the right-hand side of the balance sheet and consist of debt, preferred stock, retained earnings, and common equity. Given the accounting identity $A = L + E$ (assets equal liabilities plus equity), a net increase on the asset side of the balance sheet must be financed by an increase in one or more of the above capital components.

Each of the various components of a firm's financial structure has a unique cost for that particular type of capital. These component costs are explained in more detail below.

### 10.4.1 *Cost of debt*

The *component cost of debt* used in the calculation of the weighted average cost of capital is the marginal cost of debt (the cost of new debt), or, simply, the interest payment the firm must pay to attract investors to purchase its bonds. $K_B$ is this interest rate or yield to maturity that equates the present value of the amount borrowed with the future interest and principal repayments:

$$\mathrm{PV} = \sum_{t=1}^{N} \frac{\text{Interest}}{(1+K_B)^t} + \frac{\text{Principal}}{(1+K_B)^N} \tag{10.13}$$

where PV is the present value of the amount borrowed, and $K_B$ is the effective cost of debt.

Debt can be issued at a premium (greater than par value) or a discount (less than par value). Hence, the effective interest rate is determined by using Eq. (10.13) which takes into consideration the interest actually paid and the amount of funds the firm actually receives. The amount of funds received may differ from the par value of the debt or the face value of the principle, depending on whether the bonds were issued at a premium or at a discount. The actual component cost of debt also takes into account the corporate tax rate, because interest is a tax deductible expense. Therefore,

$$\text{Component cost of debt} = K_B(1 - \tau_c) \tag{10.14}$$

where $\tau_c$ = firm's corporate tax rate.

For example, if a firm obtains a loan at an effective interest rate of 12% and its annual tax rate is 30%, then its after-tax cost of debt is 8.4%:

$$K_B(1 - \tau_c) = 0.12(1 - 0.3) = 0.12(0.7) = 8.4\%$$

The tax adjustment must be made to the debt component cost because the component cost of the firm's equity is based on the firm's after-tax income. In effect, the federal government is subsidizing a firm for a portion of its interest charges. Therefore, the effective interest rate must be adjusted to take into account the preferential tax treatment (tax subsidy) derived from the use of debt.

### 10.4.2 *The cost of retained earnings and new equity*

The cost of debt is based on the return that bondholders require from their investment in the firm's bonds. The cost of equity through retained earnings, $K_{R/E}$, is the rate of return stockholders require on the firm's common stock. This opportunity cost concept is based on the argument that if the firm can reinvest its earnings at a rate superior to the next-best opportunity the stockholders have, then the stockholders' wealth will be increased by the firm's reinvestment of the stockholders' funds.

In equilibrium, the shareholders' required rate of return equals the expected rate of return of new investment, $K_{R/E}$. This expected rate of return on a share of common stock depends on the dividends that are paid on the stock. If these dividends are expected to grow at a constant rate, then we can use the Gordon dividend model.

$$P_o = \frac{D_1}{K_{\frac{R}{E}} - g} \tag{10.15}$$

where $P_o$ = the current price of the stock; $D_1$ = the dividend expected to be paid at end of period 1; $K_{R/E}$ = the expected rate of return; and $g$ = the growth rate of the dividend.

Equation (10.15) can be reduced to the following expression, which is the expected rate of return on common equity:

$$K_{R/E} = \frac{D_1}{P_o} + \text{Expected}\, g \tag{10.16}$$

Equation (10.16) states that investors expect to receive a dividend yield of $D_1/P_o$ (percent) and a capital gain yield of $g$, or a total expected return of $K_{R/E}$.

To illustrate, a firm's stock is currently selling at \$26 per share, with an expected dividend of \$1.50 per share and an expected growth rate of 7%. Therefore, the firm's expected and required rate of return, and hence its cost of retained earnings, would be

$$K_{R/E} = \frac{\$1.50}{\$26} + 7\% = 5.77\% + 7\% = 12.77\%$$

which is the minimum rate of return management must expect to receive from its equity-financed portion of investments to justify using the company's retained earnings rather than paying them out at as dividends to the stockholders.

The purpose for assigning an opportunity cost to retained earnings is to force the firm's managers to consider the options available to the stockholders. If the firm can use the funds more productively than the stockholders can, then stockholders would be willing to reinvest their earnings in the firm. Up to this point, we have not explicitly included the personal tax situation of each stockholder in the discussion of the cost of retained earnings and whether the mangers should pay out dividends or reinvest the firm's earnings. This complication is considered in detail in Chapter 12.

To calculate the cost of new equity, we adjust the cost of retained earnings ($K_{R/E}$) for any flotation costs associated with the issuance of the new shares of stock. Given the cost of retained earnings, the cost of new equity is

$$K_{NE} = \frac{K_{R/E}}{1 - f} \tag{10.17}$$

where $f$ is the flotation cost of the new equity issue in decimal form. For the firm whose $K_{R/E}$ was calculated at 12.77% in the previous example, if we assume flotation costs of 4% for the issuance of new equity, the cost of the new equity is

$$K_{NE} = \frac{12.77}{1 - 0.04} = 13.3\%$$

which is the minimum rate of return management must expect to earn from its investment to justify the issuance of new shares of stock.

### 10.4.3 *Cost of preferred stock*

The calculation of the *component cost of preferred stock* used in the weighted average cost of capital is similar to the formula used to calculate the cost of retained earnings. The calculation is the preferred dividend, $D_P$, divided by the issuance price, $P_o$, (the net price after deducting flotation costs) or

$$K_P = \frac{D_P}{P_o} \tag{10.18}$$

To illustrate, a firm pays a \$13 dividend per share on its preferred stock, which has a market value of \$100 per share. Issuance of new stock will incur an underwriting cost of 3.2%, or \$3.20 per share. Therefore, the net funds received by the firm would be \$96.80 per share. The cost of preferred stock would then be

$$K_P = \frac{\$13}{\$96.80} = 13.43\%$$

Unlike the cost of debt, no tax adjustments are made with the cost of preferred stock because preferred dividends, unlike interest payments, are not tax deductible.

### 10.4.4 *The logic and procedure of weighted cost of capital*

The second set of calculations needed to determine the WACC involves finding the appropriate weights for each capital component. Each component is weighted in proportion to its market value and to the total market value of the firm's assets, in accordance with the equation

$$W_i = \frac{\text{Market value of outstanding component } i}{\text{Total market value of the firm's assets}} \tag{10.19}$$

where $i$ = the $i$th particular capital component. To determine the firm's total WACC, the component costs ($K$) that were previously calculated are multiplied by the respective weights and summed for all components:

$$\text{WACC} = \sum_{i=1}^{m} W_i K_i \tag{10.20}$$

where $i$ = the $i$th capital component (convertible debt, regular debt, new preferred stock, new common stock, retained earnings, etc.) and $m$ = the total number of capital components included.

Equation (10.20) can be expanded to include other types of securities that have an impact on the firm's cost of capital, such as short-term debt, warrants, and options. However, in most cases, only long-term, permanent sources of capital are used in calculating the WACC in Eq. (10.20). This is because we are interested in getting a fairly stable measure of the marginal cost of funds.

The logic behind the weighted average cost of capital principle is that when estimating the cost of capital for any capital budgeting project, the firm should be viewed as a going concern (the firm will continue operating indefinitely for the foreseeable future). Therefore, each capital component should not be strictly considered as a separate entity, because most investments will be financed by a package of capital components rather than by a single source of financing. For a particular firm, the after-tax cost of debt is 10.5%, while its cost of equity is 14%. If a decision is made to finance its new investments by using only debt, then the firm's cost of capital would be 10.5%, or its expected cost of debt. If the firm is considered a going concern, using only debt on this investment project would decrease the firm's debt capacity. If the firm continues to expand, then at some point it will have depleted its debt capacity and must turn to equity financing. At this point, if a project is available with an expected return of 13%, the project would be acceptable in terms of debt financing but unacceptable in terms of equity financing. Hence, the linkage of specific financing to individual projects leads to suboptimal investment decisions, which reduces firm value.

To avoid this problem, the first should be viewed as an ongoing concern and use a cost of capital estimate that reflects all of the various types of funds that the firm will be using to finance its operations.

In our discussion so far, we have made two crucial assumptions: (1) market values and book values are equal, and (2) the historical capital structure is optimal and will be maintained by future financing decisions. When actually using this approach to estimate the WACC and there is a divergence between the market values of the firm's various securities and their book values, the analyst should use the market values. Likewise, if the historic capital structure is not optimal or the firm's management has decided to change the capital structure, the future target capital structure should be used instead of the historic one.

**Example 10.1.** The information in Table 10.3 is from First Chicago Corporation's annual report in 1986. The weighted average cost of capital can be easily calculated from this information, if we assume that the firm will finance its future investments in the same proportion as its current capital structure.[4] The firm's marginal tax rate is 46%. The WACC is calculated to be 8.31%.

## 10.5 The Marginal Cost of Capital (MCC)

The marginal cost of capital (MCC) is a very useful measure for the financial manager. One way of maximizing the firm value is to

[4]Such items as required reserves, liquidity reserves, processing costs, and service fees are ignored for the sake of simplicity in this example. Please note that this bank no longer exists.

Table 10.3 Components of Cost of Capital.

| Capital | Weight $W_i$ | Cost $K_i$(%) |
|---|---|---|
| Preferred stock | 0.008 | 10.00 |
| Common stock | 0.0128 | 8.80 |
| Retained earnings | 0.029 | 8.61 |
| Long-term debt | 0.200 | 8.48 |
| Time deposits | | |
| Savings | 0.068 | 5.20 |
| Other | 0.116 | 12.90 |
| Other deposits | 0.472 | 12.76 |
| Borrowed funds | 0.275 | 12.21 |
| | 1.000 | |

$$\begin{aligned}\text{WACC} = \sum_{i=1}^{m} W_i K_i &= 0.008(10\%) + (0.0128)(8.8\%) + (0.029)(8.61)\\ &+ (0.20)(8.48\%)(1-0.46) + (0.068)(5.2\%)(1-0.46)\\ &+ (0.116)(12.90\%)(1-0.46) + (0.472)(12.76\%)(1-0.46)\\ &+ (0.275)(12.21\%)(1-0.46) = 8.31\%\end{aligned}$$

minimize the firm's cost of capital. To achieve this goal, the manager must be able to measure the MCC. Another application of the MCC is to use it as the discount rate in the NPV method when making capital budgeting decisions. For regulated industries, such as utilities, cost of capital is significant in determining the fair rate that the utility can charge its customers.

*Marginal cost* can be defined as the additional cost of another unit. For example, the marginal cost of labor is the cost of adding another additional worker, the marginal cost of production is the cost of producing one more unit of goods. Similarly, the marginal cost of capital is the additional cost of obtaining a dollar of new funds. Thus, the marginal cost of capital is the cost of getting each dollar of new capital. As with other marginal costs, the marginal cost increases as more new capital is obtained.

Figure 10.2 shows a representation of the marginal cost of capital and the average cost of capital. Instead of the more familiar smooth curves representing marginal and average costs, both the MCC and the ACC are represented by discrete intervals. Initially, the MCC equals the ACC, but as the marginal cost

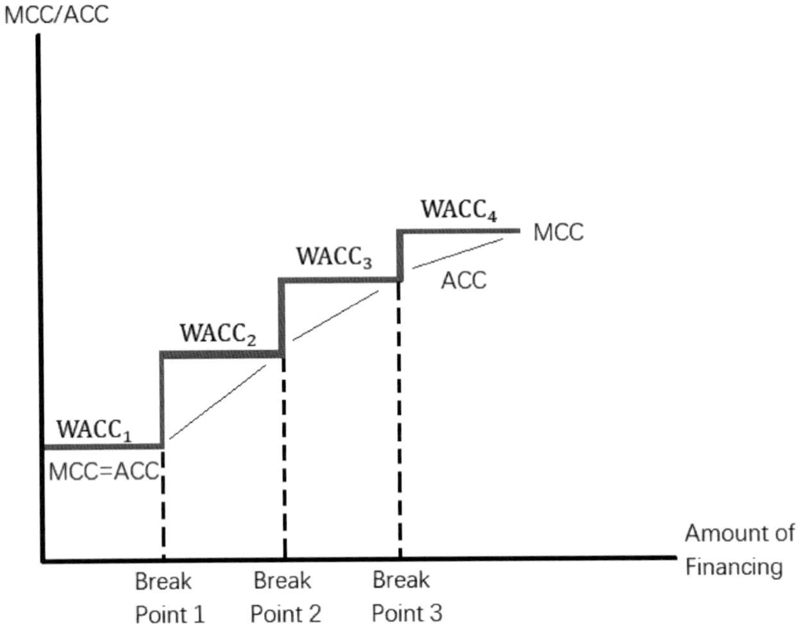


Figure 10.2 Marginal Cost of Capital (MCC) and Average Cost of Capital (ACC).

increases in discrete intervals, the average cost increases by a smaller amount. Each of the MCC intervals represents a package of financing, with component cost ($K$) weighted at the firm's optimal, or target, capital structure. In effect, we can have a WACC for each interval, as shown by $\text{WACC}_1$, $\text{WACC}_2$, etc., in Figure 10.2. Unfortunately, the WACC includes the word *average* and thus may be confused with the ACC. In reality, a more concise terminology would be *weighted average of the marginal costs of each interval.* Clearly, the WACC is different from the ACC in Figure 10.2.

Lintner (1963) showed that the differences between average earnings yield and current earnings yield is the marginal cost of capital. Current earnings yield reflects economies of scale that may result from changes in the economy or management.

To illustrate the calculation of the marginal cost of capital, we will use firm L whose capital structure and other market value data are given below.

| | | |
|---|---|---|
| Debt | \$2,500,000 | 25% |
| Preferred | 1,250,000 | 12.5 |
| Common (250,000 shares × \$25 per share) | 6,250,000 | 62.50 |
| Total value | \$10,000,000 | 100% |

For our calculations, $P_o = \$25$; $D_o = \$1.256$ (dividends per share paid in the previous period; an investor purchasing stock today would receive the next dividend, $D_1$); $g = 8\%$, the expected constant growth rate; $K_{R/E}$ = cost of retained earnings ($D_1/P_o + g = D_o(1+g)/P_o+g = \$1.356/\$25+.08 = .05+.08 = 13\%$); $K_B$ = interest rate on new debt (before tax) = 12%; $K_P$ = cost of preferred stock (before tax) = 12%; and $\tau_c = 30\%$.

Based on the above data, the weighted average cost of capital, similar to the WACC shown in Figure 10.2, is

$$\begin{aligned} WACC &= (\text{Fraction of debt}) \times (\text{Interest rate})(1 - \text{Tax rate}) \\ &\quad + (\text{Fraction of preferred capital}) \times (\text{Cost of preferred}) \\ &\quad + (\text{Fraction of common equity}) \times (\text{Cost of equity}) \\ &= 0.25(12\%)0.7) + (0.125)(12\%) + (0.625)(13\%) \\ &= 2.1\% + 1.50\% + 8.125\% = 11.725\% \end{aligned}$$

Assuming the firm's current capital structure is optimal (that is, current weights are equal to management's target weights), it calls for 25% debt, 12.5% preferred stock, and 62.5% equity. Therefore, each new marginal dollar raised will be comprised of 25 cents of debt, 12.5 cents of preferred stock, and 62.5 cents of equity. This maintains the firm's optimal capital structure in the current proportion of debt, preferred stock, and equity. As long as the firm's after-tax cost of debt remains 8.4%, cost of preferred stock at 12%, and cost of equity at 13%, its marginal cost of capital for each new dollar of capital will be constant at 11.725%. However, firm L cannot raise unlimited quantities of capital at 11.725%. As a company raises larger sums of capital, its component costs (the cost of debt, preferred stock, and common equity) rise, producing a corresponding rise in the weighted average cost of capital. Given an increase in any or all of the component costs, the cost of each new dollar will be greater than 11.725%, and the weighted average cost of capital will be $WACC_2$ as shown in Figure 10.2. Just where this point occurs is discussed next.

Suppose firm L's capital budget calls for an additional $1 million for new investment in the coming year. The capital will be raised to maintain the capital structure of 25% debt to 12.5% preferred stock and 62.5% common equity. Therefore, the company would obtain $250,000 in debt, $125,000 in preferred stock, and $625,000 in common equity. There are two sources of equity: (1) it can be raised by issuing new common stock or (2) the firm may choose to retain its earnings of the previous year.

The debt will have an after-tax cost of 8.4% (a pretax cost of 12%). The preferred stock has a cost of 12%, and the cost of common equity through retained earnings is 13%. Equity through the issuance of new common stock will be higher because of flotation costs. Suppose the flotation cost ($f$) is 7%. The cost of equity would then increase to

$$K_{NE} = \frac{K_{\frac{R}{E}}}{(1-f)} = \frac{0.13}{0.93} = 14\%$$

L's weighted average cost of capital using retained earnings or common equity is as follows:

$WACC_1$, or MCC, Using Retained Earnings of Equity

| Component | Weight | Component Cost (%) | Product (%) |
|---|---|---|---|
| Debt | 0.25 | 8.4 | 2.10 |
| Preferred | 0.125 | 12.0 | 1.50 |
| Common | 0.625 | 13.0 | 8.125 |
| | 1.00 | | 11.725 |

$WACC_2$, or MCC, Using Issuance of New Common Stock as Equity

| Component | Weight | Component Cost (%) | Product (%) |
|---|---|---|---|
| Debt | 0.25 | 8.4 | 2.10 |
| Preferred | 0.125 | 12.0 | 1.50 |
| Common | 0.625 | 14.0 | 8.750 |
| | 1.00 | | 12.35 |

The weighted average cost of capital, or the marginal cost of capital, for each new dollar is 11.725% if the firm uses its retained earnings, but jumps to 12.35% if the firm issues new common stock.

When will the company run out of retained earnings and be forced to issue new stock? This is the *break point*, which we now discuss in detail.

Suppose the firm expects earnings of \$750,000 next year and its payout ratio is 0.40; that is, it expects to pay out 40% of these earnings as dividends. This leaves \$750,000 (1 – 0.4) = \$450,000 to be added to the firm's retained earnings for the year. How much financing can the firm afford with retained earnings of \$450,000 combined with its debt and preferred stock capacity before being forced to issue new common stock? This is the break point. Since 62.5% represents the new retained earnings, then

$$0.625X = P \text{ retained earnings} = \$450{,}000 \text{ or}$$

$$X = \frac{450{,}000}{0.625} = \$720{,}000 = \text{Break point}$$

Therefore, as the firm raises \$720,000, of which \$450,000 is retained earnings and \$270,000 (720,000 – 450,000) consists of preferred stock and new debt, the firm will be able to retain its capital structure and a marginal cost of 11.725%. The \$270,000 can be broken down to its components of \$720,000 (0.125) = \$90,000 of preferred stock and \$720,000 (0.25) = \$180,000 of debt.

However, if firm L raises \$720,001 instead of \$720,000, the last dollar will require 62.5 cents derived from issuing common stock instead of from retained earnings. The resulting marginal cost is 12.35% instead of 11.725%, as calculated in the table.

Break points occur whenever a component of the cost of capital rises. Suppose firm L can only obtain \$350,000 of 12% debt. If any additional debt costs 14%, the next break point would be

$$\text{Break point for debt} = \frac{\text{Amount of lower cost debt}}{\text{Debt as percentage of capital}}$$

$$= \frac{\$350{,}000}{0.25} = \$1{,}400{,}000$$

This formula can be written in a more general form and applied to any capital component used in the calculation of the marginal

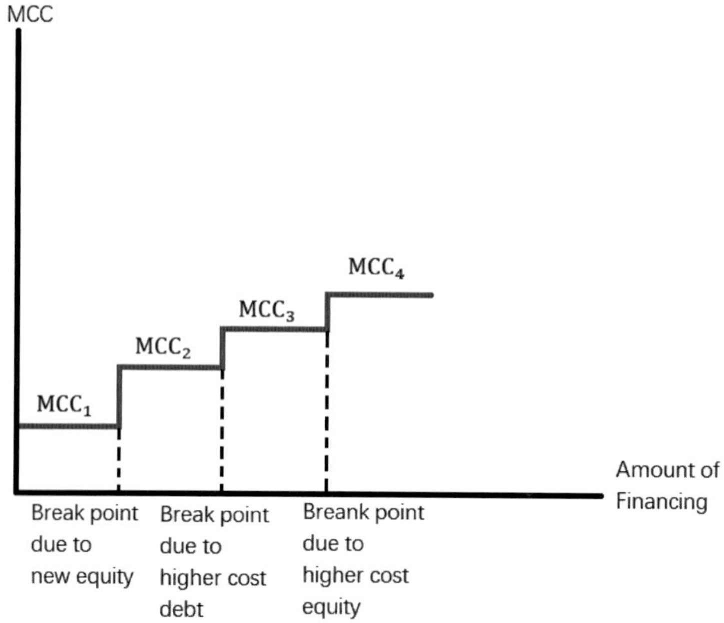


Figure 10.3 Marginal Cost Capital Schedule.

Cost of debt:

$$\text{Break point for MCC schedule} = \frac{\text{Total amount of lower cost capital component}}{\text{Percentage of total capital the component represents}}$$

Break points can occur if interest rates rise, if the costs of preferred stock rise, or the cost of issuing common stock rises with increases in the number of shares issued. An illustration of these breaks may look like Figure 10.3, which is called the *marginal cost of capital schedule.*

Conceivably, break points can occur continuously with constant new financing. In this case, the marginal cost of capital schedule would look like that shown in Figure 10.4. (A mathematical approach to the determination of the MCC is presented in Appendix 10B.)

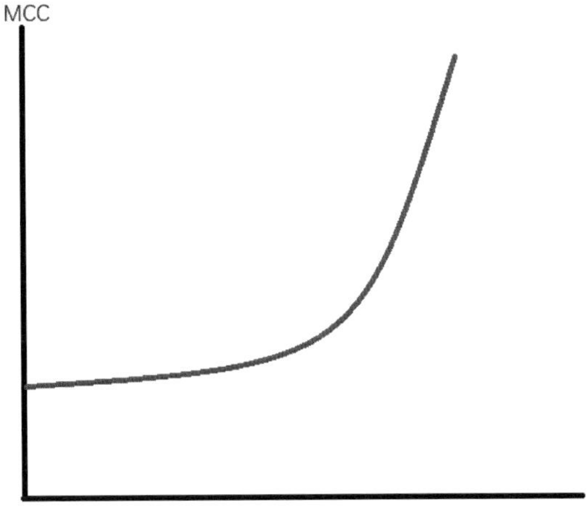


Figure 10.4 Continuous MCC Schedule.

## 10.6 The Chase Manhattan Model Approach to Cost of Equity Capital

In this section, we show how the capital asset pricing model, discussed in Chapter 8, can be combined with information on market returns and risks to calculate a firm's cost of equity capital. The Chase Manhattan model, or the Chase cost of equity capital, integrates the CAPM and M&M theories of cost of capital, thereby making them more realistically applicable in the business world.

### 10.6.1 *The CAPM approach to cost of equity capital estimation*

Because the CAPM expressed the required rate of return for an investment in terms of its level of market risk, the CAPM can also be used to determine the required rate of return (or the cost of equity capital) for a proposed investment project. The CAPM can be defined as

$$E(R_i) = R_f + [E(R_m) - R_f]\beta_i \tag{10.21}$$

where $R_i$ = the expected rate of return or cost of equity of investment $i$; $R_f$ = the risk-free rate of return; $R_m$ = the market return; and $\beta_i$ = the beta coefficient for risky asset $i$.

To use Eq. (10.21) as an estimate of cost of equity capital, we need two estimates. The first is the risk-free rate. For this we can use the short-term current interest rate on Treasury bills. The second is the market rate of return, $R_m$. Market indexes such as the Dow Jones 30, Standard and Poor's 500, or any other acceptable indicator can be used as a measure. We illustrate the use of the CAPM cost of equity capital method in Example 10.2.

**Example 10.2.** The following information is from Johnson & Johnson. For October 2018, Johnson & Johnson's computed beta (three-year monthly estimation from Yahoo Finance) was 0.7. And the market return (S&P 500 index) in the corresponding month is 2.16%, while the 4-week Treasury bill rate is 1.55%.

The cost of equity capital, as calculated by the CAPM, is

$$E(R_i) = R_f + [E(R_m) - R_f]\beta_i = 1.55\% + (2.16 - 1.55)(0.7) = 1.98\%$$

The CAPM calculates a cost of equity capital of 16.18% for First Chicago, which is a rather high estimate because it incorporates a bullish market return. This and other market assumptions are a weakness associated with the CAPM. Other assumptions include no taxes or transaction costs (perfect markets), no anticipated inflation, many buyers and sellers, and investor perception of the same efficient frontier. As is evident, transaction costs and tax costs have a great impact on the cost of equity capital an must be considered in its calculation.

### 10.6.2 *Levered beta ($\beta_L$) versus unlevered beta ($\beta_U$)*

In general, the beta obtained from the market model is influenced by the effects of leverage (long-term debt). To estimate the cost of capital without the leverage effect, Hamada (1972) and Lee (2017) have formulated the equity

$$\beta_L = \beta_U \left[1 + \frac{B}{S}(1 - \tau_c)\right] \tag{10.22}$$

where $\beta_L$ = beta coefficient with leverage effect; $\beta_U$ = beta coefficient without the leverage effect; $B/S$ = leverage ratio; $B$ = debt; $S$ = equity; and $\tau_c$ = corporate tax rate.

Given Eq. (10.22), if we calculate $\beta_L$ from the market model and obtain $B/S$ from market information, then we can solve for $\beta_U$. We can best illustrate Eq. (10.22) with an example.

**Example 10.3.** A packaging company has a beta of 1.2 and finances its investments through equity only. Its current equity market value is $1,629,200. The company needs additional funds of $1,005,900 to finance a new packaging line and plant but management feels it can no longer use equity. Therefore, these funds will be generated through debt. The company's new beta coefficient or risk measure is found as follows:

$$\beta_U = \frac{\beta_L}{[1 + \frac{B}{S}(1 - \tau_c)]} = \frac{(1.20)}{(1 + \frac{1{,}005.9}{1{,}629.2})}$$
$$= (1.2)/(1 + 0.617) = (1.2)(0.618) = 0.74$$

From Example 10.3, we can see that $\beta_U$ is less than $\beta_L$, which implies that a company that uses leverage can increase its systematic risk level and thereby increase its cost of capital. Hence, there are two types of beta coefficients: one including debt and another without debt.

In this section, we have demonstrated the indirect impact of leverage on the CAPM and its beta coefficient. Senbet and Taggart (1984) have explicitly incorporated the effects of leverage into the CAPM. Their model is based on the assumption that the corporate borrower can obtain funds at lower rates than can the individual investor. Qualitatively, Senbet and Taggart's results are identical to the models discussed in this chapter thus far. However, quantitatively, their results are much more complex, and are discussed at a more advanced level of corporate finance.

### 10.6.3 *The chase approach to cost of equity capital estimation*

The financial analysis and planning group at the Chase Manhattan Bank developed a realistic method for estimating the cost of equity capital (See Stern (1980) for details). Conceptually, the Chase method combines the M&M theories with the CAPM theory to derive a theoretical and empirical compromise for cost of equity capital estimation.

The Chase method is not only practically useful in the real world but is also a useful procedure for the beginning finance student.

To derive its estimate of the levered equity cost of capital, Chase Manhattan uses three variables:

1. A present period estimate of the long-term government bond yield.
2. The premium for risk expected to be earned on all stocks on the NYSE over the government bond yield to compensate investors for the higher risk they bear.
3. The expected beta ($\beta$) on the company's common shares. Beta is the index that measures the relative risk of a particular security or stock against the average of all stocks on the NYSE.

The first two data requirements can be met by using current information from today's financial markets or by using long-run historical information gathered over many years. The actual choice of which kind of information is most representative is left to the financial analyst. If the analyst feels that the current market condition is representative of the near future, then current market information is the best choice. On the other hand, if the analyst feels that the future will be more like long-run past trends rather than to current market conditions, then long-run historical averages are the more meaningful.

The Chase method (CM) bases its estimate of the levered equity cost of capital on both past data — by deriving a company's beta based on past market behavior — and forecasts of long-term financial data — by using long-term bond yields and risk premiums.

After obtaining the necessary company, industry, and market information, CM then uses a modified version of the M&M valuation equation to arrive at an estimate of the pure equity cost of capital. We start with an expression for the firm's value

$$V = \frac{NOPAT}{C} + \tau_c B \tag{10.23}$$

where $NOPAT$ = the unlevered net operating after-tax profit of the company; $C$ = the pure equity cost of capital; $\tau_c$ = the corporate tax rate; and $B$ = the market value of debt.

Equation (10.23) is the M&M Proposition 1 with tax case and is discussed in more detail in Appendix 10A of this chapter. However, the first term on the right-hand side of the equation is the firm's market value without leverage effects. In Chapter 5, we discussed how a firm's market value can be determined by its appropriate discount rate. Essentially, this term also assumes that the firm has no growth or leverage effects in its calculation of market value.

The second term on the right-hand side $\tau_c B$ represents the tax shield effect associated with issuing debt. Conceptually, this term is consistent with the reasoning we developed in the WACC section that debt use must be adjusted for the tax advantage of interest payments.

CM then substitutes an equivalent expression for the value of the firm ($V$):

$$V = S + B \tag{10.24}$$

where $S =$ the market value of equity. Substituting Eq. (10.23) into Eq. (10.24), we get

$$S + B = \frac{NOPAT}{C} + \tau_c B \tag{10.25}$$

or equivalently

$$NOPAT = C(S + B - \tau_c B) \tag{10.26}$$

Using Eq. (10.26), CM further defines the levered cost of equity ($Y$) as the normalized net earnings ($NE$) divided by the stockholder's equity ($S$) or

$$Y = \frac{NE}{S} = \frac{NOPAT - \bar{i}B(1 - \tau_c)}{S} \tag{10.27}$$

where $\bar{i} =$ the average rate of interest on company debt; $NOPAT =$ the income of an unlevered firm; and $NE =$ the normalized net earnings of a levered firm (interest payments on debt and tax shield adjustments). By *normalized*, or *smoothed out*, we imply that transitory components of accounting income have been removed through statistical adjustments. In other words, normalized income contains only the permanent portion of accounting earnings. We have broken down the numerator on the right-hand side of Eq. (10.27) to provide a better understanding of what the shareholders are entitled to:

$$\underset{\text{(Unlevered income)}}{\underline{NOPAT}} - \underset{\text{(Interest payment on debt)}}{\underline{\bar{i}B}} + \underset{\text{(Tax shield factor)}}{\underline{\bar{i}B\tau_c}} \tag{10.28}$$

The concept of Eq. (10.27) needs further explanation. Following the accounting identity, a levered firm's value is $V = S + B$. Therefore, the value of an unlevered firm is $V = S$. Since $NE$ has been adjusted for both leverage and tax effects, a company's market value without leverage can be defined as $NE/Y = E$. In other words, $Y$ is similar to $C$ as defined in Eq. (10.23). Substituting Eq. (10.26) into Eq. (10.27), we get

$$Y = \frac{C(S + B - \tau_c B) - \bar{i}B(1 - \tau_c)}{S} \tag{10.29}$$

Solving for $C$ results in the unlevered firm's cost of equity:

$$C = \frac{Y + (1 - \tau_c)\left(\frac{B}{S}\right)\bar{i}}{1 + (1 - \tau_c)\left(\frac{B}{S}\right)} \tag{10.30}$$

With the derivation of (10.30), we have shown how M&M Proposition 1 with tax can be combined with accounting information and other related data to determine the cost of capital with leverage effects.

We have seen that $C$ and $Y$ represent the cost of capital without and with leverage, respectively. This distinction is similar to the one in the previous section when we calculated the cost of capital using the CAPM.

In general, the CAPM approach is more acceptable in determining cost of capital because the effects of risk diversification have been directly incorporated into the CAPM.

In the calculation of Eq. (10.30), CM uses the following:

1. The marginal federal and state income tax over the previous 5 years of the company's operations.

2. The historic debt-to-equity ratio, or the average short-term plus long-term debt (including capitalized leases) divided by equity, deferred items, and minority interest during the previous 5 years.
3. To estimate $\bar{i}$, we can use average interest rate on short-term and long-term debt over the last 5 years.

To take leverage and tax effects into account for a particular project, the financial manager should first determine the company's target debt-equity ratio, then finance new projects and investments while maintaining this target ratio.

The cost of capital adjusted for tax and the target leverage effect is defined as

$$C^* = C\left[1 - (\tau_c)\left(\frac{B^*}{V^*}\right)\right] \tag{10.31}$$

where $V^*$ = the future projected capital employed; $B^*$ = the target total debt for the firm; $C^*$ = the cost of capital adjusted for tax and the target leverage effect; and $\tau_c$ = the corporate tax rate.

This equation is conceptually understandable, but its mathematical derivation can be quite tedious. For more detailed information, refer to M&M (1966) or Lee (2017). The most important implication for the cost of capital is $B^*/V^*$, which M&M (1963) refer to as "the firm's long-run target debt ratio."

So far, we have only discussed the first half of the CM approach to the cost of capital. CM also incorporates the CAPM for its cost of capital derivation. For example, if long-term government bonds are yielding 10%, the premium required for common stocks over the bond yield is 6% and the relative risk (the beta coefficient) of the stock is 0.95, then $Y$ (the cost of equity capital, including historical financial risk), is as follows:

$$E(R_i) = R_f + [E(R_M) - R_f]\beta_i \tag{10.32}$$

or

$$Y_i = R_f + (\beta_i)(PM) \tag{10.33}$$

where $Y_i$ = the cost of equity capital for the $i$th firm with leverage and $PM$ = the market risk premium. Therefore,

$$Y = 10\% + 0.95(6\%) = 15.7\%$$

This is a prediction of equity cost based on past risk characteristics. In the second step, that portion of the risk attached to the past debt ratio or financial risk is removed to determine $C$, the cost of capital based on business risk alone. This cost of equity capital is a fundamental characteristic of the risk the firm faces in its particular kind of business and will continue unless the firm's business changes significantly or assumes a different risk characteristic due to an economic or technological change. The equation that takes into account these changes is derived from the cost of equity capital given in Eq. (10.4A) of Appendix 10A, in which debt financing is the sum of the return required for business risk plus the return required for financial risk, or

$$Y = C + (1 - \tau_c)(C - \bar{i})\left(\frac{B}{S}\right) \tag{10.34}$$

where $C$ = the cost of equity capital without debt; $\tau_c$ = the marginal tax rate over the past five years; $\bar{i}$ = the average interest rate on all debt over the past five years; and $B/S$ = the average total debt to total equity over the past five years. (Debt includes capitalized leases and equity includes deferred items and minority interest.)

Equation (10.34) is the M&M Proposition 2 model with tax as is discussed in Appendix 10A. This equation states that cost of equity with debt = cost of equity without debt + risk premium associated with leverage. Equation (10.34) can be rearranged to solve for $C$. The result is Eq. (10.30):

$$C = \frac{Y + (1 - \tau_c)\left(\frac{B}{S}\right)\bar{i}}{1 + (1 - \tau_c)\left(\frac{B}{S}\right)}$$

If the marginal tax rate is 30%, $B/S$ averages 60%, and the interest rate is 9% over the last five years, then $C$ — the cost of capital for business risk alone (without any debt) — can be calculated as

$$C = \frac{15.7\% + (1 - 0.3)(0.60)(9\%)}{1 + (1 - 0.3)(0.60)} = \frac{15.7\% + 3.78\%}{1 + 0.42} = \frac{18.61}{1.42} = 13.7\%$$

Alternatively, the cost of equity without debt can be calculated directly from the CAPM, as we have shown in the previous section. Thus, $\beta_U$, calculated by Eq. 10.22, can be substituted for the beta variable in the CAPM model.

In the third step, the total cost of capital, $C$, is calculated by factoring in the projected financial risk based on the leverage debt ratio, $B^*/V^*$, which is expected in the future. The result will always be less than $C$ for prudent levels of debt, because the after-tax cost of debt (which is lower than the cost of equity) lowers the total cost of capital, $C^*$, despite the higher risk of debt financing. If $B/S$ is expected to be 40%, then $C^*$ is as follows:

$$\begin{aligned} C^* &= C\left[1-(\tau_c)\left(\frac{B^*}{V^*}\right)\right] \\ &= 13.7\%[1-(0.3)(0.40)] = 13.7\%(0.88) = 12.06\% \end{aligned}$$

The target debt ratio comprises total debt plus capitalized leases divided by total debt plus capitalized leases plus equity plus deferred items plus minority interest. This is useful information for the investor because it is important in setting the cost of capital rate, $C^*$, which the firm uses to discount future earnings to estimate the intrinsic value of the company's stock. If the company does not publicly announce its target debt ratio, the investor must decide on the debt ratio the company will have in the future. Without some knowledge of the company's intentions regarding future capital spending and dividend payouts, the investor will feel some uncertainty about the firm and will discount future earnings more heavily as a result of this uncertainty. Investors may bid up the price of the company's stock if more information about capital spending, profitability of new investment, and target debt levels are available.

The initial information needed to calculate the cost of capital is largely market determined. The estimate of the long-term government bond yield may be obtained from banks and investment houses. The risk premium for average stocks over the bond yield is judgmental and subjective, based partially on the historic premium over a period of years. However, it is also based on current opinions of the future, with its additional risks of increased government spending and higher levels of inflation. (Merrill Lynch and Value Line have computed betas for stocks listed on the New York Stock Exchange and other exchanges, which investors may purchase for a fee.)

The Chase Manhattan technique can also be used to estimate the cost of capital for a division or subsidiary of the firm. In this case, the beta for the division or subsidiary may not be directly observable, so we would need to use a pure play technique.

The pure play technique attempts to identify firms that are publicly traded and are engaged solely in the same line of business as the division or the subsidiary. The beta for the publicly traded firm is used as a proxy for the division or subsidiary, and the cost of capital is then determined. This assumes that the substitute firm has the same systematic risk and capital structure as the division or subsidiary. (For a thorough discussion of the pure play approach, see Fuller and Kerr, 1981.)

There are some problems associated with cost of capital applications. In a paper entitled, “Problems with the Concept of Cost of Capital,” Haley and Schall (HS, 1978) indicate that the concept of the cost of capital historically has served three purposes: (1) as a guide for financial decisions, (2) as a standard for investment decisions, and (3) as a link between financing and investment decisions. HS carefully investigate the conditions under which certain cost of capital concepts can become either misleading or irrelevant. By reviewing M&M’s cost of capital definitions, HS demonstrate that the weighted average cost of capital can be misleading and inefficient because income streams may not be perpetual, discount rates may change over time, and a firm’s risk class is not independent of its financial structure. In addition, HS demonstrate that there are two possible problems in using the cost of capital as an indicator for undertaking investment decisions: (1) there may be a different cost of capital for different risk levels and for different time periods, and (2) if the rate of return for an investment to be accepted differs when calculated for internal and external financing, then there is no unique cost of capital for the investment. Empirically, Lee, Linke, and Zumwalt (1981) have demonstrated that cost of capital estimates obtained from alternative methods, as discussed in this chapter, are not necessarily highly correlated.

Thus far in this text, we have talked in depth about the four major financial theories depicted in Figure 10.5. Corner A represents pre-M&M theories, or classical financial theories, such as Gordon’s models or Lintner’s models (1963). Corner B is the innovative works of M&M (1958, 1961, 1963, 1966). Corner C represents the capital asset pricing model and arbitrage pricing model, which were revolutionary in their incorporation of business and market risk.

A: Pre-M&M classical finance theories
B: M&M theories
C: CAPM & APT
D: OPM

Figure 10.5 The Four Major Financial Theories.

At corner D we have the newest financial model — the option pricing model.

In this section, with the Chase model, we have integrated corners C and B; that is, M&M theories with the CAPM. The result is a model that incorporates corporate tax rates with market and business risks to calculate cost of capital.

Cost of equity can be classified into two categories: one that includes debt, the other that excludes debt. Each of these categories has two methods of estimation, as depicted in Figure 10.6.

The purpose of the Chase method is to integrate M&M and the CAPM. Theoretically, the CAPM is better than the M&M approach. The CAPM explicitly includes the effects of diversification. However, the M&M approach can more easily accommodate accounting and other financial information. Furthermore, diversification generally is limited in the real world. In theory, investors diversify their investments to reduce risk. Many investors are prevented from

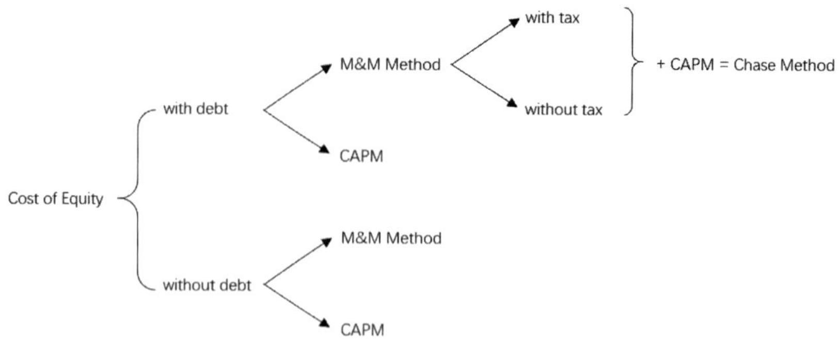


Figure 10.6 Cost of Equity Determination.

achieving this objective by the availability of funds. However, some investors make investments in mutual funds to achieve diversification.

## 10.7 Summary

In this chapter, we have discussed five approaches to calculating the cost of capital. These five approaches are: (1) the earnings yield, (2) the discounted cash flow, (3) the weighted average cost of capital, (4) the CAPM approach, and (5) the Chase Manhattan method. The marginal cost of capital was also explored.

The interrelationship among different cost-of-capital estimation methods were explored in some detail. The relative advantages between different estimation methods were also indirectly explored. The five cost-of-capital estimation methods that were discussed in this chapter give managers enough background to choose the appropriate cost-of-capital estimation method for utility-regulation determination, capital-budgeting decisions, and financial planning and forecasting. According to a surveyed paper by Graham and Harvey (2001), a firm's valuation technique depends on its size and firm risk, rather than the project's risk, and the most popular cost of capital methods include CAPM, average stock returns, and multibeta CAPM.

Overall, the cost of capital is one of the most useful and complex concepts in financial management. The beginning student of finance should strive to understand this concept and learn how to use these tools in real-world situations.

## References

Arditti, F. D. and M. S. Tysseland. "Three Ways to Present the Marginal Cost of Capital," *Financial Management* (Summer 1973, pp. 63–67).

Brennan, M. "Taxes, Market Valuation, and Corporate Financial Policy," *National Tax Journal*, 23 (1970, pp. 417–427).

Brick, I., C. F., Lee, H. Y. Chen, and C. H. Hsieh. "A Comparison of Alternative Models for Estimating Firm's Growth Rate," *Review of Quantitative Finance and Accounting*, 47(2) (2016, pp. 369–393).

Chen, A. H. "Recent Developments in the Cost of Debt Capital," *The Journal of Finance*, 23 (1978, pp. 863–877).

Chen, A. H. and E. H. Kim. "Theories of Corporate Debt Policy: A Synthesis," *The Journal of Finance*, 34 (1979, pp. 371–384).

Chen, H. Y. and Lee, C. F. "Sustainable Growth Rate, Optimal Growth Rate, and Optimal Payout Ratio: A Joint Optimization Approach," *Journal of Banking and Finance*, 37(4) (2013, pp. 1205–1222).

Chu, C. C. "Alternative Methods for Determining the Expected Market-Risk Premium: Theory and Evidence," Ph.D. Dissertation, Graduate College of the University of Illinois at Urbana, 1984.

Fuller, R. J. and H. S. Kerr. "Estimating the Divisional Cost of Capital: An Analysis of the Pure-Play Technique," *The Journal of Finance*, 36 (1981, pp. 997–1009).

Ibbotson, R. *2020 SBBI Yearbook: Stocks, Bonds, Bills, and Inflation.* (Duff & Phelps).

Graham, J. R. and C. R. Harvey. "The Theory and Practice of Corporate Finance: Evidence from the Field," *Journal of Financial Economics*, 60 (2001, pp. 187–243).

Haley, C. W. and L. D. Schall. "Problems with the Concept of the Cost of Capital," *Journal of Financial and Quantitative Analysis*, 13 (1978, pp. 847–870).

Hamada, R. S. "The Effect of the Firm's Capital Structure on the Systematic Risk of Common Stocks," *The Journal of Finance*, 27 (May 1972, pp. 435–452).

Henderson, G. V., Jr. "In Defense of the Weighted Average Cost of Capital," *Financial Management*, 8 (Autumn 1979, pp. 57–61).

Higgins, R. C. "Growth, Dividend Policy, and Cost of Capital in the Electrical Utility Industry," *The Journal of Finance*, 29 (1974, pp. 1189–1210).

Ibbotson, R. G. and R. A. Sinquefield. *Stocks, Bonds, Bills, and Inflation* (Chicago: Morningstar, 2015).

Lee, Alice and J.D. Cummins. "Alternative Models for Estimating the Cost of Equity Capital for Property/Casualty Insurers," *Review of Quantitative Finance and Accounting*, 10 (1998, pp. 235–267).

Lee, C. F. *Financial Analysis and Planning: Theory and Applications*, 3rd edn. (World Scientific: Singapore, 2017).

Lee, C. F., C. M. Linke and J. K. Zumwalt. "Alternative Cost-of-Capital Estimation Methods: An Integration of Comparison." Paper Presented at 1981 FMA Annual Meeting.

Lee, C. F., M. C. Gupta, H. Y. Chen, and A. C. Lee. "Optimal Payout Ratio under Uncertainty and the Flexibility Hypothesis: Theory and Empirical Evidence," *Journal of Corporate Finance*, 17(3) (June 2011, pp. 483–501).

Lintner, J. "The Cost of Capital and Optional Financing of Corporate Growth," *The Journal of Finance*, 18 (May 1963, pp. 292–310).

Litzenburger, R. and H. Sosin, "On the CAPM Approach to the Estimation of a Public Utility's Cost of Equity Capital," *The Journal of Finance*, 35 (1980, pp. 369–387).

Merton, R. C. "On Estimating the Expected Return on the Market," *Journal of Financial Economics*, 8(4) (December 1980, pp. 323–361).

Miller, M. H. "Debt and Taxes," *The Journal of Finance*, 32 (May 1977, pp. 261–75).

Miller, M. H. and F. Modigliani. "Some Estimates of the Cost of Capital to the Utility Industry, 1954–57," *American Economic Review* (June 1966, pp. 333–391).

Modigliani, F. and M. H. Miller. "The cost of capital, corporation finance, and the theory of investment," *The American Economic Review*, 58 (1958, pp. 261–297).

Modigliani, F. and M. H. Miller. "Dividend policy, growth, and the valuation of shares," *Journal of Business* (October 1961, pp. 411–433).

Modigliani, F. and M. H. Miller. "Corporate Income Tax and the Cost of Capital: A Correction," *American Economic Review*, 63 (1963, pp. 433–443).

Senbet, L. W. and R. A. Taggart Jr. "Capital structure equilibrium under market imperfections and incompleteness," *The Journal of Finance*, 39(1) (1984, pp. 93–103).

Stern, J. M. *Analytical Methods in Financial Planning* (Chase Manhattan Bank, New York, 1980).

Williams, J. B. *The Theory of Investment Value* (Cambridge: Harvard University Press, 1938).

## Appendix 10A — M&M Propositions 1 and 2

Modigliani and Miller modified Gordon and Lintner's classical finance theory with two papers (1958, 1963). In these papers, M&M systematically developed a financial theory through three propositions. Proposition 1 describes the market value of a firm and how it is determined. Proposition 2 is a model indicating how the cost of equity capital is determined. Proposition 3 discusses the method of evaluating investment decisions. All three propositions consider both a taxed and taxless world. Since the proposition without tax is an ideal, intellectual situation, in this appendix we discuss only cases with taxes.

Proposition 3 is a description of how the internal rate of return compares with the cost of capital method in determining whether an investment is worthwhile. Because these criteria were discussed in detail in Chapters 6 and 9, we will confine our discussion in this appendix to Propositions 1 and 2.

The equation for Proposition 1 is as follows:

$$V_L = V_U + \tau_c B \tag{10.1A}$$

where $V_L$ = the market value of a levered firm; $V_U$ = the market value of an unlevered firm ($NOPAT/C$); (NOPAT = net operating profit after tax; $C$ = cost of capital without debt); and $\tau_c B$ = tax advantage of taking on debt.

Based on the perpetual bond valuation concept discussed in Chapter 5, we can show under what condition the value of the tax deductibility of interest is equal to $\tau_c B$. If a company issues a par $B$ dollars of debt and interest rate on the debt is $i$, then each year the firm will pay $iB$ dollars of interest. Because interest payments are tax deductible, then the tax shield associated with $iB$ and the interest expense is $\tau_c iB$. If this tax shield lasts perpetually, then the value of tax deductibility is

$$\frac{\tau_c Bi}{i} = \tau_c B \tag{10.2A}$$

This supposes that the bonds are issued only at par and that the interest rate does not change.

In another paper, Miller (1977) modified the results of Eq. (10.1A) by introducing personal tax effects as well as the corporate tax effects on firm value. This alternate model became

$$V_L = V_U + \left[1 - \frac{(1-\tau_c)(1-\tau_{PS})}{1-\tau_{PB}}\right] B \tag{10.3A}$$

where $\tau_c$ = corporate tax rate for the $j$th firm; $\tau_{PS}$ = personal tax rate from capital gain income; and $\tau_{PB}$ = personal tax rate from bond income.

If we compare Eqs. (10.3A) and (10.1A), we find that the advantage of using debt in a situation involving corporate and personal taxes is less than in a situation with only corporate tax. Using Eq. (10.3A), Miller derived the extreme conditions when there are no advantages to using debt. These are (1) when $(1-\tau_c)(1-\tau_{PS}) = (1-\tau_{PB})$ and (2) when the supply rate of return equals the demand rate of return on bonds.

M&M Proposition 2 describes the cost of equity capital with leverage and its tax effects. This model was based upon M&M's Proposition 1 (1963) with tax case is defined as

$$Y = C + (1-\tau_c)(C-i)\left(\frac{B}{S}\right) \tag{10.4A}$$

where $Y$ = cost of equity with debt; $C$ = cost of equity without debt; $\tau_c$ = corporate tax rate; $i$ = interest rate; $B$ = amount of debt; and $S$ = amount of equity.

This equation, based upon Proposition 1, defines the cost of equity without debt and adjusts it for tax effects, leverage effects, and the differential between the cost of equity without debt and the interest rate of debt.

## Appendix 10B — A Mathematical Approach to MCC

This appendix relies on the article "Three Ways to Present the Marginal Cost of Capital" by Arditti and Tysseland, which appeared in *Financial Management* (Summer 1973).

The market value of the firm at $t_0$ may be represented by

$$V_0 = \frac{\bar{x}}{1+k_0} \tag{10.1B}$$

where $\bar{x}$ = the future expected income stream and $k_0$ = the firm's average cost of capital at $t_0$.

Firm value may also be represented by the summation of the market values of the various financing components:

$$V_0 = S_0 + B_0 \tag{10.2B}$$

where $S_0$ = the market value of the firm's equity at $t_0$ and $B_0$ = the market value of the firm's debt at $t_0$.

For the sake of simplicity, we assume only two forms of financing: debt and equity.

Suppose a firm is considering making an investment $I$, which has an expected rate of return $r$. If the firm makes the new investment, its value will be

$$V_1 = \frac{\bar{x} + (1+r)I}{(1+k_1)} \tag{10.3B}$$

where $V_1$ = the firm's market value at $t_0$ and $k_1$ = the firm's new average cost of capital at $t_1$.

In the spirit of Eq. (10.2B), the firm's new value is also

$$V_1 = S_0' + B_0' + I \tag{10.4B}$$

where $S_0'$ and $B_0'$ = the new values of the old debt and equity; and $I$ = either the value of new debt or new equity or a combination of debt and equity.

The project will be acceptable to the firm only if the value of the new equity is greater than or equal to the value of the old equity; that is, if

$$S_0' \geq S_0$$

Given this decision rule for acceptance, there must be some rate $r$ that satisfied this condition.

First, subtracting Eq. (10.2B) from Eq. (10.4B) yields

$$V_1 - V_0 = S_0' + B_0' - S_0 - B_0 + I$$

If we assume that the bondholders are not affected by the risk characteristics of the new investment, we have $B_0' = B_0$. Transferring $I$ to the left side of the equation yields

$$V_1 - V_0 - I = S_0' - S_0$$

However, in view of the requirement that the new value of the equity is at least as high as the old value of the equity, we have

$$V_1 - V_0 - I \geq 0$$

or

$$V_1 - V_0 \geq I$$

as the equivalent investment criterion that a prospective project must meet to be acceptable. Substituting (10.3B) for $V_1$ and (10.1B) for $V_0$,

$$\frac{\bar{x} + (1 + r)I}{(1 + k_1)} - \frac{\bar{x}}{1 + k_0} \geq I$$

With some algebraic manipulation, we get

$$\frac{\bar{x}}{1 + k_0}[(1 + k_0) - (1 + k_1)] + (1 + r)I \geq (1 + k_1)I \qquad (10.5\text{B})$$

Substituting $V_0 = \bar{x}/(1 + k_0)$, dividing through by $I$, and solving for $r$, we have

$$r \geq k_1 + \frac{V_0}{I}(k_1 - k_0) \qquad (10.6\text{B})$$

This says that the required return on an investment should be greater than or equal to the rate of expected return on all assets as shown by the right-hand side of Eq. (10.6B). Hence, $r$ should be greater than or equal to the new WACC. If the new investment, $I$, does not change the risk characteristics of the firm's income stream, then $k_1 = k_0$, and the decision rule for acceptance is that $r$ must be greater than or equal to the marginal average cost of capital, which is equivalent to the WACC (marginal cost of capital). If the new investment increases the riskiness of the firm's income stream, then $k_1 > k_0$ and $r$ should be greater than the new average cost of capital, $k_1$. In this case, the right-hand side of Eq. (10.6B) is the WACC, or marginal cost of capital. Hence, $r$ should be equal to or greater than the new WACC.

## Questions and Problems

1. Define the following:

   a. Average earnings yields versus current earnings yield
   b. Cost of retained earnings and cost of new equity
   c. Weighted cost of capital
   d. Marginal cost of capital
   e. Unlevered cost of capital

2. Discuss four possible methods for estimating the growth rate of dividends per share.
3. Discuss how the M&M theory and the CAPM can be integrated together to estimate the unlevered cost of capital.
4. Discuss five alternative methods for cost-of-capital estimation. Use the criteria of theory and practice to evaluate the relative advantages of these methods.
5. How can we integrate CAPM into the M&M valuation model to improve cost-of-capital estimation?
6. Can the weighted-average cost of capital be theoretically justifiable? Why or why not?
7. Discuss how CAPM can be used to estimate the cost of equity capital in terms of the information needed.
8. The current stock price of XYZ Company is \$100. It is expected that the company will pay a \$10 dividend per share in the next period. If growth rate of the dividend is 5%, what is the cost of equity capital?
9. Calculate the after-tax cost of debt under each of the following conditions:

   a. Interest rate = 10%; tax rate = 0%
   b. Interest rate = 10%; tax rate = 50%
   c. Interest rate = 10%; tax rate = 100%

10. The information needed to calculate cost of capital for GM is as follows:

| | |
|---|---|
| Risk-free interest rate | = 8.5% |
| Beta of GM | = 0.46 |
| Market rate of return | = 10.55% |
| D/E ratio | = 0.36 |
| Target D/E ratio | = 0.4 |
| Corporate tax rate | = 40% |
| Interest rate on all debt | = 10% |

   a. Calculate the cost of capital using the CAPM method.
   b. Calculate the cost of capital using the Chase method.

11. ABC Company's capital is as follows:

| **Capital** | **Percentage of Capital (%)** | **Cost (%)** |
|---|---|---|
| Common stock | 60 | 12 |
| Preferred stock | 2 | 14 |
| Debt | 38 | 10 |

Calculate the weighted average cost of capital for ABC Company. (Assume the marginal corporate tax rate is 40%.)

12. Sweet Food's stock sells for \$100 a share, and it is believed that the current year's dividend on the stock will be \$5 per share. The past earnings growth rate is 10%, and it is expected this will continue. The current interest rate on new debt is 8%. The firm's marginal tax rate is 40%. The firm's capital structure, considered optimal, is as follows.

| | |
|---|---|
| Debt | \$200,000 |
| Common equity | \$300,000 |

Answer these questions:

a. Calculate the after-tax cost of new debt and of common equity, assuming new equity comes only from retained earnings.
b. Find the marginal cost of capital, assuming no common stock is sold.
c. Find the marginal cost of capital if new common stock is sold with a flotation cost of 10%. (The cost of debt is constant.)

13. Walker Public Relations, Inc. has common stock which currently sells for \$40 per share. The most recent dividend was \$1.50 per share (at $t = 0$) and they are expected to grow at a 10% rate indefinitely. New common stock can be sold to net the company \$38 per share.

a. Find the cost of internal equity (retained earnings).
b. Find the cost of new common stock.

14. The XBC Company can sell debt with an 8% coupon rate, a \$1,000 par value and 10 years to maturity. The company will net

$975 per bond and has tax rate of 40%. Find the company's after tax cost of debt.

15. Jackson's Computer Corporation has preferred stock which currently sells on the market for $90 per share. It pays a dividend of 8% on a par value of $100. New preferred stock can be sold with flotation costs of $5 per share. Find the company's cost of preferred stock.
16. White's Cookie Shops, Inc. has a beta of 1.4 and a tax rate of 40%. The risk-free rate of interest is 6% and the expected return on the market is 13%. New common equity can be sold with flotation costs of 5%.

    a. Find the company's cost of internal equity.
    b. Find the company's cost of new common stock.

17. Follen, Inc. has the following optimal capital structure which is considers to be optimal:

| | |
|---|---|
| Debt | $600,000 |
| Preferred stock | 200,000 |
| Common stock | 1,200,000 |
| **Total value** | $2,000,000 |

Currently the company has $15,000 in retained earnings available for capital investments. The company's tax rate is 46%. Investors expect earnings and dividends to grow at a constant rate of 8% for the indefinite future. Follen will pay a dividend of $1 per share in the coming year ($t = 1$).
New capital can be obtained under the terms identified below:

*New Common Stock*: New common stock can be sold at the current market price of $20 per share. Flotation costs are $2 per share for the first $30,000 of new common stock sold. Any new stock sold above the $30,000 will entail flotation costs of $3 per share.
*Preferred Stock*: New preferred stock can be sold to the public at a price of $100 per share and paying an annual dividend of $10 share. Flotation costs are $5 per share regardless of the amount of preferred stock sold.

*Debt*: Debt can be sold at a before tax cost of 10%. Investors will pay $1,000 per bond with 10 years until maturity. The coupon rate on the bond is 9.6%. The cost of debt does not change as additional debt is sold.

a. Find the weights for each of the sources of financing.
b. Find the breaks in the weighted marginal cost of capital curve.
c. Find the firm's after tax cost of:
   i. Debt
   ii. Preferred stock
   iii. Internal equity (retained earnings)
   iv. New common stock.
d. How much of the company's common equity financing will come from new common stock if the company needs to raise?
   i. $30,000 in total financing.
   ii. $50,000 in total financing.
   iii. $100,000 in total financing.
e. Compute the firm's weighted marginal cost of capital schedule.
f. Compute the firm's weighted average cost of capital for $100,000 total financing.

18. Lexington, Inc. has the following capital structure which they consider to be optimal:

| | |
|---|---|
| Debt | $1,200,000 |
| Preferred Stock | 800,000 |
| Common Equity | 2,000,000 |
| **Total** | $4,000,000 |

The firm wishes to raise $900,000 in order to undertake several important investment opportunities. The following information on the cost of sources of funds has been gathered:

*Debt*: $200,000 of new 10-year bonds can be sold at $980 to net the company $960 per bond if they bear a 10% coupon rate. If more than $200,000 in debt financing is needed, the company will only net $940 per bond.
*Preferred Stock*: Preferred stock can be sold at $77 to net the company $75 per share if it carries a 7% dividend on a par value

of \$100 per share. These terms prevail regardless of how much preferred stock is sold.
*Common Equity*: Common stock is expected to pay a dividend of \$2 per share in the coming year ($t = 1$). The stock is currently selling at \$22 per share and will net the company \$20 per share. Dividends are expected to grow at 7% forever. The firm will have \$200,000 available from retained earnings this year for investment in new capital projects.
The company's tax rate is 50%.

a. Find the firm's after-tax cost of debt.
b. Find the firm's cost of preferred stock.
c. Find the firm's cost of retained earnings.
d. Find the firm's cost of new common stock.
e. Find the weights for each of the sources of financing.
f. Find the breaks in the weighted marginal cost of capital curve.
g. How much of the \$900,000 will be financed from new common stock?
h. Compute the WMCC schedule and then prepare the corresponding graph.
i. Compute the WACC of \$900,000 total financing.
j. Which projects would be accepted given the above WMCC schedule, if the company faces the following investment schedule:

| **Project** | **Cost** | **IRR** |
|---|---|---|
| A | \$100,000 | 25% |
| B | 15,000 | 20 |
| C | 50,000 | 18 |
| D | 100,000 | 15 |
| E | 125,000 | 13 |
| F | 200,000 | 10 |
| G | 100,000 | 9 |

19. Company AAA is an all equity firm with a beta of 0.8. The market risk premium is 10% and the risk free rate is 6%. The company is considering a project that will generate annual after-tax cash flow of \$320,000 at year-end for five years. The project requires an immediate investment of \$1.3 million. If the project

has the same risk as the firm as a whole, should Company AAA take the project?

20. The correlation between the returns on Company BBB and the returns on S&P 500 is 0.675. The variance of the returns on Company BBB is 0.004225 and the variance of the returns on S&P 500 is 0.001467. What is the beta of Company BBB stock?
21. Company CCC is a levered firm with a debt-to-equity ratio of 0.25. Assume that the cost of equity is 15% and cost of debt is 8%. The corporation tax rate is 30%. If a new company project has the same risk as the overall firm, what is the weighted average cost of capital for the project?
22. Company DDD has an equity beta of 1.2 and a debt-to-equity ratio of 1.2. The expected return on the market is 15% and the risk free rate is 6%. The before tax cost of debt capital is 9%. The corporation tax rate is 35%. Please calculate Company's weighted average cost of capital.
23. Calculate the weighted average cost of capital for Company EEE. The book value of Company EEE's outstanding debt is $50 million. Currently the debt is trading at 130% of book value and is priced to yield 10%. The 6 million outstanding shares of Company EEE's stock are trading at $25 per share. The required return on Company EEE's stock is 16%. The tax rate is 35%.
24. The current stock price of XYZ Company is $100. It is expected that the company will pay a $10 dividend per share in the next period. If growth rate of the dividend is 5%, what is the cost of equity capital?
25. **Calculating WACC.** The treasurer for Falcon Enterprises wants to know the weighted average cost of capital for the firm, based on the following information:

    | | |
    |---|---|
    | Target percent of equity | = 65% |
    | Target percent of debt | = 35% |
    | Cost of equity | = 14% |
    | Pretax cost of debt | = 11% |
    | Tax rate | = 34% |

    Compute Falcon's WACC for the treasurer.
26. **Calculating WACC.** Recomputing Falcon Enterprises' WACC using the information given in Problem 11, but assume that the tax rate has fallen to 25%.

27. **Calculating WACC.** You are the CFO at Mensa & Company. If the target capital structure weights are 505 debt and 50% equity, calculate the firm's WACC, based on the following information:

    Two million shares of stock outstanding;
    Current market price of stock = \$42;
    Total face value of bonds = \$80 million;
    Bonds currently sell for 90% of face value
    Bond's YTM = 10%
    Risk-free rate = 4%
    Expected return on the stock market = 15%
    Beta = 0.95
    New common stock has a 10% flotation cost
    Tax rate = 30%.

28. **Calculated Weighted Average Cost of Capital.** LMN Corporation's stock sells for \$50 per share. Its expected dividend is \$2.50 per share and the firm's growth rate is 10%. It is in the 30% tax bracket. The current rate of interest for the firm's bonds, sold at par, is 8%. New bonds can be sold with a flotation cost of \$30 per bond. The market value of the firm's capital is:

| | |
|---|---|
| Debt | \$400,000 |
| Equity | \$600,000 |
| Total capital | \$1,000,000 |

    a. What are the after-tax costs of debt and equity for this firm?
    b. What is the weighted average cost of capital (WACC) for this firm?
    c. How would this WACC change if the firm runs out of retained earnings and a new stock issue has flotation costs of 5%?

29. **Calculated Weighted Average Cost of Capital.** Q Corp has the following capital structure, which also is equal to its target capital structure:

| | |
|---|---|
| Debt | \$1,000,000 |
| Preferred Equity | 1,000,000 |
| Common Equity | 2,000,000 |
| Total capital | \$4,000,000 |

Currently, the firm has $50,000 in retained earnings available for investment. The company's tax rate is 30%. Investors expect the firm's dividend to grow at an 8% rate. It currently pays $1.00 per share in dividends. Its stock price is $15 per share.
New capital can be raised under the following conditions:

- New 20 year bonds can be sold at par with a coupon rate of 7% and a par value of $1,000. Flotation costs for new bond issues are $50 per bond.
- New preferred stock can be sold to the public at a price of $50 per share with an annual dividend of 6%. Flotation costs are 10% of the amount of preferred sold.
- New common stock can be sold at a price of $15 per share. Flotation costs are $2.00 per share for new equity.

a. What are the weights for each source of financing?
b. What are the company's cost of debt, preferred equity, retained earnings, and new common equity?
c. Where are the break points in the firm's marginal cost of capital curve?
d. How much new common equity is needed to raise:
   1. $90,000 of new capital?
   2. $150,000 of new capital?
e. What is the marginal cost of capital for each of the levels of financing in Part (d) above?
f. Draw the firm's marginal cost of capital schedule.

## Chapter 11

# Capital Structure and Valuation

**Contents**



## 11.1 Introduction

A corporation can finance its operations through the issuance of a range of different securities, such as common stock, preferred stock, and bonds of differing maturities. This mix of securities is known as the firm's capital structure. In Chapter 11, we consider the question of determining the appropriate capital structure of a company; that is, the optimal mix of debt and equity securities.

Section 11.2 begins by looking at the effect of debt on the earnings per share of the corporation. Section 11.3 proceeds to discuss taxes and debt, which is then followed by a discussion in Section 11.4 about the combination of financial leverage and operating leverage and the joint effect on EPS. Section 11.5 discusses management's target capital structure for the firm, and Section 11.6 discusses the reasons for the existence of an optimal capital structure. A chapter summary is provided in Section 11.7. Appendix 11A presents an explanation of Modigliani and Miller's Proposition 1 without tax.

## 11.2 Financial Leverage and Its Effects on Earnings per Share

Before discussing the effects of capital structure, we recall our discussion of Chapter 2 on earnings per share as related to elements of a corporation's income statement and balance sheet. A firm's net operating income, or profits from operations, is referred to as earnings before interest and taxes (EBIT). Interest payments on the corporation's debt constitute a first claim on these earnings, while corporate taxes must be paid on the remaining net income. After deducting interest and tax payments from net operating income, the remaining *net income after taxes* is available to common stockholders. Part of this amount may be paid to stockholders as dividends, and part retained to finance future business operations. *Earnings per share* is then obtained by dividing net income after taxes by the number of shares outstanding. Therefore,

$$\text{Earnings per share (EPS)} = \frac{\text{EBIT} - \text{Interest payments} - \text{Tax payments}}{\text{Number of shares outstanding}} \tag{11.1}$$

It is convenient to express this relationship algebraically. Let us denote by $A$ the value of the firm's total assets. (These assets are the sum of debt and stockholders' equity.) Suppose that, through its business operations, the corporation earns a rate of return $r$ on the assets, so that

$$\text{EBIT} = rA$$

If the value of outstanding debt is $B$, and the annual interest rate on the debt is $i$, then

$$\text{Interest payments} = iB$$

If taxes must be paid at rate $\tau_c$ on net earnings of $(rA - iB)$, then

$$\text{Tax payments} = \tau_c(rA - iB)$$

It follows that

$$\text{Net income after taxes} = rA - iB - \tau_c(rA - iB)$$

Therefore, if there are $N$ shares outstanding, corresponding to Eq. (11.1), the earnings per share of a corporation can be expressed as

$$\text{EPS} = \frac{rA - iB - \tau_c(rA - iB)}{N} \tag{11.2}$$

where $A$ = value of assets; $r$ = rate of return on assets; $B$ = value of debt; $i$ = rate of interest on debt; $\tau_c$ = rate of corporate taxation; and $N$ = number of shares outstanding.

Let us illustrate these ideas through examination of the data in Table 11.1, taken from a corporation's income statement and balance sheet. For this corporation, in millions of dollars, $A = 2{,}400$ and $B = 1{,}300$. The corporation earns a rate of return on assets ($r$)

$$r = \frac{\text{EBIT}}{A} = \frac{270}{2{,}400} = 0.1125$$

or 11.25%. The rate of interest paid on debit is

$$i = \frac{104}{1{,}300} = 0.08$$

Then, with $\tau_c = 0.40$ and $N = 40$, we solve for earnings per share using Eq. (11.2):

$$\text{EPS} = \frac{270 - 104 - 0.40(270 - 104)}{40} = \$2.49$$

Thus, earnings per share are $2.49.

Table 11.1 Financial Information on a Corporation.

| |
|---|
| Value of assets = $2,400 million |
| Value of debt = $1,300 million |
| Interest paid on debt = $104 million |
| Corporate tax rate = 40% |
| Shares outstanding = 40 million |
| Earnings before interest and taxes = $270 million |

### 11.2.1 *Impact of capital structure on earnings per share*

There are two common procedures for measuring a firm's capital structure to assess the relative size of its debt commitments. These are as follows:

1. *The balance sheet method.* The ratio of total debt to total assets provides an obvious measure of capital structure. For example, for the corporation of Table 11.1, we find

$$\frac{B}{A} = \frac{1{,}300}{2{,}400} = 0.5417$$

so that 54.17% of this corporation's total assets are financed by debt. Alternatively, total assets can be decomposed as the sum of debt and share-holder's equity ($S$), so that

$$A = B + S$$

We can then compute the debt-equity ratio, which for the corporation of Table 11.1 is

$$\frac{B}{S} = \frac{1{,}300}{2{,}400 - 1{,}300} = \frac{1{,}300}{1{,}100} = 1.1818$$

implying that the total value of debt is 118.18% of shareholders' equity.

2. *The income statement method.* Using information from a firm's income statement, it is possible to measure the extent to which earnings cover interest obligations on the debt. With this in mind, we define *times interest earned* as follows:

$$\text{Times interest earned} = \frac{\text{EBIT}}{\text{Interest paid on debt}}$$

For the corporation of Table 11.1, we find

$$\text{Times interest earned} = \frac{270}{104} = 2.5962$$

Hence, for this corporation, earnings are more than two and a half times interest payments. This provides a measure of how well the company is able to service its debt from earnings.

Our objective now is to explore the impact of a corporation's capital structure on earnings per share. For this purpose, we use the debt–equity ratio as a measure of capital structure. We will analyze this question formally, but, before doing so, let us pause to see if it is possible to anticipate what conclusion might emerge.

We look again at the corporation of Table 11.1. From the stockholders' point of view, it seems that the corporation has performed very well. It is operating partly with funds borrowed at an interest rate of 8% and has a rate of return of 11.25% on its assets. If you had the opportunity to borrow money at 8% interest and *knew* that you could achieve a rate of return of 11.25% on these funds, you would surely take it! Similarly, as a stockholder in this corporation, you would reason that if a rate of return of 11.25% could be guaranteed, the corporation could achieve higher earnings by increasing its debt at an interest rate of 8%. Indeed, we can reason that provided the rate of return is higher than the interest rate, increasing the debt will raise earnings per share. This argument suggests that debt should be increased to the point that it is no longer possible to find projects whose rate of return exceeds the interest rate that must be paid on borrowed funds.

The argument of the previous paragraph has a crucial deficiency: it ignores *uncertainty*. In practice, it is not possible to *guarantee* the rate of return that a corporation will achieve on its business operations. Of course, investors can form some estimate, or *expectation*, of returns from operations. If the expected rate of return exceeds the interest rate on debt, then we would *expect* earnings per share to increase as the debt–equity ratio is increased. However, expectations about the success of business operations may not be fulfilled, and, in this event, the corporation could achieve a rate of return that is lower than the interest rate that must be paid on the debt. Nevertheless, it will still be necessary to service this debt before making any distribution to stockholders. Therefore, a relatively high level of debt would lead to *lower* earnings per share. It follows that a higher debt–equity ratio leads to greater uncertainty, or risk, about earnings per share.

Summarizing our discussion so far, if expected returns from operations exceeds interest on debt, then raising the debt–equity ratio will produce two effects on earnings per share:

1. An increase in expected earnings
2. An increase in risk, or uncertainty, about earnings

We now proceed to demonstrate these conclusions formally. Rearranging Eq. (11.2), earnings per share can be expressed as

$$\text{EPS} = \frac{(1-\tau_c)(rA - iB)}{N} \tag{11.3}$$

The number of shares outstanding is

$$N = \frac{S}{h}$$

where $S =$ dollar value of total equity and $h =$ dollar value per share. Therefore, substituting into Eq. (11.3),

$$\text{EPS} = \frac{h(1-\tau_c)(rA - iB)}{S}$$

Next, writing

$$A = B + S$$

we find

$$\text{EPS} = \frac{h(1-\tau_c)[r(B+S) - iB]}{S} = h(1-\tau_c)\left[r + (r-i)\frac{B}{S}\right] \tag{11.4}$$

Let us examine the implications of Eq. (11.4). Suppose that the rate of return on assets exceeds the interest rate, so that $(r-i)$ is positive. It follows, then, that an increase in the debt–equity ratio, $B/S$, leads to an increase in earnings per share. Conversely, if $(r-i)$ is negative, then the higher the $B/S$, the lower the earnings per share.

To provide a numerical illustration of this, suppose that the corporation of Table 11.1 purchases 10% of its outstanding shares, financing this purchase by borrowing the necessary funds at 8% interest. There will now be 36 million shares outstanding, and shareholder equity is reduced from \$1,100 million to \$990 million. There is a

Table 11.2 Position of Corporation of Table 11.1 after Repurchase.

| |
|---|
| Value of assets = \$2,400 million |
| Value of debt = \$1,410 million |
| Corporate tax rate = 40% |
| Interest paid on debt = \$112.8 million |
| Corporate tax rate = 40% |
| Shares outstanding = 36 million |
| Earnings before interest and taxes = \$270 million |

corresponding increase of \$110 million in debt, on which additional interest of \$8.8 million must be paid. Let us assume that this corporation continues to produce earnings of 11.25% on its total assets. The corporation's new position is presented in Table 11.2.

Using Eq. (11.2), we find earnings per share:

$$\text{EPS} = \frac{270 - 112.8 - 0.40(270 - 112.80)}{36} = 2.62$$

The EPS of \$2.62 exceeds by 13 cents the EPS derived from the data of Table 11.1. Hence, we see that, as predicted, increasing the debt–equity ratio produces an increase in earnings per share.

We now return to Eq. (11.4) and incorporate into our analysis uncertainty about the rate of return, $r$, on assets. Suppose that our views about future earnings prospects can be represented by thinking of $r$ as a random variable with mean $\bar{r}_r$ and variance $\sigma_r^2$. Thus, $\bar{r}_r$ denotes the expected rate of return on assets, while $\sigma_r^2$ provides a measure of uncertainty about rates of return — the greater the uncertainty, the larger the variance. It follows, from Eq. (11.4), that expected earnings per share are

$$E(\text{EPS}) = h(1 - \tau_c)\left[\bar{r} + (\bar{r} - i)\frac{B}{S}\right] \tag{11.5}$$

Therefore, from Eq. (11.5), we see that if the expected rate of return, $\bar{r}_r$ exceeds the interest rate, $i$, on debt, an increase in the debt–equity ratio leads to an increase in expected earnings per share.

Next, writing Eq. (11.4) as

$$\text{EPS} = h(1 - \tau_c)\left[\left(1 + \frac{B}{S}\right)r - i\left(\frac{B}{S}\right)\right]$$

it follows that the variance in earnings per share is

$$\sigma_{EPS}^2 = \left[h(1-\tau_c)\left(1+\frac{B}{S}\right)\right]^2 \sigma_r^2 \qquad (11.6)$$

As a consequence of Eq. (11.6), we see that the higher the debt–equity ratio, the higher is $\sigma_{EPS}^2$, which measures uncertainty about earnings per share.

We have now demonstrated the following two conclusions about capital structure and earnings per share:

1. Provided a corporation can find projects for which the expected return is higher than the rate of interest that must be paid on debt, an increase in the debt–equity ratio leads to an increase in expected earnings per share.
2. An increase in the debt–equity ratio leads, all other things equal, to an increase in uncertainty about earnings per share.

We have seen that the choice of capital structure involves a trade-off between expected earnings and risk. This trade-off is illustrated in Figure 11.1, where we see that a greater proportion of debt in a firm's capital structure can produce higher expected earnings per share, but only at the cost of greater uncertainty about such earnings.

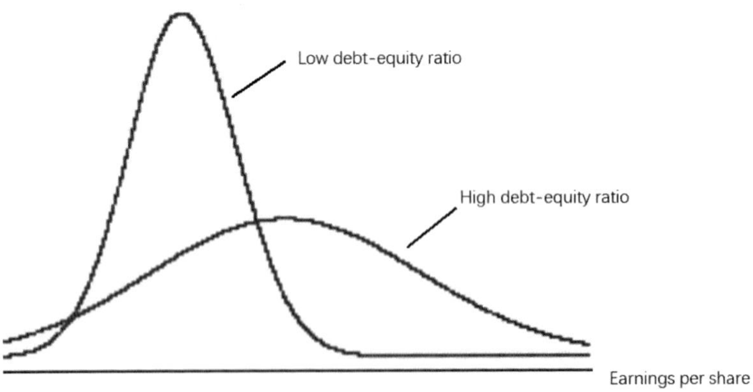


Figure 11.1 Probability Density Functions for Earnings per Share with Low and High Debt–Equity Ratios.

### 11.2.2 *Financial leverage*

The stockholder in a corporation with debt is essentially in the position of investing not only personal funds — the stockholder's equity — but also funds provided by others — the holders of the corporation's debt. The corporation's stock is called *levered equity*, and the stockholders are said to have *financial leverage*. This terminology arises from the notion that debt provides a "lever" with the potential to "jack-up" stockholders' earnings. This potential for greater returns than could be achieved through unlevered equity constitutes the benefits flowing to stockholders from financial leverage. However, as we have seen, financial leverage is not without cost to stockholders. Since interest payments on debt constitute a prior claim on earnings from business operations, financial leverage increases stockholders' risk.

In this and later chapters, we use EPS information. It is necessary to show a link between EPS measures and value maximization. This can be done in the context of the valuation models developed in Chapter 5. For example, recall the dividend return valuation approach to determine the theoretical value of a stock price:

$$P_0 = \frac{D_1}{k - g}$$

In this model, $D_1$ is the expected dividend per share (DPS), and $k$ and $g$ are the required rate of return and growth of dividend per share. EPS is an important factor in determining DPS. (In Chapter 12, we will discuss in detail various theories of dividend payment behavior.) One of the policies normally followed by corporations is a constant payout policy; that is, the ratio of DPS to EPS remains constant over time. Hence, if a corporation were following a constant payout ratio policy, the key determinant of DPS is the level of EPS. As EPS changes, the DPS also changes so that the ratio remains constant.

## 11.3 Tax and Debt

The problem we address in this chapter is the determination of the best capital structure for a firm. How much leverage, as measured by the debt–equity ratio, is appropriate? If the primary objective of management is the maximization of the firm's present value, is there an optimal capital structure? So far, we have not produced an answer to this question. In the preceding discussion, we saw that increased leverage can raise expected returns to stockholders, but only at the cost of additional risk. Is there, then, a level of debt that will place the firm at the "best possible" point on the risk-expected return trade-off curve of Figure 11.1?

These questions were addressed in two celebrated papers by Modigliani and Miller (M&M) in 1958 and 1963. Given certain assumptions, M&M answer our question about optimal capital structure. Before discussing their analysis, we set out their assumptions.

**Assumption 1.** Capital markets are *perfect*. Information is readily available at no cost to all investors; there are no brokerage costs; investors can borrow at the same rate as corporations; market participants behave rationally.

**Assumption 2.** The amount of risk in a firm's operations can be measured, and firms with the same degree of business risk can be identified and classified into "equivalent risk" classes.

**Assumption 3.** All investors form the same expectations about a firm's future earnings and the riskiness of the earnings.

**Assumption 4.** All debt is riskless, whatever the level of indebtedness.

**Assumption 5.** There are no corporate taxes.

Like most theoretical work, the analysis of M&M is based on assumptions that are simplifications of reality. Perhaps the most immediately objectionable of these is that there are no corporate taxes. This assumption is later dropped by M&M, as we will see. However, it is convenient for us to discuss the situation in a world without taxes. This allows us to create a benchmark for comparison, so that when we introduce taxes to the model we can identify the consequences of the government's tax policy.

Given the above assumptions, M&M advance the following contention, known as **Proposition 1:**

Table 11.3 Information on a Leveraged Firm.

| |
|---|
| Market value of debt = \$1,300 million |
| Market value of equity = \$1,100 million |
| Interest rate on debt = 0.08 |
| Earnings before interest and taxes = \$270 million |
| Interest paid on debt = \$104 million |

In a world with no corporate taxes, the total market value of a firm is independent of its capital structure. The total market value is the stream of expected future operating earnings, discounted at a rate appropriate to the business risk class of the firm.

We demonstrate this proposition more formally in Appendix 11A at the end of this chapter. For the present, we illustrate the line of argument with a numerical example.

Consider the leveraged company of Table 11.1. In Table 11.3 we summarize some of the pertinent information. For the sake of continuity, we assume that the market value of stockholders' equity is \$1,100 million, though in practice this typically differs from the book value, as reported in the balance sheet. To make the distinction notationally clear, we use $S$ to denote the market value of stockholders' equity. The firm's total value, $V$, is the sum of the market values of equity and debt; that is,

$$V = S + B$$

Therefore, for our corporation, we find a total market value of

$$V = 1{,}100 + 1{,}300 = \$2{,}400 \text{ million}$$

For illustrative purposes, we are in a world without corporate tax, so that any earnings remaining after interest payments are available for distribution to stockholders.

Now, suppose that you were in the happy position of owning 1% of the equity value (equal to \$11 million) of this leveraged firm. After payment of \$104 million to debtholders, you would receive a distribution of 1% of the remaining earnings, or \$1.66 million.

Suppose that you learn of the opportunity to invest in a second firm that is unlevered but otherwise identical to the first. The second firm has expected earnings of \$270 million and a degree of business risk identical to the first firm. Consider the adoption of the following strategy:

1. Sell for \$11 million your stock in the levered firm.
2. Borrow, at 8% interest, \$13 million; that is, 1% of the debt of the levered firm.
3. Purchase 1% of the equity of the unlevered firm.

How much would you expect to pay for 1% of the unlevered corporation's stock?

To answer this question, let us see what your returns will be. First, you receive 1% of the earnings of the unlevered firm; that is, \$2.7 million. However, you must subtract from this your interest payments −8% of \$13 million, which amounts to \$1.04 million. Therefore, your net return will be \$1.66 million, which is precisely the same return from the levered firm. Presumably, because the two firms are in the same business risk class, a 1% share in the unlevered firm is worth precisely 1% of the value of the levered firm; that is \$24 million. It follows that the market values of the two firms are identical. Given the assumption of perfect markets, this must be the case. For example, imagine that it were possible to purchase 1% of the unlevered firm's equity for less than \$24 million. Then, surely, stockholders in the levered firm would take advantage of the opportunity, selling stock in the levered firm and purchasing stock in the unlevered firm. This process, known as *arbitrage*, would drive down the price of the stock in the levered firm and drive up the price of stock in the unlevered firm to the point at which the market values of the two firms are equal. In economics, there is a general rule that similar goods cannot sell at different prices in the same market. This *law of one price* is the guiding principle behind the M&M arbitrage argument.

We have now demonstrated the validity of M&M's Proposition 1. In the absence of corporate taxes, a firm's total market value is unaffected by the firm's capital structure. It is instructive to reflect on how we reached such a conclusion. Recall that to invest in the unlevered company, we allowed for the use not only of our own funds, but also of borrowed funds. That way, an investor can substitute leverage from personal borrowing for that of the levered firm. It is this capability to create *homemade leverage* that renders irrelevant the extent of a firm's own financial leverage, provided individuals and firms borrow at the same interest rate.

We can now provide a simple expression for a firm's value. To keep the discussion straightforward, we assume that investors expect the firm to produce yearly net operating income of EBIT. Also, let $k$ denote the rate at which future expected earnings are discounted for firms in this risk class. If the firm is unlevered and there are no corporate taxes, the value of the earnings stream is

$$V_U = \frac{\text{EBIT}}{1+k} + \frac{\text{EBIT}}{(1+k)^2} + \cdots = \frac{\text{EBIT}}{k} \tag{11.7}$$

where $V_U$ denotes the value of the unlevered firm. Moreover, we have seen that a levered firm in the same business risk class has the same value as the corresponding unlevered firm. Hence, the levered firm's value, $V_L$ is

$$V_L = V_U + \frac{\text{EBIT}}{k} \tag{11.8}$$

### 11.3.1 *Modigliani and Miller Proposition 1 with taxes*

The conclusion of Modigliani and Miller that a firm's value does not depend on its capital structure rests on a number of assumptions, including the absence of corporate taxes. If corporate taxes with tax deductible interest are brought into the model, the picture changes. Essentially, this is because an unlevered firm must pay taxes on all of its net operating income, while the levered firm subtracts interest payments on the debt from EBIT before assessing taxes. This suggests that a levered firm will be more highly valued than an unlevered firm in the same business risk class with the same expected future earnings stream. In effect, the government is subsidizing the payment of interest by the corporation. If we consider the structure of the tax law, there is no reason why interest must be a tax-deductible expense. If interest is treated for tax purposes just like dividends — that is, both are paid after taxes — then Eqs. (11.7) and (11.8) are still true except that the numerator must be adjusted for tax payments.

Given tax-deductible interest payments, consider again the corporation of Table 11.3, but now with a corporate tax rate of 40%.

The owner of 1% of the equity of this leveraged firm received a distribution of 1% of net income after taxes; that is, 1% of 0.06(270 − 104) = \$9.6 million. Hence, the investor's holding yields \$.996 million.

Suppose that, using the proceeds from the sale of this stock together with borrowed funds, the stockholder purchases 1% of the equity of an unlevered firm in the same business risk class with the same expected earnings. In this case, the entire net operating income of \$270 million is subject to corporate tax at the rate of 40%. The stockholder's distribution then, is 1% of 0.60(270) = \$162 million, or \$1.62 million. However, if \$13 million has been borrowed at 8% interest to purchase stock in the unlevered firms, then interest payments of \$1.04 million must be made, leaving a net return of \$1.62 million −\$1.4 million = \$0.58 million. Clearly, payment of a total price of \$24 million – \$11 million worth of stock in the levered firm plus a loan of \$13 million — for a 1% interest in the unlevered firm would be a bad bargain. Therefore, we conclude that a 1% holding in the unlevered corporation has a value less than \$24 million and that the levered firm has a higher value than the unlevered firm.

Let us see if we can find by how much the levered firm's value exceeds the unlevered firm's value. To accomplish this, we ask how much an investor should be willing to pay for a 1% stake in the unlevered firm. This investor has two possible strategies:

1. Keep \$11 million in the levered firm, yielding a return of \$0.996 million.
2. Sell holdings in the leveraged firm, supplement these proceeds with borrowed funds, and purchase 1% of the unlevered firm's equity.

If the second strategy also yields a net return of \$0.996 million, the investor should be indifferent between the two strategies. This net return is simply the difference between the distribution of 1% of the unlevered firm's after-tax earnings (\$1.62 million) and the interest that must be paid on the borrowed funds. Hence, if a net return of \$0.996 million is to be obtained, we must have

$$0.996 = 1.62 - \text{Interest paid on borrowed funds}$$

so that

$$\text{Interest paid on borrowed funds} = 1.62 - 0.996 = \$0.625 \text{ million}$$

Since these funds are borrowed at an interest rate of 8%, then the total amount of borrowed funds must be

$$\text{Borrowed funds} = \frac{0.624}{0.08} = \$7.8 \text{ million}$$

We conclude that this investor can obtain an expected return of $.996 million from the purchase of 1% of the unlevered firm's equity, provided the total amount paid for this holding is $18.8 million, made up of $11 million from the sale of holdings in the levered firm and $7.8 million of borrowed funds.

This argument implies that the unlevered firm's market value is $1,880 million. Therefore, the difference in the values of the levered and unlevered firms is

$$\begin{aligned} &\text{Value of levered firm} - \text{Value of unlevered firm} \\ &= 2{,}400 - 1{,}880 = \$420 \text{ million} \end{aligned}$$

Leverage results in increased value because corporate taxes are not paid on that portion of earnings used to service debt. Therefore, we might argue that the greater the level of debt, all other things equal, the greater the firm's value. In our example, we found that the levered firm's value exceeded that of an otherwise comparable unleveraged firm by $520 million. This excess is precisely 40% (the corporate tax rate) of $1,300 million (the total value of the leveraged firm's debt). This conclusion is quite general, given our assumptions, so that we can write

$$V_L = V_U + \tau_c B \tag{11.9}$$

where $V_L$ = value of leveraged firm; $V_U$ = value of unleveraged firm; $\tau_c$ = corporate tax rate; and $B$ = value of leveraged firm's debt.

This is M&M Proposition 1 with corporate tax. It suggests that, all else equal, a firm's value can be increased by raising the amount of debt in its capital structure.

For the unlevered firm, with an expected annual net operating income of EBIT, if the corporate tax rate is $\tau_c$, then earnings available for distribution to stockholders are $(1 - \tau_c)$ *EBIT*. Therefore, if expected earnings for firms in this risk class are discounted at rate $k$, the present value of the expected stream of accruals to stockholders is

$$V_U = \frac{(1 - \tau_c)\text{EBIT}}{k}$$

From Eq (11.9), it follows that the value of a levered firm in the same risk class with the same expected earnings stream is

$$V_L = \frac{(1 - \tau_c)\text{EBIT}}{k} + \tau_c B$$

Therefore, Modigliani and Miller's Proposition 1 with tax can be stated as follows:

Given Assumptions 1–4, the value of a levered firm exceeds that of an unlevered firm in the same business risk class with the same expected earnings by an amount $\tau_c B$ where $\tau_c$ is the corporate tax rate and $B$ the value of the levered firm's debt.

### 11.3.2 *Miller's irrelevance argument*

The conclusion we have reached so far is not overly satisfactory as a description of the real world. It suggests that by increasing its debt, a corporation can infinitely increase its value. To say the least, this virtual license to print money is implausible. Moreover, corporations do not continually increase the proportion of debt in their capital structure.

One approach to this dilemma has been proposed by Merton Miller (1977). Miller's analysis brings personal taxes, as well as corporate taxes, into the discussion and rests on the notion of *equilibrium* in the corporate bond market. Miller's model is based on the following assumptions:

1. Investors hold either common equity or bonds.
2. All distributions to stockholders are capital gains or untaxed dividends. We provide some support for this by noting the following:
   - No investor has to realize a capital gain before death.
   - Capital gains and capital losses in well-diversified portfolios can offset one another.
   - 80% of dividends received by taxable corporations can be excluded from taxable income.

- Many types of investment funds, such as pension or trust funds, pay no tax at all.

3. Interest on bonds is taxed at the personal tax rate, which varies among investors from 0 for tax-exempt institutions to the top marginal rate paid by high-income earners.

Let us consider first the *aggregate* position of all firms and begin with an imaginary world in which all firms are unlevered. Managers realize the potential to increase their firm's value by increasing debt and therefore attempt to persuade investors to purchase debt by offering sufficiently attractive interest rates. Tax-exempt institutions are the most easily persuaded, because the interest payments they receive are tax-free. However, to attract bond purchasers, the interest rate must be made more attractive to compensate for the taxes that must be paid on interest received. How far will this process go? Corporations will continue to try to attract further debt, bidding up the price (interest rate) to the point at which this price is so high that issuing more debt fails to raise the firm's value. In this *equilibrium* condition, the cost of debt is such that the next dollar of debt issued has no net effect on the firm's value.

Who are the holders of debt in this model? Investors whose marginal tax rate is not higher than the corporate tax rate. Suppose that an investor has a choice between debt and equity. A dollar of operating income can accrue to this investor as either interest payment on a bond or as a distribution to stockholders. In the first case, the investor receives, *after tax*, $\$(1 - \tau_P)$, where $\tau_P$ is the personal tax rate. As a stockholder, this investor could obtain $\$(1 - \tau_c)$, where $\tau_c$ is the corporate tax rate. Clearly, bonds should be preferred if $\tau_P$ is less than $\tau_c$. For the individual investor, the point at which personal and corporate tax rates are the same represents a position of indifference between holding debt and equity. Suppose that the corporate tax rate is 40%, and that an investor pays personal tax at this marginal rate. If this investor is entitled to \$1 of the corporation's earnings, there are two possibilities:

1. As a bondholder, \$1 is received, on which 40 cents of tax are paid, leaving 60 cents after tax.
2. The corporation pays tax of 40 cents, leaving 60 cents for distribution to the stockholder.

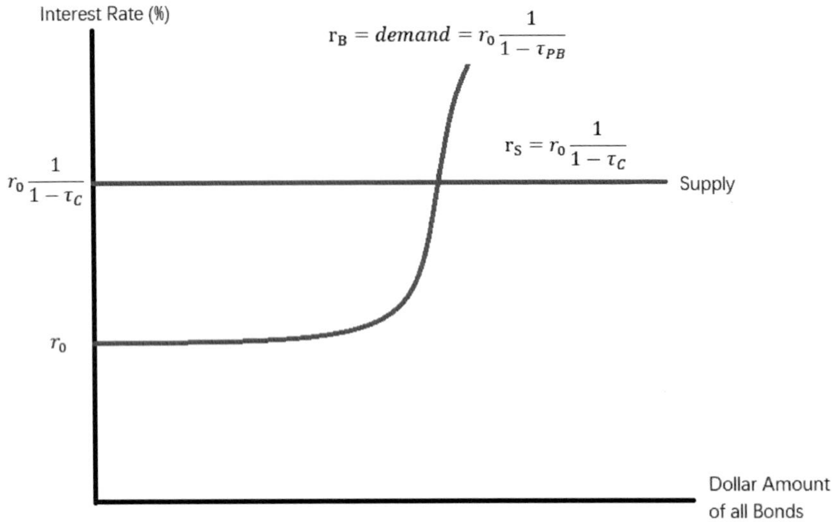


Figure 11.2 Aggregated Supply and Demand for Corporate Bonds.

We see that for this investor it is a matter of indifference whether the claim on earnings is through debt or equity.

The foregoing argument suggests that, in the aggregate, for most firms there is an optimal debt–equity ratio, as shown by Figure 11.2. However, let us now consider the position of a single firm. Whatever this firm's capital structure, the equilibrium position in the bond market is such that the price paid for debt balances the increase in the firm's value that can accrue from the corporate tax advantage of the issuance of debt. For this firm, then, the net effect is zero.

When personal income tax is taken into account along with the corporate income tax, Miller shows the gain from leverage, $G_L$, for the stockholder to be

$$G_L = \left[1 - \frac{(1-\tau_c)(1-\tau_{PS})}{(1-\tau_{PB})}\right] B \tag{11.10}$$

where $\tau_c$ is the corporate tax rate; $\tau_{PS}$ is the personal income tax rate on income from stock ownership; $\tau_{PB}$ is the market value of the firm's debt.

As we have argued, if $\tau_{PS} = 0$ and the market is in equilibrium, then $(1 - \tau_c) = (1 - \tau_{PB})$ for the margined investor, and the firm's $G_L$ from issuing debt will be 0, as can be seen by putting these values in Eq. (11.10):

$$G_L = \left[1 - \frac{(1 - \tau_c)(1 - 0)}{(1 - \tau_c)}\right] \times B = (1 - 1)B = 0$$

In reality, it is possible for the individual to defer the payment of taxes on capital gains by not selling stock. In fact, Miller argues that this can be done indefinitely. If this is correct, then it is possible for $\tau_{PS}$ to equal 0, as we have assumed in the above argument.

Under the Tax Reform Act of 1986, which went into effect in January 1987, dividends and capital gains are taxed at a maximum tax rate of 28%. This is a major change from the previous 50% rate on dividends and 20% rate on long-term capital gains. The new tax law also shifts the major tax burden to corporations and away from individuals, even though the maximum corporate tax rate is now 34%, reduced from 40%. Corporations will be paying more taxes because of the loss of the loss of the investment tax credit and the changes to the Accelerated Cost Recovery System depreciation allowances.

If we look at Eq. (11.10) and the changes of the Tax Reform Act of 1986, we can see the following:

1. The decrease of personal rates $\tau_{PS}$ and $\tau_{PB}$ will, in general, reduce the value of the tax shield.
2. The reductions in corporate tax rates will, in general, reduce the value of the tax shield.

In the aggregate, the impact of the reduction of personal and corporate tax rates will reduce the tax shield value of interest deductibility. This should reduce the amount of debt financing used by corporations, other things being equal.

The change of the tax code to make capital gains and dividends taxable at the same rate appears to make $(1 - \tau_{PB})$ equal $(1 - \tau_{PS})$. If these cancel out of Eq. (11.10), then we are left with the tax shield value on interest deductibility equal to $\tau_c B$, as first proposed by M&M. However, this is not the case. The shareholder can still defer capital earnings by not selling stock. Therefore, $(1 - \tau_{PS})$ will not equal $(1 - \tau_{PB})$ and the tax shield value will be somewhat less than the $\tau_c B$ identified by M&M.

We have come full circle, returning to M&M's Proposition 1. According to Miller's argument, even in the presence of corporate taxes, capital structure is irrelevant in determining a firm's market value. However, as a practical matter, such factors as bankruptcy and agency costs, as well as market imperfections, may make capital-structure decisions an important determinant of firm value.

## 11.4 Degree of Financial Leverage, Operating Leverage, and the Combined Effect[1]

We have seen that financial leverage can lead to higher expected earnings for a corporation's stockholders. The use of borrowed funds to generate higher earnings is known as *financial leverage*. But this is not the only form of leverage available to increase corporate earnings. Another form is *operating leverage*, which pertains to the proportion of the firm's fixed-operating costs. In this section, we discuss the combined effect of these two types of leverage. Before doing so, however, we discuss a measure of the extent, or degree, of leverage.

### 11.4.1 *Degree of financial leverage*

Suppose that a levered corporation improves its performance of the previous year by increasing its operating income by 1%. What is the effect on earnings per share? If you answered "a 1% increase," you have ignored the influence of leverage. To illustrate, consider the corporation of Table 11.1. In the current year, as we saw earlier, this firm produces earnings per share of \$2.49.

The firm's operating performance improves next year, to the extent that earnings before interest and taxes increase by 1%, from \$270 million to \$272.7 million. Other relevant factors are unchanged. Interest payments are \$104 million, and with a corporate tax rate of 40%, 60% of earnings after interest are available for distribution to stockholders. Thus, earnings available to stockholders = $0.60(272.7-104) =$ \$101.22 million. Therefore, with 40 million shares

[1]In Appendix 2C of Chapter 2, we have defined these three variables in terms of elasticity definition. In addition, we also show how Excel can use these three variables in terms of accounting data. The detailed derivations of DOL, DFL, and DCL can be found in Chapter 7 of Lee and Lee (2017).

outstanding, earnings per share next year will be

$$\text{EPS} = \frac{\$101.22}{40} = \$2.5305$$

Hence, the percentage increase in earnings per share is

$$\%\ \text{Change in EPS} = \frac{2.5305 - 2.49}{2.49} \times 100 = 1.6265\%$$

We see that a 1% increase in EBIT leads to a greater percentage increase in EPS. The reason is that none of the increased earnings need be paid to debtholders. All of this increase goes to equity holders, who therefore benefit disproportionately. The argument is symmetrical. If EBIT were to fall by 1%, then EPS would fall by 1.6265%.

The extent to which a given percentage increase in operating income produces a greater percentage increase in earnings per share provides a measure of the effect of leverage on stockholders' earnings. This is known as the *degree of financial leverage* (DFL) and is defined as

$$\text{DFL} = \frac{\%\ \text{Change in EPS}}{\%\ \text{Change in EBIT}}$$

We now develop an expression for the degree of financial leverage. Suppose that a firm has earnings before interest and tax of EBIT, and debt of $B$, on which are interest payments at rate $i$. If the corporate tax rate is $\tau_c$, then

$$\text{Earnings available to stockholders} = (1 - \tau_c)(\text{EBIT} - \text{iB}) \qquad (11.11)$$

If the firm increases operating income by 1% to 1.01 EBIT, with everything else unchanged, we have

$$\text{Earnings available to stockholders} = (1 - \tau_c)(1.01 \times \text{EBIT} - \text{iB}) \qquad (11.12)$$

Comparing Eqs. (11.11) and (11.12), the increase in earnings available to stockholders is

$$(1 - \tau_c)(1.01\,\text{EBIT} - iB) - (1 - \tau_c)(\text{EBIT} - iB) = 0.01(1 - \tau_c)\text{EBIT}$$

It follows that the percentage change in stockholders' earnings, and hence in earnings per share, is

$$\begin{aligned}\%\text{ Change in EPS} &= \frac{(0.01)(1-\tau_c)\text{EBIT}}{(1-\tau_c)(\text{EBIT}-iB)}\times 100\\ &= \frac{(0.01)\text{EBIT}}{\text{EBIT}-iB}\times 100\end{aligned}$$

Since the increase in EBIT is 1%, it follows from our definition that the degree of financial leverage is

$$\text{DFL} = \frac{(0.01)\text{EBIT}}{(\text{EBIT}-iB)0.01)} = \frac{\text{EBIT}}{\text{EBIT}-iB} = 1.6265 \qquad (11.13)$$

Thus, the degree of financial leverage can be found as the ratio of net operating income to income remaining after interest payments on debt. This is illustrated in Figure 11.3, which plots the degree of financial leverage against interest payments for a given level of net operating income. If there are no interest payments, so that the firm is unlevered, DFL is 1. That is, each 1% increase in earnings before interest and tax leads to a 1% increase in earnings per share. As interest payments increase, so does the degree of financial leverage, to the point where, if interest payments equal net operating

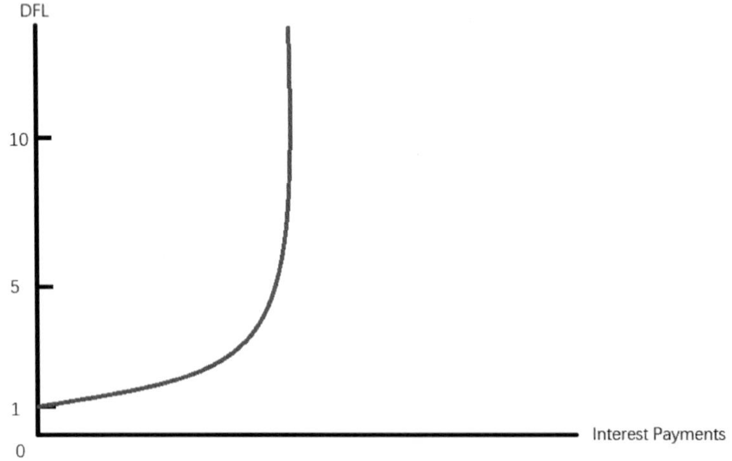


Figure 11.3 Relation between Degree of Financial Leverage and Interest Payments.

income, DFL is infinite. This is not surprising, for in this case there would be no earnings available to stockholders. Hence, any increase in net operating income would, proportionately, yield an infinitely large improvement.

### 11.4.2 *Operating leverage and the combined effect*

Net earnings are the difference between total sales value and total operating costs. We now look in detail at operating costs, which we break down into two components: fixed costs and variable costs. *Fixed costs* are costs that the firm must incur, whatever its level of production. Such costs include rent and equipment depreciation. *Variable costs* are costs that increase with production, such as wages. The mix of fixed and variable costs in a firm's total operating cost structure provides operating leverage. Let us consider a firm with a single product, under the following conditions:

- The firm incurs fixed costs $F$, which must be paid whatever the level of output.
- Each unit of output costs an additional amount $V$.
- Each unit of output can be sold at price $P$.
- A total of $Q$ units of output are produced and sold.

In Table 11.4 we display some further information on the firm of Table 11.1. This company produces parts for the automobile industry. Its current net operating income is derived from the sale of 10 million units, priced at \$150 each. Operating cost consist of \$310 million of fixed costs and variable costs of \$92 per unit.

Suppose this corporation increases its sales volume by 1% to 10.1 million units next year, with other factors unchanged. Would you

Table 11.4 Cost and Sales Data for Corporation of Table 11.1.

| | |
|---|---|
| Value of sales | \$1,500 million |
| Fixed operating costs | \$310 million |
| Variable operating costs | 920 million |
| Total operating costs | 1,230 million |
| Earnings before interest and taxes | \$270 million |
| Volume of sales | 10 million units |
| Price per unit | \$150 |

guess that earnings before interest and tax also increase by 1%? In fact, net operating income will rise by more than 1%. The reason is that while the value of sales and variable operating costs increases proportionately, fixed operating costs remain uncharged. These costs, then, constitute a source of operating leverage. The greater the share of total cost attributable to fixed costs, the greater this leverage.

The extent to which a given percentage increase in sales volume produces a greater percentage increase in earnings before interest and taxes is used to measure the degree of operating leverage.

The degree of operating leverage (DOL) is given by

$$\text{DOL} = \frac{\%\ \text{Change in EBIT}}{\%\ \text{Change in sales volume}}$$

Let us now find a measure of degree of operating leverage. If $Q$ units are sold at price $P$, then

$$\text{Value of sales} = QP$$

Total operating costs consist of fixed costs $F$ and total variable costs $QV$, so that

$$\text{Total operating costs} = \text{Fixed costs} + \text{Variable costs} = F + QV$$

Therefore, we can write

$$\begin{aligned}&\text{Earnings before interest and taxes}\\&\quad = \text{Value of sales} - \text{Total operating costs}\end{aligned}$$

So that

$$\text{EBIT} = QP - (F + QV) = Q(P - V) - F \qquad (11.14)$$

Suppose that sales volume increases by 1% from $Q$ to $1.01Q$. In this case, we have

$$\text{EBIT} = 1.01(Q(P - V) - F)$$

So that, by comparison with (11.14), the increase in EBIT is $0.01Q(P - V)$. It follows that

$$\%\ \text{Change in EBIT} = \frac{0.01Q(P - V)}{Q(P - V) - F} \times 100 = \frac{Q(P - V)}{Q(P - V) - F}$$

Since there is a 1% increase in sales volume, it follows from our definition of degree of operating leverage that

$$\text{DOL} = \frac{Q(P - V)}{Q(P - V) - F} \tag{11.15}$$

Therefore,

$$\text{DOL} = \frac{\text{Value of sales} - \text{Variable costs}}{\text{Value of sales} - \text{Variable costs} - \text{Fixed costs}}$$

Let us compute the degree of operating leverage for the firm of Table 11.4:

$$\text{DOL} = \frac{1{,}500 - 920}{1{,}500 - 920 - 310} = 2.1481$$

For this firm, each 1% increase in sales volume leads to an increase of 2.1481% in earnings before interest and taxes.

The source of operating leverage is illustrated in Figure 11.4, which plots degree of operating leverage against the proportion of total fixed costs. If there are no fixed costs, then, as is clear from Eq. (11.15), the degree of operating leverage is 1. In other words, there is no operating leverage, and a 1% increase in sales volume leads to a 1% increase in earnings before interest and taxes. As the proportion of fixed costs increases, so does the degree of operating leverage.

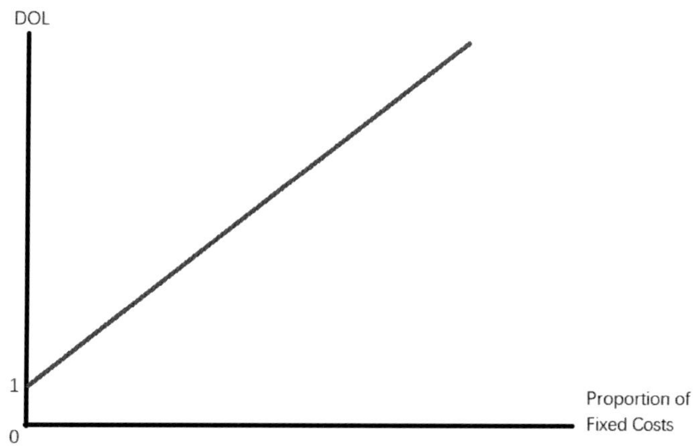


Figure 11.4 Relation between Degree of Operating Leverage and Proportion of Fixed Costs.

Operating leverage and financial leverage may act in combination, so that the impact of a change in corporate performance, as measured by volume of sales, is magnified in its effect on earnings per share. We can think of this combined leverage effect as developing through two stages:

1. To the extent that there are fixed costs in a firm's total cost structure, an increase (decrease) in sales volume produces a greater percentage increase (decrease) in earnings before interest and taxes, through the effect of operating leverage.
2. To the extent that interest payments must be made to debtholders, an increase (decrease) in earnings before interest and taxes produces a greater percentage increase (decrease) in earnings per share.

The combined leverage effect measures the extent to which a given percentage increase in sales volume leads to a greater percentage increase in earnings per share.

The *combined leverage effect* (CLE) is given by

$$\text{CLE} = \frac{\text{\% Change of EPS}}{\text{\% Change in sales volume}}$$

We can express the combined leverage effect as

$$\begin{aligned}\text{CLE} &= \frac{\text{\% Change in EPS}}{\text{\% Change in EBIT}} \times \frac{\text{\% Change in EBIT}}{\text{\% Change in sales volume}}\\ &= \text{DFL} \times \text{DOL}\end{aligned}$$

Therefore, we see that combined leverage is the product of the degrees of financial and operating leverage. For the firm of Tables 11.1 and 11.4, we find from our previous calculations that

$$\text{CLE} = (1.625)(2.1481) = 3.49$$

For this firm, each 1% increase in sales volume leads to an increase of 3.49% in earnings per share. Thus, the combined effects of operating and financial leverage produce for stockholders a magnification of variations in business performance, in the sense that percentage changes in sales volume are reflected in percentage changes of almost three-and-one-half their size in earnings per share.

We conclude this discussion by giving an algebraic expression that allows direct evaluation of the combined leverage effect. Writing earnings before interest and taxes as

$$\text{EBIT} = Q(P - V) - F$$

and using Eq. 11.13, the degree of financial leverage is

$$\text{DFL} = \frac{Q(P - V) - F}{Q(P - V) - F - iB}$$

Therefore, using Eq. (11.15), we can find the combined leverage effect:

$$\text{CLE} = \text{DFL} \times \text{DOL}$$

$$= \frac{Q(P - V) - F}{Q(P - V) - F - iB} \times \frac{Q(P - V)}{Q(P - V) - F}$$

$$= \frac{Q(P - V)}{Q(P - V) - F - iB}$$

Thus, combined leverage can be found as follows:

$$\text{CLE} = \frac{Q(P - V)}{Q(P - V) - F - iB} \tag{11.16}$$

It is the final two terms in the denominator of Eq. (11.16), acting in combination, that produce leverage. If there were no fixed operating costs and no interest payments on the debt, then there would be no leverage. Each dollar increase in either term, all else equal, produces the same leverage as a dollar increase the other. Moreover, we see that if an increase in interest payments is matched by a decrease of the same amount in fixed operating costs, then leverage will be unchanged.

We now verify Eq. (11.16) for the firm of Tables 11.1 and 11.4. For this firm, value of sales = \$1,500; variable operating costs = \$920; fixed operating costs = \$310; and interest payments on debt = \$104 (all figures are in millions of dollars). Therefore,

$$\text{CLE} = \frac{1{,}500 - 920}{1{,}500 - 920 - 310 - 104} = \frac{580}{166} = 3.49$$

confirming our earlier finding.

In Appendix 2C of Chapter 2, we used Johnson & Johnson data to calculate DOL, DFL, and CLE, which are defined in this section.

### 11.4.3 *The trade-off between business risk and financial risk*

Leverage is a two-edged sword. If stockholders know that a corporation could improve its operating performance, they would prefer a high degree of leverage. As we have just seen, a relatively small sales-growth rate can, through the combined effects of operating leverage and financial leverage, lead to a much larger proportionate increase in earnings per share. However, the economic climate in which corporations operate is too complex and unpredictable to allow such certainty in judgments. Sales could fall short of expectations, and quite possibly fall from earlier levels. In this case, leverage works against stockholders, and a small decrease in sales leads to a proportionately greater drop in earnings per share for the levered corporation. Therefore, in conjunction with leverage, it is also necessary to consider uncertainty, or risk.

Just as there are two types of leverage, we must also examine two types of risk. As discussed earlier in this book, business risk describes uncertainty about future earnings before interest and taxes. Such uncertainty can arise for a number of reasons. First, it is impossible to forecast sales demand with complete precision, so that there will be some uncertainty about future sales volume. A related issue involves the prices at which a corporation is able to sell its products. In markets where there is intense competition among firms, competitors may react to slack demand by price-cutting, offering temporary discounts, providing generous loan terms, and other inducements to potential customers. To compete successfully, our firm will probably have to match its competitors' moves, which eats into profits. A further source of uncertainty arises because production costs cannot be predicted with certainty. Prices of raw materials used by a manufacturer can fluctuate dramatically over time.

These sources of uncertainty about business conditions must be considered in the context of operating leverage. We have seen that, if the business climate is favorable for our corporation, the higher the degree of operating leverage, the higher the expected net operating income. On the other hand, the higher the degree of operating leverage, all else equal, the greater the uncertainty about earnings before interest and taxes. The typical position is illustrated in Figure 11.5,

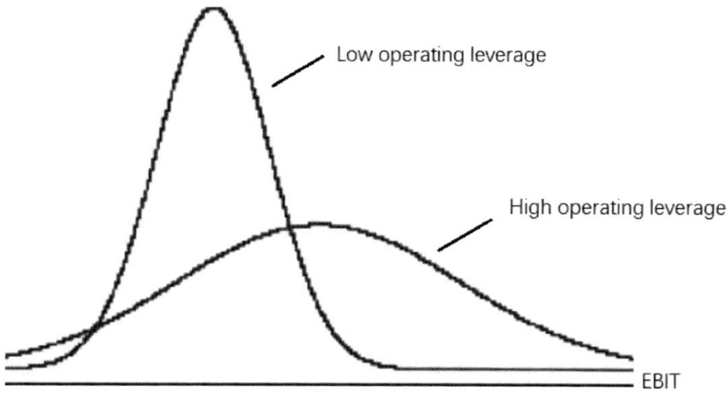


Figure 11.5 Probability Density Functions for Earnings before Interest and Taxes for Firms with Low and High Degrees of Operating Leverage.

which shows probability distributions representing likely earnings before interest and taxes for two corporations. These firms are identical, except that one has a greater degree of operating leverage. The following points emerge from this graph:

1. The mean of the EBIT distribution for the firm with the higher degree of operating leverage is greater than that for the other firm. This reflects the increase in expected EBIT that can arise from operating leverage.
2. The variance of the EBIT distribution for the firm with the higher degree of operating leverage is greater than that for the firm with less leverage; that is, the former distribution is more widely dispersed about its mean than the latter distribution. This reflects the increase in business risk associated with a high degree of operating leverage.

Next, we consider financial risk. In the first section of this chapter, we saw that a high proportion of debt in a firm's capital structure can lead to higher expected earnings per share, but also to greater uncertainty about such earnings. This uncertainty is known as financial risk. Figure 11.6 shows the probability distributions of earnings per share for two corporations. The probability distributions of EBIT are the same for these two corporations, but one firm has a higher

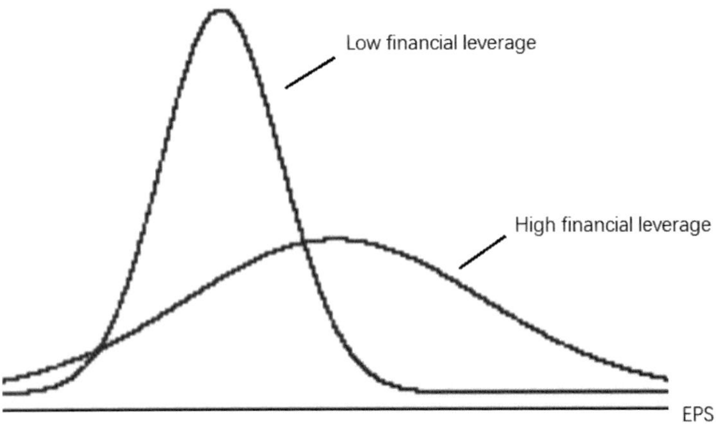


Figure 11.6 Probability Density Functions for Earnings per Share for Firms with Low and High Degrees of Financial Leverage.

degree of financial leverage than the other. From this figure, we see the following:

1. The mean of the EPS distribution for the firm with the higher degree of financial leverage exceeds the mean of the other firm. This reflects the potential for higher expected EPS resulting from financial leverage.
2. The variance of the EPS distribution is higher for the firm with the greater degree of financial leverage. This reflects the increase in financial risk resulting from financial leverage.

Thus, the overall risk faced by corporate stockholders is a combination of business risk and financial risk. We might think of the possibility of a trade-off between these two types of risk. Suppose that a firm operates in a risky business environment. Perhaps it trades in volatile markets and is highly capital-intensive, so that a large proportion of its costs are fixed. This riskiness will be exacerbated if the firm also has substantial debt, so that the firm has considerable financial risk. On the other hand, a low degree of financial leverage, and hence of financial risk, can mitigate the impact of high business risk on the overall riskiness of stockholders' equity. Management of a corporation subject to low business risk might feel more sanguine about taking on additional debt and thereby increasing financial risk.

## 11.5 Target Capital Structure

Our discussion on the proportion of debt that a corporation should have in its capital structure has yielded some important information but has not taken us to the point where we can analyze a firm to determine exactly what that proportion should be. We have discussed one theoretical model that suggests that capital structure should have no influence on a firm's value. We saw that raising the degree of financial leverage should lead to an increase in expected earnings for stockholders; however, this also results in additional financial risk. According to the models of Modigliani and Miller, these two factors should cancel out each other in the sense that capital structure is irrelevant in determining a firm's market value.

Nevertheless, in reality managers do set targets for debt levels. In this and the following section, we discuss the factors that management considers in determining such *target capital structures* and possible reasons that optimal capital structures might exist.

### 11.5.1 *Cost of capital and target capital structure*

We have examined the relationship between capital structure and stockholders' earnings. We now look at the problem in terms of a corporation's cost of acquiring capital. As we will see, these two ways of viewing capital structure and market value of the firm are related.

To develop our analysis, we begin by expressing the firm's market value as the sum of the values of debt and stockholders' equity; that is,

$$V = B + S \tag{11.17}$$

where $V$ = market value of firm; $B$ = value of debt; and $S$ = value of stockholders' equity.

Suppose that our firm has net operating income EBIT, so that earnings available for distribution to stockholders will be

$$\text{Net income after taxes} = (1 - \tau_c)(\text{EBIT} - iB)$$

where EBIT = earnings before interest and taxes; $\tau_c$ = corporate tax rate; and $i$ = interest rate on debt.

Let us now consider the rates of return achieved by this company. We can either consider the rate of return on all assets

$$r_A = \frac{(1 - \tau_c)\text{EBIT}}{V} \tag{11.18}$$

that would prevail if all earnings were taxed, or the rate of return on stockholders' equity

$$r_E = \frac{(1 - \tau_c)(\text{EBIT} - iB)}{S} \tag{11.19}$$

From Eq. (11.18), we can write

$$(1 - \tau_c)\text{EBIT} = r_A V$$

Substitution in Eq. (11.19) then yields

$$r_A = \frac{S}{V} r_E + \frac{B}{V}(1 - \tau_c)i \tag{11.20}$$

Eq. (11.20) has an important interpretation in terms of cost of capital. To understand this, let us consider the following:

- Suppose that a corporation wishes to raise capital through the sale of common stock. The quantity $r_E$ measures the rate of return on equity demanded by common stockholders. Therefore, we can view $r_E$ as the price to be paid, or the cost to the firm, of an additional dollar of stockholders' equity.
- Suppose that the firm is able to borrow funds at interest rate $i$. This is the price that must be paid to bondholders for each additional dollar borrowed. However, corporate tax, at rate $\tau_c$ is not paid on that portion of net operating income allocated to debt servicing. Therefore, the cost to a corporation of a dollar of debt is $(1 - \tau_c)i$.
- Typically, corporate capital structure consists of both equity and debt. How can we combine the individual costs of these components of capital structure to form a measure of the overall cost of capital? What we need is an average of the two costs. In forming such an average, it is natural for a firm with a high degree of financial leverage to heavily weight the cost of debt. However, if the firm has little debt, its cost of debt should not be heavily weighted in computing overall cost of capital. A natural measure is to form a weighted average in which the weight given to the cost of equity

is the proportion $S/V$ of the firm's total value attributable to the stockholders' equity value, and the weight given to the cost of debt is the proportion $B/V$ of the firm's total debt value. This is what is done in Eq. (11.20), so that we call $r_A$ the *weighted average cost of capital.*

### 11.5.2 *Weighted average cost of capital*

The weighted average cost of capital is given by

$$r_A = \frac{S}{V} r_E + \frac{B}{V}(1 - \tau_c)i$$

where $V$ = total market value of the firm; $S$ = value of stockholders' equity; $B$ = value of debt; $r_E$ = rate of return on stockholders' equity; $i$ = interest rate on debt; and $\tau_c$ = corporate tax rate.

Here, $r_E$ is the cost of equity, and $(1 - \tau_c)i$ is the cost of debt. Hence, $r_A$ is a weighted average of these two costs, with respective weights $S/V$ and $B/V$.

As can be seen from Eq. (11.18), there is a relatively simple relationship between a firm's value and its weighted average cost of capital. From that equation, we find

$$V = \frac{(1 - \tau_c)\text{EBIT}}{r_A}$$

This suggests that the debt–equity mix that maximizes a firm's value is that for which the weighted average costs of capital are lowest. As Example 11.1 illustrates, cost of capital can be used to determine an appropriate capital structure for a firm.

**Example 11.1.** A corporation with no debt is privately owned. This corporation generates average annual net operating earnings of \$5 million. Because of business risk, earnings have not been precisely at this level each year, but rather have fluctuated around this figure. The corporation pays tax on earnings at a 40%.

The owners of this corporation are planning to sell it to the public and are considering the possibility of issuing debt. To keep our calculations manageable, let us assume that debt can be issued in multiples of \$2 million, up to a maximum of \$12 million. Management

Table 11.5 Management Estimates of Interest Rate on Debt and Stockholders' Expected Return on Equity for Different Levels of Debt.

| **Debt (B) ($ millions)** | **Interest Rate on Debt (i)** | **Rate of Return on Equity ($r_E$)** |
|---|---|---|
| 0 | — | 0.120 |
| 2 | 0.100 | 0.124 |
| 4 | 0.105 | 133 |
| 6 | 0.112 | 0.145 |
| 8 | 0.125 | 0.160 |
| 10 | 0.142 | 0.180 |
| 12 | 0.165 | 0.205 |

believes that the greater the level of debt, the riskier will bondholders perceive this debt, and hence the higher rate of interest they will demand. Table 11.5 provides estimates of required interest rates as well as estimates of the rate of return expected by stockholders for different levels of debt. These rates increase with the level of debt, as stockholders require compensation for additional financial risk. The corporation expect to continue producing average net operating income at past levels, with the same level of business risk.

Given the estimates of Table 11.5, we now determine how much debt this firm should have in its capital structure to maximize its total value. In the notation we are using, for this corporation, EBIT = 5 and $\tau_c = 0.40$.

The first step is to calculate, for each level of debt, the value of stockholders' equity. We do this by writing Eq. (11.19) as

$$S = \frac{(1 - \tau_c)(\text{EBIT} - iB)}{r_E}$$

so that we have

$$S = \frac{0.60(5 - iB)}{r_E}$$

For example, if \$8 million of debt is issued, the value of stockholders' equity is

$$S = \frac{0.60(5 - 1)}{0.160} = \$15 \text{ million}$$

Next, the firm's total market value is found by adding the value of debt to the value of stockholders' equity, yielding, in the case of \$8 million of debt,

$$V = B + S = 8 + 15 = \$23 \text{ million}$$

In this case, we find a total market value of \$23 million.

The results of similar calculations for this and other possible debt levels are displayed in Table 11.6 and in Figure 11.7, where we plot the firm's total market value against the level of debt issued. From these calculations, we see that the firm's total value is maximized by selling \$2 million of debt and \$23.23 million of common equity, so that, as shown in Table 11.6, at this optimal structure, 8% of the firm's total value is attributable to debt.

In the third column of Table 11.6, we compute the cost of debt as $(1 - \tau_c)i$. The cost of equity is $r_E$, which must be combined with the cost of debt to find the weighted average cost of capital, as shown in Eq. (11.20).

Alternatively, the weighted average cost of capital, $r_A$, can be computed directly from Eq. (11.8). The results of these calculations are given in the last column of Table 11.6 and plotted in Figure 11.8, which graphs the weighted average cost of capital against the level of debt. As expected, the minimum value of $r_A$ also occurs when \$2 million of debt is issued. In this case, the cost of a dollar of debt is 0.060, the cost of a dollar of equity is \$0.124, and the weighted average cost of a dollar of capital is \$0.119.

In Example 11.1, we have examined the case of a firm for which there apparently is an optimal capital structure. How does this square with our earlier theoretical discussion suggesting that capital structure is irrelevant in the valuation of a firm? If the assumptions of the M&M analysis are correct, one answer is that the management estimates of stockholders' expected rates of return on equity, given in Table 11.5, are incorrect. However, a second answer is that in the real world we are likely to find that the assumptions of our theoretical model are invalid. This is discussed in detail later in this chapter.

### 11.5.3 *Capital structure and beta determination*

In our discussion of the capital asset pricing model, we saw that the rate of return, $R_i$, expected by holders of security $i$ could be

Table 11.6 Firm Value and Level of Debt.

| B | I | $r_E$ | Value of Equity(S) ($ millions) | Value of Firm (V) ($ millions) | B/V | $(1-\tau_c)i$ | $R_A$ |
|---|---|---|---|---|---|---|---|
| 0 | — | 0.120 | 25.00 | 25.00 | — | — | 0.120 |
| 2 | 0.100 | 0.124 | 23.23 | 25.23 | 0.08 | 0.060 | 0.119 |
| 4 | 0.105 | 0.133 | 20.66 | 24.66 | 0.16 | 0.063 | 0.122 |
| 6 | 0.112 | 0.145 | 17.91 | 23.91 | 0.25 | 0.067 | 0.125 |
| 8 | 0.125 | 0.160 | 15.00 | 23.00 | 0.35 | 0.075 | 0.130 |
| 10 | 0.143 | 0.180 | 11.93 | 21.93 | 0.46 | 0.085 | 0.137 |
| 12 | 0.165 | 0.205 | 8.84 | 20.84 | 0.58 | 0.099 | 0.144 |

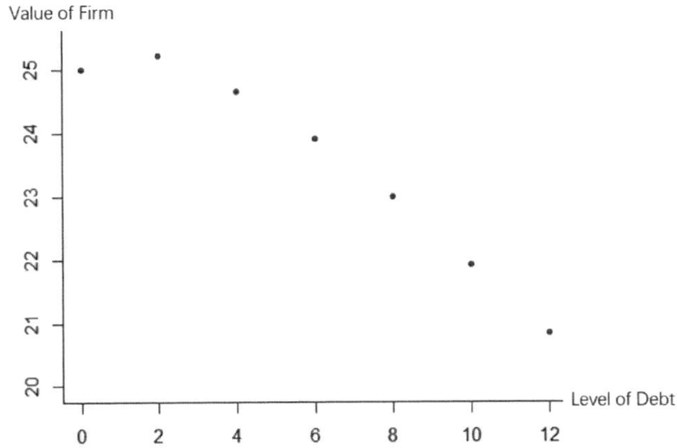


Figure 11.7 Firm Value Plotted Against Level of Debt for Data of Example 11.1.

expressed as

$$E(R_i) = R_f + \beta_i[E(R_M) - R_f]$$

where $R_f$ is the risk-free rate and $R_M$ is the rate of return on a market basket of securities. Here, $\beta_i$ (beta) is the systematic risk of security $i$.

Suppose that the security is a share in the common stock of a corporation. Let us assume that this corporation increases the proportion of deb in its capital structure, all other relevant factors remaining unchanged. How would you expect this change to affect the firm's beta? We have seen that an increase in the riskiness of stockholders' future earnings. To compensate for this additional risk, stockholders' will demand a higher expected rate of return. Therefore, from Eq. (11.2), beta must rise for this company's stock.[2] We see that, all other things equal, the higher the proportion of debt in a

[2]From the definition of beta

$$\beta_i = \frac{\rho_{iM}\sigma_i\sigma_M}{\sigma_M^2}$$

we know that $\sigma_i$ increases, therefore, we must conclude that $\beta$ must increase.

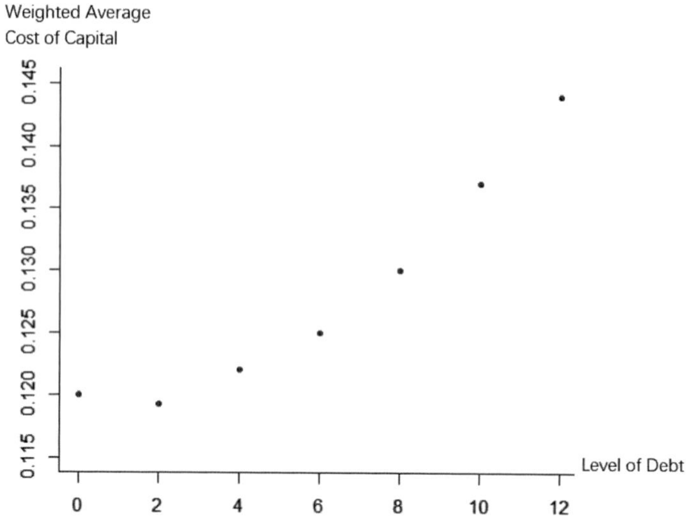


Figure 11.8 Weighted Average Cost of Capital Plotted Against Level of Debt for Data of Example 11.1.

firm's capital structure, the higher the beta of shares of its common stock.

$$\beta_L = \beta_U \left(1 + \frac{B(1-\tau_c)}{S}\right) \tag{11.21}$$

where $\beta_L$ is the leveraged beta; $\beta_U$ is the unlevered operating beta; $B$ is the amount of debt; $S$ is the amount of equity; and $\tau_c$ is the corporate tax rate.

When the market model is used to estimate a firm's beta, as in Chapter 8, the resulting estimate of the beta is the market assessment of both operating and financial risk. This is called the *leveraged beta*. Hamada (1972) and Rubinstein (1973) suggest that Eq. (11.21) can be modified to calculate the unleveraged beta. This beta is an estimate of the firm's operating, or business, risk.

From Chapters 2 and 8, we know that Johnson and Johnson's related data are $\beta_L = 0.7449$ and average $(B/S) = 1.56$. If $\tau_c = 0.40$, then Ford's unleveraged beta can be calculated as

$$\beta_U = \frac{0.7449}{[1 + (1.56)(1 - 0.40)]} = \frac{0.7449}{1.536} = 0.49$$

## 11.6 Possible Reasons for Optimal Capital Structure

Our theoretical discussion, earlier in this chapter, on optimal capital structure did not take us very far toward producing a useful prescription for practical management decision-making. We know that greater financial leverage can yield higher expected earnings per share, but that this is accompanied by greater risk. Modigliani and Miller argue that as a result of investors' ability to create homemade leverage, a firm's market value will not depend on its capital structure. However, introducing corporate taxes into their analysis provides a possible tax shield for investors. Consequently, it becomes advantageous to issue debt to increase the firm's market value, according to this model. However, according to Miller's irrelevance argument, the picture changes again when personal taxes enter the discussion. Because individual investors have differing marginal personal tax rates, the cost of aggregate corporate borrowing will be an increasing function of the total amount borrowed. Therefore, in the aggregate, there will be an equilibrium optimal capital structure all firms. However, no individual firm is sufficiently powerful for its actions alone to disturb this market equilibrium cost of capital, so that for the individual firm, capital structure is again irrelevant to its market value.

Theoretical models such as those just discussed are valuable analytical tools. However, in general, theoretical development is possible only on the basis of assumptions that, at best, are idealizations of the real world and that may altogether neglect certain realities. In this section, we explore various factors not yet considered and see that such considerations may indeed suggest the existence of an optimal capital structure for the firm.

### 11.6.1 *The traditional approach of optimal capital structure*

Durand (1952) proposed an approach to explain why there is an optimal capital structure for a firm. Called the *traditional approach*, it suggests that "moderate" amounts of debt do not noticeably increase the risks to either the debtholders or the equityholders. Hence, both cost of debt ($i$) and cost of equity ($r_E$) are relatively constant up to some point. However, beyond some critical amount of debt used, both $i$ and $r_E$ increase. These increases in both the cost of debt and equity begin to offset the decrease in the average cost of capital ($r_A$), as indicated in Eq. (11.20), initially falls and then increases. This allows for a minimum value for the average cost of capital function. If the average cost of capital is at the minimum, then the firm's value

$$V = \frac{(1 - \tau_c)\text{EBIT}}{r_A}$$

is maximized. This implies that there is an optimum capital structure for the firm.

### 11.6.2 *Bankruptcy costs*

Earlier in this chapter, we saw in the M&M analysis that in the presence of corporate taxes, the value of the levered firm ($V_L$) exceeds the value of the otherwise comparable unlevered firm ($V_U$). The difference can be viewed as an increment to present value derived from the tax shelter ($\tau_c B$). Therefore, we can write

$$V_L = V_U + \tau_c B \tag{11.22}$$

One issue not considered in deriving this result is the possibility of corporate bankruptcy. Obligations to bondholders constitute a first claim on a company's assets. However, under U.S. law, stockholders, who are the owners of public companies, have only limited liability. Their personal assets, other than holdings in the firm, are protected from the claims of bondholders. If operating performance is sufficiently poor, stockholders can avoid obligations to bondholders through the firm's declaring bankruptcy. Essentially, bankruptcy turns over the firm to its debtholders. Bankruptcy proceeds can be very costly. Heavy legal fees must be paid, assets must often be sold at "bargain basement" prices, frequently following lengthy and expensive disputes among competing claimants. Taken together, these bankruptcy costs may be far from negligible, and the possibility of their being incurred must be considered in assessing a firm's market value.

On whom do bankruptcy costs fall? After bankruptcy, the firm belongs to its creditors, who must therefore bear these costs. However, purchasers of corporate bonds will be aware of this and will charge a higher price — that is, demand a higher interest rate — for debt. This, in turn, reduces the amount of earnings available for distribution to stockholders, reducing the value of shares. Hence, before bankruptcy, costs are carried by stockholders as reductions in the value of their equity holdings.

How much does the possibility of bankruptcy lower the firm's value? Two factors must be considered: (1) the costs incurred in the event of bankruptcy and (2) the likelihood, or probability, of bankruptcy occurring. For example, suppose that bankruptcy costs are estimated at \$5 million, and it is believed that there is one chance in ten of bankruptcy occurring. Then

$$\begin{aligned}&\text{Expected bankruptcy cost}\\&\quad= (\text{Probability of bankruptcy})(\text{Bankruptcy cost})\\&\quad= (0.1)(5{,}000{,}000) = \$500{,}000\end{aligned}$$

All other things equal, the greater the amount of debt a firm has, the more likely it will fail to meet its obligations and be driven to bankruptcy. Therefore, seeing this risk, bondholders will demand higher rates of interest the larger the debt, as suggested in Example 11.1. Thus, expected bankruptcy cost is an increasing function of the proportion of debt in a firm's capital structure.

Taking into account the possibility of bankruptcy and its effect on firm value, we can augment Eq. (11.9) as follows:

$$V_L = V_U + \tau_c B - \text{Present value of bankruptcy costs} \qquad (11.23)$$

The higher the level of debt, the greater the present value of the tax shield. As we saw in Eq. (11.9), the effect is linear, in the sense that the value of the tax shield is a constant multiple $\tau_c$ (the corporate tax rate) of the debt value. However, as Eq. (11.23) indicates, we must now subtract the present value of bankruptcy cost. This, too, is an increasing function of the debt level, reflecting the increase in the probability of bankruptcy that attaches to increasing debt levels.

We have seen that increasing debt yields a positive increment to firm value through the tax shield and a negative increment through bankruptcy costs. If these factors operate in conjunction, as illustrated in Figure 11.9, then an optimal capital structure results. We see for the unlevered firm, zero values for the tax shield and bankruptcy costs. Each increases with the level of debt issued, the

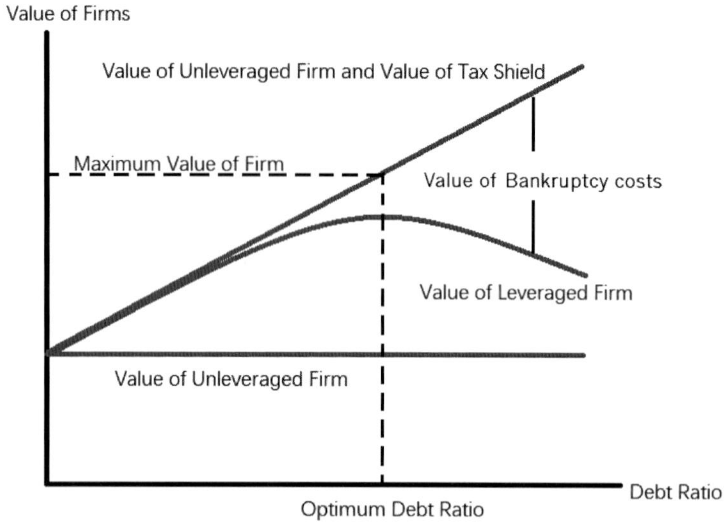


Figure 11.9 Possibility of Optimal Debt Ratio When Allowing for Present Value of Bankruptcy Costs.

net effect being a relationship between firm value and debt level that shows a maximum value for a debt level well below 100% of total value.

Myers (1984) called the optimal capital structure discussed in this section the *static trade-off theory*. He also proposed a *pecking-order theory* to contrast to the static trade-off theory. The pecking-order theory is based on the following:

1. Firms prefer internal finance.
2. Firms adapt their target dividend payout ratio to investment opportunities. (The target dividend payout ratio is discussed in Chapter 12.)
3. If internally generated cash flows are less than investment outlays, the firm first draws down its cash balance or marketable securities portfolio.
4. If external financing is required, the firm issues the safest security first. That is, the firm first issues debt, then hybrid securities such as convertible bonds, then equity as a last resort.

Looking at the behavior of firms in the marketplace, investment outlays are predominantly financed by debt issues and internally generated funds. New stock issues play a relatively small and infrequent part in raising new capital. This indicates that management follows a pecking order approach.

### 11.6.3 *Agency costs*

*Agency costs* are legal and contract costs that protect the rights of stockholders, bondholders, and management, and arise when the interests of these parties come into conflict. Such organizational conflict may lead to capital structure decisions that affect the firm's value. For example, having sold debt, stockholders may gain if the corporation abandons its low-risk projects in favor of more risky projects. If the higher-risk projects are successful, the stockholders will benefit from the high returns. On the other hand, this exposes bondholders to a higher degree of risk than they anticipated when the bonds were purchased, and thus they face a higher-than-expected chance of corporate bankruptcy.

Bondholders anticipate such possibilities and require that bonds be protected by restrictive covenants. Such covenants involve two types of costs to the firm. First, there are costs in monitoring the covenants, and second, these covenants restrict management flexibility, possibly precluding courses of action that would raise the firm's market value. These costs are borne by stockholders, resulting in a lower market value for equity.

In general, we might expect that agency costs of this sort will be greater the higher the debt. If there is little debt, bondholders will consider their investments relatively secure and demand only modest, fairly inexpensive protection of their interest. At higher debt levels, more stringent assurances will be required. Thus, agency costs affect firm value in much the same way as bankruptcy costs. The greater the debt, the greater the agency cost against firm value. This is illustrated in Figure 11.10, which extends Figure 11.9 by allowing for agency cost. At any level of debt above 0, agency cost causes a decrease in market value; the greater the debt level, the larger the agency cost factor. Hence, agency cost yields a lower optimal amount of debt in the capital structure than would otherwise prevail.

How does our discussion of bankruptcy and agency costs square with Miller's irrelevance argument? Under Miller's thesis, the competitive market will drive up the cost of debt to the point where it

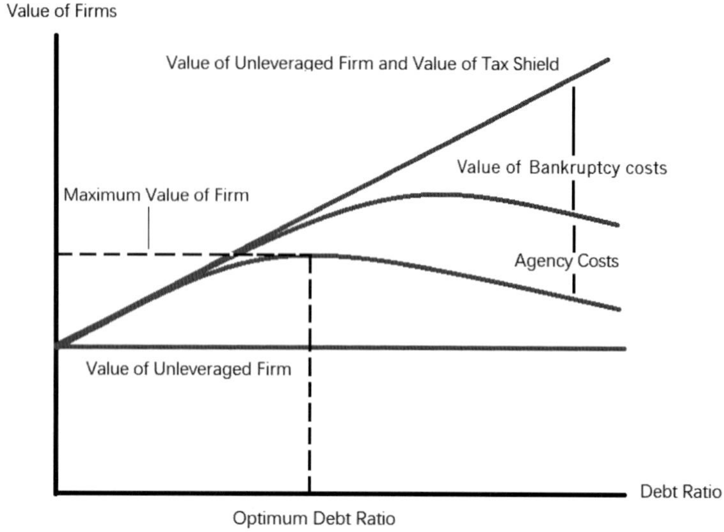


Figure 11.10 Possibility of Optimal Debt Ratio When Allowing for Present Value of Bankruptcy and Agency Costs.

balances the gain in market value derived from issuing debt. However, for the individual firm, the concept of a single price for debt may be an oversimplification. Rather, bankruptcy and agency costs will raise the price of debt as the level of debt increases. Therefore, there is indeed the possibility of an optimal capital structure.

### 11.6.4 *Imperfect markets*

The theoretical analysis of Modigliani and Miller is based on assumptions often characterized as perfect capital market behavior. In evaluating M&M's conclusions on the irrelevance of capital structure, it is natural to look for real-world departures from these assumptions. As we have seen, one important source of imperfection arises if, as a result of bankruptcy costs and agency costs, a firm must pay increasingly higher interest rates the greater the proportion of debt in its capital structure. When this negative impact of debt on firm value is taken in conjunction with the positive impact of the tax shield derived from corporate taxation, there is the possibility of an optimal capital structure.

These are the most common sources of market imperfections. Others come to mind when we recall the requirement, needed to establish the Modigliani and Miller proposition, that investors can substitute homemade leverage for corporate financial leverage. However, three factors that suggest that the two may not be perfect substitutes:

1. In practice, individuals and corporations may face different interest rates for loans. Generally, larger corporations can borrow funds at lower rates than individuals can obtain for personal loans.
2. Institutional factors may stand in the way of the creation of homemade leverage. For example, life insurance companies and pension funds, which account for a substantial portion of equity holdings, are not permitted to borrow in this way.
3. Equity holders' personal assets are protected by limited liability in the event of a corporate bankruptcy. However, when homemade leverage is created by personal borrowing, the debtor may not be protected against creditors. If the loan is not repaid, the creditor can seize personal assets, especially if the loan is collateralized by personal assets.

## 11.7 Summary

In this chapter, we discussed factors that must be considered in evaluating a firm's capital structure. We have found that theory, based on certain idealized assumptions about the real world, can provide illumination. In general, the greater the proportion of debt in a firm's capital structure, the higher the stockholders' expected earnings. On the other hand, there is greater risk, or uncertainty, attached to such earnings. Under certain idealized assumptions, Proposition 1 of Modigliani and Miller, in a world with no taxes, asserts that debt and earnings will balance one another, in the sense that firm value will be independent of its capital structure.

To provide a more accurate description of real-world institutions, we must relax the M&M assumptions. First, allowing for corporate taxes provides stockholders with a tax shield, leading to the conclusion that firm value increases as the proportion of debt in the capital structure rises. However, Miller shows that if we allow for the existence of personal taxes, with individuals paying different marginal tax rates, capital structure is again irrelevant to firm value.

Finally,consideration of market imperfections, such as bankruptcy costs and agency costs, leads to the conclusion that, for an individual corporation, there may indeed be an optimal capital structure with a debt level between 0 and 100%.

## References

Barnea, A., R. Haugen and L. Senbet. "Market Imperfections, Agency Problems, and Capital Structure: A Review," *Financial Management*, 10 (Summer 1981, pp. 7–22).

Brennan, M. and E. Schwartz. "Corporate Income Taxes, Valuation, and the Problem of Optimal Capital Structure," *Journal of Business*, 54 (January 1978, pp. 103–14).

DeAngelo, H. and R. Masulis. "Optimal Capital Structure Under Corporate and Personal Taxation," *Journal of Financial Economics*, 7 (March 1980, pp. 3–29).

Durand, D. "Costs of Debt and Equity Funds for Business: Trends and Problems of Measurement," In *Conference on Research in Business Finance* (NBER, January 1952), pp. 215–262.

Hamada, R. S. "The Effect of the Firm's Capital Structure on the Systematic Risk of Common Stocks," *The Journal of Finance*, 27 (May 1972, pp. 435–452).

Jensen, M. and W. Meekling. "Theory of the Firm: Managerial Behavior, Agency Costs and Capital Structure," *Journal of Financial Economics*, 3(4) (October 1976, pp. 305–360).

Kim, E. "A Mean Variance Theory of Optimal Capital Structure and Corporate Debt Capacity," *The Journal of Finance*, 33 (March 1978, pp. 45–63).

Lambrecht B. M., Myers S. C. "A Lintner model of payout and managerial rents," *The Journal of Finance*, 67 (2012, pp. 1761–1810).

Lee, C. F. "Investment, Financing, Dividend, and Production Policies: Review, Integration, and Extension," Working Paper (2020, Rutgers University).

Lee, C. F. and J. Lee. *Financial Analysis, Planning and Forecasting: Theory and Applications*, 3rd edn. (Singapore: World Scientific, 2017).

Lee, C. F., W. L. Liang, F. L. Lin and Y. Yang. "Applications of Simultaneous Equations in Finance Research: Methods and Empirical Results," *Review of Quantitative Finance and Accounting*, 47 (2016, pp. 943–971).

Miller, M. "Debt and Taxes," *The Journal of Finance*, 32 (May 1977, pp. 261–275).

Miller, M. and F. Modigliani. "Some Estimates of the Cost of Capital to the Electric Utility Industry, 1954–57," *American Economic Review*, 66 (June 1966, pp. 411–33).
Modigliani, F. and M. Miller. "Corporation Income Taxes and the Cost of Capital: A Correction," *American Economic Review*, 13 (June 1963, pp. 433–443).
Myers, S. C. "The Capital Structure Puzzle," *The Journal of Finance*, 39 (July 1984, pp. 575–592).
Rubinstein, M. E. "A Mean-Variance Synthesis of Corporate Financial Theory," *The Journal of Finance*, 28 (March 1973, pp. 167–187).
Senbet, L. and R. Taggert. "Capital Structure Equilibrium Under Market Imperfections and Incompleteness," *The Journal of Finance*, 39 (March 1984, pp. 93–103).

## Appendix 11A — An Explanation of Modigliani and Miller Proposition 1

In this appendix, we explain Proposition 1 of Modigliani and Miller in a world with no taxes. Consider two corporations: one with debt and the other unlevered. Assume that these two corporations are expected to generate identical earnings streams and are in the same business risk class. If $V_U$ = value of unlevered firm, $S_U$ = value of stockholders' equity in the unlevered firm, $V_L$ = value of the levered firm, $S_L$ = value of stockholders' equity in the levered firm, and $B$ = value of debt in levered firm, then the market values of the two firms are $V_U = S_U$ and $V_L = S_L + B$.

Suppose that an investor owns a proportion $p$ of the levered firm's stock, with a value $pS_L$. These holdings generate for the investor a share that is a proportion $p$ of earnings remaining after interest payments are made on the corporate debt. Hence, expected earnings are $p(EBIT - iB)$, where $i$ = interest rate on debt and $EBIT$ = expected earnings before interest and tax for each firm.

Now, consider a second investment strategy in which a proportion $p$ of the unlevered firm is purchased, this purchase being financed partly through an amount $pS_L$ raised from sale of the levered company's stock and partly through borrowing, at interest rate $i$, an amount $pB$. This investor has holdings valued at $pV_U$ less $pB$, the debt owed. Since the two holdings yield the same expected income streams, with identical risks, they must have the same value if markets are efficient. Hence, it follows that

$$pV_U - pB = pS_L$$

so that

$$V_U = B + S_L = V_L$$

and the unleveraged firm's value is equal to that of the leveraged firm.

If these two investment strategies did not yield the same expected income streams, then there would be an arbitrage opportunity. Smart investors in the marketplace, seeing that two identical strategies offered different levels of return, would pursue the strategy offering the highest expected income stream. Additionally, they would offer the lower-yielding investment strategy to less-informed market participants. This arbitrage would generate risk-free profits until the values of both strategies were equal. Hence, in an efficient market, two strategies of similar risk cannot offer different returns.

## Questions and Problems

1. Define the following terms:
   a. EPS, DPS, and PPS
   b. DOL, DFL, and CLE
   c. M & M proposition I with tax
   d. Miller's proposition
   e. Agency cost
   f. Pecking order theory
2. Discuss how optimal capital structure can be theoretically determined.
3. Here are some items from the income statement and balance sheet of ABC Company:

   Value of assets = \$2,000 million
   Value of liabilities = \$1,200 million
   Number of shares outstanding = 20 million
   Operating income = \$800 million
   Corporate tax rate = 40%
   Interest paid on debt = \$120 million

   a. Find the effective interest rate on debt.

b. Find net income and EPS.
c. Find the rate of return on assets.

4. You are going to buy either Company A's or Company B's stock. If you are risk-average and your only concern is return and risk of EPS, which company would you choose under the following conditions:

| | **Company A** | **Company B** |
|---|---|---|
| Expected return on assets ($r$) | 10% | 11% |
| VAR ($r$) | 0.3% | 0.2% |
| Price per share | \$100 | \$100 |
| Debt-equity ratio | 1/3 | 2/3 |
| Interest rate on debt | 7% | 11% |
| Corporate tax rate | 34% | 34% |

5. Calculate the degree of operating leverage, the degree of financial leverage, and the total leverage of TTT company, using the following items:

Quantity sold = 20,000
Price per unit = \$10
Variable cost per unit = \$7
Fixed cost = \$30,000
Interest payments = \$10,000.

6. The Moonglow Company has total assets of \$100 million. Given the following $B/A$ ratios and interest rates on debt, calculate Moonglow's rate of return on equity for each $B/A$ ratio. (Assume that operations income is \$25 million, and corporate tax rate is 50%.)

| ***B/A*** **Ratio (%)** | **Interest Rate (%)** |
|---|---|
| 0 | — |
| 10 | 10 |
| 30 | 12 |
| 50 | 15 |

7. Consider the following items for a fishing business:
Total market value of a firm = \$50,000
Value of debt = \$20,000

Rates of return on equity = 12%
Interest payment = \$2,000
Corporate tax rate = 34%

a. Find the value of stockholder's equity.
b. Find the weighted average cost of capital (WACC).
c. Find the net income.
d. If the firm issues more debt, what are the effects on WACC?

8. ABC Company wants to double its assets because of increased market demand. New financing alternatives are for common stock to net \$15 a share or straight debt of 10%. The current balance sheet is as follows:

**Current Balance Sheet**

| | | | |
|---|---|---|---|
| | | Debt (8%) | \$10,000 |
| | | Common stock (\$10 par) | 15,000 |
| | | Retained earnings | 5,000 |
| Total assets | \$30,000 | Total claims | \$30,000 |

EPS = \$5
Total fixed cost = \$5,000
Corporate tax rate = 34%

a. Calculate current EBIT.
b. Find expected EPS for the two alternatives.
c. Calculate DFL and DOL.

9. Financial records for ABC Company include the following:

Anticipated sales = \$600,000
Degree of financial leverage = 4/3
Variable cost = \$300,000
Combined leverage effect = 2
Quantity sold = 100,000
Profit margin = 10%
Total debt = \$200,000
Leverage ratio = 1/2
Common stock outstanding = 10,000 shares
Current price per share = \$50
Pay-out ratio = 1/3
IRR = 12%

Find the following:

a. Total interest payment
b. Total fixed cost
c. Degree of operating leverage
d. Break-even quantity
e. EAIT (Earnings After Interest and Taxes)
f. Corporate tax payment
g. Return on net worth
h. Return on total assets
i. EPS
j. P/E ratio for common stock
k. Retention rate
l. Growth rate for common stock
m. Required rate of return

10. Here is ABC Company's next year's prediction:

| Economy | Probability | ROA (%) | Debt ($) | Equity ($) | Tax Rate (%) | Interest Rate (%) |
|---|---|---|---|---|---|---|
| State 1 | 0.1 | 12 | 500 | 1,000 | 40 | 8 |
| State 2 | 0.5 | 14 | 500 | 1,000 | 40 | 8 |
| State 3 | 0.4 | 15 | 500 | 1,000 | 40 | 8 |

a. Calculate next year's expected after-tax return on equity.
b. How much is the after-tax return on equity?
c. Assume the debt prediction was wrong. Instead, debt will increase to $1,000 next year, answer Questions a and b.
d. Compare your results under each scenario. How sensitive are the results to errors in the forecasted level of debts?

11. Assume that you are in Miller and Modigliani's world of no corporate taxes with perfect capital markets. There are two companies L and U that have identical expected EBIGT (net operating income) of $10,000. Assume that the value of the shares of the levered company L is $5,000 and the value of L's debt is $5,000 which carries a 10% interest rate. The value of the shares of the unlevered company is $9,000. If an investor currently owns 1% of the shares of the levered firm, numerically demonstrate the arbitrage transactions that would take place to drive the market value of L to equal that of U.

12. Assume that the world is that of Miller and Modigliani in which corporate taxes exist, but otherwise all of the prior assumptions of

the no tax case hold. Two firms X and Y have the same expected EBIT of $10,000. However, Firm X is unlevered and the total market value of its stock is $9,500. Firm Y is levered with debt valued at $5,000. The corporate tax rate is 40%. The market is in equilibrium.

a. Find the value of the levered firm.
b. Find the value of the levered firm's stock.

13. How would your answer to the previous question change if we expand the world and allow for a personal tax rate on stock income of 30% and a personal tax rate on debt income of 30%?
14. Assume that the value of a levered firm's stock is $4,000 and that of an unlevered firm is $9,000. Also assume that the value of the debt of the levered firm is $3,000 with a 10% interest rate. The corporate tax rate is 40% and all other taxes are nonexistent. Explain the arbitrage process that will take place to drive the values of the two firms back into equilibrium if the investor owns 2% of the unlevered firm at the present time.
15. You are supplied with the following income statement for L&S, Ltd. for last year:

| | |
|---|---|
| Sales | $30,000 |
| Variable costs | 10,000 |
| Fixed operating costs | 5,000 |
| EBIT | $15,000 |
| Interest expense | 7,000 |
| Earnings before taxes | $8,000 |
| Taxes (40%) | 3,200 |
| Net income | $4,800 |

a. Find the degree of operating leverage for the above level of sales and interpret its meaning.
b. Find the degree of financial leverage and interpret its meaning.
c. Find the degree of combined leverage and interpret its meaning.
d. If L&S pays preferred dividends of $1,200 per year, what is its degree of financial leverage and its degree of combined leverage? (*Note*: To put preferred dividends on a before-tax basis so that they are comparable to interest, preferred dividends must be divided by (1-corporate tax rate)).

16. Fritzer, Inc. is trying to estimate its cost of equity by using a proxy company that has a beta of 1.2. The proxy has a 40% tax rate and $B/S$ ratio of 0.8. Fritzer's tax rate is 30%. The risk-free rate of interest is 6% and the expected return on the market is 14%.
    a. If Fritzer uses no debt financing, what is its cost of equity?
    b. If Fritzer has a $B/S$ ratio of 1.00 and before-tax cost of debt of 10%, find its cost of equity and its overall cost of capital.
17. Danco is a levered company; however, if it were unlevered the value of its stock based on operating income alone would be $10,000. The market value of its debt is $6,000, and the interest rate on debt is 10%. Its corporate tax rate is 40%, the personal tax rate on debt income is 30%, and the personal tax rate on stock income is 25%. The company's debt to equity ratio is 3.00. In the event of bankruptcy it is estimated that the associated costs will be $10,000 and the probability of bankruptcy is 0.5. Find the value of Danco.

## Chapter 12

# The Dividend Puzzle

### Contents



## 12.1 Introduction

In its efforts to maximize shareholder's wealth, the firm's corporate finance department is faced with three types of decisions: investment decisions, financing decisions, and dividend policy decisions. This chapter deals with dividend policy decisions. There are two major questions involved in formulating a firm's dividend policy: Does a firm's dividend policy have an effect on the firm's value? And if so, will the firm try to achieve an optimal payout ratio by attaining an ideal dollar payment per share? These questions have been a source of debate between financial practitioners and academicians for years. The former feel that there is indeed an optimal level of dividend payout, while factions of academics argue that dividend policy does not affect firm value at all. Still other groups of academics argue that dividends alone affect firm value.

Dividend policy is the decision a firm makes either to pay out earnings or to retain them for reinvestment in the firm, and the determination of the amount to be allocated for each. As we recall, the pricing model for common stock per share is $P_0 = D_1/(k_s - g)$. According to Gordon, if the firm increases its cash dividend, it will increase the price of its stock. But we must also consider that an increase in dividends results in lower retained earnings and a lower growth rate, $g$. This, in turn, will have the effect of decreasing the firm's stock price. Therefore, the optimal dividend policy must balance the effects of these two variables. In this chapter, we also discuss some factors that affect a firm's dividend policy, such as the difference between shareholders who are tax exempt and shareholders who must pay taxes on dividends and capital gains, stockholder preferences, and reinvestment plans.

Section 12.2 begins by discussing how dividends are paid, then Section 12.3 goes on to dividend payment determination. Stock dividends and stock splits, and stock repurchases are discussed in Section 12.4. The capital asset pricing model with dividends effects is discussed in Section 12.5, and the irrelevance of dividend policy is discussed in Section 12.6. We follow up with a critique of the irrelevance of dividend policy in Section 12.7. Finally, we summarize the chapter in Section 12.8, and, in Appendix 12A, we use JNJ data to show how dividend behavior model can be empirically estimated.

## 12.2 How Dividends are Paid

In this section, there are four issues that will be discussed. They are (i) factors influencing dividend policy, (ii) dividend forms and payment procedures, (iii) stock repurchase, and (iv) inflation accounting and corporate dividends.

### 12.2.1 *Factors influencing dividend policy*

There are two broad categories of factors to consider when developing a dividend policy. The first is the company's financial position, which encompasses market, economic, and government influences on the firm. The second is investor preferences and pertains to the influences that shareholders exert on management's decision about dividend policy. Each of these categorical conditions is discussed in more detail below.

#### Company Financial Situation.

When a firm borrows from a bank or issues a bond to the market, a common restriction or constraint is that dividends must be paid from earnings generated after the loan agreement is made. Many debt contracts also stipulate that dividends be paid only when certain safety ratios, such as the current ratio or times-interest-earned ratio, reach a certain minimal standard.

There is a legal constraint known as the *impairment of capital rule* designed to protect the firm's creditors. This rule stipulates that dividends cannot exceed the amount of retained earnings listed on the balance sheet, thus ensuring that the firm has enough capital to pay its legal obligations.

Cash dividends as such, must be paid in cash, which may be a problem for a company with liquidity difficulties. It is possible that a firm is in a profitable situation but does not have the means to make cash payments to the equity holders because of liquidity problems.

The IRS has the power to levy heavy penalties on a firm if it can be proved that the dividend payout is being held down to help wealthy shareholders avoid tax payments. However, the firm can argue that it is not paying dividends in order to reinvest earnings in new, more profitable investments.

If a firm has the flexibility to postpone or accelerate the timing of the cash flows from its investments or projects, then it will increase flexibility with its dividend policy.

When a firm is seeking equity financing, an important consideration (as we have seen in the cost of capital discussion) is its source of funds. These funds can come either from retained earnings or through the issuance of new common stock. The overall cost of issuing new common stock depends on the *flotation costs* of a new issue.

These are the accounting, legal, and other costs paid by the corporation when making a public issue. If flotation costs are high, as is likely for smaller firms, then financing through retention may be cheaper than the sale of new common stock.

For small, closely held companies, the issuance of new stock as a means of financing may mean dilution of control. If this is undesirable, then the company may choose to retain more earnings.

Another alternative in the financing decision is to choose between debt or equity. If debt costs are low, then a firm may choose to adjust its debt ratio to maintain a constant dividend payout. If the average cost of capital can be maintained within the firm's target level, then dividend policy becomes less of a factor in the firm's financing decisions.

**Investor Preferences.**

Dividends, which are considered income to the recipient, are taxed by the federal government, at the ordinary-income tax rate and also by state governments. As of 1987, capital gains were taxed as ordinary income. Therefore, investors would be indifferent between capital gains and dividend payments as far as personal taxes are concerned. The extent to which this holds true depends on the firm's shareholders, commonly called the firm's *clientele.*

Many stockholders prefer current income to future income. Retired individuals who depend on dividends as a source of income are an example. Others may not need the current income and thus may choose to reinvest their dividends; however, they must first pay personal income taxes on their dividends. Therefore, another consideration of dividend policy is the dividend *needs* of shareholders, which is another example of the clientele effect.

From empirical observation, we normally expect that when dividends increase, stock prices also increase. Similarly, a dividend cut is associated with a fall in stock price. It would seem that a dividend increase is a signal to investors that management foresees prosperity, while a dividend cut serves as a warning of weaker future earnings. Usually, management is reluctant to reduce dividends, preferring instead to maintain a stable ratio of dividends to earnings. Therefore, any reduction in dividends is a signal of bad times, whereas an increase in dividends implies confidence in the future. This illustrates the concept of *information content* in dividend announcements.

These are some of the factors that come into consideration when financial management establishes a dividend policy. Later in this chapter, we look at quantitative models used in the dividend decision and how some of these factors come into play.

### 12.2.2 *Dividend forms and payment procedures*

Dividends can be disbursed in many forms, but most commonly they are paid quarterly in cash. For example, in 1987, General Mills paid quarterly dividends of \$0.42, or a total of \$1.28 per share as the regular annual dividend. There are several steps in the dividend payment procedure.

The procedure beings with the *dividend declaration date.* On this date, the firm's directors may issue a statement declaring a regular dividend, such as "On October 30, 1988, the directors of this corporation met and declared quarterly dividends to be \$0.58 per share, payable to the holder of record on December 15, and payment will be made on January 5, 1989." On the declaration date, the dividend becomes a legally binding obligation of the corporation.

By 5 p.m. on the *holder of record date* — December 15, 1988 — investors on the corporation's list of shareholders are entitled to receive the dividend even if they sell their stock before the payment date.

**The Ex-Dividend Date.**

A slight problem arises if the shareholder decides to sell a day or two before the record date. The securities brokerage industry cannot immediately process the name of the buyer for inclusion on the stockholder list and delete the name of the previous shareholder. Therefore, the industry has arbitrarily declared that the right to the declared dividend terminates four working days before the record date. Anyone who buys the stock between four working days prior to the record date and the record date is not entitled to the dividend. Likewise. Any shareholder who sells during this period will receive the dividend. The date — four working days prior to the record date — is called the *ex-dividend date* (in Latin, *ex* means from). Essentially, the dividend has been taken from anyone who buys the stock after the ex-dividend date. In our example, the ex-dividend date is December 11, four days prior to December 15. Suppose investor A buys 200 shares of stock from investor B. To receive dividends, A must buy the stock by December 10. If investor A buys on December 11 or afterward, investor B will receive the dividend. Hence, we would expect to see the price of shares fall by the dividend amount on the ex-dividend date.

When a stock reaches the ex-dividend date, the market should reflect the decrease in the stock's value, because the purchaser of the stock is not entitled to the current dividend. The extent of the drop in stock price is open to debate and depends in part on the tax situation of the marginal investor. If the marginal investor is in the 30% tax bracket and the dividend is $1 per share, the per share price should fall by $.70 on the ex-dividend date, all else equal.

The *payment date* is when the company actually mails out dividend checks to shareholders, which in this case is January 5, 1989.

At the end of the year, the corporation mails a form 1099 to the shareholders informing them how much they received in dividends during the current year — information the shareholders can use when filing their tax returns. A copy of this form is also sent to the IRS. This system of informing the taxing authorities is unique to the U.S. Most nations require a corporation to withhold a portion of the dividend and turn these funds over to the government to settle the individual's tax liability on the dividend income.

One model has been developed to incorporate tax effects into determining the ex-dividend price[1]:

$$\frac{P_0 - P_x}{D_0} = \frac{1 - T_p}{1 - T_g} \qquad (12.1)$$

where $P_0$ = the price just before the stock goes ex; $P_x$ = the ex-dividend share price; $D_0$ = the amount of the dividend per share; $T_p$ = the relevant marginal personal tax rate; $T_g$ = the effective marginal tax rate on capital gains.

$$\text{If } T_p = T_g = 0, \quad \text{or} \quad T_p = T_g, \quad \text{then} \quad P_x = P_0 - D_0 \qquad (12.1a)$$

[1]E. Elton and M. Gruber, "Marginal Stockholder Tax Rates and the Clientele Effect," *Review of Economics and Statistics*, 52 (February 1970).

**Example 12.1.** Ex-Dividend Stock Price with Taxes

Q: An investor owns a stock that has a market price of \$50 per share and has been paid a cash dividend of \$2 per share. If this investor's $T_p = 30\%$ and $T_g = 25\%$, what is the ex-dividend stock price?

A: Substituting $P_0 = \$50$, $D_0 = \$2$, $T_p = 30\%, T_g = 25\%$ into Eq. (12.1), we obtain:

$$P_x = 50 - \frac{(1 - 0.30)\,(2)}{(1 - 0.25)} = \$48.13$$

Tax laws require the corporation to mail a copy of Form 1099 to every shareholder at the end of the year to report the amount of dividends the firm paid to that person. The firm also sends a copy of this form to the IRS to report the dividend income it paid to each shareholder during the year. This system of informing the taxing authorities is unique to the U.S. Most other nations of the world require that corporations withhold portions of stockholders' dividends and turn these funds over to the government to settle each individual's tax liability on dividend income.

**Automatic Dividend Reinvestment Plans (ADR).**

As we shall see, there is some controversy as to the value of paying dividends. One way to resolve the problem of whether shareholders want dividends or not is to give the shareholder the choice of receiving either cash dividends or shares of stock that reflect the reinvestment of the cast dividend. Many firms offer their shareholders a choice of either dividends or reinvestment through *automatic dividend reinvestment* (ADR) plans.

Although the exact details of each plan differ, the general characteristics of ADRs are fairly standard. One type of ADR is a bank-administered plan. The corporation sends the dividend of the participating shareholder directly to the trust department of a bank, which maintains accounts for each participating shareholder. The trust department purchases the firm's stock in the secondary market and credits these shares to each participant's account, less any brokerage fees or administrative costs. A second type of ADR is one that is administered by the firm itself. The firm either issues new shares to the participants or purchases its own shares in the secondary market and distributes these shares to the plan's participants.

From the firm's viewpoint, the major advantage of ADRs is that they either provide a continuous source of new equity capital to the firm or they provide buying support for the firm's common stock in the secondary market. From the shareholder's standpoint, an ADR provides for immediate reinvestment of dividends, which allows the shareholder to take full advantage of compounding. The major disadvantage of ADRs is that the participating shareholder must declare and pay taxes on the dividends that are declared, even though the shareholder receives no cash flow from the corporation. Additionally, the shareholder's ability to diversify is reduce somewhat by participation in the plan.

### 12.2.3 *Stock repurchase*

Management's use of corporate funds to repurchase the company's stock is an important decision. From the viewpoint of both management and shareholder, there are benefits to be gained by repurchase. The shares that are reacquired are designated as *treasury stock*. These treasury shares are then available for reissue to executives under stock-option plans, to employees as part of profit-sharing plans, to shareholders as stock dividends or splits, and to other firms for mergers or acquisitions.

From a management perspective, the benefits of stock repurchase may be defensive if management fears a takeover. By using up the firm's excess cash or by borrowing funds to finance the repurchase, management can reduce the attractiveness of the firm as a takeover target. Further, any dissatisfied stockholders have the opportunity to sell their shares back to the firm at a favorable price before the potential takeover company can make an offer for their stock.

Another benefit from management's viewpoint is the reduction of the mailing and processing costs of annual reports, dividends, proxy statements, and other materials. Some repurchases are aimed directly at small shareholders for precisely this reason.

There are three methods used in repurchasing stock. A *tender offer* is a public announcement by the company to all shareholders that the company will buy a certain number of shares at a specified price during a set period of time. Every shareholder has to decide whether the price offered by the company now is better than the price of the share will be when the tender offer expires. If more shares are tendered to the company than it intends to repurchase, management may elect to purchase all shares or a pro rata percentage of those offered by each shareholder. A second method of repurchase is *open-market repurchasing*. The corporation, acting through a broker, purchases shares in the secondary market just like any other investor. The corporation's intention to engage in open-market repurchasing is usually announced in advance, although the exact number of shares repurchased and the actual days of the transactions are not known. The third type of repurchase is *disproportionate repurchase*, which occurs when a firm repurchases shares from a specific shareholder or group of shareholders. This type of repurchase can be used to buy out a single large shareholder or to buy out a group of small shareholders with few shares.

The repurchase of a company's stock can be viewed as beneficial to both the corporation and the individual shareholders. There have been discussions on the repurchase of stock as a good investment in itself. Nothing can be further from the truth. It is impossible for a firm to invest in itself in the sense of making a real investment. We view a real investment as the purchase of a productive asset that produces goods and services that can be sold in the marketplace. There is no expected return or cash flow from a share repurchase or on any goods and services produced. Carried out to its logical extreme, repurchasing one's shares leads to returning the shareholders' capital and dissolving the corporation.

The financing or capital structure impact of a repurchase can be considered in light of the M&M argument presented in Chapter 11. As the firm repurchases its stock, it may very well increase EPS, but it also increases its financial leverage. The impact of repurchase on the firm depends on the amount of leverage the firm had initially and on how much the repurchase increases the firm's current financial leverage.

### 12.2.4 *Inflation accounting and corporate dividends*

A paper by Rappaport (1981) addresses the problem of the inflationary impact on the dividend decision. With the increase of inflation, many companies have adjusted their statements to reflect constant-dollar or current-cost accounting. The *constant-dollar method* adjusts historical costs according to the consumer price index to reflect changes in purchasing power. The *current-cost method* restates specific prices, such as the current cost of replacing the company's assets, to reflect the effects of inflation. However, even after adjusting income by these two methods, getting an estimate of the company's maximum affordable dividend can be difficult. Because of inflation, the corporation may find itself paying higher taxes and thereby reducing its available cash flow. Therefore, earnings should be based on economic profits or cash flow rather than on accounting profits. A company's level of affordable dividends should be based on its financing policies and projected cash flows from its planned growth investment strategies rather than based strictly on the previous year's accounting earnings. In times of high inflation, a firm may seriously overestimate its dividend-paying capacity by relying on accounting earnings.

The impact of inflation on corporate cash flow has a direct relationship to a firm's ability to pay dividends. In general, as the rate of inflation increases, the firm's ability to pay dividends from free cash flow declines. To see this effect, we look at two hypothetical companies that make the same product, sell it for the same price, and, in the process, incur the same general and administrative expenses. In a given year, both companies sell 4,000 units resulting in $1.8 million in revenues. Both companies began the year with 1,000 units of inventory. The inflation rate for each quarter was 5%. The companies differ only in their method of inventory accounting, which has a direct effect on reported profits, taxes, and cash flow. Company A uses a first-in, first-out (FIFO) method, while Company B uses a last-in, first-out (LIFO) method. Table 12.1 shows the effect of inflation and the method of accounting for inventories on cash flow and on the ability to pay dividends.

The key element of the inflationary effect on the firm's ability to pay dividends is the increased costs that may not be immediately reflected in higher prices for the product being sold. This may be magnified by the accounting method that the firm's management chooses to follow. As seen in Table 12.1, the cash flow available for dividends is reduced because taxes increase as the illusory holding-period gain in inventory is included in gross profits when the FIFO method is used. The inventory gain is inversely related to turnover: the lower the inventory turnover, the larger the inflationary impact.

There are other ways in which inflation reduces the capacity of a firm to pay dividends. Depreciation policies, classification of cash

Table 12.1 Inflation and Dividends — Impact of FIFO and LIFO on Cash Flow.

Two firms, Companies A and B, sell the same product as the same price with the same expenses.
Beginning Inventory = 1,000 units at $200/unit = $200,000
Purchase = 4,000 units (1,000/quarter)
A = FIFOB = LIFO

**Zero inflation: Company A = Company B**

| | | | Cost of Inventory |
|---|---|---|---|
| Sales | $1,800,000 | | |
| Cost of goods sold | 800,000 | | |
| Gross profit | $1,000,000 | Beginning | $200 × 1,000 Units |
| Gas | 450,000 | Purchases | +200 × 1,000 |
| Operating income | $550,000 | | +200 × 1,000 |
| Interest | 50,000 | | +200 × 1,000 |
| Taxable income | $500,000 | | +200 × 1,000 |
| Tax (46%) | 330,000 | Sales | −200 × 1,000 |
| Net income | $270,000 | | −200 × 1,000 |
| Inventory profit | 0 | | −200 × 1,000 |
| Free cash | $270,000 | | −200 × 1,000 |
| Dividend (50%) | 135,000 | Ending inventory | $200 × 1,000 = $200,000 |
| Cash available | $135,000 | | |

**5% Inflation**

| | | |
|---|---|---|
| Sales | $1,800,000 | $1,800,000 |
| Cost of goods sold | 862,030 | 905,130 |
| Gross profit | $937,970 | $894,870 |
| Gas | 450,000 | 450,000 |
| Operating income | $487,970 | $394,870 |
| Interest | 50,000 | 50,000 |
| Taxable income | $437,970 | $394,870 |
| Tax (46%) | 201,466 | 181,640 |
| Net income | $236,504 | $213,230 |
| Inventory profit | 43,100 | 0 |
| Free cash | $193,404 | $213,230 |
| Dividend | 135,000 | 135,000 |
| Cash available | $58,404 | $78,230 |

| Cost of Inventory | Cost of Inventory |
|---|---|
| 200 × 1,000 | 210 × 1,000 = $200,000 |
| 200 × 1,000 | (Ending Inventory) |
| 220.50 × 1,000 | 210 × 1,000 |
| 231.53 × 1,000 | 220.50 × 1,000 |
| 243.10 × 1,000 = $243,000 | 231.53 × 1,000 |
| (Ending Inventory) | 243.10 × 1,000 |

Company B has a smaller tax payment by $19826; hence, Company B has this much more cash. Therefore, LIFO is better.

outflows as expenditures or capital acquisitions, and the increase in cash requirements because of rising prices all tend to reduce the firm's ability to pay dividends during periods of inflation.

On balance, the reasons for lower dividends that we have discussed can be summarized as tax climate, flotation costs of new securities, investment opportunities of the corporation, and inflation.

## 12.3 Dividend Payment Determination

Dividend policy represents one of the most important financial decisions a firm makes. How much a firm chooses to pay out in the dividends and how much it chooses to retain for future investments can affect both the growth of the firm and its stock price.

### 12.3.1 *Residual theory*

The most easily understood theory of dividend payment determination is called the *residual theory.* As the name implies, this theory holds that firms pay dividends out of earnings that remain after it meets its financing needs. These are funds for which the firm has no immediate use. The procedure for a residual dividend policy follows several steps:

1. Determine the firm's optimal capital budget.
2. Determine the amount of equity needed to finance that budget.
3. To the extent possible, use the firm's retained earnings to supply the needed equity.
4. Distribute any leftover earnings as dividends.

The basic assumption of residual dividend theory is that shareholders want the firm to retain earnings if reinvesting them can generate higher rates of return than the shareholders could obtain by reinvesting their dividends. For example, if a corporation can invest retained earnings in a new venture that generates an 18% rate of return, whereas investors can obtain a return of only 10% by reinvesting their dividends, then stockholders would benefit more from the firm reinvesting its profits.

Whether firms actually practice the residual theory is a matter of question. Such a theory would simply erratic dividend payments, especially for fast-growth companies. Firms do seem to try to stabilize their dividend-payout rates, so analysts do not place much faith in the residual theory. However, two alternative theories for the dividend behavior of firms have found considerable empirical support.

### 12.3.2 *Lintner's model*

Lintner (1956) was the first to investigate the partial-adjustment model of dividend behavior. Using this model, Lintner demonstrated how dividend policy decisions can be made by using the following three steps:

*Step 1*: Compare last period's dividend with the desired level of dividends and adjust the deviation accordingly the next period.

*Step 2*: Assume the desirable dividend level is $D_t^* = PE_t$, where $P$ is the long-run payout ratio for dividends and $E_t$ is the earnings level for that period.

*Step 3*: Combining steps 1 and 2, we obtain a dividend decision model:

$$D_t = D_{t-1} + \delta(D_t^* - D_{t-1}) \tag{12.2}$$

or

$$D_t = D_{t-1} + \delta(PE_t - D_{t-1}) \tag{12.3}$$

To solve for the variable $\delta$, the partial adjustment coefficient, we use a regression model:

$$D_t = b_0 + b_1 E_t + b_2 D_{t-1} + e_t \tag{12.4}$$

where $b_1 = \delta$ and $b_2 = (1 - \delta)$. From the estimated $b_1$ and $b_2$, we can estimate $\delta$ and $P$ as follows:

$$\delta = 1 - \hat{b}_2 \tag{12.5}$$

$$P = \frac{\hat{b}_1}{1 - \hat{b}_2} \tag{12.6}$$

Equation (12.4) in terms of JNJ's EPS and DPS will be explored in detail in Appendix 12A. However, here we use the desired dividend payment, $D_t$, as a function of earnings, whereas with ratio analysis the desired ratio is a function of the industry average.

From this model, we can conclude that firms set their dividend in accordance with their level of current earnings. We can also conclude that changes in dividends over time do not correspond exactly with changes in earnings in the immediate time period, but rather are spread out over several time periods.

Another explanation for the $\delta$ coefficient is that it is the average speed of adjustment. We can interpret the quantity $(1 - \delta)$ as a safety factor that management uses to avoid increasing the dividend payment to levels that cannot be maintained.

Equation (12.4) shows the changes in dividend levels between periods rather than the absolute levels themselves. This allows us to investigate changes in the firm's dividend policy. Of the 28 firms Lintner studied, 26 appeared to have and follow a predetermined target payout ratio, $P$. On the whole, most of these firms updated their dividend policies annually. (To see how Eq. (12.4) can be used to analyze annual dividend payments, refer to Appendix 12A.)

Lee *et al.* (1987) has generalized Linter's partial adjustment model into an integrated behavior model. Lee and Lee (2017) show the integrated model includes partial adjustment adaptive expectations and residual models and special cases. Lee and Lin (2019) use 1,200 U.S. nonfinancial firms to estimate the integrated model. They found that about 55% follow the adaptive expectation model and 15% follow the partial adjustment behavior model. They also showed that the adaptive expectation model should be used instead of the partial adjustment model to study dividend smoothing behavior.

### 12.3.3 *Stable dividend policy*

The Lintner study reinforces the notion that dividend policy conveys information to investors. Many financial managers strive to maintain steady or modestly growing dividends and avoid large fluctuations or changes in dividend policies. Reducing dividend fluctuations helps reduce investor uncertainty about future dividends.

Lower risk leads to higher stock prices. Managers resist increasing dividends if they do not expect to maintain the increase in the future. This supports a predominant policy of maintaining historical dividends.

If firms hesitate to raise dividends too quickly, they positively abhor the prospect of reducing dividends, for several reasons. First, many individuals and institutions require large cash flows from their investments. For example, retired people in lower tax brackets generally covet high dividend payments. Tax-exempt institutions, such as endowment funds or pension funds, also need high current income and therefore desire high dividends. Miller and Modigliani argue that these individuals or institutions should ignore a stock's level of dividends because they always can liquidate some of their holdings in order to generate desired cash flows. Unfortunately, in real-world capital markets, this advice would generate substantial transaction costs, especially brokerage fees. In addition to the time involved in deciding to sell securities, investors may exhaust all of their principal, leaving none for future income requirements.

Second, mangers often resist reducing dividends also because a cut in dividends may be interpreted by the investment community as a signal of trouble with the firm or a result of poor management. Even if the reduction is intended to allow the firm to pursue an attractive opportunity, it may adversely affect stock prices.

A third reason that firms resist reducing dividends involves the legal list. Many large, institutional investors are bound by the prudent man rule, or by legislation, to buy only securities that are included on the legal list. One criterion of the list is a long history of continued dividend payments without dividend reductions. Therefore, a firm that reduces or omits a dividend payment faces the risk of being ineligible for purchase by certain institutional investors.

A stable dividend policy can become a sort of self-fulfilling prophecy. An unexpected rise or reduction in dividends can have an announcement effect on the firm's share price. An increase in dividends may lead investors to perceive a promising future and share price may increase. A drop in dividends may lead investors to fear a less promising future, resulting in a drop in share price. These perceptions may be accurate if managers themselves feel it is

Table 12.2 JNJ — Earnings per Share and Dividends per Share.

| Year | 2019 | 2018 | 2017 | 2016 | 2015 | 2014 | 2013 |
|---|---|---|---|---|---|---|---|
| **DPS ($)** | 3.75 | 3.54 | 3.32 | 3.15 | 2.95 | 2.76 | 2.59 |
| **EPS** | 5.72 | 5.7 | 0.48 | 6.04 | 5.56 | 5.8 | 4.92 |
| **PPS** | 145.75 | 127.27 | 139.72 | 115.21 | 102.72 | 105.06 | 92.35 |
| **Payout ratio (%)** | 16.60 | 15.78 | 14.80 | 12.11 | 11.43 | 11.01 | 9.87 |

important to avoid fluctuations, especially cuts. In such a company, investors would be correct in viewing dividend declarations as sources of information.

The dividend per share (DPS), earnings per share (EPS) and price per share (PPS) data information presented in Table 12.2 illustrates how important managers consider consistent dividends to be. Notice that JNJ's dividend continued to increase in 2015, despite a drop in earnings. When earnings fell, JNJ managers felt compelled to increase the payout ratio in order to maintain the growth in dividends that investors had come to expect. In 2017, 2018, and 2019 stronger earnings resulted in payout ratio of between 14.8% and 16.6%.

Both dividend yield and earnings yield can be used to show profitability of an investment in a stock.[2]

Using the data of Table 12.2, we can calculate the dividend yield (DPS/PPS) and earnings yield (EPS/PPS) as follows:

| Year | 2019 | 2018 | 2017 | 2016 | 2015 | 2014 | 2013 | Mean |
|---|---|---|---|---|---|---|---|---|
| **Dividend yield** | 0.026 | 0.028 | 0.024 | 0.027 | 0.029 | 0.026 | 0.028 | 0.027 |
| **Earnings yield** | 0.15 | 0.18 | 0.16 | 0.23 | 0.25 | 0.24 | 0.28 | $0.213 |

[2]Statistical analyses of the relationship between (i) DPS and EPS and (ii) dividends yield and earnings yield for J&J are to be done by students (Problem 1 of this chapter).

### 12.3.4 *Information content of dividends — A synthesis*

Many theorists and practitioners alike believe that the payment of a dividend conveys a signal to the marketplace. In effect, each dividend payment, and especially a change in dividends, carries information to investors about the company. This type of information could be made public in other ways, but managers routinely set dividends to signal to the market that they expect the firm to prosper.

### 12.3.5 *Double taxation*

Tax law complicates dividend decision by imposing the burden of *double taxation.* In effect, income that a firm pays to shareholders as dividends is taxed twice. A corporate income tax is levied on the corporation's profits, and shareholders then pay personal income taxes on the dividends they receive. This is one of the complexities of the U.S. tax laws that affects dividend policy.

The investor has no control over corporate tax effects. It is up to the corporate managers to reduce or defer tax payments as much as possible. However, the investor can influence the amount of personal taxes due on any dividend earnings. Investors can reduce or defer taxes by buying low-dividend, high-growth stocks. Or, if they are tax exempt, investors can buy dividend-paying stocks.

Personal income taxes may affect an investor's preference for dividends or capital gains. When the tax rate on capital gains is substantially lower than the tax rate on personal income, then shareholders should prefer capital gains to dividends. This increases the firm's focus on retained earnings as equity financing. Investors still can realize homemade dividends through capital gains from sales of stock.

Different investors will have different preferences between dividends can capital gains. For example, average investors may prefer dividends because of the need for additional income, while wealthy investors may prefer capital gains because they currently do not need the income. Some large, tax-exempt institutions, such as pension funds, pay no taxes on their investment income, so they may be indifferent between dividends or capital gains. Other tax-exempt institutions, such as foundations and endowments, may favor current income to help meet budget needs.

Investors can defer receiving capital gains by holding stock; gains are received and become taxable only when stock is sold at a profit. Dividends offer less flexibility. Once the firm pays a dividend, the investor must pay taxes on this income. Therefore, the ability to defer taxes on capital gains may bias the investor against cash dividend payments.

## 12.4 Stock Dividends, Stock Splits, and Stock Repurchases

Managers can use stock dividends, stock splits, or stock repurchases to change the firm's number of common shares outstanding. A *stock dividend* is a payout of dividends in the form of stock rather than cash. A stock dividend commonly is expressed as a percentage; for example, a 10% stock dividend means that a stockholder receives one new share for every ten shares currently owned. A *stock split* is essentially the same thing as a stock dividend, except that a split is expressed as a ratio instead of a percentage. Basically, a stock dividend and a stock split increase the number of shares of stock outstanding without any cash flow to the firm or increase in firm value.

A *stock repurchase* is another way to pay cash to shareholders. It occurs when management uses cash to buy back the stock of the company. As we discussed in an earlier chapter, net equity sales in the U.S. have been small or negative in recent years. This has occurred because U.S. corporations actually repurchased more stock than they sold. Stock repurchases will reduce the number of common shares outstanding in the equity markets.

### 12.4.1 *Stock dividends and stock splits*

The major difference between a stock split and a stock dividend is in their accounting treatments. The American Institute of Certified Public Accountants (AICPA) recommends treatment of an increase in shares outstanding of less than 20 to 25% as a stock dividend and treatment of any increase greater than this as a stock split. The accounting treatment for a stock dividend transfers retained earnings equal to the market value of the new shares to the common stock account. Table 12.3 shows the effect on the firm's equity account of a 10% stock dividend.

Table 12.3 Stock Dividend and the Balance Sheet.

| | |
|---|---|
| **Before Dividend:** | |
| Common stock: $40 par value, 1,000 shares issued at $43 and outstanding; | |
| Current market price $100 per share ($40 par × 1,000 shares = $40,000) | $40,000 |
| Paid in capital in excess of par | $3,000 |
| Retained earnings | $80,000 |
| **Total shareholders' equity** | **$123,000** |
| **After a 10% Stock Dividend:** | |
| Common stock: $40 par value, 1,100 shares issued and outstanding; | |
| Current market price 90.91 per share ($40 par × 1,100 shares = $44,000) | $44,000 |
| Paid in capital in excess of par | $ 9,000 |
| Retained earnings | $70,000 |
| **Total shareholders' equity** | **$123,000** |

Table 12.3 shows that major changes include a capitalization of retained earnings at the current market price of the stock and an increase in the number of shares by the amount of the stock dividend. The value of shareholders' equity, in both an accounting and an economic sense, remains the same. The total equity book value was reported as $123,000 both before and after the stock dividend. The market value of the firm stayed at $100,000 (1,000 shares × $100/share before the split; 1,100 shares at $90.91/share after the split). However, the common stock account rises by $4,000 (100 new shares × $40 per share) paid in capital excess of par becomes $3,000 +100($100 – $40) = $9,000; retained earnings' new value is $80,000 – 100($100) = 70,000.

The firm accounts for a stock split differently. Table 12.4 shows that a two-for-one stock split causes no changes in any of the equity account balances. The number of shares increases, but each shares has a lower par value. The market price of the shares also changes to reflect the increase in the number of shares outstanding.

There is no economic difference between the effects of a stock split and the effects of a stock dividend. To see why, envision a family of four having an apple pie for dessert. It doesn't matter if each member of the family gets one piece equal to one quarter of the pie or two pieces equal to one-eighth each. Stock splits and stock dividends change how the firm divides the pie, but they do not affect the percentage of ownership held by shareholders.

Stock splits or stock dividends may be of value for various reasons. For one, these techniques may help the firm maintain an optimal trading range for its stock price. This argument is based on the belief that investors are more likely to purchase a stock if its price falls within a certain range. Above the upper limit of this range, a round lot of stock may cost too much for some investors.[3] Consequently, they are forced to choose between buying odd lots and paying higher commissions, or investing in other securities. Below the trading range, some investors may consider the stock too cheap and not worthy of investment.

The institutionalization of the market casts doubt on the optimal trading range argument. Mutual funds, pension funds, and other institutions usually buy and sell in such large amounts that they care

Table 12.4 Stock and a Partial Balance Sheet.

| | |
|---|---|
| **Before Split:** | |
| Common stock: $40 par value, 1,000 shares issued and outstanding; | |
| Current market price $100 per share | $40,000 |
| Paid in capital in excess of par | $3,000 |
| Retained earnings | $80,000 |
| **Total shareholders' equity** | **$123,000** |
| **After a Two-for-One Stock Split:** | |
| Common stock: $40 par value, 2,000 shares issued and outstanding; | |
| Current market price $50 | $40,000 |
| Paid in capital in excess of par | $3,000 |
| Retained earnings | $80,000 |
| **Total shareholders' equity** | **$123,000** |

[3]Most stock trades occur in "round lots" of 100 shares. "Odd lots" are stock trades involving less than 100 shares. Because of their smaller size, transaction costs on odd-lot trades are higher on a per-share basis than round-lot trades.

little about optimal trading ranges. Stocks have performed so well in recent years, in fact, that they have attracted a lot of investor attention. Despite these anecdotal arguments, the question of an optimal trading range is still an open issue that needs to be evaluated by further empirical work.

Copeland presents an argument against stock splits and stock dividends and claims that transaction costs are higher after stock splits.[4] Some analysts favor stock splits or stock dividends, however, for the information that such announcements convey to the market. Generally, high-growth firms split their stock or issue stock dividends. If the market were to extend this trend to conclude that all stock splits or stock dividends indicate profitable, high-growth firms, then were would be some merit to the information-content argument. However, Fama, Fisher, Jensen, and Roll report negligible price impacts for stock splits or dividends, unless they are accompanied by earnings or cash-dividend increase.[5]

Until scholars improve their understanding of investor psychology, the value of stock splits and stock dividends will remain an open question. Managers will continue to offer stock splits and dividends, and some investors will readily accept them as valuable, whereas other investors will not.

A *reverse stock split*, as its name implies, is a reduction in the number of shares outstanding, with each share increasing in value to keep the total value of the firm unchanged. As with a stock split, theory gives no reason to expect any change in the underlying value of the company that engages in a reverse split. In fact, many investors regard a reverse split as an admission by management that the company faces financial difficulties. This belief is based primarily on the argument that the market price per share is too low to attract serious investors.

---

[4]T. Copeland, "Liquidity Changes Following Stock Splits," *Journal of Finance*, 34 (March 1979, pp. 115–141).

[5]E. Fama, L. Fisher, M. Jensen and R. Roll. "The Adjustment of Stock Prices to New Information," *International Economic Review* (February 1969, pp. 1–21).

**Example 12.2.** Stock Dividends and Stock Splits

Q: Use the information in the "Before Dividend" section of Table 12.3 to answer the following question:

a. If this company announces a 5% stock dividend, how will the equity account be affected?
b. Using Table 12.3, if this company announces a four-for-one stock split, how should the "After Stock Split" section of this table be presented?

A: a. The equity account will change as follows:

i. The amount added to common stock is:

$$(\$40)(5\%)(1{,}000) = \$2{,}000$$

The current stock price per share is \$95.24 (\$100/1.05).

ii. The amount added to be paid in capital in excess of par is:

$$(\$100 - \$40)(5\%)(1,000) = \$3{,}000$$

iii. Retained Earnings will be reduced by \$5,000 (\$2,000 + \$3,000)

b. The statement will be the same except the number of shares outstanding will be 4,000 shares at \$10 per share.

### 12.4.2 *Stock repurchase*

A *stock repurchase* occurs when management spends corporate funds to buy back the stock of the company. A stock repurchase can benefit both management and shareholders. The repurchased shares become treasury stock and are then available for reissue to executives under stock option plans, to employees as part of profit-sharing plans, and to other firms as part of mergers or acquisitions.

Management gains some defensive benefits by way of a stock repurchase. If managers of a cash-rich, low-debt firm fear a takeover, they may finance the stock purchase with the firm's excess cash or use debt, reducing the attractiveness of the firm as a takeover target. In addition, the repurchase program invites any dissatisfied stockholders to sell their shares back to the firm at a favorable price before a potential takeover company can make an offer for the stock.

Management also benefits from the reduction in mailing and processing costs for annual reports, dividend payments, proxy statements, and other materials. Some repurchases are aimed directly at small shareholders for precisely this reason.

Shareholders also may benefit from a stock repurchase. Stockholders who want to sell their shares can do so at a favorable price. Stockholders who choose to hold onto their shares may benefit from the reduction in the number of shares outstanding. For example, suppose someone owns 1,000 shares of a company that has 25,000 shares outstanding. This stock represents a 4% (1,000/25,000) stake in the company. If the company repurchases 5,000 of its shares from other investors, then that stockholder's stake in the company increases to 5% (1,000/20,000).

Information related to cash dividends paid, repurchases of common stock, and employee compensation and stock option plans can be found in a firm's (consolidated) statement of common stock, retained earnings, and treasury stock. Table 12.5 presents this information for JNJ, Inc. during the period from 2017 to 2019. For example, in 2017, JNJ distributed its net earnings as follows: cash dividends ($8,943 million), employee compensation and stock option plans ($1,079 million), and retained earnings ($101,793 million). In 2017, JNJ paid cash dividends of $3.32 per share. This statement also reveals that JNJ repurchased 6,358 shares of common stock in 2017.

See Notes to Consolidated Financial Statements of JNJ 1995 Annual Report.

Firms can repurchase stock by two methods. A tender offer is a publicly announced offer by the company to all shareholders to buy a certain number of shares at a specified price during a set period of time. Every shareholder has to decide whether the price offered by the company beats the price the shares will have when the tender offer expires. If stockholders tender more shares than the company intends to repurchase, management may elect to purchase pro rata percentages of the total from each shareholder.

A firm also can reacquire its stock through an *open market repurchase.* Acting through a broker, the corporation purchases shares in the secondary market just like any other investor. A corporation usually announces its intention to engage in an open market repurchase in advance, although the exact amount of shares repurchased and the actual days of the transactions are not known.

Table 12.5 Consolidated Statement of Common Stock, Retained Earnings, and Treasury Stock: 2017, 2018, and 2019 (Dollars in millions; Shares in thousands).

| Consolidated Statements of Equity — USD ($) in Millions | Total | Retained Earnings | Accumulated Other Comprehensive Income | Common Stock Issued Amount | Treasury Stock Amount |
|---|---|---|---|---|---|
| **Balance at Jan. 01, 2017** | $ 70,418 | 110,551 | (14,901) | 3,120 | (28,352) |
| Net earnings | 1,300 | 1,300 | — | — | — |
| Cash dividends paid | (8,943) | (8,943) | — | — | — |
| Employee compensation and stock option plans | 2,077 | (1,079) | — | — | 3,156 |
| Repurchase of common stock | (6,358) | — | — | — | (6,358) |
| Other | (36) | (36) | — | — | — |
| Other comprehensive income (loss), net of tax | 1,702 | — | 1,702 | — | — |
| **Balance at Dec. 31, 2017** | $ 60,160 | 101,793 | (13,199) | 3,120 | (31,554) |
| Net earnings | 15,297 | 15,297 | — | — | — |
| Cash dividends paid | (9,494) | (9,494) | — | — | — |
| Employee compensation and stock option plans | 1,949 | (1,111) | — | — | 3,606 |
| Repurchase of common stock | (5,868) | — | — | — | (5,868) |
| Other | (15) | (15) | — | — | — |
| Other comprehensive income (loss), net of tax | (1,791) | — | (1,791) | — | — |

*(Continued)*

Table 12.5 (*Continued*)

| Consolidated Statements of Equity — USD ($) in Millions | Total | Retained Earnings | Accumulated Other Comprehensive Income | Common Stock Issued Amount | Treasury Stock Amount |
|---|---|---|---|---|---|
| **Balance at Dec. 30, 2018** | $ 59,752 | 106,216 | (15,222) | 3,120 | (34,362) |
| Net earnings | 15,119 | 15,119 | — | — | — |
| Cash dividends paid | (9,917) | (9,917) | — | — | — |
| Employee compensation and stock option plans | 1,933 | (758) | — | — | 2,691 |
| Repurchase of common stock | (6,746) | — | — | — | (6,746) |
| Other | (1) | (1) | — | — | multicolumn1c— |
| Other comprehensive income (loss), net of tax | (669) | multicolumn1c— | (669) | multicolumn1c— | multicolumn1c— |
| **Balance at Dec. 29, 2019** | $ 59,471 | 110,659 | (15,891) | 3,120 | (38,417) |

The impact of a repurchase on a firm's financing or capital structure can be considered in light of the M&M argument. As the firm repurchases its stock, it may very well increase EPS, but it also increases its financial leverage. The impact of a repurchase on the firm depends on the amount of the firm's initial leverage and how much the repurchase increases this financial leverage.

## 12.5 The Capital Asset Pricing Model with Dividend Effects

The M&M analysis of firm value did not include uncertainty in order to allow the M&M models to flow smoothly. The capital asset pricing model, as developed by Sharpe, does allow for uncertainty. In both Chapters 10 and 11 we discussed how corporate and personal income taxes affect firm value. Because capital gains were once taxed at a lower rate than dividends, investors once preferred them to dividends. However, double taxation on dividend income greatly reduces the earnings value of stock for certain investors. Therefore, the basic CAPM equation without tax is

$$E(R_j) = R_f + \beta_j[(E(R_{m,t}) - R_f] \tag{12.7}$$

which can be extended to calculate firm value after corporate and personal income taxes have been taken into account. Brennan (1970) modified the original CAPM model so that a given level of risk, investors receiving higher dividends require higher rates of return because of greater taxes on dividends. Thus, the empirical CAPM becomes

$$E(R_{j,t}) = R_f + b\beta_j + \tau(d_j - R_f) \tag{12.8}$$

where $b = E(R_m) - R_f - \tau(d_m - R_f)$; $\tau$ = a positive coefficient that accounts for the taxation of dividends, interest, and capital gains; $\beta_j$ = the systematic risk on the $j$th security; $d_j$ = the dividend yield on the $j$th security; $R_f$ = the risk free rate; and $d_m$ = market dividend yield.

Litzenberger and Ramaswamy (1979) introduce a clientele who prefer dividends. For these shareholders, dividends increase their income, which increases their borrowing capacity and allows them to borrow larger amounts. In this case, $\delta$ can be negative.

From Eq. (12.8), we see that if the dividend yield factor is statistically significant, either positive or negative, then dividend policy is relevant to firm value. The coefficient sign $\tau$ will indicate which investors value the dividend payment the most.

The third term on the right side of Eq. (12.8), $\tau(d_j - R_f)$, integrates both dividend yield and corporate taxes together and thus integrates their impact on the determination of rate of return. In other words, in Eq. (12.7), a security's required rate of return depends not only on the risk-free rate, $R_f$ and the market risk premium, $b\beta_j$, but also requires an additional term associated with the tax levy, $\tau(d_j - R_f)$. Equation (12.8) has been extended and tested by Litzenberger and Ramaswamy (1979).

### 12.5.1 *Some empirical evidence*

To test the dividend effect on firm valuation, Litzenberger and Ramaswamy (1979) used the following model:

$$R_{j,t} - R_{f,t} = \gamma_0 + \gamma_1\beta_{j,t} + \gamma_2(d_{j,t} - R_{f,t}) + \epsilon_{j,t} \tag{12.9}$$

where $\gamma_0$ = constant of the regression: $\gamma_1$ = the slope associated with the market risk premium; $\gamma_2$ = the slope associated with the dividend risk premium; and $\epsilon_{j,t}$ = the error term. $R_{j,t}$, $R_{f,t}$, and $\beta_{j,t}$ are as defined in Eqs. (12.7) and (12.8).

Using data on the rates of return of individual companies along with dividend yields, market returns, and risk-free information, Litzenberger and Ramaswamy ran cross-sectional regressions on these determinants to derive the relative importance of each on the total valuation procedure. They found that $\gamma_2$ is positive and significantly different from 0. Therefore, the risk-adjusted return for a security is higher for those firms that issue higher dividend yields. The implication is that dividends are undesirable because higher returns are necessary to compensate investors for holding higher dividend-yielding stocks. This also supports the taxation argument that capital gains are preferred to dividends during the period studied.

In 1980, Litzenberger and Ramaswamy introduced the possibility that, in addition to the tax effect of dividends, the dividend payment contains other information that can be used to predict future dividends. The results of this 1980 study reaffirm the effect of dividends as noted in their 1979 study, and they found no useful linkage between information content and subsequent dividend behavior.

### 12.5.2 *Determinants of dividend policy*

The dividend policies that are available to the management of a firm are as follows:

1. A stable dollar dividend.
2. A stable dividend payout ratio.
3. Either 1 or 2 coupled with a year-end extra.
4. No dividends.

The policy that management chooses depends on its interpretation of financial theory and the impact of real-world considerations on the market price of the firm's stock. Modigliani and Miller propose that dividends are irrelevant in valuing the worth of a firm's stock. If this is true, managers and investors should not concern themselves with dividends. M&M present the argument for dividend irrelevance in a general and abstract fashion. The logic of their arguments is discussed in the following section.

## 12.6 The Irrelevance of Dividend Policy

Suppose a firm is in business for two years. During the first year, the cash flow available to management for dividends or reinvestment is \$115,000. During the second year, a cash flow of \$132,250 is paid to the shareholders as a dividend. If the firm's cost of capital is 15%, the firm's value is the present value of its future cash flows discounted at the cost of capital:

$$\text{Firm value} = \sum_{t=1}^{N} \frac{\text{Cash flow}}{(1+k)^t} = \frac{115{,}000}{1.15} + \frac{132{,}250}{1.15^2}$$
$$= \$100{,}000 + \$100{,}000 = \$200{,}000$$

The above value can be viewed as the value of the entire firm, or the analysis can be made on a per share basis. If we assume 20,000 shares outstanding, the value per share on a cash flow basis is \$10. If management decides to make no new investment during year 1, the entire \$115,000 can be paid out as a dividend for year 1.

If management decides to make a short-term investment equal to the entire amount of the first-year cash flow at the firm's cost of capital and pay no dividend in that year but pay out the entire proceeds in year 2, the firm's value would be

$$\text{Firm value} = \sum_{t=1}^{N} \frac{\text{Cash flow}((1 + \text{Return on investment})^{N-t}}{(1+k)^t}$$

$$= \frac{0}{1.15} + \frac{132{,}250}{1.15^2} + \frac{115{,}000(1 + 1.15)}{1.15^2} = \$200{,}000$$

The value per share would remain \$10. If management pays a dividend during the first year in excess of the \$115,000, the firm would have to finance the additional cash required to pay the dividend. As we have seen, there are numerous ways for the firm to raise funds. For this example, we will assume that management decides to issue new equity. The form of financing really has no effect on the argument presented by M&M, although the presentation becomes somewhat more complicated as various forms of debt financing are introduced.

Management has declared a dividend of \$150,000 to be paid the first year. The cash flow of \$115,000 and a new stock issue of \$35,000 are used to pay the dividend. The new shareholders expect to earn a 15% return on their investment, so that during year 2 they expect to receive \$40,250 in the form of a dividend and return of capital. Thus, the old shareholders will receive a dividend of \$132,250 minus \$40,250, or \$92,000. The value of the firm under these conditions will be

$$\begin{aligned}\text{Firm value} &= \text{Old shareholders value} + \text{New shareholders value}\\ &= \frac{150{,}000}{1.15} + \frac{92{,}000}{1.15^2} + \frac{40{,}250}{1.15^3}\\ &= \$200{,}000 + 35{,}000 = \$235{,}000\end{aligned}$$

The value per share remains \$10, because now there are 20,000 old shares and 3,500 new shares. Regardless of the dividend payment that management selects, firm value is unchanged in the eyes of the old shareholders. Based on this reasoning M&M conclude that the payment of dividends has no effect on firm value and is therefore irrelevant.

### 12.6.1 *Homemade dividends*

An alternative approach to the relationship between dividends and firm value can be presented from the shareholder's perspective. In the example above, the firm initially paid $115,000 in year 1 and $132,250 in year 2 as dividends for 20,000 shares, or $5.75 per share during year 1 and ^6.6125 per share during year 2. A shareholder with no immediate use for the dividend could reinvest the dividend in an equally risky investment yielding 15% and receive a cash flow from this investment yielding 15% in year 2 along with the regular dividend. The investor's cash flow would be 0 in year 1 and $6.6125 from the new investment and $6.6125 as the regular dividend, or a total cash flow of $13.225 in year 2. This is exactly the cash flow the investor would receive if the firm made the investment, while paying no dividends in year 1 and $264,500 in year 2, or $13.225 per share.

If the investor preferred a larger cash flow in year 1 than the company was paying, he or she could sell some shares in year 1 to generate a cash flow in year 1 of, say, $7.50, consisting of $5.75 worth of dividends and the sale of enough shares to generate $1.75. The sale of stock during year 1 will reduce the amount of dividends the investor is entitled in year 2 by $1.75 plus the rate of return the investor would have earned for that year, or a total of $2.0125. The dividend the investor is entitled to receive in year 2 is $6.6125 minus $2.0125, or $4.60 a share, which is exactly the amount of dividends the investor is entitled to if the corporation issues new shares in the above example. The cash flow of $92,000 in year 2 divided by 20,000 shares equals $4.60 per share.

These shareholder actions are called *homemade dividends*. The point of homemade dividends is that no matter what dividend policy the firm's managers follow, the investor — either by investing excess dividends or selling shares — can achieve different combinations of dividend flows, thereby making the corporation's dividend policy irrelevant.

### 12.6.2 *Assumptions used to obtain the conclusions of Modigliani and Miller*

Miller and Modigliani (1961) developed the theory that firm value is independent of its dividend policy in a world without taxes or transaction costs under assumptions of both certainty and uncertainty. Some other assumptions they made are as follows:

1. There are perfect capital markets.
2. Investors are rational and have homogenous expectations.
3. There is symmetric information between corporate management and shareholders.

By *perfect capital markets*, we refer to a world without taxes or transaction costs, where information is available freely to all investors in the marketplace. The market reflects all available information, and capital is channeled to areas of the economy where it will do the most good in terms of profitability. *Rational investors* refers to the preference of all investors to seek profits and be risk-averse so that, given the same set of circumstances, investors can be expected to act the same way. It is important to note that in perfect capital markets, rational investors can still be faced with uncertainty. Therefore, perfect capital markets do not necessarily imply perfect foresight on the part of rational investors. The idea that dividends convey information is not possible in the M&M argument because it assumes that management and shareholders have the same information. In a world with asymmetric information between shareholders and management, dividends can have an informational role.

Modigliani and Miller developed an algebraic approach to examine the value of the following:

1. Dividend streams
2. Earnings stream
3. Discounted cash flows
4. Investment opportunities

They did this to show that dividend policy has no effect on firm valuation in a world without taxes. The dividend stream approach to valuation implies that a firm's present market value is the present value of the future infinite stream of dividend payments, as discussed in Chapter 5. The earnings stream approach and the discounted cash flow approach assume that a firm's present market value is equivalent to the present value annuities of the earnings stream and discounted cash flows. The investment opportunity approach explicitly decomposes the market value associated with growth opportunities from the firm's perpetual market value associated with growth opportunities from the firm's perpetual value. The firm's perpetual market value is associated with its growth approaches under the other three assumptions.

In a world without taxes, a firm can choose any dividend policy without affecting the cash flows received by its investors. If dividends are paid in excess of cash flows from operations, inflows of new equity could be used to fund new investments. If the dividend payout is less than the cash flows from operations, then leftover funds can be used to repurchase outstanding shares.

The main point is that in a world without transactions costs or taxes, firm value becomes independent of dividend policy. In such a world, a firm's value depends only on the distributions of future cash flows as a result of the investments undertaken. Therefore, two firms that are identical except for their dividend policy payout will have the same present value regardless of their current dividend payout. The reason is that if dividend and investment outlays are greater than operational inflows, the situation can be remedied by issuing new equity. Although M&M's conclusions are correct under these assumptions, under real-world conditions of taxes and transactions costs, these assumptions are unrealistic. The importance of dividend policy in the real world is that transactions costs, taxes, and internally generated sources of funds for investment purposes are less costly than debt or equity issuances. Therefore, dividend policy may be an important consideration for the financial manager.

### 12.6.3 *Clientele effects*

The clientele effect was introduced by Miller and Modigliani (1961) as a market imperfection that affects dividend policy. M&M observed that corporations tend to attract clientele who are attracted by the firm's established payout ratio. Investors in higher tax brackets tend to hold stocks with a lower dividend payout and a high capital gains yield to avoid the personal tax of dividend as a source of income. On the other hand, retirees, because of their lower tax brackets, tend to invest in companies with larger yields.

As a result of the type of investors a firm attracts, management may be reluctant to change its dividend policies. Management may cause the firm's shareholders to incur unwanted transactions costs if there is a shift in payout ratios. Therefore, the tax differential favoring capital gains used to be a systematic market imperfection that produces this clientele effect.

### 12.6.4 *Dividend information content — A synthesis*

There is a belief that the payment of a dividend conveys a signal to the marketplace. In effect, each dividend payment or change in the dividend carries information to the investors about the company. The type of information conveyed could be made public in other ways. However, dividends are management's way of signaling to the market that the firm expects to do well. One way of looking at the logic behind the informational content argument is by looking at a Sources and Uses of Funds Statement, with dividends being defined as the difference between the sources of funds and the uses of funds. Table 12.6 presents the residual theory of dividends in a Sources and Uses of Funds Statement.

After all other operational investment and financing decisions have been made, any remaining funds can be paid out as dividends to the shareholders. As mentioned earlier, this is the residual theory of dividends. Management's meeting all other needs before considering how much to pay out in dividends, as in the residual approach, would be a signal to the shareholders. The information conveyed by this action would be that management has concerns that are more important than dividends. On the other hand, if management has a target dividend payment or feels it could sustain a dividend increase by manipulating the sources and uses of funds, a different kind of information would be conveyed. A discussion of the relationship between dividends and the factors that are part of the sources and uses of funds will help explain the type of information conveyed by the dividend.

Profits from operations are the main source of dividend payments. Legally, dividends must be paid out of current net income or retained earnings. Otherwise, they are considered a *liquidating dividend* or a

Table 12.6 Residual Dividends.

| |
|---|
| **Sources of funds** |
| Profits from operations |
| Depreciation |
| Sale of assets |
| Short-term and long-term borrowing |
| Sale of stock[a] |
| **Uses of funds** |
| Financing losses from operations |
| Purchase of assets |
| Repayment of short-term and long-term borrowing |
| Repurchase of stock |
| Sources − Uses = Dividends |

*Notes*: [a]According to Higgins (1972), if shareholders prefer capital gains income to dividend income in a world of differential taxes, external equity should not be used to finance investment and dividend payments. Given the changes in the 1986 Tax Law, which treats dividend income and capital gains income equally, it is now permissible to consider external equity as a source of funds.

return of the investor's capital. If the profits increase through successful investments, dividend growth may slow in the short run because of the investment required to sustain the growth in earnings. In the future, these investments are expected to generate cash flows that will enable the firm to pay higher dividends. The variability of the company's profits will also affect the amount of dividends that are paid. If a company is in a cyclical industry, we would expect to see a relatively low payout — even during periods of high profits — to ensure that the dividend is not cut when sales and profits fall to lower levels. In this case, a low dividend payout coupled with an extra dividend during more profitable times might be appropriate.

Depreciation is a recognition of the deterioration of an asset's economic worth, which affects the amount of taxes a corporation has to pay. Other things being equal, the higher the depreciation, the lower the taxable income and the lower the tax liability. If management chooses to keep the firm's productive capability intact by reinvesting, there is probably no relationship between depreciation and the ability to pay dividends. However, in an inflationary environment, when the replacement and maintenance costs of maintaining productive capability are higher than the depreciation charge, the funds needed to maintain capacity will adversely affect the ability to pay dividends.

As unprofitable subsidiaries or operations are liquidated or sold off, the cash flow available for dividends will increase, thereby allowing a dividend increase in the short run. However, if this policy of liquidating assets is followed to the extreme, the firm will, in effect, be out of business, unable to pay any dividends because there is no productive capacity to generate future profits.

When a firm borrows either short or long term, there are usually covenants in the borrowing agreements that limit the amount of dividends or the increases in dividends. This dividend restriction is placed on management to protect the firm's creditors from being disadvantaged in the event that management makes a large portion of the firm's cash available to the shareholders in the form of dividends. The severity of these covenants may indirectly convey information about how creditors perceive the company and its management and may directly limit the firm's ability to pay dividends.

When firms borrow, there are normally repayment schedules that must be met. As the firm pays off these sinking funds, the amount of cash available for dividends is reduced. Hence, any increase in borrowing may reduce the firm's ability to pay dividends because of repayment provisions.

By selling additional equity, the firm (if it intends to keep its dividend per share constant or growing at the same historic rate) will need larger cash flows to meet dividend requirements. The nature of the firm and its prospects for being able to continually issue new equity must also be considered. A firm with an established track record will have little difficulty in selling new equity easy and thus may be able to pay out a large portion of its earnings as dividends. However, a firm that is new or has a weaker record will find it more difficult to tap the equity markets for funds, so that its only available source of funds is its earnings. Hence, the firm will be required to have a lower dividend payout.

From a uses-of-funds viewpoint, if the firm expects current losses or deficits to be temporary, it may not cut the dividend. If the company becomes profitable, then we can see no relation between financing operating losses and dividends in the short run. However, if the firm's losses are persistent, then the dividend ultimately will be cut to reflect the unprofitable operations.

Based on the residual dividend idea, the purchase of assets is likely to reduce the funds available for dividends. The extent of this reduction is related to the size and timing of the new investments, as well as the firm's access to capital markets and the shareholders' preferences for dividend income. It is possible for a firm to be involved in new investments while at the same time maintain a high dividend payout through new financing. The interaction of each of these activities may be complex, but must be evaluated by management to make fundamentally sound decisions. Any reduction in liquidity by retiring debt or repurchasing stock will probably have a negative effect on the firm's ability to pay high dividends.

The sources and uses of funds that a management selects will have an impact on the level of dividends that a firm is able to sustain. The decisions affecting each of the uses and sources are not made in isolation, because each one of these decisions will influence the firm's success and provide a return to the shareholders.

It is probably an oversimplification to say that all of the decisions affecting sources and uses of funds are made and then residual cash is paid out as a dividend. Rather, there are simultaneous considerations and decisions that include dividend payment and levels of dividends as well as the other sources and uses. Hence, any dividend payment or change in dividends may be a signal of management's assessment of all of these other factors. If so, the information conveyed in the dividend payment may be one way that management indicates to the marketplace its beliefs about the future prospects of the firm's cash flows.

### 12.6.5 *Short-run versus long-run dividend effects*

Another perspective of the relationship between dividend payout and firm value involves the effect that a change in the timing of dividend payouts may have on firm value. Future dividends are riskier than current dividends, so that shareholders may prefer present payments over future payments. However, this "bind in the hand is worth two in the bush" argument has its drawbacks. Recall that firm valuation under uncertainty is determined by the riskiness of its cash flows from investment projects. Increasing the dividend payout today will not affect firm value because it does not reduce the riskiness of future cash flows.

This is true under M&M's three assumptions of perfect capital markets, rational investors, and perfect certainty. However, M&M's hypothesis does not hold true in the short run. Friend and Blume (1975) have based a study on a Department of Commerce survey of investors' attitudes on their preference for dividends. This study shows that in the short run most investors prefer dividends over capital gains. Therefore, the financial manager should consider both a company's investment opportunities as well as investor preference before making dividend policy decisions.

Practically, in the short run, dividend payments reduce the internal funds available for capital investment and reduce working capital cash flows, thereby reducing the liquidity ratio and increasing the firm's short-run financial risk. Under these circumstances, given increased risk, banks will charge higher interest premiums, creditors will require stricter covenants, and equity holders will require higher returns.

## 12.7 Critique on M&M Dividend Irrelevance of Dividend Policy

The two main reasons for Miller and Modigliani (1961) obtaining the irrelevancy of dividend policy are: i. companies pay either 100% cash dividend or pay no cash dividend and ii. they assume there are no uncertainty in their analysis framework. By relaxing these two hypotheses, DeAngelo and DeAngelo (2006) have shown there is an optimal dividend policy. By using a more rigorous model, Lee *et al.* (2011) have theoretically supported DeAngelo and DeAngelo's conclusion.

Lee *et al.* (2011) generalized the flexibility dividend hypothesis by Blau and Fuller (2008) and others. In addition, Lee *et al.* (2011) also introduced growth rate, systematic risk, and total risk variables into the theoretical model. They used data collected in the U.S. from 1969 to 2009 to investigate the impact of growth rate, systematic risk, and total risk on the optimal payout ratio in terms of the fixed-effect model. They found that based on flexibility considerations, a company will reduce its payout when the growth rate increases. In addition, Lee *et al.* (2011) found that a nonlinear relationship exists between the payout ratio and the risk. In other words, the relationship between the payout ratio and risk is negative (or positive) when the growth rate is higher (or lower) than the rate of return on total assets. Their theoretical model and empirical results can therefore be used to identify whether flexibility or the free cash flow hypothesis should be used to determine the dividend policy. Chen *et al.* (2013) studied the joint determination of sustainable growth rate, optimal growth rate, and optimal payout ratio.

## 12.8 Summary

The important question of Chapter 12 is, Are dividends valuable? According to the M&M argument, dividends are irrelevant in a perfect market. However real-world factors such as taxes, inflation, transaction costs, and personal preferences make the answer to the question less definite. There are situations when high dividends are preferred and other scenarios when no or low dividends are appropriate. The impact of inflation, the clientele effect, and the information content of dividends provide a framework for analysis of the importance of dividends, each of which may be beneficial in answering the question about the value of dividends in certain circumstances.

Overall, there appears to be no general rule that is universally applicable to management and shareholder decisions about dividends. The best that can be said is that dividend value depends on the circumstances of the decision-maker. As these circumstances change over time, a manager may be faced with dividend irrelevance at one point and, given certain changes in the environment, with a Gordon world of dividend primacy at another point.

In recent years, there have been sweeping changes in U.S. tax structure and regulation. Both managers and investors are concerned with evaluating the impact of these changes on firm value and the dividend decision. The dialogue accompanying these changes may provide some additional information on dividend value.

## References

Black, F. "The Dividend Puzzle," *Journal of Portfolio Management*, 2(2) (Winter 1976, pp. 5–8).

Black, F. and M. Scholes. "The Effects of Dividend Yield and Dividend Policy on Common Stock Prices and Returns," *Journal of Financial Economics*, 1 (May 1974, pp. 1–22).

Blau, B. M. and K. P. Fuller. "Flexibility and Dividends," *Journal of Corporate Finance* 14 (2008, pp. 133–152).

Brennan, M. "Taxes, Market Valuation, and Corporate Financial Policy," *National Tax Journal* (December 1970, pp. 417–427).

Chen, H. Y., M. Gupta, A. C. Lee and C. F. Lee. "Sustainable Growth Rate, Optimal Growth Rate, and Optimal Payout Ratio: A Joint Optimization Approach," *Journal of Banking and Finance* 37(4) (2013, pp. 1205–1222).

Copeland, T. "Liquidity Changes Following Stock Splits," *The Journal of Finance*, 34 (March 1979, pp. 115–141).

Dann, L. "Common Stock Repurchases: An Analysis of Returns to Bondholders and Stockholders," *Journal of Financial Economics*, 8 (June 1981, pp. 113–138).

DeAngelo, H. and L. DeAngelo. "The Irrelevance of the MM Dividend Irrelevance Theorem," *Journal of Financial Economics*, 79 (2006, pp. 293–315).

Fama, E. and H. Babiak. "Dividend Policy: An Empirical Analysis," *Journal of the American Statistical Association* (December 1968, pp. 1132–1161).

Fama, E., L. Fisher, M. Jensen and R. Roll. "The Adjustment of Stock Prices to New Information," *International Economic Review* (February 1969, pp. 1–21).

Friend, I. and M. Blume. "The Demand for Risky Assets," *American Economic Review*, 65 (December 1975, pp. 900–922).

Friend, I. and M. Puckett. "Dividends and Stock Prices," *American Economic Review*, 64 (September 1964, pp. 656–682).

Gordon, M. J. "Dividends, earnings, and stock prices," *The Review of Economics and Statistics*, 41(2) (1959, pp. 99–105).

Higgins, R. C. "Dividend Policy and Increasing Discount Rates: A Clarification." *Journal of Finance and Quantitative Analysis*, 7 (June 1972, pp. 1757–1762).

John, K. and J. Williams. "Dividend, Distribution, and Taxes: A Signaling Equilibrium," *The Journal of Finance*, 40 (September 1985, pp. 1053–1070).

Kalay, A. "Signaling, Information Content and the Reluctance to Cut Dividends," *Journal of Financial and Quantitative Analysis*, 15(14) (November 1980, pp. 855–870).

Lee, C. F. "Functional Form and the Dividend Effect in the Electric Utility Industry," *The Journal of Finance*, 31 (December 1976, pp. 1481–1486).

Lee, C. F. "Investment, Financing, Dividend, and Production Policies: Review, Integration, and Extension," working paper (Rutgers University, 2020).

Lee, C. F. and J. Lee. *Financial Analysis, Planning and Forecasting: Theory and Application*, 3rd edn. (World Scientific, 2017).

Lee, C.F. and J. Lin. "A New Approach to Investigate Dividend Smoothing: Theoretical and Empirical Evidence" *30th FEA Conference* (New York University, November 1–2, 2019).

Lee, C.F., C. Hu and M. Foley. "Differential Effect of Inside Debt, CEO Compensation Diversification, And Firm Investment," *Review of Quantitative Finance Accounting*, 56(2) (2021, pp. 505–543).

Lee, C.F., J. Lee and A. C. Lee. *Statistics for Business and Financial Economics*, 3rd edn. (Springer, 2013).

Lee, C. F., C. Wu and M. Djarraya. "A Further Empirical Investigation of the Dividend Adjustment Process," *Journal of Econometrics*, 35 (1987, pp. 267–285).

Lee, C. F., M. C. Gupta, H. Y. Chen and A. C. Lee. "Optimal Payout Ratio under Uncertainty and the Flexibility Hypothesis: Theory and Empirical Evidence," *Journal of Corporate Finance*, 17 (2011, pp. 483–501).

Lintner, J. "Distribution of Incomes of Corporations Among Dividends, Retained Earnings and Taxes," *American Economic Review*, 56 (May 1956, pp. 97–113).

Lintner, J. "Optimal Dividends and Corporate Growth Under uncertainty," *The Quarterly Journal of Economics* (February 1964, pp. 49–95).

Litzenberger, R. and K. Ramaswamy. "The Effect of Personal Taxes and Dividends on Capital Asset Prices: Theory and Empirical Evidence," *Journal of Financial Economics*, 6 (June 1979, pp. 163–196).

Miller, M. "Debt and Taxes," *The Journal of Finance*, 32 (May 1977, pp. 261–275).

Miller, M. and F. Modigliani. "Dividend Policy, Growth, and the Valuation of Shares," *Journal of Business*, 43 (October 1961, pp. 411–432).

Miller, M. H. and K. Rock. "Dividend Policy Under Asymmetric Information," *The Journal of Finance*, 40 (September 1985, pp. 1031–1051).

Rappaport, A. "Inflation accounting and corporate dividends," *Financial Executive* (1981, pp. 20–22).

Shefrin, H. and M. Stativan. "Explaining Investor Preference for Cash Dividends," *Journal of Financial Economics*, 13 (June 1984, pp. 253–282).

Van Horne, J. and J. McDonald. "Dividend Policy and New Equity Financing," *The Journal of Finance*, 26 (June 1971, pp. 507–519).

Woolridge, J. "Dividend Changes and Security Prices," *The Journal of Finance*, 38 (December 1983, pp. 1607–1615).

## Appendix 12A — Partial Adjustment Dividend Payment Model — JNJ as Case Study

In this appendix, we use the partial adjustment regression model introduced in this chapter as Eq. (12.3) to show how dividend payment behavior can be analyzed for a major corporation. Annual EPS and DPS data for JNJ 1988–2009 are listed in Table 12.1A and will be used to perform the following case study:

$$D_{j,t} = b_0 + b_1 E_{j,t} + b_2 D_{j,t-1} + e_{j,t} \tag{12.1A}$$

where $D_{j,t}$ = DPS for the $j$th firm in period $t$; $D_{j,t-1}$ = DPS for $j$th firm in period $t-1$; $E_{j,t}$ = EPS for $j$th firm in period $t$; $b_0$ = the intercept term; $b_1$ and $b_2$ = the regression coefficients, and $e_{j,t}$ = the error term.

By using annual EPS and DPS data from JNJ from 1988–2019 as presented in Table 12.1A.

$$\bar{R}^2 = 0.9297 \tag{12.2A}$$

$$D_{j,t} = -0.2273 + \underset{(2.60)}{0.1056E_{j,t}} + \underset{(14.06)}{0.9459D_{j,t-1}}$$

The $t$ statistics, indicated in the parenthesis, show that both estimated $b_1$ and $b_2$ are significantly different from 0 at the 95% significant level. Following Eqs. (12.4) and (12.5), the estimated partial adjustment coefficient ($\delta$) and long-term payout ($P$) can be estimated as follows:

$$\delta = 1 - 0.9459 = 0.0541$$

$$P = \frac{0.1056}{(1 - 0.9459)} = 1.9519$$

The partial adjustment coefficient reflects how fast a firm adjusts its dividend payment toward the target norm.

Most recently, Lee *et al.* (1987) have generalized the partial adjustment model of Eq. (12.1A) as

$$D_{j,t} = b_0 + b_1 E_{j,t} + b_2 D_{j,t-1} + b_3 D_{j,t-2} + \epsilon_j \tag{12.3A}$$

Table 12.1A Annual EPS and DPS Data for JNJ.

| Year | $DPS_t$ | $EPS_t$ | $DPS_{t-1}$ | $DPS_{t-2}$ |
|---|---|---|---|---|
| 1988 | 1.89 | 5.63 | — | — |
| 1989 | 1.1 | 3.19 | 1.89 | — |
| 1990 | 1.29 | 3.38 | 1.1 | 1.89 |
| 1991 | 1.51 | 4.3 | 1.29 | 1.1 |
| 1992 | 0.88 | 1.54 | 1.51 | 1.29 |
| 1993 | 1 | 2.71 | 0.88 | 1.51 |
| 1994 | 1.12 | 3.08 | 1 | 0.88 |
| 1995 | 1.25 | 3.65 | 1.12 | 1 |
| 1996 | 0.72 | 2.12 | 1.25 | 1.12 |
| 1997 | 0.83 | 2.41 | 0.72 | 1.25 |
| 1998 | 0.95 | 2.23 | 0.83 | 0.72 |
| 1999 | 1.04 | 2.94 | 0.95 | 0.83 |
| 2000 | 1.22 | 3.39 | 1.04 | 0.95 |
| 2001 | 0.66 | 1.83 | 1.22 | 1.04 |
| 2002 | 0.78 | 2.16 | 0.66 | 1.22 |
| 2003 | 0.91 | 2.39 | 0.78 | 0.66 |
| 2004 | 1.08 | 2.83 | 0.91 | 0.78 |
| 2005 | 1.26 | 3.46 | 1.08 | 0.91 |
| 2006 | 1.44 | 3.73 | 1.26 | 1.08 |
| 2007 | 1.6 | 3.63 | 1.44 | 1.26 |
| 2008 | 1.77 | 4.57 | 1.6 | 1.44 |
| 2009 | 1.91 | 4.4 | 1.77 | 1.6 |
| 2010 | 2.11 | 4.85 | 1.91 | 1.77 |
| 2011 | 2.25 | 3.54 | 2.11 | 1.91 |
| 2012 | 2.4 | 3.94 | 2.25 | 2.11 |
| 2013 | 2.59 | 4.92 | 2.4 | 2.25 |
| 2014 | 2.76 | 5.8 | 2.59 | 2.4 |
| 2015 | 2.95 | 5.56 | 2.76 | 2.59 |
| 2016 | 3.15 | 6.04 | 2.95 | 2.76 |
| 2017 | 3.32 | 0.48 | 3.15 | 2.95 |
| 2018 | 3.54 | 5.7 | 3.32 | 3.15 |
| 2019 | 3.75 | 5.72 | 3.54 | 3.32 |

The result of the estimated multiple regression model for BOA is

$$\bar{R}^2 = 0.9584 \tag{12.4A}$$

$$D_{j,t} = -0.2267 + \underset{(2.88)}{0.0933E_{j,t}} + \underset{(5.73)}{0.7934D_{j,t-1}} + \underset{(1.36)}{0.2019D_{j,t-2}}$$

The addition of the dividend per share variable lagged two years improves the forecasting power of this model. This can be seen by comparing the $\bar{R}^2$ of Eq. (12.2A) of 93% to the $\bar{R}^2$ of 96% for Eq. (12.4A). The further implication of this empirical result can be found in Fama and Babiak (1968), Lee *et al.* (1987), and Lee and Lin (2019).

Lee and Lin (2019) have used four alternative dividend behavior models, which were developed by Lee *et al.* (1987), to study dividend smoothing behavior for about 1,200 firms. They found that more than 50% of the companies use the adaptive expectation model to perform dividend smoothing and only 15% use partial adjustment model to perform dividend smoothing. This result implies that dividend smoothing research in terms of partial adjustment model is not appropriate.

## Questions and Problems

1. Define the following terms:
   a. Declaration date
   b. Record date
   c. Ex-dividend date
   d. Payment date
2. According to Gordon (1959), are dividends relevant in determining firm value? Explain. How do M&M (1961) view the relevance of dividends? Discuss their four approaches to valuation.
3. In what ways do behavioral considerations affect a firm's dividend policy? Use the partial adjustment model to answer this question.
4. How can dividend policy analysis help financial analysis and planning?
5. Jennett, Ltd. is paying a dividend with a date of record of April 5, 2021.
   a. If investor A sells the stock to investor B on April 5, 2021, which one is entitled to the dividend?
   b. If investor A sells the stock to investor B on April 1, 2021, which one is entitled to the dividend?
   c. If investor A sells the stock to investor B on March 31, 2021, which one is entitled to the dividend?

6. Does the presence of corporate taxes have any impact on the importance of a firm's dividend policy to its value? Explain.
7. If personal taxes are irrelevant to the dividend policy of the firm with respect to firm value, how much should the value of a firm's stock change on the ex-dividend date?
8. What is the general relationship between the rate of inflation and the firm's ability to pay dividends from free cash flow?
9. If a firm pays a constant dollar dividend, does this mean that there is no relationship between dividends and earnings? Explain.
10. What is a stock repurchase? By what methods can a firm repurchase shares? Explain why a stock repurchase can be beneficial to stockholders and to management.
11. Suppose XYZ Company's stock currently is selling for $100 and a two-for-one stock split is declared. What will happen to the price of the stock?
12. Briefly explain why a firm's dividend-payout record can be a source of information to the marketplace.
13. Explain the differences between a stock split and a stock dividend.
14. Evaluate the following statement: "When a stock goes ex-dividend, the price of the stock always falls by the amount of the dividend."
15. What are homemade dividends? How do Miller and Modigliani use homemade dividends?
16. What types of companies would be likely to pay little or no dividends? What companies would be likely to pay steady dividends?
17. Briefly explain why a company would choose to repurchase its own stock.
18. Briefly explain why a company might declare a stock split.
19. Suppose the Wagner Corporation has just declared a reverse 1-for-2 split of its stock. If the current price of the stock is $25, what will happen to the stock's price?
20. Explain what is meant by double taxation of dividends.
21. Why do corporations attempt to maintain a stable dividend policy? How do they accomplish this?
22. What is a DRIP? Why would a company institute a DRIP? Why would investors be interested in a DRIP?
23. What information is revealed in a dividend announcement?
24. Why are dividend decisions so important to a firm?

25. How does a firm's access to the capital markets affect its dividend policy?
26. Why would a smaller, fast-growing company be less likely to pay dividends than a larger company that is experiencing moderate growth?
27. Is there any difference between managers buying shares of their firm for themselves and the firm repurchasing its own shares?
28. In establishing a firm's dividend policy, should management consider its compensation (i.e., bonus due to earnings growth) or the need of the shareholders as the primary determinant of how much dividend to pay?
29. Briefly discuss the two competing views on the importance of dividend policy.
30. Why might some bond indentures place restrictions on dividend payments?
31. In the context of the clientele effect, explain what might stop a board of directors from making a major change in the firm's dividend policy to help finance attractive budgeting projects.
32. Kjetsaa Kat Krunchies, Inc., has announced that dividends will be paid on April 3 to holders of record on Friday, March 15.

    a. When is the ex-dividend date?
    b. If the record day is Wednesday, May 13, when is the ex-dividend date?
    c. If the record day is Monday, March 11, when is the ex-dividend date?

33. Discuss the empirical studies of CAPM with taxes and dividends. How can this finding be compared with Gordon (1959) and M&M (1961)?
34. How can option-pricing theory be used to determine the relevance of dividends to firm valuation? Explain.
35. Use the annual dividend per share (DPS), earnings per share (EPS) price per share (PPS), earning year (EY), and dividend year (DY) data of JNJ in the following table during 2008–2019 to analyze the following:

    a. The dividend-earnings relationship
    b. The dividend yield-earnings yield relationship

**EPS, DPS, PPS, EY, and DY for JNJ from 2008–2019**

| Year | EPS | DPS | PPS | EY | DY |
|---|---|---|---|---|---|
| 2008 | 4.62 | 1.795 | 58.56 | 0.079 | 0.031 |
| 2009 | 4.45 | 1.93 | 64.41 | 0.069 | 0.030 |
| 2010 | 4.85 | 2.11 | 61.85 | 0.078 | 0.034 |
| 2011 | 3.54 | 2.25 | 65.58 | 0.054 | 0.034 |
| 2012 | 3.94 | 2.40 | 69.48 | 0.057 | 0.035 |
| 2013 | 4.92 | 2.59 | 92.35 | 0.053 | 0.028 |
| 2014 | 5.8 | 2.76 | 105.06 | 0.055 | 0.026 |
| 2015 | 5.56 | 2.95 | 102.72 | 0.054 | 0.029 |
| 2016 | 6.04 | 3.15 | 115.21 | 0.052 | 0.027 |
| 2017 | 0.48 | 3.32 | 139.72 | 0.003 | 0.024 |
| 2018 | 5.7 | 3.54 | 127.27 | 0.045 | 0.028 |
| 2019 | 5.72 | 3.75 | 145.75 | 0.039 | 0.026 |

36. Tarnell Corporation has the following equity:

| | |
|---|---|
| Common stock (1,000,000 shares at $4) | $4,000,000 |
| Paid in capital | 3,000,000 |
| Retained earnings | 8,000,000 |
| Total net worth | $15,000,000 |

The current market price of the stock is $15.00.

a. If the company declares a 2-for-1 stock split:
   i. How would the above equity accounts appear?
   ii. What would the EPS be before and after the stock split?

b. If the company pays a 10% stock dividend:
   i. How would Tarnell's equity accounts appear?
   ii. What would the EPS be both before and after the stock dividend?

37. Syntas Systems follows a residual theory of dividends. For the coming year Syntas has $400,000 in new capital expenditures with rates of return above the 12% required by the company's investors. There are currently 100,000 shares outstanding.

a. If the company currently has $300,000 in internal equity and uses no debt financing, what will dividends per share be?

b. If the company currently has $500,000 in internal equity and uses no debt financing, what will dividends per share be?
c. Explain the argument against the residual theory concerning investors desire for current income.

38. Reegan's Peanut Corporation has a capital structure consisting of 50% debt and 50% equity. Earnings available to common stockholders (net income) and capital expenditure projections for the next three years are given as follows:

| Year | Net Income | Capital Requirements |
|---|---|---|
| 1 | $500,000 | $800,000 |
| 2 | 600,000 | 600,000 |
| 3 | 400,000 | 700,000 |

Find the amount of debt, external equity, and total dividends in each year if:

a. The company follows the residual theory of dividends.
b. The company follows a constant payout ratio of 30%.
c. Why is a stable dollar dividend considered by many to result in a higher value than either of the above policies?

39. **Dividend per Share.** D&G Corporation maintains a constant payout ratio of 25%. If earnings are $3 per share, what will be D&G's dividend per share?
40. **Payout Ratio.** A company has just paid a dividend of $4 per share. If earnings are $5 per share, what is the payout ratio?
41. **Dividend per Share.** Devito Corporation maintains a constant payout ratio of 45%. If earnings are $8 per share, what will be Devito's dividend per share?
42. **Retention Rate and Dividend per Share.** Lockwood Industries maintains a constant retention rate of 35%. If earnings are $4 per share, what will be Lockwood's dividend per share?
43. **Stock Split.** The LFN Corporation currently has 1-million shares outstanding with par value of $25. Suppose the company declares a 5-for-1 split.

a. How many shares will be outstanding?
b. What will the new par value be?

44. **Stock Dividend.** Use the information in the "Before Dividend" section of Table 12.3 to construct a new statement after an 8% stock dividend.
45. **Stock Splits.** Use the information in the "Before Split" section of Table 12.4 to construct a new statement for a 5-for-1 stock split.
46. **Ex-dividend Price.** with Tax Miller, Inc., has declared a \$3.00 per share dividend. Miller stock sells for \$55 per share and is about to go ex-dividend. Use Eqs. (12.1) and (12.1a) to answer the following questions:

    a. If $T_p = T_g = 0$, what is the ex-dividend price?
    b. If $T_p = T_g = 30\%$, what is the ex-dividend price?
    c. If $T_p = 30\%$ and $T_g = 20\%$, what is the ex-dividend price?

47. **Stocks Split.** Suppose ABC Company's stock currently is selling for \$75 per share and a 3-for-2 stock split is declared. What will be the new price of ABC's stock?
48. **Payout Ratio and Ex-dividend Price.** A company has just paid a dividend of \$2 per share for its stock, which has a price of \$98 per share. If earnings are \$6 per share, what is the payout ratio? What is the ex-dividend stock price if the tax effect is negligible?
49. By using DPS and EPS annual data from Merck during 1988–2009, we obtain the following partial adjustment dividend behavior equation.

$$\bar{R}^2 = 0.5110$$

$$D_{j,t} = 0.6297 + \underset{(4.33)}{0.2031 E_{j,t}} + \underset{(0.379)}{0.1463 D_{j,t-1}}$$

    a. Please calculate partial adjustment coefficient and long run payout ratio.
    b. Interpret the results.
    c. Compare the partial adjustment coefficient and long run ratio of Merck with JNJ, which was previously presented.

50. The following table presents the PPS, DPS, EPS, DY, and EY for IBM, JNJ, MRK, and PG from 1980 to 2019.

| Year | Company | PPS | DPS | Dividend Yields (DY) | EPS | Earnings Yield (EY) |
|---|---|---|---|---|---|---|
| 1980 | IBM | 16.97 | 0.86 | 0.0507 | 1.52 | 0.0899 |
| 1981 | IBM | 14.22 | 0.86 | 0.0605 | 1.41 | 0.0990 |
| 1982 | IBM | 24.06 | 0.86 | 0.0357 | 1.85 | 0.0768 |
| 1983 | IBM | 30.50 | 0.93 | 0.0304 | 2.26 | 0.0741 |
| 1984 | IBM | 30.78 | 1.02 | 0.0333 | 2.69 | 0.0875 |
| 1985 | IBM | 38.88 | 1.10 | 0.0283 | 2.67 | 0.0686 |
| 1986 | IBM | 30.00 | 1.10 | 0.0367 | 1.95 | 0.0651 |
| 1987 | IBM | 28.88 | 1.10 | 0.0381 | 2.18 | 0.0755 |
| 1988 | IBM | 30.47 | 1.10 | 0.0361 | 2.32 | 0.0761 |
| 1989 | IBM | 23.53 | 1.18 | 0.0503 | 1.62 | 0.0687 |
| 1990 | IBM | 28.25 | 1.21 | 0.0428 | 2.63 | 0.0930 |
| 1991 | IBM | 22.25 | 1.21 | 0.0544 | −0.26 | −0.0118 |
| 1992 | IBM | 12.59 | 1.21 | 0.0961 | −3.01 | −0.2388 |
| 1993 | IBM | 14.13 | 0.39 | 0.0280 | −3.50 | −0.2481 |
| 1994 | IBM | 18.38 | 0.25 | 0.0136 | 1.25 | 0.0683 |
| 1995 | IBM | 22.84 | 0.25 | 0.0109 | 1.81 | 0.0791 |
| 1996 | IBM | 37.88 | 0.32 | 0.0086 | 2.56 | 0.0676 |
| 1997 | IBM | 52.31 | 0.39 | 0.0074 | 3.09 | 0.0591 |
| 1998 | IBM | 92.19 | 0.43 | 0.0047 | 3.38 | 0.0366 |
| 1999 | IBM | 107.88 | 0.47 | 0.0044 | 4.25 | 0.0394 |
| 2000 | IBM | 85.00 | 0.51 | 0.0060 | 4.58 | 0.0539 |
| 2001 | IBM | 120.96 | 0.55 | 0.0045 | 4.69 | 0.0388 |
| 2002 | IBM | 77.50 | 0.59 | 0.0076 | 3.13 | 0.0404 |
| 2003 | IBM | 92.68 | 0.63 | 0.0068 | 4.42 | 0.0477 |
| 2004 | IBM | 98.58 | 0.70 | 0.0071 | 4.48 | 0.0454 |
| 2005 | IBM | 82.20 | 0.78 | 0.0095 | 4.99 | 0.0607 |
| 2006 | IBM | 97.15 | 1.10 | 0.0113 | 6.15 | 0.0633 |
| 2007 | IBM | 105.12 | 1.51 | 0.0144 | 7.32 | 0.0696 |
| 2008 | IBM | 84.16 | 1.90 | 0.0226 | 9.07 | 0.1078 |
| 2009 | IBM | 130.90 | 2.15 | 0.0164 | 10.12 | 0.0773 |
| 2010 | IBM | 146.76 | 2.50 | 0.0170 | 11.69 | 0.0797 |
| 2011 | IBM | 183.88 | 2.90 | 0.0158 | 13.25 | 0.0721 |
| 2012 | IBM | 191.55 | 3.30 | 0.0172 | 14.53 | 0.0759 |
| 2013 | IBM | 187.57 | 3.70 | 0.0197 | 15.42 | 0.0822 |
| 2014 | IBM | 160.44 | 4.25 | 0.0265 | 15.68 | 0.0977 |
| 2015 | IBM | 137.62 | 5.00 | 0.0363 | 13.66 | 0.0993 |
| 2016 | IBM | 165.99 | 5.50 | 0.0331 | 12.44 | 0.0749 |
| 2017 | IBM | 153.42 | 5.90 | 0.0385 | 6.17 | 0.0402 |
| 2018 | IBM | 113.67 | 6.21 | 0.0546 | 9.56 | 0.0841 |

(*Continued*)

(*Continued*)

| Year | Company | PPS | DPS | Dividend Yields (DY) | EPS | Earnings Yield (EY) |
|---|---|---|---|---|---|---|
| 2019 | IBM | 134.04 | 6.43 | 0.0480 | 10.63 | 0.0793 |
| 1980 | JNJ | 2.08 | 0.05 | 0.0223 | 0.14 | 0.0652 |
| 1981 | JNJ | 2.32 | 0.05 | 0.0229 | 0.16 | 0.0676 |
| 1982 | JNJ | 3.10 | 0.06 | 0.0195 | 0.17 | 0.0562 |
| 1983 | JNJ | 2.55 | 0.07 | 0.0263 | 0.16 | 0.0629 |
| 1984 | JNJ | 2.26 | 0.07 | 0.0325 | 0.17 | 0.0761 |
| 1985 | JNJ | 3.29 | 0.08 | 0.0242 | 0.21 | 0.0638 |
| 1986 | JNJ | 4.10 | 0.09 | 0.0210 | 0.12 | 0.0282 |
| 1987 | JNJ | 4.68 | 0.10 | 0.0215 | 0.30 | 0.0645 |
| 1988 | JNJ | 5.32 | 0.12 | 0.0225 | 0.36 | 0.0672 |
| 1989 | JNJ | 7.42 | 0.14 | 0.0188 | 0.41 | 0.0547 |
| 1990 | JNJ | 8.97 | 0.16 | 0.0183 | 0.43 | 0.0478 |
| 1991 | JNJ | 14.31 | 0.19 | 0.0134 | 0.55 | 0.0383 |
| 1992 | JNJ | 12.63 | 0.22 | 0.0176 | 0.61 | 0.0487 |
| 1993 | JNJ | 11.22 | 0.25 | 0.0225 | 0.68 | 0.0611 |
| 1994 | JNJ | 13.69 | 0.28 | 0.0206 | 0.78 | 0.0570 |
| 1995 | JNJ | 21.38 | 0.32 | 0.0150 | 0.93 | 0.0435 |
| 1996 | JNJ | 24.88 | 0.37 | 0.0148 | 1.08 | 0.0436 |
| 1997 | JNJ | 32.94 | 0.42 | 0.0129 | 1.23 | 0.0375 |
| 1998 | JNJ | 41.94 | 0.48 | 0.0116 | 1.13 | 0.0271 |
| 1999 | JNJ | 46.63 | 0.54 | 0.0117 | 1.50 | 0.0322 |
| 2000 | JNJ | 52.53 | 0.62 | 0.0118 | 1.65 | 0.0314 |
| 2001 | JNJ | 59.10 | 0.70 | 0.0118 | 1.87 | 0.0316 |
| 2002 | JNJ | 53.71 | 0.79 | 0.0148 | 2.20 | 0.0410 |
| 2003 | JNJ | 51.66 | 0.92 | 0.0179 | 2.42 | 0.0468 |
| 2004 | JNJ | 63.42 | 1.09 | 0.0173 | 2.87 | 0.0453 |
| 2005 | JNJ | 60.10 | 1.27 | 0.0212 | 3.38 | 0.0562 |
| 2006 | JNJ | 66.02 | 1.45 | 0.0220 | 3.76 | 0.0570 |
| 2007 | JNJ | 67.38 | 1.64 | 0.0255 | 3.67 | 0.0571 |
| 2008 | JNJ | 58.56 | 1.795 | 0.0307 | 4.62 | 0.0789 |
| 2009 | JNJ | 64.41 | 1.93 | 0.0300 | 4.45 | 0.0691 |
| 2010 | JNJ | 61.85 | 2.11 | 0.0341 | 4.85 | 0.0784 |
| 2011 | JNJ | 65.58 | 2.25 | 0.0343 | 3.54 | 0.0540 |
| 2012 | JNJ | 69.48 | 2.4 | 0.0345 | 3.94 | 0.0567 |
| 2013 | JNJ | 92.35 | 2.59 | 0.0280 | 4.92 | 0.0533 |
| 2014 | JNJ | 105.06 | 2.76 | 0.0263 | 5.80 | 0.0552 |
| 2015 | JNJ | 102.72 | 2.95 | 0.0287 | 5.56 | 0.0541 |
| 2016 | JNJ | 115.21 | 3.15 | 0.0273 | 6.04 | 0.0524 |
| 2017 | JNJ | 139.72 | 3.32 | 0.0238 | 0.48 | 0.0034 |

(*Continued*)

(*Continued*)

| Year | Company | PPS | DPS | Dividend Yields (DY) | EPS | Earnings Yield (EY) |
|---|---|---|---|---|---|---|
| 2018 | JNJ | 127.27 | 3.54 | 0.0278 | 5.70 | 0.0448 |
| 2019 | JNJ | 145.75 | 3.75 | 0.0257 | 5.72 | 0.0392 |
| 1980 | MRK | 2.35 | 0.07 | 0.0281 | 0.15 | 0.0654 |
| 1981 | MRK | 2.35 | 0.07 | 0.0313 | 0.15 | 0.0632 |
| 1982 | MRK | 2.35 | 0.08 | 0.0330 | 0.16 | 0.0663 |
| 1983 | MRK | 2.51 | 0.08 | 0.0315 | 0.17 | 0.0675 |
| 1984 | MRK | 2.61 | 0.08 | 0.0324 | 0.19 | 0.0714 |
| 1985 | MRK | 3.81 | 0.09 | 0.0241 | 0.21 | 0.0553 |
| 1986 | MRK | 6.88 | 0.11 | 0.0162 | 0.27 | 0.0391 |
| 1987 | MRK | 8.81 | 0.15 | 0.0170 | 0.37 | 0.0421 |
| 1988 | MRK | 9.62 | 0.23 | 0.0239 | 0.51 | 0.0528 |
| 1989 | MRK | 12.92 | 0.29 | 0.0222 | 0.63 | 0.0488 |
| 1990 | MRK | 14.98 | 0.34 | 0.0225 | 0.76 | 0.0507 |
| 1991 | MRK | 27.75 | 0.40 | 0.0143 | 0.91 | 0.0330 |
| 1992 | MRK | 21.69 | 0.48 | 0.0221 | 1.06 | 0.0489 |
| 1993 | MRK | 17.19 | 0.53 | 0.0308 | 0.93 | 0.0544 |
| 1994 | MRK | 19.06 | 0.58 | 0.0304 | 1.19 | 0.0624 |
| 1995 | MRK | 32.81 | 0.64 | 0.0195 | 1.35 | 0.0411 |
| 1996 | MRK | 39.81 | 0.74 | 0.0186 | 1.60 | 0.0402 |
| 1997 | MRK | 53.00 | 0.87 | 0.0164 | 1.91 | 0.0361 |
| 1998 | MRK | 73.75 | 0.99 | 0.0134 | 2.20 | 0.0299 |
| 1999 | MRK | 67.19 | 1.12 | 0.0167 | 2.51 | 0.0374 |
| 2000 | MRK | 93.63 | 1.26 | 0.0135 | 2.96 | 0.0316 |
| 2001 | MRK | 58.80 | 1.38 | 0.0235 | 3.18 | 0.0541 |
| 2002 | MRK | 56.61 | 1.42 | 0.0251 | 3.01 | 0.0532 |
| 2003 | MRK | 46.20 | 1.46 | 0.0316 | 2.95 | 0.0639 |
| 2004 | MRK | 32.14 | 1.50 | 0.0467 | 2.62 | 0.0815 |
| 2005 | MRK | 31.81 | 1.52 | 0.0478 | 2.11 | 0.0663 |
| 2006 | MRK | 43.60 | 1.52 | 0.0349 | 2.04 | 0.0468 |
| 2007 | MRK | 54.69 | 1.52 | 0.0278 | 1.51 | 0.0276 |
| 2008 | MRK | 30.40 | 1.52 | 0.0500 | 3.65 | 0.1201 |
| 2009 | MRK | 36.54 | 1.52 | 0.0416 | 5.67 | 0.1552 |
| 2010 | MRK | 36.04 | 1.52 | 0.0422 | 0.28 | 0.0078 |
| 2011 | MRK | 37.70 | 1.56 | 0.0414 | 2.04 | 0.0541 |
| 2012 | MRK | 40.94 | 1.69 | 0.0413 | 2.03 | 0.0496 |
| 2013 | MRK | 50.05 | 1.73 | 0.0346 | 1.49 | 0.0298 |
| 2014 | MRK | 56.79 | 1.77 | 0.0312 | 4.12 | 0.0725 |
| 2015 | MRK | 52.82 | 1.81 | 0.0343 | 1.58 | 0.0299 |
| 2016 | MRK | 58.87 | 1.85 | 0.0314 | 1.42 | 0.0241 |

(*Continued*)

(*Continued*)

| Year | Company | PPS | DPS | Dividend Yields (DY) | EPS | Earnings Yield (EY) |
|---|---|---|---|---|---|---|
| 2017 | MRK | 56.27 | 1.89 | 0.0336 | 0.88 | 0.0156 |
| 2018 | MRK | 76.41 | 1.99 | 0.0260 | 2.34 | 0.0306 |
| 2019 | MRK | 90.95 | 2.26 | 0.0248 | 3.84 | 0.0422 |
| 1980 | PG | 2.15 | 0.11 | 0.0523 | 0.25 | 0.1163 |
| 1981 | PG | 2.51 | 0.12 | 0.0485 | 0.28 | 0.1100 |
| 1982 | PG | 3.70 | 0.13 | 0.0355 | 0.31 | 0.0847 |
| 1983 | PG | 3.55 | 0.15 | 0.0422 | 0.33 | 0.0937 |
| 1984 | PG | 3.56 | 0.16 | 0.0438 | 0.29 | 0.0802 |
| 1985 | PG | 4.36 | 0.16 | 0.0373 | 0.26 | 0.0592 |
| 1986 | PG | 4.77 | 0.17 | 0.0350 | 0.28 | 0.0581 |
| 1987 | PG | 5.34 | 0.17 | 0.0316 | 0.17 | 0.0323 |
| 1988 | PG | 5.44 | 0.17 | 0.0321 | 0.41 | 0.0762 |
| 1989 | PG | 8.78 | 0.21 | 0.0235 | 0.50 | 0.0568 |
| 1990 | PG | 10.83 | 0.23 | 0.0213 | 0.61 | 0.0560 |
| 1991 | PG | 11.73 | 0.25 | 0.0213 | 0.62 | 0.0530 |
| 1992 | PG | 13.41 | 0.27 | 0.0200 | 0.63 | 0.0467 |
| 1993 | PG | 14.25 | 0.29 | 0.0205 | 0.18 | 0.0130 |
| 1994 | PG | 15.50 | 0.33 | 0.0213 | 0.85 | 0.0548 |
| 1995 | PG | 20.75 | 0.37 | 0.0181 | 0.99 | 0.0480 |
| 1996 | PG | 26.91 | 0.42 | 0.0158 | 1.14 | 0.0426 |
| 1997 | PG | 39.91 | 0.48 | 0.0120 | 1.31 | 0.0328 |
| 1998 | PG | 45.66 | 0.54 | 0.0118 | 1.44 | 0.0316 |
| 1999 | PG | 54.78 | 0.60 | 0.0110 | 1.36 | 0.0249 |
| 2000 | PG | 39.22 | 0.67 | 0.0171 | 1.34 | 0.0342 |
| 2001 | PG | 39.56 | 0.73 | 0.0185 | 1.10 | 0.0278 |
| 2002 | PG | 42.97 | 0.79 | 0.0184 | 1.84 | 0.0429 |
| 2003 | PG | 49.94 | 0.86 | 0.0173 | 2.19 | 0.0439 |
| 2004 | PG | 55.08 | 0.98 | 0.0177 | 2.62 | 0.0476 |
| 2005 | PG | 57.88 | 1.09 | 0.0188 | 2.75 | 0.0475 |
| 2006 | PG | 64.27 | 1.21 | 0.0188 | 2.98 | 0.0464 |
| 2007 | PG | 70.62 | 1.34 | 0.0190 | 3.22 | 0.0456 |
| 2008 | PG | 61.82 | 1.45 | 0.0235 | 3.86 | 0.0624 |
| 2009 | PG | 60.63 | 1.64 | 0.0270 | 4.49 | 0.0741 |
| 2010 | PG | 64.33 | 1.80 | 0.0280 | 4.32 | 0.0672 |
| 2011 | PG | 66.71 | 1.97 | 0.0295 | 4.12 | 0.0618 |
| 2012 | PG | 67.89 | 2.14 | 0.0315 | 3.82 | 0.0563 |

(*Continued*)

*(Continued)*

| Year | Company | PPS | DPS | Dividend Yields (DY) | EPS | Earnings Yield (EY) |
|---|---|---|---|---|---|---|
| 2013 | PG | 81.41 | 2.29 | 0.0281 | 4.04 | 0.0496 |
| 2014 | PG | 91.09 | 2.45 | 0.0269 | 4.19 | 0.0460 |
| 2015 | PG | 79.41 | 2.59 | 0.0326 | 2.50 | 0.0315 |
| 2016 | PG | 84.08 | 2.66 | 0.0316 | 3.80 | 0.0452 |
| 2017 | PG | 91.88 | 2.70 | 0.0294 | 5.80 | 0.0631 |
| 2018 | PG | 91.92 | 2.79 | 0.0304 | 3.75 | 0.0408 |
| 2019 | PG | 124.90 | 2.90 | 0.0232 | 1.45 | 0.0116 |

A. Please calculate mean, standard deviation, skewness, and coefficient variation for related PPS, DPS, EPS, DY, and EY.

B. Based upon the dividend earning relationships and the dividend yield earning relationships for IBM, JNJ, MRK, and PG presented in the following, compare the results among these four companies.

Solutions for B.

(1) Dividends-Earnings relationship: $DPS_t = a + bEPS_t + e_t$

a. IBM

| Regression Statistics | |
|---|---|
| Multiple $R$ | 0.0400 |
| $R$ Square | 0.0016 |
| Adjusted $R$ Square | −0.0368 |
| Standard Error | 0.3571 |
| Observations | 28.0000 |

| | Coefficients | Standard Error | $t$ Stat | $P$-value |
|---|---|---|---|---|
| Intercept | 0.7922 | 0.1024 | 7.7366 | 0.0000 |
| EPS | 0.0061 | 0.0298 | 0.2040 | 0.8399 |

b. JNJ

| **Regression Statistics** | |
|---|---|
| Multiple $R$ | 0.9944 |
| $R$ Square | 0.9888 |
| Adjusted $R$ Square | 0.9884 |
| Standard Error | 0.0492 |
| Observations | 28.0000 |

| | **Coefficients** | **Standard Error** | ***t* Stat** | ***P*-value** |
|---|---|---|---|---|
| Intercept | −0.0192 | 0.0135 | −1.4222 | 0.1669 |
| EPS | 0.3983 | 0.0083 | 47.9231 | 0.0000 |

c. MRK

| **Regression Statistics** | |
|---|---|
| Multiple $R$ | 0.9248 |
| $R$ Square | 0.8553 |
| Adjusted $R$ Square | 0.8498 |
| Standard Error | 0.2174 |
| Observations | 28.0000 |

| | **Coefficients** | **Standard Error** | ***t* Stat** | ***P*-value** |
|---|---|---|---|---|
| Intercept | 0.0234 | 0.0681 | 0.3432 | 0.7342 |
| EPS | 0.5013 | 0.0404 | 12.3989 | 0.0000 |

d. PG

| **Regression Statistics** | |
|---|---|
| Multiple $R$ | 0.9781 |
| $R$ Square | 0.9567 |
| Adjusted $R$ Square | 0.9550 |
| Standard Error | 0.0768 |
| Observations | 28.0000 |

**ANOVA**

| | *df* | *SS* | *MS* | *F* |
|---|---|---|---|---|
| Regression | 1.0000 | 3.3877 | 3.3877 | 574.1455 |
| Residual | 26.0000 | 0.1534 | 0.0059 | |
| Total | 27.0000 | 3.5411 | | |

| | **Coefficients** | **Standard Error** | ***t* Stat** | ***P*-value** |
|---|---|---|---|---|
| Intercept | 0.0503 | 0.0226 | 2.2278 | 0.0348 |
| EPS | 0.3834 | 0.0160 | 23.9613 | 0.0000 |

(2) Dividend Yields-Earnings Yields Relationship: $DY_t = a + bEY_t + e_t$

a. IBM

| **Regression Statistics** | |
|---|---|
| Multiple $R$ | 0.3584 |
| $R$ Square | 0.1285 |
| Adjusted $R$ Square | 0.0950 |
| Standard Error | 0.0212 |
| Observations | 28.0000 |

| | **Coefficients** | **Standard Error** | ***t* Stat** | ***P*-value** |
|---|---|---|---|---|
| Intercept | 0.0303 | 0.0045 | 6.7572 | 0.0000 |
| EY | −0.0959 | 0.0490 | −1.9578 | 0.0611 |

b. JNJ

| **Regression Statistics** | |
|---|---|
| Multiple $R$ | 0.8670 |
| $R$ Square | 0.7517 |
| Adjusted $R$ Square | 0.7421 |
| Standard Error | 0.0026 |
| Observations | 28.0000 |

| | Coefficients | Standard Error | *t* Stat | *P*-value |
|---|---|---|---|---|
| Intercept | 0.0024 | 0.0019 | 1.2162 | 0.2348 |
| EY | 0.3307 | 0.0373 | 8.8714 | 0.0000 |

c. MRK

| Regression Statistics | |
|---|---|
| Multiple $R$ | 0.8147 |
| $R$ Square | 0.6638 |
| Adjusted $R$ Square | 0.6509 |
| Standard Error | 0.0053 |
| Observations | 28.0000 |

| | Coefficients | Standard Error | *t* Stat | *P*-value |
|---|---|---|---|---|
| Intercept | −0.0010 | 0.0038 | −0.2539 | 0.8015 |
| EY | 0.5187 | 0.0724 | 7.1650 | 0.0000 |

d. PG

| Regression Statistics | |
|---|---|
| Multiple $R$ | 0.8695 |
| $R$ Square | 0.7560 |
| Adjusted $R$ Square | 0.7466 |
| Standard Error | 0.0058 |
| Observations | 28.0000 |

| | Coefficients | Standard Error | *t* Stat | *P*-value |
|---|---|---|---|---|
| Intercept | 0.0033 | 0.0027 | 1.2528 | 0.2214 |
| EY | 0.4033 | 0.0449 | 8.9746 | 0.0000 |

Chapter 13

# Interaction of Financing, Investment, and Dividend Policies

## Contents



## 13.1 Introduction

The purpose of this chapter is to discuss the three-way interaction between investment, financing, and dividend decisions. As was shown in previous chapters, a set of ideal conditions exists under which there will be no interaction effects between the areas of concern. However, the ideal conditions imposed by academicians to analyze the effects dividend and financing policy have on the investment decision and the value of the firm are not realistic, when one considers financial management in the real world. Thus, an overview of the interactions of financing, investment, and dividend decisions is important for those concerned with financial analysis and planning.

This chapter sequentially addresses the three interaction effects. In Section 13.2 the relation between investment and dividend policy is explored through a discussion of internal-versus-external financing, with the emphasis on the use of retained earnings as a substitute for new equity, or vice versa. The interaction between corporate financing and dividend policies will be covered in Section 13.3, where default risk on debt is recognized. Then in Section 13.4, the interaction between investment and financing policy is discussed; the role of the financing mix in analyzing investment opportunities will receive detailed treatment. Again, the recognition of risky debt will be allowed, so as to lend further practicality to the analysis. The recognition of financing and investment effects are covered in Section 13.5, where capital-budgeting techniques are reviewed and analyzed with regard to their treatment of the financing mix. In this section several numerical comparisons are offered, to emphasize that the differences in the techniques are nontrivial. Section 13.6 will incorporate a number of current issues by exploring the topic of optimal capital structure, which may be the single most important issue in financial planning. Section 13.7 will discuss the implication of different policies on systematic risk determination. A summary and concluding remarks are offered in Section 13.8.

## 13.2 Investment and Dividend Interactions

Internal financing consists primarily of retained earnings and depreciation expense, while external financing is comprised of new equity and new debt, both long- and short-term. Decisions on the appropriate mix of these two sources for a firm are likely to affect both the payout ratio and the capital structure of the firm, and this in turn will generally affect its market value. In this section, an overview of internal and external financing is provided, with the discussion culminating in a summary of the impacts that earnings retention or earnings payout (with or without supplemental financing from external sources) can have on a firm's value and on planning and forecasting.

These concerns will be outlined in further detail in later chapters, and will also play an important role in total financial management.

### 13.2.1 *Internal financing*

Changes in equity accounts between balance-sheet dates are generally reported in the statement of equity. Retained earnings are most often the major internal source of funds made available for investment by a firm. The cost of these retained earnings is generally less than the cost associated with raising capital through new common-stock issues. It follows that retained earnings, rather than new equity, should be used to finance further investment if equity is to be used and the dividend policy (dividends paid from retained earnings) does not seem to matter. The availability of retained earnings is then determined by the firm's profitability and the payout ratio, the latter being indicative of dividend policy. Thus, we find that the decision to raise funds externally may be dependent on dividend policy, which in turn may affect investment decisions.

Table 13.1 presents the composite payout ratio for S&P 500 firms. The payout ratios indicated in Table 13.1 show that, on average,

Table 13.1 Composite Payout Ratio for S&P 500 Firms (1960–2018).

| Year | Payout Ratio (%) | Year | Payout Ratio (%) | Year | Payout Ratio (%) | Year | Payout Ratio (%) |
|---|---|---|---|---|---|---|---|
| 1960 | 63.86 | 1975 | 48.42 | 1990 | 53.38 | 2005 | 29.23 |
| 1961 | 60.51 | 1976 | 43.33 | 1991 | 63.21 | 2006 | 28.55 |
| 1962 | 58.52 | 1977 | 44.71 | 1992 | 59.37 | 2007 | 34.09 |
| 1963 | 56.81 | 1978 | 44.51 | 1993 | 46.77 | 2008 | 57.46 |
| 1964 | 54.27 | 1979 | 41.02 | 1994 | 41.48 | 2009 | 38.64 |
| 1965 | 53.40 | 1980 | 42.93 | 1995 | 36.58 | 2010 | 27.04 |
| 1966 | 53.26 | 1981 | 44.96 | 1996 | 36.67 | 2011 | 27.51 |
| 1967 | 54.59 | 1982 | 50.15 | 1997 | 35.16 | 2012 | 32.28 |
| 1968 | 53.18 | 1983 | 53.60 | 1998 | 36.59 | 2013 | 33.26 |
| 1969 | 53.09 | 1984 | 46.47 | 1999 | 32.29 | 2014 | 34.04 |
| 1970 | 57.86 | 1985 | 52.29 | 2000 | 28.63 | 2015 | 43.20 |
| 1971 | 56.78 | 1986 | 56.71 | 2001 | 40.51 | 2016 | 43.01 |
| 1972 | 51.63 | 1987 | 57.16 | 2002 | 34.67 | 2017 | 39.30 |
| 1973 | 45.34 | 1988 | 40.42 | 2003 | 32.69 | 2018 | 36.14 |
| 1974 | 39.81 | 1989 | 45.48 | 2004 | 28.09 | | |

firms in the S&P 500 retain more than 50% of their earnings after 1973 rather than pay them out in dividends. This is done because of the investment opportunities available for a firm and indicates that retained earnings are a major source of funds for a firm.

### 13.2.2 *External financing*

External financing usually takes one of two forms, debt financing or equity financing. We leave the debt-versus-equity question to subsequent sections, and here, directly confront only the decision whether to utilize retained earnings or new common stock to finance the firm.

We have previously shown that the market value of the firm is unaffected by such factors if dividend policy and capital structure are irrelevant. It should also be clear that dividend policy and capital structure can affect market values. Therefore, the consideration of an optimal internal-external financing combination is important in the field of financial management. This optimal combination is a function of the payout ratio, the debt-to-equity ratio, and the interaction between these two decision variables. From this it can be shown (and this will be the topic of discussion in the following paragraphs) that different combinations of internal and external financing will have different effects on the growth rate of earnings per share, of dividends per share, and, presumably, of the share price itself.

Higgins (1977) considered the amount of growth a firm could maintain if it was subject to an external equity constraint and sought to maintain certain debt and payout ratios. He was able to show the sustainable growth rate in sales, $S^*$, to be:

$$S^* = \frac{p(1-d)(1+L)}{t - p(1-d)(1+L)} = \frac{(rr)(\text{ROE})}{1-(rr)(\text{ROE})} \tag{13.1}$$

where $p$ = Profit margin on sales; $d$ = Dividend payout ratio; $L$ = Debt-to-equity ratio; $t$ = Total asset-to-sales ratio; $rr$ = Retention Rate; ROE = Return on Equity.

The derivation of Eq. (13.1) can be found in Chapter 18 of Lee and Lee (2017).

Higgins (1977) used the 1974 U.S. manufacturing firms' composite financial statement data as an example to calculate $S^*$. Using the figures $p = 5.5\%$, $d = 33\%$, $L = 88\%$ and $t = 73\%$, he obtained:

$$S^* = \frac{(0.055)\,(1-0.33)\,(1+0.88)}{0.73-(0.055)\,(1-0.33)\,(1+0.88)} = 10.5\%$$

Using this method, we can calculate sustainable growth rate in sales for financial analysts and planning models. In Appendix 2B of Chapter 2, we have calculated the sustainable growth rate for JNJ in terms of 2019 data.

From this we can see that a firm with many valuable investment opportunities may be forced to forego some of these opportunities due to capital constraints, and the value of the firm will not be maximized as it could have been. Dividend and capital-structure decisions relate directly to investment decisions. While it may not be reasonable to assume that the firm could not issue new equity, the question is at what cost it can be raised under such a constraint.

In an even more practical vein, Higgins also incorporated inflation into his model, acknowledging the fact that most depreciation methods that serve to make the depreciation account a source of funds are founded on historical costs and not the replacement values the firm must pay to sustain operations at their current level. Introducing the new variables defined below, it is possible to define sustainable growth in real and nominal terms, the former being the item of interest here.

Let

$c$ = Nominal current assets to nominal sales;
$f$ = Nominal fixed assets to real sales;
$j$ = Inflation rate.

So real sustainable growth is

$$S_r^* = \frac{(1+j)p(1-d)(1+L)-jc}{(1+j)c+f-(1+j)p(1-d)(1+L)} \tag{13.2}$$

Using figures from the manufacturing sector and an inflation rate of 10% which at the time of writing was approximately the actual inflation rate then prevailing, it was found that real sustainable growth was only a third of that of the nominal figure; this serves to further emphasize the importance of the interaction between dividend policy and investment decisions, since the former acts as a constraint on the latter. Higgins' (1977) paper has been generalized by Johnson (1981) and Higgins (1981).

The usual caveat associated with the dividend-irrelevance proposition is that investment policy is unaffected; i.e., new equity is issued to replace those retained earnings that are paid out. Here we emphasize new equity with the intent of avoiding financing-policy questions. Knowing that the flotation costs involved with new issues could be avoided by employing retained earnings, the effect such a strategy has on firm value is largely an empirical question. Any such tests directed toward this issue must also recognize that there may be a preference for dividends that may dominate or mitigate the flotation-cost effects. With these factors in mind, Van Horne and McDonald (1971) ran cross-sectional regressions on samples of utility stocks and electronics manufacturers to see whether dividend payouts and the rates of new issues of common stocks had significant effects on price-earnings ratios. The utility industry results indicate that, at the lower end of the new-equity issue spectrum, the dividend-preference effect overshadowed the flotation-cost effect, a result that appeared to shift in direction when higher levels of new equity financing were considered. Further analysis into the dividend-preference question has been performed by Litzenberger and Ramaswamy (1979). Using a generalized capital-asset-pricing model, they examined this trade-off between dividend preference and tax effects, all in an effort to justify the contention of an optimal dividend policy. The results presented by Van Horne and McDonald were admittedly tentative (especially since the electronics industry sample yielded few corroborating results), and most of the $t$-statistics associated with the utility sample new-issue coefficients were quite low. The strongest statement that could be made following this analysis is that there appears to be little detrimental effect on firm valuation from following a strategy of maintaining a high payout rate and financing further investment with new-equity issues.

## 13.3 Interactions between Dividend and Financing Policies

If we were able to hold the capital structure of firms constant, then we would be able to determine the advantage or disadvantage of internal financing relative to external financing. Van Horne and McDonald, as briefly mentioned before, were able to empirically test for the effects created by either policy, providing the substance for a major part of the following discussion. If we were to go into more depth and specifically consider firms that issue risky debt while maintaining shareholder's limited-liability status, and still keeping to the chosen internal or external equity plan, then the interactions between financing and investment decisions can affect the relative positions of stock and bondholders. Black (1976) argued that a possible strategy a firm could follow to transfer economic resources from bondholders to stockholders is to pay as generous dividends as possible. In this way the internal–external financing plan is predetermined, since paying large dividends jeopardizes the bondholders' position as assets are siphoned away from the firm, all to the gain of the shareholders.

In this section, the interactions between dividend and financing policy will be analyzed in terms of (1) cost of equity capital, and (2) the default-risk viewpoint of debt.

### 13.3.1 *Cost of equity capital and dividend policy*

Van Horne and McDonald (1971) chose to develop a cross-sectional model to test for the significance of dividend payouts in the valuation process in the electric utility industry. The use of the electric utility industry proved to be operationally less difficult than other industries because it was desired to hold interfirm differences constant, and independent variable selection to this end was relatively straightforward. Since the authors were interested in capitalization rates, year-end P/E ratios were selected to be the dependent variables. This value was thought to be a function of three variables — growth in assets, dividend payout, and financial risk. The latter variable is considered sufficient for this sample due to the homogeneity of the other aspects of the included firm's risks. The model can be written out and more carefully defined by the following;

$$P/E = a_0 + a_1 g + a_2 p + a_3 R + u \tag{13.3}$$

where $g$ = Compound growth of assets over eight previous years; $p$ = Dividend payout ratio on an annual basis; Lev = Interest charges/[operating revenues – operating expenses]; $u$ = Error term.

While the growth and risk factors do not correspond exactly to what most capital-market theory tells us is relevant, research with respect to this particular industry lends credence to these variables as defined here (see Malkiel (1970)).

Upon regressing the data for the 86 companies included in the sample, all three independent variables are found to be statistically significant. Of the 86 firms, all of which paid dividends, 37 firms also had new equity issues. Testing to see whether the 37 firms that issued new equity came from the same population as those that did not raise new equity, the researchers found no essential difference. Since we know there are nontrivial flotation costs associated with the issuance of new equity, the finding of no difference between the sub-samples implies one of two things: either the costs associated with new issues are relatively too small compared to the total costs of the firm to be detected (despite their large absolute size, or size relative to the new issue by itself), or a net preference for dividends by holders of electric utility stocks exists which acts to offset the aforementioned expenses.

The main thrust of this paper was to assess the impact of new equity flotation costs on firm value. With the number of firms issuing new equity, Van Horne and McDonald were able to calculate new-issue ratios — that is, new issues/total shares outstanding at year-end — and separate these firms into four groups, leaving those firms issuing new equity in a separate classification, as indicated in the upper portion of Table 13.2. Adding dummy variables to Eq. (13.4), the effect of new issue rates could be analyzed:

$$P/E = a_0 + a_1(g) + a_2 p + a_3(Lev) + a_4(F_1) + a_5(F_2) + a_6(F_3) + a_7(F_4) \tag{13.4}$$

where $g$ = Compound growth rate; Lev = Financial risk measured by times interest; earned; and $F_1, F_2, F_3, F_4$ = Dummy variables representing levels of new equity financing.

We would expect negative coefficients on the dummy variables if the flotation costs were to be relevant, but in fact all coefficients were positive, though only one was significant (possibly due to small sample size and small relative differences). Empirical results are indicated in the lower portion of Table 13.2. However, by replacing the dummy variable of Group E for any one of the four dummy variables

Table 13.2 New-Issue Ratios of Electric Utility Firms.

| | ***F* Dummy Variable Grouping** | | | | |
|---|---|---|---|---|---|
| | A | B | C | D | E |
| New-issue ratio interval | 0 | 0.001–0.05 | 0.05–0.1 | 0.1–0.15 | 0.15 and up |
| Number of firms in interval | 49 | 16 | 11 | 6 | 4 |
| Mean dividend payout ratio | 0.681 | 0.679 | 0.678 | 0.703 | 0.728 |
| Dummy variable coefficient | 1.86 | 3.23 | 1.26 | 0.89 | N.A. |
| Dummy variable $t$-statistic | (1.33) | (2.25) | (0.84) | (0.51) | N.A. |

*Source*: Lee and Lee (2017). *Financial Analysis, Planning and Forecasting*, page 891.

discussed above, Van Horne and McDonald found that the estimate of its coefficient is negative.

One question pertaining to the figures presented here stems from the interpretation of the significance of the dummy variables. As it turns out, the class B dummy-variable coefficient is greater than the class A coefficient, supposedly because of a preference for dividend payout, while actually that payout was lower in class B. The question is whether the dummy that is intended to substantiate the dividend-preference claim through the new-issue ratio actually tells us that investors instead attach a higher value to higher earnings retention. The finding of higher P/E ratios resulting from earnings retention would be consistent with the Litzenberger–Ramaswamy framework cited earlier, and the new-issue effect is somewhat confounded with the dividend effect.

From the data we can see that the coefficients did decrease as the new-issue ratios increased, though they were not significant, and, not surprisingly, new-issue ratios were rather highly negatively correlated with dividend payout ratios. From this we can say, although with some hesitation, that external equity appears to be a more costly alternative compared to internal financing when pushed to rather extreme limits. Over more moderate ranges, or those more closely aligned with the industry averages, this claim cannot be made with the same degree of certainty, since we cannot be certain that the payout ratio does not have a positive influence on share price, and therefore an inverse relationship to the cost of equity capital.

### 13.3.2 *Default risk and dividend policy*

With the development of the Option Pricing Model, Black and Scholes (1973) have made available a new method of valuing corporate liabilities or claims on the firm. Chen (1978) has reviewed some developments in the theory of risky debt and also examined in a more systematic fashion the determinants of the cost of debt capital. Both Resek (1970) and Hellwig (1981) have shown that the Miller and Modigliani (1958 and 1963) arbitrage process that renders capital structure irrelevant is generally invalidated if the debt under consideration is risky and the shareholders enjoy limited liability. From this and the 1963 M&M article, we can show that there exists optimal structures for firms under the more realistic conditions mentioned above.

In the option-pricing framework the two claimants of the firm, the debt holders and the equity holders, are easily seen to have conflicting interests; thus, one group's claim can only be put forth at the expense of the other party. The assumption that the total firm value is unchanged is utilized to highlight the wealth-transfer effects, but, as we see in the following section, that need not be the case. It is now necessary to find a way to value corporate debt when default risk is introduced. If the total value of the firm is known or given (this value should be reasonably well known or approximated prior to debt valuation since the former is an upper bound on the latter), then once the debt value is established the total equity value falls out as the residual. It is also required that we know how to perform the transfer of wealth (since the stated goal of corporate finance is to maximize the shareholders' wealth), and learn of any possible consequences that could result from such attempts.

Merton (1974) sought to find the value of risky corporate debt, assuming that the term structure of riskless interest rates was flat and known with certainty. This was an indirect goal, since the true emphasis lay in finding a way to value the equity of the firm as a continuous option. The further assumption of consol-type debt was also employed, in an attempt to avoid the transactions-cost arguments involved with rolling over debt at maturity. Invoking Modigliani and Miller's Proposition I (M&M, 1958) and allowing for risky debt, we find the value of the stock to be the difference between the value of the firm as a whole and the value of the total debt financing employed to support that whole. Explicitly,

$$S = V - \frac{C}{r}(1 - L) \tag{13.5}$$

where $S$ = Total value of the firm's stock, $V$ = Total firm value, $C$ = Constant coupon payment on the perpetual bonds, $r$ = Riskless rate of interest, $L$ = A complicated risk factor associated with possible default on the required coupon payment.

The last term of Eq. (13.5) is more often represented by B, the value of the total debt claims outstanding against the firm, stated in a certainty-equivalent form. It should be apparent from this equation that by introducing a greater probability of default on the debt while maintaining firm value, the equity holders gain at the expense of the bondholders.

Rendleman (1978) took Merton's model and adapted it to allow for the tax deductibility of interest charges. As in the Merton article, debt is assumed to be of perpetual type, consols — a justifiable assumption since most firms roll over their debt obligations at maturity. The tax benefit introduced is assumed to be always available to the firm. In instances where the interest expense is greater than earnings before taxes, the carryback provision of the tax code is used to obtain a refund for the amount of the previously unused tax shield and, in the event the three-year carryback provision is not sufficient to make use of the tax shield, Rendleman suggests that a firm could sell that advantage to another firm by means of a merger or an acquisition, when the other firm involved could use the tax benefit. Thus the coupon (net) to be paid each time period is given by $C(1 - T)$.

At first glance it is apparent that the equity holders gain from this revision, as they are alleged to in the 1963 tax-corrected model of M&M. But something else is at work as well: Since the firm is subject to a lower debt-service requirement, it can build a larger asset base, which serves to act as insurance in the case of default probabilities owing to the small net coupon payment. In short, the risk premium associated with debt is reduced and the value of the stock, given in Eq. (13.5) can be rewritten as below:

$$S = V - \frac{C(1-T)}{r}(1 - L^*) \tag{13.6}$$

where all the variables are as defined before and $L^*$ is less than the $L$ given before because of the lessened default risk.

It has been argued above that the bondholders benefit when interest is tax-deductible, excluding the possibility here that an overzealous attempt to lever the firm is quickly undertaken when the tax-deductibility feature is introduced, and Eqs. (13.5) and (13.6) seem to indicate that the value of the shareholders' claim also increases, though we have not yet provided any theoretical justification for such a statement.

Rendleman's analysis gave us the $L$-value, which is the clue to this seeming problem. Management can act in a way to jeopardize the bondholders' claims by issuing more debt and thus making all debt riskier, or by undertaking projects that are riskier than the average project undertaken by the firm. This is the subject of the next section.

Another possibility is to pay large dividends so as to deplete the firm of its resources, thus paying off the shareholders but hurting the bondholders. Black (1976) goes so far as to suggest that the firm could liquidate itself, pay out the total as a dividend, and leave the bondholders holding the proverbial bag. Bond covenants, of course, prevent this sort of action (hence, agency theory), and if a firm could not sell its growth opportunities not yet exploited in the market, this may not maximize the shareholder's wealth, either, but within bounds it does seem a reasonable possibility.

In their review article, Barnea, Haugen, and Senbet (BHS, 1981) discuss the issues related to market imperfections, agency problems, and the implications for the consideration of optimal capital structures. The authors make use of M&M's valuation theory and option-pricing theory to reconcile the differences between academicians and practitioners about the relevance of financing and dividend policies. They arrive at the conclusion that, without frictionless capital markets, agency problems can give rise to potential costs. These costs can be minimized through complex contractual arrangements between the conflicting parties. Potential agency costs may help to explain the evolution of certain complexities in capital structure, such as conversion privileges of corporate debt and call provisions. If these agency costs are real, then financial contracts which vary in their ability to reduce these costs may very well sell at different equilibrium prices or yields, even if the financial marketplaces are efficient. An optimal capital structure can be obtained when, for each class of contract, the costs associated with each agency problem are exactly balanced by the yield differentials and tax exposures. Overall, BHS show that optimal capital structures can exist and that this is still consistent with the mainstream of classical finance theory.

## 13.4 Interactions between Financing and Investment Decisions

Myers (1974) has analyzed in detail the interactions of corporate financing and investment decisions and the implications therein for capital budgeting. He argues that the existence of these interaction effects may be attributable to the recognition of transaction costs, corporate taxes, or other market imperfections. Ignored in his analysis is the probability of default on debt obligations, or, as could otherwise be interpreted, changes in this default risk. As alluded to in the previous section, if we consider possible effects of default risk on the firm's investment and financing decisions, then further analysis must be performed to determine how these interactions can affect the wealth positions of shareholders and bondholders. In this section we will analyze this issue by considering both the risk-free debt case and the risky debt case.

### 13.4.1 *Risk-free debt case*

Following Myers (1974), the basic optimization framework is presented in accordance with well-accepted mathematical programming techniques, discussed in the capital-rationing segment of Chapter 6. It is presented as a general formulation; it should be considered one approach to analyzing interactions and not the final word *per se*. Specific results derived by Chambers, Harris, and Pringle (1982), will be used later to demonstrate the importance of considering alternative financing mixes when evaluating investment opportunities.

We identify a firm $Q$, which faces several investment opportunities of varying characteristics. The objective is to identify those projects that are in the stockholders' interest (i.e., they maximize the change in the firm's market value *ex*-dividend at the end of the successive time periods $t = 0, 1, \ldots, T$) and undertake them in order of their relative values. We specify relative values so that project divisibility remains possible, as was assumed by Myers. Required is a financing plan that specifies the desired mix of earnings retained, debt outstanding, and proceeds from the issuance of new equity shares.

Let $dV$ be a general function of four factors in a direct sense: (i) the proportion of each project $j$ accepted, $x_j$; (ii) the stock of debt outstanding in period $t$, $y_t$; (iii) the total cash dividends paid in period $t$, $D_t$; and (iv) the net proceeds from equity issued in period $t$, $E_t$. For future use let $Z$ be denoted as the debt capacity of the firm in period $t$, this being defined as a limit on $y_t$ imposed internally by management or by the capital markets, and $C_t$ is the expected net after-tax cash flow to the firm in time period $t$. The problem can now be written as;

$$\text{Maximize } dV(x_j, y_t, D_t, E_t) = W$$

subject to the constraints;

$$\begin{aligned}
&\text{(a) } U_j = x_j - 1 \le 0 \quad (j = 1, 2, \ldots, J) \\
&\text{(b) } U_t^F U_t^F U_t^F = y_t - Z_t \le 0 \quad (t = 1, 2, \ldots, T) \qquad (13.7) \\
&\text{(c) } U_t^C U_t^C U_t^C = -C_t - [y_t - y_{t-1}(1 + (1 - \tau)r)] + D_t - E_t \le 0
\end{aligned}$$

where $\tau$ and $r$ are the tax rates and borrowing rates, respectively. Both are assumed constant for simplicity, but in actuality both could be defined as functions of other variables. Constraints (a) and (b) specify the percentage of the project undertaken cannot exceed 100%, and the debt outstanding cannot exceed the debt capacity limit. Constraint (c) is the accounting identity, indicating that outflows of funds equal inflows, and could be interpreted as the restriction that the firm maintain no excess funds.

Constraint (b) can be used to investigate the interaction between the firm's financing and investment decisions by examining the necessary conditions for optimization. If we assign the symbols $L_j$, $L_{ft}$, and $L_{ct}$ to be the shadow prices on constraints (a)–(c), respectively, and let $A_j = dW/dx_j$, $F_t = dW/dy_t$, $Z_{jt} = dZ_t/dx_j$, and $C_{jt} = dC_t/dx_j$, we can rewrite Eq. (13.7) in Lagrangian form as the following:

$$\begin{aligned} Max\ W' = W &- L_j(x_j - 1) - L_{ft}(y_t - Z_t) \\ &- L_{ct}\{-C_t - [y_t - y_{t-1}(1 + (1-\tau)r)]\} \\ &+ D_t - E_t) \end{aligned} \tag{13.7'}$$

The necessary first-order conditions for the optimum are shown as Eqs. (13.8) through (13.11), with accompanying explanations. For each project:

$$A_j + \sum_{t=0}^{T}[L_{ft}Z_{jt} + L_{ct}C_{jt}] - L_j \leq 0 \tag{13.8}$$

This can be interpreted as follows: The percentage of a project undertaken should be increased until its incremental cost exceeds the sum of the incremental value of the project, the latter consisting of the added debt capacity and the value of the cash flows generated by that project. The incremental increase in value of the firm obtained by increasing $x_j$ to this maximum point is termed the Adjusted Present Value, APV ("adjusted" because of the consideration of interaction effects).

We can examine each of these effects in turn. For the debt constraint in each period;

$$F_t - L_{ft} + L_{ct} - L_{c,t-1}[1 + (1-\tau)r] \leq 0 \tag{13.9}$$

For the constraint implied on dividends;

$$\frac{dW}{dD_t} - L_{ct} \leq 0 \tag{13.10}$$

and for the new equity constraint:

$$\frac{dW}{dE_t} + L_{ct} \leq 0 \tag{13.11}$$

While Eqs. (13.8) through (13.11) are all of interest, the focus is on Eq. (13.8), which tells us that the NPV rule commonly put forth should be replaced by the APV rule, which accounts for interaction effects.

Specifically considering the financing constraint, Eq. (13.9), we would like to be able to find the value of this constraint, which is most easily done by assuming for the moment that dividend policy is irrelevant. Combined with Eqs. (13.8) and (13.9) and the definition of APV we obtain[2];

$$\text{APV}_j = A_j + \sum_{t=0}^{T} Z_{jt} F_t \tag{13.12}$$

which, in the spirit of the M&M with-tax firm-valuation model, tells us that the value of a project is given by the increase in value that would occur in an unlevered firm, plus the value of the debt the project is capable of supporting. This follows from the ability of the firm to deduct interest expenses for tax purposes. This procedure will be further investigated in the following section when we compare it with other well-accepted capital-budgeting techniques.

When dividend policy is not irrelevant, the standard argument arises as to whether the preference for dividends, given their general tax status, outweighs the transaction costs incurred by the firm when dividends are paid and new financing must be raised. In this framework, dividends are viewed as another cash flow and, as such, the issue centers on whether the cash flows from the project plus any increases in the debt capacity of the firm are adequate to cover the cost of financing, through whatever means.

Though we are unable to discern the effect of dividend policy on the value of the firm, it is not outside the solution technique to incorporate such efforts by including the related expenses as inputs to the numerical-solution procedure.

It is generally assumed that these interaction effects exist, so if we are to consider disregarding them, as some would insist, we must know what conditions are necessary for lack of dependence of financing and investment decisions. As Myers points out, only in a world of perfect markets with no taxes is this the case. Otherwise, the tax deductibility of the interest feature of debt suggests that the APV method gives a more accurate assessment of project viability than does the standard NPV method.

### 13.4.2 *Risky debt case*

Rendleman (1978) not only examined the risk premiums associated with risky debt, but also considered the impact that debt financing could have on equity values, with taxes and without. The argument is to some extent based on the validity (or lack thereof) of the perfect-market assumption often invoked, which, interestingly enough, turns out to be a double-edged sword.

Without taxes, the original M&M article claims, the investment decision of a firm should be made independent of the financing decision. But the financing base of the firm supports all the firm's investment projects, not some specific project. From this we infer that the future investments of a firm and the risk premiums embodied in the financing costs must be considered when the firm takes on new projects. If, for example, the firm chooses to take on projects of higher than average risk, then this may have an adverse effect on the value of the outstanding debt (to the gain of the shareholders), and the converse holds true as well. It follows that the management of a firm should pursue riskier and riskier projects to transfer some of the firm's risk from the shareholders to the bondholders, who do not receive commensurate return for that risk. If the bondholders anticipate this action on the part of management, then it is all the more imperative that management takes the action since the bondholders are requiring, and receiving, a risk premium for which they are not being forced to take the "standard" or market-consensus level of risk.

Myers (1977) presents an argument in which a firm should issue no risky debt. The rationale for this strategy is that a firm possesses certain real options, or investment opportunities, that unfold over time. With risky debt some of these investment projects available only to the firm of interest may not be undertaken if it is in the interest of the shareholders to default on a near-term scheduled debt payment. In this way risky debt induces a suboptimal investment policy and firm value is not maximized as it would be if the firm issued no risky debt. One problem here is that we do not have strict equivalence between equity-value maximization and firm-value maximizations, so investment policy cannot be thought of entirely in terms of firm-value maximization. This is a quirk associated with the option-pricing framework when applied to firm valuation, and it clouds the determination of what is suboptimal in the finance area.[3]

While we conceded that we aren't entirely sure as to how we should treat the interaction effects of financing and investment policy, we can state with some degree of certainty that, even in the absence of the tax deductibility of interest, these two finance-related decisions are interdependent and, as a result, the financial manager should remain wary of those who subscribe to the idea that financing decisions do not matter.

Allowing the tax deductibility of interest, it is ironic to note that the conclusions are not nearly as clear-cut as before. If the firm undertakes further, more risky projects, the value of debt may actually increase, if the firm does not issue further debt. The shareholders gain from the new project only on its own merits. If no additional debt financing is raised, it is impossible to obtain a larger tax shield and the debt may actually become more secure as a result of the larger asset base. If, however, the firm does issue more debt and, in that way, acts to jeopardize the currently outstanding debt, the number of considerations multiply, and analysis becomes exceedingly difficult because the value of the project by itself, plus the value of the added tax shield, need to be considered in light of the possible shifting of wealth due to transfers of risk amongst claimants of the firm. Thus, it seems that, when we allow the real world to influence the model, as it well should, the only thing we can say for certain about financing and investment decisions is that each case must be considered separately.

From this section and the previous section, we found that investment, financing, and dividend decision are interrelated. Lee *et al.* (2016) have different types of simultaneous equations estimation methods to study the interaction among these three policies. They found there exists strong interrelationships among investment, financing, and dividend decisions.

## 13.5 Implications of Financing and Investment Interactions for Capital Budgeting

This section is intended to briefly review capital-budgeting techniques and explain how each in turn neglects accounting for financing influences in investment-opportunity analysis and discuss the method by which they do incorporate this aspect of financial management into the decision process. We will draw heavily upon the work of Chambers, Harris and Pringle (1982) [CHP], in making particular distinctions between methods most often covered in corporate-finance textbooks and presumably used in practice, presenting numerical comparisons derived from varying sets of circumstances.

Chambers, Harris, and Pringle examined four standard, discounted cash-flow models and considered the implications of using each as opposed to the other three. By way of simulation, they were able to deal with differences in financing projects as well as with possible differences in the risk underlying the operating cash flows generated by each project. The problem inherent in this and any project evaluation (not to say that there are not other difficulties) is in concentrating on the specification of the amount of debt used to finance the investment project. Project debt is therefore defined as the *additional debt capacity* afforded the firm as a result of accepting the project, and can alternatively be described as the difference between the firm's optimal debt level *with* the project and *without* it. Conceptually this is a fairly concrete construct, but it still leaves some vague areas when we are actually performing the computations.

As discussed earlier, it is essential to arrive at some value estimate of the estimated cash flows of a project. The CHP analysis considered the following four methods; (i) the Equity Residual method; (ii) the "After-tax Weighted Average Cost-of-Capital" method; (iii) the "Arditti-Levy" Weighted Cost-of-Capital method; and (iv) the Myers "Adjusted Present Value" method. For simplicity, Table 13.3 contains the definitions of the symbols used in the following discussion, after which we briefly discuss the formulation of each method, and then elaborate on the way in which each method incorporates interacting effects of financing and investment decisions.

### 13.5.1 *Equity-residual method*

The equity-residual method is formulated in Eq. (13.13) in a manner that emphasizes the goal of financial management, the pursuance of

Table 13.3 Definitions of Variables.

| | |
|---|---|
| $R_t$ | = Pretax operating cash revenues of the project during period $t$; |
| $C_t$ | = Pretax operating cash expenses of the project during period $t$; |
| $dep_t$ | = Additional depreciation expense attributable to the project in period $t$; |
| $\tau_c$ | = Applicable corporate tax rate; |
| $I$ | = Initial net cash investment outlay; |
| $D_t$ | = Project debt outstanding during period $t$; |
| $NP$ | = Net proceeds of issuing project debt at time zero; |
| $r_t$ | = Interest rate of debt in period $t$; |
| $k_e$ | = Cost of the equity financing of the project; |
| $k_w$ | = After-tax weighted-average cost of capital (i.e., debt cost is after-tax); |
| $k_{AL}$ | = Weighted average cost of capital — debt cost considered before taxes; |
| $\rho$ | = Required rate-of-return applicable to unlevered cash-flow series, given the risk class of the project. |

$r$, $k_e$, and $\rho$ are all assumed to be constant over time.

the interests of shareholders:

$$\text{NPV(ER)} = \sum_{t=1}^{N} \frac{[(R_t - C_t - dep_t - rD_t)(1-\tau_c) + D_t] - (D_t - D_{t+1})}{(1+k_e)^t} - [I - NP] \qquad (13.13)$$

The formula presented above can be interpreted as stating that the benefit of the project to the shareholders is the present value of the cash flows not going to pay operating expenses or to service or repay debt obligations.

With these flows identified as those going to shareholders, it is appropriate, and rather easy, to discount these flows at the cost of equity. The only difficulty involved is identifying this cost of equity, a problem embodied in all capital-budgeting methods.

### 13.5.2 *After-tax, weighted-average, cost-of-capital method*

The after-tax, weighted-average, cost-of-capital method, depicted in Eq. (13.14), has two noticeable differences from the formulation of the equity-residual method:

$$\text{NPV} = \sum_{t=1}^{N} \frac{(R_t - C_t - dep_t)\,(1 - \tau_c) + dep_t}{(1 + k_w)^t} - I \tag{13.14}$$

First, no flows associated with the debt financing appear in the numerator, or as relevant cash flows. Second, the cost of capital is adjusted downward, with $k_w$ being a weighted average of debt and equity costs, the debt expense accounted for on an after-tax basis. In that way debt financing is reckoned with in an indirect manner. With the assumption that $r$ and $k_e$ are constant over time, $k_w$ can be affected only by the debt-to-equity ratio, a problem most often avoided by assuming a fixed debt-to-equity ratio.

### 13.5.3 *Arditti and Levy method*

The Arditti–Levy method is most similar to the after-tax weighted-average cost-of-capital method. This formulation can be written as:

$$\text{NPV(AL)} = \sum_{t=1}^{N} \frac{[(R_t - C_t - \text{dep}_t - rD_t)(1 - \tau_c) + \text{dep}_t] + rD_t}{(1 + k_{AL})^t} - I \tag{13.15}$$

It was seen as necessary to restate the after-tax, weighted-average, cost-of-capital formula in this manner because the tax payment to the government has an influence on the net cash flows, and for that reason the cash-flow figures would be misleading. To rectify this problem the discount rate must now be adjusted since the interest tax shield is reflected in the cash flows and double counting would be involved. While the after-tax, weighted-average cost of capital recognized the cost of debt in the discount rate, it was akin to the equity-residual method in considering only returns to equity. The Arditti and Levy formulas imply that a weighted average discount rate including the lower cost of debt could only (or best) be used if all flows to all sources of financing were included; hence the term $rD_t$ is found at the end of the first term. This can be rationalized if one considers the case of a firm where there is one owner. The total cash flow to the owner is the relevant figure, and the discount rate applicable is simply a weighted average of the two individual required rates of return.

### 13.5.4 *Myers adjusted-present-value method*

This method, derived in Section 13.4, is closely related to the Arditti–Levy method except for the exclusion of the interest-expense flows to the bondholders. In treating the financing mix, Myers implicitly assumes that the tax shield, created by the interest payments and afforded to the equity holders, has the same risk for the equity holders as the coupon or interest payments have for the bondholders. Instead of aggregating all factors and attempting to arrive at a suitable weighted-average discount rate, Myers found it less difficult to leave operating- and financing-related flows separated, and to discount each at an appropriate rate. This formulation can be written as:

$$\text{APV} = \sum_{t=1}^{N} \frac{(R_t - C_t - \text{dep}_t)(1-\tau_c) + \text{dep}_t}{(1+\rho)^t} - I + \sum_{t=1}^{N} \frac{\tau_c r D_t}{(1+r)^t} \tag{13.16}$$

This formulation appears to be closely related to the Modigliani and Miller with-tax firm-valuation model, and well it should, given Myers' motivation for this work. We choose not to discuss it here, but the reader should be aware that Myers' emphasis was not solely on the tax advantage of debt, as the last term in the above equation tends to imply.

The four methods are obviously comparable, but usually give different figures for the net present value. The equity-residual, after-tax, weighted-average cost-of-capital and the Arditti–Levy weighted-average, cost-of-capital formulations are comparable if the value of the debt outstanding remains a constant proportion of the remaining cash flows; this is often taken to mean a constant debt ratio. This will not guarantee that the Myers APV method will yield the same results, although the Myers method is equivalent to the other three only if the project life can be described as one period, or as *infinite with constant perpetual flows* in all periods. By way of numerical examples, we now address the task of determining the factors that create the differences in the net-present-value figures generated by each method.

**Example 13.1.** VPI Company is considering a new project with a cost of \$25,000 and a life of 5 years. The project's yearly pre-tax operating cash revenues and expenses are \$20,000 and \$9,000, respectively. The additional depreciation would be \$5,000 per year. The net proceeds from a new debt issue would be \$10,000, with a yield of 10% that is expected to remain constant over the life of the project. The corporate tax rate is 35%, and the risk-free and market rates of return are 6% and 12%, respectively. The firm's cost of equity is 15%. Debt will be repaid at the end of the five-year period. Using the above information, calculate the net present value of the new proposed project based upon: (a) Equity residual, (b) After-tax WACC, (c) Arditti–Levy WACC, and (d) Myers' APV (M&M proposition with corporate taxes).

Using the following information: I = \$25,000; $R_t$ = \$20,000; $N$ = 5 years; $C_t$ = \$9,000; $dep_t$ =\$5,000; $\tau_c$ = 35%; ND = \$10,000; $r_t$ = 10%; $k_E$ = 15%; Leverage Ratio = (10,000/25,000) = 0.40; $R_f$ = 6%; and $R_m$ = 12%, we calculate the NPVs for all four methods. They are as follows:

Step 1: Calculate alternative cash flow

(a) After tax operating cash flow: $= (R_t - C_t - dep_t)(1 - T_c) + dep_t$

Years 1–5 = (20,000 − 9,000 − 5,000)(1 − 0.35) + (5,000) = \$8,900.

(b) After Tax Debt Cash Flows: $= -r_t B_t(1 - T_c) - (B_t - B_{t-1})$

years 1–4 = −0.10(10,0001(1 − 0.35) − 0 = −\$650

year 5 = −650 − 10,000 = −\$10,650

The cash flow of the fifth year includes \$650 interest expense and \$10,000 $\text{deb}_t$ repayment.

(c) After tax equity cash flows:

Year 0 = $-I + \text{NP} = -25{,}000 + 10{,}000 = -\$15{,}000$

Years 1–4 = \$8,900 – 650 = \$8250

Year 5 = \$8,900 – 10.650 = –\$1,750

Step 2: Calculate NPV for four alternative methods

(a) Equity Residual Method:

$$\begin{aligned}\text{NPV} &= \sum_{t=1}^{N} \frac{[(R_t - C_t - \text{dep}_t - rB_t)(1 - T_c) + \text{dep}_t] - (B_T - B_{t-1})}{(1 + k_E)^t} \\ &\quad - (I - NP) \\ &= \sum_{t=1}^{4} \frac{8{,}250}{(1 + 0.15)^t} - \frac{1750}{(1 + 0.15)^5} - (25{,}000 - 10{,}000) \\ &= 8{,}250(2.8550) - 1{,}750(0.4972) - 15{,}000 = \$7{,}683.51.\end{aligned}$$

where $B_t - B_{t-1} = D_t - D_{t-1} = \text{deb}_t$ repayment in period $t$.

(b) After Tax WACC Method:

$$\begin{aligned}\text{WACC}(k_w) &= wr(1 - T_c) + (1 - w)(k_E) \\ &= 0.40(0.10)(1 - 0.35) + (1 - 0.40)(0.15) \\ &= 0.1160 \text{ or } 11.6\% \\ \text{NPV} &= \sum_{t=1}^{5} \frac{8{,}900}{(1 + 0.116)^t} - 25{,}000 \\ &= 8{,}900(3.6408) - 25{,}000 \\ &= \$7{,}402.99\end{aligned}$$

(c) Arditti–Levy Method

$$\begin{aligned}K_{AL} &= wr + (1 - w)(k_E) \\ &= (0.40)(0.10j + (1 - 0.40)(00.15) = 0.13 \text{ or } 13\%\end{aligned}$$

Please note that $K_{AL}$ is based upon pretax basis, which is higher than $k_w$, which is based upon after tax basis.

$$\begin{aligned}\text{NPV} &= \sum_{t=1}^{5} \frac{8{,}250 + 1{,}000}{(1+.13)^t} - 25{,}000\\ &= 9{,}250(3.5172) - 25{,}000\\ &= \$7{,}534.10\end{aligned}$$

(d) Myers Method

Two methods can be used to estimate $\rho$.

Method 1:

$$\rho = \frac{k_w}{(1 - wT_c)} = \frac{0.116}{1 - (0.40)(0.35)} = 0.1350 \text{ or } 13.50\%$$

Method 2:

$$\begin{aligned}K_e &= \rho + (\text{Debt to equity ratio})(1 - \rho_c)(\rho - r_t)\\ 0.15 &= \rho + \left(\frac{10{,}000}{1{,}5000}\right)(1 - 0.35)(\rho - 0.1)\\ \rho &= 0.13499\end{aligned}$$

Please note that Method 2 is based upon M&M Proposition 2 (cost equity for leverage form).

$$\begin{aligned}\text{NPV} &= \sum_{t=1}^{5} \frac{8{,}900}{(1+0.135)^t} + \sum_{t=1}^{5} \frac{350}{(1+0.10)^t} - 25{,}000\\ &= 8{,}900(3.4747) + 350(3.7908) - 25{,}000\\ &= \$7{,}251.60\end{aligned}$$

**Example 13.2.** In this example, we assume that a \$1,000 investment generates operating flows of \$300 per year for all five years of the project's life. Debt financing comprises \$600 of the project's total financing and the principal is repaid over the five time periods in equal amounts. The discount and tax rates employed are included in Table 13.4 with the results for each of the four methods.

Table 13.4 Application of Four Capital Budgeting Techniques.

**Inputs:** 1. $k_e = 0.112$; 2. $r = 0.041$; 3. $\tau_c = 0.46$; 4. $\rho = 0.0802$; 5. $w = 0.6$.

| Method | NPV Results | Discount Rates |
|---|---|---|
| 1. Equity-residual | \$230.55 | $k_e = 0.112$ |
| 2. After-tax WACC | 270.32 | $k_w = 0.058$ |
| 3. Arditti–Levy WACC | 261.67 | $k_{AL} = 0.069$ |
| 4. Myers APV | 228.05 | $r = 0.041$ and $\rho = 0.0802$ |

*Source*: Lee and Lee (2017). *Financial Analysis, Planning and Forecasting*, page 904.

Because the Arditti–Levy method recognizes the acquisition of the debt capital and uses a lower discount rate, as does the after-tax WACC, these two methods give the highest net-present-value figures. The equity-residual method recognizes only the \$400 outflow at time zero, but the higher discount suppresses the net-present-value figure. The Myers APV method, though discounting financing-related flows at the cost of debt, also attains a low net-present-value figure because the majority of the flows are discounted at a higher unlevered cost-of-equity rate.

Basically, we can speak of three differences in these methods that create the large discrepancies in the bottom-line figures. The risk factor, reflected in discount rates that may vary over time, is a major element, as was evidenced in the example presented above. The pattern of debt and debt payments will also be an important factor, particularly so when the debt repayment is not of the annuity form assumed earlier. Finally, the recognition and valuation of the debt tax shields will play an important role in net-present-value determination, especially when the constant-debt-repayment assumption is dropped and the interest expenses and associated tax shields grow larger.

In the CHP study the valuation models described earlier were employed in a simulation procedure that would allow the assessment of the investment proposal. The inputs to the capital-budgeting procedures were varied across simulations, and the effects of the changes in each input were scrutinized from a sensitivity-analysis viewpoint.

They considered, but did not dwell upon, the effects of changing discount rates over time or by some scaling factor on the bottom-line valuation figures; further discussion was deferred primarily because of the multitude of possible combinations that would be of interest. Compounding the problem, one would also be interested in different debt-equity combinations and the effects these would have with changing discount rates, since the weighting scheme of the appropriate discount rates plays an integral part in the analysis. In avoiding this aspect of the analysis, the projects evaluated in the forthcoming discussion will be viewed as being of equivalent risk, or as coming from the same risk class. Lest the reader feel shortchanged, it is suggested that one examine each method and verify for him or herself what changes would be produced in the net-present-value figures with varying debt schedules.

More in tune with the basic theme of this chapter, we go on to consider the effects that changing financing mixes, debt-payment patterns, and project lives have on the figures attained for each of the four methods considered, the first (financing mix) being the major issue involved.

In confronting mix effects, we are required to select a model for valuing debt in the Myers APV method because $\rho$ (the unlevered cost of equity capital) is unobservable. In this case we must choose between numerous alternatives, the most notable being those of Modigliani and Miller (1963), where debt provides an interest-tax shield, and that of Miller (1977), where the inclusion of personal taxes on investor interest income has the effect of perfectly offsetting the tax shield the firm receives, rendering the debt tax advantage moot. In the simulation results of CHP presented in the following paragraphs, the Myers cost of unlevered equity capital is computed using each method, with subscripts denoting the particular method used.

Four projects of varied cash-flow patterns and lives are to be presented and valued, each of which will be simulated with three different debt schedules. Brief descriptions of the projects and debt schedules can be found in Table 13.5, along with the fixed inputs to be used in the actual computations.

The projects' cash flows, as listed in the table, were actually manipulated in a predetermined way, so that the more interesting cases would be presented. Project 1 is simply a base figure,

Table 13.5 Inputs for Simulation.

| Project | Net Cash Inflows Per Year | Project Life |
|---|---|---|
| 1 | \$300 per year | 5 years |
| 2 | \$253.77 per year | 5 years |
| 3 | \$124.95 per year | 20 years |
| 4 | \$200 per year, years 1–4<br>\$792.58 in year 5 | 5 years |

For each project the initial outlay is \$1000 at time $t = 0$, with all subsequent outlays being captured in the yearly flows.

Debt Schedule

1. Market value of debt outstanding remains a constant proportion of the project's market value.
2. Equal principal repayments in each year.
3. Level debt, total principal repaid at termination of project.

| Inputs: | | |
|---|---|---|
| | $k_e = 0.112$ | $r = 0.041$ |
| | $k_w = 0.085$ | $\rho_{(M\&M)} = 0.0986$ |
| | $\rho_M = 0.085$ | $\tau_c = 0.46$ |
| | $W = 0.3$ | |

*Source*: Lee and Lee (2017). *Financial Analysis, Planning and Forecasting*, page 906.

while Project 2 has a cash-flow pattern that makes the net present value 0, when using the after-tax, weighted-average cost of capital. Project 3 has a longer life, and thus will serve as a method of determining the effects of increasing project life. Finally, Project 4 has four level payments with a larger final payment in year 5, intended to simulate an ongoing project with terminal value in year 5.

The results of the simulations are presented in Table 13.6. For purposes of comparison, the net-present-value figures of the after-tax, weighted-average cost of capital are reported first, for two reasons. The after-tax weighted-average cost of capital is probably the best-known technique of capital budgeting, and its net present value figures are insensitive to the debt schedule. The initial weights of the debt and equity used to support the project are all that are used in calculating the weighted discount rate, rendering the repayment pattern of debt irrelevant.

As indicated earlier, the after-tax weighted-average cost of capital, Arditti–Levy weighted-average cost of capital, and the equity-residual methods are all equivalent if the debt ratio is held

Table 13.6 Simulation Results.

| Project | Capital Budgeting | Net-Present-Value under Alternative Debit Schedule | | |
|---|---|---|---|---|
| | | **Constant Debt Ratio** | **Equal Principal** | **Level Debt** |
| 1 | After-tax WACC | 182 | 182 | 182 |
| | Arditti–Levy WACC | 182 | 179 | 187 |
| | Equity-Residual | 182 | 167 | 202 |
| | Myers APV (M&M) | 160 | 157 | 166 |
| | Myers APV (M) | 182 | 182 | 182 |
| 2 | After-tax WACC | 0 | 0 | 0 |
| | Arditti–Levy WACC | 0 | −1 | 7 |
| | Equity-Residual | 0 | −3 | 32 |
| | Myers APV (M&M) | −18 | −19 | −10 |
| | Myers APV (M) | 0 | 0 | 0 |
| 3 | After-tax WACC | 182 | 182 | 182 |
| | Arditti–Levy WACC | 182 | 169 | 186 |
| | Equity Residual | 182 | 128 | 194 |
| | Myers APV (M&M) | 138 | 119 | 150 |
| | Myers APV (M) | 182 | 182 | 182 |
| 4 | After-tax WACC | 182 | 182 | 182 |
| | Arditti–Levy WACC | 182 | 174 | 182 |
| | Equity Residual | 182 | 147 | 183 |
| | Myers APV (M&M) | 155 | 146 | 156 |
| | Myers APV (M) | 182 | 182 | 182 |

*Source*: Lee and Lee (2017). *Financial Analysis, Planning and Forecasting*, page 907.

constant. It is also of interest here that the Myer's APV figures, using the Miller method for determining the cost of capital, are constant over debt schedules; they are, for all intents and purposes, the same as the after-tax, weighted-average cost-of-capital figures, a finding that is reasonable if one believes that the cost of debt capital is the same as that of unlevered equity. Of all the methods cited above, the equity-residual method is the most sensitive to the debt schedule employed, with both principal and interest payments being included in the cash flows, a feature compounded by the higher discount rates included in the computations. The two methods that include the interest tax shield, the Arditti–Levy method and the Myers APV (M&M) method are also sensitive to the amount of debt outstanding, the interest tax shield being of greater value the longer the debt is outstanding. In all cases the latter method gives the lowest net-present-value figures due to the treatment of the interest tax shield.

In further simulations CHP showed (and it should be no surprise) that as higher levels of debt are employed and higher tax rates are encountered, the magnitude of the differences is amplified, and the method employed in the capital-budgeting decision takes on greater and greater importance. Even so it was argued that changes associated with changes in the inputs of the longest-lived project, where the changes in the net-present-value figures were the most pronounced, were not that great when compared with the outcomes associated with changing the estimates of the cash flows by as little as 5%. The importance of this finding is that projects that are of short duration and are financed with relatively little debt are not as sensitive to the capital-budgeting technique employed. But, in the case of longer-lived projects, the method selected can have serious implications for the acceptance or rejection of a project, particularly when higher levels of debt financing are employed. Analysts undoubtedly possess their own views as to which method is stronger conceptually, and, in the event of capital-budgeting procedures, should be aware of the debt policy to be pursued. Even in light of these views, it may be prudent to use the Myers APV method with the M&M unlevered-equity cost-determination method as the first screening device for a project or set of projects. Since this method yields the most conservative figures, any project that appears profitable following this analysis should be undertaken, and any project failing this screening can be analyzed using the methods chosen by the financial manager, if further analysis is felt to be warranted.

Since the Myers APV method is recommended, it is worthwhile for us to show the procedure for obtaining the APV, as discussed in Table 13.4. Let the information needed to establish APV be $R_t = \$4{,}000$, $C_t = \$1{,}000$, $\text{dep}_t = \$500$, $D_t = \$3600$, $E_t$ (equity financing) $= \$2800$, $I = \$7000$, $k_e = 0.15$, $r = 0.09$, $\tau_c = 0.46$, $w = D/(D+E) = \$4200/\$7000 = 0.6$, $N = 6$.

From this information, we can assemble the information needed to estimate APV as follows:

(a) Operating flows $= (R_t - C_t - \text{dep}_t)(1 - \tau_c) + \text{dep}_t$
$= (\$4000 - \$1000 - \$500)(1 - 0.46) + \$500$
$= \$1850$

(b) Financial flows $= \tau_c r D_t$
$= (0.46)(0.09)(\$3600)$
$= \$149.04$

$$\begin{aligned}
\text{(c)}\quad k_w &= wr(1-\tau_c) + (1-w)k_e \\
&= (0.6)(0.09)(1-0.46) + (1-0.6)(0.15) \\
&= (0.029) + (0.06) \\
&= 0.089
\end{aligned}$$

$$\begin{aligned}
\text{(d)}\quad \rho &= \frac{k_w}{(1-\tau_c w)} \\
&= \frac{0.089}{(1-(0.46)(0.6))} \\
&= 0.1229
\end{aligned}$$

From this information we can calculate APV as:

$$\begin{aligned}
APV &= \$1850\left(\sum_{t=1}^{6} 1/(1+0.1229)^t\right) \\
&\quad + \$149.04\left(\sum_{t=1}^{6} 1/(1+0.09^t)\right) - \$7000 \\
&= (\$1850)(4.0784) + (\$149.04)(4.4859) - \$7000 \\
&= \$1213.62
\end{aligned}$$

By using appropriate budget constraints, Lambrecht and Myers (2012) have theoretically shown that investment dividend and financing policy are inter-related. To test this theory developed by Lambrecht and Myers, Lee *et al.* investigate the interrelationship among investment, financing and dividend decisions using 2SLS, 3SLS, and GMM methods based on the U.S. listed firm annual data between 1965 and 2012. Their results are consistent with Lambrecht and Myers's (2012) theory that dividend and investment decisions are jointly determined. In addition, these three corporate decisions are co-determined and the interaction among them should be taken into account in a simultaneous equation framework.

## 13.6 Debt Capacity and Optimal Capital Structure

Contrary to the neoclassical theory of Modigliani and Miller and others, developed in the late 1950's and early 1960's, we have argued that the investment, financing, and dividend policies of a firm do interact, and by so doing can affect the market value of the firm and/or the value of the equity of the firm. By way of these interaction effects the irrelevance propositions cited earlier and so prevalent in the finance literature become themselves invalidated. In being able to outline those interaction effects we are hinting, not very subtly, that firms do have optimal capital structures and certain debt capacities, though they may not necessarily be constant through time. This section more explicitly addresses the debt-capacity issue, and in so doing strives to arrive at optimal capital decisions. Here we assume that the firm's debt capacity is defined at the margin as being the point where the advantage derived from incremental additions of debt to the capital structure of the firm is just offset, or more than offset, by the costs incurred, whether strictly monetary or risk-based costs.

The methods explored in the following discussion are not to be taken as though they were inscribed in stone and handed down from the mountain; they are instead intended to serve as a useful aid to the financial manager in the conduct of financial planning and forecasting. One particular problem embodied in the following is how risk is to be defined so that the cost-benefit analysis can be performed. Total firm risk is one term used, and risk of bankruptcy or insolvency is a viable alternative. Most of the following analysis can be viewed as though we are decomposing total firm risk into two components, business risk and financial risk. Given this and the common assumption firms aim toward target total risk levels (independent of any investor's portfolio decisions), we will be able to show how firms arrive at finance mixes that are considered optimal.

Tuttle and Litzenberger (1968) took the above assumption and applied it to the screening and ranking of investment opportunities, where each project was transformed to be of the same risk as that associated with the existing equity capital of the firm. The ability of the firm to lever or unlever itself at some known borrowing or lending rate is sufficient to allow this to be done, again without consideration of portfolio effects, but first it is necessary to see why a firm would proceed along such lines of investigation.

Let us identify a firm Q, with an expected rate-of-return on the firm's equity denoted as $R_Q$ and the standard error-of-estimate of those returns as $S_Q$. Given the numerous investment opportunities faced by the firm with expected rate-of-return $R_p$ and standard error-of-estimate of those returns as $S_p$, we can separate these projects into three groups as characterized in Table 13.7: (1) those accepted without question, (2) those indisputably rejected, and (3) those on which we cannot exercise judgment without the specification of a risk-return trade-off.

By way of a simple dominance principle the "accept" and "reject" decisions should be clear. The concern here is the valuation of those projects that fall into the third category above. Tuttle and Litzenberger allow the firm to lend or borrow at some constant known rate; in so doing the firm gains the ability to partially offset the risk of a project, making it risk-equivalent with the rest of the firm's projects. Risk being equivalent for all projects, it is a simple task to evaluate the project; the expected return is the sole consideration (if, for the time being, one assumes that the project's cash flows are perfectly correlated with the rest of the firm's cash flows).

We adopt the following notation:

$R_e$ = Expected rate of return to equity from the project;
$R_d$ = Yield to maturity on long-term debt of similar risk to that of the firm;
$R_p$ = Expected internal rate-of-return offered by the investment project; and
$W$ = 1 + the debt-to-equity ratio.

The levered residual rate-of-return to equity can be shown as:

$$R_e = WR_p - R_d(W - 1) \tag{13.17}$$

Table 13.7 Acceptance–Rejection Criteria.

| **Accept** | **Reject** | **Indeterminate** |
|---|---|---|
| $\boldsymbol{R_r \geq R_Q^*}$ and $S_p \leq S_Q$ | $R_p < R_Q$ and $S_p > S_Q$ | $R_p > R_Q$ and $S_p > S_Q$ or $R_p < R_Q$ $S_p < S_Q$ |

*Note*: *In the special instance where both relationships are strict equalities the firm is, of course, indifferent in attitude toward the project.

or, alternatively,

$$R_e = R_d + W(R_p - R_d) \tag{13.17a}$$

and the new standard error of equity returns becomes:

$$S_e = WS_p \tag{13.18}$$

By multiplying the last term of Eq. (13.17a) by $S_p/S_p$ and substituting into Eq. (13.18), we obtain Eq. (13.19):

$$R_e = R_d + \frac{S_e}{S_p}(R_p - R_d) \tag{13.19}$$

Now by differentiating with respect to the risk of equity, we find the linear trade-off between residual return to equity and standard error;

$$\frac{dR_e}{dS_e} = \frac{R_p - R_d}{S_p} \tag{13.20}$$

By itself Eq. (13.20) could be used to value projects, in much the same way that portfolio-performance measures evaluate portfolio returns on a risk-adjusted basis. In the context of this chapter, however, the task is reduced to finding the factor $W'$ that equates the risk of the equity returns of the project with that of the rest of the equity of the firm; the procedure of solving mix, $W'$, can be defined as:

$$S_{e'} = W'S_p \tag{13.18a}$$

Then the risk-adjusted rate-of-return on investment project $R_e$ can be written as:

$$R_{e'} = R_d + W'(R_p - R_d) \tag{13.21}$$

At this point, all we need to do is make a simple comparison of the project's levered, expected rate-of-return with the existing return on equity for the firm as a whole. We have therefore devised a method for solving all investment-opportunity analysis problems not covered by the dominance rule mentioned earlier.

The assumptions of debt costs being independent of the degree of leverage employed and perfect correlations between cash flows are obviously violated in practice. Tuttle and Litzenberger also showed how both of these factors work into the analysis. By allowing debt costs to be affected in some linear manner, as was the cost of equity, the cost of financing a project ($k_p$) can be expressed as:

$$k_p = \frac{1}{W'}R_p + \left(1 - \frac{1}{W'}\right) R_d \tag{13.22}$$

which, when rearranged, appears as:

$$k_p = R_d + \frac{1}{W'}(R_p - R_d) \tag{13.22a}$$

For a project, if $R_d$, $R_p$, $R_e$, $S_p$, and $S_e$ and 0.05, 0.40, 0.15, 0.60, and 0.30, respectively, then $W' = 0.30/0.60 = 0.50$ and $R_e = 0.05 + (0.50)(0.40 - 0.05) = 0.225$. Since $k_p$ is smaller than $R_p$, this investment project should therefore be accepted.

As we would expect, the required rate-of-return-to-risk trade-off assumes smaller values when risky debt is allowed. Still, this leaves the method of analysis as viable. By solving for the appropriate $W'$, we make the risk of the project equivalent to all other projects. Then we have only to compare expected rates of return with hurdle (cost of capital) rates imposed in the form of the existing return on equity. Only in the instance where so much debt has been employed to reduce the risk of a project that the cost of debt for the project exceeds the existing return-on-equity would the firm be unable to evaluate the project in this manner.

Looking at the problem from the portfolio viewpoint, we must also, when assessing its risk, consider the diversification benefits that a project yields, so that the $W'$ is properly selected. By using the equation for the variance between two random variables — the returns on the existing equity of the firm and the returns on the new project — we set the portfolio standard error equal to the existing equity's standard error and vary the financing ratio $W$ (and by so doing, vary the dollar equity investment in the project), until we achieve the stated goal. While computationally this is more difficult than the previous cases, the conclusion is the same: Some financing mix exists (in all but the most extreme instances) that will allow us to examine new projects on an equity-risk-equivalent basis, that being defined as the optimal financing mix.

To explicitly consider the effect of diversification on cost of financing, Tuttle and Litzenberger (1968) generalized Eq. (13.22a) as

$$k'_p = r_d + \frac{\rho_{pe} S_p}{S_e}(R_e - R_d) \tag{13.22a$'$}$$

where $k'_P$ = Cost of financing a project, $\rho_{pe}$ = Correlation between $R_p$ and $R_e$, $S_p$ = Estimated standard deviation of $R_p$, $S_e$ = Estimated standard deviation of $R_e$.

If $\rho_{pe} = 1$, then Eq. (13.22a′) reduces to Eq. (13.22a). Since $k'_P$ is generally smaller than $k_P$, diversification associated with capital projects will generally reduce the cost of financing.

This analysis highlights the true meaning of optimal capital structure when target risk levels are set. Optimal capital structure is not some debt-to-equity figure that allows the firm a degree of leverage deemed as safe. It is a function of the underlying risk of the projects undertaken by the firm. It is almost as though the optimal capital-structure decision is given from outside the firm, and the financial manager is the agent pursuing the maintenance of the proper financing mix, given the selection of the projects that themselves add to firm value.

In a later paper Litzenberger and Sosin (1979) [LS] investigated the capital-structure decision for regulated and deregulated firms. They maintain that optimal capital structures do exist (and that firms should actively pursue them), but that an aggressive policy by a regulated industry can be nonoptimal from the standpoint of equity investors, and for the consumers of the regulated industry's products. By virtue of being regulated with respect to rates charged, any gains derived by a company by aggressively levering the firm will be passed on to consumers in a rather short time span. If an aggressive leverage policy is followed, the equity holders incur more risk and probably do not receive commensurate return. Since leverage is closely akin to risk, the chance of bankruptcy and disrupted service is increased, and the possibility of the consumer suffering the brunt of the costs through price hikes is likewise increased. The conclusion derived from this analysis is rather straightforward: A regulated firm's debt capacity should not be pushed to its limits in terms of maximizing total firm value. Debt should be used only so long as it is riskless, and the chance of equity holder and consumer loss is minimized. In addition, LS argued that the issuance of non-default-free debt by regulated and nonregulated firms can be socially nonoptimal.

Martin and Scott (1976) adopted the insolvency definition of bankruptcy, and broke down the analyst's task into four components: estimation of the before-tax cash flows, estimation of the appropriate discount rate for pure equity streams, estimation of the additional contribution of a project to total firm debt capacity, and computation of the value of the project to the firm. Step 1 is identical to all prior capital-budgeting methods discussed, and should require no further explanation. Step 2 relies heavily on the Hamada (1972) contention that an unlevered beta ($\beta_0$) for a firm's equity can be computed as shown below:

$$\beta_0 = \beta \left( \frac{S}{S_0} \right)_{t-1} \tag{13.23}$$

where $\beta$ is levered beta, $S$ is the market value of the equity in the firm in time period $(t-1)$, and $S_0$ is the market value of the equity if the firm undertook no leverage in period $(t-1)$. In defining debt capacity, we must specify some accepted probability of insolvency, resulting from the inclusion of financial leverage. Insolvency, based on a flow concept, is defined here as the probability that the operating flows are sufficient to meet the debt financing requirements. In specifying flows, we should be aware that adjustments could be made in cash and marketable securities or in lines of credit so as to avoid insolvency, and are generally not recognized in operating flows. In essence, the argument assumes that these factors are at their optimal points, all other things held constant.

Recognizing portfolio effects, the risk a project adds to the cash-flow variability of the firm is determined by the correlation of the project's cash flows and those of the firm prior to the project's acceptance. If the project's cash flows are positively correlated with those of the firm, the higher the correlation, the less debt its operating cash-flow stream can support. Since no precise estimate exists as to the shareholders' desired leverage, the financial manager is not required to pursue an optimal debt policy by this step. The sole concern here is the establishment of the relevant risk of the project. If we allow $C$ to represent the firm's net cash flow after the financing charges, and $E$, $D$, $I$, $SF$, and $\tau$ denote earnings before interest and taxes, depreciation, interest expenses, sinking-fund requirements, and tax rates, respectively, we can form the following probability statement by assuming that $C$ is distributed normally with variance of 0.02:

$$P(C \leq 0) = P(C \leq \overline{C} - z\sigma_c) \qquad (13.24)$$

and $Z$ represents the number of standard normal deviations the expected level of cash flows lies from zero. Clearly, the validity of this procedure hinges on the power of the analysis to compute the proper standard deviation of the firm's cash-flow streams with the new project included (the form of the distribution could be varied according to the analyst's judgment).

By setting the desired insolvency-probability level associated with the firm, the amount of debt a project allows the firm to issue emerges from the analysis, since the allowable increase of interest expense is readily computed by decreasing $C$ until the probability of insolvency is set equal to the pre-specified limits. This allowable decrease in $C$ is the allowable increase in interest expense, and by virtue of knowing the required coupon rate on the firm's bond, the amount of debt that can be issued logically follows.

Step 4 of the analysis is the valuation of the project, a process broken into two parts (similar to the Myers analysis cited in earlier sections of this chapter). From the Capital Asset Pricing Model we are able to compute a beta for the project in question, and use that figure to compute a cost of equity capital for unlevered flows, this rate being used to discount the operating cash flows of the project. In knowing the required coupon payment necessary to float the firm's bonds at par, in Step 3, we know the appropriate discount rate to apply to the capitalization of the interest tax shield generated by the debt undertaken as a result of the project's acceptance. Discounting the tax shield generated by the interest payments at the cost of debt, we obtain the present value of the debt capacity attributable to the project, the summation of these two components giving the total value of the project to the firm. Again we see that debt capacity is directly related to the underlying risk of the projects accepted by the firm, and not by any subjective estimate as to what the firm's total debt to equity ratio should be, or some target to which the times-interest-earned figure should revert.

In some respects the preceding analysis viewed optimal debt capacity in the light of increasing returns to scale. The more highly uncorrelated the flows of those projects undertaken by the firm, given their absolute size, the greater is the debt capacity, or the lower the probability of insolvency. Also of interest is the implicit assumption that insolvency costs are incurred only when the actual event of insolvency occurs. Hong and Rappaport (1978) argue that debt capacity should be expressed as the amount (or percentage) of debt in the firm's capital structure at the point of optimal capital structure, and that insolvency costs are incurred prior to the event of insolvency. In this way insolvency costs act to offset the advantage of the interest tax shield attained by the amount of interest-paying debt outstanding. The rationale for claiming that insolvency costs are incurred at all levels of debt financing, regardless of the safety of the debt, is by way of agency theory, where the existence of nontrivial monitoring costs decreases the value of obtaining further interest tax shields.

From the Modigliani and Miller analysis (1963) we find few complications in specifying the value of the interest tax shield attributable to increases in debt, particularly so in the case of perpetual debt. The problem of specification arises only when we attempt to examine the insolvency-cost function. If we follow the Hong and Rappaport example and allow insolvency costs to be a linear function of the amount of debt outstanding (an assumption that probably does not generally hold in practice, but does allow for considerable ease in exposition), another term can be added to the standard M&M firm-valuation formula, as shown below:

$$V^L = \frac{\text{NOI}(1-\tau)}{k_s} + \frac{rD\tau}{r} - k_i D \tag{13.25}$$

where NOI, $\tau$, $r$, $k_s$, $D$ and $V^L$ represent net operation income, marginal corporate tax rate, coupon rate, cost of equity capital, total debt, and firm value with leverage, respectively; $k_i$ is the average insolvency cost per unit of debt. The insolvency costs are presented in present-value form. Since optimal capital structure also carries with the property that cost of capital overall is at its minimal point, we could express the value of the firm as the present value of the operating inflows discounted at this minimum cost of capital, as shown below in Eq. (13.26):

$$V^L = \frac{NOI(1-\tau)}{k_a} \tag{13.26}$$

where $k_a$ is the average cost of capital.

By rearranging Eq. (13.26) to read $V^L k_a = NOI(1-\tau)$ and substituting this into Eq. (13.25) and solving for $k_a$, we can obtain the following expression for the weighted-average cost of capital:

$$k_a = k_s + \frac{k_s D(k_i - \tau)}{V^L} \tag{13.27}$$

from which we can see that the overall cost of capital depends heavily on the rates at which $k_i$ and $\tau$ change as additional debt is employed. Differentiating with respect to changes in debt outstanding, all else held constant, we find:

$$\frac{dk_a}{dD} = \frac{k_s}{V^L}\frac{(dk_i - \tau)}{dD} \tag{13.28}$$

where $T$ is assumed constant and $k_i$, while assumed to be a linear function of the level of debt, may change as the firm attains higher degrees of financial leverage. The financial planner must specify the functional form of $k_i$ to be able to minimize $k_a$, that is, set Eq. (13.28) equal to zero.

For project valuation we must consider the optimal debt level at the new level of $V^L$, which means only that we are again interested in incremental additions of debt, but, unlike the Martin and Scott analysis, this figure is not only dependent on the ability of the firm to utilize interest tax shields; the incremental insolvency costs and the effect on the insolvency-cost function itself must be considered.

The Martin–Scott method of optimizing capital structure subject to an insolvency constraint utilized the Capital Asset Pricing Model and the Hamada procedure for obtaining unlevered-beta estimates, where the unlevered beta was subsequently used in arriving at unlevered costs of equity capital that are applied in the M&M tax-corrected firm-valuation model. As Conine (1980) points out, the Hamada method applies only when the debt employed is assumed to be risk-free, an assumption that Martin and Scott did not adhere to. This has the effect of overstating the cost of equity capital as equity assumed all of the firm's risk. This bias the total cost of capital upward and may cause incorrect reject decisions to be made when the firm is considering new investment opportunities.

To be consistent with the CAPM, Conine outlines two methods for resolving the problem: The debt can be assumed riskless, or debt could also be priced according to the CAPM, where the Hamada formulation can be rederived with the inclusion of risky debt.[5] With the first proposed solution hardly resolving the problem, Conine showed that the unlevered beta could be computed from:

$$\beta_0 = \frac{\beta S}{S_0} + \frac{D(1-\tau)\beta_D}{S_0} \tag{13.29}$$

where $\beta_0$, $\beta$, $S$, and $S_0$ have been defined in Eq. (13.23); $D$ and $\beta_D$ are risky debt and beta of risky debt respectively; $\tau$ is the marginal corporate tax rate. This equation shows that the levered beta computed from historical data, most often used as a first approximation to the beta of equity claims, and also reflects the risk of the debt of the firm. In estimating an unlevered beta with the existence of risky debt, the original Hamada method will overestimate the proper beta and should be adjusted by using the Conine method.

While not technically correct, the Martin and Scott method of capital budgeting and the two adjustments to their method provide a solid conceptual basis for evaluating projects under conditions of uncertainty and the existence of valuable tax shields. In making the suggested corrections, the financial manager should be better able to evaluate projects and simultaneously pursue an optimal capital structure. [See Conine (1980) and Martin and Scott (1980).]

To show how Martin and Scott's (1976) method can be used to estimate debt capacity and perform capital budgeting, we assume that ABC company's current cash flow is normally distributed with mean \$100,000 ($\bar{C}_1$) and a standard deviation of \$80,000 ($\sigma_{c1}$). In addition, we also have valuation information for Project X as shown in Table 13.8.

**Step 1.** We can use the CAPM discussed in Chapter 8 to calculate $k_s$:

$$k_s = 0.09 + (0.16 - 0.09)(1.5) = 0.195$$

Table 13.8 Valuation Information for Project X.

| |
|---|
| A. Project Cash-Flow Information |
| 1. NOI = \$18,000 |
| 2. Project maturity = infinity |
| 3. Marginal tax rate for ABC = 45% |
| 4. Initial cash outlay = \$800,000 |
| B. Required Return Information |
| 1. $R_f = 0.09$ |
| 2. $R_m = 0.16$ |
| 3. $\beta_0 = 1.5$ |
| C. Debt-Capacity Information |
| 1. Standard deviation in project cash flows = \$8,000 |
| 2. Correlation between firm and project cash flows = 0.5 |
| 3. Cost of new debt, $r = 0.10$ |

**Step 2.** We calculate debt capacity as follows: The combined standard deviation (the firm's cash flow + Project X) can be defined as:

$$\sigma_{c'} = ((80{,}000)^2 + 2(0.5)(80{,}000)(8{,}000) + (8{,}000)^2)^{1/2}$$
$$= \$84{,}285.23$$

Using this information $\bar{C} = \$100{,}000$, $\sigma_c = \$80{,}000$, we have

$$z = \frac{\overline{C} - 0}{\sigma_c} = \frac{\$100{,}000}{\$80{,}000} = 1.25$$

From the normal distribution table, as listed at the rear of this book, the z-value 1.25 implies that 10.56% of the area under ABC's cash-flow distribution lies in the tail beyond zero, as indicated in of Figure 13.1(a). This implies that ABC's present risk of insolvency is 10.56%. After the project is undertaken, as indicated in Figure 13.1(b),

$$\frac{\$118{,}000}{\$84{,}285} = 1.40$$

This latter $z$-value ($z'$) indicates (see Figure 13.1(b)) that the risk of insolvency for the firm has been reduced to 8.08%. The reduction

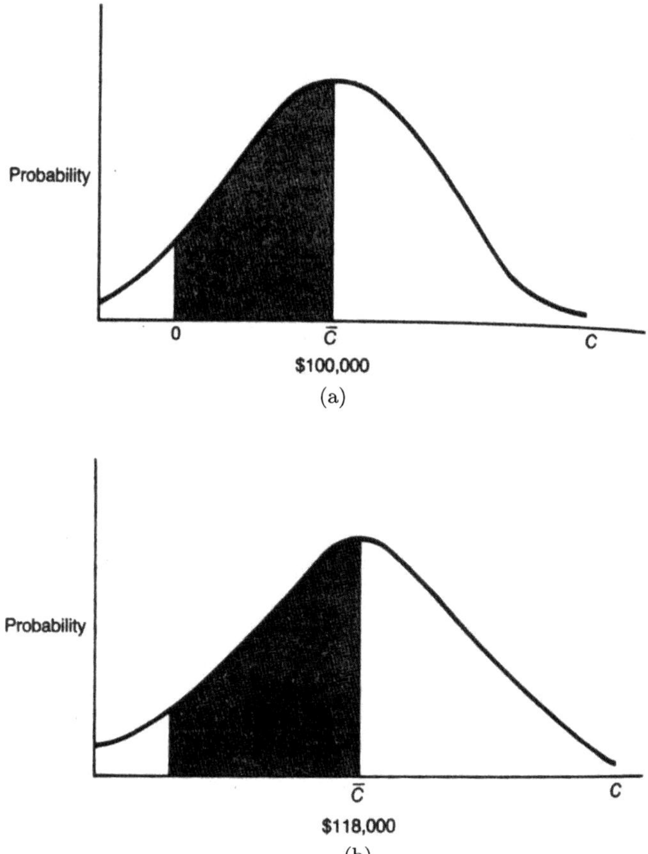


Figure 13.1 (a) Distribution of Unencumbered Cash Flows for ABC Company. (b) Distribution of Unencumbered Cash Flows after Project is Undertaken.

of insolvency risk allows the firm to issue new debt up to the point where its insolvency risk is again 10.56%.

The increase in debt capacity can be determined by computing the added interest and before-tax sinking-fund payment ABC could incur without increasing the firm risk of insolvency above its previous level of 10.56%. In this case:

$$z = \frac{(\overline{C} - C')}{\sigma_{c'}} = \frac{(118{,}000 - C')}{84{,}285} = 1.25$$

This implies that $C'$ equals $12,643.75.

The process of inputting the addition to debt capacity can be quite involved where debt has a finite maturity and unequal principal payments. If, however, it is assumed that the addition to debt capacity is permanent, debt service cost (DSC) can be composed entirely of interest expense, so that:

$$D = \text{DSC}/k_d = (\$12{,}643.75) \cdot (0.10) = \$126{,}438$$

**Step 3.** Using the above-mentioned information, we can make the capital-budgeting decision in terms of the M&M type of valuation model as defined in Eq. (13.25′):

$$V = \text{NOI}\frac{(1-\tau)}{k_s} + \frac{rD\tau}{r} \tag{13.25′}$$

Substituting the related figure into Eq. (13.25′), we obtain:

$$\begin{aligned} V &= \frac{(\$18{,}000)\,(1-0.45)}{0.195} + \frac{(126{,}438)(0.10)(0.45)}{0.10} \\ &= \$50{,}769 + \$56{,}897 \\ &= \$107{,}666 \end{aligned}$$

Thus, given Project X's internal cash outlay of \$80,000, the project is expected to produce a net present value of \$27,666.

Finally, it should be noted that Martin and Scott's model has been generalized by Gahlon and Stover (1979) to incorporate the effect of correlations among the cash flows of all proposed projects. It has been also recently integrated with Myers' (1974) APV model, as discussed in the previous section.

Alderson and Lee (1988) found the grounds for the integration of pension funding with capital structure decisions. In doing so, they argue that unfunded vested liabilities are an imperfect substitute for debt. In general, we regard pension is an inside debt.

Lee (2020) studied differential effect of inside debt on components of firm risk, and how it relates to CEO portfolio diversification to reduce firm risk exposure. They found that compensating CEOs with inside debt (e.g., pensions and other deferred compensation plans) leads to reductions in firms' systematic risk and idiosyncratic risk, but to disproportionate degrees. CEOs with larger inside debt draft and implement policies, which lead to a significantly larger reduction in the idiosyncratic firm risk and investment. They then showed that the differential effect is the result of an asymmetry in CEOs' perceived benefits of diversifying exposures to individual firm risk components. They further showed that granting excessive debt-based pay may divert executives from firm specific but productive activities (e.g., R&D investments), therefore may compromise long-run corporate success.

## 13.7 Implications of Different Policies on the Beta Coefficient

Investment, financing, dividend, and production policy are four important policies in financial management decision. In previous sections, we have discussed investment, financing and dividend policies. In addition, the beta coefficient determination has been discussed in Chapter 7. In this section, we will discuss the impacts of financing, production and the dividend policy on beta coefficient determination.

### 13.7.1 *Impact of financing policy on beta coefficient determination*

Suppose that the security is a share in the common stock of a corporation. Let us assume that that this corporation increases the proportion of debt in its capital structure, all other relevant factors remaining unchanged. How would you expect this change to affect the firm's beta? We have seen that an increase in the level of debt leads to an increase in the riskiness of stockholders' future earnings. To compensate for this additional risk, stockholders' will demand a higher expected rate of return. Therefore, from Eq. (13.30), beta must rise for this company's stock. We see that, all other things equal, the higher the proportion of debt in a firm's capital structure, the higher the beta of shares of its common stock.

$$\beta_L = \beta_U \left(1 + \frac{B\,(1 - \tau_c)}{S}\right) \tag{13.30}$$

where $\beta_L$ is the leveraged bet; $\beta_U$ is the unlevered operating beta; $B$ is the amount of debt; $S$ is the amount of equity; and $\tau_c$ is the corporate tax rate.

When the market model is used to estimate a firm's beta, the resulting estimate of the beta is the market assessment of both operating and financial risk. This is called *leveraged beta.* Hamada (1972) and Rubinstein (1973) suggest that Eq. (13.30) can be modified to calculate the unleveraged beta. This beta is an estimate of the firm's operating or business, risk.

We know that JNJ's related data are $\beta_L = 0.32$ and average $(B/S) = 0.64$. If $\tau_c = 0.4$, the JNJ's unleveraged beta can be calculated as

$$\beta_U = \frac{0.32}{[1 + (0.64)(1 - 0.4)]} = 0.23$$

### 13.7.2 *Impact of production policy on beta coefficient determination*

In this section, we will first discuss production policy. Then we will discuss implications of different policies on the beta coefficient determination. Production policy refers to how company uses different input mix to produce its products. The companies' production process can be classified into either capital intensive or labor intensive which depend upon whether capital labor ratio ($K/L$ Ratio) is larger or smaller than one. We can use either Cobb–Douglas production function or Variable Elasticity of Substitution (VES) production function to show how capital and labor affect the change of the beta coefficient. The Cobb–Douglas production function in two factors, capital ($K$) and labor ($L$) can be defined as follows.

$$Q = K^a L^b \tag{13.31}$$

where $Q$ is firm's output, $a$ and $b$ are positive parameters.

Lee *et al.* (1990) have derived the theoretical relationship between beta coefficient and the capital labor ratio in terms of the Cobb–Douglas production functions as follows in Eq. (13.32).

$$\beta = \frac{(1 + r)\,\mathrm{COV}(\tilde{e}, \tilde{R}_m)}{\mathrm{VAR}(\tilde{R}_m)\{\phi\,[1 - (1 - E)\,b]\}} \tag{13.32}$$

where $r$ = the risk-free rate; $\tilde{R}_m$ = return on the market portfolio; $\tilde{e}$ = random price disturbances with zero mean; $E = -(\partial P/\partial Q)(Q/P)$, an elasticity constant; $b$ = contribution of labor to total output; $\varphi = 1 - \lambda\text{COV}(\tilde{v}, \tilde{R}_m)$; $\lambda$ = the market price of systematic risk.

In addition, the VES production function in two factors capital ($K$) and labor ($L$) can be defined as follows in Eq. (13.33).

$$Q = K^{\alpha(1-s\rho)}[L + (\rho - 1)\, K]^{\alpha s\rho} \tag{13.33}$$

where $Q$ is firm's output and $\alpha$, $s$, and $\rho Q$ is firm's output and $\alpha$, $s$, and $\rho Q$ is firm's output and $\alpha$, $s$, and $\rho$ are parameters with the following constraints:

$$\begin{aligned} &\alpha > 0 \\ &0 < s < 1 \\ &0 \leq s\rho \leq 1 \\ &L/K > (1-\rho)/(1-s\rho)^3 \end{aligned}$$

Lee *et al.* (1995) have derived the theoretical relationship between beta coefficient and the capital labor ratio in terms of the VES production functions as follows.

$$\beta = \frac{(1+r)\{\text{COV}(\tilde{e}, \tilde{R}_m) - [\Phi(1-\mu E)\alpha s\rho\phi^{-1} - w(pQ)^{-1}(1-\rho)K]\text{COV}(\tilde{v}, \tilde{R}_m)\}}{\text{VAR}(\tilde{R}_m)\{\Phi - [\Phi(1-\mu E)\alpha s\rho - w\phi(pQ)^{-1}(1-\rho)K\}} \tag{13.34}$$

where $p$ = expected price of output; $\mu$ = reciprocal of the price elasticity of demand, $0 \leq \mu \leq 1$; $w$ = expected wage rate; $\tilde{v}$ = random shock in the wage rate with zero mean; $\Phi = 1 - \lambda\text{COV}(\tilde{e}, \tilde{R}_m)$; $r, \tilde{R}_m, \tilde{e}, E, \varphi, \lambda$ are as defined in Eq. (13.30).

### 13.7.3 *Impact of dividend policy on beta coefficient determination*

Impact of payout ratio on beta coefficient is one of the important issue in finance research. By using dividend signaling theory, Lee *et al.* (1993) have derived the relationship between the beta coefficient and payout ratio as follows.

$$\beta_i = \beta_{pi}\,[1 + \gamma F(d_i)] \tag{13.35}$$

$\beta_i$ = the firm's systematic risk when the market is informationally imperfect and the information asymmetry can be resolved by dividends; $\beta_{pi}$ = the firm's systematic risk when market is informationally perfect; $\gamma$ = a signaling cost incurred if firm's net after-tax operating cash flow $X$ falls below the promised dividend $D$; $d_i$ = firm's dividend payout ratio; $F(d_i)$ = cumulative normal density function in term of payout ratio.

Equation (13.31) implies that beta coefficient is a function of payout ratio.

In sum, this section has shown that how financing, production, and dividend policy can affect the beta coefficient. This information is important for calculating cost of capital equity. Lee (2020) has investigated the joint impact of financing, dividend, and production decision on beta coefficient in detail.

## 13.8 Summary

In this chapter, we have discussed four important policies in financial management. These four important policies are investment, financing, dividend, and production. In the determination of dividend policy, we examined the relevance of the internal-external equity decision in the presence of nontrivial transaction costs. While the empirical evidence was found to be inconclusive because of the many variables that could not be controlled, there should be no doubt in anyone's mind that flotation costs (incurred when issuing new equity to replace retained earnings paid out) by themselves have a negative impact on firm value. But if the retained earnings paid out are replaced whole or in part by debt, the equity holders may stand to benefit because the risk is transferred to the existing bondholders — risk they do not receive commensurate return for taking. Thus, if the firm pursues a more generous dividend-payout policy while not changing the investment policy, the change in the value of the firm depends on the way in which the future investment is financed.

The effect that debt financing has on the value of the firm was analyzed in terms of the interest tax shield it provides and the extent to which the firm can utilize that tax shield. In Myers' (1974, 1977) analysis we also saw that a limit on borrowing could be incorporated so that factors such as risk and the probability of insolvency would be recognized when making each capital-budgeting decisions. When compared to other methods widely used in capital budgeting, Myers' APV formulation was found to yield more conservative benefit estimates. While we do not wish to discard the equity-residual, after-tax weighted cost-of-capital method or the Arditti–Levy weighted cost-of-capital method, we set forth Myers' method as the most appropriate starting point when a firm is first considering a project, reasoning that if the project was acceptable following Myers' method, it would be acceptable using the other methods — to an even greater degree. If the project was not acceptable following the APV criteria, it could be reanalyzed with one of the other methods. The biases of each method we hopefully made clear with the introduction of debt financing.

Section 13.6 outlined practical procedures for attaining optimal capital structures subject to probability-of-insolvency constraints or costs incurred attributable to the risky debt financing. If management is able to specify the tolerance for risk, or the rate at which monitoring costs are incurred, then an upper limit on debt capacity can be stated as the amount of interest expense the firm can afford. In the case of regulated firms, we also consider capital-structure decisions, in light of the inability of the equity holders to acquire the benefits of the interest tax shield; and we concluded that regulated firms, in the best interests of their shareholders and of society, should issue debt only to the extent it does not jeopardize the equity stake or the existence of the firm. In Section 13.7, we have discussed how different policies can affect the determination of beta coefficient.

In essence, this chapter points out the vagaries and difficulties of financial management in practice. Virtually no decision concerning the finance function can be made independent of the other variables under management's control. Lambrecht and Myers (2012) have shown that investment financing and dividend decision should be jointly determined. Profitable areas of future research in this area are abundant; some have already begun to appear in the literature under the heading "simultaneous-equation planning models." Any practitioner would be well advised to stay abreast of developments in this area.

Graham and Harvey (2001) surveyed 392 CFOs about cost of capital, capital budgeting, and capital structure. What we discussed in this chapter relative to the findings of this survey is the concern for a firm's financial flexibility when issuing debt and earnings.

Furthermore, this survey analyzed how although larger firms use present value techniques and CAPM but smaller firms concentrate on the payback criterion. The pecking order theory and trade-off of capital structure hypothesis were also discussed in this survey.

## References

Alderson, M. J. and C. F. Lee. "Corporate Pension Policy and Capital Structure Decisions," *Journal of Business and Economics*, 40 (1988, pp. 209–228).

Arditti, F. D. and H. Levy. "The Weighted-Average Cost of Capital as a Cutoff Rate: A Critical Examination of the Classical Textbook Weighted Average," *Financial Management*, 6 (Fall 1977, pp. 24–34).

Barnea, A., R. A. Haugen and L. W. Senbet. "Market Imperfections, Agency Problems, and Capital Structure: A Review," *Financial Management* (Summer 1981, pp. 7–22).

Black, F. "The Dividend Puzzle," *Journal of Portfolio Management* (Winter 1976, pp. 5–8).

Black, F. and M. Scholes. "The Pricing of Options and Corporate Liabilities," *Journal of Political Economy*, 81(3) (May–June 1973, pp. 637–654).

Chambers, D. R., R. S. Harris and J. J. Pringle. "Treatment of Financing Mix in Analyzing Investment Opportunities," *Financial Management*, 11 (Summer 1982, pp. 24–41).

Chen, A. H. "Recent Development in Cost of Debt Capital," *The Journal of Finance*, 33 (1978, pp. 863–877).

Conine, T. E., Jr. "Debt Capacity and the Capital Budgeting Decision: A Comment," *Financial Management*, 9 (Spring 1980, pp. 20–22).

DeAngelo, H. and L. DeAngelo. "The Irrelevance of the MM Dividend Irrelevance Theorem," *Journal of Financial Economics*, 79 (2006, pp. 293–315).

Fama, E. F. and M. H. Miller. *The Theory of Finance* (Holt, Rinehart and Winston, New York, 1972).

Graham, J. R. and C. R. Harvey. "The Theory and Practice of Corporate Finance: Evidence from the Field," *Journal of Financial Economics*, 60(2–3) (2001, pp. 187–243).

Gupta, M. C. and A. C. Lee. "An Integrated Model of Debt Issuance, Refunding, and Maturity," *Review of Quantitative Finance and Accounting*, 26(2) (March 2006, pp. 177–199).

Gahlon, J. M. and R. D. Stover. "Debt Capacity and the Capital Budgeting Decision: A Caveat," *Financial Management*, 8 (Winter 1979, pp. 55–59).

Hamada, R. S. "The Effect of the Firm's Capital Structure on the Systematic Risk of Common Stock," *The Journal of Finance*, 27 (May 1972, pp. 435–452).
Hellwig, M. F. "Bankruptcy, Limited Liability, and the Modigliani-Miller Theorem," *The American Economic Review*, 71 (1981, pp. 155–170).
Higgins, R. C. "How Much Growth Can a Firm Afford?" *Financial Management*, 6 (Fall 1977, pp. 7–16).
Higgins, R. C. "Sustainable Growth under Inflation," *Financial Management*, 10 (Autumn 1981, pp. 36–40).
Hong, H. and A. Rappaport. "Debt Capacity and the Capital-Budgeting Decision: A Caveat," *Financial Management* (Autumn 1978, pp. 7–11).
Jensen, M. and W. Meckling. "Theory of the Firm: Managerial Behavior, Agency Costs, and Ownership Structure," *Journal of Financial Economics*, 3 (October 1976, pp. 305–360).
Johnson, D. J. "The Behavior of Financial Structure and Sustainable Growth in an Inflationary Environment," *Financial Management*, 10 (Autumn 1981, pp. 30–35).
Kim, E. H. "Miller's Equilibrium, Shareholder Leverage Clienteles, and Optimal Capital Structure," *The Journal of Finance*, 37 (May 1982, pp. 301–319).
Kim, E. H. "A Mean-Variance Theory of Optimal Capital Structure and Corporate Debt Capacity," *The Journal of Finance* (March 1978, pp. 45–64).
Kim, E. H., J. J. McConnell and P. R. Greenwood. "Capital Structure Rearrangements and Me-First Rules in an Efficient Capital Market," *The Journal of Finance*, 32 (June 1977, pp. 811–821).
Lambrecht, B. M. and S. C. Myers. "A Lintner Model of Payout and Managerial Rents," *The Journal of Finance*, 67 (2012, pp. 1761–1810).
Lee, C. F. "Investment, Financing, Dividend, and Production Policies: Review, Integration, and Extension," Working paper (Rutgers University, 2020).
Lee, C. F. and J. Lee. *Financial Analysis, Planning and Forecasting: Theory and Application* (World Scientific: Singapore, 2017).
Lee, C. F. and A. C. Lee. *Encyclopedia of Finance*, 2nd edn. (Springer, New York, 2013).
Lee, C. F., C. Wu and D. Hang. "Dividend Policy under Conditions of Capital Markets and Signaling Equilibrium," *Review of Quantitative Finance and Accounting*, 56(2) (20221, pp. 505–543).
Lee, C. F., S. Rahman and K. T. Liaw. "The Impacts of Market Power and Capital-Labor Ratio on Systematic Risk: A Cobb-Douglas

Approach," *Journal of Economics and Business* (August 1990, pp. 237–241).

Lee, C. F., K. C. Chen and K. T. Liaw. "Systematic Risk, Wage Rates, and Factor Substitution," *Journal of Economics and Business*, 47(3) (August 1995, pp. 267–279).

Lee, C. F., C. Hu and M. Foley. "Differential Effect of Inside Debt, CEO Compensation Diversification, And Firm Investment," *Review of Quantitative Finance and Accounting Accounting*, 56(2) (2021, pp. 505–543).

Lee, C. F., M. C. Gupta, H. Y. Chen and A. C. Lee. "Optimal Payout Ratio under Uncertainty and the Flexibility Hypothesis: Theory and Empirical Evidence," *Journal of Corporate Finance*, 17 (2011, pp. 483–501).

Lee, C. F., W. L. Liang, F. L. Lin and Y. Yang. "Application of Simultaneous Equation in Finance Research: Methods and Empirical Results," *Review of Quantitative Finance*, 47(4) (2016, pp. 943–971).

Litzenberger, R. H. and K. Ramaswamy. "The Effect of Personal Taxes and Dividends on Capital-Asset Prices: Theory and Empirical Evidence," *Journal of Financial Economics*, 7 (1979, pp. 163–195).

Litzenberger, R. H. and H. B. Sosin. "A Comparison of Capital-Structure Decision of Regulated and Nonregulated Firms," *Financial Management*, 8 (1979, pp. 17–21).

Malkiel, B. G. "The Valuation of Public-Utility Equity," *Bell Journal of Economics and Management Science*, 1 (Spring 1970, pp. 143–160).

Martin, J. D. and D. F. Scott. "Debt Capacity and the Capital Budgeting Decision," *Financial Management*, 5(2) (Summer 1976, pp. 7–14).

Martin, J. D. and D. F. Scott, Jr. "Debt Capacity and the Capital Budgeting Decision: A Revisitation," *Financial Management*, 9(1) (Spring 1980, pp. 23–26).

Merton, R. C. "On Pricing of Corporate Debt: The Risk Structure of Interest Rates," *The Journal of Finance*, 29 (1974, pp. 449–470).

Miller, M. H. "Debt and Taxes," *The Journal of Finance*, 32 (1977, pp. 261–275).

Modigliani, F. and M. Miller. "Corporation Income Taxes and the Cost of Capital: A Correction," *American Economic Review* (June 1963, pp. 261–297).

Modigliani, F. and M. Miller. "The Cost of Capital, Corporate Finance, and Theory of Investment," *American Economic Review* (June 1958, pp. 261–297).

Myers, S. C. "Interaction of Corporate Financing and Investment Decision," *The Journal of Finance*, 29 (1974, pp. 1–25).

Myers, S. C. "Determinants of Corporate Borrowing," *Journal of Financial Economics*, 5 (1977, pp. 147–175).

Rendleman, R. J., Jr. "The Effects of Default Risk on Firm's Investment and Financing Decisions," *Financial Management*, 7(1) (Spring 1978, pp. 45–53).

Resek, R. W. "Multidimensional Risk and the Modigliani-Miller Hypothesis," *The Journal of Finance*, 25 (1970, pp. 47–51).

Rhee, S. G. and F. L. McCarthy. "Corporate Debt Capacity and Capital-Budgeting Analysis," *Financial Management*, 11 (Summer 1982, pp. 42–50).

Rubinstein, M. E. "A Mean-Variance Synthesis of Corporate Financial Theory," *The Journal of Finance*, 28 (March 1973, pp. 167–87).

Stiglitz, J. "Some Aspects of Pure Theory of Corporate Finance: Bankruptcies and Take-overs," *Bell Journal of Economics and Management Science*, 3 (Autumn, 1972, pp. 458–482).

Tuttle, L. and R. H. Litzenberger. "Leverage, Diversification, and Capital-Market Effects on a Risk-Adjusted Capital-Budgeting Framework," *The Journal of Finance*, 23 (June 1968, pp. 427–443).

Van Horne, J. C. and J. D. McDonald. "Dividend Policy and New Equity Financing," *The Journal of Finance*, 26 (1971, pp. 507–519).

## Questions and Problems

1. Define or explain the following terms:

   a. $P/E$ ratio and dividend yield
   b. Sustainable growth in sales
   c. Levered versus unlevered beta
   d. Bond beta and equity beta
   e. APV method for capital budgeting
   f. The cost of financing for a project with portfolio effect included

2. Discuss the potential interaction between investment decisions and dividend decisions. What factors can influence the internal vs. external financing decision?
3. Briefly discuss the interaction between dividend policy and financing policy. How can they be analyzed in terms of (1) the cost of equity capital, and (2) the valuation of risky debt?
4. Discuss the interaction between financing decisions and investment decisions. How do these interactions affect capital budgeting decisions?

5. Compare the four methods used to make the capital budgeting decisions under certainty with leverage.
6. Define the concept of debt capacity, then explain how the concept of debt capacity is used in capital budgeting under uncertainty.
7. How are leveraged beta ($\beta_L$) and unleveraged beta ($\beta_U$) calculated? Also, how do risk-free and risky debt affect the estimation of $\beta_U$?
8. Using the following data, calculate the sustainable growth rate in sales.

   Profit margin of sales = 10%
   Payout ratio = 30%
   Debt-equity ratio = 50%
   Total asset-sales ratio = 55%

9. Analyze Eqs. (13.10) and (13.11) in terms of the risk-adjusted rate of return for equity and the weighted cost of capital in terms of the various applicable theories of finance.
10. Given the existence of risky debt and agency costs, explain why the maximization of shareholder value may not lead to the same decisions as the maximization of firm value.
11. Calculate the weighted average cost of capital for ABC Company, using the following information:

    Equity = 200,000 shares, at \$50 per share
    Expected rate of return on the stock = 12%
    Debt = \$10,000,000 outstanding, at book value (debt is trading at 90% of par)
    Yield to maturity = 10%
    Marginal tax rate = 40%

12. A project costs \$700,000 and has NPV of 0. Calculate this project's APV in the following cases:
    a. If the firm invests, it has to raise \$300,000 by issuing stock. Issue costs are 10% of net proceeds.
    b. If the firm invests, its debt capacity increasing by \$400,000. The present value of interest tax shields on this debt is \$60,000.
    c. If the firm invests, it sells new stock, as in Part (a), and borrows, as in Part (b).

13. The profit margin of IFCC, Inc. is 8%. The company pays out 40% of its net earnings as dividends. The total asset to sales turnover and debt-equity ratios are 60% and 50%, respectively. Calculate the firm's sustainable growth rate in sales.
14. AKM Corporation is considering a new investment proposal. The project's initial outlay is $10,000, and it has an infinite life span. Other information is as given below:

    Mean of current cash flows = $500
    Standard deviation of current CFs = $200
    Projects NOI = $50/year
    Standard deviation of project's cash flows = $10
    Risk-free rate of return = 6%
    Market rate of return = 11%
    Rate of return on equity = 13%
    Project's unlevered beta = 1.4
    Corporate tax rate = 30%
    Cost of new debt = 10%
    Correlation between the firm and new project cash flows = 0.30

    Using the Martin & Scott Method, calculate the NPV of the new investment proposal.

15. VPI Company is considering a new project with a cost of $25,000 and a life of 5 years. The project's yearly pretax operating cash revenues and expenses are $20,000 and $9,000, respectively. The additional depreciation would be $5,000 per year. The net proceeds from a new debt issue would be $10,000, with a yield of 10% that is expected to remain constant over the life of the project. The corporate tax rate is 35%, and the risk-free and market rates of return are 6% and 12%, respectively. The firm's cost of equity is 15%. Debt will be repaid at the end of the five-year period.

    Using the above information, calculate the net present value of the new proposal based on each of the following methods:

    a. Equity residual.
    b. After-tax WACC.
    c. Arditti–Levy WACC.
    d. Myers' APV (M&M proposition with corporate taxes)

16. With respect to the equity residual, after-tax WACC, Arditti–Levy WACC, and the Myer's APV methods:

a. Under what conditions does the Myers' APV model give the same answer as the other three methods?
b. Which methods are the most sensitive to the amount of debt outstanding? Explain.
c. Which method is most sensitive to the debt repayment schedule? Explain.

17. Elliot corporation has a current expected (mean) return on equity of 13% and a standard error of equity of 3%. Its current yield on debt is 8%. Elliott is currently considering four investment projects with the expected returns and standard errors of return given as follows:

| Project | Expected Return (%) | Standard Error (%) |
|---|---|---|
| A | 16 | 6 |
| B | 12 | 4 |
| C | 14 | 2 |
| D | 15 | 4 |

Respond to the following questions or problems using the Tuttle and Litzenberger method:

a. Classify the projects into one of the three categories of (1) clearly acceptable, (2) rejected without question, and (3) judgement cannot be made without consideration of the specific risk-return trade-off.
b. For those projects which can be judged only by considering the risk-return trade-off, use the risk adjusted rate-of-return assuming the project's cash flows are perfectly positively correlated with the firm's cash flows.
c. If the cash flows are not perfectly positively correlated with the firm's existing cash flows, how would your answer to Part (b) change?

# PART V

# Long-term Financing

# Chapter 14

# Long-term Debt Financing

## Contents



## 14.1 Introduction

In Chapters 14, 15, 16, and 17 we discuss various financial instruments for raising new capital. Broadly speaking, these instruments can be classified as debt or equity, or as hybrid securities involving elements of both debt and equity. In Chapter 14, we discuss long-term debt financing through the issue of corporate bonds.

We begin by discussing the formal legal aspects of the bond contract and the various types of bond issues in Section 14.2.

The attractiveness of a bond issue to investors depends not only on the bond's interest rate, but also on various provisions in the bond contract that affect the bond's perceived risk. Provisions and covenants of bonds is discussed in Section 14.3.

We then examine theories of market interest rate determination in Section 14.4. Terms of structure and yield to maturity is discussed in Section 14.5, alternative hypothesis for term structure is discussed in Section 14.6, and duration and volatility is discussed in Section 14.7. Innovations in the bond market are talked about in Section 14.8, and Section 14.9 summarizes the chapter.

## 14.2 The Bond Contract

To finance its operations, a corporation may issue many different kinds of debt. In this chapter, we discuss the most common instrument of long-term debt financing — the public issue of bonds. In effect, the purchaser of a bond is making a loan to the issuing corporation at a given interest rate for a specific period of time, which may range up to 30 years. Thus, bondholders are creditors of the issuing corporation. As such, they have an interest in the future welfare of the corporation and require some protection for their investment. This protection is generally specified in an *indenture*, which is a legal contract between the issuing corporation and the bondholders, written at the time that the bonds are issued. A *trustee*, typically a bank, is appointed to oversee the bondholders' interests, with the responsibility of verifying that the issuing corporation will continue to meet the terms of the indenture.

An indenture is a complex and lengthy legal document, and we pause here to discuss just a few of its elements. Later in the chapter, we will examine some of the more detailed provisions and covenants that may be included in an indenture.

The bond contract sets out the term of the loan, the interest payments that are to be made, and the method of payment. In the typical bond issue, interest payments of fixed amounts are made at regular intervals, often semiannually. Failure to meet a scheduled interest payment constitutes a breach of the terms of the bond contract. In such an eventuality, bondholders have the right to demand immediate repayment of the entire loan. This feature of the indenture provides considerable protection for bondholders.

In recent years, a number of variants of the usual interest rate payment structure have become popular. For example, bonds may be issued with *variable interest rates*, where the actual rate paid is related to some published index, such as the Treasury bill rate. The advantage of such an arrangement to the bondholder is its protection against declining bond value should interest rates rise. On the other hand, should interest rates fall, the issuing corporation will not be tied into a disadvantageous interest payment schedule.

The *fixed-rate noncallable bond* places all of the interest rate risk on the issuer. This means that if interest rates fall after the issuance of the bond, the corporation is stuck with paying the higher rate of interest for its debt. The *variable-rate bond* and the *callable bond* place the interest rate risk on the investor. With the variable-rate bond, if rates fall the corporation must pay the new market rates determined by the index to which the bond is tied. In the case of callable bonds, the issuer can *call* the old higher-rate issues and refinance them with new lower-rate debt.

Another instrument that has achieved some popularity in recent years is the *zero coupon bond.* This type of bond is issued at a large discount under par value and is repaid at par at the end of its term. However, no interest payments are made over the term. In effect, zero coupon bonds offer the holder a guaranteed compound interest rate over the term of the bond. Such an arrangement is particularly attractive to tax-exempt institutions, such as pension funds, because the interest rate is assured over the life of the bond and there is no need to reinvest a stream of interest payments as with regular bonds. Zero coupon bonds are less attractive to taxpayers because the Internal Revenue Service does not treat the difference between par value and purchase price as capital gains. Instead, imputed interest payments in each year are treated as ordinary income.[1]

There are several advantages of zero coupon bonds to the issuing corporation. Principal and interest do not have to be paid until

---

[1]However, the 1986 Tax Act removed the differential tax rate treatment for capital gains and ordinary income.

the bond matures. Nevertheless, interest payments may be amortized for tax purposes over the life of the bond, so that tax savings accrue in a steady flow before any payments must actually be made. Also, because of their attractiveness to tax-exempt institutions, which constitute a large segment of the market of bond purchasers, zero coupon bonds generally can be sold at a lower effective interest rate than regular bonds.

The major disadvantage of zero coupon bonds to the issuing corporation is the serious impact on cash flows that occurs when an issue of zero coupon bonds matures. This is the so-called crisis-at-maturity risk that the corporation must face by either refinancing the maturity issue or generating sufficient cash to pay off the bondholders.

### 14.2.1 *Secured bonds*

In addition to interest payment terms, bond purchasers require some protection in the bond contract against default. This could be provided by a claim on the issuing corporation's assets. An example is a *mortgage bond*, which is secured by the physical assets of the issuing corporation; in the event of default, these assets may be sold to pay off the debt. For instance, a corporation planning to build a new plant may issue bonds and pledge that plant as security. More typically, mortgage bonds provide a claim against *all* of the issuing corporation's property. Holders of this type of bond will require indenture guarantees that the corporation will carry out the necessary maintenance work to maintain the value of the property in question and will purchase insurance on that property.

### 14.2.2 *Unsecured bonds*

An *unsecured bond*, which provides no claim against specific corporate property, is called a *debenture*, and the vast majority of corporate debt issued today falls into this category. Debentures are said to be *senior* if they constitute a first claim on corporate assets in the event of default. If other creditors have priority, the debenture is said to be *subordinated*. In the event of a default, the priority of claim on corporate assets is important to bondholders and will influence (all other things equal), the interest rate demanded for purchase of debt. This is why the terms of priority in claims on assets are spelled out in the bond contract.

### 14.2.3 *Rating agencies*

The best-known and most widely accepted measure of a bond issue's credit quality is the rating assigned by various independent rating agencies. The rating given to a corporate security affects its marketability and the yield the corporation must pay to raise additional funds. Table 14.1 lists the rating systems used by the major rating agencies.

Table 14.1 Rating System Used by the Major Rating Agencies (Shaded Area Indicates Ratings Considered Below Investment Grade).

| | **New Moody's** | **Former Moody's** | **Standard & Poor's** | **Duff & Phelps** |
|---|---|---|---|---|
| Best quality, smallest degree of risk | Aaa | Aaa | AAA | 1 |
| High quality, slightly | Aa1 | Aa | AA+ | 2 |
| more long-term risk | Aa2 | | AA | 3 |
| than top rating | Aa3 | | AA− | 4 |
| Upper-medium grade, | A1 | A | A+ | 5 |
| possible impairment | A2 | | A | 6 |
| in the future | A3 | | A− | 7 |
| Medium-grade, lack | Baa1 | Baa | BBB+ | 8 |
| outstanding | Baa2 | | BBB | 9 |
| investment characteristics | Baa3 | | BBB− | 10 |
| Speculative issues, | Ba1 | Ba | BB+ | 11 |
| protection may be | Ba2 | | BB | 12 |
| very moderate | Ba3 | | BB− | 13 |
| Very speculative, may | B1 | B | B+ | 14 |
| have small assurance | B2 | | B | |
| of interest and principal payments | B3 | | B− | |
| Issues in poor standing, may be in default | Caa | Caa | CCC | |
| Speculative in a high degree, with market shortcomings | Ca | Ca | CC | |
| Lowest quality, poor | C | C | C | |
| prospects of attaining real investment standing | | | D | |

For most federally chartered financial institutions, there are regulations that limit the quality of bonds in which they can invest. Any rating Baa or above is considered investment quality, whereas any rating below this level is considered speculative (below investment grade).

A question that arises when considering the service that the rating agencies provide is, Are these rating agencies better able to identify and relate the default risk of a bond than are other market participants? The answer is based on two factors: (1) the amount and (2) the quality of the information used by the rating agencies to analyze this information and forecast the likelihood of default. Most financial executives and financial institution regulators act as if the rating agencies can perform their evaluation function better than other market participants.[2]

## 14.3 Provisions and Covenants of Bonds

When a corporation issues bonds, the indenture constitutes a legal contract with the bondholders. The *provisions* and *covenants* of that contract — together with investors' expectations about the future course of interest rates and assessments of the riskiness of the issuing corporation's operations — contribute to the perceived value of the bond and hence to the interest rate that must be offered to raise the needed capital.[3]

The provisions of a corporate bond issue stipulate when interest payments are to be made. As we have already noted, such stipulations are of value to the bondholders. Failure to make these payments constitutes default, in which case full payment of principal and accrued interest can be demanded.

Generally, long-term corporate bond indentures also contain provision for a *sinking fund* to secure the orderly retirement of a debt issue over time. Payments to this fund may be mandatory or optional. Debt retirement through a sinking fund may, at the discretion of the issuing corporation, be administered in one of two ways. The

---

[2]See Kaplan and Horwitz (1979) and Wakeman (1986) for further discussion about bond rating.

[3]See Ang (1975, 1978), Smith and Warner (1979), Malitz (1986), Finnerty (1983), and Livingston (1987) for further discussion about bond covenants and refunding.

corporation may either purchase its bonds on the open market retire a stipulated percentage of the issue, the specific bonds to be retired being determined by lottery.

The provision of a mandatory sinking funds involves one factor that enhances bond value and another that reduces bond value. As with stipulated interest payments, the requirement of sinking-fund contributions is a legal obligation, and failure to meet this obligation leads to default. Thus, a mandatory sinking fund reduces the riskiness of a bond and therefore increases its value. On the other hand, if interest rates have fallen since the issue date, so that the bond price has risen, the corporation will elect to redeem part of the issue. Investors then face the possibility of losing some of their unrealized capital gains. In general, it is not possible to determine the net effect of a mandatory sinking funds on bond value. Broadly speaking, the more secure the issuing corporation, so that the less likely the perceived probability of default, the lower the value to the bondholder of the legal obligation to make sinking-fund payments.

By contrast, the provision for optional sinking-fund payments, allowing for retirement of a percentage of the debt at the discretion of the corporation, unambiguously reduces the bond's value. The reason is that the corporation will take up such an option only if the bond price is above par.

Many bond contracts contain a *call provision* giving the issuing corporation the right to redeem the bond at specific times at premiums over par value. The size of these premiums typically depends on when the call option is exercised. The attraction to the issuing corporation of a call option is that if interest rates fall and bond prices rise over time, the call option provides the opportunity to retire high coupon debt and refinance by issuing new debt or common stock. From the bondholder's perspective, the call provision imposes ceilings on the value to which a bond can rise at particular points of time. Hence, all other things equal, a higher coupon interest rate will be required on a bond with a call provision than on a bond without such a provision.

### 14.3.1 *Bond refunding*

When management issues a callable bond, it faces the decision of deciding when to call the bond. Using the NPV format developed for capital budgeting decisions in Chapter 6, we can reformulate the

NPV equation for the bond refunding decision. The NPV of refunding an outstanding bond issue is

$$\text{NPV} = \sum_{t=1}^{N} \frac{I_C - I_B}{(1 + k_B)^t} - C \tag{14.1}$$

where $I_C$ is the current after-tax interest costs of the old bond issue; $I_B$ is the after-tax interest cost of the new bond issue, $C$ is the cost of refunding the bond issue, including transaction costs, call premiums, and other costs; and $k_B$ is the before-tax rate on new debt.

If the NPV is positive, the costs are less than the present value of the benefits and the bond issue should be refunded. If the NPV is negative, the issue should not be refunded. The cost of new debt is used in the analysis because at the time of the refunding decision all of the information about $I_C$, $I_B$, $C$, and $N$ is known with certainty.

To show how the NPV is used in this case, we present the following example. A firm has \$10 million worth of a 15% callable bond issue outstanding, with ten years to maturity. The current interest rate on similar bonds is 10%. The after-tax cost of refunding the issue is \$15 per bond. This includes the payment of the call premium and other costs required to refund the bond on an after-tax basis. The firm is in a 30% tax bracket. The NPV analysis is as follows:

$$\begin{aligned}
I_C &= (1 - \text{Tax rate}) \times \text{Interest rate of old bonds} \\
&\quad \times \text{Amount of old bond} \\
&= (1 - 0.3)(0.15)(10{,}000{,}000) = \$1{,}050{,}000 \\
I_B &= (1 - \text{Tax rate}) \times \text{Interest rate of new bond} \\
&\quad \times \text{Amount of new bond} \\
&= (1 - 0.3)(0.10)(10{,}000{,}000) = \$700{,}000 \\
C &= (\text{Amount of bonds outstanding} \div \$1{,}000 \text{ Per bond}) \\
&\quad \times \text{after} - \text{Tax cost of refunding per bond} \\
&= \frac{10{,}000{,}000}{1{,}000} \times \$15 = \$150{,}000
\end{aligned}$$

$$\text{NPV} = \sum_{t=1}^{N} \frac{I_C - I_B}{(1+k_B)^t} - C$$

$$= \sum_{t=1}^{10} \frac{(\$1{,}050{,}000 - 700{,}000)}{(1+0.1)^t} - \$150{,}000 = \$2{,}000{,}598$$

In this case, the firm should refund the existing bond issue because this would increase the firm's value by over $2 million.

Corporate bond contracts invariably contain other covenants as a result of the inherent conflicting interests of bondholders and stockholders. At the time the bond is issued, the bondholder should be able to assess the riskiness of the issuing corporation and its business environment. Therefore, it should be possible to estimate subjectively the probability of default. However, the bondholder will also want some assurance that the corporation will not subsequently take action that will increase the probability of default. Therefore, indentures typically contain *restrictive covenants* requiring the issuing corporation to meet specific standards, as verified by the trustee. These covenants may include restrictions on certain leasing arrangements or limitations on the size of future dividend payments in relation to earnings. We have seen the bondholder-stockholder conflict, or agency problems, in our discussions of capital structure in Chapter 11 and dividends in Chapter 12. All of the covenants and restrictions in the bond indenture are directly related to resolving agency problems.

As we have seen, bond value depends on the term to maturity, macroeconomic factors such as expectations about future inflation, and specific call provisions in the bond contract. It also depends on investors' perceptions about default risk, which in turn are influenced by the specific provisions and covenants of the bond contract and by the financial position of the issuing corporation. Suck risk assessment is difficult for the individual investor. However, bond rating agencies, such as Standard and Poor's and Moody's, regularly classify corporate bonds into risk categories; should circumstances change during the life of a bond, the bonds may be reclassified. Investors have access to this information so that, all other things equal, the higher the bond rating (that is, the lower the assessed riskiness), the lower the required interest rate.

## 14.4 Interest Rate Theory

A corporation issuing bonds must be concerned with the rate of interest that must be offered to raise needed capital. Accordingly, we now turn to the factors that determine interest rates. The classical treatise on this subject was published by Irving Fisher in 1930.

To begin, it is convenient to imagine a world of stable prices with no inflation. We can think of the interest rate as *the price that must be paid for borrowed funds.* As in any market, this price is determined through the interaction of demand and supply. Corporations demand borrowed funds in the expectation that these funds can be invested in profitable projects. Of course, the lower the interest rate that must be paid on new debt, the greater the number of profitable investment opportunities and hence the higher the demand for borrowed funds. Thus, demand is a function in which the quantity of borrowed funds demanded is inversely related to the level of interest.

Turning to the supply side, lenders of funds are, in effect, foregoing immediate consumption opportunities in accumulating savings. Interest earned can be viewed as the price that is paid to induce these savings. Interest earned can be viewed as the price that is paid to induce these savings. It is reasonable to expect that, all else equal, the higher the level of interest, the greater the level of savings that will be induced, and hence the higher the amount of money available for borrowing.

In Figure 14.1 we have graphed demand for and supply of borrowed funds as functions of the interest rate. Equilibrium in this market occurs at the point at which these curves intersect. Thus, the equilibrium interest rate, $r$, is the rate at which demand for borrowed funds equals the supply of these funds. This is the rate of interest that we should expect to prevail in this market. For example, suppose that the actual interest rate is at some higher level $r*$. In that case, the supply of borrowed funds available would exceed demand for those funds. Borrowers would then offer lower interest rates for the excess funds, and rates would be bid down to the equilibrium level, $r$.

Given Fisher's supply and demand model for interest rate determination, we now determine how the equilibrium interest rate might evolve over time. This rate will change if the supply or demand curve shifts. For example, consider the position in Figure 14.2, where we

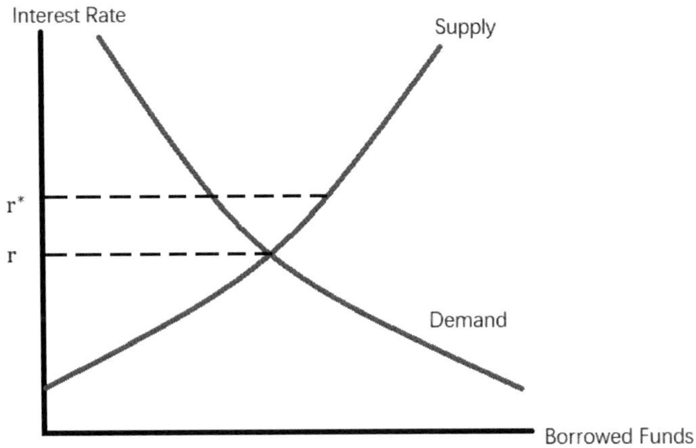


Figure 14.1 Demand and Supply for Borrowed Funds, Determining the Equilibrium Interest Rate.

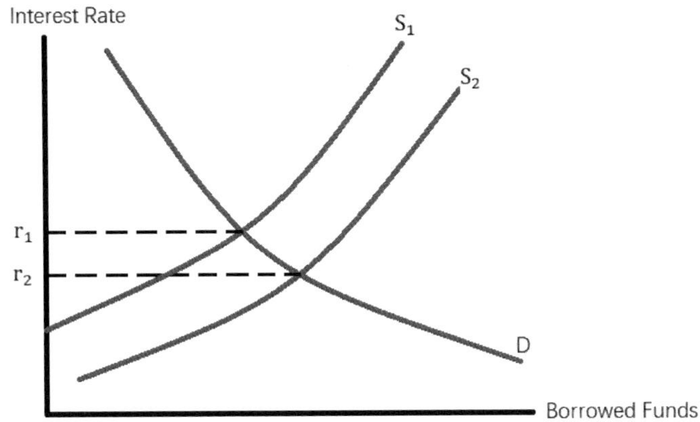


Figure 14.2 Shift in Supply Curve Inducing Change in the Equilibrium Interest Rate.

have again graphed a single demand curve, $D$. Suppose, however, that at any given level of interest rates, the supply of funds available for borrowing increases, so that the supply function shifts from $S_1$ to $S_2$. This shift induces a fall in the equilibrium interest rate from $r_1$ to $r_2$.

We have seen that a shift in the supply function leads to a change in the equilibrium interest rate. A shift in the demand function will similarly induce such a change. We now determine the factors that might cause shifts in the demand and supply functions for borrowed funds.

The aggregate demand of corporations for borrowed funds, at any given interest rate, depends on corporate perceptions of the prospects for profitable investments. Such perceptions alter with changing views about likely future levels of economic activity and also with the development of new technologies. However, over time it is reasonable to expect changes of this sort to be gradual and modest.

The aggregate supply of savings, at any interest level, depends on the wealth of the population and the distribution of that wealth among members of the population. It can also depend on demographic factors, because members of certain age groups save higher propositions of their incomes. These factors also can be expected to exhibit considerable stability from one year to the next.

Thus, as a consequence of the Fisher theory, in an inflation-free world the equilibrium interest rate changes only gradually over time.

However, we cannot be content with this conclusion as a theory about the real-world behavior of interest rates. We live in a world of inflation and, more-over, in a world in which the rate of price inflation changes considerably over the years and in which there is considerable uncertainty about future inflation levels. Therefore, the next step in our discussion is to examine Fisher's theory in the presence of inflation.

### 14.4.1 *Inflation and Fisher model*

Suppose that \$1,000 is invested for one year at an actual, or *nominal*, interest rate of 10%. At the end of this term, the investor will receive \$1,100. However, if prices increase over the year, this money will not purchase as much as it did one year earlier. For example, if the general level of prices in the economy increased by 6% over the year, a bundle of goods costing \$1,100 at the end of the year could have been purchased for 1,100/1.06 = \$1,037.74 at the beginning of the year. In this sense, we say that the *real* return to the investor is not 10% but

$$\frac{1{,}037.74 - 1{,}000}{1{,}000} \cong 0.0377$$

or 3.77%. Fisher argued that it is not the nominal rate but rather the real rate of interest on which supply and demand depend in capital markets. One difficulty with the practical interpretation of this hypothesis is that the real rate of return actually realized depends on future rates of inflation, which are not known with certainty. Rather, it is postulated that market participants form *expectations* about future inflation rates.

If \$1 is invested at nominal interest rate $r_{\text{nominal}}$ for one year, then $\$(1 + r_{\text{nominal}})$ will be received at the end of the year. However, if an inflation rate of $i_e$ is expected over the year, the purchasing power of this money at the beginning of the year would be $\$(1 + r_{\text{nominal}})/(1 + i_e)$. Thus, the real rate of return expected on this investment will be

$$\frac{1 + r_{\text{nominal}}}{1 + i_e} - 1 = r$$

from which we obtain the expression

$$1 + r_{\text{nominal}} = (1 + r_{\text{real}})(1 + i_e) \tag{14.2}$$

Returning to our previous example, if the expected inflation rate is 6% and the nominal interest rate is 10%, so that $r_{\text{nominal}} = 0.10$ and $i_e = 0.06$, then the real rate of interest perceived by market participants is

$$r_{\text{real}} = \frac{1 + 0.10}{1 + 0.06} - 1 = 0.0377$$

confirming our earlier calculations.

Returning to Eq. (14.2), we have

$$1 + r_{\text{nominal}} = 1 + r_{\text{real}} + i_e + r_{\text{real}} i_e$$

so that

$$r_{\text{nominal}} = r_{\text{real}} + i_e + r_{\text{real}} i_e$$

In practice, this expression is often simplified by noting that $r_{real}$ and $i_e$ are usually quite small, so that their product will also be small and, as an approximation, can be neglected. Thus, while acknowledging that in a highly inflationary economy such an approximation would be very crude, we write

$$r_{\text{nominal}} = r_{\text{real}} + i_e$$

so that

$$\text{Nominal rate of interest} \cong \text{Real rate of interest} + \text{Expected inflation} \qquad (14.3)$$

In Fisher's model, market participants are assumed to base decisions on the real interest rate. According to our earlier argument, this rate is expected to change only gradually over time. The implication from Eq. (14.2) in that case is that changes in the nominal rate of interest prevailing in an economy are the result of changes in expectations about future price inflation.

As we have noted, there is some difficulty in checking the validity of Fisher's theory as it applies to the real world. The classic work on this topic was done by Eugene Fama (1975), who argued that in an efficient capital market, where participants optimally predict future inflation rates, actual future inflation rates can be expressed as the difference between the nominal rate and the real rate, the latter of which should be constant, plus a random error term incorporating the difference between actual and expected inflation. Hence, we should find

$$i_a = -r_{\text{real}} + r_{\text{nominal}} + \text{Random error}$$

where $i_a$ is the actual observed inflation rate. Thus, according to Fisher's theory, in an efficient market, in the expression

$$i_a = \alpha + \beta r_{\text{nominal}} + \text{Random error}$$

we should find $\alpha$ and $\beta$ constant over time, with $\alpha$ equal to the negative of the real interest rate, and $\beta$ equal to 1. Using data on Treasury bill rates and the consumer price index, Fama employed regression methods applied to observations from January 1953 to July 1971 and found support for the Fisher hypothesis. However, this study did lead to some controversy, and Fama later (1977) accepted many of the arguments of other researchers. A particularly forceful criticism is that Fama's sample period was atypical in comparison with earlier or subsequent experience in that inflation rates were relatively stable over these years. Using an extended sample, through 1980, Newbold and Bos (1985) found a relationship between interest rates and inflation that changed quite markedly over time.

The evidence available on the Fisher hypothesis is mixed. There can be little doubt that changes in inflationary expectations induce similar changes in nominal interest rates. However, in actual markets it is far from clear that the real rate of interest is approximately constant over time. Real-world factors — such as maturity risk, default risk, and liquidity risk — may be constantly changing over time and thereby cause interest rates of change. By *maturity risk* we mean that the longer the life of the bond, other things equal, the greater the chance of default. Hence, the normal structure of the yield curve is upward-sloping. The riskier the issues of the security, the higher the interest rate because of the increase in the probability of default. During periods of recession, investors may demand a higher default premium (higher interest rate) than during periods of economic prosperity. Each bond investor has different liquidity requirements, and as we have seen, certain bonds are actively traded while others are not. Thus, the degree of liquidity of an individual issue has an effect on the interest rate of the bond.

## 14.5 Term of Structure and Yield to Maturity

In the previous section, we saw how the general level of interest rates might depend on expectations about inflation rates. In this section, we discuss the relationship between interest rates and the *term* of a bond. To illustrate, suppose you purchase for \$750 a bond with par value of \$1,000, with coupon interest payments of 6%, and eight years to maturity. For simplicity, we will assume that all payments are made annually. The stream of payments received at the end of each of the next eight years will be \$60, \$60, \$60, \$60, \$60, \$60, \$60, and \$1,060.

Suppose that in computing the present values of these payments, we use interest rates $r_1, r_2, \ldots, r_8 = 6\%$. The present value of the payments received will be

$$\begin{aligned} PV = {} & \frac{60}{(1+r_1)^1} + \frac{60}{(1+r_2)^2} + \frac{60}{(1+r_3)^3} + \frac{60}{(1+r_4)^4} + \frac{60}{(1+r_5)^5} \\ & + \frac{60}{(1+r_6)^6} + \frac{60}{(1+r_7)^7} + \frac{1{,}060}{(1+r_8)^8} \end{aligned} \tag{14.4}$$

If all market participants discount at these rates, and if the market is efficient, this present value will be the price of the bond: \$750.

In computing bond yields, dealers do not compute a series of discount rates but rather a single yield to maturity, based on the assumption that the discount rate remains unchanged over different time horizons. Thus, setting $r_i$ equal to $r(i = 1, 2, \ldots, 8)$ in Eq. (14.4) and equating present value and purchase price, we find

$$\text{PV} = \frac{60}{(1+r)^1} + \frac{60}{(1+r)^2} + \frac{60}{(1+r)^3} + \frac{60}{(1+r)^4} + \frac{60}{(1+r)^5} + \frac{60}{(1+r)^6} + \frac{60}{(1+r)^7} + \frac{1{,}060}{(1+r)^8}$$

The yield to maturity, then, is the value satisfying Eq. (14.4), which is simply the familiar internal rate of return. In fact, the solution to this equation is 0.109, so that yield to maturity for this bond is 10.9%. Many pocket calculators are equipped to make yield to maturity calculations, and bond dealers employ extensive tables for this purpose.

In spite of the fact that bond dealers concentrate much attention on yield-to-maturity calculations and the regular publication of these rates, they are of limited worth in valuing bonds. The reason is that only rarely will investors have a constant discount rate for income streams over all time horizons. In fact, if expectations about inflation rates vary in different years, then so will the discount rates demanded by investors. To illustrate, consider two bonds, both treasury securities, for which risk of default is negligible. Each bond has face value of \$1,000 and matures in two years. Further details are shown in Table 14.2.

A quick look at Table 14.2 suggests that since bond A has the higher yield to maturity, it is the better buy, or equivalently that the market is inefficient in setting these prices. However, this need not be

Table 14.2 Data on Bonds that Mature in Two Years.

| **Bond** | **Coupon Interest Rate (%)** | **Price (\$)** | **Yield to Maturity (%)** |
|---|---|---|---|
| A | 6 | 932.11 | 9.91 |
| B | 12 | 1,037.77 | 9.82 |

Table 14.3 Present Value Calculations for Two Bonds, Discounting at 7% in Year 1 and 10% in Year 2.

| | **Bond A** | | **Bond B** | |
|---|---|---|---|---|
| | **Dollar Receipts ($)** | **Present Value** | **Dollar Receipts ($)** | **Present Value** |
| Year 1 | 60 | 56.075 | 120 | 112.150 |
| Year 2 | 1,060 | 876.033 | 1,120 | 925.620 |
| Total | | 932.110 | | 1,037.770 |

the case. Suppose that in year 1, investors discount receipts at 7%, but because rapid economic expansion and accelerated inflation are expected, second year payments are discounted at 10%. Table 14.3 shows how these assumptions affect the present value calculations. For bond A, $60 is to be received in one year, and the present value of this receipt is

$$\frac{60}{(1+0.07)} = \$56.075$$

At the end of the second year, the investor receives the $1,000 face value of the bond plus a $60 interest payment. The present value is

$$\frac{1{,}060}{(1+0.10)^2} = \$876.033$$

Hence, the 3 total present value, to the nearest cent, of receipts from bond A is $932.11. Notice from Table 14.2 that this is the purchase price of the bond. In exactly the same way, we find that the total present value of receipts for bond B is its purchase price. A further look at Table 14.3 should explain why bond A has a higher yield to maturity than bond B. Notice that a higher proportion of the total receipts for bond A will be received at the end of the second year than for bond B. However, given the expectation of accelerating inflation, investors will find such an arrangement relatively unattractive.

Another way of summarizing the conclusion of our example is that two-year interest rates are higher than one-year rates. We thus conclude that in studying bond yields it is necessary to examine the term structure of interest rates, rather than just concentrate on yield to maturity only.

Table 14.4 Receipts from \$2,000 Invested in Bond A and \$1,000 in Bond B.

| | Receipts from Bond A (\$) | Receipts from Bond B (\$) | Difference (\$) |
|---|---|---|---|
| Year 1 | 120 | 120 | 0 |
| Year 2 | 2,120 | 1,120 | 1,000 |

Our example can be taken further to demonstrate how the term structure of interest rates can be inferred in an efficient market. Specifically, we will confirm from the data of Table 14.2 that if this market if efficient, the two-year rate is indeed 10%. Faced with the market described in Table 14.2, consider an investor able to purchase two units of bond A or one unit of bond B. This position is shown in Table 14.4. In either case, \$120 will be received at the end of the first year, so that the only difference is that the bond A purchaser will receive an extra \$1,000 at the end of the second year. To achieve this extra return will initially cost an extra

$$(2)(932.11) - 1{,}037.77 = \$826.45$$

Therefore, if this market is efficient, the present value of \$1,000 in two years is \$826.45. This implies a two-year interest rate $r_2$ satisfying

$$826.45 = \frac{1{,}000}{(1+r)^2}$$

so that

$$r_2 = \sqrt{\frac{1{,}000}{826.45}} - 1 = 0.10$$

This is merely a reversal of our earlier calculations. Initially, we assumed a two-year interest rate of 10% in verifying that this market is efficient. Now we have shown that market efficiency implies a two-year interest rate of 10%.

In the next section, we explore various hypotheses regarding the term structure of interest rates in efficient markets.

## 14.6 Alternative Hypothesis for Term Structure

Observation suggest that interest rates on bonds depend on the term to maturity. Most commonly, we find interest rates increasing

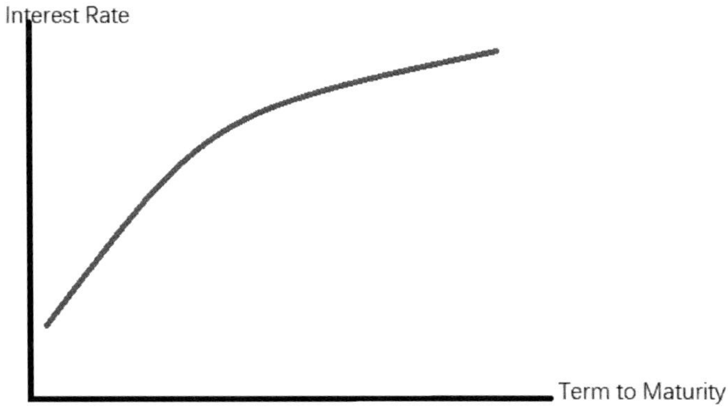


Figure 14.3 Typical Structure of Interest Rates.

with increases in terms, s depicted in Figure 14.3, where we show a situation in which interest rates increase, but at a decreasing rate, with increasing term to maturity. However, such a structure invariably does not prevail, and, on some occasions, short-term rates are higher than long-term rates.

In this section, we discuss various theories that have been advanced to explain the term structure of interest rates. Our concern here is not with the general level of interest rates in an economy, but with the dependence of rates on term to maturity. In our discussion, it will be convenient to ignore the possibility of default and also the possibility of different tax treatments of alternative investment strategies. In effect, our discussion applies strictly to Treasury bills.

### 14.6.1 *The traditional-expectations hypothesis*

Suppose that we are at time 0 and looking into the future, so that times 1, 2, etc., refer to one year ahead, two years ahead, and so on. As before, we use the notation $r_n$ = the current, or *spot rate*, or an $n$-period security.

Our aim is to explain the relationship among the spot rates $r_1, r_2, r_3, \ldots$. The *traditional-expectations hypothesis* assumes that bond-market participants look ahead and make predictions, or form expectations, about the spot rates that will prevail in the future. To represent such expectations, we employ the notation ${}_ir_k^e$ = the expected rate on a $k$-period security $i$ periods into the future.

Consider an investor with two alternatives for the same dollar investment:

1. Purchase a two-year bond and hold to maturity.
2. Purchase a one-year bond, and, when this matures, invest the proceeds in a second one-year bond.

Using the first strategy, for each dollar invested, the investor will receive $\$(1+r_2)^2$ at the end of the second year. With the second strategy, dollar receipts at the end of the second year cannot be known with certainty. However, we can ask what return will be *expected* at this time. At the end of the first year, our investor will have $\$(1+r_1)$ for the purchase of a new one-year bond. At time 0, the expected rate of return on such a bond is ${}_1r_1^e$. Hence, at the end of the second year, the expected return per each dollar initially invested is $\$(1+r_1)(1+{}_1r_1^e)$.

According to the traditional-expectations hypothesis, in an efficient bond market interest rates adjust to equilibrium levels at which the expected returns from these two strategies are equal. Therefore, we must have

$$(1+r_2) = [(1+r_1)(1+{}_1r_1^e)]^{\frac{1}{2}}$$

so that

$$(1+r_2)^2 = (1+r_1)(1+{}_1r_1^e) \tag{14.5}$$

Suppose that we observe a one-year rate of 8% and a two-year rate of 8.5%. The implication of the traditional-expectations hypothesis is that the one-year rate expected in one year's time must be such that

$$1+{}_1r_1^e = \frac{(1+r_2)^2}{(1+r_1)} = \frac{(1.085)^2}{1.08} = 1.090$$

Hence,

$${}_1r_1^e = 0.090$$

so that the expected one-year rate a year in the future is 9%. Under this hypothesis, the two-year spot rate is higher than the one-year spot rate because of market participants' expectations of a larger spot rate in a year's time. Notice that the two-year spot rate is approximately the average of the current and expected one-year rates.

Our example assumed a two-year horizon, but is easily generalized to longer holding periods. Let $n$ be any positive integer, and consider the alternatives of purchasing a single $n$-year bond, or a stream of $n$ one-year bonds. According to the traditional-expectations hypothesis, equilibrium interest rates must be

$$(1 + r_n)^n = [(1 + r_1)(1 + {}_1r_1^e)(1 + {}_2r_1^e)(1 + {}_2r_1^e) \cdots (1 + {}_{n-1}r_1^e)] \tag{14.6}$$

where ${}_tr_1^e$ is the expected one-year rate at time $t$ for $t = 1, 2, \ldots, n-1$. Therefore, in equilibrium, we find that

$$(1 + r_n) = [(1 + r_1)(1 + {}_1r_1^e)(1 + {}_2r_1^e) \cdots (1 + {}_{n-1}r_1^e)]^{\frac{1}{n}} \tag{14.7}$$

This expression is rather complicated, but to a reasonably close approximation, the $n$-year spot rate can be expressed as the average of the current one-year spot rate and the next $n - 1$ expected one-year rates; that is,

$$r_n \cong \frac{r_1 + {}_1r^e + {}_2r_1^e + \cdots + {}_{n-1}r_1^e}{n}$$

According to the traditional-expectations hypothesis, in general, long-term rates will be higher than short-term rates if market participants expect an increase in the general level of interest rates in the future. Conversely, if a decline in interest rates is expected, short-term rates should be higher than long-term rates.

To this point, our discussion of the traditional-expectations hypothesis is incomplete, as we have assumed implicitly that bonds will be held to maturity. However, such an assumption is not essential, as we now illustrate. Consider an investor with a one-year time horizon and facing the following two alternatives:

1. Purchase a one-year bond.
2. Purchase a two-year bond, and sell it at the end of the first year.

At the end of the first year, the strategy 1 will yield $\$(1 + r_1)$. Consider now the second strategy, whose yield per dollar will depend on price movements in the bond market. The expected return per dollar will be the expected present value at the end of the first year of the two-year bond. This is simply the second-year dollar return discounted at the expected one-year rate at the end of the first year.[4] Thus, we find

$$\text{Expected present value of two year bond after one year} = \frac{(1+r_2)^2}{1+{}_1r_1^e}$$

According to the expectations theory, for an efficient market in equilibrium we should find equality of expected returns for these two strategies, so that

$$1+r_1 = \frac{(1+r_2)^2}{1+{}_1r_1^e} \tag{14.8}$$

which is equivalent to the equilibrium condition of Eq. (14.5).

### 14.6.2 *Forward rates*

Even if the traditional-expectations hypothesis is not accepted, it provides us with a useful mechanism for defining *forward interest rates.* Suppose that the prevailing spot rates in a bond market are $r_1, r_2, r_3, \ldots$. Consider again the investor who can hold a two-year bond to maturity or purchase two one-year bonds in successive years. Under the first alternative, $\$(1+r_2)^2$ per dollar invested will be returned at the end of the second year. Under the second alternative, suppose that the $\$(1+r_1)$ received at the end of the first year is invested at rate ${}_1f_1$ for one year. Then, the dollar returns will be equal provided that

$$(1+r_1)(1+{}_1f_1) = (1+r_2)^2$$

or

$$1+{}_1f_1 = \frac{(1+r_2)^2}{(1+r_1)} \tag{14.9}$$

Thus, the prevailing term structure implies not only that an investor can currently secure a one-year rate $r_1$, but that by purchasing a

---

[4]In fact, in arguing this way we have made the simplifying assumption that the expected value of the reciprocal of a random variable is the reciprocal for its expectation. This is not strictly true, but should provide an adequate approximation if uncertainty about the expectation is not too great.

two-year bond, the investor can also secure in a year's time a one-year rate of ${}_1f_1$. Hence, we refer to this quantity as a *forward rate*, so that ${}_1f_1$ = one-year forward rate for year 1. More generally, we could define ${}_1f_1$ = one-year forward rate for year $t$.

Notice, by comparing Eqs. (14.5) and (14.9) that if the traditional-expectations hypothesis is correct, forward interest rates must be equal to expected spot rates, so that

$$ {}_1f_1 = {}_1r_1^e $$

Now, given current spot rates, we can compute the implied one-year forward rates. Consider the following two investment alternatives:

1. Purchase an $n$-year bond, and hold to maturity.
2. Purchase an $(n-1)$ = year bond, hold to maturity, and invest the proceeds in a one-year bond.

At maturity, the first alternative yields $\$(1+r_n)^n$ per dollar invested, while the second alternative yields $\$(1+r_{n+1})^{n-1}$ at time $(n-1)$. If this second amount can then be invested at rate ${}_{n-1}f_1$, the two end-period returns will be equal if

$$ (1+r_n)^n = (1+r_{n-1})^{n-1}(1+{}_{n-1}f_1) $$

so that the one-year forward rate at time $(n-1)$ implied by this term structure is

$$ {}_{n-1}f_1 = \frac{(1+r_n)^n}{(1+r_{n-1})^{n-1}} - 1 \tag{14.10} $$

To illustrate, suppose that spot rates are $r_1 = 0.080$, $r_2 = 0.085$, $r_3 = 0.088$, $r_4 = 0.090$, and $r_5 = 0.091$. This structure implies that the one-year forward rate in year 4 is

$$ {}_4f_1 = \frac{(1+r_5)^5}{(1+r_4)^4} - 1 = \frac{(1.091)^5}{(1.090)^4} - 1 = 0.095 $$

Employing Eq. (14.7) in this way, the one-year forward rates that can be computed from the above spot rates are ${}_1f_1 = 0.090$, ${}_2f_1 = 0.094$, ${}_3f_1 = 0.096$, and ${}_4f_1 = 0.095$.

More generally, the spot rates can be used to compute rates for terms longer than one period. We define ${}_tf_j$ = the $j$-year forward rate for year $t$. To see how these forward rates can be found, let $n$ and $k$ be two positive integers, with $n$ greater than $k$, and consider the following two investment strategies:

1. Purchase an $n$-year bond and hold to maturity.
2. Purchase an $(n-k)$-year bond, hold to maturity, and invest the proceeds in a $k$-year bond.

If ${}_{n-k}f_k$ is the $k$-year forward rate for year $(n-k)$, then

$$(1 - r_n)^n = (1 + r_{n-k})^{n-k}(1 + {}_{n-k}f_k)^k$$

so that

$${}_{n-k}f_k = \left[\frac{(1 + r_n)^n}{(1 + r_{n-k})^{n-k}}\right]^{\frac{1}{k}} - 1 \qquad (14.11)$$

which reduces to Eq. (14.9) for the special case where $k = 1$. Table 14.5 shows the forward rates computed from the spot rates given earlier. For example, to find ${}_2f_3$ we need to set $k = 3$ and $n = 5$ in Eq. (14.11). Then,

$${}_2f_3 = \left[\frac{(1 + r_5)^5}{(1 + r_2)^2}\right]^{\frac{1}{3}} - 1 = \left[\frac{(1.091)^5}{(1.085)^2}\right]^{\frac{1}{3}} - 1 = 0.095$$

Hence, the term structure, in effect, allows an investor to secure a three-year rate of 9.5% in two years by purchasing a five-year bond now.

It is generally accepted that the traditional-expectations hypothesis provides a useful contribution to our understanding of the term structure of interest rates in that the relationship between long-term and short-term rates depends to some extent on expectations about

Table 14.5 Forward Rates ${}_tf_j$ Implied by $r_1 = 0.080$, $r_2 = 0.085$, $r_3 = 0.088$, $r_4 = 0.090$, and $r_5 = 0.091$.

| **$t/j$** | **1** | **2** | **3** | **4** |
|---|---|---|---|---|
| 1 | 0.090 | 0.092 | 0.093 | 0.094 |
| 2 | 0.094 | 0.095 | 0.095 | |
| 3 | 0.096 | 0.096 | | |
| 4 | 0.095 | | | |

future interest rate movements. However, this theory is considered inadequate to provide a complete description of observed term structure. Historically, long-term rates are higher than short-term rates; indeed, the yield curve of Figure 14.1 is very common. This general tendency for yields to be an increasing function of term to maturity is an implausible consequence if the traditional-expectations hypothesis provides a full explanation of term structure, because we would have to conclude that, far more often than not, market participants expect a rise in the general level of interest rates.

To provide a better model to explain market experience, we must, while acknowledging the importance of expectations, consider uncertainty about those expectations.

### 14.6.3 *The term-preference hypothesis*

In introducing the traditional-expectations hypothesis, we first discussed the position of an investor with a two-year time horizon. This investor had the choice of purchasing a single two-year bond or two one-year bonds in consecutive years. If the traditional-expectations hypothesis is correct, the investor will be indifferent between these alternatives, provided that the term structure is such that the one-year forward rate is equal to the expected one-year rate next year; that is,

$$_1f_1 = {}_1r_1^e \qquad (14.12)$$

However, by investing in the two-year bond, assuming no default risk, this investor can be *sure* of achieving the expected return over the two-year period. On the other hand, under the other alternative, next year's one-year rate will not be known with certainty, so that it is not possible to be sure about the two-year return. This investor will prefer the sure thing, so that if Eq. (14.12) is correct, the investor will opt for the longer-term bond.

By contrast, consider our example of an investor with a one-year time horizon who is able to purchase either a one-year bond or a two-year bond with the intention of selling it after one year. Again, if the traditional-expectations hypothesis is correct, Eq. (14.12) will hold. But in the former option, the expected return can be achieved with certainty, while in the latter the investor cannot be sure of the price at which the two-year bond can be sold in a year's time.

In this case, if Eq. (14.10) provides a complete description of the term structure, this investor will prefer the shorter-term bond.

We have seen that in a market in which term structure is determined entirely by expectations about future interest rates, some investors will prefer shorter-term bonds, while others will prefer longer-term bonds. In practice, market rates depend on the aggregate term preferences of borrowers and lenders. The *liquidity-preference hypothesis* asserts that, in the aggregate, lenders prefer to lend short and borrowers to borrow long, and that, on the average, lenders may have shorter time horizons than borrowers. If this hypothesis is correct, long-term interest rates should incorporate a premium over the rates predicted by the traditional-expectation hypothesis in order for borrowers to induce lenders to purchase longer-term bonds.

One reason to expect positive premiums, increasing in size with the term to maturity of the bond, follows from our earlier discussion of Fisher's theory. If interest rates — and, consequently, bond prices — move with changes in expectations about inflation, then we must consider uncertainty about these expectations. Economic forecasting is far from an exact science. Nevertheless, we would be more confident about a prediction for next year's inflation rate than about a forecast of the inflation rate of ten years. Because of this additional uncertainty, investors will require a higher premium for the purchase of a long-term bond than for a shorter-term bond.

We now see how such *term preference* modified the traditional-expectations hypothesis. Under that hypothesis, forward rates are expectations of future spot rates, so that, for example,

$$ {}_t f_1 = {}_t r_1^e \quad (t = 1, 2, 3, \ldots) $$

However, if the term structure is to reflect investor preference for shorter-term bonds, these forward rates should also incorporate *term premiums* $(L_1, L_2, L_3, \ldots)$, which are generally positive and increase with the term. The forward rates would be

$$ {}_t f_1 = {}_t r_1^e + L_t $$

In place of Eq. (14.6), the $n$-year spot rate is

$$ \begin{aligned} &(1 + r_n) \\ &\quad = [(1 + r_n)(1 + {}_1 r_1^e + L_1)(1 + {}_2 r_1^e + L_2) \cdots (1 + {}_{n-1} r_1^e + L_{n-1})]^{\frac{1}{n}} \end{aligned} $$

This theory of term structure is attractive because it does not assert that long-term rates will be higher than short-term rates, especially if sufficiently substantial declines in spot rates are expected. However, it does suggest that rates will increase with term length.

### 14.6.4 *Market segmentation hypothesis*

Besides the traditional-expectations are the term-preference hypotheses, there is the market-segmentation hypothesis to explain the difference between short-term and long-term interest rates. According to the market-segmentation hypothesis, if more funds are available in the short-term market than in the long-term market, then interest rates will be lower in the short-term and higher in the long-term than predicted by both the traditional-expectations and the term-preference hypothesis.

## 14.7 Duration, Volatility, and Weighted-Average Term to Maturity

### 14.7.1 *Duration and its implication*

In the previous section, when discussing term structure, our examples involved bonds initially purchased at par. However, in practice, because they are initially floated at different times and different coupon interest rates, bonds of the same corporation with the same remaining terms to maturity may be priced either above or below par. Consequently, such bonds will have different payment structures over time. In this section, following Hopewell and Kaufman (1973), Lee *et al.* (2013), and Bodie *et al.* (2021), we examine the effect of this phenomenon.

In Table 14.2, we considered two bonds — one with a coupon rate of 6% and one with a coupon rate of 12%, each with two years to maturity. The respective yields to maturity of these bonds were 9.91% and 9.82%. For the bond with a 6% coupon rate, \$60 is paid at the end of the first year and \$1,060 at the end of the second year. In Table 14.6, we have discounted these payments at 9.91%, the yield to maturity, and have made similar calculations for the 12% coupon bonds.

From Table 14.6, we can see an important distinction between these two bonds. For the 6% coupon bond, a proportion

Table 14.6 Calculation of Duration for Two Bonds.

| | | **6% Coupon Bond** | | |
|---|---|---|---|---|
| **Year** | **Payment** | **Present Value (At 9.91%)** | **Proportion of Present Value** | **Proportion in Year X** |
| 1 | 60 | 54.59 | 0.0586 | 0.0586 |
| 2 | 1,060 | 877.47 | 0.9414 | 1.8828 |
| | | 932.06 | 1.0000 | 1.9414 |

| | | **12% Coupon Bond** | | |
|---|---|---|---|---|
| **Year** | **Payment** | **Present Value (At 9.91%)** | **Proportion of Present Value** | **Proportion in Year X** |
| 1 | 120 | 109.27 | 0.1053 | 0.1053 |
| 2 | 1,120 | 928.66 | 0.8947 | 1.7894 |
| | | 1,037.93 | 1.0000 | 1.8947 |

$54.59/932.06 = 0.0586$ of the total present value will be paid at the end of the first year, while the corresponding proportion for the 12% coupon bond is 0.1053. From this we would conclude that although the term to maturity is the same for both bonds, the 6% coupon bond is, in effect, a longer-term bond than the 12% coupon bond.

The timing and amount of the cash flows are incorporated in the calculation of bond *duration*, which is obtained by summing the products of proportion of present value and years to payment. For the 6% coupon bond, we find

$$\text{Duration} = (0.0586)(1) + (1.8828)(2) = 1.9414 \text{ years}$$

Similarly, the duration of the 12% coupon bond in Table 14.6 is 1.9047 years. The formula, in terms of Macaulay's (1938) paper for calculating duration, is shown in Eq. (14.13):

$$D = \sum_{t=1}^{T} \frac{(t)(PV_t)}{\sum_{t=1}^{T} PV_t} \tag{14.13}$$

where $D$ is the duration of the bond; $t$ is a specific point in time; $T$ is the number of years to maturity; and $PV_t$ is the present value of the cash flow received at time $t$. (A further definition of $PV$ is

$$PV_t = \frac{C_t}{(1+r)^t}$$

where $r$ is the interest rate and $C_t$ is the cash payment in period $t$ ($t = 1, 2, \ldots, T$)). It should be noted that $C_T$ includes annual coupon payments (coupon rate ($i$) times face value ($F$)) and bond face value ($F$). Equation (14.13) can be written as

$$D = \sum_{t=1}^{T} \frac{(t)(PV_t)}{PV} \tag{14.14}$$

where $PV$ represents the theoretical value of bond. Equation (14.14) implies that the duration ($D$) is the weighted average of maturity, $t$.

One way of looking at this calculation of duration is to treat each yearly cash flow as a separate zero coupon security. For the 6% bond with a two-year life, we can imagine that we have (1) a one-year zero coupon bond that costs \$54.59, matures in one year at \$60, and has a duration of 1, and (2) a two-year zero coupon bond that costs \$877.47, matures in two years at \$1,060, and has a duration of 2. The duration of a zero coupon bond is identical to its maturity because there is only one cash flow, which occurs at the maturity of the bond.

Further, the duration of a portfolio of bonds is equal to the weighted average of the duration of the individual bonds held in the portfolio, or

$$D_P = \sum_{i=1}^{N} wt_i D_i \tag{14.15}$$

where $D_P$ is the duration of the portfolio; $wt_i$ is the percentage of the portfolio invested in the $i$th security; and $D_i$ is the duration of the $i$th security.

Hence, in our example, the duration of the first portion of the bond is 1 with a weight of \$54.59/\$932.06 and the second portion has a duration of 2 with a weight of \$877.47/\$932.06, giving a portfolio duration of 1.9414 using Eq. (14.15).

The duration of a bond is important in assessing its riskiness. All other things equal, the longer the duration of a bond, the more sensitive the bond's price to changes in interest rates. Sensitivity of this kind is measured by *volatility*, which is the percentage change in bond price expected to result from a 1% change in interest rates. It can be shown that

$$\text{volatility} = \frac{\text{duration}}{1 + \text{yield}}$$

Thus, for the 6% coupon bond,

$$\text{volatility} = \frac{1.9414}{1 + 0.0991} = 1.7664$$

Hence, a 1% increase in interest rates should lead to a 1.7664% decrease in the price of this bond. For the 12% coupon bond,

$$\text{volatility} = \frac{1.9047}{1 + 0.0982} = 1.7344$$

Thus, the 6% coupon bond is more volatile than the 12% coupon bond. In such circumstances, all other things equal, investors will demand a higher expected rate of return as compensation for the additional uncertainty.

The traditional role of bonds as an asset category has changed over the past 15 years due to surging interest rates and the resultant price volatility during the 1970s. The use of bond maturity to reduce interest-rate risk in bond portfolios through maturity matching has become increasingly inadequate. By the 1970s, several researchers had recognized that maturity is an incomplete measure of the life and risk of a coupon bond.

In 1971, Fisher and Weil recommended a practical measurement tool that could help immunize bond portfolios against interest-rate risk, and in 1973, Hopewell and Kaufman demonstrated that it could also be used as a measure of price risk for bonds. This concept is *duration*, which has emerged as an important tool for the measurement and management of interest-rate risk. Bierwag, Kaufman, and Toevs (BKT) noted in 1983 that only the introduction of beta in the 1960s has generated as much interest in the investment community as has duration.

The purpose of this section is to review briefly the historical development of duration and to examine its potential use by investors in alternative bond-portfolio immunization strategies, as well as to look at certain reservations that should be considered when using duration to immunize bond portfolios.

In 1938, Frederick Macaulay developed the concept of duration as part of an overall analysis of interest rates and bond prices. He was attempting to develop a more meaningful summary measure of the life of a bond that would correlate well with changes in bond price; he arrived at a weighted average of the time to each bond payment, with the weights being the present values of each payment relative to the total present value of all the flows:

$$D = \frac{\sum_{t=0}^{n} t\left[\frac{C_t}{(1+k_d)^t}\right]}{\sum_{t=0}^{n} \frac{C_t}{(1+k_d)^t}} \tag{14.14a}$$

where $C_t$ = the coupon-interest payment in periods 1 through $n-1$; $C_n$ = the sum of the coupon-interest payment and the face value of the bond in period $n$; $k_d$ = the YTM or required rate of return of the bondholders in the market; and $t$ = the time period in years.

Thus, for the first semi-annual payment in the series between 0 and $n$, $t$ would equal 0.5. The denominator of this equation is equal to the current price of the bond as estimated by the present value of all future cash flows. It is obvious that Eq. (14.14a) is a different way to present duration. Eq. (14.14a) is a modified version of (14.14).

The duration of a bond with a fixed maturity date declines just as maturity with the passage of time. The duration of a coupon bond, however, is always shorter than its maturity. Only for pure discount (zero-coupon) bonds will duration equal maturity. Duration is also affected by the size of the coupon and its YTM, decreasing as either increases.

It is useful to place the concept of duration in the perspective of other summary measures of the timing of an asset's cash flow. Because the cash flows from bonds are specific, both as to timing and amount, analysts have derived a precise measure of the timing for bonds. The most commonly used timing measure is term to maturity (TM), the number of years prior to the final payment on the bond. The advantage of TM is that it is easily identified and measured. However, the disadvantage is that TM ignores interim cash flows.

Moreover, TM ignores the substantial difference in coupon rates and the difference in sinking funds.

### 14.7.2 *Weighted-average term to maturity and duration*

In an attempt to rectify the deficiency of TM, a measure that considered the interest payments and the final principal payment was constructed. The *weighted-average term to maturity* (*WATM*) computes the proportion of each individual payment as a percentage of all payments and makes this proportion the weight for the year the payment is made:

$$\text{WATM} = \frac{\text{CF}_1}{\text{TCF}}(1) + \frac{\text{CF}_2}{\text{TCF}}(2) + \cdots + \frac{\text{CF}_n}{\text{TCF}}(n) \qquad (14.16)$$

where $\text{CF}_t$ = the cash flow in year $t$; $t$ = the year when cash flow is received; $n$ = maturity; and TCF = the total cash flow from the bond.

Sample Problem (23.5) provides further illustration.

Suppose a 10-year, 4% bond will have total cash-flow payments of \$1,400. Thus, the \$40 payment in $\text{CF}_1$ will have a weight of 0.0287 (\$40/\$1,400), each subsequent interest payment will have the same weight, and the principal in year 10 will have a weight of 0.74286 (\$1,040/1,400). Therefore:

$$\begin{aligned}\text{WATM} &= \frac{\$\ 40}{\$\ 1400}(1) + \frac{\$40}{\$1400}(2) + \frac{\$40}{\$1400}(3) + \cdots \\ &\quad + \frac{\$40}{\$1400}(9) + \frac{\$1040}{\$1400}(10) = 8.71 \text{ years}\end{aligned}$$

The WATM is definitely less than the TM, because it takes account of all interim cash flows in addition to the final payment. In addition, a bond with a larger coupon has a shorter WATM because a larger proportion of its total cash flows is derived from the coupon payments prior to maturity — that is, the coupon-weighted average of the larger coupon is larger than the smaller coupon bond. The weighted-average term can be utilized to take into account sinking-fund payments, thus lowering the WATM.

### 14.7.3 *WATM versus duration measure*

A major advantage of WATM is that it considers the timing of all cash flows from the bond, including interim and final payments. One disadvantage is that it does not consider the time value of the flows. The interest payment of the first period is valued the same as the last period.

The *duration measure* is simply a weighted-average maturity, where the weights are stated in present value terms. In the same format as the WATM, duration is

$$D = \frac{\mathrm{PVCF}_1}{\mathrm{PVTCF}}(1) + \frac{\mathrm{PVCF}_2}{\mathrm{PVTCF}}(2) + \cdots + \frac{\mathrm{PVCF}_n}{\mathrm{PVTCF}}(n) \tag{14.17}$$

where $\mathrm{PVCF}_t$ = the present value of the cash flow in year $t$ discounted at current yield to maturity; $t$ = the year when cash flow is received; $n$ = maturity; and PVTCF = the present value of total cash flow from the bond discounted at current YTM.

The time in the future when a cash flow is received is weighted by the proportion that the present value of that cash flow contributes to the total present value or price of the bond. Similar to the WATM, the duration of a bond is shorter than its TM because of the interim interest payment. Duration is inversely related to the coupon of the bond. The one variable that does not influence the average TM but can affect duration is the prevailing market yield. Market yield does not affect WATM because this measure does not consider the present value of flows. Nevertheless, market yield affects more on both the numerator of WATM and TM. As a result, there is an inverse relation between a change in the market yield and a bond's duration.

Tables 14.7 and 14.8, taken from Reilly and Sidhu's (1980) article, "The Many Uses of Bond Duration," illustrate the difference between

Table 14.7 WATM (Assuming Annual Interest Payments).

| **Bond A** $1,000, 10 years, 4% | | | | **Bond B** $1,000, 10 years, 8% | | | |
|---|---|---|---|---|---|---|---|
| (1) Year | (2) Cash Flow ($) | (3) Cash Flow/TCF | (4) (1) × (3) | (5) Year | (6) Cash Flow ($) | (7) Cash Flow/TCF | (8) (5) × (7) |
| 1 | 40 | 0.02857 | 0.02857 | 1 | 80 | 0.04444 | 0.04444 |
| 2 | 40 | 0.02857 | 0.05714 | 2 | 80 | 0.04444 | 0.08888 |
| 3 | 40 | 0.02857 | 0.08571 | 3 | 80 | 0.04444 | 0.13332 |
| 4 | 40 | 0.02857 | 0.11428 | 4 | 80 | 0.04444 | 0.17776 |
| 5 | 40 | 0.02857 | 0.14285 | 5 | 80 | 0.04444 | 0.22220 |
| 6 | 40 | 0.02857 | 0.17142 | 6 | 80 | 0.04444 | 0.26664 |
| 7 | 40 | 0.02857 | 0.19999 | 7 | 80 | 0.04444 | 0.31108 |
| 8 | 40 | 0.02857 | 0.22856 | 8 | 80 | 0.04444 | 0.35552 |
| 9 | 40 | 0.02857 | 0.28713 | 9 | 80 | 0.04444 | 0.39996 |
| 10 | 1,040 | 0.74286 | 7.42860 | 10 | 1,080 | 0.60000 | 6.00000 |
| Sum | $1,400 | 1.00000 | 8.71425 | Sum | $1,800 | 1.00000 | 7.99980 |
| WATM = 8.71 years | | | | WATM = 8.00 years | | | |

*Source*: Lee and Lee (2017). *Financial Analysis, Planning and Forecasting*, page 254.

Table 14.8 Duration (Assuming 8% Market Yield).

| (1) Year | (2) Cash Flow | (3) PV at 8% | (4) PV of Flow | (5) PV as % of Price | (6) (1) × (5) |
|---|---|---|---|---|---|
| **Bond A** | | | | | |
| 1 | $40 | 0.9259 | $37.04 | 0.0506 | 0.0506 |
| 2 | 40 | 0.8573 | 34.29 | 0.0469 | 0.0938 |
| 3 | 40 | 0.7938 | 31.75 | 0.0434 | 0.1302 |
| 4 | 40 | 0.7350 | 29.40 | 0.0402 | 0.1608 |
| 5 | 40 | 0.6806 | 27.22 | 0.0372 | 0.1860 |
| 6 | 40 | 0.6302 | 25.21 | 0.0345 | 0.2070 |
| 7 | 40 | 0.5835 | 23.34 | 0.0319 | 0.2233 |
| 8 | 40 | 0.5403 | 21.61 | 0.0295 | 0.2360 |
| 9 | 40 | 0.5002 | 20.01 | 0.0274 | 0.2466 |
| 10 | 1,040 | 0.4632 | 481.73 | 0.6585 | 6.5850 |
| Sum | | | $731.58 | 1.0000 | 8.1193 |
| Duration = 8.12 years | | | | | |
| **Bond B** | | | | | |
| 1 | $80 | 0.9259 | $74.07 | 0.0741 | 0.0741 |
| 2 | 80 | 0.8573 | 68.59 | 0.0686 | 0.1372 |
| 3 | 80 | 0.7938 | 63.50 | 0.0635 | 0.1906 |
| 4 | 80 | 0.7350 | 58.80 | 0.0588 | 0.1906 |
| 5 | 80 | 0.6806 | 54.44 | 0.0544 | 0.2720 |
| 6 | 80 | 0.6302 | 50.42 | 0.0504 | 0.3024 |
| 7 | 80 | 0.5835 | 46.68 | 0.0467 | 0.3269 |
| 8 | 80 | 0.5403 | 43.22 | 0.0432 | 0.3456 |
| 9 | 80 | 0.5002 | 40.02 | 0.0400 | 0.3600 |
| 10 | 1,080 | 0.4632 | 500.26 | 0.5003 | 5.0030 |
| Sum | | | $1000.00 | 1.0000 | 7.2470 |
| Duration = 7.25 years | | | | | |

*Source*: Lee and Lee (2017). *Financial Analysis, Planning and Forecasting*, page 255.

the timing measures. These two tables show the WATM and the duration, respectively. Due to the consideration of the time value of money in the duration measurement, duration is the superior measuring technique.

WATM is always longer than the duration of a bond, and the difference increases with the market rate used in the duration formula. This is consistent with the duration property of an inverse relation between duration and the market rate.

## 14.8 Innovations in the Bond Market

During the 1980s, most of the innovative activity in finance occurred in the bond market. This is due primarily to the impact of inflation and widely variable interest rates on fixed-income securities. Issuers and creditors in the fixed-income market faced higher uncertainty and risk on interest rates, reinvestment, purchasing power, marketability, and insolvency. Each of these risks has been a cause of, or at least associated with, the innovations in the fixed-income market.

### 14.8.1 *Deep discount and zero coupon bonds*

The *deep discount bond* is tailor-made for tax-exempt investors such as pension funds, foundations, college endowments, and individual IRAs and Keoghs. The deep discount bond helps protect the investor from having to continually reinvest the interim interest flows at varying rates. Because the intermediate cash flows are small or zero (zero coupon bond), the imputed interest is automatically reinvested at the bond's yield to maturity. This characteristic of deep discount bonds can be used by financial institutions in their liability-management programs. Any intermediary that offers a fixed return on its liabilities can invest in deep discount bonds to lock in a guaranteed return for the life of the bond.

Another advantage of deep discount bonds is inherent call protection. An insurer is usually unwilling to pay par for a bond that has a positive impact on the firm's cash flow. Additionally, these bonds have no sinking fund provisions and little or no internal payments.

These benefits are offset by the major disadvantage of deep discount or zero coupon securities from both the issuer's and investor's perspective: the balloon payment required at maturity. At maturity, the firm will have to raise a large amount of cash to meet the repayment or else refinance the issue at prevailing interest rates. The potential increase in risk is evident to both the issuer and the investor. The actual economic conditions that issues will be faced with when the bonds mature will determine the success of each issue on a case-by-case basis.

A variation on the deep discount or zero coupon bond is the *compound interest bond.* These bonds are similar to zero coupon bonds in that they do not pay interest. Instead, the investor receives the principal and the compound value of the interest at maturity. Compound interest bonds are sold at par instead of at a deep discount, so that the issuer has a greater cash flow per bond. The advantages and disadvantages of the compound interest bond are the same as for zero coupon bonds.

### 14.8.2 *Floating-rate notes*

Citicorp introduced the *floating-rate note* in 1974, but it has never really gained market acceptance. Thus, these types of debt instruments are still in an innovative stage of development. A floating-rate note is a debt issue with an interest rate that fluctuates based on market conditions. The coupon rate is adjusted up or down at a predetermined interval according to a given market interest rate.

For investors, the advantage of the variable-rate note is obvious during periods of rising interest rates. Each six months, or whatever the stated period, the interest on the note is adjusted upward to reflect the higher rates, and thus the investor is protected against a decline in the investment's value. On the other hand, during periods of falling rates, the attractiveness of floating rates diminishes because the investor must accept lower rates as market rates drop. The issues have exactly the opposite perspective, which may explain why the floating note has not caught on. When most investors are interested in buying, there are few issuers; and when most issuers are interested in bring out this type of security, there are few buyers.

### 14.8.3 *Extendable notes*

*Extendable notes* are short-term securities, typically one to five years, which, at the option of the investor, may be redeemed or renewed at maturity for a similar period at a new interest rate. The attraction of extendable notes is that they alleviate some of the problems that issuers and investors have with floating notes. With extendables, investors have the option of getting their cash back at a specified rate or accepting an offer by the issuer to extend the maturity of the note at prevailing rates. This allows investors the flexibility of withdrawing their funds invested in the notes at new interest rates should market rates rise. On the other hand, issuers can often save the trouble and expense of having to issue new securities to new investors.

There are numerous variations available with extendables. Some have a predetermined redemption schedule of increasing prices at which the holder can sell the note back to the issuer. Other notes have either a set schedule for redemption (such as every five years until maturity) or a variable redemption as determined by the movement of market rates. Once some predetermined indicator reaches a certain level, the investor has the option of redeeming the bond or extending it for another period.

### 14.8.4 *Junk bonds*

A *junk bond* is a corporate bond that is rated below investment grade — a minimum of BBB by Standard & Poor's Corporation and Baa by Moody's. Junk bonds first become popular in the 1970s, when corporations involved in mergers, takeovers, and corporate restructurings began to finance these activities by issuing large amounts of junk bonds. Investors seem to ignore the higher probability of default of the issues because of their expected higher returns. Drexel Burnham and other investment banking firms have made extensive efforts to market these issues and sell the idea to the investing public. During 1986 and 1987, low quality or unrated new public offerings accounted for just over one quarter of the total public offerings of bonds. The crash of October 1987 may alert investors to the potential problems of junk bonds and reduce their popularity.

## 14.9 Summary

The issuance of debt securities is an important aspect of raising long-term capital. Knowledge of the institutional factors and an understanding of interest rates are essential for the financial manager, who must decide when to issue debt securities and how much.

An overview of the debt contract and the practice of rating debt securities is provided so that the student can form an institutional vocabulary for debt securities. Interest rate theory, based on the writings of Irving Fisher, and various explanations of the term structure of interest rates are presented to provide a theoretical foundation to understand the debt market. The basic provisions of the debt contract, as well as variations and innovations, are presented to show how adaptable the basic debt contract is to the changing market environment.

## References

Ang, J. S. "The Two Faces of Bond Refunding," *The Journal of Finance* (June 1975, pp. 869–874).

Ang, J. S. "The Two Faces of Bond Refunding: Reply," *The Journal of Finance*, 33(1) (1978, pp. 354–356).

Bodie, Z., A. Kane and A. Marcus. *Investments*, 12th edn. (McGraw-Hill Book Company, New York, 2021).

Cox, J. C., J. E. Ingersoll Jr and S. A. Ross. "Duration and the measurement of basis risk," *Journal of Business* (1979, pp. 51–61).

Fabozzi, F. J. and Pollack. *The Handbook of Fixed Income Securities*, 8th edn. (Homewood, IL: Dow Jones, Irwin, 2012).

Fama, E. F. "Short-term Interest Rates as Predictors of Inflation," *American Economic Review*, 65 (June 1975, pp. 269–282).

Fama, E. F. "Interest Rates and Inflation: The Message in the Entrails," *American Economic Review*, 67 (June 1977, pp. 487–496).

Finnerty, J. D. "Evaluating the Economics of Refunding High-Coupon Sinking-Fund Debt," *Financial Management* (Spring 1983, pp. 5–10).

Fisher, I. *The Theory of Interest: As Determined by Impatience to Spend Income and Opportunity to Invest It* (New York: Augustus M. Kelley, 1865). First published in 1930.

Hopewell, M. H. and G. G. Kaufman. "Bond Price Volatility and Term to Maturity: A Generalized Respecification," *American Economic Review* (September 1973, pp. 749–753).

Kalotay, A. J. "Sinking Funds and the Realized Cost of Debt," *Financial Management* (Summer 1978, pp. 45–55).

Kalotay, A. J. "Innovations in Corporation Finance: Deep Discount Private Placements," *Financial Management* (Spring 1982, pp. 55–57).

Kaplan, R. S. and G. Horwitz. "Statistical Methodological Inquiry," *Journal of Business* (April 1979, pp. 231–261).

Krans, A. "An Analysis of Call Provisions and the Corporate Refunding Decision," *Midland Corporate Finance Journal*, 1 (Spring 1983, pp. 46–64).

Lee, C. F. and A. C. Lee. *Encyclopedia of Finance*, 2nd edn. (Springer, New York, 2013).

Lee, C. F., J. F. Finnerty and E. A. Norton. *Foundations of Financial Management* (West Publishing Company, 1997).

Lee, C. F., J. Finnerty, J. Lee, A. C. Lee and D. Wort. *Security Analysis, Portfolio Management, and Financial Derivatives* (World Scientific, 2013).

Livingston, M. "Measuring the Benefit of a Bond Refunding: The Problem of Nonmarketable Call Options," *Financial Management*, 16 (Spring 1987, pp. 38–40).

Malitz, I. "On Financial Contracting: The Determinants of Bond Covenants," *Financial Management*, 15(2) (Summer 1986, pp. 18–25).

Macaulay, F. R. "Some Theoretical Problems of Approximating the Bond Yields and Stock Prices in the United States Since 1856," *National Bureau of Economic Research* (New York: Columbia University, 1938).

Newbold, P. and T. Bos. *Stochastic Parameter Regression Models* (Beverly Hills: Sage Publications, 1985).

Reilly and Sidhu. "The Many Uses of Bond Duration," *Financial Analysts Journal*, 36 (July/August 1980, p. 60).

Smith, C. W. and J. B. Warner. "On Financial Contracting: An Analysis of Bond Covenants," *Journal of Financial Economics*, 34(3) (June 1979, pp. 117–161).

Wakeman, L. M. "The Real Function of Bond Rating Agencies," *The Revolution in Corporate Finance*, J. M. Stein and D. H. Chew, Jr. (eds.) (New York: Basil Blackwell, 1986).

Yawitz, J. B. and J. A. Anderson. "The Effect of Bond Refunding on Shareholder Wealth," *The Journal of Finance* (December 1977, pp. 1738–1746).

Yawitz, J. B. and J. A. Anderson. "The Effect of Bond Refunding on Shareholder Wealth: Reply," *The Journal of Finance*, 34(3) (June 1979, pp. 805–809).

## Appendix 14A — Yield to Maturity and Its Application

Based upon maturity and duration, which were discussed in the text, we will discuss the concept formula of yield to maturity. In addition, we also will discuss how yield to maturity can be applied to bond portfolio management.

## 14A.1 Yield to Maturity[5]

*Yield to maturity* is an average maturity measurement in its own way because it is calculated using the same rate to discount all payments to the bondholder — thus, it is an average of spot rates over time. For example, if the spot rate for period two, $r_2$, is greater than that for period one, $r_1$, the YTM on a two-year coupon bond would be between $r_1$ and $r_2$ — an underestimate of the two-year spot rate. Likewise, the opposite condition would overestimate the two-year spot rate. With the high volatility of interest rates that has existed in recent years, the difference can be dramatic. For example, in Britain during 1977, the 20-year spot rate of interest was approximately 20%, while the YTM on 20-year coupon bonds was only 13%. The reason for the larger discrepancy was that YTM was calculated as an average of the relatively low short-term spot rates and the relatively high long-term spot rates.

Until the 1970s, when interest-rate and bond-price volatility increased dramatically, the significance of the superiority of duration over average-measurement of bond-portfolio risk was required for immunization against interest-rate risk. Studies comparing the success of portfolios immunized with a duration strategy and a maturity strategy have shown that duration outperforms maturity 75% of the time for a variety of planning periods. Duration also produces lower variances between realized and promised returns than either the maturity strategy or the naïve strategy of annually rolling over 20-year bonds.

The motivation for bond investment is to secure a fixed cash flow over a particular investment horizon. Asset and liability portfolios of financial institutions often generate future cash-flow patterns that must conform to certain solvency and profitability restrictions. For example, insurance companies and pension funds, with definite

---

[5]Malkiel (1962) and Bodie *et al.* (2021) have carefully discussed the sensitivity of bond prices to changes in market interest rate, i.e., interest rate sensitivity. They have carefully proposed several propositions to describe this kind of relationship. It is well-known that bond characteristics such as coupon rate or yield to maturity affect interest rate sensitivity. Therefore, the yield to maturity discussed in Chapter 5 and this section can be used to analysis the interest rate sensitivity of bond prices.

future commitments of funds, invest now so that their future cash-flow stream will match well with their future commitment stream. Bond-immunization strategies are designed to guarantee the investor in default-free and option-free bonds at rate of return that approximates the promised rate (or YTM) computed at the outset of the investment. Nevertheless, the YTM will be equal to the RY only if the interim coupon payments are reinvestable at the YTM. If interest rates change, the RY will be lower or higher than YTM, depending upon the relationship between the bond's measured duration $D$ and the investor's expected holding period has been shown that RY is computed as a weighted average of the YTM and the average RR available for coupon payments:

$$\text{RY} = \left(\frac{D}{H}\right)(\text{YTM}) + \left(1 - \frac{D}{H}\right)(\text{RR}) \tag{14.1A}$$

Therefore, the RY would equal the YTM only if the duration on the bond were kept equal to the time horizon of the investor. An increase in the RR would increase the return from reinvested coupons, but would at the same time decrease the bond value. Only holding the bond to maturity would prevent this value reduction from affecting the RY. Therefore, the overall impact of RR increases depends upon the extent to which the income effect offsets the value reduction. On the other hand, a decrease in the RR will decrease the return from reinvested coupons, but it will increase the bond values in the market. As shown in Eq. (14.1A), these opposite impacts on RY will exactly offset each other only when $D$ equals $H$.

If a more complete time spectrum of zero-coupon bonds of all types were readily available, bond-portfolio immunization would be a relatively simple process. Simply by choosing bonds with maturities equal to the length of an investor's investment horizon, the rate of return would always be as promised by the YTM, regardless of interest-rate changes. Beginning with Treasury-bond sales of February 15, 1985, the U.S. Treasury has been cooperating with Wall Street firms in the stripping of coupon payments from new Treasury issues through separate registration of coupon and maturity payments, thus manufacturing a series of zero-coupon issues. However, since this applies only to Treasury issues, it is still necessary for investors to use duration models to immunize portfolios of nontreasury bonds.

To immunize a bond portfolio, investors must match the duration of the portfolio with the length of their investment horizons. This must be accomplished within their assumed stochastic process of interest-rate movements and changes in the yield curve. If the yield curve changes during the holding period, the immunization process will break down and the RY will not equal the YTM as promised.

Since the hoped-for results of the passive duration-immunization method can be upset by interest-rate shifts, some investors may prefer to try to predict interest-rate changes and undertake an active immunization strategy. This would involve the formation of bond portfolios with durations intentionally longer or shorter than the investment-planning period. Since it is usually assumed that the market consensus about future interest rates is the most likely possibility, investors should pursue active strategies only if their forecasts of rates differ from those of the market. The investor, who expects the interest rate to be higher than the market forecast, should form a bond portfolio with a duration shorter than the length of the investment horizon. If successful, the income gains from reinvestment of coupons and maturing bonds will exceed the value loss on unmatured bonds: RY will exceed the YTM promised. If unsuccessful, the reinvestment return will not be enough to offset the value loss and RY will be less than YTM.

If the investor expects interest rates to be lower than the market forecast, the procedure would be the reverse of that described above — that is, to purchase a bond portfolio with a duration longer than the investment horizon. If successful, the lower reinvestment returns will be more than offset by the bond-value gains. Thus the active immunization strategy relies solely upon the ability of the investor to predict the direction of future interest-rate changes and to take full advantage of market opportunities for realized returns greater than market rates. While this provides the investor with an opportunity for substantial returns, it can also result in substantial losses. Because of this, Leibowitz and Weinberger (LW, 1981) derived a "stop loss" active immunization strategy which they called contingent immunization. In this method, the portfolio manager pursues higher returns through active management unless the value of the portfolio declines to a level that threatens a minimum target return. At this point, the portfolio is switched into a pure immunization mode designed to provide the minimum target specified at the outset. Other researchers have developed similar strategies that rely on two portfolios — one actively and the other passively immunized. Interest changes could take place that would virtually wipe out the active portfolio, but they would not greatly affect the minimum target return of the two-portfolio combination.

## 14A.2 The Macaulay Model

The duration model that is still most widely used because of its simplicity is the *Macaulay model.* However, basic limitations affect the use of this model. First, the current and forward spot rates are assumed to be equal over a specific planning horizon — that is, the yield curve is assumed to be flat. This is also one of the basic weakness of the YTM measurement. Second, this model provides an accurate measure of interest-rate risk only when there is a single parallel shift in the term of structure of interest rates — that is, there is only one shift within the holding period and it does not involve a change in yield-curve shape.

Most studies surveyed seem to indicate that the Macaulay model assumptions are unrealistic and too restrictive. Cox *et al.* (1979) noted that it does not take into account the dynamic nature of the term structure observed in the real world, in which yield curves can and do change in shape as well as location. As a result, a number of more complex duration models have been developed to measure risk when multiple term-structure shifts can affect the shape and location of the yield curve. Because the actual underlying stochastic process governing interest-rate changes is not known, only empirical analysis can determine whether the extra complexity of these models justifies their usage. Bierwag *et al.* (1982) extensively tested the Macaulay model along with four more complex duration models and found that duration-matching strategies generated realized returns consistently closer to promised yields than a maturity-matching strategy. Even more interesting, the Macaulay measure appeared to perform as well as the more complex models. Their findings suggest that single-factor duration matching is a feasible immunization strategy that works reasonably well, even with the less complex (and thus less costly) Macaulay model.

Duration appears a better measure of a bond's life than maturity because it provides a more meaningful relationship with interest-rate changes. This relationship has been expressed by Hopewell and Kaufman (1973) as:

$$\frac{\Delta P}{P} = \frac{D}{(1+i)}\Delta i = D * \Delta i \tag{14.2A}$$

where $\Delta$ = "change in"; $P$ = bond price; $D$ = duration; and $i$ = market interest rate or bond yield.

For example, a bond with five years' duration will decline in price by approximately 10% when market yield increases by 2%. Note that $\Delta P/P$ on the left-hand side of Eq. (14.2A) is the percentage change in price, and $\Delta i$ is the absolute change in yield level and not percentage change.

Other useful generalizations can be made concerning the relationships of duration to various bond characteristics, as follows.

(1) The higher the coupon, the shorter the duration, because the face-value payment at maturity will represent a smaller proportional present-value contribution to the makeup of the current bond value. In other words, bonds with small coupon rates will experience larger capital gains or losses as interest rates change. Additionally, for all bonds except zero-coupon-rate bonds, as the maturity of the bond lengthens the duration at the limit will approach $(1+\text{YTM})/\text{YTM}$. Table 14.1A shows the relationship between duration, maturity, and coupon rates for a bond with a YTM of 6%. At the limit (maturity goes to infinity), the duration will approach 17.667 (i.e., $(1+0.06)/0.06$).

As can be seen in Table 14.1A, the limit is independent of the coupon rate: it is always 17.667. However, when the coupon rate is the same as or greater than the yield rate (the bond is selling at a premium), duration approaches the limit directly. Conversely, for discount-priced bonds (coupon rate is less than YTM), duration can increase beyond the limit and then recede to the limit. In the case of the bond with the 2% coupon at a maturity of 50 years, the duration is 19.452 — and this approaches the limit as maturity keeps increasing.

Regardless of coupon size, it is nearly impossible to find bonds with durations in excess of 20 years; most bonds have a limit of about 15 years.

Table 14.1A Duration, Maturity, and Coupon Rate.

| Maturity (years) | Coupon Rate 0.02 | 0.04 | 0.06 | 0.08 |
|---|---|---|---|---|
| 1 | 0.995 | 0.990 | 0.985 | 0.981 |
| 5 | 4.756 | 4.558 | 4.393 | 4.254 |
| 10 | 8.891 | 8.169 | 7.662 | 7.286 |
| 20 | 14.981 | 12.98 | 11.904 | 11.232 |
| 50 | 19.452 | 17.129 | 14.273 | 15.829 |
| 100 | 17.567 | 17.232 | 17.120 | 17.064 |
| $\infty$ | 17.667 | 17.667 | 17.667 | 17.667 |

(2) The higher the YTM, the shorter the duration, because YTM is used as the discount rate for the bond's cash flows and higher discount rates diminish the proportional present-value contribution of more distant payments. As has been shown, at the limit duration is equal to (1 + YTM)/YTM; in Table 14.2A the relationship between duration and YTM is shown.

(3) A typical sinking fund (one in which the bond principal is gradually retired over time) will reduce duration. Duration can be reduced by the sinking-fund or call provision. A large proportion of current bond issues do have sinking funds, and these can definitely affect a bond's duration. An example will illustrate this fact. A 10-year 4% bond with a sinking fund of 10% of face value per year starting at the end of the fifth year has a duration of 7.10 years as compared to the duration of 8.12 years of a similar bond without a sinking fund. Table 14.3A provides further illustration.

The effect of a sinking fund on the time structure of cash flows for a bond is certain to the issuer of the bond, since the firm must make the payments: they represent a legal cash-flow requirement that will affect the firm's cash flow. However, the sinking fund may not affect the investor since the money put into the sinking fund may not necessarily be used to retire outstanding bonds. Even if it is, it is not certain that a given investor's bonds will be called for retirement.

(4) For bonds of less than five years to maturity, the magnitudes of duration changes are about the same as those for maturity

Table 14.2A Duration and YTM.

| **YTM** | **Duration at Limit (maturity $\to \infty$)** |
|---|---|
| 0.02 | 51 |
| 0.04 | 26 |
| 0.08 | 13.5 |
| 0.10 | 11 |
| 0.20 | 6 |
| 0.30 | 4.33 |
| 0.50 | 3 |

changes. For bonds of 5 to 15 years' maturity, changes in the magnitude of duration are considerably less than those of maturity. For bonds with more than 20 years to maturity, changes in the magnitude of duration are very small relative to changes in maturity. As can be seen in Figure 14.1A, in the range of zero to five years the relationship between duration and maturity is shown approximately by a straight line with a slope of 45 degrees. In the range of five to ten years, the slope of the line is less, indicating a smaller change in duration for a given change in maturity. And for more than 20 years, the line is almost horizontal, showing a smaller change in duration for a given change in maturity.

(5) In contrast to a sinking fund, all bondholders will be affected if a bond is called. The duration of a callable bond will be shorter than a noncallable bond.

When a bond is callable, the cash flow implicit in the YTM figure is subject to possible early alteration. Most corporate bonds issued today are callable, but with a period of call protection before the call option can be exercised. At the expiration of this period, the bond may be called at a specified call price, which usually involves some premium over par.

To provide some measure of the return in the event that the issuer exercises the call option at some future point, the yield to call is calculated instead of the YTM. This computation is based on the assumption that the bond's cash flow is terminated at the "first call date" with redemption of principal at the specified call price. The

Table 14.3A Duration with and without Sinking Funds (Assuming 8% Market Yield).

| | Cash Flow | Present-Value Factor | Present Value of Cash Flow | Weight | Duration |
|---|---|---|---|---|---|
| Bond A — No Sinking Fund | | | | | |
| 1 | $40 | 0.9259 | $37.04 | 0.0506 | 0.0506 |
| 2 | 40 | 0.8573 | 34.29 | 0.0469 | 0.0938 |
| 3 | 40 | 0.7938 | 31.75 | 0.0434 | 0.1302 |
| 4 | 40 | 0.7350 | 29.40 | 0.0402 | 0.1608 |
| 5 | 40 | 0.6806 | 27.22 | 0.0372 | 0.1860 |
| 6 | 40 | 0.6302 | 25.21 | 0.0345 | 0.2070 |
| 7 | 40 | 0.5835 | 23.34 | 0.0319 | 0.2233 |
| 8 | 40 | 0.5403 | 21.61 | 0.0295 | 0.2360 |
| 9 | 40 | 0.5002 | 20.01 | 0.0274 | 0.2466 |
| 10 | 1,040 | 0.4632 | 481.73 | 0.6585 | 4.5850 |
| Sum | | | $731.58 | 1.0000 | 8.1193 |
| Duration = 8.12 years | | | | | |
| Bond A — Sinking Fund (10% per year from fifth year) | | | | | |
| 1 | $ 40 | 0.9259 | $37.04 | 0.04668 | 0.04668 |
| 2 | 40 | 0.8573 | 34.29 | 0.04321 | 0.08642 |
| 3 | 40 | 0.7938 | 31.75 | 0.04001 | 0.12003 |
| 4 | 40 | 0.7350 | 29.40 | 0.03705 | 0.14820 |
| 5 | 140 | 0.6806 | 95.28 | 0.12010 | 0.60050 |
| 6 | 140 | 0.6302 | 88.23 | 0.11119 | 0.66714 |
| 7 | 140 | 0.5835 | 81.69 | 0.10295 | 0.72065 |
| 8 | 140 | 0.5403 | 75.64 | 0.09533 | 0.76264 |
| 9 | 140 | 0.5002 | 70.03 | 0.08826 | 0.79434 |
| 10 | 540 | 0.4632 | 250.13 | 0.31523 | 3.15230 |
| Sum | | | $ 793.48 | 1.00000 | 7.09890 |
| Duration = 7.10 years | | | | | |

*Source*: Lee and Lee (2017). *Financial Analysis, Planning and Forecasting*, page 261.

crossover yield is defined as that yield where the YTM is equal to the yield to call. When the price of the bond rises to some value above the call price, and the market yield declines to value below the crossover yield, the yield to call becomes the minimum yield. At this price and yield, the firm will probably exercise a call option when it is available. When prices go below the call price, the YTM is the minimum yield.

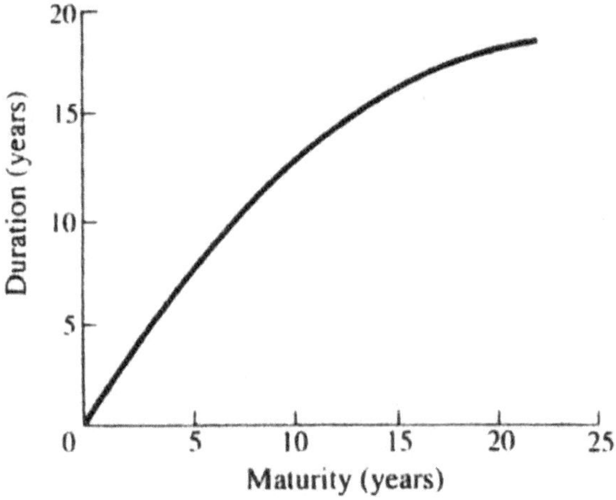


Figure 14.1A Duration versus Maturity.

To calculate the crossover yield for a 8%, 30-year bond selling at par with 10-year call protection, the annual return flow divided by the average investment can be used as an approximation for the yield. The implied crossover yield is 8.46%:

$$\text{Crossover yield: } \frac{80 + \frac{1080-1000}{10}}{\frac{1080+1000}{2}} = 8.46\%$$

In one year's time the bond's maturity will be 29 years with nine years to call. If the market rate has decline to the point where the YTM of the bond is 7%, which is below the crossover yield of 8.46%, the bond's yield to call will be 6%.

$$\text{Yield to call} = \frac{80 + \frac{1000-1123.43}{9}}{\frac{1080+1123.43}{2}} = 6\%$$

If a bond-portfolio manager ignored the call option and computed the duration of this bond to maturity at a market yield of 7%, the duration would be 12.49 years. If duration was computed recognizing the call option at a price of $1,080 and using the yield to call of 6%, it would be 6.83 years.

Since a majority of corporate bonds have a call option, the effect of the call option upon a bond's duration could have an effect on the bond manager's investment decision. Therefore, the bond's duration, both disregarding the call option and regarding the call option, must be considered in an investment decision. That is, if interest rates stabilize or continue to rise, the call-option duration is of less importance than the bond's duration disregarding the call option. If interest rates fall, the call-option duration is of more importance.

## Questions and Problems

1. Define the following terms:
   a. Indenture and bond contract
   b. Coupon bonds and zero coupon bonds
   c. Secured bonds and mortgage bonds
   d. Debenture and subordinated debenture
   e. Bond rating and rating agencies
   f. Sinking fund
   g. Call provision
   h. Restrictive covenants
   i. Equilibrium interest rate
   j. Yield to maturity
   k. Forward rate
   l. Deep discount bond
   m. Floating rate notes
   n. Extendable notes
2. How can the Fisher equation be used to determine the normal interest rate? How has Fama tested the Fisher equation?
3. Define maturity and duration. Why is the duration concept used in analyzing the longer-term bond financing decision?
4. Discuss three alternative term structure theories. How can these theories be used to make long-term bond financing decisions?
5. Suppose firm XYZ is setting up an amortized term loan. What are the annual payments for a $10 million loan under the following terms:
   a. 9%, 10 years
   b. 10%, 10 years
   c. 12%, 20 years
6. Use the following information to calculate duration:

a. $F = \$1{,}000$
b. Yield to maturity $(r) = 0.08$
c. Coupon rate $(i) = 0.10$
d. Annual coupon payments $(Fi) = (\$1,000)(0.10) = \$100$
e. Number of years to maturity $(T) = 5$ years

7. ABC Company issued $100 million worth of 20-year, 10% callable bonds five years ago. The bonds are callable today at $1,050 per bond. Each bond has a par value of $1,000. Transactions costs of calling the issue and refunding the bonds are $6 per bond. In today's market, ABC can issue a 15-year callable bond at 8%. ABC's tax rate is 30%. Should ABC refund the bond issue?
8. Rank the following securities based on yield, assuming that they are for the same company with the same maturity:

   a. Subordinated debentures
   b. Mortgage bonds
   c. Senior debentures

9. For each of the following bond ratings, identify the rating agency:

   a. Aa1
   b. AAA
   c. Aaa
   d. 14
   e. C
   f. Caa
   g. BB+

10. Explain the factors which enhance or reduce the values of bonds with mandatory sinking funds.
11. Distinguish between the cause of a change in bond yields as you move along the supply curve for bonds and that which results from a shift in the supply curve.
12. If $10,000 is invested for one year at an interest rate of 12% and the rate of inflation is 8%, what is the real interest rate in terms of approximate Fisher equation?
13. Consider an investment of $10,000 for 1 year at a nominal yield of 12%. If the expected rate of inflation is 8%, what is

the precise real rate of interest according to the exact Fisher equation, which present in Eq. (14.2)?

14. If the real rate of interest is 6%, current inflation is 3%, and expected inflation is 5%, then:
    a. What is the precise nominal interest rate?
    b. What is the approximate nominal interest rate?
15. Why is an upward sloping yield curve inconsistent with the traditional expectations hypothesis?
16. Explain why the liquidity preference theory is consistent with an upward sloping yield curve?
17. Consider the following prices, maturities, and durations of four zero coupon bonds:

| **Bond** | **T** | **Price** | **Duration** |
|---|---|---|---|
| A | 1 | $890 | 1 |
| B | 3 | 900 | 3 |
| C | 5 | 950 | 5 |
| D | 8 | 800 | 8 |

    a. Why do the years to maturity equal the bonds' durations?
    b. If an investor purchases each of the bonds for his/her portfolio, what is the duration of the portfolio?

18. Interpret the value of 1.845 for a bond's volatility and explain how this value is affected by the duration of the bond.

19(a). Please define the formula for calculating duration.

19(b). Please show that duration is equal to maturity for a zero discount bond.

20(a). The coupon rate for bond A and bond B are 4.00% and 5.00%, respectively. In addition we assume that the maturities of both bonds are 5 years. By using the market interest rate of 6.00%, please calculate duration for both bonds A and B.

20(b). If we expect the market interest rate is going to go up by 0.50%, by what percent will the bond price decrease?

21(a). By using Eq. (14.1A) on in Appendix 14A, please discuss the relationship among realized rate of return (RY), YTM, and reinvestment rate (RR). If D is equal to 3.50 years, YTM is equal to 3.00%, and the reinvestment rate is equal to 2.50%, please calculate the realized rate of return.

21(b). Please draw some implications associated with 3(a).

## Chapter 15

# Common Stock, Preferred Stock, and Financing Decisions

## Contents



## 15.1 Introduction

In this chapter, we discuss mechanisms for the issue and trading of common and preferred stock and the role of stockholders in corporate ownership.

We begin in Section 15.2 by discussing accounting rules for the balance-sheet valuation of corporate stock. Section 15.3 discusses the market for common stock, and Section 15.4 discusses procedures for issuing common stock. Corporate control and stock repurchase are discussed in Section 15.5. Agency theory is discussed in Section 15.6, and preferred stock is discussed in Section 15.7. The choice between debt, preferred stock, and equity is looked at in Section 15.8, and finally, Section 15.9 summarizes the chapter. Appendix 15A examines the relationship between inflation and the general level of stock market prices.

## 15.2 Balance Sheet Accounts

A corporation is owned by its common stockholders, and corporate management is presumed to act in the interests of this ownership. Formally, stockholders exercise their ownership rights through the election of the corporation's board of directors, who in turn appoint the senior managers responsible for the operation of the corporation's business activities. These managers are thus responsible to stockholders, and the board of directors is the instrument for monitoring this responsibility.

We have already seen that a corporation can raise capital through the issue of debt instruments. Another way to raise capital is by issuing new shares of common stock. Such an issue could dilute the ownership of existing stockholders and would require their approval.

In this section, we discuss the balance-sheet valuation, through book value per share, of common stockholders' equity in a firm. The stockholders' equity accounts of a corporation constitute total common stockholders' equity as the sum of the following three components:

1. *Par value.* In some instances, the par value of a share of corporate stock is the price per share of the corporation's first issue of common stock. However, this figure is arbitrary and has no relationship to the stock's actual market value. Legally, par value is the amount of money that has been put up by stockholders or will be required of them in the event of bankruptcy. For example, if an issue of stock with a par value of $5 is sold for $4.50 per share, then in the event of bankruptcy the holders of this stock would be required to put up an additional 50 cents per share. Because such

an issue would not be very attractive to potential purchasers, the par value is almost inevitably set below the market value. In fact, most stock is issued at either a par value of $1 or at "no par," which is possible because there is no legal requirement for a corporation to set a par value on an issue of stock.

2. *Additional paid-in capital.* Since the par value of an issue of stock will underestimate the total amount of money raised from the issue, the difference must be accounted for separately. For example, suppose that a corporation sells 100,000 additional shares of common stock, with a $1 par value per share, at $10.50 per share. The total amount raise is $1,050,000. Of this total, $100,000 is attributed in the accounts to the par value of shares outstanding, while the remaining $950,000 is recorded as additional paid-in capital. Therefore, the sum of par value and additional paid-in capital constitutes the total price paid for all the outstanding stock of a corporation *at the time the shares were issued.*
3. *Retained earnings.* Even for accounting purposes, par value plus additional paid-in capital is an incomplete assessment of stockholders' equity in a corporation. Common stock ownership entitles holders to a proportionate share of dividend distributions. However, corporations do not distribute all earnings as dividends. Earnings retained for further investment are also part of the account of stockholders' equity.

Total common stockholders' equity is the sum of par value, additional paid-in capital, and retained earnings. Book value per share is then computed by dividing this total by the number of shares outstanding, as illustrated in Table 15.1 for the XYZ Corporation. This corporation has issued 65 million shares of common stock and has stockholder approval to issue up to 15 million additional shares.

Table 15.1 Stockholder's Equity Accounts for XYZ Corporation.

| | |
|---|---|
| Common stock (80 million shares authorized, 65 million shares outstanding, $1 par) | $65,000,000 |
| Additional paid-in capital | 125,830,000 |
| Retained earnings | 474,280,000 |
| Total common stockholders' equity | $665,110,000 |

Book value per share = $665,110,000/65,000,000 = $10.23

All shares have a par value of $1. However, over the years, the money received by XYZ Corporation from the sale of stock has exceeded the par value of this stock by $125,830,000. In the aggregate, XYZ Corporation has been profitable and has accumulated a total of $474,280,000 in undistributed earnings. Of course, if in any year the corporation operates at a loss, a subtraction from total retained earnings must be recorded. Finally, in Table 15.1 we compute total common stockholders' equity and, dividing by the number of share outstanding, arrive at a figure of $10.23 for book value per share.

It is important to distinguish between the accounting concept of book value per share and the market value of common stock. The two can be quite different, and from the point of view of both management and stockholders, market value is by far the more relevant. The reason is that book value is not closely connected with the price that can be obtained for a share of stock, which depends on the interaction of supply and demand forces in the stock market. The difference between book value and market value can perhaps best be characterized by noting that book value is *backward looking* while market value is *forward looking.* Book value is based only on money raised from the sale of stock and retained earnings *over a series of past years.* On the other hand, in valuing a corporation, market participants are concerned about dividend payments that will be distributed to stockholders *in the future.* Thus, if investors judge that a corporation's business prospects are likely to improve substantially in future years, they will bid up the price of its common stock. However, this judgment will have no immediate impact on book value per share, though if expectations are realized and in future years the corporation has positive retained earnings, book value will also increase over time.

## 15.3 The Market for Common Stock

In this section, we outline the institutional arrangements for common stock ownership and trading in the U.S. In many small companies, stock is owned solely by management. There is no market for such closed, or closely owned, corporate stock, which is therefore difficult to value unless the corporation is sold or an offering is made to the public. However, the majority of the stock in most larger corporations is not owned by management. Stockholdings in such *publicly held* corporations are more or less regularly traded through institutionalized markets, where price is set through the interaction of demand for and supply of these shares. Historically, most publicly owned corporate stock had been held by individual investors. However, the last 30 years have witnessed a radical change in the constitution of stock ownership in the U.S. In this period, the growth of pension funds, life insurance companies, and mutual funds has been dramatic, so that their holdings constitute a sizable, and growing, percentage of all publicly held stock. Moreover, these institutions trade far more frequently than do individuals, on average, so that their decisions and actions dominate the market for many stocks. They also offer a number of compelling advantages for investors. First, with the growing skepticism about reliance on Social Security to provide adequate retirement income, employees have found it increasingly attractive to bargain for enhanced pension plans. Second, a large fund can spread risk at modest cost in a manner that is possible only for the wealthiest individual investors. It seems clear that institutions are likely to prove increasingly dominant in the markets for common stock in the years to come.

The secondary market is established either in an organized stock exchange or, less formally, in the over-the-counter market. The stocks of smaller publicly held corporations are generally traded on regional exchanges, while listings for larger firms are generally on national exchanges, such as the American Stock Exchange or, for major corporations, the New York Stock Exchange. Listing on these exchanges cannot be secured automatically: exchange members require some assurance that the stock will be attractive to investors and regularly traded.

A stock exchange is characterized by a physical location, a set of members who execute, for a fee, buy and sell orders, and a set of rules and procedures for the establishment of an orderly and efficient market. The genesis of the major U.S. exchange, the New York Stock Exchange, was in the 1790s, when Wall Street became an important center for the trading of stock, initially through the Tontine Coffee House. In 1817, members adopted a constitution and the name New York Stock and Exchange Board. From that time, the NYSE grew through developments in communications and data processing capabilities, and through growth in the U.S. economy and the public interest in corporate stock ownership, to its modern form.

Stocks on the NYSE and other exchanges are traded for investors by exchange members, who have paid for this right by the purchase of seats on the exchange through an auction market. For actively traded stocks, dealers will receive many buy and sell orders during any working day. Transaction prices are established through an equilibrium of bids to buy and offers to sell. An exchange will have several types of members. The two most significant are commission-house brokers and specialists. About half the members of the NYSE are commission-house brokers attached to member brokerage houses. These members execute clients' buy and sell orders and relay to senior partners information about market movements. Most of the remaining NYSE members are specialists whose primary function is to establish a market in one or two securities through trades with other members.

Unlisted stocks — that is, stocks not listed on an exchange — are traded in the over-the-counter market. Typically, these are securities for which the market is thin, so that there will not be frequent buy and sell orders. By contrast with the exchanges, the over-the-counter market consists of a small number of individual brokers who hold inventories of these stocks and are prepared at any time to quote both a bid and offer price for a stock. The prices will differ — the size of the difference depending on the thinness of the market — and this difference constitutes the return to the brokers establishing the market.[1]

## 15.4 Procedures for Issuing Common Stock

We now discuss the procedures that must be followed by a corporation that has decided to raise capital by issuing new common stock. The procedures depend on whether existing stockholders have *preemptive rights*; that is, on whether the corporation is required to

[1]For a more detailed discussion of such topics as the role of the specialist, the types of market orders, the bid-ask spread, the National Market System, and the National Associations of Security Dealers (NASD), see Bodie *et al.* (2021).

offer any new issue to existing stockholders before making a public offering. Even when there is no preemptive right, it may still be preferable to consider a rights offering to existing stockholders rather than a public offering.

The issuing corporation makes such decisions in conjunction with the investment bankers chosen to market the issue. In effect, the investment banker — either alone for smaller issues or through an underwriting syndicate for larger issues — purchases the entire issue at a price agreed on with the corporation and subsequently sells these shares to the public. The advantage of such an arrangement to the corporation lies in the assurance that an agreed on amount of capital will be raised. On the other hand, the underwriters face the risk of being unable to move the entire issue at a satisfactory price and therefore suffering some financial risk. It is to spread this risk that syndicates are formed, usually consisting of underwriters, investment bankers, and brokerage firms. Also, as compensation for underwriting risk, the offering price of the issue will likely be set below the prevailing market price of the corporation's outstanding stock.

Other costs will also be incurred in issuing new stock: the investment banker must be paid, and accounting, legal, and other costs will be involved. The mechanism for payment of the investment banker's fee is the spread between the price paid by the banker for the stock and the public offering price. This fee must be negotiated between the corporation and its investment banker.

Once an investment banker has been chosen and a decision made on whether a rights issue will be involved, a registration statement must be filed with the Securities and Exchange Commission before stock can be sold. This document, prepared by the issuing firm and its investment banker, with the assistance of legal and accounting advisers, must be scrutinized for accuracy of representation by SEC staff, a process that typically takes about 20 days.

During this waiting period, the corporation and its investment bankers can prepare a prospectus of the offering for the public. However, since the stock market could move substantially during this time, it will not be possible to set the offering price until SEC clearance has been received. This offering price, negotiated between the corporation and its investment banker, typically will be somewhat

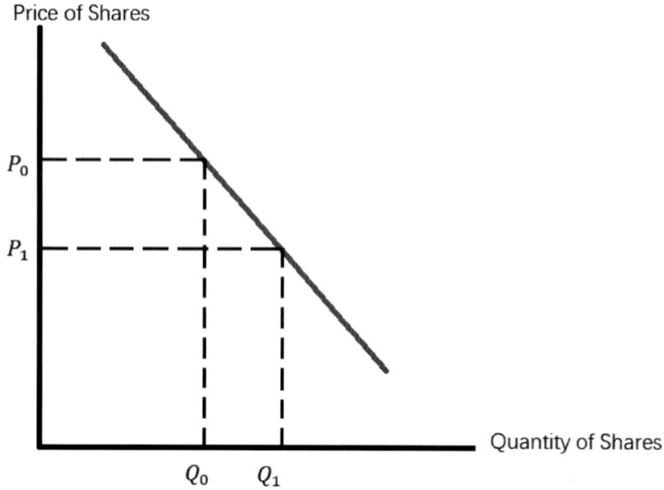


Figure 15.1 Expected Fall in Price of Shares from a New Stock Issue.

below the market price immediately before the issue.[2] To see why this is so, consider Figure 15.1 in which we have graphed the demand function, $D_0$, representing the relationship between investors' demand for the shares of a corporation and the price of those shares. Suppose that prior to the new issue, the quantity of shares outstanding is $Q_0$, so that the corresponding market price is $P_0$. If the size of the issue is $Q_1 - Q_0$ shares, so that number of shares outstanding will be $Q_1$, then, if market sentiment remains unchanged, we see from Figure 15.1 that price per share would be expected to drop from $P_0$ to $P_1$.

However, this may not be the end of the story, for it may be possible to shift out the demand curve of Figure 15.1. This could be achieved in two ways. First, the issuing corporation must mount a promotional campaign before the issue date in an attempt to

[2]The downward slope of the demand curve for the firm's stock may be caused by market pressure; that is, marginal investors require a lower price before they will purchase any additional shares. However, for some individual firms, the demand curve may be horizontal and the new issue can be sold without a reduction in price. This remains an empirical issue, which the investment banker must evaluate before making a recommendation on the price of the new shares.

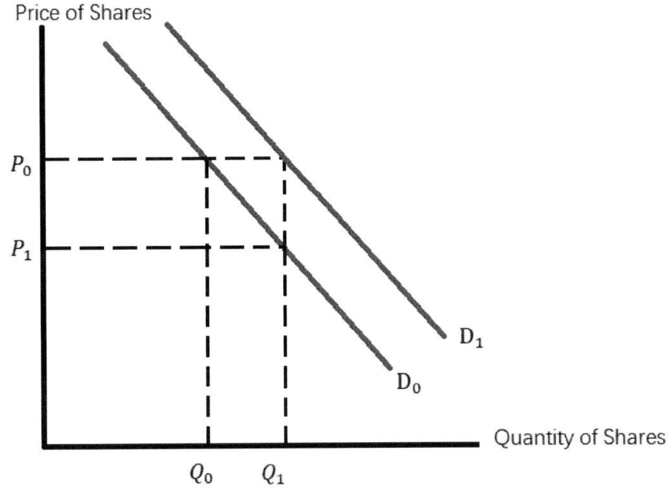


Figure 15.2 Increase in Demand for a New Stock Issue.

convince potential investors of the attractiveness of its prospects. Such a campaign would be particularly useful if new capital is being raised so that the corporation can expand in new directions. Second, members of the underwriting syndicate have the incentive to aggressively market the issue to their clients. It is possible that these strategies could shift the demand curve for the corporation's shares to the position shown in Figure 15.2. State laws called *blue sky laws* limit the amount of promotional activities the firm and the underwriter may use in trying to sell the stock. Suppose that the corporation and its underwriters are successful in increasing the attractiveness of the shares to shift the demand curve from $D_0$ to $D_1$. As can be seen in Figure 15.2, the original market price, $P_0$, still prevails. The implication in these circumstances is that the entire issue could be sold at the current market price.

In practice, the spread between the market price and the price paid by the underwriters depends on many factors, including perceptions about the corporation's prospects, the marketing campaign, and the view that is taken of the general market for new issues.

For the aggregate stock market, the demand curve for shares is downward sloping. As the stock market rises, companies are more likely to issue new shares, which will cause the market to experience downward price pressure to attract investors to purchase the new shares.

### 15.4.1 *Rule 415 shelf registration*

The traditional underwriting process for new equity issues tended to be time consuming, loaded with red tape, and costly. Rule 415 of the Securities and Exchange Commission eliminates much of the inconvenience and cost associated with bringing a new issue to market. To register under Rule 415, a firm files a relatively short form describing the securities and the firm's financing needs over the next two-year planning horizon. To receive SEC approval for a shelf registration, the firm must have submitted all required SEC documentation over the last three years, filed the latest year's SEC-required documentation, and not be in arrears on any financial obligations.

This shelf rule offers a great deal of flexibility for both the issuer and the investor. The issuer's intention to place new securities in the market is made known to the investment community. Investors can then submit bids to the issuer for all or part of the proposed securities. The issuer then has the right to accept or reject the offer, depending on the terms of the offer and the issuer's need for funds. It is also possible for the issuer to initiate the sale of the securities by asking for bids from brokers, dealers, or investors. This means that underwriters will be forced to react to the competition. Under the shelf rule, the underwriter can be bypassed as investors make bids directly to issuers, thereby reducing the time and money spent on bringing out a new issue.

There are certain drawbacks to this procedure. Some investors will worry that the amount of disclosure may be reduce, and the traditional issuer and underwriter relationship will be threatened. In effect, the firm deals directly with the investor without consulting the underwriter. Conceivably, the lack of an underwriter's advice and expertise could cause problems of control should a takeover occur.

It is not surprising that most shelf registrations take place in the issue of new debt rather than equity issues. Less than 10% of all new equity issues are brought out under shelf registration, while in excess of 50% of new bond issues are brought out under shelf registration.

### 15.4.2 *Preemptive right*

A *preemptive right* gives the existing shareholders the first choice to purchase a portion of a new issue of stock so that they can maintain their relative position of control. Depending on the laws of the state from which the corporation has received its charter, the shareholders may automatically have a preemptive right or the corporate charter must explicitly state the right of the shareholders with respect to preemptive right.

The rationale for the preemptive right is threefold: (1) it protects the existing shareholders' percentage of controlling interest, (2) it prevents the dilution of the value of the existing shareholders' investment, and (3) it maintains the existing shareholders' proportionate interest in the firm's earnings and dividends. In the first instance, we can imagine a disagreement between management and shareholders. Typically, the shareholders will vote to install a new board of directors, who in turn will replace management. To protect their jobs, the entrenched management may try to issue new shares to investors whose interest are more in line with their own and thereby reduce the voting power of the existing shareholders, making it more difficult for them to replace the management.

The second reason for the preemptive right is that it protects the value of the existing shareholders' investment. If the firm were to sell new shares at a price below the current market value, in effect there would be a transfer of wealth (value) from the old shareholders to the new shareholders. To prevent this wealth transfer, the old shareholders have the right to purchase a proportionate share of the new issue to retain the value of their initial investment.

The third reason, like the second, protects the old shareholders from a wealth transfer. If new shares are issued to new shareholders, the proportionate amount of future dividends received by the old shareholders may be reduced, which may shift future wealth from the old shareholders to the new shareholders.[3]

[3]This dilution is related to the degree that the new shares were sold at a price below the existing price of the stock before the new issue. If the proceeds of the new issue are invested in positive net present value projects, it is possible to avoid dilution as long as the impact of the positive net present value project exceeds the dilution effect.

### 15.4.3 *Issuing stock with a preemptive right*

When a new issue of stock is brought to market by a firm whose shareholders have a preemptive right, the existing shareholders have the right to purchase a share of the new issue equal to their existing percentage of ownership. If the firm's charter does not specifically allow for a preemptive right, management has the option of either first offering the new issue to existing shareholders or offering it directly to the market. Once the rights are issued to the existing shareholders, they must either exercise their rights by buying some of the new equity issue to maintain their percentage ownership of the firm, or sell the rights to someone else. If the old shareholders do not exercise their rights or sell them to someone else, they are making a costly mistake. By not doing anything and letting the rights expire worthless, they lose an amount equal to the right's value.

A *right* is a certificate, issued by the corporation to the existing shareholders, that specifies the conditions under which the shareholders may purchase shares of the new equity issue. Each shareholder receives one right for each existing share of stock owned. The right contains information about the subscription price and the number of rights required to purchase one new share. Based on this information, we can determine the theoretical value of the right for the old shareholders:

$$\begin{aligned}&\text{Value of one right}\\&\quad=\frac{\text{Market value of stock rights on} - \text{Subscription price}}{\text{Number of rights to purchase 1 share} + 1}\end{aligned} \tag{15.1}$$

The numerator measures the value created by being able to buy a share of stock at less than its market value. The lower the subscription price, the more valuable the right. The denominator takes into account the fact that when you exercise your right to buy a new share, you are entitled to receive an additional right during the *rights-on period*, which is a period between when the rights offering is announced and the holder-of-record date is set. During the right-on period, if you purchased a share of stock you would receive not only the share of stock but also one right. Hence, the market value of the stock, rights on, consists of two parts: the value of the underlying share and the value of one right. In our notation,

$$\text{Value of one right} = \frac{\begin{array}{c}\text{Market value of the stock, without the rights}\\ +\text{Value of one right} - \text{Subscription price}\end{array}}{\text{Number of rights to purchase 1 share} + 1} \quad (15.2)$$

Rearranging this formula and cancelling terms,

$$\begin{aligned}&\text{Value of one right (Number of rights to purchase 1 share)}\\ &\quad = \text{Market value of the stock without the right}\\ &\quad\quad - \text{Subscription price} \qquad (15.3)\end{aligned}$$

After a certain date, called the *holder-of-record date*, to purchase a new share you would pay the market value of the stock without the right, and the value of one right would be

$$\text{Value of one right} = \frac{\begin{array}{c}\text{Market value of the stock, without the right}\\ -\text{Subscription price}\end{array}}{\text{Number of rights to purchase 1 share}} \quad (15.4)$$

Hence, the value of the right depends on when the stock was purchased. If you are an existing shareholder and you purchased your stock before the holder-of-record date, then the value of a single right is shown in Eq. (15.1). After the holder-of-record date, the value of the right changes to the amount shown in Eq. (15.4).

Exhibit 15.1 gives a hypothetical right-valuation problem.

As can be seen in Exhibit 15.1, all that changes is the market price of the shares at the holder-of-record date. If the stock is purchased prior to the ex-right date, the new owner will receive the right, whereas if the stock is sold after the ex-right date, the seller of the stock will receive the right. The market price of the shares reflects the fact that in one case both a share of stock and a right are received before the ex-right date, and in the second case only the share of stock is received.

From the perspective of the corporation and management, there are benefits to using the rights offering to raise new capital. By offering the stock to existing shareholders, who are presumably happy

**Exhibit 15.1:** The Value of a Right.

| Market condition prior to the holder-of-record date | | Market condition after the holder-of-record date | |
|---|---|---|---|
| *Holder-of-record date* | | | |
| Market value of stock, right on | \$99 | Market value of stock, without rights | \$98 |
| Subscription price | \$96 | Subscription price | \$96 |
| Number of rights to buy one share | 2 | Number of rights to buy one share | 2 |
| Value of one right $= \frac{\$99-\$96}{2+1}$ | | Value of one right $= \frac{\$98-\$96}{2}$ | |
| Value of one right = \$1 | | Value of one right = \$1 | |

with the present firm management, the likelihood of successfully raising the amount of new capital is increased. Further, the underwriting costs of a rights offering, compared to a public offering of new stock, are substantially lower. Hence, it is normally in the firm's best interest to issue stock to a friendly, receptive audience while at the same time save the underwriting costs.

## 15.5 Corporate Control and Stock Repurchase

*Corporate control* is the right to determine the management of corporate resources, and such rights are vested in the corporation's board of directors. In theory, ownership of common stock includes the right to elect the members of the firm's board of directors, which is carried out through the *proxy system.* A *proxy* is a legal instrument that transfers, for a temporary period, the rights to vote. Typically, in the case of corporate stockholders, this period is the duration of the annual meeting of stockholders. In a company that has a wide dispersion of shareholders, the proxy system of voting places the power to elect the board of directors in the hands of incumbent management. Basically, each shareholder receives a statement prepared by the current management asking that the shareholder support the provisions put forth by management with respect to such issues as election of the board of directors, the auditing firm to be used by the corporation, the executive compensation plan, and other decisions that affect the shareholder wealth. If shareholders disagree with management proposals, they can vote no. If they agree or don't have any opinion, they can sign the proxy statement giving management the right to vote for them at the annual meeting. In most cases, the management proposals are approved.

Some companies have various classes of common stock that limit or restrict the voting rights of the shareholders. For example, a company can have a Class A voting stock and a Class B nonvoting stock that are identical except on the ability to vote. Such classified stock is used by owners of a closely held company who wish to maintain voting control. By issuing two classes of stock and selling nonvoting stock to the public, the owners can raise new capital without giving up voting control. The major stock exchanges have rules regarding the trading of nonvoting shares.

The two most common methods of voting in corporate elections are *majority voting* and *cumulative voting*. With majority voting, the candidate receiving the most votes wins. This method of voting prevents minority representation on the board of directors because an individual or a group owning or controlling over 50% of the voting shares can ensure that its candidates are elected as directors.

Cumulative voting encourages more minority representation on the board. Under cumulative voting, anyone owning 100 shares can use them to vote for as many or as few positions as desired. If there are 10 positions vacant, the shareholder can cast all 1,000 votes (100 shares $\times$ 10 positions) for a single candidate. This increases the minority shareholders' chance of electing candidates by enabling them to pool their votes in support of a limited number of candidates.

To determine the minimum number of shares required to elect one member to the board, the following relationship can be used:

$$r = \frac{S \times d}{D + 1} + 1, \tag{15.5}$$

where $r$ = the number of shares required to elect one director; $S$ = total number of voting shares; $d$ = the number of directors the shareholder wants to elect; and $D$ = the total number of directors to be elected.

If 1,000 shares are voted and 10 directors are to be elected, a minimum of 92 shares will be needed to elect one director:

$$r = \frac{1{,}000 \times 1}{10 + 1} + 1 = 92.$$

A shareholder with 100 shares can vote all 1,000 votes for a candidate to ensure the candidate's election. Hence, a person with 10% of the outstanding shares is ensured representation: in this case, 10% (1 director out of 10).

One way for majority shareholders to increase the impact of cumulative voting is to reduce the number of board positions to be filled at any one time. This can be accomplished by either reducing the size of the board or by staggering the terms of the directors.

As opposed to issuing common stock, a corporation may acquire some of its own common stock outstanding. These management-repurchased shares are called *treasury stock*. Treasury stock is not considered an investment to the corporation (that is, an asset); rather, the acquired stock reduces the firm's capitalization. There are many reasons why a firm may reacquire its own stock, as shown in Exhibit 15.2, but one reason is as an alternative to issuing dividends. If a firm acquires its own shares, assuming that earnings are not affected by the repurchase, a capital gain equal to the amount of the dividend can be realized. For example, during the past year, ABC Corporation earned $6.6 million, of which $3.3 million was to be distributed as dividends to the common stockholders. With the stock price of ABC Corporation at $30 per share and 1.1 million shares outstanding, ABC faces two alternatives as shown in Exhibit 15.3. First, ABC Corporation can distribute dividends at $3 per share, thus allocating the $3.3 million. Alternatively, ABC can use the $3.3 million to acquire 100,000 shares of its own stock through a $33 per share tender offer. Basically, this creates a capital gain of $3 per share to the shareholders. This approach has advantages and disadvantages to the shareholder depending on the tax laws regarding capital gains and dividends and whether these capital gains are realized or not.

**Exhibit 15.2:** Reasons for a Corporation to Reacquire Its Own Stock.

1. Meet employee stock compensation contracts
2. Reduce shares outstanding in hope of increasing EPS
3. Buy out a particular ownership interest
4. Attempt to make a market in the company's stock
5. Contract the operations of the business
6. Meet the stock needs of a potential merger

**Exhibit 15.3:** Alternatives Facing ABC Corporation.

$$\text{Current EPS} = \frac{\$6.6\text{ million}}{1.1\text{ million}} = \$6\text{ per share}$$

$$\text{Current}\frac{P}{E}\text{ratio} = \frac{\$30}{\$6} = 5$$

$$\text{EPS after repurchase of }100,000\text{ shares} = \frac{\$6.6\text{ million}}{1\text{ million}} = \$6.60\text{ per share}$$

Expected market price after repurchase

$$= \left(\frac{P}{E}\right)(\text{EPS}) = (5)(\$6.6) = \$33 \quad \text{per share}$$

## 15.6 Agency Theory

*Agency theory* involves the agency relationship between management and stockholders. This theory is based on the premise that ownership of capital should not be confused with ownership of the firm. Rather, each factor of production — such as land, labor, and capital — is owned by somebody. The firm is just the set of contracts covering the way inputs are joined to create outputs and the way receipts from outputs are shared among the owners of the inputs. Hence, the shareholders do not own the firm in any real sense, or at least no more than does labor, management, suppliers, or any other group that contributes to the creation of firm value.

By acting according to portfolio theory, the stockholder will hold a well-diversified portfolio of securities of many firms so as to reduce unsystematic risk. Thus, this investor has no special incentive to be concerned with the detailed operations of any single firm. Such behavior implies a large degree of separation between the ownership of capital and the control of decision-making in the individual firm.

On the other hand, the managers of the firm tie up a substantial amount of their well-being, human capital, and perhaps wealth in their firm. As a rule, managers are not diversified, in that their salary, stock options, and other payments depend on the success or failure of the firm. Hence, management has a much larger stake in the success or failure of the firm, and this is reflected in management attempts to control the selection of the board of directors through the use of the proxy system, majority voting, or stock classes.[4]

## 15.7 Preferred Stock

Preferred stockholders' claims on assets and income fall between the bondholders' and the common stockholders' claims. When classifying preferred stock as debt or equity, the final decision is based on the circumstances of the decision-maker. Like bonds, preferred stock has a stipulated fixed rate of dividend payments, which must be paid before the firm can pay dividends to the common shareholders, but after all interest and sinking fund payments have been made on the debt. Hence, creditors consider preferred stock as a portion of equity, whereas common stockholders view it as debt.

Like common stock, if the dividend on the preferred stock is not paid because the firm does not have sufficient cash flow, the firm will not be in danger of bankruptcy. In most cases of deferred payment, the preferred shareholders have the same right to vote on corporate matters as the common shareholders. In the case of a passed dividend, some preferred shareholders are given the right to select a certain percentage of the board of directors.

Unlike the arrangement for common stockholder dividends, most preferred stocks have a cumulative arrangement stipulating that all accumulated preferred dividends that have been omitted must be paid before the common shareholders can receive any dividends. The existence of a *dividend arrearage* (nonpayment of preferred dividends with a cumulative feature) causes a drop in the creditworthiness of the firm as well as a drop in the value of the common shares. If the arrearage persists for long periods, the corporation usually will make some sort of arrangement with the preferred shareholders such as offering them cash, more preferred stock, or common stock to settle preferred shareholders' claim.

From the corporation's viewpoint, a major drawback of preferred stock is that the dividend payments are not tax-deductible. Therefore, in most cases, the firm would be better off issuing tax-deductible

[4] Agency costs were discussed in Chapter 11. For a more detailed discussion agency theory, see Barnea *et al.* (1985).

debt instead of preferred stock. In certain industries, such as banking, the marginal tax rate is low so the firm can afford to issue preferred stock. In the public utility industry, where taxes are considered an expense for rate-making purposes, the lack of tax deductibility of preferred dividends is not an impediment. These two industries probably account for the majority of preferred stock that is outstanding or currently being issued.

### 15.7.1 *Floating-rate preferred stock*

*Floating-rate preferred stock* is preferred stock with a dividend payment that is changed periodically based on a specific index, such as the T-bill rate. Under current tax law, the treatment of dividend income for corporations almost guarantees the existence of preferred stock. Of all dividends received by one corporation from another, 80% are excluded from the recipient's taxable income. The remaining 20% are taxed at the corporation's marginal tax rate. For example, a corporation paying the maximum tax rate of 34% would pay an effective tax rate on dividend income of 6.8% $(0.34 \times 0.20)$. For a corporation with surplus funds to be invested in marketable securities, the tax treatment from investment in preferred stock (which pays dividends) over investments in bonds (which pay fully taxable interest) is enormous.

Exhibit 15.4 compares the tax treatment of preferred dividend and interest income from the corporate perspective.

This exhibit shows the tax advantage of preferred stock for the corporate investor. By combining a floating rate and unredeemability provisions with a tax advantage, the floating-rate preferred stock is an ideal security for both the corporate issuer and the corporate

**Exhibit 15.4:** Bond Income versus Preferred Dividend Income.

| Bond<br>Investment of $50,000<br>in a 10% bond | | Preferred<br>Investment of $50,000<br>in a 10% preferred stock | |
|---|---|---|---|
| Interest | $5,000 | Preferred dividend | $5,000 |
| Tax (0.34) | 1,700 | Tax $(0.34 \times 0.20 \times \$5000)$ | 340 |
| After-tax return | $3,300 | After-tax return | $4,660 |
| After-tax yield $\frac{\$3{,}300}{50{,}000} = 6.6\%$ | | After-tax yield $\frac{\$4{,}660}{50{,}000} = 9.2\%$ | |

investor. Issuers favor the nonredeemable feature because it provides a permanent source of financing that they never have to repay. Investors like the issue because of the tax treatment for dividends and the adjustment of the rates to market changes.

There is additional flexibility in these kinds of issues. The time period, the method of adjustment of the rate, and the target rate can be varied to meet particular circumstances. The maximum rate (cap) and minimum rate (floor) can also be adjusted to meet the needs of the issuer and the investor.

## 15.8 The Choice between Debt, Preferred Stock, and Equity

In this and the previous chapter, we discuss the sources of long-term financing available to a firm. In this section, we consider the decision-making process that allows for a reasoned and well-thought-out plan for obtaining long-term capital of one form or another.

When choosing a source of long-term financing, a firm must have particular criteria on which to base the selection. For this decision, as in other financial management decisions, the ultimate criterion is the maximization of shareholder wealth. This is not a one-dimensional concept. Many factors must be considered when choosing between debt, preferred stock, or equity. Cost, control, availability, and marketability are a few of the factors to be considered in selecting the best financing alternative.

In general, the after-tax cost of a financing alternative must be weighed against its risk. Both future and current market conditions must be considered. In addition, all terms and covenants should be evaluated in detail to ensure that management has a thorough understanding of the impact that the financing choice will have on firm value.

### 15.8.1 *Identifying financing alternatives*

In practice, it is not always easy to discern clearly the financing options available, nor is it easy to treat each financing decision independently. In fact, most firms simultaneously employ various types of financing.

The first area of concern is maturity: Does the firm need temporary or long-term financing? If the goal is to raise long-term capital, a list of available sources should be created. These sources should be classified as either debt, leasing, or equity. Various combinations of these alternatives are usually possible. For each alternative, a quantitative and qualitative analysis should be performed.

One generally accepted approach to analyzing alternatives is to calculate the after-tax cost or the after-tax cash flows associated with each source of financing. This is normally carried out through a *pro forma* analysis, which seeks to determine how a certain financing instrument will change the firm's financial perspective.

### 15.8.2 *Factors to consider about sources of financing*

Some of the significant factors that must be analyzed in choosing sources of financing are the timing of the cash flows; federal, state, and local taxes; the opportunity costs that the firm faces; the change in the firm's capital structure; and the effect on EPS and, alternately, the price of the firm's equity. From management's perspective, the impact on cash flow is one of the most important considerations in making a financing decision. Fixed servicing charges associated with debt financing may severely limit management's options for future decisions. For instance, when a zero coupon bond is issued, the corporation does not have any cash outflows (debt service) until the issue is called or matures. The attractiveness of this financing alternative is thus enhanced in the short run because it gives management a chance to use the firm's cash flows for other purposes. However, at maturity the balloon payment associated with the zero coupon issue can be burdensome, especially if the firm cannot refinance at reasonable terms at that time. This is the crisis-at-maturity problem, which one does not face with some preferred or common issues.

A second consideration is that corporate tax rates and regulations have immediate and variable impact on the type of financing that should be used. Depending on the tax regulations in effect, leasing or some other type of financing may be enough to take advantage of tax breaks and incentives. The *safe harbor* leasing arrangement used during 1981 and 1982 and the *defeasance* (debt for equity swaps) arrangements during 1981 to 1984 are good examples of this type of accommodation. Each financing decision should be evaluated in conjunction with the firm's overall tax posture to determine the best alternatives at present and to create contingency financing plans based on anticipated changes in the tax law in the near future.

Similarly, opportunity-cost factors deal with the impact that one type of financing may have on a firm's future decisions. For example, if a firm decides to issue equity, the next time the firm needs to raise funds its range of alternatives probably will be broader because of the increase in the firm's equity base or debt capacity. Conversely, if a firm decides on a debt issue, the range of financing alternatives may become somewhat limited. If a firm selects a certain type of financing today, what opportunities has it given up or created in the future?

In a related vein, the capital structure of any firm must be taken into account so that the firm's value is maximized by the degree of leverage tied to a given financing package. Numerous theoretical considerations by Modigliani and Miller argue whether there is a relationship between the degree of financial leverage and firm value. Regardless of whether the theory is correct or not, the firm's management must balance the relatively cheap after-tax cost of debt against the increase in risk and demands on cash flow associated with the issue of debt. One clear-cut signal is the bond-rating agencies' evaluation of various firms. There is a well-defined market relationship between the cost of debt or equity and the rating that a firm receives. Intra-industry comparisons also provide useful benchmarks for management when making this decision.

The impact that the proposed financing will have on equity price is also an important consideration. As we have seen in Chapter 5, the EPS can be an important determinant of a share value. The impact of the level and growth of EPS on the value of debt and equity needs to be examined in relation to historic patterns, current levels, and expected future levels and growth. In many cases, EPS increases with debt financing as long as earnings before interest and taxes are sufficient to meet the firm's fixed charges. However, the volatility of EPS is also greater with debt financing. Thus, if debt financing is selected, EPS will be greater than it would for equity financing: but for a given change in sales (increase or decrease), the change in EPS will also be greater.

The issue is whether the relatively cheap cost of debt outweighs the increase in risk. This can be evaluated in terms of expected revenue and operating profits, fixed-charge coverage, times interest earned, expected EPS, and growth tin EPS. However, the final test is the market reaction to the financing. Will the firm's P/E ratio increase, decrease, or remain the same? If we consider the following relationship:

$$P = EPS \times \frac{P}{EPS}$$

the price of a share of equity is equal to EPS times the price-earning ratio. For a given level of EPS, the market measurement of the firm's future prospects is embodied in the P/E ratio. The market makes an assessment of the trade-off between cheap debt and increased risk, and this is reflected in the P/E ratio.

Some of the factors affecting financing decisions are difficult or impossible to quantify; these factors must be identified and analyzed qualitatively, based on management's judgment and experience. The relative importance of these factors depends almost entirely on the situation. One such factor is control. While the ultimate ownership or control of the firm is vested in the shareholders, management is also in a position of control, and a certain financing alternative may influence these positions as well as the balance between shareholders and management. Suppose that a firm is to issue a block of voting equity, but there is the possibility that this equity might be picked up by unfriendly interests intent on taking over the firm. Based on the control factor alone, debt or some other form of financing would be used instead. On the other hand, if the shareholders feel that the firm has too much leverage and management is proposing a new debt issue, which will increase that leverage, they may wish to replace the present management with a more conservative group. In most cases, the control factor is not the key variable, but it still must be considered.

The nature of the firm's industry, the growth rate of revenue, the competitive situation, and the structure of existing assets may dictate the type of financing that is preferable. A company in a stable industry can probably afford to issue more debt than a firm in a highly cyclical industry. To achieve faster growth or competitive advantage, a firm may resort to debt financing. A firm's asset structure may determine not only the general class of financing debt, preferred stock, or common stock, but also the specific nature of the financing (leases or mortgages).

Current fads and market conditions may also have a role in deciding financing alternatives. If the market is paying a premium for convertible debt, the firm should give serious consideration to this type of financing. When the market is selling at high P/E ratios, equity should be given serious consideration.

Finally, factors unique to a firm or a particular economic climate should also be included in the analysis. Essentially, the decision-maker should consider all contingencies and the financial analysis should be carried out under various scenarios. This gives a more complete picture of the future and helps determine the success or failure of the financing decision.

### 15.8.3 *Ranking alternatives*

After the possible alternatives have been identified and a detailed delineation of both quantitative and qualitative factors has been performed, the next step in the financing process is to rank the various alternatives. This usually involves including the trade-offs of cost and qualitative factors.

By comparing quantitative and qualitative factors, management can establish priorities for determining the most favorable alternative or alternatives. Before making a final decision, the result of such an analysis can be used to benefit the decision-maker. The possibility of creating a tailor-made or combination financing package can be assessed by reviewing the favorable aspects of each alternative.

### 15.8.4 *Making the final decision*

Most financial managers have established a business relationship with an investment banker. The primary function of investment bankers is to provide a link between capital markets and firms. In effect, the investment banker is a middleman between the issuers and the investors. As the relationship matures, the investment banker comes to act as a financial adviser to the issuer. As such, investment bankers provide the issuer with information and suggestions regarding the type, form, and price of the security to be issued. Because the methods used to raise capital funds vary greatly and because market conditions are subject to change, the investment banker's advice generally concerns not only the needs of the issuer, but also the prevailing conditions in the capital markets and the current status of government regulations.

In most cases, the final decision on the exact form of the financing to be used is made in conjunction with the firm's investment banker. The investment banker may anticipate the firm's capital needs and bring proposals or suggestions to the financial manager. In either case, the final decision will be made in consultation with the firm's investment banker, who ultimately serves as the underwriter of the issue when it is brought to market.

At the conclusion of discussions and negotiations with the firm's investment banker, management has at its disposal the information needed to make the final decision. In the face of uncertainty and changing conditions associated with financial markets, it is not possible to ensure that the firm will always choose the best financing alternatives. Nevertheless, the use of a systematic approach to the financing decision, balanced by management's experience and judgment and the expertise of the investment bankers, should establish a solid foundation for a successful financing decision.

## 15.9 Summary

Chapters 14 and 15 present a detailed view of the main sources of long-term financing: debt, preferred stock, and common stock. The desirability of each of these types of financing depends on many factors, which must be systematically evaluated to finance the firm.

These two chapters have mapped out an approach to making informed decisions about the types of financing that a firm may undertake. The material is not meant as an exhaustive checklist to be used under all circumstances; rather, it provides a general framework that can be adapted to many different circumstances. The relative importance of specific factors depends on the firm's circumstances, along with the existing economic, regulatory, and market conditions.

## References


Barnea, A., R. A. Haugen and L. W. Senbet. *Agency Problems and Financial Contracting* (Prentice Hall, Englewood Cliffs, NJ, 1985).

Bodie, Z., A. Kane and A. Marcus. *Investments*, 12th edn. (McGraw-Hill Book Company, New York, 2021).

Elsaid, H. H. "The Function of Preferred Stock in the Corporate Financial Plan," *Financial Analysts Journal*, 25 (July–August 1969, pp. 112–117).

Furst, R. W. "Does Listing Increase the Market Price of Common Stocks?" *Journal of Business*, 43 (April 1970, pp. 174–180).

Lee, C. F. and J. Lee. *Financial Analysis, Planning and Forecasting: Theory and Applications*, 3rd edn. (Singapore: World Scientific, 2017).

Lee, C. F. and A. C. Lee. *Encyclopedia of Finance*, 2nd edn. (Springer, 2013).

Lee, C. F., J. F. Finnerty and E. A. Norton. *Foundations of Financial Management* (West Publishing Company, 1997).

Logue, D. E. and R. A. Jarrow. "Negotiation vs. Competitive Bidding in the Sale of Securities by Public Utilities," *Financial Management*, 6 (Autumn 1978, pp. 31–39).

Marks, K. R. and W. A. Law. "Hedging Against Inflation with Floating-Rate Notes," *Harvard Business Review*, 58 (March–April 1980, pp. 106–112).

Smith, C. W. "Alternative Methods for Raising Capital: Rights Versus Underwritten Offerings," *Journal of Financial Economics*, 9 (December 1977, pp. 273–307).

Stewart, S. S. "Should a Corporation Repurchase Its Own Shares?" *The Journal of Finance*, 31 (June 1976, pp. 911–926).

Summers, L. H. "Inflation, the Stock Market, and Owner-occupied Housing," *American Economic Review*, 71 (June 1981, pp. 429–434).


## Appendix 15A — Inflation and the Value of Common Stock

The price of a corporation's common stock reflects the market value of that corporation and is influenced by a great many factors. In Appendix 15A, we briefly consider the effect of inflation on the value of common stock.

First, consider an idealized world, with no taxes and no uncertainty about economic developments. Suppose that the rate of inflation is expected to rise, with a consequent increase in nominal interest rates. It might seem that this development would lower the value of corporate stock, because the future returns on which this value depends would be discounted by investors at a higher rate. However, such an argument ignores the fact that under general inflationary conditions, the prices of the goods and services produced by a corporation's assets can also be increased. In effect, this cancels out the higher discount rate, and the firm's value is unchanged. Another way of putting this is that, in our idealized world, common stocks provide a perfect hedge against inflation.

Unfortunately, this is an instance in which a model with idealized assumptions can lead us far astray in making predictions about the real world, as recent experience suggests. In the period from the mid-1960s through 1980, when inflation in the U.S. was at historically high levels, the real value of common stocks fell dramatically. One explanation for this phenomenon lies in the tax laws. Three factors in the tax laws argue that anticipated or actual high inflation is likely to lower the value of stocks.

1. In an inflationary environment, the real value of depreciation write-offs and other corporate tax deductions is reduced because allowable depreciation is based on historic cost and inventory accounting is based on FIFO. Consequently, before-tax profits will be overstated, leading to a higher effective tax rate on real profits.
2. Investors in common stocks similarly suffer from inflation. Taxes are imposed on nominal capital gains, not merely real gains. Even if the real, inflation-adjusted price of stock is lower at the time of sale than at the time of purchase, a capital gains tax is still imposed on a *nominal* increase in value.
3. Sophisticated investors are aware of the unfavorable tax position that may follow from common stock ownership in times of high inflation and will seek alternative investments that are not similarly disadvantaged. One such possibility, discussed by Lawrence Summers (1981), is owner-occupied housing. If, through inflation, the price of housing grows rapidly, then so does the implicit income of the owner-occupier as a result of the consequent growth in rents. Such imputed rents escape taxes. Moreover, most owner-occupiers

also escape capital gains liabilities on the sale of houses, through either the exemption for those owner-occupiers age 55 or over or provisions that allow rollover when another home is purchased. It can be argued that these discriminatory features of the tax laws render home ownership relatively more attractive than common stock ownership when high inflation is expected. The consequent drop in demand for stocks must lower their prices, all other things equal. The same factors also explain the explosive growth in house prices in the U.S. in the 1970s.

## Questions and Problems

1. Define the following:
    a. Book value
    b. Par value
    c. Bid-ask spread
    d. Preemptive right
    e. Corporate control
2. Compare and contrast book value per share and market value per share.
3. What are some possible scenarios that would exhibit dilution of the ownership of existing stockholders?
4. Explain the significance of having different markets for common stocks; that is, the NYSE and OTC.
5. Explain the role of the investment banker in the market for common stocks.
6. Why would the price of common stock paid by underwriters differ from the market price? When would the price be the same?
7. What is the significance of Rule 415 of the SEC?
8. Compare and contrast agency theory from the perspective of management and the perspective of the shareholders.
9. Explain the similarities and differences between preferred stock and corporate bonds. As a financial manager, what factors are important in deciding between these two forms of financing.

10. What are advantages and disadvantages for both firms and investors of the following?

    a. Preferred stock
    b. Corporate bonds
    c. Common stock

11. Outline the decision-making process in choosing between the various forms of financing (debt, preferred stock, and equity). Be sure to include economy-wide, industry-wide, and firm-specific factors that have an impact on the decision-making process.
12. ABC Company's stockholder equity on December 31, 1986, is as follows:

| | |
|---|---|
| Common stock: \$1 par (30,000,000 shares authorized, 25,000,000 shares outstanding) | \$25,000,000 |
| Additional paid-in capital | 165,000,000 |
| Retained earnings | 410,000,000 |
| On December 31, 1987: | |
| Net income | \$55,000,000 |
| Treasury stock at cost (5,000,000 shares) | 125,000,000 |

    What is the book value per common share?
13. A company has \$4 million in paid in capital, \$10 million in retained earnings, and \$4 million in par value common stock at \$1 per share. Find the book value of equity per share.
14. Distinguish between primary and secondary markets.
15. Distinguish between an over-the-counter market and an organized stock exchange.
16. How is it possible to increase the number of shares outstanding by selling new common stock and at the same time keep the price of the stock the same? (Refer to Figures 15.1 and 15.2.)
17. What are the three rationales for preemptive rights?
18. Why does a "right" have value in and of itself?
19. Allen Manufacturing is announcing a rights offering. The subscription price is \$50 and 2 rights are required to purchase one share of stock. The market value of the firm's stock rights-on is \$54.

a. Find the value of one right.
b. If the value of the stock drops to $51 after the stock goes ex-rights, what is the value of one right?

20. Tyndall, Inc. has 5,000,000 voting shares outstanding and 10 directors need to be elected. Shareholder Smith owns 500 shares.

 a. If cumulative voting is permitted, what is the maximum number of votes Smith can cast for any one director?
 b. If majority voting is permitted, what is the maximum number of votes Smith can cast for any one director?
 c. Determine the minimum number of shares required to elect any one director under cumulative voting.

21. Explain why a stock repurchase is an alternative to paying a dividend and why the former may have a tax advantage over the latter.
22. If a corporation has an effective tax rate of 30%, show the tax effects of $100,000 in preferred dividend income and of $100,000 in interest income.

 a. Would the corporation favor investing in the preferred stock or debt? Explain.
 b. What is the effective tax rate on the income from preferred dividends?

# Chapter 16

# Warrants and Convertible Securities

**Contents**



## 16.1 Introduction

A hybrid security has characteristics of both debt and equity. In Chapter 16, we discuss various types of hybrid securities and examine the factors that determine their market value. We have already discussed the valuation of bonds, stocks, and options in earlier chapters. Our approach to valuing hybrid securities is to use those valuation methods to reach an estimate of the value of a warrant or a convertible bond.

A warrant is generally issued in conjunction with a bond as a sweetener to make the debt issue more attractive to investors so that they will require a lower coupon interest rate. A warrant gives the holder the right to purchase a specific number of shares of common stock at a stipulated price for a specific period. Convertible bonds (and convertible preferred stock) are securities that can be exchanged for a stipulated number of shares of common stock during a specific period.

In effect, holders of these hybrid debt securities have made loans to the issuing corporation. However, in contrast to ordinary bondholders, they have the opportunity to profit if the firm flourishes to the extent that the market value of its common stock increases by an appreciable amount. Naturally, there is some cost associated with such an opportunity, so that convertible bonds or bonds with warrants will have lower coupon interest rates than straight (nonconvertible) debt. In this chapter, we look at how the market values such securities, which are intermediate between debt and equity. We also will see that the risk associated with hybrids in between the risk of straight debt and straight equity. We also discuss the features that render hybrid securities attractive to both the issuing corporation and the investors, and the effect of these securities on the firm's EPS.

In Section 16.2 of this chapter, we discuss hybrid securities. Section 16.3 discusses warrants and their valuations. Section 16.4 convertible bonds and their valuations. Cost of capital for convertibles and impacts of call and conversion is discussed in Section 16.5, and beta coefficients for convertible bonds is discussed in Section 16.6. In Section 16.7 we discuss earnings per share when warrants and convertibles are issued, and finally, Section 16.8 summarizes the chapter. Appendix 16A discusses the market value of a convertible bond, and Appendix 16B gives an option approach to evaluating bonds and stocks.

## 16.2 Hybrid Securities

In Chapters 14 and 15, we discussed corporate bonds and common stock in some detail. The interpretation of these two types of securities is relatively straightforward: bonds constitute a fixed claim on the corporation, while common stock confers a residual claim and a share in corporate ownership. However, corporations also raise capital through the issue of securities that are neither straight debt nor straight equity. Our purpose in this chapter is to discuss such hybrid securities. Specifically, we consider warrants and convertible securities.

A warrant is normally issued with debt and constitutes an option to purchase a specific number of shares of common stock at a stipulated price for a set period of time. Typically, a warrant is detachable, which means that it can be traded separately from the bond. Based upon our discussion of call options in Chapters 22 and 23, a warrant is essentially a call option, and its value is influenced by the same factors that influence the value of a call option.

Why would a corporation issue warrants along with bonds, and what is the attraction to investors of these securities? From the point of view of the issuing corporation, to the extent that the market puts a positive value on the warrant, the bond with a warrant will be valued more highly than an otherwise identical straight bond. Therefore, through the attachment of warrants, the corporation will be able to sell debt at a lower interest rate.

In issuing warrants, a corporation does not know how much capital will eventually be raised through the exercise of the associated options. However, the amount raised will be directly related to the extent of profitable business activity generated by the corporation over the exercise period. If the corporation is relatively unsuccessful, its stock price is likely to stagnate and the options will not be exercised. On the other hand, if the corporation is successful, and in response to this success the stock price rises, the options are more likely to be exercised, generating additional capital presumably at a time when it is most needed.

The foregoing discussion assumes that the market is not changing. Even if the firm doesn't undergo any change, the general level of market movement could affect the probability of the warrant being exercised.

Convertible securities are bonds or preferred stock that can be exchanged for a stipulated number of shares of common stock of a corporation during a specific period of time. If the price of the common stock of a corporation during a specific period of time. If the price of the common stock rises sufficiently, holders of these securities will find it profitable to exercise this conversion right. As in our discussion of warrants, this right will have some positive value in the market, so that a corporation will be required to pay a lower coupon rate on convertible bonds than on bonds with no conversion privilege.

Convertible bonds are also attractive when management prefers to raise capital through the issue of equity rather than debt, but believes that — as a result of transient influences — the common stock is temporarily undervalued by the market if this perception is correct, the stock price will rise and, as a result, debt will be converted to equity. A possible further advantage of a convertible securities issue over the issue of bonds with warrants is that management knows how much capital will be raised. The exercise of a warrant raises further capital; the conversion of a bond for shares of common stock does not raise new capital. However, there is an implicit increase of cash flow, if the conversion occurs prior to the maturity date, through the saving of future coupon payments; the conversion simply substitutes equity for debt.

A further distinction between warrants and convertible bonds is that warrants are not callable, while a convertible bond can generally be called. The bondholder can be offered conversion within a short time period or surrender of the bond at a specific cash price. As with the pricing of callable and noncallable bonds, the pricing of callable convertibles and noncallable convertibles is different. Investors demand a higher return for a callable security, and firms are willing to pay this higher price because of the increase in management flexibility.

We have seen why a corporation might find it attractive to issue hybrid securities rather than straight debt and/or equity. What of the investor? These securities may be particularly attractive in the bond market when it is difficult for investors to assess the riskiness of a corporation's future business activities. If it is feared that the corporation is about to embark on high-risk enterprises, the holder of a straight bond will be in the unappealing position of gaining nothing if these enterprises are successful and facing greatly increased default risk if they are unsuccessful. However, a more even-handed situation is established if the bonds are issued either with warrants or with a conversion privilege. Through the exercise of the option involved, the bondholder will share in any success resulting from a risky venture. In this case, it is less important to market participants to be able to assess future business risk of a corporation's activities. Hence, the payoff characteristics of convertible bonds and other hybrid securities allow for a resolution of risk determination that is considered an agency problem by Barnea, Haugen, and Senbet (1985), as discussed later in this chapter.

## 16.3 Warrants and Their Valuation

Consider an issue of 20-year bonds, with a face value of \$1,000. The issuing corporation consults its investment bankers and is advised that in order to raise the desired amount of capital, a coupon interest rate of 14% per annum would be required for a straight bond issue. However, the common stock of this corporation is currently trading at \$35 per share, and the investment bankers advise that if 20 warrants — each allowing the purchase at \$40 of a share of common stock anytime in the next ten years — are attached, the bonds can be marketed with a coupon interest rate of 10%. As is standard practice, the exercise price of the warrant would be adjusted for any future stock splits, but the warrant holder would receive no share in future dividend distributions. As is again usual, the warrants would be detachable, so that they could be traded separately.

We begin by determining the implied market value of these warrants, discussing later the factors that determine this value. The bondholder will receive a stream of 20 annual interest payments of \$100, plus the \$1,000 face value of the bond in 20 years. The investment bankers' advice is that investors discount these payments at a rate of 13% per annum. Therefore, the present value of the debt element of the bond is

$$\begin{aligned}\text{Present value of debt} &= \sum_{t=1}^{20} \frac{100}{(1.13)^t} + \frac{1{,}000}{(1.13)^{20}} \\ &= 702.50 + 87 = \$789.50 \qquad (16.1)\end{aligned}$$

Thus, it is estimated that the market values the straight debt component of this issue at \$789.50. Because it is also estimated that these bonds can be sold for \$1,000, the warrants attached to each bond are valued at \$210.50, or \$10.53 per warrant.

We now ask how this valuation of the warrant might have been derived. In effect, the warrant is an American call option (Chapter 23) with an expiration date 10 years hence. In Chapter 23, we study the relationship between the value of a call option and the price of the stock. Specifically, we see the following:

1. The value of a call option must be between two bounds. The upper bound is the market price of the stock, and the lower bound is the greater of 0 and the difference between the price of the stock and the exercise price of the option.
2. The value of the call option, all other things equal, rises at an increasing rate with increases in the stock price to the point where, when the stock price is high, the value of the option will increase at very nearly the same rate as the stock price.

These considerations suggest the relationship between warrant value and stock price shown in Figure 16.1. All other things equal, the value of a warrant is an increasing function of the price of the stock, in the manner illustrated in Figure 16.1. In addition, in Chapter 23 we note several other factors influencing the value of a call option:

1. The lower the exercise price, the higher the value of the call option.
2. The greater the volatility of the stock price, the higher the value of the call option.
3. The longer the time to the expiration date, the higher the value of the call option.
4. The higher the risk-free rate of interest, the higher the value of the call option.

In Chapters 22 and 23, we will see how these factors interact in the Black–Scholes valuation model for call options. These factors are also relevant in the valuation of warrants. However, the purchaser of warrants should also be aware of two other factors that affect the warrant value. First, the holder of a warrant does not receive dividend payments from the issuing corporation, a factor ignored in the Black–Scholes option valuation model. Whenever a dividend is paid, the value of a warrant decreases, since the price of the stock falls on the ex-dividend date. Therefore it may be better to exercise early if it is anticipated that management will increase the level of dividend payments in the future. Second, if numerous warrant options are exercised, this could lead to an appreciable increase in the number of shares outstanding. Consequently, earnings per share may be less than would otherwise have been the case. This potential dilution in earnings per share tends to lower the value of a warrant. Given a

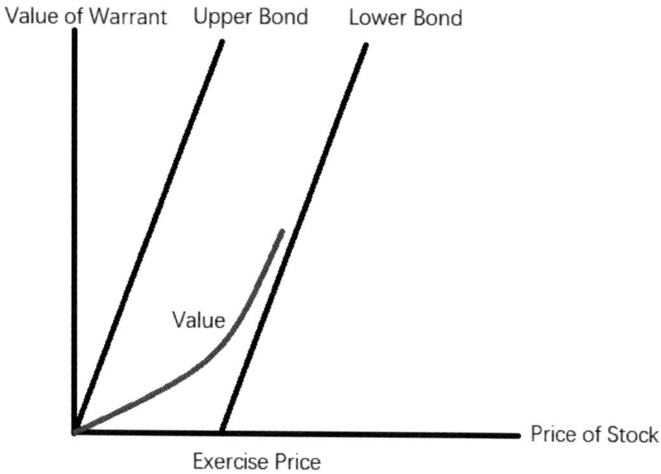


Figure 16.1 Warrant Value as a Function of Stock Price.

dilution in EPS, price per share may fall, which reduces the value of the warrant.

Let $N^b$, $P^b$ *and* $V^b$ be the before-exercise number of shares outstanding, common stock price per share before-exercise and total equity value before-exercise respectively, let $N^w$ be the number of warrants, and let $W^b$ be the value of one warrant. The value of the firm's old equity is

$$V^b = N^b P^b + N^w W^b \tag{16.2}$$

If all the warrants are exercised, then the warrants holders will pay the firm $N^w E$ ($E$ = exercise price) and the equity value will rise to

$$V^a = V^b + N^w E \tag{16.3}$$

where $V^a$ represents the total equity value after the warrants have been exercised.

The total value of the warrants after all warrants have been exercised is

$$N^w W^a = h(V^b + N^w E) - N^w E \tag{16.4}$$

where $h = \frac{N^w}{N^b + N^w}$ = the proportion of $V^a$ owned by warrant holders.

Equation (16.4) implies that the after exercise warrant value ($W^a$) is

$$W^a = \frac{V^b - N^b E}{N^b + N^w} \tag{16.5}$$

Thus the warrant holder should exercise if[1]

$$hV^b > (1 - h)N^w E \tag{16.6}$$

In this case, warrant holders gain if the old equity value exceeds the amount they pay at exercise.

If warrants are exercised, then the market price per share ($P^a$) can be defined as

$$P^a = \frac{V^b + N^w E}{N^b + N^w} \tag{16.7}$$

It is worthwhile for warrant holders to exercise the warrants $P^a > E$.

## 16.4 Convertible Bonds and Their Valuation[2]

Consider an issue of 20-year bonds with a face value of $1,000, each bond convertible to 50 shares of common stock. The current market price of the stock is $15 per share. The coupon rate on these

---

[1]Equation (16.5) implies that warrant holders should exercise if

$$V^b > N^b E \tag{a}$$

Multiplying both sides of (a) by $h$, we obtain

$$hV^b > hN^b E \tag{b}$$

Substituting $h = \frac{N^w}{(N^b + N^w)}$ into the right-hand side of equation (b) and rearranging the terms, we obtain

$$hV^b > (1 - h)N^w E$$

which is Eq. (16.6).

[2]The convertible bonds discussed in this section can be converted only into the firm's own stock. However, convertible bonds can also convert into other firms' stock. For example, the *Asian Wall Street Journal* (November 26, 1987) reported that a Taiwan Company, Yuen Fong Yu, issued a convertible bond that allows investors to convert this bond into Chung Hwa Pulp Corporation's common stock.

convertible bonds is 9.5%, while similar straight debt of the issuing corporation currently carries a rate of 12%. This issue is protected against stock splits, but can be called by the corporation, at a price of $1,050, at any time after five years.

The number of shares that can be received in exchange for each bond is called the *conversion ratio*; in our example, the conversion ratio is 50 shares to one bond. If the exchange was made immediately, a bond valued at $1,000 would be surrendered in exchange for 50 shares of common stock, so that the effective price would be $20 per share. This is known as the *conversion price*, which, in general, is

$$\text{Conversion price} = \frac{\text{Par value of bond}}{\text{Conversion ratio}} \tag{16.8}$$

Many contracts specifically state the conversion price. In this example, the conversion price exceeds the current market price of the shares by one-third. Obviously, it makes no sense to exercise this conversion privilege immediately. However, that privilege may be of some value, since holders of the convertible bond can profit if the price of the stock increases sufficiently.

Let us see how much investors are being asked to pay for the conversion privilege. As in the previous section, this calculation can be made by computing the present value of the bond's debt element. Holding the debenture of maturity, the bondholder would receive a stream of 20 annual payments of $95, plus $1,000 at the end of 20 years. These payments must be discounted at a rate of 12%, so that

$$\begin{aligned}\text{Present value of debt} &= \sum_{t=1}^{20} \frac{95}{(1.12)^t} + \frac{1{,}000}{(1.12)^{20}} \\ &= 709.6 + 103.7 = \$812.30 \end{aligned} \tag{16.9}$$

This is often called the *bond value* of the convertible bond.

We must also consider a second possibility: the instrument may be worth more if the conversion privilege is exercised. Since, at issue, the bond can be exchanged for 50 shares of common stock valued by the market at $15 per share, we say that its conversion value is $(50) \times (15) = \$750$. We see that the bond value exceeds the conversion value but is lower than the price of the bond. If the bond is issued at par, then the difference between the market value of $1,000 and the larger of the bond value or conversion value is $186.70. This represents the price that investors pay for the conversion privilege. As mentioned earlier, the conversion privilege is a call option on the shares of corporate common stock, and its value is influenced by all those factors that determine the value of call options. However, one factor should be noted in the present case. If the conversion privilege is exercised, the bond must be surrendered in exchange for stock. Therefore, the exercise price per share of the call option is the value of the convertible bond divided by the conversion ratio. Over time, market forces will cause the price of a convertible bond to vary, and so the exercise price of the implicit call option will also vary.

To see how the market values convertibles bonds, consider again bond value and conversion value. The market value of a convertible bond should be at least as high as bond value and conversion value. The bond value is simply that price at which the bond would sell if it could not be converted to common stock, and the conversion privilege cannot have negative worth. Also, if the convertible bond sold for less than its conversion value, investors could make an immediate profit by purchasing the bond, converting it, and selling the shares of stock. Investors would jump at such an opportunity, and the additional demand would drive up the price of the convertible bond. We have thus established that both the bond value and the conversion value constitute lower bounds to the value of a convertible bond.

To see what constitutes the boundary value of a convertible bond, consider the relationship between bond and conversion values and the issuing corporation as illustrated in Figure 16.2. First consider Figure 16.2(a). If the corporation is worth nothing, then so are its stocks and bonds. As corporate value increases, we can expect a proportionate increase in the value of common stock and hence in the conversion value of the convertible bond. Initially, as corporate value increases, bond value will increase more rapidly than conversion value, as investors' fears of default subside. However, at higher corporate values, the rate of increase of bond value slows rapidly, asymptotically approaching risk-free debt. Thus, as seen in Figure 16.2(a), the conversion value and bond value curves will cross at A, so that at a sufficiently high corporate value, the conversion value of a convertible bond will exceed its bond value.

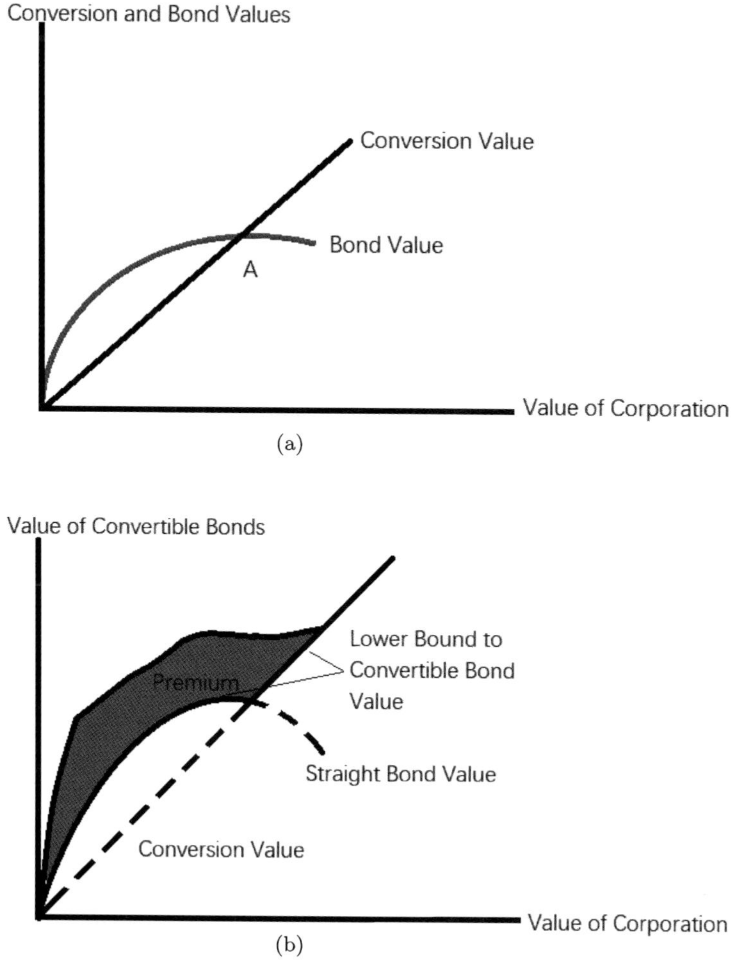


Figure 16.2 Relationship of Convertible Bond Value and Corporation Value under different conditions.

As we have seen, the value of a convertible bond must be at least as high as both its conversion value and its bond value. This lower bound to convertible bond value, as a function of the value of the corporation, is illustrated in Figure 16.2(b).

In practice, the market value of a convertible bond will usually exceed this lower bound as shown in Figure 16.2(b), the excess being the amount that investors are willing to pay for the conversion privilege (premium). The Black–Scholes option pricing model which will be discussed in Chapters 22 and 23 can be used to evaluate the market value of the premium. Along with the Black–Scholes determinants of option values, investors must also consider foregone dividends, if the conversion privilege is not exercised, and the possibility of dilution in corporate ownership. Another important consideration is any call provision in the convertible bond issue. Mikkelson (1981) showed that stock prices tend to increase dramatically prior to management's exercise of the call provision.

To illustrate some of the factors involved in convertible bond valuation, consider a newly issued 20-year convertible bond with a $1,000 face value and a coupon rate of 9.5%. This bond may be converted to 50 shares of common stock, which is selling at $15 per share. The bond can be called, at a price of $1,050, any time after five years. It is estimated that if capital were to be raised through a straight debt issue, a coupon interest rate of 12% would be required. It is believed that investors expect 10% annual growth in the value of this firm's stock. A dividend yield of 5% is currently being paid, and it is expected that this yield will be 5.5% next year. Thus, using the Gordon dividend model, common stockholders require a rate of return of 15.5%.

Since the bond can be exchanged for 50 shares of common stock, then the conversion value for this convertible bond at the time of issue is

$$\text{Conversion value} = (50)(15) = \$750 \tag{16.10}$$

This is the same bond for which we calculated a debt value of $813.30 at the beginning of this section.

Thus, at the time of issue, the debt value exceeds the conversion value of the bond. However, since the convertible bond is sold for $1,000, investors are, in effect, paying $1,000 − $813.30 = $186.70 for the conversion privilege.

We can examine this valuation by looking at the internal rate of return that is being demanded by purchasers of this bond. Consider an investor who is planning to hold this convertible bond for 5 years, during which time it is callable. Since the price of common stock is expected to grow at 10% per annum, then after 5 years,

$$\text{Expected conversion value} = (750)(1.10)^5 = \$1{,}208 \tag{16.11}$$

Hence, this investor expects to receive five annual interest payments of \$95, plus common stock valued at \$1,208 at the end of this period. Discounting these receipts at internal rate of return $r$ yields the market value of the convertible bond, so that

$$1{,}000 = \sum_{t=1}^{5} \frac{95}{(1+r)^t} + \frac{1,208}{(1+r)^5} \tag{16.12}$$

The solution of this equation, in terms of $r$, is $r = 1.27$. We thus conclude that the required internal rate of return on the convertible bond is 12.7%. Notice that this rate is between the 12% rate required by bondholders and the 15% rate required by common stockholders. This finding is to be expected because a convertible bond is less risky than common stock but riskier than a straight bond.

In summary, the basic value concepts and definitions used to value convertible bonds in terms of our example are as follows:

- Face value = market price of issuance = \$1,000
- Straight debt value = \$813.30
- Conversion value = \$1,050
- Call price = \$1,050
- Expected conversion value = \$1,208.

However, the theoretical value of this convertible bond can also be calculated by using an understandable formula; this formula and its implications are given in Appendix 16A. Lee *et al.* (2013) and Lee and Lee (2017) have discussed convertible securities in further detail.

## 16.5 Cost of Capital for Convertibles and Impacts of Call and Conversion

### 16.5.1 *Cost of capital for convertibles*

A convertible bond is equivalent to a portfolio of two securities: a bond and a warrant. The bond portion pays interest and returns the principal of maturity, and the warrant portion serves as a call on the value of the firm's equity. Hence, the value of a convertible bond is

$$CV = B + W \tag{16.13}$$

where $CV$ is the market value of a convertible bond; $B$ is the market value of a bond; and $W$ is the market value of a warrant. Therefore, the cost of capital for the convertible bond must be a weighted average of the two component securities, or

$$K_{cv} = \left(\frac{B}{B+W}\right) k_b(1-\tau_c) + \left(\frac{W}{B+W}\right) k_w \tag{16.14}$$

where $k_b(1-\tau_c)$ is the after-tax cost of the bond and $k_w$ is the total cost of the warrant. This being the case, the traditional argument for using convertibles as a form of cheap debt requires that the lower coupon rate on convertible bonds is sufficient to offset the higher cost associated with the warrant. If we look at the after-tax cost of convertible bonds compared to straight debt, we see that the $k_b(1-\tau_c)$ of the convertible bond is less than the cost of the straight debt. If the difference between $k_b(1-\tau_c)$ for the convertible bond and straight debt is greater than $k_w$, then the total cost of the convertible bond is less than the total cost of the straight debt. If the difference is less than $k_w$, then the convertible bond is more costly.

### 16.5.2 *Impacts of call and conversion*

All convertible bonds have a call features, which gives the firm the right to force the owner of the convertible to either convert the convertible bond into equity or liquidate the investment in the bond for a cash payment. Thus, firm management must have a policy for when to force conversion. The optimal call policy is that a convertible bond (preferred) should be called as soon as its conversion value is equal to or greater than the market value of the equity received on conversion or the current market price times number of shares received. To guarantee conversion, management should wait until conversion value is sufficiently greater than the call price.[3]

The call provision is equivalent to a call option written by the investor who purchases the callable convertible bond from the firm, that is, the bonds may be repurchased by the firm anytime during the life of the security at the prevailing call or exercise price.

[3]Brigham (1966) surveyed companies and found that many managers set a policy of waiting until the conversion value is at least 20% greater than the call price.

**Exhibit 16.1:** The Effects of Conversion of a Convertible Bond on Stockholder and Bondholder Wealth and Firm Value.

| Type of Change due to Conversion | Stockholder Wealth | Bondholder Wealth | Firm Value |
|---|---|---|---|
| Change in tax liabilities | – | – | – |
| Change in relative priority of outstanding claims | – | + | 0 |
| Change in incentive for management to transfer wealth | ? | + | + |
| Decrease in bankruptcy cost | + | + | + |
| Decrease in amount of conversion privileges outstanding | ? | – | – |
| Increase in shares outstanding | – | 0 | – |
| Total effect | ? | ? | ? |

If we assume perfect markets, investors should convert the bond in one of four situations: (1) at the maturity of the convertible, (2) when the convertible is called, (3) when the conversion price increases, or (4) when the current dividend yield on the equity is greater than the yield on the convertible bond. The first two situations are *forced conversions*, because it is not in the best interest of the investor to give up the convertible security at these times. In these cases, the investor can receive cash when the bond matures or can receive cash by selling the bond in the marketplace. We are assuming it is better to convert than to receive the call value. For example, if the investor takes cash, he or she must then purchase shares of stock in the market, which increases transaction costs that are usually avoided in the conversion process. The third and fourth situations are voluntary conversions because it is beneficial for the investor to give up the convertible bond for an equity position.

Mikkelson (1981) presents the implications of a call of a convertible security on shareholder wealth. The principal effects of a call and conversion of debt are a reduction in the amount of outstanding conversion privileges, a decrease in the firm's financial leverage, and an increase in the number of common shares outstanding. The investment or asset structure of the firm is unaffected by the conversion in the short run. Exhibit 16.1 presents a summary of Mikkelson's arguments concerning how a call and a conversion affect the wealth of the firm's bondholders and shareholders and the value of the firm.

From Exhibit 16.2 it is clear that the total net effect of a conversion is not easily identifiable. What is required is a case-by-case analysis of each situation to determine the relative importance of each type of change and its effect on the shareholder, the bondholder, and firm value. If managers act to maximize shareholder wealth, the net effect should be positive. A negative effect on shareholder wealth with a positive effect on firm value suggests that the bondholders or management are benefiting from the conversion of the convertible debt.

However, as a general rule, we would normally consider that the cost of convertible bond, $K_{cv}$, is higher than the cost of straight debt, $k_b$.

Barnea *et al.* (1985) have shown that convertible bonds might resolve the agency problems associated with issuing stocks and bonds. They argue that creditors have incentives to force the firm into low-risk activities, while equity holders have incentives to adopt high-risk projects.[4] If these conflicts cannot be resolved, the firm might be forced to give up profitable investment projects. Convertible bonds represent a financing package of mixed risk incentives and go a long way toward resolving the conflicts between bondholders and stockholders. Thus, convertible bonds and bonds associated with warrants will have less restrictive debt covenants than will non-convertible bonds.

## 16.6 Beta Coefficients for Convertible Bonds

Using the concept that a convertible bond is a portfolio of a bond and a warrant, Beatty *et al.* (1988) show the relationship of the systematic risk of the convertible, bond, and warrant as follows:

$$\beta_{CV} = \frac{B}{B+W}(\beta_B) + \frac{W}{B+W}(\beta_W) \qquad (16.15)$$

[4]Using the option pricing concept, it can be shown that risky projects reduce the market value of risky bonds and increase the market value of stocks. Appendix 16A provides further discussion on these arguments.

**Exhibit 16.2:** EPS Calculation for Simple Capital Structure.

**Constant Number of Shares Outstanding**

| | |
|---|---|
| Revenue | $10,000,000 |
| Less *expenses* | −7,500,000 |
| Operating income | $2,500,000 |
| Less *interest* | −300,000 |
| Taxable income | $2,200,000 |
| Less *taxes* (50%) | −1,100,000 |
| Net income | $1,100,000 |
| Less *preferred dividends* | −100,000 |
| | $1,000,000 |

Earnings available to common shareholders ($1,000,000) dividend by number of shares outstanding (1,000,000) = $1 EPS

**Varying Number of Shares Outstanding**

| Date | Share Increase (Decrease) | Total Shares | Fraction of Year That Balance Was Unchanged | Weighted Average Number of Shares Outstanding |
|---|---|---|---|---|
| 1/1/1988 | — | 1,000,000 | 2/12 | 166,666.67 |
| 2/28/1988 | 200,000 new issue | 1,200,000 | 4/12 | 400,000.00 |
| 6/30/1988 | 400,000 repurchased | 800,000 | 2/12 | 133,333.33 |
| 9/1/1988 | 200,000 new issue | 1,000,000 | 4//12 | 333,333.33 |
| 12/31/1988 | | 1,000,000 | 12/12 | 1,033,333.33 |

Earning available to common shareholders ($1,000,000) divided by weighted average of shares outstanding (1,033,333) = $.97 EPS.

where $\beta_{CV}, \beta_B$, and $\beta_W$ are the beta coefficients for the convertible, bond, and warrant.

We showed that the value of a warrant is proportional to the value of a call option, or

$$W = C(1 - g) \tag{16.16}$$

where $W$ and $C$ are the values of a warrant and a call option and $(1-g)$ is a proportionality factor that takes into account the dilution effects of the new shares issued when the warrant is exercised.

Because the return on the warrant is also proportional to the return on the call option, the systematic risk of the warrant $(\beta_W)$ must equal the systematic risk of the call option $(\beta_C)$, or

$$\beta_W = \beta_C \tag{16.17}$$

Lee and Lee (2017) has shown that the beta on the call option is related to the beta of the underlying asset, as follows:

$$\beta_C = \left(\frac{S}{C} \times \frac{\partial C}{\partial S}\right) \beta_s \tag{16.18}$$

where $S$ and $C$ are the market values of the stock and the options; $\partial C/\partial S$ is the partial derivative of $C$ with respect to $S$; and $\beta_s$ is the systematic risk of the equity. In this equation, $(\frac{S}{C} \times \frac{\partial C}{\partial S})$ measures the elasticity between the value of the call option and the value of the underlying stock.

Putting all of this together, we can show that the beta of a convertible is

$$\beta_{CV} = \frac{B}{B+W}\beta_B + \frac{W}{B+W}\left(\frac{S}{C} \times \frac{\partial C}{\partial S}\right)\beta_s \tag{16.19}$$

Thus, the systematic risk of a convertible bond is a weighted average of the systematic risk of a regular bond and the systematic risk of the firm's equity times an elasticity term. In general, the beta of a convertible bond will be less than the beta of the firm's equity and greater than the beta of its debt.

## 16.7 Earnings per Share (EPS) when Warrants and Convertibles are Issued

Warrants and convertibles have the potential to change a firm's EPS and number of shares. We now turn our attention as to how warrants and convertibles affect EPS and the number of shares outstanding.

Investors, managers, accountants, and federal and state governments are concerned with the earnings per share of a corporation. By earnings per share, we generally mean the net income after taxes less preferred stock dividends divided by the weighted average number of shares of common stock outstanding. In 1969, the Accounting Principles Board, a forerunner of the FASB, issued *APB Opinion No. 15*, "Earnings per Share." This ruling lays down the rules for calculating the earnings per share for financial reporting purposes. In 1982, the FASB issued *Statement No. 55*, "Determining Whether a Convertible Security is a Common Stock Equivalent." These accounting requirements provide alternative ways of calculating earnings per share if a company has convertible securities, warrants, stock options, or other contracts that permit the number of shares of common stock to be increased.

A simple capital structure has only one form of voting equity capital and no other forms or potential forms of equity, such as warrants or convertibles. The existence of preferred stock does not create a complex capital structure. Exhibit 16.2 shows an EPS calculation for a firm with a simple capital structure and a constant number of shares outstanding as well as an EPS calculation for a firm with a changing number of shares outstanding.

As you can see in this exhibit, the issuance or repurchase of common shares during a particular period affects the average number of shares outstanding and thereby changes the firm's EPS. In Exhibit 16.2, months were used as the denominator of the weighting fractions. However, weeks or months can also be used if this is more pertinent to the timing of the changes in the number of shares.

A corporation that has warrants, convertibles, or options outstanding is said to have a *complex capital structure*. The capital structure is complex because the measure of shares outstanding is a function of a known amount of common shares currently outstanding plus an estimate of the potential number of shares that must be issued to satisfy the holders of warrants, convertibles, and options should they decide to exercise their rights and receive new common shares. Because of the possible dilution in EPS represented by securities that have the potential to become new shares of common stock, we must consider *common stock equivalents* (CSEs). CSEs are securities that are not common stock but are equivalent to common stock because they are likely to be converted into common stock in the future. Convertible debt, convertible preferred stock, stock rights, stock options, and stock warrants are all securities that can create new common shares and thus dilute the firm's earnings per share. This dilution effect means that the CSE securities will reduce a firm's EPS.

*APB 15* provides two types of EPS for firms with a complex capital structure: primary EPS and fully diluted EPS. Primary EPS is computed by dividing adjusted earnings by the weighted average shares of common stock and common stock equivalents, or

$$\text{Primary EPS} = \frac{\begin{array}{c}\text{Income} - \text{Preferred stock dividends} + \text{After tax}\\ \text{Effect of bond interest expense if bonds are CSE}\end{array}}{\text{Weighted average of common shares and CSE}} \quad (16.20)$$

Fully diluted EPS is computed by dividing the adjusted earnings by the maximum number of potential common shares, given the requirements of *APB 15*:

$$\text{Fully diluted EPS} = \frac{\begin{array}{c}\text{Net income} - \text{Preferred stock dividends if}\\ \text{preferred stock is not a CSE} + \text{After tax effort}\\ \text{of bond interest expense if bonds are CSE}\end{array}}{\begin{array}{c}\text{Weighted average of common shares and}\\ \text{CSE assuming maximum dilution}\end{array}} \quad (16.21)$$

If all hybrid securities are considered to be dilutive CSEs, then primary EPS would be equal to fully diluted EPS. Exhibit 16.3 gives EPS calculations for both primary and fully diluted EPS.

It is interesting to speculate on whether the market will use primary EPS of fully diluted EPS in valuing shares of stock. If the market expects the common stock equivalent to be converted to new equity, then fully diluted EPS are more meaningful, whereas if the market does not expect the common stock equivalents to be converted, then it would treat convertible bonds like debt and make no

**Exhibit 16.3:** Primary EPS and Fully Diluted EPS.

*Complex Capital Structure Data*

Convertible bonds, 10% interest, $1,000 par value, issued at par $10,000,000 on 1/1/1990 at a AA bond rate of 16%, maturity on 12/32/2009, convertible into ten shares of common stock, 100,000 primary shares.

Preferred stock, 10% interest, $100 par value, 10,000 shares issued at $1,000,000.

Convertible preferred stock, 8% interest, $100 per share, 10,000 shares convertible into one share of common per share of preferred, $1,000,000 issued at a AA bond rate of 10%, 10,000 fully diluted shares.

Common stock $1 per share, outstanding 1,000,000 shares $1,000,000; 10,000 warrants outstanding, each convertible into two shares of common stock at $50 per share; current market price of the warrant is $165, current market price of stock is $105 per share, 1,020,000 primary shares.

| Primary EPS | | Fully Diluted EPS | |
|---|---|---|---|
| Operating income | $2,600,000 | | $2,600,000 |
| Less interest | −1,000,000 | | −1,000,000 |
| Taxable income | $1,600,000 | | $1,600,000 |
| Less taxes (50%) | −800,000 | | −800,000 |
| Net income | $800,000 | | $800,000 |
| Less preferred dividends | −180,000 | Less preferred stock dividends if preferred stock is not CSE | −100,000 |
| | $620,000 | | $700,000 |
| After-tax effect if bonds are CSE [1,000,000 (1 − .5)] | $500,000 | After-tax effect if bonds are CSE | +500,000 |
| | $1,120,000 | | $1,200,000 |
| $\frac{\$1,120,000}{1,120,000} = \$1$ per share | | $\frac{\$1,200,000}{1,130,000} = \$1.06$ per share | |

adjustment for new shares and use primary EPS. Convertible bonds that have no chance of being converted are called *hung convertibles. APB 15* and *FASB 55* provide EPS information under either circumstance and let the market participant choose which measure is more meaningful.

From the perspective of the financial analyst, it is important to be able to identify the difference between two firms with the same primary EPS and markedly different fully diluted EPS. In general, hybrid securities in the capital structure cause the difference.

## 16.8 Summary

Hybrid securities give both investors and financial managers greater flexibility in their interactions in the financial markets. Understanding these securities requires an understanding of option pricing.

Our knowledge of how these securities affect firm value, from a financial viewpoint, differs greatly from accounting for their existence. We need a more thorough understanding of these hybrids and how the investor values them before we can adequately define the types of information we need about these kinds of securities.

## References

Barnea, A., Haugen, R. A., and L. Senbet. *Agency Problems and Financial Contracting* (New York: Prentice-Hall, 1985).

Beatty, R. P., Lee, C. F., and K. C. Chen. "On the Nonstationarity of Convertible Bond Betas: Theory and Evidence," *Quarterly Review of Economics and Business*, 26 (Fall 1988).

Bierman, H. "The Cost of Warrants," *Journal of Financial and Quantitative Analysis* (June 1973, pp. 499–503).

Black, F. and M. Scholes. "The Pricing of Options and Corporate Liabilities," *The Journal of Political Economy*, 81(3) (May–June, 1973, pp. 637–654).

Brennan, M. J. and E. S. Schwartz. "Convertible Bonds: Valuation and Optimal Strategies for Call and Conversions," *The Journal of Finance* (December 1977, pp. 1699–1715).

Brennan, M. J. and E. S. Schwartz. "Analyzing Convertible Bonds," *Journal of Financial and Quantitative Analysis* (November 1980, pp. 907–929).

Brigham, E. F. "An Analysis of Convertible Debentures," *The Journal of Finance* (March 1966, pp. 35–54).

Chen, A. H. Y. "A Model of Warrant Pricing in a Dynamic Market," *The Journal of Finance* (December 1970, pp. 1041–1060).

Galai, D. and N. Schneller. "The Pricing of Warrants and the Value of the Firm," *The Journal of Finance* (December 1978, pp. 133–142).

Ingersoll, J. "An Examination of Corporate Call Policies on Convertible Securities," *The Journal of Finance* (May 1977, pp. 463–478).

Ingersoll, J. "A Contingent Claims Valuation of Convertible Securities," *Journal of Financial Economics* (May 1977, pp. 289–322).
Lee, C. F. and J. Lee. *Financial Analysis, Planning and Forecasting: Theory and Applications*, 3rd edn. (Singapore: World Scientific, 2017).
Lee, C. F. and A. C. Lee. *Encyclopedia of Finance*, 2nd edn. (Springer, 2013).
Lee, C. F., J. Finnerty, J. Lee, A. C. Lee, and D. Wort. *Security Analysis, Portfolio Management, and Financial Derivatives* (World Scientific Publishers, Inc., 2013).
Leung, J. "Taiwan Concern Sets Novel Issue in Bond Market," *Asian Wall Street Journal* (November 26, 1987).
Marr, N. W. and G. R. Thompson. "The Pricing of New Convertible Bond Issues," *Financial Management* (Summer 1984, pp. 31–37).
Mikkelson, A. W. H. "Convertible Calls and Security Returns," *Journal of Financial Economics* (September 1981, pp. 237–264).
Schwartz, E. S. "The Valuation of Warrants: Implementing a New Approach," *Journal of Financial Economics* (January 1977, pp. 79–83).

## Appendix 16A — Market Value of Convertible Bond

According to Brigham (1966) and Lee and Lee (2017), the market value of convertible bond can be estimated as follows:

$$P = \sum_{t=1}^{j=m} \frac{rF(1-\tau_c) + [(P_0 - F)(n-m)]\tau_c}{(1+k_i)^t} + \frac{F'}{(1+k_i)^{j-m}} \quad (16.1\text{A})$$

where $P_0$ = initial market price of convertible bond; $P$ = market value of the convertible bond; $r$ = coupon rate on the bond; $F$ = face value of the bond; $k_i$ = effective rate of interest on the bond at the end of the period $m$ (now); $n$ = original maturity of the bond; $m$ = number of periods since the bond was issued; $j$ = number of periods from the time the bond was issued until the time of conversion; $F'$ = value of the stock on date of conversion; and $\tau_c$ = marginal corporate tax rate.

The terms on the right-hand side of Eq. (16.1A) are the present value of the after-tax interest expense and the present value of the terminal cost to the company. The first term is a function of $j$, which implies that the unamortized bond discount (or premium) ceases to be deductible (or taxable) after the bond is converted to common stock. The value of $j$ is comparable to the maturity period in debt financing except that in convertible financing the period is an estimate rather than a contractual figure.

## Appendix 16B — Option Approach to Evaluating Bonds and Stocks

Using the Black and Scholes (1973) theory and put-option concepts which will be discussed in Chapters 22 and 23, we can define the market value of risky debt as[5]

$$\begin{aligned}&\text{Market value of risky debt} + \text{Put option}\\&\quad = \text{Market value of risk} - \text{Free debt} \qquad (16.1\text{B})\end{aligned}$$

Equation (16.1B) implies that put options can be used as coinsurance to make risky bonds riskless because the value of put options is determined by the same factors that determine the value of call options. Therefore, when a firm undertakes a risky project, there will be an increase in the market value of risky debt to maintain the constant market value of risk-free debt.

Following Black and Scholes, Lee and Lee (2017) derived the relationship among the market value of equity ($P_m$), the market value of a firm's assets ($V_A$), and the amount of debt owed at maturity ($D$) as

$$P_m = V_A N(d_1) - e^{-rt} DN(d_2) \qquad (16.2\text{B})$$

where $d_1 = \frac{LOG_a\left(\frac{V_A}{D}\right)+R_f t}{\sigma\sqrt{t}} + \frac{1}{2}\sigma\sqrt{t}$; $d_2 = d_1 - \sigma\sqrt{t}$; $r$ = continuously compounded annual risk-free interest rate; $\sigma$ = standard deviation of the rate of return on the firm's assets; $e = 2.71828$; and $N(d_i)$ = probability that a standard normal random variable is less than $d_i$ ($i = 1, 2$).

Following the Black and Scholes model which will be discussed in Chapters 22 and 23, we know that $P_m$ increases when $\sigma$ increases.

[5] Chapter 13 offers an alternative approach to determine the market value of risky debt. However, the results are identical.

Therefore, a firm that undertakes a risky project will increase the market value of equity ($P_m$).

Chapter 11 of Lee and Lee (2017) discussed an alternative method for evaluating convertible bonds in detail.

## Questions and Problems

1. Define the following terms:

   a. Hybrid securities
   b. Warrants
   c. Conversion ratio
   d. Conversion price
   e. Premium of convertible bond
   f. Conversion value and expected conversion value
   g. Beta coefficient of convertible bonds

2. Describe how the required internal rate of return on the convertible bond can be estimated.
3. XYZ Company has 5 million shares outstanding and an expected market value of 30 million dollars. When its warrants mature and the company wants to issue 500,000 new shares, assuming each warrant can be used to purchase one new share, what exercise price will not affect the existing shareholders' wealth?
4. How is the market value of a convertible bond determined?
5. The earnings per share for XYZ Company is \$3. XYZ's P/E ratio is 15 and its payout ratio is 1/3. Company XYZ wishes to offer \$20 million of 10%, 20-year convertible debentures with an initial conversion premium of 15% and a call price of \$110. XYZ currently has \$2 million common share outstanding and a 34% tax rate:

   a. What is the conversion price?
   b. What is the conversion ratio per \$1,000 debenture?
   c. What is the initial conversion value of each debenture?
   d. How many new shares of common stock must be issued if all debentures are converted?

6. Alice Lee is debating whether to invest \$1,200 in warrants or in common stock of XYZ Company. The current market price of XYZ's stock is \$30. She could purchase warrants that entitle her

to buy one share of stock per warrant for $25. These warrants have a market price of $3. In one year the market price of the stock may rise to $35 per share or fall to $25 per share. What do you advise her to do?

7. One of the owners of XYZ Company's warrants wonders whether it is now advantageous to exercise those warrants. The warrant allows the owner to purchase 3.5 shares of common stock at $40 per share.
   a. Should the owner exercise the warrant if the market price of common stock is $50?
   b. What is the market value of the owner's warrant when the stock price is $50?

8. A convertible bond issue of $1 million has the following characteristics:

   Par value of bond = $1,000
   Maturity of debt is 7 years
   Coupon rate (paid annually) is 13%
   Current stock price = $90
   Conversion price = $100
   Assuming that the current coupon rate of a similar straight bond is 16%, calculate the following values:

   a. Conversion ratio
   b. Bond value
   c. Conversion value
   d. Conversion premium
   e. Price of convertible bond if the stock price is:
      i. $80
      ii. $100
      iii. $125

9. VSA Corp. is issuing 12-year convertible bonds with a face value of $.25 million. The par value and annual interest would be $1,000 and $75 per bond respectively. The coupon rate of a similar bond without conversion provision is 10%. The convertible bond is callable at $1,075 any time after 6 years. The growth rate in VSA's stock prices is expected to be 8% and the current dividend yield is 10%. The current market price of the company's shares is $32. The conversion ratio is 25. Calculate the expected conversion

value at $t = 6$ and find the internal rate of return required by the investors.

10. The straight bond issue of a corporation carries a coupon rate of 11.50%. If the firm also gives 15 warrants along with each bond, the coupon rate would be 9.25%. A warrant would entitle the holder to buy one share of common stock at $12.50 during the next 3 years. Calculate the value of warrants if the par value of the convertible bond is $1,000 and the maturity is 10 years.
11. RFC currently has 90,000 shares of common stock and 10,000 warrants outstanding. A warrant holder can purchase one share at $31.50 for each warrant held. The current stock price is $40 per share.

    a. Calculate the per share loss to old shareholders if the option is exercised by the warrant holders.
    b. Find the exercise price that would result in no loss or gain to the old shareholders.

12. A warrant entitles its holder to purchase 2 shares of a company's common stock at $15 per share. Calculate the value of one warrant if the current stock price is:

    a. $13
    b. $17

13. Dave is planning to invest $500. He has two alternatives: Common stock and warrants of a blue chip company. The current market prices of stock and warrants are $20 and $2 respectively A warrant holder is entitled to buy one share of this firm at $17.50.

    a. Calculate the rate of return on the stock and warrant investments held for one year if the prices at $t = 1$ are as follows:

        i. Stock = $30; Warrants = $10
        ii. Stock = $16; Warrants = $1

    b. Explain the results of the two alternatives of investing in stock and warrants.

# Chapter 17

# Leasing: Theory and Practice

## Contents



## 17.1 Introduction

Chapter 17 explores the leasing decision. Accounting, marketing, and economic information and finance theory are used to show how managers make the decision to either buy or lease capital assets and equipment. The financial theories discussed in this chapter include the traditional, M&M, CAPM, and OPM theories, which are utilized and demonstrated as an aid to the manager for long-term and short-term evaluation of the lease versus buy decision.

The chapter begins with Section 17.2 explaining the basic definitions and types of lease arrangements. This is followed by Section 17.3 discussing accounting for leases. Section 17.4 discusses accounting updates. Section 17.5 discusses cash flow estimation and present value analysis of lease or buy alternatives. Section 17.6 discusses valuation of riskless and risky cash flows for the lease or buy decision, and Section 17.7 discusses the CAPM and lease versus buy decisions. Section 17.8 explains how options are used to evaluate salvage value in financial leases. Finally, Section 17.9 summarizes the chapter. Appendix 17A derives the discount rate for riskless cash flows, and Appendix 17B applies the APV method for leasing decision.

## 17.2 Reasons and Types of Leasing Arrangements

It is well-known that companies obtain the use of long-term operating assets through a lease rather than a purchase. In a lease, a company acquires the use of an asset — such as a copy machine, office space, or even an airplane — by financing it directly through the asset's owner. In the airline industry, about one-third of airplanes are leased. Airlines decide to lease versus buy assets for a variety of reasons, including the ability to obtain financing, reduced risk of obsolescence, or operating flexibility. For example, small, recently established airlines, which may have difficulty obtaining capital to buy large airplanes, lease planes to exploit new routes. At the end of fiscal 2016, the operating fleet of Spirit Airlines consisted of 95 airplanes of which 38% were owned and 62% were leased. Spirit also leases most of its land and buildings that it occupies, such as its aircraft maintenance base as well as various computers, cargo, flight kitchens, and training facilities.

Is there a difference in the economic substance of acquiring a long-term operating asset (such as an airplane) by issuing long-term debt or acquiring the use of an asset by signing a lease contract? In most cases, there is no real substantial difference in leasing and purchasing. The form of the contract is different, but the substance of these transactions is the same.

The main reasons for leasing an asset instead of purchasing are:

(a) True lease financing might be cheaper than borrowing or purchasing the asset. This kind of advantage is primarily due to different marginal tax rates faced by the lessor and lessee.
(b) Since leasing generally does not require the firm to make a down payment (as most lending institutions do), the effect is to conserve working capital. Although generally smaller than those required in most purchase arrangements, lease payments are prepaid and in that sense are like a down payment.
(c) Leasing may preserve the credit and debt capacity of the firm. This, as we shall see, is a result of the accounting conventions in use today.
(d) Leasing can reduce the risk of obsolescence and capital-equipment disposal problems. Almost always the term of the lease is less than the life of the asset, particularly so in the case of leases that are cancelable at certain times at the option for the lessee.
(e) Leasing is more flexible and convenient than buying an asset. Most lessors deal with leasing arrangements on a regular basis and are used to tailoring these arrangements, within reason, to their client's best interest.

There are many forms of leasing arrangements. The three most common are (1) direct leasing, (2) sale and leaseback, and (3) leveraged leasing. Each leasing type can be further broken down into accounting requirements applicable to the lessor and the lessee. The types of accounting practice required may also determine the type of lease a lessee is willing to undertake. That is, the type of lease undertaken will have different impacts on the lessee's financial statements.

### 17.2.1 *Direct leasing*

A *direct lease* gives the lessee the use of an asset while the lessor retains title and ownership of the asset. In return, the lessor receives contracted lease payments from the lessee as remuneration for the use of the asset. Frequently, direct leases contain provisions requiring the lessor to provide maintenance service; such an arrangement is called a *service lease*. The lessor may also assist in partial financing of the lessee if necessary. Another distinguishing feature of a direct lease is the *cancellation clause*, which allows the lessee to cancel the lease at period intervals.

The types of lessors are as varied as the number of lessees. Manufacturers of expensive products, such as computers and copy machines, often lease their products to firms or individuals. Trucking firms will purchase fleets of trucks in order to lease them out individually or otherwise. Some firms make a business out of leasing by purchasing and leasing items on a short-term basis. For example, financial intermediaries often purchase capital goods with the intention of leaving them out. This may not be an integral part of their business but does afford tax advantages. (The tax advantages of leasing are discussed in a later section.)

### 17.2.2 *Sale and leaseback*

In a *sale and leaseback* arrangement, a firm sells an asset (most often an asset it just purchased) to a second party and the two parties then enter into a lease in which the original owner leases back the asset from the new owner. The new owner retains title to the asset and all other benefits of ownership, such as tax credits and depreciation allowance. The lessee receives the funds from the sale of the asset along with the use of the asset.

In most cases, the asset is sold by the original owner at its fair market value, which includes consideration of trade and volume discounts as well as the current market condition. The main advantage of the sale and leaseback is its accounting treatment, which is discussed later in this chapter.

### 17.2.3 *Leverage leasing*

*Leverage leasing* involves financial leverage, which is not used in the other two forms of leasing. A third party, the lender, supplies a large portion of the funds a lessor needs to purchase an asset it intends to lease out. This type of lease is often used in situations where large capital outlays are necessary for the purchase of the asset.

For the lessee, there are no fundamental differences between a leveraged lease and the other two forms of leases. And differences to the lessee are the result of different lease payments required by the lessor due to the degree of leverage used.

The lessor, however, is in a different position. As a debtor, the lessor is required to make interest payments. The size of these payments depends on the degree of leverage employed, which, in turn, affects the size and timing of net cash flows to the lessor. Again, the accounting treatment determines whether this type of lease arrangement is advantageous to either party of the agreement. We now discuss these accounting arrangements.

## 17.3 Accounting for Leases

In the previous section, we mentioned that each form of leasing can be further distinguished by the accounting reporting methods applicable to the lessor and the lessee. In this section, we see how such distinctions are made and the effects they have on each party's financial statements. We also discuss the taxes involved in each leasing practice, which is often a decisive factor in the leasing decision.

The 1976 Financial Accounting Standard Board (FASB) *Statement No. 13* standardized the procedures for lease accounting. Before this statement was issued, lease obligations of the lessee either were not presented in the firm's financial statements or were given only cursory treatment in a footnote. Hence, leases that resembled debt-financed purchases were easily "hidden" and kept off the balance sheet. *FASB 13* required that capital leases (discussed later in this section) be shown on the lessee's financial statements as if the asset were owned by the firm. The reason for this is that if the lessee contracts for an asset in such a way as to acquire all the risks and benefits associated with the asset, then this asset should be appropriately reflected in the lessee's financial statements.

The following rules are used in the classification of capital and operating leases for lessees. However, according to Fabozzi and Nevitt (2000), even within these guidelines there is a great deal of latitude with respect to classification. From the lessee's standpoint, the lease is a capital lease if it satisfies any of the following four criteria:

1. The lease transfers ownership of the asset to the lessee prior to the expiration of the lease obligation term, including any time covered by bargain renewal options.
2. The lease contains a bargain purchase option that allows the lessee to purchase the leased asset at a price sufficiently lower than

the current expected fair market value at the time the option is exercisable.

3. The lease is equal to or greater than 75% of the remaining estimated economic life of the leased asset, unless 75% of the asset's expected life has already elapsed.
4. The present value of the minimum lease payments including any guarantee by the lessee relating to the lessor's debt and other expenses, equals or exceeds 90% of the fair value of the leased asset.

Leases that do not meet any of the four criteria listed above are classified as operating leases.

### 17.3.1 *Capital lease treatment*

For a *capital lease* (a lease that is viewed as a defacto acquisition), the accounting treatment for the lessee is the same as if the asset were actually purchased by the lessee and financed by debt. Equal entries are made in the assets and liabilities of the balance sheet. This reflects the "acquisition" or use of the asset by the firm as well as the contractual promise to make the scheduled lease payments. The only difficulty with this procedure is determining the value of the asset. *FASB 13* requires two estimates of the asset's value, as discussed below.

#### 17.3.1.1 *Discount rate estimate*

The *discount rate estimate* discounts the minimum lease payments plus any expected profits derived from the bargain purchase options included in the lease agreement and deducts any executory costs (insurance, maintenance, and taxes) that may be incurred by the lessor that are embodied in the lease payments. The discount rate that is used is the lessee's *marginal borrowing rate* ($K_B$) or the interest rate implicit in the lease. The marginal borrowing rate is the rate at the inception of the lease that the lessee would have paid to borrow the funds necessary to buy the leased asset on a secured loan with repayment terms similar to the payment schedule of the lease. The *implicit rate* is the internal rate of return that sets the net outlay for the asset (by the lessor) equal to the present value of the lease payments plus any net residual value expected to be realized by the lessor on termination of the lease. The *residual value* is the estimated fair market value of the leased property at the end of the term of the lease. The lessor often transfers the risk of loss to the lessee through a guarantee of the estimated residual value. The amount of a guaranteed residual value is the price the lessee must pay the lessor for purchase of the leased asset at the termination of the lease.

We can illustrate how the implicit interest rate is determined with an example. The city of Tiny Rock has just leased a fleet of ten buses for its new transportation system. The lease contract is to run for ten years. The fleet was recently purchased by the Metropolitan Bank; hence, the bank is the lessor. Annual lease payments prepaid each year are \$85,000, and at the end of the lease term Tiny Rock has the option to buy the fleet for \$20,000, at which time the market value of the buses is also expected to be \$20,000. Tiny Rock estimates that the buses cost the bank \$544,337.

The implicit interest rate in the lease is the value $r$ in the following equation:

$$\$544{,}337 = \$85{,}000 + \sum_{t=1}^{9} \frac{\$85{,}000}{(1+r)^t} + \frac{\$20{,}000}{(1+r)^{10}} \tag{17.1}$$

That is,

$$\begin{aligned}\text{Cash outlay} &= \text{First year lease payment}\\ &\quad + \text{Present value of lease payments of last 9 years}\\ &\quad + \text{Present value of purchase option price}\end{aligned}$$

Solving for $r$ yields 12% as the implicit interest rate on the lease.

The implicit rate on the lease may be higher, lower, or equal to the lessee's marginal borrowing rate. If the implicit rate is lower than the marginal borrowing rate, then the implicit rate must be used; otherwise, the lessor has a choice of using either the implicit rate or the marginal borrowing rate. In this case, we assume that the lessee's marginal borrowing rate is 12% and that the lessor chooses the implicit rate. The implicit interest rate in the lease may be greater than the lessee's marginal borrowing rate because the lessor is able to purchase the asset for a cheaper price than the lessee or because the lessor is in a position to use the investment tax credit if it is available (that is, if not fully passed along to the lessee in the form of lower lease payments or if currently part of the tax code).

Given that there could be a differential between these two rates of interest — both of which are relevant to the leasing arrangement — the comparison of these two rates is by no means the best method for making purchase versus lease decisions, especially since the lessor's cost figures inevitably are only estimates. Rarely will the lessor reveal the costs incurred in acquiring an asset to be leased. Note that with the lessee's marginal borrowing rate equal to 12%, the present value of the lessee's lease obligation is $544,337.

Finally, in this case, we assume that the marginal tax rate of the lease is 25%.

#### 17.3.1.2 *Fair market value estimate*

The second type of required estimate is that of the asset's fair market value at the time the lease takes effect. The lessee records a capital lease as both an asset and a liability at the lower of (1) the present value of the lease payments or (2) the fair market value of the leased asset at the beginning of the lease. For our example, we will assume that the fair market value of the buses being leased is $600,000. The lower of the two estimates — here, the $544,337 present value — is added to the asset account Capital Equipment under "leases."

A further breakdown is required before entries can be made to the liability accounts. A schedule of interest expense and a balance of the lease obligation must be computed. The amount of each lease payment that is not recorded as interest on the balance of the lease obligation (the difference between total lease payment and interest, which is similar to principle repayment on a loan) must be recorded as a current lease obligation in the period prior to its payment. The balance of the lease obligation is then carried as a noncurrent lease obligation.

Six tables give the information needed to compute the financial accounting of leases. Table 17.1 shows the depreciation schedule in terms of the sum-of-years'-digits method. The sum-of-years'-digits are defined as

$$\text{SYD} = \frac{N(N+1)}{2} \tag{17.2}$$

where $N$ = estimated years of useful life. In our case, $N = 10$, so

$$\text{SYD} = \frac{10(10+1)}{2} = 55$$

Table 17.1 City of Tiny Rock Depreciation Schedule.

Assumptions:
1. Asset value is $544,337
2. Residual value at end of year 10 is $20,000
3. Depreciation is sum-of-year's digits

| **Year End** | **Depreciation Expense** | **Capital Equipment Under Lease** |
|---|---|---|
| 0 | $0 | $544,337 |
| 1 | 95,334 | 449,003 |
| 2 | 85,801 | 363,202 |
| 3 | 76,267 | 286,935 |
| 4 | 66,734 | 220,201 |
| 5 | 57,200 | 163,001 |
| 6 | 47,667 | 115,334 |
| 7 | 38,134 | 77,200 |
| 8 | 28,600 | 48,600 |
| 9 | 19,067 | 29,530 |
| 10 | 9,533 | 20,000* |

Total depreciation = $524,337

*Note*: *Rounded by $3.

Therefore, the depreciation for each year can be calculated as follows:

First year: $(\$544{,}337 - 20{,}000) \times \frac{10}{55} = \$95{,}334$

Second year: $\$524{,}337 \times \frac{9}{55} = \$85{,}801$

.

.

.

Tenth year: $\$524{,}337 \times \frac{1}{55} = \$9{,}533$

Table 17.2 is a lease amortization schedule that includes cash payments, interest on the lease, lease obligation reductions, and outstanding lease obligations. In Table 17.2, the interest expense of the

Table 17.2 Lease Amortization Schedule.

**Assumptions:**
1. Asset value is $544,337
2. Interest rate is 12%
3. Annual lease payments of $85,000 with final payment of $20,000 on final day of year 10

| **Beginning of Year** | **(A) Cash Payment (A = B + C)** | **(B) Interest on Lease [B = (D)(12%)]** | **(C) Lease Obligation Reduction (C = A − B)** | **(D) Outstanding Lease Obligation (D = D − C)*** |
|---|---|---|---|---|
| 0 | | | | $544,337.00 |
| 1 | $85,000 | $0 | $85,000.00 | 459,337.00 |
| 2 | 85,000 | 55,120.44 | 29,879.56 | 429,457.44 |
| 3 | 85,000 | 51,534.89 | 33,465.16 | 395,992.28 |
| 4 | 85,000 | 47,519.07 | 37,480.93 | 358,511.35 |
| 5 | 85,000 | 43,021.36 | 41,978.64 | 316,532.71 |
| 6 | 85,000 | 37,983.93 | 47,016.08 | 269,516.64 |
| 7 | 85,000 | 32,342.00 | 52,658.00 | 216,858.64 |
| 8 | 85,000 | 26,023.04 | 58,976.96 | 157,881.68 |
| 9 | 85,000 | 18,945.80 | 66,054.20 | 91,827.48 |
| 10 | 85,000 | 11,019.30 | 73,980.70 | 17,846.78 |
| End of year 10 | 20,000 | 2,141.61 | 17,846.78 | 0 |

*Note*: *$544,337.00 − $85,000.00 = $459,337.00, $459,337.00 − $29,879.56 = $429,457.44.

Table 17.3 Principle Repayment Figures on an Annual Basis — Balance Sheets for 10 Years of Lease Arrangements.

**Assumptions**
1. Initial asset value of $544,337.
2. Depreciation schedule in Table 17.1 used to update asset value.
3. Outstanding lease obligations taken from Table 17.2.

| End of Year | Assets | Current Lease Obligations | Noncurrent Lease Obligations |
|---|---|---|---|
| 0 | $544,337 | $0 | $0 |
| 1 | 449,003 | 85,000 | 459,337.00 |
| 2 | 363,202 | 85,000 | 429,457.44 |
| 3 | 286,935 | 85,000 | 395,992.28 |
| 4 | 220,201 | 85,000 | 358,511.35 |
| 5 | 163,001 | 85,000 | 316,532.71 |
| 6 | 115,334 | 85,000 | 269,516.64 |
| 7 | 77,200 | 85,000 | 216,858.64 |
| 8 | 48,600 | 85,000 | 157,881.68 |
| 9 | 29,533 | 85,000 | 91,827.48 |
| 10 | 20,000 | 0 | 0 |

lease is 12% times the outstanding lease obligation; the lease obligation reduction is the cash lease payment minus interest on the lease; and the outstanding lease obligation is the lease balance minus the lease obligation reduction. The residual value of $20,000 is paid by the lessee to the lessor at the end of the tenth year to purchase the leased asset. On the balance sheet at the end of each year, both interest on the lease and lease reduction are current liabilities (current lease obligations), as presented in Table 17.3,[1] while noncurrent lease obligations are outstanding lease obligations, as presented in Table 17.3.

A decrease of the shareholders' equity account caused by the accrued interest occurs because of the accounting treatment of leases for reporting purposes. While these equity effects are purely accounting creations (that is, they affect such factors as ratios and returns),

[1]We assume that cash payment is made at the beginning of the year. If the cash payment were at the end of the year, then only lease reduction is a current liability. (See Kieso *et al.*, 2019).

Table 17.4 Income Statement Expenses on Annual Basis, Operating Lease Option.

| Year | Lease Payment |
|---|---|
| 1 | $85,000 |
| 2 | 85,000 |
| 3 | 85,000 |
| 4 | 85,000 |
| 5 | 85,000 |
| 6 | 85,000 |
| 7 | 85,000 |
| 8 | 85,000 |
| 9 | 85,000 |
| 10 | 85,000 |

they are still a real concern to shareholders, management, creditors, and others involved.

On the lessee's income statement, both depreciation and the interest expense implicit in the lease payments, as shown in Tables 17.1 and 17.2, are deductions from income. The depreciation method used depends on which of the four criteria for capital leases identified at the beginning of this section are satisfied. If rules 1 or 2 are satisfied and a bargaining purchase option and/or the lease transfers ownership, then the lessee's normal depreciation policies apply. If rules 1 or 2 are not satisfied and either rules 3 or 4 are, then the asset must be amortized over the term of the lease contract. Thus, more flexibility in depreciation expense write-off is granted to the lessor if rules 1 or 2 are satisfied.

Tables 17.4 and 17.5 present income statement expenses for our example under an operating lease option and a capital lease option. The income differential under the two different accounting treatments in presented in Table 17.6

Several reporting requirements must be disclosed in the financial statement footnotes. Total assets under lease obligations must be described by type, whether by function or by the nature of the asset. The minimum lease payment for each of the next five years must also be presented as well as the contingent lease payments incurred during the period. Finally, a general description of the leasing arrangement, including any restrictions imposed by the lease contract, must be disclosed.

Table 17.5 Income Statement Expenses on Annual Basis, Capital Lease Option.

| Year | Depreciation Expense | Interest Expense | Total Expenses |
|---|---|---|---|
| 1 | $95,334 | $55,120.44 | $150,454.44 |
| 2 | 85,801 | 51,534.89 | 137,335.89 |
| 3 | 76,267 | 47,519.07 | 123,786.07 |
| 4 | 66,734 | 43,021.36 | 109,755.36 |
| 5 | 57,200 | 37,983.93 | 95,183.93 |
| 6 | 47,667 | 32,342.00 | 80,009.00 |
| 7 | 38,134 | 26,023.04 | 64,157.04 |
| 8 | 28,600 | 18,945.80 | 47,545.80 |
| 9 | 19,067 | 11,019.30 | 30,086.30 |
| 10 | 9,533 | 2,083.17 | 11,674.61* |
| | | | $849,988.44 |

*Note*: *Excluded from the capitalized lease expense option is the purchase price of the asset.

Table 17.6 Income Differential under Capitalization and Noncapitalization.

Income figures from Tables 17.4 and 17.5 are used for comparative purposes.

| Year | Capitalized Expenses | Noncapitalized Expenses | Difference | Cumulative Difference — Capitalized Less Noncapitalized |
|---|---|---|---|---|
| 1 | $150,454.44 | $85,000.00 | $65,454.44 | $65,454.44 |
| 2 | 147,335.89 | 85,000.00 | 52,335.89 | 117,790.33 |
| 3 | 123,786.07 | 85,000.00 | 38,786.07 | 156,574.40 |
| 4 | 109,755.36 | 85,000.00 | 24,755.36 | 181,329.76 |
| 5 | 95,183.93 | 85,000.00 | 10,183.93 | 191,513.69 |
| 6 | 80,009.00 | 85,000.00 | −4,991.00 | 186,522.69 |
| 7 | 64,157.04 | 85,000.00 | −20,842.96 | 165,681.73 |
| 8 | 47,545.80 | 85,000.00 | −37,454.20 | 128,224.53 |
| 9 | 30,086.30 | 85,000.00 | −54,913.70 | 73,310.83 |
| 10 | 11,674.61 | 85,000.00 | −8,325.39 | 64,988.44 |

### 17.3.2 *Accounting for operating leases*

Operating leases require the same reporting requirements in terms of footnotes as capital leases but are not required to be included on the balance sheet. Interest expense and depreciation expense can also be excluded from the income statement.

Given the differing accounting treatments for leases, we have to wonder what difference it makes which method is employed. The difference to the financial manager is the effect on net income. Table 17.6 shows that in the short term the net income suffers but can be recouped in later years when the depreciation expense plus the interest expense becomes smaller than the uniform lease payment.

With the recent emphasis on short-term profitability, managers must arrange leases that keep lease figures out of the body of the firm's financial statements. Return on equity is an important measure for most firms and investors and adds another factor to the lease capitalization question. To the extent that the difference between the lease payment and the depreciation expense is greater than the difference between the total expenses to be deducted from income and the lease payment, the return-on-equity figure will be reduced further because of an increase in the equity account. This accrues solely as a result of the depreciation method employed and the capitalization procedure required by *FASB 13*.

We have stated that large capitalizations have an adverse effect on reported profitability measures. We now discuss the firm's liquidity and risk position as a result of a lease agreement. Because current liabilities are increased while current assets remain the same, net working capital (current assets — current liabilities) will decrease. This is also true of most of the standard liquidity ratios, making the firm appear at a higher risk. Coverage ratios, such as times interest earned and times fixed charges earned, also decrease because of the higher fixed charges incurred. All of these changes will be compounded by a lower earnings figure. Debt to equity, including capitalized leases, as a form of debt financing, will make the firm's position seem even more risky. These coverage and debt ratios should improve over time because the interest expense decreases while earnings and equity are expected to increase. Ingberman, Ronen, and Sorter (1979) have performed an extensive analysis on ratio changes due to capitalization of lease obligations.

A firm's earnings figures are important because they are often used as a measure of firm performance in a given period. Ball and Brown (1968) were early pioneers in empirical analysis of accounting information they found that at least 50% of the information used to derive market stock prices comes from the annual income figure. Hence, managers have good reason to be concerned about reported earnings and their effects on stock price.

Another important study performed by Abdel-Khalik (1981) examined the effects of capitalization on the shareholder's position. This study found that lease capitalization did not have particularly adverse effects. However, when they analyzed similar firms, some of which capitalized leases while others did not, their study showed a tendency on the part of financial analysts to lower the credit worthiness of firms that capitalized. However, the adverse effects of capitalization on shareholders are still undecided.

The ratio analysis mentioned earlier can have important implications for creditors or investors in assessing a firm's financial strength. By assessing firm risk, they are determining the firm's cost of capital. Two well-known studies, Pinches and Mingo (1973) and Pogue and Soldofsky (1969), have shown that certain ratios — such as liquidity, leverage, and profitability ratios — are highly correlated with the firm's bond ratings, and bonds are one source of long-term financing. Altman's (1968) study on bankruptcy predictors showed that these same ratios are also fairly accurate predictors of bankruptcy. Hence, if these ratios are used to evaluate a firm's performance, capitalization of leases may have adverse effects on the firm.

### 17.3.3 *Accounting for leases from the lessor's standpoint*

Accounting for leases from the lessor's standpoint is not as complex as it is from the lessee's standpoint. Capitalization of asset value and off-balance sheet reporting is not an issue to the lessor because the lessor actually owns the asset in question and it appears on the lessor's balance sheet. Therefore, the lessor must include the purchase of the asset on all relevant statements. The recorded value of the asset is determined in much the same manner for the lessor as for the lessee. As required by *FASB 13*, the only complications that may arise in recording are if the value of the asset is less than or greater than the cost of the asset, in which case the income figure must adjusted.

However, in 2016, FASB and International Accounting Standards Board (IASB) issued updates to GAAP and International Financial

Reporting Standards (IFRS) codifications that require the majority of leases to be listed as an asset along with a corresponding liability on the lessee's balance sheet. In the next section, we discuss this new update.

## 17.4 Lease Accounting Updates

Following Gordon *et al.* (2018), U.S. GAAP leasing standards were established in 1976 with the issuance of FASB 13. Recently, FASB issued FASB topic 842 in 2016, which becomes effective for public corporations in 2019 (though early adoption is permitted). Prior to this accounting update FASB Topic 840 was the accounting standard in effect. Historically, only capital leases were required to be listed on the lessee's balance sheet. Operating lease payments only had to be disclosed in the footnotes of the financial statements. However, in 2016, FASB and IASB issued updates to GAAP and IFRS codifications that require the majority of leases to be listed as an asset along with a corresponding liability on the lessee's balance sheet. These were issued in response to criticism that previous standards did not meet the needs of financial statement users because they did not always provide a faithful representation of leasing transactions. Since criticism was primarily aimed at the treatment of leases for the lessee, the treatment of lease accounting for lessors was not materially changed (though minor changes were made in order to align lessor guidance with lessee guidance).

### 17.4.1 *Key updates & changes to leasing standards under U.S. GAAP*

Under the new standards for operating leases under GAAP, a lessee is required to recognize a right-of-use asset and lease liability measured at the present value of lease payments within the balance sheet, recognize a single lease cost allocated over the lease term on a generally straight-line basis, and classify all cash payments within operating activities in the statement of cash flows. The lessee is permitted to make an accounting policy election to not recognize lease assets or liabilities if the term of the lease is 12 months or less and does not include an option to purchase the underlying asset that the lessee is reasonably certain to exercise. Notably, GAAP still retains a distinction between operating leases and finance leases. As such, the effect of leases in the income statement and the statement of cash flows is substantially unchanged from previous GAAP standards. The amendments within FASB's GAAP update are effective for fiscal years beginning after December 15, 2018 for public business entities and early application is permitted.

### 17.4.2 *Revised criteria for determination of operating versus capital lease*

Under the new GAAP standards, lessees classify leases as operating leases or finance leases. Classification as an operating lease or finance lease by the lessee depends on whether the lessee meets Group I criteria. If the lease meets any of the criteria it is classified as a finance lease. If the lessee does not meet any of the criteria it is classified as an operating lease. Under GAAP, there also exists Group II criteria, however, the criteria only has bearing on the lessor's treatment of the lease; as this section is focused primarily on the treatment on leases by the lessee, they will not be discussed. The Group I criteria are as follows:

1. The lease transfers ownership of the leased asset to the lessee at the end of the lease term.
2. The lessee has an option to purchase the asset and is reasonably certain to exercise.
3. The lease term is for a major part of the asset's life; guidance is greater than or equal to 75% of the asset's life.
4. The sum of the present value of lease payments and the present value of residual value the lessee guarantees meets the criterion of being substantially all of the asset's fair value; substantially all of the asset's fair value is defined as greater than or equal to 90% of the asset's fair value.
5. The leased asset is of a specialized nature; such an asset would be prohibitively expensive for the lessor to repurpose for use by another user or have no alternative use to the lessor.

Notice that the only difference to the Group I criteria between the old GAAP leasing standards and the new GAAP leasing standards for the lessee is the addition of the fifth criteria, that the leased asset is of a specialized nature (making it slightly more difficult to classify a lease as an operating lease). In sum, it is classified as a capital lease if the following conditions are met:

1. The title transfers.
2. If the title does not transfer, and there is a bargain purchase option than it is classified as capital lease.
3. If the title doesn't transfer, there is no bargain purchase option, and the lease term is larger than 75% of the expected useful life, than it is also classified as capital lease.
4. If the title doesn't transfer, there is no bargain purchase option, the lease term is not larger than 75% of the expected useful life, and present value of lease payments is larger than 90% of fair market value, than it is classified as capital lease.
5. If the title doesn't transfer, there is no bargain purchase option, the lease term is not larger than 75% of the expected useful life, present value of lease payments is smaller than 90% of fair market value, and the asset is of a specialized nature, than it is classified as capital lease.
6. If all conditions mentioned in items 1–5 are not followed than it is classified as operating lease.

Prior to the updated U.S. GAAP standards on leases, operating leases were kept off the balance sheet. Instead, lessees were required to list the lease obligations in the footnotes to their financial statements. As a result of the updated standards and the requirements that lessees report the present value of operating leases as an asset and corresponding liability on the balance sheet, companies are likely to appear more leveraged than previously. Stated in another way, companies' financial statements are more likely to report their actual leverage and make comparisons of firms' leverage easier for investors.

### 17.4.3 *Updates to leasing standards under IFRS*

Under the new IFRS standards for leases, the lessee does not differentiate between operating leases or finance leases. Rather, under IFRS, lessees treat all leases as if they were a U.S. GAAP finance lease, whereby lessees report interest expense and amortization expenses for all leases. There does exist Group I criteria, which are the same as the U.S. GAAP Group I criteria listed previously. However, the existence of the Group I criteria has no bearing upon the lessee and are solely for use by the lessor. Like the new U.S. GAAP standards, IFRS also maintains an exemption for reporting leases on the balance sheet if they are less than a year in duration. Additionally, under the updated IFRS standards, a lessee may elect to treat leased assets with a value of less than \$5,000 as rental agreements. For example, if a lessee leased a car with a value of \$3,000 and a useful life of 2 years, the lessee does not have to recognize a lease asset or a lease liability.

The lease figure initially reported as the amount of lease assets and lease liabilities on the balance sheet is the present value of lease payments. The associated expense with the lease will be split on the income statement, with the portion representing amortization or principal being embedded in operating income and the balance embedded within interest expense.

### 17.4.4 *Impacts of new leasing standards on financial statements & ratios*

The new leasing standards are expected to effect the statements and ratios. The most important impact from the new standards, under both IFRS and GAAP, will be the requirement to recognize a right-to-use asset along with a corresponding liability on the balance sheet. This will serve to increase reported leverage for most companies, as recognizing an asset and liability from leases will cause leverage metrics such as the debt-to-assets ratio to increase. As an illustration of the degree of the impact from the change in the treatment of operating leases under GAAP, we can analyze the impact on reported leverage ratios by capitalizing JCPenney's operating leases.

JCPenney's financial statements for the year ended February 3, 2018, disclosed the following minimum non-cancelable lease payments:

Discounting these payments at an 8% rate and assuming that the thereafter period consists of approximately 9.9 years of payments of \$170 mm, the implied asset and liability that would be reported on the balance sheet would be approximately \$1,823.9 mm. As a result, reported debt would increase to \$6,055.9 mm from \$4,232 mm (defined as long-term debt and capital lease liabilities), an increase of 43%. Correspondingly, the D/A ratio would increase to 50% to 72%.

Thus, while at first glance JCPenney seems to be highly leveraged and troubled operationally, adjusting its debt for operating leases makes it even more so. Under the updated U.S. GAAP guidance, the effect of operating leases on operating income should remain approximately the same.

Under IFRS, the reported lease liability from such payments would be similar since the regulations do away with the differentiation between operating leases and finance leases. As a result, the implied asset and liability amounts from what are currently reported operating lease payments would be brought onto the balance sheet. Since the differentiation on the balance sheet between operating leases and finance leases would disappear, all leases (with limited exceptions such as for leases with terms less than one year) would be reported on the balance sheet as finance leases. The effects on the reported leverage would be the same, with an expected increase of the Debt/Asset ratio from 50% to 72%. However, under the new IFRS guidance, operating income and cash flow operations will be higher, stemming from the fact that what were previously operating leases will be treated as finance leases.

Since what were previously operating leases will be treated as finance leases, no longer will lease payments be embedded solely into operating income and cash flows from operating activities. Instead, coinciding with the treatment of finance leases, a portion of the lease payment will be deducted from operating income, and a portion of the lease payment will be allocated as interest expense on the income statement. Conversely, on the statement of cash flows, a portion of the lease expense representing principal repayment will be reported in cash flow from financing and the portion representing interest expense may be reported under cash flows from operating activities or cash flows from financing activities. In the aggregate, companies that report under IFRS will see improvements in operating income when adoption occurs and, when compared with a hypothetical identical company but for the use of U.S. GAAP instead of IFRS, higher operating income and interest expense.

As a result, financial statement users should exhibit caution when comparing companies that use differing reporting standards. Even if two companies had an identical lease payment schedule, the company using IFRS may report higher operating income and higher interest expense while the company using U.S. GAAP may report lower

Table 17.7 JCPenney & Co. Reported Operating Lease Payments.

| Year | Operating Lease Payments | Present Value |
|---|---|---|
| 2018 | 211 | 195.4 |
| 2019 | 187 | 160.3 |
| 2020 | 169 | 134.2 |
| 2021 | 150 | 110.3 |
| 2022 | 132 | 89.8 |
| Thereafter | 1,686 | 1,134 |
| Total/Implied Debt | | $1,823.9 |

*Note*: 2020 JCPenny annual report.

operating income but lower interest expense. An analyst should keep the differences in mind and attempt to adjust for them in order to make an apples-to-apples comparison between companies.

In sum, the new accounting standards bring a greater level of transparency to financial statements than previously available and is the most significant change to leasing standards under both GAAP and IFRS. As far as transparency goes, the IFRS standards go a bit further and reflects the wide-spread practice of analysts and institutions, such as rating agencies, that capitalize operating leases and in effect turn them into finance leases by increasing assets and liabilities by the present value of the lease payments and add back imputed interest expense from operating leases to operating income. Nonetheless, the changes to lease guidance for lessees under U.S. GAAP is still a significant improvement over the previous standards and mimics the most significant change under the IFRS guidance by recognizing an asset and liability from the majority of leases on the balance sheet.

The updated guidance under both standards enables analysts and investors to compare the credit capacity and leverage metrics of companies with different financing practices much more readily and consistently by doing away with the off-balance sheet treatment of operating leases. While the new GAAP standards for leases don't exclude imputed interest expense from operating income, analysts and investors will find it much easier to adjust the operating income for imputed interest since the present value of operating leases will now be listed as an asset on the balance sheet. Presumably, analysts will be able to use the disclosure of future minimum lease payments in conjunction with the lease liability to calculate an imputed interest rate and use this information to adjust the operating income accordingly. Thus, while there are still flaws in the lease standards, they are vastly improved to the previous standards and have greatly increased the ability financial statement users to compare the health and operating metrics of companies. JCPenney & Co. Reported Operating Lease Payments during 2018 to 2022 can be found in Table 17.7.

## 17.5 Cash Flow Estimation and Present Value Analysis of Lease or Buy Alternatives

Two important considerations facing the financial analyst regarding the lease-buy decision are (1) the estimation of the timing and size of each expected cash inflow and outflow and (2) estimation of the appropriate discount rate. The leasing decision is made by comparing leasing cash flows against cash flows that would be obtained had the asset been purchased and funded entirely by debt, in this type of decision, the investment decision is made separately from the financing decision. Consequently, management may reject profitable leasing opportunities if the leasing opportunity creates a positive net present value under discounted cash flow analysis while all other opportunities are not profitable. Therefore, our analysis of the lease-buy decision recognizes that we are not necessarily choosing the best of two or more projects but rather are finding the best project overall. Again, we are assuming that the leasing package is 100% debt financed. Later we examine the implication and appropriate treatment of other valuation models.

First, however, we outline some leasing characteristics. Regardless of the accounting treatment of the lease, the only allowable deduction from taxable income is the lease payment. Depreciation and interest expenses are irrelevant for tax and cash flow determination. This should help illustrate an earlier statement that capitalization of leases has no economic consequences. The major concern over capitalization is whether the Internal Revenue Service accepts the lease arrangement as a true lease and not a disguised sale that a firm could use to write off expenses. The result would be a greater-than-normal tax shield for the acquiring firm. The specifics of what constitutes a true lease are found in IRS *Ruling 55-540*, which states that the critical criterion for a lease is that the lessee has a bargain purchase option after using the asset for most of its economic life or after having made payments totaling its estimated value.

There are two general approaches that can be used in the discounted cash flow analysis of leasing, both of which are approximately equivalent. In the first approach, the goal is to maximize the discounted after-tax cash flows. In the second approach, the goal is to find the minimum discounted cash flows under the assumption that the revenues generated under the lease or buy decision are equivalent. For reasons of computational ease, we will use the second method.

The present value method discussed in Chapter 6 can be used to analyze the lease-buy decision. According to this method, the alternative with the lowest present value is the most desirable. To illustrate, we will use the city of Tiny Rock's case, discussed previously, to show how lease-buy decisions can be made using the present value decision rule.

### 17.5.1 *Present value — Lease*

Using information from Tables 17.1 through 17.6, the schedule of cash outflows for a leasing alternative is shown in Table 17.8. In this table, the lease payments are obtained from Table 17.2. The $85,000 at the end of each of the first nine years represents a prepaid expense and is not tax deductible until the next year. However, the $20,000 payment in the tenth year is a current expense payment. The tax shield is obtained by multiplying the lease payment by the tax rate (0.25), and the cash outflow after taxes is equal to the lease payment minimum the tax shield.

Since interest payments are tax deductible, an appropriate discount rate for discounting the after-tax cash flow might be the after-tax cost of borrowing. In our example, the after-tax cost of borrowing is $12\% \ (1-0.25) = 9\%$.[2] However, this kind of discount rate has been questioned by Gordon (1974) and others. (Gordon's argument about discount rates is discussed in the next section.) The present value of

---

[2]The use of this rate assumes that the firm's future taxable income will be sufficient to fully utilize the tax shield associated with lease payment.

Table 17.8 Schedule of Cash Outflows.

| End of Year | (1) Lease Payment | (2) Tax Shield [(1) * (0.25)] | (3) Cash Outflow after Taxes [(1) − (2)] | (4) Present Value of Cash Outflows $[\frac{(2)}{(1+9\%)^t}]$ | (5) Interest Expense | (6) Tax shield [(5) * (0.25)] | (7) Cash Outflow after Taxes [(1) − (6)] | (8) Present Value of cash outflows $[\frac{(7)}{(1+9\%)^t}]$ |
|---|---|---|---|---|---|---|---|---|
| 0 | $85,000 | — | $85,000 | $85,000.00 | — | — | $85,000 | 85,000.00 |
| 1 | 85,000 | $21,250 | 63,750 | 58,486.24 | $0 | $0 | 85000.00 | 77,981.65 |
| 2 | 85,000 | 21,250 | 63,750 | 53,657.10 | 55,120.44 | 13,780.11 | 71219.89 | 59,944.36 |
| 3 | 85,000 | 21,250 | 63,750 | 49,226.70 | 51,534.89 | 12,883.72 | 72116.28 | 55,687.00 |
| 4 | 85,000 | 21,250 | 63,750 | 45,162.11 | 47,519.07 | 11,879.77 | 73120.23 | 51,800.22 |
| 5 | 85,000 | 21,250 | 63,750 | 41,433.13 | 43,021.36 | 10,755.34 | 74244.66 | 48,253.93 |
| 6 | 85,000 | 21,250 | 63,750 | 38,012.04 | 37,983.93 | 9,495.98 | 75504.02 | 45,020.58 |
| 7 | 85,000 | 21,250 | 63,750 | 34,873.43 | 32,342.00 | 8,085.50 | 76914.50 | 42,074.87 |
| 8 | 85,000 | 21,250 | 63,750 | 31,993.98 | 26,023.04 | 6,505.76 | 78494.24 | 39,393.61 |
| 9 | 85,000 | 21,250 | 63,750 | 29,352.27 | 18,945.80 | 4,736.45 | 80263.55 | 36,955.57 |
| 10 | — | 21,250 | (21,250) | (8,976.23) | 11,019.30 | 2,754.83 | (2754.83) | (1,163.67) |
| End of year 10 | 20,000 | 5,000 | 15,000 | 6,336.16 | 2,141.61 | 535.40 | 19464.60 | 8,222.06 |
| | | | $379,556.92 | | | | | $464,170.17 |

total cash outflows under the leasing alternative is \$463,903.75. This figure must then be compared with the present value of cash outflows under the borrowing alternative, which is discussed next.

### 17.5.2 *Present value — Buy*

Let us assume that the city of Tiny Rock purchases the buses using a 12% loan with loan payments payable at the beginning of each year.[3] Let us also assume that the schedule of loan payments is identical to the schedule of lease payments in Table 17.2. The loan payment, principle amount owing after payment, and annual interest are listed in Table 17.9. Table 17.10 presents schedule of cash outflows for debt alternatives. The tax shield for the buy alternative is interest expense plus depreciation. The present value of the buy alternative is \$449,499.13, which is less than the present value of the lease alternative. Therefore, it is better to buy the buses with borrowed money rather than lease them. The major difference from our example between lease and buy is that the buy alternative enjoys a depreciation tax shield.

## 17.6 Valuation of Riskless and Risky Cash Flows for the Lease or Buy Decision

The first article dealing with the theoretical issues of the leasing decision was by Gordon (1974). His paper was intended to be a teaching note to Johnson and Lewellen's 1972 paper but is now considered the first attempt at lease valuation under conditions of market equilibrium.

Gordon was concerned with four issues:

1. The correct discount rate for riskless cash flows.
2. The difference in the lives of a lease contract versus a purchase option.
3. The risk difference between each cash flow or stream of cash flows.

[3]Bower *et al.* (1966) argued that if loan payments are payable at the end of the year and lease payments payable at the beginning of the year, the earlier payments of the lease alternative will increase the firm's capacity for raising funds by other means of financing earlier than under the debt alternative.

Table 17.9 Schedule of Debt Payments.

| Year | Loan Payment | Principle Amount Owing after Payment | Annual Interest |
|---|---|---|---|
| 0 | $85,000 | $459,337.00 | $0 |
| 1 | 85,000 | 429,457.44 | 55,120.44 |
| 2 | 85,000 | 395,992.28 | 51,534.89 |
| 3 | 85,000 | 358,511.35 | 47,519.07 |
| 4 | 85,000 | 316,532.71 | 43,021.36 |
| 5 | 85,000 | 269,516.64 | 37,983.93 |
| 6 | 85,000 | 216,858.64 | 32,342.00 |
| 7 | 85,000 | 157,881.67 | 26,023.04 |
| 8 | 85,000 | 91,827.48 | 18,945.80 |
| 9 | 85,000 | 17,846.78 | 11,019.30 |
| 10 | 20,000 | 0 | 2,141.61 |

4. The financing differences between alternative acquisition plans.

Gordon performed his study of item 1 under the Modigliani and Miller (1963) equilibrium framework. That is, if a firm carries no debt in its capital structure and the expected value of its earnings is $\bar{X}$, then the value of this firm is

$$V_u = \frac{(1-\tau_c)\bar{X}}{k} \tag{17.3}$$

where $V_u$ = the total value of an all-equity firm; $(1-\tau_c)\bar{X}$ = the perpetual stream of after-tax cash flows; and $k$ = investors' required rate of return on equity.

If a firm invests solely in risk-free bonds, $M$, earnings the riskless rate of interest, $i$, then the earnings stream, $X$, becomes $(M)(i)$. Note that $i$ is equal to the return investors require after corporate income tax has been considered. The reason is that the investor could buy the same bonds directly and avoid the corporate tax. Hence, the after-tax yield at which the stock of a risk-free corporation sells is the interest rate on risk-free bonds without deducting the corporate tax.[4]

Resolutions for the remaining three issues Gordon raised are found in the following formulations of the values of buy-lease alternatives.

[4]The proof of this conclusion is given in Appendix 17A.

Table 17.10 Schedule of Cash Outflows: Debt Alternative.

| End of Year | (1) Loan Payment | (2) Interest | (3) Depreciation | (4) Tax Shield [(2) + (3)]0.25 | (5) Cash Outflow after Taxes (1) − (4) | (6) Present Value of Value of Cash Outflows (9%) |
|---|---|---|---|---|---|---|
| 0 | $85,000 | $0 | $0 | $0 | $85,000.00 | $85,000.00 |
| 1 | 85,000 | 55,120.44 | 95,334 | 37,613.61 | 47,386.39 | 43,472.27 |
| 2 | 85,000 | 51,534.89 | 85,801 | 34,333.97 | 50,666.03 | 42,645.60 |
| 3 | 85,000 | 47,519.07 | 76,267 | 30,946.51 | 54,053.49 | 41,740.11 |
| 4 | 85,000 | 43,021.36 | 66,734 | 27,438.84 | 57,561.16 | 40,776.33 |
| 5 | 85,000 | 37,983.93 | 57,200 | 23,795.98 | 61,204.02 | 39,776.49 |
| 6 | 85,000 | 32,342.00 | 47,667 | 20,002.25 | 64,997.75 | 38,785.16 |
| 7 | 85,000 | 26,023.04 | 38,134 | 16,039.26 | 68,960.74 | 37,721.25 |
| 8 | 85,000 | 18,945.80 | 28,600 | 11,886.45 | 73,113.55 | 36,695.69 |
| 9 | 85,000 | 11,019.30 | 19,067 | 7,521.57 | 77,478.43 | 35,671.07 |
| 10 | 20,000 | 2,141.61 | 9,533 | 2,918.65 | 17,081.35 | 7,215.16 |
| | | | | | | $449,499.13 |

In the case of the buy alternative, the net present value is

$$\mathrm{NPV}_P = -I_o + \sum_{t=1}^{N} \frac{(1-\tau_c)(R_t) + \tau_c \mathrm{dep}_t}{(1+k)^t} \tag{17.4}$$

where $I_o$ = net initial outlay, $\tau_c$ = applicable corporate tax rate; $R_t$ = cash flows before depreciation and taxes; $\mathrm{dep}_t$ = depreciation expenses in time $t$; $k$ = weighted discount rate, (weighted according to the risk of the component flows); and $N$ = the life of the project. The net present value for the lease alternative is

$$\begin{aligned}\mathrm{NPV}_L = {} & -L_o(1-\tau_c) - \sum_{t=1}^{j} \frac{(1-\tau_c)L_t}{(1+i)^t} + \sum_{t=1}^{N} \frac{(1-\tau_c)(R_t)}{(1+k)^t} \\ & + \sum_{t=1}^{j} \frac{(1-\tau_c)F_t}{(1+i)^t} + \frac{P_j}{(1+k)^j} + \sum_{t=j+1}^{N} \frac{\tau_c dep'_t}{(1+k)^t} \end{aligned} \tag{17.5}$$

where $L_o$ = lease payment at $t = 0$; $L_t$ = lease payment at end of time $t$; $F_t$ = executory costs paid by the lessor; $P_j$ = purchase price of asset at end of the lease term; $\mathrm{dep}'_t$ = depreciation expense in the time period $t$; $i$ = discount rate for a riskless cash flow; $k$ = discount rate for a risky cash flow; $j$ = life of lease; and $N$ = life of the asset.

By assuming that the asset will be purchased at the end of the lease term, we eliminate the problem of different lives from the lease alternative formulation. Because we have explicitly stated $k$ and $i$, we are able to decompose the total cash flows into separate streams of differing risks. In general, cash flows stipulated in a lease or debt contract are considered riskless, while flows associated with the earnings stream are discounted at a rate that incorporates risk.

However, we still need to solve the debt financing problem implicit in the lease alternative. This is most easily achieved by assuming 100% debt financing with the purchase alternative, which transforms the $I_o$ term in Eq. (17.4), the purchase equation, into the same form as the lease payment stream. Consequently, Eq. (17.4) can be rewritten as

$$\begin{aligned}\mathrm{NPV}_P = {} & -L_o(1-\tau_c) - \sum_{t=1}^{j} \frac{(1-\tau_c)(M_t - A_t) + A_t}{(1+i)^t} \\ & + \sum_{t=1}^{N} \frac{(1-\tau_c)(R_t)}{(1+k)^t} + \sum_{t=1}^{N} \frac{\tau_c \mathrm{dep}_t}{(1+i)^t} \end{aligned} \tag{17.6}$$

where $M_t$ = payment of interest and principal on the loan during period $t$; $A_t$ = the amortization of the loan for tax purposes in period $t$; and $(M_t - A_t)$ = interest payment on the loan in period $t$. By subtracting the NPV of the purchase equation ($\text{NPV}_P$) from the NPV of the lease equation ($\text{NPV}_L$), we can derive an expression for the net advantage of the lease or purchase option:

$$\text{NPV}_L - \text{NPV}_P = \sum_{t=j+1}^{N} \frac{\tau_c \text{dep}'_t}{(1+k)^t} - \sum_{t=1}^{j} \frac{(1-\tau_c)(L_t - M_t - F_t) - \tau_c A_t}{(1+i)^t} - \sum_{t=1}^{N} \frac{\tau_c \text{dep}_t}{(1+i)^t} - \frac{P_j}{(1+k)_j} \quad (17.7)$$

Hence, we find that the lease option is preferred (1) the higher the depreciation tax shield on the asset, (2) the lower the lease payments to the periodic outlays if the asset were purchased, and (3) the lower the purchase price at time $j$. Notice that items 1 and 3 are in apparent conflict and require some type of resolution, as discussed below.

Consider the special case created by imposing the following assumptions:

(a) $L_o = 0$
(b) Life of the lease = Life of the asset
(c) Straight-line depreciation
(d) Equal annual lease payments
(e) Straight-line loan amortization
(f) $F_t = 0$.

Under condition (b), $P_j = 0$; from conditions (c) and (e), $A_t$ = (total loan)$/N = \text{dep}_t$. Therefore, Eq. (17.7) reduces to Eq. (17.8):

$$\text{NPV}_L - \text{NPV}_P = \sum_{t=1}^{N} \frac{(1-\tau_c)(M_t - L_t)}{(1+i)^t} \quad (17.8)$$

Now, the following example is used to show how Eqs. (17.4–17.7) can be used to do real-world analyses.

**Example:**

Q: GKM Corporation is considering acquisition of new equipment. The specific details associated with purchasing as well as leasing the equipment are given as follows:

Purchase cost ($I$) = \$300,000
Executory costs ($F$) = \$4,000
Life of asset = 10 years
Life of lease = 5 years
Cash flows before depreciation and taxes = \$70,000
Corporate tax rate = 30%
Cost of capital ($K$) = 13%
Discount rate for riskless cash flows = 9%
Annual lease payment = \$60,000
Residual value at $j$ = \$50,000

The first lease payment will be made at $t = 0$, and the succeeding payments being made at the end of each year. Using Eqs. (17.5–17.7), calculate the NPVs of the lease and buy options. The firm can borrow \$250,000 at an interest rate of 9% to finance the purchase of the equipment, payable in five equal annual installments.

Solutions:

a. Calculation of Eq. (17.5)

$$
\begin{aligned}
\text{NPV}_L &= -L_0(1-T_c) - \sum_{t=1}^{j} \frac{(1-T_c)L_t}{(1+i)^t} + \sum_{t=1}^{N} \frac{(1-T_c)R_t}{(1+k)^t} \\
&\quad + \sum_{t=1}^{J} \frac{(1-T_c)F_t}{(1+i)^t} - \frac{P_j}{(1+k)^j} + \sum_{t=J+1}^{N} \frac{T_c \text{dep}'_t}{(1+k)^t} \\
&= -50,000(1-0.30) \\
&\quad - \sum_{t=1}^{5} \frac{(1-0.30)(60{,}000)}{(1+0.09)^t} \\
&\quad + \sum_{t=1}^{10} \frac{(1-0.30)(70{,}000)}{(1+0.13)^t} \\
&\quad + \sum_{t=1}^{5} \frac{(1-0.30)(4{,}000)}{(1+0.09)^t} - \frac{50{,}000}{(1+0.13)^5} \\
&\quad + \sum_{t=6}^{10} \frac{(0.30)(10{,}000)}{(1+0.13)^t}
\end{aligned}
$$

$$= -42{,}000 + (0.70)(3.88965)(60{,}000) + (0.70)(5.42624)(70{,}000)$$
$$+(0.70)(3.88965)(40{,}000) - (0.54276)(50{,}000)$$
$$+(0.30)(0.54276)(3.51723)(10{,}000)$$
$$= \$50{,}000.52$$

b. Calculation of Eq. (17.4)

$$\begin{aligned}
\text{NPV}_p &= -l_0 + \sum_{t=1}^{N} \frac{(1-T_c)(R_t) + T_c \text{dep}_t}{(1+k)^t} \\
&= -300{,}000 + \sum_{t=1}^{10} \frac{(1-0.30)(70{,}000) + (0.30)(30{,}000)}{(1+0.13)^t} \\
&= -300{,}000 + 324{,}721.92 \\
&= \$14{,}721.92
\end{aligned}$$

c. Calculation of Eq. (17.6)

$$\text{NPV}_p = -L_0(1-T_c) - \sum_{t=1}^{j} \frac{(1-T_c)(M_t - A_t) + A_t}{(1+i)^t} + \sum_{t=1}^{N} \frac{(1-T_c)(R_t)}{(1+k)^t} + \sum_{t=1}^{N} \frac{T_c \text{dep}_t}{(1+i)^t}$$

$$M_t = \frac{250{,}000}{\sum_{t=1}^{5} \frac{1}{(1+0.09)^t}} = \frac{250{,}000}{3.88965} = \$64{,}273.14$$

$$A_t = \frac{250{,}000}{5} = \$50{,}000$$

$$\text{dep}_t = \frac{300{,}000}{10} = \$30{,}000$$

Then,

$$
\begin{aligned}
\text{NPV}_p &= -60{,}000(1-0.30) \\
&\quad - \sum_{t=1}^{5} \frac{(1-0.30)(64{,}273.14-50{,}000)+50{,}000}{(1+0.09)^t} \\
&\quad + \sum_{t=1}^{10} \frac{(1-0.30)(70{,}000)}{(1+0.13)^t} + \sum_{t=1}^{10} \frac{(0.30)(30{,}000)}{(1+0.09)^t} \\
&= -42{,}000 - 233{,}344.77 + 265{,}885.76 + 57{,}758.97 \\
&= \$48{,}299.93
\end{aligned}
$$

d. Calculation of Eq. (17.7)

$$
\begin{aligned}
\text{NPV}_L - \text{NPV}_P = {} & \sum_{t=j+1}^{N} \frac{T_c \text{dep}'_t}{(1+k)^t} \\
& - \sum_{t=1}^{j} \frac{(1-T_c)(L_t - M_t - F_t) - T_c A_t}{(1+i)^t} \\
& - \sum_{t=1}^{N} \frac{T_c \text{dep}_t}{(1+i)^t} - \frac{P_j}{(1+k)^j}
\end{aligned}
$$

$$
\begin{aligned}
&= \sum_{t=6}^{10} \frac{(0.30)(10{,}000)}{(1+0.13)^t} \\
&\quad - \sum_{t=1}^{5} \frac{(1-0.30)(60{,}000-64{,}273.14-4{,}000)-(0.30)(50{,}000)}{(1+0.09)^t} \\
&\quad - \sum_{t=1}^{10} \frac{(0.30)(30{,}000)}{(1+0.09)^t} - \frac{50{,}000}{(1+0.13)^t}
\end{aligned}
$$

$$= 5{,}727.04 + 80{,}870.49 - 57{,}758.94 - 27{,}138$$
$$= \$1{,}700.59$$

## 17.7 CAPM and the Lease of Buy Decision

In this section, we will use CAPM to deal with other sources of uncertainty in determining the value of a lease. Using arguments presented in Miller and Upton, we can use the CAPM to determine the equilibrium rental rate and the value of the lease. Following Lee, Martin, and Senchack (1982), the OPM can be used to evaluate the salvage value in a financial lease.

The risk-adjusted equilibrium gross rental rate consists of three components:

1. The risk-free rate of interest on capital investment.
2. The risk of obsolescence or technological change on the economic value of the assets (which changes the economic depreciation).
3. The normal rate of economic depreciation.

Following the CAPM concept discussed in Chapter 8, Miller and Upton (1976) and Schallheim *et al.* (1987) defined the net equilibrium rate as

$$E(R_{it}) = E\left(\frac{L_{it}}{\pi_i}\right) - E(\text{dep}_{it}) = R_f - \beta_{it}[E(R_{mt}) - R_f] \quad (17.9)$$

where $R_{it}$ is the yield on the lease; $L_{it}$ is the lease payment in period $t$; $\pi_i$ is the cost of the asset in period $t$; $R_f$ is the risk-free rate; $\beta = \text{COV}(d_{it}, R_{mt})/\text{VAR}(R_{mt})$; $R_m$ is the market return; $\text{dep}_{it}$ $(d_{it})$ is the normal economic depreciation; and $E(.)$ is the expectation operator.

In this form, we have a CAPM-type model, which can be used to determine the rental rate or level of lease payments. The risk-free rate and the economic depreciation were explained earlier. However, the beta and the risk premium associated with obsolescence need some interpretation.

The sign associated with the risk premium, $\beta(R_m - R_f)$, in this case is negative, which indicates that as the risk of obsolescence increases, the value of the asset decreases.

The beta can take any value. If the beta equals 0, there is no relationship between the state of the economy and depreciation and hence the asset should not be priced in the marketplace. If the beta is less than 0, the owners of the asset suffer a loss in value from two sources — a poor economy and an increase in technological innovation — so that they will demand a higher lease payment to compensate for this double-barreled reduction in the asset's value is offset by the increase in overall economic activity.

In this form of lease payment model, we have assumed no risk of default by the lessee. If there is a credit risk associated with the lease arrangement, the lessor will demand a higher lease payment according to the degree of risk. In this instance, Eq. (17.9) can be rewritten as

$$E(L_{it}) = R_f E(\pi_{it}) - \beta_{it}[E(R_m) - R_f]E(\pi_{it}) + E(dep_{it})E(\pi_{it}) \tag{17.10}$$

Equation (17.10) implies that the equilibrium rental payment must compensate the owner of the asset (the lessor) for (1) the capital invested in the asset at the risk-free rate $[R_f E(\pi_{it})]$, (2) the expected loss due to expected depreciation $[E(dep_{it})E(\pi_{it})]$, and (3) the nondiversifiable risk $-\beta_{it}[E(R_m) - R_f]E(\pi_{it})$.

Because the rent payment itself is risk free, the risk borne by the lessor is the risk associated with the uncertain end-of-period residual value of the asset. Schallheim *et al.* (1987) have shown that the yield of financial leases is positively related to the risk-free interest rate and the discounted value of the covariance risk of the asset's residual value.

Another approach to analyzing the leasing decision is to use capital budgeting techniques such as those implemented for cases of uncertainty. Miller and Upton (1976) investigated the capital asset pricing model and its applicability to the leasing decision. In so doing, they divided their findings between the economist's opinion — that the financing decision is of no consequence — and the accountant's opinion — that financing is important and nonfinancial elements are irrelevant. In their analysis, Miller and Upton assumed perfectly competitive markets. Therefore, financial advantages were dismissed from the lease rental payment stream. Upton and Miller did recognize that financial advantages may indeed exist in imperfect markets.

## 17.8 Options to Evaluate Salvage Values in Financial Leases

In the last section, we used the CAPM model to evaluate financial leases under uncertainty. Here, we use the model of Lee *et al.* (1982) to show how the option model can be used to evaluate salvage values in a financial lease.

We define the initial purchases price of assets ($S_o$) to be leased as follows:

$$\begin{aligned} \mathrm{S_o} = {} & \text{Present value of after tax lease payment } [\mathrm{L}(1-\tau_c)] \\ & + \text{Present value of accounting depreciation (capital recovery)} \\ & \quad \text{tax shelter (DTS) on the asset} \\ & + \text{After tax residual value on the leased asset } [S_N(1-\tau_c)] \\ & \quad \text{at termination of the lease agreement in year } N \qquad (17.11) \end{aligned}$$

Lee *et al.* proposed an option pricing framework to evaluate the present value of the salvage value. To do this, they decompose $S_N$ as

$$S_N = \mathrm{MAX}(O, S_N - E) + \mathrm{MIN}(S_N, E) \qquad (17.12)$$

where $\mathrm{MAX}(o, S_N - E)$ = the intrinsic value of a call option to purchase the asset for an exercise price, $X$, at the end of the year $T$; $\mathrm{MIN}(S_T, E)$ = the residual component of $S_N$ after the call option's intrinsic value has been deducted; and MAX (.) and MIN (.) refer to the maximum and minimum value of the arguments.

Since valuation of a call option on a leased asset's value is analogous to the valuation of an option on a dividend payment,[5] Lee *et al.* used Geske's (1978) option pricing model with stochastic yield to evaluate the present value of $\mathrm{MAX}(o, S_N - E)$.

The term $\mathrm{MIN}(S_N, E)$ is the value of a put option. Once the value of the first term is known (call option), the value of $\mathrm{MIN}(S_N, E)$ can be determined using the put-call parity relationships. Adding these two values yields an estimate of the salvage value of the leased asset to the lessor.

[5]The Black and Scholes (1973) model which will be discussed in Chapters 22 and 23 does not take dividend payments into account.

## 17.9 Summary

In Chapter 17, we have discussed the lease-buy decision. The conventional rationale for leasing is to reduce the risk of utilizing an asset by not actually owning it, thus giving the firm greater borrowing capacity.[6] This rationale for leasing has recently come into question with the new accounting rules on lease accounting requiring public disclosure of fixed obligations on all financial statements. Thus, these quasi-debt instruments can no longer be hidden in footnotes on financial statements. There is still some question as to the effect leases have on the various financial statements, as bond covenants and other restrictions may become binding if leases, which could be treated in more than one way for accounting purposes, are not optimally utilized.

Risk is an element of lease contracts that attract considerable attention and raises the question of whether compensating returns must be made between agreeing parties. The existence of various forms of leasing arrangements indicates willingness by the parties to the lease to engage in leasing activities that involve risk transfers.

Using a lease amortization schedule, we have classified lease cash payments as current liabilities and long-term liabilities. The income statement report associated with both capital and operating leases is also discussed.

Using the appropriate discount rate, we derived the present value of the buy alternative and the present value of the lease alternative. In the area of lease valuation, we found that the risk-free rate is the minimum discount rate applicable to cash flows of a leasing scheme. Accounting treatments for both capital lease and operating lease were also discussed.

## References

Abdel-Khalik, A. R. "The Economic Effects on Lessees of FASB Statement No. 13, Accounting for Leases," *Financial Accounting Standard Board of Financial Accounting Association* (Stamford, CT, 1981).

[6] Ang and Peterson (1984) found that firms that use more debt tend to rely more on leasing. However, this finding implies that leasing allows the firm to maintain high debt capacity.

Altman, E. I. "Financial Ratios, Discriminant Analysis and the Prediction of Corporate Bankruptcy," *The Journal of Finance*, 23(4) (1968, pp. 589–609).

Ball, R. and P. Brown. "An Empirical Evaluation of Accounting Income Numbers," *Journal of Accounting Research* (1968, pp. 159–178).

Black, F. and M. Scholes. "The Pricing of Options and Corporate Liability," *Journal of Political Economy*, 81(3) (May–June 1973, pp. 637–654).

Bower, R. S., F. C. Herringer, and J. P. Williamson. "Lease Evaluation," *The Accounting Review*, 41(2) (1966, p. 257).

Fabozzi, F. and P. K. Nevitt. *Equipment Leasing*, 4th edn. (Wiley, John & Sons, Incorporated, 2000).

Geske, R. "The Pricing of Options with Stochastic Dividend Yield," *The Journal of Finance*, 33 (May 1978, pp. 617–625).

Gordon, M. "A General Solution to the Buy-or-Lease Decision," *The Journal of Finance*, 29 (March 1974, pp. 245–250).

Gordon, E. A., Raedy, J. S., and A. J. Sannella. *Intermediate Accounting*, 2nd edn. (Hoboken, NJ: Pearson, 2018).

Ingberman, M., Ronen, J., and G. Sorter. "How Lease Capitalization Under FASB Statement No. 13 Will Affect Financial Ratios," *Financial Analysts Journal* (January–February 1979, pp. 28–31).

Johnson, R. and W. Lewellen. "Analysis of the Lease versus Buy Decision," *The Journal of Finance*, 27 (September 1972, pp. 815–823).

Kieso, D. E., Weygandt, J. R., and T. D. Warfield. *Intermediate Accounting*, 17th edn. (New York: John Wiley & Sons, 2019).

Lee, C. F. and A. C. Lee. *Encyclopedia of Finance*, 2nd edn. (Springer, 2013).

Lee, W. J., Martin, J. D., and A. J. Senchack. "The Case for Using Options to Evaluate Salvage Values in Financial Leases," *Financial Management* (Autumn 1982, pp. 33–41).

Miller, M. and C. Upton. "Leasing, Buying, and the Cost of Capital Services," *The Journal of Finance*, 31 (June 1976, pp. 761–786).

Modigliani, F. and M. Miller. "Corporate Income Taxes and Cost of Capital: A Correction," *American Economic Review* (June 1963, pp. 433–443).

Myers, S. C., Dill, D., and A. Bautista. "Valuation of Financial Lease Contracts," *The Journal of Finance*, 31 (June 1976, pp. 761–820).

Myers, S. C. "Interaction of Corporate Financing and Investment Decision," *The Journal of Finance*, 29 (1974, pp. 1–25).

Pinches, G. E. and K. A. Mingo. "A Multivariate Analysis of Industrial Bond Ratings," *The Journal of Finance*, 28(1) (1973, pp. 1–18).

Pogue, T. F. and R. M. Soldofsky. "What's in a Bond Rating," *Journal of Financial and Quantitative Analysis*, 4(2) (1969, pp. 201–228).

Schallheim, J. S., R. E. Johnson, R. C. Lease, and J. J. McConnell. "The Determinants of Yield on Financial Leasing Contracts," *Journal of Financial Economics*, 19 (September 1987, pp. 45–67).

## Appendix 17A — Derivation of Discount Rate for Riskless Cash Flows

Let $\bar{X}$ be the earnings on risk assets and $M$ be the amount the firm borrows at interest rate $i$. Also, let the firm invest the borrowed money in bonds carrying the same interest rate. Using M&M Proposition 1, discussed in Chapter 11, we have

$$V_L = \frac{(1-\tau_c)\bar{X}}{k} + \frac{\tau_c M_i}{i} = V_u + \tau_c M \tag{17.1A}$$

Assuming that borrowing and lending at the same interest rate and risk conveys no liquidity advantage, doing so must increase the firm's value (its shares and debt) by an amount equal to the amount borrowed. In Appendix 17B we will use Eq. (17.1A) for adjusted present value method to perform lease versus buy decision.

By differentiating the expression for the value of the levered firm of Eq. (17.1A) with respect to $M$ and setting the result equal to 1, we can solve for $k$ through rearrangement of terms. The amount of change in firm value is equal to the change in the level of riskless bonds held by the firm.

$$\begin{aligned}\frac{\partial V_L}{\partial M} &= \frac{\partial(1-\tau_c)Mi}{k\partial M} + \left(\frac{\partial \tau_c M}{\partial M}\right)\frac{1}{1} \\ &= \frac{(1-\tau_c)i}{k} + \frac{\tau_c i}{i} = \frac{(1-\tau_c)i}{k} + \tau_c = 1\end{aligned} \tag{17.2A}$$

where $k$ is the yield investors require on the incremental after-tax earnings. Eq. (17.2A) can be rearranged to yield

$$(1-\tau_c)i = (1-\tau_c)k$$

$$i = k$$

Equation (17.1A) is based on the discounting of risk-free $M_i$ at interest rate $i$ and not $(i-\tau_i)i$.

To see what the result would be by using the after-tax cost of debt as the rate to discount the debt tax shield, we find that

$$V_L = \frac{(1-\tau_c)(M)(i)}{k} + \frac{(\tau_c)(M)(i)}{i(1-\tau_c)}$$

The first derivative of $V_L$ with respect to $M$,

$$\frac{\partial V_L}{\partial M} = \frac{(1-\tau_c)\,i}{k}\frac{\partial M}{\partial M} + \frac{(\tau_c)(i)}{i(1-\tau_c)}\frac{\partial M}{\partial M} = 1 \tag{17.3A}$$

reduces to[7]

$$(1-\tau_c)i = \frac{(1-2\tau_c)k}{(1-\tau_c)} \tag{17.4A}$$

When $\tau_c = 0.5$, the right portion of Eq. (17.4A) reduces to 0, which implies that $i$ must also be 0 for the left-hand side to equal 0 as well. However, this is not a realistic result because it implies that a riskless asset yields no return and therefore the cost of riskless debt to the firm is 0. A more unrealistic situation arises when $\tau_c$ is greater than 0.5 but less than 1. In this case, either $i$ or $k$ must be negative to satisfy the equality. It is improbable that investors will accept negative rates of return when holding cash is the more feasible alternative.

## Appendix 17B — Application of APV Method for Leasing Decision

Myers (1974) has used Modigliani and Miller's (1963) Proposition I with tax and derived adjusted present value formulation as:

$$\text{APV} = \sum_{t=1}^{N} \frac{(R_t - C_t - \text{dep}_t)(1-\tau_c) + \text{dep}_t}{(1+\rho)^t} - I + \sum_{t=1}^{N} \frac{\tau_c r D_t}{(1+r)^t} \tag{17.1B}$$

where $R_t$ = pretax operating cash revenue gathered by the project during time period $t$; $C_t$ = pretax operating cash expenses due to the project during time period $t$; $\text{dep}_t$ = additional depreciation due to the project during time period $t$; $\rho$ = the market rate of return on

---

[7]Equation (17.3A) implies

$$\frac{(1-\tau_i)_i^2 + \tau_c k}{k(1-\tau_c)} = 1$$

From this equation, we have

$$(1-\tau_i)_i^2 = k(1-2\tau_c)$$

which yields Equation (17.4A).

Table 17.1B APV Method for Leasing Decision.

| | Year 0 | Year 1 | Year 2 | Year 3 | Year 4 | Year 5 |
|---|---|---|---|---|---|---|
| Out Standing balance of | $600 | $480 | $360 | $240 | $120 | $0 |
| loan interest payment | | $24 | $19 | $14 | $10 | $5 |
| Tax deduction on interest | | $9.60 | $7.68 | $5.76 | $3.84 | $1.92 |
| After-tax interest expense | | $14.40 | $11.52 | $8.64 | $5.76 | $2.88 |
| Repayment of loan | | $120 | $120 | $120 | $120 | $120 |

unlevered flows of the indicated risk class; $r$ = the interest rate paid on debt; $\tau_c$ = corporate tax rate.

An example involves the simplest case, where a $1200 investment project generates operating flows of $400 per year for all five years of the project's life. Debt financing comprises $600 of the project's total financing and the principal is repaid over the five time periods in equal amounts. For this project, the discount rate on unlevered firm is 8%, the interest rate on debt is 4% and the tax rate is 0.4. The tax shields of levered investment are calculated in Table 17.1B. By using (17.1B), we can get the APV of the investment project is $423.40.

$$\begin{aligned}\text{APV} &= \sum_{t=1}^{N} \frac{(R_t - C_t - \text{dep}_t)(1-\tau_c) + \text{dep}_t}{(1+\rho)^t} - I + \sum_{t=1}^{N} \frac{\tau_c r D_t}{(1+r)^t} \\ &= \sum_{t=1}^{N} \frac{400}{(1.08)^t} - 1200 + \frac{9.60}{(1.04)^1} + \frac{7.68}{(1.04)^2} + \frac{5.76}{(1.04)^3} \\ &\quad + \frac{3.84}{(1.04)^4} + \frac{1.92}{(1.04)^5} \\ &= 423.40\end{aligned}$$

**Myers Adjusted-Present-Value Method to Leasing.**

We have learned that the APV of any project can be expressed as:

$$\text{APV} = \text{All-equity value} + \text{Additional effects of debt}$$

As an example of how to compute the net present value of lease relative to purchase by using Myers APV method, suppose the Docksider

Table 17.2B APV Method for Leasing Decision (Continue).

| **Lease − Buy** | **Year 0** | **Year 1** | **Year 2** | **Year 3** | **Year 4** | **Year 5** |
|---|---|---|---|---|---|---|
| **Lease** | | | | | | |
| Lease payment | | −\$12,500 | −\$12,500 | −\$12,500 | −\$12,500 | −\$12,500 |
| Tax benefit of lease payment | | \$4,250 | \$4,250 | \$4,250 | \$4,250 | \$4,250 |
| Buy (−) Cost of machine | \$50,000 | | | | | |
| Lost depreciation tax benefit | | −\$1,700 | −\$1,700 | −\$1,700 | −\$1,700 | −\$1,700 |
| Total | \$50,000 | −\$9,950 | −\$9,950 | −\$9,950 | −\$9,950 | −\$9,950 |

Corporation can spend \$50,000 purchasing a crane, for lifting sailboats in and out of the harbor. Docksider also can lease the same crane by paying \$12,500 per year for five years. The pretax interest rate and tax rate are 6.5% and 0.34. In the context of the lease-versus-buy decision, the APV method can be expressed as:

$$\begin{pmatrix}\text{APV of the lease}\\ \text{relative to the purchase}\end{pmatrix} = \begin{pmatrix}\text{NPV of the lease}\\ \text{relative to the purchase}\\ \text{when purchase is financed}\\ \text{by all equity}\end{pmatrix} - \begin{pmatrix}\text{Additional effects when}\\ \text{purchase is financed}\\ \text{with some debt}\end{pmatrix}$$

For Docksider's example, we know the all-equity value is the NPV of the cash flows discounted at the pretax interest rate. The incremental cash flows for Docksider from leasing instead of purchasing are shown in Table 17.2B. The calculation shows that the lease is preferred over the purchase by \$529.03 if the purchase is financed by all equity.

$$\text{All-Equity NPV} = \$50{,}000 - \frac{\$9{,}950}{1.065} - \frac{\$9{,}950}{(1.065)^2} - \frac{\$9{,}950}{(1.065)^3} - \frac{\$9{,}950}{(1.065)^4} - \frac{\$9{,}950}{(1.065)^5} = \$8650.99.$$

Table 17.3B APV Method for Leasing Decision (Continue).

| | Year 0 | Year 1 | Year 2 | Year 3 | Year 4 | Year 5 |
|---|---|---|---|---|---|---|
| Out Standing balance of | $50,000 | $42,195 | $34,055 | $25,566 | $16,713 | $0 |
| loan interest payment | | $3,250 | $2,743 | $2,214 | $1,662 | $1,086 |
| Tax deduction on interest | | $1,105 | $933 | $753 | $565 | $369 |
| After-tax interest expense | | $2,145 | $1,810 | $1,461 | $1,097 | $717 |
| Extra cash that purchasing firm generates over leasing firm | | $9,950 | $9,950 | $9,950 | $9,950 | $9,950 |
| Repayment of loan | | $7,805 | $8,140 | $8,489 | $8,853 | $16,713 |

If Docksider decides to finance all equity of its purchase, the relative tax shields are calculated in Table 17.3B. The additional effect of debt, NPV of tax shields is:

$$\frac{\$1,105}{1.065} + \frac{\$933}{(1.065)^2} + \frac{\$753}{(1.065)^3} + \frac{\$565}{(1.065)^4} + \frac{\$369}{(1.065)^5} = \$3,191.55$$

Because the tax shield represents interest deductions not available under the lease alternative, the NPV of tax shield must be subtracted from the NPV of the lease relative to the purchase when purchase is financed by all equity. Thus, the adjusted present value of the lease relative to the purchase is $8,650.99-$3,191.55=$5,459.44. A positive NPV of the lease relative to the purchase indicates that the leasing alternative is preferred to purchase alternative.

## Questions and Problems

1. Discuss the three types of leasing, as well as the accounting breakdown of these types of leases. What are the accounting "rules" for classifying capital and operating leases?
2. Briefly compare the accounting treatment of capital leases with that of operating leases. What assumptions and processes are involved?
3. In what ways can the capitalization of leases affect firm value?

4. Compare accounting treatments of leases from the lessor's and the lessee's standpoints. What are the implications of these treatments on financial decisions?
5. How is M&M Proposition 1 used to determine the discount rate in the leasing decision?
6. How are the CAPM and OPM used in the lease-buy decision under uncertainty?
7. Use the following information to compute the annual lease payment that a lease will require. (Lease payments made at the beginning of the year.)

   a. Purchase price of $300,000, interest rate of 15%, 6-year lease period, no residual.
   b. Purchase price of $200,000, interest rate of 10%. 10-year lease period, residual value of $20,000.
   c. Purchase price of $50,000, interest rate of 12%, 10-year lease period, residual value of $30,000.

8. ZXY Company decides to acquire a piece of equipment for $200,000. If ZXY wants to lease-finance the equipment, the manufacturer will provide such financing over 10 years. If the discount rate is 12%, what is the annual lease payment? Use this information to construct a lease amortization schedule.
9. Assume that $I_o = \$300,000$, $F_t = F = \$3,000$, $R_t = R = \$80,000$, $k = 12\%$, $N = 10$ years, $i = 10\%$, $t_c = 34\%$, and $j = 5$ years. Also, let the terms of lease option be six payments of $50,000 each, with the first payment at $t = 0$ and succeeding payments at the end of each year for five years. At the end of five years, the asset can be purchased at $50,000, which is the current estimate of the asset's value at that time. Using Eqs. (17.5–17.7), calculate related present values.
10. XYZ Reduction Company has just leased a press that calls for annual lease payments of $50,000 payable in advance. The lease period is nine years, and the leased property is classified as a capital lease. The company's incremented borrowing rate is 8%, whereas the lessor's implied interest rate is 12%. The company depreciates all of its owned assets on a straight-line basis. Using the above information, compute:

a. The value of the leased property to be shown on the balance sheet after the initial lease payment.
b. The annual lease expense in each year as it will appear on the accounting income statement.

11. The purchase price of a piece of equipment is $100,000. The interest rate is 12%. A lease on this equipment would be for 6 years. The residual value of the asset at the end of the lease is expected to be zero. Find the annual lease payments if the payments are due at the beginning of each year.
12. Rework the previous problem assuming that the equipment has a residual value of $5,000.
13. New equipment costs $50,000. The equipment can be leased for four years with five equal payments, the first being made at $t = 0$ and the subsequent ones at the end of each year for years 1 through 4. Using this information, calculate the annual lease payment and construct the lease amortization schedule. The residual value is $3,000 and the discount rate is 10%.
14. How would you answer the previous problem if the equipment had no residual value?
15. ICAI, Inc. has a lease proposal with the conditions as given below:
    Annual lease payment (advance) = $15,000
    Life of the lease = 7 years
    Marginal borrowing rate = 15%
    Residual value = $4,000

    a. Calculate the estimated value of the capital lease.
    b. If the implicit interest rate is 14%, find the value of the lease.
    c. How would your answer change if the implicit rate of interest were 16%?
    d. What is the relationship between the value of the lease and the appropriate discount rate?

16. GKM Corporation is considering acquisition of new equipment. The specific details associated with purchasing as well as leasing the equipment are given as follows:
    Purchase cost ($I$) = $300,000
    Executory costs ($F$) = $4,000
    Life of asset = 10 years
    Life of lease = 5 years

Cash flows before depreciation and taxes = \$70,000
Corporate tax rate = 30%
Cost of capital ($K$) = 13%
Discount rate for riskless cash flows = 9%
Annual lease payment = \$60,000
Residual value at $j$ = \$50, 000
The first lease payment will be made at $t = 0$, and the succeeding payments being made at the end of each year. Using Eqs. (17.5–17.7), calculate the NPVs of the lease and buy options. The firm can borrow \$250,000 at an interest rate of 9% to finance the purchase of the equipment, payable in five equal annual installments .

17. XYX Reduction Company has just leased a press that calls for annual lease payments of \$50,000 payable in advance. The lease period is 9 years and the leased property is classified as a capital lease. The company's incremented borrowing rate is 8%, whereas the lessor's implied interest rate is 12%. The company depreciates all of its owned assets on a straight-line basis. Using the above information, compute:
    (a) The value of the leased property to be shown on the balance sheet after the initial lease payment.
    (b) The annual lease expense in each year, as it will appear on the accounting income statement.
18. Company AAA is a relatively new firm. Company AAA has experienced enough losses during its early years to provide it with at least 8 years of tax-loss carryforwards. Thus, Company AAA's effective tax rate is 0. Company AAA plans to lease equipment from BBB Leasing Company. The term of the lease is 4 years. The purchase cost of the equipment is \$300,000. BBB Leasing Company is in the 35% tax bracket. There are no transaction costs to the lease. Each firm can borrow at 8%.
    (a) What is Company AAA's reservation price?
    (b) What is BBB Leasing Company's reservation price?
19. Company CCC is entering a negotiation for the lease of equipment that has a \$250,000 purchase price. Company CCC's effective tax rate is 0. Company CCC will be negotiation the lease with DDD Leasing Company. The term of the lease is 5 years. DDD Leasing Company is in the 30% tax bracket. There are

no transaction costs to the lease. Each firm can borrow at 10%. What is the negotiating range of the lease?

20. EEE Corporation wants to expand its manufacturing facilities. FFF Leasing Corporation has offered EEE the opportunity to lease a machine for $120,000 for 5 years. The machine will be fully depreciated by the straight-line method. The corporate tax rate for EEE is 20%, while FFF's corporate tax rate is 30%. The appropriate before tax interest rate is 7%. Assume lease payments occur at year end. What is EEE's reservation price? What is FFF's reservation price? What is the negotiating range of the lease?
21. An asset costs $90. Only straight-line depreciation is allowed for this asset. The asset's useful life is 3 years. It will have no salvage value. The corporate tax rate on ordinary income is 30%. The interest rate on risk-free cash flow is 10%.

    (a) What set of lease payments will make the lessee and the lessor equally well off?
    (b) Show the general condition that will make the value of a lease to the lessor the negative of the value to the lessee.
    (c) Assume that the lessee pays no taxes and the lessor is in the 34% tax bracket. For what range of lease payments does the lease have a positive NPV for both parities?

22. RTC is a furniture manufacturer that is considering installing a milling machine for $380,000. The machine will be straight-line depreciated over 7 years and will be worthless after its economic life. RTC has been financially distressed and thus the company does not appear to get tax shields over the next 7 years. ABC Leasing Company has offered to lease the machine over 7 years. The corporate tax rate of RTC is 30%. The appropriate before-tax interest rate is 8% for both firms Lease payments occur at the beginning of the year. What is RTC's reservation price? What is ABC's reservation price? What is the negotiating range of the lease?
23. WOL corporation has decided to purchase a new machine that costs $6 million. The machine will be worthless after 3 years. Only straight-line method is allowed by the IRD for this type of machine. WOL is in the 35% tax bracket. The GGG Bank has offered WOL a 3-year loan of $2 million and an interest charge of

14% on the outstanding balance of the loan at the beginning of each year. 14% is the market wide rate of interest. Both principal repayments and interest are due at the end of each year. The HHH Leasing offered to lease the same machine to WOL Lease payments of $2.1 million per year are due at the end of the 3 years of the lease.

(a) Should WOL buy the machine with the loan or lease it?
(b) What is the annual lease payment that will make WOL indifferent to whether it leases the machine or purchases it?

# PART VI

# Short-term Financing and Financial Planning

Chapter 18

# Short-term Financial Analysis and Planning

## Contents

## 18.1 Introduction

Short-term financial management and planning begins with cash. The financial manager must understand the firm's sources and uses of cash. And with an understanding of the environment in which the company operates, the manager can then apply various cash management, budgeting, and planning techniques to accomplish specific organizational goals.

The day-to-day management of a firm's cash flow is often considered a somewhat routine and low-level operation in the overall spectrum of corporate activity. However, the entire organization is directly affected by such short-term activity. Indeed, an organization's success, although helped only marginally by good short-term planning and management, can be severely affected by poor or nonexistence short-term financial analysis and planning.

Cash is only one of the critical variables that must be managed in short-term financial analysis and planning. The other components of working capital, such as accounts receivable, marketable securities, and accounts payable, must also be managed properly in the short term.

We begin Chapter 18 by discussing the components of working capital. We then show, in Section 18.3, how the concept of cash flow is used in short-term financial planning. In Section 18.4, we compare the concept of cash flow and funds flow, and in Section 18.5 we discuss ways a firm can organize for short-term financial planning. In Section 18.6 we present principles of short-term financial planning, and in Section 18.7 we explain the cash flow cycle and measurement techniques. In Section 18.8 we discuss the entire process of forecasting, budgeting, and planning. We discuss the cash budget in Section 18.9, and in Section 18.10 we talk about demand-driven, capital-driven, and cost-driven cash budgets. The use of cash forecasts and business plans are discussed in Section 18.11. In Section 18.12 we discuss planning horizons and time intervals of cash budgets, and in Section 18.13 we look at forecasting, budgeting, and planning. Section 18.14 gives a summary of the chapter. Appendix 18A presents time-series components of sales.

## 18.2 The Components of Working Capital

*Working capital* is the dollar amount of an organization's current assets, which include cash, marketable securities, accounts receivable, and inventories. These current assets are considered to be *liquid* because they can be converted into within a short period. Each of the separate components of working capital is affected by the activities of various parts of the organization. Production, pricing, distribution, marketing, wage contracts, and financing decisions are just a few of the diverse activities within the firm that can affect not only the amount of working capital but also how quickly the individual assets can be converted to cash. Additionally, the external environment in which the firm operates (product markets, investment markets, and financial markets) can also affect the amount and the rate of change of a firm's working capital. In a highly seasonal industry, the typical scenario is for inventory to increase dramatically. As demand for the product increases, inventory will decrease as accounts receivable increases. The cycle is completed when the accounts receivable are collected in cash. For many organizations, the level of working capital is subject to seasonal and cyclical forces, which can cause a high degree of variability.

Working capital can be further defined as either permanent or temporary. *Permanent working capital* is the dollar amount of working capital that remains fixed over time regardless of seasonal or cyclical variations in sales. *Temporary working capital* consists of the additional funds required to meet the seasonal or cyclical variations in sales over and above permanent working capital.

The concept of short-term financial planning is much broader than that of working capital asset management because it involves the management of current assets and current liabilities and their interrelationship. In practice, little or no distinction is made between investment decisions involving current assets and financing decisions involving current liabilities. Current assets and current liabilities are often closely related, as in the spontaneous financing of current assets such as inventory when the firm purchases goods or supplies on credit. Both asset and liability are increased simultaneously, providing financing — at least in the short run — for the investment.

*Net working capital* is the difference between current assets and current liabilities and is a financial indicator that can be used in conjunction with ratio analysis to gauge a firm's liquidity. In general, an abundance of net working capital is considered desirable because it suggest that the firm has ample liquidity to meet its short-term obligations. As we shall see, this may not always be the case. In fact, one of the objectives of short-term financial planning is to reduce

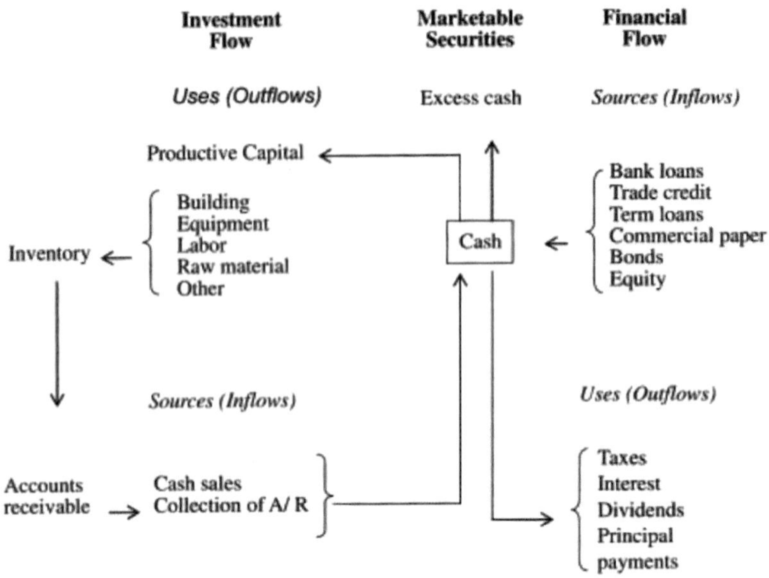


Figure 18.1 Flow of Funds.
*Source*: Lee and Lee (2017), p. 943.

excess or redundant working capital to a minimum, which in turn reduces the cost of carrying idle assets.

As the firm operates, funds flow continuously from one type of asset to another in a circular fashion. Figure 18.1 shows how funds flow through an organization. The time it takes these funds to complete a full cycle reflects the average time that the organization's cash is invested in inventory and accounts receivable, both of which are nonearnings assets. Therefore, it is in the organization's best interest to keep this cycle as short as possible while remaining competitive.

## 18.3 The Concept of Cash Flow

The nature of cash flow varies widely among different types of organizations. The controlling factors that relate cash flow to short-term financial planning are (1) projecting the cash flow cycle and (2) managing the investment and financing of working capital.

Today, one of the most critical issues for financial managers is *liquidity* — the organization's ability to pay its debts and expenses in a timely fashion. In the 1960s, financial management stressed growth and profitability. The reason is that during this period, inflation ranged from less than 1% to slightly more than 5% per year, and the prime lending rate of banks ranged from 2 1/4% to 8 1/2%. Because of the stability of the economic environment, financial managers accented growth and profitability rather than liquidity. Even less-skillful managers were able to remain in business simply by riding the economic growth curve.

However, in the mid-1970s the economic environment changed markedly. Whereas the average rate of inflation was 2.3% in the 1960s, it ranged from 3.3% to 12% in the 1970s, while the prime rate exceeded 20% at times. In the 1980s, the economic condition changed as dramatically as the 1970s. Uncertainty replaced prosperity as economic conditions changed. The significance of all of this change is that financial managers can no longer only stress growth and profitability, but must also consider liquidity. Thus, survival and liquidity are of much greater importance today, when we are facing high interest rates, uncertainty about government policy, and an increase in the magnitude of the variability of cash flows.

## 18.4 Cash Flow versus Funds Flow

Liquidity and cash flow are closely related. However, cash flow and funds flow are concepts that have origins and uses in two different disciplines: finance and accounting. The concepts of profitability, net working capital, net income, and funds flow that accountants normally deal with are not cash-based concepts. These accounting concepts are affected by the accruals and deferrals associated with the accounting cycle, which are made to match historical costs and revenues associated with a specific period. Financial managers, bankers, creditors, and investors are more interested in current or future cash flows, because they want to know how much cash will be available for reinvestment, interest, principal, and dividends.

*Profitability* involves the relationship between revenues and expenses during a given time interval and thus would seem to be a cashed-based concept. However, because revenues include credit sales and deferrals, while expenses include payables and accruals, the concept of profitability is also funds-based.

Net working capital is a funds-based concept. It is the quantity of excess current assets over current liabilities at a single point in time. Net working capital is strictly a quantitative concept that reveals nothing about the *quality* of current assets or current liabilities. Since the concept of net working capital deals with current assets, and current assets should eventually be converted into cash, there is a relationship between the firm's net working capital and its cash flow. However, this relationship can be imprecise and is a function of the timing of the conversion to cash (hence the word *flow*). Only when the timing of current assets conversion into cash or the timing of the payment of current liabilities is considered can we then discuss planning cash flow, which is a dynamic concept.

Calculating net income plus depreciation is usually a funds-based operation, although there are two cases in which net income plus depreciation equals cash flow and therefore is cash-based. The first case involves an all-cash business, such as a liquor store or a fast-food outlet. The second case involves a static firm operating on a cash or accrued basis and having no changes in any balance sheet items from one period to the next. In such a firm, net income plus depreciation equals the cash flow for the period. However, it is difficult to imagine such a static firm in the real world.

In any short-term financial analysis and planning, the financial manager must understand the difference between cash flow (a financial concept) and funds flow (an accounting-based concept). In planning short-term cash flow, the cash budget is the basic tool of analysis and provides the framework that is used for planning.

The main purposes of planning cash flow are (1) to predict what demands will be made on the organization in the future, (2) to assess the financial impact of those demands, and (3) to generate and choose from alternative courses of action to meet those demands. Certain aspects of future operations can be predicted with a great degree of accuracy. These aspects tend to be in the area of expenses. Salaries, for example, are a fairly predictable expense; if the work force is to be expanded by ten employees, the cost can be predicted with a high degree of accuracy. On the other hand, customer demand for products or services and the effect of competitors' actions on the revenue stream are not as easy to predict with any degree of accuracy. To handle these types of difficult forecasting problems, the cash flow manager must generate "what if" scenarios: What if customer demand rises 20%? What if it falls 5%? What if the chief competition cuts prices? In effect, the cash flow manager makes and tests assumptions about customer behavior and competitors actions and converts these assumptions into cash flow numbers.

After various scenarios have been identified and the appropriate cash flow statements have been prepared, planning can begin. Basically, cash flow planning deals with two areas: (1) the investment of surplus cash balances and (2) the use of short-term borrowing to meet cash flow deficits. Given the wide range of money market investments and the numerous sources and techniques of short term financing available, the cash flow manager is faced with the problem of identifying the highest return, lowest risk investments for surplus cash and the cheapest, most dependable sources of short-term financing to meet the deficit. (Chapters 19 and 20 will provide a detailed look at these issues.)

## 18.5 Organizing for Short-term Financial Planning

The way an organization structures and staffs the resources devoted to short term financial analysis and planning is primarily a question of the size of the firm. Exhibit 18.1 shows typical resources for small, medium, and large organizations. In a small organization, officers may hold dual titles, such as president and treasurer, and there may be a very small staff or no staff responsible for cash planning and management. In a medium-sized firm, specialization begins to occur, and an internal staff becomes necessary for cash management. Given that sizable amounts of money flow through large organizations, they may find it profitable to have a staff devoted exclusively to cash

**Exhibit 18.1:** Cash Planning and Management Resources.

| Size of Organization | Officers in Charge | Staff Size |
|---|---|---|
| Small | President/Treasurer<br>Vice President/Controller | 0–2 |
| Medium | Treasurer<br>Assistant Treasurer | 1–10 |
| Large | Assistant Treasurer | Over 10 |

planning and management and may even have cash managers in their regional offices.

## 18.6 Short-term Financial Planning Principles

The goals for effective short-term financial management are (1) to meet production schedules, (2) to satisfy sales demand, (3) to minimize financing costs, and (4) to provide liquidity for the firm. These goals are best achieved by matching the maturity of the financing sources of funds with the maturity of the assets being held, as indicated in Figure 18.1 and Exhibit 18.1. If the maturities are not matched, the firm will be subject to unnecessary risks and the burden of additional costs, as presented in Figure 18.2. If long-term assets are financed with short-term liabilities, the manager will have to refinance continually, which increases the risk the firm faces because the necessary cash may be unavailable or available at substantially higher costs. Additionally, repeated refinancing involves increased transaction costs in terms of dollars and executive time. On the other hand, if short-term needs are financed with long-term liabilities, the cost of long-term financing will be higher than the returns earned on the short-term asset investment, and this negative spread will adversely affect profits.

Liquidity is required and, as we have seen, is becoming more important not only to meet the firm's expected obligations, but also

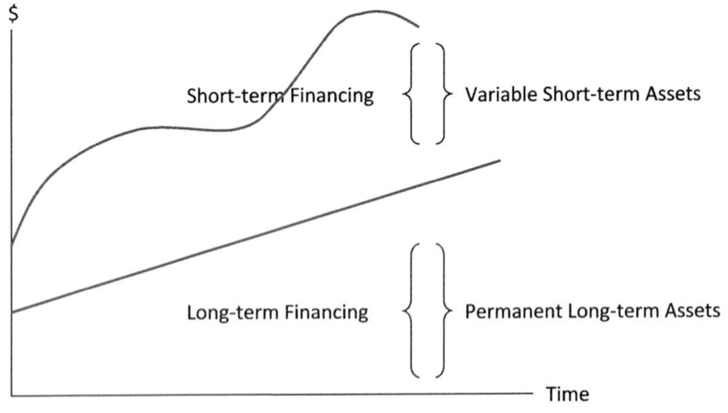


Figure 18.2 Matching Maturities of Financing Sources and Assets.

to take advantage of unforeseen opportunities. Therefore, the short-term financial planner must balance liquidity requirements against the opportunity costs of foregoing profitable working-capital investments. Exhibit 18.2 identifies the types of problems financial managers face as they try to balance liquidity and profitability.

In applying the matching principle in practice, each manager may take a somewhat different approach depending on whether the manager wants to be conservative or aggressive. In certain circumstances, deliberately creating a mismatch between current liabilities and current assets could lead to a low-cost financing plan. However, the lowering of cost usually is attendant with higher risk.

## 18.7 The Cash Flow Cycle and Its Calculation

The time it takes for cash to flow through the working capital accounts and return to cash is a measurable quantity of time called the *cash flow cycle*. Essentially, the cycle begins when the organization pays cash for investment in current assets and ends when cash flows back to the organization as payment for the goods or services rendered. To be more specific, the cash flow cycle equals the average age of current assets or inventory plus the average age of accounts receivable minus the average age of accounts payable. The first task of the short-term financial planner is to identify the firm's cash flow cycle. The next step is to focus on how to speed up the inflows and slow down the outflows in the most cost-effective fashion.

The cash flow cycle is defined as follows:

$$\begin{aligned}\text{Cash flow cycle} &= \text{Average age of inventory}\\ &\quad +\text{Average age of accounts receivable}\\ &\quad -\text{Average age of accounts payable}\\ &= \text{Number of days in the planning period}\\ &\quad \times\left(\frac{\text{Average inventory}}{\text{Cash operating expenditures}}\right.\\ &\quad +\frac{\text{Average accounts receivable}}{\text{Sales}}\\ &\quad \left.-\frac{\text{Average accounts payable}}{\text{Cost of goods sold}}\right) \qquad (18.1)\end{aligned}$$

**Exhibit 18.2:** Problems Associated with Balancing Liquidity and Profitability.

| Working Capital Component | Forms | Problem if Component is too Small | Problem if Component is too Large |
|---|---|---|---|
| Cash | Dollars<br>Demand deposits | Risk of running out of cash: illiquidity, insolvency | Loss of return from money market investments |
| Marketable securities | Money market investments (T-bills, CDs, commercial paper, etc.) | Insufficient safety margin to meet expected and unexpected cash requirements | Misuse of scarce investor capital needed for real investment |
| Accounts receivable | Open-book accounts of customers | Credit policy may be too strict and noncompetitive<br>Demand for product or services is falling | Credit policy may be over-generous<br>Collection problems<br>Costly use of resources |
| Inventory | Raw materials<br>Work in process<br>Finished goods | Inability to meet demand<br>Loss of sales<br>Production interruptions | Costs of carry: storage insurance and handling will be higher than necessary<br>Risk of obsolescence |
| Short-term financing | Bank loans<br>Lines of credit<br>Commercial paper | Not able to carry sufficient short-term assets to meet demand or operating requirements | Very costly; may be financing many idle assets that may not be productive |

where average inventory = (beginning inventory + ending inventory)/2; average accounts receivable (AR) = (beginning AR + ending AR)/2; and average accounts payable (AP) = (beginning AP + ending AP)/2.

The managerial actions that affect the duration of the various cash flow components are defined as follows:

$$\begin{aligned}
&\text{Managerial actions}\\
&\quad = \text{Inventory financing, collateral for loans, liquidation}\\
&\qquad + \text{Factoring, pledging, altering credit terms, tightening}\\
&\qquad\quad \text{collection, policies, speeding up billing procedures}\\
&\qquad - \text{Change payment requency, stretch out payables (forego}\\
&\qquad\quad \text{discounts)} \qquad (18.2)
\end{aligned}$$

To demonstrate the calculation of the cash flow cycle, we will consider a maintenance service organization called Speedy Maintenance, which provides cleaning services for offices and commercial and industrial buildings. One important aspect of this type of firm is that all work is done on the customers' premises, which means there is little need for Speedy to have a large investment in fixed assets. An administrative office and a garage to store vehicles, supplies, and equipment are all that is required. The major expense of doing business is labor. Most employees work on an hourly basis and are unskilled or semiskilled. Most of Speedy's business is rendered repetitively, usually under a flat-rate contract with extra fees for special services. Two areas of potential concern for Speedy's management are liability and casualty insurance and adequate supervision of its widely dispersed work force. These areas could have a dramatic impact on cash flow. If an employee damages or steals property in the building being cleaned, Speedy could be held liable for a large replacement cost.

Service concerns like Speedy must monitor two levels of cash flow: the *overall cash flows* from the entire operation and the *specific cash flows* from each individual contract. Speedy's financial statement for the past two years is presented in Exhibit 18.3, which provides all of the information necessary to calculate Speedy's cash flow cycle. Substituting related information from Exhibit 18.4 into Eq. (18.1), we obtain.

To estimate the cost of this cash flow cycle to Speedy, interest rates for short-term financing sources must be used. Exhibit 18.4 presents cost calculations for Speedy's cash flow cycle assuming financing interest rates of 10%, 16%, and 20% per year. These calculations reflect what the costs would be if funds had to be borrowed

**Exhibit 18.3:** Speedy Maintenance, Inc., Financial Statement.

**Balance Sheet (For year ending 31 December)**

| | 31 December 19XX | 31 December 19X1 | | 31 December 19XX | 31 December 18X1 |
|---|---|---|---|---|---|
| Cash | $10,000 | $15,000 | Wages payable | $15,000 | $15,000 |
| Marketable securities | 5,000 | 5,000 | Accounts payable | 45,000 | 55,000 |
| Accounts receivable | 65,000 | 85,000 | Mortgage payable | 25,000 | 25,000 |
| Inventory | | | Bank note payable | 130,000 | 130,000 |
| Cleaning supplies | 18,000 | 21,000 | Common stock | 50,000 | 50,000 |
| Cleaning equipment | 50,000 | 54,000 | Retained earnings | 8,000 | 25,000 |
| Trucks (net) | 80,000 | 75,000 | | | |
| Building (office and Garage) | 45,000 | 45,000 | | | |
| Total assets | $273,000 | $300,000 | Total liabilities + Equity | $273,000 | $300,000 |

**Income Statement**
(For year ending 31 December)

| | 19XX | 19X1 |
|---|---|---|
| Sales | $379,000 | $430,500 |
| Cost of services supplied | | |
| Labor | 250,222 | 290,000 |
| Supplies | 70,000 | 70,000 |
| Operating expenses | 50,000 | 50,000 |
| Taxable income | 9,600 | 20,500 |
| Income tax | 1,600 | 3,500 |
| Net income | $8,000 | $17,000 |

$$\text{Cash flow cycle} = 365\left(\frac{\frac{18{,}000 + 21{,}000}{2}}{70{,}000}\right) + 365\left(\frac{\frac{65{,}000 + 85{,}000}{2}}{430{,}500}\right)$$

$$- 365\left(\frac{\frac{45{,}000 + 55{,}000}{2}}{360{,}000}\right) = 102\text{ days} + 64\text{ days} - 51\text{ days} = 115\text{ days}$$

**Exhibit 18.4:** Financing Costs of Speedy's Cash Flow Cycle.

| | **Average Amount Invested** | **Average Investment Period in** | **Estimated Cost of Financing (Average Investment × days × Interest Rate/365)** | | |
|---|---|---|---|---|---|
| Asset | [(Begin + End)/2] | Days | 10% | 15% | 20% |
| Cleaning supplies | \$19,500 | 102 | \$545 | \$817 | \$1,090 |
| Accounts receivable | \$75,000 | 64 | 1,315 | 1,973 | 2,630 |
| Accounts payable | \$50,000 | 51 | (699) | (1,048) | (1,397) |
| Total cost to finance | | 115 | \$1,161 | \$1,742 | \$2,323 |

at these assumed rates to finance the cash flow cycle. The objective of the cash flow manager is to keep these costs to a minimum.

Calculating the cost of financing an organization's cash flow cycle is a useful starting point for the cash flow manager, who can then begin to evaluate whether the firm's resources are being used efficiently and effectively. In turn, this evaluation serves as a starting point for weighing the trade-offs between the cost of carrying a given cash flow cycle and the benefits derived from it. Suppose, for example, that Speedy's management believes the cost of maintaining accounts receivable is too high. Since most of Speedy's accounts receivable reflects services provided under contract, Speedy's management could alter the payment terms at contract renewal time to reduce the amount of funds tied up in receivables. However, this cost reduction could be outweighed by the loss of contracts that might be incurred if some customers switch to another maintenance firm. A more appropriate course of action might be to minimize this cost subject to net losing the contract. Exhibit 18.5 shows the cash flow cycle for one of Speedy's contracts, estimates the cost per month to finance the cycle, and lists the effects that several possible modifications to the contract would have on the cash flow.

As in all problem-solving and decision-making, there is more than one way to approach the situation. Short-term financial planning is no different. The cash flow cycle and cash flow planning are based on the use of a cash budgeting statement. We will now look at this approach to cash flow planning, keeping in mind that these various techniques are meant to be complementary to each other, not substitutes.

## 18.8 Cash Flow Forecasting, Budgeting, and Planning

Forecasting, budgeting, and planning are the basic components of what has come to be called the *corporate planning process.* As a general rule, planning, as broadly defined, contributes to higher profits, improved decision-making, and a reduction of critical mistakes. The three-step process of planning involves making decisions and taking action today that will affect the future of the firm. Because no one can predict the future with any consistent degree of accuracy, the planning process must be continuous and ongoing. The three steps

**Exhibit 18.5:** Speedy Maintenance Contract XYZ.

Total contract = \$120,000 for one year
Payment terms = \$10,000 on the last day of each month
Cost of supplies per month = \$2,000
Cost of labor per month = \$7,500 (Workers paid weekly)
Cash flow cycle = Average age of inventory + Average age of AR − Average age of AP

$$= 30\left(\frac{\frac{2{,}000+0}{2}}{2{,}000}\right) + 30\left(\frac{\frac{0+10{,}000}{2}}{10{,}000}\right) - 30\left(\frac{\frac{2{,}000+\frac{7{,}500}{4}}{2}}{9{,}500}\right)$$

$$= 15\text{ days} + 15\text{ days} - 6\text{ days} = 24\text{ days}.$$

| Asset | Average Amount Invested | Average Investment in Days | Estimated Cost of Period Financing at 15% |
|---|---|---|---|
| Cleaning supplies | \$1,000 | 15 | \$6.16 |
| Accounts receivable | 5,000 | 15 | 30.82 |
| Accounts payable | 1,938 | 6 | (4.78) |
| Total cost per month | | | \$32.20 |
| | | | ×12 |
| Total cost per year | | | \$386.40 |

| Yearly Cost—Suggested Modifications | Effects |
|---|---|
| Make payments weekly | Reduce A/R |
| Make payments bimonthly | Increase A/R |
| Pay workers bimonthly | Increase A/P |
| Pay workers monthly | Increase A/P |

of forecasting, budgeting, and planning must be constantly revised to fit each new situation based on the continued inflow of new information. Hence, this constantly changing environment makes for an unending task of constantly revising and reworking the plan.

Because the future changes so frequently, plans made at any one point in time should not be expected to work precisely as initially formulated. Plans should be amended to reflect new information about the firm's environment that will alter circumstances and decisions.

An environment can change yearly, quarterly, monthly, or even daily. Hence, the planner most use a flexible tool to evaluate and analyze the potentially volatile situation.

The three-step procedure of forecasting, budgeting, and planning can be viewed as a set of building blocks that are mutually supporting. We will discuss the planning process as if each of the three steps is performed in sequence. However, each step must constantly be revised in light of new information about the firm's business environment or new information from the other steps. Thus, rather than being sequential, the three steps in the planning process are dealt with simultaneously. Envision the planning process as a three-legged stool; without one of the three legs — forecasting, budgeting, planning — the stool serves no useful function.

## 18.9 The Cash Budget

A *cash budget* shows the cash flow that is anticipated in the coming planning period given various scenarios. This budget goes beyond a simple summation of cash receipts and disbursements by attempting to forecast the actual timing of the cash flows into and out of the business. The precision of the budget depends on the characteristics of the organization, the degree of uncertainty about the business environment, and the ability of the planner to accurately forecast the future cash flows.

The budget process is characterized by five steps:

1. Forecasting sales.
2. Projecting all cash inflows, including forecasted receipts.
3. Projecting all cash outflows.
4. Interrelating the inflows and the outflows subject to policy decisions of the firm's management.
5. Determining the excess or shortage of cash during the planning period.

It is Step 5 that leads from forecasting and budgeting preparation into the planning process.

All cash budgets begin with a forecast of sales, which is normally supplied to the financial planner by the firm's marketing function. However, the primary source of cash inflow is not sales, but the collection of accounts receivable. In addition, the firm may raise cash from external sources through short- or long-term financing or the sale of assets. These inflows are also part of the cash budget.

The collection history of accounts receivable is used as the starting point in estimating the cash flow from sales. If the firm has made any changes in its credit terms or policies, or if the firm's customer base has changed, then the manager must incorporate the impact of these changes in estimating cash collections. The planner must look closely at any variation from the normal collection pattern to fully understand the impact the change is having on the firm's cash flow. An example of the relationship between sales and collection of cash is shown in Table 18.1.

The arrows in Table 18.1 indicate the interrelationship between the month in which the sales are generated and the month in which the cash is actually received. For example a total of \$60,000 is collected in March. This consists of 20% cash collection of current month sales on $\$75,000 \times 0.2 = \$15,000$; 70% collection of the sales which were made in the previous month or $\$50,000 \times 0.70 = \$35,000$; and 10% collection of the sales which were made two months previous or $\$100,000 \times 0.10 = \$10,000$.

Most of the cash outflows, or disbursements, are one of four types: (1) payments for purchases of raw materials, (2) payments for wages, rent, maintenance, and other operating expenses, (3) payments to short- and long-term suppliers of financing in the form of interest, principal, and dividends, and (4) taxes.

Operating expenses may be related to the forecasted level of sales and may vary with the changes in expected revenues. The payments to the suppliers of capital, interest, and principal represent contractual obligations that must be met to avoid bankruptcy and are unrelated to sales in the short run. Hence, a portion of the cash outflow is fixed and unrelated to revenues, so that if sales fall or do not reach expected levels, the change in cash flow will usually be less than the change in revenues. Note that depreciation and other noncash expenses do not appear in the firm's cash budget. This is because they represent accrued expenses for which there is no cash outflow during the planning horizon.

Interrelating the starting level of cash, cash inflows, and cash outflows allows the financial manager to determine the amount of excess cash available or the deficit that must be financed by borrowing.

Table 18.1 Sales and Cash Flow.

| **Sales** | **Nov. $100,000** | **Dec. $100,000** | **Jan. $100,000** | **Feb. $50,000** | **Mar. $75,000** | **Apr. $100,000** | **May $100,000** |
|---|---|---|---|---|---|---|---|
| Cash sales (20% of current months sales) | | | $20,000 | $10,000 | $15,000 | $20,000 | $20,000 |
| Collection of A/R (70% of previous months) | | | 70,000 | 70,000 | 35,000 | 52,500 | 70,000 |
| Collection of A/R (10% of month $t$–2) | | | 10,000 | 10,000 | 10,000 | 5,000 | 7,500 |
| Cash from collection of Sales and A/R | | | $100,000 | $90,000 | $60,000 | $77,500 | $97,500 |

It is this surplus or deficit that will determine the type of cash management plans that are formulated for the planning period.

The final step in the planning process is the most creative, as the cash flow manager tries various strategies to meet the cash shortfall or to invest the cash surplus. If the cash deficit falls below some predetermined limit (minimum cash balance), the cash manager must take corrective action such as raising funds by borrowing, altering the firm's payment pattern, or changing the credit policy to reduce the level of accounts receivable and thereby speed up the inflow of cash. Any one or a combination of these options would allow the cash manager to meet the cash shortfall. If there is excess cash, the cash manager must invest this surplus, which raises the question of what type of investment is best.

By experimenting with various alternatives and asking the "what if" question, the cash flow planner is better able to argue convincingly for a certain course of action, whether it be with creditors or other managers within the organization. By anticipating problems before they occur or become serious, cash flow managers act in a proactive fashion that puts them in a much stronger position to perform their job effectively. Failing to foresee problems that may occur and reacting in a hasty fashion once they have occurred puts the cash flow manager in a defensive position, with little room to bargain.

Usually, the cheapest and easiest solution to meeting a cash shortage is to arrange for a line of credit of sufficient size to cover the largest cash deficit the firm might incur. This borrowing can be repaid with excess levels of cash when they occur. However, by anticipating the deficits and surpluses in advance, the cash flow planner may be able to initiate other, more positive actions that will eliminate the problem without the aid of external financing. For example, the manager may convince the marketing department that a reduction in the level of accounts receivable, accomplished through a more restrictive credit policy or tighter collection policy, will eliminate the need for external financing and be the cheapest means of meeting the cash shortfall.

In certain cases, the organization may find it cost-effective to finance "on the trade" by extending or delaying payment of its own disbursements. This strategy must be evaluated to gauge the impact that slower payment will have on the firm's overall credit rating.

Whatever strategy is chosen, the cash flow planner must work closely with other managers in the firm and with the firm's creditors, must carefully coordinate the information available, and must correctly define the problem at hand to act effectively. The major contribution of the cash flow manager to the firm's success is that he or she knows the extent, severity, and duration of the problem to be solved.

## 18.10 Demand-Driven, Capital-Driven, and Cost-Driven Cash Budgets

Budgets must be designed and implemented to suit the organization. Therefore, the approach used in developing the budget should be adapted to the environment and characteristics of the individual organization. For example, in some businesses, success or failure is more closely related to demand or revenues; for other businesses, capital expenditure is most important; for still others, the cost structure is the crucial characteristic.

A *demand-driven* business is typified by a service-oriented firm. The budgeting process begins with a sales forecast, which estimates the level and timing of the cash inflows. The cash manager takes as given the amount and timing of the flows and has freedom to experiment with various strategies on how these flows will be financed or how the expenses will be met.

A *capital-driven* business, such as a manufacturing firm, must produce substantial cash flows to service long-term financing requirements. In this case, the receipt of revenue and the disbursement for expenses is somewhat flexible, and the cash flow planner can experiment with these components of the cash budget.

A *cost-driven* business is one in which business or operating expenses are the biggest factor in determining the cash budget. Such firms tend to be labor-intensive or governmental in nature. Because such organizations have some difficulty varying the disbursement pattern because of legal or contractual obligations, expenses become the most critical element in the cash flow planning process. The major challenge in managing these organizations is controlling expenses. For example, in most government organizations the expense of the necessary service is estimated and tax legislation is then passed to cover it. Budgeting for this type of enterprise should begin with outflows, or expenses, which can then be used to justify or determine the necessary inflows.

## 18.11 Users of Cash Forecasts and Business Plans

In addition to preventing the company's cash balance from falling below an acceptable minimum level and predicting the availability of surplus cash for investment, cash forecasts serve several other purposes, including the following:

- *Using cash efficiently.* A cash manager who accurately forecasts cash balances can often use available cash efficiently and avoid borrowing heavily one week and then having a surplus the following week.
- *Financing seasonal business fluctuations.* An accurate cash forecast helps the manager predict the firm's seasonal need for cash.
- *Borrowing shot- and long-term.* By knowing cash needs in advance, a cash manager can select the best combination of short-term and long-term financing to minimize overall interest costs.
- *Paying maturing obligations.* A cash forecast includes provisions for the repayment of large loans or maturing bond issues.
- *Providing financing for expansion.* An accurate forecast helps the cast manager arrange loans and stock issues for expansion well in advance of need. The forecast can also help avoid borrowing money earlier than necessary.
- *Taking advantage of cash discounts.* A company that knows it will have surplus cash available can safely take advantage of trade discounts. A company with surplus cash may also save money by buying materials and supplies on sale or in larger-than-normal quantities, given the consideration of the overall cost impact.
- *Estimating debt capacity.* A cash forecast shows a company's ability to pay interest and therefore shows the amount of debt that company can safely incur.
- *Formulating dividend policy.* Cash forecasts help to ensure that adequate cash will be available to pay dividends to shareholders.

## 18.12 Planning Horizons and Time Intervals of Cash Budgets

Cash flow planning is essentially short term. All of the assets and liabilities that make up net working capital are also short term in that they normally turn over several times a year. The purpose of cash flow planning is to identify and deal with temporary cash shortages or surpluses. Permanent or long-term funds are the subject of the capital structure decision. Capital budgeting covers the long-term investment decision.

Few companies undertake cash flow budgeting and planning for more than a year in advance. Sometimes it is advisable to plan for more than a year, such as in the case of a construction company where projects require eighteen months to three years to complete. But for most manufacturing, trading, and service companies, on year is a sufficient planning horizon, and six months or less may well be adequate.

Since cash flow planning is concerned with fluctuations in cash balances, the time interval used for planning is often a more important consideration than the length of the overall planning period. The most common planning interval is one month; that is, a financial manager forecasts cash inflows and outflows over one month, then calculates beginning and ending cash balances. This procedure is repeated for each of the other eleven months of the year if the overall planning horizon is one year. Using a one-month time interval has the advantage of coinciding with the payment and receipt patterns of most firms. However, many companies use a shorter interval, and some large firms even use weekly or daily intervals. Why is such a short interval necessary? If the company forecasts by the month and shows adequate cash balances at the end of the month, isn't it a waste of time to use a shorter interval? The answers to the questions depend on the circumstances of the company. Suppose a firm uses a planning interval of one month. Its cash flow plan for one month might look like A in Exhibit 18.6.

Just looking at the monthly cash flow plan, everything appears to be fine. The company's cash balance stays steady at $30,000. However, if we look at the weekly cash flow interval, we see that the firm

**Exhibit 18.6:** Cash Flow Budgets and Planning Intervals.

A. Monthly Planning Interval

| | | |
|---|---|---|
| Beginning cash balance | $30,000 | |
| Cash inflows | | |
| A/R collections | 55,000 | |
| Licensing fee collections | 25,000 | |
| Sale of surplus assets | 15,000 | |
| *Total cash inflow* | $95,000 | |
| *Total cash available* | | $125,000 |
| Cash outflows | | |
| Salaries and wages | $24,000 | |
| Raw material purchases | 19,500 | |
| Supplies | 5,000 | |
| Rent | 14,000 | |
| Income tax payment | 25,000 | |
| Payroll taxes | 7,500 | |
| *Total cash outflows* | $95,000 | |
| *Cash at end of month* | | $30,000 |

B. Weekly Planning Interval

| | Week 1 | Week 2 | Week 3 | Week 4 |
|---|---|---|---|---|
| Beginning cash balance | $30,000 | ($2,250) | ($9,500) | ($2,250) |
| Cash inflows | | | | |
| A/R collections | $12,000 | $15,000 | $11,000 | $17,000 |
| Licensing fee collections | | | | 25,000 |
| Sale of surplus assets | | | 10,000 | 5,000 |
| *Total cash inflows* | $12,000 | $15,000 | $21,000 | $47,000 |
| Total cash available | $42,000 | $12,750 | $11,500 | $44,750 |
| Cash outflows | | | $600 | $6,000 |
| Salaries and wages | $6,000 | $6,000 | 4,000 | 5,000 |
| Raw material purchases | 5,500 | 5,000 | 1,250 | 1,250 |
| Supplies | 1,250 | 1,250 | 2,500 | 2,500 |
| Rent | 6,500 | 2,500 | | |
| Income tax payment | 25,000 | | | |
| Payroll taxes | | 7,500 | | |
| *Total cash outflow* | $44,250 | $22,250 | $13,750 | $14,750 |
| *Cash at end of week* | ($2,250) | ($9,500) | ($2,250) | $30,000 |

needs some short-term financing during the first three weeks of the month. In this case, the firm would do well to choose a planning interval no longer than one week, and perhaps even shorter. The reason this firm should use a weekly planning interval is to ensure that arrangements can be made to meet the cash shortfalls that occur during the first three weeks.

Several additional factors should be taken into consideration when deciding on the length of the planning interval for the cash budget. These include the following:

- *Inflation rates and opportunity costs.* When inflation rates are high, the firm wants to minimize the amount of idle cash it is holding and also minimize the amount of short-term financing that is used.
- *Size of cash flows.* Companies that plan their cash flows by the day usually have very large cash flows. For example, $1 million invested at an annual rate of 12% yields $328.75 per day, a sum that makes it worthwhile to plan to invest cash daily. In contrast, $10,000 at 12% yields $3.28 per day. A company could not justify spending valuable time and effort to earn this sum.
- *Executive time available for cash flow planning and management.* Executive time is one of the scarcest resources of most companies. Thus, the returns earned from daily cash management may not justify the time spent in achieving them. Such a situation would dictate a longer planning interval.
- *Predictability of cash flow timing and size.* The predictability of the timing and the size of cash flows will have a great impact on the appropriate planning interval. The more unpredictable the size and timing of the cash flow, the shorter should be the planning interval.
- *Size of required cash balances.* From the point of view of avoiding insolvency, the size of the minimum cash balance in relation to the cash flow has a bearing on the planning interval. If cash balances are large, temporary variations within a long planning interval are unlikely to place a firm in jeopardy. But if a company is operating on small or marginal balances, a large cash outflow over only a few days may bring balances down to unacceptable levels. In such circumstances, a short planning interval is necessary for survival, even if it is not economically justified.

## 18.13 From Forecasting to Budgeting to Planning

The first step in forecasting the cash budget is to make a detailed list of the assumptions concerning the inflows and outflows for the planning period. Exhibit 18.7 lists some common assumptions:

The second step is to develop the schedule of receipts and disbursements for at least the three scenarios of worst, most likely, and best cases. The selected estimates are then put on the schedule. The magnitude and timing of these figures will be very sensitive to the individual scenario. Any figures that appear to be out of line should be reevaluated to ensure that the figures and the assumptions make sense. Exhibit 18.8 shows the general format of the cash flow forecast for a most likely case, a worst case, and a best case.

Once cash inflows and disbursements have been forecast, the planner can then forecast the cash balances at the beginning and end of each interval in the planning period; the results appear as the top and bottom lines of the schedules. These figures, showing the cash surpluses or deficits, are the main reason for going through the forecasting exercise. They will be used by management in determining the short-term financial plan for the planning period.

If we compare the cash balances under the three scenarios, we notice that under the worst case there is no need for external financing, while the greatest cash shortage is experienced under the best case. This is quite usual for most firms because the increased level of activity during the "best" periods requires more external financing.

**Exhibit 18.7:** Assumptions for Cash Inflows and Outflows.

| | Worst Case | Most Likely | Best Case |
|---|---|---|---|
| Revenues | 5% decline | Same as last year | 10% increase |
| Credit sales | 95% of sales volume | 90% of sales volume | 85% of sales volume |
| Collection experience | 80% in 30 days | 85% in 30 days | 100% in 30 days |
| Expenses | 10% in 60 days | 10% in 60 days | |
| | 10% bad debts | 5% bad debts | |
| | 5% increase | Same as last year | 3% decline |
| Capital expenditures | $0 | $100,000 in February | $150,000 in February |

**Exhibit 18.8:** Six-Month Cash Flow Forecast.

| | Most likely case | | | | | |
|---|---|---|---|---|---|---|
| | **January** | **February** | **March** | **April** | **May** | **June** |
| Beginning cash balance | \$20,000 | \$16,000 | (\$63,000) | (\$3,000) | (\$5,000) | \$25,000 |
| Cash sales and collection of A/R | 50,000 | 65,000 | 75,000 | 65,000 | 75,000 | 65,000 |
| Insurance claims | | | 25,000 | | | |
| Dividends and interest | 5,000 | 2,000 | | 5,000 | | 2,000 |
| *Total cash inflow* | \$55,000 | \$67,000 | \$100,000 | \$70,000 | \$75,000 | \$67,000 |
| Total cash available | \$75,000 | \$83,000 | \$37,000 | \$67,000 | \$70,000 | \$92,000 |
| Cash outflow | | | | | | |
| Labor wages | \$23,000 | \$25,000 | \$25,000 | \$25,000 | \$25,000 | \$25,000 |
| Salary | 5,000 | 5,000 | 5,000 | 5,000 | 5,000 | 5,000 |
| Raw material payment | 4,000 | 16,000 | 10,000 | 15,000 | 15,000 | 10,000 |
| Dividends | 2,000 | | | 2,000 | | |
| Income taxes | 25,000 | | | 25,000 | | |
| New equipment | | 100,000 | | | | |
| *Total cash outflow* | \$59,000 | \$146,000 | \$40,000 | \$72,000 | \$45,000 | \$40,000 |
| Cash at end of month | \$16,000 | (\$63,000) | (\$3,000) | (\$5,000) | \$25,000 | \$52,000 |

(*Continued*)

**Exhibit 18.8:** (*Continued*)

| | Worst case | | | | | |
|---|---|---|---|---|---|---|
| | **January** | **February** | **March** | **April** | **May** | **June** |
| Beginning cash balance | $15,000 | $12,500 | $26,500 | $82,500 | $83,500 | $109,500 |
| Cash sales and collection of A/R | 47,500 | 62,000 | 70,000 | 62,000 | 70,000 | 62,000 |
| Insurance claims | | | 25,000 | | | |
| Dividends and interest | 5,000 | 2,000 | | 5,000 | | 2,000 |
| *Total cash inflow* | $52,500 | $64,000 | $95,000 | $67,000 | $70,000 | $64,000 |
| Total cash available | $67,500 | $66,500 | $121,500 | $149,500 | $153,500 | $173,500 |
| Cash outflow | | | | | | |
| Labor wages | $25,000 | $25,000 | $26,000 | $26,000 | $26,000 | $26,000 |
| Salary | 5,000 | 5,000 | 5,000 | 5,000 | 5,000 | 5,000 |
| Raw material payment | 3,000 | 10,000 | 8,000 | 13,000 | 13,000 | 10,000 |
| Dividends | 2,000 | | | 2,000 | | |
| Income taxes | 25,000 | | | 20,000 | | |
| New equipment | | — | | | | |
| *Total cash outflow* | $55,000 | $40,000 | $39,000 | $66,000 | $44,000 | $41,000 |
| *Cash at end of month* | $12,500 | $26,500 | $82,500 | $83,500 | $109,500 | $132,500 |

(*Continued*)

**Exhibit 18.8:** (*Continued*)

| | Best case | | | | | |
|---|---|---|---|---|---|---|
| | **January** | **February** | **March** | **April** | **May** | **June** |
| Beginning cash balance | $25,000 | $17,000 | ($112,000) | ($49,000) | ($55,000) | ($29,000) |
| Cash sales and collection of A/R | 55,000 | 70,000 | 85,000 | 73,000 | 78,000 | 73,000 |
| Insurance claims | | | 25,000 | | | |
| Dividends and interest | 6,000 | 3,000 | | 6,000 | | 3,000 |
| *Total cash inflow* | $61,000 | $73,000 | $110,000 | $79,000 | $78,000 | $76,000 |
| Total cash available | $86,000 | $90,000 | ($2,000) | $30,000 | $23,000 | $47,000 |
| Cash outflow | | | | | | |
| Labor wages | $25,000 | $27,000 | $27,000 | $27,000 | $27,000 | $27,000 |
| Salary | 5,000 | 5,000 | 5,000 | 5,000 | 5,000 | 5,000 |
| Raw material payment | 6,000 | 20,000 | 15,000 | 20,000 | 20,000 | 15,000 |
| Dividends | 2,000 | | | 3,000 | | |
| Income taxes | 25,000 | | | 30,000 | | |
| New equipment | | 150,000 | | | | |
| *Total cash outflow* | $69,000 | $202,000 | $47,000 | $85,000 | $52,000 | $47,000 |
| *Cash at end of month* | $17,000 | ($112,000) | ($49,000) | ($55,000) | ($29,000) | 0 |

The cash budget, as shown in Exhibit 18.8, serves a number of purposes. It can be used as a starting point of the cash planning process. It can act as a standard of behavior against which the performance of the company can be evaluated. It can serve as a control mechanism in that any deviation from the standard can be isolated and corrective action taken if needed. The cash budget can also be used as a starting point in "what if" or sensitivity analysis. For example, what if revenues grow at a rate different than assumed? How will this affect the amount of short-term financing required?

So far, we have been talking about cash forecasting and cash budgeting, which serve as a starting point for cash flow planning. Cash flow planning is the way the organization determines how to adjust its cash balances to an optimum level. The two steps in cash flow planning are (1) determining an appropriate cash level and (2) determining how to bring the organization's cash balance to this optimal level.

Dividing a company's need for cash into three categories yields (1) cash for day-to-day transactions, (2) reserve cash to meet contingencies, and (3) cash for compensating balance requirements. The required level of day-to-day transaction cash depends on the number, frequency, and amount of anticipated transactions. The only requirement for this element of the cash balance is that it be large enough to cover the checks written against it.

To estimate reserve cash requirements, the cash flow manager can tabulate the daily or weekly changes in the cash account. These changes will range from some very large changes to small fluctuations. Because the major problem is running short of cash, the cash flow manager is especially interested in the large decreases and thus might select a reserve balance that would allow for all but the largest cash decreases to be met.

Finally, the organization needs to maintain compensating balances required by the bank. To determine the appropriate minimum cash balance, a cash flow manager simply adds together the three segments just estimated. If the budgeted balance is significantly higher than the minimum balance, the organization can use the excess cash to purchase marketable securities. On the other hand, if the cash balance falls below the desired level, the organization can plan to borrow short-term funds or to sell marketable securities. To complete the transition from cash budget to cash flow plan, the manager must show how the cash balance will be adjusted to meet the minimum cash balance.

At this point, we have a cash flow budget, not a short-term financial plan. Planning is the mental process of visualizing a set of future events that the financial planner is determined to make happen in the future, not just a summary of what the planner expects to happen. But given the cash budget in Exhibit 18.8 and the minimum cash balance requirements, we can begin planning.

Some of the cash balances at the end of each planning interval may be higher than needed, while others may be too low or even negative. Financial planners first determine how to invest any excess cash to earn the maximum return. This decision depends on the amount of excess cash and the length of time it will be available. Next, the planner decides how to cover temporary cash shortages discovered by the forecast. We will discuss various means of doing this in detail in Chapters 19 and 20 but point out here that we are not limited to putting the money in the bank or borrowing from the bank. Other options are delaying purchases or payments until a later period, deciding to eliminate or reduce certain expenditures, selling marketable securities or other assets, and accelerating collections.

The results of this kind of planning are shown in Exhibit 18.9 for the most likely case. In this example, the planner has decided to postpone the expenditure for new equipment from February to March and to stretch out the payables for raw materials by an additional thirty days. The planner has also decided to invest cash balances in excess of $10,000 in 30-day T-bills. Any shortages of cash would be covered by establishing a line of credit with a commercial bank. Various other alternatives should also be considered before the final plan is formulated.

Through this plan, the financial planner has kept a minimum cash balance of $10,000 and reduced borrowing on the firm's line of credit to $2,469 in March. Also, the cash manager was able to invest in the money-market surplus cash balances during the months of February, March, May, and June. This is only one possible alternative that the financial planner may wish to consider before finalizing the cash flow plan. Thus, once the manager has determined how to invest excess cash and meet cash shortages, the results of these decisions are incorporated into the cash flow budget, which then becomes the cash flow plan. The manager's remaining responsibility is to ensure,

**Exhibit 18.9:** Six-Month Most-Likely Cash Flow Plan.

| | January | February | March | April | May | June |
|---|---|---|---|---|---|---|
| Beginning cash balance | $20,000 | $10,000 | $10,000 | $10,000 | $10,000 | $10,000 |
| Cash inflows | | | | | | |
| collection of A/R | 50,000 | 65,000 | 75,000 | 65,000 | 75,000 | 65,000 |
| Insurance claims | | | 25,000 | | | |
| Dividends and interest | 5,000 | 2,000 | | 5,000 | | 2,000 |
| Maturing marketable securities* | | 10,000 | 43,531 | | 498 | 30,803 |
| Total cash inflow | $55,000 | $77,100 | $143,531 | $70,000 | $75,498 | $97,803 |
| Total cash available | $75,000 | $87,100 | $153,531 | $80,000 | $85,498 | $107,803 |
| Cash outflow | | | | | | |
| Labor wages | $23,000 | $25,000 | $25,000 | $25,000 | $25,000 | $25,000 |
| Salary | 5,000 | 5,000 | 5,000 | 5,000 | 5,000 | 5,000 |
| Raw material payment | | 40,000 | 16,000 | 10,000 | 15,000 | 15,000 |
| Dividends | 2,000 | | | 2,000 | | |
| Income taxes | 25,000 | | | 25,000 | | |
| Payoff line of credit** | | | | 2,506 | | |
| New equipment | | | 100,000 | | | |
| Total cash outflow | $55,000 | $34,000 | $146,000 | $69,506 | $45,000 | $45,000 |
| Cash available | 20,000 | 53,100 | 7,531 | 10,494 | 40,498 | 62,803 |
| Minimum cash balance | 10,000 | 10,000 | 10,000 | 10,000 | 10,000 | 10,000 |
| Marketable securities at 12%/year | $10,000 | $43,100 | | $494 | $30,498 | $52,803 |
| Short-term borrowing at 18%/year | | | $2,469 | | | |

*Notes*: *It is assumed that the marketable securities are invested for one month at one percent interest (12%/12 months = 1% month) 10,000 × 1.01 = $10,100 for February.

**It is assumed that the borrowing is done for one month at 1.5% interest (18%/12 months = 1.5%/month) 2,469 × 1.015 = $2,506 for April.

to the extent possible, that this plan is put into effect and is mirrored by actual results.

The accuracy of the forecast used in preparing the cash flow plan is of critical importance first in creating the budget and then in developing a plan that is a useful management toll to implement the budget. The less reliable the forecast or the less certain the cash flow manager is about events that may affect the cash flows, the larger the minimum cash balances, lines of credit, or a combination of both that are required. GIGO (garbage-in, garbage-out) is an appropriate acronym in this case. If the planner does not have much confidence in the forecast, the resulting plan will be of little value to the organization.

## 18.14 Summary

In Chapter 18, we have identified and defined cash flow and related it to the accounting-based concept of funds flow. The short-term financial manager is much more concerned with the actual cash flowing through the first on a day-to-day basis than the longer-term funds flow perspective.

A three-scenario approach to short-term financial planning (using worst, most-likely, and best-case scenarios) is recommended because future events cannot always be forecasted with accuracy. For this reason, the initial step of the planning process involves making educated guesses about future cash flows that cover a reasonable range of possible situations. In both budgeting and planning, the cash flow manager should ask the following questions: Does this plan make sense in light of my own experience? Does it coincide with what I expect to happen during the coming year?

Throughout the planning process, there should be a feedback mechanism that enables the short-term financial planner to update the forecast in light of new information and/or a new understanding of the situation that may come about from actually preparing the budget and the plan. Cash flow managers must understand that the process itself is the most important aspect of short-term financial management. The final plan is not definitive. It serves only to guide future courses of action and decisions and is subject to continual revision.

The final part of the chapter demonstrated the interrelationship of forecasting, budgeting, and planning. Once the problems have been defined, a financial planner must generate alternatives that will lead to satisfactory solutions. The material in the next two chapters expands on the possible alternatives available to the financial planner. In most cases, there is more than one way to solve a problem. Sometimes it is worth the extra effort to look for the optimal solution; sometimes it is not. With experience, the financial manager learns when to use a satisfactory solution that may not be the best one theoretically. It makes little sense to spend a lot of time and make many improvements on a plan that will only marginally improve performance.

## References

Campbell, T. S. and L. Brendsel. "The Impact of Compensating Balance Requirements on the Cash Balances of Manufacturing Corporations," *The Journal of Finance* (March 1977, pp. 31–40).

Fabozzi, F. and L. N. Masonson. *Corporate Cash Management Technique and Analysis* (Homewood, IL: Dow-Jones, Irwin, 1985).

Frost, P. A. "Banking Services, Minimum Cash Balances, and the Firm's Demand for Money," *The Journal of Finance* (December 1970, pp. 1029–1039).

Gallinger, G. W. and P. B. Healey. *Liquidity Analysis and Management* (Reading, PA: Addition-Wesley, 1991).

Gentry, J. and C. F. Lee. "Financial Forecasting and the X-11 Model: Preliminary Evidence," *Advances in Financial Planning and Forecasting*, 2 (1987, pp. 27–49).

Lee, C. F. and A. C. Lee. *Encyclopedia of Finance*, 2nd edn. (Springer, 2013).

Sagner, J. *Working Capital Management: Applications and Case Studies* (Wiley, 2014).

Lee, C. F. and J. Lee. *Financial Analysis, Planning and Forecasting: Theory and Application*, 3rd edn. (World Scientific, 2017).

Stigum, M. and A. Crescenzi. *Stigum's Money Market*, 4th edn. (McGraw-Hill Education, 2007).

Stone, B. K. "The Use of Forecasts for Smoothing in Control-Limit Models for Cash Management," *Financial Management* (Spring 1972, pp. 72–84).

## Appendix 18A — Time-Series Components of Sales

One of the most important and difficult tasks facing the financial managers is forecasting. Since financial managers are interested in the future and are interested in making decisions about the future, they must necessarily have some meaningful estimate of future activity. The purpose of this appendix is to shed some light on how the financial planner can realistically forecast working capital requirements in a systematic fashion.

The main characteristic of a time series of numbers is that its observations have some dependency on time. There are at least three forms that this time dependency can take, as shown in Figure 18.1A.

Figure 18.1A(a) shows a time series with an upward trend; (b) shows a time series with a quarterly pattern, repeated identically every year; and (c) shows a random or irregular time series of autocorrelated or serially correlated terms (each successive value is related to the preceding value with a random disturbance element added).

If the real-world data that we are using to forecast followed only on these patterns, there would be no problem in forecasting the future patterns. However, in the real world, available information is usually a mixture of at least three components. To simplify the problem of predicting future movements, we can take any time series and separate it into its three components. One way of doing this is to use the Bureau of the Census decomposition model X-11. The X-11 program makes it possible to determine the $S, C,$and $I$ components in a time series. Additionally, the program calculates the relative percentage contribution of the $S, C,$and $I$ components to the original time series.

If future performance is in any way related to past data, then financial planning and forecasting will benefit from a better understanding of the components of the past data. Decomposing past time-series data and discovering the relative percentage contribution of the $C, S,$ and $I$ components to changes in the series may provide insight for management and financial planners.

The $C$ component reflects permanent information in both a short-run and long-run economic time series. The $S$ component represents a permanent pattern underlying the short-run time series. Although the percentage contribution of the seasonal component may be high

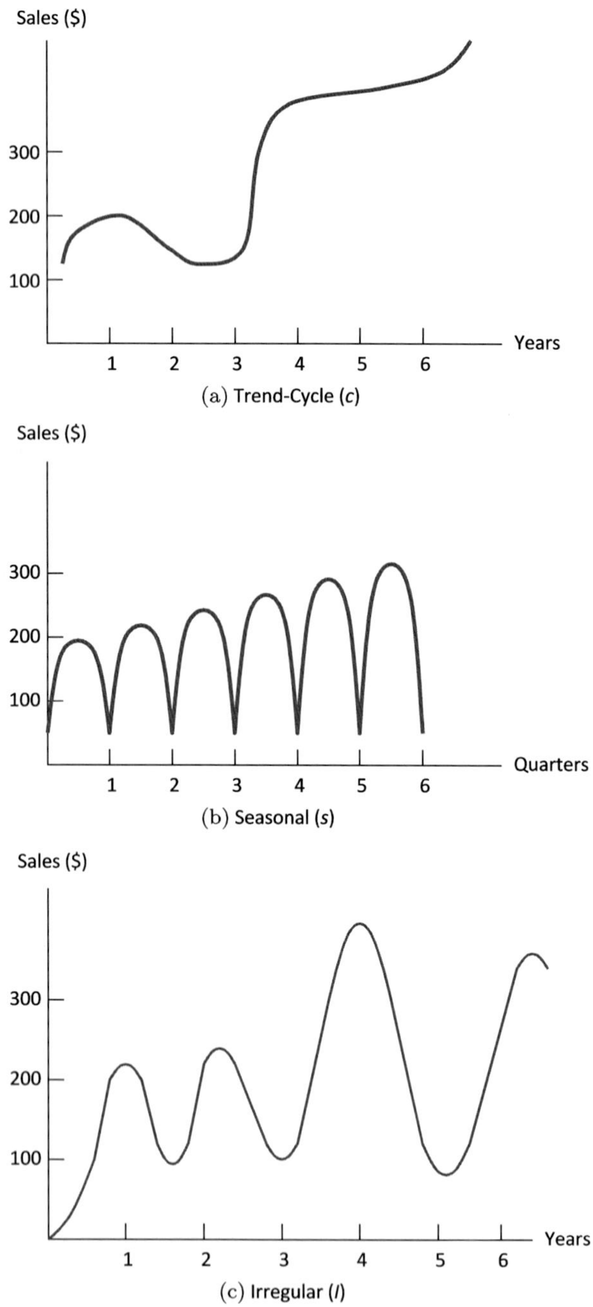


Figure 18.1A Three Time-Series Components.

in the short run, it contains permanent information that management can use for intermediate and short-run planning. The uncertainty arising from the seasonal component is relatively low. The $I$ component contains the randomness that exists in the time series for both short- and long-run analyses and can be interpreted as noise in the information. The higher the relative percentage contribution of the $I$ component in a time series, the greater the noise or uncertainty. Hence, greater forecasting errors can occur the higher the percentage contribution of $I$.

Given information concerning the relative percentage contribution each component makes to a time series, financial managers can better understand the composition of the data, evaluate the predictive quality of a financial planning variable, and assess potential causes of forecasting errors. Additionally, creating an industry index for key financial planning variables provides a quantitative measure of the relative percentage contribution of each component. The availability of this industry index information provides a benchmark against which the forecasting quality of the firm's financial planning variables can be compared. The results of these comparisons could be used to improve forecasting accuracy and usefulness.

For quarterly forecasting, the X-11 generates a seasonal forecast of the next four quarters and computes the percentage contribution of the $C, S$, and $I$ components relative to the changes in the original data. The relationship is defined as

$$\bar{O}_t^2 = \bar{I}^2{}_t + \bar{C}^2{}_t + S^2{}_t \tag{18.1A}$$

where each symbol represents the mean of the absolute quarterly changes, as follows: $\bar{O}^2{}_t$ = the original series; $\bar{I}^2{}_t$ = the random component; $\bar{C}^2{}_t$ = the trend-cycle component; and $\bar{S}^2{}_t$ = the seasonal component. The relative contribution of the changes in each component for each time span is given by the ratios $\bar{I}^2{}_t/\bar{O}^2{}_t$, $\bar{C}^2{}_t/\bar{O}^2{}_t$, and $\bar{S}^2{}_t/\bar{O}^2{}_t$. To illustrate the statistical computation of the relative contribution of each $C, S$, and $I$ component to the percentage change in the original time series, let us consider the quarterly sales of IBM from the first quarter of 1969 to the fourth quarter of 1982, as shown in Table 18.1A.

The relative contribution of each component for one quarter is calculated in the following manner. The first step is to determine the absolute change in the original sales series ($O_t$) between each

Table 18.1A Original Quarterly Sales Data for IBM, 1969 to 1982 ($ millions).

| **Original Series Year** | **1st Quarter** | **2nd Quarter** | **3rd Quarter** | **4th Quarter** | **Total** |
|---|---|---|---|---|---|
| 1969 | 1,685 | 1,832 | 1,778 | 1,903 | 7,197 |
| 1790 | 1,721 | 1,874 | 1,914 | 1,996 | 7,505 |
| 1971 | 1,870 | 1,942 | 2,082 | 2,380 | 8,274 |
| 1972 | 2,312 | 2,365 | 2,334 | 2,522 | 9,533 |
| 1973 | 2,451 | 2,547 | 2,756 | 3,240 | 10,994 |
| 1974 | 3,002 | 3,260 | 3,125 | 3,288 | 12,675 |
| 1975 | 3,272 | 3,496 | 3,600 | 4,068 | 14,436 |
| 1976 | 3,815 | 4,014 | 3,957 | 4,519 | 14,436 |
| 1977 | 4,090 | 4,419 | 4,586 | 5,038 | 18,133 |
| 1978 | 4,432 | 4,921 | 5,284 | 6,439 | 21,076 |
| 1979 | 5,295 | 5,355 | 5,384 | 6,829 | 22,863 |
| 1980 | 5,748 | 6,181 | 6,481 | 7,805 | 26,212 |
| 1981 | 6,461 | 6,895 | 6,721 | 8,993 | 29,070 |
| 1982 | 7,066 | 8,053 | 8,171 | 11,074 | 34,364 |

quarter. For example, sales in the first and second quarters ($O_t$ and $O_2$) of 1969 were $1,685 million and $1,832 million, so the absolute change in sales between the first and second quarters was $147 million ($O_1 - O_2$). The absolute difference in sales between the third and fourth quarters ($O_3 - O_4$) was $125 million ($1,778-$1,903). Thus, for the original sales series ($O_t$) the X-11 routine calculates the absolute change in sales between each of the 56 quarters; that is, $O_1 - O_2, O_2 - O_3, O_3 - O_4, \ldots, O_{54} - O_{55}, O_{55} - O_{56}$. The mean of the percent changes in the original sales series ($O_t$) was 9.25 percent, which is shown in Table 18.2A.

The X-11 routine also calculates the absolute change in the original sales for time spans of two, three, and four quarters. Because the computation methodology is similar for each time span, we will use the four-quarter time span to illustrate the technique. The absolute change in sales every four quarters is calculated by the model. All possible four-quarter time period combinations of changes in sales are

Table 18.2A Mean of the Absolute Average Percent Changes in Sales Related to Trend-Cycle, Seasonal, and Irregular Components for One-, Two-, Three-, and Four-Quarter Time Spans, 1969 to 1982 (in percent).

| Span in Quarters | Original | Trend Cycle | Seasonal | Irregular |
|---|---|---|---|---|
| 1 | 9.25 | 3.19 | 7.29 | 1.90 |
| 2 | 9.54 | 6.31 | 6.26 | 1.44 |
| 3 | 12.73 | 9.47 | 7.59 | 1.57 |
| 4 | 12.89 | 12.78 | 0.44 | 1.45 |

computed: $O_1 - O_5$, $O_5 - O_9$, $O_9 - O_{13}$, ..., $O_{45} - O_{49}$, $O_2 - O_6$, $O_6 - O_{10}$, ... , $O_{46} - O_{50}$, $O_3 - O_7$, ..., $O_{47} - O_{51}$, $O_4 - O_8$, ..., $O_{52} - O_{56}$. The same procedure is used to calculate two- and three-quarter time spans. The means of the changes in the original series ($O_t$) for two-, three-, and four-quarter time spans were 9.54%, 12.73%, and 12.89%. These values are presented in Table 18.2A.

## 18A.1 The Contribution of Each Component

The next step in the forecasting process is to calculate the mean absolute percent change in the final adjusted time series for $C, I$, and $S$. The X-11 model computes a final adjusted table for each component. We now compute the relative contribution of each component to changes in the original IBM sales series for a one-quarter time span. Using Eq. (18.1A) and the appropriate values from Table 18.2A produces

$$(\bar{O})^2 = (0.0190)^2 + (0.0319)^2 + (0.0729)^2 = (0.08076)^2$$

For a one-quarter time span, the relative contribution of each component is

$$I \text{ component} = \frac{\bar{I}^2}{(\bar{O}')^2} = \frac{0.00035}{0.006523} = 5.38\%$$

Table 18.3A Relative Contributions of Components to Changes in IBM Sales for One-, Two-, Three-, and Four-Quarter Time Spans, 1969 to 1982 (in percent).

| Span in Quarters | Trend-Cycle | Seasonal | Irregular | Total |
|---|---|---|---|---|
| 1 | 15.13 | 80.82 | 4.03 | 100 |
| 2 | 45.51 | 51.73 | 2.76 | 100 |
| 3 | 58.46 | 40.35 | 1.19 | 100 |
| 4 | 98.40 | 0.14 | 1.46 | 100 |

$$C \text{ component} = \frac{\bar{C}'^2}{(\bar{O}')^2} = \frac{0.00068}{0.006523} = 15.19\%$$

$$S \text{ component} = \frac{\bar{S}^2}{(\bar{O}')^2} = \frac{0.005180}{0.006523} = 79.42\%$$

## 18A.2 Interpretation

The above data indicates that the irregular component contributed slightly over 5% of the change in the original sales series of IBM for the period from the first quarter of 1969 to the second quarter of 1982. Additionally, 15% of the change in the original sales series was related to the trend-cycle component and 79% was represented by the seasonal component. Permanent information signals contributed 95% of the change in past quarterly sales of IBM, and random events account for 5%.

Table 18.3A shows the relative contribution of each component to changes in IBM's original sales series for one-, two-, three-, and four-quarter time spans. The irregular component went from 4.3% to 1.46% as the time spans increased. The relatively low $I$ component for the four separate time spans suggests that the size of the forecasting error should be relatively small for aggregate forecasts of IBM's sales.

For a more detailed discussion of forecasting, see "Financial Forecasting and the X-11 Model" by Gentry and Lee (1987).

## Questions and Problems

(1) Define the following:
   a. Cash flow versus funds flow
   b. Variable short-term asset
   c. Cash flow cycle
   d. Cost- versus demand-driven cash budget
   e. Trend-cycle component of sales

2. What are major problems associated with balancing liquidity and profitability?
3. Discuss the method of calculating the cash flow cycle.
4. How are cash budgets and business plans used in short-term financial management?
5. Describe the cash budgeting procedure.
6. XYZ Company's financial data for calculating the cash conversion cycle is listed below. Given this information, calculate the cash conversion cycle and related financial ratios.

| | **1983** | **1984** | **1985** | **1986** | **1987** |
|---|---|---|---|---|---|
| Sales | $1,849 | $1,645 | $1,375 | $1,254 | $1,211 |
| Cost of sales* | $1,164 | $1,023 | $846 | $771 | $756 |
| Depreciation | 13 | 12 | 11 | 10 | 9 |
| Administration and other expenses* | 623 | 533 | 446 | 389 | 356 |
| Total operating expenses | $1,800 | $1,568 | $1,303 | $1,170 | $1,121 |
| Net operating income | $49 | $77 | $72 | $84 | $90 |
| Cash and marketable securities | $46 | $31 | $50 | $34 | $33 |
| Accounts receivable | 599 | 543 | 477 | 420 | 368 |
| Inventories | 451 | 399 | 299 | 260 | 222 |
| Other | 7 | 7 | 5 | 5 | 5 |
| Total current assets | $1,103 | $980 | $831 | $719 | $628 |
| Accounts payable and accrued expenses | $104 | $104 | $116 | $105 | $95 |
| Taxes payable | 0 | 8 | 9 | 14 | 10 |
| Commercial paper | 453 | 390 | 238 | 246 | 182 |
| Total current liabilities | $557 | $502 | $363 | $365 | $287 |

*Note*: *Assumed to be cash operating expenditures.

7. Assume cash inflows and outflows are as follows:

| | Worst Case | Most Likely | Best Case |
|---|---|---|---|
| Revenue | 10% decline | Same as last year | 5% increase |
| Credit sales | 90% of sales volume | 80% of sales volume | 85% of sales volume |
| Collection experience | 80% in 30 days | 85% in 30 days | 100% in 30 days |
| | 10% in 60 days | 10% in 60 days | |
| | 10% bad debts | 5% bad debt | |
| Expenses | 5% increase | Same as last year | 3% decline |
| Capital expenditure | $0 | $100,000 in February | $150,000 in February |

*Sales last year were*

| Nov. | Dec. | Jan. | Feb. | Mar. | Apr. | May | June |
|---|---|---|---|---|---|---|---|
| 100,000 | 80,000 | 100,000 | 30,000 | 150,000 | 80,000 | 100,000 | 80,000 |

Prepare a cash budget for each of the three scenarios.

8. The following financial data have been taken from the annual report of RSM Corporation:

| Particulars | 1987 | 1988 |
|---|---|---|
| **Current assets** | | |
| Cash and marketable securities | $40,000 | $43,000 |
| Accounts receivable | 410,000 | 455,000 |
| Inventory | 280,000 | 305,000 |
| *Total current assets* | $730,000 | $803,000 |
| **Current liabilities** | | |
| Accounts payable | $215,000 | $238,000 |
| Short-term borrowings | 150,000 | 140,000 |
| *Total current liabilities* | $365,000 | $378,000 |

(*Continued*)

| **Particulars** | **1987** | **1988** |
|---|---|---|
| Sales | $1,168,000 | $1,314,000 |
| Cost of goods sold* | 760,000 | 825,000 |
| Depreciation | 25,000 | 23,000 |
| Administrative and other expenses* | 235,000 | 246,000 |
| Total operating expenses | $1,020,000 | $1,094,000 |

*Note*: *Cash operating expenses.

Using the above information, calculate the following data:

a. Average age of inventory
b. Average age of accounts receivable
c. Average age of accounts payable
d. Cash flow cycle

9. Using the date in the previous problem, calculate the cost of financing the cash flow cycle if RSM Corporation's annual rate of interest on borrowings is:

a. 10%
b. 12%
c. 15%

10. UCI Company's projected sales for the first four months in 1989 are given below:

| **Month** | **Sales** |
|---|---|
| January | $55,000 |
| February | 50,000 |
| March | 60,000 |
| April | 70,000 |

The collection schedule is as follows:

10% in cash
60% in one month
25% in two months
5% in bad debts

Sales for November and December 1988 were $50,000 and $75,000 respectively. The firm buys materials 30 days in advance; that is, the materials for consumption in January are bought by the beginning of the preceding month. December, and are paid by the end of the month (the end of December in this example). Materials costs are 60% of the sale price.

Wages for the months of January, February, and March are projected to be $5,000 per month. Wages are paid twice in the month, on 1st and 16th of each month. The wages payable as on 31 December were $2,400. Other monthly expenses amount to $5,000 per month and are paid in cash. Taxes due for an earlier quarter are paid in second month of the succeeding quarter. The taxes due for the quarter ended 31 December 1988 were $8,850.

The company plans to buy a new vehicle in January for $15,000. The old vehicle is expected to be sold for a net amount of $1,900. A note of $10,750 will be due for payment on 29 February 1989. The firm can either withdraw cash deposit or borrow to pay the note. A quarterly loan installment of $9,000 is also due for payment in March.

The opening cash balance on 1 January is $5,000. The company policy is to maintain a minimum cash balance of $5,000. If the cash flow projections show a deficit for a particular month, the firm either withdraws cash from its short-term deposit or borrows at the beginning of the month to meet the expected short fall. The interest rate on such loans is 15% per year. Interest is paid at the end of every month. Such borrowings are paid off in the next month if the funds are available. Excess cash balance (over $5,000) is put in short-term deposits paying 1% interest per month.

Determine the monthly collections and disbursements and prepare a cash budget for the next three months.

11. Raymond Corporation's yearly sales are $2 million and the average collection period is 25 days. 90% of sales are on a credit basis. Assuming a 360-day year, determine the firm's investment in accounts receivable.
12. If Raymond Corp. extends its credit period to 30 days, the sales on credit could increase by 25%.

a. Calculate the additional investment in accounts receivables.
b. Find the additional expenditure on interest if the cost of financing accounts receivable is 15% per year.

13. A firm's annual credit sales are $2.7 million. If its accounts receivables are $375,000, what is the firm's average collection period? (Use a 360-day year.)
14. Century's projected cash inflows and outflows for the second quarter in 1989 are as given below:

| **Month** | **Receipts** | **Disbursements** |
|---|---|---|
| April | $10,000 | $12,000 |
| May | 12,020 | 10,000 |
| June | 10,000 | 10,500 |

The opening cash balance is $1,000 which also is the minimum balance that the company must maintain at all times. The short-term interest rate is 12% per year and interest is paid on a monthly basis. These loans are repaid monthly to the extent that excess cash is available.

Prepare a monthly cash budget for each of the three months.

# Chapter 19

# Credit Management

## Contents



## 19.1 Introduction

Chapter 19 extends some of the generally discussed concepts of Chapter 18 into a more focused examination of a specific aspect of short-term financial analysis and planning: the management of credit. More precisely, we are going to look at the terms, costs, benefits, and methods of evaluation that relate to trade credit.

On the balance sheet of nearly any company. Accounts receivable are listed on the asset side and accounts payable on the liability side. These categories represent credit extended to other companies (accounts receivable) and credit extended by other companies (accounts payable). Thus, trade credit is a form of short-term financing for the buying company. For the selling company, trade credit is a means to increase overall sales and must be evaluated in terms of the incremental gain per unit of additional risk. Because many firms have a lot of capital tied up or extended to them in the form of trade credit, decisions involving the management of credit can have great impact on such concerns as cash flow, cost of capital, sales growth, and debt capacity.

In Section 19.2, we discuss key terms and concepts related to trade credit. In Section 19.3, we look at the cost of short-term debt and the factors that must be considered when discerning the true costs and benefits of trade credit. Section 19.4 discusses financial ratios and credit analysis, and Section 19.5 discusses the credit decision in the context of the firm's collection policies. Finally, Section 19.6 summarizes the chapter. Appendix 19A discusses two methods to estimate the discriminant function for credit-granting decisions.

## 19.2 Trade Credit

*Trade credit* is credit the seller provides the buyer by allowing the buyer to postpone payment while still taking possession of the goods or services. From an accounting point of view, this kind of credit is listed on the seller's balance sheet as accounts receivable and on the buyer's balance sheet as accounts payable.

Although there is a wide variety of arrangements for transactions involving credit between different industries, credit terms are usually based on the same logic: to induce customers to pay before the final date, it is common to offer a cash discount for prompt settlement. Thus, a company may require final payment within 20 days but offer a 2% discount to customers who pay within 10 days, an arrangement stated as 2/10, net 20.

Other arrangements for credit transactions include special terms for recurrent purchases and seasonal accounts. When a company buys many items on a recurrent basis, it is common to account for all sales during the month as occurring at the end of the month, thereby eliminating the inconvenience of requiring separate payment for each delivery. The specific terms relating to this type of arrangement are 5/10, EOM, net 60; that is, by paying the bill within 10 days of the end of the month (EOM), the customer will receive a 5% discount. Otherwise, full payment is due within 60 days of the invoice date. Manufacturers who produce seasonal goods often encourage customers to take early delivery by allowing them to delay payment until the normal order season, a type of credit arrangement known as *season dating.*

While the terms of sale stipulate the amount of credit granted, they specify nothing concerning the nature of the contract. In many instances, the contract between buyer and seller is only implicit, particularly when the two parties have a well-established relationship. These types of repetitive sales are made on open account simply involving book entries and an implicit contract so stated. However, there are many other types of contractual arrangements, due to such factors as the parties being unfamiliar with each other, the order being very large, customized orders, and international customers. These more formal types of trade-credit agreements include promissory notes, commercial drafts, bank acceptances, and irrevocable letters of credit.

Basically, a *promissory note* is an IOU, whereby the buyer promises to pay the seller a certain amount by a specified date for a designated order, all in writing and signed by the buyer.

A *commercial draft* is similar in nature to a promissory note. However, its workings are somewhat different. First, the seller draws a draft ordering payment by the customer and sends this draft to the customer's bank along with any shipping documents. This commercial draft is a *sight draft* if immediate payment is required; otherwise, it is a *time draft* on which the customer's signature and the word *accepted* must be added. In either case, the advantage of this trade-credit instrument is that the seller obtains a commitment from the buyer before any goods are delivered. This commitment is the money that the seller receives ahead of time or the trade acceptance the buyer signs, which the bank returns to the seller.

Sometimes the seller knows little of the customer's creditworthiness and thus will require a stronger guarantee of the customer's debt. Such assurance can be constructed by asking the customer to arrange for his or her bank to accept the time draft. This arrangement and the resulting more-negotiable instrument is called a *banker's acceptance.*

An *irrevocable letter of credit* may be requested by an exporter who requires greater certainty of payment. First, the customer's bank sends the exporter a letter stating that it has established a line of credit for the customer with some bank in the U.S. The exporter can then collect payment ahead of delivery from the U.S. bank, which then forwards the appropriate documents to the customer's bank. (Chapter 27 provides a more detailed discussion of all of these instruments.)

For the seller, accounts receivable is the key balance sheet item to analyze for evaluating how much net credit the company has outstanding. Moreover, the balance of accounts receivable is a multidimensional item in terms of time and composition. Current accounts receivable can be defined to satisfy the following relationship:

$$AR_t = AR_{t-1} + AR_t^N - AR_t^0 \tag{19.1}$$

where $AR_t$ = the current balance of accounts receivable outstanding; $AR_{t-1}$ = the balance of accounts receivable outstanding remaining from previous period; $AR_t^N$ = new accounts receivable added during the current period; and $AR_t^0$ = past accounts receivable collected in the current period.

Typically, this relationship is evaluated for efficiency by using the average-collection-period ratio discussed in Chapter 2. In addition, because we could expand Eq. (19.1) in terms of the $AR_{t-1}$ variable $[AR_{t-1} = AR_{t-2} + AR_{t-1}^N - AR_{t-1}^0]$, it is possible and worthwhile to examine the relative age of accounts receivable. This type of analysis can be pursued through an aging-of-accounts-receivable table, such as Table 19.1. In this table, notice a decline in the quality of accounts receivable from January to February. This sort of breakdown allows analysis of the cross-sectional composition of accounts over time. An even more in-depth determination of the risk associated with accounts receivable is a breakdown by customer, associating probabilities of payment with the dollar amount owed.

Table 19.1 Aging of Accounts Receivable.

| | **January** | | **February** | |
|---|---|---|---|---|
| **Number of Days** | **Accounts Receivable ($)** | **% of Total** | **Accounts Receivable ($)** | **% of Total** |
| 0–30 days | 250,000 | 25.0 | 250,000 | 22.7 |
| 31–60 days | 500,000 | 50.0 | 525,000 | 27.8 |
| 61–90 days | 200,000 | 20.0 | 250,000 | 22.7 |
| Over 90 days | 50,000 | 5.0 | 75,000 | 6.8 |
| Total accounts receivable | 1,000,000 | 100.0 | 1,100,000 | 100.0 |

The importance of accounts receivable goes beyond the evaluation of the firm's trade credit, to the point of having significant implications for the firm's overall risk. This impact on risk is particularly evident when accounts receivable make up a large portion of the firm's current assets. In such instances, the quality of accounts receivable can lead to misleading conclusions concerning the firm's liquidity ratios. For example, in Chapter 2, Johnson & Johnson shows accounts receivable of nearly \$7.3 billion, representing about a third of the total current assets of \$24.3 billion. With total current liabilities of \$22.3 billion, the firm shows a current ratio of 1.09 and working capital of \$2.0 billion. Yet, just as an example, if GM's accounts receivable were mostly overdue accounts with low probability for payment, then we would probably be safer in our analysis of their liquidity to disregard the short-term variability of this item as a cash equivalent. If we delete accounts receivable, GM's current ratio falls to .76 and its working capital to −\$5.3 billion. This adjustment yields a markedly less-favorable perspective of the company's liquidity position.

Another factor for the financial manager to consider is the relative costs versus the relative benefits of maintaining large accounts receivable. As previously noted, accounts receivable can favorably affect a firm's current ratio, thus making the firm appear more liquid. The effect of a higher current ratio can be multidimensional, influencing the firm's debt capacity and cost of debt, its stock price, and its credit relations with other companies. Nevertheless, the maintenance of a high current ratio by means of the accounts receivable has its costs, such as the expense of financing the larger receivable in terms of the firm's cost of capital; additional collection, investigation, and bad-debt costs; and possible the cost of tying up more of the firm's working capital in an illiquid form, hereby increasing bankruptcy risk.

The trade-credit position of the buyer can be examined in much the same light as that of the seller. For the buyer, we look to the other side of the balance sheet and evaluate the accounts payable. The analysis of this account can be pursued both cross-sectionally in terms of relative size, average payment period, and aging of accounts payable, and over time by looking at the changes in the cross-sectional characteristics.

There is considerable disagreement over the extent to which firms should utilize trade credit to finance their operations. On one side are those who associate no cost with the credit obtained through accounts payable and believe therefore that the firm should maximize its use of this cheap source of capital. In particular, advocates of this view would advise the firm to maximize the length of time between receiving the goods and paying for them. Yet, there are those in the academic and business domains who believe that using accounts payable as a source of capital involves considerable costs. As mentioned earlier, most trade-credit terms involve a discount on the purchase price for paying early. Thus, if the firm does not take this discount, it may actually be incurring an opportunity cost. The potential size of this opportunity cost can be determined as follows.

Suppose you purchase 4100 worth of goods on terms of 5/10, net 30; the cash discount allows you to pay \$95 instead of \$100. If you do not take the discount, you are essentially getting a 20-day loan from the seller. However, you would pay 5/95 = 5.26% more for your goods. By dividing 365/20 = 18.25, we get the number of 20-day periods at 5.26% per year. Thus, 5.26% per period times 18.25 periods per year = 96% per year, which is a 96% yearly cost on the original loan.

Viewed in this manner, accounts payable is not the cheap financing source it might have originally appeared to be. Surely the firm can raise capital at a lower cost than 96% per annum.

Other costs that must be considered when evaluating accounts payable are those associated with maintaining low liquidity ratios and, relatedly, bankruptcy costs. Moreover, the thorough evaluation and management of a firm's trade credit must consider accounts receivable and accounts payable together, as discussions affecting one will have consequent effects on the other. To better understand this relationship and evaluate the costs of trade credit, we now turn to a more explicit determination of the involved costs.

## 19.3 The Cost of Trade Credit

The decisions of how much trade credit to issue (seller) or use (buyer) must be made on the basis of relative costs. This section identifies the costs of trade credit and related issues in the cost estimation-determination process.

### 19.3.1 *The seller's perspective*

For the seller, the cost of granting trade credit is not a straightforward calculation. Much of what can be considered a cost related to trade credit has to be estimated or forecasted. Furthermore, the seller should really be interested in the incremental cost or, correspondingly, the incremental gain associated with increasing or decreasing trade credit.

First, let us identify the additional costs that the company would bear for extending trade credit to its customers. Changes in accounts receivable can be evaluated according to three dimensions, each related to cost. First, by either granting trade credit to new customers or easing existing terms so that current customers purchase more, the seller incurs the additional expense of financing a larger absolute size of receivables. Second, by easing credit terms, such as by lengthening the credit period, the seller can expect the average collection period to increase, thus increasing the period over which accounts receivable are financed. Third, as credit terms are eased or more trade credit is granted, there is a greater probability of having more bad accounts to write off.

Most obvious, perhaps, is the incremental gain in additional sales that will result from easing credit terms or increasing trade credit granted. We can compute this incremental change in profits that would arise from any change in the seller's credit policy, but to do so we must estimate the additional (or decremental) sales that will occur as well as the increase in the size of accounts receivable, the average collection period, and the relevant discount rate.

As an example of computing incremental cost, we will examine the impact from an increase in the credit period granted to customers. First, we will define the following terms and their initial values:

$S_0$ = Current sales = \$1 million per year.
$S$ = Incremental sales = \$250,000.
$V$ = Variable costs as a percentage of sales = 70%. $V$ includes the cost of administering the credit department and all other costs except bad-debt losses and financing costs (interest charges) associated with carrying the investment in receivables. Costs of carrying inventories are included in $V$.

$I - V$ = Contribution margin = 30% or equivalently, the percentage of each sales dollar that goes toward covering overhead and increasing profits.

$k$ = The cost of financing the investment in receivables = 12%. $k$ is the firm's cost of new capital when the capital is used to finance receivables.

$ACP_0$ = Average collection period prior to a change in credit policy = 20 days.

$ACP_N$ = New average collection period after the credit policy change = 30 days. In this example, we assume that customers pay on time, thus $ACP$ = specified collection period.

Given this information, we seek to compute values for $\Delta I$ (incremental change in the level of the firm's investment in accounts receivable) and $\Delta P$ (incremental change in profits). We can calculate $\Delta I$ as follows:

$$\begin{aligned}
\Delta I &= \text{(Increased investment in receivables associated} \\
&\quad \text{with original sales)} \\
&\quad + \text{(Additional investment in receivables associated} \\
&\quad \text{with new sales)} \\
&= \text{(Change in collection period)(Old sales per day)} + V(ACP_N) \\
&\quad \times \text{(Incremental sales per day)} \\
&= (ACP_N - ACP_0)\left(\frac{S_0}{360}\right) + \left[V(ACP_N)\left(\frac{S}{360}\right)\right] \\
&= (30 - 20)\left(\frac{1{,}000{,}000}{360}\right) + \left[0.7(30)\left(\frac{250{,}000}{360}\right)\right] = \$42{,}361
\end{aligned} \tag{19.2}$$

From this information, we can now determine $\Delta P$, the incremental profit associated with the proposed credit period change:

$$\begin{aligned}
\Delta P &= \text{(New sales)(Contribution margin)} \\
&\quad - \text{(Cost of carrying new receivables)} \\
&= \Delta S(1 - V) - k(\Delta I) = \$250{,}000(01.3) - 0.12(42{,}361) \\
&= \$69{,}917
\end{aligned} \tag{19.3}$$

The result indicates that increasing the credit period from 20 to 30 days can be expected to raise pretax profit by \$69,917. Thus, the new credit policy should be adopted.

Note that two simplifying assumptions were made in this analysis: (1) that all customers paid on time ($ACP$ = credit period) and (2) that no bad-debt losses were incurred. However, in both cases, adjustments to the calculation procedures can be made quite easily. For instance, instead of using the credit period in Eq. (19.2), we can use the present average collection period and period estimated for the new credit policy. We can also adjust for bad-debt losses by estimating the percent of total sales that they will encompass $B$ — say, 5% — and subtract this amount from $\Delta P$. Thus, we modify Eq. (19.3) as

$$\begin{aligned}\Delta P &= (\text{New sales})(\text{Contribution margin})\\ &\quad - (\text{Cost of carrying receivables})\\ &\quad -(\text{Bad} - \text{Debt losses}) = \Delta S(1 - V) - k(\Delta I) - B(S)\\ &= \$250{,}000(10.3) - 0.12(42{,}361) - 0.05(\$1{,}250{,}000) = \$7.417\end{aligned} \tag{19.4}$$

Alternatively, bad-debt losses could be estimated as a percentage of incremental sales, and this amount is then subtracted from the change-in-profit function.

### 19.3.2 *The buyer's perspective*

For the buyer, determining the cost of using trade credit can be approached from various angles, depending on one's viewpoint. For instance, some practitioners and academicians argue that there is no cost associated with using trade credit and thus it is essentially a form of free financing. That is, the buyer pays nothing extra for the purchased goods or services by waiting until the last payment day. Therefore, trade credit costs nothing to the buyer and should be used to the maximum extent possible.

Yet, as demonstrated in the previous section, it is possible to identify an opportunity cost to the buyer for not taking the offered trade discounts. In fact, as our example pointed out, foregoing this opportunity to acquire goods or services at a discount to the originally agreed-on price can be a very expensive form of financing for the buyer. Consequently, the opportunity-cost perspective would advocate taking all trade discounts to maximize profitability and, hence, firm value as long as the firm's cost of capital is less than the imputed cost of not taking the discount.

Another argument against the view that trade credit has no cost for the buyer relates to bankruptcy costs. In the case where the buyer maximized its use of accounts payable as a form of financing, increasing accounts payable and stretching out payments as much as possible, the risk of illiquidity may increase. The impact of such implicit bankruptcy risk would be to increase the cost of other sources of capital, as creditors would perceive this increased risk and expect to be compensated for it. Moreover, the buyer's extensive accounts payable position could adversely affect relations with other suppliers, resulting in less-advantageous credit terms.

At this point, there seems to be considerable support for the principle that trade credit as a source of financing involves significant costs. In fact, much has been written advocating direct comparison between the cost of trade credit, such as computed under the opportunity-cost perspective, with the cost of alternative sources of capital. However, this view fails to account for the impact of tax timing differences among firms. Brick and Fung (1984) contend that the rate at which firms turn over inventory interacts with the accounting procedure to induce a tax-timing difference between cash and credit transactions, which makes credit transactions less costly. Sagner (2014) and Sartoris and Hill (1983) have discussed cost of trade credit in further details.

## 19.4 Financial Ratios and Credit Analysis

In analyzing the credit of a potential or current customer, we can apply a range of qualitative and quantitative approaches. While a number of outside sources can provide valuable information to aid in this process, we defer our discussion of these sources until the next section. Instead, we discuss here a number of quantitative methods that the seller can use when doing credit analysis. Before going on, one important point must be stressed. Any type of quantitative methodology that is used to aid the decision process is just that — an aid — and not the sole criterion for making the decision. Quantitative methods and models rarely allow consideration of all the information relevant to a problem. Therefore, any outcome from quantitative approaches must be considered in light of aspects that cannot be modeled.

### 19.4.1 *Financial ratio analysis*

While a complete analysis of a customer's present and future financial condition is usually too expensive to conduct, significant evidence of a firm's creditworthiness can be derived from its financial statements. Using key financial ratios and some of the analytical methodology discussed in Chapter 2, the seller can make a reasonable estimate of the customer's financial status.

This investigation might focus on the liquidity ratios and their trend over time. In this case, the analyst would be trying to determine whether the firm is liquid enough to meet its short-term obligations. Additionally, calculating the relative size of the customer's accounts payable to other liabilities, as well as the change in the proportion of accounts payable//sales, should also yield information as to whether the customer will be able to pay its bills. Relatedly, the composition of current assets and their change over time is significant, because if the buying firm has low cash levels but large inventory and accounts receivable balances, it may have a cash flow problem and thereby greater credit risk. The statement of changes in financial position can reveal more detailed knowledge of the customer's cash flow and therefore might be examined as well. Finally, comparisons of the customer firm's financial ratios with industry averages can provide further discrimination of the buyer's credit status.

### 19.4.2 *Numerical credit scoring*

Using financial ratio analysis to evaluate credit risk is certainly helpful. Yet, the decision that must be made following the examination of such data can be complicated by the difficulty of interpreting conflicting ratios. Different ratios often imply different predictions for the same firm. To overcome such ambiguity, information from several financial ratios can be combined into a single index. The resulting multivariate financial model will yield a single number for classifying the firm in terms of credit risk.

When considering how to construct such a multivariate model, there are several areas of concern:

1. What form should the model take (for example, linear or multiplicative)?
2. What variables should be included?
3. What weights should be applied to the variables?

These questions have no straightforward answers, for there is no widely accepted economic theory of financial distress to serve as a guide for such decisions. However, researchers have found the statistical tools of *factor analysis* and *linear discriminant analysis* to be of great help in devising financial risk indexes.

As a technique for deriving composite financial variables to classify firms by risk group, discriminant analysis has two purposes: (1) to test for mean group differences and describe the overlap between groups and (2) to construct a classification scheme based on a set of $m$ variables in order to assign previously unclassified observations to appropriate groups. This composite financial variable by which firms are classified is sometimes called a financial *z score*. Linear discriminant analysis has been applied extensively by practitioners and academicians in financial distress determination, bankruptcy prediction, bond rating analysis, and, as we are most interested in here, credit analysis.

A number of studies have developed models to help determine a firm's trade-credit policy. Notably, Lee and Lee (2017) and Mehta (1974) proposed a two-group discriminant-analysis model to identify the "good" amount from the "bad" account. To implement this type of classification methodology, Lee and Lee utilized a linear discriminant function of the form

$$Y_i = AX_{1i} + BX_{2i} \tag{19.5}$$

where $Y_i$ = index value for the $i$th account; $X_{1i}$ = $i$th firm's quick ratio; $X_{2i}$ = $i$th firm's total sales/inventory ratio; and $A$ and $B$-parameters or weights to be determined.

To formulate the original model, Mehta suggests the following steps. First, extend open-book credit to all new credit applicants for a sample period, recording for each account the quick ratio, the total sales/inventory ratio, and whether or not the account defaults in payment after a specified period. If the new account defaults, it is

Table 19.2 Status and Index Values of the Accounts.

| Account Number | Account Status | $Y_i$ |
|---|---|---|
| 7 | Bad | .81 |
| 10 | Bad | .89 |
| 2 | Bad | 1.30 |
| 3 | Bad | 1.45 |
| 6 | Bad | 1.64 |
| 12 | Good | 1.77 |
| 11 | Bad | 1.83 |
| 4 | Good | 1.96 |
| 1 | Good | 2.25 |
| 8 | Good | 2.50 |
| 5 | Good | 2.61 |
| 9 | Good | 2.80 |

classified as a bad account and the index ($Y_i$) is assigned a value of 0; if the account pays on time, it is classified as a good account and the index is assigned a value of 1. With this information, the linear discriminant analysis can be undertaken with two independent variables. Based on the sample data of $X_{1i}$ and $X_{2i}$, the coefficients can be estimated by either of two methods. (We defer detailed discussion of these methods to Appendix 19A.)

On the derivation of the discriminant model, the minimum cutoff value must be determined. The objective here is to refuse credit to those accounts with a $Y$ value below the cutoff value and to extend credit to those with a $Y$ value above the cutoff.

To demonstrate, we can modify the work of Van Horne (2002). After calculating $Y$, twelve accounts are arranged in ascending order of magnitude, as shown in Table 19.2.

Observing the overlap area for accounts 6, 12, 11, and 4, we can thus determine that the cutoff value must lie between 1.64 and 1.96. If we arbitrarily choose the midpoint 1.80 as the cutoff value, we will misclassify accounts 11 and 12, as seen graphically in Figure 19.1. Given the cutoff value, Figure 19.1 classifies account 11 as a good account when, in fact, we know it is a bad account; account 12 is classified as a bad account when it is actually a good account. These are type I and type II classification errors, respectively.

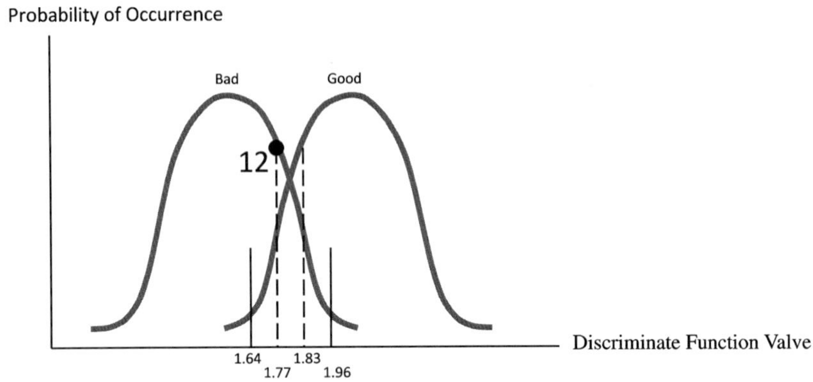


Figure 19.1 Distributions of Good and Bad Accounts.

Type I errors involve the rejection of the null hypothesis when it is actually true, while type II errors involve the acceptance of the null hypothesis when it is actually false. For the sake of practicality, the analysis should assume an area of possible misclassification for indexes between 1.64 and 1.95. Accounts or firms falling within this range require further investigation and analysis.

If the manager has reason to believe that new credit applicants will not differ significantly from past applicants, whose performance was the basis for the model formulation, then discriminant analysis can be used to select and reject credit sales customers. Moreover, by eliminating the need to spend time investigating customers with a definite reject or select classification (that is, $\leq 1.64$ and $\geq 1.96$), valuable search costs can be reduced and focused on those accounts in the range of uncertainty ($1.64 < Y_i < 1.96$).

As described by Lee and Lee (2017) and Mehta (1974), the manager faces four tasks to effectively apply linear discriminant analysis to the credit decision:

1. Determining significant factors
2. Selecting the sample
3. Assigning weights to factors to develop an index
4. Establishing cutoff values for the index

As previously mentioned, factor analysis can also be a valuable quantitative tool for credit analysis. In particular, factor analysis can be used to determine the most important or representative data relevant to the decision at hand. For credit analysis, where the analyst must choose among various feasible indicators and financial ratios in determining creditworthiness, factor analysis can simultaneously take into account all the interdependencies among the variables and help isolate those that best help explain the dependent variable.

Two key concepts related to factor analysis are factor scores and factor loadings. A *factor score* is simply a linear combination (or linear composite) of the original variables and is defined as

$$F_i = b_1Y_1 + b_2Y_2 + \cdots + b_jY_j + b_pY_p \tag{19.6}$$

where $F_i$ is the $i$th factor score; $Y_j(j = i, 1, 2, \ldots, p)$ are the original variables; and $b_1 \ldots b_p$ are the coefficients to be estimated.

A *factor loading* is simply the correlation (across objects of a set of factors with the original variables. Using the factor loading, one can identify which of the original variables correlate most closely with each of the indicative factor scores. In this way, the credit analyst could derive a general, more efficient set of explanatory variables to use in the decision-making process. Moreover, factor analysis can be combined with discriminant analysis to pinpoint, in a more objective manner, the significant factors to use, as discussed by Lee and Lee (2017) and Lee *et al.* (2013).

### 19.4.3 *Benefits of credit-scoring models*

The process of deciding whether to grant trade credit to a customer, and how much, is complicated, requiring significant information search and assimilation time and, in the end, money. Moreover, it is no easy task to identify the costs related to such a process. However, we can highlight some of the potential benefits from implementing a *credit-scoring model*, which can also make related costs easier to identify. These potential benefits are as follows:

1. Quantification of risk
2. Identification of predictor variables
3. Consistency of credit decisions
4. More efficient allocation of credit analyst's time and resources

Related to the quantification of risks in the credit decision, Foster (2008) examined the credit records of a manufacturing firm and classified the accounts into categories of "good" and "bad." Bad accounts were defined as those placed for collection with an outside agency or written off in the company's books. Based on their availability and popularity, the eventual list of predictor variables was narrowed down and modeled using a stepwise regression procedure.

From the results of his model, Ewert (1977) presented the following cumulative frequency distribution of good and bad accounts for the 200 firms in his holdout sample[1]:

| Credit Score from Scoring Model | Cumulative Frequencies | |
|---|---|---|
| | **"Goods" (%)** | **"Bads" (%)** |
| −0.200 | 0 | 0 |
| 0.208 | 0 | 35 |
| 0.226 | 2 | 36 |
| 0.245 | 3 | 40 |
| 0.356 | 6 | 58 |
| 0.543 | 16 | 76 |
| 0.577 | 17 | 82 |
| 0.596 | 20 | 85 |
| 0.699 | 34 | 97 |
| 0.763 | 49 | 99 |
| 0.898 | 75 | 100 |
| 1.200 | 100 | 100 |

From this presentation of the results, we could develop a decision rule. For example, to make a credit decision based on Ewert's model, the rule might be to extend trade credit if the score for an applicant is equal to or greater than 0.577. This cutoff point will result in approximately 18% of good and 18% of bad accounts being misclassified. From observing these percentages and the costs of each misclassification, management can make a more concrete, objective decision on the desired risk level.

[1]The holdout sample refers to the sample having not been used to estimate the empirical results.

### 19.4.4 *Outside sources of credit information*

In addition to internal methods of evaluating credit worthiness, a number of outside sources can provide valuable information. Probably the most important piece of information an outside source could offer is whether potential customers have paid their debts promptly in the past.

For a new customer, checking with a credit agency will probably be the easiest and most efficient way for the seller to evaluate credit-worthiness. The largest and most well-known of these agencies is Dun and Bradstreet: its regular reference book provides credit ratings on nearly 3 million domestic and foreign firms. Figure 19.2 shows the key for interpreting these ratings. As an additional service, Dun and Bradstreet provides a full credit report on a potential customer.

The Credit Interchange Service of the National Association of Credit Management provides a clearinghouse for the collection and dissemination of information relating to the customer experience of other firms. Of course, one could simply contact these firms directly to get this information.

Another source of credit information is the customer's bank. Usually, the seller's bank makes a credit check through the customer's bank to obtain information on the applicant's average bank balance, access to bank credit, and general reputation.

If the customer is a public company with outstanding securities on the secondary markets, the seller can check the financial community's opinion about the customer. Moody's or Standard and Poor's provide ratings for the customer's outstanding bonds. Moreover, comparing these bond prices with those of similar firms, along with an examination of recent movements in the customer's stock price, can offer additional clues to future financial performance.

## 19.5 Credit Decision and Collection Policies

So far, we have discussed how trade credit is defined for both seller and buyer, what costs should be considered and how they can be measured, and quantitative methods to facilitate the seller's decision whether to grant credit. Although the use of numerical credit-scoring methods can assist the manager in the credit-granting decision, additional facets to credit policy need to be determined.

## Key to Ratings

| ESTIMATED FINANCIAL STRENGTH | | | COMPOSITE CREDIT APPRAISAL | | | |
|---|---|---|---|---|---|---|
| | | | HIGH | GOOD | FAIR | LIMITED |
| 5A | $ 50,000,000 | and over | 1 | 2 | 3 | 4 |
| 4A | $ 10,000,000 to | 49,999,999 | 1 | 2 | 3 | 4 |
| 3A | 1,000,000 to | 9,999,999 | 1 | 2 | 3 | 4 |
| 2A | 750,000 to | 999,999 | 1 | 2 | 3 | 4 |
| 1A | 500,000 to | 749,999 | 1 | 2 | 3 | 4 |
| BA | 300,000 to | 499,999 | 1 | 2 | 3 | 4 |
| BB | 200,000 to | 299,999 | 1 | 2 | 3 | 4 |
| CB | 125,000 to | 199,999 | 1 | 2 | 3 | 4 |
| CC | 75,000 to | 124,999 | 1 | 2 | 3 | 4 |
| DC | 50,000 to | 74,999 | 1 | 2 | 3 | 4 |
| DD | 35,000 to | 49,999 | 1 | 2 | 3 | 4 |
| EE | 20,000 to | 34,999 | 1 | 2 | 3 | 4 |
| FF | 10,000 to | 19,999 | 1 | 2 | 3 | 4 |
| GG | 5,000 to | 9,999 | 1 | 2 | 3 | 4 |
| HH | Up to | 4,999 | 1 | 2 | 3 | 4 |

GENERAL CLASSIFICATION

| ESTIMATED FINANCIAL STRENGTH | | | COMPOSITE CREDIT APPRAISAL | | |
|---|---|---|---|---|---|
| | | | GOOD | FAIR | LIMITED |
| 1R | $ 125,000 | and over | 2 | 3 | 4 |
| 2R | $ 50,000 to | $ 124,999 | 2 | 3 | 4 |

**EXPLANATION**
When the designation "1R" or "2R" appears, followed by a 2,3 or 4, it is an indication that the Estimated Financial Strength, while not definitely classified, is presumed to be in the range of the ($) figures in the corresponding bracket, and while the Composite Credit Appraisal cannot be judged precisely, it is believed to fall in the general category indicated.

**ABSENCE OF RATING (--) THE BLANK SYMBOL**
A blank symbol——should not be interpreted as indicating that credit should be denied. It simply means that the information available to Dun & Bradstreet does not permit us to classify the company within our rating key and that further inquiry should be made before reaching a credit decision.

**KEY TO THE D&B PAYDEX (PAYMENT INDEX)**

| PAYDEX | PAYMENT |
|---|---|
| 100 | ANTICIPATE |
| 90 | DISCOUNT |
| 80 | PROMPT |
| 70 | SLOW TO 15 days |
| 50 | SLOW TO 30days |
| 40 | SLOW TO 60 days |
| 30 | SLOW TO 90 days |
| 20 | SLOW TO 120 days |
| UN/0 | UNAVAILABLE |

**EMPLOYEE RANGE DESIGNATIONS IN REPORTS ON NAMES NOT LISTED IN THE REFERENCE BOOK**
Certain businesses do not lend themselves to a Dun & Bradstreet rating and are not listed in the Reference Book. Information on these names, however, continues to be stored and updated on the D&B Business Information File. Reports are available on such businesses and instead of a rating they carry and Employee Range Designation (ER) which is indicative of size in terms of number of employees. No other signification should be attached.

**KEY TO EMPLOYEE RANGE DESIGNATIONS**

| | |
|---|---|
| ER1 | 1000 or more Employees |
| ER2 | 500 - 999 Employees |
| ER3 | 100 - 499 Employees |
| ER4 | 50 - 99 Employees |
| ER5 | 20 - 49 Employees |
| ER6 | 10 - 19 Employees |
| ER7 | 5 - 9 Employees |
| ER8 | 1 - 4 Employees |
| ERN | Not available |

**Dun & Bradstreet**
**Credit Services**

A company of The Dun & Bradstreet Corporation

1988

1 Diamond Hill Road
Murray Hill, N.J. 07974-0027

18B7 (8801)

Figure 19.2 Key to Dun and Bradstreet Ratings.
*Source*: Lee and Lee (2017), p. 1905.

1. If the credit request is acceptable, for what amount is it safe to grant credit?
2. Should the applicant be offered the incentive of a cash discount for early payments?
3. What collection measures are appropriate for a delinquent customer?

The initial credit-granting decision and these three additional credit policy decisions are all related and affect (1) sales level, (2) collection cost and bad-debt losses, and (3) the form of investment (inventories, accounts receivable, or cash).

The amount of credit to grant can be determined by a comparative evaluation of the new account and its related risk, to established accounts having a similar level of financial ability and willingness to pay. A more quantitative analysis can be accomplished by estimating the expected level and timing of cash flows from the new account and then determining the net present value of those cash flows. Primary considerations are the probability of delinquency or default, how this probability will increase, and its rate of increase as the amount of credit allowed is increased.

The actual credit terms, such as the length of the payment period and the size and availability of a cash discount, are generally determined by industry practices. Major deviations from these practices usually result in reprisals from competitors, low profit margins, or lost sales.

Another factor to consider when deciding whether and to what extent to grant credit is the possibility of repeat orders. In some instances, it might be profitable over the long run to take on a customer with an expected negative NPV of cash flows form the first order. Such would be the decision where the seller could estimate with a reasonable amount of certainty that the customer would eventually develop into a good, reliable account.

### 19.5.1 *Collection policy*

The actions a firm takes when an account becomes delinquent constitute its *collection policy.* A collection policy involves two dimensions to which the firm can allocate its collection efforts. The first dimension is time. When an account is not paid within the allowed credit period, it is considered delinquent. As the account becomes more delinquent, the firm intensifies its collection efforts. For example, an account in its first month of delinquency might be sent an impersonal, mild reminder. If this first notice doesn't produce results, a stronger reminder may be sent during the second month of delinquency, perhaps followed up by a phone call. If the delinquency continues, more forceful and harsh measurements may be pursued, such as turning the account over to a collection agency.

The second dimension of collection policy is about quality, which is inversely related to account risk. An account's quality risk is reflected in the probabilities of bad debt, expected future business, or both. Low risks of this nature would entail mild collection policies.

Although related, time and quality dimensions may not necessarily coincide. Marginal firms may pay early, while high-quality customers such as government agencies may be slow in their payment habits. Nevertheless, because both of these dimensions measure some aspect of risk in accounts receivable, both should be considered when formulating a collection policy.

Another important aspect regarding collection policy is that each successive step may only yield a partial degree of success. Thus, for a given category of accounts, sending the first letter may, on average, produce 50% payment on the outstanding balance. The implication is that a series of collection efforts will yield a series of partial payments. Consequently, various collection policies produce different timing of cash flows over several reporting periods. In this light, the evaluation of collection policies can be seen within the framework of a capital budgeting problem.

As discussed in earlier chapters, one of the more accepted criteria for selecting capital budgeting alternatives is the maximization of the net present value of cash flows (the NPV method). Applying this evaluation method to the collection policy decision, three related estimates must be made:

1. What relevant cash flows will arise and when?
2. How measurement or estimation will be carried out
3. What discount rate should be used?

The appropriate discount rate to use is the cost of capital, of which estimation methods were discussed in Chapter 10. Cash flow estimation techniques were explained in Chapter 6. Included among the relevant cash flows are collection receipts, collection costs, and bad-debt costs.

### 19.5.2 *Factoring and credit insurance*

*Factoring* and *credit insurance* are two other alternatives that can be considered in formulating the collection policy, particularly for the smaller firm. For the large firm, there are definite advantages in actively managing its accounts receivable. Divisions may be able to pool information on customer creditworthiness, and economies of scale may arise in the record-keeping, billing, and pursuit of delinquent accounts. But the smaller firm is perhaps disadvantaged in that it may not be able to hire or properly train someone for the specialized debt-collection function. However, the small firm (and large firms as well) can farm out a good portion of these duties to a third party called a *factor*.

Essentially, under the factoring process, the firm sells its trade credit to a factor. Initially, the factor and the client firm agree on credit limits and the average collection period for each customer, thereby allowing the factor to identify the risk involved. Next, the client firm notifies each customer that the factor has purchased the debt. From this point, the client firm sends the factor invoices from all sales, and, subsequently, the customer makes payment directly to the factor. The factor pays the selling firm on the basis of the agreed-on average collection period, regardless of whether the customer has paid. Of course, reducing the uncertainty of accounts receivable in this manner has its costs. Typically, the factor charges a fee of 1 to 2% of the value of the invoice.

An alternative route for achieving protection against bad debts and their associated costs is to obtain credit insurance. Generally, the credit-insurance company imposes a maximum amount that it will cover for accounts with a particular credit rating. In many cases, the seller can collect not only if the customer actually becomes insolvent, but also if an account is overdue.

## 19.6 Summary

The subject of Chapter 19 is the management of trade credit for both buyer and seller. For the buyer, the essential issue is to determine the cost of using trade credit as a form of financing, then compare this cost with the cost of alternative sources of capital. While some argue that accounts payable have no cost, we support the arguments against this view. That is, for the buyer, trade credit involves opportunity costs in the form of foregone discounts, implicit bankruptcy costs for taking on too much accounts payable, and costs associated with the timing of taxes and the accounting procedure used.

The grantor of trade credit, the seller, has a larger array of decisions to make. The first of these we discussed was determining the cost of granting trade credit. Next, we examined a numerical credit-scoring method via linear discriminant analysis to make the credit-granting decision more effective in terms of and related collection and bad-debt costs. Finally, we discussed the other aspects of the firm's credit policy, including the decision of how much credit to grant, on what terms, and the collection policy procedures to be pursued for delinquent accounts. We noted that the evaluation of various collection policies can be viewed and even carried out in the framework of a capital budgeting problem. Chapter 9 offers a number of methods to deal with the capital budgeting problem with uncertainty, including (1) the risk-adjusted discount rate method, (2) the certainty equivalent method, (3) the statistical distribution method, and (4) various simulation methods.

## References

Brick, I. F. and W. K. H. Fung. "The Effect of Taxes on The Trade-Credit Decision," *Financial Management* (Spring 1984, pp. 24–30).

Foster, G. *Financial Statement Analysis*, 2nd edn. (Pearson India, 2008).

Lee, C. F., Lee, J. C., and A. C. Lee. *Statistics for Business and Financial Economics*, 3rd edn. (Springer Academic Publishers, 2013).

Lee, C. -F. and Alice C. Lee. *Encyclopedia of Finance*, 2nd edn. (Springer, 2013).

Lee, C. F. and J. Lee. *Financial Analysis, Planning and Forecasting: Theory and Application*, 3rd edn. (World Scientific, 2017).

Mehta, D. R. *Working Capital Management* (Englewood Cliffs, New Jersey: Prentice-Hall, 1974).

Sagner, J. *Working Capital Management: Applications and Case Studies* (Wiley, 2014).

Sartoris, W. and N. Hill. "A Generalized Cash Flow Approach to Short-Term FinancialDecisions," *TheJournalofFinance*,38(May1983,pp. 349–60).
Van Horne, J. C. *Financial Management & Policy*, 12th edn. (Pearson Education India, 2002).

## Appendix 19A — Two Methods to Estimate the Discriminant Function

Although we discussed the linear discriminant function, Eq. (19.5), in Chapter 19, we did not show how to drive parameters $A$ and $B$. In this appendix, following Lee and Lee (2017), we demonstrate two methods to estimate the linear discriminant function: (1) the dummy regression method and (2) the eigenvalue method.

### 19A.1 Dummy Regression Method

First, let us restate Eq. (19.5):

$$Y_i = A_1X_{1i} + B_2X_{2i}$$

Then we restate this equation as

$$y_i = a_1x_{1i} + b_2x_{2i} \tag{19.1A}$$

where $y_i = Y_i - \bar{Y}_i$; $x_{1i} = X_{1i} - \bar{X}_{1i}$; and $x_{2i} = X_{2i} - \bar{X}_{2i}$.

Next, following Hamburg (1983), we can solve for $a_1$ and $b_2$:

$$\text{VAR}(x_{1i})a_1 + \text{COV}(x_{1i,}x_{2i})b_2 = \text{COV}(x_{1i}, y_i) \tag{19.2A}$$

$$\text{COV}(x_{1i}, x_{2i})a_1 + \text{VAR}(x_{2i})b_2 = \text{COV}(x_{2i}, y_i) \tag{19.3A}$$

Using the data listed Table 19.1A, $\text{VAR}(x_{1i})$, $\text{VAR}(x_{2i})$, $\text{COV}(x_{1i}, x_{2i})$, $\text{COV}(x_{1i}, y_i)$ and $\text{COV}(x_{2i}, y_i)$ are calculated as follows:

$$\begin{aligned}\text{VAR}(x_{1i}) &= \frac{\sum x_{1i}^2}{n} - \left(\frac{\sum X_{1i}}{n}\right)^2 = \frac{32 + 29.19}{n} \\ &\quad - \left(\frac{13.6 + 14.9}{n}\right)^2 = \frac{61.19}{14} - \left(\frac{28.5}{14}\right)^2 \\ &= 4.3707 - 4.144 = 0.2267\end{aligned}$$

$$\begin{aligned}\text{VAR}(x_{2i}) &= \frac{\sum x_{2i}^2}{n} - \left(\frac{\sum X_{2i}}{n}\right)^2 = \frac{2.8122}{14} - \left(\frac{6.2}{14}\right)^2 \\ &= 0.2008 - 0.196 = 0.0048\end{aligned}$$

Table 19.1A Roster of Liquidity and Leverage Ratios for Two Groups with Two Predictors and a "Dummy" Criterion Variable $y$.

| Group 1 | | | Group 2 | | |
|---|---|---|---|---|---|
| $X_{1i}$ | $X_{2i}$ | $Y_i$ | $x_{1i}$ | $x_{2i}$ | $y_i$ |
| 2.0 | 0.50 | 1 | 1.8 | 0.35 | 0 |
| 1.8 | 0.48 | 1 | 1.9 | 0.34 | 0 |
| 2.3 | 0.49 | 1 | 1.7 | 0.42 | 0 |
| 3.1 | 0.41 | 1 | 1.5 | 0.49 | 0 |
| 1.9 | 0.43 | 1 | 2.2 | 0.36 | 0 |
| 2.5 | 0.44 | 1 | 2.8 | 0.38 | 0 |
| | | | 1.6 | 0.55 | 0 |
| | | | 1.4 | 0.56 | 0 |

*Source*: Lee and Lee (2017). *Financial Analysis, Planning and Forecasting*, page 86.

$$\begin{aligned}\mathrm{COV}(x_{1i}, x_{2i}) &= \frac{\sum X_{1i}X_{2i}}{n} - (\bar{X}_{1i})(\bar{X}_{2i}) = \frac{12.424}{14} \\ &\quad - (2.0357)(0.4428) = 0.8874 - 0.9014 = -0.014 \\ \mathrm{COV}(x_{1i}, y_i) &= \frac{\sum X_{1i}Y_i}{n} - (\bar{X}_{1i})(\bar{Y}_i) = \frac{13.6}{14} - (2.0357)(0.4285) \\ &= 0.9714 - 0.8722 = 0.0992 \\ \mathrm{COV}(x_{2i}, y_i) &= \frac{\sum X_{2i}Y_i}{n} - (\bar{X}_{2i})(\bar{Y}_i) = \frac{2.75}{14} - (0.4428)(0.4285) \\ &= 0.1964 - 0.1897 = 0.00668\end{aligned}$$

Utilizing Cramer's rule, $a_1$ and $b_2$ can be estimated using a matrix, as follows:

$$a_1 = \frac{\begin{vmatrix} 0.0992 & -0.0140 \\ 0.0066 & 0.0048 \end{vmatrix}}{\begin{vmatrix} 0.2267 & -0.0140 \\ -0.0140 & 0.0048 \end{vmatrix}} = \frac{0.0047616 + 0.0000924}{0.0010886 - 0.000196}$$

$$= \frac{0.00056856}{0.0008926} = 0.63697$$

$$b_2 = \frac{\begin{vmatrix} 0.2267 & 0.0992 \\ -0.0140 & 0.0066 \end{vmatrix}}{\begin{vmatrix} 0.2267 & -0.0140 \\ -0.0140 & 0.0048 \end{vmatrix}} = \frac{0.00149 + 0.00138}{0.00108 - 0.00019} = \frac{0.00288}{0.00089} = 3.2359$$

## 19A.2 The Eigenvalue Method

In utilizing the eigenvalue method to estimate the linear discriminant function, we again start from Eq. (19.5). Following Lee and Lee (2017) Chapter 3, we set up a system of equations to solve for the $A$ and $B$ coefficients, which can be written as

$$S_{11}A + S_{12}B = D_1 \tag{19.4A}$$

$$S_{12}A + S_{22}B = D_2 \tag{19.5A}$$

Again, using Cramer's rule we obtain

$$A = \frac{S_{22}D_2 - S_{12}D_2}{S_{22}S_{11} - S_{12}^2} \tag{19.6A}$$

$$B = \frac{S_{11}D_1 - S_{12}D_1}{S_{22}S_{11} - S_{12}^2} \tag{19.7A}$$

where $S_{11}$ = variance of $X_1$; $S_{22}$ = variance of $X_2$; $S_{12}$ = covariance between $X_1$ and $X_2$; $S_{12}^2$ = the square of the covariance between $X_1$ and $X_2$; $D_1$ = the difference between the average of $X_1$'s for good accounts and the average of $X_1$'s for bad accounts; and $D_2$ = the difference between the average of $X_2$'s for good accounts and the average of $X_2$'s for bad accounts.

Using the previous calculations and those in Table 19.1A, we get the following:

$$A = \frac{(0.0048)(0.1116) - (-0.0014)(0.1116)}{(0.0048)(0.2267) - (-0.0014)^2} = 0.63697$$

$$B = \frac{(0.2267)(0.0154) - (-0.0014)(0.0154)}{(0.0048)(0.2267) - (-0.0014)^2} = 3.2359$$

which is the same solution we arrived at using the dummy regression method.

## Questions and Problems

1. Define or explain the following:
   a. Trade credit
   b. Aging of accounts receivable
   c. Credit analysis
   d. Factor score and factor loading
   e. Collection policy
   f. Factoring
   g. Type I and Type II classification errors
2. Explain the differences among the three formal types of trade-credit agreements.
3. What is the significance of an aging of accounts receivable schedule to the credit manager?
4. Calculate the annualized cost of not taking a discount if the terms are 2/10, net 30, and the purchase is for \$100. Repeat the calculation for terms of 2/20, net 30, and 2/20, net 60. Explain the relationship of the discount period and the credit period to that of the cost of not taking the discount.
5. From Problem 4, cite some possible implications on accounts receivable from the changes in the credit terms. State in terms of the size of the accounts receivable account and the timing of its cash flows.
6. Indicate the effect on sales, accounts receivable, and profits given the following changes on 2/10, net 30, credit terms:
   a. Credit manager changes credit policy to net 60
   b. Credit manager increases the discount to 5%
   c. Credit manager lengthens discount period to 20 days
7. Explain how the credit manager uses ratio analysis to assess a customer's credit risk.
8. What are the limitations of numerical credit scoring?
9. List the alternative sources of obtaining credit information.
10. Outline the interrelationship of trade credit to cash flow, cost of capital, sales growth, and debt capacity.
11. What is a discrimination function? Discuss two methods to estimate this function.
12. GTB Inc. has sales of \$2 million and a 50-day collection period and is considering loosening its credit standards, a change that is

expected to increase sales by \$1,000,000. However, the collection period is project to be 60 days, and added investigation expenses may be \$50,000. Bad-debt expenses would be around 5% of the additional sales. The firm's contribution margin is 12%, and the before-tax cost of capital is 15% (using a 360-day year).

a. What is the total marginal cost associated with a relaxation of the credit standard?
b. What is the marginal benefit of the policy change?
c. Should the change be implemented?

13. Calculate the annualized cost of not taking a discount on the purchase on the purchase of goods worth \$200 for each of the following terms of credit:

    a. 2/15, net 30
    b. 2/15, net 45
    c. 3/15, net 60
    d. 5/30, net 60

14. RAS, Inc. buys goods on the credit terms of 2/10, net 25. The firm presently does not use the facility of discount and, instead, pays after 25 days. A new policy has been suggested under which RAS would borrow equivalent money at 20% annual interest rate and use that loan to get the discount benefit. Is it a good proposal? Assume a 360-day year.
15. A company currently discounts 50% of its purchases based on the terms of 3/15, net 30; the balance (the other 50%) is paid in 30 days on the net date. The firm's credit manager has a proposal under consideration to stretch the payables and pay all purchases in 45 days. The expected purchases for next year are \$20 million. If the opportunity cost of investment is 15%, demonstrate why the company should or should not implement this policy. Assume a 360-day year.
16. RAJ Company's current annual sales are \$1.8 million and the average collection period is 30 days. If the company eases its credit terms, sales would increase to \$2.25 million and the average collection period would be 50 days. The variable costs are 80% of sales and the cost of capital is 20%. The bad debts under the new policy would be 4% of new sales. Assuming a 360-day year, calculate the following values and determine if RAJ's policy would be advantageous.

a. Additional investment in accounts receivable.
b. Extra costs associated with the new policy.
c. Incremental net profit contribution.

17. Now assume that the RAJ Company in the previous problem also incurs the following additional expenses:

    Cost of investigation = \$20,000.
    Increase in the average finished goods inventory = \$100,000 (which would be financed at an annual interest rate of 17%)

    a. Re-evaluate the decision to ease credit terms.
    b. Would the acceptability of the new policy be changed? Explain.

Chapter 20

# Cash, Marketable Securities, and Inventory Management

**Contents**



## 20.1 Introduction

Using the cash balance information from Chapter 18 and the information on credit management covered in Chapter 19, we can formulate a picture of the future level of cash balances. With this forecast of future cash balances, we now concern ourselves with determining the optimum level or range of cash balances and how to manage deviations.

Based on the firm's future cash needs, the financial manager can determine whether too much or too little cash is on hand at present. Surplus funds, if available, can be invested temporarily in short-term, high-quality securities or can be used for other corporate purpose such as dividends or inventory purchase. Conversely, a cash shortage will make it necessary for the firm to either sell current holdings of securities or borrow from the financial markets.

This process is called cash management and represents an important aspect of the firm's operations. Idle funds represent management inefficiency, as they add nothing to firm value. However, enough liquidity must be maintained for the firm to pay its bills and meet emergencies. Therefore, in examining the characteristics and processes of effective cash management,

Section 20.2 discusses the Baumol and Miller–Orr Models. Section 20.3 discusses various cash collection systems. Since there will most likely be times when the firm has short-term cash deficits, Section 20.4 discusses the uses and functioning of bank credit lines, along with a review of the determination of the costs of bank credit. Section 20.5 discusses courses of action that the financial manager can follow to effectively invest and manage surplus funds, and Section 20.6 discusses inventory management. Section 20.7 summarizes the chapter. Appendix 20A presents the derivation of optimal amount of cash holdings.

## 20.2 The Baumol and Miller–Orr Models

Like the firm's real inventories, cash is just another raw material that is needed to carry on the firm's operations. Moreover, the availability of cash determines to a significant extent the firm's liquidity position. All other assets have less liquidity than cash in the sense that their transformation into cash requires time, cost, or both. Marketable securities are considered less liquid than cash because, although they can usually be disposed of immediately, their conversion to cash requires transaction costs. The rate of return from this investment represents the opportunity cost of liquidity to the holder of cash.

Consequently, the problem of determining an optimal level for the cash balance can be considered a cost-minimization problem. That is, the financial manager's job in this area is to minimize the relative costs of having a cash surplus versus having a cash deficit. As a starting point for analyzing this problem, we turn to the application of Baumol's economic inventory ordering quantity (EOQ) model for cash management.

### 20.2.1 *Baumol's EOQ model*

The EOQ model strives to equate the two opposing marginal costs associated with ordering and holding inventory, thereby minimizing total costs. For our purposes, we can consider cash to be a manageable inventory for which we want to minimize the sum of the following costs:

1. Ordering or transactions costs from converting securities into cash and vice versa
2. Carrying or opportunity costs equal to the foregone rate of return that the holder of cash incurs

Figure 20.1 shows the relationships among transaction cost $(AB)$, opportunity cost $(CD)$, and total cost $(EF)$.

In applying the EOQ model to our optimal cash balance problem, we must be aware of the underlying assumptions about cash flows:

1. Cash outflows occur at a constant rate
2. Cash inflows occur periodically when securities are liquidated

These assumed cash flow patterns are shown in Figure 20.2.

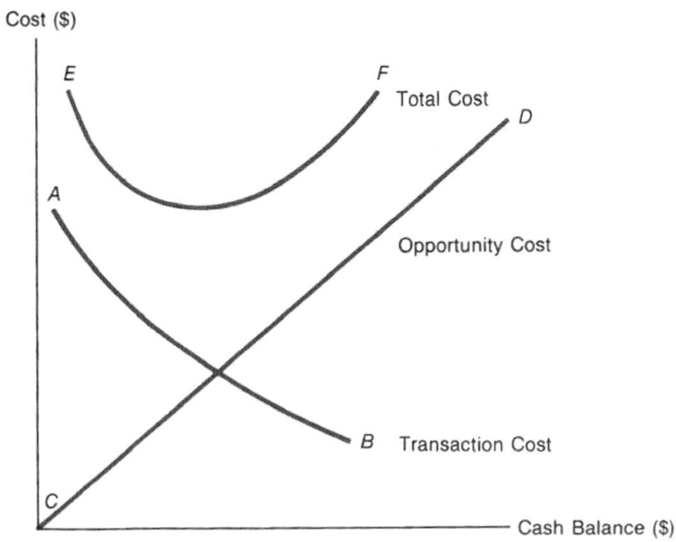


Figure 20.1 Determining the Optimal Cash Balance as a Cost-Minimization Problem.

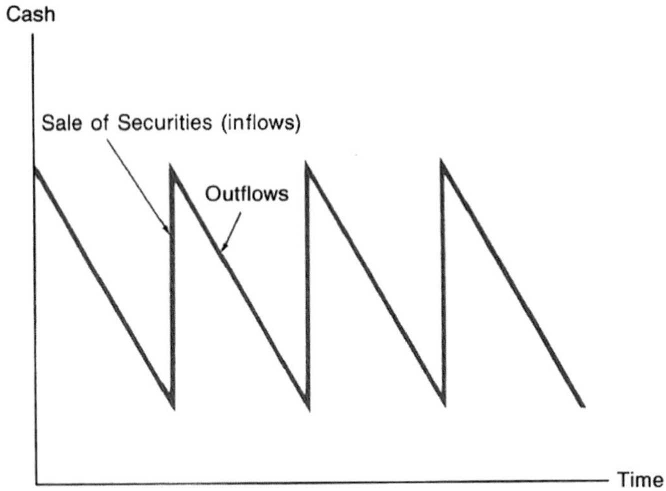


Figure 20.2 The Assumed Cash Flow Patterns Using Baumol's EOQ Model.

We now present the EOQ model, apply its mechanism to a sample problem, and interpret the result. The specific cash flow patterns we assume are (1) the firm uses cash at a steady, predictable rate, say \$1 million per week; (2) the firm's cash inflows from operations also occur at an even, forecastable rate, say \$700,000 per week, and (3) the firm's net cash outflows also occur at a similarly predictable rate of \$300,000 per week. Based on these assumptions, the EOQ model for determining the optimal cash balance, C*, can be stated as follows[1]:

$$\text{EOQ} = C^* = \sqrt{\frac{2FT}{k}} \tag{20.1}$$

where $C^*$ = optimal cash holdings to be transferred from marketable securities or borrowed; $C^*/2$ = optimal average cash balance; $F$ = fixed-transaction costs of making a securities trade or borrowing money; $T$ = total amount of net new cash needed for disbursements over the entire period (usually a year); and $k$ = the opportunity cost of holding cash (equal to the foregone rate of return on marketable securities or the cost of borrowing).

[1] Appendix 20A gives the derivation of Eq. (20.1).

EOQ is positively related to $F$ and $T$ and inversely related to $k$. By taking the square root of $FT/k$, the relationship with EOQ is less than proportionate. If the value of fixed-transactions costs ($F$) doubles, then EOQ will increase by only 1.41 times.

For example, we assume the following values: $F = \$120$; $T = 52$ weeks $\times$ \$300,000/week $=$ \$1,560,000; and $k = 12\% = 0.12$. With these values, we can calculate the value of $C^*$ as

$$C^* = \sqrt{\frac{2\,(\$120)\,(\$1{,}560{,}000)}{0.12}} = \$55{,}857$$

As the firm's cash balance approaches 0 (or some minimum acceptable level), \$55,857 worth of securities should be sold to replenish this account. The frequency with which this process should occur can be calculated as \$1,560,000/\$55,857 $= 27.9 \approx 28$ times during the year or, equivalently, $365/28 =$ every 13 days. Finally, the firm's average cash balance would be

$$\frac{C^*}{2} = \frac{\$55{,}857}{2} = \$27{,}928.50$$

While the EOQ model can be useful in that it offers some insight to the optimal cash balance determination problem, its restrictive assumptions about cash flow behavior are not particularly realistic. More likely, a firm's cash inflows will be interspersed with cash outflows and occasionally exceed the flow of outgoing payments. Thus, cash balances over a planning period will move both upward and downward at varying intervals, whereas the EOQ model implicitly assumes demand for cash (inflows) to be positive. Another problem with the EOQ framework is that the conventional model assumes production (inflows) is nonrandom and controllable while sales (outflows) are random and uncontrollable. In actuality, we can't characterize cash flows in this fashion, because control over inflows and outflows is seldom absolute.

### 20.2.2 *Miller–Orr model*

The Miller and Orr model for cash management improves on the EOQ methodology in significant ways. Miller and Orr start with the assumption that there are only two forms of assets: cash and marketable securities. Also, the Miller–Orr model allows for cash

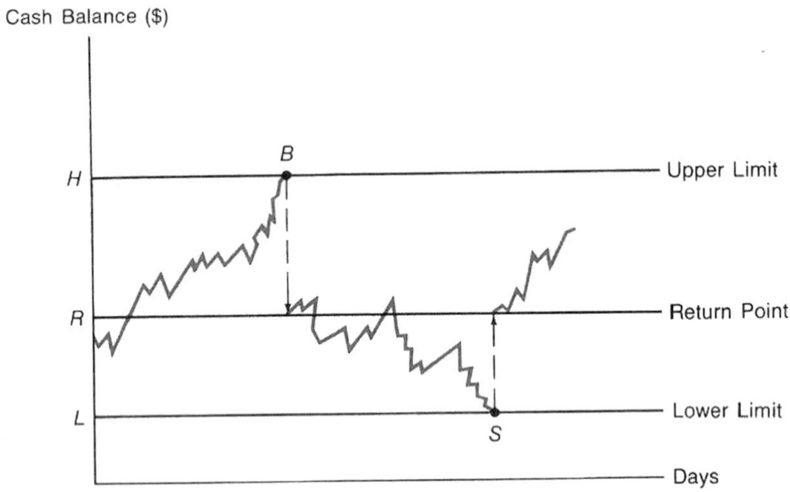


Figure 20.3 The Workings of the Miller–Orr Model.

balance movement in both positive and negative directions and for the optimal cash balance to be a range of values rather than a single point estimate. This model is even more useful for firms that are unable to predict day-to-day cash inflows and outflows.

Figure 20.3 shows the functioning of the Miller–Orr model. Notice in this figure that the cash balance is allowed to meander undisturbed as long as it remains within the predetermined boundary range shown by $H$ and $L$. However, at point $B$, the cash balance reaches the maximum allowable level. At this point, the firm could purchase marketable securities of an amount equal to the dashed line, which would lower the cash balance to the "return point" from which it is again allowed to fluctuate freely. At point $S$, the firm's cash balance reaches the minimum allowable level. At this point, the firm could sell marketable securities to investors or borrow to bring the cash level back up to the return point.

In how much of a range $(H - L)$ should the cash balance be allowed to fluctuate? According to the Miller–Orr model, the higher the day-to-day variability in cash flows and/or the higher the fixed transactions costs associated with buying and selling securities, the farther apart the control limits should be set. On the other hand, if the opportunity cost of holding cash (the foregone interest from marketable securities) is high, the limits should be set closer together. Management's objective is to minimize total costs associated with cash. By use of minimization procedures, the spread between the upper and lower cash limit ($S$), the return point ($R$), the upper limit ($H$), and average cash balance (ACB) are

$$S = 3\left[\frac{3F\sigma^2}{4k}\right]^{\frac{1}{3}} \tag{20.2}$$

$$R = \frac{S}{3} + L \tag{20.3}$$

$$H = S + L \tag{20.4}$$

$$\text{ACB} = \frac{4R - L}{3} \tag{20.5}$$

where $L$ = lower limit; $F$ = fixed-transactions cost; $k$ = opportunity cost on a daily basis; and $\sigma^2$ = variance of net daily cash flow.

The firm always returns to a point one-third of the spread between the lower and upper limits. With the return point set, the firm will likely bump up against its lower limit more frequently than its upper limit. While this lower point does not minimize the number of transactions and their resulting cost (as the middle point would), it is an optimum point in that it minimizes the sum of transactions costs and interest costs, the latter of which are incurred from holding excessive cash.

To use the Miller–Orr model, the financial manager needs to follow three steps:

1. Set the lower limit.
2. Estimate the variance of cash flows.
3. Determine relevant transactions and interest costs.

Setting the lower limit is essentially a subjective task. However, common sense and experience are helpful. Most likely, the lower limit will be some minimum safety margin above 0. An important consideration in setting this limit is any bank requirement that must be satisfied.

To estimate the variance of cash flows, one could record the net cash inflows and outflows for each of the preceding 100 days and then compute the variance of those 100 observations. This approach would require updating, particularly if net cash flows were unstable over time. One additional aspect to consider in this calculation is the impact of seasonal effects, which might also require adjustments to the variance estimate.

To determine the relevant transactions costs, the financial manager need only observe what the firm currently pays to buy or sell a security. Interest costs can be derived from current available market returns on short-term, high-grade securities. The financial manager may want to use a forecasted interest rate for the planning period if a significant change from current interest rate levels is expected.

We now demonstrate the actual calculations for the Miller–Orr model. First, assume the following:

Minimum cash balance = \$20,000
Variance of daily cash flows = \$9,000,000 (hence, the Standard deviation, $\sigma =$ \$3,000 per day)
Interest rate = 0.0329% per day
Transactions cost (average) for buying and selling one security = \$20.

Utilizing this data, we first compute the spread between the lower and upper limits:

$$\text{Spread} = 3\left(\frac{3 \times 20 \times 9{,}000{,}000}{4 \times 0.000329}\right)^{\frac{1}{3}} = \$22{,}293$$

Next, we compute the upper limit and return point:

$$\text{Upper limit} = \text{Lower limit} + \text{Spread} = \$20{,}000 + \$22{,}293 = \$42{,}293$$

$$\text{Return point} = 20{,}000 + \left(\frac{22{,}293}{3}\right) = \$27{,}431$$

$$\text{Average cash balance} = \frac{4\,(\$27{,}431) - \$20{,}000}{3} = \$29{,}908$$

Based on our assumed input values and model calculations, we can establish the following rule:

> If the cash balance rises to \$42,293, invest \$42,293 − \$27,431 = \$14,862 in marketable securities; if the cash balance falls to \$20,000, sell \$27,431 − \$20,000 = \$7,431 of marketable securities to restore the cash balance to the return point.

While the Miller–Orr model is an improvement on the EOQ model, we still must make an evaluation of its assumptions. Most important is the assumption that cash flows are random, which in many cases is not completely valid. Under certain circumstances and at particular times of the year, consecutive periods of cash flows may be dependent, the volatility of net cash flows may sharply increase, or a trend in cash balances may arise. The frequency and extent of these events will affect the Miller–Orr model's effectiveness. Actual tests using daily cash flow data for various firms indicate that the model did as well or better than the intuitive decisions of these firms' financial managers. However, other studies have shown that simple rules of thumb have performed just as well. Consequently, the Miller–Orr model can be considered more valuable because of the insight it offers concerning optimal cash balance determination rather than as an operating rule.

As a final observation, let us compare the results from the Baumol and Miller–Orr models. The Baumol EOQ model suggests that for each five-day period, 3 × \$72,111 worth of securities should be sold to cover cash needs. The average cash balance was determined to be \$36,056. The Miller–Orr model suggests the return point should be \$27,431. However, the number of transactions depends on how often the cash balance reaches the boundaries of the allowed spread (\$20,000 and \$42,293). Thus, using the Miller–Orr results, we would maintain a lower average cash balance, thus freeing up more funds to be invested. Also, allowing the balance to float within the prescribed spread should result in a smaller total number of transactions — buying or selling securities — thereby decreasing this cost relative to the EOQ's results.

## 20.3 Cash Management Systems

Another aspect to cash management involves the efficiency with which money owed to the company is collected. The sooner the company can collect its money, the sooner the money can be put to work, thereby enhancing firm value. There are a number of systems to improve the cash collection process. However, before discussing these systems, we must consider the float concept.

**Float.**

In banking terms, *float* is defined as cash items that are in the process of collection. Another way to think of float is the difference between the balance shown in a firm's (or an individual's) checkbook and the balance on the bank's books. For instance, suppose that, on average, a firm writes $10,000 worth of checks each day. If it takes five days for these checks to clear and be deducted from the firm's bank account, then the firm's checking records will show a balance $50,000 less than the bank's records. Conversely, if the firm, on average, receives $10,000 worth of checks each day, but it takes only three days for these checks to be deposited and cleared, the firm's books will show a balance of $30,000 above the balance on the bank's records. The difference between the $50,000 positive float and the $30,000 negative float, −$20,000, is called the firm's *net float.* It is conceivable that a firm could consistently have a negative cash balance on its books, as long as it can accurately forecast its positive and negative clearings.

Float management can be seen as an integral component of the cash management system. To understand how float can be analyzed and forecasted, we need to look at the five different types of float:

1. *Invoicing float* is the time it takes for a firm to bill receivables. The company's internal accounting and the efficiency of its billing procedures both affect this type of float.
2. *Mail float* is the time the firm's bill spends in the mail once it is sent to the customer and the time the customer's check spends in the mail coming back to the firm.
3. *Processing float* is the time between receipt of payment by the billing firm and deposit of the check for collection.
4. *Collection float* is the time from when the check is deposited to when the funds are made available in the firm's checking account.
5. *Disbursing float* is the time between when a check is written on available bank account funds and the check actually clears with the corresponding dollar amount deducted from the firm's bank balance.

The first four floats hinder the firm's ability to turn collection items into cash and therefore are negative floats, while the disbursing float is positive float because it reduces cash needs. The benefits of reducing float by one day or from increasing the firm's net float are particularly significant when interest rates are high. Suppose a company with annual credit sales of \$250 million can make \$684,932 available by reducing negative float by one day, (\$250,000,000/365). If the firm's borrowing cost is 15%, then \$102,740 in interest costs (before taxes) per year could be saved by the float reduction.

As discussed below, mail float is generally hard to control, but it can be controlled to some degree through the use of *lock boxes.* Processing and invoicing float can be monitored and fine-tuned for efficiency. Collection and disbursement float can be enhanced for the firm's benefit by implementing cash collection and disbursement services provided primarily by the banking system; this is an area of discussion to which we now turn.

### 20.3.1 *Cash collection and transference systems*

One way to speed up the collection of payments from customers is through *concentration banking.* Using this collection system, customers in a particular location make payment to a local branch office rather than to company headquarters. The branch office then deposits the checks into a local bank account. Surplus funds are transferred at some periodic interval to one of the firm's principal banks, called *concentration banks.*

The advantage of this system is that it reduces both mailing and collection float. However, concentration banking involves some additional costs, such as higher administrative costs, compensation to the local bank for its services, and the cost associated with transferring the funds from the local bank to the concentration bank. (Methods of cash transference are examined in a later section.)

A related cash collection technique is the combining of concentration banking with a *lock-box* system. The primary distinguishing feature of a lock-box system is that the firm pays the local bank to take on the administrative chores. Instead of customers mailing their payments to one of the company's mailing addresses, all payments are sent directly to a post office box. One or more times a day, a bank will collect checks from the box and deposit them for collection. Among the advantages of a lock-box arrangement is the potential reduction in mail float, and, significantly, processing float. More sophisticated advanced arrangements between banks and firms involve having the

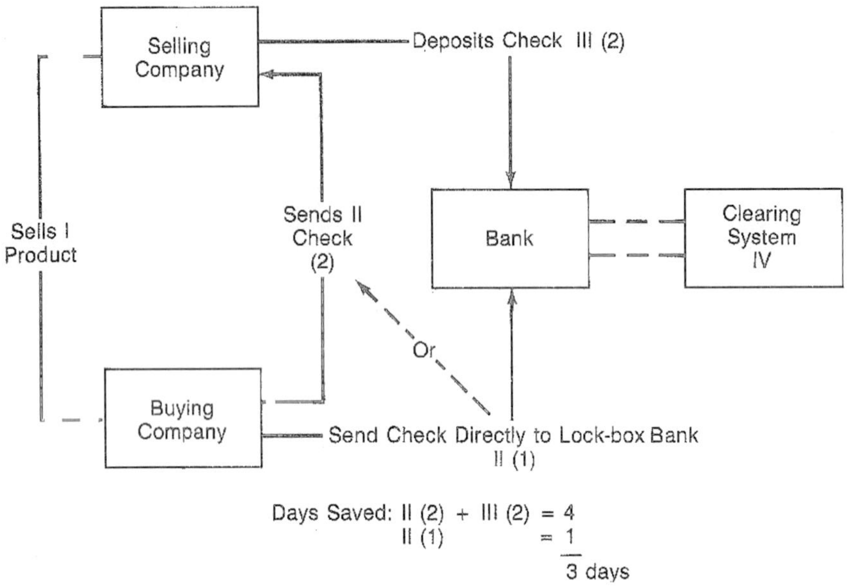


Figure 20.4 Flow Diagram of a Lock-Box System.

banks capture daily invoice data on magnetic tape and forward this data to the company's central office, thereby reducing the burden on the firm's accounts receivable staff. Figure 20.4 displays a flow diagram of the lock-box system. Numbers in parenthesis represent days of float lost to the selling company. As the figure shows, the lock-box system could save three days of float.

Another type of cash collection arrangement, which is perhaps more useful to firms such as insurance, finance, leasing, and mortgage companies, is a *preauthorized check* (PAC). The PAC is a commercial instrument that is used to transfer funds between demand deposit accounts. Through such a preauthorized indemnification agreement, the collecting firm is authorized to draw a check at specific intervals and in specified amounts on the customer's demand deposit account. In terms of float reduction, the PAC reduces both mail and collection float and ensures that the company gets its money by a specified date.

### 20.3.2 *Cash transference mechanism and scheduling*

Once the company has a cash collection system in place, it must decide how to transfer monies from the selected decentralized points as well as when to simultaneously minimize costs and maximize liquidity. There are three mechanisms for transferring money between accounts at two different banks: wire transfers, depository transfer checks, and electronic transfers.

*Wire transfers* involve an electronic bank-to-bank transfer of funds. Large cash balances can be transferred within an hour and made available to the firm immediately. While wire transfer is the fastest method available to move funds, it is also the costliest.

A *depository transfer check* (DTC) is an ordinary check restricted "for deposit only" at a designated bank. Hence, the designated collection bank completes a DTC for the daily deposits into the firm's checking account and then submits the DTC to the collection system. Although the DTC is less expensive than a wire transfer, it is also slower.

An *electronic transfer*, or automated DTC, is essentially the DTC mechanism in high-tech form. To reduce the time involved, an electronic check image is processed through automated clearinghouses rather than through a wire network. An electronic transfer is cheaper than a DTC and usually has a one-business-day clearing time.

Although probably more than 80% of the 1,200 largest industrial firms make a daily transfer of each day's reported deposits, the scheduling of when to transfer funds can be a problem. In fact, a growing number of progressive companies are realizing considerable cost savings by adopting various rules of thumb by which to manage the scheduling of cash transfers. We now discuss several of these methods: managing about a target balance, anticipation, dual balance, and weekend timing.

*Managing about a target balance* is illustrated in Figures 20.5 and 20.6. Figure 20.5 depicts daily cash transfers that leave a $20,000 target closing balance. Figure 20.6 illustrates the technique of managing about the $20,000 target balance. Initially, the account balance starts at 0 and then builds above the target up to the point where the average closing balance is $20,000 over the transfer period. However, while both schedules yield the same average balance, the schedule in Figure 20.6 involves only one-fifth the transfers.

This example has been simplified by ignoring transfer-time delays and weekends (when banks are closed and hence transactions do not occur) and assuming a uniform deposit schedule. However, it does suggest the potential for significant cost savings. Moreover,

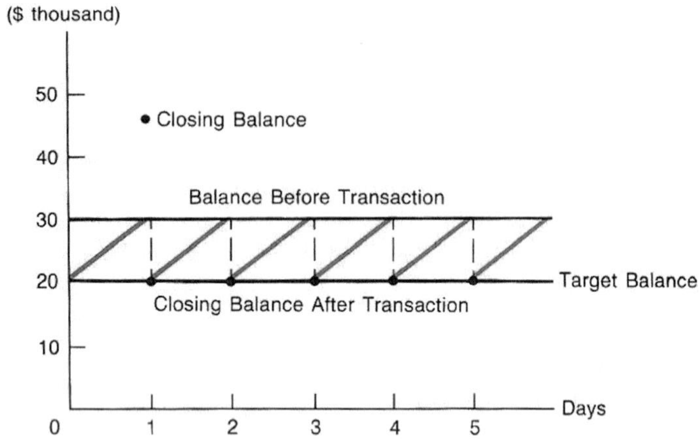


Figure 20.5 Daily Transfer of Each Day's Deposits.
*Source*: Lee and Lee (2017). *Financial Analysis, Planning and Forecasting*, page 1020.

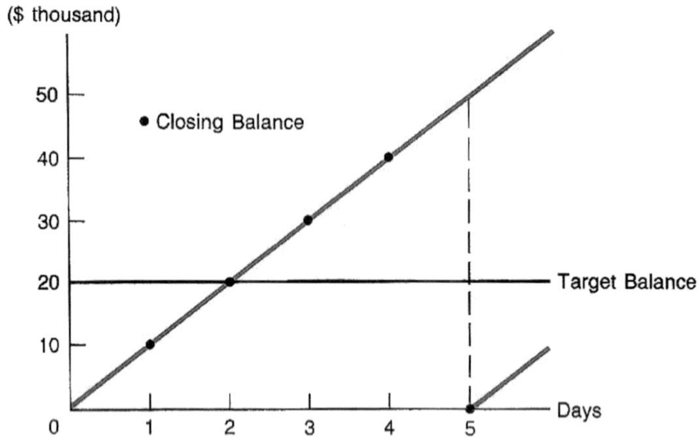


Figure 20.6 Managing About the Target Balance.
*Source*: Lee and Lee (2017). *Financial Analysis, Planning and Forecasting*, page 1021.

in addition to reducing transfers, managing about the target balance allows the firm to withdraw its initial investment in the target balance (which is replenished by the deposit flow). Thus, managing about a target means more cash sooner.

*Anticipation* is a system whereby a cash transfer is initiated before formal notice of a balance addition is received from the depository bank. The benefit of this scheduling technique is that it can eliminate delays arising from communication, processing, and/or clearing. Consequently, it can reduce or eliminate excess balances, accelerating transfers by one to three day's deposits.

To illustrate more precisely how anticipation works, we will employ an example of the *adjusted field target* technique, the most common use of anticipation. Assume that your firm wants to maintain an average field balance of $10,000. However, from communication, processing, and clearing delays, an average of $8,000 of deposits is left in the process of being transferred. Hence, the actual average balance is $18,000. To achieve the $10,000 target balance, the cash manager makes a one-time transfer of $8,000 from the field bank and goes with an adjusted field target, or *effective field target*, of $2,000. Yet, because of the $8,000 average transfer-in-process, the actual average balance is the desired $10,000 target level.

The viability and effectiveness of this technique will be limited by the variability of deposits and the cash manager's ability to accurately forecast derivations in the assumed pattern and level of deposits.

A *dual balance* effect can arise when the DTC availability time granted at the concentration bank is less than the clearing time back to the depository bank. To understand how dual balances can come about and benefit a firm, assume that a $20,000 DTC is initiated on Wednesday with one-business-day availability but two-business-day clearing. Thus, on Thursday your company receives an increase of $20,000 in its account at the concentration bank. However, the funds are not removed from your firm's depository bank until Friday. Consequently, on Thursday your company has a "dual balance" in the sense that the same funds are available cash balances in both banks.

The benefit of a dual balance can be accentuated by *weekend timing*. That is, by initiating the transfer on Thursday, the DTC would not clear until Monday, thereby making the dual balance available for an additional two days.

Each of these four scheduling techniques — managing about a target, anticipation, dual balances, and weekend timing — focuses on a different aspect of the scheduling costs arising from cash transfers.

However, trying to reap the benefits from a combination of all four systems is very complex, particularly when dozens or hundreds of depository banks are involved. Any optimal scheduling mechanism should incorporate sophisticated versions of each scheduling technique and appropriately reflect trade-offs between direct transfer costs, excess balances, and any dual balances. To handle such a task, Stone and Hill (1980) have formulated this problem in a linear programming model. Field tests of their model show it to be an effective means for achieving additional cost reduction in the scheduling of cash transfers.

Chang (2018) has studied international cash conversion cycle and corporate performance. He observed a negative relationship between the cash conversion cycle (CCC) and firm's profitability and value, supporting that an aggressive working capital policy can enhance corporate performance; however, he found that this effect reduces or reverses when firms exist at the lower CCC level. In his study, he took into account the factors of changes in macroeconomic environments, economic development status, financial crises, corporate governance, and financial constraints.

## 20.4 Credit Lines and Bank Relations

In the previous section, we examined methods by which firms can improve the efficiency of their cash collection systems. Despite such efforts, seasonal effects or other unpredictable events might cause the firm to occasionally need short-term funds to maintain day-to-day operations. Thus, arises the need for, and importance of, establishing good bank relations along with a credit line to fill in for sudden or seasonal "cash gaps." This section examines various aspects of the credit line from both the borrower's and lender's points of view, within the general framework of bank relations.

### 20.4.1 *Credit lines*

The most common type of short-term loan by banks to firms is the working capital credit line, which is extended to financially strong borrowers. The purpose of this credit line is to help firms cover cash gaps in their working capital requirements that are caused by seasonal swings or some unexpected event. Through the credit line commitment, a bank specifies its intention to honor borrowings up to the amount of the established credit line. This amount is determined on the basis of the firm's *pro forma* peak funding requirement and assures the firm of the availability of funds to finance disparities in working capital as sales expand and contract.

The cost of using or having available a line of credit usually has two components. First, loan interest is charged on only the amount actually borrowed, and the loan may be repaid as reflows of cash occur to the firm. Typically, because the loan is short term, the interest rate is fixed in the line-of-credit agreement. However, because the usual agreement requires that the firm be out of debt to the bank for some period during the year, the bank can renegotiate the terms of the agreement should interest rates change significantly. Part of this requirement is precautionary to ensure the firm's financial viability, because credit lines are often unsecured.

The second cost associated with the availability of a credit line arises when the firm is required to hold compensating balances with the bank. Compensating balances usually take the form of demand deposits or low-interest time deposits and must average an agreed-on percentage of the loan amount. From one point of view, compensating balances essentially increase the effective cost of money borrowed through a line of credit. Let us use an example.

Suppose that your firm sets up a line of credit with ABC Bank for \$1 million, available at an interest rate of 14%. However, as part of the loan agreement, ABC Bank requires your firm to maintain compensating balances in the form of demand deposits equal to 20% of the loan. This is equal to \$200,000 that your firm essentially cannot use. That is, if your company borrowed all \$800,000 for the entire year, it would incur an interest cost of \$112,000. However, there is the additional opportunity cost from having \$200,000 sit idle in the bank vault. Assuming that this money could have been put to work to earn at least the bank's interest rate of 14%, this compensating balance essentially costs the firm an additional \$28,000. Therefore, the incremental cost from the compensating balances can be calculated as follows:

$$\frac{\$112{,}000}{\$800{,}000} = 14\% \qquad \frac{0.14 \times \$200{,}000}{\$800{,}000} = 3.5\%$$

Therefore:

$$\frac{\$112{,}000 + \$28{,}000}{\$800{,}000} = 17.5\%$$

If the firm borrows the extent of the credit line for the entire year, the additional cost of the compensating balances is 3.5%. Therefore, the firm's effective interest expense is 17.5%, not 14%.

In general, we can state the following:

$$\text{Effective interest cost} = \frac{\text{Interest expense} + \text{Implicit interest expense}}{\text{Line of credit limit} - \text{Compensating balances}} \tag{20.6}$$

However, compensating balances have other uses. In particular, firms often use compensating balances to pay the bank for such services as operating lock boxes, processing the firm's checks without charge, and providing price advice on various business matters.

Before leaving our discussion of credit lines, we should mention the impact of credit lines from the bank's perspective. In general, establishing credit lines for financially sound firms is a profitable investment for the bank. In terms of current interest earned and the heightened potential for additional business from the firm in the future, the bank can view their credit lines as sound assets. However, the bank also faces a number of concerns.

In particular, an overextension of assets in the form of credit lines can bring peril to the bank's liquidity position. The nature of a credit line is short term, yet the source of funds for this investment is typically a liability with a longer maturity. This disparity in maturities between assets and liabilities is referred to as a *maturity gap*. Thus, should there be a higher-than-forecasted demand on the total available lines of credit, or if enough firms become unable to pay back their credit line to the bank, the bank will find itself in a liquidity crunch.

Another concern for the bank is to analyze how the firm plans to use the credit line. For instance, the banker might think twice about extending a credit line to a firm that plans to use the funds to attempt a leveraged buyout. Such considerations affect the terms of the credit line agreement and consequently the bank's financial health.

### 20.4.2 *Bank relations*

Large corporations that are financially sound are not necessarily so dependent on a strong bank relationship. When in need of short-term funds, these corporations can often go directly to the market and issue commercial paper at a lower interest cost. However, for smaller firms or those less financially adept, a good relationship with the bank is an important component in the cash management plan. The importance of these relations, as we have just discussed, can take the form of a credit line. Thus, the future availability of funds can be made less uncertain by establishing and maintaining good bank relations. This nurturing process can take place through such actions as maintaining compensating balances and repaying credit lines on time every year.

## 20.5 Marketable Securities Management

So far in this chapter, we have focused on determining an optimal cash balance, making cash collection more efficient, and using bank credit lines. This section looks at short-term excess cash balances and how they can be used to maximize firm value yet not endanger liquidity. We will examine criteria for investment of excess cash balances, types of marketable securities, and strategies and hedging considerations.

### 20.5.1 *Investment criteria for surplus cash balances*

When deciding on a financial instrument in which to invest short-term excess cash balances, the cash manager must realize that these funds may be needed in the near future for the firm's operations. Therefore, we suggest the following four criteria by which to evaluate investments for short-term surpluses: (1) certainty of principal, (2) maturity, (3) liquidity, and (4) yield.

First and foremost, the firm must consider the level of risk it can afford when investing surplus cash. Because these funds most likely will be needed relatively soon, the financial instrument should be high grade, short term, and liquid. In determining the value of this investment, we focus on two types of risk: default risk and interest rate risk.

*Default risk* is the possibility that the company that issues the debt will be unable to make interest payments or to repay the principal amount on schedule. For U.S. Treasury securities, default risk is considered negligible, while for some corporate issues of commercial paper it can be significant. Various rating services such as Standard and Poor's and Moody's rate bonds, commercial paper, and other debt instruments for degree of quality in terms of default risk.

*Interest rate risk* is the variation in the debt security's price arising from changes in interest rates. The degree of this risk depends on the stability of the instrument. Long-term bonds are more sensitive to shifts in interest rates than are the prices of short-term securities. To understand more clearly how interest rates can affect bond prices, recall our valuation formula from Chapter 5:

$$\text{Bond price} = \sum_{t=1}^{n} \frac{\text{Fixed interest payment}}{(1+i)^t} + \frac{\text{Principal}}{(1+i)^n}$$

As the market interest rate ($i$) increases, the present discounted value of the sum of all future interest payments and principal decreases. Moreover, the longer the remaining time before maturity, the more severely the higher $i$ will affect the bond's price by discounting future flows at a higher rate. Thus, there is a good reason for the cash manager to avoid default and interest rate risks by choosing short-term-maturity instruments.

Typically, the longer a security's term to maturity, the higher the interest rate the security will pay, for the reasons mentioned above. That is, longer-term bonds have a higher propensity for default and interest rate risks. However, because of supply and demand conditions, economic conditions, and inflation concerns, the term structure of interest rates does not always conform to the pattern. Nevertheless, the cash manager cannot afford to take on high levels of default or interest rate risk and therefore should primarily consider short-term debt instruments for investments.

Another reason for using primarily short-maturity investments is that the firm can usually sell the instrument quickly at a price close to its market value, a quality you will recognize as liquidity. Treasury bills are highly liquid — they have a broad market with many participants, low commission costs, and a price determined primarily by market interest rates. Somewhat less-liquid investments include bank-negotiable certificates of deposit and commercial paper.

An example of an illiquid investment is real estate, which typically has a thin market, high transactions costs, and prices determined to a great extent by the relative bargaining position of buyer and seller.

Finally, in maximizing the use of surplus cash, the cash manager should consider the various yields available on different marketable securities relative to the other criteria already mentioned. Since safety of principal is the primary criterion for investment of excess cash, yield should be considered only after the other criteria have been met.

### 20.5.2 *Types of marketable securities*

In classifying financial instruments as marketable securities, the distinction typically is based on maturity and, to a lesser extent, on liquidity. Investment instruments with a maturity of one year or less and that are traded to some extent in the secondary markets are called *money-market securities.* Conversely, the market for securities with more than one year to maturity, such as stocks, bonds, and mortgage bonds, is called the *capital market.*

*U.S. Treasury bills* (T-bills) are the most widely traded and, consequently, the most important money-market instrument. New issues of T-bills are auctioned off by the Federal Reserve every Monday, with maturities of 91 or 192 days. Once a month, T-bills with 365-day maturities are offered as well. Denominations range from $10,000 to $100,000 per bill. Further, all obligation for repayment rests with the U.S. government.

Although T-bills are usually the lowest yielding of all marketable securities, they are also the most riskless in terms of liquidity and default. Moreover, the weekly issuance of T-bills, along with their large outstanding quantities, enables the cash manager to choose a highly precise maturity. The price of a T-bill is determined on a discount basis; that is, its price is the face value, say $10,000, less the total value of the interest payments to be received, say $500. Thus, this T-bill would be sold by the Federal Reserve for $9,500, and its yield can be computed by applying the following equation:

$$\begin{aligned}\text{Annual yield} &= \frac{\$10{,}000 - \text{Price}}{\text{Price}} \times \frac{365\,\text{days}}{\text{Days to maturity}}\\ &= \frac{\$10{,}000 - 9{,}500}{9{,}500} \times \frac{365}{182} = 0.1055 \qquad (20.7)\end{aligned}$$

*Repurchase agreements* (repos) are not actual securities in themselves, but rather contracts to acquire immediately available funds through the sale of securities together with a simultaneous agreement to repurchase those securities at a later date. Repos are most commonly made for one business day and nearly always involve a Treasury or other government agency security.

For example, suppose your company has $1 million in excess cash available for two days. Instead of buying T-bills and then selling them two days later, your company could create a repurchase agreement with the bank, in which your company would agree to "purchase" $1 million worth of T-bills and then "sell" them back to the bank after two days for the original $1 million plus two days of interest. No actual transfer of physical securities is made; rather, the entire transaction consists of bookkeeping entries on the two parties' accounts.

There are two distinct advantages to using repos for short-term surplus cash. First, maturity can be tailored to the exact period of fund availability, from overnight to 30 days or more. Second, because the selling price of the securities is predetermined by agreement between buyer and seller, interest rate risk can be avoided. The yield on repos is similar but slightly lower than that of T-bills.

*Negotiable certificates of deposit* (CDs) are financial instruments offered by banks to customers to deposit funds for a fixed period at a fixed and prespecified rate of interest. CDs are issued in denominations of $100,000 or more, with maturities ranging from 1 to 18 months.

Yields on CDs are higher than yields of T-bills for two reasons. First, CDs are substantially less liquid than T-bills (that is, their secondary market is very thin). Second, CDs have higher default risk because they represent unsecured debt obligations of the issuing bank. However, the spread between CD and T-bill yields will vary depending on economic conditions, supply and demand forces, and investor attitudes.

*Commercial paper* is defined as the unsecured short-term promissory notes sold by large, financially sound companies. Maturities typically range from 30 to 270 days. While commercial paper is usually sold as bearer securities at a discount (like T-bills), some corporations sell paper that repays the principal plus interest at maturity.

Because of its unsecured nature and heterogeneity, commercial paper is traded infrequently on the secondary markets and hence is somewhat illiquid. However, because only the firms with the highest credit ratings are able to generate enough demand for their paper, yields on commercial paper are similar and sometimes even lower than yields on CDs.

*Banker's acceptances* are time drafts drawn on and accepted by a bank, usually to secure arrangements between unfamiliar firms. Although we discussed banker's acceptances earlier, we mention them again here because they can also be used for a firm's short-term surplus balances. After generating a banker's acceptance, a bank will typically sell it to an investor at a discount. Maturities range from 30 to 180 days, while denominations vary from \$25,000 to over \$1 million, depending on the specific transaction the banker's acceptance was originally created to finance. Again, banker's acceptances are relatively illiquid compared to T-bills and carry yields usually higher than on CDs because of their more heterogeneous characteristics.

Developed in 1973, *money-market mutual funds* offer another type of investment, yet today investment in these funds ranges around \$200 billion. By pooling investor dollars to buy money-market securities, these funds offer the small investor or firm access to higher market yields at low transaction costs with a large degree of liquidity. Most funds invest only in high-grade marketable securities.

### 20.5.3 *Hedging considerations*

In the 1970s and early 1980s, the volatility of market interest rates increased enormously because of increased uncertainty in the financial markets, which requires a higher real return on investment. Nevertheless, under these conditions, the cash manager encounters risks that are substantial in terms of interest rate changes and their resulting impact on portfolio value. How can such risks be addressed?

One aspect of this issue involves the concept of hedging (which will be discussed in Chapters 22 and 23). Hedging the current marketable securities portfolio or even some future investment implies that the cash manager is content with current market yields. Thus, hedging attempts to reduce the uncertainty of future conditions by locking-in current parameters (price, interest rate, yield, etc.) Different types of future hedge ratios can be found in Chen *et al.* (2003). Chapter 32 of Lee *et al.* (2016) has used the S&P 500 index future to show how alternative hedge ratio can be estimated in terms of different types of time series models.

There are various useful financial tools to aid the cash manager in the hedge decision. These include interest rate futures, interest rate options, and options on interest rate futures. Let us consider the application of these instruments to one type of hedge problem.

Suppose your firm holds $10 million in T-bills that it expects liquidate in 60 days on December 17. According to the forecasts of economists and the firm's cash manager, market interest rates are expected to jump by as much as 1.5% within the next two months. This large increase in interest rates will decrease the market value of the firm's T-bills, thus yielding less cash than originally anticipated. With such a variety of hedging instruments, a number of strategies could be employed. In this case, we use options on T-bill futures.

An option on a futures contract is nearly identical to an option on common stock. The obvious difference is that the underlying asset is a futures contract. By exercising a futures option, the holder enters into a long or short futures position, depending on whether the option is a call or put, respectively. Thus, the futures contract is an agreement to buy or sell the commodity at a prespecified price at some future designated time. However, in using a futures option, one need not necessarily worry about entering into a futures contract. Instead, the hedger earns an offsetting profit (or loss 0 on the value of the option alone.

For our example, the cash manager could buy the appropriate number of put options on the T-bill futures contract to protect the company against any depreciation in value of its marketable securities. The appropriate number of contracts is the hedge ratio between the option and its underlying asset (which will be discussed in Chapters 22 and 23). However, in this example we use puts, so the hedge ratio for a call option is not the same. Fortunately, there is a simple relationship:

$$\text{Put hedge ratio} = 1 - \text{Call hedge ratio} = 1 - N(d_1) \qquad (20.8)$$

where $N(d_1)$ is the cumulative normal density function of $d_1$. The $d_1$ is

$$\frac{\ln\left(\frac{P}{E}\right) + rt + \frac{\sigma^2 t}{2}}{\sigma\sqrt{t}}$$

where $P$ and $E$ represent T-bill futures price and strike price; $r$ and $t$ represent risk-free rate and time to maturity; and $\sigma$ is the variance of T-bill futures.

If the cash manager maintains this hedge ratio over time, devaluation of the firm's T-bill holdings, caused by an increase in interest rates, will be offset by the profit in the put options that were bought. On the other hand, if rates remain unchanged or trend downward, the cash manager can simply let the puts expire worthless. The sacrifice of purchase price is a small cost relative to the value and size of the insurance they offer.

## 20.6 Inventory Management

Inventories are used to link production and sales. A manufacturing firm must maintain a certain amount of inventory during production; that is, goods in process, such as raw materials, finished goods, and inventory in transit.

*Raw materials inventory* gives the firm flexibility in its purchasing. Without this inventory, the firm must exist on a hand-to-mouth basis, buying raw material strictly in keeping with its production schedule. Conversely, raw materials inventory may be bloated temporarily because the firm's purchasing department has taken advantage of quantity discounts. *Finished-goods inventory* allows the firm flexibility in production scheduling and marketing. *Inventory in transit* is inventory that is between various stages of production or storage. Management of inventory in transit permits efficient production scheduling and utilization of resources. Without this type of inventory, each stage of production would have to wait for the preceding stage to complete a unit. Resultant delays and idle time give the firm an incentive to maintain a large in-transit inventory.

Inventory management generally concerns (1) inventory loans and (2) inventory economic order quantity.

### 20.6.1 *Inventory loans*

Both accounts receivable and inventory can be used to secure short-term loans. Inventory loans come in three basic forms: blanket inventory liens, trust receipts, and field warehouse financing.

1. *Blanket inventory lien.* The firm's creditor is given a claim on all inventory held by the firm. The term *blanket* refers to the fact that all of the firm's inventory is "covered" by the lien. If the borrowing firm defaults on the loan, then the lender has the right to seize the collateral (inventory).
2. *Trust receipts.* The firm's creditor is given a claim on specific assets in that the ownership or title of the specific goods belongs to the lender until the loan is paid off. However, actual possession of the goods remains in the hands of the borrowing firm, which is able to use or sell the goods while conducting its normal business.
3. *Field warehouse financing.* In this case, the lender retains title or ownership of the inventory, as in the case of trust receipts, but a third party takes physical possession of the goods. This third party takes control of the inventory and only releases it to the borrower under certain prespecified conditions.

### 20.6.2 *Economic order quantity*

The economic order quantity for inventory is similar to the Baumol economic order quantity (EOQ) for cash. The EOQ for inventory is defined as:

$$Q^* = \sqrt{\frac{2SO}{C}} \tag{20.9}$$

where $C$ = carry cost per unit; $S$ = total usage units of an item of inventory; and $O$ = ordering cost per unit.[2]

Equation (20.9) is known as the economic, lot-size formula. To illustrate its use, suppose that for a specific inventory item, the firm orders 50,000 units during a 200-day period, ordering costs are

[2] $Q^*$ is obtained by differentiating the total inventory cost ($T$), defined as

$$T = \frac{CQ}{2} + \frac{SO}{Q}$$

where $C$, $S$, and $O$ are defined in Eq. (20.9), and $Q$ represents the number of units of inventory. The derivation procedure is the same as that used in Appendix 20A.

$200 per order, and carryings costs are $20 per unit per 200 days. The optimal economic order quantity is

$$Q^* = \sqrt{\frac{2\,(50{,}000)\,(200)}{20}} = 1{,}000 \text{ units}$$

For an order quantity of 50,000 units, the firm would order (50,000/1,000), or 50 times during the 200-day period, or every 4 days. Equation (20.9) implies that $Q^*$ varies directly with total usage ($S$) and order cost ($O$) and inversely with the carry cost ($C$). This analysis is similar to the analysis used for EOQ for cash, as discussed earlier in this chapter.

## 20.7 Summary

Chapter 20 has examined various aspects of cash and marketable security management. Two techniques were discussed that can assist in the estimation of an optimal level or range for the cash balance; these were Baumol's model and the Miller–Orr model.

To make the cash collection system more efficient, the firm can choose from various methods for collecting or transferring cash and deciding when to transfer it. Such cost minimization is ideal for linear programming applications.

The credit line offers the firm a means of handling cash variations caused by seasonal effects or unanticipated events. Establishing good bank relations is an important feature for any cash management system. However, bank services do take on a cost, typically in the form of compensating balances. While credit lines can be a good investment for a bank, they can have detrimental effects on the bank's liquidity that could intensify any maturity gap problems.

Efficient cash management ensure that surplus balances are invested in marketable securities that meet minimum standards for certainty of principal, maturity, liquidity, and yield. In Chapter 20, we considered the hedge decision from the cash manager's perspective and gave various example of hedging applications. Optimal inventory management was also briefly discussed.

## References


Chang, C. C. "Cash conversion cycle and corporate performance: Global evidence," *International Review of Finance and Economics*, 56 (2018, pp. 568–581).

Chen, S. S., C. F. Lee and K. Shrestha. "Future Hedge Ratios: A Review," *The Quarterly Review of Economics and Finance*, 43 (2003, pp. 433–465).

Gallinger, G. W. and P. B. Healey. *Liquidity Analysis and Management* (Reading, MA: Addison-Wesley, 1991).

Gitman, L. J., E. A. Moses and I. T. White. "An Assessment of Corporate Cash Management Practices," *Financial Management*, 8 (Spring 1979, pp. 32–41).

Lee, C. F. and A. C. Lee. *Encyclopedia of Finance*, 2nd edn. (Springer, 2013).

Lee, C. F. and J. Lee. *Financial Analysis, Planning and Forecasting: Theory and Application*, 3rd edn. (World Scientific, 2017).

Lee, C. F., J. C. Lee, J. C., J. R. Chang and T. Tai. *Essentials of Excel, Excel VBA, SAS and Minitab for Statistical and Financial Analyses* (Springer International Publishing, 2016).

Levin, R. I. and C. A. Kirkpatrick. *Quantitative Approaches to Management*, 7th edn. (New York: McGraw-Hill, 1989).

Mehta, D. R. *Working Capital Management* (Englewood Cliffs, New Jersey: Prentice-Hall, 1974).

Miller, M. H. and D. Orr. "A Model of the Demand for Money by Firms," *Quarterly Journal of Economics*, 80 (August 1968, pp. 413–435).

Sagner, J. *Working Capital Management: Applications and Case Studies* (Wiley, 2014).

Stone, B. K. and N. C. Hill, "Cash-transfer Scheduling for Efficient Cash Concentration," *Financial Management*, 9 (Autumn 1980, pp. 35–43).

Vander Weide, J. and S. F. Maier. *Managing Corporate Liquidity* (New York: John Wiley & Sons, 1985).

Yong-hak, K. *Advances in Working Capital Management* (Emerald Publishing, 1991).


## Appendix 20A — Derivation of Eq. (20.1)

From Eq. (20.1), the total costs of cash balances are defined as

$$\text{Total costs} = \text{Holding cost} + \text{Transaction cost} = \frac{C}{2}(k) + \frac{T}{C}(F) \tag{20.1A}$$

where $C$ is the amount of cash reinvested by borrowing or selling marketable securities, and $k$ and $T$ are as defined by Eq. (20.1).

To minimize the total cost, we take the partial derivative of Eq. (20.1A) with respect to $C$ and set the derivative equal to 0:

$$\frac{\partial(\text{total cost})}{\partial C} = \frac{k}{2} - \frac{(T)F}{C^2} = 0 \tag{20.2A}$$

From Eq. (20.2A), we solve for $C^*$, the optimal cash transfer, as

$$\frac{k}{2} = \frac{(FT)}{C^2}; \quad C^* = \sqrt{\frac{2FT}{k}}$$

This is Eq. (20.1).

## Questions and Problems

1. Define or explain the following:
   a. Baumol's EOQ model
   b. Invoicing float and disbursing float
   c. Lock-box system
   d. Cash scheduling
   e. Credit line
   f. Effective interest cost
   g. CD
   h. Put hedge ratio versus call hedge ratio
2. Show how Miller–Orr's stochastic EOQ model is derived.
3. Briefly discuss cash management systems.
4. Explain how cash managers can hedge the interest rate risk when managing the marketable securities.
5. Given that $F = \$2{,}000$, $T = 52$ weeks $\times$ \$600,000/week $=$ \$3,120,222, and $k = 15\%$, use the Baumol model to calculate the EOQ of cash balance.
6. The standard deviation of JAV Company's daily net cash flows is \$100. The firm pays \$15 in transactions costs to transfer funds into and out of commercial paper that pays 9.5% annual interest. JAV's financial manager uses the Miller–Orr model to set the target cash balance. In addition, JAV decides to maintain a \$20,000 minimum cash balance (lower limit). What are JAV's

(a) target balance, (b) upper and lower limits, and (c) expected average cash balance?

7. Consider the following inventory and storage cost information:

   Orders must be placed in multiples of 100 units
   Requirements for the 50-week year are 50,000 units
   Carrying cost per unit per year is $0.50
   Ordering cost per order per year is $20

   What is the EOQ of inventory? What is the optimal number of orders to be placed during the year?

8. A firm has the following information regarding its cash flows:

   Fixed transaction costs = $5 per transaction
   Monthly needed for cash = $1,000
   Opportunity cost of cash = 12%

   Using the Baumol's EOQ Model, compute the optimal cash borrowings or withdrawals and optimal average cash balance.

9. The following data pertains to IRC, Inc.:

   Minimum cash balance = $10,000
   Annual interest rate = 14.6% (daily rate = 0.04%)
   Variance of daily cash flows = $1,000,000
   Average transaction cost to buy and sell securities = $15.

   Using the above information and the Miller–Orr Model, calculate:

   a. The spread between the upper and lower limits ($S$)
   b. The return point ($R$)
   c. The upper limit ($H$)
   d. The average cash balance (ACB).

10. Given the results in the previous problem, establish the decision rules for the management of IRC's cash flows.
11. A company writes checks for $50,000 per day. A customer takes about four days to present these checks to the firm's bank and collect the money. Similarly, the company receives checks of $60,000 every day, and it takes three days to deposit and clear them. Find the positive, negative and net floats for this firm.
12. MNC International's annual credit sales are $36.5 billion. If the company is able to reduce negative float by 2 days, how much

money would be released? If MNC's cost of financing is 13.5%, calculate the interest expense savings.

13. The Federal Reserve is selling 91-day T-bills with a face value of $100 for $96.50. Compute the annualized yield on these T-bills if an investor holds them until maturity.
14. HAL, Inc. has a $10 million line of credit with the Oriental Bank of Commerce. The bank charges an annual interest rate of 13.5%. One of the conditions of the credit line is for HAL to maintain a compensating balance in the form of demand deposits equal to 10% of the loan. If the company utilizes its full borrowing capacity, what is the effective interest cost of borrowing?
15. BHEL presently handles all its credit customers from its New York City office. Annual credit sales are $72 million. The company is analyzing the desirability of establishing a lock-box system in selected areas to reduce the negative float. Studies carried out by BHEL's consultants indicate that the lock-box system could possibly reduce float by 4 days. Assuming a 360-day year, find the following:

    a. The extra cash made available by the lock-box system.
    b. If the interest rate is 12.50%, and the charge for the new system is $80,000 per year, should BHEL adopt this system?

16. Hyper International earns 7.50% interest annually on its investments in marketable securities. If the company adopts a draft disbursing system, disbursement float can be increased by 2 days. Next year's purchases are estimated at $3.6 million. Individual payments average $1,000. Assume that there is a 360-day year and that purchases are distributed evenly over 360 days.

    a. Calculate the amount of cash made available by the new proposal.
    b. If each draft issued costs $0.10, what would be your answer?

17. A firm operates for 240 days out of the year. The total annual consumption of raw materials is 100,000 units. Fixed cost per order is $180, and the annual, per unit carrying cost of inventory has been estimated at $9.

    a. Find the optimal economic order quantity.
    b. How many orders would be placed by the firm during the entire period?

18. Assume in the previous problem that the per order cost is \$225 and the cost of carrying one unit is \$20. Compute the optimal EOQ and explain why the results are so different.
19. A company is holding \$5 million in T-bills, which are to be sold after 45 days on October 15. The firm's treasurer expects an increase of 2% in the market interest rates over the next four to six weeks. Such an increase would lower the market price of T-bill's and would cause a loss to the company.

    What strategy would you suggest to avoid this loss? Assume that the company uses options on T-bills and the hedge ratio is known.

## Chapter 21

# Financial Planning and Strategy

**Contents**



## 21.1 Introduction

Chapter 21 covers alternative financial planning models and their use in financial analysis and decision-making. The approach taken in this chapter gives the student an opportunity to combine information (accounting, market, and economic), theory (classical, M&M, CAPM, and OPM), and methodology (regression and linear programming).

We begin by presenting the procedure for financial planning and analysis in Section 21.2. This is followed by a discussion of the Warren and Shelton algebraic simultaneous equations planning model in Section 21.3. Section 21.4 discusses the importance of sensitivity analysis and its application to Warren and Shelton's financial planning model, Section 21.5 discusses the application of linear programming (LP) to financial planning and analysis, Section 21.6 discusses the application of econometric approaches to financial planning and analysis, and Section 21.7 offers a summary of the chapter. Appendix 21A shows how the simplex method is used in the capital rationing decision. Appendix 21B is a description of parameter inputs used to forecast Johnson & Johnson's financial statements and share price. Appendix 21C shows the procedure of how to use Excel to implement the FINPLAN program. Appendix 21D presents an outline for a project.

## 21.2 Procedures for Financial Planning and Analysis

Before discussing the various financial planning models, we must first be sure of our understanding of what the financial planning process is all about. Otherwise, we run the risk of too narrowly defining financial planning as simply data gathering and running computer programs. In reality, financial planning involves a *process* of analyzing alternative dividend, financing, and investment strategies, forecasting their outcome and impact within various economic environments, and then deciding how much risk to take on and which projects to pursue. Thus, financial planning models are merely tools to improve forecasting as well as to help managers better understand the interactions of dividend, financing, and investment decisions.

More formally, we can outline the financial planning process as follows:

1. *Utilize* the existing set of economic, legal, accounting, marketing, and company policy information.

2. *Analyze* the interactions of the dividend, financing, and investment choices open to the firm.
3. *Forecast* the future consequences of present decisions to avoid unexpected events as well as to aid in understanding the interaction of present and future decisions.
4. *Decide* which alternatives the firm should undertake, the explicit outline for which is contained in the financial plan.
5. *Evaluate* the subsequent outcome of these decisions once they are implemented against the objectives set forth in the financial plan.

So where does the financial planning model come in? To clarify its role in this process, look at Figure 21.1, which presents a flowchart of a financial planning model. The inputs to the model are economic and accounting information (discussed in Chapter 2) and

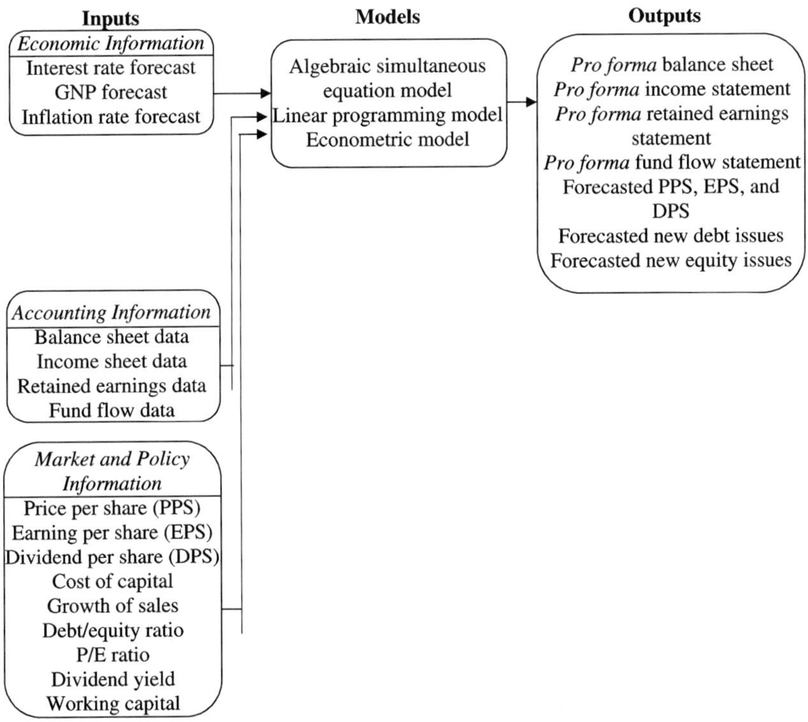


Figure 21.1 Inputs, Models, and Outputs for Financial Planning and Forecasting Models.

market and policy information (discussed in Chapters 3–20). Three alternative financial planning, analysis, and forecasting models are (1) the algebraic simultaneous equations model, (2) the linear programming model, and (3) the econometric model.[1] The outputs of the financial planning and forecasting model are pro forma financial statements, forecasted PPS, EPS, and DPS, new equity issued, and new debt issued. Essentially, the benefit of the model is to efficiently and effectively handle the analysis of information and its interactions with the forecasting of future consequences within the planning process.

Hence, the financial planning model efficiently improves the depth and breadth of the information the financial manager uses in the decision-making process. Moreover, before the finalized plan is implemented, an evaluation of how well subsequent performance stands up to the financial plan provides additional input for future planning actions.

A key to the value of any financial planning model is how it is formulated and constructed. That is, the credibility of the model's output depends on the underlying assumptions and particular financial theory the model is based on, as well as its ease of use for the financial planner. Because of its potentially great impact on the financial planning process and, consequently, on the firm's future, the particular financial planning model to be used must be chosen carefully. Specifically, we can state that a useful financial planning model should have the following characteristics:

1. The model results and assumptions should be credible.
2. The model should be flexible so that it can be adapted and expanded to meet a variety of circumstances.
3. The model should improve on current practice in a technical or performance sense.

[1]This chapter discusses three alternative financial planning models. The simultaneous equation model can be found in Lee and Lee's (2017) Chapter 24. The linear programming model can be found in Chapters 22 and 23. Finally, the econometric type of financial planning model can be found in Chapter 26. This chapter has discussed the simultaneous equation model in detail; however, the other two models have only been briefly discussed. For further information on these two models, see Lee and Lee (2017).

4. The model inputs and outputs should be comprehensible to the user without extensive additional knowledge or training.
5. The model should take into account the interrelated investment, financing, dividend, and production decisions and their effect on the firm's market value.
6. The model should be fairly simple for the user to operate without extensive intervention of nonfinancial personnel and tedious formulation of the input.

On the basis of these guidelines, we now present and discuss the simultaneous equations, linear programming, and econometric financial planning models, which can be used for financial planning and analysis.

## 21.3 The Algebraic Simultaneous Equations Approach to Financial Planning and Analysis

In this section, we present the financial planning approach of Warren and Shelton (1971), which is based on a *simultaneous equations* concept. The model, called FINPLAN, deals with overall corporate financial planning as opposed to just some are of planning, such as capital budgeting. The objective of the FINPLAN model is not to optimize anything, but rather, to serve as a tool to provide relevant information to the decision-maker. One of the strengths of this planning model, in addition to its construction, is that it allows the user to simulate the financial impacts of changing assumptions regarding such variables as sales, operating ratios, price-to-earnings ratios, retention rates, and debt-to-equity ratios.

The advantage of utilizing a simultaneous equation structure to represent a firm's investment, financing, production, and dividend policies is the enhanced ability for the interaction of these decision-making areas. The Warren and Shelton (WS) model is a system of 20 equations which are listed in Table 21.1. These equations are segmented into distinct subgroups corresponding to sales, investment, financing, and per share (return to investors) data. The flowchart describing the interrelationships of the equations is shown in Figure 21.2.

Table 21.1 Warren and Shelton Model.

**Section 1 — Generation of Sales and Earnings before Interest and Taxes for Period $t$**

(1) $SALES_t = SALES_{t-1}(1 + GSALS_t)$

(2) $EBIT_t = REBIT_t SALES_t$

**Section 2 — Generation of Total Assets Required for Period $t$**

(3) $CA_t = RCA_t SALES_t$

(4) $FA_t = RFA_t SALES_t$

(5) $A_t = CA_t + FA_t$

**Section 3 — Financing the Desired Level of Assets**

(6) $CL_t = RCL_t SALES_t$

(7) $NF_t = (A_t - CL_t - PFDSK_t) - (L_{t-1} - LR_t) - S_{t-1} - R_{t-1}$
$-b_r\{(1 - T_t)[EBIT_t - i_{t-1}(L_{t-1} - LR_t)] - PFDIV_t\}$

(8) $NF_t + b_t(1 - T_t)[i_t^e NL_t + U_t^1 NL_t] = NL_t + NS_t$

(9) $L_t = L_{t-1} - LR_t + NL_t$

(10) $S_t = S_{t-1} + NS_t$

(11) $R_t = R_{t-1} + b_t\{(1 - T_t)[EBIT_t - i_t L_t - U_t^1 NL_t] - PFDIV_t\}$

(12) $i_t = i_{t-1}\left(\dfrac{L_{t-1} - LR_t}{L_t}\right) + i_t^e \dfrac{NL_t}{L_t}$

(13) $\dfrac{L_t}{S_t + R_t} = K_t$

**Section 4 — Generation of Per Share Data for Period $t$**

(14) $EAFCD_t = (1 - T_t)[EBIT_t - i_t L_t - U_t^1 NL_t] - PFDIV_t$

(15) $CMDIV_t = (1 - b_t)EAFCD_t$

(16) $NUMCS_t = NUMCS_{t-1} + NEWCS_t$

(17) $NEWCS_t = \dfrac{NS_t}{(1 - U_t^s)\,P_t}$

(18) $P_t = m_t EPS_t$

(19) $EPS_t = \dfrac{EAFCD_t}{NUMCS_t}$

(20) $DPS_t = \dfrac{CMDIV_t}{NUMCS_t}$

*Notes*: There are 20 equations and 20 unknowns for this model. The unknowns are listed and defined in Table 21.2. In addition, Table 21.2 lists and defines parameters (inputs).

*Source*: Lee and Lee (2017). *Financial Analysis, Planning and Forecasting*, page 1166.

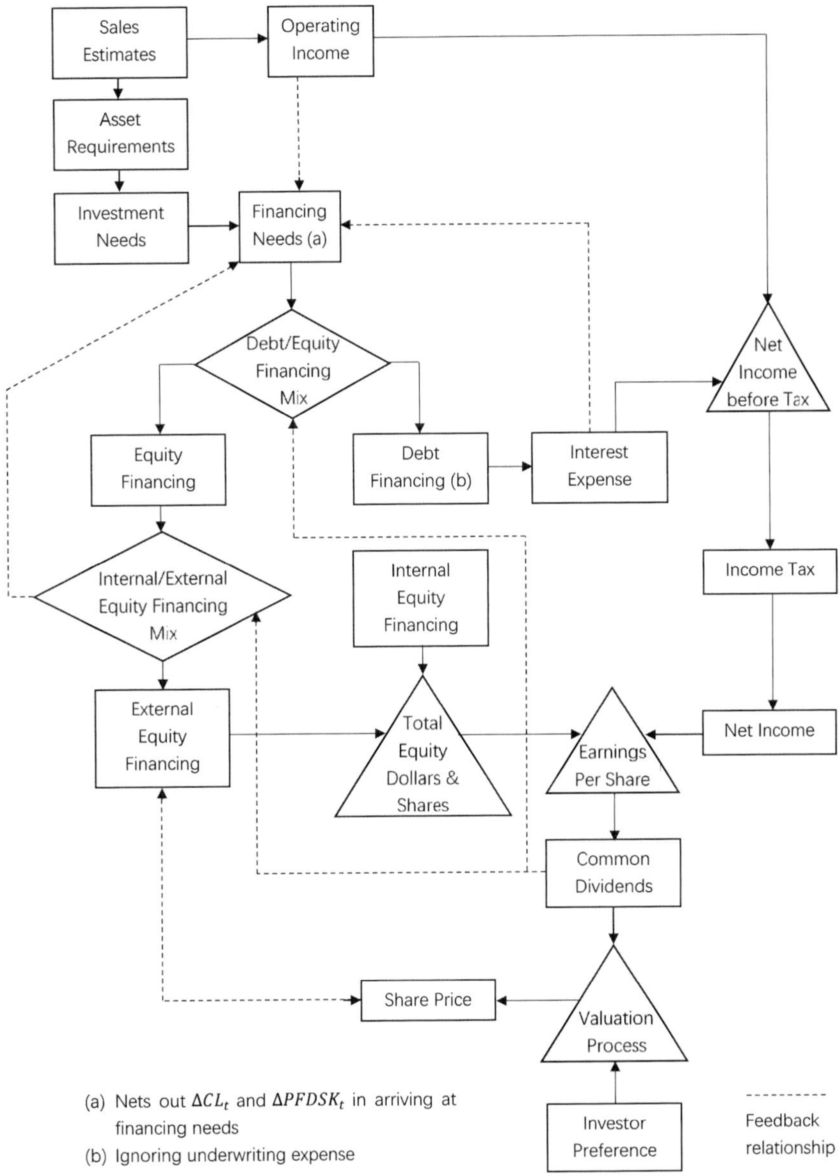


Figure 21.2 Flow Chart of a Simplified Financial Planning Model.

The key concepts of the interaction of investment, financing, and dividends, as explained in Chapter 13, are the basis of the FINPLAN model, which we now consider in some detail. *First*, we discuss the inputs to the model; *second*, we delve into the interaction of the equations in the model; and *third*, we look at the output of the FINPLAN model.

The inputs to the model are shown in Table 21.2. The driving force of the WS model is the sales growth estimates ($\text{GSALS}^t$). Equation (1) in Table 21.1 shows that sales for period $t$ is the product of sales in the prior period multiplied by the growth rate in sales for period $t$. EBIT is then derived, by expressing EBIT as a percentage of sales ratio, as in Eq. (2) of Table 21.1. Current and fixed assets are then derived in Eqs. (3) and (4) of the table through use of the CA/SALES and FA/SALES ratios. The sum of CA and FA is total assets for the period.

Financing of the desired level of assets is undertaken in Section 3 of the Table. In Eq. (6), current liabilities in period $t$ are derived from the ratio of CL/SALES multiplied by *SALES*. Equation (7) represents the funds required ($\text{NF}^t$). FINPLAN assumes that the amount of preferred stock is constant over the planning horizon. In determining what funds are needed and where they are to come from, FINPLAN uses a source-and-use-of-funds accounting identity. For instance, Eq. (7) shows that the assets for period $t$ are the basis for the firm's financing needs. Current liabilities, as determined in the prior equation, are one source of funds and therefore are subtracted from asset levels. As mentioned above, preferred stock is a constant and therefore must be subtracted also. After the first term in Eq. (7), $(A_t - \text{CL}_t - \text{PFDSK}_t)$, we have the financing that must come from internal sources (retained earnings and operations) and long-term external sources (debt and stock issues). The term in the second parenthesis, $(L_{t-1} - \text{LR}_t)$, takes into account the remaining old debt outstanding, after retirements, in period $t$. Then the funds provided by existing stock and retained earnings are subtracted out. The last quantity is the funds provided by operations during period $t$.

Once the funds needed for operations are defined, Eq. (8) specifies that new funds, after taking into account underwriting costs and additional interest costs from new debt, are to come from long-term debt and new stock issues. Equations (9) and (10) simply update the debt and equity accounts for the new issues. Equation (11) updates

Table 21.2 List of Unknowns and List of Parameters Provided by Management.

| | |
|---|---|
| *A. Unknowns* | |
| 1. $\mathrm{SALES}_t$ | Sales |
| 2. $\mathrm{CA}_t$ | Current assets |
| 3. $\mathrm{FA}_t$ | Fixed assets |
| 4. $A_t$ | Total assets |
| 5. $\mathrm{CL}_t$ | Current payables |
| 6. $\mathrm{NF}_t$ | Needed funds |
| 7. $\mathrm{EBIT}_t$ | Earnings before interest and taxes |
| 8. $\mathrm{NL}_t$ | New debt |
| 9. $\mathrm{NS}_t$ | New stock |
| 10. $L_t$ | Total debt |
| 11. $S_t$ | Common stock |
| 12. $R_t$ | Retained earnings |
| 13. $I_t$ | Interest rate on debt |
| 14. $\mathrm{EAFCD}_t$ | Earnings available for common dividends |
| 15. $\mathrm{CMDIV}_t$ | Common dividends |
| 16. $\mathrm{NUMCS}_t$ | Number of common shares outstanding |
| 17. $\mathrm{NEWCS}_t$ | New common shares issued |
| 18. $P_t$ | Price per share |
| 19. $\mathrm{EPS}_t$ | Earnings per share |
| 20. $\mathrm{DPS}_t$ | Dividends per share |
| *B. Provided by Management* | |
| 21. $\mathrm{SALES}_{t-1}$ | Sales in previous period |
| 22. $\mathrm{GSALS}_t$ | Sustainable growth rate |
| 23. $\mathrm{RCA}_t$ | Current assets as a percent of sales |
| 24. $\mathrm{RFA}_t$ | Fixed assets as a percent of sales |
| 25. $\mathrm{RCL}_t$ | Current payables as a percent of sales |
| 26. $\mathrm{PFDSK}_t$ | Preferred stock |
| 27. $\mathrm{PFDIV}_t$ | Preferred dividends |
| 28. $L_{t-1}$ | Debt in previous period |
| 29. $\mathrm{LR}_t$ | Debt repayment |
| 30. $S_{t-1}$ | Common stock in previous period |
| 31. $R_{t-1}$ | Retained earnings in previous period |
| 32. $b_t$ | Retention rate |
| 33. $T_t$ | Average tax rate |
| 34. $i_{t-1}$ | Average interest rate in previous period |
| 35. $\mathrm{i}_t^e$ | Expected interest rate on new debt |
| 36. $\mathrm{REBIT}_t$ | Operating income as a percent of sales |
| 37. $U_t^1$ | Underwriting cost of debt |
| 38. $U_t^s$ | Underwriting cost of equity |
| 39. $K_t$ | Ratio of debt to equity |
| 40. $\mathrm{NUMSCS}_{t-1}$ | Number of common shares outstanding in previous period |
| 41. $s_t$ | Price-earnings ratio |

*Source*: Lee and Lee (2017). *Financial Analysis, Planning and Forecasting*, page 1168.

the retained-earnings account for the portion of earnings available to common stockholders from operations during period $t$. Specifically, $b^t$ is the retention rate in period $t$ and $(1 - T^t)$ is the after-tax percentage, which is multiplied by the earnings from the period after netting out interest costs on both new and old debt. Since preferred stockholders must be paid before common stockholders, preferred dividends must be subtracted from funds available for common stockholders. Equation (12) calculates the new weighted-average interest rate for the firm's debt. Equation (13) is the new debt-to-equity ratio for period $t$.

Section 4 of Table 21.1 applies to the common stockholder; in particular, dividends and market value. Equation (14) represents the earnings available for common dividends and is simply the firm's after-tax earnings. Correspondingly, Equation (15) computes the earnings to be paid to common stockholders. Equation (16) updates the number of common shares for new issues.

As Eq. (17) shows, the number of new common shares is determined by the total new stock issue divided by the stock price after discounting for issuance costs. Equation (18) determines the price of the stock through the use of a price–earnings ratio $(m^t)$ of the stock purchase. Equation (19) determines EPS, as usual, by dividing earnings available to common stockholders by the number of common shares outstanding. Equation (20) determines dividends in a similar manner.

Tables 21.3– 21.5 illustrate the setup of the necessary input variables and the resulting output of the pro forma balance sheet and income statement for the Exxon Company. As mentioned, the WS equation system requires values for parameter inputs, which for this example are listed in Table 21.3. The first column represents the value of the input, while the second column corresponds to the variable number. The third and fourth columns pertain to beginning and ending periods for the desired planning horizon.

From Tables 21.4 and 21.5 you can see the type of information the FINPLAN model generates. With 2016 as a base year, planning information is forecasted for the firm over the period 2017–2020. Based on the model's construction, its underlying assumptions, and the input data, the WS model reveals the following:

1. The amount of investment to be carried out.
2. How this investment is to be financed?

Table 21.3 FINPLAN Inputs.

| | **Value of Data** | **Variable Number** | **Beginning Period** | **Last Period** |
|---|---|---|---|---|
| The Number of Years to be Simulated | 4 | 1 | 0 | 0 |
| Net Sales at $t$–1=2018 | 81,581 | 2 | 0 | 0 |
| Sustainable Growth Rate | 0.1076 | 3 | 1 | 4 |
| Current Assets as a Percent of Sales | 0.5643 | 4 | 1 | 4 |
| Fixed Assets (Total – Current) as a Percent of Sales | 1.3106 | 5 | 1 | 4 |
| Current Payables as a Percent of Sales | 0.3828 | 6 | 1 | 4 |
| Preferred Stock | 0 | 7 | 1 | 4 |
| Preferred Dividends | 0 | 8 | 1 | 4 |
| Long Term Debt in 2018 | 27,684 | 9 | 0 | 0 |
| Long Term Debt Repayment (Reduction) | 1,555 | 10 | 1 | 4 |
| Common Stock in 2018 | 3,120 | 11 | 0 | 0 |
| Retained Earnings in 2018 | 106,216 | 12 | 0 | 0 |
| Retention Rate = 1 – Payout Ratio | | | | |
| Payout Ratio = Dividend Per Share/Earnings Per Share | 0.3794 | 13 | 1 | 4 |
| Average Tax Rate (Income Taxes/Pretax Income) | 0.1501 | 14 | 1 | 4 |
| Average Interest Rate in 2018 | 0.0363 | 15 | 0 | 0 |
| Expected Interest Rate on New Debt | 0.0368 | 16 | 1 | 4 |
| Operating Income as a Percentage of Sales | 0.2329 | 17 | 1 | 4 |
| Underwriting Cost of Debt | 0.02 | 18 | 1 | 4 |
| Underwriting Cost of Equity | 0.01 | 19 | 1 | 4 |
| Ratio of Long-term Debt to Equity | 1.5598 | 20 | 1 | 4 |
| Number of Common Shares Outstanding | 2,681.50 | 21 | 0 | 0 |
| Price-Earnings Ratio | 22.3099 | 22 | 1 | 4 |

Table 21.4 Pro Forma Balance Sheet (2018–2022).

| | 2018 | 2019 | 2020 | 2021 | 2022 |
|---|---|---|---|---|---|
| **Assets** | | | | | |
| Current assets | 0.00 | 50984.99 | 56469.69 | 62544.40 | 69272.60 |
| Fixed assets | 0.00 | 118423.00 | 131162.32 | 145272.08 | 160899.69 |
| Total assets | 0.00 | 169407.99 | 187632.01 | 207816.48 | 230172.28 |
| Liabilities and net worth | | | | | |
| Current liabilities | 0.00 | 34589.56 | 38310.52 | 42431.77 | 46996.35 |
| Long term debt | 27684.00 | 82151.15 | 90988.54 | 100776.61 | 111617.63 |
| Preferred stock | 0.00 | 0.00 | 0.00 | 0.00 | 0.00 |
| Common stock | 3120.00 | −59003.12 | −59711.16 | −60495.93 | −61365.70 |
| Retained earnings | 106216.00 | 111670.40 | 118044.10 | 125104.03 | 132924.00 |
| Total liabilities and net worth | 0.00 | 169407.99 | 187632.01 | 207816.48 | 230172.28 |
| Computed DBT/EQ | 0.0000 | 1.5598 | 1.5598 | 1.5598 | 1.5598 |
| Int. rate on total debt | 0.0363 | 0.0366 | 0.0367 | 0.0367 | 0.0367 |
| **Per share data** | | | | | |
| Earnings | 0.0000 | 6.4109 | 7.5057 | 8.3296 | 9.2440 |
| Dividends | 0.0000 | 3.9789 | 4.6584 | 5.1697 | 5.7372 |
| Price | 0.0000 | 143.0258 | 167.4510 | 185.8335 | 206.2330 |

Table 21.5 Pro Forma Income Statement (2018–2022).

| | 2018 | 2019 | 2020 | 2021 | 2022 |
|---|---|---|---|---|---|
| Sales | 81581.00 | 90357.06 | 100077.19 | 110842.97 | 122766.88 |
| Operating income | 0.00 | 21048.35 | 23312.62 | 25820.47 | 28598.10 |
| Interest expense | 0.00 | 3010.16 | 3335.63 | 3696.05 | 4095.19 |
| Underwriting commission — debt | 0.00 | 1120.44 | 207.85 | 226.86 | 247.92 |
| Income before taxes | 0.00 | 16917.74 | 19769.15 | 21897.56 | 24254.99 |
| Taxes | 0.00 | 2539.68 | 2967.73 | 3287.25 | 3641.15 |
| Net income | 0.00 | 14378.06 | 16801.41 | 18610.31 | 20613.85 |
| Preferred dividends | 0.00 | 0.00 | 0.00 | 0.00 | 0.00 |
| Available for common dividends | 0.00 | 14378.06 | 16801.41 | 18610.31 | 20613.85 |
| Common dividends | 0.00 | 8923.67 | 10427.71 | 11550.39 | 12793.87 |
| Debt repayments | 0.00 | 1555.00 | 1555.00 | 1555.00 | 1555.00 |
| Actual funds needed for investment | 0.00 | −6100.97 | 9684.35 | 10558.30 | 11526.24 |

3. The amount of dividends to be paid.
4. How alternative policies can affect the firm's market value?

Even more important, as we will explore later in this chapter, this model's greatest value (particularly for FINPLAN) arises from the sensitivity analysis that can be performed.[2] That is, by varying one or several of the input parameters, the financial manager can better understand how his or her decisions interact and, consequently, how they will affect the company's future. (Sensitivity analysis is discussed in greater detail later in this chapter.)

We have shown how we can use Excel to solve 20 simultaneous equation systems as presented in Table 21.1, and the results are presented in Table 21.4 and Table 21.5. Now, we will discuss how we can use the data from Table 21.3 to calculate by hand the unknown variables in terms of JNJ's 2018 annual report.

*Section 1: Generation of Sales and Earnings before Interest and Taxes for Period t*

$$\begin{aligned}\text{Sales}_t &= \text{Sales}_{t-1} \times (1 + \text{GSALS}_t)\\ &= 81{,}581 \times 1.1076\\ &= 90{,}359.1156 \qquad (1)\\ \text{EBIT}_t &= \text{REBIT}_{t-1} \times \text{Sales}_t\\ &= 0.2329 \times 90{,}359.1156\\ &= 21{,}044.64 \qquad (2)\end{aligned}$$

*Section 2: Generation of Total Assets Required for Period t*

$$\begin{aligned}\text{CA}_t &= \text{RCA}_{t-1} \times \text{Sales}_t\\ &= 0.5643 \times 90{,}359.1156\\ &= 50{,}989.65 \qquad (3)\end{aligned}$$

[2]The Excel version of the FINPLAN program can be found in Chapter 24 of Lee and Lee (2017). It might be useful for the reader to go through the FINPLAN program by themselves.

$$\begin{aligned}\mathrm{FA}_t &= \mathrm{RFA}_{t-1} \times \mathrm{Sales}_t\\ &= 1.3106 \times 90{,}359.1156\\ &= 118{,}424.66 \qquad (4)\\ \mathrm{A}_t &= \mathrm{CA}_t + \mathrm{FA}_t\\ &= 50{,}989.65 + 118{,}424.66\\ &= 169{,}414.31 \qquad (5)\end{aligned}$$

*Section 3: Financing the Desired Level of Assets*

$$\begin{aligned}\mathrm{CL}_t &= \mathrm{RCL}_{t-1} \times \mathrm{Sales}_t\\ &= 0.3828 \times 90{,}359.1156\\ &= 34{,}589.47 \qquad (6)\\ \mathrm{NF}_t &= (\mathrm{A}_t - \mathrm{CL}_t - \mathrm{PFDSK}_t) - (\mathrm{L}_{t-1} - \mathrm{LR}_t) - \mathrm{S}_{t-1} - \mathrm{R}_{t-1} - b_t\\ &\quad \times \{(1 - T_t)[\mathrm{EBIT}_t - i_{t-1}(\mathrm{L}_{t-1} - \mathrm{LR}_t)] - \mathrm{PFDIV}_t\}\\ &= (169{,}414.31 - 34{,}589.47 - 0) - (27{,}684 - 1{,}555)\\ &\quad - 3{,}120.0 - 106{,}216 - 0.3794 \times \{(1 - 0.1501)\\ &\quad \times [21{,}044.64 - 0.0363 \times (27{,}684 - 1{,}555)] - 0\}\\ &= -7{,}120.21. \qquad (7)\end{aligned}$$

Please note that we solve the first seven equations step-by-step; however, Eq. (8) through Eq. (13) are interrelated. Therefore, we need to solve these equations in terms of simultaneous equation system approach. To solve this six-equation system, we first start with Eq. (12) as follows. We substitute parameters into Eq. (12) and obtain the following result.

$$\begin{aligned}\mathrm{i}_t\mathrm{L}_t &= \mathrm{i}_{t-1}(\mathrm{L}_{t-1} - \mathrm{LR}_t) + \mathrm{i}^e_{t-1} \times \mathrm{NL}_t\\ &= 0.0363 \times (27{,}684 - 1{,}555) + 0.0363 \times \mathrm{NL}_t\\ &= 948.4827 + 0.0363 \times \mathrm{NL}_t. \qquad (12)\end{aligned}$$

We then substitute related parameters into Eqs. (8–11) and (13) to create new a simultaneous equation system to solve unknowns $\mathrm{NL}_t$,

$\mathrm{NS}_t$, $\mathrm{L}_t$, $\mathrm{S}_t$, $\mathrm{R}_t$, and $\mathrm{i}_t$.

$$\begin{aligned}&\mathrm{NF}_t + b_t(1-T)[i_{t-1} \times \mathrm{NL}_t + \mathrm{U}_t^L \times \mathrm{NL}_t]\\ &\quad = \mathrm{NL}_t + \mathrm{NS}_t - 7{,}120.21 + 0.3794 \times (1 - 0.1501)\\ &\quad\quad \times (0.0363 \times \mathrm{NL}_t + 0.02 \times \mathrm{NL}_t) = \mathrm{NL}_t + NS_t\\ &\quad\quad - 7{,}120.21 + 0.01815 \times \mathrm{NL}_t = \mathrm{NL}_t + \mathrm{NS}_t \end{aligned} \tag{8}$$

$$\mathrm{NS}_t + 0.98185\mathrm{NL}_t = -7{,}120.21 \tag{a}$$

$$\mathrm{L}_t = \mathrm{L}_{t-1} - \mathrm{LR}_t + \mathrm{NL}_t \tag{9}$$

$$\mathrm{L}_t = 27{,}684 - 1{,}555 + \mathrm{NL}_t$$

$$\mathrm{L}_t - \mathrm{NL}_t = 26{,}129 \tag{b}$$

$$S_t = S_{t-1} + NS_t \tag{10}$$

$$-NS_t + S_t = 3{,}120.0 \tag{c}$$

$$\begin{aligned}\mathrm{R}_t &= \mathrm{R}_{t-1} + b_t\{(1-\mathrm{T}_t)[\mathrm{EBIT}_t - i_t L_t - U_t^L NL_t] - \mathrm{PFDIV}_t\}\\ &= 106{,}216 + 0.3794 \times \{(1 - 0.1501)\\ &\quad \times [21{,}044.64 - i_t L_t - 0.02 \times \mathrm{NL}_t] - 0\}\end{aligned} \tag{11}$$

Substitute (12) into (11)

$6480.047315952 - 0.018154050978\mathrm{NL}_t$

$$\begin{aligned}R_t &= 110{,}551 + 0.3794 \times \{0.8499 \times [21{,}044.64\\ &\quad - (948.4827 + 0.0363 \times \mathrm{NL}_t) - 0.02 \times \mathrm{NL}_t]\}\\ &= 117{,}031.04731 - 0.01815\mathrm{NL}_t\end{aligned}$$

$$117{,}031.04731 = R_t + 0.01815\mathrm{NL}_t \tag{d}$$

$$\begin{aligned}L_t &= (S_t + R_t)K_t\\ L_t &= 1.5598S_t + 1.5598R_t\end{aligned} \tag{13}$$

$$L_t - 1.5598S_t - 1.5598R_t = 0 \tag{e}$$

$$26{,}129 = 1.5598S_t + 1.5598R_t - \mathrm{NL}_t \quad ((\mathrm{b}) - (\mathrm{e}) = (\mathrm{f}))$$

$$21{,}262.424 = 1.5598NS_t - \mathrm{NL}_t + 1.5598R_t$$
$$((\mathrm{f}) - 1.5598\ (\mathrm{c}) = (\mathrm{g}))$$

$$-\mathrm{NL}_t + 1.5598NS_t - 0.0283\mathrm{NL}_t = -161{,}282.6036$$
$$-161{,}282.6036 = 1.5598\mathrm{NS}_t - 1.0283\mathrm{NL}_t$$
$$((\mathrm{g}) - 1.5598\ (\mathrm{d}) = (\mathrm{h}))$$

$$-1.0283\mathrm{NL}_t - 1.5315\mathrm{NL}_t = -150{,}176.5$$
$$\mathrm{NL}_t = 150{,}176.5/2.5598 = 58667.279$$
$$((\mathrm{h}) - 1.5598\ (\mathrm{a}) = (\mathrm{i}))$$

Substitute $\mathrm{NL}_t$ in (a)

$$\mathrm{NS}_t = -64{,}722.677$$

Substitute $\mathrm{NL}_t$ in (b)

$$L_t = 84{,}796.279$$

Substitute $\mathrm{NS}_t$ in (c)

$$S_t = -61{,}602.677$$

Substitute $\mathrm{NL}_t$ in (d)

$$R_t = 118{,}095.8584$$

Substitute $\mathrm{NL}_t L_t$ in (12)

$$i_t = 0.0363$$

*Section 4: Generation of Per Share Data for Period t*

$$\begin{aligned}\mathrm{EAFCD}_t &= (1 - \mathrm{T}_t)(\mathrm{EBIT}_t - i_t L_t - \mathrm{U}_t^L \mathrm{NL}_t) - \mathrm{PFDIV}_t \\ &= (1 - 0.1501) \times [21{,}044.64 - 0.0363 \times 84{,}796.279 \\ &\quad - 0.02 \times (58667.279)] - 0 \\ &= 14{,}272.532 \qquad (14)\end{aligned}$$

$$\begin{aligned}\mathrm{CMDIV}_t &= (1 - b_t)\mathrm{EAFCD}_t \\ &= (1 - 0.3794) \times (14{,}272.532) \\ &= 8{,}857.533 \qquad (15)\end{aligned}$$

Please note that we solve Eqs. (14) and (15) step-by-step; however, there are simultaneous equation relationships among Eqs. (16–20). Now we show how this five-equation system can be used to solve $\text{NUMCS}_t$, $\text{NEWCS}_t$, $\text{P}_t$, $\text{EPS}_t$, and $\text{DPS}_t$.

$$\text{NUMCS}_t = X_1 = \text{NUMCS}_{t-1} + \text{NEWCS}_t$$

$$X_1 = 2{,}681.50 + \text{NEWCS}_t \tag{16}$$

$$\text{NEWCS}_t = X_2 = \text{NS}_t/(1 - \text{U}_t^E)\text{P}_t$$

$$X_2 = -64{,}722.677/(1 - 0.01)P_t \tag{17}$$

$$P_t = X_3 = m_t\text{EPS}_t$$

$$X_3 = 22.3099(\text{EPS}_t) \tag{18}$$

$$\text{EPS}_t = X_4 = \text{EAFCD}_t/\text{NUMCS}_t$$

$$X_4 = 14{,}272.532/\text{NUMCS}_t \tag{19}$$

$$\text{DPS}_t = X_5 = \text{CMDIV}_t/\text{NUMCS}_t$$

$$X_5 = 8{,}857.533/\text{NUMCS}_t \tag{20}$$

(A) = For (18) and (19), we obtain

$$\begin{aligned} X_3 &= 22.3099(14{,}272.532/\text{NUMCS}_t) \\ &= 318{,}418.76166/X_1 \end{aligned}$$

Substitute (A) into Eq. (17) to calculate (B)

$$(\text{B}) = X_2 = -64{,}722.677/[(1 - 0.01) \times 318{,}418.76166/X_1]$$

$$(\text{B}) = X_2 = -0.2053X_1$$

Substitute (B) into Eq. (16) to calculate (C)

$$(\text{C}) = X_1 = 2{,}681.50 - 0.2053X_1$$

$$(\text{C}) = X_1 = 2224.7573 = \text{NUMCS}_t$$

Substitute (C) into (B)

$$(\text{B}) = X_2 = -456.74 = \text{NEWCS}_t$$

From Eqs. (19) and (20) we obtain $X_4$, $X_5$

$$X_4 = 6.42 = \mathrm{EPS}_t$$

$$X_5 = 3.98 = \mathrm{DPS}_t$$

From Eq. (18) we obtain $X_3$

$$X_3 = 143.2296 = P_t$$

Now we summarize the forecasted variables for 2019 as follows:

- Sales = \$90,359.1156
- Current Assets = \$50,989.65
- Fixed Assets = \$118,424.66
- Total Assets = \$169,414.31
- Current Payables = \$34,589.47
- Needed Funds = (\$7,120.21)
- Earnings before Interest and Taxes = \$21,044.64
- New Debt = \$58,667.279
- New Stock = (\$64,722.68)
- Total Debt = \$84,796.279
- Common Stock = (\$61,602.677)
- Retained Earnings = \$118,095.86
- Interest Rate on Debt = 3.63%
- Earnings Available for Common Dividends = \$14,272.532
- Common Dividends = \$8,857.53
- Number of Common Shares Outstanding = 2,224.76
- New Common Shares Issued = (456.74)
- Price Per Share = \$143.23
- Earnings Per Share = \$6.42
- Dividends Per Share = \$3.98

The above forecasted variables are almost identical to the numbers for 2019 presented in Tables 21.4 and 21.5. We use mean absolute deviation error criteria to compare these forecasted numbers with actual numbers, and the results are presented in Table 21.6.

## 21.4 Sensitivity Analysis

The efficiency of the financial planning and forecasting model will depend solely on how it is used. This section looks at alternative

Table 21.6 Mean Absolute Deviation Errors for Comparing Actual versus Forecasted Numbers for 2019.

| | 2019 Forecast | 2019 Actual | Mean Absolute Deviation Error for Forecast Variables (%) |
|---|---|---|---|
| Sales | 90,357.06 | 82,059 | 10.11 |
| Operating income | 21,048.35 | 23,416 | 10.11 |
| Interest expense | 3,010.16 | 318 | 846.59 |
| Income before taxes | 16,917.74 | 17,328 | 2.37 |
| Taxes | 2,539.68 | 2,209 | 14.97 |
| Net income | 14,378.06 | 15,119 | 4.90 |
| Preferred dividends | 0 | 0 | 0.00 |
| Common dividends | 14,378.06 | 9,917 | 44.98 |
| Debt repayments | 1,555 | 2,823 | 44.92 |
| **Assets** | | | |
| Current assets | 50,984.99 | 45,274 | 12.61 |
| Fixed assets | 118,423 | 17,658 | 570.65 |
| Total assets | 169,407.99 | 157,728 | 7.41 |
| **Liabilities and net worth** | | | |
| Current liabilities | 34,589.56 | 35,964 | 3.82 |
| Long term debt | 82,151.15 | 26,494 | 210.07 |
| Preferred stock | 0 | 0 | 0.00 |
| Common stock | −59,003.12 | 3,120 | 1991.13 |
| Retained earnings | 111,670.4 | 110,659 | 0.91 |
| Total liabilities and net worth | 169,407.99 | 176,237 | 3.87 |
| Computed DBT/EQ | 1.56 | 1.65 | 5.58 |
| Int. rate on total debt | 0.04 | 0.01 | 233.3 |
| **Per share data** | | | |
| Earnings | 6.4109 | 5.72 | 12.08 |
| Dividends | 3.9789 | 3.75 | −6.10 |
| Price | 143.0258 | 145.75 | 1.87 |

uses of financial planning models to improve their information dissemination. One of the most advantageous ways to use these financial planning models is to perform *sensitivity analysis.* The purpose of sensitivity analysis is to hold all but one or perhaps a couple of variables constant and then analyze the impact of their change on the predicted outcome.

Financial planning models are merely forecasting tools to help the financial manager analyze the interactions of important company decisions with uncertain economic elements. Since we can never be precisely sure what the future holds, sensitivity analysis stands out as a desirable manner of examining the impact of the unexpected as well as of the expected.

The simultaneous equations approach, as embodied in Warren and Shelton's FINPLAN, offers the best method for performing sensitivity analysis. By changing the parameter values, we can compare new outputs of the financial statements with those such as in Tables 21.4 and 21.5. The difference between the new statement and the statements in Tables 21.4 and 21.5 reflects the impact of potential changes in such areas as *economic conditions* (reflected in the interest rate, tax rate, and sales growth estimates) and *company policy decisions* (reflected in the maximum and minimum limits specified for the maturity and amount of debt and in the dividend policy as reflected in the specified payout ratio).

To perform sensitivity analysis, we change growth in sales (variable 3), operating income as a percentage of sales (variable 17), the P/E ratio (variable 22), the expected interest rate on new debt (variable 16), and long-term debt-to-equity ratio (variable 20). The new parameters are listed in Table 21.7. Summary results of the alternative sensitivity analyses for EPS, DPS and price per share (*PPS*) are listed in Table 21.8. The results indicate that changes of key financial decision variables will generally affect EPS, DPS, and PPS.

Table 21.7 Sensitivity Analysis Parameters.

| Model Variable Number | Parameter | Alternative Values | Sensitivity Analysis Number |
|---|---|---|---|
| 3 | Growth in sales | 0.20 | 1 |
| | | 0.15 | 2 |
| 20 | Long-term debt-to-equity ratio | 0.10 | 3 |
| | | 0.5 | 4 |
| 17 | Operating income as a percentage of sales | 0.20 | 5 |
| | | 0.50 | 6 |
| 22 | Price-to-earnings ratio | 5 | 7 |
| | | 30 | 8 |
| 16 | Expected interest rate on new debt | 0.005 | 9 |
| | | 0.05 | 10 |

Table 21.8 Summary Results of Sensitivity Analysis for EPS, DPS, and PPS (2017–2020).

| **Original Analysis** | **2017** | **2018** | **2019** | **2020** |
|---|---|---|---|---|
| EPS | 6.73 | 7.18 | 7.63 | 8.10 |
| DPS | 3.51 | 3.74 | 3.97 | 4.22 |
| PPS | 128.29 | 136.96 | 145.45 | 154.48 |
| Sensitivity Analysis #1 | | | | |
| EPS | 7.35 | 8.66 | 10.15 | 11.91 |
| DPS | 3.83 | 4.51 | 5.29 | 6.21 |
| PPS | 140.23 | 165.17 | 193.68 | 227.12 |
| Sensitivity Analysis #2 | | | | |
| EPS | 5.89 | 5.40 | 4.94 | 4.52 |
| DPS | 3.07 | 2.81 | 2.58 | 2.36 |
| PPS | 112.38 | 103.00 | 94.25 | 86.23 |
| Sensitivity Analysis #3 | | | | |
| EPS | 6.90 | 7.71 | 8.58 | 9.55 |
| DPS | 3.60 | 4.02 | 4.47 | 4.98 |
| PPS | 131.58 | 147.03 | 163.62 | 182.10 |
| Sensitivity Analysis #4 | | | | |
| EPS | 7.07 | 8.05 | 9.03 | 10.14 |
| DPS | 3.68 | 4.20 | 4.71 | 5.29 |
| PPS | 134.82 | 153.56 | 172.34 | 193.42 |
| Sensitivity Analysis #5 | | | | |
| EPS | 4.88 | 5.41 | 5.96 | 6.56 |
| DPS | 2.54 | 2.82 | 3.10 | 3.42 |
| PPS | 93.01 | 103.17 | 113.62 | 125.14 |
| Sensitivity Analysis #6 | | | | |
| EPS | 12.34 | 14.04 | 15.93 | 18.08 |
| DPS | 6.43 | 7.32 | 8.30 | 9.42 |
| PPS | 235.39 | 267.81 | 303.88 | 344.82 |
| Sensitivity Analysis #7 | | | | |
| EPS | 8.36 | 9.22 | 10.11 | 8.36 |
| DPS | 4.36 | 4.80 | 5.27 | 4.36 |
| PPS | 41.82 | 46.08 | 50.53 | 41.82 |

(*Continued*)

Table 21.8 (*Continued*)

| **Original Analysis** | **2017** | **2018** | **2019** | **2020** |
|---|---|---|---|---|
| Sensitivity Analysis #8 | | | | |
| EPS | 6.88 | 7.75 | 8.69 | 9.74 |
| DPS | 3.58 | 4.04 | 4.53 | 5.08 |
| PPS | 206.26 | 232.42 | 260.65 | 292.32 |
| Sensitivity Analysis #9 | | | | |
| EPS | 7.15 | 8.09 | 9.09 | 10.21 |
| DPS | 3.73 | 4.22 | 4.74 | 5.32 |
| PPS | 136.48 | 154.27 | 173.38 | 194.74 |
| Sensitivity Analysis #10 | | | | |
| EPS | 7.00 | 7.85 | 8.76 | 9.79 |
| DPS | 3.65 | 4.09 | 4.57 | 5.10 |
| PPS | 133.53 | 149.73 | 167.15 | 186.65 |

EPS = Earning per share; DPS = Dividend per share; PPS = price per share.

## 21.5 The Linear Programming Approach to Financial Planning and Analysis

In this section, we will discuss how linear programming techniques can be used to (i) solve profit maximization problems, (ii) to perform capital rationing problems, and (iii) to perform financial planning and forecasting.

An alternative approach to financial planning is based on using the optimization technique of linear programming. Using linear programming to do financial planning, the decision-maker sets up an objective function, such as to maximize firm value based on some financial theory. Hence, the model optimizes this objective function subject to certain constraints, such as maximum allowable debt/equity and payout ratios.

To use the linear programming approach for financial decisions, the problem must be formulated using the following three steps:

1. Identify the controllable decision variable of the problem.
2. Define the objective to be maximized or minimized, and define this function in terms of the controllable decision variables. In general, the objective is usually to maximize profit or minimize cost.

3. Define the constraints, either as linear equations or inequalities of the decision variables.

Several points need to be noted concerning the linear programming model. The variables representing the decision variables are divisible; that is, a workable solution would permit the variable to have a value of 1/2, 3/4, etc. If such a fractional value is not realistic (that is, you cannot produce 1/2 of a product), then a related technique called *integer programming* can be used.[3]

In this section, we apply linear programming to profit maximization, capital rationing, and financial planning and forecasting.

### 21.5.1 *Profit maximization*

XYZ, a toy manufacturer, produces three types of toys: King Kobra (KK), Pistol Pete (PP), and Rock Coolies (RC). To produce each toy, the plastic parts must be molded by machine and then assembled. The machine and assembly times for each type of toy are shown in Table 21.9.

Variable cost, selling prices, and profit contributions for each type of toy are presented in Table 21.10.

XYZ finances its operations through bank loans. The covenants of the loans require that XYZ maintain a current ratio of 1 or more; otherwise the full amount of the loan must be immediately repaid. The balance sheet of XYZ is presented in Table 21.11.

For this case, the objective function is to maximize the profit contribution for each product. From Table 21.10, we see that the profit

Table 21.9 Production Information for XYZ Toys.

| **Toy** | **Machine Time (hours)** | **Assembly Time (hours)** |
|---|---|---|
| KK | 5 | 5 |
| PP | 4 | 3 |
| RC | 5 | 4 |
| Total hours available | 150 | 100 |

[3]Both linear programming and integer programming are generally taught in the MBA or undergraduate operation-analysis course. See Hillier and Lieberman, *Introduction to Operation Research,* for discussion of these methods.

Table 21.10 Financial Information for XYZ Toys.

| Toy | Selling Price ($/unit) | Variable Cost ($/unit) | Profit Contribution ($/unit) |
|---|---|---|---|
| KK | 11 | 10 | 1 |
| PP | 8 | 4 | 4 |
| RC | 8 | 5 | 3 |

Table 21.11 Balance Sheet of XYZ Toys.

| Assets | | Liabilities and Equity | |
|---|---|---|---|
| Cash | $100 | Bank loan | $130 |
| Marketable securities | 100 | Long-term debt | 300 |
| Accounts receivable | 50 | Equity | 70 |
| Plant and equipment | 250 | | |
| | $500 | | $500 |

contribution for each product is KK = \$1, PP = \$4, and RC = \$3. We can multiply this contribution per unit times the number of units sold to identify the firm's total operating income. Thus, the objective function is

$$MAX\ P = X_1 + 4X_2 + 3X_3 \tag{21.1}$$

where $X_1, X_2, X_3$ are the number of units of KK, PP, and RC.

We can now identify the constraints of the linear programming problem. The firm's capacities for producing KK, PP, and RC depend on the number of hours of available machine time and assembly time. Using the information from Table 21.9, we can identify the following capacity constraints:

$$5X_1 + 4X_2 + 5X_3 \leq 150\,\text{hours} \quad \text{(Machine time constraint)} \tag{21.2}$$

$$5X_1 + 3X_2 + 4X_3 \leq 100\,\text{hours} \quad \text{(Assembly time constraints)} \tag{21.3}$$

There is also a constraint on the number of Pistol Petes (PP) and Rock Coolies (RC) that can be produced. The firm's marketing department has determined that 10 units of PPs and RCs are the maximum amount that can be sold; hence

$$X_2 + X_3 \leq 10 \quad \text{(Marketing constraint)} \tag{21.4}$$

Finally, the bank covenant requiring a current ratio greater than 1 must be met. Thus,

$$\frac{\text{Cash} + \text{Marketable securities} + \frac{A}{R} - \text{Cost of production}}{\text{bank loan}} \geq 1$$

$$\frac{100 + 100 + 50 - 10X_1 - 4X_2 - 5X_2}{130} \geq 1 \tag{21.5}$$

$$10X_1 + 4X_2 + 5X_3 \leq 120 \quad \text{(Current ratio constraint).}$$

Since production of each toy must, at minimum, be 0, three nonnegative constraints complete the formulation of the problem:

$$X_1,\ X_2,\ X_3 \geq 0 \quad \text{(Nonnegative constraint)} \tag{21.6}$$

Combining the objective functions and constraints yields

$$MAX\ X_1 + 4X_2 + 3X_3 \tag{21.7}$$

subject to $5X_t + 4X_2 + 5X_3 \leq 150$
$5X_1 + 3X_2 + 4X_3 \leq 100$
$X_2 + X_3 \leq 10$
$10X_1 + 4X_2 + 5X_3 \leq 120$
and
$X_1 \geq 0,\ X_2 \geq 0,\ X_3 \geq 0$

Using the simplex method to solve this linear programming problem, we derive the three simplex method tableaus in Table 21.12. Tableau 1 presents the information of objective function and constraints as derived in Eq. (21.7). Since there are constraints for four resources, there are four slack variables: $S_1, S_2, S_3$, and $S_4$. The initial tableau implies that we produce neither KK, PP, nor RC. Therefore, the total profit is 0, a result that is not optimal because all objective coefficients are positive. In the Tableau 2, the firm produces ten units of PP and generates a \$40 profit. But this result also is not optimal because one of the objective function coefficients is positive. Tableau 3 presents the optimal situation because none of the objective function coefficients is positive. (Appendix 21A presents the method and procedure for specifying Tableau 1 and solving Tableaus 2 and 3 in terms of a capital rationing example.)

Table 21.12 Simplex Method Tableaus for Solving Eq. (21.7).

Tableau 1

| | Real Variables | | | Slack Variables | | | | |
|---|---|---|---|---|---|---|---|---|
| | **X1** | **X2** | **X3** | **S1** | **S2** | **S3** | **S4** | |
| S1 | 5 | 4 | 5 | 1 | 0 | 0 | 0 | 150 |
| S2 | 5 | 3 | 4 | 0 | 1 | 0 | 0 | 100 |
| S3 | 0 | 1 | 1 | 0 | 0 | 1 | 0 | 10 |
| S4 | 10 | 4 | 5 | 0 | 0 | 0 | 1 | 120 |
| *Objective Function Coefficients* | | | | | | | | |
| Profit | 1 | 4 | 3 | 0 | 0 | 0 | 0 | 0 |
| Total Profit: 0 | | | | | | | | |

Tableau 2

| | Real Variables | | | Slack Variables | | | | |
|---|---|---|---|---|---|---|---|---|
| | **X1** | **X2** | **X3** | **S1** | **S2** | **S3** | **S4** | |
| S1 | 5 | 0 | 1 | 1 | 0 | −4 | 0 | 110 |
| S2 | 5 | 0 | 1 | 0 | 1 | −3 | 0 | 70 |
| X2 | 0 | 1 | 1 | 0 | 0 | 1 | 0 | 10 |
| S4 | 10 | 0 | 1 | 0 | 0 | −4 | 1 | 80 |
| *Objective Function Coefficients* | | | | | | | | |
| Profit | 1 | 0 | −1 | 0 | 0 | −4 | 0 | −40 |
| Total Profit: 40 | | | | | | | | |

Tableau 3

| | Real Variables | | | Slack Variables | | | | |
|---|---|---|---|---|---|---|---|---|
| | **X1** | **X2** | **X3** | **S1** | **S2** | **S3** | **S4** | |
| S1 | 0 | 0 | 0.5 | 1 | 0 | −2 | 0.5 | 70 |
| S2 | 0 | 0 | 0.5 | 0 | 1 | −1 | 0.5 | 30 |
| X2 | 0 | 1 | 1 | 0 | 0 | 1 | 0 | 10 |
| X1 | 1 | 0 | 0.1 | 0 | 0 | −0.4 | 0.1 | 8 |
| *Objective Function Coefficients* | | | | | | | | |
| Profit | 0 | 0 | −1.1 | 0 | 0 | −3.6 | −0.1 | −48 |
| Total Profit: 48 | | | | | | | | |

In Tableau 3, the solution values for variables $X_1$ and $X_2$ are found in the right-hand column. Thus, $X_1 = 8$ units and $X_2 = 10$ units. Since $X_3$ doesn't appear in the final solution, it has a value of 0. The slack variables indicate the amount of XYZ's unused resources. For example, $S_1 = 70$ indicates that the firm has 70 hours of unused machine time. To produce 8 units of $X_1$ requires 40 hours, and to produce 10 units of $X_2$ requires 40 hours, so our total usage of machine time is 80 hours. This is 70 hours less than the total hours of machine time the firm has available. $S_2 = 30$ indicates that there are additional assembly hours available. $S_3 = 0$ (it is not in the solution) implies that the constraint to make 10 units of $X_2 + X_3$ is satisfied. $S_4 = 0$ implies that the current ratio constraint is also satisfied and that financing, or, more precisely, the lack of financing, is limiting the amount of production. If the firm can change the bank loan covenant or increase the amount of available funds, it will be able to produce more. The maximum total profit contribution is \$48 given the current production level.

### 21.5.2 *Linear programming and capital rationing*

Linear programming is a mathematical technique that can be used to find the optimal solution to problems involving the allocation of scarce resources among competing activities. Mathematically, linear programming can best solve problems in which both the firm's objective is to be maximized and the constraints limiting the firm's actions are linear functions of the decision variables involved. Thus, the first step in using linear programming as a tool for financial decision-making is to model the problem facing the firm into a linear-programming form. To construct the programming model involves the following steps.

First, identify the controllable decision variables. Second, define the objective to be maximized or minimized and formulate that objective into a linear function with controllable decision variables. In finance, the objective generally is to maximize profit and market value or to minimize production costs. Third, the constraints must be defined and expressed as linear equations (equalities or inequalities) of the decision variables. This usually involves determining the capacities of the scarce resources involved in the constraints and then deriving a linear relationship between these capacities and the decision variables.

For example, suppose that $X_1, X_2, \ldots, X_N$ represents output quantities. Then the linear programming model takes the general form:

Maximize (or Minimize)

$$Z = c_1X_1 + c_2X_2 + \cdots + c_NX_N$$

Subject to

$$\begin{aligned}
a_{11}X_1 + a_{12}X_2 + \cdots + a_{1N}X_N &\leq b_1 \\
a_{21}X_1 + a_{22}X_2 + \cdots + a_{2N}X_N &\leq b_2 \\
\vdots \qquad \vdots \qquad\qquad \vdots \quad &\quad \vdots \\
a_{M}X_1 + a_{N2}X_2 + \cdots + a_{MN}X_N &\leq b_M \\
X_j \geq 0, \quad (j = 1, 2, \ldots, N)&
\end{aligned}$$

$Z$ represents the objective to be maximized or minimized (that is, profit, market value, or (cost)); $c_1, c_2, \ldots, c_N$ and $a_1, a_2, \ldots, a_{MN}$ are constant coefficients relating to profit contribution and input, respectively; and $b_1, b_2, \ldots, b_N$ are the firm's capacities of the constraining resources. The last constraint ensures that the decision variables to be determined are positive or zero.

Several points should be noted concerning the linear programming model. First, depending on the problem, the constraints may also be stated with equal (=) signs or greater than ($\geq$) or less than ($\leq$) signs. Second, the solution values of the decision variables are divisible, such that a solution would permit $X(1) = 1/2, 1/4$, etc. If such fractional values are not possible, the related technique of integer programming (yielding only whole numbers as solutions) can be applied. Third, the constant coefficients are assumed known and deterministic (fixed). If the coefficients have probabilistic distributions, then one of the stochastic programming methods must be used.

In Chapter 6, we have discussed how to use the linear programming technique to perform capital rationing for a three projects case. As an extended example, we apply linear programming to the area of capital rationing to a four projects case. We assume that a firm has a 12% cost of capital and \$15 million in resources for investment opportunities. Management is considering four investment projects, with financial information as listed in Table 21.13.

Restating the problem in linear programming equations, the objective is to select the projects that yield the largest total net present value; that is, to invest in optimal amounts of alternative projects such that

$$\text{NPV} = 34.72X_A + 41.34X_B + 27.81X_C + 60.88X_D$$

is maximized, where $X_A$, $X_B$, $X_C$, and $X_D$ represent amounts to be invested in Project A, Project B, Project C, and Project D.

Table 21.13 Financial Information for Firm Investment Projects.

| Cash Flow ($ millions) | | | NPV at 12% ($ millions) | | |
|---|---|---|---|---|---|
| **Project** | **C₀** | **C₁** | **C₂** | **C₃** | |
| A | −15 | +45 | +7.5 | +5 | +34.72 |
| B | −7.5 | +7.5 | +35 | +20 | +41.34 |
| C | −7.5 | +7.5 | +22.5 | +15 | +27.81 |
| D | 0 | −60 | +90 | +60 | +60.88 |

The projects are subject to several constraints. For one, the total cash outflow in period 0 cannot be more than the $15 million ceiling. That is

$$15X_A + 7.5X_B + 7.5X_C + 0X_D < 15$$

Another constraint is that not more than one project can be purchased or can a negative amount be purchased:

$$0 \leq X_A \leq 1$$

$$0 \leq X_B \leq 1$$

$$0 \leq X_C \leq 1$$

$$0 \leq X_D \leq 1$$

Collecting all these equations together forms the linear program:

Maximize

$$34.72X_A + 41.34X_B + 27.81X_C + 60.88X_D \qquad (21.8)$$

Subject to

$$15X_A + 7.5X_B + 7.5X_C + 0X_D \leq 15$$

$$0 \leq X_A \leq 1 \quad 0 \leq X_B \leq 1 \quad 0 \leq X_C \leq 1 \quad 0 \leq X_D \leq 1$$

To obtain a solution, we can use either linear or integer (zero-one) programming. Integer programming is a linear program that limits $X$'s to whole integers. This is especially important in this type of business decision because we might not accept a fraction of a project, which is what the constraint $0 \leq X \leq 1$ is likely to produce.

The best integer solution is to accept Projects B and C ($X_B = 1$ and $X_C = 1$), which yields the maximum NPV of $69.15.[4]

### 21.5.3 *Linear programming approach to financial planning*

Carleton (1970) and Carleton, Dick, and Downes (CDD, 1973) have formulated a financial planning model within a linear programming framework. Their objective function is based on the dividend stream model as expressed in Eq. (21.9):

$$\frac{P_0}{N_0} = \sum_{t=0}^{T-1} \frac{D_t}{N_t (1+k)^t} + \frac{P_T}{N_T (1+k)^T} \tag{21.9}$$

where $N_0$ = total common shares in period 0; $P_0$ = total equity value in period 0; $P_T$ = aggregate market value of the firm's equity at the end of period $T$; $N_t$ = number of common shares outstanding at the beginning of period $t$; $D_t$ = total dividends paid by the firm in period $t$; $k$ = cost of equity capital, assuming constant risk and a constant $k$; and $N_T$ = number of common shares outstanding in period $T$.

This objective function attempts to maximize the present value of the owners' equity, which includes all future dividends and long-term growth opportunities. (This model formulation is simply a rearranged version of the Gordon theory discussed in Chapter 5.)

Equation (21.9) is a nonlinear function in terms of $N_t$. To apply the linear programming method to this objective function, the function should be linearized. Following Lee and Lee (2017), a three-period linearized objective function for Eq. (21.9) can be defined as

$$\begin{aligned}\frac{D_0}{P_0} = \frac{D_0}{N_0} + \frac{D_1}{N_0(1+k)} - \frac{\Delta E_1^n}{N_0(1+k)(1-c)} + \frac{D_2}{N_0(1+k)^2} \\ - \frac{\Delta E_2^n}{N_0(1+k)^2(1-c)} - \frac{\Delta E_3^n}{N_0(1+k)^3(1-c)} + \frac{P_3}{N_0(1+k)^3}\end{aligned} \tag{21.10}$$

[4]The best linear programming solution for this problem is to accept only Project B ($X_B = 2$), which yields the maximum NPV of $82.68. The procedure of solving this problem can be found in the Appendix 21A.

where $D_0, P_0, N_0$, and $k$ are as defined in Eq. (21.9); $\Delta E_1^n$, $\Delta E_2^n$, $\Delta E_3^n$ represent the new equity issued in periods 1, 2, and 3; $D_1$ and $D_2$ represent dividend payments in periods 1 and 2; $c$ is an estimate of the portion of equity lost to underpricing and transaction costs; and $P_3$ is the total market value of equity in the third period. To use this model, $P_3$ should be forecast first. Since both $D_0/N_0$ and $P_3$ are predetermined, they can be omitted from the objective function without affecting the optimization results. If $N_0 = 49.69$, $c = 0.10$, and $k = 16.5\%$, then the objective function without $D_0//N_0$ and $P_3$ can be written as

$$MAX\, 0.018D_1 - 0.020\Delta E_1^n + 0.015D_2 - 0.017\Delta E_2^n - 0.014\Delta E_3^n.$$

Using this objective function and the constraints listed in Table 21.14, this model can be used to forecast important variables related to key pro forma financial statements. In Table 21.14, the constraint of available earnings for the common equity holders pertains to the amount of net income available to common equity holders. The constraint of sources and uses of funds involves the relationship among the investments, dividend payments, new equity issued, and new debt issued.

Policy constraints pertain to financing policy and dividend policy as described in Chapters 3, 9, 12, and 13. Financing policy can be classified into interest coverage and maximum leverage limitation. The dividend-related constraints can be classified into prefinancing limitations to avoid accumulating excess cash, minimum dividend growth, and payout restrictions. (More detailed discussion of these constraints can be found in Lee and Lee (2017, Chapter 16)).

The maximization of the Carleton or CDD objective function of the linear programming planning model is subject to legal, economic,

Table 21.14 Constraints Involved in the Linear Programming Model.

| |
|---|
| *Definition Constraints* |
| Available earnings for common equity holders |
| Sources and uses of funds |
| *Policy Constraints* |
| Leverage-ratio related |
| Dividend-payment related |

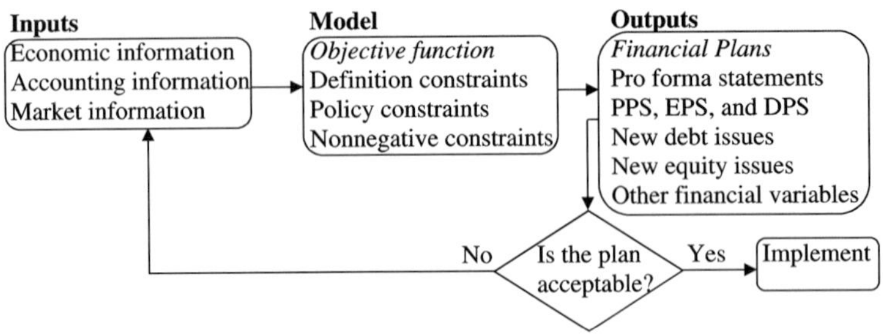


Figure 21.3 Flowchart of Carleton's Long-term Planning and Forecasting Model.

and policy constraints. Thus, the LP approach blends financial theory with the idiosyncrasies of market imperfections and company preferences. The objective function and the constraints are inputs to the planning model. The rest of the input information for the CDD financial planning model includes base information and forecasts of the economic environment. *Base information* is simply the most recent fiscal-year results.

Figure 21.3 is a flowchart of Carleton's long-term financial planning model. This flowchart implies that the results of financial plans should be carefully evaluated before they are implemented. If the outputs are not satisfactory, both the inputs and the model should be reconsidered and modified.

Output from the LP model consists of the firm's major financial planning decisions (dividends, working capital, financing). The use of linear programming techniques allows these decisions to be determined simultaneously.

Carleton and CDD emphasize the importance of the degree of detail included in their model's forecasted balance sheets and income and funds-flow statements. That is, these statements are broken down into the minimum number of accounts consistent with making meaningful financial decisions: capital investment, working capital, capital structure, and dividends. Complicating the interpretations of the results with myriad details can diminish the effectiveness of any financial planning model.

In comparing the LP and simultaneous equations approaches to financial planning, the main difference between the two is that the linear programming method optimizes the plan based on classical finance theory while the simultaneous equations approach does not.

However, in terms of ease of use, particularly for doing sensitivity analysis, the simultaneous equations model has the upper hand.

## 21.6 The Econometric Approach to Financial Planning and Analysis

The econometric approach to financial planning and analysis combines the simultaneous equations technique with regression analysis. The econometric approach models the firm in terms of a series of predictive regression equations and then proceeds to estimate the model parameters simultaneously, thereby taking account of the interactions among various policies and decisions.

To investigate the interrelationship between investment, financing, and dividend decisions, Spies (1974) developed five multiple regressions to describe the behavior of five alternative financial management decisions. Spies used a simultaneous equations technique to estimate all the equations at once.[5] He then used this model to demonstrate that investment, financing, and dividend policies generally are jointly determined within an individual industry.

Through the partial-adjustment model, the five endogenous variables (dividend payments, net short-term investment, gross long-term investment, new debt issued, and new equity issued), as defined in Table 21.15, are determined simultaneously through the use of the "uses equals sources" accounting identity. This identity ensures that the adjustment of each component of the budgeting process (the endogenous variables) depends not only on the component's distance from its target, but also on the simultaneous adjustment of the other four decision variables.[6]

### 21.6.1 *A dynamic adjustment of the capital budgeting model*

The capital budgeting decision affects the entire structure of the corporation. By its nature, the capital budgeting decision determines

[5]This technique takes into account the interaction relationship among investment, financing, and dividend policies (discussed in Chapter 13).

[6]It is assumed that there are targets for all five decision variables. In Table 21.11, $X^*_{1,t}$, $X^*_{2,t}$, $X^*_{3,t}$, $X^*_{4,t}$, $X^*_{5,t}$ represent the targets of $X_{1,t}$, $X_{2,t}$, $X_{3,t}$, $X_{4,t}$, $X_{5,t}$.

Table 21.15 Endogenous and Exogenous Variables.

Endogenous Variables

(a) $X_{1,t} = D/V_t$ = cash dividends paid in period $t$
(b) $X_{2,t} = IST_t$ = net investment in short-term assets during period $t$
(c) $X_{3,t} = ILT_t$ = gross investment in long-term assets during period $t$
(d) $X_{4,t} = -DF_t$ = minus the net proceeds from new debt issued during period $t$
(e) $X_{5,t} = -EQF_t$ = minus the net proceeds from new equity issued during period $t$

Exogenous Variables

(a) $Y_t = \sum_{i=1}^{5} X_{i,t} = \sum_{i=1}^{5} X_{i,t}^*$
where $Y$ = net profits + depreciation allowance (a reformulation of the sources = uses identity)
(b) RCB = corporate bond rate
(c) $\text{RDP}_t$ = average dividend-price ratio (or dividend yield)
(d) $\text{DEL}_t$ = debt-equity ratio
(e) $R_t$ = the rates of return the corporation could expect to earn on its future long-term investment (or internal rate of return)
(f) $CU_t$ = rates of capacity utilization (used by Francis and Rowell (1978) to lag capital requirements behind changes in percent sales; used here to define the $R_t$ expected)

*Source*: Lee and Lee (2017). *Financial Analysis, Planning and Forecasting*, page 1278.

the firm's very essence and thus has been discussed at great length in both finance literature in general and in this book. In Chapter 13, we recognized that the components of the capital budget are determined jointly. The investment, dividend, and financing decisions are tied together by the "uses equals sources" identity, a simple accounting identity that requires all capital invested or distributed to stockholders be accounted for.[7] However, despite the obviousness of this relationship, few attempts have been made to incorporate it into an econometric model. In this section, we describe Spies' (1974) econometric capital budgeting model, which explicitly recognizes the "uses equals sources" identity.

[7]This constraint also plays an important role in both Warren and Shelton's model and Carleton's model, as discussed previously.

In his empirical work, Spies divided the capital budgeting decision into five basic components: dividends, net short-term investment, gross long-term investment, new debt financing, and new equity financing. The first three components are uses of funds, while the latter two components are sources of funds. The dividends component includes all cash payments to stockholders and must be nonnegative. Net short-term investment is the net change in the corporation's holdings of short-term financial assets, such as cash, government securities, and accounts receivable. This component of the capital budget can be either positive or negative. Gross long-term investment is the change in gross long-term assets during the period. For example, the replacement of old equipment is considered a positive long-term investment. Long-term investment can be negative, but only if the sale of long-term assets exceeds replacement plus new investment.

As for sources of funds, the debt-financing component is simply the net change in the corporation's liabilities, such as corporate bonds, bank loans, taxes owed, and other accounts payable. Since a corporation can either increase its liabilities or retire existing liabilities, this variable can be either positive or negative. Finally, new equity financing is the change in stockholder equity minus the amount due to retained earnings. This should represent the capital raised by the sale of new shares of common stock. Although corporations frequently repurchase stock already sold, this variable is almost always positive when aggregated.

The first step is to develop a theoretical model that describes the optimal capital budget as a set of predetermined economic and financial variables. The first of these variables is a measure of cash flow: net profits plus depreciation allowances. This variable, denoted by $Y$, is exogenous as long as the policies determining production, pricing, advertising, taxes, and the like cannot be changed quickly enough to affect the current period's earnings. Since quarterly data are used in this work, this seems a reasonable assumption. It should also be noted that the "uses equals sources" identity ensures the following:

$$\sum_{i=1}^{5} X_{i,t} = \sum_{i=1}^{5} X_{i,t}^{*} = Y_t \tag{21.11}$$

where $X_{1,t}$, $X_{2,t}$, $X_{3,t}$, $X_{4,t}$, $X_{5,t}$, $X_{1,t}^*$, and $Y_t$ are defined in Table 21.12.[8]

The second exogenous variable in the model is the corporate bond rate, $RCD_t$, which was used as a measure of the corporations' borrowing rate. In addition, the debt-equity ratio at the start of the period, $DEL_t$, was included to allow for the increase in the cost of financing due to leverage. The average dividend-price ratio for all stocks, $RDP_t$, was used as a measure of the rate of return demanded by investors in a no-growth, unlevered corporation for the average-risk class. The last two exogenous variables, $R$ and $CU_t$, describe the rate of return the corporation could expect to earn on its future long-term investment. The ratio of the change in earnings to investment in the previous quarter should provide a rough measure of the rate of return to that investment. Spies used a four-quarter average of that ratio, $R_t$, to smooth out the normal fluctuations in earnings. The rate of capacity utilization, $CU_t$, was also included to improve this measure of expected rate of return. Finally, a constant and three seasonal dummy variables were included. The exogenous variables are summarized in Table 21.12.

### 21.6.2 *Simplified Spies model*

The simplified Spies model[9] for dividend payments ($X_{1,t}$), net short-term investments ($X_{2,t}$), gross long-term investments ($X_{3,t}$), new debt issues ($X_{4,t}$) and new equity issues ($X_{5,t}$) is defined as

$$\begin{aligned} X_{i,t} = a_{0i} &+ a_{1t}Y_t + a_{2i}RCB_t + a_{3i}RDP_t + a_{4i}DEL_t \\ &+ a_{5i}R_t + a_{6i}CU_t + a_{7i}X_{i,t-1} \end{aligned} \qquad (21.12)$$

[8]Expanding Eq. (21.11), we obtain $X_{1,t}+X_{2,t}+X_{3,t}+X_{4,t}+X_{5,t} = X_{1,t}^*+X_{2,t}^*+X_{3,t}^*+X_{4,t}^*+X_{5,t}^* = Y_t$.

[9]The original Spies model and its application can be found in Lee and Lee (2017). In addition, Taggart (1977) has proposed an alternative econometric model for financial planning and analysis. Readers who are interested in this model, please see Lee and Lee (2017) Chapter 26 for further detail.

where $i = 1, 2, 3, 4, 5$, etc. Equation (21.12) implies that dividend payments, net short-term investments, gross long-term investments, new debt issues, and new equity issues all can be affected by new cash inflow ($Y_t$), the corporate bond rate ($RCB_t$), average dividend yield ($RDP_t$), debt-equity ratio ($DEL_t$), rates of return on long-term investment ($R_t$), rates of capacity utilization ($CU_t$), and $X_{i,t-1}$ (the last period's dividend payment, net short-term investment, etc.). These empirical models simultaneously take into account theory, information, and methodologies, and they can be used to forecast cash payments, net short-term investment, gross long-term investment, new debt issues, and new equity issues.

## 21.7 Summary

Chapter 21 has examined three types of financial planning models available to the financial manager for use in analyzing the interactions of company decisions: the algebraic simultaneous equations model, the linear programming model, and the econometric model. We also have discussed the benefits of sensitivity analysis for determining the impact on the company from changes (expected and unexpected) in economic conditions.

The student should understand the basic functioning of all three models, along with the underlying financial theory. Moreover, it is essential to understand that a financial planning model is an aid or tool to be used in the decision-making process and is not an end in and of itself.

The computer-based financial modeling discussed in this chapter can be performed on either a mainframe computer or a PC. An additional dimension is the development of electronic spreadsheets. These programs simulate the matrix or spreadsheet format used in accounting and financial statements. Their growing acceptance and popularity is due to the ease with which users can make changes in the spreadsheet. This flexibility greatly facilitates the use of these programs for sensitivity analysis.

## References

Carleton, W. T. "An Analytical Model for Long-range Planning," *The Journal of Finance*, 25 (1970, pp. 291–315).

Carleton, W. T., C. L. Dick, Jr. and D. H. Downes. "Financial Policy Models: Theory and Practice," *Journal of Financial and Quantitative Analysis*, 8 (1973, pp. 691–709).

Francis, J. C. and D. R. Rowell. "A Simultaneous Equation Model of the Firm for Financial Analysis and Planning," *Financial Management*, 7 (Spring 1978, pp. 29–44).

Harrington, D. R. *Case Studies in Financial Decision-Making* (Chicago, IL: the Dryden Press, 1985).

Hillier, F. S. and G. J. Lieberman. *Introduction to Operation Research* (Oakland, CA: Holden-Day, 1986).

Lee, C. F. and J. Lee. *Financial Analysis and Planning: Theory and Application*, 3rd ed. (Singapore, World Scientific, 2017).

McLaughlin, H. S. and J. R. Boulding. *Financial Management with Lotus 1-2-3* (Englewood Cliffs, NJ: Prentice-Hall, 1986).

Myers, S. C. "Interaction of Corporate Financing and Investment Decisions," *The Journal of Finance*, 29 (March 1974, pp. 1–25).

Myers, S. C. and G. A. Pogue. "A Programming Approach to Corporate Financial Management," *The Journal of Finance*, 29 (May 1974, pp. 579–599).

Spies, R. "The Dynamics of Corporate Capital Budgeting," *The Journal of Finance*, 29 (June 1974, pp. 829–845).

Stern, J. M. "The Dynamics of Financial Planning," *Analytical Methods in Financial Planning* (1980, pp. 29–41).

Taggart, R. A., Jr. "A Model of Corporate Financing Decisions," *The Journal of Finance*, 32 (December 1977, pp. 1467–1484).

Warren, J. and J. Shelton. "A Simultaneous Equations Approach to Financial Planning," *The Journal of Finance*, 26 (September 1971, pp. 1123–1142).

## Questions and Problems

1. According to Warren and Shelton (1971), what are the characteristics of a good financial planning model?

2. Briefly discuss the Warren and Shelton model of using a simultaneous equations approach to financial planning. How does this model compare with the Carleton model?
3. Discuss the basic concepts of simultaneous econometric models. How can accounting information be used in the econometric approach to do financial planning and forecasting?
4. Briefly discuss the use of econometric models to deal with dynamic capital budgeting decisions. How are these kinds of capital budgeting decisions useful to the financial manager?
5. Briefly compare programming models, simultaneous models, and econometric models. Which type of model seems better for use in financial planning?
6. Discuss and justify the WS model.
7. Discuss how linear programming can be used in financial planning and forecasting.
8. How can investment, financing, and dividend policies be integrated in terms of either linear programming or econometric financial planning and forecasting?
9. Using information in Tables 21.3 and 21.12, use the FINPLAN program enclosed in the instructor's manual to solve empirical results as listed in Tables 21.4, 21.5, and 21.14.
10. a. Identify the input variables in the Warren and Shelton model which require forecasted values and those which are obtained directly from current financial statements.
    b. Discuss how the analyst can obtain values for the forecasted values.
    c. Why is sensitivity analysis so important and beneficial in this model?
11. a. List and define the five basic components of the capital budgeting decision of the Spies model.
    b. Identify which of the components are sources of funds and which are uses.
    c. Identify the exogenous variables in this model.

12(a). Please use the 21 inputs indicated in Table A to solve Warren and Shelton model discussed in this chapter by both Excel and hand calculations.

Table A Inputs for Warren and Shelton Model.

| Data | Variable | Description |
|---|---|---|
| 47,348.0 | $SALE_{t-1}$ | The net sales (revenues) of the firm at the beginning of the simulation. $t-1=2004$ |
| 0.0687 | $GCALS_t$ | Growth rate in sales during period $t$. |
| 0.5770 | $RCA_{t-1}$ | Expected ratio of current assets (CA) to sales in $t$. |
| 0.2204 | $RFA_{t-1}$ | Expected ratio of fixed assets (FA) to sales in $t$. |
| 0.2941 | $RCL_{t-1}$ | Current Payables as a Percent of Sales |
| 0.0 | $PFDSK_{t-1}$ | Preferred Stock |
| 0.0 | $PFDIV_{t-1}$ | Preferred Dividends |
| 2,565.0 | $L_{t-1}$ | Debt in Previous Period |
| 395.0 | $LR_{t-1}$ | Debt Repayment |
| 3,120.0 | $S_{t-1}$ | Common Stock in Previous Period |
| 35,223.0 | $R_{t-1}$ | Retained Earnings in Previous Period |
| 0.6179 | $b_{t-1}$ | Retention Rate |
| 0.3372 | $T_{t-1}$ | Average Tax Rate |
| 0.0729 | $i_{t-1}$ | Average Interest Rate in Previous Period |
| 0.0729 | $i^e_{t-1}$ | Expected Interest Rate on New Debt |
| 0.2754 | $REBIT_{t-1}$ | Operating Income as a Percentage of Sales |
| 0.05 | $U^L$ | Underwriting Cost of Debt |
| 0.05 | $U^E$ | Underwriting Cost of Equity |
| 0.6464 | $K_t$ | Ratio of Debt to Equity |
| 2,971.0 | $NUMCS_{t-1}$ | Number of Common Shares Outstanding in Previous Period |
| 19.9 | $m_{t-1}$ | Price-Earnings Ratio |

12(b). Please interpret the results of Warren and Shelton model in terms of the input data presented in 12(a).

$$SALES_t = 47348(1+0.0687) = 50600.81 \quad (1)$$

$$EBIT_t = 50600.81(0.2754) = 13935.46 \quad (2)$$

$$CA_t = 0.577(50600.81) = 29196.67 \quad (3)$$

$$CA_t = 0.2204(50600.81) = 11152.42 \quad (4)$$

$$A_t = 29196.67 + 11152.42 = 40349.08 \quad (5)$$

$$CL_t = 0.2941(50600.81) = 14881.7 \quad (6)$$

$$\begin{aligned} NF_t &= (40349.08 - 14881.7) - (2565 - 395) - 3120 - 35223 \\ &\quad - 0.6179\{0.6628[13935.46 - 0.0729(2565 - 395)]\} \\ &= -20688.02 \end{aligned} \tag{7}$$

$$\begin{aligned} &-20688.02 + 0.6179\{0.6628[0.0729(NL_t) + 0.05(NL_t)]\} \\ &\quad = NL_t + NS_t \\ &0.9497NL_t + NS_t = -20688.02 \end{aligned} \tag{8a}$$

$$L_t = 2565 - 395 + NL_t = 2170 + NL_t \tag{9b}$$

$$S_t = 3120 + NS_t \tag{10c}$$

$$R_t = 35223 + 0.6179\{0.6628[13935.46 - i_tL_t - 0.05NL_t]\} \tag{11}$$

$$\begin{aligned} i_tL_t &= 0.0729(2565 - 395) + 0.0729NL_t \\ &= 158.193 + 0.0729NL_t \end{aligned} \tag{12}$$

Substituting (12) into (11) yields

$$R_t = 40865.4 - 0.05NL_t \tag{d}$$

$$L_t = (S_t + R_t)0.6464 \tag{13e}$$

(b)–(e) yields

$$(S_t + R_t)0.6464 - NL_t = 2170 \tag{f}$$

(f)–0.6464(c) yields

$$0.6464R_t + 0.6464NS_t - NL_t = 153.232 \tag{g}$$

And (g)–0.6464(d) yields

$$0.6464NS_t - 1.0323NL_t = -26262.16 \tag{h}$$

Finally, (h)–0.6464(a) yields

$$NL_t = 7829.756$$

Substitute $NL_t$ in (a) yields

$$NS_t = -28123.94$$

Substitute $NL_t$ in (b) yields

$$L_t = 9999.756$$

Substitute $NS_t$ in (c) yields

$$S_t = -25003.94$$

Substitute $NL_t$ in (d) yields

$$R_t = 40473.91$$

Substitute $NL_t$ in (12) yields

$$i_t L_t = 158.193 + 0.0729 NL_t = 211.39$$

$$\begin{aligned} EAFCD_t &= 0.6628[13935.46 - 211.39 - 0.05(7829.756)] \\ &= 8836.84 \quad (14) \\ CMDIV_t &= 0.3821(8836.84) = 3376.56 \quad (15) \\ NUMCS_t &= 2971 + NEWCS_t \quad (16) \\ NEWCS_t &= \frac{-28123.94}{(1-0.05)P_t} = \frac{-29604.15}{P_t} \quad (17) \\ P_t &= 19.9(EPS_t) \quad (18) \\ EPS_t &= EAFCD_t/NUMCS_t = 8836.84/NUMCS_t \quad (19) \end{aligned}$$

From (18) and (19) we know that

$$P_t = 175853.12/NUMCS_t$$

Substitute $P_t$ in (17) yields

$$NEWCS_t = \frac{-29604.15}{P_t} = -0.1684 NUMCS_t$$

Substitute $NEWCS_t$ in (16) yields

$$NUMCS_t = 2971 - 0.1684NUMCS_t$$
$$\Rightarrow NUMCS_t = 2542.79$$

Consequently we know that

$$NEWCS_t = -0.1684(NUMCS_t) = -428.21$$

And

$$EPS_t = 8836.84/2542.79 = 3.475$$
$$DPS_t = CMDIV_t/NUMCS_t = 3376.56/2542.79 = 1.328 \quad (20)$$

Finally the price per share is equal to

$$P_t = 175853.12/NUMCS_t = 69.158$$

12(c). Recalculate 12(b) when $b_{t-1}$ is equal to 0.8 and $m_{t-1}$ is equal to 15.

## Appendix 21A — The Simplex Algorithm for Capital Rationing

The procedure of using the simplex method in capital rationing to solve Eq. (21.8) is as follows:

*Step 1*: Convert equality constraints into a system of equalities through the introduction of slack variables $S_1$ and $S_2$, as follows:

$$\begin{aligned} 15X_1 + 7.5X_2 + 7.5X_3 + S_1 &= 15 \\ -45X_1 - 7.5X_2 - 7.5X_3 + 60X_4 + S_2 &= 20 \end{aligned} \quad (21.1A)$$

where $X_1 = X_A$; $X_2 = X_B$; $X_3 = X_C$; and $X_4 = X_D$ (each of these is a separate investment project).

*Step 2*: Construct a tableau or tableaus for representing the objective function and equality constraints. This has been done for 4 tableaus in Table 21.1A. In Tableau 1, the figures in columns 2 through 6 are the coefficients of $X_1, X_2, X_3, X_4, S_1$, and $S_2$, as specified in the two equalities in Eq. (21.1A). Below these figures are the objective

Table 21.1A Simplex Method Tableaus.

**Tableau 1**

| | Real Variables | | | | Slack Variables | | |
|---|---|---|---|---|---|---|---|
| | **$X_1$** | **$X_2$** | **$X_3$** | **$X_4$** | **$S_1$** | **$S_2$** | |
| $S_1$ | 15 | 7.5 | 7.5 | 0 | 1 | 0 | 15 |
| $S_2$ | −45 | −7.5 | −7.5 | 60 | 0 | 1 | 20 |
| *Objective Function Coefficients* | | | | | | | |
| *NPV* | 34.72 | 41.34 | 27.81 | 60.88 | 0 | 0 | |
| Total *NPV*: 0 | | | | | | | |

**Tableau 2**

| | Real Variables | | | | Slack Variables | | |
|---|---|---|---|---|---|---|---|
| | **$X_1$** | **$X_2$** | **$X_3$** | **$X_4$** | **$S_1$** | **$S_2$** | |
| $S_1$ | 15 | 7.5 | 7.5 | 0 | 1 | 0 | 15 |
| $X_4$ | −0.75 | −0.125 | −0.125 | 1 | 0 | 0.017 | 0.333 |
| *Objective Function Coefficients* | | | | | | | |
| *NPV* | 80.38 | 48.95 | 35.42 | 0 | 0 | −1.015 | −20.2933 |
| Total *NPV*: 20.2933 | | | | | | | |

**Tableau 3**

| | Real Variables | | | | Slack Variables | | |
|---|---|---|---|---|---|---|---|
| | **$X_1$** | **$X_2$** | **$X_3$** | **$X_4$** | **$S_1$** | **$S_2$** | |
| $X_1$ | 1 | 0.5 | 0.5 | 0 | 0.067 | 0 | 1 |
| $X_4$ | 0 | 0.25 | 0.25 | 1 | 0.05 | 0.017 | 1.083 |
| *Objective Function Coefficients* | | | | | | | |
| *NPV* | 0 | 8.76 | −4.77 | 0 | −5.359 | −1.015 | −100.673 |
| Total *NPV*: 100.673 | | | | | | | |

**Tableau 4**

| | Real Variables | | | | Slack Variables | | |
|---|---|---|---|---|---|---|---|
| | **$X_1$** | **$X_2$** | **$X_3$** | **$X_4$** | **$S_1$** | **$S_2$** | |
| $X_2$ | 2 | 1 | 1 | 0 | 0.133 | 0 | 2 |
| $X_4$ | −0.5 | 0 | 0 | 1 | 0.017 | 0.017 | 0.583 |
| *Objective Function Coefficients* | | | | | | | |
| *NPV* | −17.52 | 0 | −13.53 | 0 | −6.527 | −1.015 | −118.193 |
| Total *NPV*: 118.193 | | | | | | | |

function coefficients. Note that only $S_1$ and $S_2$ are listed in the first column of Tableau 1. This indicates that $S_1$ and $S_2$ are basic variables in Tableau 1 and that remaining variables $X_1, X_2, X_3$, and $X_4$ have been arbitrarily set equal to 0.

With $X_1, X_2, X_3$, and $X_4$ all equal to 0, the remaining variables assume the values in the last column of the tableau; that is, $S_1 = 15$ and $S_2 = 20$. The numbers in the last column represent the values of basic variables in a particular basic-feasible solution.

*Step 3*: Obtain a new feasible solution. The basic-feasible solution of Tableau 1 indicates zero profits for the firm. Clearly, this basic-feasible solution can be bettered because it shows no profit, and profit should be expected from the adoption of any project.

The fact that $X_4$ has the largest incremental NPV indicates that the value of $X_4$ should be increased from its present level of 0. If we divide the column of figures under $X_4$ into the corresponding figures in the last column, we obtain quotients $\infty$ and 1/3. Since the smallest positive quotient is associated with $S_2$, then $S_2$ should be replaced by $X_4$ in Tableau 2.

The figures in Tableau 2 are computed by setting the value of $S_1$ to 0, $S_2$ to 1, and NPV to 0. The steps in the derivation are as follows: To eliminate the nonzero terms, we first divide the second row in Tableau 1 by 60 and thus obtain the coefficients indicated in the second row of Tableau 2. We then multiply this row by –60.88 and combine this result with the third row, as follows:

$$\begin{aligned}
&[34.72 + (-60.88) \times (-0.75)]\, X_1 + [41.34 + (-60.88) \times (-0.125)]\, X_2 \\
&\quad + [27.81 + (-60.88) \times (-0.125)]\, X_3 + [60.88 - (60.88) \times 1]\, X_4 \\
&\quad + [0 + (-60.88)\,(0)]\, S_1 + [0 + (-60.88)\,(0.017)]\, S_2 \\
&= (-60.88)\left(\frac{1}{3}\right) \qquad (21.2\text{A})
\end{aligned}$$

The objective function coefficients of Eq. (21.2A) are listed in the third row of Tableau 2. Tableau 2 implies that the company will undertake 1/3 units of Project 4 ($X_4$) and that the total NPV of

$X_4$ is \$20.2933. All coefficients associated with objective function are positive, which implies that the NPV can be improved by replacing $S_1$ with either $X_1, X_2, X_3, X_4$.

Using the same procedure mentioned above, we can now obtain Tableau 3. In Tableau 3, the only positive objective function coefficient is $X_2$. Therefore, $X_2$ can replace either $X_1$ or $X_4$ to increase the NPV.

Once again, using the procedure discussed above, we now obtain Tableau 4. In Tableau 4, none of the coefficients associated with objective function are positive. Therefore, the solution in this tableau is optimal. Tableau 4 implies that the company will undertake 2 units of Project 2 ($X_2$) and 0.583 units of Project 4 ($X_4$) to maximize its total NPV.

From Tableau 4, we obtain the best feasible solution:

$$X_1 = 0, \quad X_2 = 2, \quad X_3 = 0 \quad \text{and} \quad X_4 = 0.583$$

Total NPV is now equal to $(21.2)(41.34) + (60.88)(0.583) = \$118.193$.

Although there are computer packages that can be used for linear programming, we can use the simplex method to hand-calculate the optimal number of projects and the maximum NPV in order to understand and appreciate the basic technique of derivation.

## Appendix 21B — Description of Parameter Inputs Used to Forecast Johnson & Johnson's Financial Statements and Share Price

In our financial planning plan program, there are 20 equations and 20 unknowns. To use this program, we need to input 21 parameters. These 20 unknowns and 21 parameters can be found in Table 21.2.

We use 2018 as the initial reference year and input the 21 parameters, the bulk of which can be obtained or derived from the historical financial statements of JNJ. The first input is $\text{SALE}_{t-1}$ (\$81,581), defined as fiscal 2018 net sales and can be obtained from the income statement of JNJ. The second input is $\text{GCALS}_{t-1}$. This parameter can be calculated by either the percentage change method: $\text{Sales}_{t-1} - \text{Sales}_{t-2}/\text{Sales}_{t-2} = 6.71\%$ or sustainability growth rate: $\text{ROE}_{t-1} * b_{t-1}/1 - \text{ROE}_{t-1} * b_t - 1 = 10.76\%$.

The third input is $RCA_{t-1}$ (56.43%), defined as current assets divided by total sales, and the fourth input is $\text{RLA}_{t-1}$ (1.3106), defined as total asset minus current asset divided by net sales. The next parameter is $\text{RCL}_{t-1}$ (38.28%), defined as current liabilities as a percentage of net sales. The sixth parameter is preferred stock issued (PKV), with a value of 0, as JNJ does not currently have any preferred stock outstanding. The inputs for the aforementioned three parameters are all obtained from the JNJ's fiscal 2018 balance sheet. The seventh input is JNJ's preferred stock dividends, and since there is no preferred stock outstanding, it is correspondingly 0. The eighth input is $\text{LR}_{t-1}$ (\$27,684), defined as long-term debt, coming from the balance sheet of JNJ for the fiscal year 2018, and the ninth input is $\text{LR}_{t-1}$ (\$−1,555), defined as long-term debt retirement, from the 2018 statement of cash flows.

The tenth input is $S_{t-1}$ (\$3,120), which represents common stock issued, and the eleventh input is retained earnings ($R_{t-1} = \$106{,}216$). Both of these two variables can be found in the balance sheet for JNJ's fiscal year 2018. The twelfth input is the retention rate ($b_{t-1} = 37.94\%$), defined as $1 - \text{Dividend payout}_{t-1}/\text{Net income}_{t-1}$. The thirteenth input, the average tax rate ($T_{t-1}$), is assumed to be 15%. The fourteenth input is the weighted average effective interest rate ($I_{t-1} = 3.63\%$), which is the interest expense divided by long-term debt for JNJ's fiscal year 2018. The fifteenth input is expected interest on new debt (i.e., $t - 1 = 3.68\%$), calculated as the average of the weighted average interest rates in previous two periods.

The next input is $\text{REBIT}_{t-1}$ (23.29%), defined as operating income as a percentage of sales. However, JNJ does not list explicitly list operating income in its income statements. Thus, we defined operating income as JNJ's earnings before provision for taxes on income, with interest expense added back and interest income subtracted out. We also adjusted for nonrecurring expenses and added back other income/losses (related primarily to hedging activities, write-downs, and restructuring charges) to get to an adjusted and normalized operating income figure.

The seventeenth input is the underwriting cost of debt ($U^L$) that we assume to be 2%, and the eighteenth parameter is the underwriting cost of equity ($U^E = 1\%$). The nineteen input is the ratio of long-term debt to equity ($K_{t-1} = 155.98\%$), defined as debt divided by total equity. The twentieth input is the number of common shares outstanding ($NUMCS_{t-1} = 2{,}681.5$) listed in the JNJ's Earnings Statement for fiscal year 2018. The last input is P/E ratio ($m_{t-1} = 22.309$) which is calculated as JNJ's closing share price on the last trading day of 2018 divided by fiscal 2018 net income.

## Appendix 21C — Procedure of Using Excel to Implement the FINPLAN Program

This appendix describes the detailed procedure of using Excel to implement the FINPLAN program. There are four steps to use the FINPLAN program.

*Step 1.* Open the Excel file of FINPLAN Example.

| | A | B | C | D | E |
|---|---|---|---|---|---|
| 1 | FINPLAN input | | | | |
| 2 | 2018 | | | | |
| 3 | Value of Data | Variable | Beginning | Last | |
| 4 | | Number | Period | Period | Value |
| 5 | 4 | 1 | 0 | 0 | The number of years to be simulated |
| 6 | 81,581 | 21 | 0 | 0 | Net Sales at t-1=2018 |
| 7 | 0.1076 | 22 | 1 | 4 | Growth in Sales |
| 8 | 0.5643 | 23 | 1 | 4 | Current Assets as a Percent of Sales |
| 9 | 1.3106 | 24 | 1 | 4 | Fixed Assets as a Percent of Sales |
| 10 | 0.3828 | 25 | 1 | 4 | Current Payables as a Percent of Sales |
| 11 | 0 | 26 | 1 | 4 | Preferred Stock |
| 12 | 0 | 27 | 1 | 4 | Preferred Dividends |
| 13 | 27,684 | 28 | 0 | 0 | Long Term Debt in Previous Period |
| 14 | 1,555 | 29 | 1 | 4 | Long Term Debt Repayment (Reduction) |
| 15 | 3,120 | 30 | 0 | 0 | Common Stock in Previous Period |
| 16 | 106,216 | 31 | 0 | 0 | Retained Earnings in Previous Period |
| 17 | 0.3794 | 32 | 1 | 4 | Retention Rate |
| 18 | 0.1501 | 33 | 1 | 4 | Average Tax Rate (Income Taxes / Pretax Income) |
| 19 | 0.0363 | 34 | 0 | 0 | Average Interest Rate in Previous Period |
| 20 | 0.0368 | 35 | 1 | 4 | Expected Interest Rate on New Debt |
| 21 | 0.2329 | 36 | 1 | 4 | Operating Income as a Percentage of Sales |
| 22 | 0.0200 | 37 | 1 | 4 | Underwriting Cost of Debt |
| 23 | 0.0100 | 38 | 1 | 4 | Underwriting Cost of Equity |
| 24 | 1.5598 | 39 | 1 | 4 | Ratio of Debt to Equity |
| 25 | 2,681.50 | 40 | 0 | 0 | Number of Common Shares Outstanding in Previous Period |
| 26 | 22.3099 | 41 | 1 | 4 | Price-Earnings Ratio |
| 27 | | | | | |
| 28 | | | | | |

Sheet1 | sensitivity analysis | Sheet3

*Step 2.* Click the "Tools" and see "Macros." Another way to find it is under "View" and see "Macros."

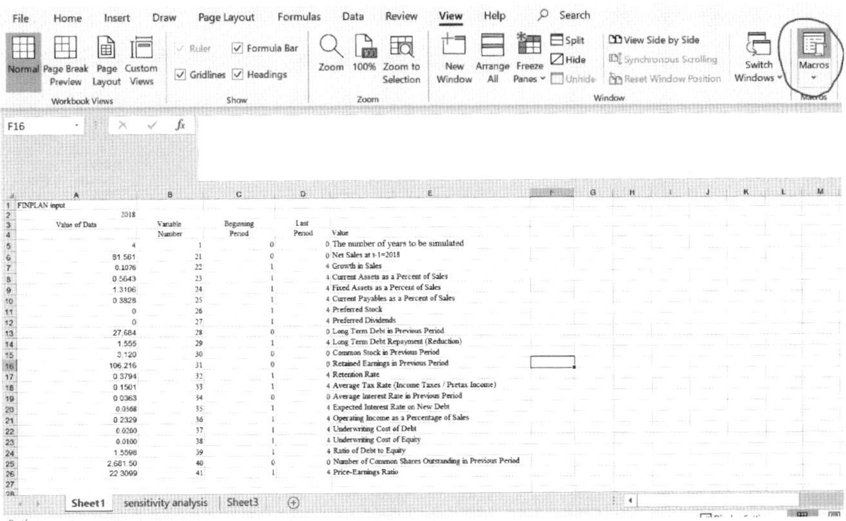


| | A | B | C | D | E |
|---|---|---|---|---|---|
| 1 | FINPLAN input | | | | |
| 2 | 2018 | | | | |
| 3 | Value of Data | Variable | Beginning | Last | |
| 4 | | Number | Period | Period | Value |
| 5 | 4 | 1 | 0 | 0 | The number of years to be simulated |
| 6 | 81.561 | 21 | 0 | 0 | Net Sales at t-1=2018 |
| 7 | 0.1076 | 22 | 1 | 4 | Growth in Sales |
| 8 | 0.5643 | 23 | 1 | 4 | Current Assets as a Percent of Sales |
| 9 | 1.3106 | 24 | 1 | 4 | Fixed Assets as a Percent of Sales |
| 10 | 0.3828 | 25 | 1 | 4 | Current Payables as a Percent of Sales |
| 11 | 0 | 26 | 1 | 4 | Preferred Stock |
| 12 | 0 | 27 | 1 | 4 | Preferred Dividends |
| 13 | 27,684 | 28 | 0 | 0 | Long Term Debt in Previous Period |
| 14 | 1,555 | 29 | 1 | 4 | Long Term Debt Repayment (Reduction) |
| 15 | 3,120 | 30 | 0 | 0 | Common Stock in Previous Period |
| 16 | 106,216 | 31 | 0 | 0 | Retained Earnings in Previous Period |
| 17 | 0.3794 | 32 | 1 | 4 | Retention Rate |
| 18 | 0.1501 | 33 | 1 | 4 | Average Tax Rate (Income Taxes / Pretax Income) |
| 19 | 0.0363 | 34 | 0 | 0 | Average Interest Rate in Previous Period |
| 20 | 0.0368 | 35 | 1 | 4 | Expected Interest Rate on New Debt |
| 21 | 0.2329 | 36 | 1 | 4 | Operating Income as a Percentage of Sales |
| 22 | 0.0200 | 37 | 1 | 4 | Underwriting Cost of Debt |
| 23 | 0.0100 | 38 | 1 | 4 | Underwriting Cost of Equity |
| 24 | 1.5598 | 39 | 1 | 4 | Ratio of Debt to Equity |
| 25 | 2,681.50 | 40 | 0 | 0 | Number of Common Shares Outstanding in Previous Period |
| 26 | 22.3099 | 41 | 1 | 4 | Price-Earnings Ratio |

*Step 3.* Choose "Macros" and then click "Run."

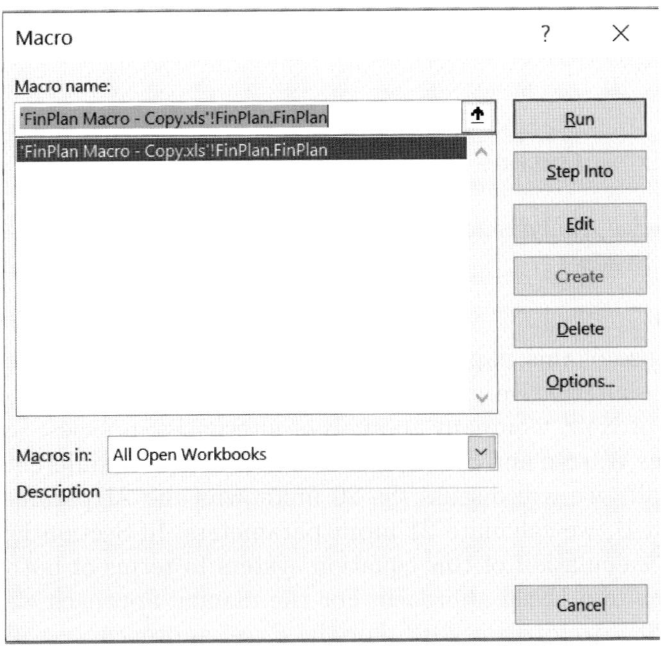

*Step 4*. Excel will show the solutions of the simultaneous equations.

**Pro forma Income Statement**

| | 2018 | 2019 | 2020 | 2021 | 2022 |
|---|---|---|---|---|---|
| Sales | 81581.00 | 90356.22 | 100075.35 | 110839.91 | 122762.36 |
| Operating income | 0.00 | 21048.16 | 23312.19 | 25819.76 | 28597.05 |
| Interest expense | 0.00 | 3010.14 | 3335.56 | 3695.94 | 4095.04 |
| Underwriting commission -- debt | 0.00 | 1120.43 | 207.83 | 226.84 | 247.89 |
| Income before taxes | 0.00 | 16917.59 | 19768.80 | 21896.98 | 24254.12 |
| Taxes | 0.00 | 2539.66 | 2967.68 | 3287.16 | 3641.01 |
| Net income | 0.00 | 14377.93 | 16801.12 | 18609.81 | 20613.10 |
| Preferred dividends | 0.00 | 0.00 | 0.00 | 0.00 | 0.00 |
| Available for common dividends | 0.00 | 14377.93 | 16801.12 | 18609.81 | 20613.10 |
| Common dividends | 0.00 | 8923.59 | 10427.52 | 11550.08 | 12793.41 |
| Debt repayments | 0.00 | 1555.00 | 1555.00 | 1555.00 | 1555.00 |
| Actl funds needed for investment | 0.00 | -6102.16 | 9682.96 | 10556.67 | 11524.35 |

**Pro forma Balance Sheet**

| | 2018 | 2019 | 2020 | 2021 | 2022 |
|---|---|---|---|---|---|
| **Assets** | | | | | |
| Current assets | 0.00 | 50984.52 | 56468.65 | 62542.67 | 69270.04 |
| Fixed assets | 0.00 | 118421.91 | 131159.91 | 145268.07 | 160893.76 |
| Total assets | 0.00 | 169406.43 | 187628.55 | 207810.74 | 230163.81 |
| **Liabilities and net worth** | | | | | |
| Current liabilities | 0.00 | 34589.24 | 38309.82 | 42430.60 | 46994.62 |
| Long term debt | 27684.00 | 82150.39 | 90986.87 | 100773.83 | 111613.52 |
| Preferred stock | 0.00 | 0.00 | 0.00 | 0.00 | 0.00 |
| Common stock | 3120.00 | -59003.55 | -59712.07 | -60497.36 | -61367.70 |
| Retained earnings | 106216.00 | 111670.35 | 118043.94 | 125103.68 | 132923.37 |
| Total liabilities and net worth | 0.00 | 169406.43 | 187628.55 | 207810.74 | 230163.81 |
| Computed DBT/EQ | 0.0000 | 1.5598 | 1.5598 | 1.5598 | 1.5598 |
| Int. rate on total debt | 0.0363 | 0.0366 | 0.0367 | 0.0367 | 0.0367 |
| Per share data | | | | | |
| Earnings | 0.0000 | 6.4108 | 7.5056 | 8.3295 | 9.2437 |
| Dividends | 0.0000 | 3.9788 | 4.6583 | 5.1696 | 5.7371 |
| Price | 0.0000 | 143.0249 | 167.4487 | 185.8295 | 206.2269 |

After we obtain the forecasted values from the model, we compare them with the actual data of JNJ in 2019 via calculating the absolute percentage change of error.

## Appendix 21D — Outline for a Project

Alternative Policies Analysis and Share Price Forecasting: XYZ Company as a Case Study

*A. Introduction*

The main purpose of this paper is to use XYZ Company as a case study to analyze alternative policies. In Section B, we use the cash flow statement of XYZ Company to analyze alternative policies. In Section C discuss Warren and Shelton model in terms of four different sections, especially we will discuss the 20 unknowns and 21 parameters. In Section D, we calculate 21 input parameters. In Section E, we perform the calculation of this equation system in terms of both manual approach and Excel approach. For the manual approach we use data from 2017 to forecast 2018. For the Excel approach we will forecast 2018, 2019, and 2020. In Section F, we will perform sensitivity analysis by changing growth rate, debt equity ratio, and P/E ratio.

*B. Investment, Financing, Dividend, and Production Policy for XYZ Company*
In this section students should use the information from the cash flow statement which contains information about all four policies. In addition, students should use these policies which have been learned in the class, which include Chapters 7, 13, 14, 17, and 18 to do some meaningful analysis.

*C. Warren and Shelton Model*
Warren and Shelton Model is a 20-equation model with 20 unknowns and 21 parameters to be input into the model. This model includes the following four sections:

1. Generating of Sales and Earnings Before Interest and Taxes for Period $t$.
2. Generating of Total Assets Required for Period $t$.
3. Financing the Desired Level of Assets.
4. Generation of Per Share Data for Period $t$.

*D. Calculate 21 Input Parameters (Definitions of these Variables can be Found on page 1168 of the Textbook.)*
It should be noted that most of the parameters have already been calculated in the first project. In addition, for students to calculate these parameters, they should extensively search for information from the four financial statements.

*E. Perform the Calculation of 20 Unknown Variables*

1. Manual approach.
2. Excel approach.

*F. Sensitivity Analysis of Forecasting Stock Price Per Share and Important Financial Statement Items*
In this section you should change growth rate, debt equity ratio, and P/E ratio.

*G. Summary and Concluding Remarks*

*References*

# PART VII

# Options, Futures, and Corporate Finance

Chapter 22

# Options, Futures, Swaps, and Risk Management

## Contents



## 22.1 Introduction

For those not familiar with their characteristics and uses, derivative securities such as futures, options, and swaps can appear to be highly speculative — that is, risky — investments. News stories in recent years informed the public of the escapades of highly speculative investments made by personnel at organizations such as Barings Bank PLC; Procter & Gamble; Orange County, California; Gibson Greetings; and Metallgesellschaft.

On the contrary, proper use of derivatives helps companies, as well as investors, to *reduce* risk. Firms that use oil, metals, or grain as production inputs can use derivatives to "lock in" prices today to reduce the risk of future price fluctuations. Financial derivatives can reduce firms' financing costs and can help corporate treasurers reduce the risk of future changes in interest rates or exchange rates.

The seventies and eighties can be regarded as truly revolutionary for financial markets and financial theory. During these decades, derivative securities, such as futures, options, warrants, and swaps, literally caused the markets to explode. It is said that the value of derivatives now traded generally exceeds the value of the New York Stock Exchange by a factor of 10. Much of the growth of these derivatives can be attributed to increased volatility in the financial markets. In addition, with the theoretical development of the Black–Scholes Option pricing model, the way that financial analysts consider risk and return has changed. The main purpose of this chapter is to introduce these relatively new ideas by briefly discussing futures, options, and swaps and applying them to the valuation of option-like securities and the management of corporate risk.

In the next five sections, we will go into more detail concerning the topics Futures, Options, Option-Like Securities, Swap Contracts, and Risk Management. In Section 22.2, we take a deeper look at futures contracts, and how entering futures contracts can hedge exchange rate risks. In Section 22.3, we define what an option contract is, and how to value option contracts. In Section 22.4, we will learn about other securities that act like options, for example warrants, convertible securities, callable bonds, and risky corporate debt. We will then learn the benefits of using interest rate swaps and currency rate swaps to hedge risk in Section 22.5. In Section 22.6, we will describe the importance of managing risk for investors through the various strategies of futures contracts, option contracts, swaps, warrants, convertible bonds, and other hedging procedures. Finally, in Section 22.7 we will provide a summary of the chapter.

## 22.2 Futures Contracts and Hedging

This section defines futures contracts. In the first Section 22.2.1, we define what a futures contract is and explain the terminology associated with futures contracts. Section 22.2.2 provides a brief background on the history of Futures Exchanges both domestically and internationally. In Section 22.2.3, the importance of margin requirements in respect to futures contracts is described. After we discuss maintenance requirements, we will look at Section 22.2.4 and learn about the regulation surrounding the futures markets. In Section 22.2.5, we learn about the advantages of using futures to hedge out risk, especially exchange rate risk. This section will provide a large overview of futures contracts and how futures can be used to hedge risk for investors.

### 22.2.1 *Nature of contracts*

Many types of securities share similar characteristics with options, which we will discuss in the next section. Perhaps the most significant is a *futures contract.* The International Money Market (IMM) of the Chicago Mercantile Exchange (CME) began trading futures contracts on foreign exchange currency in 1972. In 1982, a market similar to the IMM opened in London. This market, called the London International Financial Futures Exchange (LIFFE), trades futures contracts that are similar to the IMM contracts. In this section, we focus on currency futures. However, several other futures also exist, such as futures on grains and oilseeds, futures on metals and petroleum, and futures on interest rates. Table 22.1 presents futures price quotations of corn futures as examples for these markets.

A *forward contract* is a tailor-made agreement between a corporate customer and a bank that specifies an amount, a place, a date, and an exchange rate for the exchanged of one currency for another. These forward contracts are very useful because they can be tailored to fit any situation, but they are very expensive. Unlike a forward contract, a *futures contract* is a standardized financial instrument with a stated amount and specific maturity that is traded on an organized exchange and is resalable up to the close of trading or settlement date. The futures contract defines what asset is to be bought or sold, and how, when, where and in what quantity it is to be delivered. The terms also specify the currency in which the contract will trade, minimum tick value, and the last trading day and expiry or delivery month. Futures contracts tend to be smaller than forward contracts and are not as flexible in meeting hedging needs.

Table 22.1 is composed of futures quotes provided by the Wall Street Journal for the commodities corn, gold, and crude oil on the date December 3, 2014. The underlying asset of the futures contract,

Table 22.1 Futures quotes for select commodities from the Wall Street Journal on December 3, 2014.

| | Open | High | Low | Last Trade | Prior Settlement | Change | Volume | Open Interest |
|---|---|---|---|---|---|---|---|---|
| ***Corn, 5,000 bushels, cents per bushel*** | | | | | | | | |
| Dec., 2014 | 367′4 | 368′4 | 364′2 | 367′2 | 367′4 | −0′4 | 4112 | 24,040 |
| Mar, 2015 | 381′4 | 382′2 | 377′2 | 380′0 | 391′2 | −1′2 | 50891 | 662,693 |
| May, 2015 | 389′6 | 390′6 | 386′0 | 388′6 | 389′6 | −1′0 | 7407 | 151,237 |
| July, 2015 | 396′4 | 397′4 | 392′6 | 395′4 | 396′6 | −1′2 | 5550 | 136,085 |
| Sep, 2015 | 401′2 | 401′4 | 397′6 | 401′0 | 401′4 | −0′4 | 2795 | 29,316 |
| Dec., 2015 | 410′0 | 410′6 | 406′2 | 409′6 | 409′8 | −0′2 | 3865 | 153,588 |
| ***Gold, 100 oz, $ per oz*** | | | | | | | | |
| Dec., 2014 | 1198.1 | 1213.7 | 1196.1 | 1209.3 | 1199.2 | 10.1 | 369 | 2,249 |
| Jan., 2015 | 1196.6 | 1214.8 | 1194.4 | 1210.4 | 1199.2 | 11.2 | 980 | 666 |
| Feb., 2015 | 1197.6 | 1215.0 | 1193.5 | 1210.7 | 1199.4 | 11.3 | 114302 | 232,811 |
| Apr., 2015 | 1196.7 | 1215.3 | 1194.7 | 1211.0 | 1199.9 | 11.1 | 1481 | 44,443 |
| June, 2015 | 1198.4 | 1214.8 | 1196.9 | 1211.5 | 1200.4 | 11.1 | 1236 | 32,368 |
| Aug, 2015 | 1200.4 | 1208.0 | 1199.4 | 1206.0 | 1200.8 | 5.2 | 539 | 9,102 |
| ***Crude Oil, 1,000 barrels, $ per barrel*** | | | | | | | | |
| Jan., 2015 | 67.60 | 68.23 | 66.88 | 67.20 | 66.88 | 0.32 | 174480 | 319,555 |
| Feb., 2015 | 67.70 | 68.32 | 67.00 | 67.31 | 67.00 | 0.31 | 24323 | 121,625 |
| Mar, 2015 | 67.80 | 68.43 | 67.15 | 67.47 | 67.15 | 0.32 | 19196 | 136,119 |
| Apr., 2015 | 68.25 | 68.61 | 67.36 | 67.62 | 67.39 | 0.23 | 8403 | 48,702 |
| May, 2015 | 68.38 | 68.83 | 67.63 | 67.88 | 67.64 | 0.24 | 5443 | 41,828 |
| June, 2015 | 68.65 | 69.00 | 67.86 | 67.99 | 67.86 | 0.13 | 16355 | 142,552 |

*Source*: Wall Street Journal, Market Data Center, December 3, 2014. http://online.wsj.com/mdc/public/page/mdc_commodities.html?mod=mdc+topnav_2_3000.

the contract size, and the way the price is quoted is shown at the top of each section. For the commodity corn, the size of the contract is 5,000 bushels, quoted at cents per bushel. The expiration month of each contract is also listed in the first column. Futures terms related to Table 22.1 are defined in Table 22.2.

The table indicates the opening price, the highest price in trading thus far during the trading day, and the lowest price thus far during the trading day. The opening price represents the prices at which the contracts were trading immediately at the start of trading on December 3, 2014. For the May 2015 Crude Oil contract, the opening price was \$68.38 per barrel, with a high of \$68.83 per barrel and low of \$67.63 per barrel.

The Last Trade column represents the most recent trading price for the contract on the current trading day. The Change column represents the change of the current price of the contract from the previous day's settlement price. The settlement price is the price used to calculate the daily gains and losses and margin requirements. We calculate it as the price at which the contract traded immediately before the day's trading session ended. For the June 2015 Gold contract, the last trade was at \$1211.5 per ounce. This price is \$11.1 greater than the settlement price from yesterday. Therefore, we see that the prior settlement for the June 2015 Gold contract was $\$1200.4(\$1211.5 - 11.1 = 1200.4)$. Since the change is positive, we subtract the change from the last trade value. If the change was negative, we would add that to the last trade number to find the prior settlement price. We add when the change is negative since the prior settlement price had a higher price than the current's day last trade, meaning the prior settlement price needs to be larger than the current day's last trading price.

The second to last column in Table 22.1 represents the volume. This column gives the trading volume, or the number of contracts traded in a day, for the given futures contract. It can be contrasted with the open interest, which is the number of contracts outstanding, or in other words, the number of long positions or the number of short positions. If there is a large amount of trading by day traders, then the volume of trading may be greater than the beginning open interest or the closing open interest.

The price fluctuations of a futures contract are limited by the rules of the exchange on which it trades. The parties (buyer and seller) to the futures contract typically do not know each other. However, neither faces any chance of default on the futures contract because an exchange clearinghouse stands ready to ensure performance of the contract. The major limitations of the futures contract from the viewpoint of corporations or hedgers are the relatively small sizes and the standardized maturities of available contracts.

After expiry, each futures contract will be settled, either by physical delivery (typically for assets underlying commodities) or by a

Table 22.2 Futures Terms.

| | |
|---|---|
| **Open** | The price for the day's first trade, registered during the period designated as the opening of the market. |
| **High** | Highest price at which the futures contract sold during the day. |
| **Low** | Lowest price at which the futures contract sold during the day. |
| **Settle** | Since each contract is marked to market each day, the settlement price or the marking to market price is very important to investors. The settlement price is a figure determined by formula from within the range of closing prices or it may be the closing price. |
| **Change** | The amount the settlement price changed from the previous day. |
| **Lifetime high or low** | The highest and lowest prices recorded for each contract maturity from the first day it was traded to the present. |
| **Open interest** | The quantity of open long positions at the exchange's clearinghouse for each contract. |
| **Volume** | The number of contracts actually traded on the exchange for a given trading session. |

cash settlement (typically for financial underlyings). The contracts ultimately are not between the original buyer and the original seller, but between the holders at expiry and the exchange. Since contracts potentially pass through many different hands between the point of creation and sale, settling parties often do not know with whom they have ultimately traded.

Table 22.2 presents the definition of futures contract terms.

### 22.2.2 *Futures exchanges*

Futures Exchanges are able to provide risk insurance to producers with risky output and provide insurance to commodity stockholders at low cost. Speculators in the market absorb some of the risk but hedging appears to drive most commodity markets. The equilibrium futures price can be either below or above the (rationally) expected future price.

One of the earliest written records of futures trading is found in *Aristotle's Politics.* Aristotle tells the story of Thalesa, a poor philosopher from Miletus who developed a "financial device, which involves a principle of universal application." Thales used his skill in forecasting and predicted that the olive harvest would be exceptionally good the next autumn. Confident in his prediction, he made agreements with local olive-press owners to deposit his money with them to guarantee him exclusive use of their olive presses when the harvest was ready. Thales successfully negotiated low prices because the harvest was in the future and no one knew whether the harvest would be plentiful or pathetic and because the olive-press owners were willing to "hedge" against the possibility of a poor yield. When the harvest-time came, and a sharp increase in demand for the use of the olive presses outstripped availability of the presses, he sold his future-use contracts of the olive presses at a rate of his choosing and made a large quantity of money. It should be noted, however, that this is a very loose example of futures trading and, in fact, more closely resembles an option contract because Thales was not obligated to use the presses if the yield turned out to be pathetic.

The first modern organized futures exchange began in 1710 at the Dojima Rice Exchange in Osaka, Japan.

The London Metal Market and Exchange Company (London Metal Exchange) was founded in 1877, but the market traces its origins back to 1571 and the opening of the Royal Exchange, London. Before the exchange was created, business was conducted by traders in London coffee houses, using a makeshift ring drawn in chalk on the floor. At first, only copper was traded but later followed by lead and zinc (although they were only made official in 1920.) The exchange was closed during WWII did not re-open until 1952. The range of metals traded was extended to include aluminum, nickel, tin, aluminum alloy, steel, cobalt, and molybdenum. The exchange ceased trading plastics in 2011. The total value of the trade is around $11.6 trillion annually.

Chicago has the largest future exchange in the world, the Chicago Mercantile Exchange. Chicago is located at the base of the Great Lakes, close to the farmlands and cattle country of the Midwest, making it a natural center for transportation, distribution, and trading of agricultural produce. Gluts and shortages of these products caused chaotic fluctuations in price, and this led to the development of a market enabling grain merchants, processors, and agriculture companies to trade in "to arrive" or "cash forward" contracts to insulate them from the risk of adverse price change and enable them to hedge. In March 2008 the Chicago Mercantile Exchange announced its acquisition of NYMEX Holdings, Inc., the parent company of the New York Mercantile Exchange and Commodity Exchange. CME's acquisition of NYMEX was completed in August 2008.

For most exchanges, forward contracts were standard at the time. However, most forward contracts were not honored by both the buyer and the seller. For instance, if the buyer of a corn forward contract made an agreement to buy corn, and at the time of delivery the price of corn differed dramatically from the original contract price, either the buyer or the seller would back out. Additionally, the forward contracts market was very illiquid and an exchange was needed that would bring together a market to find potential buyers and sellers of a commodity instead of making people bear the burden of finding a buyer or seller.

In 1848 the Chicago Board of Trade (CBOT) was formed. Trading was originally in forward contracts; the first contract (on corn) was written on March 13, 1851. In 1865 standardized futures contracts were introduced.

Following the end of the postwar international gold standard in 1972, the CME formed a division called the International Monetary Market (IMM) to offer futures contracts in foreign currencies: British pound, Canadian dollar, German mark, Japanese yen, Mexican peso, and Swiss franc.

In 1881 a regional market was founded in Minneapolis, Minnesota, and in 1883 introduced futures for the first time. Trading continuously since then, today the Minneapolis Grain Exchange (MGEX) is the only exchange for hard red spring wheat futures and options.

The 1970s saw the development of the financial futures contracts, which allowed trading in the future value of interest rates. These (in particular the 90-day Eurodollar contracts introduced in 1981) had an enormous impact on the development of the interest rate swap market.

In June 2001, InterContinental Exchange (ICE) acquired the International Petroleum Exchange (IPE), now ICE Futures, which operated Europe's leading open-outcry energy futures exchange. Since 2003, ICE has partnered with the Chicago Climate Exchange (CCX) to host its electronic marketplace. In April 2005, the entire ICE portfolio of energy futures became fully electronic.

In 2005, The Africa Mercantile Exchange (AfMX®) became the first African commodities market to implement an automated system for the dissemination of market data and information online in real-time through a wide network of computer terminals. As at the end of 2007, AfMX® had developed a system of secure data storage providing online services for brokerage firms. The year 2010, saw the exchange unveil a novel system of electronic trading, known as After®. After® extends the potential volume of processing of information and allows the Exchange to increase its overall volume of trading activities.

In 2006 the NYSE teamed up with the Amsterdam-Brussels-Lisbon-Paris Exchanges "Euronext" electronic exchange to form the first transcontinental futures and options exchange. These two developments as well as the sharp growth of internet futures trading platforms developed by a number of trading companies clearly points to a race to total internet trading of futures and options in the coming years.

In terms of trading volume, the National Stock Exchange of India in Mumbai is the largest stock futures trading exchange in the world, followed by JSE Limited in Sandton, Gauteng, South Africa.

### 22.2.3 *Margin*

Whenever someone enters into a contract position in the futures market, a security deposit, commonly called a *margin requirement*, must be paid. While the futures margin may seem to be a partial payment for the security on which the futures contract is based, it only represents security to cover any losses that may result from adverse price movements. The meaning of the word margin is often quite confusing. We have profit margin, NYSE margin requirement, and so on. Each of these usages of the word margin has a specialized meaning. It is helpful to go over the various definitions of the word margin to ensure that any confusion is avoided.

The minimum margin requirements set by the exchange must be collected by the clearing member firms (members of the exchange involved in the clearinghouse operations) when their customers take positions in the market. In turn, the clearing member firms must deposit a fixed portion of these margins with the clearinghouse. At the end of each trading day, every futures-trading account is incremented or reduced by the corresponding increase or decrease in the value of all open interest positions. This daily adjustment procedure is applied to the margin deposit and is called *marking to market.* For example, if an investor is long on a yen futures contract and by the end of the day its market value has fallen $1,000, he or she would be asked to add an additional $1,000 to the margin account. Why? Because the investor is responsible for its initial value. For example, if a futures contract is executed at $10,000 with an initial margin of $1,000 and the value of the position goes down $1,000, to $9,000, the buyer would be required to put in an additional margin of $1,000 because the investor is responsible for paying $10,000 for the contract. If the investor is unable to comply or refuses to do so, the clearing member firm that he or she trades through would automatically close out the position. On the other hand, if the contract's value was up $1,000 for the day, the investor might immediately withdraw the profit if he or she so desired. The procedure of marking to market implies that all potential profits and losses are realized immediately.

Due to the difficulty of calling all customers whose margin accounts have fallen in value for the day, a clearing member firm usually will require that a sum of money be deposited at the initiation of any futures position. This additional sum is called *maintenance margin.* In most situations, the original margin requirement may be established with a risk-free, interest-bearing security such as a T-bill. However, the maintenance margin, which must be in cash, is adjusted for daily changes in the contract value.

As the clearing house is the counterparty to all their trades, they only have to have one margin account. This is in contrast with OTC derivatives, where issues such as margin accounts have to be negotiated with all counterparties.

### 22.2.4 *Regulation*

Each exchange is normally regulated by a national governmental (or semi-governmental) regulatory agency:

- In Australia, this role is performed by the Australian Securities and Investments Commission.
- In the Chinese mainland, by the China Securities Regulatory Commission.
- In Hong Kong, by the Securities and Futures Commission.
- In India, by the Securities and Exchange Board of India and Forward Markets Commission (FMC).
- In Japan, by the Financial Services Agency.
- In Pakistan, by the Securities and Exchange Commission of Pakistan.

- In Singapore by the Monetary Authority of Singapore.
- In the UK, futures exchanges are regulated by the Financial Services Authority.
- In the USA, by the Commodity Futures Trading Commission.
- In Malaysia, by the Securities Commission Malaysia.
- In Spain, by the Comisión Nacional del Mercado de Valores (CNMV).
- In Brazil, by the Comissão de Valores Mobiliários (CVM).
- In South Africa, by the Financial Services Board (South Africa).
- In Mauritius, by the Financial Services Commission (FSC).

### 22.2.5 *Hedging with futures*

Markets that permit individuals, corporations, and banks to protect themselves from foreign exchange risk are necessary during periods of fluctuating exchange rates. A comparison of forward and futures markets is summarized in Table 22.3.

Foreign exchange futures also can be used to hedge exchange rate risk. For example, a German firm that exports its products to the U.S. will receive U.S. dollar payments in the near future. The financial manager of the German firm can sell the deutsche mark currency futures to hedge potential devaluation of the U.S. dollar relative to the deutsche mark. The deutsche mark currency futures will result in a gain if the value of the dollar falls against the deutsche mark.

## 22.3 Options

In this section, we will learn what option contracts are and how they also can be used to manage risk. In Section 22.3.1, the basic definitions concerning options are provided, and a brief explanation on the history of option contracts is provided. In Section 22.3.2, we describe what is meant by a call and put option, as well as American versus European options. In Section 22.3.3, we discuss the different exchanges that exist for the trading of options. In Section 22.3.4, we look at a partial listing of option contracts and learn how to pull out important information from exchange quotes. Section 22.3.5 expands on how to value both call and put options, using Eqs. (22.1) and (22.2). In addition, we learn how option contracts are influenced by

Table 22.3 Comparison of Forward and Futures Markets.

| Specification of Contracts | Forward Contracts | Future Contracts |
|---|---|---|
| **Size of contract** | Tailored to individual needs | Standardized |
| **Delivery Date** | Tailored to individual needs | Standardized |
| **Method of Transaction** | Established by the bank via telephone contact with limited number of market participants | Specification among many buyers and sellers on the exchange floor |
| **Participants** | Banks, brokers, corporations, and central banks; public speculation not encouraged | Banks, brokers, corporations; public speculation encouraged |
| **Commissions** | Set by spread between bank's buy and sell prices; not easily determined by consumer | Small brokerage fee and negotiated rates on block trades |
| **Security Deposit** | None, but compensating bank balances required | Small security deposit required |
| **Clearing Operation** | Handling contingent upon individual banks and brokers | Handled by exchange clearinghouse, daily settlements marked to market |
| **Marketplace** | Communications network | Central exchange floor |
| **Economic Justification** | Facilitate world trade by providing a hedge mechanism | Risk sharing with public participation |
| **Accessibility** | Limited to very large customers | Open to anyone |
| **Regulation** | Self-regulating | Commodity Futures Trading Commission |
| **Price Fluctuations** | No daily limit | Daily limit imposed by exchange |
| **Contract Liquidity** | None | Daily trading |

the market price of the stock, exercise price of the option, volatility of the stock price, and time until option expiration.

### 22.3.1 *Basic concepts of options*

In general, there are three types of options based on equity securities: (1) warrants, (2) publicly traded options, and (3) executive stock options. A *warrant* is a financial instrument issued by a corporation that gives the purchaser the right to buy a fixed number of shares at a set price for a specified period. There usually is a secondary market where existing warrants may be traded. It must be noted that a warrant is more difficult to price than a traded option. This is because when warrants are exercised, the underlying company changes; it receives a cash inflow and its capital structure is less levered. When a publicly traded option is exercised, on the other hand, the only thing that happens is that ownership of some shares changes hands.

There are two major differences between a warrant and a publicly traded option. First, the warrant normally matures in three to five years, whereas the maturity of a publicly traded option is normally less than nine months. The second difference is that the warrant is an agreement between the corporation and the warrant's buyer. If the warrant's owner decides to exercise the right to purchase stock, the corporation issues new shares and receives the cash from the sales of those shares. A *publicly traded option* is an agreement between two individuals who have no relationship with the corporation whose shares underlie the option. When a publicly traded option is exercised, money and shares are exchanged between the individuals and the corporation receives no funds.

*Executive stock options* provide stock purchase rights as compensation for corporate employees. For services rendered, the manager or the employee has the right to buy a specific number of shares for a set price during a given period. Unlike warrants and publicly traded options, executive stock options cannot be traded. The option's owner has only two choices: exercise the option or let it expire. Like a warrant, should the owner decide to exercise the option, the corporation receives money and issues new shares.

The use of executive stock options for management compensation raises an interesting agency question. The firm's managers may make investment and financing decisions that increase the firm's risk in order to increase the value of their stock options. (As we will see, the value of an option is directly related to the variability or riskiness of the underlying asset, which in this case is the firm.) Such an action could have a detrimental effect on the bondholders and other creditors of the firm.

Publicly traded options are probably the most widely known of the three types of equity option instruments. In 1973, the Chicago Board of Options Exchange (CBOE) was founded to provide a market in these securities. Although it was possible to trade options over the counter before that time, trading volume was relatively low. The opening of the CBOE marked the beginning of a phenomenal growth in the popularity of options as financial instruments. Indeed, in terms of the value of the securities traded, the Chicago Board Options Exchange is challenging the New York and Tokyo Stock Exchanges as the world's largest securities market. There are now five options-trading centers in the U.S. — the CBOE, the American Stock Exchange, the Philadelphia Stock Exchange, the Pacific Stock Exchange, and the New York Stock Exchange — and these exchanges receive steady streams of proposals for new listings.

### 22.3.2 *Option terminology*

There are two basic types of publicly traded options: calls and puts. A *call option* gives the holder the right to buy a particular number of shares of a designated common stock at a specified price, called the *exercise price* (or striking price), on or before a given date, known as the *expiration date.* On the Chicago Board Options Exchange, options typically are created for three-, six-, or nine-month periods. All have the same expiration date: the Saturday following the third Friday of the month of expiration. The owner of the shares of common stock can write, or create an option and sell it in the options market, in an attempt to increase the return or income on a stock investment. A more venturesome investor may create an option in this fashion without owing any of the underlying stock. This *naked option writing* exposes the speculator to unlimited risk because he or she may have to buy shares at some point to satisfy the contract at whatever price is reached. This is a serious if the value of the underlying asset has a high degree of variability.

A *put option* gives the holder the right to sell a certain number of shares of common stock at a set price on or before the expiration date of the option. In purchasing a put, the owner of the shares has bought the right to sell those shares by the expiration date at the exercise price. As with calls, one can create, or write, a put, accepting the obligation to buy shares.

The owner of a put or call is not obligated to carry out the specified transaction, but has the *option* of doing so. If the transaction is carried out, it is said to have been *exercised*. For example, if you hold a call option on a stock that is currently trading at a price higher than the exercise price, you may want to exercise the option to purchase stock at the exercise price and then immediately resell the stock at a profit. This call option is said to be *in the money*. On the other hand, if the call option is *out of the money* — that is, the stock is trading at a price below the exercise price — you certainly would not want to exercise the option, as it would be cheaper to purchase stock directly. *At the money* means that the stock price is trading at the exercise price of the option.

An *American option* can be exercised at any time up to the expiration date. A *European option* can be exercised only on the expiration date; this makes it simpler to analyze because its term to maturity is known. Because of this simplifying factor, we will concentrate on the valuation of European options. The factors that determine the values of American and European options are the same; all other things being equal, however, an American option is worth more than a European option because of the extra flexibility it grants the option holder.

Although our discussion in this section is limited to options on equities, many other kinds of securities underlie publicly traded options. For example, people also trade options to buy or sell stock indexes, Treasury bonds, futures contracts, foreign currencies, and agricultural commodities. Table 22.4 summarizes the terms introduced in this section.

### 22.3.3 *Option exchanges*

In 1973, the Chicago Board Options Exchange (CBOE) was founded to provide a market for options. The opening of the CBOE created exponential growth in the popularity of options as financial

Table 22.4 Definitions of Option Terminology.

| **Call** | **An Option to Purchase a Fixed Number of Shares of Common Stock** |
|---|---|
| **Put** | An option to sell a fixed number of shares of common stock |
| **Exercise price** | The price at which the underlying security specified in an option contract may be traded |
| **Expiration date** | The time by which the option transaction must be carried out |
| **Exercise an option** | Carry out a transaction specified in an option contract |
| **American option** | An option that can be exercised any time up to the expiration date |
| **European option** | An option that can be exercised only on the expiration date |
| **At the money** | A call or put option with an exercise price equal to the current stock price |
| **In the money** | A call option with an exercise price below the stock price, or a put option with an exercise price above the stock price |
| **Out of the Money** | A call option with an exercise price above the stock price, or a put option with an exercise price below the stock price |
| **Naked options** | The writing of a call or put option without owning the underlying asset |

instruments. Most of the trading for options is done on electronic exchanges. Most derivatives exchanges are now fully electronic, so there is no need for traders to physically meet. The International Securities Exchange launched the first all-electronic options market for equities in May 2000. In addition, over 95% of the option orders handled at the Chicago Board Options Exchange are handled electronically. The remaining 5% are complex or large institutional orders that require the skill and knowledge of floor traders.

Today, the amount of option exchanges in the U.S. and around the world have increased. In addition to CBOE and the International Securities Exchange, there is BATS Option Market, Boston (BOX) Options Exchange, C2 Options Exchange, ISE Gemini, MIAC Options Exchange, NASDAQ OMX BX, NASDAQ OMX PHLX,

Philadelphia Stock Exchange, NASDAQ Options Market, NYSE, AMEX Options (American Stock Exchange), and NYSE Arca Options.

### 22.3.4 *Option price information*

Table 22.5 presents options quotations for Johnson & Johnson. The price of Johnson & Johnson shares on this date was $70.96. The first column gives the *expiration month* for each option. We have included listings for call and put options with exercise prices ranging from $67.50 to $72.50 per share, and with expiration dates in December 2012, and January and March 2013.

The next columns provide the closing prices, its change from the previous trading day, bid price, asked price, trading volume, and open interest (outstanding contracts) of each option. Column 4 shows the Bid, or the latest price offered by a market maker to buy a particular option. The *Ask* price in column 5 is the latest price offered a market maker to sell a particular option. For example, the first contract traded on the December 2012 expiration call with exercise price of $67.50. The last trade was at $3.50, meaning that an option to purchase one share of Johnson & Johnson at an exercise price of $67.50 sold for $3.50. Each option contract (on 100 shares) therefore costs $350.

Notice that the prices of call options decrease as the exercise price increases. For example, the December 2012 expiration call with exercise price $70 costs only $1.03. This makes sense, because the right to purchase a share at a higher exercise price is less valuable. Conversely, put prices increase with the exercise price. The right to sell a share of Johnson & Johnson at a price of $67.50 in December 2012 costs $0.03 while the right to sell at $70 costs $0.09.

Option prices also increase with time until expiration. Clearly, one would rather have the right to buy Johnson & Johnson for $70 at any time until January 2013 rather than at any time until December 2012. Not surprisingly, this shows up in a higher price for the January 2013 expiration options. For example, the call with exercise price $70 expiring in January 2013 sells for $1.42, compared to only $1.03 for the December 2012 call.

Table 22.5 Option Quotes for Johnson & Johnson, December 17, 2012.

**December 17, 2012**
**JNJ Underlying Stock Price: 70.96**

| | Call | | | | | | | Put | | | | | |
|---|---|---|---|---|---|---|---|---|---|---|---|---|---|
| **Expiration** | **Last** | **Chg** | **Bid** | **Ask** | **Volume** | **Open Int.** | **Strike** | **Last** | **Chg** | **Bid** | **Ask** | **Volume** | **Open Int.** |
| Dec 2012 | 3.50 | +0.35 | 3.45 | 3.55 | 3 | 626 | 67.50 | 0.03 | 0.00 | 0.02 | 0.04 | 1 | 9402 |
| Dec 2012 | 1.03 | +0.28 | 1.04 | 1.10 | 10293 | 15316 | 70.00 | 0.09 | -0.08 | 0.09 | 0.10 | 735 | 7237 |
| Dec 2012 | 0.03 | −0.03 | 0.03 | 0.01 | 99 | 10240 | 72.50 | 1.57 | -0.39 | 1.53 | 1.59 | 113 | 1399 |
| Jan 2013 | 3.57 | +0.37 | 3.55 | 3.65 | 287 | 23980 | 67.50 | 0.11 | -0.02 | 0.10 | 0.12 | 240 | 72991 |
| Jan 2013 | 1.42 | +0.21 | 1.41 | 1.43 | 313 | 70004 | 70.00 | 0.46 | -0.15 | 0.46 | 0.47 | 444 | 10940 |
| Jan 2013 | 0.27 | +0.03 | 0.25 | 0.27 | 1188 | 33215 | 72.50 | 1.82 | -0.32 | 1.78 | 1.83 | 308 | 7645 |
| Mar 2013 | 6.20 | +0.65 | 6.05 | 6.15 | 3 | 2418 | 65.00 | 0.26 | -0.07 | 0.25 | 0.26 | 235 | 25415 |
| Mar 2013 | 3.85 | +0.30 | 3.80 | 3.85 | 53 | 47303 | 67.50 | 0.57 | -0.14 | 0.56 | 0.58 | 179 | 12726 |
| Mar 2013 | 1.92 | +0.20 | 1.89 | 1.92 | 416 | 13686 | 70.00 | 1.34 | -0.18 | 1.31 | 1.33 | 120 | 5866 |

### 22.3.5 *Option valuation*

Let's begin with a simple question. How much is a call option worth on its expiration date? The question is simple because the imminent expiration makes the uncertain future movements of the price of the stock irrelevant. The call must be exercised immediately or not at all. If a call option is out of the money on its expiration date, it will not be exercised; it will become a worthless piece of paper.

On the other hand, if the call option is in the money on its expiration date, it will be exercised. The owner can purchase stock at the exercise price and immediately resell if at the market price, if desired. The option value is the difference between these two prices. On the call option's expiration date, its value is either zero or some positive amount equal to the difference between the market price of the stock and the exercise price of the option.

*Basic model*

Symbolically, let $P$ equal the price of the stock and $X$ equal the exercise price of the option. The value of the call, $V_c$, equals the maximum of zero or $P$ minus $X$. This relationship can be written as:

$$V_c = \text{Max}(0, P - X) \tag{22.1}$$

where Max denotes the larger of the two bracketed terms. For a put option ($V_p$), $V_p = X - P$ if $X > P$, and $V_p = 0$ if $X \leq P$. This can be written as:

$$V_p = \text{Max}(0, X - P) \tag{22.2}$$

The call position is illustrated in Panel (a) of Figure 22.1, which considers a call option with an exercise price of \$50, the call option is worthless, $V_c = 0$. The option's value increases as the stock price rises above \$50. If, on the expiration date, the stock is trading at \$60, then the call option is worth \$10.

Panel (b) of Figure 22.1 is the mirror image of Panel (a); it shows the position of the write of the call option. If the stock is trading below the exercise price on the expiration date, the call option will not be exercised and its seller will incur no loss. However, stock is trading at \$60, the seller of the call option will be required to sell

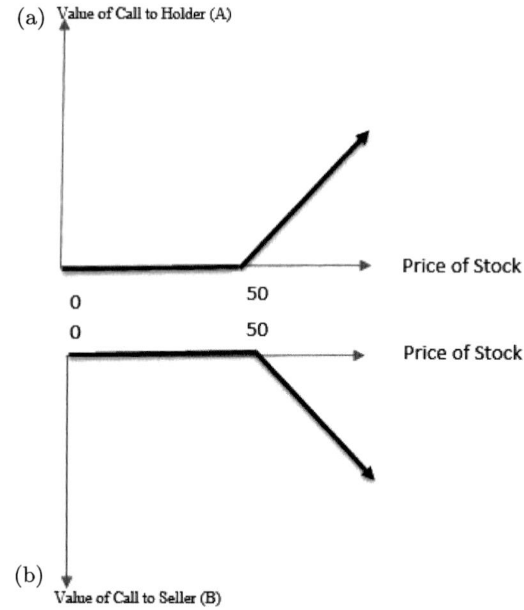


Figure 22.1 Value of $50 Exercise Price Call Option (a) to Holder, (b) to Seller.

this stock for $50, that is, $10 below the price that could be obtained on the market.

We have seen that once a call option has been purchased the holder of the option may obtain gains but cannot incur losses beyond the initial premium payment. Correspondingly, the writer of an option may incur losses but cannot achieve any more gains after receiving the premium. In both cases, the *premium* represents the current value of the option. Further, there is not net gain; the profit gained by one balances the loss of the other. Thus, options are zero-sum securities; they transfer wealth, rather than create it. To acquire this instrument, the buyer must pay the premium to the writer. This value is the price paid to acquire the chance of future profit, and therefore, it will reflect uncertainty about future market prices of the common stock. Several factors that influence call option values are discussed in the next section. The real value or attractiveness of options has to do with how options can transform risks. So it is not wealth creation that gives options value but rather the risk transformation factor.

### 22.3.6 *Variables that influence call option value*

Five factors influence the value of a call option: the market price of the stock, the exercise price of the option, the risk-free interest rate, the volatility of the stock price, and the time that remains before the option's expiration date. We'll examine the impact of these factors on call value next.

**Market Price of the Stock.** AE in Figure 22.2 shows the curvilinear relationship between a call option's value and the market price of the underlying stock. As already noted, the slope of this relationship increases as market price becomes higher; eventually, each dollar increase in the price of the stock translates into an increase in the value of the call option. In Figure 22.2, AB and CD represent the maximum and the minimum value for the call option, respectively.

**Exercise Price of the Option.** Offered two otherwise identical call options on the same stock, you would prefer the one with the lower exercise price. It would generate larger gains from any favorable movement in the price of the stock than the option with the higher exercise price. Therefore, a lower exercise price implies a

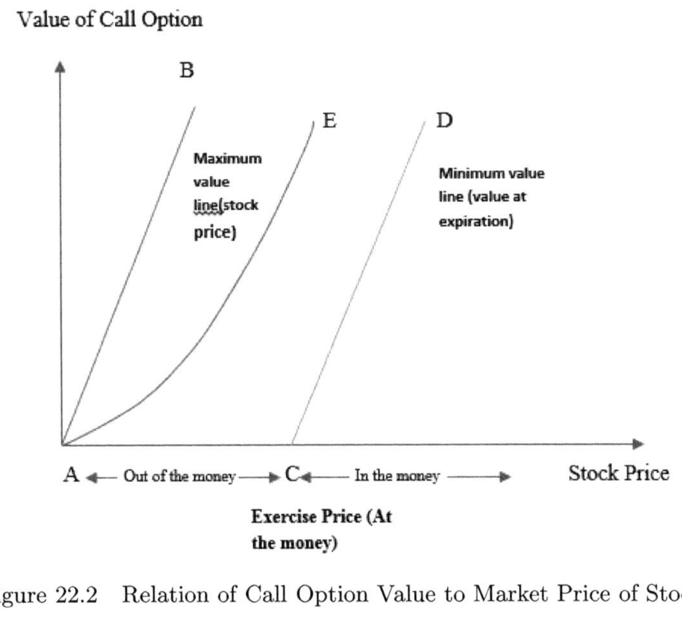


Figure 22.2 Relation of Call Option Value to Market Price of Stock.

higher call-option value, all other things being equal. In Figure 22.2, C represents the exercise price. In addition, the locations of at the money, in the money and out of the money prices are also presented.

**Risk-Free Interest Rate.** If a call option is eventually exercised, the holder of the option will reap some of the benefits of an increase in the market value of the stock. The option holder will enjoy this gain without having to pay the exercise price immediately. This payment will be made only at some future time, when the call option is actually exercised. In the meantime, this money can be invested in government securities to earn a no-risk return.

This opportunity confers an increment of value on the call option. All else being equal, a higher risk-free interest rate should cause a greater call option value. Moreover, postponing the exercise of the option for a longer time should increase the risk-free interest earnings. Accordingly, the risk-free interest rate should help to determine a call option's value in conjunction with the time remaining before the expiration date.

**Volatility of the Stock Price.** Suppose that you can purchase call options on either Stock A or Stock B each with an exercise price of \$50. Table 22.6 lists probabilities ($PR_i$) for different market prices ($P_i$) on the expiration date for each stock. Both mean expected future prices are \$52.[1] However, the price of Stock B is far more likely to

Table 22.6 Probabilities for Future Prices of Two Stocks.

| **Less Volatile for Stock A** | | | **More Volatile for Stock B** | | |
|---|---|---|---|---|---|
| **Future price ($P$)** | **Prob ($PR$)** | **($P$) ($PR$)** | **Future price ($P$)** | **Prob ($PR$)** | **($P$) ($PR$)** |
| 42 | 0.10 | 4.2 | 32 | 0.10 | 3.2 |
| 47 | 0.20 | 9.4 | 42 | 0.20 | 8.4 |
| 52 | 0.40 | 20.8 | 52 | 0.40 | 20.8 |
| 57 | 0.20 | 11.4 | 62 | 0.20 | 12.4 |
| 62 | 0.10 | 6.2 | 72 | 0.10 | 7.2 |
| | **1.00** | **52.0** | | **1.00** | **52.0** |

[1]Mean expected future price (MEFP) is calculated by the following formula: $\text{MEFP} = \sum_{i=1}^{n}(P_i)(PR_i)$.

differ substantially from the mean than the price of Stock A. The price of such a stock is said to be more volatile.

Following Eq. (22.1), the expected payoff (EP) on the expiration date for a call option can be defined as:

$$\mathrm{EP} = \sum_{i=1}^{n} (\mathrm{PR}_i) \times \mathrm{Max}(0, P_i - X) \tag{22.3}$$

where $P_i$ is the stock price per share at the $i$th state of nature, $X$ is the exercise price, and $\mathrm{PR}_i$ is the probability at the $i$th state of nature.

The expected payoff on the expiration date for a call option on the more volatile stock is higher than the expected payoff for a call option on the less volatile stock. The option on the less volatile stock will not be exercised at a price below \$50; for the three prices above \$50, it exercise will result in payoff of \$2, \$7, and \$12. Therefore, following Eq. (22.3), the expected payoff for the call option on the less volatile stock ($EP_A$) is:

$$\begin{aligned}\mathrm{EP}_A &= (0.10)(0) + (0.20)(0) + (0.40)(2) + (0.20)(7) \\ &\quad + (0.10)(12) = \$3.40\end{aligned}$$

Similarly, for a call option on the more volatile stock, $\mathrm{EP}_B$:

$$\begin{aligned}\mathrm{EP}_B &= (0.10)(0) + (0.20)(0) + (0.40)(2) + (0.20)(12) \\ &\quad + (0.10)(22) = \$5.40\end{aligned}$$

where $\mathrm{EP}_B$ is the \$5.40 expected payoff from the call option on the more volatile stock.

Although the mean expected future price is the same for the two stocks, the expected payoff from a call option on the more volatile stock is higher. This conclusion is quite general. For example, it does not require that the exercise price must fall below the expected future stock price.

**Time Remaining to Option's Expiration.** The above discussions of the risk-free interest rate and stock price volatility both suggest that a longer time remaining before an option's expiration date should accompany a higher call option value, all else being equal. Extra time allows larger gains from postponing payment of the exercise price, and it permits greater volatility in price movements of the stock. These two considerations operate together to increase the value of a call option.

Following the five variables just mentioned, Black and Scholes derived the well-known option pricing model presented in Appendix 22B. In the following section, we will use these option concepts to discuss option-like securities in some detail.

## 22.4 Option-Like Securities

Some corporate bond and stock issues take on the characteristics of options. Bonds constitute a fixed claim on the corporation, while common stock confers a residual claim and a share in corporate ownership. However, corporations also raise capital by issuing securities that are neither straight debt nor straight equity. In this section, we will discuss the following option-like securities: warrants, callable bonds, convertible securities, and risky corporate debt.

### 22.4.1 *Warrants*

As mentioned earlier, a *warrant* constitutes an option to purchase a specific number of shares of common stock at a stipulated price for a set period of time directly from the issuing corporation. Typically, a warrant accompanies a bond issue, but it is detachable; it can be traded separately from the bond. A warrant is essentially a call option written by the company that issues the stock. Its value is influenced by the same factors that influence the value of a call option.

In this context, the value of a warrant at expiration ($V_w$) is defined by the following equation:

$$V_w = \text{Max}[0, NP - NX] \tag{22.4}$$

where $P$ and $X$ are as defined in Eq. (22.1) and $N$ is the number of shares obtainable with each warrant.

### 22.4.2 *Convertible securities*

A *convertible security* is a bond or preferred stock issue that typically gives its holder the right to exchange it for a stipulated number of shares of common stock of the issuing corporation during a specified period of time. Therefore, convertible bonds and convertible preferred stock represent options to the security holder. If the price of common stock rises sufficiently, holders of these securities will find it profitable to exercise their conversion rights. As for a warrant, such a right will have some positive value in the market, so the market will accept a lower coupon rate on the corporation's convertible bonds then it would demand for a bond with no conversion privilege.

Convertible bonds are especially attractive when management prefers to raise capital by issuing equity rather than debt, but believes that transient influences have led the market to temporarily undervalue its common stock. If this perception is correct, the stock price will rise and, as a result, debt will be converted to equity. A convertible bond issue may offer an advantage over a bond issue with warrants since managers can predict how much capital the issue will raise.

The exercise of a warrant raises further capital for the firm; conversion simply substitutes equity for debt. The conversion of a bond issue for shares of common stock does not raise new capital, but it does implicitly increase cash flow if the conversion occurs prior to the bond's maturity date, by reducing future coupon payments.

A further distinction between warrants and convertible bonds is that warrants are not callable, while the issuer generally can call a convertible bond. The bondholder can be offered the option of converting it within a short time period or surrendering it at a specific cash price. As with all callable bonds, investors demand higher returns for callable, convertible securities. Firms are willing to pay this higher price in exchange for management flexibility.

We have seen why a corporation might want to issue a hybrid security rather than straight debt and/or equity. What about the investor? These securities may be particularly attractive when investors have trouble assessing the riskiness of a corporation's future business activities. If the corporation embarks on a high-risk enterprise, holders of straight bonds will be in the unappealing position of gaining nothing if the enterprise succeeds and facing greatly increased default risk if it fails.

Warrants or conversion privileges can restore some balance. By exercising a warrant or converting a bond to stock, the bondholder can share in any success resulting from a risky venture. This reduces the importance of assessing the future business risk of a corporation's activities. Now we will discuss how the conversion privilege can be determined.

Consider an issue of 20-year bonds with face values of \$1,000. Each bond is convertible to 50 shares of common stock and the current market price of the stock is \$15 per share. The coupon rate on these convertible bonds is 9.5%, while straight debt of the issuing corporation with similar terms currently carries a rate of 12%. This issue can be called by the corporation, at a price of \$1,050, at any time after five years. How much do investors pay for the conversion privilege?

The number of shares that can be received in exchange for each bond is set by the *conversion ratio*; the conversion ratio of the issue described above is 50 shares to one bond. Immediate conversion would exchange a bond valued at \$1,000 for 50 shares of common stock, so that the effective price of the stock would be \$20 per share. This *conversion price*, in general, equals:

$$\text{Conversion price} = \frac{\text{Par value of bond}}{\text{Conversion ratio}}$$

Many convertible bond contracts specifically state conversion prices. The conversion price of the example bond exceeds the current market price of the shares by one-third. Obviously, it makes no sense to exercise this conversion privilege immediately. However, that privilege may have some value due to the profit that holders of the convertible bond can expect to earn if the price of the stock increases sufficiently.

The value of the conversion privilege is determined by computing the present value of the bond's debt element. Holding the bond to maturity, the bondholder would receive a stream of 20 annual payments of \$95, plus \$1,000 at the end of Year 20. Discounting these payments at a rate of 12% gives a present value of debt, $\text{PV}_D$, of:

$$\begin{aligned}\text{PV}_D &= \sum_{t=1}^{20} \frac{\$95}{(1.12)^t} + \frac{\$1{,}000}{(1.12)^{20}} \\ &= \$95 \times \text{PVIFA}(12\%, 20\,\text{years}) \\ &\quad + \$1{,}000\text{PVIF}(12\%, 20\,\text{years}) \\ &= \$709.60 + \$103.67 = \$813.27\end{aligned}$$

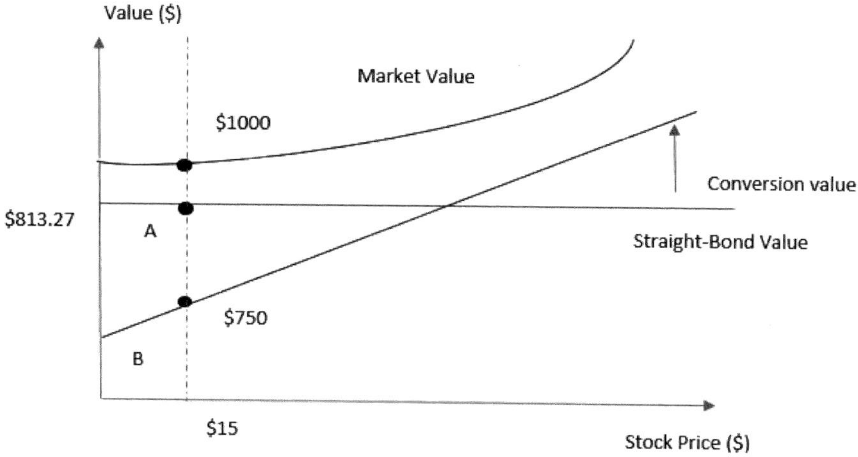


Figure 22.3 Market Value of a Convertible Bond.

This often is called the *straight bond value* of the convertible bond. The market value of a convertible bond is somewhat above the higher of the conversion or straight bond value, as shown in Figure 22.3.

Remember, however that the instrument may be worth more if the conversion privilege is exercised. Since, at issue, the bond can be exchanged for 50 shares of common stock valued by the market at $15 per share; its conversion value is 50 times $15 or $750. The bond value exceeds the conversion value, but it is lower than the price of the bond. If the bond is issued at par, then the difference between the market value of $1,000 and the larger of the straight bond value (line A in Figure 22.3) or conversion value is $186.73. This represents the *conversion premium*, or the price (line B in Figure 22.5) that investors pay for the conversion privilege.

As mentioned earlier, the conversion privilege is essentially a call option on shares of common stock, so its value is influenced by all those factors that determine the value of call options. However, one additional factor also has an effect. If the conversion privilege is exercised, the bond must be surrendered in exchange for stock. Therefore, the exercise price per share of the call option is the market price of the convertible bond divided by the conversion ratio. Over time, market forces will cause the price of the convertible bond to vary, so the exercise price of the implicit call option also will vary.

### 22.4.3 *Callable bonds*

Corporate bonds often are issued with call provisions that entitle the issuer to buy back the bond from bondholders at some later date, at a specified price. These securities are called callable bonds. We can view the call provision as a call option held by the issuer of the bond. In this case, the excise price is equal to the price at which the bond can be repurchased. In order for bondholders to allow the firm to hold a call option on the security they own, they must be compensated with a higher coupon rate.

### 22.4.4 *Risky corporate debt*

Sometimes, options are used to value risky corporate debt. Because of the limited liability of stockholders, money borrowed by the firm is back, at most, by the total value of the firm's assets. One way to view this agreement is to consider that stockholders have sold the entire firm to debt holders but hold a call option with an exercise price equal to the face value of the debt. In this case, if the value of the firm exceeds the value of the debt, stockholders exercise the call option by paying off the bondholders. If the value of the firm is less than the value of the debt, shareholders do not exercise the call option, and all assets are distributed to the bondholders.

Black and Scholes (1973) have used the option pricing model to discuss the relationship between stock, bonds, and firm values.

### 22.4.5 *Earnings per share with warrants and convertibles*

Warrants and convertible securities can change a firm's earnings per share (EPS) and number of shares outstanding. Investors, managers, accountants, and federal and state government agencies all watch the earnings per share of a corporation. Earnings per share generally means net income after taxes, less preferred stock dividends, divided by the weighted average number of shares of common stock outstanding. In 1969, the Accounting Principles Board, a forerunner of the FASB, issued APB Opinion No. 15, "Earnings Per Share." This ruling laid down the rules for calculating the earnings per share for financial reporting purposes. In 1982, the FASB issued Statement

No. 55, "Determining Whether a Convertible Security Is a Common Stock Equivalent." The accounting requirements set out in these rulings provide alternative ways of calculating earnings per share if a company has outstanding convertible securities, warrants, stock options, or other contracts that permit it to increase the number of shares of common stock.

The EPS for a firm with a simple capital structure is called basic EPS. A simple capital structure has only one form of voting capital and includes no potential equity, such as warrants or convertibles. The existence of nonconvertible preferred stock does not create a complex capital structure.

A corporation that has warrants, convertibles, or options outstanding is said to have a *complex capital structure*. The complexity comes from the difficulty of measuring the number of shares outstanding. This is a function of a known amount of common shares currently outstanding plus an estimate of the number of shares that may be issued to satisfy the holders of warrants, convertibles, and options should they decide to exercise their rights and receive new common shares.

Because of the possible dilution in EPS represented by securities that have the potential to become new shares of common stock, the EPS calculation must account for *common stock equivalents* (CSEs). CSEs are securities that are not common stock, but are equivalent to common stock because they are likely to be converted into common stock in the future. Convertible debt, convertible preferred stock, stock rights, stock options, and stock warrants all are securities that can create new common shares and thus dilute (or reduce) the firm's earnings per share. APB No. 15 mandates the calculation of two types of EPS for a firm with a complex capital structure: primary EPS and fully diluted EPS. It is useful to review the basic accounting concepts dealing with income recognition and ownership at this point.

1. *Basic EPS.* The earnings available to stockholders are divided by the average number of shares actually outstanding during the period.
2. *Primary EPS.* The earnings available to stockholders are divided by average number of common shares plus the common stock equivalents (CSEs).

3. *Fully diluted EPS.* Earnings are handled in a manner similar to primary EPS, but all warrants and convertibles are assumed to be exercised or converted. In other words, EPS is assumed to be at maximum dilution.

The relationship between these three types of EPS can be presented as follows:

**Primary EPS**

EPS = Basic EPS – Impact of CSE – CSE impact of all other dilutive securities

Fully Diluted EPS

It is interesting to speculate on whether the market will use primary EPS or fully diluted EPS in valuing shares of stock. If the market expects holders of common stock equivalents to convert them into new equity, then fully diluted EPS is likely to be more meaningful. If the market does not expect conversion, then it is likely to treat convertible bonds like straight debt and focus on primary EPS with no adjustment for new shares. In other words, the market is likely to use basic EPS in such cases.

Convertible bonds that have no chance of being converted are called *hung convertibles.* The idea here is that if investors don't wish to convert their bonds into the firm's equity, the conversion price is hung. The bond is worth more as a bond than it is worth converted into equity. APB No. 15 and FASB No. 55 require a firm to provide EPS information under either circumstance and let the market participant choose which measure is more meaningful.

The financial analyst needs to identify the difference between two firms with a similar primary EPS value and markedly different fully diluted EPS values. In general, hybrid securities in the capital structure cause the difference.

## 22.5 Swap Contracts and Hedging

In addition to using forward, futures, and option contracts to hedge transactions or transaction exposure, many corporations are engaging in what are called *swap transactions* to accomplish this. A *swap contract* is a private agreement between two companies to exchange a specific cash flow amount at a specific date in the future. If the specific cash flow amount is interest payments, then the contract is an *interest rate swap*; if the specific amount of cash flows is currency payments, then the contract is a *currency swap*. The first swap contract was negotiated between IBM and the World Bank in the early eighties. Since that time, the swap market has grown to over $10 trillion.

### 22.5.1 *Interest rate swaps*

An *interest rate swap* is a financial transaction in which two borrowers exchange interest payments on a particular amount of principal with a specified maturity. The swap enables each party to alter the characteristics of the periodic interest payments that it makes or receives.

The exchange might involve swapping a fixed-rate payment for a variable rate payment or one type of floating rate for another. All swaps trade only interest payments made on underlying note values; no principal payments need to change hands with a simple interest rate swap.

Figure 22.4 shows the cash flows of a simple interest rate swap for each of the parties involved. The two primary parties to the swap are called *counterparties*. Usually, although not always, a financial institution serves as an intermediary between the counterparties.

In this example, Company A exchanges a variable-rate debt for a fixed-rate debt. Company B trades its fixed-rate debt for a variable-rate debt. The intermediary has no exposure to interest rate movements and earns a fee of 0.1%, which is spread between the payments and the receipts of A and B.

In the typical interest rate swap, the counterparty with the fixed-rate debt pays a premium over the rate the other counterparty initially paid on its variable-rate debt. This premium is based upon factors such as terms of the swap, the creditworthiness of the counterparties, and the conditions in the market for fixed rate and variable-rate debt.

It is unusual for two companies to arrange an interest rate swap themselves. In most cases, intermediaries act as brokers, dealers, or principals to the transaction. As a broker or dealer, the intermediary serves to bring A and B together and collects an arrangement fee. However, in most swaps the intermediary acts as a principal to both counterparties, assuming the credit risk in the event that one

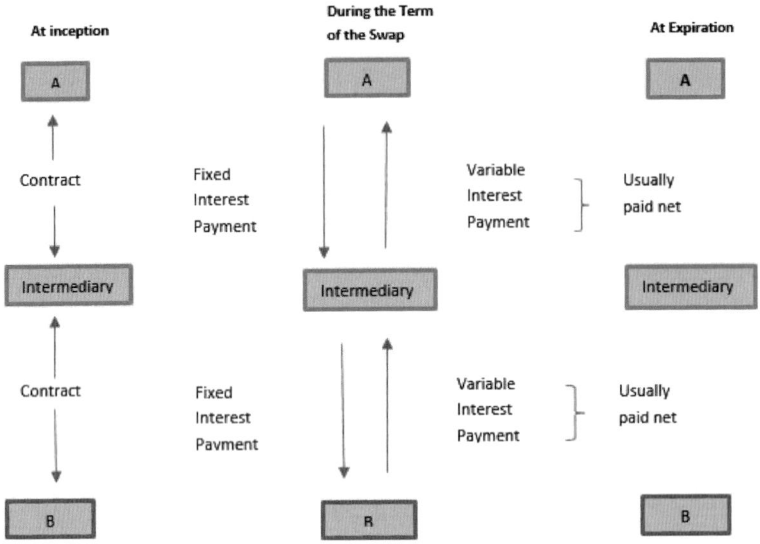


Figure 22.4 Cash Flows from a Simple Interest Swap.

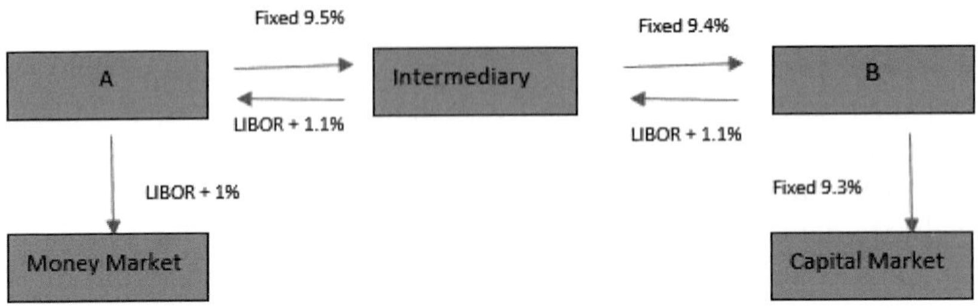


Figure 22.5 Costs of an Interest Rate Swap.

counterparty defaults. When the intermediary acts as the principal to a swap, its compensation is in the form of an arrangement fee and/or the spread between the terms of these two counterparties.

Firm A has a variable-rate debt with an interest rate of LIBOR (London Interbank Offer Rate) + 1%, which is borrowed from the money market; Firm B has a fixed-rate debt with a fixed rate of 9.3%, which is borrowed from the capital market. Through the intermediary, Firm A swaps its variable-rate debt for Firm B's fixed-rate debt at interest payment dates. This interest rate swap flowchart is presented in Figure 22.5.

The analysis of this swap is now presented in more detail.

From the information given in Figure 22.5, the interest rate cost of Firm A and Firm B and the fee of the intermediary can be calculated as follows:

| | **Firm A** | **Intermediary** | **Firm B** |
|---|---|---|---|
| Pays | Fixed 9.5% | Fixed 9.4% | Fixed 9.3% |
| | LIBOR + 1% | LIBOR + 1.1% | LIBOR + 1.1% |
| Receives | LIBOR + 1.1% | Fixed 9.5% | Fixed 9.4% |
| | Fixed 9.4% | LIBOR + 1% | LIBOR + 1.1% |
| Net Payment (Income) | (0.1%) | | |

After the swap, Firm A owns a fixed-rate debt with an interest rate of 9.4% and Firm B owns a variable-rate debt with an interest rate of LIBOR + 1%. The intermediary earns a fee of 0.1%. Due to this swap, Firm A has eliminated its interest rate exposure risk.

Firm A has entered into the swap, it has three sets of cash flows:

1. It pays FIXED 9.5% to Intermediary
2. It pays LIBOR + 1% to Money Market
3. It receives LIBOR + 1.1% from Intermediary

For Firm B, the swap could have the effects of transforming a fixed-rate loan into a floating-rate loan. After it has entered into the swap, it has three sets of cash flows:

1. It pays FIXED 9.3% to Capital Market
2. It pays LIBOR +1.1% to Intermediary
3. It receives FIXED 9.4% from Intermediary For intermediary, there are four cash flows:

1. It pays LIBOR +1.1% to Firm A
2. It pays FIXED 9.4% to Firm B
3. It receives FIXED 9.5% from Firm A
4. It receives LIBOR +1.1% from Firm B

By using the interest rate swap theory and method discussed in this section, we will discuss different swapping strategies that are available to bond portfolio managers. Swapping strategies in portfolio management can be classified: (1) pure yield-pickup swap, (2) interest-rate anticipations, (3) intermarket swap, and (4) substitution swap. Substitution swap attempts to profit from a change in yield spread between two nearly identical bonds. The trade is based upon a forecasted change in the yield spread between the two bonds, holding the coupon and maturity equal for both bonds. Intermarket Swap works on trading between sector-quality coupon categories, based upon a forecasted change in yield spread between two different categories. In this method, the most common forecasting method is to observe historical yield spreads at various points in the interest-rate cycle, and then adjust them for current supply-demand effects.

Interest-rate anticipation swaps are geared toward the investor who believes the level of interest rate is going to change and wants to benefit from this change. This type of swap is highly speculative, and time as a factor works heavily against the swapper. In a pure yield-pickup swap there is no expectation of market changes, but a simple attempt to increase yield. Essentially, two bonds are examined to establish their difference in yield to maturity (YTM), with a further adjustment to consider the impact of interim reinvestment of coupons at an assumed rate or return between now and the maturity date.

### 22.5.2 *Currency swaps*

In a *currency swap*, two firms agree to exchange an equivalent amount of two different currencies for a specified period of time.

As an example of a typical currency swap, suppose a company from the UK would like to borrow U.S. dollars to finance a foreign investment, but the firm is not known outside the UK. Similarly, a U.S. firm needs British Pounds for its UK subsidiary, but the cost of borrowing in the U.S. is cheaper than the cost of borrowing in UK for this firm. Both firms face a similar problem. They can borrow at favorable rates, but not in the desired currency. In this case, a currency swap presents one solution. A bank acting as an intermediary can bring these two firms together and arrange a swap of British Pounds for dollars. The UK firm agrees to pay the U.S. Company principal and interest on its dollar borrowings in U.S., while the U.S. firm agrees to pay the costs of the pound borrowings for its UK

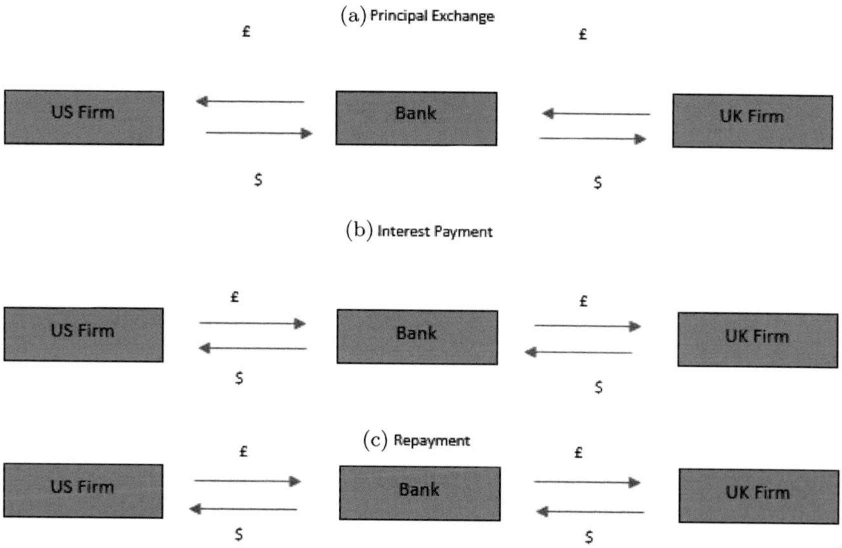


Figure 22.6 Currency Swap.

subsidiaries. Each firm thus obtains the best possible rate and eliminates exposure to exchange rate changes by agreeing to exchange currencies. Figure 22.6 illustrates the workings of a currency swap.

Figure 22.6 can be used to explain this action as: (a) principal exchange, (b) interest payment, and (c) repayment. In this case, U.S. firm and UK firm agree to exchange an amount of U.S. dollars for an equivalent amount of British Sterling. In a principal exchange, the UK firm pays the U.S. firm an amount of British Sterling and U.S. firm equivalent amount of U.S. dollars.

Consider a hypothetical five-year currency swap agreement between a U.S. firm and a UK firm entered into on March 1, 2014. We supposed the U.S. firm pays a fixed rate of interest of 4% in sterling and receives a fixed rate of interest of 5% in dollars from the UK. Interest rate payments are made once a year and the principal amounts are \$20 million and £15 million. This is termed a fixed-for-fixed currency swap because the interest rate in each currency is at a fixed rate. The swap is shown in Figure 22.6. Initially, the principle amounts flow in the opposite direction to the arrows in Figure 22.6. At the outset of the swap, the U.S. firm pays \$20 million and receives £15 million. Each year during the life of the swap

Table 22.7 Cash Flows to U.S. Firm in Currency Swap.

| Date | Dollar Cash Flows (millions) | Sterling Cash Flows (millions) |
|---|---|---|
| March 1, 2014 | −20.00 | +15.00 |
| March 1, 2015 | +1.00 | −0.60 |
| | +1.00 | −0.60 |
| March 1, 2016 | | |
| March 1, 2017 | +1.00 | −0.60 |
| March 1, 2018 | +1.00 | −0.60 |
| March 1, 2019 | +21.00 | −15.60 |

contract, the U.S. firm receives \$1 million (= 5% ∗ \$20 million) and pays £.60 million (= 4% ∗ \$15 million). At the end of the life of the swap, its pays a principal of £15 million and receives principal of \$20 million. We show these cash flows in Table 22.7

## 22.6 Risk Management

In Sections 22.2 and 22.4, we discussed how futures and swaps can be used to hedge interest rate risk and exchange rate risk. In this section, we briefly summarize how options, futures, and swaps can be used in corporate risk management.

Unexpected changes in interest rates, exchanges rates, and prices can lead to serious economic consequences for a corporation. For example, changing exchange rates can impact the price that a U.S. importer pays for goods. Because of the great volatility in the financial markets in the last decade, corporations have been devoting a great deal of effort to managing or hedging these types of financial risks. Many of these risk management strategies incorporate the use of options, futures, and swaps.

The basic idea of hedging is to take a position in a derivative security (options, futures, or swaps) so that losses in the spot market will be offset by gains in the derivatives security. For example, a corporation that will be using commercial paper to raise short-term funds in four months may be concerned that interest rates will rise and thus increase the cost of these funds. Because a rise in interest rates will reduce the amount the corporation receives from the issue, it may try to hedge a reduction in the price of its issue. This corporation can hedge the risk of a price decrease caused by an increase in interest rates by buying a futures contract on money market instruments such as Treasury bills or Eurodollars. If interest rates do rise, at least a portion of the losses will be offset by gains from the futures contract.

As another example, a corporation that has borrowed a significant amount of funds at variable interest rate may be concerned about rising short-term interest rates. Rising interest rates will increase the firm's interest costs significantly, and may adversely affect its financial well-being. To reduce its interest rate exposure, the corporation may engage in an interest rate swap in which some of the interest payments on the floating rate debt are exchanged for interest payments at a fixed rate. This allows the corporation to reduce its short-term interest rate exposure.

## 22.7 Summary

In this chapter, we discussed the basic concepts of futures, options, and swaps and how these instruments can be used to hedge risk. In addition, the concept of options was used to illustrate the mechanics of a number of securities that have option-like properties. Corporate securities, such as warrants, convertible bonds, convertible preferred stock, callable bonds, and risky corporate debt all can be analyzed using the basic principles of options. We also discussed the calculation of earnings per share for a company issuing warrants and convertibles. We also discussed gold futures and another important hedging instrument, the swap, including both interest rate swaps and currency swaps.

The main ideas discussed in this chapter are summarized as follows:

1. Futures contracts such as currency futures have similar characteristics as forward contracts. Both forward and futures contracts can be used to hedge risk.
2. Two basic types of options are call option and put option. The value of call option depends on the following five factors:

a. current stock price per share
b. exercise price of the option
c. risk-free interest rate
d. volatility of the stock price
e. time remaining to option's expiration date

3. Firms frequently issue option-like securities. For example, warrants are long-term call options issued by the firm; convertible bonds give the investor the right to buy the firm's stocks in exchange for the value of the underlying bonds. Callable bonds give the option right to the issuing firms instead of investors.
4. Risky corporate debt issued by a firm can be regarded as an option contract. We can consider that stockholders have sold the entire firm to debt holders but hold a call option with an exercise price equal to the face value of the debt.
5. Swap contracts allow firms to exchange one series of future payments for another. Both interest rate and currency swaps can be used to do risk management for a firm.

## References

Black, F. and M. Scholes. "The Valuation of Options and Corporate Liabilities," *Journal of Political Economy*, 81(3) (1973, pp. 637–654).

Hull, J. C. *Fundamentals of Futures and Options Markets*, 9th edn. (Pearson, 2017).

Hull, J. C. *Options, Futures, and Other Derivatives*, 10th edn. (Pearson, 2018).

Lee, C. F. and A. C. Lee. *Encyclopedia of Finance*, 3rd edn. (Springer, 2022).

Lee, C. F., J. C. Lee and A. C. Lee. *Statistics for Business and Financial Economics*, 3rd edn. (Springer, 2013).

Lee, C. F., J. C. Lee and A. C. Lee. *Intermediate Futures and Options* (World Scientific, 2023).

Lee, C. F., J. C. Lee and M. Lee. *Corporate Finance and Strategy: An Active Learning Approach*, 2nd edn. (World Scientific Publishing Co., 2022).

Lee, C. F., J. C. Lee, J. R. Chang and T. Tai. *Essentials of Microsoft Excel, VBA, SAS, and MINITAB for Statistical and Financial Analyses* (World Scientific, 2016).

Lee, C. F., J. Finnerty, J. C. Lee, A. C. Lee and D. Wort. *Security Analysis, Portfolio Management, and Financial Derivatives*, 3rd edn. (World Scientific, 2013).

## Appendix 22A — Single Stock Futures

In this appendix, we will learn about Single Stock Futures (SSF) and how these alternate securities can be used by investors to increase their profitability while managing their exposure. Single Stock futures possess many of the same qualities of traditional futures contracts, yet also have their differences. We will look more into the nature of Single Stock Futures, as well as their advantages in this appendix.

Single stock futures are futures contracts on individual stocks. There are currently over 80 well-known stock futures such as IBM, eBay, and Philip Morris. These futures products provide investors with a cost effective vehicle for participating in U.S. equities markets.

A stock futures contract is an agreement to deliver shares of a specific stock at a designated date in the future, called the expiration date. Most stock futures contracts are not held until expiration because traders typically offset their position — selling if the trader is long or buying if the trader is short.

The price of an equity futures typically tracks the price of the underlying instrument nearly tick for tick, so trading strategies followed in the stock market are generally transferable to the stock futures market. Single stock futures may therefore be used with a broad range of trading strategies and for a variety of portfolio management needs.

When a stock future is traded, both the buyer and seller put up a good faith deposit called margin. The margin requirement for security futures is generally 20% of the underlying value of the securities, although this requirement may be lower if the investor also holds certain offsetting positions in cash equities, stock options, or other security futures in the same securities account.

### 22A.1 Nature of SSF Contracts

Each single stock futures contract represents 100 shares of underlying stock. That is the contract size used at the London International Financial Futures Exchange (LIFFE) and by the Chicago Board Options Exchange (CBOE) for equity options. There are no daily price limits for SSF contracts. Like other securities that are exchange traded, physical delivery of underlying security takes place on the third business day following the Expiration Day.

In Figure 22.1A, we see the market quotes for Single Stock Futures from OneChicago for November 24, 2014. Both tables show the trading of SSF on the OneChicago Exchange, the bottom table just representing what stocks experience more frequent trading. The first column represents the *symbol* for each of the SSF. In the bottom table, we see that there are quotes on Allstate (ALL1C), Cisco Systems (CSCO1C), American Express (AXP), and many others. The second column, *expiration month,* states the month of expiration for each of the stock futures depicted, in this case either March or December. The third column, *days to expiration*, expands on column 2 and provides a quantitative measure of the days left in the futures contract. The fourth and seventh columns, *Future Bid Size and Future Ask Size* describe the size of the futures contract in question. As we can see for the EA1D futures contract in the second table, there is a bid/ask size of 10. The *Future Bid* illustrates the price that people are willing to buy the SSF contracts at, and the *Future Ask* is the price at which people are willing to sell. Looking at the *Dividend* column, we see that most of the stocks do not offer a dividend, except for ALL1C. In the following section we will see that when pricing single stock futures, we need to account for dividends by subtracting them out of the equation due to the fact that SSF contract holders are not entitled to a dividend. The last column represents the *time* at which each trade occurred.

## 22A.2 Pricing Single Stock Futures

Single stock futures values are priced by the market in accordance with a theoretical pricing model based on a formula:

$$\text{Futures price} = \text{Underlying stock price X}$$
$$(1 + \text{Annualized interest rate}) - \text{Dividend})$$

For stocks that contain a dividend we get the following equation:

$$F = S\cdot(1 + r) - \text{Div} \tag{22.1A}$$

| Symbol | Expiration Month | Days to Expiration | Future BID Size | Future BID | Future ASK | Future ASK Size | Dividend | Time |
|---|---|---|---|---|---|---|---|---|
| **ONECHICAGO ETF Futures on 11-24-2014** | | | | | | | | |
| XLF1D | Dec | 27 | 100 | 242.26000 | 24.3400 | 100 | 0.0000 | 11:23:59 |
| XLE1D | Dec | 27 | 100 | 88.1500 | 88.2400 | 100 | 0.0000 | 11:24:00 |
| SPY1D | Dec | 27 | 10 | 206.7000 | 207.3100 | 10 | 0.0000 | 11:23:31 |
| QQQ1D | Dec | 27 | 50 | 104.3600 | 104.4400 | 50 | 0.0000 | 11:23:59 |
| IWM1D | Dec | 27 | 10 | 117.2100 | 117.3600 | 10 | 0.0000 | 11:23:50 |
| DIA1D | Dec | 27 | 100 | 117.6700 | 177.8000 | 100 | 0.0000 | 11:24:00 |
| **Top 10 Most Active Futures at ONECHICAGO on 11-24-2014** | | | | | | | | |
| EA1D | Mar | 118 | 10 | 43.3300 | 44.2200 | 10 | 0.0000 | 10:06:33 |
| AA1C | Dec | 27 | 0 | 0.0000 | 0.0000 | 0 | 0.0000 | 09:55:37 |
| ALL1C | Dec | 27 | 0 | 0.0000 | 0.0000 | 0 | 0.2799 | 09:55:10 |
| AUY1D | Mar | 118 | 500 | 4.0300 | 4.1000 | 500 | 0.0000 | 11:23:08 |
| AXP1C | Dec | 27 | 0 | 0.0000 | 0.0000 | 0 | 0.0000 | 09:56:00 |
| CCL1C | Dec | 27 | 0 | 0.0000 | 0.0000 | 0 | 0.0000 | 09:56:31 |
| COH1D | Dec | 27 | 10 | 37.4100 | 37.4900 | 10 | 0.0000 | 11:24:00 |
| COST1C | Dec | 27 | 0 | 0.0000 | 0.0000 | 0 | 0.0000 | 11:16:40 |
| CS1D | Dec | 27 | 30 | 26.7600 | 26.8900 | 30 | 0.0000 | 11:23:38 |
| CSCO1C | Dec | 27 | 0 | 0.0000 | 0.0000 | 0 | 0.0000 | 09:57:22 |

Figure 22.1A SSF Quotes from OneChicago.

where $F$ is the single-stock futures contract price, $S$ is the underlying stock price, $r$ is the annualized interest rate, and $Div$ is the expected dividend.

Another valuation of single stock futures can be found through the following:

$$F = [S - PV(\text{Div})]{\cdot}e^{r\cdot}(T - t) \tag{22.2A}$$

where $F$ is single stock futures contract price, $S$ is the underlying stock price, $PV(Div)$ is the present value of any dividends entitled to the holder of the underlying between $T$ and $t$, $r$ is the interest rate, and $e$ is the base of the natural log.

For stocks that do not contain a dividend we can price SSF using the following equation:

$$F = S{\cdot}(1 + r) \tag{22.3A}$$

where $F$ is the single-stock futures contract price, $S$ is the underlying stock price, $r$is the annualized interest rate.

Another valuation of single stock futures can be found through the following:

$$F = S \cdot e^{r\cdot(T-t)} \tag{22.4A}$$

where $F$ is single stock futures contract price, $S$ is the price of the underlying (the stock price), $T - t$ is the days to expiration, $r$ is the interest rate, and $e$ is the base of the natural log.

Most of the time, single stock futures will trade at a premium to the stock price adjusted for the broker loan rate. The premium reflects the interest earned on the capital saved by not posting the full value of the underlying stock. Since futures holders are not entitled to collect dividends, the futures price must be adjusted downward by the expected amount of dividend payments prior to expiration. In the case where a large dividend payment is expected, the futures contract may theoretically trade at a discount to the actual cash price.

## 22A.3 Advantages of Single Stock Futures

There are many advantages to an investor who chooses to use Single Stock Futures. Some of these advantages are as follows:

**Selling A Stock Short.**
One advantage to selling a stock short is the ease and diminished expense of taking a short position in a single stock. Selling a stock short in the stock market is relatively complicated and expensive. A short sale in a stock necessitates locating the shares to borrow and paying the broker loan rate of interest. You must then wait for an uptick to sell the stock short. Waiting for an uptick to sell a stock short in a declining market can be frustrating and costly. By the time a particular stock upticks, it could be substantially below the price at which you wanted it sold. However, in the futures market with the SSF contract, you can sell a stock short just as easily as you can buy one. When you sell a stock short using an SSF contract, you don't have to wait for an uptick. You can sell when you want, without going to the trouble of finding the stock and without the expense of paying the broker loan rate of interest on the shares borrowed.

**Risk Management.**
Selling SSF contracts can also greatly contribute to risk management in an investor's portfolio with possible tax benefits. Instead of selling specific stocks in one's portfolio during market downturns, an investor could sell an equal amount of shares in SSF as a hedge against his or her stock position. The ability to hedge a particular stock facilitates holding onto the underlying position in the stock market for longer periods of time, thereby potentially providing investors substantial tax savings in long-term versus short-term gains.

**Speculation.**
An investor without owning any stock could use SSF to speculate outright on an anticipated increase or decrease in the price of a stock.

**Margins.**
One major difference between stocks and futures centers on the role of margins. For stocks, margins, which are set by the Federal Reserve's Regulation T, have been at 50% for retail investors and 15% for dealers since 1974. A stock investor buying on margin borrows the difference, and can either pay the loan down, or offset it when the security is sold. Futures margins, which are set by the exchange, don't represent a down payment on an asset — but are rather a performance bond from the investor to the exchange clearinghouse.

Margins vary quite widely as a percentage of the underlying asset, but generally are quite low. For example, the underlying value of the S&P 500 future is hovering around $335,000, but the initial margin for a speculator is only $23,438, or less than 7%. The futures investor doesn't have to pay interest on the remaining 93%; indeed, futures investors can deposit T-bills and earn interest on 90% of the deposit with a 10% haircut in their margin accounts.

**Cost Advantage.**
SSF are traded in 100-share blocks, virtually mirroring the price movement in the single stock on which the futures contract is based. A $1 move in an individual stock equals $100 in an SSF contract. There is a big cost advantage here. In order to control shares in a stock, you need to post at least 50% margin and pay interest on the balance. In SSF, all that is required is approximately 20%, or less than half the margin required in the stock market. Additionally, there is no interest charge on buying or selling a stock on margin in SSF. Essentially, you will earn or lose the same in an SSF contract as you would when buying 100 shares of stock.

**Commission Savings.**
In all probability, the transaction costs in buying or selling a SSF contract amounts to less than buying or selling the same 100 shares of stock in the stock market.

**Spread Differentials.**
SSF offers investors additional investment strategies. For example, if an investor feels the price of one stock will decline or rise in relation to another stock he or she can buy a SSF contract on one stock and sell a SSF contract on another, hoping to profit from the spread differential between the two stocks anytime up to the contract's expiration.

**No Clearing Fees on Foreign Markets.**
Investor can also gain cross border exposure without the expense of going through foreign clearing systems. Will circumvent many of the difficulties faced by investors attempting to trade across jurisdictional boundaries by providing access to UK, European and U.S. shares on a single trading platform.

Universal Stock futures transactions will be clear of costs of accessing settlement systems across international borders.

**Greater Versatility.**
SSF allows a trader to potentially profit no matter what direction the market moves. If a trader is of the opinion that the stock market is going to fall, a trader can sell a contract. A profit will be made if the trader then buys that contract back later when the price decreases. This avoids the hassle of stock borrowing.

## Appendix 22B — The Black–Scholes Option Pricing Model

Black and Scholes came up with a mathematical model to determine the value of an option. In this appendix, we present an intuitive explanation of the model. The model can be understood in terms of the following steps.

*Step 1*: The future stock price is constant over time.
Following Eq. (22.1B), if the stock price is constant over time, then the value of the call, $V_c$, is the current price of the stock, $P$, less the present value of the exercise price, $X$. Mathematically, the value of the call option is:

$$V_c = P - \frac{X}{(1+r)^t} \tag{22.1B}$$

Equation (22.1B) assumes discrete compounding of interest. If continuous compounding is assumed, then Eq. (22.1B) becomes:

$$V_c = P - X_e^{-rt} \tag{22.2B}$$

where $e$ is a constant approximately equal to 2.71828.

Step 2: Assume the price of the stock fluctuates over time. In this case, we need to adjust Eq. (22.2B) for the fluctuation associated with the uncertainty. IF we assume that the stock's returns follow a normal distribution, then both $P$ and $X$ in Eq. (22.2B) can be adjusted for the uncertainty factor associated with the fluctuation of the stock's price over time. The call option pricing model thus becomes:

$$V_c = PN(d_1) - X_e^{-rt}N(d_2) \tag{22.3B}$$

where $d_1 = \frac{[\ln(\frac{P}{X})+(r+0.5\sigma^2)t]}{\sigma\sqrt{t}}$; $d_2 = d_1 - \sigma\sqrt{t}$; $r =$ risk – free interest rate; $t =$ time until the option expires (in years).

Equation (22.3B) is the well-known Black–Scholes option pricing model. The adjustment factors $N(d_1)$ and $N(d_2)$ represent the cumulative standard normal distribution function. $N(d_1)$ and $N(d_2)$ are probabilities that a random variable with a standard normal distribution takes on a value less than $d_1$ and $d_2$ respectively. The values for $N(d_1)$ and $N(d_2)$ can be found by using a standard normal distribution table as presented at the end of the book, in Appendix B on page 1122.

Equation (22.3B) can be used to find the theoretical value on January 12, 1995, of JNJ's call option expiring in July 1995. In this case, we have $X = \$55, P = \$54.875, \sigma = 0.1434, r = 0.0563$, and $t = 0.52$ (years). Using this information we can solve for $d_1$ and $d_2$.

$$
\begin{aligned}
d_1 &= \frac{[\ln\left(\frac{54.875}{55}\right) + (0.0563 + 0.5(0.1434)^2)(0.52)]}{(0.1434)\sqrt{0.52}} \\
&= 0.313 \\
d_2 &= 0.313 - (0.1434)\sqrt{.52} \\
&= 0.21
\end{aligned}
$$

To find the values for $N(d_1)$ and $N(d_2)$, we need to use the table in Appendix B. To find the cumulative normal distribution function, we need to add the probability that $Z$ is less than zero to the value given in the table in Appendix B. Because the standard normal distribution is symmetric around zero, we know that the probability that $Z$ is less than zero is 0.5, so $N(d_1)$ and $N(d_2)$ can be computed as:

$$
\begin{aligned}
N(d_1) &= P(Z < d_1) = P(Z < 0) + P(0 < Z < d_1) \\
&= 0.5 + 0.1231 \\
&= 0.6231 \\
N(d_2) &= P(Z < d_2) = P(Z < 0) + P(0 < Z < d_2) \\
&= 0.5 + 0.0832 \\
&= 0.5832
\end{aligned}
$$

Plugging this data into the Black–Scholes formula, we get:

$$V_c = 54.875(0.6231) - (55)(0.5832)e^{-(0.0563)(0.52)} = \$3.04$$

The actual price of the option on January 12, 1995, was $2.75, as reported in *The Wall Street Journal* on January 13, 1995.

## Self-Test Problems

1. **Analyzing the Value of Convertible Bond.**
JoLee Corp. has a $1 million, $1,000 par value, 9% semiannual convertible bond that is maturing in 5 years. The conversion price for the equity is $20 per share. Today, the common stock is selling for $18 per share. Similar convertibles have a stated nominal rate (APR) of 10%.

Calculate the conversion ratio, the conversion value, and the minimum price of the bond. As an investor, what would you do with this bond? What is the value of the conversion privilege if the bond is selling at $1,000?

$$\begin{aligned} \text{A: Conversion ratio} &= \frac{\text{Par value}}{\text{Conversion price}} \\ &= \frac{\$1{,}000}{\$20/\text{share}} \\ &= 50 \text{ shares} \end{aligned}$$

$$\begin{aligned} \text{Conversion value} &= \text{Conversion ratio} \times \text{Price per share} \\ &= 50 \text{ shares} \times \$18/\text{share} \\ &= \$900 \end{aligned}$$

APR of 10% corresponds to a semiannual periodic rate of 5%

$$\begin{aligned} \text{Bond value} &= \sum_{t=1}^{n} \frac{\text{Interest}}{(1+r)^t} + \frac{\text{Par}}{(1+r)^n} \\ &= \$45 \times \text{PVIFA}\,(5\%, 10\,\text{periods}) \\ &+ \$1{,}000 \times \text{PVIF}\,(5\%, 10\,\text{periods}) \\ &= \$347.48 + \$613.91 \\ &= \$961.39 \end{aligned}$$

If the market price is below \$900 per bond, you would buy the bond and convert it into common shares. The value of the conversion privilege is the difference between \$1,000 and the larger of bond value or conversion value: \$1,000 – \$961.39 = \$38.61.

2. **Calculating the Value of a Warrant.**
On the expiration date of a warrant, the common stock of a firm is selling at \$10 per share. The warrant gives the holder the right to buy two shares of stock for \$18. What is the value of the warrant at expiration?
A: Using Eq. (22.4), we obtain:

$$\begin{aligned} V_w &= \text{Max}(0, NP - NX) \\ &= \text{Max}\,(0, 2(\$10) - \$18) \\ &= \$2.00/\text{warrant} \end{aligned}$$

The stock is valued at \$10 per share, or \$20 for two shares. The exercise of the warrant to get two shares costs \$18; therefore, the warrant is worth \$2.

## Questions and Problems

### Part A: Questions

1. Define the following terms:
   a. executive stock option
   b. call option
   c. put option
   d. exercise price
   e. option premium
   f. expiration date
   g. naked option writing
   h. in the money
   i. out of the money
   j. at the money
2. Distinguish between an American option and a European option.
3. What happens to the number of shares of stock outstanding when a call option is exercised?
4. What is the major difference between an option and a futures contract?

5. What is a convertible bond? Why would a corporation issue a convertible bond?
6. What is an interest rate swap?
7. Briefly explain how options are valued.
8. What is the relationship between the conversion ratio and the conversion price for a convertible bond?
9. Why will a convertible bond usually sell at a price above its value as equity or debt?
10. What is the difference between a warrant and a convertible bond?
11. What factors determine the value of a warrant?
12. Describe a situation in which a firm should consider issuing a convertible bond.
13. Describe a situation in which a firm should consider issuing warrants.
14. What is the conflict of interest when a manager with executive stock options is making capital budgeting decisions concerning risky projects?
15. What is the problem with a corporate treasurer speculating with options and/or futures in order to increase shareholder wealth?
16. Bankers do not need to explain the risks of using derivative instruments to sophisticated corporate treasurers. Comment on the arguments for and against this statement.

## Part B: Problems

1. **Calculating Expected Value of Call Options.**
   Find the expected value of a call option with an exercise price of \$100 at the end of the period, given the following information (current stock price is \$100):

| Probability | Stock Price |
|---|---|
| 0.4 | \$150 |
| 0.6 | 80 |

2. **Calculating Value of Call Options.**
If a call option has an exercise price of \$50, how much will it be worth on its exercise date (assuming no transaction costs) if the price of the underlying stock is:
   a. \$30?
   b. \$50?
   c. \$80?
3. **Call Option Value for Buyer and Seller.**
If a call option has an exercise price of \$60 and the price of the stock is \$40, what is the value of the call:
   a. to the holder of the option?
   b. to the seller of the option?
4. **Expected Value of Call Options.**
Allison Merrick is considering two call options, each with an exercise price of \$20 and identical in all other respects except for the distribution of underlying stock values. The distribution of the values of the underlying stocks of Companies J and K are given below:

| **Companies J** | | **Companies K** | |
|---|---|---|---|
| **Future Stock Price** | **Probability** | **Future Stock Price** | **Probability** |
| \$10 | 0.2 | \$5 | 0.1 |
| 18 | 0.3 | 17 | 0.3 |
| 22 | 0.3 | 25 | 0.4 |
| 25 | 0.2 | 35 | 0.2 |

Find the expected payoff for each call option and explain which one you would prefer.
5. **Conversion Price of a Bond.**
LMW Company has issued convertible bonds that have a conversion ratio of 20 shares to one bond. Compute the conversion price for a bond with a par value of \$1,000. If the current market price for the stick is \$75 per share, does it make sense to convert? Why?

6. **Price Conversion Privilege.**
Jones and Smith Company has just issued convertible bonds that have a coupon rate of 10% and a conversion ratio of 25 shares to one bond. They mature in 20 years and pay semiannual coupons. If similar straight debt has a nominal return of 14%, what price will investors pay for the conversion privilege if the bonds currently are selling in par?
7. **Price Conversion Privilege.**
The IKC Corporation has convertible bonds outstanding. The bonds have a coupon rate of 8% and a conversion ratio of 50 shares to one bond. They mature in 10 years and pay semiannual coupons. If similar straight debt has a nominal return of 10%, what price will investors pay for the conversion privilege if the bonds currently are selling at par?
8. **Calculating the Value of a Warrant.**
On the expiration date of a warrant, the common stock of a firm is selling at $25 per share. The warrant gives the holder the right to buy five share of stock for $90. What is the value of the warrant at expiration?

# Chapter 23

# Option Pricing Theory and Firm Valuation

## Contents



## 23.1 Introduction

In previous the chapter, we have discussed the basic concepts of options, futures, and swap. In this chapter, we will discuss option pricing theory and firm valuation. The emergence of options and option pricing theory is one of the more important financial events of recent times. In Chapter 23, we discuss several types of options and how their value is determined. We begin by looking at the basic concepts of options, then go on to discuss factors that affect the value of options, hedging and the hedge ratio, and how option pricing theory is used to investigate the capital structure question. We close the chapter with a look at a type of option called the warrant.

In Section 23.2 we discuss the basic concepts of options. In Section 23.3, we look at factors affecting option value. In Section 23.4, we determine the value of options. In Section 23.5, we discuss option pricing theory and capital structure, and in Section 23.6, we discuss warrants. Finally, in Section 23.7, we summarize the chapter.

## 23.2 Basic Concepts of Options

In general, there are three types of equity options: (1) warrants, (2) executive stock options, and (3) publicly traded options. A *warrant* is a financial instrument issued by a corporation that gives the purchaser the right to buy a fixed number of shares at a set price for a specific period. There are two major differences between a warrant and a publicly traded option. The first is that the maturity of the warrant is normally between three to five years, whereas the maturity of a publicly traded option is normally less than nine months. The second difference is that the warrant is an agreement between the corporation and the warrant's buyer. This means that if the warrant's owner decides to exercise his right and purchase stock, the corporation issues new shares and receives the cash from the sale of those shares. The *publicly traded option* is an agreement between two individuals who have no relationship with the corporation whose shares are being optioned. When the publicly traded option is exercised, money is exchanged for shares between individuals and the corporation received no funds, only a new owner.

*Executive stock options* are a means of compensation for corporate employees. For services rendered, the manager or the employee has the right to buy a specific number of shares for a set price during a given period. Unlike warrants and publicly traded options, executive stock options cannot be traded. The option's owner has only two choices: exercise the option or let it expire. Like a warrant, should the owner decide to exercise the option, the corporation receives money and issues new shares.

The use of executive stock options for management compensation raises an interesting agency question. The firm's managers may make investment and financing decisions that increase the firm's risk in order to increase the value of their stock options. Such action could have a detrimental effect on the bondholders and other creditors of the firm. Thus, we will see that the value of an option is directly related to the variability or riskiness of the underlying asset, which in this case is the firm.

Publicly traded options are probably the most widely known of the three types of equity option instruments. An important date in the history of these options is 1973, when the Chicago Board Options Exchange was founded. Although it was possible to trade options over the counter before that time, trading volume was relatively low. This date marks the beginning of a phenomenal growth in the popularity of options as a financial instrument. Indeed, in terms of the value of securities traded, the Chicago Board Options Exchange is running neck and neck with the New York and Tokyo stock exchanges as the world's largest securities market. There are now five options — trading centers in the U.S. — the Chicago Board Options Exchange, the American Stock Exchange, the Philadelphia Stock Exchange, the Pacific Stock Exchange, and the New York Stock Exchange — and there is a steady stream of proposals for new listings on these exchanges.

The share volume of trading and the general acceptance of these financial instruments renders options valuation an important subject for study. However, even more significant for our purposes, the theory of options valuation has important applications in financial management and in the valuation of other financial instruments. Black and Scholes (1973) point out that corporate securities can be viewed as options or contingent claims on firm value. In viewing a firm's securities as options, we need to evaluate the interdependencies of bonds and stocks. As we have seen, a bond's price is the present value of future interest and principal payments, and a stock's price is determined by future dividends. The contingent-claims approach to security valuation differs in that it considers the valuation of all of the firm's classes of securities simultaneously. Bonds and stocks are valued in terms of the value placed on the firm's assets; that is, their value is contingent on the firm's assets or investments.

Banz and Miller (1978) developed an approach to making capital budgeting decisions based on a contingent claim's framework. They created a method for calculating the NPV of an investment based on estimates derived from using an option valuation model. In this chapter, we consider the question of option valuation and how options are used to make financial management decisions. However, before doing so, we must become acquainted with some of the terminology of options trading.

There are two basic types of options: puts and calls. A *call* gives the holder the right to buy a particular number of shares of a designated common stock at a specified price, called the *exercise price* (or striking price), on or before a given date, known as the *expiration date.* Hence, the owner of shares of common stock can create an option and sell it in the options market, thereby increasing the return or income on his or her stock investment. Such an option specifies both an exercise price and an expiration date. On the Chicago Board of Options Exchange, options are typically created for three, six, or nine months. The actual expiration date is the third Saturday of the month of expiration. A more venturesome investor may create an option in this fashion without owning any of the underlying stock. This is called *naked option writing* and can be very risky, especially if the value of the underlying asset has a high degree of variability.

A *put* gives the holder the right to sell a certain number of shares of common stock at a set price on or before the expiration date of the options. In purchasing a put, the owner of shares has bought the right to sell these shares by the expiration date at the exercise price. As with calls, the creator can own the underlying shares (covered writing) or not (naked writing).

The owner of a put or call is not obligated to carry out the specified transaction but has the *option* of doing so. If the transaction is carried out, it is said to have been *exercised.* For example, if you hold a call option on a stock that is currently trading at a price higher than the exercise price, you may want to exercise the option to purchase stock at the exercise price, because the stock could be immediately resold at a profit. (Or you could sell the option or hold it in the hope of further gains.) This call option is said to be "in the money." On the other hand, if the call option is "out of the money" — that is, the stock is trading at a price below the exercise price — you certainly would not want to exercise the option, as it would be cheaper to purchase the stock directly.

An American option can be exercised at any time up to the expiration date. A simpler instrument to analyze is the European option, which can only be exercised on the expiration date. In this case, the term to maturity of the option is known. Because of this simplifying factor, we will concentrate on the valuation of the European options.

The factors determining the values of the two types of options are the same, although, all other things equal, an American option is worth more than a European option because of the extra flexibility permitted the option holder.

Although our discussion is limited to equity options, many kinds of publicly traded options are available. Those include options on stock indexes, options on treasury bonds, options on future contracts, options on foreign currencies, and options on agricultural commodities.

The preceding discussion presented quite a lot of new terminology. For convenience, we list and define those terms below.

*Call*: An option to purchase a fixed number of shares of common stock.
*Put*: An option to sell a fixed number of shares of common stock.
*Exercise price*: Trading price set for the transaction as specified in an option contract.
*Expiration date*: Time by which the option transaction must be carried out.
*Exercise of option*: Carrying out the transaction specified in an option.
*American option*: An option in which the transaction can be carried out at any time up to the expiration date.
*European option*: An option in which the transaction can only be carried out on the expiration date.
*Call option "in the money"*: If the stock price is above the exercise price.
*Put option "in the money"*: If the stock price is below the exercise price.
*Call option "out of the money"*: If the stock price is below the exercise price.
*Put option "out of the money"*: If the stock price is above the exercise price.

### 23.2.1 *Option price information*

Exhibit 23.1 presents options quotations for Johnson & Johnson. The price of Johnson & Johnson shares on this date was around \$170. The first column gives the **expiration month** for each option. We have included listings for call and put options with exercise prices ranging

**Exhibit 23.1:** Option Quotes for Johnson & Johnson (Underlying stock price: \$170), May 25, 2021.

| | Call | | | | | Put | | | |
|---|---|---|---|---|---|---|---|---|---|
| **Expiration** | **Last** | **Chg** | **Bid** | **Ask** | **Strike** | **Last** | **Chg** | **Bid** | **Ask** |
| Aug-21 | 8.70 | – | 8.45 | 8.70 | 165.00 | 3.34 | 0.05 | 3.35 | 3.50 |
| Aug-21 | 5.52 | (0.40) | 5.40 | 5.60 | 170.00 | 5.36 | 0.16 | 5.30 | 5.45 |
| Aug-21 | 3.25 | (0.35) | 3.25 | 3.30 | 175.00 | 8.15 | 0.35 | 8.00 | 8.25 |

from \$165 to \$175 per share, and with expiration dates in August 2021.

The next columns provide the closing prices, its change from the previous trading day, bid price, asked price, trading volume, and open interest (outstanding contracts) of each option. Column 4 shows the Bid, or the latest price offered by a market maker to buy a particular option. The *Ask* price in column 5 is the latest price offered a market maker to sell a particular option. For example, the first contract traded on the August 2021 expiration call with exercise price of \$165. The last trade was at \$8.70, meaning that an option to purchase one share of Johnson & Johnson at an exercise price of \$165 sold for \$8.70. Each option contract (on 100 shares) therefore costs \$870.

## 23.3 Factors Affecting Option Value

How much should you pay for a put or call option? The answer is not easy to determine. However, it is possible to list the various factors that determine option value.

We begin with a simple question. How much is a call option worth on its expiration date? The question is simple because we are in a deterministic world. The uncertain future movement of the price of the stock in question is irrelevant. The call must be exercised immediately or not at all. If a call option is out of the money on its expiration date, it will be exercised. Stock can be purchased at the exercise price, and immediately resold at the market price, if so desired. The option value is the difference between these two prices. On the call option's expiration date, its value will be either 0 or some positive amount equal to the difference between the market price of the stock and the exercise price of the option. Symbolically, let $P =$ price of stock, $V_c =$ value of call option, and $E =$ exercise price. Then $V_c = P – E$ if $P \geq E$, and $V_c = 0$ if $P < E$. This relationship can be

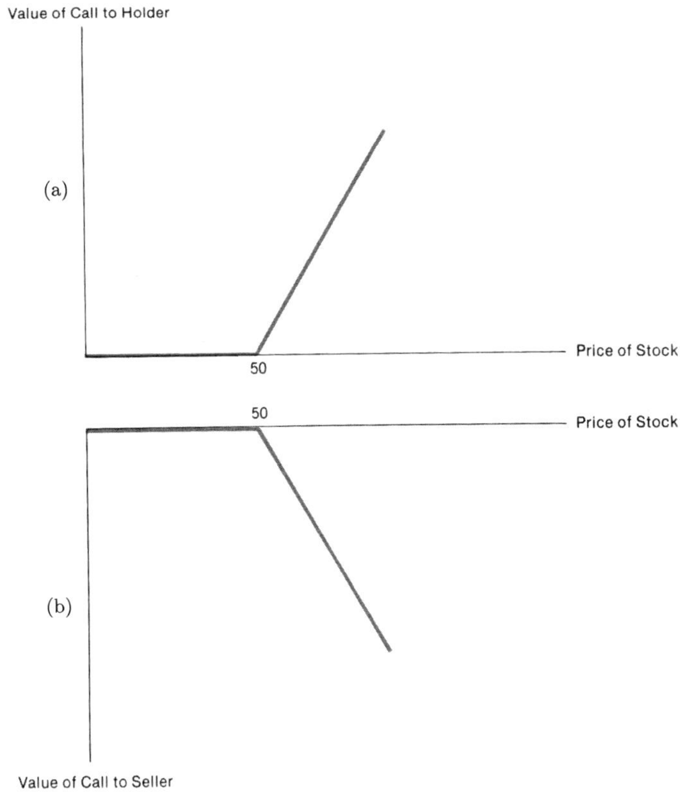


Figure 23.1 Value of \$50 Exercise Price Call Option (a) to Holder, (b) to Seller.

written as

$$V_c = \text{MAX}(0, P - E)$$

where MAX denotes the larger of the two bracketed terms. For a put option ($V_P$), $V_P = E–P$ if $E > P$, and $V_P = 0$ if $E \leq P$. This can be written as

$$V_P = \text{MAX}(0, E - P)$$

The call position is illustrated in Figure 23.1(a), where we consider a call option with an exercise price of \$50. The figure shows the option value as a function of the stock price to the option holder. For any price of the stock up to \$50, the call option is worthless and its value is 0. The option's value increases as the stock price rises above \$50. Hence, if on the expiration date the stock is trading at \$60, the call option is worth \$10.

Figure 23.1(b), which is the mirror image of (a), shows the option position from the viewpoint of the writer of the call option. If the stock is trading below the exercise price on the expiration date, the call option will not be exercised and its seller incurs no loss. However, if the stock is trading at $60, the seller of the call option will be required to sell this stock for $50, which is $10 below the price that could be obtained on the market.

We have seen that once a call option has been purchased, the holder of the option has the possibility of obtaining gains but cannot incur losses. Correspondingly, the writer of the option may incur losses but cannot achieve any gains after receiving the premium. Further, there is no net gain in the sense that the profit incurred by one will balance the loss of the other. Thus, options are zero sum securities — they merely transfer wealth rather than create it. To acquire this instrument, a price must be paid to the writer, and it is this price that corresponds to the call value. This value is the price paid to acquire the chance of future profit and will therefore reflect uncertainty about future market prices of the common stock. We will now discuss how to determine the value of an option before its expiration date.

### 23.3.1 *Determining the value of a call option before the expiration date*

Suppose that you are considering the purchase of a call option, with an exercise price of $50, on a share of common stock. Let us try to determine what factors should be taken into account in trying to assess the value of such an option prior to the expiration date. As we have seen, the problem is trivial at the expiration date. However, determining the value of an option prior to expiration is more complex.

An important factor in this determination is the current price per share of the stock. Indeed, it is most straightforward to think of option value as a function of market price. Given this framework, we can see fairly quickly how to set bounds on the value of a call option.

*Lower bound: The value of a call cannot be less than the payoff that would accrue if it were exercised immediately.* We can think of

Figure 23.1 as showing the payoff from immediate exercise of a call as a function of the current price of the stock. In our example, this payoff is zero for any market price below \$50 and equal to the market price less for the \$50 exercise price when market price is above \$50. Suppose that the current stock price is \$60 per share, and you are offered a call option for \$8. This is certain to be profitable because you could immediately exercise the call and then resell the stock at a \$10 gain. Subtracting the cost of the call option would yield a profit of \$2. Of course, market participants are well aware of this, so that the excess of demand over supply for such a call option would quickly drive up the price to at least the level where such immediate profits are unattainable.

*Upper bound: The value of a call cannot be more than the market price of the stock.* Suppose that, at the same cost, you are offered two alternatives:

(a) Purchase a share of stock
(b) Purchase an option on the same share of stock.

Looking into the future, option (b) will either be exercised or discarded as worthless. If the option is exercised, its value will be the difference between the future stock price less the exercise price. This will be less than the future stock price, which is the value derived from option (a). Similarly, if the option turns out to have no value, this cannot be preferable to holding the stock, which, while it may have fallen in price, will have retained some value. Therefore, option (b) cannot be preferable to (a), so that the option value cannot exceed the market price of the stock.

These conclusions are illustrated in Figure 23.2, which related the call-option value to the market price of the stock. The $ACD$ line shows the payoff that would be obtained if the option were exercised immediately. The $AB$ line is the set of points at which the call value equals the market price of the stock. The call value must lie between these boundaries; that is, in the shaded area depicted in Figure 23.2.

So far, we have been able to determine a fairly wide range in which the option value must lie for any given value of the market price of the stock. Let us now see if we can be more precise in formulating the shape of the relationship between call-option value and market price

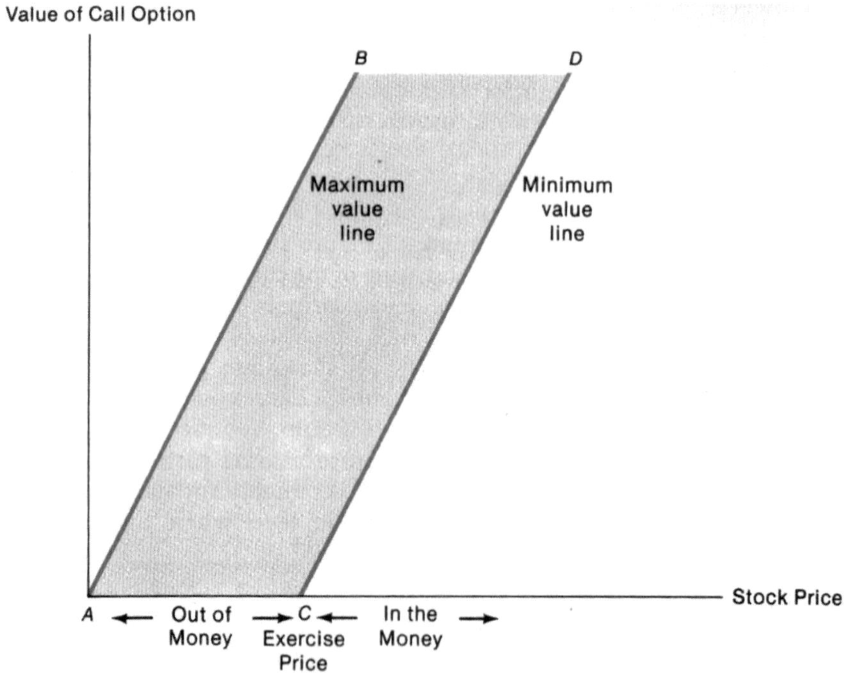


Figure 23.2 Value of Call Option.

of stock. The following considerations should help in forming the appropriate picture of Figure 23.3.

1. *If the market price of the stock is 0, the call value will also be 0, as indicated by point A*. This extreme case arises only when there is no hope that the stock will ever have any value, for otherwise investors would be prepared to pay some price, however small, for the stock. It follows, in such circumstances, that the call option will never be exercised, and so it too has no value.
2. *All other things equal, as the stock price increases, so does the call value (see lines* AB *and* CD). A call with an exercise price of $50 would be worth more if the current market price were $40 than if it were $35, all else equal. The probability that the market price will eventually exceed the exercise price by any given amount is higher in the former case than in the latter, and so, consequently, is the payoff expected from holding the call.

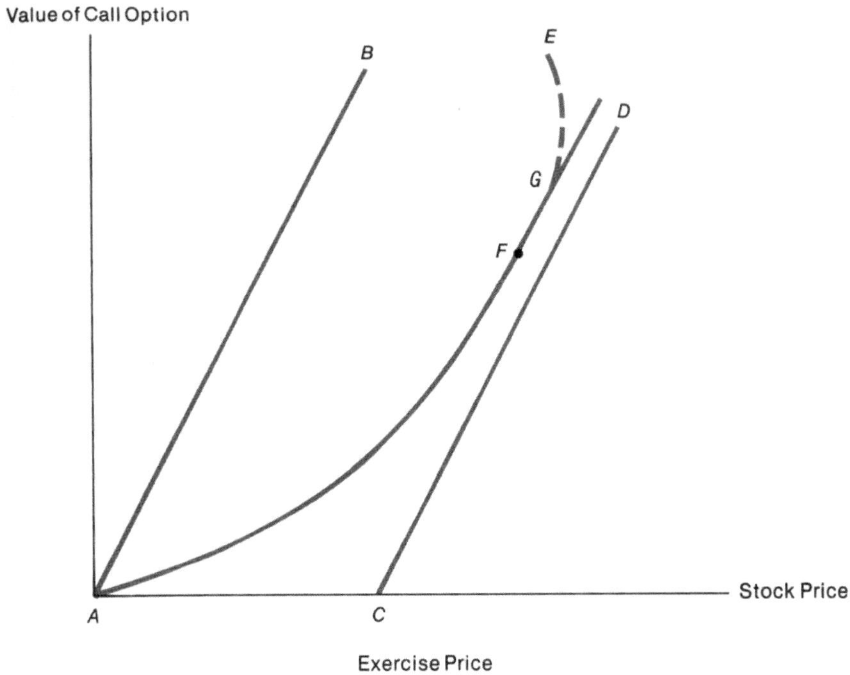


Figure 23.3 Call Option Value as a Function of Stock Price.

3. *If the price of the stock is high in relation to the exercise price, each dollar increase in price induces an increase of very nearly the same amount in the call value (shown by the slope of the line at point* F). Suppose that the market price of the stock exceeds the exercise price of a call by such a large amount that it is virtually impossible for the stock price to fall below the exercise price before the expiration date. Then, any change in stock price will induce a change of the same amount in the payoff expected from the call, since it is certain that the option will be exercised. The point is that if it is known that an option will eventually be exchanged for stock, this is tantamount to already owning the stock. The call holder has effectively purchased the stock without paying the full amount for it right away. The balance owned is the exercise price to be paid at the expiration date. It follows that the value of the call option is the market value of the stock less the present value of the exercise price. Notice that in our previous notation,

this will exceed $P$–$E$ if the exercise price does not have to be paid until some time in the future, because of the time value of money.

4. *The call value rises at an increasing rate as the value of the stock price rises, as shown by curvature* AFG. The segment $AF$ shows that as the stock price increases, the call value increases by a lesser amount. The segment $FE$ shows the call price increasing by a larger amount than the increase in the stock price. Theoretically, this is impossible, because if it occurred, eventually the call price would exceed the price of the underlying stock.

Putting these four considerations together, we show in Figure 23.3 a typical curve relating call-option value to the market price of a stock. Beginning at the origin, when both quantities are 0, the curve shows call value increasing as market price increases. Eventually, the curve becomes virtually parallel to the two 45-degree lines, forming the boundaries of the possible-values region. This is a result of the fourth consideration listed above.

The curve graphed in Figure 23.3 shows the relationship between the call-option value and the market price of the stock, when all other relevant factors influencing call-option value are constant. Next, we must try to see what these other factors might be and assess their impact on call value.

We consider, in turn, five factors that influence the value of a call option:

1. *Market price of the stock*: In Figure 23.3, we have seen the curvilinear relationship between call-option value and market price of the stock. All other things equal, the higher the market price, the higher the call-option value on the stock. As already noted, the slope of this relationship increases as market price becomes higher, to the point where, eventually, each dollar increases in the stock price translates into an increase of about the same amount in the call-option value on that stock.
2. *The exercise price*: Offered two otherwise identical call options on the same stock, you would prefer the call with the lower exercise price. This would involve larger gains from any favorable movement in the price of the stock than would an option with a higher exercise price. Therefore, we can conclude that the lower the exercise price, the higher the call-option value, all other things equal.

3. *The risk-free interest rate*: If a call option is eventually exercised, the holder of the option will reap some of the benefits of an increase in the market value of the stock. However, the holder will do so without having to immediately pay the exercise price. This payment will only be made at some future time when the call option is actually exercise. In the meantime, this money can be invested in government securities to earn a no-risk return. This opportunity confers an increment of value on the call option; the higher the risk-free rate of interest, the greater this incremental value or lower the present value of the exercise price. Therefore, we would expect to find, all else equal, that the higher the risk-free rate of interest, the greater the call-option value. Moreover, the longer the exercise of the option is postponed, the greater the risk-free interest earnings. Accordingly, we would expect the risk-free interest rate to determine call-option value in conjunction with the time remaining before the expiration date.
4. *The volatility of the stock price*: Suppose that you are offered the opportunity to purchase one of two call options, each with an exercise price of \$50. Table 23.1 lists probabilities for different market prices on the expiration date for each of the two stocks. In each case, the mean (expected) future price is the same. However, for the second stock, prices that differ substantially from the mean are far more likely than for the first stock. The price of such a stock is said to be relatively volatile. We now show that the expected payoff on the expiration date is higher for a call option on the more volatile stock than for a call option on the less volatile stock. For the less volatile stock, the option will not be exercised for prices below \$50, but for the three higher prices its exercise will result

Table 23.1 Probabilities for Future Prices of Two Stocks.

| **Less Volatile Stock** | | **More Volatile Stock** | |
|---|---|---|---|
| **Future Price (\$)** | **Probability** | **Future Price (\$)** | **Probability** |
| 42 | 0.10 | 32 | 0.15 |
| 47 | 0.20 | 42 | 0.20 |
| 52 | 0.40 | 52 | 0.30 |
| 57 | 0.20 | 62 | 0.20 |
| 62 | 0.10 | 72 | 0.15 |

in payoffs of \$2, \$7, and \$12. Therefore, we find

$$\begin{aligned}&\text{Expected payoff from call option on less volatile stock}\\&= (0)(0.10) + (0)(0.20) + (2)(0.40) + (7)(0.20) + (12)(0.10)\\&= \$3.40\end{aligned}$$

Similarly, for a call option on more volatile stock,

$$\begin{aligned}&\text{Expected payoff from call option on more volatile stock}\\&= (0)(0.15) + (0)(0.20) + (2)(0.30) + (12)(0.20) + (22)(0.15)\\&= \$6.30\end{aligned}$$

We find, then, that although the expected future price is the same for the two stocks, the expected payoff is higher from a call option on the more volatile stock. This conclusion is quite general. For example, it does not depend on our having set the exercise price below the expected future stock price. The reader is invited to verify that the same qualitative finding would emerge if the exercise price were \$55. We can conclude that, all other things remaining the same, the greater the volatility in the price of the stock, the higher the call-option value on that stock.

One useful way to measure volatility is through the *variance* in day-to-day changes in the stock price. Figure 23.4 illustrates our assertion about the influence of stock-price volatility on call-option value. The figure shows the relationship between call value and current market price for three stocks. The three curves have the same general form depicted in Figure 23.3. However, notice that for any given current market price of the stock, the higher the variance of day-to-day price changes, the greater the call-option value.

The notion of volatility in future stock market prices is related to the length of the time horizon being considered. Specifically, if the variance of day-to-day changes is $\sigma^2$, the variance in the change from the present to $t$ days is $\sigma^2 t$ if the price changes are serially independent. Therefore, the further ahead is the expiration date, the greater the volatility in price movements. This suggests that for a European option, which can only be exercised on the expiration date, the relevant measure of volatility is $\sigma^2 t$, where $t$ is the number of days remaining to the expiration date. The larger is this quantity, the greater the call-option value.

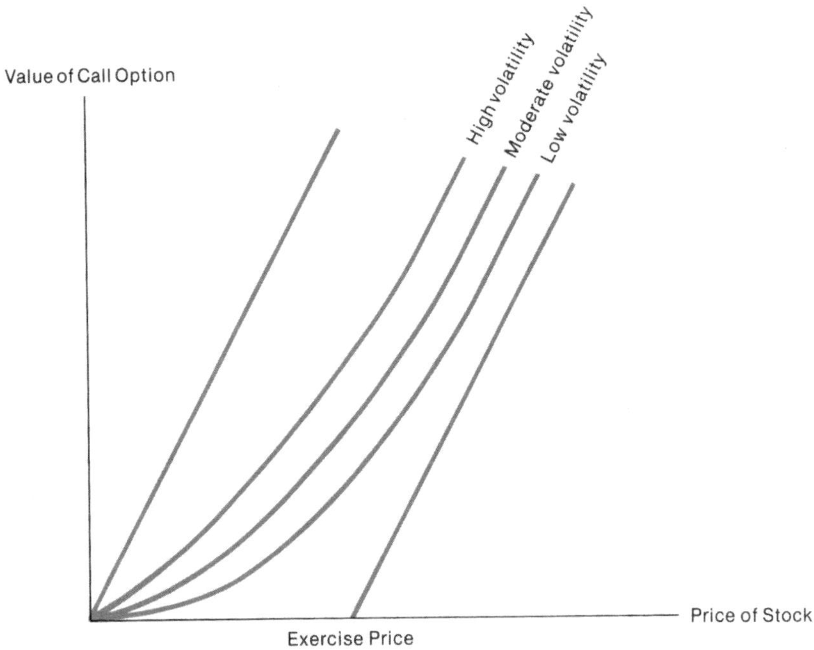


Figure 23.4 Call-Option Value as Function of Stock Price for High-, Moderate-, and Low-Volatility Stocks.

5. *Time remaining to expiration date*: We have seen in factors 3 and 4 above two reasons to expect that the longer the time remaining before the expiration date, the higher the call-option value, all else equal. The reason is that the extra time allows larger gains to be derived from postponing payment of the exercise price and permits greater volatility in price movements of the stock. These two considerations both operate in the same direction — toward increasing the call-option value.

## 23.4 Determining the Value of Options

We have seen that five factors influence the value of a call option. The interaction of these various factors in determining option value is rather complex.[1] We present a formula that, under certain

[1]Compared to the CAPM, the option pricing model (OPM) is a relative pricing approach. In the CAPM, the major determinants are risk and return. In the OPM, the return of the asset or the market does not affect the option value.

assumptions, can be shown to determine a call-option value as a function of these five parameters. However, before proceeding to this somewhat complicated relationship, we discuss a simple situation in which option valuation is more straightforward. This is useful in explaining further the dependence of option value on the risk-free rate of interest.

Our aim here is to show, for a special set of assumptions, that an investor can guarantee a particular return from a combined strategy of holding shares in a stock and writing call options on that stock, even though there is some uncertainty about the future price of the stock. The essential simplifying assumption required to generate this result is that there are only two possible values for the future price per share of the stock. In addition, for convenience we will use European options, with an expiration date in one year. Further, we assume that the stock pays no dividend and that there are no transactions costs.

Within this framework, consider the factors in Table 23.2. An investor can purchase shares of $100 each and write European call options with an exercise price of $100. There are two possible prices of the stock on the expiration date, with uncertainty as to which will materialize.

In Table 23.3, we list the consequences to the investor for the two expiration-date stock prices. If the higher price prevails, each share of stock will be worth $125. However, the call options will be exercised, at a cost per share to the writer of the difference between the stock price and the exercise price. In Table 23.3, this is a negative value

Table 23.2 Data for a Hedging Example.

| | |
|---|---|
| Current price per share: | $100 |
| Future price per share: | $125 with probability 0.6 |
| | $85 with probability 0.4 |
| Exercise price of call option: | $100 |

Table 23.3 Possible Expiration-Date Outcomes for Hedging Example.

| **Expiration-Date Stock Price** | **Value per Share of Stock Holdings** | **Value per Share of Options Written** |
|---|---|---|
| $125 | $125 | −$25 |
| $85 | $85 | $0 |

of \$25 from having written the call option. If the lower of the two possible stock prices materializes on the expiration date, each share owned will be worth \$85, and it will have cost nothing to write the option because it will not be exercised.

Suppose that the investor wants to form a *hedged portfolio* by both purchasing stock and writing call options, so as to guarantee as large a total value of holdings per dollar invested as possible, whatever the stock price on the expiration date. The hedge is constructed to be riskless, since any profit (or loss) from the stock is exactly offset with a loss (or profit) from the call option. This is called a *perfect* or *riskless hedge* and can be accomplished by purchasing $H$ number of shares for each option written. We now determine $H$. If $H$ shares are purchased and one option written, the total value on the expiration date will be \$125$H$ – \$25 at the higher market price and \$85$H$ – \$0 at the lower price. Suppose we choose $H$ so that these two amounts are equal; that is,

$$125H - 25 = 85H$$

$$H = \frac{25}{40} = \frac{5}{8}$$

Then, the same total value results whatever the stock's expiration-date market price. This ratio is known as the *hedge ratio* of stocks to options, the implication being that a hedged portfolio is achieved by writing eight options for each five shares purchased. More generally, it follows from the above argument that the hedge ratio is given by

$$H = \frac{P_U - E}{P_U - P_L}$$

where $P_U$ = upper share price; $P_L$ = lower share price; $E$ = exercise price of option; and $E$ is assumed to be between $P_U$ and $P_L$.

Returning to our example, suppose that five shares are purchased and an option on eight shares is written. If the expiration-date price is \$125, then the total value of the investor's portfolio is

$$(5)(125) - (8)(25) = \$425$$

If the expiration-date stock price is \$85, total value is

$$(5)(85) + (8)(0) = \$425$$

As predicted, the two are identical, so that this value is assured.

Next, we must consider the investor's income from the writing of call options. Let $V_c$ denote the price per share of a call option. Then, the purchase of five shares costs \$500, but $\$8V_c$ is received from writing call options on eight shares, so that the net outlay will be $\$500 - \$8V_c$. For this outlay, a value one year hence of \$425 is assured. However, there is another simple mechanism for guaranteeing such a return. An investment could be made in government securities at the risk-free interest rate. Suppose that this rate is 8% per annum. On the expiration date, an initial investment of $\$500 - \$8V_c$ will be worth $\$1.08(500 - 8V_c)$. If this is to be equal to the value of the hedged portfolio, then

$$(1.08)(500 - 8V_c) = 425$$

so that

$$V_c = \frac{(1.08)(500) - 425}{(1.08)(8)} = \$13.31$$

Therefore, we conclude that if the price per share for the call option is \$13.31, the hedging strategy will yield an assured rate of return equal to the risk-free interest rate.

In a competitive market, this is the price that will prevail, and therefore is the value of the call option. Suppose that the price of the call option was above \$13.31. By forming a hedged portfolio in the manner just described, investors could ensure a return in excess of the risk-free rate. Such an opportunity would attract many to sell options, thus driving down the price. Conversely, if the price of the option was below \$13.31, it would be possible to achieve a return guaranteed to be in excess of the risk-free rate by both purchasing call options and selling short the stock. The volume of demand thus created for the call option would drive up its price. Hence, in a competitive market, \$13.31 is the only sustainable price for this option.

Our example shows that a hedged portfolio can achieve an assured rate of return of 8%. Notice that our analysis depends on the level of the risk-free rate. If that rate is 10% per annum, the call-option value is \$14.20. This illustrates the dependence of call-option value on the risk-free interest rate.

### 23.4.1 *Expected value estimation*

A higher *expected rate of return*, as compared with the hedged portfolio, can be achieved by the exclusive purchase either of shares or of call options. Suppose that a single share is purchased for \$100. One year hence, the expected value of that share is

$$\text{Expected value of share} = (0.6)(125) + (0.4)(85) = \$109$$

Hence, the expected rate of return from a portfolio consisting entirely of holdings of this stock is 9%. Similarly, suppose that a call option is purchased for \$13.31. The expected value of this option on the expiration date is

$$\text{Expected value of call} = (0.6)(25) + (0.4)(0) = \$15$$

Hence, the expected rate of return is

$$\text{Expected rate of return on call} = \frac{15 - 13.31}{13.31} \times 100 = 12.7\%$$

The increased expected rates of return from holding exclusively these two types of securities should not be surprising. They simply represent increases required by investors for assuming additional risk.

We have shown how call-option valuation can be determined within a simple framework in which only two values for the future market price of a stock are possible. We must move on to more realistic situations that involve a range of future market prices.

The value of a put option is determined by the same factors that determine the value of a call option, except that the factors have different relationships to the value of a put than they have to the value of a call. Figure 23.5 shows the relationship between put-option value and stock price.

The value of a put option is

$$V_P = \text{MAX}(E - P, 0)$$

where $V_P$ = value of the put; $E$ = exercise price; and $P$ = value of the underlying stock.

The maximum value of a put is equal to the exercise price of the option when the stock price is 0. This is shown by the line "Maximum value of the put" in Figure 23.5. The minimum value of the put is 0, which occurs when the stock price exceeds the exercise price.

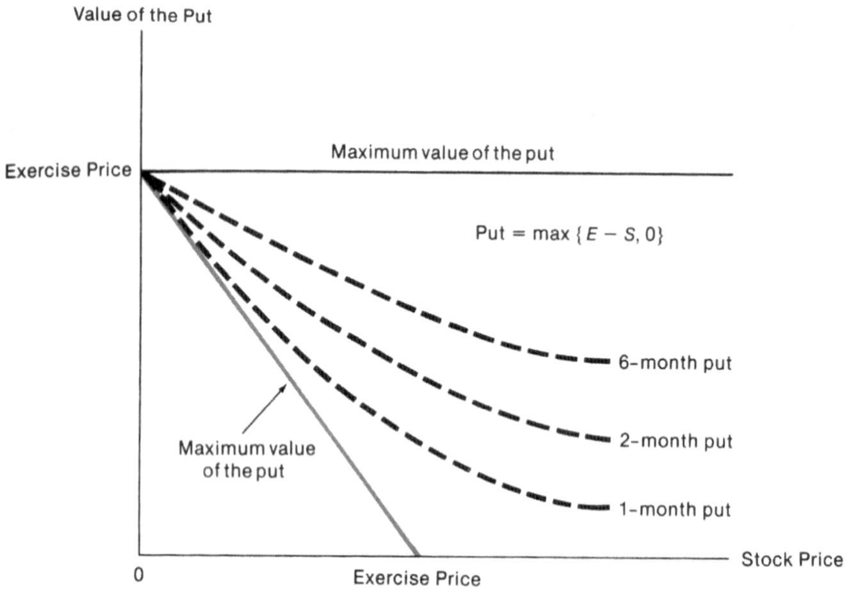


Figure 23.5 Put-Option Value.

### 23.4.2 *The Black–Scholes option pricing model*

The notion that the price of a call option should be such that the rate of return on a fully hedged portfolio is equal to the risk-free rate of interest has been used by Black and Scholes (1973) to derive a more generally applicable procedure for valuing an option. The assumption that only two future prices are possible is dropped for a more realistic view of future price movements. The complete set of assumptions on which the Black–Scholes formula is based are given below.

- Only European options are considered.
- Options and stocks can be traded in any quantities in a perfectly competitive market; there are no transactions costs and all relevant information is freely available to market participants.
- Short-selling of stocks and options in a perfectly competitive market is possible.
- The risk-free interest rate is known and is constant up to the expiration date. Market participants are able to borrow or lend at this rate.

- No dividends are paid on the stock.
- The stock price follows a random path in continuous time such that the variance of the rate of return is constant over time and known to market participants. The logarithm of future stock prices follows a normal distribution.

Under these assumptions, Black and Scholes show that the call-option value on a share of stock is given by

$$V_c = P[N(d_1)] - e^{-rt}E[N(d_2)] \tag{23.1}$$

where $V_c$ value of option; $P$ = current price of stock; $r$ = continuously compounded annual risk-free interest rate; $t$ = time in years to expiration date; $E$ = exercise price; $e = 2.71828\ldots$ is a constant; and $N(d_i)$ = probability that a standard normal random variable is less than or equal to $d_i$ $(i = 1, 2)$, with

$$d_1 = \frac{\ln(\frac{P}{E}) + rt + \sigma^2\frac{t}{2}}{\sigma\sqrt{t}} \tag{23.2a}$$

and

$$d_2 = \frac{\ln(\frac{P}{E}) + rt - \sigma^2\frac{t}{2}}{\sigma\sqrt{t}} = d_1 - \sigma\sqrt{t} \tag{23.2b}$$

where $\sigma^2$ = variance of annual rate of return on the stock, continuously compounded; and logarithms are to base $e$.

Although the specific form of the Black–Scholes option pricing formula is complicated, its interpretation is straightforward. The first term of Eq. (23.1) is the value of an investor's right to that portion of the probability distribution of the stock's price that lies above the exercise price. This term equals the expected value of this portion of the stock's price distribution, as shown in Figure 23.6.

The second term in Eq. (23.1) is the present value of the exercise price times the probability that the exercise price will be paid (the option will be exercised at maturity). Overall, the Black–Scholes model involves the present value of a future cash flow, a common concern in finance. The Black–Scholes model equates option value to the present expected value of the stock price minus the present value of the cost of exercising the option. More important for our purposes than the particular formula is the manner in which the model relates

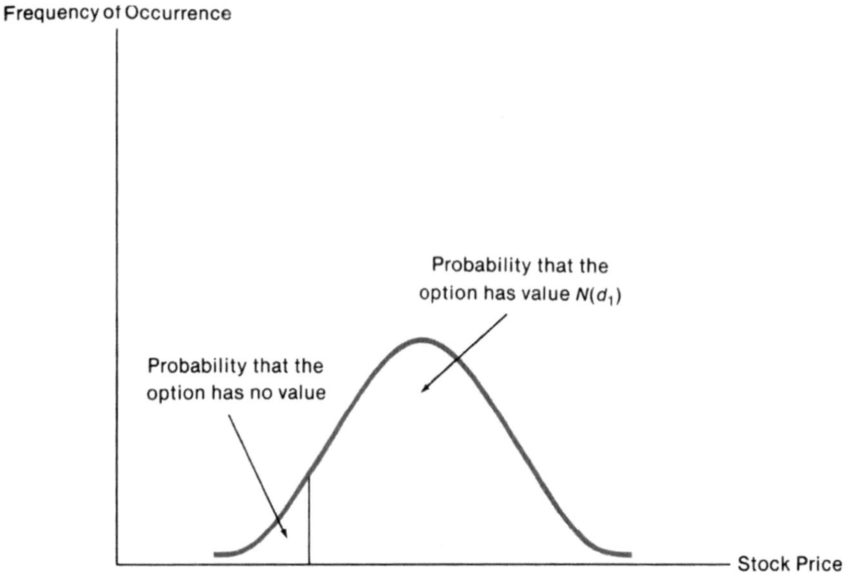


Figure 23.6 Probability Distribution of Stock Prices.

option value to the five factors discussed in the previous section. These relationships are as follows:

1. All other things equal, the higher the current market price of the stock, the higher the call-option value.
2. All other things equal, the higher the exercise price, the lower the option value.
3. All other things equal, the higher the risk-free interest rate, the higher the option value.
4. All other things equal, the greater the time to the expiration date, the higher the option value.
5. All other things equal, the greater the volatility of the stock price (as measured by $\sigma^2$), the higher the option value.

According to the Black–Scholes model, although the call-option value depends on the variance of rate of return, it does not depend on the stock's expected rate of return. This is because a change in expected rate of return affects stock price but not the relative value of the option and the stock. Recall from our earlier discussion that formation of the hedged portfolio was independent of expected return.

For example, changing the two probabilities in Table 23.2 has no effect on call-option value.

The following example illustrates the computation of option value using the Black–Scholes formula.

**Example 23.1.** Suppose that the current market price of a share of stock is \$90 and an option is written to purchase the stock for \$100 in six months. The current risk-free rate of interest is 8% per annum. Since the time to the expiration date is half a year, we have, in the notation of the Black–Scholes model, $P = 90$; $E = 100$; $r = 0.08$; and $t = 0.50$.

All of this information is readily available to market participants. More problematic is an assessment of the likely volatility of returns on the stock over the next six months. One possible approach is to estimate this volatility using data on past price changes. For instance, we could compute the variance of daily changes in the logarithm of price (daily rate of return) over the last 100 trading days. Multiplying the result by the number of trading days in the year would then yield an estimate of the required variance on an annual basis.[2] For this stock, suppose that such a procedure yields the standard deviation

$$\sigma = 0.6$$

This value or some alternative (perhaps developed subjectively) can then be substituted, together with the values of the other four factors, in Eq. (23.1) to obtain an estimate of the market value of the call option. We now illustrate these calculations.

First, we need the natural logarithm of P/E. This is

$$\ln\left(\frac{P}{E}\right) = \ln(0.9) = -0.1054$$

It follows that

$$\begin{aligned} d_1 &= \frac{\ln\left(\frac{P}{E}\right) + rt + \sigma^2\frac{t}{2}}{\sigma\sqrt{t}} = \frac{-0.1054 + (0.08)(0.50) + \frac{1}{2}(0.36)(0.50)}{0.6\sqrt{0.50}} \\ &= 0.06 \end{aligned}$$

[2]If we use monthly rate of return to calculate the variance, then the annualized variance will be 12 times the monthly variance.

and

$$d_2 = \frac{\ln\left(\frac{P}{E}\right) + rt - \sigma^2\frac{t}{2}}{\sigma\sqrt{t}} = \frac{-0.1054 + (0.08)(0.50) - \frac{1}{2}(0.36)(0.50)}{0.6\sqrt{0.50}}$$
$$= -0.37$$

Using the table of the cumulative distribution function of the standard normal distribution in the appendix at the back of this book, we find the probability that a standard normal random variable less than 0.06 is

$$N(d_1) = N(0.06) = 0.5239$$

and the probability that a standard normal random variable is less than −0.37 is

$$N(d_2) = N(-0.37) = 0.3557.$$

These numbers represent the probability that the stock price will be at least equal to the exercise price — 52% of the time over the life of the option — and the probability of exercise — 35%. We also require

$$e^{-rt} = e^{-(0.08)(0.5)} = 0.9608$$

Finally, on substitution into Eq. (23.1), we find

$$V_c = PN(d_1) = e^{-rt}EN(d_2) = (90)(0.5239)$$
$$-(0.9608)(100)(0.3557) = \$12.98$$

Therefore, according to the Black–Scholes model, the call option should be priced at $12.98 per share.

A further implication of the Black–Scholes model is that the quantity $N(d_1)$ provides the hedge ratio for a hedged portfolio of stocks and written options. We see, then, that to achieve such a portfolio, .5239 shares of stock should be purchased for each option written.

### 23.4.3 *Taxation of options*

The taxation of option gains, losses, and income are a fairly complex and constantly changing part of the tax law. However, tax treatment can have a large impact on the usefulness of option for the individual investor. Income (premiums) received by the option writer is taxed as normal income, just as if the option writer were providing a service.

Options can be used to defer gains into the future, which reduces the investor's current tax liability. For example, an investor with a short-term gain on a stock can purchase a put to protect against a drop in the stock price. This allows the investor to hold the stock and not realize the gain until sometime in the future, perhaps the next year, thereby deferring the payment of tax from the present until some future period. Hence, the tax position of the investor is also a factor in determining the value or usefulness of options. However, because we do not have a homogenous tax structure, it is difficult to incorporate the tax effect into a formulation such as the Black–Scholes model.

### 23.4.4 *American options*

In our analysis of options, we have assumed the options are European and thus may only be exercised on the expiration date, and that no dividends are paid on the stock before the expiration date. Merton (1973) has shown that if the stock does not pay dividends, it is suboptimal to exercise an American call option before the expiration date. Therefore, if American and European call options on a nondividend-paying stock are otherwise identical, they should have the same value.

The effect of dividends on a call option depends on whether the firm is expected to pay dividends before the option's expiration date. Such action should reduce the option's value — the greater the expected dividend, the larger the reduction in option value. The reason is that a dividend payment amounts to the transfer to stockholders of part of the firm's value, a distribution in which option holders do not share. The larger this reduction in firm value, all other things equal, the lower the expected future price of the stock, because that price reflects firm value at any point in time. Therefore, the higher the dividend, the smaller the probability of any gains from exercising a call option on common stock and, hence, the lower the value of the option. The extreme case occurs if the firm is liquidated and the entire amount of funds realized from the liquidation is distributed as dividends to common stockholders. Once such a distribution is made, the stock and the call option have zero value.

If the firm pays dividends, the value of an American call option on its stock will exceed that of an otherwise identical European option.

The reason is that the holder of the American call can exercise the option just before the exdividend date and thus receive the dividend payment. If the benefits from such an exercise outweigh the interest income that would have been earned on the exercise price had the option been held to the expiration date, it benefits the holder of an American call to exercise the option. Since this opportunity is not available to the holder of a European option, the American option should have a higher value.

The solution to valuing an option on a stock that pays dividends can be approximated by replacing $P$, the stock price in the Black–Scholes formula, with the stock price minus the present value of the known future dividend. This is justified because if the option is not exercised before maturity, the option holder will not receive the dividends, in which case the holder should subtract the present value of the dividend from the stock price.

## 23.5 Option Pricing Theory and Capital Structure

In this section we show how option pricing theory can be used to analyze the value of the components of a firm's capital structure. Suppose that management of an unlevered corporation decides to issue bonds. For simplicity, we assume these to be zero coupon bonds with face value $B$ to be paid at the maturity date.[3] When the bonds mature, bondholders must be paid an amount $B$, if possible. If this money cannot be raised, bondholders have a first claim on the firm's assets and will be paid the firm's entire value, $V_f$, which in this case will be less than $B$. Let us look at this arrangement from the point of view of the firm's stockholders. By using debt, stockholders can be regarded as having sold the firm to bondholders, with an option to purchase it back by paying an amount $B$ at the maturity date of the bonds. Thus, the stockholders hold a call option on the firm, with expiration date at the date of maturity of the bonds. If the firm's value exceeds the value of the debt on the expiration date, the debt will be retired, so that stockholders will have exercised their call option.

[3]These bonds will sell for less than the face value, the difference reflecting interest to be paid on the loan.

On the other hand, if the firm's value is less than the face value of the debt, stockholders' limited liability allows them to leave the firm in the hands of the bondholders. The call option will not be exercised, so that the stock will be worth nothing. However, stockholders will have no further obligations to bondholders. Therefore, on the date of expiration, the value of this call option, or, equivalently, the value of stockholders' equity, will be $V = V_f - B$ if $V_f > B$ and 0 if $V_f < B$. Thus, we can write

$$V = \text{MAX}(0, V_f - B) \tag{23.3}$$

where $V$ = value of stockholders' call option on the firm; $V_f$ = value of the firm; and $B$ = face value of debt.

This relationship is shown in Figure 23.7. As we can see, this is exactly the relationship shown in Figure 23.1(a) for the value of a call option.

We see, then, that the theory of options can provide us with insights into the valuation of debt and stockholders' equity. This analysis indicates that the stockholders own a call option on the

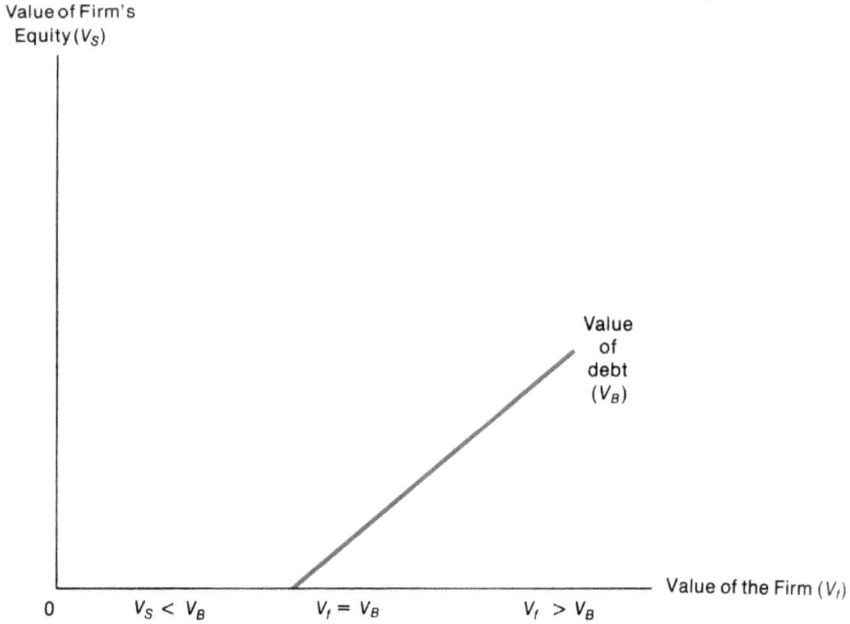


Figure 23.7 Option Approach to Capital Structure.

firm's assets. At any time, they could exercise this option by delivering the face value of the bonds to pay off the bondholders and realize the value of their option. This point is illustrated in the following example, where we employ the Black–Scholes model.

**Example 23.2.** An unlevered corporation is valued at \$14 million. The corporation issues debt, payable in six years, with a face value of \$10 million. The standard deviation of the continuously compounded rate of return on the total value of this corporation is 0.2. Assume that the risk-free rate of interest is 8% per annum.

In our previous notation, the current market price of the asset (in this case, the firm) is \$14 million, and the exercise price of the option is the face value of the debt. Therefore, we have $P = 14$, $E = 10$, $r = 0.08$, $t = 6$, and $\sigma = 0.2$, where we are measuring value in units of a million dollars. We will use the Black–Scholes formula, Eq. (23.1), to compute the value of stockholders' equity; that is, the value of the stockholders' call option on the firm. First, we require the natural logarithm of $P/E$, so that

$$\ln\left(\frac{P}{E}\right) = \ln(1.4) = 0.3365$$

Next, we find

$$d_1 = \frac{\ln\left(\frac{P}{E}\right) + rt + \sigma^2 \frac{t}{2}}{\sigma\sqrt{t}} = \frac{0.3365 + (0.08)(6) - \frac{1}{2}(0.2)(6)}{0.2\sqrt{6}} = 1.91$$

and

$$d_2 = \frac{\ln\left(\frac{P}{E}\right) + rt - \sigma^2 \frac{t}{2}}{\sigma\sqrt{t}} = \frac{0.3365 + (0.08)(6) - \frac{1}{2}(0.2)(6)}{0.2\sqrt{6}} = 1.42$$

From tabulated values of the cumulative distribution function of the standard normal random variable, we find

$$N(d_1) = N(1.91) = 0.9719$$

and

$$N(d_2) = N(1.42) = 0.9222$$

We also require

$$e^{-rt} = e^{-(0.08)(6)} = 0.6188$$

On substitution in Eq. (23.1), we find the value of stockholders' equity.

$$V = PN(d_1) - e^{-rt}EN(d_2) = (14)(0.9996)$$
$$- (0.6188)(5)(0.9977) = \$10.91\,\text{million}$$

Therefore, the value of the debt is

$$\text{Value of debt} = 14 - 10.91 = \$3.09\,\text{million}$$

In Table 23.4, we compare, from the point of view of bondholders, the cases where the face values of issued debt are \$5 million and \$10 million. We see from the table that increasing the proportion of debt in the capital structure decreases the value of each dollar of face value of debt. If all the debt is used at one time, this phenomenon, which simply reflects the increase in bondholders' risk as debt increases, will result in the demand for correspondingly higher interest rates. As our example illustrates, if the corporation sells only \$5 million of face-value bonds, a price of \$618,000 per million dollars in face value will be paid for these bonds. However, if bonds with face value of \$10 million are to be issued, this price will fall to \$610,000. In such a case, the market for bonds operates such that the risk to bondholders of future default is considered in establishing the price of the zero coupon bonds, or, more generally the interest rate attached to any bonds.

Suppose, however, that our company issues bonds with face value of \$5 million, at a cost to bond purchasers of \$3.09 million. One year later, this corporation decides to issue more debt. In valuing

Table 23.4 Effect of Different Levels of Debt on Debt Value.

| **Face Value of Debt (\$ millions)** | **Actual Value of Debt (\$ millions)** | **Actual Value per Dollar Debt Face Value of Debt** |
|---|---|---|
| 5 | 3.09 | \$0.618 |
| 10 | 6.10 | \$0.610 |

this new debt, potential purchasers of bonds will assess the risk of default. One factor taken into consideration will be the *total* level of debt of the corporation; that is, the amount of existing debt as well as the size of the new issue. Hence, the market price for the new bonds will reflect riskiness. Consider, however, the position of existing bondholders. The interest rates to be paid to these holders of old debt has already been established. The issue of new debt is going to increase the chance of default on all loans. Consequently, the value of existing bonds must fall when new bonds are issued. Therefore, the issue of new bonds entails a decrease in the wealth of existing bondholders. The beneficiaries are the stockholders of the company whose wealth increases by a corresponding amount. We see, then, that there is a conflict of interest between existing bondholders and holders of common stock. All other things equal, existing bondholders will prefer that no further debt be issued, while stockholders will prefer to see more debt issued. This provides an illustration of the agency problem discussed in Chapter 11. Purchasers of bonds will require covenants restricting the freedom of action of corporate management in order to protect the value of their investment.

### 23.5.1 *Riskiness of business operations*

Let us return to the corporation of Example 23.2, which is about to issue debt with face value of $10 million. Leaving the other variables unchanged, suppose that the standard deviation of the continuously compounded rate of return on the corporation's total value is 0.4, rather than 0.2. This implies that the corporation is operating in an environment of greater business risk. Setting $\sigma^2 = 0.4$, with all other relevant variables as specified in Example 23.2, we find $d_1 = 1.32$ and $d_2 = 0.34$, so that $N(d_1) = 0.9066$ and $N(d_2) = 0.6331$. From Eq. (23.1), we find the value of stockholders' equity to be

$$V = PN(d_1) - e^{-rt}EN(d_2) = (14)(0.9066) - (0.6188)(10)(0.6331) = \$8.77 \text{ million}$$

Thus, the value of the debt is

$$\text{Value of debt} = 14 - 8.77 = \$5.23\,\text{million}$$

Table 23.5 summarizes the comparison between these results and those of Example 23.2. We see that this increase in business risk,

Table 23.5 Effect of Different Levels of Business Risk on the Value of $10 Million Face Value of Debt.

| Variance of Rate of Return | Value of Equity ($ millions) | Value of Debt ($ millions) |
|---|---|---|
| 0.2 | 7.90 | 6.10 |
| 0.4 | 8.77 | 5.23 |

with its associated increase in the probability of default on the bonds, leads to a reduction from $6.10 million to $5.23 million in the market value of the $10 million face value of debt. To the extent that potential purchasers of bonds are able to anticipate the degree of business risk, the higher interest rate on the bonds reflects the risk involved. The greater the degree of risk, the higher the interest rate that must be offered to sell a particular amount of debt.

However, suppose that having issued debt, corporate management embarks on new projects with a higher level of risk than could have been foreseen by the purchasers of the bonds. As we have just seen, this will lower the value of existing bonds. This decrease in bondholders' wealth accrues as a gain in wealth to holders of common stock. Once again, we find a conflict of interest between stockholders and bondholders. Once debt has been sold, it will be in the interests of stockholders for the firm to operate with a high degree of business risk, while bondholders will prefer lower levels of risk. Thus, the degree of business risk represents another example of an agency problem. Bondholders will want protection against the possibility that management will take on riskier than anticipated projects, and will demand protective covenants against such actions. Because of this factor, the issue of a large volume of debt is likely to be accompanied by constraints on the freedom of management action in the firm's operation.

## 23.6 Warrants

A *warrant* is an option issued by a corporation to individual investors to purchase, at a stated price, a specified number of the shares of common stock of that corporation. Warrants are issued in two principal sets of circumstances:

1. In raising venture capital, either to start a new company or to substantially increase the scope of operations of an existing company, warrants are often issued to lenders as an additional inducement to the promised interest payments or to purchasers of new stock issues.
2. Often, when issuing bonds, a company will increase the bonds' attractiveness by attaching warrants. Thus, as well as receiving interest payments on the bonds, their purchasers obtain an option to buy stock in the corporation at a specified price. As we have seen, such options will have some value, and so their attachment to bonds should lead to a lowering of the interest rate paid on a fixed quantity of bonds or an increase in the number of bonds that can be sold at a given interest rate.

Since a warrant is essentially a call option on a specified number of shares of common stock, the principles underlying the valuation of call options are also applicable to the valuation of warrants. Suppose that a warrant entitles its holder to purchase $N$ shares of common stock at a total cost $E$. If, at the expiration date, the price per share of common stock is $P$, then shares of total value $NP$ can be purchased at cost $E$. If $NP$ exceeds $E$, the option to purchase will be exercised, and the difference between these quantities is the value of the warrant. On the other hand, if $NP$ is less than $E$, it will not pay to exercise the option, so that the warrant will be worthless. The warrant's value on the expiration date can then be expressed as

$$V_w = \text{MAX}(0, NP - E)$$

where $V$ = value of warrant; $N$ = number of shares that can be purchased; $P$ = market price per share of stock; and $E$ = exercise price for the purchase of $N$ shares of stock.

Prior to the expiration date, for reasons discussed earlier in this chapter, the warrant's value will exceed this theoretical value. The same factors affecting the value of an ordinary call option are also relevant here. Thus, all other things equal, warrant value will increase with increases in the volatility of the stock price, in the risk-free interest rate, and in the time to the expiration date. However, the basic version of the Black–Scholes model generally will not be directly applicable, as it pertains to the valuation of warrants. The reason is that, generally, warrants differ in important respects from ordinary call options. The factors are as follows:

1. The life of a call option typically is just a few months. However, the life of a warrant is several years. While it may not be unreasonable to expect volatility of rate of return to remain constant for a few months, it is less likely that it will do so for several years.
2. Over a period of several years, it is likely that dividends will be paid. As we have seen, dividend payments, which do not accrue to warrant holders, reduce the value of options to purchase stock.
3. For many warrants, the exercise price is not fixed to the expiration date, but changes at designated points in time. It may well pay to exercise the option to purchase shares immediately before such a change.
4. It may be that the number of shares that all warrant holders are entitled to purchase represents a considerable fraction of the total number of share of the corporation. Thus, if these options are all exercised, and total earnings are unaffected, then earnings per share will be diluted.

Let us look at this last point in more detail. Since by using warrants, a corporation can extract more favorable terms from bondholders, it follows that, in return, the company must have transferred something of value to these bondholders. This transfer can be visualized as giving the bondholders a stake in the corporation's equity. Thus, we should regard equity comprising both stockholdings and warrant value. We will refer to this total equity, prior to the exercise of the options, as *old equity* so that

$$\text{Old equity} = \text{Stockholders' equity} + \text{Warrants}$$

Suppose that the warrants are exercised. The corporation then receives additional money from the purchase of new shares, so that total equity is

$$\text{New equity} = \text{Old equity} + \text{Exercise money}$$

We denote by $N$ the number of shares outstanding and by $N_w$ the number of shares that warrant holders can purchase. If the options are exercised, there will be a total of $N + N_w$ shares, a fraction

$N_w/(N_w + N)$ of which is owned by former warrant holders. These holders then own this fraction of the new equity; that is,

$$H(\text{New equity}) = H(\text{Old equity}) + H(\text{Exercise money})$$

where

$$H = \frac{N_w}{N_w + N}$$

Thus, a fraction, $N_w/(N_w+N)$, of the exercise money is effectively returned to the former warrant holders. In fact, they have really spent $[1–N_w/(N_w + N)] = N/(N_w + N)$ of the exercise money to acquire a fraction, $N_w/(N_w + N)$, of the old equity. Therefore, in valuing the warrants, the Black–Scholes formula must be modified. We need to make the appropriate substitutions in Eq. (23.1) for the current stock price, $P$, and the exercise price of the option, E.

$$P = \left(\frac{N_w}{N_w + N}\right) \quad \text{(Value of old equity)}$$

$$E = \left(\frac{N}{N_w + N}\right) \quad \text{(Exercise money)}$$

It also follows that the appropriate measure of volatility, $\sigma^2$, is the variance of rate of return on the total old equity (including the value of warrants), not simply on stockholders' equity.

Suppose that a firm has one million shares outstanding, currently selling at \$100 per share. There are also 500,000 warrants with an exercise price of \$80 per share. The warrants are worth \$20, or the current stock price, \$100, less the exercise price of \$80. The value of the old equity is

$$\text{Old equity} = 100(1\text{m}) + (20)(0.5\text{m}) = \$110\,\text{million}$$

If the warrants are exercised, the firm will receive \$40 million (\$80 $\times$ $0.5m$) of new equity, so that the new equity is

$$\text{New equity} = \$110\text{m} + \$40\text{m} = \$150\,\text{million}$$

When they exercise their warrants, the warrant holders will own 1/3 of the shares outstanding; that is,

$$H = \frac{N_w}{N_w + N} \quad \text{or} \quad \frac{500{,}000}{500{,}000 + 1{,}000{,}000}$$

and the old shareholders will own the remaining 2/3 of the shares outstanding.

The warrant holders now have an investment worth $50 million, or

$$\frac{1}{3}(150\text{m}) = \frac{1}{3}(110\text{m}) + \frac{1}{3}(40\text{m}) = \$50\,\text{million}$$

It makes sense for the warrant holders to exercise their warrant; they spend $40 million for shares that are worth $50 million. In terms of the warrant value, the market should be willing to pay $20 per warrant for 500,000 warrants, or $10 million.

In Chapter 16, we discuss convertible bonds. A *convertible bond* is a security that gives its owner the right to exchange it for a given number of shares of common stock any time before the maturity date of the bond. Hence, a convertible bond is actually a portfolio of two securities: a bond and a warrant. The value of a convertible bond is the value of the bond portion of the portfolio plus the value of the warrant. The option approach to evaluate warrant and convertible bonds can be found in Hull (2018) and Lee *et al.* (2013).

## 23.7 Summary

In Chapter 23, we have discussed the basic concepts of call and put options and have examined the factors that determine the value of an option. One procedure used in option valuation is the Black–Scholes model, which allows us to estimate option value as a function of stock price, option-exercise price, time-to-expiration date, and risk-free interest rate. The option pricing approach to investigating capital structure is also discussed, as is the value of warrants.

## References

Banz R. and M. Miller. "Prices for State Contingent Claims: Some Estimates and Applications," *Journal of Business*, 51 (1978, pp. 653–672).

Black, F. and M. Scholes. "The Pricing of Options and Corporate Liabilities," *Journal of Political Economy*, 31 (May–June 1973, pp. 637–659).

Cox, J. C. and M. Rubinstein. *Option Markets* (Englewood Cliffs, NJ: Prentice-Hall, 1985).

Eun, C. and B. Resnick. *International Financial Management*, 8th edn. (McGraw-Hill, 2018).
Galai, D. and R. W. Masulis. "The Option Pricing Model and the Risk Factor of Stock," *Journal of Financial Economics*, 3 (1976, pp. 53–81).
Hull, J. C. *Options, Futures, and Other Derivatives*, 10th edn. (Pearson, 2018).
Lee, C. F., J. E. Finnerty, A. C. Lee, J. Lee, and D. H. Wort. *Security Analysis, Portfolio Management, and Financial Derivatives* (World Scientific Publishers, Inc, 2013).
Merton, R. C. "The Theory of Rational Option Pricing," *The Bell Journal of Economics and Management Science*, 4 (1973, pp. 141–183).
Rendleman, R. J., Jr. and B. J. Barter. "Two-State Option Pricing," *The Journal of Finance*, 24 (1979, pp. 1093–1110).

## Questions and Problems

1. Find the expected value of an option with an exercise price of \$100 at the end of the period, given the following information. (Current stock price is \$100.)

| Probability | Outcome | Stock Price |
|---|---|---|
| 0.4 | S1 | \$150 |
| 0.6 | S2 | \$80 |

2. A riskless hedge position can be constructed by buying a stock and writing options on the stock. Using the information in Problem 1: (Assume the risk-free interest rate is 10%.)
   a. Find the optimal hedge ratio.
   b. Find the equilibrium option price.
3. The price of Goodsell Company stock on January 1 is \$100 per share. A call option maturing on April 1 has a \$100 exercise price. The standard deviation of Goodsell stock is 20% per year. What is the call option value if the risk-free rate is 10%?
4. Suppose an unleveraged firm is valued at \$10 million. The firm issues debt, payable in nine years, with a face value of \$7 million. The standard deviation of the rate of return on the total

value of this firm is 0.4, and the risk-free interest rate is 8% per annum. Using the option valuation model, calculate the value of stockholders' equity.

5. How does the price of a call option respond to the following changes, other things equal?

   a. Stock price increase
   b. Exercise price increase
   c. Risk-free interest rate increase
   d. Extension of the expiration date
   e. Volatility of the stock price increase

6. If a call option has an exercise price of $50, then over what stock price range would it be:

   a. Out of the money?
   b. In the money?

7. If a put option has an exercise price of $50, then over what stock price range would it be:

   a. Out of the money?
   b. In the money?

8. Would an American option generally sell at a price higher or lower than a European option? Explain.
9. If a call option has an exercise price of $50, how much will it be worth on its exercise date (assuming no transaction costs) if the price of the underlying stock is:

   a. $30
   b. $50
   c. $80

10. If a call option has an exercise price of $60 and the price of the stock is $40, what is the value of the call option to the

    a. Holder of the option
    b. Seller of the option

11. Allison Merrick is considering two call options, each having exercise prices of $20 and being identical in all other respects except for the distribution of underlying stock values. The distribution of the values of the underlying stocks of Companies J and K are given below:

| Company J | | Company K | |
|---|---|---|---|
| **Future Stock Price** | **Probability** | **Future Stock Price** | **Probability** |
| $10 | 0.2 | $5 | 0.1 |
| 18 | 0.3 | 17 | 0.3 |
| 22 | 0.3 | 25 | 0.4 |
| 25 | 0.2 | 35 | 0.2 |

Find the expected payoff for each and explain which one you would prefer.

12. The current price per share is $80 which can either go up to $100 or down to $60. The probabilities of upward and downward movement of the stock price is 0.6 and 0.4, respectively. Given an exercise price of $80 on a call option and an optimal hedge ratio of 0.4:

    a. Find the lower bound of the stock price.
    b. Find the expected value of the call option.
    c. Demonstrate that the hedged portfolio is riskless.

13. The standard deviation of the return on the stock of Company A is 0.5 per year. A call option written on this stock is maturing six months from now and has an exercise price of $80. If the current stock price is $80 and the risk-free rate of interest in 8%, find the optimal hedge ratio for a portfolio of stocks and options using the Black–Scholes model. (*Note*: This is equivalent to finding $N(d_1)$ in the Black–Scholes model.)
14. A firm has outstanding debt of $12 million which matures in 0.5 years from now. The standard deviation of the rate of return of the firm's value is 0.3. The value of another otherwise identical firm with zero debt is $20 million. Find the value of the firm's outstanding debt, given that the risk free interest rate is 8%.

# Chapter 24

# Portfolio Insurance and Synthetic Options

## Contents



## 24.1 Introduction

Portfolio insurance is a strategy that may allow portfolio managers and investors to limit downside risk while maintaining upside potential. In this context, the word *insurance* is somewhat misleading: portfolio insurance is not a true form of insurance, where the insured pays a premium to someone who accepts the risk of some adverse event. Rather, portfolio insurance is an asset-allocation or hedging strategy that allows the investor to alter the amount of risk he or she is willing to accept by giving up some return. This chapter looks at the basic concept of portfolio insurance, the various alternative methods available to the portfolio manager to hedge the portfolio, the impact of portfolio insurance on the stock market, and the pricing of equity securities and market regulation, and finally, empirical studies of portfolio insurance.

In this chapter Section 24.2 discusses the basic concepts of portfolio insurance. Section 24.3 discusses the strategies and implementations of portfolio insurance, and Section 24.4 is a comparison of alternative portfolio insurance strategies. Section 24.5 presents empirical studies of portfolio insurance, and finally Section 24.6 summarizes the chapter.

## 24.2 Basic Concepts of Portfolio Insurance

*Portfolio insurance* refers to any strategy that protects the value of a portfolio of assets. It can be used for stock, bonds, or real assets. If the value of the asset declines, the insurance or hedge will increase in value to help offset the decline in price of hedged assets. If the price of the asset increases, the increase of the insured portfolio will be less than the increase in the asset but will nevertheless still increase.

Table 24.1 illustrates how portfolio insurance works. In this example, the underlying asset is purchased for \$95 and \$5 is spent on portfolio insurance. The minimum amount that the insured investor can realize is \$95, but the uninsured portfolio can fall in value to a low of \$75 if the market falls. If the value of the asset increases, the value of the insured portfolio will increase, but at a smaller rate. Figure 24.1 illustrates the profit and loss of the insured and uninsured portfolio.

Rubinstein (1985) stated that the portfolio shown in Figure 24.1 has the three properties of an insured portfolio.

(1) The loss is limited to a prescribed level.
(2) The rate of return on the insured portfolio will be a predictable percentage of the rate of return on the uninsured portfolio.
(3) The investments of the portfolio are restricted to a market index and cash. The expected return on the market index is above the expected return from holding cash, and the insurance is fairly priced. This guarantees that the insured portfolio has a higher expected return than the uninsured portfolio.

Portfolio insurance allows market participants to alter the return distribution to fit investors' needs and preferences for risk. From

Table 24.1 Mechanics of Portfolio Insurance: An Example.

| | |
|---|---|
| Initial investment | \$100.00 |
| Cost of portfolio insurance | −\$5.00 |
| Amount of Investment going toward securities | \$95.00 |
| Amount invested=\$100 | |

| **Value of Portfolio at Year End (\$)** | **Return on Uninsured Portfolio (%)** | **Value of Insured Portfolio (\$)** | **Net Return on Insured Portfolio (%)** |
|---|---|---|---|
| 75.00 | −25 | 95.00 | −5 |
| 80.00 | −20 | 95.00 | −5 |
| 85.00 | −15 | 95.00 | −5 |
| 90.00 | −10 | 95.00 | −5 |
| 95.00 | −5 | 95.00 | −5 |
| 100.00 | 0 | 95.00 | −5 |
| 105.00 | 5 | 100.00 | 0 |
| 110.00 | 10 | 105.00 | 5 |
| 115.00 | 15 | 110.00 | 10 |
| 120.00 | 20 | 115.00 | 15 |
| 125.00 | 25 | 120.00 | 20 |
| 130.00 | 30 | 125.00 | 25 |

column 2 and column 4 of Table 24.1, it is clear that the expected return of an uninsured portfolio is smaller than the expected return of an insured portfolio. It should be noted that in an efficient market at a fair price the insurance will be used until the expected return on insured and uninsured portfolios are the same.

The uninsured portfolio has greater upside potential as well as greater downside risk, whereas the insured portfolio limits the downside loss to the cost of the hedge. The upside potential of the insured portfolio is always below that of the uninsured portfolio. The cost of the insurance is the lower return for the insured portfolio should prices increase. While some investors would prefer the greater upside potential that the uninsured portfolio offers, risk-averse investors would prefer the limited-risk characteristics that the hedged portfolio offers.

In general, portfolio insurance can be thought of as holding two portfolios. The first portfolio can be viewed as the safe or riskless portfolio with value equal to the level of protection desired. This level

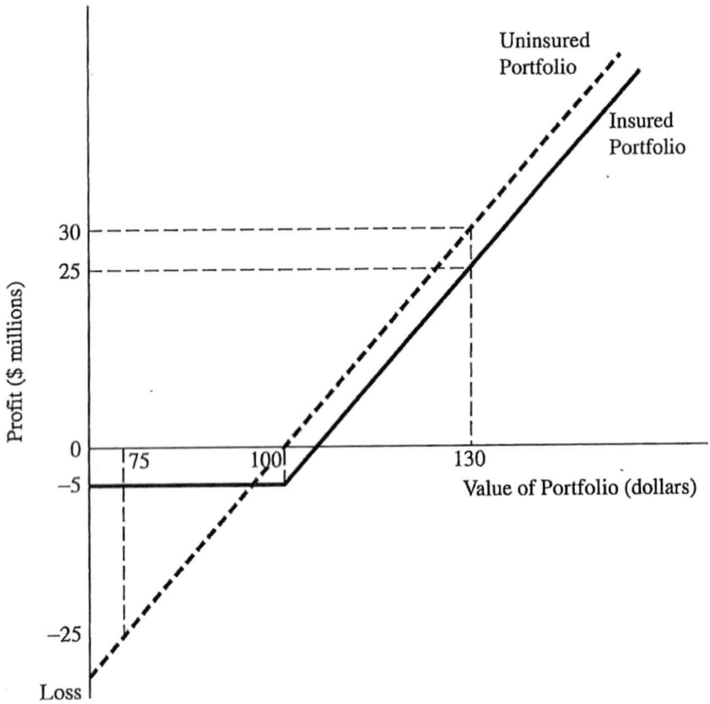


Figure 24.1 Gains and Losses of Insured and Uninsured Portfolios: An Example.

is called the *floor* and is the lowest value the portfolio can have. For certain strategies this can be held constant or allowed to change over time as market conditions or needs change. The second portfolio consists of the difference between the total value of the portfolio and the floor, commonly called the *portfolio cushion.* These assets consist of a leveraged position in risky assets. To insure the portfolio, the cushion should be managed so as to never fall below zero in value because of the limited-liability property of common stock. Figure 24.2 shows the relationship between the total value of the portfolio, the cushion, and the floor. The actual investment or allocation of the portfolio funds between risky and risk-free assets is determined by changing market conditions or the changing requirements of the portfolio manager.

A simple example of changing the mix between risky and risk-free assets in response to market changes offers the opportunity to demonstrate the dynamic nature of portfolio insurance. As shown in Figure 24.2, half the current portfolio is invested in risky assets

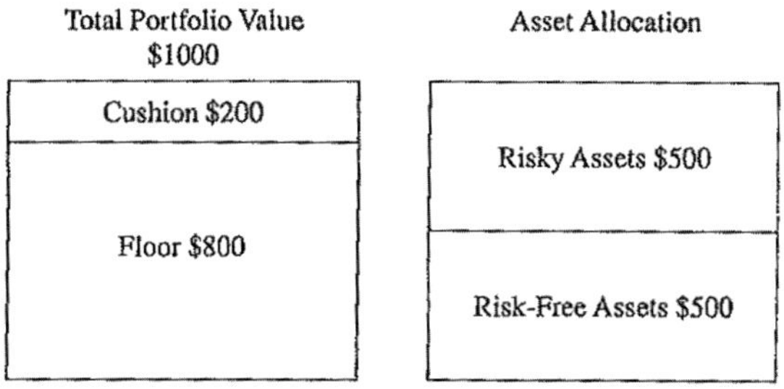


Figure 24.2 Components of an Insured Portfolio Valued at $1,000.

and half in risk-free assets. The exposure at this point is $500. The cushion is $200. If this is a reasonable relationship that the portfolio manager wishes to maintain, the relationship between these two, defined as the *multiple*, can be calculated:

$$\text{Multiple} = \frac{\text{Exposure}}{\text{Cushion}} \tag{24.1}$$

$$m = \frac{e}{c}$$

$$= \frac{500}{200} = 2.5 \tag{24.2}$$

As the market for the risky assets changes, the exposure and the cushion value change, causing a change in the multiple. Given a predetermined trigger or change in multiple, the portfolio manager can trade to restore the balance between the cushion and the exposure. If, for example, the market value of the risky asset rises 20%, the value of the cushion increases to $300 and the value of the risky assets rises to $600. The total value of the portfolio is the value of the risky assets plus the value of the risk-free assets ($500 + $600, or $1,100). The value of the floor remains at $800 so that the cushion goes to $300 ($1,100 – $800). The multiple has fallen to

$$m = \frac{e}{c} = \frac{600}{300} = 2 \tag{24.3}$$

If the target multiple is 2.5, an adjustment must be made by the portfolio manager, who must sell some of the risk-free assets and purchase risky assets until the multiple is 2.5. Hence, the manager needs to rebalance the portfolio so that $750 is invested in risky

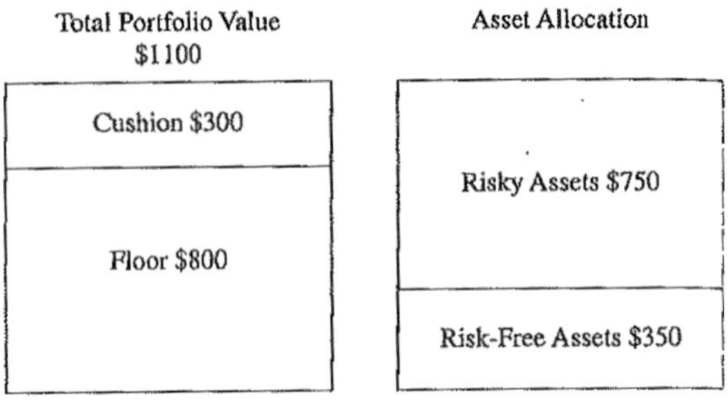


Figure 24.3 Components of an Insured Portfolio Rebalanced after a Market Rise.

assets and $350 is invested in risk-free assets. This mix will restore the multiple to the desired level of 2.5:

$$m = \frac{e}{c} = \frac{750}{300} = 2.5 \tag{24.4}$$

Figure 24.3 shows the portfolio after rebalancing.

Increasing the portfolio's risky assets as the market rises allows the manager to participate in the bull market. As long as the market continues its rise, the manager continues to shift assets to the risky-asset portfolio to participate in the market gain. However, when the market turns bearish and begins to go down, the manager needs to sell off risky assets and invest in risk-free assets. For example, if the market declined by 16 2/3% back to its original level at the beginning of this example, the value of the risky assets would be $625 ($750 × 0.8333). At this new level, the multiple would be

$$m = \frac{e}{c} = \frac{625}{175} = 3.56 \tag{24.5}$$

The target multiple of 2.5 is below the actual multiple of 3.56, so the portfolio manager must sell some of the risky assets and place the proceeds into risk-free assets. The total value of the portfolio has fallen to $975 ($625 + $350). The value of the cushion has fallen to $175 ($975 − $800). In order to have a multiple of 2.5 the risky assets have to be reduced to

$$m = \frac{e}{175} = 2.5$$

$$e = \$437.50 \tag{24.6}$$

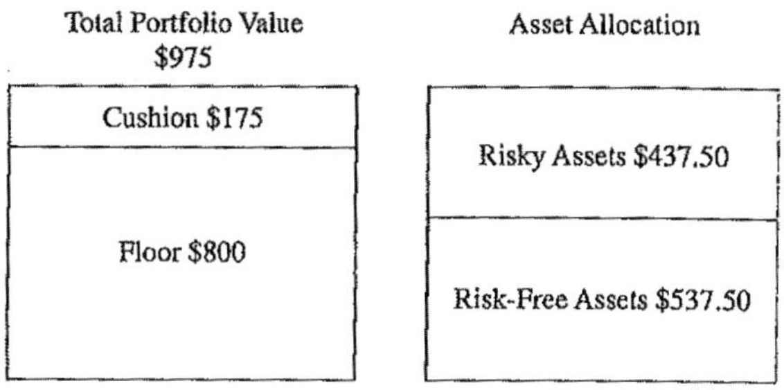


Figure 24.4 Components of an Insured Portfolio Rebalanced after a Market Fall.

Hence $187.50 of the risky assets must be sold and this amount must be invested in the risk-free assets. The position of the insured portfolio after this rebalancing is shown in Figure 24.4.

As the market falls, the portfolio manager sells off risky assets and invests the proceeds in risk-free assets, thereby reducing exposure to a falling market. In general, this strategy can best be described as "run with your winners and cut your losses." *Underlying this discussion are the assumptions that the rise and fall of the market takes place over a time interval long enough for the portfolio manager* to *rebalance the position, and that the market has sufficient liquidity to absorb the value of the risky assets.* This may not always be the case, however. October 19, 1987, commonly called Black Monday, and October 26, 1987, commonly called Blue Monday, as well as October 13, 1989, are examples of a rapid fall in prices in a very illiquid market for risky assets.

This general discussion of portfolio insurance is based on an article by Perold (1986). The simplicity of this approach makes it an ideal way to explain the general way of accomplishing portfolio insurance or portfolio hedging. Perold has called this *constant-proportion portfolio* insurance (CPPI). As has been seen, it involves holding the risk-free asset in an amount equal to the level of protection desired (floor), plus holding the remainder of the portfolio in a risky asset. The multiple of the risky asset to the cushion is then held in a constant proportion.

As will be seen, there are a number of ways of insuring or hedging a portfolio to keep the multiple constant. These are discussed in the next section.

## 24.3 Strategies and Implementation of Portfolio Insurance

Portfolio insurance allows the investor to participate in the appreciation of value of a risky portfolio while limiting the potential losses of the portfolio. This is very similar to the features available from an investment in options. There are four basic strategies to implementing a portfolio-insurance program: (1) the use of stop-loss orders, (2) the purchase of exchange-traded put options, (3) the creation of synthetic put options, and (4) dynamic hedging using futures contracts. All of these strategies are detailed below.

### 24.3.1 *Stop-loss orders*

A *stop-loss order* is a conditional market order to sell portfolio stock if the value of the stock drops to a given level. For example, if you held an index portfolio when the market index is at $100 and you expected the market to rise, you could limit your downside risk by placing a stop-loss order at $95. If the market fell to $95, your stop-loss order would become a market sell order, and the portfolio would be sold at the prevailing market price. The use of a stop-loss order does not guarantee that you would get exactly $95; you could get more or less. Still, you would begin to liquidate your position at a predetermined level. As you can see, the placement of stop-loss orders is a kind of crude portfolio insurance in that it allows you to make money if the market goes up and cuts your losses (approximately) to a predetermined level should the market fall.

As pointed out by Rubinstein (1985), the major problem of using stop-loss orders to approximate portfolio insurance is the path dependence of this technique — that is, if the market falls, the stop-loss order is executed, and the portfolio is sold, the portfolio manager needs to make a decision about when to get back into the market. The worst thing that could happen would be for the market to rebound immediately after the execution of the stop-loss order and sale of the portfolio. In such a case, the portfolio would consist of 100% cash. Because of this cash position, the portfolio would not benefit from the increase in stock price as the market rises. On the other hand, if the market were to continue to fall after the execution of the stop-loss order, the portfolio manager with 100% cash would be in a position enhanced by the portfolio insurance — that is, 100% cash in a falling market. Hence, the success of the portfolio-insurance strategy is dependent on the subsequent market movement. Ideally, portfolio insurance should work regardless of the subsequent movement of the market; thus it should be *path independent.* Clearly, in the case of stop-loss orders it is path dependent, and this strategy is not a very useful form of portfolio insurance.

### 24.3.2 *Portfolio insurance with listed put options*

Put options can be purchased on a stock index on various exchanges and used for creating an insured portfolio. Table 24.2 lists the indexes and exchanges on which options are available. If the market falls, the drop in the value of the portfolio will be offset by the gain in value of the put option. On the other hand, if the market increases in value, the portfolio will increase in value but the premium paid for the put option will be lost. For example, a portfolio manager with a $100-million portfolio purchases 4,000 Major Market Index (MMI) options with an exercise price of $250 with the cost of each option at $500. If the market value of the portfolio declines by $10 million by the expiration date of the option and the MMI index drops to $225, the portfolio manager can exercise the puts to offset the losses on the stock portfolio. The portfolio manager delivers the 4,000 put options

Table 24.2 Listed Options on Market Indexes.

| **Chicago Mercantile Exchange** | **Chicago Board Options Exchange** | **American Stock Exchange** |
|---|---|---|
| S&P 500 Index | S&P 100 Index<br>S&P 500 Index | Major Market Index<br>Computer<br>Technology Index<br>Oil Index<br>Institutional Index |
| **Philadelphia Stock Exchange** | **New York Stock Exchange** | **Pacific Exchange** |
| Utilities Index<br>Value Line Index<br>National OTC Index | NYSE Composite Index<br>NYSE Beta Index | Financial News<br>Composite Index |

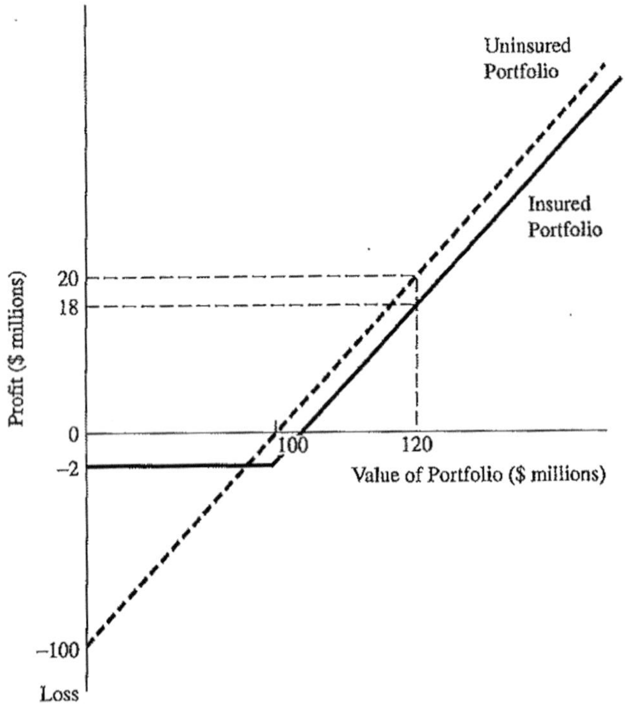


Figure 24.5 Gains and Losses of Insured and Uninsured Portfolios.

and receives \$10 million. Since the puts cost \$2 million, the net gain on the puts is \$8 million. The \$8 million gain on the puts offsets some of the \$10 million loss on the portfolio, for a net loss of \$2 million. If the portfolio increases in value by \$20 million and the MMI index closes above \$250, the net gain on the portfolio will be \$20 million from the increase in equity value minus the \$2 million premium paid for the options — a net gain of \$18 million. The portfolio returns for this example are depicted in Figure 24.5.

A perfect hedge is usually not possible because the correlation between the market index and the portfolio may not be perfect. This is called the *tracking problem*. The greater the correlation between the portfolio and the index, the more effective the hedge. The lower the correlation, the less effective the hedge as a portfolio insurance strategy.

In the example it was assumed that the beta coefficient between the portfolio and the MMI was equal to one. If the beta in reality were not equal to one, more or less put contracts would be needed to insure the portfolio. For a beta less than one fewer puts would be needed, and for a beta greater than one more puts would be needed. For example, if the portfolio had a beta of 1.20, 20% more put options would be needed to hedge the portfolio.

The price change of the market index and the value of the portfolio, as well as the movement of the price of the option on the index, are all related. The success of a portfolio-insurance strategy depends on correct determination of the hedge ratio. The hedge ratio is the ratio of the value of the portfolio to the value of the options contracts used to hedge the portfolio:

$$\text{Hedge ratio} = \frac{\text{Number of contracts} \times \text{Face value of contracts}}{\text{Face value of portfolio}}$$

In discussing the use of put options for portfolio insurance, two characteristics were assumed about the nature of the options used.

(1) They are available with long maturities or with maturities that match the portfolio manager's investment horizon.
(2) They are exercisable only at maturity — that is, they are European-type options.

Unfortunately, all the index options listed in Table 24.2 are American options. American options can be exercised at any time before expiration, hence have higher values to certain investors. This is so because American options have all the advantages of European options plus the privilege of early exercise. The portfolio manager who uses American options for portfolio insurance finds that he or she is paying for the early exercise privilege when in fact he or she does not really need it. Second, listed options are not protected against normal cash-dividend payments. When a firm's stock goes ex-dividend, the price of the stock is expected to fall by the amount of the dividend payment. This expected fall in the price of the stock is not offset by any changes in the option contract; hence the market price of the option will be affected by the ex-dividend behavior of the stock's price. As a result, options can be used to insure the capital-appreciation component of the stock return but not the dividend component. Third, all listed options have a maximum maturity of nine months, with most of the trading taking place in the near contracts with maturities of three months or less. Given these problems, the usefulness of index put options for portfolio insurance is somewhat questionable.

### 24.3.3 *Portfolio insurance with synthetic options*

Rubinstein and Leland (1981) suggest a strategy that replicates the returns on a call option by continuously adjusting a portfolio consisting of stock and a risk-free asset (T-bill, cash). This is called a synthetic call-option strategy; it involves increasing the investment in stock by borrowing when the value of stocks is increasing, and selling stock and paying off borrowing or investing in the risk-free asset when market values are falling. The key variable in this strategy is the delta value, which measures the change in the price of a call option with respect to the change in the value of the portfolio of risky stocks (see also Chapter 23). For deep-in-the-money options, the delta value will be close to one because a $1 change in the stock value will result in approximately a $1 change in the option value. Thus to replicate the option with cash and stock, almost one share must be purchased and the amount borrowed will be approximately equal to the exercise price. For deep out-of-the-money options, the value of the delta will be close to zero, and the replicating portfolio will contain very few shares and little or no borrowing. Hence in its simplest form, the delta value largely depends on the relationship between the exercise price and the stock price. As the market moves to new levels, the value of the delta will change; hence the synthetic option portfolio must be rebalanced periodically to maintain the proper mix between equity and borrowing or cash.

In a similar manner, a portfolio manager can create replicated put options through a combination of selling short the asset and lending. The amount of stock sold short is equal to the delta value minus one. As the market decreases in value, more of the equity is sold (the short position increases), with the proceeds invested at the risk-free rate. If the market increases in value, money is borrowed to buy the stock and reduce the short position.

### 24.3.4 *Portfolio insurance with dynamic hedging*

As a practical matter, rather than buying, selling, or short selling stocks, a portfolio manager may trade (buy or sell) stock-index futures to adjust the exposure of a portfolio. If the stock market is declining, futures contracts are sold to effectively reduce the position in the portfolio. The selling of stock-index futures has the same effect on the portfolio as the sale of stocks and the investment in a risk-free asset. As the market turns around and begins to go up in value, the portfolio manager purchases futures contracts to cover the short position by liquidating the investment in the risk-free asset. This procedure is called *dynamic hedging*. Whether it works depends upon a high degree of correlation between the value of index-futures contracts and the value of the underlying index. For most time periods there is a very high degree of comovement between the index and the futures contract. However, this may not always be the case.

Suppose that a portfolio manager wishes to insure a portfolio of well-diversified stocks with a value of \$1 million, and the portfolio beta is 1.1 when measured relative to the S&P 500. (This means that if the S&P 500 goes up or down by 1%, the change in the value of the portfolio will be 1.1%.) If the portfolio manager is worried about a market decline, he or she can insure his or her portfolio by selling S&P 500 index futures contracts. By selling futures contracts, the fall in value of the portfolio would be offset by gains in the futures market. If the strategy for portfolio insurance incorporates the beta, the following relationship is necessary to determine the number of contracts required to insure the portfolio:

$$\text{Number of contracts} = \frac{\text{Value of portfolio}}{\text{Value of futures contracts}} \times \beta \qquad (24.7)$$

Assume the S&P 500 index is selling at \$110, and the portfolio is worth \$1 million on day 1. If the market falls by 10%, the value of the portfolio falls 11% to \$890,000, the value of the S&P 500 futures contract falls to \$99, and the scenario is as follows.

(1) The portfolio has lost \$110,000.
(2) Each S&P 500 futures contract sold can be repurchased for \$99 × 500 or \$49,500, for a gain of \$5500 (\$55,000 – \$49,500).

In order to have a perfect hedge, the portfolio manager would need \$110,000/5500 = 20 contracts. Using Eq. (24.7), we see that adjusting the number of contracts for the volatility or beta of the portfolio yields:

$$\text{Number of contracts} = \frac{\$1{,}000{,}000}{\$110 \times 500} \times 1.1 = 20\,\text{contracts}$$

This result of a perfect hedge is dependent upon two critical assumptions.

(1) The relationship of the volatility of the portfolio to the volatility of the index remains the same or the beta does not change; and
(2) The movement of the price of the futures contract is in lock step with the movement of the index; they are perfectly correlated.

In spite of the problems for portfolio insurance associated with the validity of these critical assumptions, the use of futures contracts for portfolio hedging is widespread. The main reason why futures have been accepted as a trading vehicle for portfolio insurance is the low trading costs. This and the reasons below have led to rapid growth in the use of futures contracts for insuring portfolios during the early part of the 1980s.

(1) Low trading costs allow for rapid and frequent adjustments in implementing the portfolio strategy.
(2) Futures markets are liquid enough for insurance programs for large institutional portfolios.
(3) The use of futures allows for independence between management of the risky assets in the portfolio and the portfolio insurance.

## 24.4 Comparison of Alternative Portfolio-Insurance Strategies

This section compares alternative portfolio-insurance strategies — that is, synthetic options, listed put options, and dynamic hedging.

### 24.4.1 *Synthetic options*

As previously discussed, *synthetic options* are not options but a strategy for allocating assets that replicates the return on a call option. There are four advantages to using a dynamic-hedging strategy instead of synthetic-option approach. First, the futures contracts have lower transaction costs than stocks. Kidder, Peabody reports that index funds pay one-way transaction costs of $125 for $100,000 of stock, or 0.125% (they assume a commission of $0.05 per share at an average price of \$40), and institutional clients pay approximately \$0.06 per share.[1] In contrast, one-way futures transaction costs for institutional investors are \$15 per \$100,000, or 0.015%. Thus the transaction costs for futures are one-eighth to one-tenth of the cost of trading stocks, thereby reducing the cost of dynamic hedging compared with synthetic options. Second, liquidity is much greater in the futures market than in options or stock markets. For example, during the large downside movement in the stock market on September 11–12, 1986, the consulting from of Leland O'Brien Rubinstein Associates sold more than \$500 million of stock-index futures.[2] Such large transactions could not be made in options markets.

The third advantage is that futures contracts are highly levered and less cash is necessary to carry out a dynamic-hedging strategy. As little as \$2,000 can control each futures contract. The fourth advantage is that because stocks are not sold, the management of the stock portfolio is independent of the portfolio insurance. In contrast, managers must be active when implementing a synthetic option because the underlying stock is bought or sold to replicate the returns on an option.

The main disadvantage of dynamic hedging with respect to synthetic options is the tracking error that might occur because the futures are not perfectly correlated with the stock. This is not a problem with synthetic options because the stock itself is purchased or sold.

Another disadvantage of implementing either a dynamic-hedging or synthetic-option strategy is that they require continuous monitoring to insure that the delta of the replicated put equals the delta of a theoretical option. The replicated put must be rebalanced at certain intervals to maintain a proper mix of stock and futures. Here a tradeoff results: the more frequent the rebalancing, the better the replication of the theoretical put; however, more frequent rebalancing also results in higher transaction costs. Thus determining when to rebalance the portfolio is a major decision when implementing

[1]Hill, J. M. *Portfolio Insurance: Volatility Risk and Futures Mispricing* (New York: Kidder Peabody Financial Futures Department, 1987).
[2]Anders, G. "Investors Rush for Portfolio Insurance." *The Wall Street Journal* (October 14, 1986, p. 6).

a synthetic-option or dynamic-hedging strategy in the presence of transaction costs.

There might be a price advantage or disadvantage to a dynamic-hedging strategy due to futures mispricing. When shorting futures for hedging purposes, the manager hopes that the futures sell at a premium and the basis (the cash price minus the futures price) widens. By selling futures when they are expensive and buying them back at a lower price, a profit results on the hedge. On the other hand, losses on the hedge will probably result if "cheap" futures are sold for hedging purposes. The following example illustrates these concepts. Suppose that a manager holds a portfolio worth \$250 and shorts futures on the same portfolio that are worth \$260. The basis is $\$250-\$260 = -\$10$. Because the basis is equal to zero at expiration, the negative basis will have to increase.

In this example the investor makes a profit of \$10 on the hedge, regardless of how the portfolio performs. The profit is a result of selling "expensive" futures and waiting for the basis to increase. Table 24.3 presents the results of this case. In contrast, suppose that an investor with a portfolio worth \$250 shorts futures worth \$245. In this example, the investor will lose money if he waits until expiration, because the basis will decrease. The result of this case can be found in Table 24.4.

Table 24.3 Profit or Loss of Expensive Futures.

| **Value of Stock at Expiration of Futures** | **Value of Futures at Expiration** | **Profit or Loss on Stock** | **Profit or Loss on Futures** | **Profit or Loss** |
|---|---|---|---|---|
| \$270 | \$270 | +\$20 | −\$10 | +\$10 |
| \$230 | \$230 | −\$20 | +\$30 | +\$10 |

Table 24.4 Profit or Loss of Cheap Futures.

| **Value of Stock at Expiration of Futures** | **Value of Futures at Expiration** | **Profit or Loss on Stock** | **Profit or Loss on Futures** | **Profit or Loss** |
|---|---|---|---|---|
| \$270 | \$270 | +\$20 | −\$25 | −\$5 |
| \$230 | \$230 | −\$20 | +\$15 | −\$5 |

Here, the basis decreases and losses result for the hedger. Cheap futures will increase the costs of implementing a dynamic-hedging strategy and expensive futures will reduce the costs. The dynamic hedger hopes to sell futures selling at a premium and buy the futures at a discount.

The synthetic-call approach is usually used when implementing a portfolio-insurance strategy without futures. Thus, more of the risky asset is purchased when performance is favorable and the stock is sold when the asset declines. When implementing a dynamic-hedging strategy, the underlying stocks are not bought or sold, but rather stock-index futures are shorted to create a put option on the portfolio. In both cases, insurance is created for the portfolio, but the methods are different. In the synthetic-option case, the underlying portfolio behaves like a call option. For the dynamic-hedging case, the portfolio is not altered, only the futures position is changed to create a put option. A further discussion of the synthetic-call approach can be found in Becker (1988).

### 24.4.2 *Listed put options*

Portfolio insurance with *listed put options* does not require continuous monitoring because the delta of the listed option is automatically changed when the price of the underlying asset changes. Because of the automatic adjustment of the delta value, a listed-put strategy requires less monitoring and lower trading frequency than a synthetic-option or dynamic-hedging strategy.

There are a number of problems with using stock-index puts for portfolio insurance. First, because index options have at most a nine-month life, an investor may have to buy these short-term options even though the planning horizon might be much longer. These cumulative purchases of puts would result in a much greater cost than a longer-term option. This is due to the fact that for the long-term one-year put to be in the money, the market price must be below the exercise price after one year. In contrast, the value of the short-term options will have a positive value if the market price finished below the exercise price after nine months.

Second, the purchaser of portfolio insurance is not interested in exercising the option early, because this would leave the portfolio uninsured. The purchaser of insurance would prefer European options over American options because European options are cheaper. (However, the most popular index option, the OEX S&P 100, is American.) This early-exercise feature is of no value to the purchaser of portfolio insurance and adds to the cost of the insurance.

The third problem is that large-portfolio managers cannot purchase put options for insurance purposes because options markets do not provide the liquidity necessary to purchase large amounts of put options. Low liquidity might be even more of a problem for deep in- or out-of-the-money options or options that expire in the six- to nine-month range of maturities.

Like futures, there might be a lacking problem between the underlying stock or stocks and the instrument underlying the portfolio.

A replicated-option approach requires more management than a listed put-option strategy. The dynamic-hedging approach uses the highly liquid futures market to rebalance the portfolio. On the other hand, portfolio managers of large portfolios cannot purchase listed puts for portfolio insurance because of lack of liquidity in the options market. Futures mispricing will increase or decrease the cost of dynamic hedging; if the short hedger shorts expensive futures, profits will result from the hedges. If expensive futures are shorted, losses will be incurred. Bodie *et al.* (2021) have discussed this issue in some detail.

### 24.4.3 *Dynamic hedging and listed put options*

The first difference between dynamic hedging and listed put options for portfolio insurance is that the delta value of a put option changes automatically while it must be adjusted continuously in a dynamic-hedging framework. Thus, dynamic hedging requires continuous monitoring and more frequent trading than listed puts.

Second, insurance costs (the premium paid for the option) for a listed-put strategy are known and paid up front. After the put is purchased, no more adjustments or monitoring are necessary. In contrast, insurance costs are unknown at the beginning of the period and are realized as the dynamic-hedging strategy is implemented. The cost of a dynamic-hedging strategy is the forgone profits that result from shorting futures. For example, suppose that a portfolio consists of $10,000 of stock and that $50,000 of futures contracts are shorted to replicate a put option (assume that this is one futures contract).

Table 24.5 Dynamic Hedging.

| | Portfolio Value | Futures Value | Profit on Portfolio | Loss on Futures | Profit on Insured Portfolio |
|---|---|---|---|---|---|
| **Period 1** | \$100,000 | \$50,000 | | | |
| **Period 2** | \$120,000 | \$60,000 | \$20,000 | −\$10,000 | +\$10,000 |

In the second period, the value of the portfolio increased to \$120,000, whereas the value of the futures contract appreciated to \$60,000. If no futures were held, profit on the portfolio would be \$20,000; however, the dynamic hedger lost \$10,000 on the futures. Thus the cost of the dynamic-hedging strategy is the gain on the insured portfolio minus the gain on the uninsured portfolio (\$10,000 − \$20,000 = −\$10,000). All these results are presented in Table 24.5.

Another difference is that listed-option strategy is confined to fixed-interval exercise prices. In contrast, a dynamic-hedging strategy can be implemented around any exercise price.

Changing volatility can affect the cost of a portfolio-insurance strategy. For options, the cost of put protection is higher if the volatility declines. This is because the purchaser of the put locks in the volatility at the time of purchase. Thus, if the volatility declines, the put value declines. In contrast, an increase in volatility lowers the cost of put protection because the price of the put increases.

With a dynamic-hedging strategy, costs are lowered if volatility declines because the delta value will be reduced and not as many futures will be sold.

A replicated-option approach can be used for any asset-portfolios of stocks, various types of bonds, agricultural commodities, currencies, or metals. Since options markets are limited, replicated options must be created to simulate the returns of these investments.

## 24.5 Empirical Studies of Portfolio Insurance[3]

Much of the early research on portfolio insurance focused on simulation models to see whether synthetic-option strategies could

[3]Part of this section is from the "Portfolio Insurance Strategies" by L. C. Ho, in *Encyclopedia of Finance* 3rd edn. (Forthcoming, 2022).

successfully limit losses on portfolios of risky assets. In the early to mid-1980s, most of the empirical research on portfolio insurance was conducted by financial institutions such as Drexel, Burnham, Lambert and Salomon Brothers. However, more articles on the subject have appeared recently in journals such as *The Financial Analyst's Journal* and *Journal of Portfolio Management.*

### 24.5.1 *Leland (1985)*

Leland (1985) developed a replication strategy in the presence of transaction costs and tested this approach by using a simulation. As Leland pointed out, because transaction costs increase without limit as the revision period becomes shorter, it may be very costly to assure a given level of accuracy in the synthetic option. In addition, "transaction costs associated with replicating strategies are path-dependent: they depend not only on the initial and final stock prices, but also on the entire sequence of stock prices in between." Another problem with trying to create portfolio insurance in the presence of transaction costs is that transaction costs are correlated with the market. Leland poses the question, "In the presence of transaction costs, is there an alternative to the Black–Scholes replicating strategy which will overcome these problems?"

Leland proposed a procedure that adjusts upward the volatility estimate to the replicating procedure. The modification is a positive function of transaction costs and the replication period. This increase in the volatility estimate is due to the fact that each time a transaction occurs, the associated trading costs cause the purchase cost to be higher and the selling proceeds to be lower than without these costs. With transaction costs, the cost of purchasing stock is higher than without these costs; similarly, the price of selling the stock is lower, inclusive of these costs. "This accentuation of up or down movements of the stock price can be modeled as if the volatility of the actual stock price was higher." The adjustment to volatility is

$$\sigma_A^2 = \sigma^2\left(1 + \frac{\sqrt{2/\pi}k}{\sigma\sqrt{t}}\right) \tag{24.8}$$

where $\sigma_A^2$ = the transaction-cost adjusted volatility; $\sigma$ = the annualized standard deviation of the natural logarithm of the price; $k$ = round-trip transaction costs as a proportion of the volume of transaction; and $t$ = the revision interval as a proportion of a year.

The modification to the volatility estimate has the following characteristics.

(1) Transaction costs remain bounded as the revision period becomes short.
(2) The strategy replicates the option return inclusive of transaction costs, with an error that is uncorrelated with the market and approaches zero as the revision period becomes short.
(3) Expected turnover and associated transaction costs of the modified replicating strategy can easily be calculated, given the revision interval. Since the error inclusive of transaction costs is uncorrelated with the market, these transaction costs put bounds on the option prices.

The delta value of this strategy takes into account transaction costs and will be higher than without transaction costs. As can be seen from Eq. (24.8), the volatility estimate increases as the revision period and transaction costs increase. Leland believes that the modified replication strategy is superior to following the Black–Scholes strategy and paying transaction costs that result from the strategy because the expected error is negative, "reflecting the fact that transaction costs are not 'covered' by the initial option price." He assumes that the Black–Scholes strategy will result in higher turnover than the modified strategy because the latter "is based on a higher volatility which tends to 'smooth' the required trading."

Leland uses a simulation to determine the effectiveness of this strategy. The risk-free rate in the simulation is 10%; the expected return for the stock is 16%, with a standard deviation of 20%. Leland uses rebalancing periods of one week, four weeks, and eight weeks to replicate options expiring in three months, six months, and twelve months. Here $H$ is the difference between the listed call and the synthetic option after the revision period, $\Delta t$.

$$\Delta H = \Delta C - [C_s S + r(C - C_s S)] \tag{24.9}$$

where $\Delta C$ is the change in the listed call option over the revision period, $C_s$ is the delta value and is the number of shares in the replicated portfolio, and $r$ is the interest rate over the revision period. If the replicated option perfectly matches the changes in the listed option, $\Delta H$ will equal zero. For each of the revision periods, the mean and standard deviation of the errors is calculated.

Using simulated data with no transaction costs, the Black–Scholes strategy replicates the option with mean errors equal to zero for a revision period of one week. The standard deviation increases as the time until expiration decreases. As expected, the mean error increases as the revision period increases, with the greatest error occurring for the eight-week rebalancing period.

Leland uses his modification to the volatility estimate to calculate the accuracy of option replication with transaction costs. He compares the errors from the modified strategy with a Black–Scholes replicating scheme in which delta values and borrowing amounts are derived from the Black–Scholes model and then transaction costs are added on. In every case, the preciseness of the modified strategy exceeds the accuracy of the Black–Scholes design when round-trip transaction costs of 1% are used.

### 24.5.2 *Asay and Edelsburg (1986)*

Asay and Edelsburg used Monte Carlo simulations to determine how closely a synthetic-option strategy can match the returns on options on Treasury-bill futures. They state that there are three objections to a synthetic-option plan. First, changing delta values mean that positions must be continuously adjusted for the returns to be similar. However, rebalancing may not be possible if prices change overnight. If the position changes, too few or too many shares will be held in the underlying asset and the returns will not be the same as in the option position. The second problem with a synthetic strategy is that transaction costs may be significant, particularly if the rebalancing period is short.

The third problem is that the position could be whipsawed. *Whipsawing* occurs when the underlying asset increases enough to trigger rebalancing. After more shares are added, the underlying asset decreases in value and the additional shares are sold at a lower price than what was paid for them. A common remedy for this problem is to use a larger adjustment gap or filter rule; however, the wrong number of shares could be held if the filter rule was increased, particularly if the stock moved in a linear manner. Whipsawed positions commonly occur when the asset fluctuates around a constant level. Asay and Edelsburg used a Monte Carlo simulation of an option on a Treasury-bill future to determine if these and other problems would cause a divergence between the theoretical and synthetic positions. Profits and losses on the synthetic option are compared with those that would be earned through the purchase and sale of the option at the theoretical price if it were held to maturity. The profit on the replicated option is equal to the value of the option at maturity minus the price paid for option. They use adjustment gaps of 5–50 basis points in the simulated one-year interest-rate futures to trigger rebalancing.

Fifty simulations on six-month options were run. The option prices generated by the synthetic approach were very close to the options purchased at their theoretical values. Larger adjustment gaps proved more accurate when the futures traded in a narrow range, but the larger gaps were "disastrous" when the futures moved in one direction. Thus, they were unable to recommend a best adjustment gap. Asay and Edelsburg found the transaction cost of the replicating strategy to be insignificant.

To determine the amount of mispricing due to using an incorrect volatility estimate, they used a "correct" volatility measure for the listed option and an "incorrect" measure for the synthetic option. They found that input of a wrong estimate into the option-pricing model seems "to have only a minimal effect through the resulting incorrect hedge ratio." The authors concluded that problems such as transaction costs, whipsawing, and frequent rebalancing do not negate the effectiveness of the synthetic option on Treasury-bill futures.[4]

### 24.5.3 *Eizman (1986)*

The purpose of Eizman's paper is to determine which rebalancing strategy is the most effective in a dynamic-hedging portfolio-insurance framework. He considered three rebalancing disciplines:

[4]Part of this section is from the "Portfolio Insurance Strategies" by L. C. Ho in *Encyclopedia of Finance* 3rd edn. (Forthcoming, 2022).

(1) to fully rebalance the required stock/cash mix at discrete time intervals, (2) to fully rebalance every time the market changes by a specified percentage, and (3) to rebalance only when the actual mix lags the required mix by more than a specified lag factor in either direction, "and then rebalance only to the extent of bringing the actual mix up to a lag factor away from the required mix...."

Log normal returns to generate one-year puts are obtained using a multiyear Monte Carlo simulation. Eizman assumes a standard deviation of 13%, an interest rate of 8%, futures transaction costs of 0.15%, and a dividend yield of 4%. Put premiums and delta values for the synthetic put were generated by the Black–Scholes model. Then average annual transaction costs and average annual replication errors are calculated. In all three strategies, there is a tradeoff between transaction costs and accuracy; the liberal adjustment strategies had lower transaction costs and higher replication errors.

For the discrete-time adjustment strategy, he rebalanced monthly, weekly, semiweekly, daily, and hourly. The transaction costs increased and replication errors decreased as the rebalance periods shortened. He used a utility function of Min $(X+Y)$, where $X$ is average annual transaction costs and $r$ is average annual replication error, to determine the most effective rebalance period. Using this criterion, the best method is the weekly method, with the semiweekly strategy coming in second.

For the second strategy, market moves from 5% to 0% were used to trigger rebalancing. Again, larger percentage rebalance periods lead to lower transaction costs and larger errors. The third discipline, in which the portfolio is rebalanced only if the actual futures/stock mix lags the required mix by more than a prescribed percentage, works the best, according to Eizman. Under this method, the adjustment is made so that the actual mix is brought up to the 3% boundary and not up to the required mix. The lag that provided the best cost/error tradeoff was 3%.

### 24.5.4 *Rendleman and McEnally (1987)*

This study addresses the issue of portfolio-insurance cost. It tries to answer the following questions.

(1) What is the probability that the portfolio will earn no more than its insured floor return?

(2) What are the expected returns and utilities of return of the insured portfolio versus those of a reasonable alternative strategy?
(3) What are the probabilities that the insured portfolio or the alternative will have the higher return?
(4) Over the long run, how will the accumulation of value from the insured portfolio stack up against the alternative?

They used a Monte Carlo simulation with a 16% expected return and a 10% interest rate. The Black–Scholes model is used to derive delta values for the put option. In addition, a logarithmic utility function is specified to measure the utility of a portfolio-insurance strategy. Rendleman and McEnally simulate one- and three-year put options using minimum returns of 5%, 0%, and −5%, stock volatility of 20% and 18%, and interest rates of 10% and 6%. Various simulations are run and the costs of the put positions are calculated along with expected utility for the insured portfolio and an uninsured portfolio.

Probability distributions are generated to determine the probability that the insured and uninsured portfolios have a return greater than the minimum floor. They concluded that the "insured portfolio is ... more likely than the optimal portfolio to achieve only the guaranteed minimum return." In addition, they found that portfolio insurance strategies "... suffer in comparison with an 'optimal' portfolio designed to maximize the rate of growth of portfolio value over time." Using the various inputs on the simulations, they determined that the insured portfolio can expect to have a lower return than a similar optimal portfolio. They concluded that portfolio-insurance strategies are optimal only when investors are highly risk averse.

### 24.5.5 *Garcia and Gould (1987)*

The main goal of this article is to compute the costs of a synthetic-call portfolio-insurance strategy. They do not deal with dynamic hedging because "... sufficient historical experience is not yet available to simulate meaningfully the results from long equities/short futures implementations." They use closing prices of the S&P 500 index from January 1, 1963 to December 31, 1983. They generate returns for 240 overlapping years by taking 20 January to January returns, then 20 February to February returns, and so on. This is the first published portfolio-insurance study to use real data as opposed to simulated data.

The returns for hedged and unhedged portfolios were calculated. Over the period of study, the arithmetic mean of the unhedged S&P 500 returns was 9.63% with a standard deviation of 16.22%; the mean return for a portfolio insurance strategy with a 0% floor and 0.5% transaction costs was 7.08 with a lower standard deviation of 9.33%. The mean return for the strategy with a −5% floor was 8.18% with a standard deviation of 11.80%.

Opportunity costs of the portfolio insurance were calculated. If the return on the unhedged portfolio was 10% and the return on the hedged portfolio was 0.10%, the opportunity cost is 5%. They conclude that with a zero floor insurance investors gain 10.27% in a down year. When the market is up, hedged portfolios forgo 7.21%.

They concluded that the cost of portfolio insurance is 170 basis points for zero-floor insurance and 83 basis points for a −5% strategy, and that a dynamically balanced portfolio will not outperform a buy-and-hold (BH) portfolio.

### 24.5.6 *Zhu and Kavee (1988)*

They evaluated and compared the performances of the two traditional portfolio strategies, the synthetic-put approach of Rubinstein and Leland (1981) and the constant-proportion approach of Black and Jones (1987). They employed a Monte Carlo simulation methodology, assuming log-normally distributed daily returns with an annual mean return of 15% and paired with different values for market volatility, in order to discover whether these strategies can really guarantee the floor return and how much investors have to pay for the protection.

Both strategies are able to reshape the return distribution so as to reduce downside risk and retain a certain part of the upside gains. However, they demonstrated that a certain degree of protection can be achieved at a considerable cost. There are two types of costs in implementing a portfolio insurance strategy. The first is the explicit cost, that is, the transactions costs. The other is the implicit cost, which is the average return forgone in exchange for protection against the downside risk. When the market becomes volatile, the protection error of the synthetic-put approach increases, and the transaction costs may be unbearable. On the contrary, while the constant proportion approach may have lower transactions costs, its implicit cost may still be substantial.

### 24.5.7 *Perold and Sharpe (1988)*

Using simulated stocks and bills prices, they examined and compared how the four dynamic asset allocation strategies, namely, the BH, constant mix (CM), CPPI, and option-based portfolio insurance (OBPI), perform in bull, bear, and flat markets and in volatile and not-so-volatile markets.

CPPI and OBPI strategies sell stocks as the market falls and buy stocks as the market rises. This dynamic allocation rule represents the purchase of portfolio insurance and has a convex payoff function, which results in a better downside protection and a better upside potential than a BH strategy. However, they do worse in relatively trendless, volatile markets.

On the contrary, a CM strategy — holding a constant fraction of wealth in stocks — buys stocks as the market falls and sells them as it rises. This rebalancing rule effectively represents the sale of portfolio insurance and has a concave payoff function, which leads to less downside protection than, and not as much upside as, a BH strategy. However, it does best in relatively trendless and volatile markets.

They suggested that no one particular type of dynamic strategy is best in all situations. Financial analysts can help investors understand the implications of various strategies, but they cannot, and should not, choose a strategy without a substantial understanding of an investor's circumstances and desires.

### 24.5.8 *Rendleman and O'Brien (1990)*

They addressed the issue that the misestimation of volatility input can have a significant impact on the final payoffs of a portfolio using a synthetic put strategy. In an OBPI strategy, the daily portfolio adjustments depend on the delta of the put option on the risky asset. In the original Black and Scholes (1973) valuation equation, the delta at each day is a function of the following variables:

$$D_t = f(S_t, \bar{k}_0, \bar{r}_0, \sigma_0, T) \tag{24.10}$$

where $S_t$ is the price of the risky asset at date $t$, $k_0$ the strike price, $r_0$ the annual continuously compounded riskless rate of interest, $\sigma_0$ the *ex-ante* volatility parameter at the beginning of the insurance period, and $T$ the maturity of the option.

Assume that at the beginning of the insurance period, one manager predicts a high-volatile market and a 20% annualized volatility, while a second manager believes a low-volatile market and a 10% volatility. The delta for the first manager is higher which means he would buy more insurance and allocate less to a position in the risky asset. Assume that the *ex-post* volatility turns out to be 10%. The second manager will have made the proper allocation between risky and riskless assets. In contrast, the high-estimate manager will have invested too little in the risky asset. This misallocation would lose the opportunity of participating in the price appreciation in a strong market. Thus, a manager who underestimates volatility will typically end up buying less insurance than is necessary to ensure a given return, while a manager who overestimates volatility will buy more insurance than is necessary and forgo gains.

As for the issue of portfolio rebalancing, they examined adjustment frequencies by time intervals, namely, daily, weekly, monthly, and bimonthly. The effect (error) is measured as the difference of the horizon insurance values between noncontinuous and continuous trading. They suggested that weekly rebalancing produces an amount of error that appears to be tolerable by most portfolio managers.

More importantly, they addressed the biggest potential risk of implementing portfolio insurance strategies — the gap risk, by simulating the performance of the OBPI strategy over the period of the October 1987 market crash. They indicated that most insured portfolios would have fallen short of their promised values because the managers would not be able to adjust the portfolio in time before a big drop in the market. The gap risk will be discussed further in the financial stability section.

### 24.5.9 *Loria, Pham, and Sim (1991)*

They simulated the performance of a synthetic-put strategy using futures contracts based on the Australian All Ordinaries Index for the period from April 1984 to March 1989. Their study contains 20 consecutive nonoverlapping three-month insurance periods whose expiration dates coincide with the expiration dates of each SPI futures contract traded on the Sydney Futures Exchange. Four implementation scenarios are examined: a zero floor versus 5% floor which correspond to a portfolio return of 0% and −5% per annual, respectively; and a realized volatility versus Leland's (1985) modified volatility. They reported that there is no perfect guarantee of loss prevention under any scenario. Even in the scenario with a 5% floor and modified volatility, two out of 20 contracts do not meet the desired floor. In addition, the OBPI strategy is most effective under severe market conditions. In other periods characterized by insignificant market declines, the value of the insured portfolio is below that of the market portfolio. They suggested futures mispricing may be one potential culprit for this outcome.

### 24.5.10 *Do and Faff (2004)*

This empirical paper is an extension of Loria *et al.* (1991). They examined two approaches (the OBPI and CPPI) and conducted simulations across two implementation strategies (via Australia stock index and bills, and via SPI futures and stock index). Furthermore, they considered the use of implied volatility as an input into the model, and the use of a zero floor versus 5% floor. The dataset consists of 59 nonoverlapping three-month insurance periods, which span from October 1987 to December 2002. Thus, their key contributions relative to Loria *et al.* (1991) are the examination of a futures-based CPPI, a fine-tuned algorithm that allows for dividend payments, the consideration of *ex ante* volatility information, and more up-to-date data.

In terms of floor protection, the futures-based portfolio insurance implementation generally dominates its index-and-bill rival in both floor specifications, which reflects the low transaction costs in the futures market. Furthermore, the perfect floor protection is possible when implied volatility is used rather than using *ex post* volatilities. From the cost of insurance perspective, the futures-based strategy generally induces a lower cost of insurance than its index-and-bill rival in both floor specifications, which reflects the same reason as above. However, the cost of insurance is higher when implied volatility is used compared to *ex post* volatilities. The possible explanation is that the implied volatility is often higher than the same period *ex post* volatility, which results in over-hedging. As for the performances between the OBPI and CPPI approaches, there is no strong evidence to distinguish between them. Within the futures-based implementation, the synthetic put appears to dominate the CPPI with respect to floor protection, while the latter appears to slightly outperform in terms of upside participation.

They also examined whether portfolio insurance strategies work under stress conditions by assessing the strategies' effectiveness during tranquil and turbulent periods. Tranquil periods are defined as ones that return more than −4% and have a realized volatility of less than 15%; violation of either one or both of these conditions is regarded as indicating a turbulent period. All portfolio insurance strategies achieve 100% floor protection during tranquil periods, whereas the futures-based OBPI approach records the highest portfolio return. During turbulent times, futures-based portfolio insurance continues to perform quite well. The 1987 stock market crash makes the assessment difficult because of trading halts. However, assuming the futures continued to trade during that crisis, from the algorithm's perspective, the futures-based CPPI maintains a positive return, while the OBPI results in a negative return.

### 24.5.11 *Cesari and Cremonini (2003)*

This study is an extensive comparison of a wide variety of traditional portfolio insurance strategies. There are basically five dynamic asset allocation strategies: (1) BH, (2) CM, (3) constant proportion (without and with the lock-in of profits, CP and CPL), (4) the option-based approach (with three variations, BCDT, NL, and PS), and (5) technical strategy (with two kinds of stop-loss mechanism, MA and MA2); therefore, nine strategies in total are considered.

For each strategy, eight measures for risk, return, and risk-adjusted performance are calculated, namely, mean return, standard deviation, asymmetry, kurtosis, downside deviation, Sharpe ratio, Sortino ratio and return at risk. The strategies are then compared in different market situations (bear, no-trend, bull markets) and with different market volatility periods (low, medium, and high periods), taking into account transaction costs and discrete rebalancing of portfolios. The three market situations are defined accordingly if market average returns fall into the three ranges: (−30%, −5%), (−5%, +5%), (+5%, +30%), and the three ranges for the volatile periods are: (10%, 15%), (15%, 25%), (25%, 30%). Transaction costs are treated in two ways: a proportional cost to the value traded, and a correction to the Leland's (1985) option volatility. Two main rebalancing disciplines are used: a time discipline with weekly adjustment and a price discipline with adjustment only when prices are increased/decreased by 2.5% with respect to the previous rebalance time.

Monte Carlo simulations of MSCI World, North America, Europe, and Pacific stock market returns show that no strategy is dominant in all market situations. However, in bear and no-trend markets, CP and CPL strategies appear to be the best choice. In a bull market or in no-trend but with high volatility market, the CM strategy is preferable. If the market phase is unknown, CP, CPL, and BCDT strategies are recommended. In addition, these results are independent of the volatility level and the risk-adjusted performance measure adopted.

### 24.5.12 *Herold, Maurer, and Purschaker (2005)*

By constructing a fixed income portfolio, in which the risky asset is the JPMorgan government bond index and the riskless asset is cash (one-month yield), they compared the hedging performances between the traditional CPPI strategy and the risk-based (specifically, VaR-based) strategy with a one-year investment horizon that begins at each year from 1987 to 2003. CPPI avoids losses in the bear years of 1994 and 1999. The mean return is inferior to (about 40 bp below) that of the risk-based strategy. CPPI also produces a higher turnover.

### 24.5.13 *Hamidi, Jurczenko, and Maillet (2007)*

Although they proposed a conditional CPPI multiplier determined either by VaR or by ES, only a VaR-based measure is studied in this empirical work, and the ES measure is absent for future research.

The data set contains 29 years of daily returns of the Dow Jones Index, from January 2, 1987 to May 20, 2005, 4,641 observations in total. They used a rolling window of 3,033 returns to estimate the VaR, and there are 1,608 VaRs in the out-of-sample period.

They resorted to eight methods of VaR calculation: one nonparametric method using the historical simulation approach; three parametric methods based on distributional assumptions, namely, the normal VaR, the RiskMetrics VaR based on the normal distribution, and the GARCH VaR based on the Student-$t$ distribution; four semiparametric methods using quantile regression to estimate the conditional autoregressive VaR (CAViaR), namely, the symmetric Absolute Value CAViaR, the Asymmetric Slope CAViaR, the IGARCH(1,1) CAViaR, and the Adaptive CAViaR.

According to the 1,608 back-testing results, the Asymmetric Slope CAViaR is the best model to fit the data. After having calculated the VaR values, the conditional multipliers can be determined. The estimations spread between 1.5 and 6, which are compatible with multiple values used by practitioners in the market (between 3 and 8).

Using the time-varying CPPI multipliers estimated by different methods, and a "multi-start" analysis — the fixed one-year investment horizon beginning at every day of the out-of-sample period, they found that the final returns of these insured portfolios are not significantly different.

### 24.5.14 *Ho, Cadle, and Theobald (2008)*

This empirical study presents a complete structure of comparing traditional portfolio insurance strategies (OBPI, CPPI) with modern risk-based portfolio insurance strategies (VaR-, ES-based RBPI). By constructing a currency portfolio, in which the risky asset is the Australian dollar and the riskless asset is a U.S. dollar overnight deposit, they compared the dynamic hedging performances between the traditional and the modern strategies with a one-year investment horizon that begins at each year from 2001 to 2007.

When implementing the OBPI strategy, the delta is calculated based on the modified Black–Scholes formula, $D_t = f(S_t, \bar{k}_0, r_t, \sigma_t, T)$. That is, daily annualized historical volatilities are used as inputs in the put-replication process instead of the constant *ex ante* or the implied volatility in the original model to mitigate the volatility misestimation problem. Besides, the latter two parameters would make the portfolio daily returns more volatile. The interest rates are also updated daily for the same reason. When CPPI is implemented, the possible upper bounds of the multiplier are examined via the extreme value theory, which ranges from 4 to 6 corresponding to different confidence levels. When risk-based approaches are employed, both a historical distribution and a normal distribution with exponentially weighted volatility of risky asset returns are assumed. A daily rebalancing principle is adopted in their research without any modification to show the original results of hedging.

The performances are evaluated from six differing perspectives. In terms of the Sharpe ratio and the volatility of portfolio returns, the CPPI is the best performer, while the VaR based upon the normal distribution is the worst. From the perspective that the return distribution of the hedged portfolio is shifted to the right and in terms of both the average and the cumulative portfolio returns across years, the ES-based strategy using the historical distribution ranks first. Moreover, the ES-based strategy results in a lower turnover within the investment horizon, thereby saving transaction costs.

## 24.6 Summary

This chapter has discussed basic concepts and methods of portfolio insurance for stocks. Strategies and implementation of portfolio insurance have also been explored in detail. Other issues related to portfolio insurance and dynamic hedging have also been studied.

Portfolio insurance was described not as an insurance technique but rather as an asset-allocation or hedging technique. The general methods of portfolio insurance — (1) stop-loss orders, (2) market-traded index options, (3) synthetic options, and (4) futures trading were discussed.

## References

Anders, G. "Investors Risk for Portfolio Insurance," *The Wall Street Journal* (October 14, 1986, p. 6).

Asay, M. and C. Edelsburg. "Can a Dynamic Strategy Replicate the Returns of an Option?" *The Journal of Futures Markets*, 6 (Spring 1986, pp. 63–70).

Becker, K. "Rebalancing Strategies for Synthetic Call Options," Doctoral dissertation (University of Illinois, 1988).

Benninga, S. and M. Blume. "On the Optimality of Portfolio Insurance," *The Journal of Finance*, 40 (December 1985, pp. 1341–1352).

Bertrand, P. and J. L. Prigent. "Portfolio Insurance Strategies: OBPI versus CPPI," *Finance*, 26(1) (2005, pp. 5–32).

Black, F. and R. Jones. *Simplifying Portfolio Insurance* (New York: Goldman Sachs, 1986).

Black, F. and R. Jones. "Simplifying Portfolio Insurance," *Journal of Portfolio Management*, 14 (1987, pp. 48–51).

Black, F. and M. Scholes. "The Pricing of Options and Corporate Liabilities," *Journal of Political Economy*, 81 (1973, pp. 637–659).

Blume, M. E., A. C. Mackinlay and B. Terker. "Order Imbalances and Stock Price Movements on October 19 and 20, 1987," *The Journal of Finance*, 44 (September 1989, pp. 827–848).

Bodie, Z., A. Kane, and A. J. Marcus. *Investments*, 12th edn. (McGraw-Hill, 2021).

Brennan, M. J. and R. Solanki. "Optimal Portfolio Insurance," *Journal of Financial and Quantitative Analysis*, 16 (September 1981, pp. 279–300).

Cesari, R. and D. Cremonini. "Benchmarking, Portfolio Insurance and Technical Analysis: A Monte Carlo Comparison of Dynamic Strategies of Asset Allocation," *Journal of Economic Dynamics & Control*, 27 (2003, pp. 987–1011).

Do, B. H. and R. W. Faff. "Do Futures-Based Strategies Enhance Dynamic Portfolio Insurance?" *Journal of Futures Markets*, 6 (June 2004, pp. 591–608).

Dreher, W. "Does Portfolio Insurance Ever Make Sense?" *Journal of Portfolio Management*, 14 (Summer 1988, pp. 25–32).

Eizman, E. S. "Rebalance Disciplines for Portfolio Insurance," *Journal of Portfolio Management*, 13 (Fall 1986, pp. 59–62).

Finnerty, J. and H. Park. "Stock Index Futures: Does the Tail Wag the Dog?" *Financial Analysts Journal*, 43 (March/April 1987, pp. 57–61).

Finnerty, J. and H. Park. "How to Profit from Program Trading," *Journal of Portfolio Management*, 14 (Winter 1988, pp. 40–46).

Garcia, C. B. and F. J. Gould. "An Empirical Study of Portfolio Insurance," *Financial Analysts Journal*, 43 (July/August 1987, pp. 44–54).

Grossman, S. "An Analysis of the Implications for Stock and Futures Price Volatility of Program Trading and Dynamic Hedging Strategies," *Journal of Business*, 61 (July 1988, pp. 275–298).

Grossman, S. "Insurance Seen and Unseen: The Impact on Markets," *Journal of Portfolio Management*, 14 (Summer 1988, pp. 5–8).

Hamidi, B., E. Jurczenko and B. Maillet. "An extended expected CAViaR approach for CPPI." Working Paper (Variances, University of Paris-1, 2007).

Herold, U., R. Maurer and N. Purschaker. "Total Return Fixed-Income Portfolio Management: A Risk-Based Dynamic Strategy," *Journal of Portfolio Management*, 31 (Spring 2005, pp. 32–43).

Hill, J. *Portfolio Insurance: Volatility Risk and Futures Mispricing* (New York: Kidder, Peabody, and Co., 1987).

Ho, L. C., J. Cadle and M. Theobald. "Portfolio Insurance Strategies: Review of Theory and Empirical Studies," in *Handbook of Quantitative Finance and Risk Management*, C. F. Lee, A. C. Lee and J. Lee (eds.) (New York: Springer, 2010, pp. 319–332).

Ho, L. C. "Portfolio Insurance Strategies," in *Encyclopedia of Finance*, C. F. Lee and A. C. Lee (eds.), 3rd edn. (New York: Springer, 2022, Forthcoming).

Ho, L. C., J. Cadle and M. Theobald. "An Analysis of Risk-Based Asset Allocation and Portfolio Insurance Strategies," in *Encyclopedia of Finance*, C. F. Lee and A. C. Lee (eds.), 3rd edn. (New York: Springer, 2022, Forthcoming).

John, L. M., L. M. Donald, E. P. Jerald and W. M. Dennis. *Managing Investment Portfolios: A Dynamic* Process, 3rd edn. (CFA Institute, 2007).

Kritzman, M. "What's Wrong with Portfolio Insurance?" *The Journal of Portfolio Management*, 13 (Fall 1986, pp. 13–16).

Lee, C. F. and A. C. Lee. *Encyclopedia of Finance*, 3rd edn. (Springer, 2022, forthcoming).

Leland, H. E. "Who Should Buy Portfolio Insurance," *The Journal of Finance*, 35 (May 1980, pp. 581–594).

Leland, H. E. "Option Pricing and Replication with Transaction Costs," *The Journal of Finance*, 40 (December 1985, pp. 1283–1307).

Loria, S., T. M. Pham and A. B. Sim. "The Performance of a Stock Index Futures-Based Portfolio Insurance Scheme: Australian Evidence," *Review of Futures Markets*, 10(3)(1991, pp. 438–457).

Luskin, D. *Portfolio Insurance: A Guide to Dynamic Hedging* (Wiley, 1988).

Malkiel, B. "The Brady Commission Report: A Critique," *Journal of Portfolio Management*, 14 (Summer 1988, pp. 9–13).

Nolan E., M. A. Sola, and S. Crouch. *The Insured Portfolio: Your Gateway to Stress-Free Global Investments* (Wiley, 2010).

O'Brien, T. "The Mechanics of Portfolio Insurance," *Journal of Portfolio Management*, 14 (Spring 1988, pp. 40–47).

Perold, A. F. "Constant Proportion Portfolio Insurance," Working Paper (Harvard Business School, 1986).

Perold, A. R. and W. F. Sharpe. "Dynamic Strategies for Asset Allocation," *Financial Analysts Journal*, 44 (1) (1988, pp. 16–27).

"Presidential Task Force on Market Mechanisms," *Tire Brady Report* (Washington, DC: U.S. Government Printing Office, 1988).

Rendleman, R. J. and R. W. McEnally. "Assessing the Cost of Portfolio Insurance," *Financial Analysts Journal*, 43 (May/June 1987, pp. 27–37).

Rendleman, R. J. Jr. and T. J. O'Brien. "The Effects of Volatility Misestimation on Option-Replication Portfolio Insurance," *Financial Analysts Journal*, 46(3) (1990, pp. 61–70).

Rubinstein, M. "Alternative Paths to Portfolio Insurance," *Financial Analysts Journal*, 41 (July/August 1985, pp. 42–52).

Rubinstein, M. and H. Leland. "Replicating Options with Positions in Stock and Cash," *Financial Analysts Journal*, 37 (July/August 1981, pp. 63–72).

Singleton, C. and R. Grieves. "Synthetic Puts and Portfolio Insurance Strategies," *Journal of Portfolio Management*, 10 (Spring 1984, pp. 63–69).

Tilley, J. A. and G. O. Latainer. "A Synthetic Option Framework for Asset Allocation," *Financial Analysts Journal*, 41 (May/June 1985, pp. 32–41).

Zhu, Y. and R. C. Kavee. "Performance of Portfolio Insurance Strategies," *Journal of Portfolio Management*, 14(3) (1988, pp. 48–54).

## Questions and Problems

1. What is portfolio insurance? Identify and explain the various strategies that can be used to insure a portfolio.
2. What is the difference between hedging and portfolio insurance?
3. A manager is running a $10-million portfolio. She has decided to allocate $5 million to risky assets and $5 million to risk-free assets. She has set the floor of the portfolio at $7 million.

   (a) What is the cushion for this portfolio?
   (b) What is the exposure for this portfolio?
   (c) What is the multiple for this portfolio?

4. Given the information in question 3, if the market for risky assets increases by 30%:

   (a) What is the value of the total portfolio?

(b) What is the new multiple?
(c) What should the portfolio manager do to restore the portfolio to its target multiple?

5. Given the information in question 3, if the market for risky assets decreases by 10%:

   (a) What is the value of the total portfolio?
   (b) What is the new multiple?
   (c) What should the portfolio manager do to restore the portfolio to its target level?

6. What does the term *path dependence* mean? Why is it important for portfolio-insurance strategies to be path independent?
7. Define a synthetic option. Explain how the option position is adjusted in a rising or falling market.
8. What is a delta value? Why is it important?
9. A portfolio manager has $10 million invested in a well-diversified portfolio of common stock with a portfolio beta of 0.9 measured relative to the S&P 500. How many S&P 500 futures contracts are needed to insure the portfolio if the futures are currently selling for $105?
10. How could the strategy of hedging with futures contracts not provide a perfect hedge?
11. Compare and contrast portfolio insurance with options to portfolio insurance with futures.
12. Identify and discuss the linkage between trading futures contracts for portfolio insurance and market volatility. Does the tail wag the dog?
13. What is the difference between margin on equities and margin on futures?

# PART VIII
# Other Topics

# Chapter 25

# Mergers and Divestitures: Theory and Evidence

## Contents



## 25.1 Introduction

In Chapter 25 we begin the discussion of mergers and divestitures with a brief historical overview of the merger movements that have occurred in the U.S. In Section 25.2, we classify the various types of business combinations and in Section 25.3, we discuss the methods of business combinations. In Section 25.4 we discuss the tax, accounting, and legal considerations involved in mergers. Section 25.5 examines the theoretical rationale for mergers as well as the empirical evidence about them. Section 25.6 presents a cost-benefit analysis of business combinations from the perspective of the firm. Section 25.7 looks at the related topics of divestitures and spin-offs, and finally Section 25.8 provides a summary. Appendix 25A shows exchange ratio, Appendix 25B shows empirical studies of the beneficiaries of business combinations, and Appendix 25C discusses the effects of divestitures on firm valuation.

## 25.2 Classification of Business Combinations

One of the central problems of financial planning and management is expansion. Firms undergo internal expansion in the normal course of operations in order to meet increasing product demand, replace old or obsolete equipment, or establish new product lines or service areas. Internal expansion is characterized by the acquisition of assets, as discussed in Chapters 6 and 9 on capital budgeting. Firms also experience *external expansion*, which is characterized by the acquisition of business operations. *Business combination* refers to external expansions in which substantially all of the operations of two firms are combined under a single ownership. Business combinations are the topic of this chapter.

There are several ways to classify business combinations, and the terminology is often imprecise. We will classify these combinations by either corporate structure or by structure of economic and financial relationship.

### 25.2.1 *Classification by corporate structure*

Assume there are only two firms, A and B. One possible business combination results in only firm B surviving. This type of combination is known as a *merger*, and B is called the *acquiring firm* and A is the *acquired firm*. Another possible business combination results in the formation of a new firm, C, which has the assets of both A and B; this is a *consolidation*. A third form is an *acquisition*, in which firm A buys firm B and both firms remain in existence, with A as the *parent* firm and B the *subsidiary*. Note that one, both, or neither of the firms survives in its original form after a business combination.

The terms merger, consolidation, and acquisition are often used interchangeably, even though technically they have different meanings. Table 25.1 illustrates these three types of business combinations.

### 25.2.2 *Classification by structure of economic and financial relationship*

Another useful way of classifying business combinations is by the economic relationship of the firms before the combination. If the two firms perform a similar function in the production or sale of goods and services, the combination is said to be *horizontal*.

Prior to a horizontal combination, the firms are competitors, or at least have the potential to be. Another type of combination involves two firms in a supplier-customer relationship; such a combination is said to be *vertical*. A third type of combination involves firms that have little, if any, product market similarities; this is known as a *conglomerate* combination. However, the term conglomerate is generally reserved for firms that have engaged in several conglomerate combinations. Horizontal, vertical, and conglomerate combinations can also be undertaken for financial reasons. A financial merger tries to improve the combined firms' financial strength with respect to improving access to financial markets, taking advantage of tax subsidies, improving the firms' financial structure, and reducing the variability of the firms' cash flows.

Caughan (2011) has classified historical merger waves into six waves. Caughan classified the first wave as horizontal mergers (1897–1904), the second wave as vertical mergers (1916–1929), and the third wave as conglomerate mergers (1960s). In addition, he classified the fourth wave as big deals decade and LBOs and hostile takeovers. He classified the fifth wave as strategic mergers, and finally, he classified the sixth wave as the emergence of hedge funds and private equity.

Most recently, Poniachek (2019) has identified the main influences of merger waves as:

- Favorable economic conditions
- Technological innovation
- Conducive financial environment
- Favorable regulatory changes

Table 25.1 Largest Mergers, Acquisitions, and LBO's (1998–2015).

| Rank | Date Announced | Acquirer Name | Target Name | Value of Transaction ($mm) |
|---|---|---|---|---|
| 1 | 11/14/1999 | Vodafone AirTouch PLC | Mannesmann AG | 202,785.13 |
| 2 | 01/10/2000 | America Online Inc | Time Warner | 164,746.86 |
| 3 | 06/26/2015 | Altice Sa | Altice Sa | 145,709.25 |
| 4 | 09/02/2013 | Verizon Communications Inc. | Verizon Wireless Inc. | 130,298.32 |
| 5 | 08/29/2007 | Anheuser-Busch Inbev | Philip Morris Intl Inc. | 107,649.95 |
| 6 | 09/16/2015 | SA/NV | SABMiller PLC | 101,475.79 |
| 7 | 04/25/2007 | RFS Holdings BV | ABN-AMRO Holding NV | 98,189.19 |
| 8 | 11/04/1999 | Pfizer Inc | Warner-Lambert Co. | 89,167.72 |
| 9 | 12/01/1998 | Exxon Corp | Mobil Corp. | 78,945.79 |
| 10 | 01/17/2000 | Glaxo Wellcome PLC | SmithKline Beecham PLC | 75,960.85 |
| 11 | 10/28/2004 | Royal Dutch Petroleum Co. | Shell Transport & Trading Co. | 74,558.58 |
| 12 | 03/05/2006 | AT&T Inc. | BellSouth Corp. | 72,671.00 |
| 13 | 04/06/1998 | Travelers Group Inc. | Citicorp | 72,558.18 |
| 14 | 07/08/2001 | Comcast Corp. | AT&T Broadband & Internet Svcs | 72,041.15 |
| 15 | 04/08/2015 | Royal Dutch Shell PLC | BG Group PLC | 69,445.02 |
| 16 | 11/17/2014 | Actavis PLC | Allergan Inc. | 68,445.40 |
| 17 | 01/26/2009 | Pfizer Inc. | Wyeth | 67,285.70 |
| 18 | 10/12/2015 | Dell Inc. | EMC Corp. | 65,999.78 |
| 19 | 09/29/2014 | UBS AG | UBS AG | 65,891.51 |
| 20 | 05/11/1998 | SBC Communications Inc. | Ameritech Corp. | 62,592.54 |
| 21 | 12/11/2015 | The Dow Chemical Co. | DuPont | 62,141.06 |
| 22 | 04/13/1998 | NationsBank Corp, Charlotte, NC | BankAmerica Corp. | 61,633.40 |
| 23 | 02/25/2006 | Gaz de France SA | Suez SA | 60,856.45 |
| 24 | 01/15/1999 | Vodafone Group PLC | AirTouch Communications Inc. | 60,286.87 |

(*Continued*)

Table 25.1 (*Continued*)

| Rank | Date Announced | Acquirer Name | Target Name | Value of Transaction ($mm) |
|---|---|---|---|---|
| 25 | 01/26/2004 | Sanofi-Synthelabo SA | Aventis SA | 60,243.38 |
| 26 | 01/26/2000 | Shareholders | Nortel Networks Corp. | 59,973.57 |
| 27 | 07/15/2002 | Pfizer Inc | Pharmacia Corp. | 59,515.02 |
| 28 | 09/30/2010 | Preferred Shareholders | American International Group | 58,977.17 |
| 29 | 01/14/2004 | JPMorgan Chase & Co. | Bank One Corp, Chicago, IL | 58,663.15 |
| 30 | 06/14/1999 | Qwest Commun Intl Inc. | US WEST Inc. | 56,307.03 |

- Favorable infrastructure changes
- Globalization
- Industry organization
- Economies of scale and scope.

## 25.3 Methods of Business Combination

### 25.3.1 *Negotiation and determination of an exchange ratio*

Actual business combinations may take many forms, and several methods may be used. One method used in many combinations is direct negotiation between the management and boards of directors of the two firms. After negotiations have been worked out, the plans are presented to the shareholder groups of both firms for approval. Items to be negotiated include the identification of what is to be exchanged, the prices, and the method of payment. Assume firms A and B negotiate so that B acquires all the assets (except cash) of A and pays for these assets with cash. Now A has cash as its only asset, and it may pay off its creditors and distribute any remaining cash as a liquidating dividend to its shareholders. However, if B pays for the assets of A with B stock, then A may sell B's stock for cash or distribute it to A's shareholders. The effects of these negotiations on B's balance sheet are an increase in the asset accounts to reflect the acquired assets and a decrease in the cash or increase in the capital accounts to reflect the method of payment.

Assume now that B acquires A's common stock (and not the assets directly). B may acquire the shares for cash or in exchange for some of its own shares or by some other plan. In the extreme case in which A's shareholders surrender all their shares for shares of B, firm A ceases to exist and firm B assumes all the assets and liabilities of A. State laws specify that once a certain percentage of A's shareholders agree to an exchange of shares, all shareholders must comply. Holdout shareholders of A may go to court to earn a fair price for their shares in the event they are not satisfied with the negotiated price.

In a less extreme case, B may acquire fewer than all of A's shares and maintain an interest in A. In this case, A's shares are listed as an investment on B's balance sheet.

The main point in the above two paragraphs is the distinction between the acquisition of assets and acquisition of stock. The method of payment is more important for accounting and tax treatments.

### 25.3.2 *Exchange ratio*

One of the more common results of negotiation is the agreement to exchange shares of common stock. In these cases, the determination of the price paid for the acquired firm is actually the determination of an exchange ratio. Larson and Gonedes (1969) presented a model for exchange ratio determination. Their analysis of exchange ratios involves making assumptions about the pre- and post-combination earnings streams and $P/E$ (price-earnings) ratios. For example, assume the information of net income, shares, earnings per share (EPS), price per share (PPS) and $P/E$ ratio about firms A and B as shown in Table 25.2. Let $ER$ be the exchange ratio, which is defined as the number of traded shares of firm B divided by the number of traded shares of firm A. The earnings per share after the combination is given by

$$\text{EPS}^* = \frac{5{,}000{,}000}{[2{,}000{,}000 + (1{,}000{,}000)\text{ER}]} = \frac{5}{2 + \text{ER}}$$

Table 25.2 Net Income, EPS, PPS, and PE Ratio for Firms A and B.

| Firm | Net Income | Shares | EPS | PPS | P/E Ratio |
|---|---|---|---|---|---|
| A | $1,000,000 | 1,000,000 | $1 | $10 | 10 |
| B | 4,000,000 | 2,000,000 | 2 | 40 | 20 |

and the post-combination price is

$$P^* = \frac{5}{2 + \text{ER}} P/E^*$$

where $P/E^*$ is the post-combination P/E ratio.

For the shareholders of firm B to be as well off after the negotiation as before, then $P^* \geq P_B$; that is,

$$\frac{5}{2 + \text{ER}} P/E^* \geq 40$$

This will occur when

$$\text{ER} \geq -2 + \frac{P/E^*}{8}$$

Assume that P/E* is 18, then the exchange ratio is 01.25 or 1/4. In other words, each share of A's stock is exchanged for 1/4th of B's stock.

And for the shareholders of firm A to be as well off, then $P^* \geq P_A/\text{ER}$, or

$$\frac{\frac{5}{2 + \text{ER}} P}{E^*} \geq \frac{10}{\text{ER}}$$

which will occur when

$$\text{ER} \geq \frac{4}{P/E^* - 2}$$

Hence, the acceptance of the negotiated exchange ratio depends on expectations about the post-combination $P/E$ ratio. Graphically, these requirements imply that the range of negotiation lies in the area labeled $I$ in Figure 25.1. The agreed-on exchange ratio will depend on the relative bargaining positions of the two firms.[1]

[1]An empirical test of the exchange ratio model has been conducted by Conn and Nielson (1977) on a sample of 131 combinations over the period from 1960

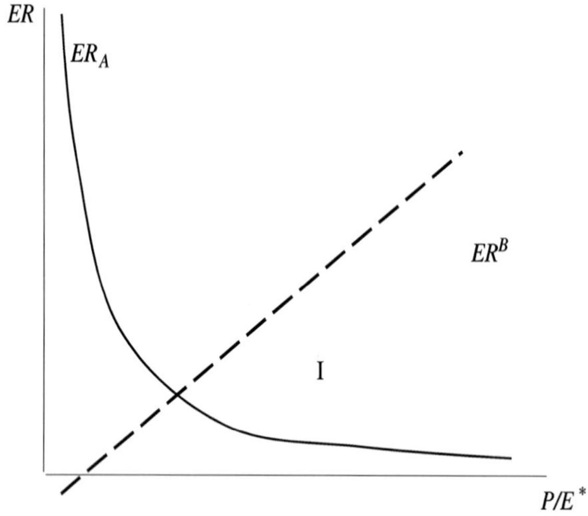


Figure 25.1 The Relationship ER and $P/E$.

Now we will define general equations for the example discussed in the previous section.

Assume Firm A and Firm B are the acquired firm and the acquiring firm, respectively. Let the exchange ratio (ER) be defined as the number of traded shares of Firm B to be exchanged for the one traded share of Firm A. LG defined the post-combination price ($p^*$) as:

$$p^* = \left[\frac{\mathrm{NI}_A + \mathrm{NI}_B}{\mathrm{N}_B + (\mathrm{ER})(\mathrm{N}_A)}\right](\mathrm{PE}^*) \tag{25.1}$$

where $\mathrm{NI}_A$ and $\mathrm{NI}_B$ represent net income for Firm A and Firm B, respectively, and $\mathrm{N}_A$ and $\mathrm{N}_B$ are the number of shares outstanding for Firm A and Firm B, respectively. $\mathrm{PE}^*$ is the post-combination price/earnings ratio. By comparing $p^*$ with price per share before the combination of Firm A ($\mathrm{P}_A$) and Firm B ($\mathrm{P}_B$), we find the following exchange ratio will affect the shareholders of both Firm A and Firm B as follows:

---

through 1969. They found that the exchange ratio model was supported by the tests, but that there were cases when the shareholders of the acquired firm benefited at the expense of the shareholders of the acquitting firm.

(i) The shareholder of Firm A are as well off after the combination as before if:

$$\mathrm{ER} \geq \frac{\mathrm{N}_B\mathrm{P}_B}{(\mathrm{NI}_A + \mathrm{NI}_B)(\mathrm{PE}^*) - \mathrm{N}_A\mathrm{P}_A} \tag{25.2}$$

(ii) The shareholder of Firm B are as well off after the combination as before if:

$$\mathrm{ER} \leq \frac{(\mathrm{PE}^*)(\mathrm{NI}_A + \mathrm{NI}_B)}{(\mathrm{N}_A)(P_B)} - \frac{\mathrm{N}_B}{\mathrm{N}_A} \tag{25.3}$$

**Example 25.1.** Exchange Ratio Determination
Q: Related financial information prior to a business combination presented as follows:

| Firm | Net Income | Shares | EPS | Price | *P/E* |
|---|---|---|---|---|---|
| A | $1,000,000 | 1,000,000 | $1.00 | $10 | 10 |
| B | 4,000,000 | 2,000,000 | 2.00 | 40 | 20 |

If the $P/E$ ratio after the business combination is 18, what is the exchange ratio that will make the shareholders of Firm B as well off after the combination as before?

For any $P/E$ greater than or equal to 10, the shareholders of Firm B will always be better off. Therefore, the only $P/E$s of interest are those less than 20.

A: Substituting the above information in Eq. (25.3), we obtain:

$$\begin{aligned}\mathrm{ER} &= \frac{(18)(5{,}000{,}000)}{40{,}000{,}000} - \frac{2{,}000{,}000}{1{,}000{,}000}\\ &= 2.25 - 2 = 0.25, \text{ or } 1/4\end{aligned}$$

If the exchange ratio is 1/4 , then the shareholders of Firm B will be as well off after the combination as they were before. This result is consistent with the result presented before. In Appendix 25A, we have discussed exchange ratio in terms of different methods and examples.

### 25.3.3 *The tender offer*

Another method used in business combinations is the *tender offer*, in which the acquiring firm makes its offer directly to the shareholders of the firm it wishes to acquire. Tender offers are usually made through the financial press. The acquiring firm offers to pay a fixed amount per share to each shareholder who then "tenders" his or her shares. The amount per share is usually set far enough above the current market price to entice the shareholders of the target firm.

Tender offers are often made when negotiations break down or as a surprise move by the acquiring firm to catch the management of the target firm off guard. Tender offers may take the form of either a cash or stock bid for a block of shares of the target firm. In many large corporations, effective control can be gained with ownership of less than 50% of the shares. Hence, an acquiring firm can make a tender offer, gain control, and then proceed with negotiation for the remainder of the shares.

Tender offers have generated a new vernacular. Some of the frequently encountered terms are as follows:

- *White knights.* In 1982, 29 major firms were targets of hostile takeover bids, and only 12 of these firms were able to resist the unwelcome bids. Of these 12 firms, only 2 were "saved" by white knights, which are firms that offer friendly takeover terms.
- *Shark repellents.* These are antitakeover amendments firms use in their corporate charters to protect themselves from unfavorable takeovers. Two such strategies are (1) *supermajority rules*, which generally require 95% approval for tender offers, and (2) *fair-price amendments*, which require that the stock be acquired at essentially one price. Fair-price amendments help shareholders to protect against two-tier acquisitions in which the acquiring firm buys one block of stock at a high price and then the remaining shares at a substantially lower price.
- *Pac-man strategy.* In this strategy, the target firm tries to take over the hostile bidder.
- *Golden parachutes.* Companies often provide their top executives with substantial severance benefits, or golden parachutes, in the event of a hostile takeover. Arguably, these benefits may have some economic justification because top management faces a dilemma in light of a hostile threat. If management resists the takeover

attempt, even if it believes such resistance is in the shareholders' best interests, the top managers are likely to be dismissed if the attempt is successful. Hence, with the golden parachute there is some incentive to acquiesce to hostile but strong suitors.

State and federal laws place several legal requirements on tender offers. The bids for shares must remain open for at least 20 days. Moreover, shares that are tendered during this period may be withdrawn during the period. And if the original offer price is raised, shares tendered under the original offer are also entitled to the higher price. Also, after one firm makes a tender offer, other firms may also enter the battle for a target firm.

**The Effect of a Tender Offer on Stock Price.**

The market price of the shares of a target firm generally rises following the announcement of the tender offer. Table 25.3 shows some examples of these price effects.

There are several options a shareholder might take after a tender offer has been made: accept the bid and tender the shares; continue to hold the shares; or sell the shares on the market. If a shareholder decides to hold the shares and the offer is successful, he or she may end up a minority shareholder facing an inactive market and the possible delisting of the shares. Shareholders who are not happy with the offered price can resort to a court valuation under state laws, which is often accomplished by means of a class-action suit.

The effect of tender offers on the returns to shareholders has been studied empirically. It is important to distinguish the tender-offer tests from tests of completed mergers (these tests are discussed later in this chapter) because the tender offer can succeed or fail. Empirical studies have attempted to estimate the market's reaction to both successful and unsuccessful tender offers. These tests are important because they reflect the market's expectation about the value of the merger. If mergers or acquisitions are preceded by a tender offer, then the first public announcement of the tender offer is an appropriate date to use in the study of benefits to shareholders. An important consideration for firms attempting takeovers by tender offers is the probability of success. To consider only the returns to shareholders through successful offers ignores the unsuccessful attempts and the market's reaction to those attempts.

Table 25.3 A Selected Companies that Received Offers in 1981.

| | | | | At Acquisition Closing Date | | | |
|---|---|---|---|---|---|---|---|
| **Acquired Company** | **Line of Business** | **Acquired By** | **Pre-Bid Price** | **Price** | **% Premium over Pre-Bid Price** | **Price-to-Book Value** | ***P/E* Ratio** |
| American Microsystems | Semiconductors | Gould | 23 | 39 5/8 | 73 | 3 | 39.4 |
| Applicon | Graphics | Schlumberger* | 27 | 33 3/4 | 25 | 12.8 | 43.3 |
| Bache Group | Brokerage | Prudential Insurance Co. | 20 | 32 | 60 | 2 | 11.4 |
| Barton's Candy | Candy | American Safety Razor | 2 | 4 | 100 | 0.9 | d |
| Beckman Instruments | Health care, analytical instruments | SmithKline | 28 | 50 1/2 | 80 | 3.3 | 28.7 |
| Buffalo Forge | Machine tools | Ampco-Pittsburgh | 16 | 37 1/2 | 134 | 1.9 | 13 |
| Bunker Ramo | Electrical components, data systems | Allied Corp. | 39 | 55 | 41 | 2 | 13 |
| Caldor | Discount stores | Associated Dry Goods | 13 | 36 5/8 | 182 | 3 | 13.8 |
| Cavitron | Dental supplies | Cooper Laboratories | 31 | 36 1/2 | 18 | 4.6 | 21.5 |

| | | | | | | | |
|---|---|---|---|---|---|---|---|
| Coldwell, Banker | Real estate, mortgage, brokerage | Sears, Roebuck | 21 | 39 3/8 | 88 | 4 | 29.2 |
| Copeland | Refrigerator, air conditioning equip. | Hillman Co. | 27 | 38 1/2 | 43 | 2.2 | 11.3 |
| Danty Machine | Stamping presses | Ogden | 32 | 70 | 119 | 1.5 | 10.1 |
| Dean Witter | Brokerage | Sears, Roebuck | 27 | 50 | 85 | 2.1 | 14 |
| Diamond International | Packaging and forest products | Generale Occidentale, S.A. | 35 | 44 1/2 | 27 | 1.2 | 16.6 |
| Fischer Scientific | Laboratory equipment | Allied Corp. | 49 | 55 | 12 | 2.6 | 17.1 |
| Franklin Mint | Specialty minting, collectibles | Warner Communications | 19 | 27 1/2 | 45 | 2.2 | 14.3 |
| GDV | Homebuilding | City Investing | 14 | 20 | 43 | 1.3 | 11 |
| GK Technologies | Electronic components | Penn Central | 41 | 50 | 22 | 2.5 | 9.4 |
| General Steel Industry | Metal process | Walco National | 14 | 19 | 36 | 1.5 | 16.5 |
| Gino's | Restaurants | Marriott Corp. | 7 | 18 | 157 | 1.7 | 10.8 |

(*Continued*)

Table 25.3 (*Continued*)

| Acquired Company | Line of Business | Acquired By | At Acquisition Closing Date | | | | |
|---|---|---|---|---|---|---|---|
| | | | Pre-Bid Price | Price | % Premium over Pre-Bid Price | Price-to-Book Value | $P/E$ Ratio |
| Gray Drug Stores | Drug and discount department stores | Sherwin Williams | 10 | 21 | 110 | 1.1 | d |
| Hobart Corp. | Food preparation equipment | Dart & Kratt | 19 | 40 | 111 | 2.2 | 13.8 |
| Iowa Beef Processors | Beef processor | Occidental Petroleum | 55 | 73 | 33 | 2.5 | 14.1 |
| Kennecott Corp. | Copper | Standard Oil of Ohio | 24 | 62 | 158 | 1.3 | 22.2 |
| Kent Moore | Specialty tools, equipment | Sealed Power | 23 | 38 | 65 | 1.8 | 13.5 |
| Lightolier | Lighting fixtures | Bairnco | 17 | 28 | 65 | 1.4 | 15.5 |
| Ludlow | Packaging, furniture | Tyco Laboratories | 17 | 27 1/2 | 62 | 1.9 | 22.4 |
| Macdonald (E. F.) | Incentive programs | Carlson | 7 | 10 | 43 | 1.7 | 9.8 |
| Mallinckrodt | Chemicals | Avon Products | 38 | 50 | 32 | 2 | 13.1 |
| Mayer (Oscar) | Processed meats | General Foods | 16 | 29 | 81 | 1.6 | 21 |

| | | | | | | | |
|---|---|---|---|---|---|---|---|
| Memorex | Computer equipment | Burroughs | 11 | 14 | 27 | 0.7 | d |
| Metpath | Laboratory tests | Corning Glass | 15 | 23 | 53 | 2.4 | 11.5 |
| Nat'l Health Enterprises | Health care | National Medical Enterprises* | 13 | 22 1/2 | 73 | 2.3 | 12.8 |
| Morris Industries | Building | Kohlberg, Kravis | 30 | 43 | 44 | 1.7 | 17.6 |
| Richardson Co. | Batteries, chemicals | Witco Chemical | 17 | 27 1/2 | 62 | 1.2 | 35.3 |
| Russell Stover Candles | Candies | Ward Paper | 15 | 20 | 33 | 1.6 | 10 |
| St. Joe Minerals | Coal, lead, zinc | Fluor | 27 | 44 1/4 | 64 | 2.1 | 17 |
| Sante Fe International | Drilling, oil, and gas | Kuwait Petroleum | 23 | 51 | 122 | 4.3 | 27.6 |
| Schaefer (F. M.) | Brewing | Stroh Brewery | 4 | 7 3/8 | 85 | NA | 3 |
| Shearson Loeb Rhodes | Brokerage | American Express | 52 | 62 3/8 | 20 | 3.9 | 8.9 |
| Sperry & Hutchinson | Trading stamps | Baldwin United | 18 | 36 | 100 | 2.3 | 16.7 |
| Sterndent | Dental supplies | Cooper Laboratories | 13 | 22 1/2 | 73 | 2.3 | 30.8 |
| Sunbeam | Home appliances | Alleghany International | 21 | 41 | 95 | 1.6 | 13 |

(Continued)

Table 25.3 (*Continued*)

| Acquired Company | Line of Business | Acquired By | At Acquisition Closing Date: Pre-Bid Price | Price | % Premium over Pre-Bid Price | Price-to-Book Value | *P/E* Ratio |
|---|---|---|---|---|---|---|---|
| Teleprompter | CATV systems | Westinghouse | 33 | 38 | 15 | 33.33 | 7.2 |
| Twentieth Century-Fox | Film producer, distributor | TCF Holdings | 53 | 68 5/8 | 30 | 62.4 | 14 |
| United Guaranty | Mortgage guaranty insurance | American International Group | 29 | 36 | 24 | 1.8 | 11.7 |
| Wallace Murray | Building products | Household International | 30 | 50 | 67 | 1.7 | 10 |

*Notes*: D = deficit; NA = not available; * = Master Fisk stock; + = based on latest full-year earnings.
*Source*: Standard and Poor's, *The Outlook*(March 1982, pp. 876–79). Reprinted by permission.

One particular study by Dodd and Ruback (1977) used a sample of firms involved in 172 tender offers and classified these firms as follows:

| | Successful | Unsuccessful |
|---|---|---|
| Bidding firm | 124 | 48 |
| Target firm | 136 | 36 |

They assume that returns are generated by the market model

$$R_{jt} = \alpha_j + \beta_j R_{mt} + \epsilon_{jt} \tag{25.4}$$

where $R_{jt}$ is the rate of return on security $j$ over period $t$; $R_{mt}$ is the rate of return on a value-weighted market index; $\epsilon_{jt}$ is a disturbance term with $E(\epsilon_{jt}) = 0$; $\alpha_j$ is the intercept term; and $\beta_j$ is a measure of the systematic risk of security $j$.

To test for possible shifts in risk that a tender offer might induce, Dodd and Ruback used a dummy variable technique and data from months −73 through −14 and from months 14 through 73, where month 0 is the month of the first public announcement of the tender offer. (This test assumes the risk shift occurs at the announcement date.) Evidence was found of significant changes in $\beta_j$ in 34 out of 184 cases. The Fama, Fisher, Jensen, and Roll (1969) technique was used to calculate average monthly residuals for each month as well as the cumulative average residuals. The results indicate that the stockholders of target firms earn large positive abnormal rates of return in the month of the first public announcements of the tender offer. The average residual in the month of tender offer is 20.58% for successful offers and 19.96% for unsuccessful target firms. However, the average residuals for both successful and unsuccessful bidding firms are 0, indicating no abnormal returns, in addition to the effects of the tender-offer announcement. For both successful and unsuccessful bidding firms, there is evidence of significant positive abnormal returns in the 12 months before the tender-offer announcement and normal returns in the months after the announcement (insignificant and negative). For target firms involved in tender offers, there is evidence of positive returns in the 12 months before the tender offer and a normal return in the 5 years following the offer, which indicates that the price changes that occurred in the month of the tender offer are permanent. Dodd and Ruback's study indicates there are gains from takeovers that could be attributed to the expectations of future gains from the combination.

Baron (1983) provides a model of tender offers based on management preference for control. There are two basic arguments for resisting tender offers: (1) the offer may be inadequate relative to the true value, and (2) management may have a preference for control that may diverge from the best interest of the shareholders. Baron's model shows that as more information about the target firm becomes available, firms whose managers have a preference for control would be expected to incur a decrease in market value. Baron's results show that targets of unsuccessful tender offers that receive future offers maintain their gains (the true value exceeds the bid) while those that do not receive future offers lose their gains (the preference for control reduces market value).

### 25.3.4 *Holding companies*

In addition to the negotiation of terms and the tender-offer technique, parties to a business combination may form a *holding company*, which is a corporation that owns sufficient voting stock of another firm (or several firms) to have effective control. This method is used extensively in the financial services and banking industries. Typically, a new corporation is formed and the shareholders of the firms to be combined exchange their current shares for shares of the holding company. This type of transaction is advantageous because effective control can be gained with as little as 10 or 20% of the outstanding stock, which means that a smaller investment is required. Also, a holding company can take advantage of legal loopholes in state and federal laws and taxes.

### 25.3.5 *Leveraged buyout*

Another method of business combination is the *leveraged buyout* (LBO). In a leveraged buyout, the buyer borrows a major portion of the purchase price, using the purchased assets as collateral for the loan. The buyer may be an outside group of investors, another company, or the manager of the division that is being sold. Once the assets are purchased, the cash flow from their operation is used to pay the principal and interest of the loan. In some cases, an LBO can be used to take the firm out of public ownership into private ownership, which is known as *going private.*

The use of the LBO can present an agency problem between the firm's managers and its public shareholders, in that the managers usually have more and better information about the firm's value than do the shareholders.

Typically, the "leverage" arises from the arrangement that certain payments for the business are made to the seller (or to a lender) for the actual earnings of the acquired firm.

This type of acquisition-merger method usually requires that the target firm either be cash-rich, generate a heavy cash flow, or sell for less than its asset value. Additionally, forecasts of future cash flows for the target firm are necessary to estimate the riskiness of the deal over time.

For example, some years ago Rollins purchased Orkin Exterminating Company. From the seller's point of view, the transaction was a sale involving over $50 million in cash paid over a short period. However, from the purchaser's standpoint, the cash flow from the purchased business of Orkin more than paid back all the purchaser's bank loans in the first five years after acquisition.

### 25.3.6 *Joint ventures*

*Joint ventures* are partial business combinations. Two or more entities form a business venture as a corporation or partnership. This provides an opportunity to combine resources in optimal proportions rather than in the fixed portfolio portions dictated by a merger or a tender offer. Thus, the participants in a joint venture are partners rather than an acquirer and a target as in mergers or acquisitions.

Joint ventures are popular for many reasons, including facilitating technological transfer, developing market structure, and international diversification. Some countries require that investment be made as part of a joint venture and some companies use the joint venture as a means to avoid government regulations against foreigners.

The nature of joint ventures raises many of the same legal issues associated with mergers. In *U.S. versus Penn-Olin Co.* (1964), it was construed that Section 7 of the Clayton Act applies to joint ventures, the FTC applying provisions that are similar to those relating to whole-unit combination. Also, it has been noted that

> Joint ventures continue to constitute one of the most perplexing subjects in antitrust law. An inquiry into joint venture theory must encompass an analysis of both structural (merger) and conduct (collusion) elements of antitrust. Utilized in the past to effectuate domestic and international cartels, joint ventures may also promote economic efficiency.[2]

Caves (1982) discusses the impact of U.S. antitrust policy on the multinational firm:

> A series of cases after World War II attacked joint ventures that U.S. multinational enterprises (MNEs) had formed with their overseas competitors. Some of these deals simply implemented agreements to divide markets and exclude foreign competitors from the U.S., in which case domestic economic welfare was the main issue. However, other joint ventures had bolstered U.S. MNE's ability to extract rents from foreign markets. The courts specifically rejected the contention that laws allowing U.S. producers to collude in export sales justified joint or collusive behavior in establishing subsidiaries overseas. In short, U.S. antitrust has taken appreciable chances of losing rent from foreign markets in order to promote competition in the domestic economy.

Joint venture formation also raises significant issues in labor law. As succession applies to merger and divestiture, it also applies to joint venture. However, the issues are less settled, and considerable attention to resolution can be expected in the future.

Much has been written in economics and finance about the impact of joint ventures on market structure, competition, and technological transfer. Patterns of joint venture formations have been analyzed, as has the impact of organizational form on accounting-based measures of rate of return. Armour and Teece (1978) studied the effects of a multidivisional organization on return on equity in the oil industry. They found a slight positive relationship between return on equity and the adoption of multidivisional organizational form.

[2]FTC Bureau of Competition, *Merger Policy Series* (May 10, 1979).

To the extent that joint ventures facilitate multidivisional organizations, their results suggest a positive impact of joint venture. Berg and Friedman (1981) addressed domestic joint ventures and, in order to concentrate on the nature of the joint venture, partitioned their sample into two categories, "knowledge acquisition" and "other." Using return on equity as the dependent variable, they found that "knowledge acquisition" is associated with lower return on equity, while "other" elements are associated with higher return on equity.

Caves (1982) presents the arguments for and against a multinational organization forming a joint venture. Arguments for this arrangement include (1) economizing on managerial or other human contributions, (2) minimizing the risk of extremely risky investment, (3) diversifying supply sources, (4) overcoming large initial investments, (5) overcoming lack of certain skills or expertise, (6) conforming to government requirements, and (7) economizing on information requirements of expertise about foreign investments. Arguments against the formation of joint ventures include (1) the possession of an intangible asset puts the expertise, (2) joint control may be troublesome, (3) the "free-rider" problem (receiving a benefit without paying for it), (4) the overall corporate perspective may be too broad, (5) transfer-pricing problems may be encountered, and (6) host government regulations may be formidable.

Weighing the costs and benefits and the pros and cons of forming a joint venture is an active area of study. However, the fact remains that many firms have elected the joint venture form.

In recent years, the size and frequency of joint ventures between U.S. corporations and foreign companies has increased dramatically. In 1984, General Motors and Toyota formed a joint venture to produce the popular Japanese compact car in California. And in 1983, American Motors signed a joint venture with Peking Automobile Factory to produce the Jeep in China.

## 25.4 Tax, Accounting, and Legal Considerations of Business Combinations

### 25.4.1 *Tax and surplus fund motives*

In addition to economic and financial motivations for business combinations, both the acquiring and acquired firm must consider the tax consequences of a business combination. Notably, all exchanges are taxable to the seller unless specifically exempted by the Internal Revenue Code. Section 368 of the code provides for the determination of tax consequences in business combinations. Code provisions that give tax-free status to the seller restrict both the type of acquisition and the terms of payment. The guiding principle in the code is whether equity interest has been maintained.

To establish tax-free status, three conditions must prevail. First, the acquisition must be for business purposes and not solely for tax reasons, the latter of which may jeopardize the legality of the combination. Second, there must be some continuity of the acquired enterprise; that is, the acquired firm must continue to operate in some identifiable form. Third, shareholders of the acquired firm must receive a significant continuing interest in the purchasing corporation. This third condition has been interpreted by the Internal Revenue Service to mean that at least 50% of the consideration must be in voting stock.

Hence, in addition to the various other items to be negotiated, the decision to structure a business combination on a taxable or nontaxable basis requires the balancing of two tax factors: (1) the recognition and nonrecognition of gain or loss to the seller versus an increase or decrease in the tax basis to the acquiring firm, and (2) the seller's request to receive the purchase price in cash or stock versus the acquiring firm's ability to pay with cash or its own stock.

### 25.4.2 *Accounting treatment*

The appropriate accounting treatment of business combinations is determined by analyzing the provisions of the negotiated agreement and factual circumstances involved in the combination. The two primary accounting procedures that pertain to business combinations are the pooling of interests method and the purchase method. Pooling of interests is appropriate when neither shareholder group assumes a dominant position in the combination, while the purchase method is appropriate when one shareholder group emerges in a dominant position, APB Opinion 16 lists a precise set of criteria to be used to distinguish poolings and purchases. A combination that meets the pooling criteria must be accounted for as a pooling; if it does not meet those criteria, then it must be accounted for as a purchase.

One of the major requirements to use the pooling method is that the method of payment must involve common stock in exchange for substantially all of the voting common stock of the acquired firm. Both methods are summarized below.

*Pooling of interests.* The general concept motivating the pooling treatment is that the business combination was *not* a purchase-sale transaction but rather a combining of interests. Hence, the prior accounting valuations are maintained and merely added together for the combined firm. Moreover, from an accounting standpoint, the two firms are considered to have been joined from day one, and the accounting reports are restated as if they had been so joined.
*Purchase method.* The purchase method of accounting for business combinations corresponds to the basic accounting principles for the acquisition of assets. However, in the case of business combinations, the procedure is complicated because several assets and liabilities may be acquired and more than cash may be given.

Consolidated statements are the relevant accounting reports when one firm has acquired an interest in the common stock of another firm. The affiliation of parent and subsidiary is treated as a single economic unit, and the accounting statements reflect the summations of individual assets and liabilities as well as revenues and expenses.

As an example of the differences between accounting treatments, consider the precombination balance sheets of firms A and B:

| **Firm B** | | | |
|---|---|---|---|
| Working capital | 100 | Long-term debt | 50 |
| Net plant | 300 | Equity | 350 |
| Total assets | 400 | Total liabilities and equity | 400 |

| **Firm A** | | | |
|---|---|---|---|
| Working capital | 50 | Long-term debt | 20 |
| Net plant | 150 | Equity | 180 |
| Total assets | 200 | Total liabilities and equity | 200 |

Assume a merger is negotiated in which firm B exchanges shares of its stock for the net assets of firm A, and the exchange qualifies as a pooling of interests. Now just add the respective accounts to reflect the combination, so that the postcombination balance sheet is as follows:

| **Firm BA** | | | |
|---|---|---|---|
| Working capital | 150 | Long-term debt | 70 |
| Net plant | 450 | Equity | 530 |
| Total assets | 600 | Total liabilities and equity | 600 |

Now assume that the criteria for a pooling of interests is not met, as would be the case if firm B raises capital by issuing new long-term debt to buy the shares of firm A with cash. Assume firm B issues debt to raise $150 to buy the stock with a (new) market value of $200 and uses $50 of excess cash in working capital. The balance sheet of the combined firms will be as follows:

| **Firm B** | | | |
|---|---|---|---|
| Working capital $(100 - 50 + 50)$ | 100 | Long-term debt $(50 + 20 + 150)$ | 220 |
| Net plant $(300 + 150)$ | 450 | Equity | 350 |
| Goodwill | 20 | | |
| Total assets | 570 | Total liabilities and equity | 570 |

Note that nothing happens to the equity account of firm B. As for firm A, its equity is gone and its shareholders have pocketed $200. The $20 of goodwill on firm B's balance sheet is the result of the book value of A's assets being equal to their fair market value on the date of combination.

Most managers prefer to pool interests when they can because the period amortization charges required under the purchase method must be deducted from reported income. Although this accounting phenomenon has no cash consequences, the surface effect of reducing reported income is usually undesirable. Nevertheless, because there are no actual cash differences between the pooling and purchase methods, the choice between the two should have no effect on the market value of the merged firms. A study by Hong, Mandelker, and Kaplan (1978) tested this proposition and found no evidence that acquiring firm's market performance was better under pooling than under purchase accounting.

Another important issue in business combinations is the effect on financial ratios. Ratios play an important role in the planning and control of financial resources, and a business combination can cause a major change in their levels, trends, or relationship to industry averages. The basic issue is to determine the appropriate way to evaluate the surviving firm(s) using pre- and post-combination data.

### 25.4.3 *Legal considerations*

Anytime a firm contemplates increasing its size and market power through the acquisition of a company within its business domain, it faces the possibility of a confrontation with federal antitrust law. Three principal statues constitute the bulk of these legal constraints. The first of these is the Sherman Act of 1890, which declares that "every contract, combination ··· or conspiracy, in restraint of trade" is prohibited and that "every person who shall ··· attempt to monopolize ··· any part of ··· commerce" is acting illegally. The Federal Trade Commission Act of 1914 prohibits "unfair methods of competition," and by amendment, "unfair or deceptive acts or practices." The third and most important antitrust law is the Clayton Act of 1914. The most powerful portion of this statute is Section 7, which forbids the acquisition of assets of stock where "in any line of commerce 'or' in any section of the country" the effect "may be substantially to lessen competition, or to tend to create a monopoly." Most prosecution has occurred under Section 7 of the Clayton Act because of its extension to the prohibition of potential restraints of trade.

The antitrust intent of the Justice Department is often interpreted to be "antibusiness" because most antitrust actions occur in cases where one or all of the firms are large. Nevertheless, antitrust actions are not instigated because of the absolute size of the principals, but rather because of the relative size and number of companies in the industry after the combination. Thus, the real intent of antitrust law, as applied to mergers, is to restrain movements away from two essential tenets of competition: (1) many competitors, with (2) none being so large that its actions dominate the market.

Defining the probability of antitrust actions is difficult because many proposed combinations have such unique features that it is hard to classify why one was approved and another not. However, there are general guidelines with which firms can assess their chances of regulatory approval.

For horizontal mergers — that is, where two firms from the same industry attempt to combine — a considerable amount of scrutiny will most likely be applied by the regulatory agency. Some of the prerequisite conditions for approval include (1) a large number of competitors in the field, (2) relatively small market shares between the two principals, (3) no substantial barriers for entry into the industry, (4) the number of competitors in the industry is not declining, and (5) one of the firms involved in the merger is in financial distress.

An additional criteria for the evaluation of a "within"-industry combination is the Herfindal index (H index), which the Department of Justice included among the merger guidelines set forth in June 1982. The Herfindal index measures the degree of diversification using the Standard Industrial Classification (SIC) system.[3] The larger the H index, the greater the degree of concentration and the more likely the Justice Department will disallow the merger. Sales figures for each firm segment are used in the computation of the segment's share of total sales. The $H$ index is defined as[4]

$$H = \sum_{j=1}^{n} {S_j}^2$$

where $S_j$ is the portion of total sales of the SIC industry segment $j$. The previous benchmark of "undue concentration" in a particular industry or market was when four or fewer firms accounted for 40% or more of total sales. The idea behind the H Index is that one or more firms with relatively high market shares is of even greater concern than the share of the largest four firms. To see this idea

[3]The SIC system is a means of identification used by the government for identifying specific types of industry segments.

[4]Montgomery (1982) has modified the H index as

$$H' = 1 - \frac{H}{(\sum_{j=1}^{n} S_j^2)^2}$$

to measure the degree of diversification for an industry.

more clearly, consider the following example. For a particular market. Four firms each hold a 12.5% market share and the remaining 50% is held by 50 firms, each with a 1% market share. The H Index would be calculated as

$$H_1 = 4(12.5)^2 + 50(1)^2 = 675$$

Now, consider another market in which one firm holds a 47% market share and the remaining 53% is shared equally by 53 other firms. As with the first case, the four largest firms control 50% of the market; however, the H index is now:

$$H_2 = 1(47)^2 + 53(1)^2 = 2{,}262$$

Hence, the *H* index quantitatively considers inequality as well as the degree of concentration.[5]

Vertical combinations can be susceptible to antitrust actions whenever they lessen competition between companies in buyer–seller-related industries. Most importantly, antitrust law is concerned with the effect of excluding competitors from competitive access to supply of customer markets. Relatedly, vertical mergers that could potentially result in reciprocal dealing are also prohibited. *Reciprocal dealing* occurs among firms that are vertically aligned in buyer–supplier relationships. If we assume that firms A and C wish to combine into company AC, this new company AC could then insist that firm B purchase C's (now AC's) original product or else AC would no longer buy B's product. If AC represents a large portion of B's market, B will feel pressure to diminish any ties with other suppliers (such as D and E) and buy primarily from AC. Vertical business combinations that create such situations are prohibited by antitrust law.

As the world marketplace has become more integrated, the definition of *market* in recent years has been extended to include global competition. This broader redefinition of *market* has served to make more mergers possible in terms of their anticompetitive effects and may explain the nature of the business combination environment in the 1980s, which witnessed a massive increase in the frequency and number of approved mergers.

---

[5]The term *inequality* refers to the number of firms holding a large share of the market. In the first case, four firms control 50% of the market, whereas in the second case one from controls 47% of the market.

## 25.5 Theoretical Rationale and Evidence

Theories to justify the merger phenomenon have been advanced by both economic and financial researchers. The most recent efforts by academicians in these fields focus on integrating their respective theoretical rationales.

Among the myriad reasons proposed to explain merger activity, the more prominent are economies of scale, market power, diversification and debt capacity, tax considerations, undervalued assets, and agency problems. With this base of merger theories, we will now explain the underlying rationales and summarize some of the major empirical results testing their validity.

### 25.5.1 *Economies of scale*

Economists generally assume the main goal of a firm is to maximize its profits. In light of this assumption, mergers and acquisitions can be analyzed in terms of (1) operating gains and (2) the effect on earnings. In particular, one theoretical justification (Silberston, 1972) is based on economies of scale, which relate to the average cost of unit output as the output level increases. There is general evidence of U-shaped average cost curves so that, up to some level, average costs fall as output increases and then remain constant for a range of output levels and eventually increase as diseconomies occur. Sources of these economies of scale include economies in capital costs, specialization of labor and plant, and the linking of successive stages of production. Thus, such economies of scale can arise from horizontal or vertical acquisitions. With vertical acquisitions, certain efficiencies arise from the ability to stabilize sources of supply or demand, in addition to any specific cost savings.

For horizontal mergers, economies of scale involve "indivisibilities," such as people, overhead, and equipment, for which returns are increased if spread over a larger number of units of output. Additional economies can arise from combining the research, marketing, and finance functions with those of another firm. Moreover, acquisitions of firms just approaching the size where they need to add corporate staff would increase the utilization of the acquiring firm's staff by making it possible for the acquired firm to avoid adding more corporate personnel.

A converse but related proposition is that firms experiencing increasing diseconomies of scale will undertake a merger to externally induce growth back into their earnings. For instance, once a firm has matured and increased in size to a point where its scale economies have been exhausted, any further increase in size will result in diseconomies. However, mergers and acquisitions may provide the acquiring firm the ability to show growth in its assets and earnings. However, this is not growth in the social sense unless there is some sort of synergy or other economies of scale.

### 25.5.2 *Market power*

Another economic justification for mergers involves the issues of market power and market share. These issues are the crux of the arguments the Justice Department advances against mergers. The basic defense is that mergers do not result in an increase in the level of competition and are only organizational changes that should leave competing forces the same. However, many mergers are opposed or blocked by the Justice Department on the grounds that they "effectively limit" competition. The question is whether the business combination results in undue concentration in an industry, because such a concentration may result in monopoly returns to the firms even in the absence of any synergy or economies of scale.

The precise relationship between economies of scale and market share is not known. One argument is that increases in market share lead to economies of scale. This would be relevant for a firm that is moving down the average cost curve as quantity (market share) increases. Another argument is that economies of scale lead to increased market share because competitive forces reward the more-efficient firms.

Another point of conjecture to the market power theory is who benefits from the supposedly higher profits of powerful firms. By measuring profitability as the ratio of net income to the book value of equity and adjusting for risk differences, Sullivan (1977) found that firms with market power earn superior returns on the book value of equity. However, with respect to the rate of return on common stock, it appears that the monopoly profits are fully capitalized in share prices.

Another test of the relationship of profits and market structure uses market value to determine whether market structure implies an ability on the part of the firm to maintain excess profits in the future. Thomadakis (1976), using an argument similar to Myers (1977), considered assets in place and the value of growth opportunities. After empirically testing 158 firms, Thomadakis found that industry concentration levels play a key role in the determination of expected excess profits from currently held assets and profits expected from the firm's investment options.

Hence, the evidence indicates that market power does lead to higher profitability on assets, but also that the market is efficient at capitalizing these profits so that no excess returns to shareholders are available on a risk-adjusted basis.

Although the economic arguments for economies of scale or market power can be used to explain horizontal and vertical combinations, the argument for conglomerate mergers is less clear. The 1972 Staff Report of the U.S. Federal Trade Commission concluded that conglomerate mergers are generally dispersed across several industries and involve relatively small market shares. This report suggests that conglomerate combinations do not benefit their shareholders.

Another possible explanation for conglomerate mergers is that these mergers benefit the managers. According to this argument, managers are motivated to assume less-than-optimal projects (with respect to shareholder interest) in order to increase their firm's size. It is questionable how long the managers of a firm can follow such a policy and retain their positions. Although this theory is based on the idea that the manager's benefits and salary are proportional to the firm's size, it is doubtful whether this relationship is true. A widely held view is that management compensation is related to the firm's profitability rather than size.

### 25.5.3 *Diversification and debt capacity*

A common assumption of financial theorists is that management's goal is to maximize shareholder wealth or firm value. Hence, decisions should be evaluated on the basis of how they affect firm value and, more directly, on how they affect the cash flow stream accruing to the owners and the uncertainty of those cash flows.

One line of financial theories of business combinations that has been used to explain conglomerate mergers involves the diversification effect. The basic argument follows from portfolio theory:

the joining together of two less-than-perfectly correlated income streams will reduce the relative variability of the streams. However, it has been conversely argued that in a perfect capital market no economic advantage can be gained by a purely conglomerate merger. That is, a merger does not create diversification opportunities beyond what was available to an individual investor before the merger.

Financial theory offers two other possible sources of gains through conglomerate mergers. The first source of gain arises from finding undervalued firms and acquiring them at or above their current market value but below their intrinsic value. The second source of gain arises from an increase in debt capacity and hence, all else the same, lower costs of capital. These gains are based on the portfolio effect, or diminished relative variability, which results from combining less-than-perfectly correlated income streams. Thus, lenders will establish new borrowing limits, which can only exceed the sum of the original limits; hence, increased debt capacity. When two firms merge, there are two debt-related effects: (1) the impact of the merger on the value of the existing debt and (2) the impact of the merger on the capacity of the firm to issue future debt.

A related argument suggests that in perfect capital markets the opportunities for investor diversification make firm diversification redundant, so that a value additivity principle must hold:

$$V_{AB} = V_A + V_B$$

where $V$ represents the value of the income stream accruing to the firm ($A$ or $B$). Schall (1972) provides an arbitrage argument that holds in a multiperiod world with taxes, to show that business combinations cannot be justified on the basis of diversification effects alone.

Another approach to the diversification question is from the bondholders' point of view. In the absence of any synergistic effects, the diversification argument implies a wealth transfer from the shareholders to the bondholders. Using a paired sample and 39 conglomerates, Kim, McConnell, and Greenwood (1977) found that conglomerates use a greater amount of leverage. In addition, by estimating abnormal returns through the use of a two-index model for bond returns (a bond index and a stock index), it was also found that bondholders do not earn abnormal returns around the time of the business combination. Hence, it is argued that if any gains are available in a conglomerate merger, they do not go to the bondholders.

Other researchers have suggested that what conglomerates may have earned in terms of risk reduction through the portfolio effect, they may also have lost by utilizing the higher debt capacity. Using a matched-sample approach and 37 conglomerate mergers between 1969 and 1975, Gahlon and Stover (1979) confirmed this hypothesis.

The above arguments approach debt capacity in terms of the surviving entity. A different approach by Shrieves and Stevens (1979) using empirical evidence suggests that one motive for merging is the desire of one firm to avoid bankruptcy. Hence, the act of merging can be viewed as having two effects on value: (1) the avoidance of bankruptcy and the savings of bankruptcy costs as well as the reduction in bankruptcy risk, and (2) a gain in aggregate debt capacity. The Shrieves–Stevens study limits itself to the first of these effects, yet was restricted in making a complete analysis because of the lack of data on bankruptcy costs and merger savings from bankruptcy avoidance. Hence, this study focuses on the incidence of financially distressed firms involved in mergers. Shrieves and Stevens (1979) concluded that the fact that most firms acquired in a merger are financially sound does not rule out the bankruptcy avoidance motive for some mergers. To determine which firms are on the verge of bankruptcy, they apply Altman's (1968) multiple discriminate analysis of financial ratios to predict bankruptcy:

$$Z = 0.0f12x_1 + 0.014x_2 + 0.033x_3 + 0.006x_4 + 0.99x_5$$

where $x_1$ = working capital/total assets; $x_2$ = retained earnings/total assets; $x_3$ = earnings before interest and tax/total assets; $x_4$ = market value of equity/book value of debt; and $x_5$ = sales/total assets.

Altman's results provide a reliable means to classify firms as likely bankruptcy candidates in the year before their merger. Shrieves and Stevens applied Altman's model to 112 acquired firms and 112 nonacquired firms chosen on a paired-sample basis with the acquiring group. The mergers occurred during the period from 1948 to 1971. The Altman model for predicting bankruptcy was based on a smaller sample of firms with a limited range of asset size. To test for differences in the predictive model due to size, Shrieves and Stevens used a sub-sample of firms with the same asset size as Altman used to test the model's appropriateness. Their results show that for data for the year prior to merger, Altman's model predicts that 17 of 112 firms in the merging group were near bankruptcy, a rate much greater than the failure rate of large firms over the period (15.2% compared to 2.8%). The model predicted bankruptcy for 5 of 112 firms in the control group, and in three of these firms financial reorganization subsequently occurred. In one instance, the firm apparently survived, and in another, the firm actually acquired a firm to improve its financial condition. Hence, the Shrieves and Stevens study provides evidence consistent with a bankruptcy avoidance rationale for some mergers.

### 25.5.4 *Tax considerations*

Another economic rationale to support merger activity is based on tax differentials. For instance, by acquiring a growth firm with little or no dividend payout and then later selling it, the acquiring firm can realize capital gains and thus attain a lower tax rate. In another scenario, firm growth may have slowed to the point where earnings retention cannot be justified to the Internal Revenue Service. Hence, there arises an incentive for the sale of this low-growth firm to another, in order to capitalize its future earnings and therefore avoid having to pay out future earnings as dividends, which are subject to a higher tax rate. Such would be the incentive for closely held firms.

In another case, the unused tax shield of one firm may be a merger incentive to another more-profitable firm. However, a business purpose must be established for such an acquisition to be allowed by the IRS. If other methods of achieving equivalent tax benefits are, in a relative sense, less costly and involve fewer problems, then the argument of tax differentials as a motivation for mergers will not retain much validity.

### 25.5.5 *Undervalued assets*

There are various reasons why a company may be undervalued. One is an ineffective management group that is not operating the company to its potential. Another, which could be a source of motivation for merger, is that potential acquirers have inside information that would increase the asset's value. Relatedly, firms involved in natural-resource industries, such as oil or mining, must estimate the value of their in-ground reserves. The approximating nature of valuing these types of assets allows for a considerable degree of alternative estimation or speculation by other firms as to their real worth. Such a situation arose in the U.S. Steel-Marathon Oil merger. Although U.S. Steel paid a substantial premium over market value for Marathon Oil, Marathon shareholders threatened suit because independent appraisals had estimated the current value of Marathon assets at more than double the price paid by U.S. Steel.

### 25.5.6 *Agency problems*

Two corporate situations that have an effect on merger activity are (1) executive stock options and (2) golden parachutes. Both are related to the emerging field of agency theory, which involves the interrelationship between various corporate groups — in this case, shareholders and management.

If the management of a firm has considerable executive stock options, it is more likely to act in the best interest of the firm's shareholders because its own interests are compatible with the shareholders' interests. For example, if an outside party makes a bid for the firm's shares at \$20 a share when the current market price is \$15 a share, management is more likely to be supportive of the merger if the managers own executive stock options in the firm's shares. If they do not have any executive stock options, they have little to gain by supporting the merger and may view the merger as a threat to their job security.

Along this line of reasoning, a number of firms have adopted a policy of golden parachutes for their managers in case of job termination. Again, if management and shareholder interests are compatible, the managers are less likely to resist the merger — and possible loss of their job — if they receive severance payments under the golden parachute provisions.

## 25.6 Cost–Benefit Analysis of Business Combinations[6]

### 25.6.1 *Synergy*

Assuming that managers are economically rational, no firm would attempt to acquire another unless it could estimate that the benefits

[6]In this section, we theoretically analyze the cost-benefit analysis of business combinations. In Appendix 25B, we have discussed two alternative methods for investigating empirical evidence of business combinations.

from acquiring the other firm less the costs of doing so would equal some positive amount. Moreover, the financial manager of the acquiring firm, say firm A, is particularly interested in whether a resulting economic gain will ensue from any merger activity. An economic benefit occurs when the combined value of two firms is greater than the simple addition of their values; thus,

$$\text{Benefit} = -(PV_A + PV_B) > 0$$

So, if firm A acquires firm B and the combined firm's present value is greater than the sum of the individual firms' present values, then the financial manager of firm A would have an economic justification for A's action. This benefit represents the synergy effect of merger.

### 25.6.2 *Source of synergy*

As with any capital budgeting decision, a firm is most interested in taking on projects or purchasing new assets that will increase its value after acquisition costs. Applying such a net present value criterion to a proposed acquisition is relevant as well. Hence, to improve our analysis we can state the cost of acquisitions, assuming payment is made in the form of cash, as follows:

$$\text{Cost} = \text{Cash} - \text{PV}_B$$

Subtracting the cost of acquisition from any economic benefits, we arrive at a net present value for the potential combining of firms:

$$\text{NPV} = \text{Benefit} - \text{Cost} = \text{PV}_{\text{AB}} - (\text{PV}_A + \text{PV}_B) - (\text{Cash} - \text{PV}_B)$$

Thus, if NPV is positive, traditional capital budgeting criteria would support the proposed acquisition.

More explicitly, we define $\Delta CF_t$ as the difference between the cash flows at date $t$ of the combined firm and the sum of the cash flows of the two separate firms. From Chapters 6 and 9, we know that the cash flow in any period $t$ can be written as:

$$\Delta\text{CF}_t = \Delta\text{Rev}_t - \Delta\text{Costs}_t - \Delta\text{Taxes}_t - \Delta\text{Capital Requirements}_t$$

where $\Delta\text{Rev}_t$ is the incremental revenue of the acquisition; $\Delta\text{Costs}_t$ is the incremental costs of the acquisition; $\Delta\text{Taxes}_t$ is the incremental acquisition taxes; and $\Delta\text{Capital Requirements}_t$ is the incremental new investment required in working capital and fixed assets.

It follows from our classification of incremental cash flows that the possible sources of synergy fall into four basic categories: Revenue enhancement, cost reduction, lower taxes, and lower capital requirements. Improvements in at least one of these four categories create synergy. Each of these categories will be discussed in the following paragraphs.

a) Revenue enhancement
Revenue enhancement can come from marketing gains, strategic benefits, or market or monopoly power. Market power was previously discussed in detail in Section 25.5.2.
b) Cost reduction
Cost reduction can be due to economies of scale, economies of vertical integration, technology transfer, complementary resources, or elimination of inefficient management. Economies of scales has been discussed in detail in Section 25.5.1.
c) Lower taxes
Lower taxes can be due to the use of tax losses, the use of unused debt capacity, or the use of surplus funds. Debt capacity was previously discussed in detail in Section 25.5.3, tax consideration was discussed in Section 25.5.4.
d) Lower capital requirements
Lower capital requirements refer to duplicate facilities when two firms merge. For example, when two firms merge there would be no need for two headquarters, so they could move their operations into one building and sell the other.

The advantage of stating the merger criterion in this manner, Brealey *et al.* (2017) point out, is that it illuminates two significant points. First, when estimating the potential gains, the focus is on whether any economic benefits will arise from the merger. Second, the estimation of cost narrows the concern as to how any benefits would be divided between the two firms. To illustrate, suppose firm A is contemplating an acquisition of firm B. The present value of A is $1 million and of B is $200,000. Firm A's financial manager estimates that the acquisition of B would create economies of scale with a present value, after tax-cost savings, of $70,000. Thus, the economic benefit from the merger of A with B would be

$$\text{Benefit} = 1{,}270{,}000 - (1{,}000{,}000 + 200{,}000) = \$70{,}000$$

Further assume that firm B can be purchased for \$220,000 in cash. The cost of this acquisition is

$$\text{Cost} = 220{,}000 - 200{,}000 = \$20{,}000$$

The stockholders of firm B are \$20,000 ahead, which is their gain from firm A's cost. In fact, firm B has captured \$20,000 of the \$70,000 economic benefit firm A expected to reap. Because the calculation of NPV from A's viewpoint is essentially that portion of the benefit that goes to A's stockholders, the NPV is

$$\text{NPV} = 70{,}000 - 20{,}000 = \$50{,}000$$

or

(Net gain to A's stockholders) = (Overall benefit of acquisition) – (Portion of benefit captured by B's stockholders).

## 25.7 Divestiture and Spin-Offs

We have discussed how business combinations are important steps in a firm's external growth. Equally important is the disposition of assets through external transactions involving ownership rights. We now consider nonroutine dispositions such as the disposal of a division, product line, or subsidiary. Routine dispositions, such as the selling of worn-out equipment, can be analyzed using capital budgeting techniques because such dispositions generally involve the replacement of an old asset with a new asset. Nonroutine dispositions may be major decisions for a firm and may result in drastic changes in the firm's product market and the types and sources of inputs the firm demands. Appendix 25C discusses the effects of divestiture on firm valuation.

The distinction between divestitures and spin-offs can be made on the basis of ownership rights. In a *divestiture*, one firm sells a segment of its operations to another firm. No new corporate entity is created. The selling firm gives up the operational cash flows associated with the divested assets and in return receives a cash flow from the buying firm. Arguably, decisions to divest a segment of operations can be made in a capital budgeting framework. (See Robichek and VanHorne, 1967). On the other hand, a *spin-off* involves a parent firm distributing all shares of a wholly owned subsidiary to its shareholders, thus creating a new corporate entity (same owners, same percentages, different firm). In the case of a spin-off, the "new" stock may be that of an existing subsidiary or it may be newly created stock representing ownership in the disposed unit.

### 25.7.1 *Accounting for divestiture and spin-offs*

*APB Opinion 30* requires separate reporting for the operations of a business segment that has been or will be discontinued. The purpose is to provide income statement information about those operations that are ongoing and those that are, or will be, terminated by disposition. Savage and Siegel (1978) discuss the issues relevant to this topic, which are (1) what constitutes a segment and (2) how the gain or loss from a segment's operations should be measured. They note that the assets and results of operations for a segment must be clearly distinguishable physically and operationally from those of the continuing operations. The profits or losses from a segment should also include the appropriate consideration of relevant expenses. Costs and other expenses are only to be allocated to the segment to the extent that they will be reduced after the disposal.

### 25.7.2 *Tax consequences*

The Internal Revenue Code, Section 355, permits tax-free spin-offs by one corporation of stock or securities in another corporation to shareholders with respect to their stock, provided there was legal control before the distribution (defined as 80% of the voting shares and 80% of the shares of any other classes of stock) and that there were two active business after the distribution. In the case of a divestiture, the transaction is treated as an ordinary sale and capital gains or losses recognized accordingly. In the case of a spin-off, a new corporate entity is created without raising any new capital and possibly with no tax consequences to the disposing firm.

### 25.7.3 *Theory and evidence*

A parent firm may divest or spin-off a part of its operations because those operations do not earn their normal risk-adjusted required rate of return. This may be due to management ineffectiveness, a loss (or lack) of synergistic effects, or a decline (or lack) of growth opportunities. However, there are reasons why a parent firm might dispose of a portion of its operations even if they did earn their required rate of return. These reasons include the fact that firms may use divestiture as a source of cash during periods of high interest rates or to retire debt or repurchase shares. Another reason is to reduce the scope/diversity of operations.

Another situation in which a firm may dispose of some of its operations is when the government (usually the Federal Trade Commission through the Clayton Act) forces a firm to dispose of part of its operations because otherwise "competition could be substantially lessened." These involuntary disposals have different implications for shareholders. If shareholders believe managers act in the shareholders' best interest (that is, make decisions to maximize shareholder wealth), then the announcement of a voluntary divestiture or spin-off should be considered positive and have a positive effect on shareholder wealth.

Boudreaux (1975) investigated 138 voluntary divestitures and 31 involuntary divestitures from 1965 to 1969. He used the FFJR (Fama, Fisher, Jensen, and Roll) technique of residual analysis and five years of monthly data surrounding the announcement date to test for any abnormal returns with respect to these announcements. His hypothesis was that the divestiture announcement constitutes good news and positive residuals are anticipated. His data indicated positive abnormal returns were available from three months before the announcement to one month after the announcement. In the 31 cases of involuntary divestiture, the wealth implications are reversed. Indeed, if the FTC complaint was appropriate, then divestiture would result in a loss of monopoly power and have a negative effect on shareholder wealth. In the case of involuntary divestment, the appropriate date to measure residuals could be (1) the date of the FTC complaint, (2) the date of the court decision, or (3) the date of divestment. Boudreaux's results indicate negative cumulative average residuals (CARs) in the months of the first two of these events.

Kummer (1978) also investigated the consequences of involuntary dispositions. He used residual analysis on monthly data for a two-factor model and, to allow for any changes in systematic risk, updated the betas in his model on a monthly basis. Kummer noted that a forced divestment may have a negative effect on shareholder wealth, even in the absence of any decline in monopoly or market power or loss of synergism, because there are real costs of divestment. Accordingly, his sample of 58 firms from 1952 to 1967 is divided into different groups based on the type of acquisition preceding the forced divestiture. Kummer's results show that horizontal acquisitions followed by a forced divestiture result in significant negative abnormal returns. In the cases of vertical and conglomerate organizations, no such abnormal returns were found surrounding forced divestiture of horizontal acquisitions. The absence of any abnormal returns in the vertical and conglomerate cases implies that either (1) the market did not value any abnormal benefits at the time of acquisition, so the disposition did not result in any loss, or (2) the market did not expect any regulatory action, so there were no systematic results.

Kudla and McInish (1981) investigated the changes in risk and return surrounding Georgia Pacific's forced spin-off of Louisiana Pacific in January 1973. They found that GP's beta increased significantly, from 0.94 to 1.75, surrounding the spin-off. Other similar firms (plywood producers) also had an increase in systematic risk, but none so drastically or significantly. Kudla and McInish also used the FFJR residual technique to measure any abnormal returns and found negative returns from the month of the FTC complaint until the month of spin-off, and positive returns following the spin-off. However, this study involves only one item in the sample.

### 25.7.4 *Analysis of the divestment decision*

Alberts and McTaggart (1979) analyzed voluntary dispositions in light of the shareholder wealth maximization criteria. Given a valuation model such as

$$V = \sum_{t=0}^{\infty} \frac{D_t}{(1+K)^t}$$

the important concerns of a disposition are (1) what are the incremental cash flows, (2) what will be done with any proceeds, and (3) how will the stochastic characteristics of the cash flows change after the decision? Alberts and McTaggart suggested that the analysis consider both the present and future profitability of the tentative disposition as well as the other opportunities available to the firm.

They also suggested that the appropriate measure of profitability is whether the return on equity committed to the division exceeds the cost of that equity. In the case of divestiture, the net proceeds from the disposition consist of the disposal value less the relevant current liabilities and allocated long-term debt. In the case of tax-free spin-offs, there are no cash proceeds to be employed elsewhere. Obviously, tax considerations are important in planning dispositions and require weighing the reinvested cash proceeds and related tax consequences against the tax-free exchange and inability to generate any real cash flows because of the requirements of the IRS for tax-free status.

Finally, it should be noted that spinning off "a jewel from the corporate crown" (Blumstein, 1983) is a possible way to increase the parent company's stock price. By publicizing a fashionable division of a diversified firm and spinning off a fraction of that subsidiary's shares, a parent firm may enhance its own stock price and not lose the tax, income statement, and balance sheet benefits the subsidiary may provide. This financial strategy may or may not have any long-term benefits, and there are costs to undertaking such a strategy. These costs involve the transaction costs as well as the indirect costs of dealing with a possibly new board of directors and the release of information about the business operations and profitability of a division of the firm.

In summary, divestitures and spin-offs constitute a major event for the firm, which may have consequences to the shareholders. The particular type of disposition must be considered in each instance.

## 25.8 Summary

Chapter 25 has provided an overview to the types, methods, and theories of business combinations, along with an empirical examination of some of the unsolved issues in this area.

With the understanding that a business combination represents an external expansion of a firm's business operations, three primary classifications of combinations were defined: (1) mergers, (2) consolidations, and (3) acquisitions. Thus, although merger is the more generally used term, as opposed to business combination, to designate such activities, it actually represents only one particular type.

Methods of combination included negotiation, tender offers, holding-company formation, and leveraged buyouts. Empirical studies of the effect of tender offers on the returns to the target and bidding firms indicate that shareholders from both firms tend to earn excess returns, at least up to the takeover date.

A number of tax implications were cited; in particular, the differentiation between taxable and nontaxable mergers and acquisitions. Two accounting practices prevail for the accounting of business combinations — the pooling of interest method and the purchase method, the former of which tends to be preferred by managers because of the less-adverse effects it has on reported net income. Legal considerations were discussed; however, the depth and complexity of this topic limits the effective amount of information this text can offer on the subject.

Financial and economic theories of business combinations were discussed as to their rationale, along with some of the existing empirical support. Although a number of reasons were presented from each academic field, perhaps the most intriguing theory from the economies field is the economics of scale argument, while the diversification and debt capacity rationale is the most prominent theory from the finance area.

Next, a simplified explanation and estimation of the economic benefits and costs of business combinations was developed. Following this we presented an examination of some of the empirical results concerning the beneficiaries of business combinations.

## References

Alberts, W. W. and J. M. McTaggart. "The Divestiture Decision: An Introduction," *Mergers and Acquisitions* (Fall 1979, pp. 18–30).

Altman, E. "Financial Ratios, Discriminant Analysis, and the Prediction of Corporate Bankruptcy," *The Journal of Finance*, 23 (September 1968, 589–609).

Armour, H. O. and D. J. Teece. "Organizational Structure and Economic Performance: A Test of the Multidivisional Hypothesis," *The Bell Journal of Economics* (1978, pp. 106–122).

Ball, R. and P. Brown. "An Empirical Evaluation of Accounting Income Numbers," *Journal of Accounting Research* (Autumn 1968, pp. 159–178).

Baron, D. P. "Tender Offers and Management Resistance," *The Journal of Finance*, 38(2) (1983, pp. 331–343).

Berg, S. V. and P. Friedman. "Impacts of Domestic Joint Ventures on Industrial Rates of Return: A Pooled Cross-section Analysis, 1964–1975," *The Review of Economics and Statistics* (1981, pp. 293–298).
Blumstein, M. "Selling a Jewel from the Corporate Crown," *New York Times* (October 9, 1983).
Boudreaux, K. J. "Divestiture and Share Prices," *Journal of Financial and Quantitative Analysis* (November 1975, pp. 619–626).
Brealey, R. A., Myers, S. C., and F. Allen. *Principles of Corporate Finance*, 12th edn. (New York: McGraw-Hill, 2017).
Carleton, W. T., D. K. Guilkey, R. S. Harris and J. F. Stewart. "An Empirical Analysis of the Role of the Medium of Exchange in Mergers," *The Journal of Finance*, 38 (June 1983, pp. 813–826).
Caughan, P. A. *Mergers, Acquisitions, and Corporate Restructuring*, 5th ed. (Wiley, 2011).
Caves, R. E. *Multinational Enterprise and Economic Analysis.* (Cambridge: Cambridge University Press, 1982).
Conn, R. and J. Nielsen. "An Empirical Test of the Larson–Gonedes Exchange Ratio Determination Model," *The Journal of Finance*, 32 (June 1977, pp. 749–760).
Dennis, D. K. and J. McConnell. "Corporate Mergers and Security Returns," *Journal of Financial Economics* (June 1986, pp. 132–187).
Dodd, P. and R. Ruback. "Tender Offers and Stockholder Returns: An Empirical Analysis," *Journal of Financial Economics* (December 1977, pp. 351–373).
Duhaime, I. M. and J. H. Grant. "Factors Influencing Divestment Decision-making: Evidence from a Field Study," *Strategic Management Journal*, 5(4), (1984, pp. 301–318).
Elgers, P. and J. Clark. "Merger Types and Shareholder Returns: Additional Evidence," *Financial Management* (Summer 1980, pp. 66–72).
Fama, E. and J. MacBeth. "Risk, Return, and Equilibrium," *Journal of Political Economy* (May 1973, pp. 607–636).
Fama, E., L. Fisher, M. Jensen, and R. Roll. "The Adjustment of Stock Prices to New Information," *International Economic Review* (February 1969, pp. 1–21).
Gahlon, J. and R. Stover. "Diversification, Financial Leverage, and Conglomerate Systematic Risk," *Journal of Financial and Quantitative Analysis* (December 1979, pp. 999–1013).
Galai, D. and R. W. Masulis. "The Option Pricing Model and the Risk Factor of Stock," *Journal of Financial Economics*, 3(1–2) (1976, pp. 53–81).
Gilmour, S. C. "The Divestment Decision Process," Unpublished doctoral thesis (Harvard University, 1973).

Halpern, P. "Empirical Estimates of the Amount and Distribution of Gains to Companies in Mergers," *Journal of Business* (October 1973, pp. 554–75).

Halpern, P. "Corporate Acquisitions: A Theory of Special Cases? A Review of Event Studies Applied to Acquisitions," *The Journal of Finance*, 38 (May 1983, pp. 297–317).

Haugen, R. and J. Udell. "Rates-of-Return to Stockholders of Acquired Companies," *Journal of Financial and Quantitative Analysis* (January 1972, pp. 1387–1398).

Hogarty, T. "The Profitability of Corporate Mergers," *Journal of Business* (March 1970, pp. 317–327).

Hong, H. G. Mandelker and R. S. Kaplan. "Pooling versus Purchase: The Effects of Accounting for Mergers on Stock Prices," *Accounting Review*, 53 (January 1978, pp. 31–47).

Jain, P. "The Effect of Voluntary Sell-off Announcements on Shareholder Wealth," *The Journal of Finance*, 40 (March 1985, pp. 209–224).

Jensen, M. and R. Ruback. "The Market for Corporate Control: The Scientific Evidence," *Journal of Financial Economics* (1983, pp. 5–50).

Kim, E. and J. McConnell. "Corporate Mergers and the Co-insurance of Corporate Debt," *The Journal of Finance*, 32 (May 1977, pp. 349–363).

Kim, E. H., J. J. McConnell, and P. R. Greenwood. "Capital Structure Rearrangements and Me-first Rules in an Efficient Capital Market," *The Journal of Finance*, 32(3) (1977, pp. 789–810).

Kudla, R. J. and T. H. McInish. "The Microeconomic Consequences of an Involuntary Corporate Spin-off," *Sloan Management Review* (Summer 1981, pp. 41–46).

Kummer, D. R. "Valuation Consequences of Forced Divestiture Announcements," *Journal of Economics and Business* (Winter 1978, pp. 130–136).

Langetieg, T. "An Application of a Three-factor Performance Index to Measure Stockholder Gains from Merger," *Journal of Financial Economics* (December 1978, pp. 365–384).

Larson, H. and N. Gonedes. "Business Combinations: An Exchange-ratio Determination Model," *Accounting Review*, 43 (October 1969, pp. 720–728).

Lee. C. F. and J. Lee. *Financial Analysis, Planning & Forecasting: Theory Application* (Singapore: World Scientific, 2017).

Linke, C. M. and J. K. Zumwalt, "A theoretical analysis of the AT&T divestiture," *Mimeo* (Unpublished paper, The University of Illinois at Urbana-Champaign, 1983).

Mandelker, G. "Risk and Return: The Case of Merging Firms," *Journal of Financial Economics*, 1(4) (1974, pp. 303–335).
McConnell, J. J. and T. J. Nantell. "Common Stock Returns and Corporate Combinations: The Case of Joint Ventures," *The Journal of Finance*, 40 (June 1985, pp. 519–536).
Miles J. A. and J. Rosenfeld. "The Effect of Spin-off Announcements on Shareholder Wealth," *The Journal of Finance*, 38 (December 1983, pp. 1597–1606).
Montgomery, C. A. "The Measurement of Firm Diversification: Some New Empirical Evidence," *Academy of Management Journal*, 25 (June 1982, pp. 299–307).
Meyers, S. "Determinants of Corporate Borrowing," *Quarterly Journal of Economics* (November 1977, pp. 147–175).
Myers, S. C. "Determinants of Corporate Borrowing," *Journal of Financial Economics*, 5(2) (1977, pp. 147–175).
Pastena, V. and W. Ruland. "The Merger/Bankruptcy Alternative," *The Accounting Review* (April 1986, pp. 288–301).
Poniachek, H. A. *Mergers and Acquisitions* (Singapore, World Scientific, 2019).
Raphael, A. and Joshua Livnat. "Divestification, Capital Structure, and Systematic Risk: An Empirical Investigation," *Journal of Accounting, Auditing & Finance*, 3 (Winter 1988, pp 19–43).
Robichek, A. and J. C. VanHorne. "Abandonment Value and Capital Budgeting," *The Journal of Finance*, 22 (December 1967, pp. 577–589).
Rosenfeld, J. D. "Additional Evidence on the Relation between Divestiture Announcements and Shareholder Wealth," *The Journal of Finance*, 39 (December 1984, pp. 1437–1448).
Ross, S. A., R. W. Westerfield, J. Jaffe and B.D. Jordan. *Corporate Finance*, 11th edn. (McGraw-Hill Education, 2016).
Savage, L. and J. Siegel. "Disposal of a Segment of a Business," *CPA Journal* (September 1978, pp. 32–27).
Schall, L. "Asset Valuation, Firm Investment, and Firm Diversification," *Journal of Business* (January 1972, pp. 11–28).
Shick, R. "The Analysis of Mergers and Acquisitions," *The Journal of Finance*, 27 (May 1972, pp. 45–52).
Shick, R. and F. Jen. "Merger Benefits to Shareholders of Acquiring Firms," *Financial Management* (Winter 1972, pp. 45–53).
Shrieves, R. and D. Stevens. "Bankruptcy Avoidance as a Motive for Merger," *Journal of Financial and Quantitative Analysis* (September 1979, pp. 501–516).
Silberston, A. "Economies of Scale in Theory and Practice," *Economic Journal*, 82 (March 1972, pp. 369–391).

Sullivan, T. "A Note on Market Power and Returns to Stockholders," *Review of Economics and Statistics* (February 1977, pp. 108–113).
Thomadakis, S. "A Model of Market Power, Valuation, and the Firm's Return," *Bell Journal of Economics* (Spring 1976, pp. 150–162).
U.S. Federal Trade Commission. *Staff Report: Economic Report on Conglomerate Merger Performance* (November 1972).

## Appendix 25A — Exchange Ratio

One of the more common results of negotiation is the agreement to exchange shares of common stock. In these cases, the determination of the price paid for the acquired firm is actually the determination of an exchange ratio. Larson and Gonedes (1969) presented a model for exchange ratio determination. Their analysis of exchange ratios involves making assumptions about the pre- and post-combination earnings streams and $P/E$ (price-earnings) ratios. For example, assume the information of net income, shares, earnings per share (EPS), price per share (PPS) and $P/E$ ratio about firms A and B as shown in Table 25.1A. Let ER be the exchange ratio, which is defined as the number of traded shares of firm B divided by the number of traded shares of firm A. The earnings per share after the combination is given by

$$\text{EPS}^* = \frac{5{,}000{,}000}{[2{,}000{,}000 + (1{,}000{,}000)\text{ER}]} = \frac{5}{2 + \text{ER}}$$

and the post-combination price is

$$P^* = \frac{5}{2 + \text{ER}} P/E^*$$

where $P/E^*$ is the post-combination $P/E$ ratio.

Table 25.1A Net Income, EPS, PPS, and PE Ratio for Firms A and B.

| Firm | Net Income | Shares | EPS | PPS | P/E Ratio |
|---|---|---|---|---|---|
| A | $1,000,000 | 1,000,000 | $1 | $10 | 10 |
| B | 4,000,000 | 2,000,000 | 2 | 40 | 20 |

For the shareholders of firm B to be as well off after the negotiation as before, then $P^*$ $P_B$; that is,

$$\frac{5}{2+\text{ER}}P/E^* \geq 40$$

This will occur when

$$\text{ER} \geq -2 + \frac{P/E^*}{8}$$

Assume that $P/E^*$ is 18, then the exchange ratio is 01.25 or 1/4. In other words, each share of A's stock is exchanged for 1/4th of B's stock.

And for the shareholders of firm A to be as well off, then $P^* \geq P_A/\text{ER}$, or

$$\frac{\frac{5}{2+\text{ER}}P}{E^*} \geq \frac{10}{\text{ER}}$$

which will occur when

$$ER \geq \frac{4}{P/E^* - 2}$$

Hence, the acceptance of the negotiated exchange ratio depends on expectations about the post-combination $P/E$ ratio. Graphically, these requirements imply that the range of negotiation lies in the area labeled $I$ in Figure 25.1. The agreed-on exchange ratio will depend on the relative bargaining positions of the two firms.[7]

Now we will define general equations for the example discussed in the previous section.

Assume Firm A and Firm B are the acquired firm and the acquiring firm, respectively. Let the exchange ratio (ER) be defined as the

[7]An empirical test of the exchange ratio model has been conducted by Conn and Nielson (1977) on a sample of 131 combinations over the period from 1960 through 1969. They found that the exchange ratio model was supported by the tests, but that there were cases when the shareholders of the acquired firm benefited at the expense of the shareholders of the acquitting firm.

number of traded shares of Firm B to be exchanged for the one traded share of Firm A. LG defined the post-combination price ($p^*$) as:

$$p^* = \left[\frac{\text{NI}_A + \text{NI}_B}{N_R + (\text{ER})(N_A)}\right](\text{PE}^*) \tag{25.1A}$$

where $\text{NI}_A$ and $\text{NI}_B$ represent net income for Firm A and Firm B, respectively, and $N_A$ and $N_B$ are the number of shares outstanding for Firm A and Firm B, respectively. $\text{PE}^*$ is the post-combination price/earnings ratio. By comparing $p^*$ with price per share before the combination of Firm A ($P_A$) and Firm B ($P_B$), we find the following exchange ratio will affect the shareholders of both Firm A and Firm B as follows:

(i) The shareholder of Firm A are as well off after the combination as before if:

$$\text{ER} \geq \frac{N_B P_B}{(\text{NI}_A + \text{NI}_B)(\text{PE}^*) - N_A P_A} \tag{25.2A}$$

(ii) The shareholder of Firm B are as well off after the combination as before if:

$$\text{ER} \leq \frac{(\text{PE}^*)(\text{NI}_A + \text{NI}_B)}{(N_A)(P_B)} - \frac{N_B}{N_A} \tag{25.3A}$$

**Example 25A.1.** Exchange Ratio Determination

Q: Related financial information prior to a business combination presented as follows:

| **Firm** | **Net Income** | **Shares** | **EPS** | **Price** | ***P/E*** |
|---|---|---|---|---|---|
| A | $1,000,000 | 1,000,000 | $1.00 | $10 | 10 |
| B | 4,000,000 | 2,000,000 | 2.00 | 40 | 20 |

If the $P/E$ ratio after the business combination is 18, what is the exchange ratio that will make the shareholders of Firm B as well off after the combination as before?
For any $P/E$ greater than or equal to 10, the shareholders of Firm B will always be better off. Therefore, the only $P/E$s of interest are those less than 20.

A: Substituting the above information in Eq. (25.3A), we obtain:

$$\mathrm{ER} = \frac{(18)(5{,}000{,}000)}{40{,}000{,}000} - \frac{2{,}000{,}000}{1{,}000{,}000} = 2.25 - 2 = 0.25 \text{ or } \frac{1}{4}$$

If the exchange ratio is 1/4, then the shareholders of Firm B will be as well off after the combination as they were before. This result is consistent with the result presented before.

## Appendix 25B — Empirical Studies of the Beneficiaries of Business Combinations

The emphasis in the arguments above has been on a diversification theory of business combinations. Another line of financial research has investigated the issues of when and to whom benefits of business combinations accrue. These empirical studies have examined the nature of the benefits as well as the efficiency of the market with respect to mergers. An early study of Hogarty (1970) compared the investment performance of 43 firms engaged in mergers between 1953 and 1964 with that of their respective industries using annual data. Hogarty found that only 10 of 43 firms were successful in outperforming their industries. Additionally, he compared the growth of earnings per share of these merging firms with that of their respective industries and found that 16 of 37 firms did better than their industries. Such results yielded the tentative conclusion that we cannot determine whether mergers are profitable. Moreover, Hogarty's study laid the groundwork for the many studies that followed. Similar results have also been found by other researchers in this area.

Another area of interest to the determination of whether mergers are beneficial is the effect of business combinations on the shareholders of the acquired companies. Using 44 conglomerate mergers and 44 nonconglomerate mergers between 1961 and 1967, Haugen and Udell (1972) compared monthly closing prices of the acquired firms with a stock index. The evidence indicates that the shareholders of firms acquired by conglomerates fared better than those acquired by nonconglomerates, but that both fared better than the market as a whole. As to the timing of this gain, most of it accrued at the time of the merger because of the substantial premium paid by acquirers.

Halpern (1973) attempted to improve the methodology used to study the benefits of mergers and investigated the size and distribution of gains to the merging firms. He noted that there are two problems in estimating the benefits of a merger: (1) choosing the correct dates from which to measure benefits and (2) eliminating the general market influence so that only the merger benefits can be estimated.

The sample in this study consisted of 78 successful mergers of NYSE-listed firms between January 1950 and July 1965. Additionally, it was required that the method of payment used in the combination be the exchange of common stock or the exchange of common stock for assets. According to Halpern, "if the stock market is efficient, the sum of the changes in the values of equity of the companies in the merger will be the market's estimate of the expected economic gain of the merger," thus ignoring any effect in the market values of any debt. The calculation of the gain to each shareholder group is the change in their stock's price between some base date and the actual date of the merger and should exclude the market and industry effects. To do this, a two-factor model was employed:

$$R_{it}^{k} = \alpha + \beta_1 R_{mt}^{k} + \beta_2 R_{It}^{k} + \epsilon_{it} \tag{25.1B}$$

where $R_i^k$, $R_m^k$, and $R_I^k$ are the $k$-period price relatives for the security ($i$), a market index ($m$), and an industry index ($I$). The market index excludes companies in the same industry as the company, and the industry index is based on the price relatives of other companies in the industry. Using the two-digit SIC industry classification resulted in 18 industry indexes based on 10 or more companies. There were 8 industries with an insufficient number of firms to form an index, and for these the single-index market model was used.

The model was estimated for all periods up to 7 months before the merger announcement and then used to calculate residuals for each company from 23 months before the announcement to the announcement date. To eliminate other individual firm factors, cross-section average residuals for each month were calculated as was the cumulative average residual. The residual technique was used to identify the average date that information about an impending merger was reflected in security prices; this date was the 17th month before the announcement. The end of the eighth month before the announcement was used as the base date to measure merger benefits. Next, the gain from the base date to the announcement date was measured and evidence emerged of positive gains to both the shareholder groups involved in the merger. The mean gain in dollars to the larger firm is approximately four times that for the smaller firms using unadjusted prices and approximately the same using the market adjustment. This downward adjustment after removing the market effect is used because mergers usually occur in rising markets. In terms of annualized rates of return, the evidence indicates that both firms in a merger have positive returns over the period between seven months before the announcement to the announcement. However, the gain to the smaller firms exceeds the gain to larger firms in terms of rates of return.

This research argues that such results are consistent with a synergistic effect, or the replacement of inferior management. One of the major methodological developments of this study is the use of the residual technique to identify the appropriate base date from which to measure merger benefits.

Later research by Mandelker (1974) provided a smaller but more complete analysis using a CAPM approach, while considering two basic questions: (1) Does the basic risk-and-return trade-off hold for merging firms, or are there abnormal returns associated with mergers? And (2) is the capital market efficient with respect to merger information? Using the market model

$$R_{jt} = \gamma_{ot} + \gamma_{1t}\beta_{jt} + \epsilon_{jt} \tag{25.2B}$$

to describe the return-generating process for the rate of return of security $j$, data for the years 1926 to 1929 are used to estimate $\beta_j$ for each stock on the NYSE. Each stock is then allocated to one of 20 portfolios by beta ranking. Betas are next recomputed for all firms for the period 1930 to 1934, and these are used to compute to beta for each of the 20 portfolios. For each portfolio, the monthly returns are computed for the period 1935 to 1938. Then the month-by-month returns of the 20 portfolios are regressed against the portfolio beta estimates as follows:

$$R_{pt} = \gamma_{ot} + \gamma_{1t}\beta_{pt-1} + U_{pt} \quad (p = 1, 2, \ldots, 20) \tag{25.3B}$$

to determine the estimates for the coefficients. These steps are repeated for other periods by using seven years of data to form the portfolios, five years to compute the initial portfolio beta, and then four years to estimate the coefficients. Finally, the rates of $R_{ot}$ and $\alpha_{1t}$ are used to compute the residuals, which are defined as

$$\epsilon_{jt} = R_{jt} - \hat{\gamma}_{ot} - \hat{\gamma}_{1t}\beta_{jt} \tag{25.4B}$$

where $\beta_{jt}$ is the $j$th security's beta using the prior 60 months' data. (This is the Fama–MacBeth (1973) methodology). This estimating procedure accounts for any change in risk. By defining each firm's merger date as month 0, the residuals for each month can be averaged and cumulated over some period. The sample of mergers consists of 241 acquiring firms and 252 acquired firms between 1941 and 1962.

The results of the preceding study indicate that there are positive abnormal returns to the shareholders of the acquiring firms before the merger and negative returns after the merger. Moreover, the systematic risk of the acquiring firms declines over the pre- and post-merger period. For the acquired firms, the cumulative average residuals indicate a larger positive-abnormal gain during the seven months before the merger. Also, the beta of the acquiring firms increases during the period between –100 and –20 months and decreases in the period –20 months to the event month and continues to decrease in the period from the event month to month +40. It was suggested that these changes in beta may bias the estimates of abnormal returns, and hence Mandelker uses a set of beta estimates for months –30 to +30 (that is, past and future data). These betas cause the cumulative average residuals to reach only half the level of those using only past information. The general results of this study imply that the shareholders of the acquired firm earn abnormal gains in the period prior to the merger.

Langetieg (1978) used a three-factor model to measure the gains from business combinations. The objective of this study was to compare the merged firm with an identical nonmerged firm using factors for (1) the market, to account for systematic risk, (2) the industry, to account for any industry-specific factors, and (3) a control group of matched nonmerging firms. In the single-factor market model, the residual represents the influence of all extramarket factors including industry effects and firm-specific effects such as mergers. Ideally, any merger analysis by a residual technique should first begin by removing all nonmerger influences. Hence, an industry index based on the two-digit SIC industry classifications was employed along with a procedure similar to Ball and Brown (1967):

$$R_{It} - R_{ft} = \alpha_I + \beta_I(R_{mt} - R_{ft}) + \epsilon_{It} \tag{25.5B}$$

Now assume the firm's residuals are linearly related to the industry residuals as follows:

$$\epsilon_{it} = C_i\epsilon_{It} + \mu_{it} \tag{25.6B}$$

Using this residual relationship in the single-index model results in

$$\begin{aligned} R_{it} - R_{ft} &= \alpha_i + \beta_i(R_{mt} - R_{ft}) + \epsilon_{it} \\ &= \alpha_i' + \beta_i(R_{mt} - R_{ft}) + C_i(\epsilon_{It} - \alpha_I) + \mu_{it} \end{aligned} \tag{25.7B}$$

where $\alpha_i' = \alpha_i + C_i\alpha_I$. We can now write merger-related excess returns as

$$\epsilon_{it} = \alpha'_i + \mu_{it} \tag{25.8B}$$

Another factor introduced by Langetieg is a well-matched sample of nonmerging firms where the matching is based on the correlation of the residuals in the market model. Hence, these control firms are similar to the merging firms over the period observed.

Using 149 mergers of NYSE firms listed on the tapes of the Center for Research in Security Prices (CRSP), Langetieg made estimates of the abnormal performance for the acquired, acquiring, and combined firms over three periods. Although various models were applied to the data, little difference was discerned among the cumulative excess return estimates. The general results indicated that the acquired firms have significantly negative cumulative average excess returns over the period between 72 and 19 months before the merger and a significantly positive gain over the period between 6 and 1 months prior to the merger. For the acquiring firm, the empirical results are not so clear — the gain to the shareholders of the acquiring firm is positive but substantially less than the gain to the acquired firm's shareholders. This study concludes that the merger produces only a slightly positive abnormal return. In terms of the multiple-factor model versus the single-factor model, it appears that inclusion of the industry factor makes a substantial difference in the results. For the combined firm after the merger, it was determined that after adjusting for the control group the excess returns are insignificantly different from 0, indicating a normal rate of return to the shareholders of the combined firm.

A study by Shick and Jen (1972) uses a different approach to the analysis of mergers and does not rely on the market model or any multiple-factor model to describe the normal return-generating process. Shick and Jen examined the benefits to shareholders of acquiring firms involved in horizontal acquisitions. They pointed out that the merger benefit to the shareholders of the acquiring firm is the difference between the return those shareholders earn with the merger and the return they would have earned without the merger. However, this difference has two elements: (1) the actual merger benefit and (2) any compensation for the change in risk. Hence, to measure the merger benefit, the risk compensation must be removed. To accomplish this, the actual rate of return for a merging firm was first computed for the three one-year periods following the merger by using market data. Using annual accounting data over one-year horizons, this study sought to minimize any risk changes. The next step was to calculate the return that would have been earned without the merger. Several alternatives are available, such as the CAPM approach used in the studies cited above or the use of average industry returns or average returns for an interindustry sample of nonmerging firms. To determine the hypothetical dividends and stock price, a common stock valuation model based on Gordon's model was used:

$$P = \frac{D}{K - g} \tag{25.9B}$$

where $P$ is the stock price; $D$ is the dividend; $K$ is the investors' required rate of return; and $g$ is the dividend growth rate. However, this model assumes a perpetual constant growth in dividends. (Modigliani and Miller allowed for various reinvestment rates.) The model used here is for both short-term and long-term growth. Specifically, a logarithmic model is utilized of the form

$$\ln P = \beta_0 + \beta_1 \ln D + \beta_2 \ln \left( \frac{g_0}{g_1} \right) + \beta_3 \ln g_1 + \beta_4 \ln h$$
$$+ \beta_5 \ln V + \beta_6 \ln A + \beta_7 \ln F + \epsilon \tag{25.10B}$$

where $g_0$ and $g_1$ are the short- and long-term growth rates; $h$ is a leverage measure based on debt and preferred stock over the common equity; $V$ is a measure of earnings variability based on ten years of data for EBIT/book value of equity; $A$ is a size variable; and $F$ is a firm-specific variable based on an exponentially weighted average of the four preceding residuals from the equation without the firm effect term. This model was estimated on a cross-sectional basis for each industry (supplemented with data for nonmerging firms in the same industry) and had an average $R^2$ equal to 0.82. The merger benefits were then measured as the difference between the actual return and the return that would have been earned by using the firm-specific variable in the estimated model. The sample of firms in this study includes 24 acquiring firms, from three industries, involved in horizontal mergers between 1958 and 1966. The results indicate a significant positive merger benefit of 9.6% during the first year following the merger. Merger benefits for the next two years were –2.68% and 2.68%, both of which were insignificant. Hence, mergers may be beneficial to the shareholders of the acquiring firm, but the market is quite efficient in evaluating the merger information and hence benefits do not persist for long.

Other related research indicates abnormal gains to acquired firms over the pre-merger period. Moreover, conglomerate mergers have shown superior gains for both shareholder groups compared to non-conglomerate mergers. Thus, a major finding of this research was that the debt capacity issue does not distinguish conglomerate from other merger types. More recent efforts have indicated that merged firms tend to incur increases in their systematic risk level.

In summary, the vast literature and empirical research on business combinations indicates that there is no strong evidence of operating gains from business combinations. With respect to the capital market effects, the evidence suggests shareholders of the acquired firm earn abnormal returns because of the (anticipated) premium paid by the acquirers, while the acquiring firm's shareholders earn a normal risk-adjusted return. Moreover, no wealth transfer occurs between shareholders and bondholders. The unresolved issue is the integration of the operating effects and the capital market effect. Business combinations occur for many reasons, and what we need is an integration of the various reasons and their effects on the risk and return combinations offered to the capital markets.

## Appendix 25C — Effects of Divestiture on Firm Valuation

From a theoretical standpoint, divestment can be defined as the disposal of a portion of a firm's assets. Usually divestments deal with whole business units or divisions of a firm. The usual reason for divestment is that the business unit or division is unprofitable. However, economic, behavioral, and business-portfolio factors may also influence divestment decisions.

Gilmour (1973) thought that behavioral factors influenced the divestment decision. He found that a change in top management preceded divestitures. Duhaime and Grant (1983) found that divisional performance as well as the performance of parent firms in comparison to industry averages were important influences on such decisions. Other influences they found included relationships among a firm's businesses and the size of divested units in relation to their parent firms.

The conventional theory in regard to a divestiture says that holding the return of the firm constant, the divestiture *should* increase the variability in earnings and cause the value of the firm to increase according to Galai and Masulis (1976).

Galai and Masulis use the option-pricing model to argue that "the stockholders have 'stolen away' a portion of the bondholders' collateral since they no longer have any claim on the assets of the new firm."

We can show that:

$$\dot{V}_t^G = \dot{V}_t^A + \dot{V}_t^B \quad (0 \leq t \leq T) \tag{25.1C}$$

where $\dot{V}_t^G$ = Value of combined firm G; $\dot{V}_t^A$ = Value of division A; $\dot{V}_t^B$ = Value of division B.

This implies:

$$V_0^G = V_0^A + V_0^B \tag{25.2C}$$

If division B is divested, this leaves only division A. Therefore, the debtholders of A, who are the debtholders of firm G after the divestiture, find that their claim on assets has been reduced. If $C$ is the face value of debt, the leverage of the firm $(V/C)$ has gone up due to the loss in assets. The variance of the firm's rate of return will change. If we assume that the variance is constant, we see that:

$$D_0^A \leq D_0^G \tag{25.3C}$$

where $D_0^G$ = Value of $G'$s debt; $D_0^A$ = Value of A$'$s debt, and combining this with Eq. (25.2A)

$$S_0^A + S_0^B > S_0^G \tag{25.4C}$$

where $S_0^A$ = Value of A$'$s Equity; $S_0^B$ = Value of B$'$s Equity; $S_0^G$ = Value of G$'$s Equity.

All of this means that the value of the holdings of the equity holders of G, who are equity holders of A and B, increases at the expense of the debtholders of G, who are the debtholders of A, as a result of the divestiture.

If this divestment decision had been anticipated by the market, there would be no redistribution of wealth. If the market over anticipated the decision, the redistribution of wealth would be reversed from the above case.

With the changing economic and legislative environment of the last few years, divestiture has become an option that has gained in prominence in a firm's decision-making process. The primary reason for divesting a business unit is to get rid of an unprofitable unit.

Finally, the AT&T divestiture was finalized January 1, 1984. How this divestiture can be analyzed in accordance with the theory and methods discussed in this chapter and Chapter 11 is an interesting issue. Interested readers can refer to Linke and Zumwalt (1983).

## Questions and Problems

1. Define the following:
   a. Exchange ratio
   b. White knights
   c. Shark repellents
   d. Supermajority rules
   e. Pac-Man strategy
   f. Golden parachutes
   g. Leveraged buyout
   h. Joint venture

2. Discuss the various methods and forms of business combinations. Distinguish between the acquisition of assets and the acquisition of stock. How is the exchange ratio determined?
3. Discuss the process involved in a tender offer. What legal restrictions are there? What effects can a tender offer have on shareholders?
4. Discuss the tax implications and consequences of business combinations. What criteria must be met to qualify a business combination as a nontaxable merger?
5. Discuss the accounting methods used for mergers. What are the effects of these methods on the structure of financial statements?
6. Discuss and compare economic and financial theories used to justify business combinations. How can these theories be used by managers to make their decisions?
7. Briefly discuss the effects of divestiture on firm value.
8. Distinguish between the technical meanings of mergers and consolidations.
9. Distinguish among horizontal, vertical, and conglomerate acquisitions.
10. Compare the excess returns to shareholders in the following cases:

    a. The bidding firm in successful tender offers
    b. The bidding firm in unsuccessful tender offers
    c. The target firm in successful tender offers
    d. The target firm in unsuccessful tender offers
    e. The target firm in successful mergers
    f. The acquiring firm in successful mergers.

11. Discuss the advantage of acquiring control of another company via a holding company.
12. What agency problem is entailed in leveraged buyouts when the buyer is management?
13. Why can LBO's produce very large returns on a buyer's equity investment?
14. How does a joint venture differ from an acquisition through merger? Why would a company enter into a joint venture rather than just purchasing the partner company?
15. List the arguments for and against joint ventures.

a. Compute the Herfindal Index for an industry in which six firms each hold 10% of the market share and two firms each hold 20%.
b. Compute the Herfindal Index for an industry in which one firm holds 40% of market share and two other firms each hold 30%.
c. Interpret the relative differences between your answers in Part (a) and (b).

17. What are the two debt-related effects of conglomerate mergers?
18. Explain the bankruptcy motive for mergers and the empirical evidence on the validity of this motive.
19. How do golden parachutes and executive stock options induce management to act in the best interests of shareholders?
20. Distinguish between the effects on a parent's cash flow and its market value as a result of spinning off versus selling off corporate units.
21. Assume that firm X is acquiring firm Z. The present value of firm X is \$250,000 and that of firm Z is \$800,000. The financial manager of X estimates that the acquisition of Z would create economies of scale with a present value of after-tax savings of \$500,000. Assume that firm Z can be purchased for \$900,000.

    a. Find the economic benefit from the merger of X with Z.
    b. Find the cost of the acquisition.
    c. What are the acquisition gains to the stockholders of Z?
    d. What are the acquisition gains to the stockholders of X?

22. Briefly explain why a firm that is losing money may be a target for a takeover.
23. Briefly explain why the management of a firm may choose to use a leveraged buyout to take the firm private.
24. Why is the Justice Department concerned about business combinations?
25. What are economies of scale? What part do they play in business combinations?
26. What is the justification for conglomerate mergers?
27. A financial analyst discovers that Firm A and B are going to merge and buys the stock of both firms in anticipation of the price rising. Discuss why such activity interferes with the operation of markets.
28. Offer some reasons why two firms might be interested in merging.

29. What is a horizontal combination? Why would a firm be interested in a horizontal combination?
30. What is a vertical combination? Why do vertical combinations occur?
31. Briefly explain why a firm that is losing money may wish to purchase a firm that is making money.
32. Best Hotels is negotiating a merger with the Dove Inn motel chain. Given the following information,

| | EPS | DPS | g (%) | $P_o$ | Number of Common Shares |
|---|---|---|---|---|---|
| Best Hotels | 2 | $1.25 | 8 | $51 | 4 million |
| Dove Inn | 1 | 0.75 | 4 | 13 | 1 million |

where $g$ represents the annual growth rate and $P_o$ the current price per share, establish the appropriate exchange ratio:

a. Based on current EPS
b. Based on EPS in five years
c. Based on current market values
d. To maintain Best Hotels' current EPS
e. To maintain Dove Inn's current EPS

Note: For Part (d) and (e), assume that incremental earnings attributable to synergy are $2 million.

33. The Gold Star Corporation plans a merger with the Lucky Company through a $6 million cash purchase. Since Lucky has no debt in its capital structure, Gold Star will acquire it by issuing $6 million of long-term debt at 10% to finance the acquisition plus the expansion. Current financial and accounting data are given below:
Using the M&M $V_L = V_u + \tau_c D$ equation, as discussed in Chapter 9, determine the incremental value Gold Star will gain by acquiring Lucky. Gold Star has EBIT f $1 million and is in a 34% tax bracket, while Lucky's EBIT of $500,000 is subject to a 34% tax rate. Also, assume that the capitalization rate of operating earnings ($k$, for an unlevered firm) is 12.5% for each company.
34. The Pinewood Corporation plans a merger with the Redbark Company through a $6-million cash purchase. Since Redbark

**Gold Star Corporation**

| | | | |
|---|---|---|---|
| Current assets | $7,000,000 | Debt (10%) | $4,000,000 |
| Fixed assets | 3,000,000 | Equity | 6,000,000 |
| Total assets | $10,000,000 | Total claims on assets | $10,000,000 |

**Lucky Company**

| | | | |
|---|---|---|---|
| Current assets | $4,000,000 | Debt (10%) | $ 0 |
| Fixed assets | 2,000,000 | Equity | 6,000,000 |
| Total assets | $6,000,000 | Total claims on assets | $6,000,000 |

has no debt in its capital structure, Pinewood will finance the acquisition by issuing $6 million of long-term debt at 10%.

**Pinewood Corporation Balance Sheet**

| | | | |
|---|---|---|---|
| Current assets | $7,000,000 | Debt (10%) | $4,000,000 |
| Fixed assets | 3,000,000 | Equity | 6,000,000 |
| Total assets | $10,000,000 | Total claims on assets | $10,000,00 |

**Redbark Company Balance Sheet**

| | | | |
|---|---|---|---|
| Current assets | $4,000,000 | Debt(10%) | $0 |
| Fixed assets | 2,000,000 | Equity | 6,000,000 |
| Total assets | $6,000,000 | Total claims on assets | $6,000,000 |

Using the M&M valuation model, $V_L$ (market value of leveraged firm) equals $V_U$ (market value of unleveraged firm) plus $V_D$(value of the tax shield), as discussed in Chapter 13. Determine the incremental value Pinewood will gain by acquiring Redbark. Pinewood has EBIT of $1 million and is in a 34% tax bracket, while Redbark's EBIT of $500,000 also is subject to a 34% tax rate. Assume that the capitalization rate of operating earnings ($k_u$ for an unleveraged firm) is 12.5% for each company.

35. Company A has a market value of $600 million and 30 million shares outstanding. Company B has a market value of $400 million and 40 million shares outstanding. Now, Company A is attempting to acquire Company B. Company A's CFO concludes

that the combined firm will have $1.5 billion synergy and Company B can be acquired at a premium of $200 million.

a. If Company A offers $15 million shares to exchange for the 40 million shares of Company B, what will the after-acquisition stock price of Company A be?
b. To make the value of a stock offer equivalent to a cash offer of $300 million, what would be the proper exchange ratio of the two stocks?

36. Company A is analyzing the possible acquisition of Company B. Neither firm has debt. The forecasts of Company A show that the purchase would increase its annual after-tax cash flow by $1 million indefinitely. The current market value of Company B is $15 million. The current market value of Company A is $40 million. The appropriate discount rate for the incremental cash flows is 8%. Company A is trying to decide whether it should offer 15% of its stock or $10 million in cash to acquire Company B.

a. What is the synergy from the merger?
b. What is the value of Company B to Company A?
c. What is the cost to Company A of each alternative?
d. What is the NPV to Company A of each alternative?
e. Which alternative should Company A use?

37. Company A is considering making an offer to purchase Company B.

Securities analysts expect the earnings and dividends of Company B to grow at a constant rate of 5% per year. Current dividend of Company B is $1.5 per share. Company A predicts the acquisition would provide Company B with some economies of scale that would improve this growth rate to 8% per year.

| **Variables** | **Company A** | **Company B** |
|---|---|---|
| Price-Earnings Ratio | 18 | 15 |
| Number of Shares Outstanding | 2,000,000 | 300,000 |
| Earnings | $2,000,000 | $900,000 |

a. What is the value of Company B to Company A?

b. If Company A were to offer 750,000 of its shares in exchange for the outstanding stock of Company B, what would the NPV of the acquisition be?
c. Should the acquisition be attempted, and if so, should it be a cash or stock offer?
d. Company A's management thinks that 8% growth is to optimistic and that 6% is more realistic. How does change your previous answers?

## Answer to Question/Problem 37

a. The value of Company B before the merger is \$4,500,000 (300,000 × 15).
Recall that the discounted value of *CF*'s growing at a constant rate is given by

$$\text{PV} = \frac{CF(1+g)}{r-g}$$

where $r$ is the risk-adjusted discount, and $g$ is the growth rate. We can use this to determine the effect of the changed growth rate, but first we must find the value of $r$ for Company B. Since the value of Company B is also the value of the expected future dividends, we can write using the above:

$$\$4.5 \text{ million} = \frac{\$1.5(300{,}000)(1.05)}{(r-0.05)}$$

and solving for $r$, find $r = 0.155$.
Then, applying the new growth rate, find the value of Company B after the merger is

$$\text{Value} = \frac{(\$1.5)(300,000)1.08}{(0.155-0.08)} = \$6.48\,\text{million}.$$

This is the value of Company B to Company A.

b. If Company A offers stock, the value of Company B to Company A is the same, but the cost differs:

Value of the combined firm = (Value of Company A before merger) + (Value of Company B to Company A)

$$= \$18(2,000,000) + \$6.48\,\text{million}$$
$$= \$42.84\,\text{million}$$

Cost = (Fraction of combined firm owned by Company B.'s stockholders) $*$ (Value of the combined firm)

$$\text{Fraction of ownership} = \frac{750{,}000}{2{,}000{,}000 + 750{,}000}$$
$$= 0.273$$

$$\text{Cost} = 0.273^{*}\$42.84\,\text{million}$$
$$= \$11.59\,\text{million}$$
$$\text{NPV} = \$6.48\,\text{million} - \$11.59\,\text{million}$$
$$= -\$5.11\,\text{million}$$

c. If Company A offers $20 in cash for each outstanding share of Company B, the NPV of the acquisition would be

$$\text{NPV} = \text{Gain} - \text{Cost}$$
$$= \text{Value of Company B} - (\text{Price}^{*}\#\text{shares})$$
$$= \$6.48\,\text{million} - (\$20 * 300,000)$$
$$= \$0.84\,\text{million}$$

Thus

$$\text{NPV(cash offer)} = \$0.84\,\text{million}$$
$$\text{NPV(stock offer)} = -\$5.11\,\text{million}$$

Therefore, the acquisition should be attempted with a cash offer since it provides a positive NPV instead of a negative NPV.

d. If the company adjust its estimate for the growth rate downward to 6%, then the value of Company B to Company A is less than $4.5 million and rest of the analyses change according to this downward adjusted estimate.

# Chapter 26

# Bankruptcy, Workouts, and Corporate Reorganization

## Contents



## 26.1 Introduction

Bankruptcy claims many firms, large and small, each year. Although the immediate reason why a firm may file for bankruptcy protection is financial, that is usually the symptom rather than the cause, which may include poor management, bad marketing, excess costs, outdated products, and so on. Some firms are able to work out their problems, restructure their finances, and remain a going concern. Others whose root problems run too deep or who are in too big of a financial hole end up selling their assets and disappearing from the business pages. In this chapter, we'll learn about the process, the problems, and the issues that are involved in bankruptcy and corporate reorganizations.

Ideally, the management, shareholders, employees, and other stakeholders in a firm, given the choice, would like to see the firm stay in existence as a profitable entity. However, firms do fail for a variety of macro- and microeconomic reasons. Regardless of the reason for failure, all of the stakeholders are losers. The main objective of this chapter is to present an overview of the bankruptcy procedure. We begin with a look at what constitutes financial distress and failure. The terms *insolvency* and *illiquidity* are defined and are shown to lead to bankruptcy. The legal forms of bankruptcy then are discussed. Bankruptcy and reorganization are a very technical legal process governed by federal and state laws. Therefore, legal advice is mandatory during these processes.

In Section 26.2 we discuss financial distress and failure. Voluntary restructuring and corporate focus is discussed in Section 26.3. The basic concepts and procedures of bankruptcy is detailed in Section 26.4. Out-of-court settlement and private workout arrangement is discussed in Section 26.5. An analysis of bankruptcy and financial distress is provided in Section 26.6, and Section 26.7 summarizes the chapter. Appendix 26A discusses bankruptcy and financial distress analysis for financial institutions.

## 26.2 What is Financial Distress and Failure?

*Financial distress* is surprisingly hard to define precisely. This is true partly because of the variety of events befalling firms under financial distress. For example, these events can include: (i) Dividend reductions, (ii) Plant closings, (iii) Losses, (iv) Layoffs, (v) CEO resignations, and (vi) plummeting stock prices.

*Financial distress* means that a firm's short-run operating and financial cash inflows are less than its outflows. This may be good or bad. Table 26.1 shows the quarterly sources and uses of funds for two firms, Firm A and Firm B.

As can be seen in Table 26.1, neither firm is currently failing; each has a positive net income of $10. Yet we might wonder if Firm A is facing financial distress because it is selling assets and not making any investments for future operations. Firm B, although paying only

Table 26.1 Quarterly Sources and Uses of Funds.

**Firm A**

| **Sources** | | **Uses** | |
|---|---|---|---|
| Net income | $10 | Loss | $0 |
| Depreciation | 5 | Dividends | 22 |
| Sell assets | 5 | Buy assets | 0 |
| Borrow | 1 | Pay off debt | 0 |
| Issue stock | 1 | Repurchase stock | 0 |
| Total sources | $22 | Total uses | $22 |

**Firm B**

| **Sources** | | **Uses** | |
|---|---|---|---|
| Net income | $10 | Loss | $0 |
| Depreciation | 5 | Dividends | 11 |
| Sell assets | 0 | Buy assets | 11 |
| Borrow | 6 | Pay off debt | 0 |
| Issue stock | 1 | Repurchase stock | 0 |
| Total sources | $22 | Total uses | $22 |

half as much in dividends as Firm A, appears to be in better financial shape. It has the ability to raise capital in the debt market and it is investing for future growth and profitability.

If Firm A were to continue to operate in this fashion, eventually the financial distress would lead to insolvency and/or failure. *Insolvency* means that the firm does not have sufficient cash inflows to meet all of its cash outflows. If Firm A continues to sell assets and borrow, eventually it will have no assets left to sell and no operating plant and equipment to produce a product. At this point, it is bankrupt, out of business. Prior to going bankrupt, Firm A will have become insolvent, without cash inflows from operations to meet legally binding outflows. On the other hand, because of its investments (indicated by the line "Buy assets" in Table 26.1), Firm B will have the capacity in the future to manufacture a product to generate operating cash flows that can be used to meet its obligations.

*Financial failure* has much more to do with the legal concept of bankruptcy than does financial distress. Financial failure means that the firm's assets are smaller than its liabilities. The firm has a negative net worth. A negative net worth implies that the firm cannot meet its legal obligations, so it is bankrupt. These definitions raise two important and related issues: illiquidity and insolvency. One is a cash flow concept, and the other is a legal term related to the balance sheet.

### 26.2.1 *Illiquidity*

The term *liquidity* can be defined as the ease with which assets can be converted into cash at a fair price in a reasonable amount of time. Liquidity is the most important factor that the financial manager must deal with on a day-to-day basis. By supplementing cash inflows from investment with financing inflows, the financial manager ensures the survival of the firm. *Illiquidity* is the opposite of liquidity. Either an asset cannot be converted into cash (e.g., a leased machine cannot be sold for $1 million, but the best offer from another buyer is $100,000). In the latter case, if the firm keeps the asset and uses it, it is worth ten times more than the amount of cash it could raise in a sale in the market.

In the short run, many firms may be illiquid, that is, they may lack cash. They remedy this situation by short-term borrowing. A firm borrows cash to meet its current obligations, knowing that is cash flow will improve in the future. This kind of illiquidity is transitory and is not associated with insolvency or bankruptcy. On the other hand, if a firm faces illiquidity with no expectation of future cash flow improvement, illiquidity may lead to insolvency and bankruptcy.

### 26.2.2 *Insolvency*

Although all businesses expect to succeed, many do not. Various financial indications of serious difficulty often are apparent. Cash shortages may cause illiquidity, borrowing may increase, accounts may be overdrawn, and maintenance of plant and equipment may be delayed. Careful observation of either profit or cash receipt and disbursement trends may signal pending financial troubles. However, frequently occurring illiquidity can make the difficulty so acute that the problem can no longer be ignored.

### 26.2.3 *Kinds of insolvency*

Cash flow problems can create either technical or legal insolvency. *Technical insolvency* is the inability of the firm to meet cash payments on contractual obligations. The lack of cash to meet accounts payable, wages, taxes, interest, and debt retirement will constitute technical insolvency, even if the enterprise has adequate assets and generates both economic and accounting profits.

When assets are plentiful in relation to liabilities, a financial manager usually can plan ahead and arrange for sufficient cash through various sources to prevent any embarrassment. Most liquidity problems can be overcome by borrowing or through the planned liquidation of certain assets. A sound, profitable business should have no difficulty in this regard, and reasonably intelligent planning should ward off the danger of technical insolvency. However, if the firm is technically insolvent because of successive losses, poor management, or insufficient investment in working capital, then lenders will be less willing to place funds at its disposal.

The financial manager also should be aware of the potential for variability in the availability of funds. Even a willing lender often is hesitant during periods of tight money, great financial uncertainty, or panic.

*Legal insolvency* is a more serious financial problem than technical insolvency. Legal insolvency exists when a firm's recorded assets amount to less than its recorded liabilities. This condition arises when successive losses create a deficit in the owners' equity account, rendering it incapable of supporting the firm's legal liabilities. The firm may be legally insolvent even when it is liquid and has plenty of cash to pay its current bills. Outsiders may not be aware of the insolvency as long as the liquidity of the firm enables it to meet its cash obligations. A protracted period of legal insolvency usually leads to bankruptcy.

Violation of a bond indenture agreement also may prove a source of financial insolvency for a firm. A bond indenture is the contract between the firm and its bondholders. A third-party trustee acts to represent the collective interests of the bondholders to monitor compliance with the indenture. Besides giving bondholders a contractual claim to interest payments, the indenture may require the firm to may annual payments to a sinking fund along with certain other provisions designed to protect the security of the bondholders.

If a firm fails to make a sinking fund payment, or to meet any other obligation under the indenture, the trustee is responsible for undertaking appropriate action. Pressure by the trustee on the firm usually will do little to alleviate a problem already in the advanced stage.

However, the trustee can warn bondholders of the difficulties and help to form a bondholders' committee to be activated in the event of in-court or out-of-court adjustments. Usually by the time a creditors' committee has been formed, the hope of getting all — or even any — of the creditors' money back is quite small.

**Example 26.1.** Consider two identical firms, Firm A and Firm B; both are having liquidity problems. The balance sheets of both firms are the same and are shown in the table below. If the long-term debt of Firm A has no restrictions, and the indenture of the long-term debt of Firm B requires net working capital to be greater than zero, are the firms illiquid? Insolvent?

**Financial Statement of Firms A and B**
**Firm A, Firm B**
**Balance Sheet**
**31 December 2021**

| | | | |
|---|---|---|---|
| Cash | $100 | Accounts payable | $1,250 |
| Accounts receivable | 1,000 | Bank loan | $1,250 |
| Inventory | 1,000 | Long-term debt | 7,500 |
| Fixed plant and equipment | 10,000 | Equity | 2,100 |
| Total assets | $12,100 | Total liabilities and equity | $12,100 |

*Solution*: If we look at the net working capital of both firms, we see it is negative. Current assets ($2,100) minus current liabilities ($2,500) equals −$400. Depending on the cash flow from accounts receivable and the payment dates of accounts payable and the bank loan, both firms are facing illiquidity problems. The long-term debt of Firm A has no restrictions, whereas the indenture of the long-term debt of Firm B requires that working capital be greater than zero. In this case, both firms are illiquid, but Firm B also is insolvent.

**Responses to Insolvency.** A firm that finds itself in financial distress due to one of the above states of insolvency or failure to satisfy a bond indenture has several alternatives:

1. Do nothing, but hope something will come along to save the situation.

2. Attempt to sell out. The firm can try to find a buyer, but buyers of troubled firms may be few. Even if one can be found, the seller frequently feels fortunate to walk away with any portion of the original equity.
3. Seek adjustments with creditors outside of the judicial process, commonly called a workout. Some arrangements between the firm and its creditors may permit it to keep operating with the hope that it can work its way out of trouble. Such adjustments usually take the form of extensions of repayment schedules and/or compositions of credit, as described in the section below.
4. Seek court relief in bankruptcy proceedings in the form of a reorganization or liquidation.
5. Assign assets to a third party for liquidation.
6. Liquidate.

## 26.3 Voluntary Restructuring and Corporate Focus

Firms sell assets to other firms — a process referred to as restructuring — for three reasons. First, the asset is worth more to the buyer than the seller. Second, the divested asset interferes with the seller's operations. Third, the buyer is willing to overpay for the asset.

Selling unrelated assets leads to a more efficient operation of the firm's remaining core businesses. The motives for selling the asset include the elimination of negative synergies with the divested assets and/or increased efficiency arising from better allocation of management time and other resources. Once a firm has sold the unrelated assets, whether the decision is the correct one or not depends upon how well management focuses on the remaining assets. Improved corporate performance occurs only if the business' focus is more sharply defined on the remaining assets.

Today, management has three basic approached to voluntary restructuring. *Carve outs* occur when the parent sells a partial interest in a subsidiary through an IPO. The carve out may increase the selling firm's value due to benefits from restructuring the asset composition of the firm. Again, value is enhanced if the manager focuses more on the remaining assets. *Spin-offs* occur when the parent transfers complete ownership of a subsidiary to the existing shareholders. The spin-off allows the shareholders to retain control over a given asset base while allowing management to focus on a smaller segment of the firm's assets. Finally, *sell offs* involve the direct sale of assets to a third party. The selling firm receives cash, which can be used for debt repayment or reinvestment in the remaining assets. Management in this case cannot only refocus on the main line of core business but also now has the wherewithal to finance any necessary changes.

Any of these voluntary approaches may be used by managers of troubled firms in order to fend off the legal complications stemming from bankruptcy.

## 26.4 Bankruptcy

Most corporations that fail, do so because of inappropriate management oversight, although firms also fail for a wide range of other reasons, as shown in Table 26.2. When corporations fail either due to repeated illiquidity or bad management, the firm must go through the legal process of *bankruptcy*.

Bankruptcy includes a range of court procedures in the U.S. that may result in the firm being liquidated or financially reorganized to continue operations. This may occur voluntarily if the firm permits a petition for bankruptcy, or a creditor's petition may force the firm into the courts. Such a petition by a creditor charges the firm with committing one of the following *acts of bankruptcy*: (1) committing fraud while legally insolvent, (2) making preferential disposition of firm assets while legally insolvent, (3) assigning assets to a third party for voluntary liquidation while insolvent, (4) failing to remove a lien on the firm within 30 days while insolvent, (5) appointment of a receiver or trustee while insolvent, or (6) written admission of insolvency. As an example, the Revel, a casino in Atlantic City, New Jersey, cost $2.4 billion to build and opened on April 2, 2012. It filed for bankruptcy less than a year later in February 2013 and then again in September 2014.

### 26.4.1 *Agency problems*

A company's shareholders and its creditors usually get along. As long as the firm is profitable, shareholders receive dividends and creditors

Table 26.2 Reasons for Corporate Failure.

1. An imbalance of skills within the top echelon. A manager tends to attract other managers of similar skills. For example, corporation management may consist principally of individuals with sales backgrounds who lack production experience.
2. A chief executive who dominates a firm's operations without regard for the advice of peers.
3. An inactive or ill-informed board of directors. For instance, the board of directors for Penn Central, even including the members who were bankers, supposedly did not become aware of the firm's impending financial disaster until a few weeks before its declaration of insolvency.[1]
4. A deficient finance function within the firm's management. Not infrequently, the only substantial input provided by the financial officer occurs when the budget is submitted back to the board. A company may have an effective financial information system; however, this information is of no avail if it does not flow to the board through a strong financial officer.
5. An absence of responsibility for the chief executive officer. Although all other managers within a company are responsible to a superior, the chief executive seldom must account for the increased separation of management and stockholders, this link may be tenuous or even lacking altogether.
6. Extremely variable sales for a capital-intensive product.

get their interest payments. If a firm becomes insolvent, the interests of shareholders and creditors quickly diverge. Creditors care nothing about the firm's ongoing business, as long as they get their money; to assure this, they are willing to sell the assets of the firm. Shareholders are desperate to keep the firm going for as long as possible in hopes that the firm can be turned around and made profitable, thereby saving their investment.

Many legal systems around the world don't try to resolve these divergent viewpoints; most try to protect one side or the other. A law that backs the creditors might make the liquidation of the firm easy, allowing a good firm to be destroyed before it has a chance to work through bad times. On the other hand, when the law backs the equityholders by making liquidation difficult, it may penalize the creditors by depriving them of their legal right to payments of interest and principal. This, in turn, will make creditors less willing to lend

[1]R.F. Murray, "The Penn Central Debacle: Lessons for Financial Analysis," *The Journal of Finance*, 26(2) (May 1971, pp. 327–332).

and will raise the cost of borrowing. The second "Capital Ideas" box in this chapter presents an example of the problems faced by both stockholders and creditors when a business has financial difficulties.

U.S. law tries to give equal weight to the concerns of creditors and shareholders. Its various chapters govern difficult bankruptcy situations. When a firm files under Chapter 11 of the U.S. Bankruptcy Code, any reorganization plan must be approved by both creditors and shareholders.

### 26.4.2 *Chapter 11*

*Chapter 11* of the Federal Bankruptcy Reform Act of 1978 tries to allow for a planned restructuring of the corporation while providing for payments to the creditors. Chapter 11 proceedings begin when a petition is filed by the corporation or by three or more creditors. A federal judge either approves or disapproves the petition for protection under Chapter 11. During the petition period, the judge protects the managers and shareholders from creditors and tries to negotiate a rescue plan between the shareholders and creditors. During this time, the corporation continues to do business.

Once in Chapter 11, the firm's management has 120 days to submit a reorganization plan, which usually includes debt rescheduling and the transfer of equity rights. Anyone has the right to submit a plan, but only very rarely does anyone but management submit a reorganization plan. The plan must secure the agreement of two-thirds of the shareholders and two-thirds of each *class* of creditors; for example, senior creditors whose debt is secured and junior creditors whose debt is unsecured are considered separate classes.

**Reorganization.** Current law allows the bankrupt firm to be reorganized under Chapter 11. The general objective of reorganization is to keep the firm alive while settling creditor's claims and attracting new capital into the firm.

**Example 26.2.** Reorganization

A firm that is undergoing reorganization under Chapter 11 has the balance sheet shown in Table A. The firm's creditors are in agreement that the present value of the firm's earnings will exceed the liquidation value of the firm and the firm's cash flow can support a debt structure of $50 million. The short-term creditors agree to a 50% settlement, as shown in Table B.

**Table A**

**Balance Sheet for Firm Prior to Reorganization**

**A Firm**
**Balance Sheet**
**1 July 2021 (Before reorganization)**

| **Assets** | **Liabilities and Equity** | |
|---|---|---|
| | Accounts Payable | $6 |
| | Notes payable | 16 |
| | First mortgage | 28 |
| | Debentures | 50 |
| | Total debts | $100 m |
| | Equity | |
| | Common stock | 10 |
| | Retained earnings | (60) |
| | Total liabilities and equity | $50 m |
| Total assets $50 m | | |

**Table B**
**Reorganization Plan**

| **Creditors** | **Amount of Claim** | **Claim After Reorganization** |
|---|---|---|
| Account payable | $6 | $3 (50%) |
| Notes payable | 16 | 8 (50%) |
| First mortgage bond | 28 | 28 (fully converted) |
| Debentures | 50 | 11 (residual) |
| Total debt | | $50 m |

Within the required 120 days, the firm's management has submitted the reorganization plans shown in Table B, along with the plan for issuing new securities shown in Table C.

**Table C**
**New Securities for Reorganization Plan**

| Old Security | New Security | Amount |
|---|---|---|
| Accounts payable | Accounts payable | \$1.5 m |
| | Common stock | 1.5 m |
| Notes payable | Preferred stock | 4.0 m |
| | Common stock | 4.0 m |
| First mortgage bond | First mortgage bonds | 14.0 m |
| | Debentures | 14.0 m |
| Debentures | Common stock | 11.0 m |
| New total capital | | \$50 m |

The creditors and shareholders approve the plan and the bankruptcy court confirms it. After the reorganization, what is the firm's capital structure?

**Solution:** Using the information in Table C, we obtain:

**Table D**
**Capital Structure After Reorganization**
**A Firm**
**Balance Sheet**
**15 October 2021 (After reorganization)**

| Assets | Liabilities and Equity | |
|---|---|---|
| | Accounts payable | \$1.5 m |
| | First mortgage bonds | 14 |
| | Debentures | 14 |
| | Preferred stock | 4 |
| | Equity | |
| | Common stock | 16.5 |
| | Total liabilities and equity | \$50 m |
| Total assets \$50m | | |

**Reforming Chapter 11.** Some critics argue that Chapter 11 is flawed and needs reform because it favors shareholders over creditors and junior creditors over senior creditors. They claim it is unfair that shareholders and junior creditors can vote to approve the reorganization plan as equals with the senior creditors.

Also, time works against creditors in Chapter 11. Upon approval of a reorganization plan by the court, interest payments to creditors stop and legal fees begin to erode the remaining value of the firm. Often senior creditors settle for less than their full debts simply to save time. Shareholders, on the other hand, wish to draw out the reorganization period as long as possible hoping for a turnaround; they have little or nothing left to lose.

In general, this delay is bad for the company. IF a firm's managers know they can default on debts and still keep their jobs, they may tend to abuse creditors. This could cause shareholders to require larger returns on their capital and creditors to be less willing to risk their funds.

Critics have presented two basic ideas for reforming Chapter 11: (1) increase the bureaucracy, and (2) allow the market to decide. The first proposes setting time deadlines after which independent arbitrators (more bureaucracy) decide a firm's fate. This would put bankruptcy more firmly in the hands of bureaucrats. The second reform proposal involves creating opportunities for creditors and owners to sell their positions to each other or third parties at prices determined competitively in the market. This market-based solution would encourage whoever ends up with equity control to make the firm as valuable as possible.

### 26.4.3 *Liquidation*

Bankruptcy law favors reorganization through Chapter 11, but if the firm cannot be preserved as a going concern, the law requires *liquidation.* Liquidation involves selling the firm's assets and distributing the proceeds to the creditors in order of the priority of their claims. *Chapter 7* of the Bankruptcy Reform Act of 1978 covers liquidation of a firm.

In determining whether or not to liquidate a firm, the law asks: Is the firm worth more dead than alive? In other words, is the net present value of the liquidated parts of an enterprise greater than the present value of the firm as a going concern? If the answer is *yes*, the firm's assets are sold and the creditors are paid off. If the answer is *no*, then Chapter 11 proceedings usually are followed.

Once the liquidation of assets has begun, it usually becomes painfully clear that few, if any, assets except cash bring their balance sheet values. Indeed, a significant reduction in asset values is to be expected. Because of this, not all claims on these assets will be satisfied in full; no liquidation generates enough cash to cover all claims.

In this event, available cash must be allocated to the various claims according to a rule called the *absolute priority of claims.* This rule requires satisfaction of certain claims prior to the satisfaction of other claims. The priority of claims in liquidation or reorganization typically takes the following order;

1. *Special current debt*, which includes trustee expenses, unpaid wages that employees have earned in the 90 days preceding bankruptcy (not to exceed $2,000 for any one case), and contributions to employee benefit plans that have fallen due within the 180 days preceding bankruptcy.
2. *Consumer claims* on deposits not exceeding $900 per claim.
3. *Tax claims.*
4. *Secured creditors' claims*, such as mortgage bonds and collateral trust bonds, but only to the extent of the liquidating value of the pledged assets.
5. *General creditors' claims*, including amounts owed to unsatisfied secured creditors and all unsecured creditors, but only to the extent of their proportionate interest in the aggregate claims of their classes.
6. *Preferred stockholders' claims*, to the extent provided in their contracts, plus unpaid dividends.
7. *Residual claims* of common stockholders.

**Example 26.3.** Absolute Priority of Claims

To illustrate the application of the absolute priority of claims, Table A shows the balance sheet for Dead Beat, Inc., a bankrupt firm. The book value of the company's assets is $100 million, but this is substantially larger than the liquidation value of $30 million. What will be the distribution of the funds received from liquidation?

**Table A**
**Balance Sheet of Bankrupt Firm**
**Dead Beat, Inc.**
**Balance Sheet**
**31 Aug 2021**

| **Assets** | **Liabilities and Equity** | |
|---|---|---|
| | Accounts payable | $2 m |
| | Accrued wages | 2 |
| | Accrued taxes | 2 |
| | Mortgages (secured by fixed assets) | 50 |
| | Debentures | 30 |
| | Preferred stock | 20 |
| | Equity | |
| | Common stock | 14 |
| | Retained earnings | (20) |
| Total Assets $100 m | Total liabilities and equity | $100 m |

In addition, the accrued wages are all within three months of the bankruptcy and are all less than $2,000 per claim. There are no customer deposits to return. The proceeds from the sale of assets related to the mortgage are $5 million. The costs of administering the bankruptcy are $1 million.

**Solution:** The asset liquidation value is only $30 million, which is much smaller than the book value of the company's total assets. Based upon the rule of absolute priority claim, the company should first distribute to the claims of:

| | |
|---|---|
| Cost of administering bankruptcy | $1 m |
| Accrued wages | 2 |
| Accrued taxes | 2 |
| Proceeds from sale of mortgaged building | 5 |
| Total prior claims | $10 m |

There are $20 million ($30 m – $10 m) available to general creditors.

Total claims for general creditors are:

| | | |
|---|---|---|
| Account payable | | \$2 m |
| Mortgage | $50 - 5 =$ | 45 |
| Debenture | | 30 |
| | | \$77 m |
| Percentage of payment to general creditors is | | $\frac{\$20\text{ m}}{\$77\text{ m}} = 25.97\%$ |

Based upon 25.97%, the distribution of \$20 to general creditors are:

| | |
|---|---|
| Account payable | $2 \times 25.97\% =$ \$.52 m |
| Mortgage | $45 \times 25.97\% =$ 11.69 |
| Debenture | $30 \times 25.97\% =$ 7.79 |
| | \$20 m |

There is nothing left for both preferred and common shareholders.

## 26.5 Out-of-Court Settlement and Private Workout Arrangement

Many financially embarrassed firms avoid bankruptcy by some sort of "workout" arrangement with their creditors. A creditor may not wish to sue for satisfaction of a claim if it seems likely to recover less than the full value of its claim, assuming the firm's financial difficulties appear temporary. The workout requires the agreement of almost all creditors and the loss of some of all management control by the owners. Small creditors frequently try to hold up workout agreements and thus force major creditors to advance funds to pay off small claims in full or in proportions greater than those received by other creditors. A successful workout may provide major creditors full satisfaction of their claims, while avoiding bankruptcy proceedings and the attendant court costs.

### 26.5.1 *Extensions*

Sometimes creditors will agree to *extensions* of the maturity dates of loans for which the principal payments currently are past due. Although this does not correct a fundamental disorder in a firm's finances, it does give the firm more breathing room; it allows the firm to make other adjustments in its financial resources without the burden of immediate repayment of the principal of the loan. Creditors don't give extensions without cost, however. They may impose restrictions on a firm's dividends; ask major owners of a small firm to put up more money, or preclude future borrowing except through subordinated debt.

### 26.5.2 *Composition*

Composition is another way a firm can adjust its capital sources. This method involves recomposing the debt of the firm in such a way that the creditors receive partial payment for their claims, say 60 cents for each dollar. Creditors may find it more expedient to follow this route than to take the troubled firm to court to seek full satisfaction. In court, they would run the risk of receiving less than they would through composition. Moreover, court appearances require various legal costs, which may more than offset the possible gains achieved by going to court.

### 26.5.3 *Creditors' committee*

A third method of adjusting a capital structure without bankruptcy proceedings involves the operation of the enterprise by a group of creditors, called a *creditors' committee.* These representatives manage the firm until it gathers sufficient liquid capital to satisfy existing claims or until an acceptable composition is found.

There is no legal compulsion for any creditor to accept an out-of-court adjustment. Any creditor can delay the process if it is dissatisfied with a proposal by the majority (or minority) of creditors to relieve the financial burden on the firm. The unhappy creditor can refuse the arrangement and insist that a claim be met in full; if it is not, the creditor can take the firm to court to be liquidated or reorganized.

**Example 26.4.** The Absolute Priority of Claims Doctrine
XYZ Corporation has just completed the sale of all of its assets for $1 million. Following the absolute priority of claims doctrine, show how these proceeds should be distributed to the creditors and owners of XYZ Corporation.

**XYZ Corporation**
**Liabilities and Equities**
**31 December 2021**

| | |
|---|---|
| Wages payable[a] | $300,000 |
| Consumer claims payable[b] | 25,000 |
| Taxes payable | 100,000 |
| Accounts payable | 75,000 |
| **Total current liabilities** | **$500,000** |
| Mortgage payable[c] | 400,000 |
| Debentures | 100,000 |
| **Long-term liabilities** | **$500,000** |
| Common stock | 400,000 |
| Paid-in capital | 100,000 |
| **Equity** | **$500,000** |
| ***Total liabilities and equity*** | **$1,500,000** |

*Notes*: [a]All less than $2,000 per individual. [b]All less than $900 per claim. [c]Assets sold by for $250,000.

**Solution to Example 26.4.** The liquidation of asset value is $1 million which is equal to the book value of creditors' claim. However, there is nothing left for equity holders. The distribution of proceeds can be presented as follows:

| | |
|---|---|
| Liquidation of assets value | \$1,000,000 |
| Absolute priority of claims | |
| 1. Wages payable | 300,000 |
| 2. Taxes payable | 100,000 |
| 3. Consumer claims payable | 25,000 |
| 4. Mortgage payable[a] | 250,000 |
| Total prior claims | \$675,000 |
| Amount available to creditors | 325,000 |
| Accounts payable | 75,000 |
| Mortgage payable | 150,000 |
| Debentures | 100,000 |
| Total paid to creditors | 325,000 |
| Amount available for stockholders | 0 |
| Common stockholders | 0 |
| Excess funds | 0 |

*Note*: [a]From sale of mortgaged building.

**Example 26.5.** The Absolute Priority of Claims Doctrine
ABC Corporation has just completed the sale of all its assets for \$1 million. Following the absolute priority of claims doctrine, show how the proceeds should be distributed to the creditors and owners of ABC Corporation.

**ABC Corporation**
**Liabilities and Equities**
**31 December 2021**

| | |
|---|---|
| Wages payable[a] | \$200,000 |
| Taxes payable | 50,000 |
| Accounts payable | 100,000 |
| **Current liabilities** | **\$350,000** |
| Mortgage payable[b] | 250,000 |
| Debentures | 700,000 |
| **Long-term liabilities** | **\$950,000** |
| Common Stock | 500,000 |
| Paid-in capital | 500,000 |
| **Equity** | **\$1,000,000** |
| ***Total Liabilities and Equity*** | **\$2,300,000** |

*Notes*: [a]\$150,000 is less than \$200,000 per employee; \$50,000 is exceed over \$2,000 per employee. [b]Assets sold for \$200,000.

**Solution to Example 26.5.** The liquidation of asset value is $1 million which is smaller than the $2.3 million book value of the company's total assets. Based upon the rule of absolute priority claim, the prior claims are:

| | |
|---|---|
| Wage payable | $150,000 |
| Taxes payable | 50,000 |
| Mortgage payable | 250,000 |
| | $450,000 |

Amount available to creditors is $1,000,000 − $450,000 = $550,000.
The unsatisfied claims total $850,000:

| | |
|---|---|
| Wage payable | $50,000 |
| Accounts payable | 100,000 |
| Debentures | 700,000 |
| | $850,000 |

The firm can pay $550,000/$850,000 = 64.706% of the creditor's claims. Based upon the above-mentioned information, distribution of proceeds can be presented as follows:

| | | |
|---|---|---|
| Liquidation of asset value | | $1,000,000 |
| Absolute priority of claims: | | |
| Wages payable | | 150,000 |
| Taxes payable | | 50,000 |
| Mortgage payable | | 250,000 |
| Total prior claims | | 450,000 |
| Amount available to creditors | | $550,000 |
| Wages payable | 50,000 × 64.706% = | 32,353 |
| Accounts payable | 100,000 × 64.706% | 64,706 |

| | | |
|---|---|---|
| Debentures | 700,000 × 64.706 | 452,941 |
| Total claims of creditors | 850,000 Total paid to creditors | $550,000 |
| Unsettled claims: | | |
| Wages payable | $17,647 | |
| Accounts payable | 35,294 | |
| Debentures | 247,059 | |
| Stockholders | 1,000,000 | |
| | $1,300,000 | |

### 26.5.4 *Private workout or bankruptcy*

In the previous two sections we have discussed bankruptcy and private workout. Now, we will briefly compare the relative advantage between these two approaches.

In both cases new financial claims are exchanged for old financial claims and senior debt is replaced with junior debt, while junior debt is replaced with equity. However, there are differences between the two. Typically, firms that utilize private workouts experience a stock price increase. The direct cost of a private workout is also less for a firm when compared to the cost of bankruptcy. In terms of job security, top management can lose pay or their job when a firm chooses either a private workout or bankruptcy.

Based on these facts private workout is better; however, bankruptcy is still used most of the time. Now, we will briefly discuss why bankruptcy is better than private workouts.

1. Tax Advantages
   Bankruptcy allows firms to issue debt, debtor in possession (DIP), that is considered senior to any previously incurred debt. Firms also experience some tax advantages in bankruptcy. They do not lose tax carryforwards and interest on pre-bankruptcy unsecured debt stops accruing.
2. Bankruptcy is better for the Equity Holder than it is for the Creditor
   Since DIP debt and the stoppage of pre-bankruptcy interest on unsecured debt favors stockholders, the equity investors are able to hold out and wait for a better deal in the bankruptcy. Absolute

priority rule (APR), as indicated in Table 26.3, is generally violated in bankruptcies.

3. Private Workout is too Complex
   If a firm's capital structure is too complex, for example if a firm has secured and trade creditors, it will be extremely difficult to reach a decision in a private workout with each different type of creditor.
4. Lack of Information
   When equity investors and creditors have incomplete information about a firm's financial troubles it can complicate the situation. For example, when a firm experiences its first shortage of cash flow it may not be able to tell if it's temporary or permanent. If the shortfall is permanent creditors will want a formal reorganization or liquidation; however, if it's only temporary equity investors will insist that reorganization or liquidation is not necessary.

The complexity and lack of information play a major role in the cost of a firm's financial distress. If the complexity of the firm's capital structure is high and there is a lack of information than private workouts will be more expensive.

Table 26.3 Absolute Priority Rule (APR).

The absolute priority rule states that senior claims are fully satisfied before junior claims receive anything.

**Deviation from Rule:**

| | |
|---|---|
| Equity holders | Expectation: No payout<br>Reality: Payout in 81% of cases |
| Unsecured creditors | Expectation: Full payout after secured creditors<br>Reality: Violation in 78% of cases |
| Secured creditors | Expectation: Full payout<br>Reality: Full payout in 92% of case |

**Reasons for Violations:**

Creditors want to avoid the expense of litigation. Debtors are given a 120-day opportunity to cause delay and harm value.
Managers often own equity and demand to be compensated.
Bankruptcy judges like consensual plans and pressure parties to compromise.

*Source*: Lawrence A. W. "Bankruptcy Resolution: Direct Costs and Violation of Priority of Claims," *Journal of Financial Economics* 27 (1990).

## 26.6 Bankruptcy and Financial Distress Analysis

Banks, insurance companies, and other potential lenders use credit scoring models to assess the creditworthiness of prospective borrowers. The general idea is to find factors that enable the lenders to discriminate between good and bad credit risks. In other words, lenders want to identify attributes that can be used to predict default or bankruptcy. Altman *et al.* (2019) and Lee and Lee (2017) have discussed related concepts and models in detail.

For the past 50 years, academicians and practitioners have used the linear discriminant function to analyze bankruptcy and financial distress for both industrial and financial firms. In this section we will discuss Altman's (1968) bankruptcy analysis for industrial firms. In Appendix 26A we will discuss Sinkey's (1975) study of identifying problem banks from nonproblem banks.

Altman's study included 33 manufacturers who filed bankruptcy petitions under Chapter X of the Bankruptcy Act during 1946–1965. These 33 firms were paired with 33 nonbankrupt firms on the basis of similar industry and asset size. Asset size ranged between \$1 million and \$25 million. For each firm, 22 variables were initially chosen for analysis on the basis of their popularity in the literature and their potential relevance to the study. These ratios were classified into five categories: liquidity, profitability, leverage, solvency, and activity. One ratio from each category was chosen for inclusion in the discriminant model. The variables used to obtain the final results are:

$$X_1 = \text{Working capital/Total assets;}$$

$$X_2 = \text{Retained earnings/Total assets;}$$

$$X_3 = \text{EBIT/Total assets;}$$

$$X_4 = \text{Market value of equity/Book value of total debt; and}$$

$$X_5 = \text{Sales/Total assets.}$$

The mean ratios of the two groups of firms one year prior to the filing for bankruptcy are listed in Table 26.4. From Table 26.4 we found that the average bankruptcy group means of these five ratios are substantially worse than nonbankruptcy group means.

Table 26.4 Mean Ratios of Bankrupt/Nonbankrupt Firms.

| Ratio | Bankrupt Group Mean | Nonbankrupt Group Mean |
|---|---|---|
| $X_1$ | −0.061 | 0.414 |
| $X_2$ | −0.626 | 0.355 |
| $X_3$ | −0.318 | 0.153 |
| $X_4$ | 0.401 | 2.477 |
| $X_5$ | 1.500 | 1.900 |

*Source*: Lee and Lee (2017). *Financial Analysis, Planning and Forecasting*, page 116.

Altman's final estimated discriminant function is

$$Y_i = 0.012X_1 + 0.014X_2 + 0.033X_3 + 0.006X_4 + 0.999X_5 \quad (26.1)$$

His results show that this discriminant function has done well in predicting nonbankrupt firms.

Using (i) the formula for the overall cost of misclassification (E) and (ii) the expected error rate as discussed in the previous chapters, Altman classified the initial sample. He concluded that all firms having a $z$-score greater than 2.99 clearly fall into the nonbankrupt sector, while those firms having a $z$-score below 1.81 are all bankrupt. The area between 1.81 and 2.99 will be defined as the zone of "ignorance" or the "*gray*" *area*.

Altman's original $Z$-score model requires a firm to have publicly traded equity and be a manufacturer. He uses a revised model to make it applicable for private firms and nonmanufacturers. The resulting model is this:

$$Z = 6.56\frac{\text{Net working capital}}{\text{Total assets}} + 3.26\frac{\text{Accumulated retained earnings}}{\text{Total assets}} + 1.05\frac{\text{EBIT}}{\text{Total assets}} + 6.72\frac{\text{Book value of equity}}{\text{Total liabilities}} \quad (26.2)$$

Table 26.5 Financial Ratio for JNJ (2018) ($ in millions).

| | | |
|---|---|---|
| $\frac{\text{Net working capital}}{\text{Total assets}}$ | $= \frac{\$14{,}803}{\$152{,}954}$ | $= 0.0967807315$ |
| $\frac{\text{Accumulated retained earnings}}{\text{Total assets}}$ | $= \frac{\$15{,}297}{\$152{,}954}$ | $= 0.100010461$ |
| $\frac{\text{EBIT}}{\text{Total assets}}$ | $= \frac{\$19{,}004}{\$152{,}954}$ | $= 0.124246505$ |
| $\frac{\text{Book value of equity}}{\text{Total liabilities}}$ | $= \frac{\$59{,}752}{\$93{,}202}$ | $= 0.641102122$ |

where $Z < 1.23$ indicates a bankruptcy prediction, $1.23 \leq Z \leq 2.90$ indicates a gray area; and $Z > 2.90$ indicates no bankruptcy.

Now we will calculate the financial $Z$-score for JNJ based upon their financial statements from 2018.

The first step is to determine the value of each of the financial statement variables and apply them in the $Z$-score value model as indicated in Eq. (26.2).

The second step is to calculate the $Z$-score. Substitute the four financial ratios in Table 26.5 into Eq. (26.2), then we obtain the following $Z$-score.

$$Z = 6.56(0.0967807315) + 3.26(0.100010461) + 1.05\,(0.124246505) + 6.72\,(0.641102122) = 5.39958079159 \doteq 5.4$$

JNJ's $Z$-score in terms of 2018 is approximately equal to 5.4, which is substantially above 2.9. Therefore, we conclude that JNJ's credit risk is very small. By using this information, JNJ's lender can give a favorable lending rate to them.

## 26.7 Summary

In this chapter, we have presented an overview of the current state of the U.S. bankruptcy laws, especially Chapter 11 and Chapter 7 of the Federal Bankruptcy Reform Act of 1978. Debate continues as to whether or not this act is doing its job to strengthen the economy in the long term by providing the legal mechanism needed to liquidate or reorganize inefficient or failing firms. Critics of the current bankruptcy laws argue that:

1. The firm's management is entrenched in its position. Most managers stay with the firm through bankruptcy proceedings.
2. Most companies that go through bankruptcy are liquidated.
3. There is no incentive for the bankruptcy process to be handled in a timely fashion.

In addition, we also have discussed how to calculate Altman's financial $Z$-score in terms of JNJ's 2018 balance sheets and earnings statement data. Appendix 26A discussed how financial ratios of the banking industry can be used to analyze problem banks and nonproblem banks.

## References

Altman, E.I. "Financial ratios, discriminant analysis, and the prediction of corporate bankruptcy," *The Journal of Finance*, 23 (1968).

Altman, E.I., Hotchkiss, E., and W. Wang. *Corporate Financial Distress, Restructuring, and Bankruptcy: Analyze Leveraged Finance, Distressed Debt, and Bankruptcy*, 4th edn. (Wiley, 2019).

Lee, C. F. and J. Lee. *Financial Analysis and Planning: Theory and Application* (Singapore: World Scientific, 2017).

Sinkey, J.F. "A multivariate statistical analysis of the characteristics of problem banks," *The Journal of Finance*, 30 (1975, pp. 21–36).

## Appendix 26A — Bankruptcy and Financial Distress Analysis for Financial Institutions

In Section 26.6 we discussed Altman's (1968) financial $Z$-score analysis for industrial firms. In this appendix we will discuss how Sinkey's (1975) study of problem banks is another example of the use of a discriminant function in financial analysis. Sinkey draws a profile of characteristics associated with banks that may be in danger of failing, in an attempt to develop an early warning system to help predict problem banks. The Federal Deposit Insurance Corporation wants to predict problem banks as early as possible in order to be able to

Table 26.1A Three Classes of Problem Banks.

| **Class** | **Size of Sample** | **Definition** |
|---|---|---|
| 1. PPO | 2(1.8%) | Serious problem-potential payoff. An advanced problem bank that has at least 50% chance of requiring financial assistance in the near future. |
| 2. SP | 14(12.7%) | Serious problem. A bank whose financial condition threatens ultimately to obligate financial outlay by the FEIC unless drastic changes occur. |
| 3. OP | 94(85.5%) | Other problem. A bank with some significant weakness, with vulnerability less than class 2, but still calling for aggressive supervision and extraordinary concern by the FEIC. |
| Total 110(100%) | | |

*Source*: Lee and Lee (2017). *Financial Analysis, Planning and Forecasting*, page 117.

advise banks of necessary financial-management changes in time for them to maintain solvent operations. "Problem" banks are categorized according to the likelihood of their needing financial assistance. The three classes of problem banks and the composition of the firms studied are presented below.

Of the 110 banks analyzed, 90 were identified as "problems" in 1972 and 20 in 1973. Each problem bank was matched with a nonproblem bank similar to it by: (1) geographic market area, (2) total deposits, (3) number of banking offices, and (4) Federal Reserve membership status.

Over 100 variables were initially examined to see if there was a significant difference between the ratios of problem and nonproblem banks on a univariate basis. Table 26.2A presents a profile analysis (mean ratios for each group) of five ratios found to be highly significant over the 1969–1972 period. These five variables represent the following dimensions of bank finances: (1) loan volume, represented by loans/assets; (2) capital adequacy, by loans/capital plus reserves; (3) efficiency, by operating expense/operating income; (4) sources of revenue, by loan revenue/total revenue; and 5) uses of revenue, by other expenses/total revenue.

Table 26.2A Profile Analysis for Problem Banks.

| Financial Ratio | 1969 | 1970 | 1971 | 1972 |
|---|---|---|---|---|
| **Loans/Assets** | | | | |
| 1. Problem bank | 53.9 | 55.4 | 56.9 | 56.0 |
| 2. Nonproblem bank | 49.3 | 48.9 | 47.8 | 47.8 |
| **Loans/Capital plus Reserves** | | | | |
| 1. Problem bank | 648.3 | 692.2 | 768.9 | 838.6 |
| 2. Nonproblem bank | 564.5 | 562.5 | 562.4 | 577.5 |
| **Operating Expense/Operating Income** | | | | |
| 1. Problem bank | 83.9 | 85.5 | 89.3 | 94.1 |
| 2. Nonproblem bank | 78.5 | 78.6 | 81.8 | 82.4 |
| **Loan Revenue/Total Revenue** | | | | |
| 1. Problem bank | 64.7 | 65.8 | 68.8 | 69.8 |
| 2. Nonproblem bank | 59.3 | 59.2 | 59.9 | 59.6 |
| **Other Expenses/Total Revenue** | | | | |
| 1. Problem bank | 15.8 | 16.0 | 16.3 | 16.4 |
| 2. Nonproblem bank | 12.3 | 13.0 | 13.2 | 13.7 |

*Source*: Lee and Lee (2017). *Financial Analysis, Planning and Forecasting*, page 118.

Sinkey then applied the multiple-discriminant-analysis technique to classify the banks on the basis of their financial ratios. Separate discriminant functions were estimated for each year from 1969 through 1972. In general, six or seven variables were included in each function. Recall that a type I error represents the prediction of a problem bank as a nonproblem one, and that a type II error represents the prediction of a nonproblem bank as a problem one. Obviously, from the viewpoint of financial outlay, a type I error is more costly to the FDIC. The prediction results for each year are presented below.

In the years closer to a bank's classification as a problem bank, the discriminant model becomes better able to classify banks that were termed problems in 1971 and 1972. It is apparent that the potential exists for the banking agency to more efficiently allocate resources and analyze pre-examination data through the implementation of an effective early warning system.

From Section 26.6, we conclude that financial ratios for industrial firms are very useful to calculate financial $Z$-score, which

| Year | Type I error (%) | Type II error (%) | Total error (%) |
|---|---|---|---|
| 1969 | 46.36 | 25.45 | 35.91 |
| 1970 | 42.73 | 27.27 | 35.00 |
| 1971 | 38.18 | 24.55 | 31.36 |
| 1972 | 28.15 | 21.36 | 24.76 |

can be used to describe the financial risk for industrial firms. This appendix shows that financial ratios for banks can be very useful to distinguish problem banks from nonproblem banks. It is well known that discriminant analysis, which can be found in Chapters 3 and 4 of Lee and Lee (2017), is very useful for performing the related analysis which has been discussed in Section 26.6 and Appendix 26A.

## Questions and Problems

1. Explain in your own words the following terms:
   a. financial distress
   b. illiquidity
   c. insolvency
   d. bankruptcy
2. What is the difference between reorganization and liquidation?
3. What is a creditors' committee? What type of power does a creditors' committee have?
4. Identify the major difference between technical insolvency and legal insolvency.
5. According to Table 26.2, what are the major reasons for corporate failure? Do those reasons make sense to you? Can you find examples in *The Wall Street Journal* to illustrate those reasons?
6. Explain the difference between a cash flow view of bankruptcy and an accounting view of bankruptcy.
7. How are the rights of bondholders protected in the event of financial distress?
8. What are the basic arguments given for the need to reform Chapter 11?

9. What are some ways that a bankruptcy can be settled out of court?
10. Briefly explain how a bond indenture agreement can affect the solvency of a firm.
11. What actions can a firm that is in financial distress take to satisfy a bond indenture?
12. Provide some of the reasons for corporate failure.
13. What is composition?
14. If a firm is liquidated, what claim do stockholders have on the assets of the firm?
15. What effect does the conflict between stockholders and bondholders have on the probability of bankruptcy?
16. Should bankruptcy law favor creditors over owners, managers, or employees?
17. What problems might arise between stockholders and bondholders in a firm that is experiencing financial distress?
18. Please discuss how Altman's financial $Z$-score is developed.
19. **The Absolute Priority of Claims Doctrine.**
    The DEFG Corporation has just completed the disposal of all of its assets for $2 million. Following the absolute priority of claims doctrine, show how the proceeds should be distributed to the creditors and shareholders.

| **DEFG Corporation<br>Liabilities and Equities<br>31 December 1996** | |
|---|---|
| Liquidation expenses payable | $25,000 |
| Wages payable | 300,000 |
| Taxes payable | 75,000 |
| Accounts payable | 600,000 |
| **Current liabilities** | **$1,000,000** |
| Long-term bonds | 1,000,000 |
| Subordinate debentures | 1,000,000 |
| **Long-term liabilities** | **$2,000,000** |
| Equity | |
| Common Stock | 1,000,000 |
| **Liabilities and equity** | **$4,000,000** |

20. **The Absolute Priority of Claims Doctrine.**
CDE Corporation has just completed the disposal of all of its assets for $1.5 million. Of this amount, $500,000 was realized from the sale of a building that had a $1 million mortgage against it. Following the absolute priority of claims doctrine, show how the proceeds should be distributed to creditors and shareholders.

| **CDE Corporation<br>Liabilities and Equities<br>31 December 1996** | |
|---|---|
| Wages payable | $300,000 |
| Taxes payable | 300,000 |
| Accounts payable | 400,000 |
| **Current liabilities** | **$1,000,000** |
| Mortgage payable | 1,000,000 |
| Long-term bonds | 1,000,000 |
| **Long-term liabilities** | **$2,000,000** |
| Equity | |
| Common stock | 1,000,000 |
| **Liabilities and equity** | **$4,000,000** |

21. **Balance Sheet for a Reorganization Plan.**
The capital structure of No Go is:

| | |
|---|---|
| Accounts payable | $2 m |
| Notes payable | 4 m |
| First mortgage bonds | 8 m |
| Debenture | 16 m |
| Preferred stock | 10 m |
| Equity | |
| Common stock | 10 m |
| Retained earnings | (30 m) |
| **Total liabilities and equity** | **$20 m** |

The firm's assets are valued at $20 million. The first mortgage bonds are fully covered. The short-term creditors have agreed to share the loss at 50%. The debenture-holders will be residual, and the preferred-holders will get nothing. Develop a reorganization plan for No Go. What is No Go's balance sheet if your plan is accepted?

22. Please use Eq. (26.1) to calculate Altman's financial $Z$-score in terms of financial statements of JNJ for 2019, 2020, 2021, 2022 and compare these three results.

## Chapter 27

# International Financial Management

**Contents**



## 27.1 Introduction

The technological revolution in communication, transportation, and information processing has greatly reduced the geographical barriers and greatly expanded the market horizon for business firms. The scope of financial decision-making in the international arena is an extension of domestic concerns and includes decisions involving working capital, capital budgeting, short- and long-term financing, valuation, cost of capital, capital structure, and dividends. International financial decision-making varies from domestic primarily in that the financial manager faces a greater range of options and variables, such as different legal systems and currencies.

International financial management is neither qualitatively different nor quantitatively the same as domestic financial management. The firm's strategic goals remain the same, as do the risk-aversion attitudes and overall management philosophy of the owners and managers, but the number of variables increases, and the decision complexity is greater because there are more alternatives to be considered. In the next paragraph, we will discuss the major content of this chapter.

Section 27.2 provides an introduction to the foreign exchange market, Section 27.3 discusses international financial markets, and Section 27.4 the international capital market. Accounting for foreign exchange exposure is discussed in Section 27.5 and the different types of exposure are discussed in Section 27.6. The international investment and financing decision is discussed in Section 27.7, and the political risk and exchange rate risk dimension is discussed in Section 27.8. A currency option valuation model is presented and examined in Section 27.9. Finally, Section 27.10 summarizes the chapter. Appendix 27A explores the relationship between exchange rates and interest rates.

## 27.2 The Foreign Exchange Market

The foreign exchange market is not a geographic place; it consists of a communications network through which many participants throughout the world agree to buy or sell currencies. The foreign exchange market includes a wide variety of smaller markets for immediate exchanges (spot trading), agreements for later exchanges (forward trading), and contracts based on exchange rates (futures and options trading).

Given the worldwide dispersion of the foreign exchange market, exchange trading never opens or closes. Markets around the world are interconnected by communication links so that it is possible to trade in the foreign exchange market somewhere in the world 24 hours a day, 7 days a week. This interconnection of diverse market segments also provides very competitive prices, which usually are within one-hundredth of a cent of each other.

Suppose JNJ, a large pharmaceutical company located in New Brunswick, New Jersey, wants to purchase several state-of-the-art pharmaceutical machine tools from a firm in Germany. Not surprisingly, the German firm quotes its prices in Euro area Euros and expects to be paid in the Euro market. JNJ's treasurer will have to make arrangements with the firm's local bank to convert U.S. dollars to Euros; in the foreign exchange market, this is an example of a *retail currency market* transaction. However, JNJ's bank may not have German currency available to sell; in this case, the bank will purchase Euros from another bank in the *interbank*, or *wholesale market*, and then sell them to JNJ in the retail market.

### 27.2.1 *Foreign exchange spot rates*

Every major newspaper with a financial section prints a daily list of exchange rates. Table 27.1 shows the exchange rates for major currencies as they appeared in *The Wall Street Journal* on March 1, 1996; they are the market exchange rates for the previous day, February 29, 1996.

An *exchange rate* is the price of one currency in terms of another currency. For example, Table 27.1 indicates that on deutsche mark could purchase 0.6786 U.S. dollars and one U.S. dollar could purchase 1/0.6786 or 1.4735 deutsche marks (DM 1.4736). This is the spot exchange rate; the *spot exchange rate* represents the exchange rate for an immediate exchange of two currencies. The actual exchange of one currency for another occurs on the *settlement date*, up to two days later. Settlement is handled by an association of 12 New York banks called CHIPS (Clearing House Interbank Payments System).

Exchange rate quotations can easily cause confusion. The market convention is to use *indirect quotes*; that is, a statement of units of foreign currency per U.S. dollar (for example, DM 1.4736/dollar). Thus, when economists expect the U.S. dollar (\$) to strengthen against the yen (¥), they expect the indirect quote (¥/\$) of the exchange rate to rise, so the U.S. dollar will purchase more Japanese yen. A weakening U.S. dollar means the dollar will purchase less yen, so the indirect quote will fall.

**Example 27.1.** Using Exchange Rates

Q: Using the spot exchange rates quoted in Table 27.1, how many French francs could a trader buy with \$1,000 on February 29, 1996? How many U.S. dollars could 100 British pounds purchase?

Table 27.1 U.S. Dollar Foreign Exchange Rates in Late New York Trading 18 December 2020.

| | In U.S.$ | | U.S.$ Versus % CHG | | Per U.S.$ | |
|---|---|---|---|---|---|---|
| | **Fri** | **Thurs** | **1-Day** | **Ytd** | **Fri** | **Thurs** |
| **Americas** | | | | | | |
| Argentina peso | 0.0121 | 0.0121 | **0.06** | 38.2 | 82.7654 | 82.7147 |
| Brazil real | 0.196 | 0.1977 | **0.87** | 26.9 | 5.1025 | 5.0585 |
| Canada dollar | 0.7821 | 0.7861 | **0.5** | −1.6 | 1.2786 | 1.2722 |
| Mexico peso | 0.0501 | 0.0505 | **0.67** | 5.4 | 19.9451 | 19.8128 |
| **Asia-Pacific** | | | | | | |
| Australian dollar | 0.7621 | 0.7624 | **0.04** | −7.9 | 1.3122 | 1.3116 |
| China yuan | 0.153 | 0.1531 | **0.06** | −6.1 | 6.537 | 6.5332 |
| Hong Kong dollar | 0.129 | 0.129 | . . . | −0.5 | 7.7524 | 7.7525 |
| India rupee | 0.01359 | 0.0136 | **0.08** | 3.1 | 73.58575 | 73.52645 |
| Japan yen | 0.00968 | 0.0097 | **0.21** | −4.9 | 103.32 | 103.1 |
| Malaysia ringgit | 0.2475 | 0.2478 | **0.12** | −1.2 | 4.0405 | 4.0355 |
| New Zealand dollar | 0.7137 | 0.715 | **0.18** | −5.7 | 1.4011 | 1.3986 |
| Philippines peso | 0.0208 | 0.0208 | **0.02** | −5.2 | 48.078 | 48.066 |
| Singapore dollar | 0.7532 | 0.7543 | **0.14** | −1.4 | 1.3276 | 1.3257 |
| South Korea won | 0.0009095 | 0.0009141 | **0.5** | −4.8 | 1099.52 | 1094.01 |
| Taiwan dollar | 0.0355 | 0.03552 | **0.06** | −5.8 | 28.17 | 28.15 |
| Thailand baht | 0.03351 | 0.03358 | **0.2** | 0.3 | 29.84 | 29.78 |
| **Europe** | | | | | | |
| Denmark krone | 0.1648 | 0.1649 | **0.07** | −8.9 | 6.0693 | 6.065 |
| Euro area euro | 1.2258 | 1.227 | **0.1** | −8.5 | 0.8158 | 0.815 |
| Norway krone | 0.1167 | 0.1168 | **0.06** | −2.4 | 8.5691 | 8.5637 |
| Russia ruble | 0.01362 | 0.01371 | **0.66** | 18.3 | 73.429 | 72.948 |
| Sweden krona | 0.1211 | 0.1209 | **−0.21** | −11.8 | 8.2569 | 8.274 |
| Switzerland franc | 1.1322 | 1.1308 | **−0.12** | −8.7 | 0.8832 | 0.8843 |
| U.K. pound | 1.3531 | 1.3583 | **0.38** | −2 | 0.739 | 0.7362 |
| **Middle East/ Africa** | | | | | | |
| Egypt pound | 0.0637 | 0.0636 | **−0.03** | −2.1 | 15.709 | 15.7143 |
| Israel shekel | 0.309 | 0.3084 | **−0.2** | −6.3 | 3.2363 | 3.2428 |
| Kuwait dinar | 3.288 | 3.2885 | **0.02** | 0.3 | 0.3041 | 0.3041 |
| South Africa rand | 0.0688 | 0.0683 | **−0.68** | 3.9 | 14.5442 | 14.6434 |

*Source*: Tullett Prebon.

A: According to Table 27.1, the spot rate quote for French francs (FF) was FF 5.0520/dollar. Since each \$1 can purchase FF 5.0520, we could convert the \$1,000 into $\$1,000 \times \text{FF}5.0520 =$ FF

5,0520.00. The indirect quote for British pounds (£ ) on February 29, 1996, was £ 0.6533/dollar; therefore, as shown in Table 27.1, one British pound would purchase 1/0.6533 or 1.5306 U.S. dollars. £100 × 1.5306 equals 153.06, so £100 could be exchanged for $153.06.

A *direct quote* states an exchange rate in terms of the amount of U.S. dollars that equal one unit of foreign currency, such as $0.6786/DM. An exchange rate also may be quoted as a *cross-rate*, the rate of a non-U.S. dollar currency expressed in terms of another non-U.S. dollar currency. For example, Table 27.1 shows that 0.6533 British pounds could be exchanged for one U.S. dollar, which could then be exchanged for 5.0520 French francs. Therefore, the cross-rate between the pound and the franc was (FF 5.0520/dollar)/(£0.6533/dollar), or FF 7.7330/British pound. In terms of the franc, the cross-rate was 1/FF 7.7330 or £0.1293/FF.

By trading dollars, pounds, and francs, we could have obtained an exchange rate of FF 7.7330/British pound; should the actual franc/pound exchange rate be different, appropriate trading of currencies could result in arbitrage profits. *Arbitrage* is when traders buy and sell virtually identical assets in two different markets in order to profit from price differences between those markets.

In the real world, this process is complicated by trading commissions, taxes on profits, and government restrictions on currency transfers. The vigorous activity in the foreign exchange markets and the number of traders actively seeking risk-free profits prevents arbitrage opportunities based on cross-rate mispricing from persisting for long.

### 27.2.2 *Foreign exchange forward rates*

Time delays are frequent in international trade. The seller must run a credit check on the buyer, the goods must be transported, and shipments must be verified. It is not unusual for three to six months to elapse between acceptance of an order and final payment. Spot exchange rates can rise or fall during this period. If left at the mercy of fluctuating spot rates, the buyer may pay more U.S. dollars than he or she originally expected, or the seller's profit may be wiped out by an adverse move in exchange rates. *Forward exchange rates* can be used to control the risk of fluctuating spot rates over a specified time period. Forward rates allow a participant to "lock in" an exchange rate today for a transaction that will occur sometime in the future. The forward markets allow users to *hedge*, or reduce the risk of, adverse currency fluctuations.

A *forward contract* is an agreement between a commercial bank and a corporate customer to exchange a specific amount of one currency for another on a specific future date at a specific price or exchange rate. At the initiation of the agreement, no money changes hands; the actual exchange of funds takes place on the future date specified in the forward contract.

Along with spot exchange rates, Table 27.2 also quotes forward exchange rates for the most frequently traded currencies. For example, the spot rate for deutsche marks was DM 1.4736/dollar on February 29, 1996; the 30-day forward rate on deutsche marks was DM 1.4709/dollar, the 90-day forward rate was DM 1.4667/dollar and the 180-day forward rate was DM 1.4595/dollar. The rates quoted for the 30-day, 90-day, and 180-day forward contracts are only meant to be representative; corporate customers who buy forward contracts can set different maturities to match their own requirements. Therefore, the actual rate agreed upon by the corporation and the bank for a forward contract will be determined by the specific maturity and the amount of currency that the customer requires.

The forward rate either will be at a discount or a premium to the spot rate. A currency is selling at a *discount* if it can be purchased more cheaply in the forward than in the spot market. Or, in other words, using indirect quotes, a dollar that is selling at a discount can buy fewer units of the foreign currency in the forward market than in the spot market. A currency is selling at a *premium* if it can purchase more units of foreign currency in the forward market. As you can see, thee forward rates for the deutsche mark are less than the spot rates in Table 27.2. Since it can purchase fewer deutsche mark in the forward market, the U.S. dollar is selling at a discount. Conversely, the deutsche mark is selling at a premium since it can purchase more dollars in the forward market.

As an example of the use of the forward market, suppose a U.S. firm needs to pay an invoice in a foreign currency 90 days from now. The firm can purchase the needed foreign currency on the forward markets and lock in the exchange rate for that transaction. If forward hedging is not done, the corporation faces the risk of a weaker dollar

Table 27.2 Forward Exchange Rate for USD/Taiwan, Hong-Kong/Taiwan, British Pound/Taiwan, Euro/Taiwan, China Yen/Taiwan, Swiss Franc/Taiwan, Canadian Dollar/Taiwan, Singapore Dollar/Taiwan.

| | USD/Taiwan | | Hong-Kong/ Taiwan | | British Pound/ Taiwan | |
|---|---|---|---|---|---|---|
| | **Buying** | **Selling** | **Buying** | **Selling** | **Buying** | **Selling** |
| **Forward- 10 Days** | 28.405 | 28.511 | 3.639 | 3.7 | 38.28 | 38.687 |
| **Forward- 30 Days** | 28.392 | 28.505 | 3.638 | 3.7 | 38.281 | 38.702 |
| **Forward- 60 Days** | 28.384 | 28.503 | 3.638 | 3.7 | 38.28 | 38.702 |
| **Forward- 90 Days** | 28.373 | 28.5 | 3.637 | 3.699 | 38.279 | 38.7 |
| **Forward- 120 Days** | 28.362 | 28.497 | 3.636 | 3.699 | 38.271 | 38.705 |
| **Forward- 150 Days** | 28.351 | 28.495 | 3.635 | 3.699 | 38.263 | 38.71 |
| **Forward- 180 Days** | 28.342 | 28.493 | 3.634 | 3.699 | 38.255 | 38.716 |

| | Euro/Taiwan | | Chinese Yen/ Taiwan | | Swiss Franc/ Taiwan | |
|---|---|---|---|---|---|---|
| | **Buying** | **Selling** | **Buying** | **Selling** | **Buying** | **Selling** |
| **Forward- 10 Days** | 34.664 | 35.077 | 4.3306 | 4.3825 | 32.048 | 32.305 |
| **Forward- 30 Days** | 34.673 | 35.112 | 4.3219 | 4.3775 | 32.065 | 32.335 |
| **Forward- 60 Days** | 34.687 | 35.131 | 4.3107 | 4.3692 | 32.086 | 32.356 |
| **Forward- 90 Days** | 34.698 | 35.144 | 4.3019 | 4.3621 | 32.107 | 32.376 |
| **Forward- 120 Days** | 34.707 | 35.169 | 4.2912 | 4.3549 | 32.123 | 32.404 |
| **Forward- 150 Days** | 34.715 | 35.195 | 4.2805 | 4.3477 | 32.139 | 32.433 |
| **Forward- 180 Days** | 34.723 | 35.221 | 4.2699 | 4.3404 | 32.155 | 32.462 |

(*Continued*)

Table 27.2 (*Continued*)

| | Japanese Yen/ Taiwan | | Canadian Dollar/ Taiwan | | Singapore Dollar/ Taiwan | |
|---|---|---|---|---|---|---|
| | **Buying** | **Selling** | **Buying** | **Selling** | **Buying** | **Selling** |
| **Forward-10 Days** | 0.2731 | 0.2772 | 22.218 | 22.422 | 21.355 | 21.541 |
| **Forward-30 Days** | 0.2731 | 0.2774 | 22.213 | 22.426 | 21.346 | 21.544 |
| **Forward-60 Days** | 0.2731 | 0.2775 | 22.212 | 22.425 | 21.343 | 21.541 |
| **Forward-90 Days** | 0.2731 | 0.2775 | 22.21 | 22.422 | 21.341 | 21.539 |
| **Forward-120 Days** | 0.2731 | 0.2776 | 22.203 | 22.423 | 21.335 | 21.541 |
| **Forward-150 Days** | 0.2731 | 0.2777 | 22.195 | 22.424 | 21.33 | 21.542 |
| **Forward-180 Days** | 0.2731 | 0.2778 | 22.188 | 22.425 | 21.324 | 21.544 |

90 days from now in the spot market, which will increase the amount of U.S. dollars it will require to satisfy the debt. Corporations use the forward markets as a form of insurance against unfavorable movements in exchange rates.

**Example 27.2.** Moving Forward

Q: The spot rate is DM 1.4736/dollar while the 90-day forward rate is DM 1.4667/dollar, as shown in Table 27.2 Alderson Company, a U.S. importer, must pay its German supplier DM 1 million in 90 days. (a) Suppose that economic forecasters predict a stronger U.S. dollar in 90 days; they predict the spot rate will be DM 1.5000/dollar. What is the cost of locking in an exchange rate now, versus waiting 90 days to convert currencies? (b) Suppose, instead that forecasters project a weaker dollar with a future spot rate of DM 1.3900/dollar. What is the cost of locking in an exchange rate now rather than waiting 90 days?

A: (a) Buying a forward contract today will lock in the exchange rate for 90 days from now at DM 1.4667/dollar. As the importer must pay DM 1 million, the value of the forward contract will be (DM 1 million)/(DM 1.4667/dollar) = \$681,802.70. If the importer waits

90 days to acquire the currency in the spot market, and if the economic forecast is correct, the value of the transaction will be (DM 1 million)/(DM 1.5000/dollar) = \$666,666.67. Thus, using the forward market to lock in a rate would increase the cost of the transaction by \$15,136.03. The importer faces a tradeoff; the forward market can eliminate the importer's worries about adverse moves in exchange rates, buy at an explicit cost of over \$15,000.
(b) As before, the value of locking in an exchange rate in the forward market is \$681,820.70. If the dollar weakens to DM 1.3900/dollar, the value of DM 1 million in 90 days will be (DM 1 million)/(DM 1.3900/dollar) = \$719,424.46. In this situation, the importer has a strong incentive to use a forward market contract; not only would it remove uncertainty about the exchange rate, but it also would appear to make the purchase cheaper in the face of the weaker dollar forecast. If the predictions about future trends in exchange rates were to prove valid, the importer would save \$37,603.76 by locking in the exchange rate in the forward market.
The foreign exchange market consists of many participants throughout the world who communicate instantaneously over great distances in order to buy or sell currencies. There is no one geographical location where the trading occurs; rather, the market is actually a communication network. There is a wide variety of foreign exchange markets: a retail market for spot trading, an interbank market for spot and forward trading, a wholesale market for spot and forward trading, a market for futures trading, a wholesale market for spot and forward trading, a market for futures trading, and a market for options trading. The structure of foreign exchange markets is shown in Figure 27.1.

Given the worldwide dispersion of the foreign exchange market, there are no opening and closing times for foreign exchange trading. Markets around the world are interconnected by communication links so that it is possible to trade foreign exchange somewhere in the world 24 hours a day, 7 days a week. This interconnection of the diverse market segments also provides competitive prices, which are usually within 1/100 of a cent of each other.

The three largest participants in the foreign exchange market are governmental central banks, commercial banks, and corporations. In

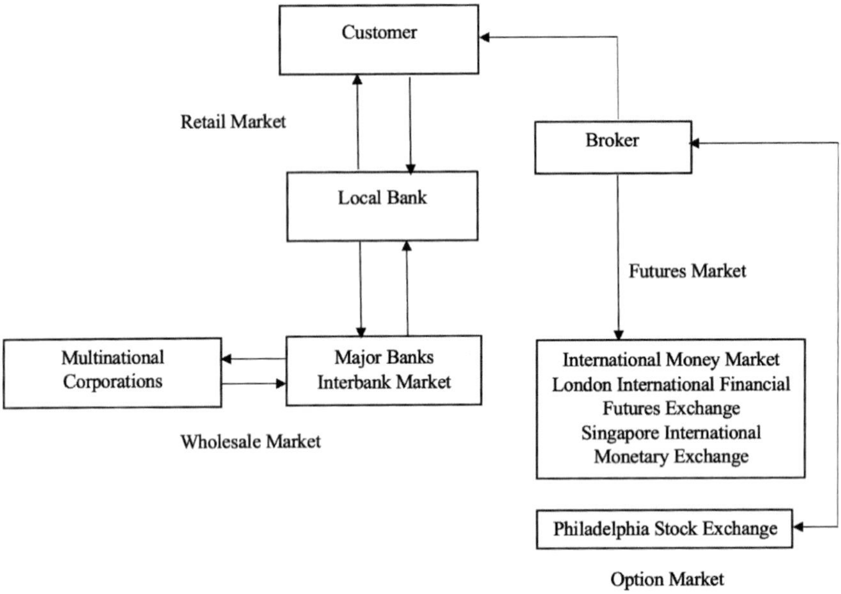


Figure 27.1 The Structure of Foreign Exchange Markets.

the interbank market, the world's large commercial banks actually create the market by trading with each other. In the wholesale market, banks provide corporations the opportunity to hedge the firm's transaction exposure. Transaction exposure of a firm's cash flow is caused by the fluctuation of exchange rates. For example, if a firm is to receive 1 million pounds in one month, the dollar value of this cash flow is dependent on the relationship between the dollar and the pound in one month. The central banks intervene in the market when they feel that their currency is mispriced. Their objective is to ensure order and stability in the marketplace.

The major world currencies are traded in the spot market and the forward market. In the *spot market*, the currencies are traded for immediate delivery; that is, on the same day that the transaction is initiated. The settlement of these transactions is handled by an association of twelve New York banks called CHIPS (Clearinghouse Interbank Payments System). In the *forward market*, an agreement is reached between a commercial bank and a corporate customer to exchange one currency for another at a fixed future date for a specific amount at a fixed price. At the initiation of the agreement, no money changes hands. The actual exchange of funds occurs on the date specified in the forward contract.

The rates quoted for the forward contract — 30, 90, and 180 days — are only meant to be representative. Most corporate customers who buy forward contracts require different maturities depending on their own requirements. Therefore, the actual rate agreed on by the corporation and the bank for a forward contract is determined for the specific maturity and the amount of currency that the customer requires.

There are various reasons why corporations buy or sell a foreign currency forward. A U.S. exporter who ships goods to Germany may receive payment in deutsche marks (DM) in 30 days. By entering into a forward agreement, the exporter assures that the value of those deutsche marks is set in terms of U.S. dollars, thereby avoiding the risk that the value of the DM will fall and on conversion fewer dollars will be received. Likewise, a U.S. importer who must pay for a shipment of goods in foreign currency in 50 days can buy a forward contract, which sets the price the importer must pay for the foreign currency regardless of what happens to the exchange rates during the 50-day period. This use of forward contracts to set a price for the future exchange of currencies, related to specific payments for goods and services, is called a *transaction-based hedge.*

Another use of forward contracts, which may or may not be economically justifiable, is called a *translation hedge*, which occurs when the financial statements of a foreign subsidiary are converted into dollars according to *Financial Accounting Standard Board* (*FASB*) *Statement 52.* Volatile exchange rates, coupled with differing degrees of inflation around the world, have caused the annual translation of financial statements to produce increase or decreases in the value of the parent firm's investment in the foreign entity. Changes caused by this consolidation of financial statements are called *translation adjustments.* These translation adjustments do not affect net income but instead are accumulated as a separate component of retained earnings. They affect net income only when the foreign investment is sold or substantially or completely liquidated by the parent firm. Should management decide to reduce or offset these translation changes, a forward contract could be used as a hedge. However, in general it is not good to hedge an accounting-based loss because the hedge involves incurring real costs to protect the firm from a noncash flow translation loss.

Until recently, the interbank, retail, and wholesale markets were the only channel through which foreign exchange was traded. However, the past 15 years have produced major changes in foreign exchange trading concurrent with the switch from the fixed-exchange-rate regime established by the Bretton Woods Agreement of 1944 to the floating- or flexible-exchange-rate regime established by the Smithsonian Agreement of 1971.

The International Money Market (IMM) of the Chicago Mercantile Exchange began trading futures contracts on foreign exchange in 1972. Unlike a forward contract, a futures contract is a standardized financial instrument with a stated amount and a specific maturity, traded on an organized market, that is resalable up to the close of the trading or settlement date. Futures contracts tend to be smaller than forward contracts and are not as flexible in meeting hedging needs.

The price fluctuations of the futures contract are controller by the rules of the exchange. The parties (buyer and seller) to the futures contract typically do not know each other. However, there is no chance of default on the futures contract because there is a clearinghouse of the exchange that stands ready to ensure performance of the contract.

The major limitation of the futures contract from the viewpoint of corporations or hedgers is the relatively small size and the standardized terms of the contract with respect to maturity. Only by chance will the standardized size and maturity of the futures contract exactly meet the firm's hedging needs. Hence, risk reduction is limited futures contracts are used to hedge a spot or cash position. To illustrate, consider the following example of a U.S. firm facing a transaction exposure. If the firm expects to receive 3,333,333 DMs in 45 days, the underlying value of the firm's position in terms of dollars is determined by the spot exchange rate between DMs and dollars in 45 days. Figure 27.2(a) shows the effect on the value of this position as the exchange rate changes.

To minimize exposure to foreign exchange fluctuations, the firm can sell a forward contract for 3,333,333 DMs at 45 days for the current forward rate, which we assume to be 3 DMs to the

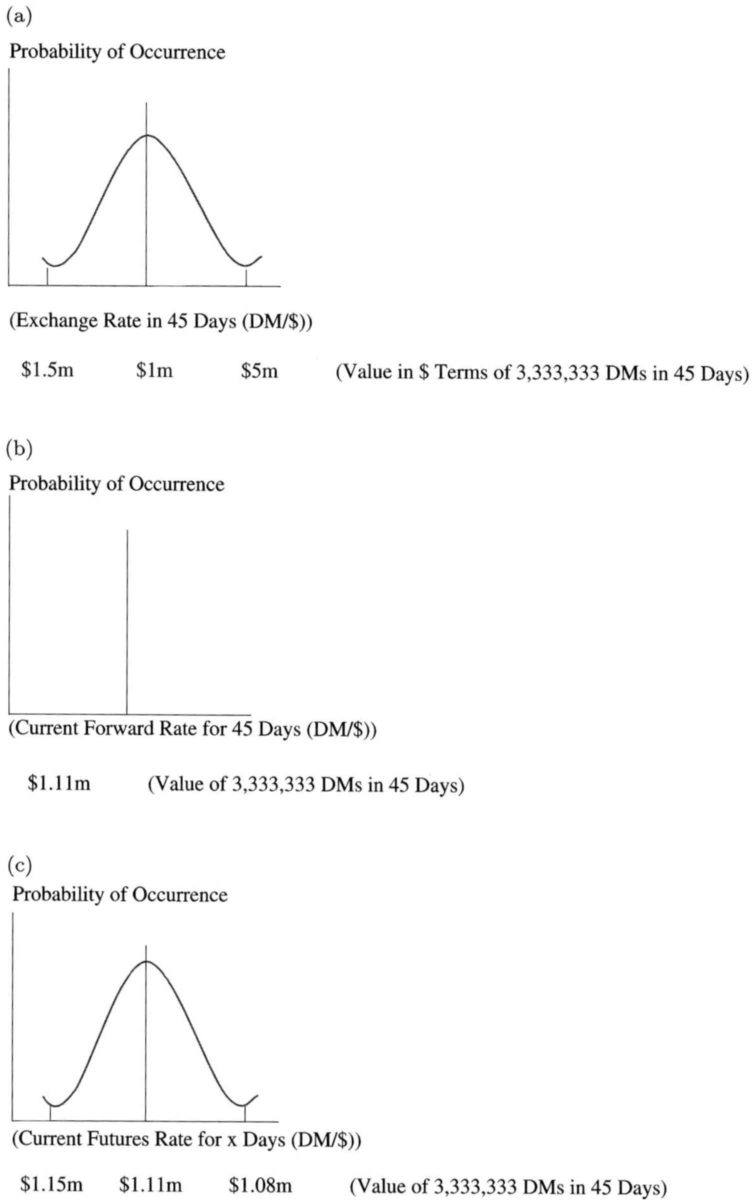


Figure 27.2 Foreign Exchange Rate Distribution (a) without Hedge, (b) Hedge with Forward, and (c) Hedge with Futures.

dollar (DM/$). This will change the situation from the one depicted in Figure 27.2(a) to the situation in Figure 27.2(b). As we can see by comparing the unhedged position in (a) to the hedge position in (b), the value of the 3,333,333 DMs is certain once the forward contract is undertaken. That is, if the firm hedges, it is certain to receive $1.11 million, whereas if it doesn't hedge it may receive between $500,000 and $1.5 million.

If the firm were to use futures to hedge the same position, it would have to sell 26.6 DM contracts to hedge the 3,333,333 DMs because the DM trades in a standardized contract amount of 125,000 DMs. In this case, the firm will either sell contracts and face the risk of purchasing 41,667 DMs at the current spot price in 45 days or sell 26 contracts and face the risk of selling 83,333 DMs at the current spot price in 45 days. In addition to this risk — the unknown price that the DM/$ will be in 45 days — the firm also will be buying a standardized contract for more or less than the 45 days, since the DM futures contracts only mature in March, June, September, or December, thereby exposing the firm to additional uncertainty because of the maturity mismatch. These factors cause the hedged position to look like that in Figure 27.2(c), which shows that there is a chance the firm will receive DMs worth between $1.08 million and $1.5 million.

In comparing hedging using forward or futures contracts, we can see that the forward contract reduces the risk of fluctuation to 9, while the futures contract reduces the risk (the range of outcomes is reduced) but does not totally eliminate it. Table 27.3 compares the characteristics of forward and futures markets.

A market similar to the IMM opened in London in 1982. This market, called the London International Financial Futures Exchange (LIFFE), trades futures contracts that are similar to the IMM contracts.

A new type of foreign exchange instrument was introduced by the Philadelphia Stock Exchange in 1982. This was an options contract giving one the right to buy or sell spot currencies at a predetermined price for a set period. The major difference between LIFFE contracts and the IMM options contracts is that when a call option on a LIFFE futures contract is exercised, the holder receives a futures contract that can be held to maturity to receive the foreign exchange. Alternatively, the IMM call currency option provides its holder with

Table 27.3 Comparison of Forward and Futures Markets.

| | **Forward** | **Futures** |
|---|---|---|
| Size of contract | Tailored to individual needs | Standardized |
| Delivery date | Tailored to individual needs | Standardized |
| Method of transaction | Established by the bank via telephone contract with limited number of market participants | Determined by open auction among many buyers and sellers on the exchange floor |
| Participants | Banks, brokers, corporations and central banks; public speculation not encouraged | Banks, brokers, and corporations; qualified public speculation encouraged |
| Commissions | Set by spread between bank's buy and sell prices; not easily determined by the consumer | Published small brokerage fee and negotiated rates on block trades |
| Security deposit | None as such, but compensation bank balances required | Published small security deposit required |
| Clearing operation (financial integrity) | Handling contingent on individual banks and brokers | Handled by exchange clearinghouse; daily settlements mark to market |
| Marketplace | Communications network | Central exchange floor |
| Economic justification | Facilitate world trade by providing a hedge mechanism | Risk sharing with public participation |
| Accessibility | Limited to very large customers | Open to anyone |
| Regulation | Self-regulating | Commodity Futures Trading Commission (CFTC) |
| Frequency of delivery | More than 90% of contracts settled by actual delivery | Theoretically, no deliveries in a perfect market; in reality, less than 1% of contracts actually delivered |
| Price fluctuations | No daily limit | Daily limit imposed by exchange |
| Contract liquidity | None | Daily trading |

the foreign exchange when the option is exercised. (A currency option valuation model is presented at the end of this chapter.)

In terms of hedging, the options contract provides a different result from hedging with a forward or a futures contract. As we have seen, the forward contract reduces the variability of the expected outcome to 0, while the futures contract reduces but does not eliminate the variability of the expected outcomes. The options contract does not affect the variability of the outcome but rather changes the shape of the distribution, as shown in Figure 27.3.

The advantages of currency futures is that the investor may transact in small amounts for reasonable transaction costs. Moreover, the market for certain currencies is quite liquid. The margins are less than on the interbank market, and the procedure of marking to market allows an investor to realize a profit or loss immediately rather than having to wait until delivery. By *marking to market* we mean the cash payment or receipt that occurs at the close of the market each day. The closing or settlement price of each day is used to determine whether the contract's owner must make a cash payment or is entitled to receive cash.

Assume that a customer buys a Swiss franc December contract and puts up an initial cash margin of $15,000. The next day, the futures price moves down and the contract loses $500. This $500 is taken from the customer's account, and the customer must deposit $500 to retain the cash balance of $15,000. If the price moves up, the customer could withdraw an amount of cash equal to the increase in the accounts value.

Markets that permit individuals, corporations, and banks to protect themselves from foreign exchange risk are necessary during periods of fluctuating exchange rates. However, it is uncertain whether all of the foreign exchange contracts currently available will survive as viable hedging vehicles.

In addition to using these markets to hedge transaction or translation exposure, many corporations engage in *swap transactions.* A swap transaction can take many forms. One example of a swap is a corporation that sells or buys a currency at the spot rate and, at the same time, reverses the transaction in the forward market at the forward rate. From the corporation's viewpoint, the net effect of this swap is to receive one currency as cash for a specific period in trade for another currency. Swaps are a way of transferring funds on an intercompany basis for a short period, allowing working capital to

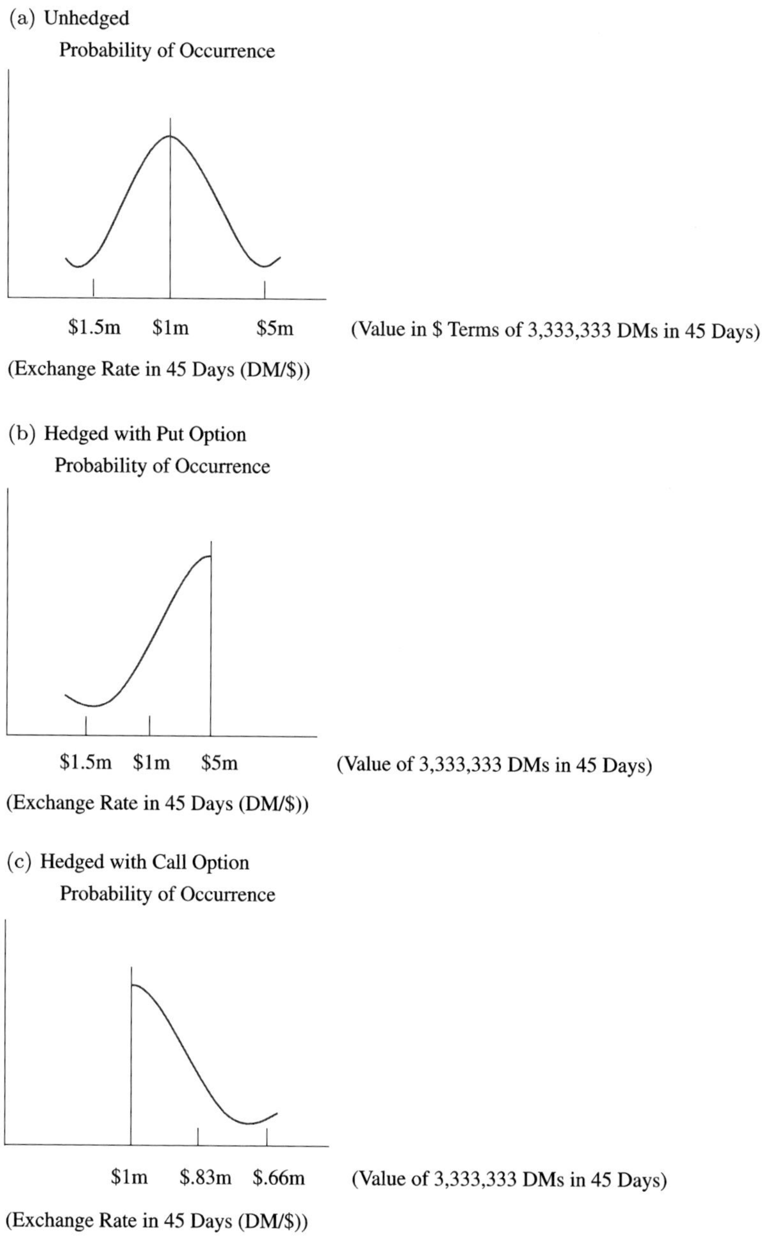


Figure 27.3 Hedging with Foreign Exchange Option Contracts.

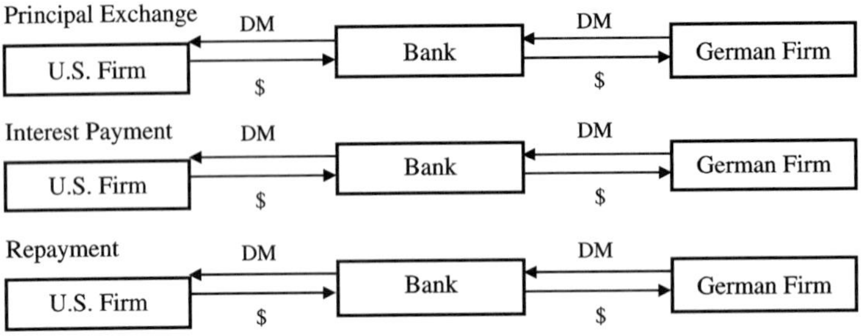


Figure 27.4 Currency Swap.

be borrowed at a fixed cost in the needed currency and for investing excess funds for a short period to earn a return unaffected by the exchange rate.

As an example of a typical currency swap, a German Company would like to borrow U.S. dollars to finance a foreign investment, but the firm is not known outside Germany. Similarly, a U.S. firm needs DMs for its German subsidiary, but the cost of borrowing in the U.S. is cheaper than the cost of borrowing in Germany. A bank acting as an intermediary can bring these two firms together, arranging a swap of DMs for dollars. The German firm agrees to pay the U.S. company principal and interest on dollar borrowings in the U.S., while the U.S. firm agrees to pay the DM borrowings of the German firm. A diagram of the swap transaction is shown Figure 27.4.

This practice of swapping by corporations and banks leads to consideration of raising short-term funds or investing excess funds intermittently in the international money market, which is the subject of the next section.

## 27.3 The International Money Market

An important aspect of the international financial system is the relationship between interest rates and exchange rates. If real rates of interest are approximately equal among nations, nominal interest rates will differ only by differences in the respective rates of inflation. The *purchasing power parity theory* related the changes in exchange rates to the relative differences in the respective rates of inflation among nations. For example, if the expected inflation rate in England is 10% and the expected inflation rate in the U.S. is 5%, one would expect the interest rate in England to be 5% higher than a comparable rate in the U.S. Likewise, one would expect the English pound sterling to depreciate by 5% relative to the U.S. dollar. Without these relationships, an arbitrageur could make a riskless profit by buying or selling a spot currency in the foreign exchange market, investing in the money market with the more favorable interest rate, and hedging these transactions by selling or buying the currency forward for a similar time period. This procedure, called *interest rate arbitrage*, links the foreign exchange market to the money market.

The degree to which this linkage takes place between national money markets is affected greatly by the actions of the governments involved. If a government has currency controls, convertibility restrictions, or other regulations, the linkage between the exchange market and the money market will be negligible. However, in the international money market, which is outside of the regulatory control of any one nation-state, the linkage between exchange rates and interest rates should be quite high.

The international money market is a free market, and interest-rate parity usually prevails. Currency spot and forward rates and interest rates in various countries are related through *interest rate parity*; that is, in the absence of market imperfections, risk-adjusted expected returns on financial assets in different countries should be equal. This is usually true in the Eurocurrency markets.

The relationships between spot and forward rates and interests rates are shown in Figure 27.5. The vertical axis gives the interest rate differential in favor of the home country. The horizontal axis plots the forward discount or premium on the foreign currency relative to the home currency. The interest rate parity line joins those points at which the forward exchange rate is in equilibrium with the interest-rate differential.

Point $A$ indicates a situation of disequilibrium. In this case, the forward premium is 2% while the interest differential is 1%. The transfer of funds out of the home country to the foreign country with exchange risks covered will yield an additional return of 1%. At point $B$, the forward premium is again 2%, but the interest differential increases to 3%. At this point it is profitable to reverse the flow of funds. The higher interest rate in the home country makes up for

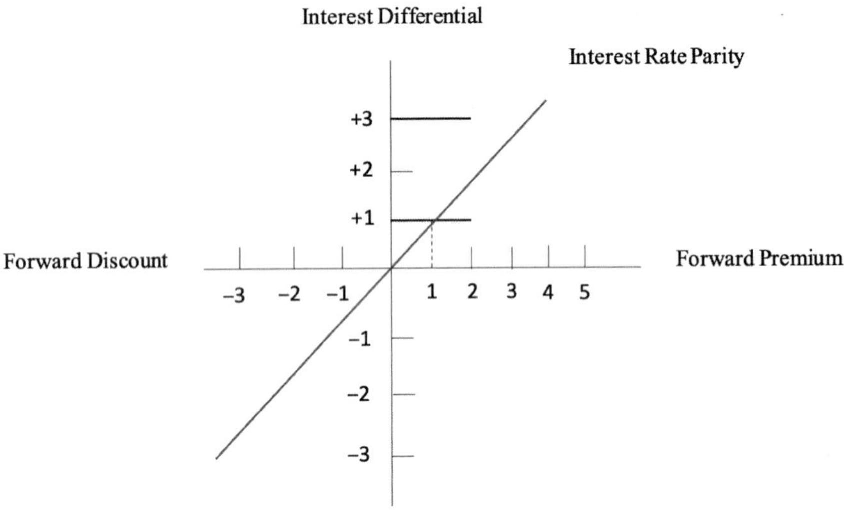


Figure 27.5 Interest Rate Parity.

the loss on the forward exchange transaction, causing a 1% increase. In either case, if investors could gain this 1% increase, they would do so. The act of covered-interest arbitrage would result in an adjustment to the interest rates and the exchange rates. When the interest rate differential equals the forward premium or discount, we have interest rate parity. Thus, when deciding to borrow or lend in various Eurocurrencies, the corporate treasurer must adjust the nominal interest rate for any premium or discount in the foreign exchange market.

Spot rates, forward rates, and interest rates must be linked in a predetermined fashion; otherwise, arbitrage opportunities will arise. This link is interest-rate parity (interest rate differences = forward premium or discount), which must hold in unregulated markets. For example, to illustrate how the arbitrage could be accomplished, consider the following information:

Spot rate FF/\$ = 8
One-year forward rate FF/\$ = 8.08
French interest rate = 14%
U.S. interest rate = 10%

In this situation, an arbitrageur could borrow dollars at 10% for one year and convert them to French francs (FF) at the spot rate.

These francs could be invested in France at 14% for 1 year. When the dollars are converted into francs, the arbitrageur simultaneously purchases a forward contract to convert the francs back into dollars in 1 year's time. If the arbitrageur started with $1 million, this transaction would produce a profit of $28,713, as shown below.

1. Borrow $1 million for 1 year at 10%. The principal repayment and interest at the end of year 1 is $1,100,000.
2. Convert $1 million to francs in the spot market and receive 8 million francs.
3. Invest 8 million francs for 1 year at 14% and receive principal and interest of 9.12 million francs.
4. Convert the 9.12 million francs to dollars by means of a forward contract at a forward rate of 8.08 francs/dollar and receive $1,128,712.80. Thus,

| | |
|---|---|
| Return | $1,128,712.80 |
| Cost | 1,100,000.00 |
| Arbitrage profit | $28,712.80 |

*Eurocurrency* refers to a time deposit in a bank that is outside of the monetary control of the country whose currency is used to denominate the deposit. For example, a *Euromark* is a deposit held in a bank outside of German monetary control but still denominated in deutsche marks. The U.S. dollar, Swiss franc, Japanese yen, and British pound are the currencies normally used in Euromarket transactions. Further, in addition to Europe, international money markets have evolved in Asia (Hong Kong and Singapore), the Caribbean (Bahamas and Netherlands Antilles), and the Middle East. Hence, the prefix *Euro* does not generally mean a geographical location but rather an external money market outside the control of national monetary authorities.

The absence of monetary control is the principal reason why Euromarkets have been so successful. The rate structure offered by Eurobanks is such that their rates will always be more competitive than rates available in the domestic money market. This structure is shown in Figure 27.6.

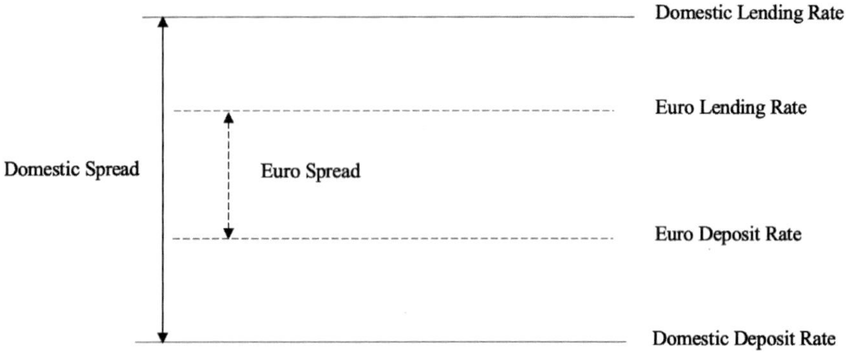


Figure 27.6 The Comparative Structure of Domestic Rates and Euromarket Rates.

The spread between deposit rates and loan rates is always smaller in the Euromarket than in the domestic market because there are no monetary regulations in the Euromarket. Regulations impose higher costs on domestic financial institutions, thereby requiring them to operate with a larger spread in order to be profitable.

The Eurocurrency lending rates are based on the London Interbank Offered Rate (LIBOR). Most of the Euro loans have a floating rate that is linked to LIBOR; these loans are usually called *floating rate notes* (FRN). The interest rate on the FRN is usually reset every six months. The actual rate is usually set at a spread over the LIBOR where the size of the spread is a function of the issuer's creditworthiness. Deposits are generally for 1, 3, or 6 months, and the deposit rates are highly competitive because the linkage to the foreign exchange market allows for the creation of offsetting positions and arbitrage.

Corporations enter the Euromarket to invest excess working capital or to finance short-term needs. Additionally, because the investment on borrowing can be in various currencies, firms often pursue hedging opportunities. A Eurocurrency deposit can be used for investing surplus cash, for compensating balances or collateral, or in expectation of the strengthening of a currency. Euromarket loans are normally used for working-capital requirements in currencies that do not have a broad money market or where government policy makes domestic borrowing more expensive or unavailable.

The international money market is a short-term market where financial intermediaries (Eurobanks) bring together borrowers and savers in an environment free of governmental regulation. The long-term Euromarket is different from the Eurocurrency or short-term market is that instead of financial intermediation, the market is structured as a direct placement market where borrower and lender deal at arm's length.

## 27.4 The International Capital Market

The long-term international financial market is almost exclusively a debt market. Corporations can issue bonds outside of their home countries in various currencies to investors worldwide. Two types of bonds are issued: foreign bonds and Eurobonds. A *foreign bond* is an international bond issued by foreign borrower denominated in the currency of the country in which it is placed. For example, a U.S. firm may issue a bond in the London capital market that is underwritten by British banks and denominated in pounds. The issue is purchased by English investors and may be traded in the secondary English bond market. A *Eurobond* is an international bond handled by an international syndicate and sold in countries other than the country of the currency in which the issue is denominated. The Eurobond is truly an international undertaking in that the borrower may be of one nationality but the investors are from all over the world and thus the currency or currencies of denomination vary widely.

From the investor's perspective, the advantages of Eurobonds are tax avoidance and anonymity. If a Swiss investor invests in a Eurobond in Luxembourg, the advantages of no domestic tax, no withholding tax, and no regulations would explain the investor's willingness to accept what the issuer might consider a competitive rate.

From the issuer's perspective, simplicity, speed, privacy, and lower cost are all attractive features of Eurobond issues. The bond offer *simplicity* because there are no government regulations with which to comply; *speed* because the time it takes to complete an issue is usually measured in weeks instead of months, as in the domestic market; *privacy* because there are few or no disclosure requirements for the issuer; and *lower cost* because the overall underwriting costs plus the interest rate are usually less than cost of a domestic issue.

The issuers and underwriters of Eurobonds tend to be creative and innovative in putting together new issues. (The first zero coupon bonds were issued in the Euromarket.) Multiple-currency issues are also becoming popular. A multiple currency bond can take either of two forms. The first is *option issue*, which allows the investor to request payment of principal and interest in any of several currencies, thus reducing the bondholder's exchange risk. The second type of multiple-currency issue has been called a *currency cocktail*, which is a bond that pays the investor a predetermined mixture of several different currencies usually related to the SDR, or *special drawing right*, which involves five different currencies, or to the European unit of account, which involves nine different currencies. The special drawing rights are a currency "cocktail" issued by the International Monetary Fund (IMF) and composed of a weighted average of the exchange rates of the U.S., West German, British, French, and Japanese currencies. The *European currency unit* (ECU) is a basket of currencies based on the currency values of the countries that are members of the European Common Market. In this case, the exchange-rate risk is shared between the issuer and the investor.

Another innovation is the *multiple-currency convertible bond.* For this security, the investor has the choice of receiving principal and interest in one or more currencies or converting the bond into equity at a predetermined rate denominated in another currency. The value of this convertible bond, like its domestic counterpart, is a function of interest rates and underlying equity performance, with the added dimension of exchange-rate changes.

Most Eurobond issues have call features as well as sinking-fund provisions, because the secondary market for trading Eurobonds is very thin. The existence of a sinking fund adds liquidity to the issue, which most investors require. However, there does appear to be an increase in the amount and frequency of secondary transactions as an increasing number of large institutions are investing in Eurobonds for trading purposes.

The Eurobond market continues as a capital market because it remains largely unregulated and untaxed. The borrowers have greater flexibility when issuing securities and pay lower interest costs. The investors receive tax-free interest income, which is paid to the bearer of the securities. The unregulated feature allows the investors to avoid taxes and government regulations.

The financial manager operating in the international marketplace must be familiar with the international financial market environment. Decisions to accept or hedge the foreign exchange risk exposure attendant with international operations are critical to the firm's financial well-being. During the 1970s, the change from fixed to floating exchange rates and changes in accounting rules on valuation of international assets, liabilities, and income increased both the complexity and the importance of the hedging decisions. We now turn our attention to the accounting issues raised by the adoption of *FASB 8* and its subsequent repeal and the issuance *FASB 52*.

## 27.5 Accounting for Foreign Exchange Exposure

Understanding and managing the interrelationship between the accounting description of international operations and the economic reality of these operations presents the financial manager with an important challenge. The roots of this problem lie in the nature of the U.S. accounting system, inflation, changing exchange rates, and measurement of economic value.

Prior to the issuance of *FASB 8* in October 1975, the accountant and financial executive had considerable leeway not only in accessing the degree of foreign exchange exposure, but also in how they could report this exposure in their financial statements.

*FASB 8* had a U.S. dollar orientation and required the accountant and financial executive to account for all transactions (domestic and international) as if they had occurred in dollars. All monetary assets (cash, marketable securities, accounts receivable) and liabilities denominated in foreign currencies had to be revalued in light of exchange rate changes. This resulting revaluation was then included in the income statement as if the firm had actually experienced a gain or loss in the current period, when in fact economic value had not changed or had changed in the opposite direction.

*FASB 8* was not well received and became the object of widespread dissatisfaction and criticism. In May 1978, the FASB began the process to rescind *FASB 8* and create a new ruling. The new ruling, *FASB 52*, became effective after December 1982. In essence, the new standard recognizes the fluctuating foreign exchange rates affect various foreign operations differently. When a foreign operation is relatively self-contained within a country, all its assets and liabilities are translated at current exchange rates. In these circumstances, adjustments arising from the translation of foreign currency financial statements are taken directly to a separate translation-adjustment account in stockholders' equity. However, in other instances, *FASB 52* recognizes that fluctuating rates affect cash flows. This would be the case, for example, when foreign operations are an extension of the parent firm's domestic operations or when an entity has receivables or payable in a currency other than its own. In these cases, the adjustments are reported as gains or losses on the income statement.

## 27.6 Types of Exposure

*Transaction exposure* to exchange risk occurs when a cash flow either leaves or is received by a firm and that cash flow is denominated in a currency other than the home currency of the firm. There are two basic ways that transaction exposure can occur: (1) receipt of payment for a commercial or financial transaction, and (2) receipt of dividends or other inflows from subsidiary. Figure 27.7 depicts these two cases of transaction exposure.

In either of the cases depicted in Figure 27.7, the U.S. corporation suffers a loss of economic value, and this loss would appear on the firm's income statement according to *FASB 52*. By *economic value* we mean the present value of future cash flows discounted at some risk-adjusted discount rate. A transaction exposure will affect either the cash flows or the risk-adjusted discount rate, or both the numerator and the denominator. Hence, from a financial point of view, we can identify the realized change in economic value caused by the revaluation or devaluation of the foreign currency.

In addition to transaction exposure, there is *accounting exposure,* or *translation exposure.* The book value of a firm is measured by assets minus liabilities. When we measure the book value of a foreign subsidiary, we must translate the value of the foreign assets and the value of the foreign liabilities into dollars at some exchange rate. The choice of the correct exchange rate has been a controversial issue, as evidenced by *FASB 8* and *FASB 52.* In a simplified

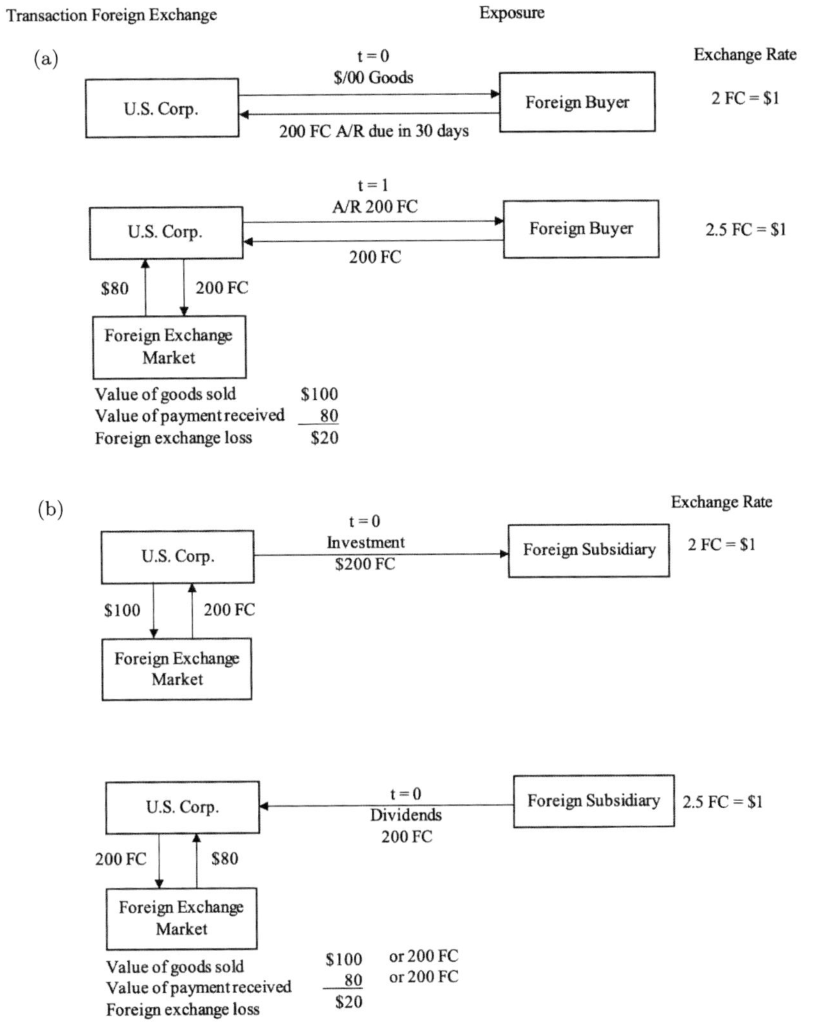


Figure 27.7 Transaction Exposure to Exchange Rate Risks. (a) Commercial or Financial Transactions and (b) Dividends or Other Inflows from a Subsidiary.

example, Table 27.4 depicts the problem of translating foreign balance sheets and income statements into dollars by various exchange rates. If all assets, liabilities, and equities were instantaneously put in place at the same historic exchange rates, there would be no exchange gain or loss as shown in Table 27.4(B). On the other hand, if the current exchange rate is used for the translation, then the

Table 27.4 Translation of Foreign Exchange Exposure.

| (A) | | B/S | | Income Statement | |
|---|---|---|---|---|---|
| Current assets | 100 FC | Current Liabilities | 120 FC | Revenue | 100 FC |
| | | | | –Expenses | 10 FC |
| Fixed assets | 200 FC | L/T debt | 40 FC | | 60 FC |
| | | | | Operating income | 30 FC |
| | | | | –Taxes | 15 FC |
| Total assets | 300 FC | Equity | 140 FC | Net Income | 15 FC |
| | | Total liabilities and equity | 300 FC | | |

| (B) | At Historic Rate 2 FC = $1 B/S | | | Income Statement | | Foreign exchange gain or loss 0 |
|---|---|---|---|---|---|---|
| CA | $50 | CL | $60 | R | $50 | |
| FA | 100 | L/TD | 20 | | | |
| TA | $150 | E | 70 | –E | | |
| | | TL+E | $150 | OI | $15 | |
| | | | | – | 7.5 | |
| | | | | Net income | $7.50 | |

(*Continued*)

Table 27.4 (*Continued*)

| (C) At Historic Rate 2 FC = $1 B/S | | | | Income Statement | | Foreign exchange gain or loss 0 | |
|---|---|---|---|---|---|---|---|
| CA | $40 | CL | $48 | R | $40 | The loss of $30 in total assets was | |
| FA | 80 | L/TD | 16 | – | | shared by the short- and long-term | |
| TA | $120 | E | 56 | E | | creditors and the equity holders as | |
| | | TL + E | $120 | | | follows: | |
| | | | | OI | $12 | Short-term creditors | $12 |
| | | | | – | 6 | Long-term creditors | 4 |
| | | | | Net income | $6 | | 14 |
| | | | | | | | $30 |
| –Foreign exchange loss of equity holders | | | | | 14 | | |
| Net loss | | | | | ($8) | | |

amount exposed to exchange risk is equal to the equity account, as shown in Table 27.4(C), where the translation loss is \$14.0.

The problem becomes more complicated when we consider that most accountants and financial analysts agree that financial accounts (cash, receivables, and payables) should be translated at current exchange rates because exchanging these accounts into dollars would involve current exchange rates and thus their dollar value would decrease (increase) with a devaluation (revaluation) of the foreign currency. For the longer-term assets and equity (inventory, fixed assets, long-term debt, and equity), there is agreement that these should be translated at historic rates because they are carried at historical costs. Hence, the actual translation loss will be somewhere between 0 (everything at the historic rate) and \$14 (everything at current rate), with the actual amount depending on the mix of the asset and liability accounts.

This state of affairs has been resolved, at least for the present, by *FASB 52*, which requires financial statements to provide information that is generally compatible with the expected economic effects of an exchange rate change on the company's cash flows and equity. It also endeavors to cause consolidated financial statements to reflect the financial results and relationship of the individual entities as measured in their own currencies, in conformity with generally accepted U.S. accounting principles.

We now turn to a discussion of the long-range implications for firm valuation involving capital budgeting and financing decisions in an international environment.

## 27.7 The International Investment and Financing Decision

A primary justification for the existence of the multinational corporation is based on imperfections in the international product, factor (raw materials), and financial markets. In the product and factor markets, the imperfections arise because it is nearly impossible for the firm to export, license, or sell its intangibles such as patents, managerial skill, engineering ability, and product development experience. Thus, the firm must have a physical presence in the foreign marketplace if it wishes to capitalize on its managerial or technical abilities. In the financial marketplace, it has been well documented by Solnik, Lessard, and others that international portfolio diversification can significantly reduce the riskiness of portfolio returns. If capital markets are segmented or if investors are unable to take advantage of gains from international diversification for some other reason, then the multinational firm may be able to provide this benefit. *Segmented capital markets* refers to government intervention in domestic financial markets to restrain the growth of loanable funds, to make certain types of borrowing more or less expensive, or to devote funds to certain sectors of the economy. In addition, local borrowers may receive a preferred rate compared to foreign borrowers.

In an article entitled "The Effects of International Operations on the Market Value of the Firm: Theory and Evidence," Errunza and Senbet use the Modgliani and Miller valuation framework to show that the existence of imperfections in the product and factor markets *per se* is not sufficient to justify direct foreign investment. However, these imperfections must give the multinational firm a systematic advantage over domestic corporations to be a valid reason for international investment. However, these imperfections must give the multinational firm a systematic advantage over domestic corporations to be a valid reason for international investment. Errunza and Senbet argue that two similar firms with different degrees of international involvement will differ in their current market valuation only if the market values international investment. For example, firm M, the multinational firm, and firm D, the domestic firm, are identical except that firm M plans to invest abroad. The value of these firms is

$$V_M = V_D + V_I = V_D + \int_0^{\infty} P(s)Z(s)[V_I(s) - I]d_s \tag{27.1}$$

where $V_D$ = the market value of the domestic firm and the current market value of firm M's assets; $V_I$ = the value of an option for future foreign direct investment; $P(s)$ = the current price of a dollar delivered in the next period if a particular state of the world $(s)$, occurs; $Z(s)$ = the decision variable where $Z(s) = 1$ means to proceed with the investment if $V_1(s) \geq I$, or not to invest if $Z(s) = 0$; $V_I(s)$ = the present value of a foreign investment's cash flows if a particular state $(s)$ occurs; $I$ = the amount of foreign investment; and $V_I(s)$–$I$ = the net present value of the foreign investment.

For $V_I$ to be positive, the NPV of the foreign investment must be positive, which implies a foreign direct investment that is expected to yield a return in excess of the opportunity cost of capital. The value of $V_I$ is 0 if all the product and factor markets are perfectly competitive. If there are barriers to entry or nonmarketable managerial skills, then the multinational firm will be able to enhance its value by accepting foreign projects with a positive NPV.

The argument can also be applied to financial markets. If the multinational firm can take advantage of opportunities not available to the individual investor, then the diversification effect of risk reduction will increase the multinational's value. On the other hand, if investors can achieve the gain of risk reduction by themselves, there is no reason for the multinational firm to provide the same service.

Therefore, we can justify the existence of the multinational organization if the product, factor, and capital markets are not perfectly competitive. This directs management to emphasize or use their managerial skills, product differentiation, or competitive pricing to the multinational's advantage in the international product markets. In the factor markets, multinationals should emphasize patents, technology, production efficiencies, managerial skills, and economies of scale. Government regulation, taxes, and capital market segmentation also offer profitable opportunities for multinationals. Exploitation of these opportunities will allow the multinational to increase its value.

Errunza and Senbet point out that taxes can affect both real and financial decisions. Given two identical firms, one domestic and one binational, if the binational firms is levered by borrowing both domestically and internationally, the binational firm's value can be shown to equal the domestic firm's value plus the real tax effect of foreign investment plus the financial tax effect of the government subsidy of debt financing. This relationship is shown in Eq. (27.2) in a Modigliani and Miller tax-adjusted domestic firm valuation framework.

$$V_{B,L} = V_U + \alpha_F V_U \left( \frac{\tau_D - \tau_F}{1 - \tau_D} \right) + \tau_D B + \theta_F B(\tau_F - \tau_D) \qquad (27.2)$$

where $V_{B,L}$ = the value of the levered binational firm; $\tau_D$ and $\tau_F$ = the proportional domestic and foreign corporate taxes, respectively; $B$ = the market value of debt; $V_U + \tau_D B$ = the value of the levered domestic firm; $\alpha_F$ = the fraction of income attributable to foreign investment; and $\theta_F B$ = the value of foreign borrowing.

Errunza and Senbet derive the model under differential taxes, differential interest rates, and foreign exchange risks. The term $\alpha_F V_U(\frac{\tau_D - \tau_F}{1-\tau_D})$ represents the after-tax effect of foreign investment on the firm's value, assuming the foreign income is subject either to foreign taxes only or to domestic taxes only, with full credit for foreign taxes. The term $\theta_F B(\tau_F - \tau_D)$ represents the foreign government tax subsidy for debt financing. If the domestic tax rates equal the international tax rates ($\tau_F = \tau_D$), then both terms are unnecessary. If $\tau_D > \tau_F$, then the second term increases in value as $\alpha_F$ increases and the last term decreases in value as $\theta_F$ increases. For $\tau_D < \tau_F$, the opposite is true. Hence, the firm should try to balance the amount of income it generates in high-tax countries with the amount of subsidized borrowing in order to maximize the sum of these two terms.

## 27.8 Political Risk and Exchange Rate Risk Dimension

Attendant with the decision to spend or invest internationally is the increase in political risk that such activity entails. These risks take many forms, including currency controls, taxation, and government expropriation of assets. Each of these governmental actions interferes with the firm's business activity. The manager must have knowledge of the foreign government's regulations and must consider future governmental actions in order to make sound valuation and investment decisions.

To incorporate political risk into financial decision-making, we can consider political risk to be an additional element of uncertainty. As discussed in previous chapters, the financial decision-maker can handle uncertainty by adjusting the discount rate or the cash flows in the valuation models. The type of business or investment that the firm is contemplating greatly influences the degree of political risk that the firm will encounter. Projects that are labor-intensive and contribute to the growth of the country's economy may receive more favorable treatment than extractive projects that are detrimental to the country's environment.

The point is that political risk will have different meaning, importance, and interpretation for each firm and each investment project and hence must be handled on a case-by-case basis. However, for most projects, there are three phases involved in managing political risk:

1. Planning for political risk before the foreign investment is made
2. Managing the political risk during the life cycle of the foreign investment
3. Divestiture, expropriation, or nationalization of the foreign investment

Investments outside one's borders are exposed to exchange rate risk and political risk. The result of this exposure is that dollar returns may be higher or lower than the foreign country's local currency returns, depending upon exchange rate fluctuations or political decisions to block/unblock currencies.

In general, a stronger dollar lowers the overseas investment returns to a U.S. investor. For example, suppose the spot exchange rate today is $1 = ¥100. We convert $1 million into ¥100 million and invest it in the Japanese stock market. Over the course of a year, let's assume our investment gains 10% in terms of the yen, so our Japanese investment is worth ¥110 million. But if the U.S. dollar strengthens so that now one-dollar purchases 105 yen, the value of our ¥110 million converts to (¥110 million/ ¥105/$) or $1,047,619 — a U.S. dollar return of only 4.76%. If the dollar had strengthened even further to, say, ¥115 to the dollar, our 10% local currency gain would convert to (¥110 million/¥115/$) or $956,521.74 — a *loss* of over 4.3% in U.S. dollar terms. A stronger dollar can obliterate positive local currency returns. This can happen in both financial market and real asset investments, such as those in overseas subsidiaries.

What helps to increase overseas investment returns in U.S. dollar terms above their local currency returns in a *weaker* dollar. In the above example, if the dollar had weakened to ¥90/$, our ¥110 million would convert to $1,222,222.22. The local currency return of 10% would have resulted in a U.S. dollar gain of over 22%.

## 27.9 Currency Option Valuation Model

Based on the Black and Scholes (1973) assumptions discussed in Chapters 22 and 23, a closed-form equation for the price of a foreign currency call option can be defined as

$$c = e^{-r_f t}[SN(d_1) - Xe^{r_d t}N(d_2)] \tag{27.3}$$

where

$$d_1 = \frac{ln\left(\frac{S}{X}\right) + \left(r_d - r_f + \frac{\sigma^2}{2}\right)t}{\sigma\sqrt{t}}$$

and $d_2 = d_1 - \sigma\sqrt{t}$; $r_d$ = the instantaneous domestic risk-free rate; $r_f$ = the instantaneous foreign risk-free rate; $\sigma$ = the instantaneous standard deviation of the spot rate; $t$ = the time to expiration; $X$ = the exercise price; and $S$ = the exchange rate (domestic/foreign). Equation (27.3) is in terms of the current spot rate. The value of the call option can also be written as a function of the forward rate on the futures exchange rate. Based on the interest rate parity theorem, the forward rate can be written as

$$F = Se^{(r_d - r_f)t} \tag{27.4}$$

Substituting this relationship into the pricing equation for the call option, we derive the option premium on a foreign currency based on the forward rate:

$$C = e^{-r_d t}[FD(d_3) - XN(d_4)] \tag{27.5}$$

where

$$d_3 = \frac{ln\left(\frac{F}{X}\right) + \left(\frac{\sigma^2}{2}\right)t}{\sigma\sqrt{t}}$$

and $d_4 = d_3 - \sigma\sqrt{t}$.

A European-type option on either the spot exchange rate or the forward exchange rate should have the same value if interest-rate parity holds. For example, assume the three-month sterling is selling at a forward rate of \$1.90 to the pound. Also assume the current U.S. T-bill rate is 12%, the standard deviation of the sterling is 0.12565, and the exercise price of a call option is \$1.92 to the pound. Thus, our variables are defined as $F = \$1.90/£$, $X = \$1.92/£$, $\sigma = 0.12565$, $t = 0.25$, and $r = 0.12$. To calculate the value of the call option, we first find $d_3$ and $d_4$ using the above information as follows:

$$d_3 = \frac{\ln\left(\frac{1.90}{1.92}\right) + \left(\frac{0.12565^2}{2}\right)0.25}{0.12565\sqrt{0.25}} = -0.13526$$

$$d_4 = -0.13526 - 0.12565\sqrt{0.25} = -0.19809.$$

Using the standard normal distribution table in the back of this book, we calculate $N(d_3)$ and $N(d_4)$ as

$$N(d_3) = N(-0.13526) = 0.4404$$
$$N(d_4) = N(-0.19809) = 0.4207$$

Therefore,

$$C = e^{-0.12(0.25)}[(\$1.90/£)(0.4404) - (\$1.92/£)(0.4207)] = \$.0282$$

Thus, a three-month call option with an exercise price of \$1.92/£ would be priced at about \$0.03/£ when the forward premium (\$1.92/£–\$1.90/£ ) is \$0.02/£.

## 27.10 Summary

The financial management decisions of a multinational firm involve a thorough understanding of both the domestic decision-making process and the international financial marketplace as well as the additional dimension of foreign political risk. With this understanding and an appreciation of the political environment and the additional risks involved, the financial manager of a multinational firm can make valuation, financing, and investment decisions, although somewhat more complex, by applying basic modern financial theory. Chapter 27 introduces the more complex multinational environment into the financial decision-making process and shows how the basic techniques and theories of financial decision-making can be applied.

## References

Black, F. and M. Scholes. "The Pricing of Options and Corporate Liabilities," *Journal of Political Economy*, 81 (1973, pp. 637–659).

Chang, R. P., Koveos, P. E., and S. G. Rhae. "Financial Planning for International Long-term Debt Financing," *Advances in Financial Planning and Forecasting,* 6 (JAI Press, 1990).

Chrystal, K. A. *A Guide to Foreign Exchange Market* (Federal Revenue Bank of St. Louis, March 1984).

Dufey, G. and I. Giddy. *The International Money Market,* 2nd edn. (Pearson, 1994).

Eiteman, D. K., Stonehill, A. I., and M. H. Stonehill. *Multinational Business Finance*, 15th edn. (Pearson, 2019).

Errunza, V. and L. Senbet. "The Effect of International Operations on the Market Value of the Firm: Theory and Evidence," *The Journal of Finance*, 36 (May 1981, pp. 401–417).

Errunza, V. and L. Senbet. "International Corporate Diversification, Market Valuations, and Size-adjusted Evidence," *The Journal of Finance*, 39 (July 1984, pp. 727–743).

Eun, C. and B. Resnick. *International Financial Management,* 8th edn. (McGraw-Hill, 2018).

Lee, C. F., Chiou, W. J. P., and A. C. Lee. "Stock Return, Risk and Legal Environment around the World," *International Review of Economics and Finance*, 19 (2010, pp. 95–105).

Lee, C. F., Chiou, W. J. P. and A. C. Lee. "Variation in Stock Return Risks: An International Comparison," *Review of Pacific Basin Financial Markets and Policies*, 12 (2009, pp. 245–266).

Solnik, B. and D. McLeavey. *International Investments,* 5th edn. (Pearson, 2004).

Sweeney, R. J. and E. J. Q. Lee. "Trading Strategies in Foreign Exchange Markets," *Advances in Financial Planning and Forecasting,* 6 (JAI Press, 1990).

Van Horne, J. C. "The Two-Tier Setting of International Planning and Research," *Advances in Financial Planning and Forecasting,* 6 (JAI Press, 1990).

## Appendix 27A — The Relationship between Exchange Rates and Interest Rates

Exchange rates react to differences in interest rates, inflation rates, and income growth rates between countries. In addition, central bank intervention and trade barriers also influence exchange rates. Fluctuating exchange rates affect returns from overseas investments. This will be true for the company investing in an overseas subsidiary or an individual wanting to buy securities in a foreign market.

In domestic markets, there are two main sources of return: income, such as bond interest or stock dividends) and capital gains or losses from asset price changes. When investing overseas, there is a third source of risk and return: the risk of converting foreign currency into domestic currency. If exchange rates vary over time, or currency conversion is blocked by the host country, the returns on foreign investments can be substantially affected. Therefore, changes in exchange rates should be considered before investing overseas.

For example, U.S. corporate treasurers want to invest excess cash in low-risk investments that offer the highest returns. In a global market, treasurers can look beyond Treasury bills or high-quality bank CDs. Suppose the French government offers higher interest rates on its short-term debt than the T-bill rate. U.S. corporate treasurers will use their excess cash to buy francs at the spot rate and invest them at the higher French interest rates. To protect their investment returns from the risk of adverse exchange rate changes, U.S. treasurers will enter into forward market agreements. This allows them to lock in the exchange rate at which they can convert francs back into dollars when the debt instruments mature. The U.S. treasurer will generally be indifferent between investing excess funds in the U.S. or in France if the extra interest earned by investing at higher French rates is offset by a foreign exchange market loss caused by the difference between the spot and forward market exchange rates.

When this occurs, we have *interest rate parity*. Under interest rate parity, investors are indifferent between investing at home or abroad as far as expected return is concerned; any existing nominal risk-free interest rate disparity is offset by spot and forward exchange rate differentials. When interest rate parity exists, the following relationship is true.

$$\frac{S_0 \times (1 + R_{FC})}{F_1} = (1 + R_{US}) \qquad (27.1A)$$

The left-hand side of Eq. (27.1A) reflects the return from converting dollars at the spot rate ($S_0$), investing them at the foreign rate ($1 + R_{FC}$), and then converting the currency back into dollars at the forward rate ($F_1$). The right-hand side reflects the return from investing the dollars in the U.S.

For example, assume that the spot exchange rate is FF 5.2870/dollar, the one-year-forward rate is quoted as FF 5.4930/dollar, and the U.S. and French one-year interest rates are 4% and 8%, respectively. For every \$1 invested in the U.S., the return is \$1 $(1 + 0.4)$ or \$1.04.

In this example, there is interest rate parity. The benefits of investing in France (the left-hand side of Eq. (27.1A)) equal the benefits of investing in the U.S. (the right-hand side of Eq. (27.1A)). Both choices lead to a return of \$1.04 for every \$1 invested.

Rearranging Eq. (27.1A), we obtain the equilibrium relationship between nominal risk-free interest rates, spot rates, and forward rates:

$$F_1 = S_0 \frac{(1 + R_{FC})}{(1 + R_{US})} \tag{27.2A}$$

Of course, the nominal risk-free interest rates and forward rate must all refer to the same period of time. The above example used one-year interest rates and a one-year forward rate. Shorter or longer time frames also could be used, as long as all the variables used them consistently.

Some forecasters use Eq. (27.2A) as a means to forecast future exchange rates; that is, they assume the future spot rate will equal the current forward rate.

[1]The adjustment process of funds flowing into or out of the U.S. in order to achieve this equilibrium is called *covered interest arbitrage.* The term "covered" refers to the fact that the difference between the current and possible future exchange rate is "locked in" by entering into a forward contract.

## Questions and Problems

1. Define or explain the following:
   a. Forward rate
   b. Spot rate
   c. Eurodollar
   d. Currency option
   e. International money market
   f. LIBOR

g. FASB 52
h. Transaction exposure
i. Translation exposure

2. You have $1 million to invest for one month. The annual interest rate in the U.S. is 6%. The interest rate in Germany is 10%. The spot exchange rate is $.40/DM and the one-month forward rate is $.3987/DM. Should you invest in Germany or in the U.S.? How much more do you make?
3. What are the advantages and disadvantages of forward and futures contracts? Explain how forward and futures contracts can be used to minimize foreign currency fluctuations and how a future option contract can be used to reduce exposure to foreign currency fluctuations.
4. When would the financial manager use a foreign currency futures contract as opposed to a foreign currency option contract?
5. Explain the effect on exchange rate variability in terms of hedging with options, futures, and forward contracts.
6. What elements are necessary for swap transactions to occur?
7. How does interest rate arbitrage link the foreign exchange market to the money market?
8. Compare the purchasing power parity theory with interest rate parity.
9. How do Euromarkets compete with domestic markets?
10 Compare and contrast foreign bonds with Eurobonds. What are the advantages to the financial manager for issuing Eurobonds as opposed to domestic bonds?
11. Explain the basic treatment of *FASB 8* and *FASB 52* on the financial reporting of the firm.
12. Compare and contrast transaction exposure with accounting exposure. Which of these types of foreign currency exposures is the financial manager likely to hedge, and why?
13. What is the significance of political risk on the investing and financing decisions of the multinational firm?
14. Atlas Trucking has entered into a contract to buy ten trucks from a German manufacturer. The contract requires that in two months Atlas must pay 600,000 DM and take delivery of the trucks. The company's forecasts for the future spot rate range from 3 DM/$ to 1 DM/$.

a. The 2-month forward rate is 2 DM/$.

   i. If the company hedges this transaction by buying a forward contract, how much will Atlas pay for the trucks in dollars?
   ii. If the company does not hedge this transaction, determine the minimum and maximum prices in dollars that Atlas can expect to pay.
   iii. Is hedging the most profitable approach? Explain.

b. Assume that a call option to buy DMs in the spot market currently costs $300 for a single contract size of 62,500 DM. The strike price of an option is $.40/DM.

   i. If the spot price is 3 DM/$ in two months, will the option be exercised? Explain.
   ii. If the spot price is 2.5 DM/$ in two months, will the option be exercised? Explain.
   iii. If the spot price is 1 DM/$ in two months, will the option be exercised?
   iv. What is the advantage of using options relative to (a) using the forward contracts or (b) operating in the spot market?

15. Consider the following information:

    Spot rate: DM/$=3.000
    Forward rate: DM/$= 2.950
    German interest rate = 10%
    U.S. interest rate = 13%

    Explain the covered interest arbitrage that will take place under these circumstances.
16. Interest rates in the U.S. are 10% and the U.S. inflation rate is 4%. In contrast, interest rates in France are 14%.

    Explain whether or not purchasing power parity holds in each of the following cases. In those where it does not hold, state to which country capital would flow.

    a. Inflation in France is 8%.
    b. Inflation in France is 10%.
    c. Inflation in France is 4%.

17. The value of an unlevered binational firm is $2 million and 20% of the company's income is from foreign investments. The domestic

tax rate is 40%. A company that is identical in all respects to the unlevered one except that it is levered, using $250,000 of foreign debt financing (borrowing) and $750,000 of domestic debt financing.

a. If the foreign tax rate is 30%, what is the value of the levered firm?
b. If the foreign tax rate is 40%, what is the value of the levered firm?
c. If the foreign tax rate is 50%, what is the value of the levered firm?
d. Explain the differences in the value of the firm based on varying tax rates.

18. Consider the following information:

Spot rate: Pounds Sterling/$ = 1,4500
Forward rate: Pounds Sterling/$ = 1.4800
English interest rate = 12%
U.S. interest rate = 10%

Explain the covered interest arbitrage that will take place under these circumstances.

19. **Foreign Investment**. (1990 CFA Level II exam) FI is a wholly owned foreign subsidiary of USDS; it is located in the country of Lumbaria. The local currency of Lumbaria is the pont. You are the Treasurer of USDS. One USDS board member has suggested that most of FI's cash be invested in one-year U.S. Treasury bills to reduce exposure to the pont.

On January 1, 1990, the yield on one-year U.S. Treasury bills was 7.1%, while the comparable yield on one-year Lumbaria Treasury bills was 14.6%; the exchange rate was 4 ponts per one U.S. dollar. FI's cash position was such that 60-million ponts could be invested for one year without concern that this money would be required for operations.

Assume that your economist's exchange rate forecast of a 5% decline in the value of the pont (vs. the U.S. dollar) by year-end 1990 proves to be correct. Calculate the proceeds to maturity, in U.S. dollars, of a 60-million pont investment in U.S. Treasury bills versus the same investment in Lumbarian Treasury bills.

**20. Foreign Investment.** Given the information below, compute the percentage change in the spot exchange rate during 1995.

| | Percent Returns in Terms of: | |
|---|---|---|
| **Country** | **Local Currency(%)** | **U.S. Dollar(%)** |
| Venezuela | +25.84 | +25.73 |
| Ireland | +14.17 | +19.61 |
| Denmark | +2.52 | +14.13 |
| Portugal | −11.82 | −5.45 |
| Philippines | −11.67 | −17.14 |

**21. Foreign Investment.** Given the information below, compute the U.S. dollar percentage return.

| | Percentage Returns | Percentage Change |
|---|---|---|
| **Country** | **Local Currency (%)** | **In the Spot Rate(%)** |
| Yelstinia | +10.5 | −18.6 |
| Thatcherland | +5.1 | +12.3 |
| Georgemark | −12.52 | +14.3 |
| Canalistan | −12.8 | −4.5 |

**22. Foreign Investment.** With the following sets of expectations, what U.S. interest rate is needed on a similar maturity instrument in order to convince overseas investors to invest in the U.S. security?

| | Home Country Interest Rate (%) | Expected Spot Rate Change (%) |
|---|---|---|
| (a) | 8 | 5 |
| (b) | 12 | −3 |
| (c) | 2 | −7 |
| (d) | 15 | 6 |

# Appendix A: Projects

## Project 1: Financial Analysis: XYZ Company versus Johnson and Johnson

Use Johnson & Johnson's and XYZ Company's 2020 annual report and stock price year-end data from Yahoo Finance to complete the following project.

A. Introduction:
The main purpose of this project is to perform financial analysis for both XYZ Company and Johnson and Johnson. In Section B calculate 26 financial ratios, DOL, DFL, and DCL for your company and perform a brief analysis. Next, in Section C calculate the 26 financial ratios, DOL, DFL, and DCL for J&J. In Section D, compare the data from Section B and C by incorporating 2 tables. Table One is composed of the 26 ratios for XYZ Company and J&J using the two years of data. Table Two has DOL, DFL, and DCL for XYZ Company and J&J. Finally, Section E, is the summary.

B. Financial analysis for XYZ Company

B1. Briefly describe company

B2. 26 Financial Ratios for XYZ Company

B3. DOL, DFL, and DCL for XYZ Company

C. Financial analysis for J&J

C1. Briefly describe J&J

C2. 26 Financial Ratios for J&J

C3. DOL, DFL, and DCL for J&J

D. Financial Analysis: XYZ Company versus J&J

D1. 26 Financial Ratios: XYZ Company versus J&J

D2. DOL, DFL, and DCL: XYZ Company versus J&J

E. Summary and Concluding Remarks

## Project 2: Valuation of Bond and Common Stock for Johnson & Johnson Inc.

1. Use Johnson & Johnson's 2020 annual report to discuss how much external sources of fund are from common stock and bond.
2. Use bond valuation model, which was discussed in Chapter 5, to determine the theoretical value of the bond.
3. Use the stock valuation model, which was discussed in Chapter 5, to evaluate stock price per share.
4. Use the summary statistic, which was presented in Johnson & Johnson's 2020 annual report, to discuss the change of P/E ratio over time.

## Project 3: Portfolio Analysis, CML, SML, and Cost of Capital: XYZ Company versus Johnson & Johnson Inc.

Use Johnson & Johnson's, one other manufacturer company's and S&P 500's monthly rate of return from 2015 to 2020 to complete this project. All these monthly rates of return can be found in Yahoo Finance.

A. Introduction

The main purpose of this project to perform portfolio analysis to estimate CML, SML, and cost of capital for XYZ Company and Johnson & Johnson. Section B is to perform portfolio analysis in terms of monthly rates of return of J&J, XYZ Company, and market rate of return. Section C is to estimate leveraged beta and cost of equity capital for J&J and XYZ Company. Section D is to estimate Sharpe, Treynor, and Jensen performance measures for J&J, XYZ Company, and S&P 500. Section E summarizes the results.

B. Portfolio Analysis of JNJ, XYZ Company, and market rate of return

1. Mean, variance, skewness, and kurtosis
2. 3 by 3 variance covariance metrics
3. Two alternative optimal portfolios in terms of two securities using the methods below.

a. Calculate optimal portfolio in terms of minimum-variance approach
b. Calculate optimal portfolio in terms of maximizing the Sharpe performance measure

C. CML, SML, Cost of Capital

C1. Beta estimation and classifications

a. Leveraged beta versus unlevered beta

$$\beta_L = \beta_U \left(1 + \frac{B(1 - \tau_c)}{S}\right)$$

b. Adjusted beta versus unadjusted beta

C2. Calculate the cost of capital for both JNJ and XYZ Company

a. DCF approach
b. CAPM approach
c. Chase Cost of Capital

i. Unleveraged Cost of Equity
ii. The Firm's Cost of Total Capital

D. Sharpe, Treynor, and Jensen Performance Measures
Calculate 3 alternative performance measures for XYZ Company and JNJ, then compare the performance among XYZ Company, JNJ, and the market portfolio.

E. Summary and Concluding Remarks

## Project 4: Cost of Capital, Capital Structure, and Dividend Policy for Johnson & Johnson Inc.

1. Use Johnson & Johnson's financial statement analysis, which we obtained in Project I, to discuss the financing policy and dividend policy for Johnson & Johnson.

2. Use the beta coefficient estimate, which we obtained in Project III, to discuss how this information can be used to perform capital budgeting decision for Johnson & Johnson.
3. Use the 2020 cash flow statement of Johnson & Johnson to discuss investment policy, financing policy, dividend policy, and production policy for Johnson & Johnson.
4. Use Johnson & Johnson's summary statistic, which is presented in Johnson & Johnson's 2020 annual report, to forecast EPS, payout ratio, and other related financial information.

## Project 5: Short-term Financial Management for Johnson & Johnson Inc.

Using Johnson & Johnson's 2020 annual report, which can be obtained from Yahoo Finance, answer the following questions:

1. Discuss the situation of Johnson & Johnson's liquidity and capital resources.
2. Use Johnson & Johnson's consolidated statement of cash flows to analyze the change of cash and cash equivalents during 2018 to 2020.
3. Discuss Johnson & Johnson's trade credit risk.
4. Discuss how the fair value of Johnson & Johnson's securities has been evaluated.
5. Discuss Johnson & Johnson's borrowing strategy.
6. What are Johnson & Johnson's inventories comprised of? How is the value of inventories determined?

## Project 6: Alternative Policies Analysis and Share Price Forecasting: XYZ Company as a Case Study

Use XYZ company's 2021 annual report to complete the following project.

A. Introduction

The main purpose of this paper is to use XYZ Company as a case study to analyze alternative policies. In Section B, we use the cash flow statement of XYZ Company to analyze alternative policies.

In Section C discuss Warren and Shelton model in terms of four different sections, especially we will discuss the 20 unknowns and 21 parameters. In Section D, we calculate 21 input parameters. In Section E, we perform the calculation of this equation system in terms of both manual approach and Excel approach. For the manual approach we use data from 2020 to forecast 2021. For the Excel approach we will forecast 2021, 2022, and 2023. In Section F, we will perform sensitivity analysis by changing growth rate, debt equity ratio, and P/E ratio.

B. Investment, Financing, Dividend, and Production Policy for XYZ Company

In this section students should use the information from the cash flow statement which contains information about all four policies. In addition, students should use these policies which have been learned in the class.

C. Warren and Shelton Model

Warren and Shelton Model is a 20-equation model with 20 unknowns and 21 parameters to be input into the model. This model includes the following four sections:

1. Generating of Sales and Earnings Before Interest and Taxes for Period $t$
2. Generating of Total Assets Required for Period $t$
3. Financing the Desired Level of Assets
4. Generation of Per Share Data for Period $t$

D. Calculate 21 Input Parameters (Definitions of these variables can be found in Chapter 21 of the textbook.)

It should be noted that most of the parameters have already been calculated in the first project. In addition, for students to calculate these parameters, they should extensively search for information from the four financial statements.

E. Perform the calculation of 20 Unknown Variables

1. Manual approach.
2. Excel approach.

F. Sensitivity Analysis of Forecasting Stock Price Per Share and Important Financial Statement Items.

In this section you should change growth rate, debt–equity ratio, and P/E ratio.

G. Summary and Concluding Remarks

References

## Project 7: Acquisitions, Divestitures, and Risk Management for Johnson & Johnson Inc.

1. Use the 2020 annual report, which can be obtained from Yahoo Finance, to discuss Johnson & Johnson's acquisitions and divestitures activities.
2. Use the 2020 annual report to discuss Johnson & Johnson's international sales and operations and their related foreign exchange and interest rate risk.
3. Use the 2020 annual report to discuss how Johnson & Johnson hedges its interest rate and currency risk.
4. How does Johnson & Johnson report its hedging activities and its derivatives positions?

From my teaching experience, I found that assigning Projects 1, 3, and 6 to students is sufficient to help them have an active learning experience. The other four projects can be treated as large homework assignments.

# Appendix B

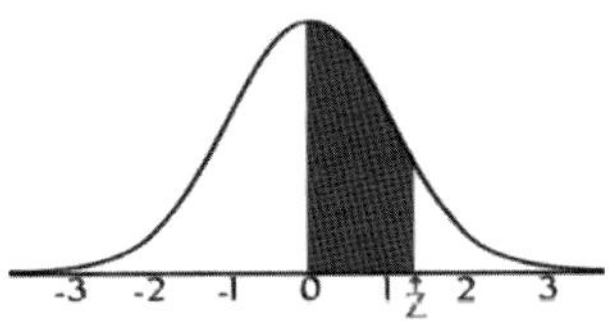


## STANDARD NORMAL TABLE (Z)

Entries in the table give the area under the curve between the mean and $z$ standard deviations above the mean. For example, for $z = 1.25$ the area under the curve between the mean (0) and $z$ is 0.3944.

| z | 0.00 | 0.01 | 0.02 | 0.03 | 0.04 | 0.05 | 0.06 | 0.07 | 0.08 | 0.09 |
|---|---|---|---|---|---|---|---|---|---|---|
| **0.0** | 0.0000 | 0.0040 | 0.0080 | 0.0120 | 0.0160 | 0.0190 | 0.0239 | 0.0279 | 0.0319 | 0.0359 |
| **0.1** | 0.0398 | 0.0438 | 0.0478 | 0.0517 | 0.0557 | 0.0596 | 0.0636 | 0.0675 | 0.0714 | 0.0753 |
| **0.2** | 0.0793 | 0.0832 | 0.0871 | 0.0910 | 0.0948 | 0.0987 | 0.1026 | 0.1064 | 0.1103 | 0.1141 |
| **0.3** | 0.1179 | 0.1217 | 0.1255 | 0.1293 | 0.1331 | 0.1368 | 0.1406 | 0.1443 | 0.1480 | 0.1517 |
| **0.4** | 0.1554 | 0.1591 | 0.1628 | 0.1664 | 0.1700 | 0.1736 | 0.1772 | 0.1808 | 0.1844 | 0.1879 |
| **0.5** | 0.1915 | 0.1950 | 0.1985 | 0.2019 | 0.2054 | 0.2088 | 0.2123 | 0.2157 | 0.2190 | 0.2224 |
| **0.6** | 0.2257 | 0.2291 | 0.2324 | 0.2357 | 0.2389 | 0.2422 | 0.2454 | 0.2486 | 0.2517 | 0.2549 |
| **0.7** | 0.2580 | 0.2611 | 0.2642 | 0.2673 | 0.2704 | 0.2734 | 0.2764 | 0.2794 | 0.2823 | 0.2852 |
| **0.8** | 0.2881 | 0.2910 | 0.2939 | 0.2969 | 0.2995 | 0.3023 | 0.3051 | 0.3078 | 0.3106 | 0.3133 |
| **0.9** | 0.3159 | 0.3186 | 0.3212 | 0.3238 | 0.3264 | 0.3289 | 0.3315 | 0.3340 | 0.3365 | 0.3389 |
| **1.0** | 0.3413 | 0.3438 | 0.3461 | 0.3485 | 0.3508 | 0.3513 | 0.3554 | 0.3577 | 0.3529 | 0.3621 |
| **1.1** | 0.3643 | 0.3665 | 0.3686 | 0.3708 | 0.3729 | 0.3749 | 0.3770 | 0.3790 | 0.3810 | 0.3830 |
| **1.2** | 0.3849 | 0.3869 | 0.3888 | 0.3907 | 0.3925 | 0.3944 | 0.3962 | 0.3980 | 0.3997 | 0.4015 |
| **1.3** | 0.4032 | 0.4049 | 0.4066 | 0.4082 | 0.4099 | 0.4115 | 0.4131 | 0.4147 | 0.4162 | 0.4177 |
| **1.4** | 0.4192 | 0.4207 | 0.4222 | 0.4236 | 0.4251 | 0.4265 | 0.4279 | 0.4292 | 0.4306 | 0.4319 |
| **1.5** | 0.4332 | 0.4345 | 0.4357 | 0.4370 | 0.4382 | 0.4394 | 0.4406 | 0.4418 | 0.4429 | 0.4441 |
| **1.6** | 0.4452 | 0.4463 | 0.4474 | 0.4484 | 0.4495 | 0.4505 | 0.4515 | 0.4525 | 0.4535 | 0.4545 |
| **1.7** | 0.4554 | 0.4564 | 0.4573 | 0.4582 | 0.4591 | 0.4599 | 0.4608 | 0.4616 | 0.4625 | 0.4633 |
| **1.8** | 0.4641 | 0.4649 | 0.4656 | 0.4664 | 0.4671 | 0.4678 | 0.4686 | 0.4693 | 0.4699 | 0.4706 |
| **1.9** | 0.4713 | 0.4719 | 0.4726 | 0.4732 | 0.4738 | 0.4744 | 0.4750 | 0.4756 | 0.4761 | 0.4767 |
| **2.0** | 0.4772 | 0.4778 | 0.4783 | 0.4788 | 0.4793 | 0.4798 | 0.4803 | 0.4808 | 0.4812 | 0.4817 |
| **2.1** | 0.4821 | 0.4826 | 0.4830 | 0.4834 | 0.4838 | 0.4842 | 0.4846 | 0.4850 | 0.4854 | 0.4857 |
| **2.2** | 0.4861 | 0.4864 | 0.4868 | 0.4871 | 0.4875 | 0.4878 | 0.4881 | 0.4884 | 0.4887 | 0.4890 |
| **2.3** | 0.4893 | 0.4896 | 0.4898 | 0.4901 | 0.4904 | 0.4906 | 0.4909 | 0.4911 | 0.4913 | 0.4916 |
| **2.4** | 0.4918 | 0.4920 | 0.4922 | 0.4925 | 0.4927 | 0.4929 | 0.4931 | 0.4932 | 0.4934 | 0.4936 |
| **2.5** | 0.4938 | 0.4940 | 0.4941 | 0.4943 | 0.4945 | 0.4946 | 0.4948 | 0.4949 | 0.4951 | 0.4952 |
| **2.6** | 0.4953 | 0.4955 | 0.4956 | 0.4957 | 0.4959 | 0.4960 | 0.4961 | 0.4962 | 0.4963 | 0.4964 |
| **2.7** | 0.4965 | 0.4966 | 0.4967 | 0.4968 | 0.4969 | 0.4970 | 0.4971 | 0.4972 | 0.4973 | 0.4974 |
| **2.8** | 0.4974 | 0.4975 | 0.4976 | 0.4977 | 0.4977 | 0.4978 | 0.4979 | 0.4979 | 0.4980 | 0.4981 |
| **2.9** | 0.4981 | 0.4982 | 0.4982 | 0.4983 | 0.4984 | 0.4984 | 0.4985 | 0.4985 | 0.4986 | 0.4986 |
| **3.0** | 0.4987 | 0.4987 | 0.4987 | 0.4988 | 0.4988 | 0.4989 | 0.4989 | 0.4989 | 0.4990 | 0.4990 |
| **3.1** | 0.4990 | 0.4991 | 0.4991 | 0.4991 | 0.4992 | 0.4992 | 0.4992 | 0.4992 | 0.4993 | 0.4993 |
| **3.2** | 0.4993 | 0.4993 | 0.4994 | 0.4994 | 0.4994 | 0.4994 | 0.4994 | 0.4995 | 0.4995 | 0.4995 |
| **3.3** | 0.4995 | 0.4995 | 0.4995 | 0.4996 | 0.4996 | 0.4996 | 0.4996 | 0.4996 | 0.4996 | 0.4997 |
| **3.4** | 0.4997 | 0.4997 | 0.4997 | 0.4997 | 0.4997 | 0.4997 | 0.4997 | 0.4997 | 0.4997 | 0.4998 |

# Appendix C: Some Useful Formulas

1. Present Values (Chapter 4)
   The discounted value of $N$ future cash flows.

$$PV = \frac{C_1}{1+r} + \frac{C_2}{(1+r)^2} + \cdots + \frac{C_N}{(1+r)^N}$$
$$= \sum_{t=1}^{N} \frac{C_t}{(1+r)^t}$$

2. Net Present Values (Chapter 4)
   Present value minus initial costs

$$\text{NPV} = \text{PV} - \text{Cost}$$
$$C_0 = -\text{Cost}$$
$$\text{NPV} = -C_0 + \sum\nolimits_{t=1}^{N} \frac{C_t}{(1+r)^t}$$

3. Perpetuity (Chapter 4)
   The value of $C$ received each year, forever.

$$\text{PV} = \frac{C}{r}$$

4. Annuity (Chapter 4)
   The value of $C$ received each year for $N$ years

$$\text{PV} = C\left[\frac{1 - \frac{1}{(1+r)^N}}{r}\right]$$

5. Growing Perpetuity (Chapter 5)
The value of a perpetuity that grows at rate $g$, where the first payment is C

$$P_0 = \frac{d_1}{(k-g)}$$

6. Growing Annuity (Chapter 5)
The value of a $N$-period annuity that grows at the rate $g$, where the first payment is C

$$\text{PV} = C\left[\frac{1}{r-g} - \frac{1}{r-g}X\left(\frac{1+g}{1+r}\right)^N\right]$$

7. Expected Return on a Portfolio of n Assets (Chapter 7)

$$\overline{R}_p = \sum_{i=1}^{n} W_i\overline{R}_i \quad \text{where} \quad \left(\sum_{i=1}^{n} W_i = 1\right)$$

8. Variance of a Portfolio of Two Assets (Chapter 7)

$$\begin{aligned}\sigma_P^2 &= \text{VAR}(W_1R_{1t} + W_2R_{2t})\\ &= \frac{1}{N}\sum_{t=1}^{N}[(W_1R_{1t} + W_2R_{2t}) - (W_1\overline{R}_1 + W_2\overline{R}_2)]^2\\ &= W_1^2\sigma_1^2 + W_2^2\sigma_2^2 + 2W_1W_2\text{COV}(R_1, R_2)\end{aligned}$$

$$\sigma_P = \sqrt{\frac{1}{N}\sum_{t=1}^{N}(R_{pt} - \overline{R}_P)^2}$$

9. Beta of a Security (Chapter 8)

$$\beta_i = \frac{\text{COV}(R_i, R_m)}{\text{VAR}(R_m)} = \frac{\rho_{i,m}\sigma_i\sigma_m}{\sigma_m^2} = \frac{\rho_{i,m}\sigma_i}{\sigma_m}$$

10. Capital Market Line (Chapter 8)

$$E(R_p) = R_f + [E(R_m) - R_f]\frac{\sigma_p}{\sigma_m}$$

11. Capital Asset Pricing Model (Chapter 8)

$$E(R_i) = R_f + \beta_i[E(R_m) - R_f]$$

12. $k$-Factor Model (Chapter 8)

$$E(R_{it}) = a + b_{j1}(factor\,1) + b_{j2}(factor\,2) + \cdots + b_{jk}(factor\,k)$$

13. Levered Beta versus Unlevered Beta (Chapter 10)

$$\beta_L = \beta_U[1 + \frac{B}{S}(1 - \tau_c)]$$

14. Value of the Firm under Corporate taxes (Chapter 11)

$$V_L = V_U + \tau_c B$$

15. Weighted Average Cost of Capital (Chapter 10)

$$\text{WACC} = \sum_{i=1}^{m} W_i K_i$$

where $i$ = the $i$th capital component (convertible debt, regular debt, new preferred stock, new common stock, retained earnings, etc.) and $m$ = the total number of capital components included.

16. Black–Scholes Model (Chapter 22)

$$V_c = PN(d_1) - X_e^{-rt} N(d_2)$$

where $d_1 = \frac{[\ln(P/X)+(r+01.5\sigma^5)t]}{\sigma\sqrt{5}}$; $d_2 = d_1 - \sqrt{t}$; $r$ = risk-free interest rate; $t$ = time until the option expires (in years).

17. Hedge Ratio (Chapter 24)

$$\text{Hedge ratio} = \frac{\text{Number of contracts} \times \text{Face value of contracts}}{\text{Face value of portfolio}}$$

# Appendix D: Solutions to Select End-of-Chapter Problems

**Chapter 2**

| | | | |
|---|---|---|---|
| 2.4 | a. 25,000 | b. 5,000 | |
| 2.5 | 4,000 | | |
| 2.7 | a. 667 | b. 360 | |
| 2.8 | a. 1.33 | b. 125,000 | |
| 2.13 | a. 14.2% | b. 18.9% | c. 23.6% |

**Chapter 4**

| | | |
|---|---|---|
| 4.4 | 869.57 | |
| 4.5 | b. 124.96 | |
| 4.6 | a. $4,422.14 | b. $6,856.62 |
| 4.9 | a. 67.59 | b. $175.41 |
| 4.10 | 20.11 | |
| 4.12 | a. 1,500 | b. $941.45 |
| 4.13 | $552.56 | |
| 4.14 | $1,000 | |

### Chapter 5

| | | | |
|---|---|---|---|
| 5.31 | a. $1,059.73 | b. $1,000.00 | c. 962.09 |
| 5.32 | a. 100 | b. 12% | |
| 5.33 | a. 40% | b. 160 | c. 80 |
| | d. 12% | e. 7.55 | |
| 5.34 | 42 | | |
| 5.35 | a. 749.06 | b. 240 | |
| 5.36 | a. 14.41% | b. $1079.85 | |
| 5.37 | 6.75% | | |
| 5.39 | 5.74 | | |
| 5.40 | $88.89 | | |

### Chapter 6

6.16 a. 55% b. 50% c. 50%

6.17 a. 2 years b. 2 2/3 years c. 5/6 years

6.19. $\gamma_A = 53.63\%$, $\gamma_B = 27.09\%$

6.20 a. 6.22 b.−99,490.4

6.22 −99.490.4

6.25 $5,000

### Chapter 7

| | | | |
|---|---|---|---|
| 7.4 | 0.0492 | | |
| 7.6 | a. 64.1% | b. 0.00283 | c. 0.2686 |
| 7.7 | a.0.126 | b. 0.258 | |
| 7.11 | a. 15.4 | b. 3.904 | |
| 7.12 | 4.88 | | |
| 7.18 | a. 60% | b. 12% | |
| 7.23 | a. 0.7083 | b. 0.725 | |

## Chapter 8

| | | | |
|---|---|---|---|
| 8.4 | a. 6% | b. 18% | c. 14% |
| 8.5 | a. 18% | b. 39.38% | c. 6.5% |
| 8.6 | 10% | | |
| 8.8 | \$94.34 | | |
| 8.12 | a. 0.385 | b. 8.38% | |
| 8.14 | 60.14 | | |

## Chapter 9

| | | | |
|---|---|---|---|
| 9.4 | 11.28 | | |
| 9.5 | a. 17.6% | b. −11.72 | c. 237.26 |
| 9.6 | a. 347.83 | b. 2079.35 | |
| 9.8 | 333.33 | | |
| 9.14 | a. \$307.45 | b. 429.75 | |

## Chapter 10

| | | | |
|---|---|---|---|
| 10.8 | 15% | | |
| 10.9 | a. 10% | b. 5% | c. 0 |
| 10.11 | 9.7% | | |
| 10.12 | a. 4.8% | b. 10.92% | |
| 10.13 | a. 14.13% | b. 14.34% | |
| 10.15 | a. 8.89% | b. 9.36% | |
| 10.16 | a. 15.8% | b. 16.63% | |
| 10.19 | −\$201,440 | | |
| 10.20 | 0.982 | | |
| 10.21 | 0.1209 | | |
| 10.22 | 16.8% | | |
| 10.24 | 15% | | |

## Chapter 11

| | | | |
|---|---|---|---|
| 11.5 | a. 2 | b. 1.5 | c. 3 |
| 11.7 | a. 30,000 | b. 9.5% | c. 11.1% |
| 11.10 | a. 18.9% | b. 189 | c. 23% |
| 11.12 | a. $11,000 | b. $6,500 | |
| 11.13 | $11,500 | | |
| 11.15 | a. 1.333 | b. 1.87 | c. 3.33 |
| 11.17 | $7,143 | | |

## Chapter 12

12.41 $.75

12.42 $80%

12.43 $3.6

12.44 $2.60

12.45 a. 5 million b. $5

12.48 a. $22 b. $52 c. $52.375

## Chapter 13

13.8 2.36%

13.11 9.16%

13.12 a. $33,333 b. 60,000 c. 26,667

13.13 13.6%

## Chapter 14

14.5 a. $1,558,200 b. $1,6527,454 c. $1,338,788

14.6 4,205

14.7 1,6699.793

14.12 4%

14.13 4%

14.14 a. 11.3% b. 11%

**Chapter 15**

15.12 $26.5

15.13 $4.5

15.19 a. $1.33 b. 0.50

15.20 454,545

15.22 a. $6,000 b. 6%

**Chapter 16**

16.3 $4

16.7 $35

16.9 a. $50.78 b. 11%

16.10 $8.65

16.11 a. –$0.85 b. $36

16.12 a. 0 b. $4

**Chapter 17**

17.7 a. 68,930.65 b. 28,449.47
c. 63,746.64

17.9 a. $126,120 b. 138, 367.36
c. –12,247

17.11 $21,716.56

17.12 $21,116.45

17.15 a. 73,271 b. 74,928.60

17.16 a. $50,000.52 b. $14,721.92
c. $48,299.93 d. $1,700.59

## Chapter 18

| | | |
|---|---|---|
| 18.8 | a. 100 days | b. 120 days |
| | c. 100 days | d. 120 days |
| 18.11 | $125,000 | |
| 18.12 | a. $150,000 | b. $37,500 |
| | c. 781.25 | |
| 18.13 | 50 days | |

## Chapter 19

| | | | |
|---|---|---|---|
| 19.4 | 37.23%, | 74.48%, | 18.62% |
| 18.12 | a. $130,133.30 | b. $120,000 | |
| 19.13 | a. 49.6% | b. 24.8% | c. 25.06% |
| | d. 63.7% | | |
| 19.14 | 49% | | |
| 19.16 | a. 150,000 | b. $48,000 | c. $42,000 |

## Chapter 20

| | |
|---|---|
| 20.5 | $288.454 |
| 20.7 | 2,000 |
| 20.8 | $1,000, $500 |
| 20.11 | $200,000, $180,000, $20,000 |
| 20.17 | a. 2,000 units, 50  b. 1,500 units, 67 |

## Chapter 22

| | | | |
|---|---|---|---|
| 22.1 | $20 | | |
| 22.2 | a. 0 | b. 0 | c.30 |
| 22.3 | a. 0 | b. 0 | |

22.4 a. \$1.6 b. \$5

22.5 \$50

22.8 \$35

## Chapter 23

23.1 \$20

23.2 a. 5/7 b. 19.48

23.3 \$5.29

23.4 \$7,226,444

23.9 \$0, \$0, \$30

23.12 a. 50 b. 12 c. 2/5

23.13 0.57

23.14 \$7.72 million

## Chapter 24

24.3 a. \$3 million b. \$5 million c. 12/3

24.4 a. 6.5 million b. 45 c. 7.5 million

24.9 172

## Chapter 25

25.16 a. 1,400 b. 3,400

25.32 a. ½ b. .424 c. 255
d. 1.5 e. 7

25.33 $V_L = 5,360,000$
$V_U = 7,290,000$

25.37 a. 6.48 b. −5.11 million
c. \$0.84 million, −\$5.11 million

## Chapter 27

27.2 5,000, 5056.25

27.14 a. 1. \$300,000, 2. \$200,000, 3. \$600,000

b. 1. \$4,416.67, 2. −300, 3. 37,200

27.15 \$114

27.17 a. \$2.342 million b. \$2.3 million

c. \$1.948 million

27.18 a. \$1,000,000 b. 1,450,000

c. \$1,627,000 d. 1,097,297.30

e. −\$2,702.70

# Author Index

**T**



**U**



**V**



**W**



**Y**



**Z**

# Subject Index

## S

## Y



## Z